Ref 920 Enc v.11
Encyclopedia of world biography /

CYF $64.41

ENCYCLOPEDIA OF WORLD BIOGRAPHY

11

ENCYCLOPEDIA OF WORLD BIOGRAPHY

SECOND EDITION

Michael
Orleans

11

GALE

DETROIT • NEW YORK • TORONTO • LONDON

Staff

Senior Editor: Paula K. Byers
Project Editor: Suzanne M. Bourgoin
Managing Editor: Neil E. Walker

Editorial Staff: Luann Brennan, Frank V. Castronova, Laura S. Hightower, Karen E. Lemerand, Stacy A. McConnell, Jennifer Mossman, Maria L. Munoz, Katherine H. Nemeh, Terrie M. Rooney, Geri Speace

Permissions Manager: Susan M. Tosky
Permissions Specialist: Maria L. Franklin
Permissions Associate: Michele M. Lonoconus
Image Cataloger: Mary K. Grimes

Production Director: Mary Beth Trimper
Production Manager: Evi Seoud
Production Associate: Shanna Heilveil
Product Design Manager: Cynthia Baldwin
Senior Art Director: Mary Claire Krzewinski

Research Manager: Victoria B. Cariappa
Research Specialists: Michele P. LaMeau, Andrew Guy Malonis, Barbara McNeil, Gary J. Oudersluys
Research Associates: Julia C. Daniel, Tamara C. Nott, Norma Sawaya, Cheryl L. Warnock
Research Assistant: Talitha A. Jean

Graphic Services Supervisor: Barbara Yarrow
Image Database Supervisor: Randy Bassett
Imaging Specialist: Mike Lugosz

Manager of Data Entry Services: Eleanor M. Allison
Data Entry Coordinator: Kenneth D. Benson

Manager of Technology Support Services: Theresa A. Rocklin
Programmers/Analysts: Mira Bossowska, Jeffrey Muhr, Christopher Ward

Copyright © 1998
Gale Research
835 Penobscot Bldg.
Detroit, MI 48226-4094

ISBN 0-7876-2221-4 (Set)
ISBN 0-7876-2551-5 (Volume 11)

Library of Congress Cataloging-in-Publication Data

Encyclopedia of world biography / [edited by Suzanne Michele Bourgoin and Paula Kay Byers].
    p. cm.
    Includes bibliographical references and index.
    Summary: Presents brief biographical sketches which provide vital statistics as well as information on the importance of the person listed.
    ISBN 0-7876-2221-4 (set : alk. paper)
    1. Biography—Dictionaries—Juvenile literature. [1. Biography.]
I. Bourgoin, Suzanne Michele, 1968- . II. Byers, Paula K. (Paula Kay), 1954- .
CT 103.E56 1997
920' .003—dc21
                                     97-42327
                                         CIP
                                         AC

Printed in the United States of America
10 9 8 7 6 5 4 3

ENCYCLOPEDIA OF WORLD BIOGRAPHY

11

Michael VIII

Michael VIII (1224/1225-1282) was Byzantine emperor from 1259 to 1282. An ambitious and unscrupulous usurper, he founded Byzantium's last dynasty.

Belonging to one of the most powerful Byzantine aristocratic families, Michael rose to prominence under the Lascarid rulers, who had built, in the Empire of Nicaea, the chief of the Greek successor states after the Fourth Crusade captured Constantinople. The Lascarids' ultimate goal of restoring Byzantine government in Constantinople had eluded them up to the accession (1258) of the last of the family, John IV, a boy of 8. A restless and untrustworthy noble, Michael had several times outraged John IV's father and grandfather with his machinations. But he was popular with the other aristocrats. Michael soon had himself made the young emperor's guardian; he was then given the title of Despot, and, by the beginning of 1259, he was finally proclaimed emperor. Thereafter, he systematically pushed John IV into the background.

Ruthless in seeking power, Michael was able in exercising it. In the autumn of 1259, at the important battle of Pelagonia, his armies defeated the dangerous coalition of King Manfred of Sicily, the Latin prince of Achaea, and Michael's Greek rival, the despot of Epirus. Then, in July 1261, by unexpected good luck, one of his generals succeeded in slipping into Constantinople and expelling the Latin regime. So Michael achieved the glorious Byzantine restoration in the old capital, which he entered triumphantly on Aug. 15, 1261. Having himself recrowned there, he associated his son with him in power, and at the end of the year had little John IV blinded, thus completing the Palaeologan replacement of the Lascarid house.

Michael was determined to recover old Byzantine territories in Europe, especially in the Peloponnesus, from the Latin regimes there. Western leaders, regarding Michael as a schismatic as well as a usurper, wished to drive him out of Constantinople. After numerous diplomatic shiftings, a powerful new Western coalition against Michael was organized in 1267 by the Treaty of Viterbo between the Pope, the former Latin emperor of Constantinople, the Latin prince of Achaea in the Peloponnesus, and Charles of Anjou. Taking advantage of hostility toward Charles of a new pope, Gregory X (reigned 1271-1276), Michael cultivated the Pontiff as a buffer to Angevin ambitions. But the Pope's price was the submission of the Eastern Church to Rome in full union. Michael was forced to accept an official union dictated at the Council of Lyons (1274). This union with the hated Latins provoked uproar and factionalism among his subjects. The Emperor was therefore forced to forestall implementation of the union, and the pro-Angevin pontiff Martin IV renewed papal support for Charles and his allies against Michael. With disaster in the offing, Michael pulled his last diplomatic trick by helping to promote the "Sicilian Vespers" rising of 1282, which expelled the Angevins and introduced Michael's ally Pedro III of Aragon (reigned 1276-1285) as ruler of the island. Charles's power was shattered as a result, and he died in 1285, his ambitions against Byzantium unrealized.

Meanwhile, Michael's forces continued to make progress in the Peloponnesus, widening Byzantine power there. But his fears of the independent aristocrats, who were the bulwarks of the Eastern frontiers, only further weakened the Byzantine position there and opened the way for subsequent Turkish expansion during the next century. In his internal policies Michael attempted to restore the economy, but his heavy expenses for his diplomacy, wars, and rebuilding of Constantinople placed such strains on the revenues that a drastic cutback was required under his son and successor, Andronicus II, who was also obliged to heal the fierce ecclesiastical strife which Michael's hated Church policies had enflamed. Michael died on Dec. 11, 1282, while campaigning in Greece.

Further Reading

The most recent scholarly study of Michael is Deno J. Geanakoplos, *Emperor Michael Palaeologus and the West, 1258-1282* (1959), a solid, though selective account. Michael's place in international affairs is shown in Steven Runciman, *The Sicilian Vespers* (1958). Good general accounts are in *The Cambridge Medieval History* planned by J. B. Bury, vol. 4 (1923; 2d ed., pt. 1, 1966), and George Ostrogorski, *History of the Byzantine State* (trans. 1956; rev. ed. 1969). □

Michelangelo Buonarroti

Michelangelo Buonarroti (1475-1564) was the greatest sculptor of the Italian Renaissance and one of its greatest painters and architects.

Michelangelo Buonarroti was born on March 6, 1475, in Caprese, a village where his father was briefly serving as a Florentine government agent. The family, of higher rank than most from which artists came in Florence, had been bankers, but Michelangelo's grandfather had failed, and his father, too genteel for trade, lived on the income from his land and a few official appointments. Michelangelo's mother died when he was 6.

After grammar school, Michelangelo was apprenticed at the age of 13 to Domenico Ghirlandaio, the most fashionable painter in Florence. That this should have happened is surprising, and no satisfactory explanation has been proposed. Michelangelo's implication in his old age that he had to overcome his family's opposition is likely to be mythical in part. In any case, after a year his apprenticeship was broken off, and an even odder arrangement followed: the boy was given access to the collection of ancient Roman sculpture of the ruler of Florence, Lorenzo de' Medici, dined with the family, and was looked after by the retired sculptor who was in charge of the collection. This arrangement was quite unprecedented at the time.

Michelangelo's earliest sculpture, a stone relief executed when he was about 17, in its composition echoes the Roman sarcophagi of the Medici collection and in its subject, the *Battle of the Centaurs,* a Latin poem a court poet read to him. Compared to the sarcophagi, Michelangelo's work is remarkable for the simple, solid forms and squarish proportions of the figures, which add intensity to their violent interaction.

Soon after Lorenzo died in 1492, the Medici fell from power and Michelangelo fled the city. In Bologna in 1494

he obtained a small but distinguished commission to carve the three saints needed to complete the elaborate tomb of St. Dominic in the church of S. Domenico. They too show dense forms, which contrast with the linear forms, either decorative or realistic, then dominant in sculpture, but are congruent with the work of Nicola Pisano, who had begun the tomb about 1265. On returning home Michelangelo found Florence dominated by the famous ascetic monk Savonarola. Michelangelo was in contact with the junior branch of the Medici family, and he carved a *Cupid* (lost) which he took to Rome to sell, palming it off as an ancient work.

Rome, 1496-1501

In Rome, Michelangelo next executed a *Bacchus* for the garden of ancient sculpture of a banker. This, Michelangelo's earliest surviving large-scale work, shows the god teetering, either drunk or dancing. It is his only sculpture meant to be viewed from all sides; all the others, generally set in front of walls, possess to some extent the visual character of reliefs.

In 1498, through the same banker, came Michelangelo's first important commission: the *Pietà* now in St. Peter's. The term pietà refers to a type of image in which Mary supports the dead Christ across her knees; Michelangelo's version is today the most famous one. In both the *Pietà* and the *Bacchus* the effects of hard polished marble and of curved yielding flesh coexist. Over life size, the *Pietà* has mutually reinforcing contrasts: vertical and horizontal, cloth and skin, allude to the living and the dead, female and male, but the unity of the pyramidal composition is strongly imposed.

Florence, 1501-1505

On his return to Florence in 1501 Michelangelo was recognized as the most talented sculptor of central Italy, but his work was still in the early Renaissance tradition, as is the marble *David,* commissioned in 1501 for Florence Cathedral but when finished, in 1504, more suitably installed in front of the Palazzo Vecchio. (The original is now in the Accademia; the statue at the original site is a copy.) It shares the clear and strong but bland presence of the *Pietà.* Before he finished the *David,* Michelangelo's style had begun to change, as indicated by his drawing of a very different bronze *David* (lost) and by other works, particularly the *Battle of Cascina.* All these works resulted from the city fathers' desire to revive monumental public art, characteristic of the period before the Medici early in the 15th century. The new Council Hall of the Palazzo Vecchio was to have patriotic murals that would also show the special skills of Florence's leading artists: Leonardo da Vinci and Michelangelo.

Michelangelo's *Battle of Cascina* was commissioned in 1504; several sketches and a copy of the cartoon exist. The central scene shows a group of muscular nudes, soldiers climbing from a river where they had been swimming, to answer a military alarm. Inevitably Michelangelo felt the influence of Leonardo and his evocation of continuous flowing motion through living forms. Michelangelo's greatness lay partly in his ability to absorb Leonardo's innovations and yet not reduce the heavy solidity and impressive dignity of his earlier work. This fusion of throbbing life with colossal grandeur henceforth was the special quality of Michelangelo's art.

From then on too Michelangelo's work consisted mainly of very large projects that he never finished because of his inability to turn down the vast commissions of his great clients which appealed to his preference for the grand scale. Of the 12 Apostles he was to execute for Florence Cathedral, he began only the *St. Matthew;* this was the first monumental sculpture suggesting a Leonardesque agitation.

Tomb of Julius II

The project of the Apostles was put aside when Pope Julius II called Michelangelo to Rome in 1505 to design his tomb, which was to include about 40 life-size statues. This project occupied Michelangelo off and on for the next 40 years. Of it he wrote, "I find I have lost all my youth bound to this tomb." In 1506 a dispute over funds for the tomb led Michelangelo, who had spent almost a year at the quarries in Carrara, to flee to Florence. A reconciliation between Julius II and Michelangelo took place in Bologna, which the Pope had just conquered, and Michelangelo modeled a colossal bronze statue of Julius for S. Petronio in Bologna, which he completed in 1508 (destroyed).

Sistine Chapel

In 1508 Julius commissioned Michelangelo to decorate the ceiling of the chief Vatican chapel, the Sistine. This work was relatively modest at first, and Michelangelo felt he was being pushed aside by rival claimants on funds. But he soon was able to alter the traditional format of ceiling painting, whereby only single figures could be represented, not scenes calling for dramas in space; his introduction of dramatic scenes was so successful that it set the standard for the future.

The elaborate program with hundreds of figures was arranged in an original framing system that was Michelangelo's earliest architectonic design. He approached the ceiling as a surface on which to attach planes built up in various degrees of projection, like a relief sculpture except that its basic units are blocks rather than malleable forms. The many planes and painted architectural framework make the many categories of images so easily readable that the framing system tends to pass unnoticed, but its rich, heavy ornament is typical of the High Renaissance. The chief figural elements of the program are the 12 male and female prophets (the latter known as sibyls) and the nine stories from Genesis. Michelangelo began painting at the end of the story, with the three Noah scenes and the adjacent prophets and sibyls, and in 4 years worked through the three Adam stories to the three Creation stories at the other end of the ceiling.

Michelangelo paused for some months halfway along, and when he returned to the ceiling, he made the prophets more monumental (in keeping with the fewer and hence bigger figures in the nearby Creation scenes). At that point his style also underwent a shift. He had begun with a manner reverting to his sculptural style in the *Pietà* and *David,* as if he was uncertain when facing the unfamiliar task of painting on such a scale. The first prophets are harmonious but static, as is the *Flood* scene. But soon there develops a forceful grandeur, with a richer emotional tension than in any previous work. This is well illustrated in the *Ezekiel,* whose massive torso seems to be in tension with the centrifugally twisted head and legs. The prophet peers questioningly into the unknown.

After the pause, Michelangelo began the second half of the ceiling with a newly acquired subtlety of expression, as in the *Creation of Adam.* The images become freer and more mobile in the last parts painted, such as the *Separation of Light and Darkness,* but the mood remains introspective.

As soon as the ceiling was completed in 1512, Michelangelo returned to the tomb of Julius and carved for it (1513-1514) the *Moses* (S. Pietro in Vincoli, Rome) and two *Slaves* (Louvre, Paris), using the same types he employed for the prophets and their attendants painted in the Sistine ceiling. The *Moses* seems to represent a final synthesis of all those variants, although it is more restrained owing to the sculptural medium. It was meant to be placed above eye level, and some of its dramatic force would probably have been mitigated when seen from the intended distance. Julius's death in 1513 halted the work on his tomb.

From now on the successive popes determined Michelangelo's activity, as they were all anxious to have work by the recognized greatest maker of monuments for themselves, their families, and the Church. Pope Leo X, son of Lorenzo de' Medici, proposed a marble facade for the family parish church of S. Lorenzo in Florence, to be decorated with statues by Michelangelo, but his project was canceled after four years of quarrying and designing.

Medici Chapel

In 1520 Michelangelo was commissioned to execute a tomb chapel for two young Medici dukes. The Medici Chapel (1520-1534), an annex to S. Lorenzo, is the most nearly complete large sculptural project of Michelangelo's career. The two tombs, each with an image of the deceased and two allegorical figures, are placed against elaborately articulated walls; these six statues and a seventh on a third wall, the *Madonna,* are by Michelangelo's own hand. The two saints flanking the *Madonna* are by assistants from his clay sketches. Four river gods were planned but not executed.

The interior architecture of the Medici Chapel develops the treatment seen in the painted architectural framework of the Sistine ceiling; the walls are treated as relief sculptures, with intersecting moldings and pillars on many planes, giving a loose freedom typical of a non-professional approach to architecture. Whimsical reversals of what is proper—trapezoidal windows and capitals smaller than their columns—introduce what is now called mannerism in architecture.

The allegories on the curved lids of the tombs are also innovative: *Day* and *Night* recline on one tomb, *Morning* and *Evening* on the other. The choice of imagery was left to the artist, and these figures seem to symbolize the endless round of time leading to death. Michelangelo said that the death of the dukes cut off the light of the times of day, and such courtly adulation, which is hard to accept as Michelangelesque, is also suggested in the dukes' fancy costumes and idealized representations. Political absolutism was growing at the time, and Michelangelo's statues were often used as precedents in formulating new types of royal portraiture. A similar style is seen in the sinuous *Victory* overcoming a tough old warrior. This statue, Michelangelo's last serious contribution to the tomb of Julius, also embodied the artist's interest in Neoplatonism, a philosophy that urged man to rise above his body into the spiritual plane.

The architecture of the Medici Chapel has a fuller analog in the library, the Biblioteca Laurenziana, built at the same time on the opposite side of S. Lorenzo to house Leo X's books. The reading room has functional suggestions in its window and pillar system and refined ornament on floor and ceiling. But the entrance hall and staircase are Michelangelo's most astonishing illustration of capricious paradox, with recessed columns resting on scroll brackets set halfway up the wall and corners stretched open rather than sealed.

His Poetry

Most of Michelangelo's 300 surviving poems were written in the 1530s and 1540s and fall into two groups. The earlier poems are on the theme of Neoplatonic love and are full of logical contradictions and conceits, often very intricate. They belong to an international trend best known in the work of Luis de Góngora and John Donne and make an interesting parallel to mannerist architecture. The later poems are Christian; their mood is penitent; and they are written in a simple, direct style. These match a phase of Michelangelo's plastic art that slightly precedes them.

"Last Judgment"

In 1534 Michelangelo left Florence for the last time, settling in Rome. The next 10 years were mainly given over to painting for Pope Paul III, who is best known for convening the Council of Trent and thus organizing the Catholic Reformation.

The first project Michelangelo executed for Paul III is the huge *Last Judgment* (1536-1541) on the end wall of the Sistine Chapel. It revives a medieval approach to the same theme in using an entire end wall in an undivided field and in the composition of the parts. The design functions like a pair of scales, with some angels pushing the damned down to hell on one side and some pulling up the saved on the other side, both directed by Christ, who "conducts" with both arms; in the two top corners are the cross and other symbols of the Passion, which serve as his credentials to be judge.

The flow of movement in the *Last Judgment* is greater than in the medieval tradition, with the two streams of figures tending to shear against each other, but it is slower compared to Michelangelo's own earlier work. The colors, blue and brown, are simple, as are the bodies. The figure type is new, with thick, waistless torsos and loosely connected limbs. The new sobriety seems to parallel the ideas of the Counter Reformation, with whose leaders Michelangelo had intimate contact through his admired mentor, the devout widow Vittoria Colonna, the addressee of many of his poems.

Michelangelo's frescoes in the Pauline Chapel in the Vatican (1541-1545) are similar to the *Last Judgment,* but here he added a remarkable technical novelty by exploring perspective movement and coloristic subtlety as major expressive components. He may have turned to these typically painterly concerns because the Pauline frescoes were the first ones he executed on a normal scale and eye level. The only sculpture of these years, the *Rachel* and the *Leah,* executed so that a small amended version of the tomb of Julius could at last be erected, are so neat and unemphatic that they are often disregarded or not accepted as Michelangelo's work.

Works after 1545

Michelangelo devoted himself almost entirely to architecture and poetry after 1545. For Paul III he planned the rebuilding of the Capitol area, the Piazza del Campidoglio, a pioneering scheme of city planning that gave monumental articulation to an area traditionally used for civic ceremonies. The geometry is dynamic, marked by a trapezoidal plan (determined by the site) formed by three buildings and an oval pavement; the airy breadth of the piazza produces a relatively gentle effect of a special theatrical locus. The chief emphasis is on the facades of the two new side buildings, executed to Michelangelo's plans after his death. Two-story pilasters mark the front plane, unifying the open porch on the lower story and the closed upper one, thus mingling suggestions of compressed power and clear skeletal construction.

Michelangelo's approach to architecture was growing richer and more three-dimensional, as in the Palazzo Farnese, which he completed after the death of Antonio da Sangallo the Younger in 1546. In Michelangelo's third story of the courtyard, a second row of wide pilasters set behind the front level of narrow ones causes the wall of which they are all part to suggest a wavy continuum.

Paul III appointed Michelangelo to take over the direction of the work at St. Peter's after Sangallo died. Here Michelangelo had less respect for his predecessor's plan, returning instead to the concepts that the first architect, Donato Bramante, had proposed in 1506. The enormous church was to be an equal-armed cross in plan, concentrated on a huge central space beneath the dome surrounded by a series of secondary spaces and their containing structures. The edge thus became a complex outline of changing convex curves, and from that Michelangelo built the wall straight up, producing a very active rhythm, all on such a monumental scale that we can never see more than a fragment at one time. Its surface alternates colossal pilasters with stacks of three vertical windows compressed between them, providing a measure of the vast scale and also binding the wall into vertical unity. By the time Michelangelo died, a considerable part of St. Peter's had been built in the form in which we know it, and the drum of the dome was finished up to the springing.

The essentially three-dimensional concept of St. Peter's, inherently architectonic and original, gave way in Michelangelo's last years to a gleaming, almost dematerialized approach to the wall, suggested in the plans (ca. 1559) for the unexecuted church of S. Giovanni dei Fiorentini and a city gate, the Porta Pia (begun 1561).

Michelangelo's sculpture after 1545 was limited to two Pietàs that he executed for himself. The first one (1550-1555, unfinished), which is in the Cathedral of Florence, was meant for his own tomb. This Pietà employs the body type of the *Last Judgment* in the Christ and its shearing up and down thrusts in the interrelationships of the figures. His late architectural style has a parallel in his last sculpture, the *Rondanini Pietà* in Milan, which is cut away to an almost abstract set of curves. Michelangelo began this sculpture in 1555, and he was working on it on Feb. 12, 1564. He died six days later in Rome and was buried in Florence.

Michelangelo's impact on the younger artists who encountered his successive styles throughout his long life was immense, but it tended to be crushing. The great baroque artists of the next century, such as Peter Paul Rubens and Gian Lorenzo Bernini, were better able at a distance to study his ideas without danger to their artistic autonomy.

Further Reading

The Complete Poems and Selected Letters of Michelangelo was translated by Creighton Gilbert and edited by Robert N. Linscott (1963). Charles de Tolnay, *Michelangelo* (5 vols., 1938-1960), is opinionated but indispensable; and Frederick Hartt's *Michelangelo* (1965), *Michelangelo: The Complete*

Sculpture (1969), and *Michelangelo Drawings* (1970) are also strongly personal but more current. Both deal only with the painting, sculpture, and drawings. James S. Ackerman, *The Architecture of Michelangelo* (2 vols., 1961), is outstanding for this aspect of his work. Ludwig Goldscheider, *Michelangelo: Paintings, Sculptures, Architecture* (4th ed. 1963), provides a reasonably complete set of good illustrations. Creighton Gilbert, *Michelangelo* (1967), is the most succinct survey. Still valid for biography is John Addington Symonds, *The Life of Michelangelo* (1893); many reprints. ☐

Jules Michelet

The French historian Jules Michelet (1798-1874) wrote the "Histoire de France" and "Histoire de la Révolution française," which established him as one of France's greatest 19th-century historians.

Jules Michelet was born on Aug. 21, 1798, in Paris. His father was a printer by trade, and his mother's family was from peasant stock. The family was poor, especially after Napoleon ordered the closing of his father's press. This family background prompted Michelet's initial sympathy with the French Revolution.

In 1822 Michelet began his long and devoted career as a teacher, becoming professor of history and philosophy at the École Normale Supérieure in 1827. In one of his earliest works, a translation of Giovanni Battista Vico's *Scienza nuova,* Michelet introduced such ideas as the importance of myth and language in historical understanding and the ability of man to forge his own history. His first volumes of French history treated the Middle Ages; already he revealed a passionate adherence to the role of the common people in history.

When Michelet joined the faculty at the Collège de France in 1838, his writing became more liberal and more oriented toward contemporary issues. Collaboration with a colleague, Edgar Quinet, on a book against the Jesuits raised the Church's suspicions. In addition, Michelet was waking up to the *esclavage* (slavery) of classes in an industrial society, a concern he expressed in his moving book *Le Peuple* (1846). Thus Michelet and other writers of the period, encouraged by the revolutionary spirit growing since 1830, were attracted to the French Revolution. Michelet's seven-volume *Histoire de la Révolution française* illustrates his famous concept of history as a resurrection of the past in its spontaneous entirety. Although in this immense achievement the portraits of certain revolutionaries are masterfully drawn, Michelet is more sympathetic when narrating crowd scenes, for example, the fall of the Bastille.

The failure of the 1848 revolutions, Louis Napoleon's coup d'etat of 1851, and the proclamation of the Second Empire in 1852 profoundly disturbed Michelet. Although he was not exiled, he spent the following year in Italy.

Worn by arduous work and depressing historical events, Michelet discovered new life in his second marriage with 20-year-old Atanaïs Mialaret. Inspired by her love of

nature, he wrote four poetical studies: *The Bird* (1856), *The Insect* (1857), *The Sea* (1861), and *The Mountain* (1867). These fecund later years saw two other outstanding books: one on the medieval witch (*La Sorcière,* 1862) and the other on world religions, including an attack on Christianity (*La Bible de l'humanité,* 1864). Michelet finally completed his history of France in 1867. Working continuously, he had written three volumes on 19th-century France up to the time of his death on Feb. 9, 1874, when he suffered a heart attack at Hyères.

Further Reading

A study of Michelet's thought is Ann Reese Pugh, *Michelet and His Ideas on Social Reform* (1923). An excellent profile and analysis appears in Pieter Geyl, *Debates with Historians* (1955; rev. ed. 1958). Michelet is also considered at length in George Peabody Gooch, *History and Historians in the Nineteenth Century* (1913; 2d ed. 1952; with new preface, 1959). See also Fritz Stern, ed., *The Varieties of History* (1956).

Additional Sources

Haac, Oscar A., *Jules Michelet,* Boston: Twayne Publishers, 1982.

Kippur, Stephen A., *Jules Michelet, a study of mind and sensibility,* Albany, N.Y.: State University of New York Press, 1981.

Orr, Linda, *Jules Michelet: nature, history, and language,* Ithaca, N.Y.: Cornell University Press, 1976.

Williams, John R. (John Raymond), *Jules Michelet: historian as critic of French literature,* Birmingham, Ala.: Summa Publications, 1987. □

Michelozzo

The Italian architect and sculptor Michelozzo (ca. 1396-1472) designed the Palazzo Medici-Riccardi in Florence, which set the standard for Renaissance palace architecture in Tuscany for the next century.

Born in Florence, Michelozzo, also known as Michelozzo Michelozzi, served from about 1417 to 1424 as assistant to the sculptor Lorenzo Ghiberti. In 1425 Michelozzo became the partner of the sculptor Donatello and designed the architectural elements for the tombs of the antipope John XXIII (1425-1427) in the Baptistery of Florence and Cardinal Brancacci (1427-1428) in Naples and for the outdoor pulpit (1433-1438) of the Cathedral at Prato.

With his commission to rebuild the monastic church of St. Francesco in Mugello, called Bosco ai Frati (ca. 1427), Michelozzo became the architect of Cosimo dé Medici, for whom he worked for at least 30 years. Several of the Medici villas near Florence, beginning with the Castello di Trebbio (ca. 1427-1436) and including buildings at Cafaggiolo (ca. 1451) and Careggi (ca. 1457), were converted by Michelozzo from fortified country houses. The Medici villa he designed at Fiesole (1458-1461) lacks any aspect of fortification and in its openness and elegance is a modest forerunner of a type of architecture important in Renaissance Italy.

Michelozzo accompanied Cosimo during his exile in Venice from 1433 to 1434 and on his return rebuilt Cosimo's favorite retreat, the monastery of St. Marco in Florence (1436-1443) with its impressive library. Michelozzo's most important building is the Palazzo Medici-Riccardi in Florence (1444-1464). The massive, block–like residence, lengthened in the 17th century, has three stories of graded rustication, from the heavy, rough stone of the ground floor to smooth ashlar above capped by a large cornice. The interior court with a ground-floor arcade on Composite columns recalls the architecture of the great, contemporary architect Filippo Brunelleschi.

In 1466 Michelozzo succeeded Brunelleschi as *capomastro* of the Cathedral of Florence and completed the details, including the lantern of the great dome. The church of St. Maria delle Grazie in Pistoia, for which Michelozzo furnished the design (from 1452), although it was completed by others with changes, reveals the influence of Brunelleschi in its square tribune with a saucer dome flanked by barrel-vaulted arms. However, the pendentives of the dome supported only by freestanding columns create an open spaciousness more suggestive of later-15th-century architecture.

In 1462 Michelozzo was in Ragusa (modern Dubrovnik, Yugoslavia) as engineer for the city walls, and in 1464 he prepared a design for rebuilding the Palazzo dei Rettori there, but the work was carried out with no reference to his style. He died in Florence and was buried in St. Marco on Oct. 7, 1472.

Further Reading

There is no monograph or important consideration of Michelozzo in English. He is discussed in Nikolaus Pevsner, *An Outline of European Architecture* (1943; 5th rev. ed. 1957), and John Pope-Hennessy, *Italian Renaissance Sculpture* (1958). □

Robert Michels

The German sociologist Robert Michels (1876-1936) wrote on the political behavior of intellectual elites and on the problem of power and its abuse.

Robert Michels was born on Jan. 9, 1876, in Cologne. He studied in England, at the Sorbonne in Paris, and at universities in Munich, Leipzig (1897), Halle (1898), and Turin.

While teaching at the University of Marburg, Michels became a Socialist. He was active in the radical wing of the German Social Democratic party and attended its party congresses in 1903, 1904, and 1905. Although he left the party in 1907, government opposition to his activities limited his academic career in Germany. He went to the University of Turin, Italy, where he taught economics, political science, and sociology until 1914, when he became professor of economics at the University of Basel, Switzerland, a post he held until 1926. He spent his last years in Italy as professor of economics and the history of doctrines at the University of Perugia and occasionally lectured in Rome, where he died on May 3, 1936.

Michels's involvement in German revolutionary causes gave him insights into trade unions, party congresses, demagogues, and the role of the intellectual in politics. His widely translated book *Political Parties* (German ed. 1911; English ed. 1949) is an analysis of prewar socialism in Germany, with examples also drawn from political protest movements in France, Italy, England, and the United States. In this and other writings he developed the hypothesis that organizations formed to promote democratic values inevitably develop a strong oligarchic tendency. His view on the nature of leadership was that, despite the original commitment to democracy, the demands of the organization compel the leader to rely on a bureaucracy of paid professional staff and to centralize authority. This process causes displacement of the original democratic goals by a conservative tendency to retain power at all costs as well as an unwillingness to have that power challenged by free elections. Michels called this theory the "iron law of oligarchy," He is criticized for failing to define "oligarchy," which some of his adherents have equated with the term "ruling class."

Michels compared working-class societies in Germany, Italy, and France and wrote about the political culture of Italy. He analyzed the Tripolitan War of 1911-1912 in terms of the suffering it caused and the impact of war propaganda. Italian imperialism, he believed, resulted from demographic pressure and from the social and cultural loss caused by overseas migration. His writings in the 1920s and 1930s dealt with nationalism, Italian socialism and fascism, elites and social mobility, the role of intellectuals, and the history of the social sciences. He often returned to the problem of oligarchy and democracy. Some critics describe him as a disappointed democrat whose disillusionment led him to an elitist point of view and made him comfortable with Italian fascism.

Further Reading

Seymour M. Lipset's introduction to Michels's *Political Parties* (1962) discusses the sociologist's work. Michels figures in general works on sociology, such as James Burnham, *The Machiavellians: Defenders of Freedom* (1943), which contains a chapter on his work, and Robert A. Nisbet, *The Sociological Tradition* (1966). □

Albert Abraham Michelson

The American physicist Albert Abraham Michelson (1852-1931) is important for his determination of the velocity of light and the study of optical interference.

Albert Michelson was born on Dec. 19, 1852, in German Poland. The family emigrated to the United States in 1854. He took the competitive examinations for congressional appointment to the U.S. Naval Academy. Although he qualified for the appointment, the place was awarded to another boy. Young Michelson traveled to Washington, was unsuccessful in getting President Grant to appoint him to the academy, but then persuaded the commandant to accept him.

Michelson graduated from the Naval Academy in 1873. Two years later he was appointed instructor in physics and chemistry there. He resigned his commission in 1880 and spent 2 years studying in Berlin, Heidelberg, and Paris. He was then appointed to the Case School of Applied Science at Cleveland, Ohio, as professor of physics. In 1889 he moved to Clark University as professor of physics, and in 1892 he was invited to head the department of physics at the new University of Chicago, a position which he held until 1931.

With few exceptions, all of Michelson's work bore directly on problems involved in the study of light; he was thus specialized to a degree that was unique among Americans at the end of the 19th century. While serving at Annapolis, he hit upon a slight but vital modification to a method then being used to measure the speed of light. With his simple device, consisting essentially of two plane mirrors, one fixed and one revolving at the rate of about 130 turns per second from which light was to be reflected, Michelson succeeded in obtaining a measure closer than any that had been obtained to the presently accepted figure—186,508 miles per second.

Michelson performed his most famous experiment at Cleveland in collaboration with the chemist Edward W. Morley. Light waves were regarded as undulations of the ether which filled all space. If a light source were moving through the ether, the speed of the light would be different for each direction in which it was emitted. In the Michelson-Morley experiment two beams of light, sent out and reflected back at right angles to each other, took the same amount of time. Thus the notion of a stationary ether had to be discarded.

Even though his own work helped touch off a revolution in physics, Michelson never realized the fundamental nature of the change. Basically a brilliant experimenter, he saw the future development of physics only as one of further precision and newer instruments which would bring the accuracy of scientific measurements to the ultimate degree. He never understood the more mathematical and theoretical approach which came to dominate physics toward the end of his life.

Michelson's contributions were numerous. He developed, as a by-product of his interference experiments, the first spectroscope having sufficiently high resolution to disclose direct optical evidence of molecular motion; gave the scientific world a new fundamental standard of length when he calibrated the international meter in terms of wavelengths of cadmium; and, using a variation of his interferometer, became the first man to measure the diameter of a star. He received the Nobel Prize in 1907, the first American to be so honored. He died on May 9, 1931, while at work on a still more refined measurement of the velocity of light.

Further Reading

A good account of the major work of Michelson's life is in Bernard Jaffe, *Michelson and the Speed of Light* (1960). There is a useful biographical memoir of Michelson by Robert A. Millikan in National Academy of Sciences, *Biographical Memoirs*, vol. 19 (1938), and another profile of his life and work is in Royal Society of London, *Obituary Notices of Fellows of the Royal Society*, vol. 1 (1932-1935). The Nobel Foundation, *Nobel Lectures: Physics, 1901-1921* (1964), has a biographical sketch. □

Thomas Middleton

The English playwright Thomas Middleton (1580-1627) was one of the most productive and talented playwrights of the Jacobean period. His best work was done in "city comedy"—comedy of intrigue with emphasis on the more lurid features of contemporary London.

Thomas Middleton was born the son of a fairly prosperous London bricklayer. He began writing early and had published at least three nondramatic pieces before he was 20. He attended Oxford in 1598 but apparently left without a degree. By 1602 he was in London, actively engaged in writing plays, first as a collaborator and then independently.

Some of Middleton's most successful work as a dramatist was done between 1602 and 1608, when he wrote a series of lively realistic comedies of London life. These include *The Family of Love* (ca. 1602), *The Phoenix* (ca. 1603), *Michaelmas Term* (1605), *A Mad World My Masters* (1605), and *Your Five Gallants* (ca. 1607). *A Chaste Maid in Cheapside* (1611), probably Middleton's most widely read comedy today, is a play of the same kind.

Most of Middleton's early work was written for performance by one or another of the companies of boy actors which were flourishing at this time. After 1608, as the popularity of the children's companies waned, he seems to have written almost exclusively for adult actors. His most notable plays from this later period are *The Changeling* (1622; written in collaboration with William Rowley) and *A Game at Chess* (1624).

The Changeling, one of the most powerful tragedies of the Jacobean period, traces the developing engagement to evil on the part of the beautiful and wealthy Beatrice-Joanna. Her sudden and inexplicable attraction to Deflores, a servant whom she had always found repulsive, initiates an exciting career of deception, lust, and murder. The highly unusual *A Game at Chess* has characters designated only as chess pieces: the White King, the Black Bishop, and so on. The action of the play, however, was clearly based on contemporary political events and caused a great sensation. The Spanish ambassador took offense and persuaded the English authorities to suppress the play for a time. Middleton apparently went into hiding to escape punishment.

In addition to his work for the professional stage, Middleton produced a number of civic pageants. In recognition of his abilities in this kind of entertainment, he was appointed city chronologer of London in 1620. He held this lucrative post until his death. He was buried in the Newington section of London, where he had resided during most of his adult life.

Further Reading

A full-length study of Middleton is Richard Hindry Barker, *Thomas Middleton* (1958). See also Samuel Schoenbaum, *Middleton's Tragedies: A Critical Study* (1955), which treats at length certain problems of authorship associated with the Middleton canon.

Additional Sources

Barker, Richard Hindry, *Thomas Middleton*, Westport, Conn.: Greenwood Press, 1974, 1958.

Mulryne, J. R., *Thomas Middleton,* Burnt Mill Eng.: Published for the British Council by Longman Group, 1979. □

Mary Burton Midgely

Modern British philosopher Mary Burton Midgely (born 1919) wrote widely on topics involving freedom and determinism, the philosophy of human nature, and the nature of morality. Her work focused primarily on human nature in relation to animal

behavior and the philosophy of human motivation and ethics.

Mary Midgely was born Mary Burton in London, England, on September 13, 1919, the daughter of Canon Tour and Evelyn (Scrulton) Burton. She was educated at Sommerville College, Oxford (first class honors, 1942). She taught at the University of Reading in Great Britain, 1949-1950, and after 1951 at the University of Newcastle upon Tyne, also in Great Britain. Here she began as a part-time lecturer, later becoming a senior lecturer in philosophy. She also served as a visiting professor in the United States. Meanwhile, in 1950 she married Geoffrey Midgely, also a university lecturer. They raised three sons.

In addition to her teaching, Mary Midgely's contributions to contemporary philosophy were wide ranging, but in two areas she made important contributions to current thought: the philosophy of human nature and moral philosophy.

Midgely criticized much 20th-century philosophy of human nature for failing to take the systematic study of animal behavior seriously as a basis for constructing a philosophical understanding of human beings. Existentialism is especially guilty of this offense. Jean-Paul Sartre and Albert Camus, the leading exponents of existentialism in the 20th century, argued that human beings create or define themselves and, as a result, it is necessary to view humans as radically free. For Sartre and Camus radical freedom means that humans "have no nature" and that humans are infinitely plastic in the sense that they can take on any shape they choose. For Sartre and Camus, humans can be free only if we assume there are no fundamental restraints on what humans can become. For the existentialists, if human nature exists then persons cannot be free.

Midgely rejected this image of humanity because it rejected the major assumption of evolutionary theory, namely that humans are on a continuum of development with animals. For Midgely, existentialism is ultimately grounded on a false dualism between humans and the animal kingdom; nearly all scientific research since Darwin rejects this radical dualism. But more important, if humans were radically free, then society would be able to shape us in any way it saw fit, and this belief flies in the face of history and experience. For Midgely, human variation or plasticity was broad and deep but it was not infinite.

But while Midgely rejected the view that humans are disembodied "choosers" who can form themselves in any way they decide, she also rejected the polar opposite of this view, namely that humans are completely determined by their genetic and biological history. If humans were completely determined by their genetic heritage, then we would be machines. A machine is something whose parts and purposes and behavior can be read off an engineering diagram or schema. But, according to Midgely, human behavior and motivation is simply too complex, unpredictable, and environmentally fixed to satisfy this condition. In short, to say that humans have a nature does not imply that humans are fully determined. Men and women can powerfully determine the course of their own lives, but their ability to define themselves is not historically and biologically unbounded. Human nature is continuous with the animals in the sense that there exists a set of inborn, active, and social tendencies that shape human behavior. However, these tendencies do not determine the details of human behavior.

An example of a natural tendency is altruism. Altruism is the ability to do good for others. The classical egoists argued that men and women were always acting for their own interests and were incapable of acting for others. Altruism was inconsistent with human nature. But animal behavior undermines this egoistic vision of humanity. Animals are constantly dying for their young. They are constantly defending the members of their group. For Midgely, animals do what "doesn't pay," and if we are to understand humans as being on a continuum with animals, then we must see human altruism not only as possible but also as being fundamental to human survival.

Midgely argued that moral theory must go hand in glove with ethology and evolutionary theory. She rejected the idea that there is a complete separation between facts and values. For example, we cannot demand or require people to do that which is inconsistent with their human nature, but this does not mean that we cannot oblige them to be altruistic in some situations. Biology and evolutionary theory can help us understand the limits and extent of altruism, and it is therefore essential. However, while these disciplines are necessary to morality, they are not by themselves replacements for ethics and moral philosophy. The facts of evolutionary theory can assist but they cannot substitute for a philosophy of value.

We can apply these ideas to social philosophy. Many philosophers such as Karl Marx have argued that we should create a social and economic order that requires men and women to work for others. Classical communism maintained that men and women are only apparently selfish because they were taught to be selfish by the greedy society in which they were raised. Communism attempted to create a society that would allow persons to be fully altruistic. One was only permitted to act for the "good of the proletariat." Midgely would argue that communism is a radical form of altruism that attempts to develop an ethic that is incompatible with human nature. But strict capitalism is also incompatible with human nature. Strict capitalism assumes that men and women are always selfish and that altruistic behavior is impossible. But altruism is present throughout the animal kingdom. As noted earlier, animals regularly die for their offspring, and primates are constantly acting in ways that benefit their group. In short, the major economic philosophies of humans are both incompatible with our knowledge of the animal kingdom.

For Midgely, animals point the way toward a more coherent social structure for men and women.

Further Reading

Among Mary Midgely's best known works are *Beast and Man* (1978), *Evolution as a Religion* (1985), and *Wickedness: A Philosophical Essay* (1989). Another book which explores her views on the theory of knowledge and information is *Wis-*

dom, Information and Wonder: What Is Knowledge For (London, 1989). □

Ludwig Mies van der Rohe

Ludwig Mies van der Rohe (1886-1969), German-born American architect, was a leading exponent of the International Style. His "skin and bones" philosophy of architecture is summed up in his famous phrase "less is more."

Ludwig Mies van der Rohe was born in Aachen on March 27, 1886. He attended the cathedral school until he was 13 years old and spent the next 2 years at a trade school. He had no formal architectural training but acted as a draftsman for a manufacturer of decorative stucco, and from 1905 to 1907 he was employed by Bruno Paul, the Berlin furniture designer.

In 1908 Mies joined Peter Behrens (the employer of Le Corbusier and Walter Gropius), who was one of several enlightened German architects attempting to link the ideals of the British Arts and Crafts movement, as propagated in Germany by Hermann Muthesius, to machine production. Behrens designed buildings and products for the German electrical industry AEG but also reverted to the esthetics, concepts, and architectural expression of the early-19th-century neoclassicist Karl Friedrich Schinkel. Thus it is not surprising that Mies's early domestic architecture, notably the Perls House (1911) at Zehlendorf near Berlin, with its hipped roof and axial plan, could have been designed by Behrens, or even by Schinkel a hundred years earlier. Mies supervised the construction of the German Embassy in St. Petersburg before leaving Behrens's office in 1912.

Early Work

During 1910 and 1911 Frank Lloyd Wright's architectural projects were published by Ernst Wasmuth of Berlin. Mies acknowledged his debt to Wright ("The encounter [of Wright] was destined to prove of great significance to the European development."), but he was also strongly influenced after World War I by the de Stijl movement of Theo van Doesburg and Gerrit Rietveld. This Dutch movement had developed from the cubistderived tradition of painters Paul Klee and Wassily Kandinsky. Mies's brick country house project (1923) and his brick monument to Karl Liebknecht and Rosa Luxemburg (1926; destroyed) in Berlin were essays in the de Stijl idiom. Even the plan of the German Pavilion (1929; destroyed) at the International Exposition in Barcelona, Spain, had the geometry of a de Stijl painting. The travertine podium, chrome-plated steel structural columns, green marble dividers, and gray glass of the pavilion, as well as the reflecting pool with a sculpture by George Kolbe and the famed Barcelona chair, stool, and table by Mies, gave the building a timeless quality of inexorable perfection.

Mies also designed the furniture for some of his other buildings, such as the tubular dining and lounge chairs for the second Deutscher Werkbund Exposition of 1927 in Stuttgart. He was director of this exposition and broad-mindedly invited Behrens, Le Corbusier, Gropius, J. J. P. Oud, Bruno Taut, Hans Poelzig, and others to contribute. "I have refrained," said Mies, "from laying down a rigid program, in order to leave each individual as free as possible to carry out his ideas." His own contribution was a row of apartments, steel-framed, finished in stucco, and with horizontal bands of windows.

In 1930 Mies designed the Tugendhat House at Brno, Czechoslovakia—a house evolved from the Barcelona pavilion—and for it he created the Tugendhat chair and the Brno chair. That year he became director of the Bauhaus, the famed German school of art which revolutionized 20th-century design. The growing strength of Nazism in Germany during the early 1930s forced the Bauhaus to move from Dessau to Berlin. Mies closed the school in 1933 but stayed on in Germany, trying to effect a change in the country's politics.

The American Years

Forced to flee Nazi Germany in 1937, Mies went to the United States; he became an American citizen in 1944. His work, and that of other modern architects, had been introduced to the American architectural scene by Philip Johnson and Henry-Russell Hitchcock in an exhibition held in 1932 at New York City's Museum of Modern Art and in its catalog, *The International Style: Architecture since 1922.*

Mies's philosophy of architecture, which was to dominate his designs in the United States, was exemplified in his revolutionary projects of 1919 and 1920-1921 for glass skyscrapers in Berlin. They were to be "new forms from the very nature of new problems." His 1922 project for a rein-forced-concrete office building epitomized all the ideals of the International Style; volume rather than mass, simplicity of surface treatment with no ornamentation, and horizontal emphasis (except in tall structures). Mies stated, "Reinforced concrete structures are skeletons by nature. No gingerbread. No fortress. Columns and girders eliminate bearing walls. This is skin and bones construction."

In 1938 Mies became director of architecture of the Illinois Institute of Technology (formerly the Armour Institute), an office he held until he resumed private practice in 1958. In his brief inaugural address he stated that "true education is concerned not only with practical goals but also with values. . . . Education must lead us from irresponsible opinion to true responsible judgment. . . ." He ended by quoting St. Augustine: "Beauty is the splendor of Truth."

A grid of 24-foot squares was the basis of Mies's Illinois Institute of Technology campus plan (1939-1940). Vincent Scully (1961) described it as a veritable "Renaissance townscape . . . conceived . . . upon a modular system of fixed perspectives" and compared it to a streetscape by the mannerist architect Giacomo da Vignola. The horizontal lines of perspective and the low vertical structural rhythm are common to both Renaissance spaces. Mies considered Crown Hall (completed 1956) on the campus, which houses the School of Architecture and Design, with its main floor an undivided space measuring 120 by 220 feet, his finest creation.

Particularly noteworthy among the residences and apartments that Mies built in and near Chicago are the Farnsworth house (1950) in Plano, Ill., and the pair of glass-sheathed apartment towers (1949-1951) on Lake Shore Drive in Chicago. He also designed Federal Center (1964), a three-building complex in the heart of Chicago's commercial area. In New York City he collaborated with Philip Johnson on the Seagram Building (1956-1958), a 38-story tower of gray and bronze glass, which was the ultimate realization of Mies's 1919 project for a glass-walled skyscraper. He died in Chicago on Aug. 18, 1969.

Mies, Frank Lloyd Wright, and Le Corbusier are the paternal triumvirate of 20th-century architecture. Mies's Werkbund apartment block of 1927 was a low-cost housing project of high-caliber design that has rarely been equaled even in the 1960s and early 1970s, when architects were desperately trying to solve the pressing need of well-designed housing. His Barcelona pavilion of 1929 was an esthetic contribution to 20th-century spatial design, comparable to Frank Lloyd Wright's Robie house and Le Corbusier's Villa Savoye.

Further Reading

A selection of drawings by Mies van der Rohe from the collection of the Museum of Modern Art is in *Ludwig Mies van der Rohe: Drawings* (1969). Biographies include Philip C. Johnson, *Mies van der Rohe* (1947; rev. ed. 1953); Ludwig Hilberseimer,

Mies van der Rohe (1956); and Arthur Drexler, *Ludwig Mies van der Rohe* (1960). Mies van der Rohe is discussed in Peter Blake, *The Master Builders* (1960; rev. ed. 1963); Vincent Scully, *Modern Architecture* (1961); and John Jacobus, *Twentieth-century Architecture: The Middle Years, 1940-65* (1966). □

Mi Fei

The Chinese painter, calligrapher, and critic Mi Fei (1051-1107) created the "Mi style" of ink-wash landscape painting. He was one of the four greatest calligraphers of the Sung dynasty and among the most influential art critics in Chinese history.

Mi Fei, also called Mi Fu, was born in Hsiang-yang, Hupei Province. He was known as a man of Wu, that is, the south-central region of China called Chiang-nan, "South of the (Yangtze) River." During the reign of Emperor Shentsung (1068-1086), Mi's mother served the future empress, and young Mi was therefore granted special "protégé appointment" to the civil service.

For the next 10 years Mi served in a variety of minor provincial posts, probably devoting most of his energy to the study of calligraphy and the collections of art his travels enabled him to see. During this period he began the connoisseur's notes on painting and calligraphy which would later be published as *Hua shih* (Painting History) and *Shu Shih* (Calligraphy History). While he did not begin to paint until years later, he was already a brilliant calligrapher.

Literati Esthetics

In 1081 Mi Fei met Su Shih, the great poet, calligrapher, and art theorist. This was the beginning of the formation of a circle of some of the most brilliant artists in history. Other members were Li Kung-lin, painter and antiquarian; Huang T'ing-chien, poet and calligrapher; and Chao Ta-nien, painter and art collector. Su Shih's cousin, the bamboo painter Wen T'ung, who had died in 1079, was also a key figure through his art and his influence on Su Shih.

Out of this association came the theory and practice of *wen-jen-hua*, or literati painting, which in all its manifestations has continued until the present to be the most dynamic and creative branch of the art. In place of the long-dominant view that painting was a public art, subject to public standards, scholar-painters held to the view expressed by Li Kung-lin: "I paint, as the poet sings, to give expression to my nature and emotions, and that is all."

Artists' Appreciation

The T'ang poet Tu Fu, now universally regarded as "China's greatest poet," was largely ignored until discovered by these 11th-century scholars. The two greatest scholar-painters of earlier centuries, Ku K'ai-chih and Wang Wei, were rescued from obscurity and lifted to the eminence and esteem they have ever since enjoyed. It is thus scarcely possible to overestimate the esthetic and critical impact of the late Northern Sung literati on the fate of the three greatest arts of Chinese civilization. Indeed, the poetry of Su Shih, the figure painting of Li Kung-lin, and the calligraphy of Mi Fei became standards against which men would be judged for the next 500 years.

Crucial to an understanding of the flavor of life and art in this great age is an appreciation of the quality of personal relationships within this artistic and intellectual circle. Art was nothing without personality, and personality was almost an art—not, however, in the sense of deliberate eccentricity, but as a nourishing of the innate qualities of strength of character, will, honesty, creativity, mental curiosity, and integrity. When Su Shih and Mi Fei met again later in their lives, they were well aware that they were cultural heroes. They took pride in this knowledge and found the keenest creative stimulation in it.

Mi's Figure Painting

Mi said that he did not begin to paint until 7 years before his death, but it is possible that he had tried landscape painting slightly earlier. At the time, the T'ang figure painter Wu Tao-tzu was universally praised as the "standard for all time," and his followers were legion. Mi Fei rejected this image, in no small part doubtless because it was so popular, and declared that he admired only the "lofty antiquity" of the long-neglected first master of figure painting, Ku K'ai-chih. Mi Fei claimed to paint only the "loyal and virtuous men of old." Vigorous precedent for this view had come in 1060, when Su Shih had written a poem after looking at paintings by Wu Taotzu and Wang Wei. Wu Tao-tzu, he wrote, while heroic beyond compare, could finally be judged only in terms of the craft of painting, that is, by technique and formal likeness. Wang Wei, in contrast, "was basically an old poet" who "sought meaning beyond the forms."

To these men anything that smacked of mere craft, divorced from personal expression, was to be rejected. Their most obvious foils were the imperial academicians and professional painters who commanded a large popular audience. Mi Fei, a caustic and relentless critic, generally described their art as "fit only to defile the walls of a wine shop." He even accused the academy of murdering one of its members who had been too gifted and original and thus had threatened the status quo.

At an opposite extreme were the "untrammeled" masters of the 9th and 10th centuries, who had broken every rule and defied every classical model in their quest for artistic freedom, even going so far as to paint with their hair and hands, or their naked bodies. The "untrammeled" masters won the admiration of Mi Fei and his friends but were far too uncontrolled and eccentric to be emulated. Instead, it was the "primitive" and forgotten masters of the orthodox heritage to which they turned.

The only remnant of Mi Fei's figure painting, of which he was so proud, is an engraving on the "Master of the Waves" cliff at Kuei-lin, Kuang-hsi. It is said to be a 13th-century copy of Mi's self-portrait and is a strangely archaic, boldly and simply conceived image as if from centuries past, and quite possibly intended to evoke Ku K'ai-chih.

His Landscape Painting

It was Mi's landscape painting, however, for which he was so admired in later centuries. In it, too, he displayed his utter rejection of dominant tendencies and his dependence upon neglected older innovations. In the late 11th century the influence of the brilliant 10th-century landscape master Li Ch'eng was at its peak. Mi Fei criticized Li Ch'eng for achieving "more ingenuity than a sense of reality" and displayed only contempt for his followers. He advocated, instead, the "natural and unassertive" qualities of the all but forgotten 10th-century master Tung Yüan. It is highly significant that Mi Fei, who was a man of Chiang-nan, turned back to the two greatest native masters of Chiang-nan, Ku K'ai-chih and Tung Yüan, for inspiration. Regional pride and identity were major issues.

The landscape style that Mi Fei developed from Tung Yüan placed emphasis on the misty, amorphous aspect of nature that created "inexhaustible mystery." His technique is described as "Mi dots." Starting with very pale ink, he began painting on a slightly wet paper or silk, amassing clusters of shadowed forms, then adding darker ink gradually, building up amorphous, drifting mountain silhouettes bathed in wet, cloaking mist. The style is best seen in a large hanging scroll, the *Tower of the Rising Clouds*. On the painting is an inscription: "Heaven sends a timely rain; clouds issue from mountains and streams." This manner had an incalculable effect on later painters. From the 14th century on, every painter worth his salt could create a Mi Fei-style landscape at the slightest provocation.

A more difficult manner is seen in several paintings attributed to Mi, including *Spring Mountains and Pine Trees*. Archaism, as in Mi's figure painting, is the dominant mode. The mountains are conceived in the primeval state as three triangles side by side, just as the word "mountain" was written as triangles on the oracle bones of the 2d millennium B.C. The pines are similarly conceived, as roots growing into the earth, trunk and branches stretching into the sky. In such works, Mi Fei appears to be attempting to free himself of all cliché and mannerism and to paint as if no one had ever painted before him.

Mi Fei's eldest son, Mi Yu-jen, was also an excellent painter and continued his father's tradition.

Further Reading

A good discussion of Mi Fei is in Osvald Sirén, *Chinese Painting: Leading Masters and Principles* (7 vols., 1956-1958). ☐

Barbara Mikulski

Barbara Ann Mikulski became the first Democratic woman elected to the United States Senate to hold a seat not previously held by her husband.

Barbara Ann Milulski is known as the feisty senator from Baltimore, she is also the first Democratic woman ever to have served in both Houses of Congress, and the first woman ever to win a statewide election in her home state of Maryland.

"We elected a Democratic woman named Barbara and somebody named Mikulski, and the Senate won't be the same from now on!" said Mikulski after capturing the seat left open by the retirement of Republican Charles McC. Mathias, Jr., in November of 1986. Described by *Time* magazine as "a four-foot-11-inch bundle of energy with a voice like a Baltimore harbor foghorn," Mikulski swept past her Republican opponent, Linda Chavez, with 61 percent of the vote. Then-president Ronald Reagan, who had campaigned in Maryland to defeat her, called Mikulski a "wily liberal," but, as *Time* reported, he was only half right. "Wily is about the last word Marylanders would apply to Mikulski. Blunt, outspoken and feisty would describe her better. She is a fierce debater, with a fondness for pointed quips." "I define public service as not only to be a help but to be an advocate. . . . In the Senate, I plan to use the good mind, the good mouth, the good heart that God gave me," said Mikulski in *Time*.

The granddaughter of Polish immigrants, Mikulski can certainly be called liberal. The unabashed feminist backs a nuclear freeze and consistently votes for increased social spending. She is a staunch supporter of organized labor and supports protectionist legislation to save American jobs. While serving as a United States congresswoman, Mikulski was a harsh critic of the Reagan administration's defense

and foreign policies, and voted to cancel the MX missile project and cut off aid to Nicaraguan contras. "I just don't take an issue because it's popular," Mikulski said in *Business Week.* "I'm a fighter." In an article in the *Washington Post,* Mikulski maintained she still has the soul of a street organizer. "Nobody would ever use the term mellow to describe me. . . . I'm not caffeine-free, that's for sure." Indeed, a Capitol Hill staff member told *Business Week,* "When she walks into a room, it's like a brawler came in."

Mikulski got her start in politics in 1968 with the organization of a coalition of black, Polish, Greek, Lithuanian, and Ukrainian Americans to block construction of a 16-lane highway that would have destroyed areas of East Baltimore, including parts of Fells Point that boasted the first black home ownership neighborhood in the city. Called SCAR (Southeast Council Against the Road), the neighborhood group fought against an entrenched Democratic political organization at City Hall that supported the highway project. Despite the strength of the opposition, SCAR, led by Mikulski, was successful in blocking the highway proposal.

That battle whetted Mikulski's appetite for getting involved on a more formal political basis. In 1971, she ran for a seat on the Baltimore City Council. Campaigning as an outsider taking on established political machines, she wore out five pairs of shoes and knocked on 15,000 doors to spread her message throughout the Highlandtown neighborhood she grew up in. Potential constituents were told that "by being part of a group whether it's a PTA, a neighborhood association, a coalition against toxic waste, working together can make a change," as Mikulski later recalled in *Ms.* magazine. "For a woman, with no previous political experience, to run out there was a tremendous accomplishment," observed Peter N. Marudas, a political advisor to Maryland Senator Paul S. Sarbanes, in the *Washington Post.*

Mikulski's penchant for community organizing came as no surprise to her parents. William and Christine Mikulski operated a grocery store, Willy's Market, across the street from their home. Barbara, the eldest of three daughters, attended Catholic grade school and high school. The *Washington Post* noted that even as a little girl, "Barbara showed a special talent. While other kids were more athletic and agile than the klutzy, chubby Barbara, she had an uncanny ability to control situations. Tired of skinning her knees trying to jump rope 'double dutch,' Barbara coaxed her little cousins and friends into taking part in plays and shows in her parents' garage, shows in which she served as playwright, producer and director."

Mikulski considered becoming a nun, but concluded that she was too rebellious to accept the discipline of a religious order. Instead, she trained as a social worker, earning her bachelor's degree at Mount St. Agnes College in Baltimore, then continuing her studies at the University of Maryland. She graduated in 1965 with a master's degree in social work.

Mikulski first worked for the Associated Catholic Charities and then the Baltimore Department of Social Services. By 1966, she was an assistant chief of community organizing for the city social services department, working on a plan to decentralize welfare programs. While serving these organizations, primarily in cases of child abuse and neglect, Mikulski developed the deep concern for the rights of children and families that she later took to Washington.

Mikulski expressed many of her concerns in an essay titled "Who Speaks for Ethnic America?" for the *New York Times* in September of 1970. Ethnic immigrants who came to the United States at the turn of the century, she wrote, "constructed the skyscrapers, operated the railroads, worked on the docks, factories, steel mills and in the mines. Though our labor was in demand, we were not accepted. Our names, language, food and cultural customers were the subject of ridicule. We were discriminated against by banks, institutions of higher learning and other organizations controlled by the Yankee Patricians. There were no protective mechanisms for safety, wages and tenure." Mikulski maintained that it was smarter for these groups to organize than to fight, "to form an alliance based on mutual issues, interdependence and respect."

During her five years on the Baltimore City Council, Mikulski became known as an effective, hands-on representative of the people. Her campaign literature said she "got things done," and she did—from potholes to public education, when Baltimoreans had problems or needed help, they knew they could depend on Mikulski.

In 1976, Congressman Paul S. Sarbanes, of Maryland's Third Congressional District (Baltimore), announced his candidacy for the United States Senate. Mikulski was one of six people to join the race to take his place in the United States House of Representatives. Using her vast network of community supporters and volunteers, Mikulski won the Democratic primary and went on to represent the third district in the United States House of Representatives.

When she arrived on Capitol Hill in January of 1977, Mikulski got an appointment to the Merchant Marine & Fisheries Committee, where she could work on legislation affecting the Port of Baltimore, one of the state's largest employers. She also became the first woman ever appointed to the powerful House Energy & Commerce Committee, which gave her a platform to lobby on issues including railroads, telecommunications, and health care. She was a prime mover behind the 1984 Child Abuse Act and a major proponent of the Equal Rights Amendment, and she helped establish the Congressional Women's Caucus. "She's been a real stalwart, a feisty spark plug on women's issues, especially fighting for insurance reform," said Congresswoman Pat Schroeder (a Democrat from Colorado), in *Ms.*

After five terms as congresswoman, in 1986 Mikulski set her sights on the United States Senate seat being vacated by retiring Senator Charles McC. Mathias, Jr. Her opponent was Linda Chavez, a former staff director of the United States Commission on Civil Rights, who was a well-spoken and well-connected Republican.

Chavez apparently thought the "frumpy, loud and sometimes rude" Mikulski would be a pushover, wrote *People.* However, Chavez made the "mistake of trying to smear Barbara's hometown image. She called Mikulski a 'San Francisco-style Democrat' who ought to 'come out of the closet,' and accused one of Mikulski's aides of promoting 'fascist feminism' and 'anti-male attitudes,'" wrote *Ms.*

in 1987 when the magazine named Mikulski a ''Woman of the Year.''

To beat Chavez, Mikulski sought out her supporters from her days as an activist social worker, arranging meetings with business and civic leaders and longtime feminist allies. She also hired pollster Harrison Hickman, who had developed a method for analyzing ''the woman factor,'' she told *Ms.* ''We wanted to be sure that people's positive feelings toward me weren't just 'Gosh, isn't this fun? A woman Senator.'''

To compete with Chavez's polished image, Mikulski hired Lillian Brown, a makeup advisor to presidential candidates, to show her how to use low-gloss makeup to make her appear more attractive on television. ''Mikulski replaced her old, dark-framed glasses with a pair of rimless, glare-proof bifocals. She experimented with different color dresses and varying hemlines so she wouldn't look dumpy. And she learned how to sit properly and take advantage of camera angles to enhance her looks on television,'' the *Washington Post* reported. By the time Mikulski was sworn in as a United States senator, she had lost more than 40 pounds through vigorous dieting and exercise, and had toned down her East Baltimore street lingo. The *Washington Post* noted that she had ''cooled her street-fighter style to make her way in the (Senate) club.''

The Democratic party's congressional leadership showed her off by temporarily assigning Mikulski to Harry Truman's old seat on the Senate floor. According to the *Washington Post,* since her arrival her Senate colleagues ''have watched closely—and they have been impressed. The former street organizer and 'Queen of the Ethnics' has become more than a mere member of the club. She is well on her way to becoming a major player.''

Mikulski, with help from her colleague Senator Paul S. Sarbanes (Democrat-Maryland) and Majority Leader Robert C. Byrd (Democrat-West Virginia), landed four of the best committee assignments of any freshman senator. The top prize was her appointment to the Senate Appropriations Committee, the political equivalent of hitting a home run the first time at bat, since all budget bills come before the committee. She also became a member of the Senate Labor and Human Resources Committee, which handles most major welfare reform legislation; the Environment and Public Works Committee, with jurisdiction over road and bridge construction; and the Small Business Committee. She also serves on numerous subcommittees, a full schedule that has forced her to carefully pick the issues she gets involved in.

In her first term as senator, Mikulski pushed through various initiatives on behalf of Maryland, including money for the Beltsville Agricultural Research Center and Maryland's oyster beds, $24 million in urban mass transit funds for the state, and continued operation of a weather station on Maryland's eastern shore. Mikulski, who delivered a rousing speech early in the course of the Democratic National Convention in July of 1992, was reelected to another term that year and continued her high-profile involvement. *Science* magazine commented that Mikulski has ''more influence over nonmilitary R&D [research and development] than perhaps anybody else now on Capitol Hill.''

Mikulski's influence affects budgets for the National Science Foundation (NSF), National Space and Aeronautics Space Administration (NASA), and the Environmental Protection Agency (EPA), among others. In 1994, she was largely responsible for pushing through the largest congressional funding increase that the National Science Foundation had seen in 11 years. She was also aggressive in pushing for funding to modernize the offices of the Food and Drug Administration (FDA), housed in her home state. In an interview in *Science,* Mikulski noted the importance of funding projects that are linked to practical issues, although the long-term benefits may not be apparent to some. When deciding between affordable housing for the elderly and a space station, for instance, many may not see why space exploration is necessary. ''Those are the choices,'' Mikulski remarked, ''and I think it's going to be very tough.''

In addition to her political career, Maluski wrote a political mystery novel, *Capitol Offense* (published in 1996), with Marylouise Oates. While attending the Democratic Convention in Chicago, she and her co-author held a book signing to promote the new book.

Further Reading

Business Week, August 11, 1986.
Ms., January 1987; September 1988.
People, November 3, 1986.
Science, April 8, 1994, pp. 192-194; July 22, 1994, p. 469.
Time, November 17, 1986.
Washington Post, August 28, 1996.
Washington Post Magazine, June 14, 1987. □

Luis Milán

Luis Milán (ca. 1500-c. 1561) was the earliest Spanish composer to publish a collection of secular music.

Luis Milán was born of noble parents at Valencia and presumably died there. His *Libro de música de vihuela de mano; Intitulado El Maestro* (1535/1536) was the first of the seven vihuela tablature books published in 16th-century Spain. He also published two other books: a book on parlor games for gallants and their ladies to play, *Libro de motes de damas y caualleros; Intitulado el juego de mandar* (1535), and *El Cortesano* (1561; *The Courtier*), an imitation of Baldassare Castiglione's popular etiquette book, *Il Cortegiano* (1528).

Like the other Spanish vihuela tablatures, *El Maestro* purports to be a self-instructing manual, easy pieces filling book I, hard ones book II. But unlike the others, it contains no transcriptions of other masters' works, and the top line of the six horizontal lines in the tablature refers to the highest-pitched course rather than the lowest. Dedicated to the Portuguese king João III, *El Maestro* is the only Spanish tablature that contains any Portuguese songs. In addition it includes *six villancicos* (polyphonic songs) and four romances in Spanish and six Italian *sonetos*. Although free of religious pieces, *El Maestro* does end with an elaborate explanation of the church modes in polyphonic music.

Forty fantasias, four *tentos* (alternately called fantasias, a word which for Milán means simply "product of the imagination"), and six pavanes interlard the vocal music in *El Maestro*. Alternate settings of ten of the vocal pieces allow the singer to improvise long virtuoso runs between lines of the text. Milán's pavanes, especially those on Italian lines, are the most transcribed and performed Spanish vihuela music of the Golden Age.

Milán's *El Cortesano* (dedicated to Philip II) pictures life a generation earlier at the Valencian court of Germaine de Foix and her third husband, Ferdinand, Duke of Calabria. In retrospect, Milán sees himself as *arbiter elegantiarum* at their polyglot court, where nearly everyone was a poetaster idling his time in hunts, biting repartee, jests, masquerades, and amorous escapades. Juan Fernández de Heredia, his defeated rival in one such escapade (described in *El Cortesano*, 1874 ed.), was the most famous Valencian poet of the time. In return for the snipings scattered through every day of the six into which *El Cortesano* is divided, Fernández de Heredia advised Milán to stick with the only art of which he was a master, vihuela playing (*Obras*, 1955 ed.). Dance pieces were his forte, not singing, and as a teacher Milán was guilty of neglect or even cruelty, claimed Fernández de Heredia.

Further Reading

Milán's *El Maestro* has been edited and translated by Charles Jacobs (1971) and has also been published in modern notation in an Italian edition (1965). Milán is discussed in John M. Ward, *The Vihuela de Mano and Its Music, 1536-1576,* New York University Ph.D. dissertation (1953). □

Nelson Appleton Miles

Nelson Appleton Miles (1839-1925), American soldier, participated in many of the campaigns against the western Indian tribes.

Nelson A. Miles was born on Aug. 8, 1839, at Westminster, Mass. After completing his schooling at the age of 17, he moved to Boston, where he became a clerk and studied military tactics at night. At the outbreak of the Civil War he used his savings and borrowed money to raise a company of volunteers and was commissioned a lieutenant. He was able to transfer to the 61st New York Volunteers as a lieutenant colonel in September 1862. His rise to prominence was then meteoric, and he emerged from the war a major general of volunteers and recipient of the Medal of Honor. He married Mary Hoyt Sherman in 1868 (a niece of Gen. William T. Sherman and of Senator John Sherman of Ohio). Family influence brought him a colonelcy in the Army and command of the 40th Infantry Regiment.

After the Civil War, Miles served extensively in the Indian wars of the American West. In 1875 he helped defeat the Comanche, Kiowa, and Cheyenne on the South Plains. Transferred north, he aided in driving Sitting Bull and the Sioux into Canada in 1876, and the following year he received the surrender of Chief Joseph of the Nez Percé after marching his troops 160 miles through wintry cold. In 1880 he was promoted to brigadier general and given command of the Department of the Columbia. In 1885 he was given command of the Department of the Missouri but was transferred to the Department of Arizona in April 1886. There he secured Geronimo's surrender.

In 1890, after his promotion to major general, Miles suppressed the "ghost dance" craze (prompted by a messianic cult) of the Sioux Indians. Four years later, following orders from President Grover Cleveland, he quelled the Pullman strike in Chicago. For these feats he was made commanding general of the Army in 1895, a post he held until his retirement in 1903. His record during the Spanish-American War was not brilliant, but in 1901 he was given the coveted promotion to lieutenant general. He had not, however, achieved the goal he most desired. In every election following 1888, he had expected a presidential nomination. Following his retirement, he lived in Washington, D.C., where he died on May 15, 1925. He was buried with military honors at Arlington National Cemetery.

Further Reading

Hoping his life story would gain him the presidential nomination, Miles wrote his autobiography twice: *Personal Recollections*

and Observations of General Nelson A. Miles (1896) and *Serving the Republic: Memoirs of the Civil and Military Life of Nelson A. Miles* (1911). Virginia W. Johnson, *The Unregimented General: A Biography of Nelson A. Miles* (1962), is sympathetic if uncritical, while Newton F. Tolman, *The Search for General Miles* (1968), is of minor value.

Additional Sources

Amchan, Arthur J., *The most famous soldier in America: a biography of Lt. Gen. Nelson A. Miles, 1839-1925,* Alexandria, Va.: Amchan Publications, 1989.

Miles, Nelson Appleton, *Nelson A. Miles, a documentary biography of his military career, 1861-1903,* Glendale, Calif.: A.H. Clark Co., 1985.

Wooster, Robert, *Nelson A. Miles and the twilight of the frontier army,* Lincoln: University of Nebraska Press, 1993. □

Darius Milhaud

The French composer and teacher Darius Milhaud (born 1892) was the main champion of polytonality in the 20th century.

D
arius Milhaud was born on Sept. 4, 1892, in Aix-en-Provence. His family, descended from a line of Jews established in the region for generations, had the time and means to encourage their son's musical interests: violin lessons at age 7, participation in the quartet organized by his violin teacher at age 13, and studies at the Paris Conservatory (1909-1912) mark the well-planned stages of his student career. Typical of his generation, he voiced a strong distaste for the music of Richard Wagner and an equally strong admiration for Modest Mussorgsky and Claude Debussy. Sensing, nevertheless, the dangers of impressionism for his own development—"too much fog," "too many perfumed breezes"—Milhaud resolved to "break the spell" of Debussy, although "my heart always remained faithful."

Anti-impressionism was undoubtedly one of the two major factors uniting, just after World War I, the group of composers known as Les Six; the author Jean Cocteau was the other. Not a musician and therefore, by his own designation, not eligible for "membership" in the group, Cocteau was nevertheless its guiding spirit. His collaboration with Milhaud resulted in *Le Boeuf sur le toit* (1919), *Le Train bleu* (1924), and *Le Pauvre matelot* (1926). Cocteau also seems to have been responsible for stimulating Milhaud's interest in jazz, which resulted in one of his most enduring works, *La Création du monde* (1923).

Yet, for all their success, the Cocteau works do not reveal the essential Milhaud. Before Cocteau there had been the experience of yet deeper formative influence: that of the writer Paul Claudel. On first reading Claudel, in 1911, Milhaud was struck by a "force which shakes the human heart . . . like an element of nature." The two artists began a long collaboration, which Milhaud said was "the best thing of my life as a musician." They collaborated on *Agamemnon* (1913), *Les Choéphores* (1915), *Les*

Euménides (1917-1922), *Christophe Colomb* (1928), *Maximilien* (1932), *Bolívar* (1952-1953), and *David* (1954).

Claudel was minister of France to Brazil (1917-1919) and took Milhaud along as his secretary. In Rio de Janeiro, Milhaud worked out the details of the technique which, rightly or wrongly, came to be particularly identified with his style: polytonality. What had been a "superimposition of chords proceeding by masses" in *Les Choéphores* was to become in *L'Enfant prodigue* (1918) a polytonality residing "no longer in chords but in the meetings of lines."

If polytonality was a unifying factor for Milhaud's style, his origins served to define his esthetic: "*Latinity, Mediterranean* are words which have a deep resonance in me." The locales of his stage works—Greece, Palestine, Mexico, and Brazil—are significant for their strong affinities with his native Provence, and the music of these places furnished him with many melodic and rhythmic ideas. The themes of southern landscape and popular life are so omnipresent in his vocal works that they have tended to obscure his image as a composer of absolute music, that is, music free from extramusical implications.

The number of symphonies (16), concertos (31), and chamber works (about 60) that Milhaud composed is considerable; indeed, in 20th-century terms his production of over 400 works is enormous, a fact which engendered some negative criticism about his work, such as unevenness in quality, inattention to detail, and signs of haste. Such accusations ignore Milhaud's basic motivation as a composer, namely, that the act of creation is more important than the thing created. His production was all the more remarkable in view of his teaching schedule. From 1948 on he spent alternate years in Paris and at Mills College, Calif.

Further Reading

Milhaud's own account is *Notes without Music: An Autobiography* (1949; trans. 1953). Biographical information on Milhaud is also in Edward Burlingame Hill, *Modern French Music* (1924; rev. ed. 1970), and David Ewen, *The World of Twentieth Century Music* (1968). □

Pavel Nikolayevich Miliukov

The Russian historian and statesman Pavel Nikolayevich Miliukov (1859-1943) supported the Westernization and modernization of Russia while criticizing the ruthlessness and authoritarianism of its government.

Pavel Miliukov was born on Jan. 27, 1859, into a middle-class family in Moscow. He manifested an early interest in both history and politics. As a consequence of his independent views, he was suspended for a period of one year from the University of Moscow in 1881. He completed his formal training in the historical-philosophical faculty of Moscow University in 1886 and began the extensive archival research on his magisterial thesis, *National Economy in Russia in the First Quarter of the XVIIIth Century and the Reforms of Peter the Great,* which he defended successfully and published in 1892. In the meantime he began his teaching career as lecturer at the University of Moscow and as a secondary school teacher.

In the mid-1890s Miliukov became progressively more concerned with what may be called the political implications of his theoretical position as historian. As a Westernizer and liberal, Miliukov supported in-depth Westernization of the Russian national economy as well as public involvement in governmental decision making. These views, together with his efforts to encourage formation and activity of middle-class liberal organizations, were regarded by the czarist government as a direct challenge to established authority.

Miliukov was dismissed from the University of Moscow in 1895 and forbidden to teach in the Russian Empire; in addition, the Ministry of Internal Affairs arranged for his exile, first from Moscow and ultimately from the Russian Empire. Thus, in 1895, he left to accept a teaching position in Serbia and did not return to Russia until 1899. He was arrested once more, in 1900, for his liberal public utterances. After this he embarked on a series of exiles, which he characteristically combined with professional activities as a teacher and writer. He spent parts of 1901 and 1902 in England and parts of 1903, 1904, and 1905 in the United States. Miliukov continued his historical research and writing at an unabated pace, publishing no fewer than four major works in Russian history, including his classic *Out-*

lines of the History of Russian Culture (3 vols., 1896-1903) as well as an edition of his lectures at the University of Chicago, *Russia and its Crisis* (1905). In the meantime, police harassment did not prevent him from becoming a principal contributor to the left-wing journal of the liberal movement, *Osvobozhdeniie* (Liberation).

With the outbreak of the Revolution of 1905, Miliukov returned to Russia to participate in the organization of the Constitutional Democratic (Kadet) party and to accept the editorship of the party organ, *Rech'* (Speech). He played a leading role in his party's delegation to the Third and Fourth Dumas (1907-1912, 1912-1916). He strongly supported the extension of private ownership of property, rapid development of industrial technology, and close political ties with western Europe. As a corollary to these views, he continued to support the concepts of broadly based electoral franchise and representative government, both of which were honored more in the breach than in fact in the interval between 1906 and 1917.

With the outbreak of World War I, Miliukov, while supporting the war aims of the government, became more critical of the actual prosecution of the war. In 1916 he participated in the so-called Progressive Bloc, which demanded a reorganization of the government to reflect party representation in the Duma. Typically, when the Revolution of 1917 broke out, Miliukov seems to have interpreted the events as resulting especially from a lack of public confidence in the handling of the war. Thus, as principal liberal critic of the war, Miliukov was invited to become minister of foreign affairs of the new provisional government, which the Duma took responsibility for organizing.

A rush of events during the spring and summer of 1917 proved the inadequacy of Miliukov's analysis, not only of the motivation for the Revolution but also of the relevance of the entire liberal position to the political crisis in which Russia found itself. By late spring Miliukov's position in the spectrum of political pressures to which the provisional government was subject was untenably conservative. Under fire from the workers' organizations (the soviets) and the socialist parties, he resigned from the Cabinet. After the October Revolution, he left European Russia to join the Volunteer Army in the south. By 1918 the position of the counterrevolution seemed hopeless, and he left Russia for the West.

A close student of Russian history and a participant in Russian politics, Miliukov was fated to observe some of the most significant political events in his country's history from Paris. A principal contributor to, and then editor of, the emigrant newspaper *Poslednye novosti* (Latest News), Miliukov continued his work as a commentator on the Russian political scene but without being able to influence it significantly. He died at Aix-les-Bains, France, on March 31, 1943.

Further Reading

Fascinating as period history as well as informative on Miliukov's career is his *Political Memoirs, 1905-1917* (2 vols., 1955; trans., 1 vol., 1967). A full-length study of Miliukov is Thomas Riha, *A Russian European: Paul Miliukov in Russian Politics* (1969). Studies of Miliukov also appear in Anatole G. Mazour, *Modern Russian Historiography* (1939; 2d ed. 1958), and Bernadotte E. Schmitt, ed., *Some Historians of Modern Europe: Essays in Historiography* (1942). □

Harvey Bernard Milk

Harvey Milk (1930-1978), a San Francisco city politician, helped open the door for gays and lesbians in the United States by bringing civil rights for homosexuals, among many other issues, to the political table. Since Milk's murder in 1978, he has remained a symbol of activism.

Although there are still relatively few openly gay politicians in the United States, their numbers would be even fewer had it not been for Harvey Milk. His 1977 election to San Francisco's Board of Supervisors brought a message of hope to gays and lesbians across the country. Milk served as a city supervisor for less than a year before being murdered along with Mayor George Moscone by a rival politician, but he was instrumental in bringing the gay rights agenda to the attention of the American public. Milk was not a one-issue politician, however. For him, gay issues were merely one part of an overall human rights perspective. During his tragically short politi-

cal career, Milk battled for a wide range of social reforms in such areas as education, public transportation, child-care, and low-income housing. Milk's murder—and the surprisingly light sentence his killer received by virtue of the famous "Twinkie Defense"—made him a martyr to members of gay communities throughout the United States.

Harvey Bernard Milk was born on May 22, 1930 in Woodmere, New York, a town on Long Island. His grandfather, an immigrant from Lithuania, had worked his way up from a simple peddler to owner of a respected department store. Milk's father, William, was also involved in the retail clothing trade. By his early teens, Milk was already aware of his homosexuality, but he chose to keep it to himself. In high school, he was active in sports, and was considered a class clown. He also developed a passion for opera, and would frequently go alone to the Metropolitan Opera House.

Tried Hand at Several Careers

Following his graduation in 1947, Milk entered New York State College for Teachers in Albany. He received his college degree in 1951. Three months later, Milk joined the navy. He served as a chief petty officer on a submarine rescue ship during the Korean War, and eventually reached the rank of junior lieutenant before his honorable discharge in 1955. Returning to New York, Milk took a job teaching high school. By this time, Milk was living openly with his lover, Joe Campbell, though he still kept his homosexuality hidden from his family. After a couple of years, Milk became disenchanted with teaching. He tried his hand at a number of other occupations before landing a job with the Wall

Street investment firm Bache and Company in 1963. At Bache, Milk discovered that he had a knack for finance and investment, and his ascent of the corporate ladder was swift.

In spite of his unconventional lifestyle, Milk's political and social values were conservative through the early 1960s. He even campaigned for Barry Goldwater in the 1964 presidential election. As the decade progressed, however, his views gradually began to change. Milk's new romantic interest, Jack Galen McKinley, worked in theater, and through him Milk became involved as well. He was particularly interested in the experimental work of director Tom O'Horgan. Since the presence of gays in the theater world was very visible, Milk began to come to terms more completely with his homosexual identity. At the same time, his overall world view began to evolve into a more left-leaning, countercultural one.

In 1968 McKinley was hired as stage director for O'Horgan's San Francisco production of the musical *Hair*. Milk decided to move with McKinley to California, where he got a job as a financial analyst. Eventually, the conflict between his personal and professional lives became to much for Milk. During a 1970 protest of the American invasion of Cambodia, Milk burned his BankAmericard in front of a crowd of people. He was fired from his job later that day. His ties to mainstream life now broken, Milk returned to New York and theater work. By this time, he was sporting the long-hair and a beard, and looked more or less like an aging hippie. In 1972 he moved with his new partner, Scott Smith, back to San Francisco. The pair opened a camera shop on Castro Street, in the heart of what was emerging as the city's most recognizably gay neighborhood.

Pushed toward Politics by Watergate

Milk entered the political arena for the first time in 1973. Angered by the Watergate scandal and by a variety of local issues, he decided to run for a spot on the Board of Supervisors, San Francisco's city council. Using the gay community as his base of support, Milk sought to forge a populist coalition with other disenfranchised groups, including several of the city's diverse ethnic groups. His campaign slogan, "Milk has something for everybody," reflected this approach. Of the 32 candidates in the race, Milk came in tenth, not a bad showing for a long-haired, openly gay Jewish man with no political experience and relatively meager campaign funds. Though he lost the election, he gained enough support to put him on the city's political map. Because of his popularity in his own largely gay district, he became known as the "Mayor of Castro Street."

Milk spent much of the next year preparing for his next election campaign. He cultivated a more mainstream look and gave up smoking marijuana. He also revitalized the Castro Village Association as a powerful civic organization, and launched the popular Castro Street Fair. In addition, he conducted a voter registration drive that brought 2,000 new voters onto the rolls, and he began writing a newspaper column for the *Bay Area Reporter*.

Milk ran for supervisor again in 1975, this time wearing a suit and short hair. Although he gained the support of

several important labor unions, he lost again, this time placing seventh, just behind the six incumbents. In recognition of Milk's growing power base, however, newly-elected Mayor George Moscone appointed Milk to the Board of Permit Appeals, his first public office. After just a few weeks, however, Milk announced his intention to run for the state assembly. That disclosure led to his removal from his city post. Running against the entrenched Democratic party apparatus on the campaign theme "Harvey Milk vs. the Machine," Milk lost yet again, by a mere 4,000 votes. By this time, however, he had established a formidable political machine of his own, the San Francisco Gay Democratic Club. In 1977, on his third try, Milk was finally elected to the Board of Supervisors, becoming the first openly gay elected official in the city's history.

Emphasized Neighborhood and Individual Rights

Several key themes characterized Milk's successful campaign, as well as his short tenure as a city official. One was his demand that government be responsive to the needs of individuals. Another was his ongoing emphasis on gay rights. A third theme was the fight to preserve the distinctive character of the city's neighborhoods. As city supervisor, Milk was the driving force behind the passage of a gay-rights ordinance that prohibited discrimination in housing and employment based on sexual orientation. At his urging, the city announced an initiative to hire more gay and lesbian police officers. He also initiated programs that benefited minorities, workers, and the elderly. On top of that, Milk gained national attention for his role in defeating a state senate proposal that would have prohibited gays and lesbians from teaching in public schools in California.

On November 27, 1978, Milk and Mayor Moscone were shot to death in City Hall by Dan White, a conservative former city supervisor who had quit the Board to protest the passage of the city's gay rights ordinance. In his trial for the killings, White's attorneys employed what came to be known as the "Twinkie Defense." They claimed that the defendant had eaten so much junk food that his judgment had become impaired. Amazingly, White was convicted only of voluntary manslaughter, meaning he would receive the lightest sentence possible for a person who has admitted to intentionally killing somebody. The verdict, which appeared to signal that society condoned violence against gays, outraged homosexuals and their supporters across the United States. In San Francisco, riots erupted, resulting in hundreds of injuries, a dozen burned police cars, and about $250,000 in property damage. The following night, thousands of people flocked to Castro Street to celebrate what would have been Milk's 49th birthday.

Since his death, Milk has become a symbol for the gay community of both what has been achieved and what remains to be done. He has been immortalized in the names of the Harvey Milk Democratic Club (formerly the San Francisco Gay Democratic Club), Harvey Milk High School in New York, and San Francisco's annual Harvey Milk Memorial Parade. In 1985 the film *The Times of Harvey Milk* won the Academy Award for Best Documentary. Ten years later,

Harvey Milk, an opera co-commissioned by the Houston Grand Opera, the New York City Opera, and the San Francisco Opera, premiered in Houston. Although he is best remembered in the gay community, Milk's message of empowerment has served as an inspiration for people of all ethnicities and orientations.

Further Reading

Shilts, Randy, *The Mayor of Castro Street,* St. Martin's Press, 1982.

Weiss, Mike, *Double Play: The San Francisco City Hall Killings,* Addison-Wesley, 1984.

Foss, Karen A., "Harvey Milk: "You Have to Give Them Hope," in *Journal of the West,* April 1988, pp. 75-81.

New York Times, November 28, 1978, p. 33. □

James Mill

The Scottish philosopher and journalist James Mill (1773-1836) implemented and popularized utilitarianism. Although possessing little originality of thought, he indirectly influenced the development of one of the main currents of 19th-century philosophy through the sheer force of his personality.

James Mill's father was a shoemaker in the small village of Northwater Bridge, where James was born and attended the local school. His mother, Isabel, was quite ambitious for the social advancement of her first son, and James, unlike his younger sister and brother, was forbidden manual labor so that he could devote himself exclusively to education and become a gentleman. Through Isabel's intervention and his own intelligence and self-discipline, Mill secured the patronage of the local lord, Sir John Stuart. He entered the University of Edinburgh to study for the ministry. He was impressed by the lectures of Dugald Stewart, leader of the Scottish school of "commonsense" philosophy.

Mill was licensed to preach in 1798 and for the next 4 years earned his living mainly by tutoring. In 1802 he traveled to London in order to take up journalism. He translated, wrote reviews, and edited two journals. In 1805 he married Harriet Burrow, and they later had nine children. His first son, John Stuart Mill, was born in 1806, the year he began his *History of India,* which was completed 11 years later. This 10-volume work became a standard reference and earned its author a permanent position with the East India Company. Mill's achievement was to interpret historical events in terms of political, economic, and sociological factors.

In 1808 Mill met Jeremy Bentham and became closely associated with his other disciples, including the historian George Grote, the jurist John Austin, and the economist David Ricardo. Under Ricardo's influence, Mill wrote *Elements of Political Economy* (1821). His other important works include *Analysis of the Phenomena of the Human Mind* (1829) and several influential contributions to the

Encyclopaedia Britannica which applied utilitarian principles to social questions ranging from law to education.

Practical Applications of Utilitarianism

According to the principles of utility, man's happiness consists exclusively in gaining pleasure or, more practically, in avoiding pain. Mill's psychology, following David Hume and David Hartley, explains all the data of mental life in terms of association. Thus, he source of individual pleasure is, by and large, the result of associations that the individual has learned. It follows that education should be directed toward forming the appropriate associations, that is, identifying a man's pleasure with that of his fellowmen, just as the function of government is to promote "the greatest happiness of the greatest number." As a result of his own practical efforts in behalf of utilitarianism, Mill lived to see many of the utilitarians' commonsense attitudes toward law, voting, and education incorporated within the Parliamentary Reform Bill of 1830. But undoubtedly the most significant contribution he made was the strict application of these principles to the education of his eldest child. Mill completely supervised his son's early childhood and adolescence. Although the son later acknowledged that his father's system was deficient in cultivating normal emotions, he credited his remarkable education with giving him a 25-year advantage over his contemporaries.

Further Reading

Mill's books have not been collected in standard editions or reissued. For a study of his life see Alexander Bain, *James Mill* (1882). Of great interest is the portrait of James Mill by his son John Stuart Mill in the *Autobiography* (1873; many editions). Useful background studies are Leslie Stephen, *The English Utilitarians* (3 vols., 1900), and Élie Halévy, *The Growth of Philosophic Radicalism* (1928; new ed. 1934; repr. with corrections 1952).

Additional Sources

Mazlish, Bruce, *James and John Stuart Mill: father and son in the nineteenth century,* New Brunswick, USA: Transaction Books, 1988, 1975. □

John Stuart Mill

The English philosopher and economist John Stuart Mill (1806-1873) was the most influential British thinker of the 19th century. He is known for his writings on logic and scientific methodology and his voluminous essays on social and political life.

John Stuart Mill was born on May 20, 1806, in London to James and Harriet Burrow Mill, the eldest of their nine children. His father, originally trained as a minister, had emigrated from Scotland to take up a career as a freelance journalist. In 1808 James Mill began his lifelong association with Jeremy Bentham, the utilitarian philosopher and legalist. Mill shared the common belief of 19th-century psychologists that the mind is at birth a *tabula rasa* and that character and performance are the result of experienced associations. With this view, he attempted to make his son into a philosopher by exclusively supervising his education. John Stuart Mill never attended a school or university.

Early Years and Education

The success of this experiment is recorded in John Stuart Mill's *Autobiography* (written 1853-1856). He began the study of Greek at the age of 3 and took up Latin between his seventh and eighth years. From six to ten each morning the boy recited his lessons, and by the age of 12 he had mastered material that was the equivalent of a university degree in classics. He then took up the study of logic, mathematics, and political economy with the same rigor. In addition to his own studies, John also tutored his brothers and sisters for 3 hours daily. Throughout his early years, John was treated as a younger equal by his father's associates, who were among the preeminent intellectuals in England. They included George Grote, the historian; John Austin, the jurist; David Ricardo, the economist; and Bentham.

Only later did Mill realize that he never had a childhood. The only tempering experiences he recalled from his boyhood were walks, music, reading *Robinson Crusoe,* and a year he spent in France. Before going abroad John had never associated with anyone his own age. The year with Bentham's relatives in France gave young Mill a taste of normal family life and a mastery of another language, which

made him well informed on French intellectual and political ideas.

When he was 16, Mill began a debating society of utilitarians to examine and promote the ideas of his father, Bentham, Ricardo, and Thomas Malthus. He also began to publish on various issues, and he had written nearly 50 articles and reviews before he was 20. His speaking, writing, and political activity contributed to the passage of the Parliamentary Reform Bill in 1830, which culminated the efforts of the first generation of utilitarians, especially Bentham and James Mill. But in 1823, at his father's insistence, Mill abandoned his interest in a political career and accepted a position at India House, where he remained for 35 years.

The external events of Mill's life were so prosaic that Thomas Carlyle once disparagingly described their written account as "the autobiography of a steam engine." Nonetheless in 1826 Mill underwent a mental crisis. He perceived that the realization of all the social reforms for which he had been trained and for which he had worked would bring him no personal satisfaction. He thought that his intellectual training had left him emotionally starved and feared that he lacked any capacity for feeling or caring deeply. Mill eventually overcame his melancholia by opening himself to the romantic reaction against rationalism on both an intellectual and personal level. He assimilated the ideas and poetry of English, French, and German thought. When he was 25 he met Harriet Taylor, and she became the dominant influence of his life. Although she was married, they maintained a close association for 20 years, eventually marrying in 1851, a few years after her husband's death. In his *Autobiography* Mill maintained that Harriet's intellectual ability was superior to his own and that she should be understood as the joint author of many of his major works.

"System of Logic"

The main purpose of Mill's philosophic works was to rehabilitate the British empirical tradition extending from John Locke. He argued for the constructive dimension of experience as an antidote to the negative and skeptical aspects emphasized by David Hume and also as an alternative to rationalistic dogmatism. His *System of Logic* (1843) was well received both as a university text and by the general public. Assuming that all propositions are of a subject-predicate form, Mill began with an analysis of words that constitute statements. He overcame much of the confusion of Locke's similar and earlier analysis by distinguishing between the connotation, or real meaning, of terms and the denotation, or attributive function. From this Mill described propositions as either "verbal" and analytic or "real" and synthetic. With these preliminaries in hand, Mill began a rather traditional attack on pure mathematics and deductive reasoning. A consistent empiricism demanded that all knowledge be derived from experience. Thus, no appeal to universal principles or a priori intuitions was allowable. In effect, Mill reduced pure to applied mathematics and deductive reasoning to "apparent" inferences or premises which, in reality, are generalizations from previous experience. The utility of syllogistic reasoning is found to be a training in logical consistency—that is, a correct method for deciding if a particular instance fits under a general rule—but not to be a source of discovering new knowledge.

By elimination, then, logic was understood by Mill as induction, or knowledge by inference. His famous canons of induction were an attempt to show that general knowledge is derived from the observation of particular instances. Causal laws are established by observations of agreement and difference, residues and concomitant variations of the relations between A as the cause of B. The law of causation is merely a generalization of the truths reached by these experimental methods. By the strict application of these methods man is justified in extending his inferences beyond his immediate experience to discover highly probable, though not demonstrable, empirical and scientific laws.

Mill's logic culminates with an analysis of the methodology of the social sciences since neither individual men nor patterns of social life are exceptions to the laws of general causality. However, the variety of conditioning factors and the lack of control and repeatability of experiments weaken the effectiveness of both the experimental method and deductive attempts—such as Bentham's hedonistic calculus, which attempted to derive conclusions from the single premise of man's self-interest. The proper method of the social sciences is a mixture: deductions from the inferential generalizations provided by psychology and sociology. In several works Mill attempted without great success to trace connections between the generalizations derived from associationist psychology and the social and historical law of three stages (theological, metaphysical, and positivist or scientific) established by Auguste Comte.

Mill's Reasonableness

The mark of Mill's genius in metaphysics, ethics, and political theory rests in the tenacity of his attitude of consistent reasonableness. He denied the necessity and scientific validity of positing transcendent realities except as an object of belief or guide for conduct. He avoided the abstruse difficulties of the metaphysical status of the external world and the self by defining matter, as it is experienced, as "a permanent possibility of sensation," and the mind as the series of affective and cognitive activities that is aware of itself as a conscious unity of past and future through memory and imagination. His own mental crises led Mill to modify the calculative aspect of utilitarianism. In theory he maintained that men are determined by their expectation of the pleasure and pain produced by action. But his conception of the range of personal motives and institutional attempts to ensure the good are much broader than those suggested by Bentham. For example, Mill explained that he overcame a mechanical notion of determinism when he realized that men are capable of being the cause of their own conduct through motives of self-improvement. In a more important sense, he attempted to introduce a qualitative dimension to utility.

Mill suggested that there are higher pleasures and that men should be educated to these higher aspirations. For a democratic government based on consensus is only as good as the education and tolerance of its citizenry. This argument received its classic formulation in the justly famous essay, "On Liberty." Therein the classic formula of liberalism is stated: the state exists for man, and hence the only warrantable imposition upon personal liberty is "self-protection." In later life, Mill moved from a laissez-faire economic theory toward socialism as he realized that government must take a more active role in guaranteeing the interests of all of its citizens.

The great sadness of Mill's later years was the unexpected death of his wife in 1858. He took a house in Avignon, France, in order to be near her grave and divided his time between there and London. He won election to the House of Commons in 1865, although he refused to campaign. He died on May 8, 1873.

Further Reading

Information on Mill from primary sources is in his *Autobiography,* four volumes of letters in his *Collected Works,* and *John Stuart Mill and Harriet Taylor: Their Correspondence,* edited by F. A. Hayek (1951). Biographies of Mill are M. J. Packe, *The Life of John Stuart Mill* (1954), and a brief, sympathetic treatment by Ruth Borchard, *John Stuart Mill, the Man* (1957). Maurice Cowling, *Mill and Liberalism* (1963); Ernest Albee, *A History of English Utilitarianism* (1902); Leslie Stephen, *The English Utilitarians* (3 vols., 1900); and Élie Halévy, *The Growth of Philosophic Radicalism* (1928; new ed. 1934; repr. with corrections 1952), are excellent studies. □

Sir John Everett Millais

Sir John Everett Millais (1829-1896), an English painter of great technical brilliance, was a founder member of the Pre-Raphaelite Brotherhood.

John Everett Millais was born in Southampton. His parents recognized his precocious talent and moved to London when John was 9. That year he won the Silver Medal for drawing from the Royal Society of Arts. At the age of 11 he entered the Royal Academy Schools and won a succession of prizes, including the Gold Medal in 1847.

At this time Millais's close friend William Holman Hunt was formulating new ideas under the influence of John Keats's poetry and John Ruskin's *Modern Painters.* Dante Gabriel Rossetti, Millais, and Hunt founded the Pre-Raphaelite Brotherhood in 1848. Inspired by this new approach, Millais painted *Lorenzo and Isabella* (1849), from Keats's *Isabella,* and *Christ in the House of His Parents* (1850). The latter painting was exhibited in the academy in 1850; Charles Dickens said it showed "the lowest depths of what is mean, repulsive, and revolting," but it was strongly defended by Ruskin, who subsequently became a close friend of Millais. Their friendship ended in 1855, when Millais married Mrs. Ruskin a year after the annulment of her marriage.

Millais's *Huguenot* and *Ophelia,* exhibited in 1852, were immediate public successes, and in 1853 Millais was elected an associate of the Royal Academy. The Pre-Raphaelite Brotherhood began to break up, and Millais's last works in this style, the *Blind Girl* and *Autumn Leaves* (both 1856), although among his best, were not well received. His former serious sense of purpose now gave way to a more direct popular appeal. *The Black Brunswicker* was a deliberate and successful attempt to repeat the popularity of the *Huguenot*. In 1863 he was elected a royal academician and became established as a fashionable artist.

During the 1860s Millais abandoned his earlier meticulous technique and developed a more fluent style, often painting directly onto the canvas, with few preparatory drawings, and rendering detail with almost impressionistic freedom. Outstanding among his many distinguished portraits is that of Mrs. Bischoffsheim, which illustrates the technical virtuosity that won him many honors and such acclaim at European exhibitions. Perhaps his most widely known portrait was of his grandson "Bubbles"; its enormous popularity as an advertisement infuriated the artist.

Apart from rather sentimental genre subjects, such as the *Yeomen of the Guard* (1876), Millais painted a series of remarkable landscapes, beginning with *Chill October* (1870), and his *St. Stephen* (1894) is an example of the religious themes to which he returned at the end of his life.

In 1885 Millais was created a baronet. He was elected president of the Royal Academy in February 1896 and died in August.

Further Reading

The standard biography of Millais is M.H. Spielmann, *Millais and His Works* (1898), which was slightly amplified by John Guille Millais, *The Life and Letters of Sir John Everett Millais* (2 vols., 1899; 3d ed. 1902). A good general background is in Robin Ironside and John Gere, *Pre-Raphaelite Painters* (1948), and Graham Reynolds, *Victorian Painting* (1966).

Additional Sources

Millais, John Everett, Sir, bart., *Sir John Everett Millais,* London: Academy Editions; New York: distributed by Rizzoli International Publications, 1979.

Watson, J. N. P., *Millais: three generations in nature, art & sport,* London: Sportsman's Press, 1988. □

Edna St. Vincent Millay

Edna St. Vincent Millay (1892-1950) was an American lyric poet whose personal life and verse burned meteorically through the imaginations of rebellious youth during the 1920s.

Edna St. Vincent Millay was born in Rockland, Maine, on Feb. 27, 1892, and was educated in her native state. One of her juvenile poems appeared in *St. Nicholas,* and she delivered a verse essay at high school graduation. "Renascence," a long poem written when she was 19, appeared in *The Lyric Year* (1912), an anthology, and remains a favorite. A wealthy friend, impressed with Edna's talent, helped her attend Vassar College.

Following her graduation in 1917, Millay settled in New York's Greenwich Village and began to support herself by writing. Her impact was immediate with her first volume, *Renascence* (1917). She also wrote short stories under the pseudonym Nancy Boyd. *A Few Figs from Thistles* appeared in 1920. In 1921 she issued *Second April* and three short plays, one of which, *Aria da Capo,* is a delicate but effective satire on war.

In 1923 Millay published *The Harp Weaver and Other Poems,* which won the Pulitzer Prize, and married Eugen Jan Boissevain, and affluent Dutchman. In 1925 they bought a farm near Austerlitz, N.Y. Millay participated in the defense of the alleged anarchists Sacco and Vanzetti. In 1925 she was commissioned to write an opera with composer Deems Taylor; *The King's Henchman* (1927) was the most successful American opera to that time. That year, after the final sentencing of Sacco and Vanzetti, she wrote "Justice Denied in Massachusetts," a poem, and also contributed to *Fear,* a pamphlet on the case.

Millay issued *Buck in the Snow* (1928), *Fatal Interview* (1931), and *Wine from These Grapes* (1934). She tried a dramatic dialogue on the state of the world in *Conversation at Midnight* (1937), but the subject was beyond her grasp. She returned to the lyric mode in *Huntsman, What Quarry* (1939). Carelessly expressed outrage at fascism detracted from *Make Bright the Arrows* (1940); *The Murder of Lidice*

(1942) was a sincere but somewhat strident response to the Nazis' obliteration of a Czechoslovakian town. She was losing her audience; *Collected Sonnets* (1941) and *Collected Lyrics* (1943) did not win it back.

Millay's last years were dogged by illness and loss. Friends died, and her husband's income disappeared when the Nazis invaded Holland. In 1944 a nervous breakdown hospitalized her for several months. Her husband died in 1949; on Oct. 19, 1950, she followed him. Some of her last verse appeared posthumously in *Mine the Harvest* (1954).

Miss Millay's virtues were in her poems speaking frankly about sex, the liberated woman, and social justice. Though she wrote in traditional forms, her subject matter, her mixed tone of insouciance, disillusionment, courage, and intensity and her lyric gifts were highly appreciated in her time.

Further Reading

A. R. Macdougall edited the *Letters of Edna St. Vincent Millay* (1952). Biographies include Miriam Gurko, *Restless Spirit: The Life of Edna St. Vincent Millay* (1962), and Jean Gould, *The Poet and Her Book* (1969). Other studies are Elizabeth Atkins, *Edna St. Vincent Millay and Her Times* (1937); Vincent Sheean, *The Indigo Bunting* (1951); and Norman A. Brittin, *Edna St. Vincent Millay* (1967). Van Wyck Brooks, in *New England: Indian Summer* (1940), discusses Miss Millay's place in literary history; and Edmund Wilson, in *Shores of Light* (1952), retains his youthful personal affection for her and his high opinion of her literary merit. □

Arthur Miller

Arthur Miller (born 1915), American playwright, novelist, and film writer, is considered one of the major dramatists of 20th-century American theater.

Arthur Miller was born on Oct. 17, 1915, in New York City. His father ran a small coat-manufacturing business; during the Depression it failed, and in 1932, after graduating from high school, Miller went to work in an auto-parts warehouse. Two years later he enrolled in the University of Michigan. Before graduating in 1938, he won two Avery Hopwood awards for playwriting.

Miller returned to New York City to a variety of jobs, writing for the Federal Theater Project, the Columbia Workshop, and the Cavalcade of America. Because of an old football injury, he was rejected for military service, but he toured Army camps to collect material for a movie, *The Story of GI Joe,* based on a book by Ernie Pyle. His journal of this tour was titled *Situation Normal* (1944). That same year the Broadway production of his *The Man Who Had All the Luck* opened and closed almost simultaneously, though it won a Theater Guild Award. In 1945 his novel, *Focus,* a diatribe against anti-Semitism, appeared.

With the opening of *All My Sons* on Broadway (1947), Miller's theatrical career burgeoned. The Ibsenesque tragedy won three prizes and fascinated audiences across the country. Then *Death of a Salesman* (1949) brought Miller a Pulitzer Prize, international fame, and an estimated income of $2 million. The words of its hero, Willy Loman, have been heard in at least 17 languages as well as on movie screens everywhere. By the time of his third Broadway play, *The Crucible* (1953), audiences were ready to accept Miller's conviction that "a poetic drama rooted in American speech and manners" was the only means of writing a tragedy out of the common man's life.

In these three plays Miller's subject was moral disintegration. His shifting from contemporary life in *Salesman* to the Salem witch hunt of 1692 in *The Crucible* hardly disguised the fact that he had in mind Senator Joseph McCarthy's investigations of Communist subversion in the United States and the subsequent persecutions and hysteria. When Miller was called before the House Committee on Un-American Activities in June 1956, he argued, "My conscience will not permit me to use the name of another person and bring trouble to him." He was convicted of contempt of Congress; the conviction was reversed in 1958.

Two one-act plays, *A View from the Bridge* and *A Memory of Two Mondays* (1955), were social dramas focused on the inner life of working men; neither had the power of *Salesman.* Nor did his film script, *The Misfits* (1961). His next play, *After the Fall* (1964), was a bald excursion into self-analysis. His second wife, Marilyn Monroe, was the model for the heroine. *Incident at Vichy* (1965), a long one-act play based on a true story out of Nazi-occupied France, examined the nature of racial guilt and the

depths of human hatreds; it is discursive exercise rather than highly charged theater.

In *The Price* (1968) Miller returned to domestic drama in a tight, intense confrontation between two brothers, almost strangers to each other, brought together by their father's death. It is Miller at the height of his powers, consolidating his position as a major American dramatist.

But *The Price* proved to be Miller's last major Broadway success. His next work, *The Creation of the World and Other Business,* was a series of comic sketches first produced on Broadway in 1972. It closed after only twenty performances. All of Miller's subsequent works premiered outside of New York. Miller staged the musical *Up From Paradise* (1974, an adaptation of his *Creation of the World*), at his alma mater, the University of Michigan. Another play, *The Archbishop's Ceiling,* was presented in 1977 at the Kennedy Center in Washington, D.C. In the 1980s, Miller produced a number of short pieces. *The American Clock* was based on author Studs Terkel's oral history of the Great Depression, *Hard Times,* and was structured as a series of vignettes that chronicle the hardship and suffering that occurred during the 1930s. *Elegy for a Lady* and *Some Kind of Story* were two one-act plays that were staged together in 1982. Miller's *Danger, Memory!* was composed of the short pieces *I Can't Remember Anything* and *Clara.* All these later plays have been regarded by critics as minor works. In the mid-1990s, Miller adapted *The Crucible* for the Academy Award-nominated film starring Daniel Day-Lewis and Joan Allen.

Despite the absence of any major success since the mid-1960s, Miller seems secure in his reputation as a major figure in American drama. He has won the Emmy, Tony, and Peabody awards, and in 1984 received the John F. Kennedy Award for Lifetime Achievement. Critics have hailed his blending of vernacular language, social and psychological realism, and moral insight. As the commentator June Schlueter has said, "When the twentieth century is history and American drama viewed in perspective, the plays of Arthur Miller will undoubtedly be preserved in the annals of dramatic literature."

Further Reading

Miller's *Collected Plays* was published in 1957, and a collection of his short stories, *I Don't Need You Any More,* in 1967. His *Collected Plays, Volume II* was published in 1980. *The Portable Arthur Miller,* which includes several of his major plays, was published in 1971. S.K. Bhatia's study *Arthur Miller* was published in 1985. See also C.W.E. Bigsby's *A Critical Introductiion to Twentieth-Century American Drama,* published in 1984. Partly biographical is Benjamin Nelson, *Arthur Miller: Portrait of a Playwright* (1970), although the focus is on the plays. Useful critical studies are Dennis Welland, *Arthur Miller* (1961); Sheila Huftel, *Arthur Miller: The Burning Glass* (1965); Leonard Moss, *Arthur Miller* (1967); and Edward Murray, *Arthur Miller, Dramatist* (1967). In addition to these sources, there are numerous Internet web sites devoted in whole or in part to Miller's life and works. □

Henry Miller

American author Henry Miller (1891-1980) was a major literary force in the late 1950s largely because his two most important novels, prohibited from publication and sale in the United States for many years, tested Federal laws concerning art and pornography.

Born December 26, 1891 in Brooklyn, New York City, Henry Miller grew up in Brooklyn and briefly attended the City College of New York. From 1909 to 1924 he worked at various jobs, including employment with a cement company, assisting his father at a tailor shop, and sorting mail for the Post Office. While in the messenger department of Western Union, he started a novel. Throughout this period he had a troubled personal life and had two unsuccessful marriages (throughout his life he married five women and divorced all of them). Determined to become a writer, Miller went to Paris, where, impoverished, he remained for nearly a decade. In 1934 he composed *Tropic of Cancer* (United States ed., 1961), a loosely constructed autobiographical novel concerning the emotional desolation of his first years in Paris. Notable for its graphic realism and Rabelaisian gusto, it won praise from T. S. Eliot and Ezra Pound. Many were outraged by the sexual passages, however, and the author had to go to court to lift a ban on his work. The controversy caused it to become a best-seller, although critics continued to debate its literary merits. *Black Spring* (1936; United States ed., 1963) and *Tropic of Capri-*

corn (1939; United States ed., 1962) are similar in style and feeling, drawing from the experiences of Miller's boyhood in Brooklyn and formative years as an expatriate.

In 1939 Miller visited his friend the British novelist Lawrence Durrell in Greece. *The Colossus of Maroussi* (1941), depicting his adventures with the natives of the Greek islands, and one of the finest modern travel books, resulted. Returning to the United States in 1940, Miller settled permanently on the Big Sur coast of California. His acute and often hilarious criticisms of America are recorded in *The Air-conditioned Nightmare* (1945) and *Remember to Remember* (1947). *The Time of the Assassins* (1956), a provocative study of the French poet Arthur Rimbaud, states eloquently Miller's artistic and philosophic credo. *Big Sur and the Oranges of Hieronymus Bosch* (1958) deals with Miller's California friends.

Miller's major fiction of this period was the massive trilogy *The Rosy Crucifixion,* including *Sexus* (1949), *Plexus* (1953), and *Nexus* (1960). These retell his earlier erotic daydreams but lack the earlier violence of language. Miller's correspondence with Durrell was published in 1962 and his letters to Anaïs Nin in 1965. His *The World of Lawrence: A Passionate Appreciation* (1980) is about the life and career of his literary compatriot, D. H. Lawrence. *Opus Pistorum* (1984) is a novel reputedly written by Miller in the early 1940s when he needed money; most critics consider the work to be pure pornography and some question whether Miller was the actual author.

In his later years Miller was admired mainly for his role as prophet and visionary. Denouncing the empty materialism of modern existence, he called for a new religion of body and spirit based upon the ideas of Friedrich Nietzsche, Walt Whitman, and D. H. Lawrence. Miller's novels, despite sordid material and obscene language, at their best are intensely lyrical and spiritually affirmative. With his freedom of language and subject he paved the way for such Beat Generation writers as Jack Kerouac and Allen Ginsberg. Miller lived his final years in seclusion pursuing his lifelong interest of watercolor painting. He died on June 7, 1980 in Pacific Palisades, California.

Further Reading

For more on Miller's life and work, see J.D. Brown's *Henry Miller* (1986). Book-length critical studies are Edwin Corle, *The Smile at the Foot of the Ladder* (1948), and Ihab Hassan, *The Literature of Silence: Henry Miller and Samuel Beckett* (1967). For equally valuable insights and biographical information see Alfred Perles, *My Friend Henry Miller* (1955); Lawrence Durrell and Alfred Perles, *Art and Outrage: A Correspondence about Henry Miller* (1959); Annette K. Baxter, *Henry Miller, Expatriate* (1961); Kingsley Widmer, *Henry Miller* (1963); and William A. Gordon, *The Mind and Art of Henry Miller* (1967). The largest collection of critical essays is George Wickes, ed., *Henry Miller and the Critics* (1963). □

Joaquin Miller

American writer Joaquin Miller (1837-1913), a self-styled built a temporary reputation on literary opportunism and a fortuitous London reception.

Joaquin Miller was born Cincinnatus Hiner Miller on a farm near Liberty, Ind., on Sept. 8, 1837. His parents set out for the West in 1852 and settled in the Willamette Valley, Ore. Within 2 years their restless son left for the California gold mines. For a time Miller lived with northern California Indians near Mt. Shasta. He was implicated in the massacre of the Pit River Indians, attended college briefly, and operated a pony-express service between the Idaho mines and the West Coast.

In 1862 Miller became editor of the *Democratic Register* in Eugene, Ore. Before the year was over he had married and had founded a new paper, the *Eugene City Review.* Later Miller settled in a mining camp in Canyon City, Ore. He practiced law, worked a claim of his own, fought Indian harassment, and was elected judge of Grant County in 1866 for a 4-year term. In 1869 the Millers were divorced.

For the next 10 years Miller pursued a literary career. His first book of verse was *Specimens* (1868). It was followed by *Joaquin et al* (1869), a collection of 11 poems signed Cincinnatus Hiner, mostly sentimental doggerel and bad imitations of Edgar Allan Poe. His work had little success in America, so he sailed for London, a ''passionate pilgrim'' determined to sell his verses of life in the Far West. He printed *Pacific Poems* (1871) privately. An English pub-

lisher brought out *Songs of the Sierras* (1871), which launched Miller socially and commercially as the Kit Carson of poetry. His fame, however, was short-lived and his talent essentially thin. *Songs of the Sun-lands* followed (1873), along with the partially autobiographic *Life among the Modocs*. A tour of Italy produced a curious novel, *The One Fair Woman* (1876), and *Songs of Italy* (1878).

By 1879 Miller was back in New York, married to Abigail Leland, a hotel heiress, and seeking a new career in the theater. Of the four plays he preserved, *The Danites of the Sierras* (1881), an obvious melodramatic story of the Mormons, was the most popular and made him a small fortune. In 1887, without his wife, he settled on 75 acres of barren hillside in Oakland, Calif., to write more poetry and finish his utoplan romance, *The Building of the City Beautiful* (1893). He died at his beloved ''Hights'' in February 1913.

Further Reading

The best collection of Miller's work is *The Poetical Works of Joaquin Miller* (1923), edited and with an informative introduction by Stuart P. Sherman. Two polar estimates of Miller's work are Martin Severin Peterson, *Joaquin Miller: Literary Frontiersman* (1937), a flattering analysis, and M. Marion Marberry, *Splendid Poseur: Joaquin Miller, American Poet* (1953), a devastating interpretation. O. W. Frost, *Joaquin Miller* (1967), seeks an objective view.

Additional Sources

Lawson, Benjamin S., *Joaquin Miller*, Boise, Idaho: Boise State University, 1980. ☐

Perry Miller

Perry Miller (1905-1963) was the most famous interpreter of the meaning of the New England Puritanism of the 17th century.

Perry Miller was born in Chicago in 1905, received his formal undergraduate and graduate education at the University of Chicago in the 1920s, and joined the Harvard University faculty in 1931, where he taught in the English Department until his death in 1963.

Miller was the most influential figure in a scholarly movement during the 1920s and 1930s which reinterpreted 17th-century New England Puritanism. The dominant image of the Puritan had been that of a narrow-minded bigot, a reactionary kill-joy whose legacy to American history was sexual repression, alcohol prohibition, and hypocrisy. Several scholars between the two world wars published research which replaced that image with a more complex, balanced, and sympathetic one. Perry Miller's articles and books analyzed Puritan ideas in unprecedented depth.

The New England Mind: The Seventeenth Century (1939) was one of the most abstract works of American intellectual history ever written. In it Miller analyzed the nature of Puritan piety and intellect. He explained characteristic Puritan logic, epistemology, natural philosophy, rhetoric, literary style, ideas of government, and theory of human nature as well as theology. Miller's description was of a highly rational Puritan mentality attempting to make rules to live by in a world created by God's caprice. Changes in thought over time were not investigated in *The New England Mind: The Seventeenth Century*, but they were in *Orthodoxy in Massachusetts, 1630-1650* (1933) and in *The New England Mind: From Colony to Province* (1953). *Orthodoxy* was Miller's first published book, and in it he explained how the Puritans managed intellectually to become independent congregationalists while insisting that they had not separated from the mother Church of England. *From Colony to Province* tells the story of the interaction between the ideas of the Puritan establishment imported from England and the new American environment. If the tension of *The Seventeenth Century* is between the heart's piety and the head's reason, the tension of *From Colony to Province* is between the ideals of Puritanism at the onset and the consequent ironic realities of the ideals in action. The Puritans came to Massachusetts pursuing the goal of a religious utopia, but succeeded in creating a materialistic society.

Ideas were studied at length by Miller because he believed them to be important in expressing life's meaning and in influencing human behavior. His interpretation that Puritanism was a coherent and powerful body of ideas caused early New England history to become intellectual history to a significant degree. Miller's emphasis upon Puritan ideas was part of a rejuvenation of colonial American scholarship during and after the 1930s, and it coincided with the rise of American intellectual histories. During the 1940s and 1950s Americans tried to understand the roots of their nation's identity and democratic commitments. Earlier American ideas were frequently traced as the sources of later values and behavior.

The inevitable historiographical pendulum swing occurred toward the end of Miller's life and after his death, as younger scholars minimized the coherence and causal importance of Puritanism in New England. Criticisms of Miller for over-intellectualizing New England colonists and for imputing elite characteristics to the population as a whole became common as social historians took over a scholarly field previously dominated by historians of ideas.

Perry Miller was writing about 19th-century America late in his life, but he did not live to impose a broad synthetic interpretation on the later history of the country. *The Life of the Mind in America: From the Revolution to the Civil War* (1965) was edited after his death.

Further Reading

For biographical background on Miller, and for interpretation of his works, see the memorial issues of *Harvard Review 2* (1964) and Robert Middlekauff, "Perry Miller," in Marcus Cunliffe and Robin Winks, editors, *Pastmasters, Some Essays on American Historians* (1969).

An example of the typical interpretation of Puritanism prior to Perry Miller can be found in Vernon Louis Parrington, *Main Currents in American Thought,* vol. 1, "The Colonial Mind" (1927). Examples of the type of social history written following Miller's death include Darrett Rutman's *Winthrop's Boston* (1965), John Demos' *A Little Commonwealth: Family Life in Plymouth Colony* (1970), and Philip Greven, *The Protestant Temperament: Patterns of Child-Rearing, Religious Experience and the Self in Early America* (1977). Some commentators have suggested that Perry Miller can be said to have had an "ironic" interpretation of the long sweep of American history. See Gene Wise, *American Historical Explanations* (1973) and Richard Reinitz, *Irony and Consciousness* (1980). □

Samuel Freeman Miller

Samuel Freeman Miller (1816-1890), American jurist, was an associate justice of the U.S. Supreme Court.

Samuel F. Miller was born on April 5, 1816, in Richmond, Ky. He earned his medical degree at Transylvania University in 1838. While serving as a country doctor, he read law and was admitted to the bar in 1847. A Whig and a member of a Kentucky group advocating the end of slavery by gradual emancipation, Miller hoped the state constitutional convention of 1849 would advance this goal; instead, the institution of slavery was strengthened. In 1850 he left Kentucky and set up his law practice in Keokuk, Iowa.

Miller became a Republican and strongly supported Abraham Lincoln in the 1860 election. When a U.S. Supreme Court vacancy occurred, Iowa Republicans sought the first west-of-the-Mississippi seat. Miller, an affable politician with no experience as a judge, was appointed in July 1862.

Like his colleagues on the Court, Miller did not seek to assert leadership in the critical Reconstruction racial issues, leaving those matters to Congress. However, his opinion in the *Slaughter-House Cases* (1873), which sustained an act of the Louisiana Legislature regulating the butchering business in New Orleans, was a landmark in the field of civil rights. The claim was made that the 14th Amendment protected individual butchers from having to agree to the rules of a state-authorized monopoly. Miller upheld the state government, stating that the 14th Amendment pertained only to the newly freed Negroes, who needed protection.

Soon, however, those who sought to curtail the advancement of Negroes reinterpreted Miller's decision. If a state could regulate the affairs of citizens who were butchers, they could do the same for citizens who were black. Once Southern legislatures had come back into the hands of racial conservatives, the *Slaughter-House* doctrine became a bastion of white supremacy. In *Slaughter-House* Miller had, somewhat unwittingly, given a new direction to American history: Reconstruction and Negro advancement faltered, while business interests were given strong impetus.

In a less ambiguous civil rights decision, *Ex parte Yarbrough* (1884), Miller upheld, under the 15th Amendment, the right of a Negro to vote in a Federal election.

Miller unsuccessfully sought the chief justiceship in 1873. He was considered a Republican presidential possibility in both 1880 and 1884. He married twice and was the father of two children. He died on Oct. 13, 1890, in Washington, D.C., while still serving on the bench.

Further Reading

Charles Fairman, *Mr. Justice Miller and the Supreme Court, 1862-1890* (1939), is a fine, occasionally uncritical biography. Miller is somewhat overpraised by William Gillette in Leon Friedman and Fred L. Israel, eds., *The Justices of the United States Supreme Court, 1789-1969*, vol. 2 (1969). □

William Miller

William Miller (1782-1849), American clergyman, founded a movement which involved thousands in eagerly awaiting the Second Coming of Christ.

William Miller was born on Feb. 15, 1782, near Pittsfield, Mass. His family soon moved to western New York, where he received a rudimentary education. Battle experience during the War of 1812 aroused his concern with religious questions. Converted from deism by a revival meeting in 1816, he became a Baptist. Gradually, the subject of the Second Coming attracted his attention, and eventually, after laborious biblical investigation, he concluded that Christ would reappear about 1843.

Most enthusiastic Christians of the period were seeking to establish the date of the Second Advent. Doctrinally orthodox, Miller made only one innovation, suggesting that Christ would appear before (rather than after) the millennium. A reserved, somewhat shy man, he hesitated to publish his convictions, but the nearness of the event made it urgent to save as many souls as possible by publishing his news to the world. As a boy preacher, he discovered an unexpected eloquence, and in 1833 the Baptist Church ordained him as a minister.

Miller's message attracted increasing attention in New England and western New York. In 1838 he published *Evidence from Scripture and History of the Second Coming of Christ about the Year 1843*. Two years later another Baptist cleric, the Reverend Joshua Himes, seeing Miller as a tool to further the cause of evangelism, took over management of Miller's campaign.

Miller's enthusiasm, plus the pressures of an economic depression, drew thousands of converts. As his following grew, so did controversy over his activities. Orthodox ministers condemned but could not silence him. Miller had avoided naming a day for the Advent, but, as 1843 approached, pressures for a precise prediction increased. He chose March 1843. When March passed, he still insisted

that 1843 was the fateful year. Others in his movement chose October 22 as the last day; Miller agreed. Some people sold their goods, not expecting to need them after October 22; others took a holiday to watch the Millerites gather to await the Advent. According to older accounts, the undisturbed arrival of October 23 drove some of the faithful to suicide and others to insanity; recent scholars have discounted such tales. Meanwhile, the Baptist Church disowned Miller, and he joined others to form the Advent Society, ancestor of several modern Adventist churches. He died on Dec. 20, 1849, in Hampton, N.Y.

Further Reading

The principal source for Miller's life is Sylvester Bliss, *Memoirs of William Miller* (1853). Alice Felt Tyler, *Freedom's Ferment: Phases of American Social History from the Colonial Period to the Outbreak of the Civil War* (new ed. 1962), accepts traditional views emphasizing the bizarre aspects of Millerite behavior. Whitney R. Cross, *The Burned-over District: The Social and Intellectual History of Enthusiastic Religion in Western New York, 1800-1850* (1950), gives a broader view of the movement based on additional sources, including Miller's own papers at Aurora College.

Additional Sources

Gale, Robert, *The urgent voice: the story of William Miller*, Washington: Review and Herald Pub. Association, 1975.

Gordon, Paul A., *Herald of the midnight cry*, Boise, Idaho: Pacific Press Pub. Association, 1990.

White, Ellen Gould Harmon, *William Miller: herald of the blessed hope,* Hagerstown, MD: Review and Herald Pub. Association, 1994. □

Jean François Millet

Jean François Millet (1814-1875) was one of the French artists who worked in Barbizon, a village near the forest of Fontainebleau. He specialized in rural and peasant scenes.

Jean François Millet was born in Gruchy near Gréville on Oct. 4, 1814. His parents were peasants, and he grew up working on a farm. In 1837 Millet moved to Paris to study painting. To learn the traditions of classical and religious painting, he entered the studio of Paul Delaroche, a successful academic imitator of the revolutionary romanticist Eugène Delacroix. But Delaroche severely criticized the unsophisticated Millet, and the young artist's official schooling soon ended. He nevertheless stayed on in Paris, supporting himself by making pastel reproductions of rococo masters, occasional oil portraits, and commercial signs.

In 1841 Millet married Pauline Ono, who died in 1844. In 1845 the artist married Catherine Lemaire. During these years Millet continued to develop his painting, and like nearly all of his contemporaries, he sought recognition in the annual Parisian Salons. One of his portraits was accepted by the Salon of 1840; two pictures were included in the Salon of 1844; and he received special praise for the *Winnower* in the Salon of 1848. An 1845 exhibition at Le Havre was also moderately successful for the artist.

During the 1840s Millet's painting gradually shifted from classical and religious subjects to scenes of the rural and peasant life with which he was familiar. As it did, he gained increasing support and recognition from other painters in his generation. Among these were Narcisse Diaz de la Peña and Théodore Rousseau, two landscape painters who were instrumental in forming the loose association of artists known as the Barbizon school. Millet and the other Barbizon artists resisted the grand traditions of classical and religious painting, preferring a direct, unaffected confrontation with the phenomena of the natural world. During the 1830s and 1840s their works were generally regarded as crude, unfinished, and unacceptable to the official tastes of the Parisian Salons. After mid-century, however, the Barbizon artists slowly gained increasing recognition, and their achievement became an important inspiration for the younger generation of impressionists.

Millet moved to Barbizon in 1848. The picturesque village became his home for the rest of his life, and he died there on Jan. 20, 1875. During that period he produced his most mature and celebrated paintings, including the *Gleaners* (1857), the *Angelus* (1857-1859), the *Sower* (1850), and the *Bleaching Tub* (ca. 1861). The works are characterized by breadth and simplicity; they generally depict one or two peasant figures quietly engaged in earthy or domestic toil. With sweeping, generalized brushwork and a monumental sense of scale, Millet consistently dignified his characters and transformed them into heroic pictorial beings.

During the late 19th century Millet's paintings became extremely popular, particularly among American audiences and collectors. As more radical styles appeared, however, his contribution became partially eclipsed; to eyes accustomed to impressionism and cubism, his work appeared sentimental and romantic. But these are the vicissitudes of taste, and they should not obscure the deep feelings about man and soil that his masterpieces continue to express.

Further Reading

A comprehensive survey of the Barbizon school and Millet's relation to it is Robert L. Herbert, *Barbizon Revisited* (1962). □

Kate Millett

Author and sculptor Kate Millett (born 1934) was one of the leading theorists of the feminist movement of the second half of the 20th century.

Katherine Murray Millett was born in St. Paul, Minnesota, on September 14, 1934, the second of three daughters. Her father, a contractor, abandoned the family when Kate was 14 years old. Although college educated, her mother at first had to support the family by demonstrating potato peelers, but eventually worked as an insurance agent.

Worked as Artist

Born into an Irish Catholic background, Millett attended parochial elementary and high schools. In 1956 she received her B.A. degree *magna cum laude* and phi beta kappa from the University of Minnesota. She majored in English. After graduation she attended St. Hilda's College at Oxford University and in 1958 received first class honors in English literature. In the fall of that year she returned to the United States to teach English at the University of North Carolina at Chapel Hill, but resigned after several weeks and moved to New York City. There she began painting and sculpting, supporting herself by working as a file clerk and kindergarten teacher. She lived in a loft on the Bowery.

In 1961 she went to Japan to continue her sculpture. During her two year stay there she taught English at Wasada University and exhibited her art work in a one-woman show in Tokyo. While in Japan she met Fumio Yoshimura, a sculptor, whom she later married (in 1965).

Wrote Feminist Manifesto

On her return to the United States she continued her art, exhibiting her furniture sculpture at a New York gallery in March 1967. She also taught English at Barnard College, and in the fall of 1968 she entered the graduate program in English and comparative literature at Columbia University. She received her Ph.D. with distinction in 1970.

Millett's doctoral dissertation began as a feminist manifesto on "sexual politics" presented at a meeting of a women's liberation group in the fall of 1968. During the 1960s Millett had become increasingly politically active in the antiwar and civil rights movements. By the mid-1960s she had joined the then-nascent women's movement, and in 1966 she became chairwoman of the education committee of the newly-formed National Organization for Women (NOW). In December 1968, because, she claimed, she "wore sunglasses to faculty meetings and took the student side during the strikes," Millett was fired from her Barnard teaching post.

The doctoral thesis was completed in September 1969, successfully defended in March the following year, and published as *Sexual Politics* in August 1970. The work was an immediate sensation (within months it had sold 80,000 copies), and Millett herself became something of a media star. Despite this superficial recognition, the book remains a classic statement of radical feminist theory. Its central thesis is stated succinctly in the original 1968 manifesto: "When one group rules another, the relationship between the two is political. When such an arrangement is carried out over a long period of time it develops an ideology (feudalism, racism, etc.). All historical civilizations are patriarchies: their ideology is male supremacy." *Sexual Politics* includes a wealth of historical and anthropological information, as well as one of the most important critiques of misogynistic aspects of Freudianism. It concludes with the first extended feminist literary analysis, which focuses on the degraded images of women found in such male authors as D. H. Lawrence, Henry Miller, and Norman Mailer.

Explored Women's Realities in Male-Dominated World

In 1970 Millett produced a low-budget documentary film, *Three Lives,* which depicted the everyday lives of three women from a feminist point of view. *The Prostitution Papers* first appeared in 1971 as part of *Woman in Sexist Society,* edited by Gornick and Moran; in that version it was a formally experimental work that presented four female voices, one of them Millett's and two of them prostitutes', exploring the realities of their lives as women in a male-dominated world. The work was published as a book in 1973 and again in 1976. In her 1971 preface Millett stressed the importance of understanding the differences among women and not masking them beneath a "fraudulent 'sisterhood.'" She urged, "Loving someone is wanting to know them."

It is this drive to understand that appears to have motivated many of Millett's succeeding works that explore increasingly extreme human experiences, a direction that culminated in her long essay *The Basement* (1979), which is about a grotesque case of an Indiana girl who was tortured and murdered in the early 1960s. Millett learned of it in 1965, and apparently it haunted her imagination for years; it became the obsessive theme of her sculpture, for a decade a series of cages. Millett came to see the girl, Sylvia Likens, as symbolic of all women in patriarchal society who are always at risk of rape and death because their sexuality is feared and condemned.

Flying, along with *Sexual Politics* probably Millett's most important work, appeared in 1974. A dazzling psychological chronicle of the speeded-up life she lived in the wake of *Sexual Politics,* it is an autobiographical confessional that stands with the greats in the genre. In particular, *Flying* focuses on the complexities of her lesbian relationships with women named Celia and Claire, as well as her bond with her husband, Fumio. *Sita* (1977) is a similar, if less successful, autobiographical exploration of the dissolution of a lesbian relationship.

In 1981 Millett published *Going to Iran,* which was a new journalistic account of a trip she made to Iran in March 1979 to address Iranian feminists on International Women's Day. The Shah of Iran had just abdicated, and the Ayatollah Khomeini had not yet fully consolidated his power. Nevertheless, Millett was soon expelled by the fundamentalist government for her feminist views. The chronicle is recorded in the rigorously honest style of her earlier works.

Later works include *The Politics of Cruelty: An Essay on the Literature of Political Imprisonment* published in 1994. Here, Millet uses her writing to sound a wake-up call to the world. She states, "Knowledge of torture is itself a political act, just as silence or ignorance of it can have political consequence." *A.D.,* published in 1995, is defined as a memoir of her Aunt Dorothy.

Further Reading

Background on the contemporary women's movement is found in Sara Evans, *Personal Politics* (1979), a useful history, and in Josephine Donovan, *Feminist Theory: The Intellectual Traditions of American Feminism* (1985), which locates Millett's theory within its intellectual context. Millett later wrote in opposition to pornography. One of these articles appears in *Pleasure and Danger,* edited by Carole S. Vance (1984). See also *Ms.* Sept./Oct. 1995; March/April 1994. □

Robert Andrews Millikan

The American physicist Robert Andrews Millikan (1868-1953) measured the charge of the electron, proved the validity of Albert Einstein's photoelectric effect equation, and carried out pioneering cosmic-ray experiments.

The second son of a Congregational minister of Scotch-Irish ancestry, R. A. Millikan was born on March 22, 1868. He entered the preparatory department of Oberlin College in 1886.

The only physics Millikan studied during his first 2 years at Oberlin was in a 12-week course, which he later described as "a complete loss." It therefore came as a complete surprise when his Greek professor asked him to teach the elementary physics course. Encouraged by the professor's remark that "anyone who can do well in my Greek can teach physics," Millikan accepted the challenge and spent the summer reading an elementary textbook and working the problems in it. This was Millikan's real introduction to physics and the origin of a conviction he held throughout life: that the most effective way of learning physics is by problem solving and not by passively listening to lectures, which he regarded as "a stupid anachronism—a holdover from pre-printing-press days."

Millikan obtained his bachelor's degree in 1891 and his master's in 1893, at the same time continuing to teach elementary physics. He received his doctorate from Columbia in 1895 and then spent a year abroad, visiting the universities of Jena, Berlin, and Göttingen. He met many prominent physicists, who discussed with him the recent and startling discoveries of x-rays and radioactivity. In 1896 he became an assistant in physics at the University of Chicago.

Chicago: The First 12 Years

When Millikan assumed his duties in 1896, American physics was in its infancy. He therefore immediately found himself dividing his 12-hour work day equally between research and the writing of introductory textbooks and the organization of courses. He was convinced that lectures should be largely replaced by laboratory and problem-oriented activities, and between 1903 and 1908 he authored or coauthored several very influential textbooks compatible with that philosophy. In 1902 he married Greta Blanchard; they had three distinguished sons.

By 1907 Millikan decided to start working intensively on research. The problem he chose—the measurement of the charge of the electron—would gain him a full professorship (1910), the directorship of Chicago's Ryerson Physical Laboratory (1910), membership in the National Academy of Sciences (1914), and an international reputation.

Millikan intuitively sensed that the most fruitful approach to the problem would be to eliminate the sources of error in a method developed by J. S. E. Townsend (1897), J. J. Thomson (1903), and H. A. Wilson (1903) at the Cavendish Laboratory in Cambridge, England. In Wilson's experiments, air was compressed in a cloud chamber, ionized with x-rays, and then rapidly expanded, causing tiny water droplets to condense on the ions and form a mist. These droplets were allowed to fall, either under the influence of gravity alone or under the influence of gravity plus an electric field. By observing their velocities of fall in the first case, Wilson used Stokes' law to calculate their radii; by observing their velocities in the second case, he could then calculate the magnitude of the charge they carried—which Wilson found to vary between wide limits. The atomicity, or definiteness, of the charge of the electron was therefore still very much in doubt.

Millikan first attempted to eliminate the error introduced into Wilson's experiments by the gradual evaporation, and hence change in radii, of the water droplets. Thinking that he could measure the rate of evaporation, he decided to apply the electric field in a direction opposite to the force of gravity, balance it, and suspend the electron-laden droplets in midair. When he turned on the electric field, however, the entire mist disappeared—with the exception of a few individual drops which remained within the field of view of his observing telescope. Millikan realized immediately that he had discovered the key to the entire problem: to make precision measurements, he should observe single droplets using this balancing-field technique. Repeated observations revealed that the charge carried by a given droplet was always a multiple of a definite, fundamental value—the charge of the electron. Millikan created a great stir when he reported these results in 1909 at a professional meeting in Canada.

On his return trip to Chicago, Millikan suddenly realized that he could discard the cloud chamber entirely, that he could replace the evaporating water droplets with non-evaporating oil droplets, which could pick up electrons by passing through air ionized by x-rays (or gamma rays). This was the refinement required to make Millikan's experiment extraordinarily precise, and for several years he made countless determinations of the electronic charge. The values he reported in 1913 and 1917 stood for two decades, until it became known that a slight error had been introduced owing to a slightly incorrect value Millikan had assumed for the viscosity of air.

Einstein's Photoelectric Effect Equation

In 1912 Millikan went to Europe for six months to be able to analyze a mass of data uninterrupted by his many duties at the university. As on all of his many trips abroad, he visited a host of physicists and exchanged ideas with them. In Berlin he was forcefully reminded of the chaotic experimental situation regarding Einstein's famous 1905 equation of the photoelectric effect. Millikan was familiar with the great experimental difficulties from some work he had carried out in 1907. He also knew that subsequent work by other physicists had been extremely inconclusive. Once again he succeeded but it took him three years (1912-1915) of intensive work.

Capitalizing on an accidental observation, Millikan discovered that the alkali metals are sensitive to a very wide range of radiant frequencies. That was the key to the problem, but it was only the beginning: numerous ingenious experimental techniques, for example, a rotating knife inside the apparatus to clean the metal surface, had to be invented. By the time he was finished he considered it "not inappropriate to describe the experimental arrangement as a machine shop *in vacuo*." His efforts were rewarded: he established beyond doubt the validity of Einstein's linear relationship between energy and frequency, as well as all other predictions of Einstein's equation. This work, together with his measurement of the charge of the electron, won for Millikan the presidency of the American Physical Society (1916-1918) as well as many other honors, medals, and prizes, the highest of which was the Nobel Prize in 1923.

War Work; National Research Council

Millikan participated in the war effort in Washington (1917-1918) as third vice-chairman, director of research, and executive officer of the recently formed National Research Council. Most of his activities centered on the development of submarine detection and destruction devices: few goals were as urgent as that of breaking the back of the German U-boat menace.

One of Millikan's greatest services to the nation during this period was the role he played in establishing the National Research Council fellowships. He recommended the establishment of a fellowship program capable of supporting for two to three years the top 5 percent of recent American recipients of doctoral degrees in physics and chemistry. Millikan, who believed passionately in a decentralized university structure, hoped that the net result of this program would be not only to provide America with highly competent scientists but also to stimulate American universities to develop programs sufficiently competent to attract these very able students. From the start the program was a huge success, and it was soon extended to mathematics and the biological sciences.

Transfer to Caltech; Cosmic-Ray Researches

After the war Millikan returned to the University of Chicago, where he immediately began several research projects. In 1921, however, he went to the California Institute of Technology (Caltech) as chairman of its Executive Council and director of the recently established Norman Bridge Laboratory of Physics.

At Caltech, Millikan soon fostered a wide variety of research, on everything from earthquakes to pure mathematics, but he himself took the greatest interest in the phenomenon known as "field emission" and particularly in cosmic rays. These radiations had been discovered in 1912 by V. F. Hess, who argued that they came from outer space. At first, Millikan was skeptical of this conclusion, but by the mid-1920s he was convinced of its accuracy, mostly as a result of high-altitude measurements. He coined the term "cosmic rays," a name retained to this day.

Millikan's convictions regarding the nature of the primary cosmic radiation—that which is incident on the earth's atmosphere—produced some of his stormiest days as a physicist. He argued convincingly that, in the vast hydrogen clouds in interstellar space, hydrogen atoms were being continually fused together to produce helium and heavier elements, thereby releasing a large amount of energy in the form of photons (light quanta). He concluded that these photons were the cosmic rays. This hypothesis, which was widely accepted, met its first serious challenge in 1929, and eventually Millikan was forced to abandon his photon hypothesis. It is now known that primary cosmic rays consist mostly of hydrogen and helium nuclei.

Millikan: The Educator and Man

At Caltech, Millikan found a unique opportunity to implement his educational philosophy and, in general, influence American education. Under his guidance, Caltech grew from obscurity to a position of preeminence. The major educational policies he implemented were twofold: first, substantial emphasis on the humanities; and second, close ties between "pure sciences" such as physics and chemistry and the engineering disciplines.

"The secret of his success," wrote a friend about Millikan, "lay to a large extent in the simple virtues instilled in his upbringing. He had a single minded devotion to all that he was doing, and he put his work above his personal desires and aspirations." At the zenith of his powers, he was America's foremost experimentalist. He attracted and inspired a large number of exceptionally capable students, many of whom subsequently became his colleagues. Millikan, who died in Pasadena on Dec. 19, 1953, had a personal credo of great simplicity—and great beauty: "It is so to shape my own conduct at all times as, *in my own carefully considered judgment,* to promote best the well-being of mankind as a whole; in other words, to start building on my own account that better world for which I pray. *The sum of all such efforts will constitute at least a first big step toward the attainment of that better world.*"

Further Reading

The most complete source of information on Millikan is his *Autobiography* (1950). A brief account of his life and work by L. A. DuBridge and Paul S. Epstein is in the *Biographical Memoirs of the National Academy of Sciences,* vol. 33 (1959). For information on various aspects of Millikan's work see David L. Anderson, *The Discovery of the Electron* (1964); Bruno Rossi, *Cosmic Rays* (1964); and Max Jammer, *The Conceptual Development of Quantum Mechanics* (1966). □

C. Wright Mills

American sociologist and political polemicist C. Wright Mills (1916-1962) argued that the academic elite has a moral duty to lead the way to a better society by actively indoctrinating the masses with values.

On Aug. 28, 1916, C. Wright Mills was born in Waco, Tex. He received his bachelor's and master's degrees from the University of Texas and his doctorate from the University of Wisconsin in 1941. Subsequently, he taught sociology at the University of Maryland and Columbia University and during his academic career received a Guggenheim fellowship and a Fulbright grant. At his death, Mills was professor of sociology at Columbia.

Mills has been described as a "volcanic eminence" in the academic world and as "one of the most controversial figures in American social science." He considered himself, and was so considered by his colleagues, as a rebel against the "academic establishment." Mills was probably influenced very much in his rebellious attitude by the treatment his doctoral mentor, Edward Allsworth Ross, had received at Stanford. Ross was fired from Stanford in 1900, largely, it is thought, because he urged immigration laws against bringing Chinese coolies into America to work on railroad building. (Stanford was funded primarily by monies from a railroad which employed such labor.) The firing of Ross spurred the movement for academic freedom in the United States under the leadership of E.R.A. Seligman of Columbia University. Ross then went on to Wisconsin, where, together with John R. Gillin, he built up one of the broadest sociology departments in the nation and where Mills was one of his early doctoral students.

Mills emerged as an acid critic of the so-called military-industrial complex and was one of the earliest leaders of the New Left political movement of the 1960s. Against the overwhelming number of academic studies, Mills insisted—and this is the central thesis of virtually all of his works—that there is a concentration of political power in the hands of a small group of military and business leaders which he termed the "power elite." Essentially, what he proposes as a cure for this immoral situation is that this power be transferred to an academic elite, a group of social scientists who think as Mills does.

As to how the power is to be transferred, Mills is not too clear, as he died before he was able to complete a final synthesis of his thought. In general, he maintains that the academic elite already wields the power but that it is subservient to a corrupt military-industrial complex which it unthinkingly serves simply because it is the going system, the establishment. The task, then, is to convert the academic elite through moral suasion or a kind of "theological preaching," as one sympathetic critic has commented. A major reason why the academic elite unwittingly serves this complex is the elite's behavioral approach, its commitment to value-free social science. In the past, conservatives have attacked the academic intelligentsia on the same grounds, that it has been immoral not to inculcate moral values.

Now Mills and the New Left made the same criticism, although in the interest of rather different moral values. Mills and his followers argued that the so-called value-free commitment to analyze "what is," that is, the existing system, automatically buttresses that system and—since the system is wrong—is thus immoral. In a sense, then, as one commentator has observed, what Mills's program amounts to is: "Intellectuals of the world, unite!"

Mills's analysis of political influence has received a much more favorable response. Mills, like a number of other, earlier writers, as far back as Plato and as recent as Walter Lippmann, perceptively pointed out that eminence in one field is quickly transformed into political influence, especially in a democracy, where public opinion is so crucial. Thus, movie stars, sports stars, and famous doctors use their fame to secure elections or political followings. How-

ever, there is no rational basis for this, since competence is related to function. If one functions as a film actor or doctor, that does not mean that he has political wisdom. Mills thus advocated his social science elite to replace such corrupt manifestations of the existing system, thereby calling into question many of the fundamental assumptions of democracy. He advocated a community of social scientists, similar to Plato's philosopher-kings, throughout the world, but especially in the United States, and this elite would wield power through knowledge.

Further Reading

For a sympathetic assessment of Mills see the work by the American Marxist theoretician Herbert Aptheker, *The World of C. Wright Mills* (1960), and Irving L. Horowitz, ed., *The New Sociology: Essays in the Social Science and Social Theory in Honor of C. Wright Mills* (1964). Criticism of Mills is in Daniel Bell, *The End of Ideology* (1960; new rev. ed. 1961); various works by Robert Dahl, particularly *Who Governs?* (1961); and Raymond A. Bauer and others, *American Business and Public Policy: The Politics of Foreign Trade* (1963). □

Robert Mills

Robert Mills (1781-1855), American architect, helped popularize the Greek revival style in the United States.

Robert Mills was born in Charleston, S.C., on Aug. 12, 1781. He studied at Charleston College. After moving to Washington, D.C., in 1800, he became an apprentice of the builder-architect James Hoban. Shortly thereafter Mills met Thomas Jefferson, who brought him to Monticello to study architecture and in 1804 sent him on a tour of the eastern states to visit new construction.

Mills worked for Benjamin H. Latrobe, architect of the Capitol, from 1804 to 1808. Concurrently, Mills began his own practice, designing Sansom Street Church in Philadelphia (1804) with a circular auditorium and covering dome, the first church dome in America. In 1808 he established his own practice as an architect and engineer in Philadelphia. Here he built row houses (1809), a Unitarian church (1811-1813), wings on Independence Hall (1812), and the Upper Ferry Bridge (1812; destroyed), whose single arch spanning 360 feet was the longest in the world. His designs for the prison at Burlington, N.J. (1808), several fine houses in Richmond, Va., and courthouses in many southern cities spread his fame and the Greek revival style. His best-known early work is the Washington Monument in Baltimore (1814-1829).

In 1817 Mills moved to Baltimore. He designed churches and became chief engineer for the city waterworks. His *Treatise on Inland Navigation* (1820) demonstrated his competence in the important field of transportation. He returned to Charleston in 1820 and worked for a decade on public buildings. He designed the State Hospital for the Insane in Columbia (1822) and the

Additional Sources

Liscombe, R. W., *Altogether American: Robert Mills, architect and engineer, 1781-1855,* New York: Oxford University Press, 1994. ☐

David Brown Milne

David Brown Milne (1882-1953), Canadian painter and etcher, was a pioneer of postimpressionism in Canadian art. He developed a personal style almost Oriental in its economy of means.

David Milne was born in January 1882 near Paisley, Ontario, and began his career as a country schoolteacher. About 1904 he went to New York to study at the Art Students' League, but after 6 months he had to turn to commercial art for a living. In his spare time he painted the urban scene in the strong outlines and broad color areas of the Fauves. He exhibited five canvases in the famous Armory Show of 1913.

In 1915 Milne settled at Boston Corner in the Berkshire Hills. At the end of 1917 he joined the Canadian army as a private; a year later he was appointed as a war artist to record places where the Canadians saw action. From 1919 to 1928 he spent winters at Boston Corner and summers in the Adirondacks. In 1923 the National Gallery of Canada bought six of his watercolors. His paintings were included in the Canadian sections of the British Empire Exhibitions in England in 1924 and 1925.

In 1928 Milne returned to Canada to stay and lived in small centers near Toronto, such as Palgrave and Uxbridge. From 1932 to 1939 he lived in a cabin on Six-mile Lake near Georgian Bay. He died on Dec. 26, 1953.

From 1934, when Milne had his first one-man show in Toronto, he was encouraged by a small but discerning group of patrons, of whom the most constant over the years was Douglas Duncan, moving spirit of the Picture Loan Society. In spite of his life of seclusion, Milne contributed regularly to the exhibition of Canadian art societies, and he was one of the four artists representing Canada in its first showing at the Venice Biennale, in 1952.

Milne found his subject matter wherever he happened to be; the streets of New York, the Berkshire Hills and lakes in the Adirondacks, the sleepy villages of rural Ontario, the rocks of Georgian Bay, or perhaps a cupful of waterlilies with the weekend comics as a background. During the 1940s an element of whimsy appears in a series of watercolors such as *Snow in Bethlehem, The Saint,* and *King, Queen and Jokers.*

As Milne's personal style developed, his color became more limited and line increasingly important. Open space took on a more active role. This tendency also appeared in the color drypoint etchings he produced from 1922 on, and one may perhaps see in this fastidious medium the source of his sensitive painting style.

fireproof Record Building in Charleston (1822). He also wrote three important treatises: *Internal Improvement of South Carolina* (1822), *The Atlas of the State of South Carolina* (1825), and *Statistics of South Carolina* (1826).

Mills was back in Washington, D.C., in 1830. He published two more useful books: *The American Pharos, or Lighthouse Guide* (1832) and *A Guide to the Capitol of the United States* (1834). From 1836 until 1851 he was the official "architect of public buildings." He erected the new Treasury Building (1836-1839), the Patent Office (1836-1840), and the Post Office (1839), monumental works featuring classical colonnades, porticoes, and decorations. The Patent Office is Greek Doric, like the Parthenon in Athens, and the Treasury colonnade is Ionic, copying the Erechtheum in Athens. In 1836 Mills won the competition for the Washington Monument in Washington, D.C., but construction did not begin until 1848 and was not completed until 1884.

Further Reading

One work on Mills is H. M. Pierce Gallagher, *Robert Mills: Architect of the Washington Monument, 1781-1855* (1935), which offers new information but is not definitive. Talbot Hamlin, *Greek Revival Architecture in America* (1944), devotes half a chapter to Mills, postulating that Mills and William Strickland, both pupils of Latrobe, brought the Greek revival style to maturity.

Further Reading

Background material on Milne is in Graham McInnes, *Canadian Art* (1950), and in Donald W. Buchanan, *The Growth of Canadian Painting* (1950). □

Alfred Milner

The British statesman Alfred Milner, 1st Viscount Milner (1854-1925), served as high commissioner of South Africa and later as a Cabinet member. A public servant of great ability, he is closely associated with British imperialism.

Alfred Milner was born on March 23, 1854, at Giessen, Hesse-Darmstadt (Germany). He lived part of his youth in Germany and part in England. His parents were English, and his mother insisted that he be educated in English schools. Young Milner distinguished himself at King's College School, London, and at Balliol College, Oxford.

Milner started out on a legal career but then turned to journalism. He was interested in many facets of economic policy and political administration. Because of his known ability he moved about in influential government circles and held a variety of official assignments. In 1884 he took the job of private secretary to G. J. Goschen. The next year Milner helped Goschen win a seat in the House of Commons, but Milner himself lost a hard-fought contest for another constituency. Later, when Goschen was chancellor of the Exchequer, Milner became his official private secretary. He went from there to a financial position in Egypt under Sir Evelyn Baring (later Lord Cromer). In 1892 Goschen brought Milner back to England to become chairman of the Board of Inland Revenue, where under both Liberals and Conservatives he was widely acclaimed.

Anglo-Boer trouble in South Africa was approaching a deadlock when Milner was chosen to go there as high commissioner in 1897. He believed in British imperialism and the necessity of protecting British interests. Before many months had passed, he became convinced that war was unavoidable. Milner refused to alter Britain's policy, and he could not believe that the Boers were acting in good faith when they sought a peaceful compromise. The Boer War was the result, and it came to dominate the entire British political scene. The long war ended with British military victory; Milner was one of the signers of the peace treaty. He then put his efforts into rebuilding South Africa after the war's destruction. He is remembered for his part in the war and for his work in building up the country's physical and economic base. In both he was a party to controversial programs: concentration camps for civilians during the war and the importation of Chinese workers to solve the labor shortage following the war. Conditions of life in both instances led to widespread condemnation by humanitarian groups in England and around the world.

Milner went back to England in the spring of 1905 after his tenure in South Africa. He was respected for his abilities by leaders of both parties, but he was always associated with the unpopular events in South Africa. Although he was not a party politician, Milner's policy was closely linked with that of the Conservatives, who were overwhelmingly defeated in the election of 1906. Milner sat in the House of Lords after having been made a viscount in 1902. There he opposed much of the legislation sponsored by the Liberals.

When the crisis of World War I came, Milner was called on again, first to increase food production and then to be a member of Prime Minister David Lloyd George's five-man War Cabinet, which ruled England from 1916 to 1918. In the latter post he was active in every aspect of wartime planning. He became war secretary in April 1918 and colonial secretary in December 1918.

Milner retired in February 1921 after long service and at a time when his views on imperialism were waning in popularity. He died on May 13, 1925.

Further Reading

Milner's own record of events in South Africa is lucidly presented in *The Milner Papers: South Africa,* edited by Cecil Headlam (2 vols., 1931-1933). His work on the problems of governing Egypt in the Cromer era is *England in Egypt* (1894; last rev. ed. 1970). The best complete biography of Milner is John Evelyn Wrench, *Alfred Lord Milner: The Man of No Illusions, 1854-1925* (1958). Milner's public career is recorded in a substantial scholarly work that uses private papers and public documents: Alfred M. Gollin, *Proconsul in Politics: A Study of Lord*

Milner in Opposition and in Power (1964). Milner as a leading imperialist is the subject of several works which emphasize his views and experiences in South Africa: Lionel Curtis, *With Milner in South Africa* (1951); Edward Crankshaw, *The Forsaken Idea: A Study of Viscount Milner* (1952); and Vladimir Halperin, *Lord Milner and the Empire: The Evolution of British Imperialism* (1952).

Additional Sources

Marlowe, John, *Milner: apostle of Empire: a life of Alfred George, the Right Honourable Viscount Milner of St James's and Cape Town, KG, GCB, GCMG, 1854-1925,* London: Hamilton, 1976.

O'Brien, Terence Henry, *Milner: Viscount Milner of St. James's and Cape Town, 1854-1925,* London: Constable, 1979. □

Slobodan Milosevic

Slobodan Milosevic (born 1941) became president of Serbia in 1989. He won two subsequent presidential elections (1990, 1992) and retained his post.

Slobodan Milosevic was born on August 20, 1941, in Pozarevac, a small town on the outskirts of Belgrade, capital city of the former Yugoslavia. His ancestors belonged to the Vasojevici clan from Montenegro. His father finished Orthodox seminary in Cetinje (Montenegro) and studied at the School of Theology in Belgrade. His mother was a teacher in Pozarevac. People remember her as a strict, diligent woman and a fervent communist.

Milosevic finished his primary and secondary education in Pozarevac. According to his teachers and classmates, young Slobodan was an outstanding high school student always sitting in the first row neatly dressed. Although rather quiet and solitary, he was politically active and published several pieces in the local high school journal. While still in high school, Milosevic met his future wife, Mirjana (Mira) Markovic, whose family ranked among the most prominent communists in Serbia. Her father was a hero from World War II; her uncle later became one of the leading politicians in postwar Serbia; and her aunt was a personal secretary of Josip Broz Tito. The young couple's contemporaries did not doubt that the love between Mirjana and Slobodan was sincere and genuine—a covenant of two similar souls rather than a marriage of interest. They raised two children.

In 1960 Milosevic became a law student at the University of Belgrade. He was an excellent student and active in the university section of the League of Communists (official name for the Communist Party) where he met Ivan Stambolic, a nephew of one of the most powerful Serbian communist leaders. Many people think that it was Stambolic who elevated the political career of Milosevic. In 1964, after graduating from the university, Milosevic was appointed as an economic counselor and a coordinator of the informational service in the administration of the City of Belgrade. In 1968 he became a deputy director of a state-owned gas conglomerate, Tehnogas. After Stambolic left Tehnogas in 1973 and became the prime minister of Serbia,

Milosevic rose to the post of director. Five years later he became president of the powerful Belgrade bank Beobanka. In 1982 he became a member of the collective presidency of the League of Communists of Serbia, and two years later a chief of the City of Belgrade Party Organization. The collective presidency of the League of Communists of Serbia elected Milosevic as its president in 1986.

On a personal level many people described Milosevic as a very pleasant and witty person, well organized, and a sophisticated politician. While his political speeches were plain and simple, he dressed well, smoked expensive cigars, and did not hesitate to use his fluent English.

On April 24, 1987, Milosevic visited Kosovo Polje, a suburb of the capital of the autonomous province of Kosovo, attempting to appease the mass of Serbs and Montenegrins protesting a continuous mistreatment by the Albanian majority. When an excited crowd tried to enter the building and talk directly to Milosevic, they were beaten back by the local police. Milosevic strode out and shouted to the crowd: "No one has the right to beat you!" These simple words changed the milieu of Serbian politics. Shortly after, in a series of steamy sessions of the League of Communists of Serbia, Milosevic succeeded in removing Stambolic and his associates from the Serbian political arena. In 1989 Milosevic became president of Serbia.

The internal disagreement among Serbia's communists over Kosovo province shook the already crumbling Yugoslav federation. After Serbia reinstated its authority over the autonomous provinces of Kosovo and Vojvodina, the prospect of Serbian domination fueled a nationalist frenzy in Slovenia and Croatia and bolstered secessionist movements in these republics. Following the collapse of the League of Communists of Yugoslavia in 1990, multiparty elections were held in each of six Yugoslav republics. While Milosevic and his Socialist Party retained power in Serbia, forces that openly advocated secession from Yugoslavia came into power in almost all other republics (with the exception of Montenegro). The nationalist hysteria that spread all over Yugoslavia invoked gruesome memories among Serbs who were subjected to genocide by the Croatian Nazi regime during World War II. Milosevic, who had already established himself as the foremost champion of Serbian rights, was the natural ally to more than two million Serbs living outside the borders of Serbia. When the negotiations among the various republics were called off in 1991, the violent breakup of Yugoslavia became imminent.

The collapse of Yugoslavia and the ensuing civil war among the break-away nations focused new attention on Milosevic. In the fighting that began in April 1992 Milosevic seemed to stay removed from personal involvement, leaving Serbian militias to carry out attacks against the newly established nations of Croatia and Bosnia Herzegovina. Nevertheless, many critics, particularly in the West, portrayed him as a ruthless despot intent upon overseeing the creation of a Greater Serbia. At the same time, Milosevic and his Socialist Party seemed secure in their Belgrade headquarters.

By late 1995, U.N.-imposed sanctions had demolished the Serbian economy and Milosevic agreed to a Balkan peace plan forged during negotiations at an air base in Dayton, Ohio. He has been attempting to rebuild his image, since he was once thought to be the reason behind military crimes, war crimes, and millions of deaths. Milosevic began making strides at winning a more favorable public opinion, calling for tolerance among ethnic groups and portraying himself as a heroic and peace-promoting defender of Serbs against annihilation. Despite the near-40 percent unemployment and the overall decline in lifestyle among the Serbs, he did retain supporters.

In 1997 Milosevic's second and final term as president was to run out, but he hoped to prolong his tenure with a technicality. On July 23, 1997, he changed his title from president of Serbia to president of the Yugoslav federation in an attempt to circumvent the term limit.

Further Reading

Slobodan Milosevic is discussed in the *Christian Science Monitor* (throughout October 1988), *Time* (June 8, 1992), and numerous references in periodicals such as the *Washington Post* (May 4, 1994), *Wall Street Journal,* and the *New York Times.* For information regarding the 1997 political race, see Calabresi, Massimo, "So Unhappy Together" in *Time* (June 23, 1997). □

Czeslaw Milosz

The Polish author and poet Czeslaw Milosz (born 1911), winner of the 1980 Nobel Prize for Literature, explored in his work both the rebirth of Christian belief and the corruption of thought by ideology.

Czeslaw Milosz is one of the most important writers and poets to have emerged in Poland since World War II. Terence De Pres stated that Milosz' poetry deals "with the central issues of our time: the impact of history upon being, the search for ways to survive spiritual ruin in a ruined world." He was born on June 30, 1911 in Szetejnie, Lithuania then in Tsarist Russia, to Polish-Lithuanian parents. His father, Alexander, was a road engineer and was recruited by the Tsar's army during World War I. Young Milosz and his mother traveled with Alexander on the dangerous bridge-building expeditions to which he was dispatched near Russian battle zones.

His family returned to Lithuania in 1918, and Milosz began a strict formal education in his hometown of Wilno, the capital of Polish Lithuania. In his early 20s, he published his first volume of poems, *A Poem on Frozen Time.* In 1934, he graduated from the King Stefan Batory University, and in 1936 his second volume of poetry appeared. He earned a scholarship to study at the Alliance Française in Paris, where he also met up with his distant cousin, Oscar Milosz, a French poet who became his mentor.

Milosz returned to Poland to work for the Polish State Broadcasting Company up to the outbreak of World War II. He stayed in Warsaw during the Nazi occupation, where he joined the underground resistance movement. Milosz was inclined toward socialism, and had an uneasy relationship with the Communist government that came to power in Poland in 1946. Milosz had an anthology of anti-Nazi poetry, *The Invincible Song* published by underground presses in Warsaw, where he also wrote "The World (A Naive Poem)" and the cycle *Voices of Poor People.* When Warsaw was destroyed, he lived for a bit outside of Cracow, whose state publishing house brought out his collected poems in a volume called *Rescue.*

At the end of World War II, Milosz worked as a cultural attaché for the Polish communist government, serving in New York and Washington. He left his position with the Polish Foreign Service in 1951 and sought (and received) political asylum in France. Milosz spent ten years in France, and he found himself having difficulty with the strongly pro-socialist and communist intellectual community. He penned two novels during his time in Paris, *Seizure of Power* and *The Issa Valley.* His most famous book, *The Captive Mind* (1953) was a bitter attack on the manner in which the Communist Party in Poland progressively destroyed the independence of the Polish intelligentsia.

He continued to speak out against the Polish intellectuals, comparing them to Charlie Chaplin in *The Gold Rush,* bustling about in a shack poised on a cliff. Too often his contemporaries would end up agreeing with their new masters, while secretly believing that they could in some way maintain at the same time an area of their own intellectual autonomy. This phenomenon he termed "Ketman" and he saw the downfall of a free intelligentsia in Poland. In a novel entitled *The Usurpers* (1955) that graphically described the communist seizure of power, he wrote of a rather pathetic classical scholar, Professor Gill, who had been deprived of a chair at the university. Gill was busy translating Thucydides for a small edition for the state publishing house as a means, he hoped, of keeping some idea of classical culture alive.

Milosz' early writing was strongly shaped by the culture of his adopted city, Wilno, which was a major center of both Catholic and Jewish learning before 1939. Milosz considered himself to be both a poet and an intellectual. His poetry at this time reflected a mood of youthful romanticism as well as recognition that kingdoms rise and fall. As his poem "Hymn" put it in 1935, "Forms come and go, what seems invincible crumbles." This world of Milosz' youth did, indeed, crumble after the German invasion. He saw Warsaw destroyed by the Germans in 1944 after the failure of Stalin's advancing armies to rescue the Polish partisans. Milosz came increasingly to distrust Marxist ideology and its ideal of a classless millennium.

Milosz saw many of his intellectual contemporaries compromising their ideals in the interest of naked power politics. He came to treat the intellectual generally with suspicion, writing in *Native Realm* (1968) that he was "not sure that all intellectual talents are not like orchids, which nourish themselves on the rotten wood of decaying trees."

With such strong opinions, Milosz found his poetry banned in Poland, but was published in Paris by the Instytut Literacki.

Milosz ultimately felt that the only way to maintain his own intellectual autonomy, claiming to be "imprisoned as I am in my I," was an exile in the West. He regretted that works like *The Captive Mind* came to be used as Cold War propaganda and hoped that Eastern Europe would be able to regenerate its culture once the wave of communism was passed. He remembered his cousin, Oscar, castigating Eastern Europeans for simply imitating other "centres of culture" instead of creating one themselves. It was a memory he did not forget.

Milosz continued his exile even further West. At age 50, he began a new career as a professor of Slavic languages and literature at the University of California at Berkeley in 1961 (some sources say 1960). He was initially an unknown member of a small department; but eventually became popular for his courses on Dostoyevsky, and known to those outside the university as a translator of the poems of Zbigniew Herbert. In the poetry he wrote after going into exile, Milosz consciously sought to build on his earlier romanticism by stressing the true meaning of words that had become corrupted by political ideology. "Yes I would like to be a poet of the five senses," he wrote in *In Milan* (1955). "That's why I don't allow myself to become one./Yes, thought has less weight than the word *lemon*/That's why in my words I do not reach for fruit." At the same time identification with nature allowed him to maintain an identity even in exile. As the poem in *Throughout Our Lands,* written in 1961 while at Berkeley, put it,

> Wherever you are, you touch the bark of trees
> testing its roughness different yet familiar,
> grateful for a rising and a setting sun
> Wherever you are, you could never be an alien.

By the 1970s, Milosz' poetry and fiction was increasingly attracting the attention of Western critics. In 1976, he was awarded a Guggenheim fellowship. In 1978, he published *Bells in Winter,* for which he received the Neustadt International Literature Prize. In 1980, he was awarded the Nobel Prize for Literature. By this time, many of his poems had become infused with a more orthodox and settled Christianity. There was also a growing sadness and premonition of oncoming death, especially after the death of his wife Janina in 1986. This was frequently a difficult and obscure poetry that was burdened by a sense of the oncoming collapse of civilization. Milosz' poetry, though, did not contain any premonition of the collapse of the Eastern European Communist régimes.

After winning the Nobel Prize, Milosz published many volumes of prose and poetry. His prose collections include *Visions from San Francisco Bay, Beginning With My Streets, The Land of Ulro,* and his Charles Eliot Norton Lectures from Harvard, *The Witness of Poetry.* In 1988, his *Collected Poems* were published, followed most recently by another collection entitled *Provinces.*

Milosz chronicled his life in 1988. This diary became the book *A Year of the Hunter,* published in 1994. A review in the *Boston Book Review* called it "an elegiac, autumnal work—a reassessment of a long and complicated career, marriage and exile." After returning to Lithuania in the spring of 1989, Milosz was flooded with sentiment about is childhood in the Issa River Valley. In this collection, Milosz explores "the nature of imagination, human experience, good and evil—and celebrates the wonders of life on earth," an abstract from Ecco press noted. David Biespiel's review of the collection notes that Milosz, as always, speaks to his readers "with a passionate mixture of lament, rage, joy, resignation, and *officium landis,* despite his self-questioning: "Did I fulfill what I had to, here, on earth?" Despite being afflicted with asthma and declining health, Milosz managed to also release another volume of poetry in 1995, *Facing the River.* In 1997, his correspondence with poet and monk Thomas Merton was published, a speculative epistolary history of their inner worlds.

Milosz' confrontation with both a revival of Christian belief (he feels chosen by God, he told Biespiel, to transform what he's experienced into art) and the corruption of thought by ideology has made him a figure of our time. He resides in the Berkeley hills, overlooking San Francisco Bay, with his wife, Carol, and a cat named Tiny.

Further Reading

Additional information on Czeslaw Milosz and his work can be found in Adam Czernjawski (editor), *The Burning Forest: Modern Polish Poetry* (Newcastle Upon Tyne: 1988); Edward Mozejko (editor), *Between Anxiety and Hope: The Poetry and Writing of Czeslaw Milosz* (Edmonton: 1988); and Czeslaw Milosz, *The Collected Poems, 1931-1987* (1988) and *Native Realm* (1989).Online sources include "The Art of Poetry: Czeslaw Milosz," http://www.voyagerco.com/PR/winter94/milosz2html; "Czeslaw Milosz," http://www.poetry.books.com/nmilosz.htm; "Hungry Mind Review: Facing The River," http://www.bookwire.com/HMR/Poetry/read.Review$1721; "Facing the River: New Poems," http://www.wwnorton.com/ecco/884547.htm; "Boston Book Review: A Year of the Hunter," http://www.bookwire.com/BBR/Life-&-Letters/read.Review$1325; and "Czleslaw Milosz (1911 Szetejinie, Lithuania)," http://sunsite.unc.edu/dukki/poetry/milosz/mil-bio. Periodical references include *America* (February 1, 1997); *Library Journal* (December 1996); *New York Review of Books* (August 13, 1992; March 23, 1995); and *Poetry* (February 1997). □

Miltiades

Miltiades (ca. 549-488 B.C.) was a brilliant Athenian military strategist and statesman who successfully brought about Athenian victory over the Persians at the Battle of Marathon.

Son of Cimon, an Athenian aristocrat, Miltiades was chief magistrate under the tyranny at Athens in 524 B.C., and in 516, with the tyrants' support, he went to seize power in the Chersonese area of Thrace. Shortly afterward he captured Lemnos. But the advancing power of Persia arrested this portion of his adventuresome career. When Darius invaded Europe and campaigned in Scythia, Miltiades entered Persian service; according to Herodotus, Miltiades wished to destroy the bridge over the Danube and cut off Darius's retreat.

By 510 Miltiades was back in Athens, driven out of the Chersonese by raiding Scythians. When the Ionians rose in revolt against Persia, Miltiades returned to the Chersonese at the invitation of the native people and ruled from 496 to 493. He withdrew when the Ionians were finally defeated.

As leader of the Philaid clan, Miltiades had many opponents at Athens. They brought him to trial on a charge of tyrannical rule in the Chersonese. But he was acquitted. Because of his unrivaled experience in Persian warfare, the people elected him one of the 10 generals who took office in July 490, when the Persian fleet was already on the way.

Battle of Marathon

When the Persian army landed at the Bay of Marathon, Miltiades proposed in the Assembly that the Athenians provide themselves with supplies and set out and meet the enemy at once instead of holding Athens and waiting for help from Sparta. His proposal was adopted. On the evening after the Persian landing, heavily armed Athenian infantry moved into the Plan of Marathon and blocked the Persian advance. The following day the Persian army moved into position and offered battle.

By this time 1,000 Plataeans had joined the 10,000 or so Athenians, and it was not known whether aid was com-

ing from Sparta; yet Miltiades advised engagement. The voting of the 10 generals was equal, but the polemarch, Callimachus, broke the tie in favor of Miltiades. While Miltiades waited for an opportunity to meet the enemy under favorable terms, news came that the Spartans would march out when the moon was full. But before the Spartans arrived, Miltiades saw a good opportunity and at dawn ordered an attack. He used the tactics of a weak center and strengthened wings against a superior infantry force and was successful.

The hero of the day, Miltiades took command of a naval offensive in the Cyclades in 489. In an unsuccessful attack on Paros, he was wounded. On his return he was impeached, condemned, and fined. He died soon afterward as a result of his wound.

Further Reading

The ancient sources for the study of Miltiades are Herodotus and Cornelius Nepos. Among modern works which deal with Miltiades are Andrew Robert Burn, *Persia and the Greeks: The Defence of the West, ca. 546-478 B.C.* (1962), and N.G.L. Hammond, *A History of Greece to 322 B.C.* (2d ed. 1967). □

John Milton

The English poet and controversialist John Milton (1608-1674) was a champion of liberty and of love-centered marriage. He is chiefly famous for his epic poem "Paradise Lost" and for his defense of uncensored publication.

The lifetime of John Milton spanned an age of sophistication, controversy, dynamism, and revolution. When he was born, England was illuminated by the versatile genius of Francis Bacon, William Shakespeare, William Byrd, Orlando Gibbons, and Inigo Jones. Christopher Wren was at the height of his powers when Milton died in 1674. At that date Henry Purcell was the major composer; Isaac Newton dominated in mathematics and physics; and literature enjoyed the varied talents of John Dryden, Andrew Marvell, John Bunyan, and Samuel Pepys.

In the middle period of Milton's life, England, after two revolutionary wars, became a republic and then a protectorate under Oliver Cromwell. When monarchy and the Anglican Church were restored in 1660, mercantilist capitalism had been firmly established, and the foundations of the British Empire and navy were laid.

Background and Education

The poet's father, John Milton, Sr., emerged from a line of obscure Roman Catholic yeomen in Oxfordshire, was educated as a chorister, went to London, and became a scrivener—a profession that combined moneylender, copyist, notary, and contract lawyer. About 1600 he married Sara Jeffrey, the wealthy daughter of a merchant-tailor. Three of their children survived infancy: Anne; John, born

on Dec. 9, 1608; and Christopher. Their father was not only an able man of business but a musician. He composed madrigals, choral pieces, and some hymns that are still sung. From him young John derived the love of music that pervades his works.

According to Milton's own account in his *Second Defense* (1654), "My father destined me while still a child for the study of humane letters, which I took up so eagerly that, from the age of twelve on, I hardly ever took to bed from my intense studies before midnight." After private tutoring, about 1620 he entered St. Paul's School, where he studied Sallust, Virgil, and Horace and the New Testament in Greek.

"After I had thus been taught several languages and had tasted the sweetness of philosophy, my father sent me to Cambridge." Admitted to Christ's College at the age of 15, he intended to become a Church of England priest. Because of a disagreement with his tutor, he was "rusticated" (temporarily expelled) in 1626. From home he wrote a Latin poem to his best friend, Charles Diodati, about the joys of exile—reading, plays, walks, and girl watching.

Back at Cambridge about April 1626, Milton was assigned a different tutor and resumed the study of logic, ethics, Greek, Latin, and Hebrew. He composed Latin poems on the deaths of prominent men, some antipopish epigrams, and *In quintum Novembris* (On the Fifth of November), a melodramatic little epic on the Gunpowder Plot. In 1628 his first major English poem, "On the Death of a Fair Infant, Dying of the Cough," was occasioned by the death of his sister's baby. A year later, in images of light and music, "On the Morning of Christ's Nativity" celebrated the harmonizing power of divine love.

In one of his *Prolusions* (college orations), Milton digressed into English verse, beginning "Hail native language." Thereafter he wrote Latin verse occasionally and a series of sonnets in Italian, but he composed increasingly in English, his tone ranging from the humor of a mock epitaph, "On the University Carrier," to somber dignity in "An Epitaph on the Marchioness of Winchester." The companion poems "L'Allegro" and "Il Penseroso" contrasted the pleasures of the "joyful man" with the more serious ones of the "contemplative man," thus revealing the complementary sides of Milton's own nature.

The Graceful Thirties

After receiving the bachelor of arts and the master of arts degrees in 1629 and 1632, Milton lived in his family's suburban home in Hammersmith and then at its country estate in Horton, Buckinghamshire, continuing studies in theology, history, mathematics, and literature but participating in social and cultural life in London and the country. The presence of his "On Shakespeare" in the 1632 folio of Shakespeare's plays suggests that Milton was in touch with actors. In his sonnet "How Soon hath Time," Milton modestly lamented his lack of accomplishments in 23 years; but he was soon writing lyrics for his *Arcades,* an entertainment. In 1634 *A Mask* (better known as *Comus*) was performed at Ludlow Castle, with music by Henry Lawes. This mixture of song, dance, pageantry, and poetry is imbued with youthful charm and glorifies the purity of chastity with exquisite lyricism; but with his characteristic readiness to do justice to opposing viewpoints, Milton did not neglect to put an attractive case for seduction into the mouth of his epicurean villain. Thus Milton began his concentration on temptation themes.

Milton's themes were both particular and universal. *Lycidas* (1637), a pastoral elegy occasioned by the death of a promising young acquaintance, dealt with why God allows the good to die young and asked if, instead of dedicating one's self to study and writing, it would not be better to do as others do and "sport with Amaryllis in the shade." Milton's answer was that "laborious days" are not wasted: eternal life lies ahead. In 1639, when he learned that his friend Diodati had died, he penned a moving Latin elegy, finding solace in Christian hope and resolution for his grief in esthetic expression. The poem also served as an outlet for a condemnation of negligent clergymen. Though Milton had abandoned the idea of entering the ministry, he was dedicated to making the Church of England more Protestant.

In 1638-1639 Milton toured France and Italy. His short but well-formed body, long auburn hair, blue eyes, and fair skin enhanced his intellectual vivacity and graceful manners. His earnest enthusiasms and versatility in languages also conduced to his being welcomed into polite society abroad. He intended to go to Greece, but news of the growing political and religious crisis in England led him to return to London so that he could help to advance liberty if

his talents were needed. In the meantime he tutored his nephews and other students.

Crucial Decades, 1640-1660

It was by writing prose that Milton found opportunity to serve his God and country. In 1641-1642 he poured out tracts opposing the bishops' control over religion. In his judgment, their powers were based on `man-made traditions, self-interest, and a combination of ignorance, superstition, and deliberate falsification.

Part of what Milton regarded as episcopal tyranny was the regulation of marriage by canon law and the bishops' courts. In his *Commonplace Book* (classified notes based on his reading), he had already shown interest in divorce, before Mary Powell became his wife about May 1642. She was about half his age and came from an Oxfordshire family. A few months later, while she was on a visit to her parents, the civil war between King and Parliament erupted. Her family were royalists living in royalist territory, whereas Milton's attacks on the bishops had committed him to the rebels. Accordingly, she failed to return to him despite his urgings. Under these circumstances his publishing a series of pamphlets on divorce (1643-1645) was hardly tactful; but if Mary read them, she discovered that, instead of urging England to follow Protestant example abroad and permit divorce for adultery, desertion, and nonconsummation, Milton emphasized the spiritual and mental aspects of marriage: he held that what is essential is neither physical nor sacramental nor contractual but lies in marital love, in the union of what distinguishes human beings from animals— their rational souls. Milton taught that if such compatibility was lacking and could not be achieved after sincere effort, all concerned should recognize the right of divorce, inasmuch as God had not joined such an ill-yoked couple. However, it is doubtful that Milton regarded his own marriage in such a light, for in 1645 he forgave a repentant Mary—she blamed her mother—and as far as is known they lived contentedly together until she died in 1652.

In 1644 Milton's "Of Education" dealt with another kind of domestic freedom, how to develop in schoolboys discipline, reasonableness, broad culture, all-round ability, and independence of judgment. The same year saw *Areopagitica,* his defense of man's right to free speech and discussion as the best means of advancing truth. To this end he opposed prepublication censorship though admitting that if a book or those responsible for it broke clear and reasonable laws against libel, pornography, blasphemy, or sedition, the work could be repressed or those responsible for it could be fairly tried and punished if found guilty. Milton advocated neither licentiousness or avoidable interference with individuals but, rather, responsible freedom under just laws and magistrates.

The divorce tracts made Milton undeservedly notorious as a fanatic libertine advocate of free love. Readers of his collected *Poems* (1645) were therefore probably surprised to find the charming seriousness of an author who, had he died then, might have been ranked with George Herbert and Robert Herrick as an Anglican poet. The volume contained not only the poems mentioned above but also exquisite lyrics such as "On a May Morning" and "At a Solemn Musick." Milton also put new life into the sonnet genre, investing it with wider subject matter.

As the civil war drew to a close, Milton turned from defending the liberty of religion, marriage, and publication to condemning royal tyranny. *The Tenure of Kings and Magistrates* (1649) argued that men have a natural right to freedom and that contracts they make with rulers are voluntary and terminable. Soon after its publication he began a decade as the revolutionary government's secretary for foreign tongues: his chief duty was to put state letters into choice Latin. His next pamphlet, *Eikonoklastes* (1649), answered "The King's Book," a self-justification attributed to Charles I. This was followed by two *Defenses of the English People* (1651, 1654) to explain why they revolted and a *Defense of Himself* (1655) against various attackers. These works were in Latin: Milton was the revolution's chief international propagandist.

For some years Milton had been losing his eyesight, and by early 1652 he was totally blind. Reflecting that this could prevent the use of his talent in God's service, he composed the sonnet "When I consider how my light is spent" with its famous conclusion, "They also serve who only stand and wait."

In 1656, four years after his first wife's death, Milton married Kathrine Woodcock. Two years later she died as a result of childbirth, and he tenderly memorialized her in a sonnet, "To my late departed Saint."

Despite adversities Milton heroically persisted. During the crisis preceding restoration of the monarchy he dictated several tracts. In *A Treatise of Civil Power* (1659) he again urged toleration and separation of Church and state. *Ready and Easy Way* (1660) argued for preservation of a republic.

Triumph in Defeat

Inevitably the eloquent defender of monarchy's overthrow was in acute danger when Charles II, son of the executed Charles I, regained the throne in 1660. Milton was harassed and imprisoned; his seditious books were publically burned; but he was included in a general pardon. In 1663 he married Elizabeth Minshell. In 1667, *Paradise Lost,* his long-planned epic on the fall of man, was published. In 1671 its sequel, *Paradise Regained,* appeared in one volume with *Samson Agonistes,* a tragedy modeled on Greek drama and the Book of Job. Milton also published some previously written prose works on grammar, logic, and early British history; his *Prolusions* with some familiar letters; and an enlarged edition of his earlier *Poems.* In 1673 he reentered public controversy with *Of True Religion,* a brief defense of Protestantism. Before his death about Nov. 8, 1674, he was planning to publish writings that appeared posthumously: his Latin state papers (1676) and a short history of Moscovia (1682). In 1694 his nephew Edward Phillips published a life of his uncle with an English translation of the state papers.

In the early 19th century the Latin manuscript of Milton's *Christian Doctrine* was discovered and translated (1825). In it he systematically set out to disencumber scriptural interpretation from misinterpretation by discovering what the Bible itself said on such matters as predestination, angels, and saving faith. One of his central convictions was that what God accommodated to limited human understandings was sufficient and that man should not impose on what God left vague a precision unjustified by what He revealed.

Paradise Lost was not suspected of unorthodoxy by centuries of Protestant readers, and, except for a few jabs at Roman Catholicism, it has universally appealed to Christians. However, because Satan is portrayed with a rebelliousness against the nature of things that dissidents find attractive, the poets William Blake and Percy Bysshe Shelley and other "Satanists" alleged that Milton was knowingly or unknowingly on the side of the devils. Their notion is evidence of the epic's tremendous imaginative power. In majestic blank-verse paragraphs it relates the whole of history from the Son's generation, through the war in heaven, the fall of the rebel angels, the creation, and man's fall, to a vision of the future, Satan's final defeat, and the establishment of Christ's kingdom. Milton did not intend most of it to be taken literally: it is largely a product of his imagination, inspired by, but not directly based on, the Bible. *Paradise Lost* is a fictionalized, imaginative attempt to dramatize approximations of complex truths. Underlying the fictive is Milton's effort to convey to his fellowmen some insight into God's wisdom and providence.

Paradise Regained, a far shorter epic, treats the rejection by Jesus of Satan's temptations. Its central point is that the true hero conquers not by force but by humility and faith in God. Like the two epics and *Comus, Samson Agonistes* treats the theme of temptation, dramatizing how the Hebrew strong man overtrusted himself and, like Eve and Adam, yielded to passion and seeming self-interest.

Reputation and Influence

For a few decades after his death, Milton was damned as a rebel and divorcer. But since then reformers and revolutionaries have been inspired by his works, especially *Areopagitica.* His influence on poets has been tremendous, though not always beneficial. John Dryden partially based his Achitophel on Milton's Satan and so admired *Paradise Lost* that he recast it as an opera, *The Fall of Man.* Joseph Addison in the *Spectator* demonstrated that Milton ranked with Homer and Virgil. Alexander Pope delightfully satirized some features of *Paradise Lost* in *The Rape of the Lock.* In *The Lives of the Poets* Samuel Johnson somewhat grudgingly conceded Milton's achievement as a poet but was so prejudiced by his royalist, Anglican sympathies that he portrayed Milton as a domestic tyrant. In general, 18th-century poets lauded him for sublimity. William Blake and Percy Bysshe Shelley exalted his Satan as a romantic rebel. William Wordsworth, viewing the poet as a liberator, wrote, "Milton, thou shouldst be living at this hour." Samuel Taylor Coleridge in his critical writings praised Milton's artistry and profundity. John Keats and Alfred, Lord Tennyson, were perhaps overinfluenced by his poetry. The Victorians put *Paradise Lost* alongside the Bible in their parlors for Sunday reading; and Milton's great 19th-century biographer, David Masson, transformed him into Victorian solidity.

Milton's poetic reputation remained high until the 1920s, when there was an adverse reaction from T.S. Eliot and other poet-critics. Somewhat oddly, they condemned his verse chiefly because of its influence. But the academic critics came to the rescue, and since about 1930 Milton studies have been revolutionized. He has been restored to a high eminence, though both his personality and works are still much controverted. Indeed, he has been extraordinarily successful in his aim of stimulating seminal discussion. However, the notion that he was sour and puritanical dies slowly. As a corrective, it is well to remember how his own daughter remembered him: ''She said He was Delightful Company, the Life of the Conversation, and That on Account of a Flow of Subject and an Unaffected Chearfulness and Civility.''

Further Reading

The standard biography is *Milton: A Life* (2 vols., 1968), by William Riley Parker. The most inclusive edition is *The Works,* prepared by general editor Frank Allen Patterson (18 vols., 1931-1938), known as *The Columbia Milton.* However, for the nonpoetic writings, *Complete Prose Works,* prepared by general editor Don M. Wolfe (8 vols., 1953 and later), is more reliable. For the poetry, the most accurate texts are provided in editions by Helen Gardner (2 vols., 1952-1955), Douglas Bush (1965), John Carey and Alastair Fowler (heavily annotated, 1968), and John T. Shawcross (rev. ed. 1971). *The Prose,* edited by J. Max Patrick (1967), includes generous selections, a survey of all the prose works, and annotations. *The Student's Milton,* edited by F.A. Patterson (1930), gives all the poetry and most of the prose in one volume with few notes (1930). *The Complete Poems and Major Prose,* edited by Merritt Y. Hughes (1957), is widely used as a textbook.

A brief, sound entree for the beginner is Douglas Bush, *John Milton: A Sketch of His Life and Writings* (1964). The general reader may prefer *John Milton, Englishman,* by James Holly Hanford (1949), but students will find wider guidance in *A Milton Handbook* by Hanford and James A. Taafe (5th ed. 1970).

The best treatment of Milton's prose in its intellectual context is *Milton and the Puritan Dilemma* by Arthur E. Barker (repr. 1956); he edited *Milton: Modern Essays in Criticism* (1965), an excellent introduction to 20th-century approaches to the poetry, with guidance for further reading. *Milton's Epic Poetry,* edited by C.A. Patrides (1967), contains a variety of essays and an annotated reading list.

Except for Shakespeare, more scholarship and criticism is devoted to Milton than to any other English author. In general, works published before about 1930 have been superseded. Among the best are the books by James Holly Hanford, John M. Steadman, Joseph Summers, Stanley Fish, Merritt Y. Hughes, Kester Svendsen, Don Cameron Allen, E. M. W. Tillyard, Rosemond Tuve, William Riley Parker, A. S. P. Woodhouse, F. Michael Krouse, Louis Martz, and Barbara Lewalski; however, this list is highly selective. The biographies, guides, and editions listed above usually suggest further reading. For fuller guidance see Calvin Huckabay, *John Milton: An Annotated Bibliography* (rev. ed. 1969). □

Queen Min

The Korean Queen Min (1851-1895), whose Korean title was Myngsng Hwanghu, was the strong-willed consort of King Kojong and manipulated court politics in the last turbulent decades of the Yi period.

Queen Min the daughter of Min Ch'irok, a government official. Her parents passed away when she was 9, leaving her a poor orphan who had to live with the Mins of Yju, the place of her birth. She was made the royal consort in 1866 at the urging of Lady Min, consort of Hungsn Taewngun and mother of King Kojong. A court lady named Yi, however, was then enjoying the royal affection and gave birth to Prince Wanhwa.

Queen Min's resentment and hatred was soon directed mostly at Taewongun, who exercised governmental powers as the regent and appeared overjoyed at the birth of the prince. Queen Min's jealousy was intensified when her own child, Wnja, died only 5 days after birth in 1871. The distressed queen now concentrated on having members of the Min family appointed to key financial, personnel, and military positions of the Korean government to oppose the rule of the regent.

As the many political blunders of the regent Taewngun became evident, Queen Min helped King Kojong inaugurate his personal rule, which was to be dominated by the Mins, who were already occupying key positions in the central administration. Followers of Taewngun were summarily removed from power positions, and the government suddenly reversed the isolationist policy pursued by Taewngun. Formal diplomatic relations between Korea and Japan were consequently established.

Queen Min now wielded political power in the name of the lackluster king and through the numerous Mins who owed their positions to her. The rule of the Mins proved to be arrogant, inefficient, and corrupt. The Political Upheaval of the Kapsin Year of 1884 drove the Mins out of power temporarily. The ''progressive'' Cabinet that displaced the Mins, however, was in turn driven out of Seoul through the interference of Ch'ing China. Meanwhile, the Japanese penetration into Korea was intensified and resulted in a short-lived pro-Japanese Cabinet led by Kim Hong-jip.

As it appeared that the Russian legation in Seoul was also being drawn into the power struggles, the Japanese precipitated the Incident of the Ulmi Year of 1895, in which a band of Japanese and Koreans, said to be led by the Japanese minister to Korea, Miura, stabbed the Queen to death. This unprecedented murder of a queen by a band of ruffians which included foreigners bent on the destruction of the ruling family took place on August 20 in the Knch'ng Palace.

Further Reading

A chapter on Min, ''Events Leading to the Assassination of Queen Min,'' is in Clarence Norwood, ed., *Hulbert's History of Korea*

(1962). See also Charles Patrick Fitzgerald, *A Concise History of East Asia* (1966). ☐

Mindon Min

Mindon Min (reigned 1852-1878) was the most able—and modern—of the Konbaung kings, the last Burmese dynasty. Eight years after his death, however, that portion of Burma still under Burmese rule fell to Britain as a result of the Third Anglo-Burmese War.

Half brother of King Pagan Min, who occupied the throne at the start of the short Second Anglo-Burmese War in 1852, Mindon Min was opposed to the war and, with others, displaced Pagan and sought to achieve an honorable settlement with the British and to minimize the possibility of further Burmese territory falling under British control. The 1852 war had resulted from provocative behavior by the governor of a Burmese province and had given the British just the pretext they wanted to extend their presence in Burma.

Mindon Min, who had left the Buddhist monkhood for the throne in a sincere bid for peace, signalized his goodwill by releasing all Europeans imprisoned by the Burmese. Such a gesture hardly halted the momentum of dynamic British imperialism, however, and Britain acquired as a consequence of its second war with the Burmese the rest of Lower Burma (to add to what it had obtained in the First Anglo-Burmese War a quarter century earlier) including the delta region and territory extending beyond Prome and Toungoo.

The spirit of the Burmese in Burmese-and British-ruled Burma was much sapped by the loss of so much territory in two successive wars. King Mindon Min sought to counter this loss of morale by three means: pursuit of correct and nonprovocative relations with the British, modernization of his backward country's economy, and establishment of the Burmese-ruled portion of Burma as a major world center of the Buddhist faith.

In 1871, Mindon Min, scholarly as well as devoutly religious in his Buddhism, convened at Mandalay (to which he had moved the Burmese capital) the fifth international synod, or council, of the world's Theravada (Hinayana) Buddhists—which further heightened his stature in the eyes of his countrymen. He also modernized the administration of government by establishing a European-style system of fixed salaries in place of the traditional way of assigning districts for the upkeep of officials. And he inaugurated a coinage system and improved communications.

The murder of the heir apparent to the Burmese throne in 1866 caused King Mindon not to designate another successor, and in a country without an orderly monarchical succession pattern, this was probably the greatest mistake of his regime. When Mindon Min died in 1878, a palace plot placed on the throne the extraordinarily unqualified Prince Thibaw, whose incompetence was to be a factor in the

replacement of the Burmese Konbaung dynasty in 1885 by the extension of British colonial rule to all parts of Burma.

Further Reading

The Burmese historian Maung Htin Aung treats Mindon Min sympathetically but faithfully in two books, *The Stricken Peacock: Anglo-Burmese Relations, 1752-1948* (1965) and *A History of Burma* (1967). The greatest of the Konbaung monarchs is also viewed favorably by the English historian D. G. E. Hall in two of his works, *Burma* (1950; 3d. ed. 1960) and *Europe and Burma* (1945). Mindon Min's rule is described and evaluated, too, by John F. Cady in *A History of Modern Burma* (1958) and by Dorothy Woodman in *The Making of Burma* (1962). ☐

Cardinal József Mindszenty

József Cardinal Mindszenty (1892-1975), primate of Hungary, was sentenced to life imprisonment in 1948 for his opposition to secularization of Catholic schools and his refusal to recognize the new government. Freed in 1956, he sought refuge at the American embassy after the Soviet invasion of Hungary. He left the country in 1971.

József Mindszenty was born on March 29, 1892, in Mindszent in western Hungary. His parents owned a farm and raised wine grapes and other crops. His father had been village magistrate and head of the parish council and of the school committee. During his school years, Mindszenty was active in the Catholic Youth Movement. After his graduation he entered the seminary in Szombathely. He was ordained a priest on June 12, 1915, and became assistant to the pastor of Felsöpàny. During this period his book on spiritual problems, *Az Édesanya* (The Mother), was published. In 1917 he was asked to teach religion at the state high school in Zalaegerszeg, a major city in western Hungary. He had to teach Latin as well since part of the teaching staff was in the army.

In 1918 World War I came to an end and the Austro-Hungarian Empire collapsed. In October King Charles IV withdrew and Count Kàrolyi took command of the revolutionary government in Budapest. In 1919 the Kàrolyi government prepared for elections in the new nation. Mindszenty assumed the leadership in his area of the newly founded Christian Party. He launched a campaign against the socialistic Kàrolyi party in both the towns and the countryside. On February 9, 1919, he was arrested and interned in the episcopal palace. The bishop himself, also hostile to the government, had been placed under house arrest. The supervision was loose, so Mindszenty had the opportunity to go to the offices of the daily newspaper, where he worked out a program for the spring elections.

On March 21, 1919, the Communists took over and proclaimed the dictatorship of the proletariat. Mindszenty was transferred to jail. He was released on May 15, 1919,

but was not allowed to teach or participate in any political activity against the state. On October 1, 1919, after the collapse of the dictatorship of the proletariat, he was assigned to the parish of Zalaegerszeg. In 1927 he was appointed administrator of the Zala region of the diocese. He was responsible for founding new places for priests, establishing schools, and furthering pastoral activity in all areas.

Pope Pius XII appointed him diocesan bishop of Veszprém on March 4, 1944. He was consecrated bishop in Esztergom on March 25, 1944. Six days earlier the German military forces occupied Hungary "in order to prevent it from concluding a separate peace with the Allies."

On October 31, 1944, the Catholic bishops of western Hungary addressed a memorandum to Premier Szálasi, pointing out the perils to Hungary's cultural sites and population if western Hungary were made a battleground resisting the Russian invasion as Hitler and the Hungarian Arrow Cross men were insisting. Mindszenty personally brought the memorandum to Budapest. On November 27 he was arrested and later transferred to the Köhida jail.

Hungary was liberated by the Red Army on April 4, 1945. Mindszenty was able to return to Veszprém. The agrarian reform carried out by the Communists removed the material basis that supported many ecclesiastical institutions. In the meantime, the Church was given subsidies but the Catholic press was restricted.

On September 16, 1945, Pope Pius XII appointed Mindszenty as archbishop of Esztergom and primate of Hungary. In October 1945 the first episcopal conference was held in Budapest. Mindszenty criticized the land reform and the government's anti-Church actions.

The Communists called for a unified school system, pointing out the necessity of reforms. They argued that church schools were anti-democratic and reactionary. Mindszenty suggested the possibility of acting in conjunction with the Protestants on the school question. In April 1948 the minister of religion and education came forth with a proposal for the nationalization of the Catholic schools. Mindszenty asked teachers and parents to stand by their schools. He demanded that secularization of the schools be dropped from the agenda. In the summer of that year the government decided on secularization. Later that summer the government invited the Catholic bishops to negotiate but insisted that the Hungarian Republic be recognized. The Catholic bishops refused such recognition. In an open letter dated December 8 Cardinal Mindszenty pointed out that archbishops and cardinals in other people's democracies were being persecuted, which followed from the nature of materialistic atheism. Therefore, recognition of the present power relationship was impossible.

On December 26 Cardinal Mindszenty was arrested and taken to jail in Budapest. He was charged with treason and conspiracy and tried in February 1949. He was sentenced to life imprisonment. In the summer of that year the Catholic college of bishops arrived at an agreement with the government; the Church drew subsidies and obtained the return of several schools.

Following the 1956 Hungarian revolution, Cardinal Mindszenty was freed on October 30. On November 3 he addressed an appeal to the Hungarian people in which he warned Hungarians "not to give way to party struggle and disagreement." "We are for private ownership," he said and assured the Catholics that every trace of violence would be removed. In the meantime, Soviet troops moved into the country and occupied strategically important points. Cardinal Mindszenty sought refuge at the American embassy, where he stayed until September 29, 1971. Then he left the country and, after a visit to Rome, settled in Vienna. He made several trips, including one to the United States. He died on May 6, 1975.

Further Reading

Cardinal Mindszenty's autobiography, *Memoirs* (1974), contains texts of his letters, statements, appeals, sermons, speeches, and other selected documents. *Cardinal Mindszenty Speaks* (1949), an authorized white book, provides a translation of papers selected from those sent from Hungary by Cardinal Mindszenty. *Mindszenty, Jozsef Cardinal: " . . . the world's most orphaned nation"* (1962) presents selected writings of Cardinal Mindszenty. Additional information can be found in George Nauman Shuster, *In Silence I Speak: the Story of Cardinal Mindszenty Today and of Hungary's "New Order"* (1956) and in Stephen K. Swift, *The Cardinal's Story: The Life and Work of Jozsef Cardinal Mindszenty* (1950).

Additional Sources

Cardinal Mindszenty: confessor and martyr of our time, Chicester: Aid to the Church in Need (UK); Chulmleigh: Augustine, 1979.

Mindszenty, József, *Memoirs,* New York: Macmillan, 1974. □

Beatrice Mintz

Beatrice Mintz is an embryologist who has been responsible for a number of advances in the understanding of cancer while working in the laboratories at the Institute for Cancer Research in Philadelphia. She has published over 150 papers on a wide range of experimental approaches in the field of developmental biology, helping to establish the role of genes in differentiation and disease.

Beatrice Mintz developed new strains of mice with a genetic predisposition to melanoma, thus offering the first experimental opportunity to analyze the progression of this disease, which is the fastest growing cancer among young people in the United States. In one experiment, she successfully accomplished the hereditary transmission of human skin melanoma cells to transgenic mice. In another experimental approach, she injected the human betaglobulin gene into fertilized mouse eggs, and this gene was then transmitted by that generation of mice to their offspring in a Mendelian ratio.

Mintz was born in New York City on January 24, 1921 to Samuel and Janie Stein Mintz. She attended Hunter College and received her A.B. in 1941; she graduated *magna cum laude,* and a member of Phi Beta Kappa. In the following year she did graduate work at New York University and then transferred to the University of Iowa where she received an M.S. in 1944 and a Ph.D in 1946. She served as a professor of biological science at the University of Chicago from 1946 to 1960. Since then, she has devoted her efforts to investigations at the Institute for Cancer Research.

Mintz has made her most important contributions to cancer research with her experiments on the embryos of mice. The techniques she has developed to manipulate the embryos have made it possible to establish the genetic transmission of certain kinds of cancer, such as melanoma, a dangerous skin cancer. She has utilized a number of delicate laboratory techniques, such as injecting a few individual cells into the blastocysts—or early embryos—of mice in vitro, and then surgically transferring these early embryos into surrogate mothers, who then gave birth to mice whose traits were traceable. She has managed to inject the liver cells of fetal mice into the placental circulation of other mouse fetuses, thus ultimately developing a new pool of donor-strain stem cells for red and white blood cells. She has also developed techniques for in-vitro freezing of cells in liquid nitrogen before culturing them. She concluded from her investigations that human DNA could be assimilated into the germ line of mice for in-vivo research into the regulation of genetic diseases .

In the early 1960s, Mintz pioneered techniques for producing mammalian chimeras using mouse embryos. Chimera is a word from Greek mythology which describes an animal with a goat's head, a lion's body, and a serpent's tail. The mammalian chimeras Mintz produced were also composites, though they were merely the composites of genetic strains from different mice. She invented methods to develop them from more than one fertilized egg; she would take as many as fifteen embryos of different strains of mice and push them together until the cells aggregated into a single large blastocyst, which was then implanted into a foster mother. The offspring of these mice often reveal differing patterns of pigmentation and skin graft reactions.

In another experiment, Mintz succeeded in producing individuals with four, rather than two, parents. Early embryos consisting of only a few cells were removed from pregnant mice and placed in close contact with similar cells of genetically unrelated embryos to form a composite, unified embryo; this was then surgically implanted in the uterus of a mouse, which gave birth to a mouse that was a cellular mosaic—its tissues comprising genetically different kinds of cells. This technique is particularly valuable for tracing the tissue site of specific genetic diseases. In addition, Mintz established that when mouse embryo cells from a malignant tumor known as tetracarcinoma were combined with normal mouse embryo cells, the cancer cells developed into normal cells.

Mintz was awarded a Fulbright research fellowship at the universities of Paris and Strasbourg in 1951, and she has continued to receive many honors and awards, including the Papanicolaou Award for Scientific Achievement in 1979, and an Outstanding Woman in Science citation from the New York Academy of Sciences in 1993. She was also the recipient of two other honors, the Genetics Society of America Medal in 1981, and the Ernst Jung Gold Medal for Medicine in 1990. Five colleges, including her alma mater, have awarded her honorary doctorate degrees. She has been invited to deliver over twenty-five special lectureships, including the Ninetieth Anniversary Lecture at the Woods Hole Marine Biological Laboratory in 1978, and the first Frontiers in Biomedical Sciences Lecture at the New York Academy of Sciences in 1980. She is a member of the National Academy of Sciences, a senior member of the Institute for Cancer Research, Fox Chase Cancer Center, Philadelphia, and serves on the editorial boards of various scientific journals. In 1996, she and Ralph Brinster, Professor of Reproductive Biology at the University of Pennsylvania School of Veterinary Medicine, won the first March of Dimes Prize in Developmental Biology. Working independently, Mintz and Brinster were honored for contributions in developing transgenic mice, now a staple in labs worldwide. She continues to strive to carry out creative and original scientific work, designing experiments that have the potential for raising new and unforseen questions.

Further Reading

McGraw-Hill Encyclopedia of Science and Technology, Volume 3, McGraw-Hill, 1992, p. 5593.
Hawkes, Nigel, "A Weapon to Change the World," in *Times,* (London), March 2, 1993, p. 16.
A Transgenic First, "http://www.the-scientist.library.upenn.edu/ yr1996/apr/notebook-960429.html," July 22, 1997.
Runkle, Guy, and Arlene J. Zaloznik, "Malignant Melanoma," in *American Family Physician,* Volume 49, January, 1994, p. 91.
☐

Peter Minuit

Peter Minuit (1580-1638) was director general of the New Netherland colony in America and founder of New Amsterdam. He later became first governor of New Sweden.

O f Huguenot Walloon descent, Peter Minuit was born in Wesel on the German Rhine. Growing up in his native city and apparently becoming a merchant there, he was deacon in the local Dutch Reformed congregation. In 1624 Spanish troops occupied Wesel; Minuit fled to Holland and then to the Dutch West India Company's American colony of New Netherland. In 1625 he was appointed to the governor's council of William Verhulst, but he soon returned to Amsterdam. Early 1626 found him once more in the colony, perhaps only as supercargo for the company; yet on September 23 the New Netherland council deposed Verhulst and proclaimed Minuit his successor.

Presumably Minuit had not planned to stay in America, for he sent for his wife only after his appointment as first director general. One of his earliest official acts was to convene Indian leaders of the region and to purchase Manhattan Island from them for trinkets valued at $24. This gave the company a semblance of legality for its occupation of the island, and its New Netherland headquarters was moved to Manhattan.

Upon completing a fort, warehouse, and mill, Minuit made his town of New Amsterdam the concentration point for scattered Dutch settlements in the colony. When regular church services commenced at New Amsterdam in 1628, Minuit and his brother-in-law (the company's storekeeper) served pastor Jonas Michaëlius as elders.

Missing records limit historical information on Minuit's administrative activities. It is known he opened both diplomatic and commercial relations with Plymouth Colony in Massachusetts in 1627. He also became involved in a bitter quarrel with Johan Van Remunde, secretary of the company in New Netherland; Michaëlius sided with the secretary and soon attacked Minuit as hypocritical, cruel, and dishonest. Both Minuit and Remunde were recalled to Holland for an investigation. After prolonged inquiry Minuit was discharged while Remunde returned to the colony.

Minuit retired to Emmerich, Duchy of Cleves. But in 1635 a company director recommended him to Sweden's chancellor as ideally qualified to establish a colony in America on the Delaware River. A meeting at The Hague (1637) resulted in the formation of a Swedish trading and colonizing company. Minuit, present at the organizational session, provided one-eighth of the 24,000 guilders capital.

Departing in late autumn with two shiploads of Swedish and Finnish colonists, Minuit reached Delaware Bay in March 1638. Late that month, having purchased a tract along the right bank of the river from neighboring Indian chiefs, he proclaimed "New Sweden" and erected Ft. Christina (present-day Wilmington). After completing the fort and leaving a subordinate in charge, Minuit sailed in June 1638 to the Caribbean to trade for tobacco. Visiting a Dutch merchantman in St. Christopher, he was drowned when a hurricane struck the island.

Further Reading

Data concerning Minuit are scattered and incomplete. For his life in New Netherland the best authorities are J. Franklin Jameson, ed., *Narratives of New Netherland, 1609-1664* (1909); I. N. Phelps Stokes, *The Iconography of Manhattan Island, 1498-1909,* vol. 1 (1915); and Albert Eckhof, *Jonas Michaëlius: Founder of the Church in New Netherland* (1926). There is some account of his role in New Sweden in Amandus Johnson, *The Swedish Settlements on the Delaware,* vol. 1 (1911), and Christopher Ward, *New Sweden on the Delaware* (1938). ☐

Comte de Mirabeau

The French statesman and author Honoré Gabriel Victor de Riqueti, Comte de Mirabeau (1749-1791), was a key leader of the French Revolution in its first years. He sought an alliance of the Crown and the Third Estate against his own class, the nobility.

orn at Bignon near Nemours on March 9, 1749, Honoré Gabriel de Riqueti, later Comte de Mirabeau, was the son of a distinguished physiocratic author, Victor de Riqueti, Marquis de Mirabeau, known as the "friend of the people" for his reform proposals. Mirabeau's career began as a cavalry officer in 1767, but he was soon sent to prison on the Island of Ré for his escapades. He was released in 1769 to join the French expeditionary force that quelled rebellious Corsica. After retirement the next year with the rank of captain, he married Émilie de Marignane (1772) at his father's wish but quickly fell out with his unloved wife. His father, enraged by Mirabeau's notorious debauches and spendthrift habits, had him repeatedly interned by *letters de cachet,* in 1773 in Manosque, then in the fastnesses of the Château d'If in Marseilles harbor in 1774, and finally in the fortress of Joux near Pontarlier in 1775.

In Joux, Mirabeau wrote the *Essay on Despotism* and won the heart of the young wife of the elderly Marquis de Monnier. Under the name of Sophie de Ruffey, she fled with him in 1776 to Switzerland and then to Amsterdam. There he earned his living as a writer of vitriolic pamphlets against the Old Regime in France, many blatantly plagiarized. He soon gained a European reputation.

In May 1777 Mirabeau was arrested and turned over to the French police. Imprisoned at Vincennes until 1780, he used this time to read widely and to write various works, including the *Essay upon Letters de Cachet,* published 2 years after his release. His liaison with Sophie de Monnier now ended, he obtained a divorce from his wife in a notorious trial (1783). He then lived with the illegitimate daughter of a Dutch statesman, Willem van Haren, her identity transparently disguised by the name of Henriette Amalie de Nerah. After 2 years in London (1784-1785) he returned to Paris to wage a pamphlet war against Charles Alexandre de Calonne and Jacques Necker, the reforming ministers of finance, on behalf of a group of Parisian bankers. Nonetheless the government sent him on a secret diplomatic mission to Berlin (1786-1787), which was of little importance in itself but gave him an opportunity to study Prussian absolutism, with its bureaucratic and militaristic apparatus, at firsthand and to write a penetrating book on the Prussian monarchy.

French Revolution

The convocation of the Estates General in 1789 brought Mirabeau's career to its climax. His own order, the nobility, scorned to elect him as a deputy, but he was chosen by the Third Estate of Aix-les-Bains in Savoy. Now all his talents, especially his eloquence and his skill in political maneuver, found their opportunity, and he became the leader of the Third Estate despite wide personal antipathy to him. His policy, despite tactical shifts, remained the same: to use the impact of the Third Estate to break the resistance of the privileged estates to reform, at the same time seeking to persuade the Crown to accept the transformation of the government into a constitutional monarchy as its only salvation. Although personally opposed to the consolidation of the three estates on June 17, he upheld the legality of the newly created National Assembly in the famous reply he gave to the royal master of ceremonies on June 23: "Tell those who send you that we are here by the will of the people and will leave only by the force of bayonets." Yet he considered the proclamation of the Declaration of the Rights of Man in August to be ill-timed, opposed the transfer of the government from Versailles to Paris, and argued for the King's right of absolute veto in the new constitution.

Mirabeau's hope to become prime minister was dashed when the National Assembly forbade its members to hold ministerial posts. Beginning in May 1790, he accepted secret payments from the Crown to support the monarchy in the Assembly but did not cease his efforts to persuade the King to abandon absolutism as a lost cause and to work with the nation's representatives. Although most of his fellow deputies suspected his corrupt financial practices, they continued to follow him politically. In December 1790 Mirabeau was elected to the presidency of the Jacobin Club, before its turn to radical extremism, and in February 1791 he was elected president of the National Assembly. He died in Paris on April 2, before the failure of his policies—due to the refusal of the King to accept the limitations imposed by the new constitution and the upsurge of popular violence under the impact of hunger and war—became clear.

Mirabeau was personally and politically a paradox but not an enigma. Extraordinary ugliness resulting from small-pox at the age of 3 did not keep him from involvement in numerous amorous scandals, which, with his reckless spending and stinging political writings, brought him repeated confinement in French prisons. A foe both of absolute monarchy and of the ministers who sought to save it by limited fiscal reforms in the last years of the reign of Louis XVI, he was nonetheless entrusted with secret diplomatic missions. After the beginning of the Revolution, he represented the Third Estate with great oratorical talents, but his political wiles served not only his private interests but also the cause of constitutional monarchy. His personal corruptness was matched by an ultimate honesty of political principle.

Further Reading

Two interesting biographies of Mirabeau are Eric Rede Buckley, *The Prisoner of Vincennes: The Early Life of Mirabeau* (1930), and Antonia Vallentin, *Mirabeau* (trans. 1948). The best modern study of his career is Oliver J.G. Welch, *Mirabeau: A Study of a Democratic Monarchist* (1951).

Additional Sources

Luttrell, Barbara, *Mirabeau,* Carbondale: Southern Illinois University Press, 1990.

Ortega y Gasset, Jose, *Mirabeau, an essay on the nature of statesmanship,* Manila: Historical Conservation Society, 1975. □

Francisco de Miranda

Francisco de Miranda (1750-1816) was a Latin American patriot who advocated independence of the Spanish colonies, and although he did not see the fulfillment of his dreams, he was willing to pay the price these efforts demanded.

Francisco de Miranda was born in Caracas on March 28, 1750, the son of a Spaniard from the Canary Islands. Early in life he entered the Spanish army and went to Madrid supplied with ample funds and letters of introduction. He bought a captaincy and began to keep the diary which in time became the nucleus of an immense archive. His military career was not fortunate. Accused of neglect of duty, he was eventually cleared and was sent to Cuba, where he again fell out with the authorities. In 1783 he left the Spanish service and fled to the United States.

Henceforth, Miranda was in open rebellion against the Spanish crown. Spurred by the example of the 13 colonies that had achieved independence from England, he aspired

to set up an independent empire in Hispanic America. Among his friends in the United States were such men as Washington, Hamilton, and Thomas Paine. Constantly hounded by Spanish agents, he visited England, Prussia, Austria, Italy, Turkey, and Russia. Catherine the Great took a liking to him and allowed him to wear the Russian uniform and use a Russian passport.

In 1790 Spain and England disputed the rights to Nootka Sound, and Miranda hoped to convince the younger William Pitt that the time had come to set up an independent empire in Hispanic America where England might enjoy a trade monopoly. He was unsuccessful, but not discouraged, and offered his services to France. He fought in its wars, and his name was later inscribed at the Arch of Triumph, but France had as little use for his schemes as England. He survived imprisonment and the Terror and, in 1797, fled to England, where he found more encouragement for his projects. In 1806 he attempted to invade Venezuela, but the authorities had been forewarned and he was repulsed. Defeated but undaunted, he awaited his hour in London.

Two years later, rebellion in the Spanish Empire seemed to improve Miranda's chances. In 1810 he met the envoy of revolutionary Venezuela, Simón Bolívar, who had gone to Great Britain in an effort to win support for the colonies. Bolívar induced Miranda to return to his native country, and after 40 years of absence, the aging conspirator again set foot in his homeland. In the turmoil that swept Venezuela he was appointed commander in chief, but the challenge to lead a country in revolt and to organize an

army from untrained civilians proved too much for him. Rather than plunge Venezuela into civil war, he concluded an armistice with the Spanish counterrevolutionary Monteverde. His officers suspected his motives and threw him into prison. The victorious Monteverde sent him to Spain, where in 1816 he died in Cadiz in the fortress of the Four Towers.

Miranda had both extraordinary gifts and great weaknesses in his private as well as in his public life. But his failures cannot obscure the fact that he was one of the first to raise the banner of liberty in Hispanic America, and though he did not reach his goal, he pointed the way. It is for this reason that he is called "El Precursor."

Further Reading

Two biographies of Miranda are William S. Robertson, *The Life of Miranda* (2 vols., 1929; repr. 1969), and Joseph F. *Thorning, Miranda: World Citizen* (1952). Miranda's role in the South American independence movement of the early 1800s is treated in Irene Nicholson, *The Liberators: A Study of Independence Movements in Spanish America* (1969). □

Joan Miró

The Spanish painter Joan Miró (1893-1983), one of the first surrealists, developed a highly personalized pictorial language derived from prehistoric and naive sources.

Joan Miró was born on April 20, 1893, in Montroig near Barcelona. At the age of 8 he was drawing regularly. His sketchbooks of 1905 contain nature studies from Tarragona and Palma de Majorca. He attended the Lonja School of Fine Arts (1907-1909) and the Gali School of Art (1912-1915) in Barcelona, after which he produced portraits and landscapes in the Fauve manner. He had his first one-man show in Barcelona in 1918. That year he became a member of the Agrupacio Courbet, to which the ceramist Joseph Llorenz Artigas belonged.

In 1919 Miró made his first trip to Paris, and thereafter he spent the winters in Paris and the summers in Montroig. He met members of the Dada group and took part in Dada activities. His first one-man show in Paris was held in 1921. His paintings of this period reflect cubist influences; *Montroig* (*The Olive Grove*; 1919), for example, has a frontal, geometric pattern derived from cubism.

The *Tilled Field* (1923-1924) marked the turning point in Miró's art toward a personal style. In the midst of a rustic landscape with animals and delicately drawn objects are a large ear and eye; thus the person of the painter comes into the picture. The change in his art was furthered by his encounter with the works of Paul Klee, Wassily Kandinsky, and Jean Arp.

Miró's aim was to rediscover the sources of human feeling, to create poetry by way of painting, using a vocabulary of signs and symbols, plastic metaphors, and dream images to express definite themes. He had a genuine sense of humor and a lively wit, which also characterized his art. His chief consideration was social, to get close to the great masses of humanity. He was deeply convinced that the art of our age can make a genuine appeal only when returning to the roots of experience. In this respect his attitude can be compared to that of Klee.

Miró was connected with the surrealists from 1924 to 1930. Surrealism was a source of inspiration to him, and he made use of its methods; however, he never accepted any surrealist "doctrine." Rather, his art, like Klee's, belongs to modern fantastic art. Under the impact of surrealism Miró painted the *Harlequin's Carnival* (1924-1925) with its frantic movement of semiabstract forms. In 1926 he collaborated with Max Ernst on the sets and costumes for Sergei Diaghilev's ballet *Roméo et Juliette*.

In 1928 Miró visited the Netherlands; inspired by the Dutch masters, he executed the series of "Dutch Interiors." In his *Dutch Interior II* (1928) objects are endowed with a fantastic animation and personality and float in ambiguous space. In 1928-1929 he made his first collages and *papiers collés* (pasted papers). He married in 1929, and his daughter, Dolores, was born in 1931. Important exhibitions of Miró's work took place in Paris in 1928, 1930, 1931, and 1932 and in New York in 1932. He designed the scenery and costumes for Léonide Massine's ballet *Jeux d'enfants* in 1932.

In 1936 Miró fled the Civil War in Spain and lived in Paris. The following year he executed a large mural, the

Reaper, for the Spanish Pavilion at the International Exposition in Paris. He settled in Palma de Majorca in 1940. The series of gouaches entitled "Constellations" (1940-1941) are full of delicate beauty and gaiety. In 1944 he produced his first ceramics with Artigas's assistance and also executed a series of paintings on irregular pieces of canvas. The following year Miró painted a number of large compositions. His work achieved great power through increased simplicity, intensified color, and abstraction, as in the *Bull-fight* (1945), *Woman and Bird in Moonlight* (1949), and *Painting* (1953). He was awarded the Grand Prix International at the Venice Biennale for his graphic work.

Miró's most famous monumental works are the two ceramic walls (1957-1959), *Night and Day,* for the UNESCO building in Paris, executed with Artigas; the mural painting (1950) and the ceramic mural (1960) for Harvard University, Cambridge, Massachusetts; and the ceramic mural (1967) for the Guggenheim Museum in New York City. In 1975 Miró demonstrated his devotion to his native country with the donation of the Miró Foundation to the city of Barcelona. The building, which houses his works and the exhibitions of other artists, was designed by the artist's great friend, Josep Lluis Sert. One exhibition room was dedicated to the showing of works by young artists who had not yet been discovered by the public. Miró died in 1983 at the age of 90.

Miró enjoyed international acclaim during his long and innovative career. He was one of the many outstanding Spaniards—including Pablo Picasso, Juan Gris, Salvador Dali, Julio González, and Francis Picabia—who, by belonging to the School of Paris, helped to establish the high esteem in which it was held during the first half of the 20th century. And like many of those other artists, Miró continued to energetically produce his art and to experiment with form and subject long after the years of his initial celebrity had passed.

Further Reading

The most comprehensive study of Miró is Jacques Dupin, *Miró* (trans. 1962), which contains a classified catalog and bibliography. The first monograph on the artist was written by James Johnson Sweeney, *Joan Miró* (1941). See also Rosa Maria Malet's *Joan Miró* (1983) and James Thrall Soby's *Joan Miró* (1980). Other monographs are Clement Greenberg, *Joan Miró* (1948), and Sam Hunter, *Joan Miró: His Graphic Work* (1958). In addition, there are numerous Internet web sites devoted in whole or in part to Miró and his works. □

Yukio Mishima

Yukio Mishima (1925-1970) was a Japanese novelist and playwright. He wrote in a multitude of styles, from ornate to plain, and dealt with a variety of subjects drawn from both literary sources and contemporary life.

Born and raised in Tokyo, Yukio Mishima attended the Peers School before enrolling in the Law Department of Tokyo University. Upon his graduation in 1947 he worked as an official in the government's Finance Ministry. He resigned his position within a year in order to devote his energies totally to writing. After a highly successful yet controversial career he committed suicide in 1970.

Exceedingly well read in both classical Japanese and Western literature, Mishima produced works of intellectual brilliance and stylistic diversity. Certain of his novels and stories directly portray contemporary life; other works—his modern Nō plays, for example—draw on various literary and philosophical writings for context. Some critics single out certain works by Mishima as thinly disguised autobiography. The author himself, however, usually denied these claims.

Mishima published several promising stories as a high school and university student. Before his career was really underway he had also won the patronage of Yasunari Kawabata, a leading novelist who would eventually receive the only Nobel Prize for Literature awarded to a Japanese writer to that time. Mishima's first full-length novel, *Kamen no Kokuhaku* (*Confessions of a Mask,* 1949), appeared shortly after he left government service. A latent homosexual narrates the story. Though his sexual orientation is evident to the reader, the narrator himself, while describing his reactions with clarity, never draws any conclusion about his sexuality. Seldom erotic, the work is primarily an exact portrayal of an extremely self-enclosed personality.

During the 1950s Mishima extended his exploration into various types of love. *Ai no Kawaki* (*Thirst for Love*, 1950), dealt with a farm widow caught up in a turmoil of love and hate. The mistress of her own father-in-law, Etsuko the widow feels intensely attracted to a young farmer in the region. In the climactic scene of the novel, however, she brutally kills the farmer just as he becomes aware of her feelings and attempts to caress her. Mishima's ability to shift direction is strikingly demonstrated in his next notable work, *Shiosai* (*The Sound of the Sea*, 1954). In this instance a young couple in a Japanese fishing village overcome their shyness and eventually recognize their love for one another. The tale is conspicuous in the Mishima canon for its simplicity and optimism.

The 1960s might be termed the "political" phase of Mishima's life and career. After *Utage no Ato* (*After the Banquet*, 1960), a somewhat disguised account of certain aspects of an actual campaign, Mishima eventually organized a movement to restore the imperial authority and martial discipline that Japan had lost through defeat in World War II. He founded and led the Tate no Kai (The Shield Society), a group somewhat quixotically dedicated to the defense of the emperor. In the late 1960s he also wrote a controversial play entitled *Waga Tomo Hittorā* (*My Friend Hitler*, 1968), and a turgid treatise on the mystique of the body, *Taiyō to Tetsu* (*Sun and Steel*, 1968).

During the last five years of his life Mishima also immersed himself in the composition of a tetralogy of novels with the overall title *Hōjō no Umi* (*The Sea of Fertility*). This quartet of books is held together principally by the theme of reincarnation and by the continued presence of one character, a schoolboy in the initial novel, *Haru no Yuki* (*Spring Snow*, 1965-1967), and an aging lawyer in the final work, *Tennin Gosui* (*The Decay of the Angel*, 1970-1971). Honda, the character in question, is the epitome of rationality and empiricism. His sceptical nature is, however, severely tested by clear evidence that the reincarnation of his boyhood friend is actually taking place.

The second novel of the tetralogy, *Homba* (*Runaway Horses*, 1967-1968), is notable for its emphasis on martial discipline, especially the ritual suicide that occurs in the final scene. In conjunction with similar scenes, especially in the notorious short story "Yūkoku" ("Patriotism," 1960), this depiction of ritualistic suicide came to appear to be a harbinger of the author's own death. On November 25, 1970, after haranguing an assembly of self-defense personnel on imperial loyalty and military discipline, Mishima disemboweled himself with a sword, exactly as a samurai warrior in medieval Japan might have done.

Yukio Mishima was the first Japanese writer of the postwar generation to attain international fame. Before his sensational death he was generally considered the most likely Japanese writer to win the Nobel Prize for Literature.

Further Reading

Three biographies of Mishima in English are: John Nathan, *Mishima* (1974); Henry Scott-Stokes, *The Life and Death of Yukio Mishima* (1974); and Marguerite Yourcenar (translated from the French by Alberto Manguel), *Mishima* (1986). Criti-cism is available in a number of sources, such as Makoto Ueda, *Modern Japanese Writers* (1976); Masao Miyoshi, *Accomplices of Silence* (1974); and Donald Keene, *Landscapes and Portraits* (1971). □

Gabriela Mistral

Gabriela Mistral (1889-1957) was a Chilean poet and educator. Her poetry earned her the Nobel Prize for literature in 1945.

Gabriela Mistral was born Lucila Godoy Alcaya on April 6, 1889, at Vicuña, a small town in northern Chile. Her parents were schoolteachers, but her father abandoned the family when she was 3. Tutored by her mother and a stepsister, also a teacher, she began instructing in 1904, achieving success in numerous high schools. In 1922 the Mexican minister of education, José Vasconcelos, invited her to assist in his reform program, and the apex of this career came the following year, when she was awarded the Chilean title "Teacher of the Nation." In 1925 she retired but remained active.

Gabriela Mistral devoted much time to diplomatic activity, serving as honorary consul at Madrid, Lisbon, Nice, in Brazil, and at Los Angeles. She also served as a representative to the League of Nations and the United Nations. In fulfillment of these responsibilities, she visited nearly every major country in Europe and Latin America. She also continued her early literary pursuits.

First literary recognition came in 1914 with *Sonnets on Death* (*Sonnets de la muerte*). The suicide in 1909 of her first love occasioned the poem, and shortly afterward her second love married someone else, causing her early poetry to reflect personal anguish.

In 1922 Gabriela Mistral's first book, *Desolation* (*Desolación*), a collection of poems previously published in newspapers and magazines, was released through the efforts of Federico de Onís, Director of the Hispanic Institute of New York. Motherhood, religion, nature, morality, and love of children are present with an overriding theme of personal sorrow. Thus, her international reputation was established, and critics marked her poetry—direct and simple without adornment—as a turn from modernism in Latin America.

Two years later her second book, *Tenderness* (*Ternura*), appeared; it contained some of the poems from *Desolation* and several new ones. Fourteen years passed before the next, *Felling* (*Tala*), appeared. It was much happier in tone, containing among other themes American scenes, "lullabies" for children, and a metaphysical acceptance of death—all written in a much more polished style than that of the works previously noted.

Her last book, *Wine Press* (*Lagar*), in 1954, dealt with most of the subjects previously treated but in a different manner. The winning of the Nobel Prize for literature in 1945 did not assuage the loss by suicide of her nephew,

adopted and raised as her son, and of her good friends Stefan Zweig and his wife. Furthermore, by 1944 she had developed diabetes. The tone of much of her last poetry was that of one patiently awaiting death with complete faith in God.

Gabriela Mistral went to the United States for medical aid in 1946, living in various locales and, after her appointment to the United Nations, moving to Long Island. It was there that she died of cancer on Jan. 10, 1957.

Further Reading

Margot Arce de Vázquez, *Gabriela Mistral: The Poet and Her Work,* translated by Helene Masslo Anderson (1964), contains a portion on the life of the poet, and other biographical data are contained in her critical analysis of the works. Arturo Torres Rioseco, *Gabriela Mistral* (1962), presents a personal view of his friend of some 30 years. Additional biographical sketches in English appear in standard anthologies of Latin American literature.

Additional Sources

Castleman, William J., *Beauty and the mission of the teacher: the life of Gabriela Mistral of Chile, teacher, poetess, friend of the helpless, Nobel laureate,* Smithtown, N.Y.: Exposition Press, 1982.
Gazarian-Gautier, Marie-Lise, *Gabriela Mistral, the teacher from the Valley of Elqui,* Chicago: Franciscan Herald Press, 1975.
□

George John Mitchell

A popular Maine Democrat, George John Mitchell (born 1933) was the majority leader in the U.S. Senate from 1989 to 1994.

George John Mitchell was born in Waterville, Maine, on August 20, 1933. He was the fourth of five children (one daughter and four sons) of Mary Saad and George Mitchell. His mother had emigrated as a young girl from Lebanon and was a factory worker in mills in the Waterville area. His father was the orphan son of Irish immigrants and worked as a laborer.

Young Mitchell was a student at St. Joseph's grammar school and Waterville High School. A scholarship permitted him to earn a higher education. He graduated from Bowdoin College in 1954 with a degree in history. Shortly thereafter he served in the U.S. Army until 1956 and was an officer in the Counter-Intelligence Corps in Berlin, Germany. Returning from active military duty, he enrolled in the Georgetown University Law Center in Washington, D.C. He attended night school and worked during the day as an insurance claims adjuster. With a law degree, earned in 1960, Mitchell became a trial lawyer in the Antitrust Division of the Justice Department in Washington, D.C. He became a member of the bar associations in Maine and the District of Columbia.

In 1962 Mitchell was appointed executive assistant to Senator Edmund S. Muskie of Maine. His association with Muskie was to alter his career and political future. "About everything good I know, I learned from Ed Muskie," he once said. Although Mitchell returned to Portland from Washington, D.C. to work for the private law firm of Jensen, Baird, Gardner and Henry, he remained active in politics. He served as the state chair for the Maine Democratic Party from 1966 to 1968. Mitchell became deputy campaign manager for Muskie's vice presidential race in 1968 and for Muskie's effort to win the presidential nomination in 1972.

In the early 1970s, Mitchell went back to his law practice job, also serving as an assistant county attorney for Cumberland County part-time in 1971. Mitchell balanced his legal workload with volunteer activity in partisan politics. He was active in the Maine Democratic Party, serving as state chairperson from 1966 to 1968. During the following nine years he served on the Democratic National Committee.

The first attempt to win an elected office for himself was a failure. Mitchell was the Democratic nominee for governor of Maine in 1974. He lost the election to an Independent in a three-candidate race.

With Muskie's backing Mitchell was appointed the U.S. attorney for Maine by President Jimmy Carter in 1977. In 1979, again with Muskie's backing, he was appointed U.S. district court judge in northern Maine. Although the judgeship was a lifetime position, he held it for only a short while.

In 1980 Mitchell accepted an appointment to the U.S. Senate to complete the unexpired term of Muskie (resigned to become secretary of state), who had recommended him to fill the vacancy. This was the start of Mitchell's 14-year career in the United States Senate. Mitchell faced Maine's voters in 1982, seeking election to a full Senate term. He won office with 61 percent of the vote, having made extensive use of television advertisements and travel throughout the state.

Mitchell was selected to chair the Democratic Senatorial Campaign Committee, responsible for getting the party's candidates elected in 1984. He was spectacularly effective. The Democrats recaptured control after a six-year period of being the minority party in the Senate. As a reward, the Democrats gave Mitchell the honorary title of deputy Senate president pro tempore.

In the Senate Mitchell served on the Veterans Affairs Committee and was interested in health care issues. He served on the Environment and Public Works Committee and was active in seeking legislation on clean air issues related to acid rain and toxic cleanups. As a member of the Finance Committee, he worked on welfare reform and the 1986 tax reform act. His other legislative interests included foster care and child care, trade relations, fisheries, indoor air pollutants, endangered species, and preservation of historic lighthouses.

Mitchell attracted attention as a member of the U.S. Senate Select Committee on Secret Military Assistance to Iran and the Nicaraguan Opposition (popularly known as the Iran-Contra Committee). This special congressional panel investigated a covert arms-for-hostages deal with Iran and financial support for Nicaraguan rebels during the Ronald Reagan presidency. The senator proved to be a skilled questioner, with a knowledge of facts and a belief that the acts of some White House staff members were wrong. His performance during the 1987 televised committee hearings and his subsequent broadcast response to President Reagan's addresses brought him favorable notice from the American public and other congressional members. In one of the most memorable moments of the Iran-Contra Affair, Mitchell warned Oliver North to "please remember, that it is possible for an American to disagree with you on aid to the Contras and still love God, and still love his country, just as much as you do. Although He is regularly asked to do so, God does not take sides in American politics."

In November 1988 Mitchell was elected to his second full term as senator. He won with an overwhelming 81 percent of the votes cast. It was the highest percentage ever received by a candidate in a state-wide election in Maine history.

The high point of his legislative career came when the Democrats elected Mitchell as Senate majority leader. He took the post at the start of the 101st Congress in 1989. As majority leader, he managed the administration and legislative process of the Senate and tended to the proceedings and legislative schedule on the Senate floor. Mitchell quickly developed a reputation as an accommodating, consensus-oriented, and consultative leader. He also was thought of as an effective spokesperson for the Democrats. However, even with a majority in the Senate, the Democrats were unable to overturn any of President Bush's first 23 vetoes.

Late in 1991, Mitchell and Oregon Republican Mark Hatfield took on the task of instating a 12-month moratorium on nuclear testing in the Nevada desert. The Senate was able to win the support of 53 cosponsors, a Senate majority. Still butting heads with the opposition, the Senate continued negotiations which lead to a final deal: the moratorium was shortened to nine months and the Energy Department would have to end all testing by September 1996. Until that date, the administration would be permitted to conduct up to 15 tests, primarily for safety reasons, the *Bulletin of the Atomic Scientists* reported in 1992.

In March 1994, Mitchell announced his retirement from the Senate at the end of his term. Within a month of Mitchell's announcement, Supreme Court Justice Harry A. Blackmun announced his retreat as well. Mitchell, who was a federal judge before taking over for Edmund Muskie in the Senate, was named as one of President Bill Clinton's choices as replacement. Clinton could have easily kept the position that of a liberal judge by replacing Blackmun with Mitchell. Mitchell turned down the offer, however, citing several reasons, saying he'd like to "live a little," *Newsweek* reported, and not spend so much time at work. He also said he felt it would not be proper to have been Senate majority leader over the same senators who would be voting on his confirmation to the Supreme Court. Speculation also abounded that Mitchell, a serious baseball fan, was holding out for the job of baseball commissioner, where he would earn approximately $1 million a year while watching games all over the country.

Vanity Fair also noted that it was around this time that he became seriously involved with Heather MacLachlan, whom he would marry. In a June 1994 issue of *Fortune,* Daniel Seligman and Patty de Llosa noted that Mitchell's retirement was financially timely: it came three years after the Senate pay raise of 1991, resulting in a salary boost from $113,400 a year to $148,400 at the time of his retirement; the congressional pension plan, which he would most likely receive, would include annual payments of two-and-a-half percent of the average of the three highest years' pay for each year served with the legislature. He would presumably collect an annual pension of $84,595, and, Seligman and de Llosa calculated, based on the life expectancy of a white male his age and a four percent inflation rate over those years, he would stand to collect $2,895,248.

Before his retirement, however, Mitchell continued to work on massive health care reform proposals. His intention was to help Americans without insurance and provide security for those who do so. Mitchell's 1400-page bill called for, among other things, a new subsidy plan to help people buy insurance, including a government voucher system to cover wholly the cost of health care for pregnant women and children under 19 if they met certain low-income requirements. He wanted "community rating zones" to prevent insurers from canceling coverage and require insurance companies to cover those with pre-existing medical conditions. The problems Mitchell encountered with his proposal was the role of government: how could it increase benefits but cut costs? Mitchell had hoped for historic reform with his bill, but was lucky to get a humble bill out of his ordeal.

Even after his retirement, George Mitchell maintained a high political profile. In 1995, he became special counsel to the firm of Verner, Liipfert, Bernhard, McPherson and Hand in Washington, D.C. That same year, Clinton named him to head a committee negotiating the reinstatement of the cease-fire in Northern Ireland. Mitchell's commission wrote a report, the *Economist* reported, that was "scrupulously balanced and meticulously written," recommending that the Irish Republican Army and British unionists begin talks and dispose of terrorist weapons simultaneously. It was rejected by then-Prime Minister John Major, who wanted weapons disposed before negotiations even began, complicating Mitchell's attempts at a breakthrough. Mitchell's impressive report was all for naught, regardless of Major's disapproval, when the IRA blew London docklands apart, killing two people and injuring over 100 during a Friday rush hour. Apparently, the IRA began planning its attack on the day Mitchell presented his commission report. Later that year, Mitchell was elected to the board of directors of the Xerox Corporation. Besides his seats on boards of Federal Express, UNUM, and Walt Disney, his duties at Xerox involved serving on the finance and nominating committee.

The White House looked for Mitchell's help again in 1996, to prepare President Clinton in his upcoming presidential debates with Bob Dole. *Newsweek* noted that Clinton aides said Mitchell was skilled at mimicking Dole's senatorial style after observing him for 15 years. After Clin-

ton's re-election and Secretary of State Warren Christopher's resignation, Clinton considered Mitchell to take over, at Christopher's recommendation, although he chose Madeleine Albright instead.

Mitchell was divorced from his wife, the former Sally L. Heath, after almost 30 years of marriage and one daughter, Andrea. He wed Heather MacLachlan on December 10, 1994, a former agent for tennis pros.

Further Reading

Mitchell lacks a published biography in book form. Mitchell's political and legislative activities and record can be researched through the following weekly services: *Facts On File* and *Congressional Quarterly: Weekly Report.* See also Michael Barone and Grant Ujifusa, *The Almanac of American Politics,* which relates the electoral activities and voting ratings of Maine's national officials. The U.S. Government Printing Office publishes a biennial *Official Congressional Directory,* which lists Senate members' addresses, committee assignments, and biographical sketches. Mitchell and Senator William S. Cohen (Republican of Maine) coauthored *Men of Zeal: A Candid Inside Story of the Iran-Contra Hearings* (1988). These two authors wrote their observations, experiences, thoughts, and conclusions about the covert operations scandal. The book also presents Mitchell's views on democratic governmental operations. Periodical references include *Bulletin of the Atomic Scientists* (October 1992); *Economist* (January 27, 1996); *Fortune* (June 27, 1994);*National Review* (September 12, 1994; March 11, 1996); *New Republic* (December 16, 1996); *New Yorker* (April 25, 1994);*Newsweek* (March 28, 1994; April 25, 1994; August 15, 1994; September 26, 1994; November 23, 1995; September 16, 1996; November 18, 1996); *U.S. News and World Report* (March 14, 1994); and *Vanity Fair* (March 1995). For online sources, see "News From Xerox," http://www.xerox.com/PR/NR950710-Mitchell and "The George J. Mitchell Papers at Bowdoin College," http://www.bowdoin.edu/dept/library/arch/mitchell/bio.htm. □

John Mitchell

John Mitchell (1870-1919) was one of the most respected American labor leaders in the early years of the 20th century.

John Mitchell was born on Feb. 4, 1870, in Braidwood, Ill., a coal mining village. Orphaned at the age of 6, he was raised by a strict Presbyterian stepmother. Economic circumstances compelled him to enter the mines at an early age. In 1886-1887 he tried mining in Colorado and Wyoming but returned to Illinois frustrated and penniless.

Mitchell decided coal miners could achieve a better and more secure life by organizing. He joined a Knights of Labor local, but its unsuccessful strikes convinced him to enter the United Mine Workers of America (UMWA) at its founding in 1890. A year later he married Katherine O'Rourke, a miner's daughter, and began to read law and study social and economic problems. Mitchell rose rapidly within the union; in September 1898 he became the UMWA president.

President Theodore Roosevelt intervened in a strike in 1902 by the anthracite miners of northeastern Pennsylvania and assisted the strikers in gaining several aims. Mitchell's leadership of the strike won public acclaim for his moderate and restrained approach to industrial relations. Roosevelt said of him, "There was only one man in the room who behaved like a gentleman, and that was not I." Mitchell had also demonstrated that the southern and eastern European immigrants (the majority of anthracite miners) could be effectively organized into unions.

A slight, wiry man of conservative dress and a sober, thoughtful disposition, Mitchell wrote two books, *Organized Labor* (1903) and *The Wage Earner* (1913), expressing his basic idea that there need not be hostility between capital and labor and the prosperity of both were linked. His outlook led him to associate with the National Civic Federation, an organization of employers and labor leaders dedicated to establishing harmonious relations between businessmen and unions. But Mitchell's growing conservatism estranged the UMWA's members. After stepping down as UMWA president in 1908, Mitchell served as head of the Civic Federation's trade-agreement department while remaining second vice president of the American Federation of Labor (AFL).

In 1911 militants within the UMWA forced Mitchell to choose between the union and the Civic Federation; he resigned from the federation. In 1915 he was appointed

chairman of the New York State Industrial Commission, a position he held until his death on Sept. 9, 1919.

Further Reading

The best biography of Mitchell is Elsie Gluck, *John Mitchell, Miner: Labor's Bargain with the Gilded Age* (1929). Mitchell's relationship with immigrant miners is dealt with in Victor R. Greene, *The Slavic Community on Strike: Immigrant Labor in Pennsylvania Anthracite* (1968). For his contacts with the National Civic Federation see Marguerite Green, *The National Civic Federation and the American Labor Movement, 1900-1925* (1956), which is detailed and objective. The only history of the UMWA is the old and unsatisfactory one by Chris Evans, *History of United Mine Workers of America* (2 vols., 1918-1920). □

Margaret Mitchell

Author of *Gone With the Wind*, the most popular novel ever written, Margaret Mitchell (1900-1949) was born on November 8 in Atlanta, Georgia, the burning of which became a spectacular scene in the immensely successful motion picture made from the book.

As a child Margaret Mitchell was saturated with stories of the Civil War told to her by family members who had lived through it. They indoctrinated her so effectively that Mitchell was ten years old before she learned that the South had lost the war. Her venturesomeness as a young woman, which included a year at Smith College and a subsequent career in Atlanta journalism, reflected the influence of her mother, Maybelle, an ardent supporter of woman suffrage. After her mother's death of influenza during the epidemic of 1918 Mitchell returned to Atlanta. Four years later she married Berrien Kinnard Upshaw, an attractive, romantic, but violent and unstable man who is often regarded as the prototype of *Gone With the Wind*'s Rhett Butler. Their marriage lasted only three months, although they were not divorced until 1924. The following year Mitchell wedded John Marsh, a union that would last her lifetime.

Mitchell had become a feature writer for the *Atlanta Journal* in 1922, and by the time she resigned in 1926 she was considered the paper's leading feature writer. These years were, she would later say, the happiest of her life. Yet, despite her success and the pleasure she took in her work, Mitchell bowed to the still powerful convention that a wife should be supported by her husband, leaving the *Journal* as soon as John's finances permitted. Childless and with no outside obligations, Mitchell turned her hand to fiction and was soon writing what would become *Gone With the Wind*. She had largely completed the novel in 1935 when Harold Latham, an acquisitions editor at Macmillan, arrived in Atlanta looking for manuscripts. Mitchell served as his guide, and when Latham departed he took with him the huge, unpolished manuscript Mitchell had stuffed into nu-

merous envelopes. Although it was in the worst physical condition of any manuscript he had ever seen, Latham was the first of millions to find it compulsively readable despite its length—which would come to 1,037 printed pages.

Gone With the Wind tells the story of Scarlett O'Hara, whose father owns a plantation named Tara during the Civil War and Reconstruction. At its start she falls in love with Ashley Wilkes, a neighbor, who loves and marries the virtuous Melanie Hamilton rather than herself. Out of spite, Scarlett marries Melanie's brother, Charles, who soon dies of various diseases after enlisting in the Confederate Army. Scarlett, now a mother, spends most of the war with Melanie in Atlanta, from which Scarlett and her son and Melanie and her newborn child barely escape when the city is fired, making their way to Tara. In order to save the ruined plantation Scarlett marries again, and is again widowed when her husband is slain leading a Ku Klux Klan attack on the Black section of Atlanta, where Scarlett had been molested by a freedman. After this she marries Rhett Butler, a dashing and dangerous man who has loved her for years and whose wealth will ensure her ownership of Tara. Eventually she realizes that it is Butler she loves after all, not Wilkes, but as by this time she has thoroughly alienated Butler he leaves her with the line immortalized by Clark Gable in the film version: ''My dear, I don't give a damn.''

Gone With the Wind was a Book-of-the-Month Club main selection even before it was published in 1936. The movie rights were quickly purchased by Selznick-International for $50,000, an immense sum during the Great Depression. In 1937 Mitchell was awarded the Pulitzer Prize

for fiction. Two years later David Selznick's brilliant film adaptation opened in Atlanta to rapturous acclaim, not just in the South but everywhere. Like the book, which had sold eight million copies as of 1949, *Gone With the Wind* became one of the most popular and durable motion pictures every made. It won ten Academy Awards in 1940 and was the world's highest grossing picture for over 20 years.

Mitchell never wrote again, refusing even to collaborate on the screenplay despite Selznick's entreaties. During World War II she threw herself into defense-related activities, but otherwise spent the rest of her life shepherding her book through many foreign editions, protecting her financial and copyright interests, and answering her extensive fan mail. Considering her extraordinary fame and the fortune her book brought her, happiness seems to have eluded Mitchell. She was subject to bouts of depression. Her last years were clouded by her husband's invalidism following a near-fatal heart attack. Unexpectedly, she died first on August 16, 1949, after being struck by a drunk driver while crossing an Atlanta street.

Among critics *Gone With the Wind* has always been controversial. Few regard it as great literature, but beginning with the Pulitzer Prize Committee many critics have admired Mitchell's gift for storytelling and the breadth of her canvas. The book has been hailed as a contribution to feminism, held up as an allegory for the development of the United States, and condemned as racist and even sadomasochistic. Racist it unquestionably is—almost inevitably so, given the time and place of its composition. Beyond that, it gives powerful support to damaging stereo-types that for long helped sustain racial segregation. It romanticizes the slave-owning class, and, except perhaps for D.W. Griffith's classic *Birth of a Nation,* no work has done more to misrepresent Reconstruction as a cruelty visited upon an innocent white South—whereas today historians generally agree that it was an honest, if flawed, attempt to bring real democracy to a region that had never known it. In light of the book's continuing sales the controversy over it seems destined to persist, like *Gone With the Wind* itself.

Further Reading

The longest biography is Anne Edwards, *Road to Tara: The Life of Margaret Mitchell* (1983). A good critical study is Elizabeth I. Hanson, *Margaret Mitchell* (1991). Although Mitchell's papers were destroyed after her death, she wrote thousands of letters, a selection of which was published by Richard Harwell, ed., as *Margaret Mitchell's Gone With the Wind Letters, 1936-1949* (1976).

Additional Sources

Edwards, Anne, *Road to Tara: the life of Margaret Mitchell,* New Haven Conn.: Ticknor & Fields, 1983.

Pyron, Darden Asbury, *Southern daughter: the life of Margaret Mitchell,* New York: Oxford University Press, 1991. □

Maria Mitchell

The American astronomer and educator Maria Mitchell (1818-1889) was the first woman in America to become a professional astronomer. She discovered a new comet and worked out its orbit and added several new nebulae to sky maps.

Born in Nantucket, Mass., on Aug. 1, 1818, Maria Mitchell was the daughter of an amateur astronomer who made a living by rating chronometers brought to him by returning ships' captains. She learned astronomy and mathematics while working as her father's helper and continued her private study for 20 years while working as librarian of the town of Atheneum.

Her discovery of a new comet in 1847 brought Mitchell worldwide recognition from other astronomers and scientists and a gold medal from the King of Denmark. In 1848 she became the first woman to be elected an honorary member of the American Academy of Arts and Sciences, was appointed a computer for the American Ephemeris and Nautical Almanac, and was presented with a new telescope by a group of American women in recognition of her achievement. In 1857-1858 she traveled abroad in order to visit observatories and meet European scientists, some of whom she had been corresponding with earlier.

After the death of her mother in 1861, Mitchell and her father moved to Lynn, Mass., the same year that plans began to be laid for the founding of Vassar College, the first institution in America dedicated to the higher education of women. In 1865, after some initial reluctance, she accepted the invitation of Matthew Vassar to become the first professor of astronomy at Vassar. The only member of the original faculty widely known both at home and abroad, she has been credited with a major role in the success of the institution both by her name, which inspired confidence in the college, and by her remarkable teaching ability.

In 1869 Mitchell received a further honor by being elected a member of the American Philosophical Society. She was also the recipient of honorary degrees from several universities. She died June 28, 1889, at Lynn, where she had retired to work in her small private observatory. In 1908 the Maria Mitchell Astronomical Observatory, built on Nantucket Island by a fund raised by American women, was dedicated to the memory of Maria Mitchell, who had become a symbol of what a woman could accomplish in the scholarly world when given opportunity and encouragement.

Further Reading

A well-written biography by a writer thoroughly versed in astronomy is Helen Wright, *Sweeper in the Sky: The Life of Maria Mitchell, First Woman Astronomer in America* (1949). See also Mrs. Phebe Mitchell Kendall, comp., *Maria Mitchell: Life, Letters, and Journals* (1896), and Mary King Babbitt, *Maria Mitchell as Her Students Knew Her: An Address* (1912).
□

Wesley Clair Mitchell

The American economist Wesley Clair Mitchell (1874-1948) was one of the most prominent contributors to the study of business cycles and was also among those who first recognized the importance of sound empirical research in economics.

Born on Aug. 5, 1874, in Rushville, Ill., Wesley C. Mitchell was the eldest son of a Civil War veteran. Despite material difficulties, Mitchell completed his college and graduate education at the University of Chicago, receiving his doctorate in 1899. He married Lucy Sprague in 1912. His main activities, research and teaching, were only briefly interrupted, mainly for government service. During one such interlude, in 1914, Mitchell wrote a highly influential monograph, *The Making and Using of Index Numbers,* for the U.S. Bureau of Labor Statistics.

Analyzing the Business Cycles

Mitchell's major treatise, *Business Cycles* (1913), represents a pioneering effort to provide an "analytic description" of the pervasive and recurrent but also complex and changing fluctuations that are observed in the modern, highly developed, and interdependent "money economies." He developed a concept of the business cycle as a self-generating process whose continuity and diffusiveness are due mainly to institutional responses of the economic system to a variety of unpredictable changes. The lags in these responses, for example, the lags of expenditures behind receipts, of selling prices behind buying prices, or of investment expenditures and deliveries behind investment decisions, are of strategic significance in the dynamics of the cycle. A central issue is the dependence of tides in business activity upon the prospects of profits or, as in times of crisis, the quest for solvency.

As cofounder, and from 1920 to 1945 as director, of the National Bureau of Economic Research, a private, nonprofit institution, Mitchell effectively promoted the testing of his ideas and findings, which was essential for understanding and solving many basic economic problems. The first book that resulted from this reexamination was *Business Cycles: The Problem and Its Setting* (1927), which drew on a much larger mass of evidence than was previously accessible and which confirmed many of Mitchell's earlier impressions about the basic nature of business cycles and the methods appropriate for their study. A full account of these methods was presented in *Measuring Business Cycles* (1946), a volume written jointly by Mitchell and Arthur F. Burns. In his last major work, *What Happens during Business Cycles: A Progress Report* (published posthumously in 1951), Mitchell showed how the cycles consist not only of roughly synchronous rises and falls in many activities but also of numerous specific rises (falls) that start while expansion (contraction) is still dominant in the economy at large. This work paved the way for research on uses of cyclical indicators in the analysis of current business conditions and short-term forecasting.

Mitchell served by presidential appointment on national committees on social trends (1929-1933), cost of living (1944), and others. He had strong humanitarian sympathies and believed that advances in economics and other social sciences can and should help to reduce such defects of the economic system as recurrence of depressions and unemployment, inequality of opportunity, concentration of power, and material insecurity. Mitchell died on Oct. 29, 1948.

Further Reading

The best collection of essays on Mitchell is Arthur F. Burns, ed., *Wesley Clair Mitchell: The Economic Scientist* (1952), which contains a comprehensive list of Mitchell's publications. Further background on Mitchell's role in economic thought is in Paul T. Homan, *Contemporary Economic Thought* (1928); Henry W. Spiegel, ed., *The Development of Economic Thought: Great Economists in Perspective* (1952); and Joseph Dorfman, *The Economic Mind in American Civilization*, vol. 5 (1959). □

Bartolomé Mitre

Bartolomé Mitre (1821-1906) was Argentina's first constitutional president and the leading historian of the country.

Son of a middle-rank Buenos Aires military officer, Bartolomé Mitre grew up in the disturbed era when dictator Juan Manuel de Rosas ruled Argentina. His father's changing assignments and the instability of the times prevented Mitre from receiving much formal education, but from his early years he showed a strong attachment to books and studies.

The family moved to Montevideo, Uruguay, and Mitre entered a military academy there. As a cadet, he fought in the recurring civil wars. More importantly, he joined the circle of exiles called the Generation of 1837, which sought the ouster of Rosas. Still in his teens, Mitre wrote poetry, literary criticism, essays, and drama, as well as polemical articles against Rosas. Political turmoil in Montevideo forced his departure, and he lived briefly in Bolivia and Chile, earning his living as a journalist. He finally returned to Buenos Aires in 1852, a member of the army which overthrew Rosas.

Mitre rapidly climbed to eminence in Argentina. The defeat of Rosas did not bring immediate stability, as leading figures disagreed over the form and content of the new government. Mitre leagued himself with those called *porteños,* who insisted that the great port city of Buenos Aires must have the leading role in controlling the nation. Others, the *provincianos,* wanted a government free from *porteño* influence. During a decade of strife Mitre's influence grew, and finally in 1861 he led the *porteño* army in victory over the *provincianos* in the battle of Pavón. For the first time since gaining independence from Spain, Argentina was a unified nation under one government. In 1862 Mitre

was chosen as first constitutional president of the Argentine Republic.

Mitre set about the task of nation building—constructing a central government, providing for schools and courts of law, promoting railroads and roads, and improving commercial and fiscal affairs—attempting to remedy 50 years of national neglect. Unfortunately, his administration was plagued by a costly war with Paraguay which slowed national progress. Mitre was frequently absent from his capital, personally commanding the army. His 6-year term ended with many difficulties unresolved.

Still young and vigorous, Mitre served several terms in Argentina's legislature, undertook crucial diplomatic missions, and founded a leading newspaper, *La Nación*. He also pursued a primary interest, the writing of history. Believing that history must be based on extensive research and documentation, Mitre strove to tell his stories with as much accuracy as possible. He felt that a true portrayal of the glories of Argentina's past would spur coming generations to even greater accomplishments. His major efforts were the still useful multivolume biographies of the independence figures Manuel Belgrano and José de San Martín.

Further Reading

The best biography of Mitre in English is William H. Jeffrey, *Mitre and Argentina* (1952). Myra Cadwalader Hole, *Bartolomé Mitre: A Poet in Action* (1947), delves into the personality of Mitre, using his correspondence extensively. A penetrating analysis of Mitre's place in Argentine history is found in Donald E. Worcester, *Makers of Latin America* (1966).

Additional Sources

Robinson, John L., *Bartolomé Mitre, historian of the Americas,* Washington, D.C.: University Press of America, 1982. □

François Mitterrand

The French politician and statesman François Mitterrand (1916-1996) served in different governments under the Fourth Republic (1946-1958) and became a major opponent of Charles de Gaulle under the Fifth Republic beginning in 1958. In 1981 he was elected president of France and served for 14 years—longer than any other head of state in the five Republics since the Revolution of 1789.

François Maurice Adrien Marie Mitterrand was born into a middle-class Catholic family on October 26, 1916, in Jarnac, a small town in southwestern France near Cognac. During his childhood Mitterrand was influenced by his parents' concern for the plight of the poor. In 1934 he traveled to Paris where he entered the University of Paris and pursued degrees in political science and law. The rise of European fascism in the 1930s during his university years attracted Mitterrand to attend demonstrations orga-

nized by the pro-fascists in 1935 and 1936. After obtaining his degree in law and letters and a diploma from the Ecole Libre des Science Politiques, Mitterrand began his mandatory military service in 1938.

Serving as a sergeant in the war, he was wounded and captured near Verdun in May of 1940 by the Germans. After three escape attempts, he fled his Nazi captors and returned to France. There he worked as a minor government official in Marshall Petain's Vichy government which collaborated with the Nazis. In 1943 he enlisted in the French Resistance movement when it became clear that the Nazis would lose the war. He used his position with the government for the Resistance while he headed the National Movement of War Prisoners and Deportees to forge the necessary papers needed in the resistance. Mitterrand claimed that his government job had been a cover for his Resistance activities all along. He was awarded the Rosette de la Resistance for his efforts

. At the end of the war he became secretary general for war prisoners and deportees in the provisional government of Gen. Charles de Gaulle. In 1945 Mitterrand was one of the founders of the Democratic and Socialist Resistance Union, a moderate political party with a strong anti-Communist bent.

Legislative and Executive Positions

With the founding of the Fourth Republic (1946-1958), Mitterrand actively entered politics and gained valuable parliamentary experience, being elected a deputy to the

National Assembly (1946-1958) and serving in 11 different governments. Under the Fourth Republic his ministerial appointments included minister of war veterans (1947-1948), minister for information (1948-1949), minister for overseas territories (1950-1951), minister of state (1952), minister for the Council of Europe (1953), minister of the interior (1954-1955), and minister of justice (1956-1957).

The founding of the Fifth Republic in 1958 by de Gaulle in the midst of the Algerian independence movement pushed Mitterrand into the opposition and, subsequently, his political thought and leanings gravitated toward the left. He opposed de Gaulle's founding of the Fifth Republic and charged that the general's "new republic" represented a permanent *coup d'etat*. During the first 23 years of the Fifth Republic, Mitterrand dedicated himself to opposing de Gaulle and his heirs. While no longer holding a ministerial post, he was elected to the Senate (1959-1962) and to the Chamber of Deputies (beginning in 1962). (He was also mayor of Château-Chinon beginning in 1959.) In time Mitterrand came to realize that to defeat de Gaulle the non-Communist left needed to be revitalized and an alliance established with the French Communist Party (PCF).

In the presidential election of 1965 Mitterrand opposed de Gaulle and ran as the candidate of the Federation of the Democratic and Socialist Left (FGDS), an alliance of non-Communist leftist parties. Realizing the advantages of electoral cooperation, the Communists backed Mitterrand in this election. Though he was defeated by de Gaulle, in the final round of the presidential contest Mitterrand obtained 44.8 percent of the vote.

Rise of the "Red Rose" Party

The popular appeal of the left, however, was set back by the momentous student-worker revolt of 1968 (the Events of May) and de Gaulle's manipulation of the crisis. Then, partially as a result of the disastrous outcome of the June 1968 legislative elections for the left, Mitterrand resigned as chairman of the FGDS and decided not to run in the 1969 presidential elections. From 1970 to 1971 he headed a political grouping known as the Convention of Republican Institutions. In 1971 he was chosen first secretary of a new Socialist Party (PS) founded in the aftermath of the 1968 revolt and created to replace the old bankrupt Socialist Party (SFIO). The PS, symbolized by a clenched first holding a red rose, eventually catapulted Mitterrand and his Socialist colleagues to power in 1981.

Shortly after assuming the leadership of the PS, Mitterrand and the Socialists agreed to support the Common Program (1972), an electoral alliance and program comprised of the Socialists, the Communists, and the left radicals (MRG). After signing the Common Program, the membership of Mitterrand's new party increased from 75,000 in 1972 to 200,000 in 1981. These numbers encouraged Mitterrand's hope of constructing a large non-Communist left in France. Several days after signing the Common Program, in fact, he declared at an international Socialist congress in Vienna that he wanted "to reconquer an important part of the communist electorate." This bold statement foreshadowed the competition that would develop between the PS and the PCF.

In addition to the competition with the PCF, Mitterrand also had to deal with rivalries developing within the PS itself, a catch-all party that cut across class lines and had three major tendencies or groupings: the radical tradition represented by Mitterrand, the revolutionary socialism of Jean-Pierre Chevènement, and the social democracy of Michel Rocard. After the founding of the PS, Mitterrand adroitly played one tendency against another to maintain his leadership of the party.

Third Try for Presidency Succeeds

After 1972 the rising popularity of Mitterrand's PS encouraged the Socialists but worried the PCF and the majority in power. In the 1973 legislative election the Socialists captured a respectable 18.9 percent of the vote, while the PCF garnered 21.4 percent. Then, in the 1974 presidential elections Mitterrand ran as the standard bearer of the left and almost defeated Valéry Giscard d'Estaing by winning 49.19 percent of the vote in the final round. In the cantonal elections of 1976 the PS became the first party of the French left by capturing 30.8 percent of the vote, while the PCF received only 17.3 percent. Fearing that the Socialists would make even further gains in the 1978 legislative elections at the expense of the PCF, the Communists sabotaged the Common Program on the eve of the elections. Consequently, instead of taking a majority of seats in the Chamber of Deputies as predicted earlier, the leftist parties suffered a setback due to their own disunity.

Between 1978 and 1981 the discord between the Socialists and Communists continued, revolving around both domestic and international issues (for example, the crisis in Poland and the Soviet invasion of Afghanistan). As a result of this breakdown of leftist unity, the PS and the PCF ran separate candidates in the 1981 presidential elections: the Socialists backed Mitterrand and the Communists supported Georges Marchais, head of the PCF. However, Marchais' poor showing in the first round of the elections convinced the PCF to back Mitterrand in the second round. Aided by Communist support and disunity now on the right, Mitterrand toppled Giscard by winning 51.75 percent of the vote. Mitterrand was aided, however, by a number of other factors: Giscard's so-called imperial image, the need for economic and social reform, and the twin problems of unemployment and inflation.

The April/May presidential elections were hailed as historic in France because they ended 23 years of right-wing government under the Fifth Republic. The elections also proved that *alternance*, or a change in government, was possible under the institutions of the Fifth Republic—a republic that Mitterrand had rejected earlier. The legislative elections held in June of 1981 constituted another historic dimension. In these elections Mitterrand's Socialist Party won an absolute majority of seats in the National Assembly. The year 1981 marked the first time since the French Revolution of 1789 that the left had captured the executive and the legislative branches of government.

An Administration of Reforms

In forming his new government Mitterrand took some noteworthy steps. He chose Pierre Mauroy, the Socialist mayor of Lille, as prime minister. To reward the Communists for their backing and to maintain leftist unity, Mitterrand included four Communist ministers in his government. He also created a Ministry for the Rights of Women and staffed his new ministry with Yvette Roudy, a long-time feminist activist.

Now in power, Mitterrand's government launched a series of reforms designed to change France. A nationalization program was carried out that extended state control over nine industrial groups, including electronics, chemical, steel, and arms industries. Social reforms were also made: the work week was reduced to 39 hours; workers received more rights at their workplace; the retirement age was reduced to 60 years of age; the vacation period was extended to five weeks of paid vacation instead of four; allocations for the elderly, for women that live alone, and for the handicapped were increased; the minimum wage was substantially increased; reimbursement for abortions was provided; a wealth tax was imposed; and approximately 100,000 jobs were created in the public sector.

The Mitterrand government also adopted a number of reforms to strengthen justice for its citizens and residents by abolishing the death penalty, striking down the old *ad hoc* state security court, amending laws against homosexuals, and trying to regularize the status of France's four million immigrant workers. In addition, the government launched a decentralization program designed to transfer some of the power and decision making from Paris to local regions. Year One of Mitterrand's Socialist experiment was a year of reforms, but an expensive one.

During the first year in power the Mitterrand government pursued a neo-Keynesian reflationary economic policy, believing that "pump priming" would help pull France out of the recession so troubling to the Western world. Yet this policy, coupled with the expensive reforms of the first year, only exacerbated the economic problems in France. Consequently, in June of 1982 Mitterrand was forced to announce that his government would pursue an austerity program. This program involved a second devaluation of the franc, a four-month-long wage and price freeze, an attempt to hold down the public debt, and a cap placed on state expenses. Such a change in economic policy meant that France was now focusing on reducing inflation instead of unemployment. The June 1982 austerity program was followed by even more rigorous austerity measures in March of 1983.

Trouble for the Socialist Government

While Mitterrand and his government enjoyed a "state of grace" during their first year, the austerity programs of 1982 and 1983, accompanied by rising unemployment, contributed to growing opposition in France and decline in the popularity of Mitterrand and his government. The Socialist government also sparked opposition with its educational policy, namely its attempt to gain more control over the 10,000 private, mainly religious, schools in France.

Concerns over educational reform as well as a climate of general discontent led to a massive demonstration on June 24, 1984, by more than one million protesters at the Bastille in Paris, constituting the largest public demonstration in France since liberation.

Facing this mounting opposition, plus a setback in the European Parliament elections of June 17, 1984, Mitterrand began to move his government towards the center. The French president made a major television address on July 12, 1984, announcing that he would renegotiate the proposed reform for private schools and that he wished henceforth to consult the French on questions of public liberties through referendums. Then, only six days later the Mitterrand government announced several key resignations from the cabinet. Mitterrand picked Laurent Fabius, a young loyal *Mitterrandiste*, as his new prime minister. Shortly thereafter, Fabius announced that the government would continue the austerity program in an effort to redress the economic crisis and to modernize France. More austerity, coupled with declining popularity at the polls, led the Communists to refuse to participate in Fabius' cabinet. Mitterrand hoped that these changes would help to defuse the opposition and also prepare the PS for the upcoming 1986 legislative elections and the 1988 presidential elections.

In foreign policy, where the French president exercises enormous power, Mitterrand was both pragmatic and Gaullist in his approach. Strongly anti-Soviet, Mitterrand supported the *North Atlantic Treaty Organization* (NATO) decision to begin the deployment of almost 600 new Pershing II and Cruise missiles in Western Europe in 1983. While Mitterrand tried to promote solidarity with members of the NATO alliance, especially West Germany, he closely guarded French autonomy on foreign policy matters. At the same time, Mitterrand supported the idea of a strong and more independent Europe. He, too, tried to encourage a North-South dialogue between the rich and the poor nations and attempted to develop and to strengthen French spheres of influence in the Third World.

The 1986 legislative elections were a blow to the Socialists. They lost their majority in the National Assembly to the rebuilt Gaullist Party, now called the Rally for the Republic (RPR). As a result Mitterrand had to give the office of prime minister to the RPR leader, Jacques Chirac. It was the Fifth Republic's first government divided between a Socialist president and a conservative legislature (called "cohabitation" in France).

Mitterand's most ambitious and visible projects were to order the construction of $6 billion of public buildings and in 1986 to a work with Great Britain to build the Channel Tunnel ("Chunnel") linking Europe's mainland with Great Britain. Scandal and accusations of corruption plagued the Mitterand presidency. His private presidential police force was accused of illegally tapping the phones of judges, journalists, senior officials, and even the prime minister. A 1994 biography *Une Jeunesse Francaise* (*Youth of a Frenchman*) brought his early career back to haunt him. In particular he was criticized for maintaining his friendship with Rene

Bousquet, the Vichy police chief who deported thousands of French Jews to Germany's death camps.

Although he married Danielle Gouze, whom he had met while working for the Resistance, in 1944, Mitterand was rumored to have several mistresses. The Mitterands had two sons. In 1994 it was revealed that Mitterand's mistress and their daughter had been living at state expense in an annex to the Elysee Palace.

In 1992 Mitterand discovered he had prostate cancer. After undergoing chemotherapy, he managed to complete his term in office, but decided not to seek a third term. He died on January 8, 1996 at age 79.

Further Reading

A critical assessment of Mitterrand's political ascendancy in France can be found in Wayne Northcutt, *The French Socialist and Communist Party Under the Fifth Republic, 1958-1981: From Opposition to Power* (1985). For a sympathetic biography of Mitterrand, see Denis MacShane, *François Mitterrand: A Political Odyssey* (1982). The most authoritative biography in French on Mitterrand is Franz-Olivier Giesbert's *François Mitterrand: ou la tentation de l'histoire* (1977). An excellent analysis of Mitterrand's Socialism in action is found in Philip G. Cerny and Martin A. Schain (editors), *Socialism, the State and Public Policy in France* (1985).

Prior to assuming the presidency, Mitterrand authored a number of books, mainly political memoirs and essays: *Aux frontières de l'Union française* (*At the Frontiers of the French Union,* 1953); *Le Coup d'Etat Permanent* (*The Permanent Coup d'Etat,* 1964); *Ma part de vérité* (*My Part of the Truth,* 1969); *Changer la vie* (*Change the Way of Life,* 1972); *La Paille et le grain* (*The Wheat and the Chaff,* 1975); *Politique, 1938-1981,* 2 vols. (*Politics,* 1977 and 1981); *L'Abeille et l'architecte* (*The Bee and the Architect,* 1978); and *Ici et maintenant* (*Here and Now,* 1980). See also *French Revolutionary Life,* February 1996. □

Isaac Mizrahi

A premier American designer, Isaac Mizrahi (born 1961) established womenswear and menswear businesses noted for their uncluttered, witty designs before he was 30 years old.

I saac Mizrahi was born in Brooklyn, New York, October 14, 1961, the youngest child and only son of Zeke and Sarah Mizrahi. He grew up in Ocean Parkway, New Jersey, in the tightknit Syrian Jewish community. Zeke Mizrahi worked in the garment industry, first as a pattern cutter on Wooster Street and later as a childrenswear manufacturer. Isaac's mother was instrumental in exposing him to fashion at an early age. A devoted fashion lover, Sarah Mizrahi exposed young Isaac to the genius of designers Balenciagas, Chanel, and Norman Norell. He would often accompany his mother on shopping trips to Saks Fifth Avenue and Bergdorf Goodman. She would also take Isaac to the ballet and to movies.

When Isaac was eight, his family moved to the middle-class Midwood section of Brooklyn. He contracted spinal meningitis during this time and his confinement was spent eating junk food and viewing television, especially old movies. The 1961 remake of *Back Street,* about an affair between a fashion designer and a married man, was a pivotal event in Mizrahi's development. The glamour of the fashion industry depicted in the movie became an inspiration to him to design clothes. When Isaac was 10 years old, Zeke Mizrahi bought a sewing machine for him. Isaac set up a workroom in the basement and created clothes for puppets for neighborhood birthday parties. At 13, Isaac was designing clothes for himself, his mother, and a close friend of his mother, Sarah Haddad.

Mizrahi was expelled several times from the strict Yeshiva school he attended for impersonating rabbis and scribbling fashion sketches in his Bible. At six years old, the school required him to begin psychotherapy or they would not let him return. One Yeshiva teacher encouraged him to audition for Manhattan's High School of the Performing Arts—the school used as a basis in the movie and television series *Fame.* He was accepted and took diction, speech, singing, dance, and academic classes. He had a small role in *Fame* and wore a costume of his own design. At 15, while attending the Performing Arts High School, Mizrahi produced clothing under his first label, IS New York. His financial mentor for IS New York was Sarah Haddad.

When Sarah Haddad's husband fell ill, IS New York closed. Mizrahi continued to sketch his ideas. Zeke Mizrahi showed the sketches to a childrenswear designer, Ellie Fish-

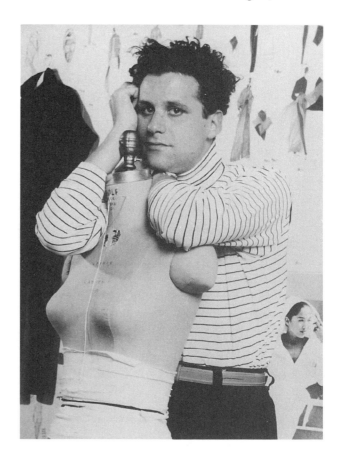

man, who suggested that Isaac should attend the Parson's School of Design.

After graduating from the Yeshiva in 1979 he enrolled in Parsons full time. By his junior year at Parsons Mizrahi was an outstanding student. His junior collection, a final project, was videotaped by the school to show to future classes. Mizrahi got a job at Perry Ellis for the summer following his junior year. Perry Ellis was Mizrahi's first industry mentor, the man he called "my guardian angel." He continued to work for Ellis part-time during his senior year and was hired after his graduation. In 1983 Ellis fell ill from AIDS. During this time Isaac's father died. After working at Perry Ellis for two years after graduation, Mizrahi left the company and joined Jeffrey Banks to help spearhead a new womenswear collection.

He remained at Jeffrey Banks for a short time due to the withdrawal of financial backing by the parent company. Mizrahi then joined Calvin Klein, but remained there for less than a year because of personnel changes. During his short time at Calvin Klein he created one of the company's most interesting collections, highlighted by streamlined red suits.

After leaving Calvin Klein, in June 1987 he and Sarah Haddad-Cheney pooled $50,000 each and opened Mizrahi's own womenswear company. They occupied a loft on Greene Street in SoHo. Seven stores bought the first season's collection. By the first collection show in April 1988 Haddad-Cheney had secured additional financing from the owners of Gitano Jeans company. In 1990 the company's workrooms and showroom moved to an expanded space on Wooster Street. Mizrahi's menswear collection premiered in April 1990.

In 1995, Douglas Keeve directed a 79-minute documentary entitled *Unzipped* in which home movie clips of Mizrahi's childhood are pieced together with excerpts of his influences (including Mary Tyler Moore and the 1922 documentary *Nanook of the North*) which won the Audience Award at the 1995 Sundance Film Festival and was praised for being "funny, succinct and modestly instructive about a fairly recondite business," Martha Duffy commented in her article for *Time*. The film presented a thorough portrayal of Mizrahi, the man—so fearful of rejection he hovers near depression. Viewers even see a few temper tantrums. His hard work and success, however, surge him out of dejection and one appreciates Mizrahi, the artist—a designer with a flamboyant personality. Audiences also learn a good deal about the fashion world from drawing board to catwalk. Besides the praise Keeve garnered for his documentary, viewers previously unfamiliar with Isaac Mizrahi learned that he doesn't take his success for granted, maintaining both a sense of humor and perspective. Audiences saw real-life footage of Mizrahi as a hyperactive baby, sketching fur pants while in bed, teasing supermodel Naomi Campbell about her navel ring, and crying when he reads about Jean-Paul Gaultier beating Mizrahi to the runway with a fashion first.

Unzipped seemed to be the extra spark in Mizrahi's fire. Although his company had been earning $10 million a year, a 1995 *Newsweek* article noted that he had yet to turn a profit. After Mizrahi made his debut on the silver screen, his popularity and recognition became even more prominent. When Mizrahi launched a new collection in February 1996 in New York, he also broadcast it live via satellite to locations outside the state. His new "Isaac" label featured two pink stars instead of A's, declaring, "Our motto is, Inside every woman is a star.'" He's been tapped as star material himself, being called the Calvin Klein of Generation X.

The year 1997 proved to be a milestone in Mizrahi's career. He announced an unprecedented deal with three major Asian markets in Japan, Singapore, and Korea which included freestanding stores, in-store shops, wholesale distribution, manufacturing, and sublicenses in Japan and shops and distribution in Southeast Asia, an online ABC source reported. The deal was estimated to generate at least $150 million in retail sales by the year 2000.

In 1989, after two collections, Mizrahi received his first award, the Council of Fashion Designers of America's Perry Ellis Award for new fashion talent. In 1990 Mizrahi received the coveted CFDA Designer of the Year Award. He was also named best designer of 1990 by the Fashion Footwear Association of New York, and Crain's New York Business included him in their annual "40 Under 40" award for great strides in business at a young age.

Mizrahi stated that his inspiration came from "food and fun" and "motion and movies." "Le Miz," "Le Wiz," or "The Miz," as he was nicknamed, was compared with such design greats as Claire McCardell, Geoffrey Beene, Halston, and Norman Norell. His creations have been referred to as "classics, with a twist," "a blend of ease and elegance," and "simple shapes, clear colors and unlabored touches of wit"—all hallmarks of American style.

Further Reading

Several periodicals of the early 1990s feature Mizrahi and his designs: "A Conversation With My Alter Ego," *Harper's Bazaar* (March 1993); "Mizrahi Unzipped," *Newsweek* (July 24, 1995); "Life Along the Catwalk," *Time* (August 14, 1995); "Mizrahi Loves Company," *Entertainment Weekly* (March 8, 1996); "Movement—That's What Design Is All About," *ELLE Magazine* (June 1990); "The Great Hip Hope," Michael Gross, *New York Magazine* (October 1, 1990); "The New Smash Hit: Le Miz," *Gentlemen's Quarterly* (August 1990); "Nobody Beats The Miz," *Vogue Magazine* (February 1989); and "Shooting Stars, Isaac Mizrahi," Sarah Mower, *British Vogue Magazine* (September 1989). Online sources include "Media savvy Mizrahi beams himself up to launch line," http://www.detnews.com/menu/stories/34751.htm; "Mizrahi's Asian Coup," http://www.wwd.com/samples/today/Thursday/014.html; "'Unzipped' follows fall & rise of designer Mizrahi," http://www.cis.yale.edu/ydn/paper/9.23/9.23.95storyno.DB; "Unzipped," http://www.panix.com/~bfrazer/flicker/unzipped.html; and "Unzipped," http://www.mogul.co.nz/reviews/unzipped/unzipped.html. For a book on fashion facts see Lynn Schnurnberger, *Let There Be Clothes* (1991). ☐

Ratko Mladic

Ratko Mladic (born 1943) led the Bosnian Serb fight in the Balkan war against Muslims, Croatians, and Serbians which began in 1991. Mladic's savage leadership is reported to have resulted in the deaths of thousands of soldiers and civilians alike, and he has been charged with war crimes.

General Ratko Mladic's forces led the assault on Sarajevo and the "ethnic cleansing" atrocities committed against Muslims. The region's history is marked by conflict among its inhabitants, and after the death of communist leader Tito who held the various ethnic groups together with his party apparatus, the nation known as Yugoslavia gradually eroded into hostilities.

Raised in Military Tradition

Born in the tiny village of Bozinovici, 25 miles south of Sarajevo in Eastern Bosnia, on March 12, 1943, Ratko Mladic grew up in an environment filled with passionate nationalistic sentiments and a tradition of war. On his second birthday, Mladic's father, Nedja, died while fighting Ustasa forces, units of Croats and Muslims who fought alongside the Germans at Bradina, southwest of Sarajevo. Years later, in a verbal exchange with a United Nation's commander in the Balkans, Mladic defended his unrelenting pursuit of war against Bosnian Muslims saying, "My son

is the first in many generations to know his father. Because there have been so many attacks on the Serbian people, children do not know their fathers."

Growing up fatherless, Mladic attended an army school on the outskirts of Belgrade. At age 15 he entered the nation's military academy and upon graduation in 1965, he joined the Communist Party. Serving in Europe's fourth largest army in Macedonia, Mladic climbed the ranks, moving from commander of a platoon to commander of a tank battalion, then a brigade. In January 1991, he assumed the position of deputy commander of the army corps in the Kosov province. As turmoil ensued after the break-up of Yugoslavia in 1991, Mladic traveled to Knin in the Krajina region and assumed the rank of colonel and command of the former Yugoslavian army.

Amidst the chaos in Krajina, Mladic used his charm, ambition, and fearlessness to advance his military career. Without uniforms or defined battle grounds, enemies often failed to recognize each other and innocent civilians lost their lives and homes. Mladic thrived in this environment, crossing between sides by using identification papers of Croat officers he had known. Even when confronted boldly by a Croatian soldier who recognized him, Mladic convinced the man that he was in fact the Croatian whose identity papers he carried. In another infamous incident, Mladic climbed aboard a bus rigged with explosives and cut the detonator wires after other special units were unable to do so. These and other actions consolidated Serbian positions in Krajina and earned Mladic the title of general in April of 1992.

Raised to Command of Bosnian Serb Army

In May of 1992, Bosnian Serb leaders read about Mladic in a Croatian newspaper and identified him as the man to lead their war initiatives, transferring him from the Yugoslav army to the new Bosnian Serb Forces. Early actions revealed Mladic's ruthless military style. "The dominant shape of armed conflict for me is attack," Mladic told a *New York Times* correspondent. "I have an offensive character, and that's highly acceptable to the high command of the army of the Republic of Serbians." Arguing his actions safeguarded a Serbian minority threatened by a Muslim-dominated government, Mladic ordered the unrelenting shelling of Sarajevo. When the Bosnian government forces moved to secure a road link between Sarajevo and Tuzla, Mladic's troops resisted an attack from three sides, killing close to 1,000 government troops, according to United Nations officials. Within months of his appointment as the first commander of the Bosnian Serb Army, Mladic consolidated control of 70 percent of the country, an area about the size of West Virginia.

Mladic and his armies fought bitterly while political leaders in Europe and the rest of the world watched, downplaying the conflict as a minor civil struggle amongst centuries-old combatants. President Clinton remarked, "It's tragic. It's terrible. But their enmities go back 500 years. Do we have the capacity to impose a settlement on people who want to continue fighting?" The war steadily escalated, fueled by sentiment such as Mladic's when he said, "There will be no peace in the Balkans until all Serbs join forces and live in a single country. Serbs should never give up their goal, even if it means another world war," quoted the *St. Petersburg Times.*

By December of 1992, the world listened in horror to reports by the Bosnian government and international human rights groups of ethnic cleansing which left 150,000 to 200,000 Muslims dead and over a million homeless. When a reporter asked Mladic for a response to a British newspaper calling him "ethnic-cleanser-in-chief," he responded, "It's not a crime to defend one's people, it's a holy duty." Yet Mladic and other Bosnian leaders fell under intense scrutiny when a tribunal closely examined the thousands of allegations of war crimes against the Serbian military. In the official indictment published by the U.N. group working from the Hague, Netherlands, Mladic and Karadzic were held responsible for "the unlawful confinement, murder, rape, sexual assault, torture, beating, robbery and inhumane treatment of civilians; the targeting of political leaders, intellectuals and professionals; the unlawful deportation and transfer of civilians; the unlawful shelling of civilians; the unlawful appropriation and plunder of real and personal property; the destruction of homes and businesses; and the destruction of places of worship."

Military Decisions Yielded Consequences

Mladic experienced personal loss as a result of the conflict. In May of 1992, the house he shared with his brother in Pofalici, a borough of Sarajevo, burned to the ground. On March 24, 1994, Mladic's daughter, Ana, a 23-year-old medical student, died in Belgrade of an apparent suicide. Her friends said she took her own life after reading a strongly worded attack on her father written by the former editor of a monthly magazine *People's Army,* Gajo Petkovic. In the article, Petkovic stated that Mladic was "carried away with rage and brutality" and held "undoubted responsibility for the crimes of members of the army he led." Mladic, raised Communist and atheist, attended his daughter's funeral at the Serbian Orthodox church with his wife, Bozana, and their son.

In December, 1992, the United States formally listed possible war criminals and Mladic was close to the top at number three, below the two leading Serbian political officials. Mladic accused the United States of interfering with and prolonging the war by offering aid to the Croats and Muslims at critical times and consistently used interviews to make anti-American statements, usually through innuendo and indirect criticism. A senior United Nations official who engaged in negotiations with Mladic compared him to Sadaam Hussein, saying, "He has the same cunning and the same urge to take on the Americans and show what a tough guy he is."

In 1995, an international tribunal established by the United Nations indicted Mladic and 51 others suspected of participating in the atrocities committed during the four years of war in the former Yugoslavia. In meetings following the Dayton Peace Accord, Serbian President Slobodan Milosevic promised to hand over some officers wanted for questioning before the tribunals but American officials were able to say only that they left the meetings "with the expectation" that Mladic would also be handed over in time. Mladic himself, however, in a March 15, 1996, interview with the BBC said, "I shall probably remain (army chief) for as long as my people need me . . . I was not ready to and did not follow any dictates from the West to be appointed as adviser of the president of the republic, and thus removed by order of some foreign intelligence circles, because they did not appoint me to my current function in the first place, so they cannot remove me, nor can their agents in politics in the region do that either. Finally, the assessment of my aides and the military is that I am still needed, that I can still be useful, at least with my good advice, if nothing else."

Despite Mladic's apparent responsibility for many of the most brutal atrocities and inhumane policies which brought mass destruction to the country and his attempts to thwart the peace process in the former Yugoslavia, efforts to bring peace to the region appeared in early 1996 appeared to be taking hold. Mladic seems to be stepping away from active responsibility and may succumb to intense political pressure and retire. Facing imminent prosecution and the loss of political power and influence, Mladic's role in the rebuilding process shows signs of being a minor one. Never lacking for words, Mladic responded to questions about his possible arrest saying, "They have to understand one fact: I am too costly, and people are protecting me. I am protected by my reputation, my honesty, and personal sacrifice in this war." On November 27, 1996, Mladic finally stepped down as military leader under pressure from political leaders. He had been dismissed by the Bosnian-Serb president on November 9, but Mladic and his supporters had refused to follow the order.

Further Reading

American Lawyer, September, 1995, p.5.

British Broadcasting Summary of World Broadcasts, March 18, 1996.

International Herald Tribune, February 21, 1996; March 23, 1996.

New Republic, Vol. 211, December 19, 1994, p. 12; Vol. 213, August 7, 1995, p. 6.

New York Times, August 8, 1993, p. 1–14; September 4, 1994, p. 6–26; April 17, 1994, p. 1–12; May 30, 1996, p. A7; November 28, 1996, p. A3.

Rocky Mountain News, April 12, 1994, p. A23.

St. Petersburg Times, July 26, 1995, p. A2.

Washington Post, January 23, 1995, p. A10; September 7, 1995, p. A1; February 18, 1996, p. A33. □

Mobutu Sese Seko

Mobutu Sese Seko (1930-1997) was the second president of the Congo (at one time called Zaire, now known as the Democratic Republic of the Congo), taking office in late 1965.

Mobutu Sese Seko was born Joseph Désiré Mobutu on Oct. 14, 1930, at Lisala. (He later abandoned those names in favor of African names.) Although his ascendancy was Ngbandi (a non-Bantu tribe of Sudanese origin), he grew up among the Bantu-speaking riverine peoples of the Congo who are commonly referred to as Bangala. He attended a secondary school run by Catholic missionaries at Coquilhatville (later Mbandaka) and after being dismissed for insubordination was drafted into the Force Publique in 1950.

Because of his educational qualifications, Mobutu was trained as a noncommissioned officer and given a desk job as an accountant. He also tried his hand at journalism by writing a few pieces for army periodicals, and when he left the Force Publique in 1956, he became a stringer and then a regular staffer in Léopoldville, rising to the post of editor of the weekly *Actualités Africaines*. He received further training at the official Congo Information Office and then at a Brussels school of journalism.

During that period, Mobutu met Patrice Lumumba and became his representative in Belgium, while reportedly serving as an informer for the Belgian security police. Lumumba brought him back to the Congo in 1960, made him a presidential aide, and raised him to the rank of colonel and chief of staff of the Congolese army.

Within 2 months of his appointment, Mobutu used his position to unseat Lumumba and to install the College of Commissioners, made up of graduate students (Sept. 20, 1960). Mobutu consolidated his hold over a segment of the

army, particularly over a commando battalion which he organized with the help of a right-wing Moroccan general serving in the UN force, turning it into a praetorian guard to control the capital city. He was instrumental in the decision to turn Lumumba over to the Katanga regime and thus bears a major responsibility for the death of the man who had been his political protector.

Thereafter, Mobutu concentrated his efforts on reunifying the fragmented army under his command and even managed to have Moïse Tshombe subscribe to his nominal paramountcy over Katanga forces after securing his release from the brief captivity into which the secessionist leader had allowed himself to be ensnared (June-July 1961).

Although civilian rule was officially restored in August 1961 under Premier Cyrille Adoula, Mobutu remained a major power broker. The army's position—and indirectly that of Mobutu—became seriously weakened as a result of its disastrous performance in attempting to control the Congo rebellion in 1963-1965. When Tshombe returned to the Congo as prime minister, Mobutu supported his decision to make use of foreign military support (foreign technicians had in any case been working with the Congolese army since 1960); and he maintained this position when Joseph Kasavubu, sensing international hostility to the presence of white mercenaries in the Congo, announced his intention to dismiss them in October 1965.

On Nov. 25, 1965, the army took power (officially for a period of 5 years), and Mobutu became president. Rather than follow Tshombe's policy of open subservience to Western interests, however, Mobutu assumed—at least initially—a nationalistic pose, rehabilitated Lumumba's memory, and challenged Belgian economic control of the Katanga mining industry. His confrontation with the Union Minière eventually led to a face-saving compromise, and his attempts to organize a mass party under the name of MPR (Mouvement Populaire de la Révolution) turned out to be somewhat less than impressive, but he was successful in beating back all attempts to unseat him.

Two such attempts (aiming at Tshombe's restoration) took the form of mutiny by Katanga forces and white mercenaries, leading to the latter group's final expulsion from the Congo at the end of 1967. Thereafter, the Mobutu regime gradually inflected its course in a conservative direction (as witnessed by the October 1968 execution of rebel leader Pierre Mulele, who had returned to the Congo following assurances of amnesty) and had to face growing disaffection and unrest on the part of student circles.

Diplomatically, Mobutu tried to strengthen the Congo's influence on the African scene. He was consistently favorable to the United States and indeed was often accused of rising to power with CIA help and of being a Trojan horse for American influence in central Africa. In December 1971 he changed his country's name to Zaïre.

Like Stalin in the Soviet Union and Saddam Hussein in Iraq, Mobutu consolidated his power by developing a cult of his own personality. Pictures of him were printed by the tens of thousands and sent to every part of the country. His every word was recorded; his was the only official voice to speak for Zaire; orchestrated crowds cheered his speeches;

and the Zairian media, all of it state censored, sang his praises and enlarged his stature in an unceasing bombardment. As historian Michael Schatzberg noted, "Scarcely a day passed when the press did not hail even his most banal activities as the magnanimous paternal gestures of a man intent only on the well being of his children, the people of Zaire. Zairian television began its broadcasts with a surrealistic vision of Mobutu descending from the cloud-filled heavens."

Mobutu beat back threats from outside Zaire in the 1970s that took the form of invasions from Shaba (formerly Katanga) Province by rebels, some of whom were former Tshombe supporters from the independence era; others were refugees from Mobutu's terror. Mobutu almost lost control of the mining districts for a while in 1978 during a second rebel offensive, and again was forced to offer vocal anti-Communist sentiments in order to obtain aid from American President Jimmy Carter, who was repelled by Mobutu's cynical approach to human rights.

Mobutu mishandled his nation's economy almost from the beginning. Once secure in power, he tried to exploit Zaire's natural mineral riches, but he and his backers lacked the personnel, infrastructure, and business ethos to make it work. Even worse, his decision in 1973 to nationalize all other economic assets owned by foreigners led to a catastrophic decline in national productivity and wealth. Humiliated by his financial woes, Mobutu returned farms and factories to their original owners, but a fall in the world price of copper further devasted the Zairian economy.

Through the 1980s and into the 1990s, Mobutu grew ever more entrenched and corrupt and ever more suspicious of attempts to liberalize his rule. He made some halfhearted concessions toward free speech and democracy in the early '90s, but was unable to yield any real power.

The 1994 genocide in Rwanda and the breakdown of order in Burundi that began in 1993 indirectly helped cause Mobutu's final downfall. More than one million refugees fled into Zaire's eastern border regions, unsettling the local population and reviving dormant feuds. Out of this uncertainty another rebellion emerged led by the enigmatic Laurent Kabila. This rebel movement proved surprisingly successful and in mid-1997 succeeded in pushing to the outskirts of the capital. Kabila became president and changed the name of the country to the Democratic Republic of the Congo. Mobutu, ailing with prostate cancer (he had undergone surgery on August 22, 1996) fled with his family and close supporters to Togo. On September 7, 1997, about four months after he left the Congo, Mobutu died in Morocco.

Mobutu's long hold on power had disastrous consequences for his people. The Nigerian playwright Wole Soyinka referred to Mobutu as Africa's leading "toad king," a monarchical ruler who lived in grotesque splendor while his people starved. Mobutu's Zaire was also the distressing model for novelist V.S. Naipaul's *A Bend in the River* (1979), a chilling account of life in an African dictatorship. Indeed, it would be hard to think of Zaire under Mobutu as a developing country. Rather, it was a deteriorating society held together only by the iron-fisted and corrupt rule of its dictator.

Further Reading

Studies of Motubu and his place in Congolese politics and history are in Michael Schatzberg, *Mobuto or Chaos? The United States & Zaire, 1960-1990* (1991); Alan P. Merriam, *Congo: Background of Conflict* (1961); Catherine Hoskyns, *The Congo since Independence, January 1960-December 1961* (1965); and Crawford Young, *Politics in the Congo: Decolonization and Independence* (1965). Events surrounding Mobutu's fall are covered in Peter Rosemblum, "Endgame in Zaire," *Current History*, May 1997; R.W. Apple Jr., "U.S. Influence Over Zaire Appears Limited," the *New York Times* (May 17, 1997); and "How New a Man is Kabila?," the *Economist* (May 24, 1997). □

Paula Modersohn-Becker

Paula Modersohn-Becker (1876-1907) was the first German painter to assimilate the Post-Impressionist currents she discovered for herself in Paris and to forge a very personal style, creating some unquestioned masterpieces during her brief career.

Paula Becker was born on February 8, 1876, into a cultured middle-class family in Dresden which moved to Bremen in 1888. Her father, a government railroad official in early retirement and failing health and concerned about his six children's financial security, insisted that the young Paula complete a two-year teachers' training program before allowing her to study at the school for women artists in Berlin. In September 1898 she settled in the nearby artists' colony of Worpswede to work with its celebrated figure painter, Fritz Mackensen. The Worpswede peasant women, often with their infants, and the old women and children from the poor house became her favorite models, and she recorded the picturesque landscape, the dark moors and stormy skies, fields with thatched cottages, woods of slender birch trees, and canals for transporting peat moss to Bremen.

But she soon looked beyond Worpswede to Paris. She went there from January to June 1900, studying at the Académie Colarossi, visiting the Louvre museum, and seeing new art shown by dealers and at the International Exposition. Even after her marriage in May 1901 to the Worpswede landscapist Otto Modersohn—recently widowed and with a young daughter—she escaped to Paris again for five weeks in the spring of 1903 and for two months in February-April 1905, now studying at the Académie Julian. In February 1906 she left her husband to devote herself exclusively to art, but he followed her to Paris and persuaded her to return in March 1907 to married life in Worpswede. She gave birth to their daughter Tille on November 2nd; on November 20, 1907, she died of an embolism and heart attack. She was 31 years old.

Modersohn-Becker produced some 1,000 drawings and 400 paintings during her brief career and documented her thoughts and experiences in her journals and extensive correspondence. Her earliest work reveals her artistic beginnings in Worpswede naturalism, but she soon recognized its limitations. Her teacher Mackensen was too much oriented to the past, too "conventional" (letter of early May 1900); his work was "not broad enough . . . too genre-like" (December 1, 1902). In her journal she clarified her artistic goal: to "strive for the greatest simplicity together with the most intimate observation" and "to achieve grandeur through simplicity". The masterpieces in the Louvre, which she frequently sketched, became her best teachers, and then the Post-Impressionist masters: Vincent van Gogh, Paul Cézanne, and Paul Gauguin, whose innovations she absorbed and transformed into her personal style.

She had visited the van Gogh retrospective in March 1905, and we can recognize the impact of his rich color harmonies and emphatic outlines in her masterful painting *Old Peasant Woman Praying*—her one major picture in an American museum, in Detroit. The old woman, with weathered yellow skin against luminous green foliage, is portrayed with respect and sympathy, in no way romanticized or sentimentalized. Cézanne she had discovered as early as 1900, in Vollard's art gallery, but his influence becomes most evident in some magnificent still lifes of 1905 and 1906, and in the simplified color planes of her late figure studies.

She mentions Gauguin in letters of 1905 and certainly visited his memorial exhibition in the autumn of 1906. The deep, exotic colors of *Self-Portrait with Camellia Branch* may be indebted to Gauguin. Its hieratic frontality and mysterious sense of otherworldliness also are derived from late Classical, Coptic mummy portraits that she admired in museums and in a volume of reproductions she received for her thirty-first birthday. She painted many other memorable self-portraits. Having promised herself "to amount to something" by age 30, she duly marked that milestone with a unique and daring self-portrait painted on her wedding anniversary in 1906. She stands half nude and as if pregnant— the traditional role she had abandoned (or merely postponed) to nurture her artistic self. In another late self-portrait that exists in two versions, in Bremen and Basel, she again appears half nude against a leafy background and with flowers in her hair, like the Tahitian women of Gauguin's natural paradise and the very image of youthful vitality and creativity.

We can also follow Modersohn-Becker's stylistic growth in another theme for which she is known and admired, that of mother and child. Her early maternities of 1903 and 1904 are realistic in the Worpswede tradition, although they are simplified and already painted in a broader manner. In 1906 in Paris she found an Italian model with an infant who posed for some of her greatest paintings: a beautiful *Reclining Mother and Child,* lying naked on the ground and curled protectively around her baby, or the *Kneeling Mother and Child,* which suggests an ancient fertility goddess. Like much of her art, they are compelling images of both personal and universal meanings. Many of

these paintings can be seen in the Bremen museum devoted to her work, the Paula Becker-Modersohn Haus (Ludwig Roselius Collection).

Modersohn-Becker was an exceptional young woman who wanted to dedicate herself to art rather than conventional domesticity despite pressure from family and friends. She worked alone, unaware of the beginnings of German Expressionism in Dresden, Munich, and Berlin—although she has been considered a precursor of that movement. Furthermore, she differed from many of these near-contemporaries and their aggressive emotionalism by her greater emphasis on formal values. Having absorbed the lessons of Post-Impressionism, she flattened her pictorial space or structured Cézannesque color planes into modernist styles that parallel or even anticipate Picasso's primitivism and first Cabist experiments of 1906 through 1908.

Further Reading

The best book about the artist is one of her own writings, finally available in English: *Paula Modersohn-Becker: The Letters and Journals* (1983) translated by Arthur S. Wensinger and Carole Clew Hoey from the new and enlarged German edition (1979) compiled by Günter Busch and Liselotte von Reinken. A briefer version, *The Letters and Journals of Paula Modersohn-Becker* (1980), translated by J. Diane Radycki from the incomplete German edition of 1925, is also available. Both have helpful prefaces and notes. Gillian Perry has written a well-documented biography (with 25 color plates of uneven quality), *Paula Modersohn-Becker: Her Life and Work* (1979). The three books are reviewed in *Woman's Art Journal,* fall 1981/winter 1982 and fall 1984/winter 1985. For general background, see the exhibition catalogues *Expressionism: A German Intuition, 1905-1920* (1980) and *Women Artists: 1550-1950* (1976) by Ann Sutherland Harris and Linda Nochlin.

Additional Sources

Perry, Gillian, *Paula Modersohn-Becker, her life and work,* London: Women's Press, 1979. □

Amedeo Modigliani

Amedeo Modigliani (1884-1920), an Italian painter and sculptor, was one of the most fascinating personalities of the School of Paris in its heroic years and a mannerist with a personal touch.

Amedeo Modigliani was born on July 12, 1884, in Leghorn to a distinguished, well-to-do Italian-Jewish family. He first studied under Guglielmo Micheli, a minor painter in the Macchiaioli group, and then at the academies of Florence and Venice, where he was greatly influenced by the art of the Renaissance. All his work echoes the painting of the Sienese 14th century, Sandro Botticelli, and the mannerists.

In 1907 Modigliani arrived in Paris, where, in the Montmartre district, he lived a truly bohemian life. He met the avant-garde young artists at the Bateau-Lavoir, an old building where many of them had their studios, and took part in their discussions. His closest friends were Chaim Soutine and Jules Pascin, and at one time he worked with the painter Moise Kisling. Aristocratic, good-looking, and melancholy, Modigliani undermined his health through alcoholism, drugs, and an uninhibited amorous way of living.

Modigliani exhibited at the Salon des Indépendants of 1908. His first sculptures were produced in 1909. That year he went back to Leghorn, returning to Paris in 1910, where he lived for the rest of his life. He moved restlessly from one apartment to another and finally transferred from Montmartre to Montparnasse in 1913, where he continued his bohemian life. He could be found regularly at the Café de la Rotonde or at the Dôme. Although he came from a rich bourgeois background, he had a genuine feeling for social responsibility. In Paris he was known as Modi, from which abbreviation, by linguistic corruption, the French referred to him (and also to Pascin, Soutine, and Maurice Utrillo) as *peintre maudit* (cursed painter).

The classically balanced character of Paul Cézanne's mature work impressed itself early (1909) and decisively on Modigliani's sensitive mind. His distinctive style resulted from a combination of his predilection for a musical outline, a thoroughgoing simplification of form, and the impact of African sculpture (to which he was introduced by his friend Constantin Brancusi) with Cézanne's manner of applying thin, translucent paint to canvas. Modigliani's sculptures of 1909-1915 also owe something to African tribal styles.

Modigliani was predominantly a painter of nudes and portraits, first working under the influence of Henri de Toulouse-Lautrec, whom he admired and in whose favorite places he was frequently seen at night. The infinite variety of the human face, its expression as type and individual, the sinuous contours of the female nudes, their ingenious placement within the framework of the picture, the new and unexpected angles from which they were visualized—all these were Modigliani's favorite themes. He was extraordinarily gifted in inventing novel aspects of his subject matter, a great master of variety.

Modigliani's masterpieces were created between 1915 and 1919. It seems that he had matured all at once. In 1918 he took part in a group show at the Berthe Weill Gallery; his nudes provoked a scandal and the police closed the show. The dealer Leopold Zborowski made great sacrifices to enable Modigliani to paint, and at one time the English poet Beatrice Hastings supported him generously. Although helped to some extent by his family, Modigliani was often near starvation, owing to the excesses of his style of living.

Modigliani's health was delicate, and he had to spend the winter of 1918/1919 in Cannes. He returned to Paris in the spring of 1919 for the birth of a daughter borne by his young mistress and model Jeanne Hébuterne. The following winter he contracted tuberculosis and was taken to a hospital, where he died in a charity ward on Jan. 25, 1920.

Modigliani is considered by many to be the greatest Italian artist of the 20th century. Among his masterpieces of painting are the *Yellow Sweater* (ca. 1919) and *Reclining Nude* (*Le Grand nu;* ca. 1919). His portraits are of uniformly high quality, for example, the one of Zborowski. (1916) and the series of Beatrice Hastings and Jeanne Hébuterne. His work, although involved in the advanced developments of Paris, nevertheless remained a direct continuation and fulfillment of the classical Italian tradition. As painter, sculptor, and draftsman, Modigliani had a leading place in the modern movement and was among the few truly great masters of the School of Paris.

Further Reading

James Thrall Soby, *Modigliani: Paintings, Drawings, Sculpture* (1951), gives a general picture of the life and art of the artist. A useful introduction to Modigliani, with good color reproductions and detailed descriptions of the plates, is Alfred Werner, *Amadeo Modigliani* (1966). Werner's *Modigliani, the Sculptor* (1962) is an important specialized study. A penetrating biography in depth is Pierre Sichel, *Modigliani: A Biography of Amadeo Modigliani* (1967). For general background see James Thrall Soby, *Twentieth Century Italian Art* (1949).

Additional Sources

Mann, Carol, *Modigliani,* New York: Thames and Hudson, 1991.
Rose, June, *Modigliani, the pure bohemian,* New York: St. Martin's Press, 1991.
Roy, Claude, *Modigliani,* New York: Rizzoli, 1985. □

Thomas Mofolo

Thomas Mofolo (1876-1948) was a Lesothoan writer whose historical novel "Chaka" encouraged a vernacular literary movement in South Africa.

Thomas Mofolo was born in Khojane on Dec. 22, 1876. He was educated in the local schools of the Paris Evangelical Missionary Society and obtained a teacher's certificate in 1898. While he was working at the book depot in Morija, some of the missionaries encouraged him to write what was to become the first novel in Southern Sotho, *Moeti oa bochabela* (1907; *The Traveler of the East*). The edifying story of a young Sotho chieftain's conversion to Christianity, it is cleverly interwoven with traditional myths and praise poems. Its success prompted other young teachers to try their hand at fiction writing, thus launching one of the earliest literary movements in sub-Saharan Africa.

Mofolo's next book, *Pitseng* (1910), is built on a rather clumsy love plot in imitation of European fiction. It contains perceptive descriptions of native mores in Lesotho and in South Africa and a thoughtful, by no means encomiastic, appraisal of the influence of Christianity on traditional marriage customs.

Mofolo then composed *Chaka,* a fictionalized account of the Zulu conqueror who built a mighty empire during the first quarter of the 19th century. Under Mofolo's pen, the eventful career of Chaka (Shaka) becomes the epic tragedy of a heroic figure whose overweening ambition drives him to insane cruelty and ultimate ruin. The earliest major contribution of black Africa to the corpus of modern world literature, *Chaka* is a genuine masterpiece; the narrative follows the austere curve of growth and decline which controls the structure of classic tragedy at its best; psychological motivation is sharply clarified at all points; and the author has cleverly manipulated the supernatural element, which is endowed with true symbolic value.

Although the missionaries were sensitive to the high literary quality of *Chaka,* the pictures of pre-Christian life that the book contains made them reluctant to publish it. In his disappointment, Mofolo left for South Africa in 1910 and gave up writing. For several years he was a labor agent, recruiting workers for the gold mines of Transvaal and the plantations of Natal. After 1927 he bought a store in Lesotho; in 1937 he acquired a farm in South Africa but was evicted under the Bantu Land Act. In 1940, a broken and sick man, he returned to Lesotho, where he died on Sept. 8, 1948.

Further Reading

The fullest account of Mofolo is found in Albert S. Gérard, *Four African Literatures* (1970). For background on Mofolo's literary output see Daniel P. Kunene's brief *The Works of Thomas Mofolo: Summaries and Critiques* (1967). Additional information on his place in the history of African literature is in Claude Wauthier, *The Literature and Thought of Modern Africa* (1964; trans. 1966); Judith Illsley Gleason, *This Africa: Novels by West Africans in English and French* (1965); and Janheinz Jahn, *Neo-African Literature* (1966; trans. 1968). □

Peter Mogila

The Russian Orthodox churchman and theologian Peter Mogila (1596-1646) is known for his restoration of Orthodox institutions.

Peter Mogila was born in Moldavia, now part of Romania, the son of Symeon, head of an aristocratic family. Political turmoil forced Symeon to flee to Poland, where his family had numerous and influential ties with the nobility. Peter studied there and then in Holland and in Paris. He served as an officer in the Polish army but at the age of 30 decided to become a monk at the famous Pechersky Lavra Monastery. He received minor orders and made his vows in 1627. Ordained a priest sometime later, he became archimandrite and in 1632 metropolitan of Kiev.

Peter's first interests lay with the fortunes of the Orthodox Church, then under strong social and economic pressure from Catholic nobility and clergy. Political and social pressures were violent. His first achievement was to take possession of Kiev's St. Sophia Cathedral and thus oust the Catholics. He restored it and the Pechersky Lavra, the monastery of Vydubetsky, and numerous other monasteries and churches, including the famous "Tenpart Church," which contained the tomb of St. Vladimir. Peter's main distinction, and the source of his difficulties, was his knowledge and appreciation of the West and of the Latin Church. He had a deep knowledge of Latin and of the Western system of seminary and university education. As an archimandrite at Pechersky Lavra, he had founded a school where Slavic and Greek studies were poorly represented. The school's academic program was fashioned on Western models, Latin being the predominant language taught there. This mixture of Western elements did not sit well with his coreligionists. He himself had been schooled in his early years at Lvov Brotherhoods School. As archimandrite, he had united the Brotherhoods School with his own at Pechersky Lavra. When he became metropolitan, he renamed this school the Collegium. Some 15 years later the Collegium became an educational and intellectual center for the Ukraine and Poland.

The writings of Peter were very important. In 1637 he published an exegetical edition of the Four Gospels. In 1646 he revised and published Orthodox Church ritual in his *Evlogion,* known also as the *Great Trebnik.* He authored, about the same time, *Short Scientific Essays about Points of the Faith.* He planned an edition of the Bible and a *Lives of the Saints,* but he died on Dec. 31, 1646, at Kiev.

Peter's greatest work was the *Orthodox Confession of the Catholic and Apostolic Eastern Church.* He wrote it to counteract the work of the Jesuits and the Reformers, both of whom were struggling for victory in Poland. It had great success, being approved by the provincial Synod of Kiev in

1640. In 1672, after his death, it was adopted as the Orthodox Standard Catechism by the Synod of Jerusalem. It was not merely a manual of instruction; it was much more a vindication of Orthodox primacy in doctrine and Church jurisdiction, in opposition to the claims of both Reformers and Counter Reformers. Because of its handy form and clarity, the *Confession* was never superseded.

Further Reading

There is scant material on Mogila in English. A good biographical sketch is in George Vernadsky, *A History of Russia,* vol. 5 (1969). For general historical background see the classic study by V. O. Kliuchevsky, *A Course in Russian History: The Seventeenth Century* (trans. 1968). □

Mohammad Reza Shah Pahlavi

Mohammad Reza Shah Pahlavi (1919-1980) was king of Iran and second in the Pahlavi dynasty. A revolution, led by the Ayatollah Khomeini in 1979, forced him into exile.

Mohammad Reza was born on Oct. 27, 1919. His father, who was then an officer in the Persian Cossack regiment, later became shah of Iran as Reza Shah Pahlavi. Upon his coronation in April 1926, his 6-year-old son, Mohammad Reza, was proclaimed crown prince. While at home he was carefully educated for his future role by his imposing and stern father. In 1931 he was sent to Switzerland and attended LeRosey school for boys. He returned to Iran in 1936 and entered the military school. He was married to Princess Fawzia of Egypt. He developed into a sportsman, enjoying soccer and skiing, and later became a licensed pilot.

World War II

In the fall of 1941 Mohammad Reza's father was forced to abdicate the throne by the British and Russian forces who had occupied the country after a short struggle. On Sept. 27, 1941, he succeeded his father as Mohammad Reza Shah Pahlavi. This was a most confused and perilous period for Iran. Not only was there a global war, but Iran was squeezed between the traditionally bitter rivalry of Russia and Britain. To this was added the lure of the vast resources of oil in Iran, which were eagerly sought by the Russians, Americans, and British.

Furthermore, the Soviet pressure on Iran had an ideological dimension which sought revolutionary change in the country. The young Shah was caught in the midst of this struggle between the pro-Soviet Tudeh party, which wanted social revolution without the Shah, and the pro-British National Will party, which wanted the Shah but no social change. The Shah himself was not happy with either.

The Soviet Union refused to evacuate Iran after World War II as it had promised and instead stayed to help a branch of the Persian Communist party set up a separate government in the northwest province of Azarbayjan. Iran complained to the fledgling United Nations organization. After much negotiations the Soviet Union evacuated Azarbayjan on May 9, 1946, and the Shah entered the province in the midst of popular jubilation.

Internal Unrest

But this did not bring tranquility, for the oil problem had not been solved. The new National Front party, formed under the leadership of Dr. Mohammad Mosaddeq, followed a philosophy of "negative neutralism." This stated that, since Iran had refused to give oil concessions to the Soviet Union, it should take them away from the British.

The country was plunged into such a crisis that by 1953 communication broke down between the Shah and Prime Minister Mosaddeq and also among the prime minister, his cabinet, and the parliament. The crisis, in which the Tudeh party was daily gaining the upper hand, forced the Shah and Sorayya (his second wife) to leave the country. Nine days later Mosaddeq was overthrown, and the Shah returned in triumph.

Mohammad Reza Shah returned with a new resolve. Whereas he had tried to reign as a constitutional monarch, he decided to rule under the constitution. He had distributed his land among the peasants, hoping that other landlords would follow his example, but they ignored the hint and dubbed him the "Bolshevik Shah." It was then that he started what later was called the "White Revolution." After distributing the land among the peasants, he nationalized forests and water, established profit-sharing plans for the workers, emancipated women, and established literacy, sanitation, and development corps, in which educated men spent 2 years of their time in lieu of military service. New industries were created, and Iran became one of the most stable countries in the Middle East.

On Oct. 27, 1967, his forty-eighth birthday, and after 26 years as king, he was crowned as His Imperial Majesty Mohammad Reza Pahlavi Aryamehr, Shahanshah of Iran. What made this coronation a unique one in the annals of Persian history was that his third wife, Farah, was crowned as empress, the first since the coming of Islam in the 7th century. Their 6-year-old son, Reza, was declared crown prince.

During the 1970s, oil-exporting countries such as Iran exercised much world power. It was also the strongest military country in the Middle East. However, the Shah was an autocratic ruler who saw his popularity decreasing, especially among the conservative Muslims who were followers of the Ayatollah Ruhollah Khomeini. The Ayatollah led a revolution in 1979, forcing the Shah and his family into exile. Mohammed Reza Pahlavi died in Cairo on July 27, 1980.

Further Reading

The best accounts in English of Mohammad Reza Shah are those written by the Shah himself, *My Mission for My Country* (1961) and *The White Revolution of Iran* (1967). The first full-length biography of the Shah in English is Ramesh Sanghvi, *The Shah of Iran* (1969). A scholarly treatment is E. A. Bayne, *Persian Kingship in Transition: Conversations with a Monarch Whose Office is Traditional and Whose Goal is Modernization* (1968).

Additional Sources

Karanjia, Rustom Khurshedji, *The mind of a monarch,* London: G. Allen & Unwin, 1977.

Laing, Margaret Irene, *The Shah,* London: Sidgwick & Jackson, 1977.

Mohammed Reza Pahlavi, Shah of Iran, *Answer to history,* New York: Stein and Day, 1980.

Mohammed Reza Pahlavi, Shah of Iran, *The Shah's story,* London: M. Joseph, 1980.

Shawcross, William, *The Shah's last ride: the fate of an ally,* New York: Simon and Schuster, 1988.

Taheri, Amir, *The unknown life of the Shah,* London: Hutchinson, 1991.

Zonis, Marvin, *Majestic failure: the fall of the Shah,* Chicago: University of Chicago Press, 1991. □

Mohammed

Mohammed (ca. 570-632) was the founder of the religion of Islam and of a political unit at Medina that later developed into the Arab Empire, or Caliphate, and a multitude of successor states.

Arabia lay on the periphery of the two empires, the Byzantine and the Persian (Sassanian), which in the early 7th century controlled most of the region from the eastern Mediterranean to India. During the 6th century each made many efforts to gain advantages in Arabia at the expense of the other. From 572 until 628 there was almost constant war between the two, and this left the Byzantine Empire exhausted and the Persian on the point of collapse. This factor contributed largely to the rapidity of the Arab military advance into Persia, Iraq, Syria, and North Africa between 634 and 650.

The town of Mecca, where Mohammed was born about 570, was a commercial center which by 600 had gained monopolistic control of the caravan trade passing up and down the west coast of Arabia, conveying luxury goods from India and East Africa to Syria. In their own business interests the merchants of Mecca had remained neutral toward the two empires. Growing prosperity had led to a malaise among the inhabitants of Mecca, accompanied by religious questioning. Mohammed's clan of Hashim, like most of the Meccan clans, gained a livelihood by commerce, but some of the other clans had been more successful and were now wealthier.

Call To Be a Prophet

Mohammed's personal situation made him keenly aware of the tensions in Mecca. He was born posthumously, and his grandfather, Abdu-l-Muttalib, and his mother both died when he was a child. As a minor, he was unable by Arab custom to inherit anything. He was thus relatively poor

until about 595, when a wealthy woman, Khadija, asked him to go to Syria as steward of her merchandise and, on the successful accomplishment of the mission, offered marriage. From this time onward Mohammed was comfortably off, but he began to spend time in solitary reflection on the problems of Mecca.

During a period of solitude about 610 Mohammed had two visions in which he beheld a supernatural being who said to him, ''You are the Messenger of God'' (this being the title more frequently given to him by Moslems than that of prophet). He also found certain words ''in his heart'' (that is, his mind). Friends helped to convince him that he was called to convey messages from God to the Arabs as Moses and Jesus had done to the Jews and Christians. He continued to receive such messages from time to time until his death. They were collected into chapters, or suras, partly during Mohammed's lifetime and definitively about 650, and constitute the Koran (Qur'ān). The Koran, though mediated by Mohammed's consciousness, is held by Moslems to come from God and should not be referred to as being of Mohammed's composition.

Meccan Preacher

At first Mohammed communicated these messages only to sympathetic friends, but from 612 or 613 he proclaimed them publicly. Many people in Mecca, especially among the younger men, became followers of Mohammed and Moslems, or adherents of his religion of Islam (submission, namely to God). In the course of time, however, opposition to Mohammed appeared among the leading merchants of Mecca, and he and his followers were subjected to various petty forms of persecution. Apparently to escape from such persecution some 80 of his followers emigrated for a time to Ethiopia. About 616, pressure in the form of a boycott was placed on the clan of Hashim to make it cease protecting Mohammed, but until after the death of the head of the clan, Mohammed's uncle Abu-Talib, about 619, it was felt that to abandon him would be dishonorable.

The new head, Abu-Lahab, however, found a way of justifying abandonment, and it became virtually impossible for Mohammed to continue preaching in Mecca. An attempt to move to the neighboring town of Taif proved abortive; but in September 622, after secret negotiations over the previous 2 years, he settled in the oasis of Medina, 200 miles to the north, where 70 of his followers had already gone. This ''emigration'' (rather than ''flight'') is the Hijra (Latin, *hegira*), on which the Islamic era is based.

First Years at Medina

The Arab clans of Medina mostly acknowledged Mohammed's prophethood and entered into alliance with him and the emigrants from Mecca. At first the emigrants depended on Medinese hospitality, but soon small groups of them began to attempt raids on Meccan caravans. Later the Moslems of Medina also joined in. This was a variant of the common Arab practice of the razzia. At first the raids had little success, but in March 624 a larger band of just over 300, led by Mohammed himself, after failing to intercept a caravan, decisively defeated a supporting force of perhaps

800 Meccans with heavy losses. This was a serious blow to Meccan prestige, and the Moslems felt that God was vindicating Mohammed.

To teach Mohammed a lesson, the Meccans in March 625 invaded the Medinese oasis with about 3,000 men. Mohammed, obliged to fight by some supporters, stationed his force of 1,000 on the lower slopes of Uhud, a hill in the north of the oasis, where they were safe from the Meccan cavalry. An attack of the Meccan infantry was repulsed by the Moslems, but as they pursued the fugitives, the cavalry managed to attack them on the flank. Many were killed before they could regain the safety of the hill. Militarily this was not a serious reverse for Mohammed, since the Meccans had also suffered casualties and retreated immediately without following up their advantage; but the reverse shook the belief that God was vindicating him, and confidence was only gradually restored.

Though the Moslems were now making several smaller razzias each year with a measure of success, the next major event was the siege of Medina by 10,000 Meccans and allies in April 627. Mohammed protected the central part of the oasis by a trench which foiled the cavalry, and after a fortnight the alliance broke up and the siege was raised. The Meccans had now shot their bolt and failed to dislodge Mohammed. When he went to Mecca in March 628 with 1,600 men, ostensibly to perform traditional pilgrimage rites, the Meccans turned him back but concluded the Treaty of al-Hudaybiya with him.

Though the terms of the treaty slightly favored the Meccans, the signing of it was a triumph for Mohammed. In the following months many nomadic tribesmen and a few leading Meccans went to Medina to join Mohammed and become Moslems. When the treaty was denounced in January 630 after an incident involving allies of each side, Mohammed was able to march on Mecca with 10,000 men. There was virtually no resistance, and Mohammed entered Mecca in triumph. A few persons guilty of hostile or objectionable acts were proscribed, but the Meccans in general were leniently treated. A fort-night later 2,000 joined Mohammed's army in opposing a concentration of tribesmen east of Mecca and shared in the victory of Hunayn.

New Religion

By 630 the religion of Islam had attained a definite form. In the earliest parts the Koran had emphasized God's goodness and power and had called on men to acknowledge this in worship. It had also asserted the reality of the Day of Judgment, when men would be assigned to paradise or hell in accordance with their attitude to God's revelation, their generosity with their wealth, and similar points. These matters were relevant to the tensions of Mecca, which were seen as arising from the merchants' overconfidence in their wealth and power. After the appearance of opposition to Mohammed, the Koran contained attacks on idols and an insistence that ''there is no deity but God.''

The religious practices of the Moslems included communal worship or prayers several times a day, in which the climax was prostration, the touching of the ground with the forehead in acknowledgement of God's majesty. They also gave alms in the form of a kind of tithe. At Medina the fast from sunrise to sunset during the month of Ramadan was introduced; and when circumstances made it possible, some of the ceremonies of the traditional pilgrimage to Mecca became a duty for Moslems.

Years of Triumph

In 622 Mohammed, though recognized as prophet in Medina, had been only one clan chief among nine. His power and authority grew, however, with the success of the razzias and other expeditions undertaken by the Moslems, especially those against the Meccans. There were Jewish clans in Medina, wealthy but now politically subordinate to the Arab clans, and these made damaging criticisms of Mohammed's religious teaching and sometimes intrigued with his enemies. On suitable occasions in 622, 624, and 625 he attacked the three main clans and expelled them. In the last case all the men were put to death.

Beyond Medina a system of alliances was gradually built up with the nomadic Arab tribes. As Mohammed grew stronger, he came to insist that those wanting an alliance should become Moslems. After the conquest of Mecca and the victory at Hunayn in January 630, he was the strongest man in Arabia, and deputations came from tribes or parts of tribes in eastern, central, and southern Arabia, seeking alliance with him. When he died on June 8, 632, he was in effective control of a large part of Arabia, but it is impossible to define exactly the area he ruled, since we do not know how important in the tribe or local community was the group allied to Mohammed.

His Personality and Achievement

Mohammed is said to have been a fast walker, of sturdy build, with a prominent forehead, a hooked nose, large brownish-black eyes, and a pleasant smile. He showed great tact in his dealings with people and, when appropriate, gentleness and even tenderness. Medieval Europe, however, on the defensive against Arab armies and Islamic culture, came to look on him as a monster or demon. Even scholars depicted him as treacherous and lecherous and an impostor. The last he certainly was not, for as Thomas Carlyle pointed out in 1840, a great religion cannot be founded on imposture.

At time Mohammed was indeed harsh to those in his power, but this was not out of keeping with the age. His marital relations—at his death he had nine wives and one concubine—must also be judged in the context of the age. A political purpose can be traced in all his marriages, and he was also creating a new family structure to replace older matrilineal family structures associated with undesirable polyandric practices. For his time he was a social reformer.

Politically his great achievement was to create the framework which made possible the uniting of the Arab tribes and was capable of being developed to include an empire. Mohammed was aware at least by 627 that it would be necessary to expand beyond Arabia, since tribes allied to him could not raid other allies and must direct their energies further afield. He thus devoted special attention to the tribes on the route to Syria and to a lesser extent on the route to Iraq. He was also to win over to his cause his chief Meccan opponents, and their administrative skills were later invaluable in conquering and ruling numerous provinces. The growth of the Arab Empire, and with it of the religion of Islam, was made possible by favorable circumstances; but the opportunity would not have been grasped but for Mohammed's gifts as visionary, statesman, and administrator.

Further Reading

The most recent full account of Mohammed is contained in the two works by W. Montgomery Watt, *Muhammad at Mecca* (1953) and *Muhammad at Medina* (1956). These volumes are briefly summarized in Watt's *Muhammad: Prophet and Statesman* (1961). Tor Andrae, *Mohammed: The Man and His Faith* (trans. 1936), is chiefly concerned with the religious aspect. Rather slighter is the section on Mohammed in Francesco Gabrieli, *Muhammad and the Conquests of Islam* (1967; trans. 1968). The primary Arabic biography is translated by Alfred Guillaume as *The Life of Muhammad: A Translation of Ishaq's Sirat Rasul Allah* (1955).
Norman Daniel, *Islam and the West: The Making of an Image* (1960), discusses the medieval distortions. The best of the numerous translations of the Koran are those by George Sale, *Selections from the Kur-an* (1734; 5th ed. 1855), and Arthur J. Arberry, *The Koran Interpreted* (1955). Richard Bell, *Introduction to the Qur'an* (1953; rev. ed. 1958), is also recommended. For general background see G. E. von Grunebaum, *Classical Islam: A History, 600 A.D.-1258 A.D.* (1971), and P. M. Holt, Ann K. S. Lambton, and Bernard Lewis, eds., *The Cambridge History of Islam* (2 vols., 1971). □

Mohammed II

Mohammed II (1432-1481), called Faith or Conqueror, was the Ottoman Turkish sultan from 1451 to 1481. His conquest of Constantinople in 1453 guaranteed the consolidation of the Ottoman Empire.

The son of Sultan Murad II (reigned 1421-1451), Mohammed II assumed full sovereignty on his father's death in February 1451. His predecessors had conquered much of the southern Balkans and had subjected the bulk of Asia Minor as well; but the continued independence of Constantinople and of other Greek territories both prolonged the life of the faded Byzantine Empire and deprived the new Turkish power of its logical capital while also posing the danger of some Christian counteroffensive from this strategic center. The ambitious young sultan therefore was determined that the final conquest of Constantinople should be his first major achievement, and he launched his great siege of this city in early April 1453.

Despite heroic resistance under the last Byzantine emperor, Constantine XI, Constantinople was taken by storm on May 29. Mohammed II quickly restored the city's splendor and prosperity, making it the capital of an imperial Turkish regime whose coherent scale and systematic scope were the results of his own massive reorganization. In 1460

Mohammed completed the annexation of the Byzantine Peloponnesus, and in the following year he conquered the truncated empire of Trebizond, thus eliminating the last remnants of independent Greek authority.

Meanwhile, Mohammed expanded Turkish power in the Balkans. He carried out the final annexation of Serbia by 1459. His siege of Belgrade was foiled, however, in 1456 by the Hungarian hero John Hunyadi. The Hungarians further attempted, with only minimal success, to prevent the Turkish conquest of Bosnia and Herzegovina. Mohammed also subdued Walachia. He was unable to conquer Moldavia; but in 1475 he seized Caffa, Tana, and Azov, securing control of the Crimea and the northern Black Sea areas. In Albania, Mohammed carried on the struggle his father had launched; only in the late 1470s was he able to occupy the key fortresses of Albania. Alone and isolated, however, the sturdy Montenegrins resisted Turkish conquest.

Mohammed, more than any other sultan, made good the Turkish domination of Asia Minor. During the 1460s he conquered the long-independent emirate of Karaman. When Uzun Hasan, the Turkoman ruler, attempted to challenge Mohammed in eastern Asia Minor, the Sultan defeated him in the decisive battle of Otluk-beli near Terdshan on the upper Euphrates in 1472. The victory guaranteed Mohammed's Asiatic power and freed him for further conquests in Europe.

To the West, Mohammed was a source of anguish and terror. Stung by his capture of Constantinople, successive popes talked of crusades against the Turk and exhorted the

European powers to join the common cause. Although such plans foundered, Mohammed faced a strong Western foe in Venice, which found Turkish disruption of its Levantine commerce intolerable. From 1463 to 1479 Venice made war on Mohammed, supporting the Albanians and the Turkomans against him and attacking his coasts. But in 1470 the Venetians lost Negroponte (Euboea), and a few years later Mohammed's forces, victorious in Albania, menaced Venice itself around the Adriatic headlands. The republic was therefore forced to accept disadvantageous peace terms. On the other hand, when Mohammed attempted to seize the island of Rhodes in 1480, it was successfully defended by the knights of St. John (Hospitalers).

But Mohammed's most daring stroke was also executed in 1480. Taking advantage of Italy's internal disorganization, he sent a fleet to the peninsula's southern shores. In August it seized Otranto and held it for a month. The panic-stricken Italian powers saw this act as the prelude to a serious effort by the Sultan, who had boasted that he would match his conquest of the "new Rome" (Constantinople) by taking the old one. But the alarm was groundless: during the following year, as he prepared a new expedition against Rhodes, Mohammed suddenly fell ill and died on May 3, 1481, leaving his empire to a period of slackness and division under his weak son and successor, Bayazid II (reigned 1481-1512).

Further Reading

A contemporary biography by an admiring Greek supporter, Kritoboulos, who concentrates on the conquest of Constantinople, was translated by Charles T. Riggs as *History of Mehmed the Conqueror* (1954). The only full-length study is in German. There is no comprehensive account of Mohammed's entire career in English, but a concise general treatment can be found in A. W. Ward and others, eds., *The Cambridge Modern History*, vol. 1 (1903). His major role in the capture of Constantinople is discussed in such accounts of that episode as Edwin Pears, *The Destruction of the Greek Empire and the Story of the Capture of Constantinople by the Turks* (1903; repr. 1968), and Steven Runciman, *The Fall of Constantinople, 1453* (1965). □

Mohammed V

Mohammed V (1911-1961), also known as Mohammed Ben Youssef, was the first king of independent Morocco. He succeeded in conciliating divided forces of Moroccan nationalism and helped to forge national unity around the throne.

Nothing at the birth of Mohammed, in Fez, predestined that he would rule over Morocco. He was only the third son of Moulay Youssef, the brother of the ruling sultan, Moulay Hafid. But in 1912, when the French occupied Morocco, Moulay Youssef replaced his brother as sultan. Mohammed Ben Youssef grew up in the royal palaces of Fez and Meknes, where an Algerian teacher tutored him. He received a traditional education based on the Koran plus some elements of modern culture, but he never formally studied French.

The Sultan

On Nov. 18, 1927, at the age of 16 Mohammed was chosen by the college of ulemas (religious scholars) to succeed his father. This choice was influenced by the French protectorate authorities, who hoped that this timid and docile youth would remain removed from the affairs of state. Isolated in his palace, Mohammed V, during the initial years of his reign, seemed to accept his unimportant role. During this same period the first nationalists organized a movement which led to the formation of the *Istiqlal,* or Independence party, in 1944. Already by the late 1930s the Sultan (who assumed the title of king in 1956) had secretly collaborated with some of these nationalists.

During World War II, however, Mohammed remained loyal to France, but in January 1943 at the Conference of Anfa, a suburb of Casablanca, the Sultan dined with U.S. president Franklin Roosevelt, who opened up the perspective of an independent Morocco if the Sultan would aid the Allies in recruiting Moroccan troops for action on the European front. In 1947, during a speech at Tangiers, Mohammed Ben Youssef departed from the written text which the French authorities had approved and openly sided with the nationalist cause.

The crisis in Franco-Moroccan relations intensified after the war. It was aggravated by the attitude of conservative resident generals who repressed the nationalist party. Stripped of real power, Mohammed V was often forced to condemn the Istiqlal officially while secretly he encouraged its leaders. Beginning in 1947 the situation deteriorated. Encouraged, even pushed, by the preponderant colonialist groups, the French authorities in Rabat tightened their direct control over the administration, an act which further diminished the Sultan's authority. The latter resisted by the only legal means at his disposal and refused as often as he could to countersign laws and decrees. He also attempted to bring the growing abuse of his powers to the attention of the French government, but all of his attempts to change the protectorate status failed.

Deposition and Exile

Tension mounted in Morocco during the 1950s. As the French in Morocco attacked the Sultan, his popularity grew. The French, allied with an important feudal chief of the south, the Glaoui of Marrakesh, and other traditionalist leaders hostile to the reformist and nationalistic elites of the Istiqlal, tried to play off one side against the other. Riots in Casablanca at the end of 1952 ushered in the era of mass politics, and the Sultan was accused of being one of the main causes for the deteriorating situation. By Aug. 20, 1953, despite the opposition of Paris, the French in Morocco deposed the Sultan, who refused to abdicate his throne. He and his family were exiled to Madagascar, where they remained for 3 years.

In Morocco the failure of the royal deposition became quickly clear. The Moroccans considered the new puppet sultan, Moulay Arafa, a usurper. Acts of terrorism multiplied, and insecurity spread throughout the country. The French in Morocco retaliated with repression and violence, while liberal politicians in Paris actively worked for a solution. When the Glaoui rallied to the cause of Mohammed V, all opposition to the exile's return melted away, and on Nov. 16, 1955, the Sultan regained Morocco and was greeted by delirious crowds. On March 2, 1956, Morocco received its independence. Mohammed V became the chief of state, and his son Moulay Hassan took command of the army.

Independent King

When Morocco became independent, Mohammed V was 45 years old. He had two sons and four daughters, all of whom had received a modern education. His poor health gave him a fragile appearance, accentuated by a natural pallor. But his gaze was attentive, and he possessed an ironic sense of humor that he revealed to friends and relatives. The early rigidity which characterized his personality as sultan gradually gave way to self-confidence as king. But he never lost the reserve and dignity which characterized his dynasty's style. Through courteous manners and down-to-earth simplicity, when he so chose, he charmed his opponents into working for him.

Mohammed's legendary exile, during which time the Moroccan nation took form, gained enormous prestige for him, and he used this to full advantage. He combined in his person the religious authority of a sharif (descendant of the prophet Mohammed) and the martyrdom of an exile, and in his presence both modernists and traditionalists, Berbers and Arabs, found unity.

Although a theocratic king who was endowed with absolute authority, Mohammed exercised his powers more as an arbiter than as a despot, which fact added to his prestige. His character and his studies of Moroccan dynastic history aided him to maneuver his opponents rather than confront them. He was a master at balancing forces, speaking to all sides and giving everyone the impression that he heeded advice; but in the end he did what was best for the palace and his dynasty. By weakening the opponents to the throne, he strengthened royal institutions and became the indispensable symbol of national unity.

Without schooling in political science, Mohammed V nevertheless had a flair for politics. He was fully aware of the contradictory realities of his country, which had to undergo the profound transformation from a medieval kingdom to a modern nation-state. His aim throughout his last years was to help the traditional society adjust to this new, modern state. He died unexpectedly of heart failure after a minor operation on Feb. 26, 1961. His son Hassan II succeeded him as king.

Further Reading

Information on Moroccan dynastic history and the role of Mohammed V is in Nevill Barbour, *Morocco* (1965). For detailed descriptions of his political role see Douglas E. Ashford, *Political Change in Morocco* (1961), and Stéphane Bernard, *The Franco-Moroccan Conflict, 1943-1956* (trans. 1968). ☐

Mohammed Ali

An Ottoman pasha of Egypt, Mohammed Ali (1769-1849) was often known as the father of modern Egypt because of the economic, social, and political changes set in motion during his almost half century of personal rule.

Mohammed Ali, the son of humble Turkish parents, was born in the Aegean seaport of Kavalla in Macedonia. His father was a town watchman. The young Mohammed Ali worked as a tax collector and tobacco merchant before becoming an officer in an Albanian regiment which the Ottoman sultan sent to Egypt in 1799 to repulse Napoleon's invasion and occupation.

Mohammed Ali, with the support of his Albanian troops, acted skillfully and shrewdly in balancing his Ottoman and Mamluk rivals for power in the several years of anarchy following the withdrawal of the European troops. He secured the support of native Egyptian religious, notable, and guild leaders, had himself proclaimed pasha in 1805, and left the reluctant sultan with little alternative but to recognize him as governor of Egypt.

Reforms as Pasha

The new pasha, however, was no Egyptian nationalist. He sought to utilize the country for his own political ambitions for power in the eastern Mediterranean. Egypt was important for what it could do for him, and yet his efforts to unify, strengthen, and modernize Egypt have made Mohammed Ali one of its greatest rulers.

Mohammed Ali effected his control over Egypt by eliminating his Mamluk opponents in a massacre, justified with contrived reasons, in 1811, by centralizing government administration in Cairo, and by building a new army. The army played a crucial part in his other political plans and ambitions; most of the resources he squeezed out of Egypt and its fellahin (peasant farmers) went to the training and modernization of the army. He assumed titular ownership of all the land, controlled the buying and selling of all agricultural products, and directed the collection of all rents and taxes.

This vastly increased the money available for Mohammed Ali's plans but at the same time improved the fellahin's existence by reestablishing law and order and by eliminating tax farmers and many rapacious landlords. His agricultural policies added a million acres to cultivation, cleaned and improved the vital canal system, and encouraged production of long-staple cotton. Mohammed Ali also took an interest in modern factory methods, particularly in using local cotton for military uniforms, but it proved frustrating and very costly with the little experience and few skilled laborers at his command.

Mohammed Ali relied heavily on the loyalty and military skill of his talented eldest son, Ibrahim Pasha. Brilliant campaigns in the Sudan, western Arabia, Greece, and Syria demonstrated the value of the French-trained Egyptian army and the potential power of Egypt under its new pasha. He was successful only to a point, however, since his efforts to boost the importance of Egypt (and hence himself) could only be at the expense of the Ottoman Empire, already unstable and in decline. On several occasions the major European powers intervened to check Mohammed Ali and to prop up the weak empire. The British in particular feared the further development of a powerful state in such a strategic area, one which would be pro-French and might also restrict British commercial interests in favor of its own.

Hereditary Pasha

Following Ibrahim's overwhelming defeat of the Sultan's supposedly new army on the border of Anatolia in 1839, the European powers, except France, forced Egyptian withdrawal from all of Syria, which Ibrahim had occupied and ruled for a decade. The Treaty of London of 1841 recognized Mohammed Ali's aim for the position of pasha as hereditary in his family. It still left Egypt under Ottoman suzerainty and with definite restrictions on the Egyptian army so that it could not again threaten Ottoman integrity. Mohammed Ali died in Cairo on Aug. 2, 1849, just after the death of Ibrahim, who in fact had ruled as pasha in place of his apparently tired and senile father for the last year.

Mohammed Ali had begun the transformation of Egypt from a traditional to a modern society, but it was still administered primarily by and for nonnative Egyptians. He had built up the strength and virtual independence of the country, but he left a potentially dangerous situation to his less capable successors which in the context of increasing European imperialism led to British occupation in 1882.

Further Reading

The best books on Mohammed Ali are Henry H. Dodwell, *The Founder of Modern Egypt: A Study of Muhammad Ali* (1931), and Helen Anne B. Rivlin, *The Agricultural Policy of Muhammad Ali in Egypt* (1961). For his ambitions outside Egypt see Richard L. Hill, *Egypt in the Sudan, 1820-1881* (1959). Tom Little, *Modern Egypt* (1967), and John Marlowe, *A History of Modern Egypt and Anglo-Egyptian Relations, 1800-1956* (2d ed. 1965), provide good background information on 19th century Egypt. □

László Moholy-Nagy

The Hungarian painter, designer, and teacher László Moholy-Nagy (1895-1946) was one of the leading figures in the Bauhaus and was highly instrumental in bringing its ideas to the United States.

László Moholy-Nagy was born on July 20, 1895, in Bacsbarsod. He studied law before becoming interested in painting. In 1919 he discovered the work of the Russian constructivists El Lissitzky and Kasimir Malevich, whose lifelong influence can be seen in Moholy-Nagy's paintings with the characteristic severe patterns of rectangles and other geometric shapes scattered sparsely over a plain background.

In 1921 Moholy-Nagy moved to Berlin. His paintings were now completely nonobjective, and he began to study the function and effect of light, which became one of his main continuing interests. Combined with this was his enthusiasm for the potential uses of the new plastic materials. Like Marcel Duchamp, he began to question the traditional involvement of the artist's hand in his own work. In 1922 Moholy-Nagy came up with a brilliant and audacious idea: he had five paintings made for him by a factory. He telephoned the factory and described what he wanted, using the factory's color chart and graph paper. As Duchamp did with his ready-mades, Moholy-Nagy claimed the five paintings as his because he had thought of them rather than actually made them by his own hand.

Moholy-Nagy's interests in a new relationship between the artist and his art, his investigations into the use of light, and his use of new materials made him a very suitable member of the Bauhaus, where he went to teach in 1923. The Bauhaus had been founded in 1919 by Walter Gropius to provide a new sort of artistic training, where the artist no

Lazlo Moholy-Nagy (bottom, right)

longer had to choose between art and design but was instead given an all-round education which would allow him to use his knowledge of art and materials to make a more functional art, often involved in industrial design.

Moholy-Nagy taught the introductory course at the Bauhaus and helped turn it away from its preoccupation with mysticism and intuitive philosophy and toward a more practical and tightly controlled emphasis on materials and their potential and function. He was peculiarly adept at fusing theory and practice and was thus highly successful at both teaching and writing. In 1928 he left the Bauhaus and executed stage designs in Berlin, using his Bauhaus-evolved ideas of space and light. During a short stay in London he produced a number of documentary films.

In 1937 Moholy-Nagy went to Chicago, where he directed the New Bauhaus for a year and then set up his own School of Design, which he ran on Bauhaus principles until his death in Chicago on Nov. 24, 1946. An extraordinarily idealistic man, he passionately believed in his own concepts of design and teaching and worked feverishly to accomplish his aims. It is in large part owing to him that the Bauhaus ideas so thoroughly infused American design.

Further Reading

Moholy-Nagy's own writings are very epigrammatic and perhaps provide a more exciting picture of the potential of his ideas than do his artistic productions. His *The New Vision* (1928) and *Vision in Motion* (1947) give a fine sense of his liveliness of mind and wide-ranging interests. An extremely touching and very informative book is the biography by his wife, Sibyl Moholy-Nagy, *Moholy-Nagy: Experiment in Totality* (1950; 2d ed. 1969).

Additional Sources

Kaplan, Louis, *Laszlo Moholy-Nagy: biographical writings,* Durham: Duke University Press, 1995. □

Daniel Arap Moi

Daniel arap Moi (born 1924) first became president of Kenya, by appointment, following the death of Kenya's first president, Jomo Kenyatta.

Daniel arap Moi first became president of Kenya in 1978. For most of his years as president, Moi and the ruling party have had absolute authority over the country's political and judicial systems. Moi is a tough, experienced fighter, with "country boy cunning" and craftiness in exploiting tribal divisions. As the pro-government *Sunday Times* said: "Moi may not have studied politics at anyone's university, but he has proved himself a real 'Professor of politics' in the practical sense." In 1982 Moi pushed legislation through making Kenya a *de jure* (by right) one-party state, although it had been a *de facto* (actual) one-party state since 1969, when the opposition was banned and KANU had begun overriding Parliament in decision-making matters.

Domestically, the Kenyan government had repressed pressure for political change by detentions, torture, and killings, and by control of the media and the courts. Internationally, demands for a more just society only came in the early 1990s, with the collapse of the eastern European bloc countries and the Soviet Union. Western donor countries, alarmed by misappropriation of aid money and human rights abuses, began exerting pressure on the Kenyan government to legalize opposition parties and hold multiparty elections. U.S. State Department officials estimated that President Moi had accumulated a personal fortune equal to that of Zairean President Mobutu Sese Seko, who is reported to have $4 billion outside the country, according to Blaine Harden in *Africa: Dispatches from a Fragile Continent.* The pressure from other governments seemed to take its toll, and Moi held multiparty elections in late 1995. The democracy was short-lived, however: Moi suspended the entire Parliament one day after they were seated.

Moi's formal educational background consisted of mission and government schools. He received further training at a teacher training college. From there he went on to teach at government training schools. Before he entered politics, his last posting in education was as assistant principal of Tambach Government African Teachers' College.

Moi's father died when Moi was young. His mother raised the family single-handedly but they were poor. Moi's paternal uncle, Senior Chief Kiplabet, arranged for Moi to attend mission schools. Born Toroitich arap Moi, he took the name Daniel when he was baptized at the Karbatonjo mission school. Moi took menial jobs at the mission schools

and during his school holidays he herded cattle. He passed his London Matriculation Examination and also got a certificate in public accounting from London through a correspondence course.

Moi's introduction to politics came in 1955 when he was selected to be an African representative to the British colonial Legislative Council, or Legco. In March of 1957 Moi and seven other African members of the Legco formed a lobby group, the African Elected Members' Organisation. Others in the parliamentary pressure group included nationalists Tom Mboyo, Oginga Odinga, and Musinde Muliro.

In 1960 as members of Legco, Moi and other nationalists participated in the constitutional talks held in London in preparation for Kenya's independence from Britain. On their return, they formed the political party Kenya Africa National Union (KANU). Eventually Moi and others from minority tribal groups broke away from KANU because it represented the interests of the dominant tribes, the Luo and the Kikuyu, and formed a multi-tribal coalition, the Kenyan African Democratic Union (KADU) as an alternative to KANU. Moi became chair of the new party.

In the transition period to independence Moi was appointed parliamentary secretary in the ministry of education in 1961. In this position he represented Kenya at the UNESCO Conference in Addis Ababa, Ethiopia, and he traveled to India. In the pre-independence coalition government Moi was appointed minister for education and later minister for local government.

In pre-independence national elections in 1963, KADU failed to present enough candidates to challenge KANU, now headed by nationalist leader Jomo Kenyatta. As a result, Kenyatta became president of the new republic in 1964, and Moi lost his ministerial portfolio. To bring the opposition into his government Kenyatta appointed Moi minister of home affairs after KADU dissolved itself in November of 1964.

No sooner had the new legislature had been sworn in than Moi set his government on a confrontational course with the opposition. With his power as executive, he suspended Parliament indefinitely and told the legislators to return to their constituencies. Many of the opposition parliamentarians are articulate, independent-minded professional people who will challenge the ruling party, if given the opportunity. Several opposition publications were confiscated and editors of two publications, one church-sponsored, were charged with sedition for publishing articles critical of Moi.

Moi is a Kalenjin from the Rift Valley, a minor tribe in ethnically divided Kenya. His tribal heritage has been a significant factor in his political career. Jomo Kenyatta, Kenya's first independence president in 1964 and a Kikuyu, selected Moi as vice president in 1967 partly because Moi lacked a powerful political base and was not a participant in the Luo-Kikuyu fight.

As vice president, Moi was perceived as bland and unassuming. But, as political rival Oginga Odinga related in his 1967 biography, *Not Yet Uhuru,* Moi was like "a giraffe with a long neck that saw from afar." As minister of home affairs, a position Moi retained when he became vice president, he was "responsible for the prisons, the police force, and the immigration department, [and he] made friendships which were to stand him in good stead in later years," according to *Africa Confidential* of June 1990. "His responsibility for issuing passports brought him into close touch with the Asian business community. His job of issuing work permits brought him equally close to British business houses. It was Moi's responsibility too as the minister of home affairs to make appointments throughout the police, prisons and immigration services. This was to be useful in later years when the police services were riddled with Moi appointees."

When Kenyatta died in August 1978, Moi became president with the consent of KANU and the help of powerful Kikuyus like attorney general Charles Njonjo. Moi named Kibaki, a Kikuyu, vice president, and other influential Kenyatta people retained their positions and parliamentary seats. Moi stressed continuation of Kenyatta's policies in his theme of "Nyayoism," or "footsteps."

As president, one of the first things Moi did was to travel the country to rural areas, visiting every tribal group. He introduced free milk programs for school children, released all political detainees, and abolished land-buying companies that had been gouging small land holders. Popular appeal, however, was not enough for Moi to hold power, especially as he came from an insignificant power base. Moi began rewarding loyalty and, as a consequence, the government became enormously corrupt. Kickbacks demanded on major government projects jumped from between 5 and 10 percent under Kenyatta to between 10 and 25 percent under Moi, according to a Kenyan economist cited by Harden in *Africa: Dispatches from a Fragile Continent.* "Under Kenyatta, a spending project would be approved because it was a sound project and then it would be padded," the economist said. "Under Moi, there were a number of projects that would not and should not have been approved except for corruption."

Official corruption and abuse of powers, plus a deteriorating economy, exploded in a 1982 coup attempt by Kenya air force officers, most of them Luos, dissatisfied with their people being excluded from power and access to the national treasury. The army remained loyal to Moi and put down the coup. The president then detained most of the 2,100-strong air force, and created a totally new force. He eliminated Kikuyu and Luo officers from the military and put in Kalenjin and non-ethnic challengers; for instance, he named General Mahmoud Mohammed—and ethnic Somali—army chief of general staff. Government handouts co-opted military leaders. Officers above the rank of major got free farms, gifts of the government. Moi gave the military plentiful reasons to remain loyal to him.

On the grassroots level, the KANU youth wing conducted a massive membership recruitment drive, which reported to have attracted four million new members and raised millions of dollars for the ruling party. Even at the market level, buyers and sellers could not trade without a party card. The general services unit, a paramilitary wing of the police force with a reputation for brutality, quashed pro-democracy activities and demonstrations.

As part of his effort to rid the inner circles of government of Kikuyus, Moi orchestrated the spectacular fall from power of his Kikuyu attorney general and backer Charles Njonjo in mid-1983. Moi arranged for Kenya's byzantine political network to brand Njonjo a traitor to the nation, forcing him to resign from the Cabinet and Parliament. "You know a balloon is a very small thing," Moi said to Harden in explaining his control over political cronies. "But I can pump it up to such an extent that it will be big and look very important. All you need to make it small again is to prick it with a needle."

In July of 1991 Africa Watch, a human rights organization with offices in New York and London, published a scathing attack on the Moi government, accusing it of committing torture and gross human rights violations. In *Kenya: Taking Liberties,* Africa Watch documented incidents of torture and deaths of political detainees and pro-democracy advocates by the security forces.

Pressures for change were building for other reasons as well. In 1990, Minister of Foreign Affairs Robert Ouko was brutally murdered shortly after returning from a trip with Moi for meetings with U.S. State Department officials in Washington, D.C. Moi's head of internal security Hezekiah Oyugi and Minister of Energy Nicholas Biwott were prime suspects in Ouko's murder. Moi stopped investigations into the murder, leaving widespread belief among Kenyans that he covered up the crime by his two top associates. As much as anything else, that provoked an outpouring of domestic and international demands for an end to Moi's one-party autocracy and the holding of multiparty elections.

As demands for elections increased, the government stepped up its repression: opposition leaders and university students were detained and tortured, their families beaten, their homes burned; publications were removed from the newsstands; and an outspoken cleric died in suspicious circumstances. On July 7, 1990 (in Swahili the date is Saba Saba for 7-7), security forces brutally put down a rally held by the opposition in defiance of a police order banning the meeting. Police charged 1,000 people with "riot-related offenses." Officials said 20 people died.

In November of 1991 the international lending agencies suspended payment of $350 million in aid to the Kenyan government. With the economy in poor condition, tourism declining, and low export commodity prices, Moi and the ruling party bowed to the pressure. He ordered Parliament to amend Kenya's constitution to allow the establishment of political parties other than KANU and to permit multiparty elections.

If the opposition parties had united behind a single candidate they could have defeated Moi, even in rigged elections. But the opposition parties, legalized only in December 1991, were divided amongst themselves. The divisions tended to break down along tribal lines. For instance, former Vice President Jaramogi Oginga Odinga (in his 80s) headed the Forum for the Restoration of Democracy (FORD Kenya). Odinga belongs to the Luo, one of the largest tribal groups in the country. Mwai Kibaki, another former vice president and a Kikuyu, lead the Democratic Party. Wealthy Kikuyu businessman Charles Matiba was the presidential candidate for FORD Asili ("original"), a spin-off from FORD Kenya. Thus, the opposition was split between two of the largest language groups, and the largest of these groups, the Kikuyu, was further divided. The egoism of the opposition leaders played neatly in Moi's favor.

Once the campaigning began, KANU distributed money to woo supporters through its youth wing, Youth for Kanu '92. Some of these funds were diverted from the National Social Security Fund, according to *Africa Confidential* in its October 1992 issue. The government flooded Nairobi with newly printed currency during the election campaign. Local newspapers reported the government nearly doubled the nation's money supply by distributing new Kenya shilling notes worth about $1.5 billion.

On December 29, 1992, in the first multiparty elections in Kenya in 26 years, incumbent Moi was elected president by a minority of voters. Moi took just over 34 percent of the popular vote and the three major opposition candidates split nearly 64 percent of the vote. The ruling party won 100 parliamentary seats and the opposition 88.

The elections that returned President Moi and the ruling national party, the Kenya Africa National Union (KANU), were marked by violence and intimidation. Shortly before the elections, tribal fighting occurred in the Rift Valley between the Kalenjin—Moi's people—and the Kikuyu, Kenya's largest tribal group, leaving approximately 700 people dead and 10,000 homeless. In 16 of the Rift Valley constituencies, no opposition candidates for Parliament ran against the ruling party. KANU supporters physically prevented either the candidates or their agents from submitting their registration papers. The deaths and registration intimidation support opposition parties' claims that Moi and KANU employed violence and threats to win the elections.

International election monitors brought in at the request of the opposition parties refused to certify the elections as free and fair. In their report on the elections, the Commonwealth Observer Group criticized KANU for not curbing the "worst excesses of their supporters," for "widespread bribery, a lack of transparency on the part of the Electoral Commission, intimidation, administrative obstacles and violence . . . and the reluctance of the government to delink itself" from KANU. Despite all these reservations, the Commonwealth observers said the election "results in many instances directly reflect, however imperfectly, the expression of the will of the people."

In December of 1995 elections were held and a new multiparty Parliament was elected. One such opposition party was led by the famous paleoanthropologist Richard Leakey, who was born in Kenya and used to head the Kenya Wildlife Service, with Moi's backing until they had a fallout. On January 27, however, one day after being seated, the government was prorogued, or suspended by decree. The country's disarray continues, meanwhile, with violent bandit attacks on the rise and tribal fighting causing hundreds of deaths. Garbage collection is piling up in the cities, and electricity is sporadic. Rwandan Hutu refugees, many accused of the genocide in that country, have fled to asylum in

Kenya with the support of Moi. Although Moi figured that elections would lead donor governments to resume aid, it doesn't appear that reconciliation with foreign powers is near.

With an election looming in 1997, Kenya's opposition parties continue to be crippled by infighting, unable to unite behind a single candidate or agree on an agenda with which to challenge Moi. Furthermore, violence against opponents of President Moi and against the press has escalated to pre-1988 levels. Opposition leader Leakey has traveled to South Africa, London, and the US in search of international support, while Moi remains unwilling to implement constitutional reform.

Further Reading

Days, Drew S., and others, *Justice Enjoined: The State of the Judiciary in Kenya,* Robert F. Kennedy Memorial Center for Human Rights, 1992.
Harden, Blaine, *Africa: Dispatches from a Fragile Continent,* W. W. Norton, 1990.
Christian Science Monitor, March 5, 1997, p.19.
Kenya: Taking Liberties, Africa Watch, July 1991.
Africa Confidential, June 1, 1990; December 6, 1991.
News Release (Nairobi), Commonwealth Observer, January 1, 1993.
New York Times, September 29, 1996, p. 1–14.
The Standard (Nairobi), January 5, 1993.
Sunday Times (Nairobi), December 27, 1992. □

Molière

The French dramatist Molière (1622-1673) wrote comedies that range from simple farces to sophisticated satires. The master of French comedy, he was both the product and the critic of the French classical period.

As author, director, producer, manager, and actor, Molière lived fully the life of a man of the theater. His adventures can be understood only in this context, for his medium of expression, the theater, was also that which best gives expression to his life. The Paris of his day was alive with theatrical activity. Not only did the public attend his plays, but it also took sides for or against the playwright. His friends and enemies were divided along literary, rather than social, lines. Since he put a little of himself into each character he created, he was not exempt from personal attack when he offended the sensibilities of certain groups. Many of his enemies were powerful members of the court, and only because a number of his friends were also powerful figures was he able to continue writing and presenting his works. His comedies, which often dealt with exaggerated passions, evoked equally passionate responses from his audience. Against such a backdrop, the life of Molière was played out amidst intrigues and financial concerns both on and off the stage.

Molière, born Jean Baptiste Poquelin, was baptized in the church of St-Eustache in Paris on Jan. 15, 1622. His father, a member of the rising bourgeoisie, purchased the post of official furnisher (*tapissier ordinaire du Roi*) at the court. The young Jean Baptiste grew up in the shadow of the court, the most lively section of Paris. Like many of the great writers of his time, he was educated at the Collège de Clermont, a Jesuit institution. There he received a solid classical background, and he may have known some of the future libertine thinkers, such as Pierre Gassendi and Cyrano de Bergerac. After finishing his secondary education, he studied law briefly and was admitted to the bar in 1641.

Choice of Vocation

At this point Molière was to take over his father's post at the court, but such was not to be the case. Ever since he was a small boy, he had been attracted to the theater. Tradition affords the image of the little boy grasping his grandfather's hand as they both watched the farces and tragedies at the Hôtel de Bourgogne or at the fair at Saint-Germain. When Tiberio Fiorelli, called Scaramouche, came to Paris in 1640, Molière struck up a warm friendship with the Italian actor-mime. He also met at this time a young actress, Madeleine Béjart, with whom he was to be associated until her death in 1672.

In 1643 Molière renounced the hereditary post his father held and chose instead the theater. Since the life of the theater was not considered very respectable, he assumed the name "Molière" in order to spare embarrassment

to his family. That same year he signed on with the family of Madeleine Béjart and nine other actors, who formed a troupe known as the Illustre Théâtre. As the most recent of three Parisian companies, Molière and his friends fared very badly. In 1944, ridden by debts and having served two terms in debtors' prison, Molière was forced to abandon this venture. He and the Béjarts joined another company, whose tours were to take them all over France for the next 13 years. In 1650 Molière became the head of the troupe, and he managed to secure the patronage of the Prince of Conti.

Although little factual evidence of his travels and tribulations is available, it is certain that Molière and his itinerant players learned much in the provinces. Molière was a hard worker. The short, stocky man with a large head and melancholy eyes frequently acted, sometimes under a harlequin mask, with the troupe he managed. Rhythm and mime, learned from the Italians, were an important part of their style. When the company was finally called to give a performance before Louis XIV in 1658, it was Molière's farce, *Le Docteur amoureux,* that most amused the King. The King's brother became patron of the troupe, and Molière returned to the city of his birth.

First "Cause Célèbre"

In December 1662 Molière presented his latest comedy, *L'École des femmes,* in five acts and in verse, before the King. It was to be his greatest success. The play centers about Arnolphe, a bourgeois who delights in watching the signs of cuckoldry all around him. In order to spare himself the same shameful fate, he chooses for his bride a child whom he then raises in total ignorance. The principal comic device of the plot rests upon the fact that his young rival, ignorant of Arnolphe's identity, tells him exactly how he plans to steal Agnès from under his nose. The play gave rise to a storm of protest, known as the "Quarrel of *L'École des femmes.*" Molière's enemies, jealous of the King's favor toward the playwright, attacked him on grounds of irreligion, vulgarity, plagiarism, and immorality. Rather than answer his enemies directly, Molière chose to vindicate himself by writing a response in the form of a play. His *Critique de l'École des femmes,* presented in June 1663, dramatized the controversy by introduction and discussion on stage of both the critics and the criticisms. The *raison d'être* of the play may be summed up in the celebrated formula pronounced by the character Dorante: "Je voudrais bien savoir si la grande règle de toutes les règles n'est pas de plaire, et si une pièce de théâtre qui a attrapé son but n'a pas suivi un bon chemin (Is it not true that the greatest of all rules is to be pleasing, and if a play has attained that end, has it not followed the right road?)."

The "Quarrel" served a purpose much larger than the comedy on which it was centered. In fact, it served to put comedy on an equal footing with tragedy as a legitimate literary form. Until that time it had been considered a humble stepchild of great French classical tragedy, exemplified by many of the works of Pierre Corneille. Molière proved that the passions and vices ridiculed through comedy were just as deeply rooted and universal as those that lent themselves to the creation of tragedy. In an age firmly committed to the superiority of tragedy and the dictates of Aristotle's *Poetics,* Molière reestablished comedy in a place of honor.

Battle of *Tartuffe*

In May 1664 Louis XIV organized at Versailles a splendid celebration called *Les Plaisirs de l'Île Enchantée.* It was here that Molière was invited to perform *Tartuffe ou l'Imposteur.* The play's title has become synonymous in French with hypocrite and, in particular, a hypocrite in matters of religion. The plot centers on the household of Orgon and its plight after the head of the house has taken in a spiritual adviser who is an impostor and a rogue. Only Orgon and his mother are too blind to see through the mask of piety; the other members of the household are aware of Tartuffe's hypocrisy. The latter group must resort to extraordinary means in order to convince Orgon of his error. In the final version of the play, intervention of the King himself, through an emissary, is necessary to dispose of Tartuffe.

It is not surprising that the play incurred the wrath of the powerful Society of the Holy Sacrament. This order of puritan religious devotees advocated restraints and assumed postures not unlike those of Tartuffe. Although the King harbored no love for the puritans, even he was ineffective in lessening their hold over a segment of the aristocracy. For 5 long years Molière struggled for the right to perform his play—even in amended form—but to no avail. Finally, in 1669, the "Peace of the Church" put an end to the powerful group, and *Tartuffe* was revived with great success at the Palais Royal.

Dom Juan

The interdiction of *Tartuffe* in 1664 left Molière with a gap in his repertory program. In spite of the fact that *Dom Juan* was composed hastily and in prose, a growing number of critics regard it as one of his greatest plays. Certainly, the popularity of the Don Juan legend attests to the compelling nature of the protagonist.

Molière did not originate the legend and, in fact, borrowed from a variety of sources. Nevertheless, his *Dom Juan* bears the stamp of its creator. Like his predecessors, this Dom Juan is struck down by a statue, but only after he has assumed the mask of the hypocrite. As long as he asserts his liberty from outside the social framework, he remains free and invulnerable. His downfall becomes possible, however, when he seeks to subvert society from within. There is a significant difference between the hypocrisy of Tartuffe and that of Dom Juan. Whereas the former is a servile and often vulgar hypocrite, the latter maintains the aloofness and superiority of the aristocrat.

Dom Juan was presented in February 1665 and was favorably received. After Easter, however, the play was mysteriously removed from the boards, and it was not published until after Moilère's death. It remained almost unknown until the 20th century.

Le Misanthrope

Molière first presented *Le Misanthrope* in June 1666. Although he had been granted the personal patronage of the King, illness, marital problems, and melancholy had left their mark on the playwright. Yet, during this unhappy period, Molière conceived and presented a work that attests to his mastery and genius.

Alceste, the misanthrope of the title, is at war with the aristocratic society of which he is a member. Like many other characters in the dramatic universe of Molière, he seeks to impose his own imperfect vision upon society. He will settle for nothing less than absolutes in a world governed by relative values. Because of this attitude he is basically a comic figure, and all the more so when he asserts in the final scene that only by leaving aristocratic society will he become the perfect aristocrat.

Last Years

Le Misanthrope pleased a small number of admirers, but it lacked the popular appeal necessary to make it a financial success. *L'Avare,* presented 2 years later, failed miserably, and Molière faced grave monetary problems. It required a comedy-ballet, *Le Bourgeois gentilhomme* (1670), to bring in the public once again.

Not the least of Molière's hardships was a hacking cough, which he tried to mask as a comic device. When overcome by a coughing spell onstage, he made it seem voluntary and exaggerated. In his last years, however, his condition worsened greatly. He had little faith in medicine, and one might argue, justifiably—for doctors had been unable to help him. In 1671 he gave *Les Fourberies de Scapin,* a bright comedy reminiscent of his early farces. But the best commentary on his condition was the biting work that was to be his last: *Le Malade imaginaire.* During the fourth performance, on Jan. 17, 1673, Molière was seized by convulsions. He died that same night, attended only by two nuns, having been refused the right to see a priest.

Further Reading

Much of the immense Moilère bibliography is in French. Biographies in English which merit particular attention are John L. Palmer, *Molière* (1930), and Ramon Fernandez, *Molière: The Man as Seen through the Plays,* translated by Wilson Follett (1958). Other biographies include Henry M. Trollope, *The Life of Molière* (1905); H. C. Chatfield-Taylor, *Molière: A Biography* (1906); D. B. Wyndham Lewis, *Molière: The Comic Mask* (1959); and Mikhail Bulgakov, *The Life of Monsieur de Molière* (trans. 1970), a lively fictionalized biography.

An important critical study of Molière's works and a forerunner of much recent criticism is Will G. Moore, *Molière: A New Criticism* (1949). Judd D. Hubert, *Molière and the Comedy of Intellect* (1962), is a more psychologically oriented study. Lionel Gossman, *Men and Masks: A Study of Molière* (1963), also reflects modern trends. A more varied critical perspective appears in Jacques Guicharnaud, ed., *Molière: A Collection of Critical Essays* (1964). Recommended for general historical background are Henry Carrington Lancaster, *A History of French Dramatic Literature in the Seventeenth Century* (5 vols., 1929-1942), and P. J. Yarrow, *The Seventeenth Century, 1600-1715* (1967). □

Miguel de Molinos

The writings of the Spanish priest Miguel de Molinos (1628-1696) formed the basis of the Quietist movement in the Roman Catholic Church. Both his works and the movement were condemned by Rome.

Born in Muniesa near Saragossa on June 29, 1628, Miguel de Molinos received a doctorate in theology from the University of Valencia. In 1663 he was sent to Rome as promoter for the canonization of a Valencia citizen. The case fell through, but Molinos stayed in Rome and became widely known as a spiritual director.

Molinos's major work, *Spiritual Guide,* appeared in 1675 and immediately created a sensation. Only the contemplative attitude (that is, the one of passive prayer), it argues, leads to the perfection of spiritual life. The attitude is opposed to all strenuous ascetic efforts, even the need to fight one's evil nature. The emphasis is entirely on inner quiet, resignation, and abandonment to the will of God. His doctrine had, to some extent, been anticipated by the Alumbrados, the Enlightened Ones, a spiritual movement in 16th-and 17th-century Spain which he must have known.

Although Molinos's book displayed all the customary signs of ecclesiastical approval, it was immediately denounced by the Jesuits, whose method of "spiritual exercises" was diametrically opposed to his pure passivity. Yet several powerful dignitaries came to his rescue, and his adversaries saw their own attacks placed on the Index. Just when victory seemed complete, the powerful archbishop of Naples, Caracciolo, warned the Pope against the dangers of "those quietists" (the first time the term was used). In 1685 Molinos was arrested, and his writings, including 12,000 letters, were thoroughly examined by the Holy Office. Persistent rumors have it that the French cardinal D'Estrée, representative of Louis XIV, was behind the entire scheme. At any rate, Molinos was declared guilty not only of doctrinal errors but also of immoral conduct. The latter accusation has continued to intrigue students of Church history, since the man had always been known for his exemplary life. Chances are that the charges were trumped up on the basis of a malevolent interpretation of certain passages in the letters.

A public session was organized in Rome on Sept. 3, 1687, and Molinos admitted the 68 errors with which he was charged. In front of a hostile crowd the tribunal condemned him to life imprisonment. He died in prison on Dec. 28, 1696. However, Quietism did not die with him. While Molinos was in prison, it even entered the very court of France that may have been responsible for his condemnation. One of his disciples, Madame Guyon, ardently publicized Quietist spirituality in France and through the King's favorite, Madame de Maintenon, enjoyed all the marks of royal approval. When Madame Guyon in turn came under fire, Bishop François Fénelon rose to her defense and expanded the Quietist doctrine.

Further Reading

The standard study of Molinos is in French. An older English study is John Bigelow, *Molinos the Quietist* (1882). Molinos is discussed in Ronald Arbuthnott Knox, *Enthusiasm: A Chapter in the History of Religion, with Special Reference to the XVII and XVIII Centuries* (1950). The influence of Quietism and Molinos is analyzed in Katharine Day Little, *François de Fénelon: Study of a Personality* (1951), and Michael de la Bedoyere, *The Archbishop and the Lady: The Story of Fénelon and Madame Guyon* (1956). □

Vyacheslav Mikhailovich Molotov

The Soviet statesman Vyacheslav Mikhailovich Molotov (1890-1986) was second in command during Stalin's regime and served as the chief Soviet diplomat in World War II.

Vyacheslav Molotov was born on March 9, 1890, in the village of Kukarka (now Sovetsk) in what is now the Kirov Oblast. His family name was Scriabin, and he was distantly related to the famous composer of the same name. His family sent him to the gymnasium (high school) in Kazan, and it was there, as a teen-ager, that he first became involved in the revolutionary movement, taking a minor part in the Revolution of 1905. The following year he joined the Bolsheviks and, to avoid police harassment, changed his name to Molotov (literally, "of the hammer").

In 1909, just prior to his graduation, he was arrested for political agitation and exiled for 2 years to Vologda Province. Instead of returning to Kazan, he made his way to St. Petersburg, where he studied briefly at the Polytechnic Institute. More importantly, living in the capital afforded him the opportunity for involvement in the new Bolshevik newspaper *Pravda* and for establishing his first contact with Joseph Stalin.

Unlike most other Bolsheviks, Molotov spent no time abroad, and when World War I broke out, he was still in Russia. In June 1915 he was again arrested and exiled, this time to the distant Siberian province of Irkutsk. Late in 1916 he escaped from Siberia and managed to get back to the capital, now renamed Petrograd, where he rejoined the revolutionary movement. He was one of the few Bolsheviks of any prominence who were in Petrograd when the monarchy was overthrown, and he became immediately involved in issuing the rejuvenated *Pravda*. He also joined the Petrograd Soviet, becoming perhaps the most important Bolshevik in that organization until the election of Leon Trotsky to its presidency. After the Bolshevik seizure of power in November 1917, he assumed a variety of government tasks, most of them away from the center of power.

In 1921, probably at the behest of Stalin, Molotov was chosen a candidate member of the Central Committee, and from that time his fortunes were irrevocably tied to Stalin's.

In the intraparty struggle he identified even more closely with Stalin and was elevated to the Politburo in 1926. In 1928 he was made first secretary of the Moscow Party Committee and proceeded to purge it of non-Stalinists.

In 1930 Molotov's work was rewarded with his appointment as chairman of the Council of People's Commissars (that is, prime minister) of the Soviet Union. He held this post for over a decade, adding the foreign affairs post in 1939. In the latter post he acquired an international reputation, first negotiating the infamous Nazi-Soviet Pact of 1939 but later serving as Stalin's top representative at the various wartime conferences: Teheran (1943), Yalta (1945), and Potsdam (1945), and at the founding conference of the United Nations in 1945.

In 1949 Molotov yielded the Foreign Ministry to Andrei Vishinsky but continued as vice-chairman of the Council of Ministers. Upon Stalin's death in March 1953, he emerged as potentially one of the strongest leaders, reassuming control over the Foreign Ministry and forming, with Lavrenty Beria and Georgi Malenkov, an ephemeral triumvirate that presumably controlled the Bolshevik party. Though he outlasted both of his partners, by 1955 it was apparent that Molotov had lost considerable power.

The Twentieth Party Congress of February 1956 and the resultant anti-Stalin line ruined Molotov's chances as he was so closely identified in the public eye with the Stalinist heritage. Later that year, Dmitri Shepilov replaced him as foreign minister. In the summer of 1957 Molotov and others of the "antiparty" group were expelled from the Central

Committee. Molotov himself was made emissary to Outer Mongolia, roughly the equivalent of exile, and was forced to remain there until 1960. Then he made a small comeback by becoming the Soviet representative to the International Atomic Energy Conference in Vienna. In 1961 at the Twenty-second Party Congress a renewed denunciation of Stalin led to new cries for punishment for Molotov, but he escaped banishment or any serious penalty and retired from public life. In 1984 he was reinstated to the party, but died in Moscow on November 8, 1986.

Further Reading

Molotov's views as a foreign minister can be seen in some anthologies of his speeches, for example, *Problems of Foreign Policy* (trans. 1949). Molotov was sufficiently bland to defy biographers, but there is Bernard Bromage, *Molotov: The Story of an Era* (1956). Most studies of Stalin devote some attention to Molotov, notably Isaac Deutscher, *Stalin: A Political Biography* (1949; rev. ed. 1966). □

Count Helmuth Karl Bernard von Moltke

The Prussian soldier Count Helmuth Karl Bernard von Moltke (1800-1891) was the military architect of the wars of German unification. He served as chief of the Prussian general staff from 1857 to 1888.

Helmuth von Moltke was born on Oct. 26, 1800, in Parchim, Mecklenburg, to German-Danish parents impoverished by the Napoleonic Wars. Educated in the Copenhagen Royal Cadet Corps (1811-1817), Moltke began Danish service in 1819 but in 1822 transferred to Prussia as an infantry lieutenant. He did little regimental duty, attending the Berlin Kriegsakademie from 1823 to 1826 and working in the general staff's topographical office from 1828 to 1831. Moltke wrote technical studies, histories, translations, and fiction in attempts to advance his career, which in 1829 he diagnosed as suffering from his own weakness of character. In 1833 he became a first lieutenant in the general staff and in 1835 a captain.

In September 1835 Moltke became an adviser to the Turkish army, which he joined for the calamitous 1839 campaign in Syria. Moltke's maps, sketches, and watercolors of the Near East all showed versatility. After his 1840 reentry into Prussian service, the 1841 publication of his *Turkish Letters* established him as an author of some popularity.

Domestically happy in his childless marriage (1842-1868) to an English wife, Marie Burt, Moltke served on the Coblenz staff and the transport section and general staff at Berlin, then briefly headed the Magdeburg staff. Royal unwillingness to use the Prussian army during the Revolution of 1848 briefly caused Moltke to consider migrating to Australia as a farmer. However, service as adjutant to Prince Henry in Rome, and later to Crown Prince Frederick William, gave Moltke diplomatic experience, more rapid promotion, the material for more "travel books," and the soubriquet of "the man who knows how to be silent in seven languages."

Chief of Staff

On Oct. 29, 1857, Maj. Gen. Moltke became chief of staff. He changed little in staff organization but emphasized modern technology in all sections. General strategy and a two-front war plan produced in 1860 occupied much of Moltke's personal attention.

The Austro-Prussian attack on the Danes over Schleswig-Holstein in 1864 was so mismanaged by Baron F. H. E. von Wrangel's chief of staff, Eduard Vogel von Falckenstein, that the latter was superseded by Moltke, who soon brought the Danes to terms. This promotion to a field post was then accounted the climax of Moltke's career, as well as a triumph of "staff" over "regulars."

In the Austro-Prussian War of 1866 King William I and Minister-President Otto von Bismarck entrusted the deployment of forces to Moltke, who telegraphed laconic "general directives" from Berlin for the rapid convergence of 85 percent of the Prussian army against Austrian and Saxon forces in Bohemia. In the July 3 battle of Sadowa (Königgrätz) King William relied entirely on Moltke's judgment through a closely contested, but finally decisive, engagement. The Austrian infantry was routed and demoralized, and the Hapsburgs hastened to agree to

Bismarck's terms. This blitzkrieg campaign made Moltke famous.

In the 1870-1871 war against France, Moltke detrained the 2d Army on the Rhine, expecting to win a defensive battle there before marching on Paris. The conversion of this deployment into a German invasion of France was a measure of Prussian staff capacity, Moltke's confidence and adaptability, and French strategic passivity. The German army units cohered in a general advance, while the French units collapsed into pockets of local resistance. The surrender of Napoleon III at Sedan (Sept. 2, 1870) and Marshal Achille Bazaine at Metz (Oct. 28) opened the way to a siege of Paris. Moltke attended the proclamation of the German ''Reich'' (Jan. 18, 1871), followed by the January 28 armistice and May 10 Treaty of Frankfurt. In June 1871 ''der Grosse Schweiger,'' or ''the Great Silent One,'' as Moltke was called, was promoted to field marshal.

As chief of staff, Moltke consistently discounted the chances of complete success in a two-front war. A defensive victory on the Rhine or Vistula, followed by an offensive and a negotiated peace, was the essence of his strategy for conflict against France and Russia. Moltke's view that ''perpetual peace is a dream, and not even a beautiful one'' must be set against his opinion that ''a war, even the most victorious, is a national misfortune'' to begin to grasp the breadth of his military thinking. After his retirement in 1888, he took an increasingly critical view of Kaiser William II. Moltke continued to be politically active, however, until his death in Berlin on April 24, 1891.

The lank, bewigged, half-Danish Moltke has been called a ''general on wheels'' as distinct from his military predecessors on horseback. This expression grasps only the particular form—railway deployment—most salient in Moltke's emphasis on modern technology as part of the totality of a military enterprise. It was the breadth and versatility of his mind that gave dimension to Moltke's personal motto: ''First weigh, then wage.'' Moltke thus considered every strategic problem ''simply common sense,'' but his method of analysis was so demanding that Paul von Hindenburg accounted Moltke ''unlike all the other German generals.'' If the German general staff proved unable to inherit Moltke's strategic system, the German army for a time was inspirited by his motto for its officers: ''Be more than you seem.''

Further Reading

A primary source for Moltke's life is *Moltke: His Life and Character, Sketched in Journals, Letters, Memoirs, a Novel, and Autobiographical Notes,* translated by Mary Herms (1892). Further biographical information is in William O'Connor Morris, *Moltke: A Biographical and Critical Study* (2d ed. 1894); Friedrich August Dressler, *Moltke in His Home* (trans. 1906); and Frederick Ernest Whitton, *Moltke* (1921). □

Jöurgen Moltmann

Jöurgen Moltmann (born 1926) was professor of systematic theology at the University of Tubingen. Dur-

ing the mid-1960s he achieved international prominence as the leading exponent of the ''theology of hope.'' This, along with subsequent works in Christology, anthropology, and ethics, established him as one of Germany's most important Protestant theologians of the 20th century.

Jöurgen Moltmann was born in 1926 in Hamburg, Germany. His childhood and pre-university education were lived during the years of the Nazi regime. In 1944 he was sent off to war and was captured (in February 1945) by the British. Although the war ended three months later, he was held as a prisoner of war for more than three years in Scotland and England. These were formative years for Moltmann. He spoke of the guilt and inconsolable grief he felt over the crimes of his country and the necessity of standing up to it all. Then an army chaplain gave him a New Testament with Psalms. His previous experience with the Bible and religion had been indifferent and inconsequential. But, he related that ''these Psalms gave me the words for my own suffering.''

Studied Theology

Abandoning his previous plans to study physics and mathematics, Moltmann returned to Germany to study theology at the University of Gottingen, where the leading faculty (especially Otto Weber) had belonged to the Confessing Church, independent from the national church and opposed to Hitler. Upon graduation in 1952 he became pastor of a parish church in Wasserhorst. His doctoral dissertation, written under Weber and completed in 1957, resulted in a teaching position in a seminary of the Confessing Church at Wuppertal. He says that he took the position uncertain there was anything more for theologians to say after the monumental *Church Dogmatics* of Karl Barth. But important university positions, for a brief time at Bonn (where Barth had once taught) and then at Tubingen, soon opened for him.

Began Formulating ''Theology of Hope''

At the dawn of the 1960s the theme of hope was in the air. Politically, there was John F. Kennedy's American ''Camelot,'' and in Prague there was to appear Alexander Dubcek's ''Socialism with a human face.'' Religiously, there was the *aggiornamento* of Pope John XXIII and the civil rights movement of Martin Luther King, Jr. But it was decisively the reading of *Das Prinzip Hoffnung* (The Principle of Hope) by Ernst Bloch—the free thinking Marxist philosopher from the former East Germany (later a refugee to the West, and Tubingen)—that stimulated Moltmann to formulate a ''theology of hope.'' Bloch argued with persuasive scholarly insight that what is essentially and characteristically human is neither enchantment with the past (Freud and behaviorism) nor preoccupation with the present (existentialism, mysticism, and platonism), but anticipation of the future. He developed an ontology of ''not yet being'' in which the future, like a vacuum, draws the present away from the grips of the past and toward an ever new and potentially better future.

For Moltmann this was secular confirmation of what scholars had been saying since the turn of this century about Biblical anthropology and eschatology. From the promises made to Abraham to the message of the prophets, from Jesus' preaching about the Kingdom of God to John's vision of a new heaven and a new earth, an orientation toward the future, with anticipation and hope, is central to the self understanding of both Old and New Testament writers. Where Biblical thought and Moltmann differ from Bloch is in their insistence that standing on the horizon of the future is not a vacuum but the "God of hope."

Writings Explored Christian Doctrine

Moltmann's book *Theology of Hope* (German edition 1964, English 1967) is probably the most articulate and creative work of theology written during the second half of the 20th century. He was not, however, the only theologian of hope, and he worked in cordial relations with his contemporary from Gottingen days, Wolfhart Pannenberg, and with the Roman Catholic theologian Johannes B. Metz. Furthermore, Moltmann was not the captive of his own popularity as a theologian of hope. His writings explore and contribute to the full spectrum of Christian doctrine. In *The Crucified God* (1974) he returned to the theme of his prisoner-of-war days: defeat, despair, and death. He proposed that the cross of Christ is revelatory of the life of God and that, as Dietrich Bonhoeffer and historic patripassionism have suggested, "only a suffering God can help us."

But Moltmann insisted that the resurrection of Christ is God's decisive word to us and that this hope requires an appropriate response in social, economic, and political life. Faith shows its "hope for the life that defeats death in . . . protest against the manifold forms of death"—the economic death of the starving, the political death of the oppressed, the social death of the handicapped, the technological death of the war-torn. The theology of hope is, therefore, political theology, defying the forces of death and practicing confidence not in circumstances or in feelings but in the promises of God.

Other works by Moltmann include *Trinity and the Kingdom* (1980), *God in Creation* (1985), and *The Way of Jesus Christ* (1989). In *Trinity and the Kingdom,* critics noted the surfacing of Moltmann's ideas on tritheism—the idea that each aspect of the Trinity is a separate God—beginning to emerge. *Trinity* also hinted at panentheism—the view that God and the world are connected—which was becoming part of his theology. This idea was carried further in *God in Creation* and *The Way of Jesus Christ.*

Further Reading

In addition to *Theology of Hope* and *The Crucified God, Experiences of God* (1980) provides a good introduction and contains a helpful autobiographical essay. *The Church in the Power of the Spirit* (1977) provides a profound study of mission for the modern church. *The Trinity and the Kingdom* (1981) further develops the doctrine of God. See also *The Power of the Powerless* (1983) and *On Human Dignity: Political Theology and Ethics* (1984). (Dates are for the English editions.) For evaluations, see Martin E. Marty and Dean G. Peerman (editors), *New Theology No. 5* (1968) and *New Theology No. 6* (1969); Frederick Herzog, *The Future of Hope: Theology as Eschatology* (1970); M. Douglas Meeks, *Origins of the Theology of Hope* (1974); and Christopher Morse, *The Logic of Promise in Moltmann's Theology* (1979). See also *Christianity Today* January 11, 1993; *The Future of Theology: Essays in Honor of Jéurgen Moltmann,* Eerdmans, 1996; Moltmann, Jéurgen, *Love [videorecording]: The Foundation of Hope—A Celebration of the Life and Work of Jéurgen Moltmann and Elisabeth Moltmann-Wendel,* Harper & Row, 1988. □

N. Scott Momaday

N. Scott Momaday (born 1934) is recognized as one of the premier writers in the United States. In 1969, his novel *House Made of Dawn* was awarded the Pulitzer prize for fiction.

One of the most distinguished Native-American authors writing today, N. Scott Momaday is chiefly known for novels and poetry collections that communicate the fabulous oral legends of his Kiowa heritage. In 1969 he became the first American Indian to win the Pulitzer Prize in fiction for his novel *House Made of Dawn,* which had a tremendous impact on the development of Native-American literature in the United States. Published during a time of heightened cultural awareness in the late 1960s and early 70s, *House Made of Dawn* not only influenced but also brought attention to other gifted Indian writers, including Vine Deloria Jr., Leslie Silko, and James Welch.

Born in a Kiowa Indian hospital in Lawton, Oklahoma, on February 27, 1934, Navarre Scott Momaday was the only child of Kiowa artist Alfred Morris Momaday and teacher Mayme Natachee Scott Momaday. A descendant from early American pioneers, Momaday's mother derived her middle name from a Cherokee great-grandmother, Natachee. His father inherited the Kiowa family name "Mammedaty" from Momaday's grandfather. "At that time," Momaday explains in an essay which appears in *Something about the Author,* Volume 48, "people had but one name. That was the name that was given to him as a child, and that was the only name he had. But during his lifetime the missionaries came in, and the Indians adopted the Christian tradition of the surname and the Christian name. And so my grandfather was given the name John, and he became known as John Mammedaty, and Mammedaty simply became the surname of his family. It was passed down. Some of my relatives in Oklahoma still use that spelling, but my father abbreviated it to Momaday."

Growing up on Indian reservations in the American Southwest, Momaday attributes many of his childhood and lifetime memories to his parents. "Some of my mother's memories have become my own. This is the real burden of the blood; this is immortality," he relates in *The Names: A Memoir.* Born of mixed blood, Natachee began to identify

with her Indian heritage around the age of sixteen. A beautiful girl, she called herself "Little Moon" while her cousins referred to her as "Queen of Sheba"—both of which pleased her mightily. To pursue a degree and to learn more about her Indian heritage, Natachee attended the Haskell Institute, the Indian school at Lawrence, Kansas, in 1929. Her intense love of books and English literature was a great pleasure that she passed on to her son. Through their shared experiences, Momaday learned to develop a mental repository for his vast collection of memories. As Momaday recalls, "Memories . . . qualify the imagination, to give it another formation, one that is peculiar to the self. I remember isolated, yet fragmented and confused, images—and images, shifting, enlarging, is the word, rather than moments or events—which are mine alone and which are especially vivid to me."

Cultivates Vivid Early Memories

Momaday remembers that the first notable event in his life occurred when he was just six months old and he accompanied his parents on a journey to the Black Hills in Wyoming to see Devil's Tower. Referred to in Kiowa as Tsoai ["Rock Tree"], Devil's Tower became the source of Momaday's Kiowa name, Tsoai-talee, given to him by Pohd-lohk ["Old Wolf"], a Kiowa elder. Pohd-lohk had in his possession a ledger which he had secured from the Supply Office at Fort Sill and which depicted the calendar history of the Kiowa people from 1833. Momaday would later derive much of his knowledge about the origin of his people from that book.

Being an only child, Momaday learned at an early age to give free reign to his imagination, or as he states, "to create my society in my mind. And for a child this kind of creation is accomplished easily enough." Momaday's mother encouraged him to learn English as his native language, and this circumstance sometimes led the boy to experience brief periods of cultural dislocation. In describing these strange incidents, Momaday relates that he was able to see "Grendel's shadow on the walls of Canyon de Chelly, and once, having led the sun around Hoskinini Mesa, saw Copperfield at Oljeto Trading Post." When he was twelve, his family moved to the Pueblo village of Jemez. Momaday remembers "not being able to imagine a more beautiful or exotic place," and Jemez offered the boy a child's natural delight full of canyons and mountains. In Momaday's interpretive mind, Jemez became a landscape full of mystery and life, and many of his descriptive details of those childhood days can be found in his later writings. Once referring to Jemez as having "horses in the plain and angles of geese in the sky," Momaday later reflected on this image when writing *Angle of Geese and Other Poems* (1974).

Embarks on a Writing Career

Uncertain about his future after graduating from high school, Momaday contemplated attending West Point before deciding to enroll in the University of New Mexico in 1952. He earned a bachelor's degree in Political Science in 1958, while distinguishing himself as a public speaker and creative writer. Taking a one year break from his studies, Momaday taught school on the Jicarilla Apache reservation before pursuing a graduate studies program in literature. By this time, he had received his first academic recognition as a talented writer when he was awarded the John Hay Whitney Fellowship in creative poetry writing and the Stanford Wilson Dissertation Fellowship at Stanford University. While at Stanford, Momaday met Yvor Winters, who later became a close friend and adviser. Momaday obtained his Master's degree in 1960 and his Ph.D. three years later. In 1965 he published his first book, *The Complete Poems of Frederick Goddard Tuckerman,* which was based on his doctoral dissertation. Momaday credits Winters for his decision to analyze the writings of Tuckerman, a reclusive New England naturalist. According to the 1971 edition of the *Penguin Companion to World Literature,* Momaday's thesis led to an increased awareness of Tuckerman's poems on the part of poets and critics alike.

Following his graduate studies, Momaday joined the faculty of the University of California at Santa Barbara in 1963 as assistant professor of English. Further literary research led him to pursue a Guggenheim Fellow at Harvard University during the 1966-67 academic year, after which he returned to Santa Barbara to resume teaching. Two years later, he was named professor of English at the University of California, Berkeley, where he taught creative writing and introduced a new curriculum centered around American Indian literature and mythology. Also during this period, Momaday published his influential novel *House Made of Dawn* (1968). The story follows the adventures of Abel, a disenchanted Native-American World War II veteran who attempts to balance his identity between culturally disparate native and non-native worlds. Unable to exist peacefully in either world, Abel gradually reaches the conclusion that he is lost, and he returns to the reservation to heal his shattered psyche. In an analysis of *House Made of Dawn* published in the June 9, 1968, *New York Times Book Review,* Marshall Sprague observes that "while mysteries of culture different from our own cannot be explained in a short novel," nevertheless Momaday's book is "as subtly wrought as a piece of Navajo silverware." The next year, Momaday was accorded one of literature's highest honors when he was named the recipient of the Pulitzer Prize in fiction for *House Made of Dawn.*

In his next novel, *The Way to Rainy Mountain* (1969), Momaday incorporated several Kiowa myths and legends into a quasi-fictional account of the 300-year-old migration of the Kiowa tribe from their place of origin in the Yellowstone region to the plains, where they learned to domesticate horses and developed into a sophisticated society. Relating the legend of how the Kiowas came into the world through a hollow log, Momaday explains that the Kiowas are a small tribe because when they entered the log "there was a woman whose body was swollen up with child, and she got stuck in the log. After that, no one could get through, and that is why the Kiowas are a small tribe in numbers." *The Way to Rainy Mountain* features illustrations by Momaday's father, Alfred, and it has been characterized by a reviewer for *Choice* (September 1969) as "a beautiful book—honest, unique, dignified, and told with a simplicity that approaches the purest poetry.... It is a book for all seasons, for all readers."

In subsequent years, Momaday's reputation has ascended to the international level. In 1979 he was awarded Italy's highest literary award, the Premio Letterario Internationale "Mondello." Moreover, in 1990 Momaday was selected to be a keynote speaker in Moscow before the Conference on Environment and Human Survival, the Global Forum and the Supreme Soviet. That same year, he was asked to be a member of the Pulitzer Prize Jury in Fiction. The father of four daughters, Momaday continues to write and teaches classes on oral tradition at the University of Arizona.

In 1993, Momaday published *In the Presence of the Sun.* This book includes 70 poems and 16 new stories about the "great tribal shields of the Kiowas and a strange, arresting section on Billy the Kid," according to *The New York Times Book Review*'s Barbara Bode. Bode further says that "the reader will not find here the 'political' Indian, the Indian as 'victim' or the romanticized Indian. Rather, we hear the voices of people like Otters Going On and the woman Roan Calf, of people raided and killed, worshipped and wept. Yet the images, the voices, the people are shadowy, elusive, burning with invention, like flames against a dark sky."

The following year saw the publication of *Circle of Wonder.* The is a poetic story that "skillfully blends Christian and Native American traditions," according to *Publishers Weekly.* The book also features Momaday's artwork.

Further Reading

Shubnell, Matthias, *N. Scott Momaday: The Cultural and Literary Background,* Norman, University of Oklahoma Press, 1985.
Something about the Author, volume 48, edited by Anne Commire, Detroit, Gale, 1987; 158-162.
Twentieth Century Western Writers, second edition, edited by Geoff Sadler, Chicago, St. James Press, 1991; 470-471.
Woodward, Charles, *Ancestral Voice: Conversations with N. Scott Momaday,* Lincoln, University of Nebraska Press, 1989.
Review of *The Way to Rainy Mountain, Choice,* September 1969.
Sprague, Marshall, review of *House Made of Dawn,* June 9, 1968. □

Theodor Mommsen

The German historian and philologist Theodor Mommsen (1817-1903) ranks among the greatest of 19th-century historians. Most of his work was devoted to the study of ancient Rome.

Theodor Mommsen, the son of a poor but scholarly Protestant minister, was born at Garding in the duchy of Schleswig on Nov. 30, 1817. After receiving his early schooling at home and at a gymnasium in Altona near Hamburg, he attended the University of Kiel (1838-1843), studying law. Mommsen was much influenced by the lectures of Otto John and by the writings of Friedrich Karl von Savigny; his interests became focused on the classical world, and he wrote his dissertation on Roman associations and made a study of Roman tribes.

In 1843 Mommsen received a traveling scholarship from the Danish government and a small grant from the Berlin Academy for study in Italy. There he became acquainted with Bartolommeo Borghesi, an outstanding scholar of Latin inscriptions, who had a profound influence on Mommsen's future. During this time the plans for the monumental collection of Latin inscriptions (*Corpus inscriptionum Latinarum*) took shape, and it was published under the auspices of the Berlin Royal Academy of Science after 1861. As a sample for this task, Mommsen collected the Samnite inscriptions and the *Inscriptions of the Neapolitan Kingdom,* which he published in 1852, dedicated to Borghesi.

In 1847 Mommsen returned to Schleswig, where he supported the independence struggle of the Elbe duchies from Denmark by editing and writing for the *Schleswig-Holsteinische Zeitung,* an organ of the provisional government. After the failure of this independence movement he accepted the chair of Roman law at the University of Leipzig (1848) but was dismissed from his position in 1851 for his support of the liberal cause during the revolution.

Before leaving Leipzig for an appointment at the University of Zurich in 1852, Mommsen had come to the attention of the publisher Karl Reimer, who persuaded him to write a popular but scholarly *Roman History.* The first three volumes, in addition to monographs on Roman Switzerland, were begun in Zurich and completed at the University

of Breslau, where Mommsen taught from 1854 until 1858. This work, published between 1854 and 1856, describes the history of the Roman Republic to the advent of Caesar's dictatorship and made Mommsen's name famous throughout Europe. Plans for a fourth volume on the imperial period were never carried out. Instead he published a fifth volume, *Roman Provinces under the Empire* (1884), utilizing the Latin inscriptions collected for the *Corpus inscriptionum.*

Appointed editor for the *Corpus inscriptionum* in 1854, Mommsen received a professorship at Berlin (1858), where he remained for the rest of his life. These 45 years were filled with scholarship of stupendous proportions but of the highest quality. In addition to his continuing work on the *Corpus inscriptionum,* Mommsen published *Römisches Staatsrecht,* 3 vols. (1871-1888; *Roman Constitutional Law); Römisches Strafrecht* (1899; *Roman Criminal Law); Reden und Aufsätze* (1905; *Speeches and Essays);* and *Gesammelte Schriften,* 7 vols. (1905-1910; *Collected Writings);* and he participated in the *Monumenta Germaniae,* in studies on the *Roman Limes* and on numismatics, and in the *Thesaurus linguae Latinae.* In 1902 his unique position in the world of scholarship was recognized by the award of the Nobel Prize for literature; he was the first German to achieve this honor.

In public life Mommsen intermittently served in the Prussian Parliament (1863-1866 and 1873-1879) and in the German Reichstag (Imperial Diet) (1881-1884) and was a cofounder of and contributor to the *Preussischen Jahrbücher,* one of the most influential German political journals. A political liberal and patriot, he found much to criticize, both in his own country and abroad. He was torn

between despising Bismarck and taking pride in his national accomplishments.

Mommsen died at Charlottenburg, a suburb of Berlin, on Nov. 1, 1903.

Further Reading

An excellent modern, although abridged, translation of the third volume of Mommsen's *Roman History* is in Dero A. Saunders and John H. Collins, *The History of Rome: An Account of Events and Persons from the Conquest of Carthage to the End of the Republic* (1958), which contains a good introduction to and evaluation of that work. Studies in English on Mommsen's life and work are in W. Warde Fowler, *Roman Essays and Interpretations* (1920), which describes Fowler's personal acquaintance with Mommsen, and in James Westfall Thompson and Bernard J. Holm, *A History of Historical Writing,* vol. 2 (1942), which includes a good bibliography. □

John Monash

Sir John Monash (1865-1931) was an outstanding Australian soldier, engineer, and administrator.

On June 27, 1865, John Monash was born at West Melbourne, Victoria, the only son of Louis Monash and his wife Berthe, née Manasse, Jewish migrants from East Prussia (Poland). After schooling at Jerilderie, New South Wales, where his father kept a store, John attended Scotch College, Melbourne, of which he was equal dux (equalled the highest marks made by others in his courses) and won the mathematics exhibition at the 1881 public examinations.

Monash failed the first year of his arts and engineering course at the University of Melbourne, being engrossed in private reading, the theater, and loss of religious faith. He then completed two years, though preoccupied with editing the *Melbourne University Review,* piano performances, and chess. But, deeply distressed by his mother's death, he abandoned his course in 1885. He obtained employment building bridges, then in control of construction of a suburban railway, followed by employment with the Melbourne Harbor Trust. He resumed his university work part time, completing his B.A., B.E. in 1891, and LL.B. in 1893. On April 8, 1891, he married Hannah Victoria Moss, by whom he had one daughter.

After militia experience from 1884 in the university company, quickly rising to sergeant, he joined the North Melbourne Battery, Garrison Artillery, which he was to command from 1896 to 1908 as major.

Monash formed a civil engineering partnership in 1894 with J. T. N. Anderson. They made only a precarious living until Monash began appearing in the courts as an advocate on engineering matters and later was employed as an adviser and negotiator by large contractors. The firm also built bridges. They lost all their capital, however, after an eccentric legal judgment in favor of a defaulting client, and until 1905 Monash remained deeply in debt. He was eventually

saved by developing his local rights to the Monier patent for reinforced concrete construction. The companies for major building construction which he now formed and managed became highly profitable. By 1912 Monash was a well-to-do Melbourne businessman at the head of his profession, a radical president of the Victorian Institute of Engineers, a university councillor, and a part-time lecturer.

From 1908 Monash was Victorian commandant of the Australian Intelligence Corps (militia). He became closely involved in staff work and educated himself further on all matters military. In 1913 and 1914 he commanded an infantry brigade as colonel. On the outbreak of World War I he was appointed to command the 4th Infantry Brigade, Australian Imperial Force. During the Gallipoli campaign his record was not especially distinguished, but few senior officers did better. He was promoted to major general in command of the 3rd Australian Division, trained it in 1916, and led it ably in 1917 at Messines and in the battles leading up to Passchendaele, and in early 1918 led it in combatting the German offensive. From May, as lieutenant-general, he was corps commander during the battle of Hamel and the succession of great victories from August 8, including Mont St. Quentin, until the breaking of the Hindenburg line.

Monash's reputation remains as the greatest Australian soldier, remarkably unexposed to adverse criticism. He was fortunate in taking over a superb Australian corps at the decisive turning-point of the war, but his task could hardly have been better done. His particular qualities were his capacity to work harmoniously with staff, to assert forcefully requirements to superiors, to fight for recognition for the

A.I.F., and to demonstrate to the troops that, so rarely in that war, he was right behind them. He was articulate in explaining battle plans, with extraordinary attention to detail and provisions for avoiding unnecessary risks. His military achievement, given his background as a civilian Jew of Prussian origin, remains astounding. He has sometimes been spoken of as the outstanding Allied general, but he was never tested at the highest levels of command. In 1919 he wrote *The Australian Victories in France in 1918;* some of his war letters were published in 1934. He was promoted to general in 1929.

After the war Monash was chairman of the State Electricity Commission of Victoria with the task of harnessing brown coal for the use of industry, then one of the most important national tasks. He succeeded triumphantly, building an institution which for a long time was an outstandingly successful state instrumentality. He was the unchallenged spokesman for returned soldiers; in charge of the Special Constabulary Force during the police strike of 1923 and chairman of the subsequent royal commission; university vice chancellor from 1923; Jewish spokesman and an active Zionist. He brusquely dismissed requests around 1930 to lead a right-wing coup. Monash died on October 8, 1931. His funeral was the most largely attended Australia had known.

In the 1920s Monash was unquestionably regarded as the greatest living Australian—a tall poppy who was never cut down. Essentially he was a most gifted administrator; a man of extraordinarily wide knowledge, experience, and scientific and cultural interests; devoted to public service; and eventually, nearly all ambitions achieved, a man who wore his distinction modestly.

Further Reading

Additional information and a bibliography can be found in G. Serle, *John Monash. A Biography* (Melbourne, 1982). □

George Monck

The English general and statesman George Monck, 1st Duke of Albemarle (1608-1670), was instrumental in the restoration of Charles II to the English throne in 1660.

George Monck, or Monk, who was born on Dec. 6, 1608, of an old Devonshire family of modest means, chose the vocation of soldier while only 17. He served with English expeditions to the Continent, and later with Dutch forces—a not uncommon practice for a soldier of fortune in those days. Subsequently, he commanded his own regiment in Ireland after the rebellion began there in 1641 against the English. He was captured by the parliamentary forces and imprisoned for 2 years in England, but because of his reputation as an excellent soldier, little concerned with politics, he was released and accepted command under the Puritan regime. Still later, after Oliver Cromwell defeated the Scots, Cromwell appointed Monck commander in chief of English forces in Scotland.

Soon afterward, Monck was recalled by Parliament and given command in the Dutch War of 1652-1654 as a "general of the fleet." Though without naval experience, he learned quickly, and the trust that Parliament had placed in him was vindicated in his victory over the Dutchman Maarten Tromp on July 29-31, 1652.

The most important chapter in Monck's life began with his return in 1653 to Scotland, where, serving as a commander in chief of parliamentary forces, he suppressed royalist counterrisings. After the death of Cromwell in 1658 and the short-lived rule of his ineffective son, Richard, and then rule by the army, men of various political factions turned to Monck, who had remained aloof from politics. He was taciturn by nature, and his views had always remained a mystery, though it is likely that he was a moderate Presbyterian whose loyalty to the regime and to Parliament was unquestioned. Tension mounted as he marched his army south into England. With the utmost caution, he entered London in February 1660. He soon proclaimed the return of Parliament, which had not been permitted to meet for several months and which, it was known, would now ask for the return of the King. His achievement was the bloodless restoration of the monarchy. A grateful Charles II rewarded him with the title, among others, of Duke of Albemarle.

Monck occupied a prominent naval command once more in the Dutch War of 1665-1667, with rather mixed

results. Afterward, he retired more and more from public affairs. He died on Jan. 3, 1670, revered as a national hero.

Further Reading

Monck seldom has been a subject for biographers, most of whom must rely heavily on a contemporary account by Monck's chaplain, Dr. Thomas Gumble, *The Life of General Monck* (1671). Both Sir Julian Corbett's short biography, *Monk* (1889), and John D. G. Davies's longer work, *Honest George Monck* (1936), besides being somewhat inaccessible, tend to be extremely laudatory. Oliver Martin Wilson Warner, *Hero of the Restoration: A Life of General George Monck* (1936), is a useful study. Monck figures prominently in two works by Godfrey Davies, *The Early Stuarts, 1603-1660* (1937; 2d ed. 1959) and *The Restoration of Charles II, 1658-1660* (1955). His career after 1660 is briefly recounted in George Clark, *The Later Stuarts, 1660-1714* (1934; 2d ed. 1955). □

Walter. F. Mondale

Active in politics throughout his adult life, Walter F. (Fritz) Mondale (born 1928) served consecutively as Minnesota attorney general, U.S. senator, and U.S. vice president under Jimmy Carter. He lost the 1984 presidential election to incumbent Ronald Reagan, carrying only 13 electoral votes.

Born on January 5, 1928, in Ceylon, Minnesota, Walter Frederick Mondale was the second son of the marriage of Theodore and Claribel (Cowan) Mondale. A Methodist clergyman, the elder Mondale moved his family to a succession of small Minnesota towns before settling in 1937 in Elmore, near the Iowa border. The Mondales' home life was marked by strong moral and religious standards, but also by a tolerant and optimistic spirit.

In school Walter Mondale starred on the football, basketball, and track teams; was an accomplished debater and singer; and was president of his class. Upon graduation in 1946 he enrolled at Macalester College, working in summers as a farm laborer to help pay his tuition. In 1949, when his father died, he left school temporarily in order to earn enough to pay all the costs of his education.

Getting Started in Politics

While a college freshman Mondale became involved in the activities of Minnesota's prospering Democratic-Farmer-Labor (DFL) Party. He volunteered to help in the Minneapolis mayoral campaign of young Hubert Humphrey in 1947 and then, a year later, in Humphrey's successful Senate campaign. Having successfully organized a Macalester campus chapter of Students for Democratic Action (an affiliate of the strongly anti-Communist Americans for Democratic Action), Mondale in 1949 accepted a paying position as Washington-based executive director of SDA. He held that position until leaving in 1950 to resume his education at the University of Minnesota.

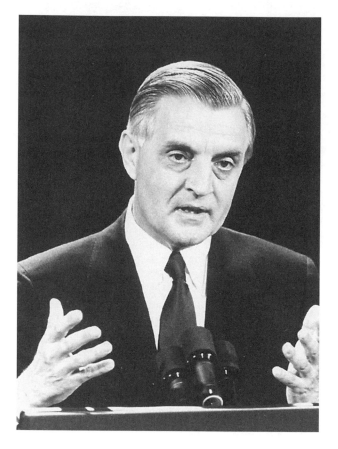

With a new sense of purpose, Mondale graduated *cum laude* from Minnesota in 1951; spent a two-year Army hitch at Fort Knox, Kentucky; and then enrolled in the University of Minnesota Law School. In 1956 he graduated in the top one-fourth of his class and was admitted to the Minnesota State Bar. Meanwhile, on December 27, 1955, Mondale married Joan Adams, a refined young woman with a strong interest in the arts. They were to have three children: Theodore Adams, Eleanore Jane, and William Hall.

On returning to Minnesota in 1950, Mondale had reentered DFL politics, helping in Orville Freeman's unsuccessful campaign for attorney general. After law school he was able to immerse himself in partisan activities. While engaged in establishing a new law firm with his friend Harry McLaughlin, Mondale served as de facto campaign manager for Freeman's gubernatorial re-election campaign in 1956 and then as official campaign manager for Freeman two years later. By the late 1950s Mondale was a respected party tactician and, as state finance director for the DFL, enjoyed extensive political contacts throughout the state.

From Attorney General to the Senate

Mondale's payoff came in May 1960. Having served since 1958 as a special assistant to the state attorney general, Miles Lord, Mondale was appointed to succeed Lord when the latter resigned. He made the most of this opportunity. Capitalizing on publicity resulting from a dramatic investigation of corruption in the Sister Elizabeth Kenny Foundation, he was easily elected attorney general in his

own right in 1960. Two years later he was re-elected with one of the largest majorities in Minnesota history.

As attorney general Mondale demonstrated a commitment to the "underclasses" of society that was to mark his entire political career, initiating a number of anti-trust, civil rights, and consumer protection actions. Most dramatic was his drafting of a brief in the landmark Gideon case, then (1962) before the Supreme Court. This brief, supporting the right of indigent defendants to counsel, was eventually co-signed by the attorneys general of more than 20 other states.

Mondale's emergence as a leading figure in the Minnesota DFL, his legal expertise, and his consistent attachment to liberal principles won him a key role at the 1964 Democratic National Convention. A member of the convention credentials committee, he was selected to head a five-member mediating commission to determine the fate of a claim by the predominantly Black Mississippi Freedom Democratic Party that its delegates should be awarded the state's seats on the convention floor rather than the segregationist regular Democrats. Aware that his efforts would decide whether the vice presidential nomination would go to Hubert Humphrey (to whom President Lyndon Johnson had delegated the overall responsibility to resolve the dispute), Mondale brought the "no-win" situation to conclusion by clever maneuvering and eloquent argument.

The compromise—while it did not satisfy the principal antagonists—passed the test of political expediency: Johnson was pleased, Humphrey received the vice presidential nomination, and—after the Democratic ticket won in November—Mondale was appointed by Minnesota's Democratic governor to complete Humphrey's unexpired term. In January 1965 Mondale became a senator in the Eighty-ninth Congress, which was to become a virtual rubber stamp for Johnson's Great Society programs.

Looking toward the 1966 election, Mondale established himself as one of LBJ's most reliable supporters, amassing impeccable liberal credentials as measured by interest groups such as ADA and the American Federation of Labor-Congress of Industrial Organizations (AFL-CIO). He strongly backed the 1965 Voting Rights Act and was among the strongest proponents of an anti-poll-tax amendment that nearly passed. He also quickly became identified with the cause of farmers, and, especially through co-sponsoring a 1966 law requiring automakers to notify consumers of defects in cars they had purchased, he won the reputation of an advocate for consumers. In November 1966, repeating the pattern of his experience as Minnesota attorney general, he won election in his own right, securing nearly 54 percent of the vote.

A Leading Liberal in the Senate

During the late 1960s—difficult years for the Democratic Party—Mondale enhanced his image as spokesperson for the "powerless"—especially minorities, the very young, and the elderly. He was instrumental in securing passage of an amended Open Housing Act in 1968 which capped off the legislative civil rights revolution of the decade and unsuccessfully backed a mortgage subsidy program for low-income citizens. On the crucially important Vietnam War issue, however, Mondale waffled, drawing criticism from the left. A loyal adherent of Johnson's Vietnam policy until the Tet offensive in early 1968, he kept his doubts about the war largely to himself through the tumultuous period preceding that year's Democratic convention, supporting his old friend Hubert Humphrey for the presidential nomination in opposition to many party liberals. Finally, in September 1968—over a month before Humphrey did so—Mondale broke from LBJ's policies, calling publicly for an unconditional halt to bombing over North Vietnam. Thereafter he strongly opposed the war, as well as any other American intervention in Southeast Asia. He later claimed that supporting the war for so long was his worst political mistake.

After Richard Nixon's election in 1968 Mondale became less conciliatory, abandoning the tendency to compromise that had marked his earlier career. A harsh critic of both the war and Nixon's domestic policies, Mondale gained added stature and visibility through his work on the Special Senate Committee on Aging and the Select Committee on Nutrition and Human Needs. His primary legislative success—a comprehensive child-care measure passed by the Senate in 1971—was vetoed by Nixon. Others of his efforts met with greater success.

By 1972 Mondale had emerged as a sufficiently significant figure in the party to be asked by George McGovern to be his running mate—an offer Mondale refused. Seeking re-election to the Senate instead, he won with 57 percent of the vote despite Nixon's landslide re-election.

With the benefit of more important and prestigious committee assignments (Finance, Budget, and the Select Committee on Intelligence), Mondale branched into new areas of concern in the mid-1970s. He championed tax reform and vigorously criticized abuses of power by the CIA and FBI. Appalled by the excesses of the Nixon administration, in 1975 he published an indictment of the "imperial" presidency, *The Accountability of Power: Toward a More Responsive Presidency.*

Meanwhile, Mondale had developed presidential aspirations of his own. In the fall of 1974 he launched a brief pre-campaign, dropping out within a few weeks because, he said, he lacked "the overwhelming desire to be President, which is essential for the kind of campaign that is required." The eventual winner of the 1976 Democratic nomination, Jimmy Carter, overlooked this seeming lack of commitment, however, selecting Mondale as his vice presidential running mate.

Vice President and After

In agreeing to join Carter on the 1976 ticket, Mondale made clear he would expect to be an "activist" vice president, serving as all-purpose adviser to the president. Beginning immediately after their narrow electoral victory in November, he worked closely with Carter in selecting the cabinet and setting policy priorities. Once in office, Mondale served as both general adviser and emissary for the president. During his four years as vice president, he handled 13 foreign assignments, including sensitive missions to Europe, the Middle East, the Far East, and Africa. Mondale

frequently disagreed with Carter in private. Publicly, however, Mondale was unfailingly loyal to Carter. He played a significant role in winning support from Democratic interest groups and legislators for some of Carter's less orthodox measures. The Mondales were also the first family to reside in the new official home for the vice president on the grounds of the Naval Observatory.

After he and Carter were defeated for re-election in 1980 Mondale found himself out of public office for the first time in 20 years. He immediately signed on with the Washington office of Winston and Strawn, a prestigious Chicago law firm. From his law firm salary and numerous speaking honoraria he earned a substantial income for the first time: over $1.1 million within two years. By late 1981, however, he had decided to run for the presidency himself in 1984. Starting out behind Edward (Ted) Kennedy in the polls, he became the front-runner for the Democratic nomination when Kennedy announced in late 1982 that he would not run. After a marathon candidacy in which he was nearly derailed by Sen. Gary Hart, Mondale won the 1984 nomination, and, in a historic move, selected as his running mate the first female vice presidential candidate on a major party ticket, Geraldine Ferraro, a congresswoman from New York.

The Mondale-Ferraro ticket never really had a chance running against the popular incumbent, Ronald Reagan. After a desultory campaign in which Mondale was portrayed by his foes as an "old-style" tool of interest groups, Reagan scored an overwhelming triumph. Mondale received only 41 percent of the vote and 13 electoral votes, the fifth greatest landslide in American history. His presidential aspirations probably permanently dashed, Mondale decided to rejoin Winston and Strawn, at least temporarily, but in a short time was again speaking out against Reagan's policies. A relatively young man, Mondale seemed unlikely to depart altogether from the world of politics—a world in which he had lived since his early college days. He went back to work in a private law firm for a time, while assisting with Democratic party politics on the state level. In 1993 he was named U.S. ambassador to Japan by President Bill Clinton.

Further Reading

A full-scale biography on Mondale was written by Finlay Lewis, titled *Mondale,* published initially in 1980 and in revised form in 1984, in time for his run for the presidency. A shorter tract is Tom Schneider, *Walter Mondale: Serving All the People* (1984). Mondale's contributions as vice president are covered in the memoirs of several participants in the Carter administration, most notably Jimmy Carter's own *Keeping Faith: Memoirs of a President* (1982) and Zbigniew Brzezinski, *Power & Principle: Memoirs of the National Security Adviser, 1977-1981* (1983). Most useful on Mondale's unsuccessful presidential campaign against Ronald Reagan are Jules Witcover and Jack W. Germond, *Wake Us When It's Over: Presidential Politics of 1984* (1985) and Peter Goldman and Tony Fuller, *The Quest for the Presidency 1984* (1985). Mondale published a critique of the "imperial" presidency of the early 1970s, *The Accountability of Power: Toward a Responsible Presidency* (1975). □

Eduardo Chivambo Mondlane

The Mozambican educator and nationalist Eduardo Chivambo Mondlane (1920-1969) was the leading figure in his country's independence movement from 1962 to 1969.

Eduardo Mondlane was born on June 20, 1920, in the Gaza district of southern Mozambique. The son of a Tsonga chief and the only member of his large family to receive even a primary education, he later attributed his educational drive to the vision of a ''very determined and persistent'' mother. The colonial school system was almost exclusively for Europeans, but Mondlane gained entry into a Swiss mission school and went from it to an American Methodist agricultural school. He then served for 2 years instructing African peasants in techniques of dry farming.

Next Mondlane obtained a scholarship and admission to a Presbyterian secondary school in the Transvaal, South Africa, and in 1948 he was admitted to Witwatersrand University of Johannesburg, the first African from Mozambique to enter a South African university. In 1949 the South African government declared him an unwanted ''foreign native'' in a white university and revoked his student permit. Returned to Lourenço Marques in Mozambique, Mondlane was arrested and interrogated about his role in the formation of a local African student association.

In June 1950 Mondlane entered the University of Lisbon as the only African student from Mozambique pursuing a higher education in Portugal. After a year during which he complained of harassment by the political police, his Phelps Stokes scholarship was transferred to the United States, where he entered Oberlin College in Ohio at the age of 31. After earning a bachelor's degree from Oberlin in 1953, he undertook graduate work at Northwestern University in Illinois and received a doctorate in 1960.

By this time Mondlane had become Mozambique's best-known, best-educated, and most watched African. The uniqueness of his position can be appreciated when one notes that perhaps 10 out of nearly 6 million Africans in Mozambique were attending secondary schools in 1955, while slightly over 200 were enrolled in technical schools or seminaries.

Researcher and Scholar

In 1957, after a year as a visiting scholar at Harvard, where he worked on role conflict (the subject of his dissertation), Mondlane joined the trusteeship section of the United Nations Secretariat in New York as a research officer. In this capacity he went to West Africa in 1960 as part of a UN team preparing and supervising a plebiscite in the British Cameroons. From the Cameroons, following an absence of 11 years and accompanied by his American wife and family, he revisited Mozambique in early 1961. After renewing and expanding a wide assortment of personal contacts on his tour of Mozambique, he returned to the United States, resigned his post at the UN, and accepted a teaching position within the East African program at Syracuse University. At the same time he began lecturing and writing on Portuguese colonialism and politicoeconomic conditions in Mozambique.

Politician and Revolutionary

In June 1962 Mondlane flew to Dar es Salaam, Tanzania, where he helped to unite several groups of exiled Mozambique nationalists into the Mozambique Liberation Front (FRELIMO). He was confirmed as the movement's first president at a congress held that September in Tanzania. He then returned to America to complete his obligations at Syracuse University. During this last semester of teaching he delivered a paper at the first American Negro Leadership Conference on Africa (Harriman, N.Y., November 1962). Early in 1963 he and his family moved to Dar es Salaam, where Mondlane assumed his new role as a revolutionary leader.

For some years Mondlane had worked with American Protestants and others to funnel scholarship funds to Africans wishing to attend secondary school in Mozambique and to study abroad. It was only consistent, therefore, that he made education a principal concern of FRELIMO. He founded the Mozambique Institute in Dar es Salaam to receive refugee students, to obtain scholarships, and, ultimately, to develop a new Mozambique primary and secondary school curriculum.

FRELIMO sent volunteers for military training to Algeria and the United Arab Republic and to camps in Tanzania. By September 1964 Mondlane had a cadre of some 250 trained men, and guerrilla operations were launched that month in the northern Cabo Delgado and Niassa districts of Mozambique. By 1969 several thousand FRELIMO guerrillas were operating in those areas. To equip and feed them, Mondlane circled the globe, raising funds and seeking arms. Money and training were made available by various African states, the Organization of African Unity (OAU), the Soviet Union, and China, and educational and humanitarian funds by the World Council of Churches (Geneva), Scandinavian countries, and various private groups in the United States.

Although a new FRELIMO military front was opened in the Tete district of northwest Mozambique during 1968, Mondlane still warned soberly of a long, costly fight ahead. His leadership came under attack within the movement by would-be rivals and dissidents of the key northern Maconde community. In the face of Portuguese intransigence and military support for Portugal from Western countries, the struggle for independence was proving more costly and slower than some had hoped. Despite criticism related to the difficulties and intrigues of exile politics, the Central Committee convened the second FRELIMO congress inside the Niassa district in July 1968. There Mondlane was re-elected president by an overwhelming majority.

A sunny, didactic man with an open life-style, Mondlane was an easy target for political enemies. On Feb. 3, 1969, he was killed by a bomb mailed to him marked as a book. His assassins remain unknown. Leaving behind a wife and three children and a weakened Mozambique liberation movement, Eduardo Mondlane immediately became a martyred symbol of the continuing African struggle for national independence. He was succeeded as president of FRELIMO by the movement's military commander, Samora Machel, while his wife, Janet Mondlane, continued as director of the Mozambique Institute.

Further Reading

Mondlane's *The Struggle for Mozambique* (1969) was completed just before his death. He was a contributor to Calvin W. Stillman, ed., *Africa in the Modern World* (1955), and to John A. Davis and James K. Baker, *Southern Africa in Transition* (1966). Recommended for general background are James Duffy, *Portugal in Africa* (1962), and Ronald H. Chilcote, *Portuguese Africa* (1967). □

Piet Mondrian

The Dutch painter Piet Mondrian (1872-1944) created a geometrical abstract style known as neoplasticism, which had widespread influence on modern painting, architecture, and design.

Piet Mondrian was born on March 7, 1872, in Amersfoort. His father, a schoolteacher, wished Piet to become a teacher, and he earned his diploma for teaching. But in 1892 he entered the Academy of Fine Arts in Amsterdam, where he studied for several years and was encouraged by artists of The Hague school, who continued the landscape tradition of Charles Daubigny and the Barbizon painters. Mondrian's early pictures are mostly of such subjects as meadows with farms and cows or windmills. Although a few of his works from about 1900 show some influence of Claude Monet and symbolism, he continued working in a very conservative tradition for a number of years.

Development of His Style

In 1908 Mondrian became deeply involved in the latest developments in art, and in the course of the next 10 years or so he developed with astonishing rapidity through a succession of styles. He began to use pure, glowing colors and expressive brushwork under the influence of pointillism and Fauvism in pictures which are almost like those of Vincent Van Gogh in their vivid colors and intensity of expression. Motifs such as church towers and windmills were painted in a blaze of color with staccato, pointillist brushstrokes. But Mondrian soon turned to a more monumental and simplified treatment in which the motif was depicted close up, in isolation, dominating the picture area symmetrically, and the pointillist brushstrokes were replaced by large unmodulated areas of color. Although these pictures were still usually based on some definite motif, they show an attempt to go beyond realism to a sort of symbolic superreality, an attitude which partly reflects Mondrian's

growing preoccupation with theosophy. The works of this period include some very poetic landscapes of deserted dunes in Zeeland.

By the time Mondrian moved to Paris in 1912, he had already seen a few cubist pictures and had begun to be influenced by cubism. But at a time when Georges Braque and Pablo Picasso were turning back to figuration, Mondrian decided to carry cubism through to what seemed to him its logical culmination of pure abstraction. Although he continued until as late as 1916 to make some reference to such subjects as trees and the facades of buildings, he gradually eliminated all traces of figuration. He quickly assimilated the cubist idiom of Braque and Picasso, working in grays or ochers and sometimes using an oval composition, but over the following years his compositions became more and more clarified, with a concentration on vertical and horizontal lines.

This development became particularly marked after Mondrian returned in 1914 to Holland, where, because of the outbreak of war, he remained until 1919, living mainly in the artists' colony at Laren. It can be seen, for instance, in various paintings and drawings of the sea in which the movement of waves is evoked by short horizontal and vertical lines (his so-called plus-and-minus compositions).

Contacts with the Dutch painters Bart van der Leck and Theo van Doesburg at this time led to further developments in Mondrian's art. Van der Leck had begun to work exclusively with white and black and with flat planes of the three primary colors: red, blue, and yellow; Van Doesburg founded in 1917 the periodical *De Stijl* and the art movement of the same name. In 1917 Mondrian began to paint completely nonfigurative works composed of rectangles of different colors and sizes against a neutral white ground. At first these color rectangles (some upright, some horizontal) were situated at varying intervals in depth, with a certain amount of overlapping, but overlapping was soon avoided, and he began to bring the color areas more and more into the same plane, in a shallower picture space. In 1918 he introduced a grid of vertical and horizontal lines which divided the composition into a number of rectangles of different sizes, each painted a uniform color; in this way the color rectangles were integrated into an overall framework. (Although he had begun to work toward the use of the three primary colors and white and black, he still mixed his colors to some extent and tended to achieve a muted effect.)

Advent of Neoplasticism

Only after Mondrian's return to Paris in 1919 did this tendency reach its culmination in the style to which he gave the name neoplasticism. From 1922 on he worked exclusively with vertical and horizontal lines and with white, black, and the three primary colors—the strongest and purest possible contrasts. In all but a few of his last works, he divided his pictures asymmetrically by a grid of heavy black vertical and horizontal lines, with certain rectangles painted a uniform intense red, blue, or yellow and all the other areas left a brilliant white. But within these limitations he achieved a wide range of effects by varying the proportions, the choice and distribution of the colors, and so on. Although he painted some pictures on canvases of square format hung diagonally, he always kept the lines strictly vertical and horizontal and indeed resigned from de Stijl in 1925 because Van Doesburg had introduced diagonal lines.

Mondrian lived in Paris from 1919 to 1938 and in London from 1938 to 1940; then he settled in New York. Stimulated by the tempo and dynamism of New York City and by jazz, in his last works he used colored lines instead of black ones and even broke up the lines into a lively mosaic of different colors. He died in New York City on Feb. 1, 1944.

Further Reading

Mondrian's own writings were republished in an edition entitled *Plastic Art and Pure Plastic Art, 1937, and Other Essays, 1941-43* (1945). The most comprehensive work on Mondrian is Michel Seuphor, *Piet Mondrian: Life and Work* (1957). Another important study is Frank Elgar, *Mondrian* (trans. 1968). A brief introduction to Mondrian is L. J. F. Wijsenbeek, *Piet Mondrian* (trans. 1969). ☐

Claude Monet

The French painter Claude Monet (1840-1926) was the seminal figure in the evolution of impressionism, a pivotal style in the development of modern art.

The second half of the 19th century witnessed profound and disrupting shifts within the larger course of Western art. Many artistic attitudes which had prevailed since the beginning of the Renaissance gave way to approaches which differed radically from the practices of the Old Masters. In painting, for instance, illusionism was one of the fundamental Renaissance values: paintings were regarded as windows through which one viewed the natural world. But in the 19th century a new approach gradually replaced the illusionist aim: paintings became increasingly two-dimensional, openly declaring flatness as an intrinsic feature of their identity. They became events in themselves, phenomena to be confronted rather than windows to be seen through.

Impressionism occupies a crucial, yet paradoxical, position in the 19th century's changing interpretation of the painting enterprise. In the hands of Claude Monet, Pierre Auguste Renoir, Camille Pissarro, and others, the new style (it was not called impressionism until 1874) was initially conceived in the spirit of illusionism. As it evolved, however, certain of its tenets emerged as being, in effect, anti-illusionist. Monet's art reveals both the complexities and the paradoxes of this historical phenomenon. In addition, it reveals how impressionism constitutes a turning point in the development of modern art.

Monet was born in Paris on Nov. 14, 1840. In 1845 his family moved to Le Havre, and by the time he was 15 Monet had developed a local reputation as a caricaturist. Through an exhibition of his caricatures in 1858 Monet met Eugène Boudin, a landscape painter who exerted a profound influ-

ence on the young artist. Boudin introduced Monet to outdoor painting, an activity which he entered reluctantly but which soon became the basis for his life's work.

By 1859 Monet was determined to pursue an artistic career. He visited Paris and was impressed by the paintings of Eugène Delacroix, Charles Daubigny, and Camille Corot. Against his parents' wishes, Monet decided to stay in Paris. He worked at the free Académie Suisse, where he met Pissarro, and he frequented the Brasserie des Martyrs, a gathering place for Gustave Courbet and other realists who constituted the vanguard of French painting in the 1850s.

Formative Period

Monet's studies were interrupted by military service in Algeria (1860-1862). The remainder of the decade witnessed constant experimentation, travel, and the formation of many important artistic friendships. In 1862 he entered the studio of Charles Gleyre in Paris and met Renoir, Alfred Sisley, and Jean Frédéric Bazille. During 1863 and 1864 he periodically worked in the forest at Fontainebleau with the Barbizon artists Théodore Rousseau, Jean François Millet, and Daubigny, as well as with Corot. In Paris in 1869 he frequented the Café Guerbois, where he met Edouard Manet.

At the outbreak of the Franco-Prussian War in 1870, Monet traveled to London, where he met the adventurous and sympathetic dealer Paul Durand-Ruel. The following year Monet and his wife, Camille, whom he had married in 1870, settled at Argenteuil, which became a semipermanent home (he continued to travel throughout his life) for the next 6 years.

Monet's constant movements during this period were directly related to his artistic ambitions. The phenomena of natural light, atmosphere, and color captivated his imagination, and he committed himself to an increasingly accurate recording of their enthralling variety. He consciously sought that variety and gradually developed a remarkable sensitivity for the subtle particulars of each landscape he encountered. Paul Cézanne is reported to have said that "Monet is the most prodigious eye since there have been painters."

Relatively few of Monet's canvases from the 1860s have survived. Throughout the decade, and during the 1870s as well, he suffered from extreme financial hardship and frequently destroyed his own paintings rather than have them seized by creditors. A striking example of his early style is the *Terrace at the Seaside, Sainte-Adresse* (1866). The painting contains a shimmering array of bright, natural colors, eschewing completely the somber browns and blacks of the earlier landscape tradition.

Monet and Impressionism

As William Seitz (1960) wrote, "The landscapes Monet painted at Argenteuil between 1872 and 1877 are his best-known, most popular works, and it was during these years that impressionism most closely approached a group style. Here, often working beside Renoir, Sisley, Caillebotte, or Manet, he painted the sparkling impressions of French river life that so delight us today." During these same years Monet exhibited regularly in the impressionist group shows, the first of which took place in 1874. On that occasion his painting *Impression: Sunrise* (1872) inspired a hostile newspaper critic to call all the artists "impressionists," and the designation has persisted to the present day.

Monet's paintings from the 1870s reveal the major tenets of the impressionist vision. Along with *Impression: Sunrise, Red Boats at Argenteuil* (1875) is an outstanding example of the new style. In these paintings impressionism is essentially an illusionist style, albeit one that looks radically different from the landscapes of the Old Masters. The difference resides primarily in the chromatic vibrancy of Monet's canvases. Working directly from nature, he and the impressionists discovered that even the darkest shadows and the gloomiest days contain an infinite variety of colors. To capture the fleeting effects of light and color, however, Monet gradually learned that he had to paint quickly and to employ short brushstrokes loaded with individualized colors. This technique resulted in canvases that were charged with painterly activity; in effect, they denied the even blending of colors and the smooth, enameled surfaces to which most earlier painting had persistently subscribed.

Yet, in spite of these differences, the new style was illusionistically intended; only the interpretation of what illusionism consisted of had changed. For traditional landscape artists illusionism was conditioned first of all by the mind: that is, painters tended to depict the individual phenomena of the natural world—leaves, branches, blades of grass—as they had studied them and conceptualized their existence. Monet, on the other hand, wanted to paint what he saw rather than what he intellectually knew. And he saw not separate leaves, but splashes of constantly changing light and color. According to Seitz, "It is in this context that we must understand his desire to see the world through the eyes of a man born blind who had suddenly gained his sight: as a pattern of nameless color patches." In an important sense, then, Monet belongs to the tradition of Renaissance illusionism: in recording the phenomena of the natural world, he simply based his art on perceptual rather than conceptual knowledge.

Works of the 1880s and 1890s

During the 1880s the impressionists began to dissolve as a cohesive group, although individual members continued to see one another and they occasionally worked together. In 1883 Monet moved to Giverny, but he continued to travel—to London, Madrid, and Venice, as well as to favorite sites in his native country. He gradually gained critical and financial success during the late 1880s and the 1890s. This was due primarily to the efforts of Durand-Ruel, who sponsored one-man exhibitions of Monet's work as early as 1883 and who, in 1886, also organized the first large-scale impressionist group show to take place in the United States.

Monet's painting during this period slowly gravitated toward a broader, more expansive and expressive style. In *Spring Trees by a Lake* (1888) the entire surface vibrates electrically with shimmering light and color. Paradoxically, as his style matured and as he continued to develop the sensitivity of his vision, the strictly illusionistic aspect of his paintings began to disappear. Plastic form dissolved into colored pigment, and three-dimensional space evaporated into a charged, purely optical surface atmosphere. His canvases, although invariably inspired by the visible world, increasingly declared themselves as objects which are, above all, paintings. This quality links Monet's art more closely with modernism than with the Renaissance tradition.

Modernist, too, are the "serial" paintings to which Monet devoted considerable energy during the 1890s. The most celebrated of these series are the haystacks (1891) and the facades of Rouen Cathedral (1892-1894). In these works Monet painted his subjects from more or less the same physical position, allowing only the natural light and atmospheric conditions to vary from picture to picture. That is, he "fixed" the subject matter, treating it like an experimental constant against which changing effects could be measured and recorded. This technique reflects the persistence and devotion with which Monet pursued his study of the visible world. At the same time, the serial works effectively neutralized subject matter per se, implying that paintings could exist without it. In this way his art established an important precedent for the development of abstract painting.

Late Work

Monet's wife died in 1879; in 1892 he married Alice Hoschedé. By 1899 his financial position was secure, and he began work on his famous series of water lily paintings. Water lilies existed in profusion in the artist's exotic gardens at Giverny, and he painted them tirelessly until his death there on Dec. 5, 1926. Still, Monet's late years were by no means easy. During his last two decades he suffered from poor health and had double cataracts; by the 1920s he was virtually blind.

In addition to his physical ailments, Monet struggled desperately with the problems of his art. In 1920 he began work on 12 large canvases (each measuring 14 feet in width) of water lilies, which he planned to give to the state. To complete them, he fought against his own failing eyesight and against the demands of a large-scale mural art for which his own past had hardly prepared him. In effect, the task required him to learn a new kind of painting at the age of 80. The paintings are characterized by a broad, sweeping style; virtually devoid of subject matter, their vast, encompassing spaces are generated almost exclusively by color. Such color spaces were without precedent in Monet's lifetime; moreover, their descendants have appeared in contemporary painting only since the end of World War II.

Further Reading

An excellent monograph on Monet is William C. Seitz, *Claude Monet* (1960). The most comprehensive survey of Monet's art in relation to impressionism is John Rewald, *The History of Impressionism* (rev. ed. 1961). A well-written and well-illustrated but less scholarly survey is Phoebe Pool, *Impressionism* (1967). □

Mongkut

Mongkut (1804-1868) was king of Thailand as Rama IV. He founded modern Thai Buddhism and as king took a leading role in opening his kingdom to the West.

Born on Oct. 18, 1804, Mongkut was the forty-third child of King Rama II (reigned 1809-1824), but he was the first son to be born of Queen Suriyen and thus was favored to succeed to the throne. He had just entered the Buddhist monkhood for a short period, as was customary, when his father died in 1824 and the royal accession council chose his older and more experienced half brother to reign as King Nangklao (Rama III, reigned 1824-1851).

As much for political safety as any other reason, Mongkut remained a monk during his brother's reign. An unusually gifted young man, Mongkut spent several years seeking intellectual and religious satisfaction in traditional Buddhism, trying first mental exercises and meditation and then orthodox scholarship, neither of which kindled his enthusiasm. Then he encountered a monk from Burma who inspired his return to the strict discipline and teachings of early Buddhism, shorn of local Thai custom and noncanonical beliefs.

Becoming abbot of a monastery in Bangkok, Mongkut developed a lively home for intellectual discourse in the 1830s and 1840s, when he gained adherents to his new teachings and invited American and French missionaries to teach Western languages, arts, and sciences. His brother monks ultimately were to found the modernist Dhammayutta sect, a major force in the life of modern Thailand.

Others who joined his circle were among the leading princes and young nobles of Bangkok society, and this group, led by Phraya Suriyawong (Chuang Bunnag)—eldest son of the leading minister of Rama III—was responsible for placing Mongkut on the throne when Rama III died on April 2, 1851. These young liberals had come to understand the nature of Western power and Siam's weakness, profiting from the example of Western warfare against China (in the Opium War, 1839-1842) and Burma (1824-1826 and 1851-1852).

Upon consolidating their power the liberals signified their willingness to come to terms with Western demands and signed treaties, beginning with Britain in 1855, which removed all barriers to trade and established extraterritoriality for European subjects in Siam. Mongkut and Suriyawong, who became his chief minister, set a pattern of accommodation to the West which came to assure Siam's survival as an independent state through the 19th-century thrust of European imperialism.

Described by European envoys as thin and austere, Mongkut was extraordinarily lively, excited by ideas, and colorfully expressive in English. Though the conservatism of his nobles precluded fundamental reforms, he educated his sons to understand the value of national independence and the necessity for reform, which alone could ensure survival. He died on Oct. 1, 1868, and was succeeded by his son, Prince Chulalongkorn.

Further Reading

The best available biography is Abbot Low Moffat, *Mongkut, King of Siam* (1961). An excellent contemporary account is Sir John Bowring, *The Kingdom and People of Siam* (2 vols., 1857).

Additional Sources

Bristowe, W. S. (William Syer), *Louis and the King of Siam,* New York: Thai-American Publishers, 1976. □

Thelonious Monk

Along with Charlie Parker and Dizzy Gillespie, Thelonious Monk (1917-1982) was a vital member of the jazz revolution which took place in the early 1940s. Monk's unique piano style and his talent as a composer made him a leader in the development of modern jazz.

When Thelonious Monk began performing his music in the early 1940s, only a small circle of New York's brightest jazz musicians could appreciate its uniqueness. His melodies were angular, his harmonies full of jarring clusters, and he used both notes and the absence of notes in unexpected ways. He flattened his fingers when he played the piano and used his elbows from time to time to get the sound he wanted. Critics and peers took these as signs of incompetency, giving his music "puzzled dismissal as deliberately eccentric," as *Jazz Journal* noted. "To them, Monk apparently had ideas, but it took fleshier players like pianist Bud Powell to execute them properly." The debate over his talent and skill continued as the years passed, but Monk eventually found himself with a strong following. By the time of his death in 1982 he was widely acknowledged as a founding father of modern jazz.

Aspects of his compositions that once were ridiculed are now analyzed at colleges and universities throughout the country. Amateur and professional pianists continue to cite him as a major influence in their styles. Many of his works, which number over 60, are jazz classics. "Round Midnight" is considered "one of the most beautiful short pieces of music written in twentieth-century America," as record producer Orrin Keepnews noted in *Keyboard Magazine.*

Though his career was beset by personal and societal obstacles, Monk always believed in his music. He never spoke to his audiences end rarely granted interviews, preferring to let his music speak for itself. Aside from his wife and two children, his music was his life. "So absorbed was he in

jazz," commented *Keyboard,* "that he would walk the New York streets for hours or stand still on a corner near his apartment on West 63rd Street, staring into his private landscape and running new songs and sounds through his mind. As he himself succinctly explained it, 'I just walk and dig.'"

Because Monk's music was beyond the grasp of most listeners, the media tended to look for peripheral details to write about. They had plenty of material; as the *New York Post* wrote, Monk was "one of jazz's great eccentrics." During concerts and recording sessions he would rise from his bench every so often and lunge into a dance, emphasizing the rhythm he wanted from his bandmembers with his 200-pound frame. With his strange hats, bamboo-framed sunglasses, and goatee, he became an obvious subject for Sunday supplement caricatures. There was also the way he talked: He and his peers—saxophonist Charlie Parker, trumpeters Dizzy Gillespie and Miles Davis, drummer Max Roach, and tenor saxophonist Sonny Rollins—were known for popularizing such expressions a "groovy," "you dig, man," and "cool, baby." But most Americans first heard of him in the early 1950s when he and a couple of friends were arrested for allegedly possessing drugs—for Monk, one among other instances of legal harassment that would create severe obstacles in his work.

Surprisingly, there are no biographies in book form on Monk. There is, however, the excellent 1989 film documentary, *Straight, No Chaser* (Warner Bros.), which combines footage shot in the late 1960s with more recent interviews with his son, Thelonious Monk, Jr., tenor saxophonist Charlie Rouse, and others. According to a *New York Times* interview, the film features "some of the most valuable jazz ever shot. Closeups of Monk's hands on the keyboard reveal a technique that was unusually tense, spiky and aggressive. Other scenes show him explaining his compositions and chord structures, giving instructions in terse, barely intelligible growls that even his fellow musicians found difficult to interpret." The film also provides glimpses into the emotional turbulences in his personal life. He was "acutely sensitive and moody and perhaps a manic-depressive," according to the same review. "Illness eventually made it impossible for him to perform."

Teaches Self to Read Music

Thelonious Sphere Monk was born October 10, 1917, in Rocky Mount, North Carolina. The first musical sounds he heard were from a player piano that his family owned. At the age of five or six he began picking out melodies on the piano and taught himself to read music by looking over his sister's shoulder as she took lessons. About a year later the family moved to the San Juan Hill section of New York City, near the Hudson River. His father became ill soon afterward and returned to the South, leaving Thelonious's mother, Barbara, to raise him and his brother and sister by herself. Mrs. Monk did all she could to encourage her young son's interest in music. Though the family budget was tight, she managed to buy a baby grand Steinway piano, and when Thelonious turned 11 she began paying for his weekly piano lessons. Even at that young age it was clear that the instrument was part of his destiny. "If anybody sat down and

played the piano," he recalled in *Crescendo International,* "I would just stand there and watch 'em all the time."

As a boy Thelonious received rigorous training in the gospel music style, accompanying the Baptist choir in which his mother sang and playing piano and organ during church services. At the same time he was becoming initiated into the world of jazz; near his home were several jazz clubs as well as the home of the great Harlem stride pianist James P. Johnson, from whom Thelonious picked up a great deal. By the age of 13 he was playing in a local bar and grill with a trio. A year later he began playing at "rent" parties (parties thrown to raise money for rent), which meant holding his own among the pianists who would each play in marathon displays of virtuosity. He gained further distinction at the Apollo Theater's famous weekly amateur music contests, which he won so many times that he was eventually banned from the event. At 16 he left school to travel with an evangelical faith healer and preacher for a year-long tour that indoctrinated him into the subtleties of rhythm and blues accompaniment.

Upon returning to New York, Monk began playing non-union jobs. In 1939 he put his first group together. His first important gig came in the early 1940s, when he was hired as house pianist at a club called Minton's. It was a time of dramatic innovation in jazz. Swing, the music of older jazzmen, was clearly inadequate for the new postwar society. In its place, a faster, more complex style was developing. The practitioners of this new music, called bebop, created it virtually on the spot, "in jam sessions and discussions that stretched past the far side of midnight," as *Keyboard* wrote. "According to jazz folklore, this activity centered on Minton's, and as the house pianist there, Monk was at the eye of what would become the bebop hurricane."

Yet while Monk was pivotal in inspiring bebop, his own music had few ties to any particular movement. Monk was Monk, an undisputed original, and the proof was in his compositions. "More than anyone else in the Minton's crowd, Monk showed a knack for writing," *Keyboard* remarked. "Years before his piano work would be taken seriously, he would be known for his composing. In fact, most of the classic Monk tunes, such as 'Blue Monk,' 'Epistrophy,' and ''Round Midnight,' were written during his gig at Minton's or before 1951."

Composes "Fast-thinking" Music

"I was about nineteen to twenty, I guess, when I started to hear my music in my mind," Monk told *Crescendo International.* "So I had to compose music in order to express the type of ideas that I had. Because the music wasn't on the scene. It had to be composed. . . . All the musicians that were thinking liked my music—and wanted to learn how to play the different songs that we were playing. And the most talented ones used to be on the scene. Like Charlie Parker and Dizzy. They were about the fastest-thinking musicians. And so they would come and play all the time, and I would teach 'em the songs, you know, and the chords. They didn't just *hear* it. I had to tell 'em what it was. . . . They got themselves together by playing a lot with me. . . . I wasn't

trying to create something that would be hard to play. I just composed music that fit with how I was thinking. . . . I didn't want to play the way I'd heard music played all my life. I got tired of hearing that. I wanted to hear something else, something better."

As the 1940s progressed and bebop became more and more the rage, Monk's career declined. "By 1948," *Keyboard* noted, "he was only doing occasional nights at Birdland, and days were often spent sitting in his room, writing tunes, gazing silently at the television, or staring for long hours at a pictured Billie Holiday taped to his ceiling. . . . Nellie, his wife, helped keep food on the table with outside work during his periods of moody immobility." In 1951 he was arrested with pianist Bud Powell on an extremely questionable charge of narcotics possession. Not only was he confined for 60 days in prison but the New York State Liquor Authority rescinded his cabaret card, without which he could not get hired for local club dates. For the next several years he survived only with the help of his good friend and patron the Baroness de Koenigswarter.

By the mid-1950s, though, his fortune took a turn for the better. In 1954 he gave a series of concerts in Paris and cut his first solo album, *Pure Monk* (now out of print). A year later he began recording for the Riverside label. His following grew, and as *Keyboard* reported, his mystique grew as well. "Program notes for the Berkshire Music Barn Jazz Concert in 1955 read, 'Monk is the Greta Garbo of jazz, and his appearance at any piano is regarded as a major event by serious followers of jazz.'" In 1957 he opened an engagement at New York's Five Spot, leading a powerful quartet with a jazz newcomer named John Coltrane on saxophone. The gig, which lasted eight months, was pivotal for Monk. "Monk found himself at the center of a cult," wrote *Keyboard.* "Audiences lined up to see his unpredictable performances, his quirky, quietly ecstatic dances during horn solos, his wanderings through the room." Several masterful albums he recorded for Riverside in the late 1950s— *Brilliant Corners, Thelonious Himself,* and *Thelonious Monk with John Coltrane*—increased his notoriety, rendering him "the most acclaimed and controversial jazz improviser of the late 1950s almost overnight." It didn't hurt that both Coltrane and Sonny Rollins were acknowledging him as their guru. "With men as highly regarded as those acknowledging his mastery," Keepnews commented in *Keyboard,* "the rest of the jazz world was quick to follow. . . . I could not [without] both satisfaction and amusement [describe] the quick change in his *down beat* record reviews from lukewarm or less to their top 5-star rating."

Eccentric Behavior Causes Trouble

The strange behavior that Monk displayed in public sometimes got him into trouble. In 1958 he was arrested, undeservedly, for disturbing the peace, and his cabaret license was revoked a second time. Forced to take out-of-town gigs, he was separated from his two main sources of stability—New York City and his wife Nellie—and his eccentricities thus intensified. During one episode in 1959 in Boston, state police picked him up and brought him to the Grafton State Hospital, where he was held for a week.

"From that point on," *Keyboard* wrote, "when asked about his eccentricities, Monk would answer, 'I can't be crazy, because they had me in one of these places and let me go.'" Around 1960 his cabaret club card was restored and he returned to playing the New York clubs. Now when he played a gig his wife accompanied him; when she couldn't make it, he telephoned her during breaks.

Nellie and Thelonious Monk shared a deep intimacy. They "believed their marriage was made in heaven," according to *Keyboard*. "They had first seen each other as children on a playground; though six months would pass before they actually met, both sensed a deep connection with that initial contact, and Monk would later surprise her by correctly recalling everything she was wearing that day." His love for her is reflected in "Crepuscile With Nellie," a beautiful tune that he labored over for a month during a time when she was hospitalized. But despite their bond, when Monk was in one of his depressions not even Nellie could communicate with him.

Toward the end of the 1950s Monk began to receive the prestige he had for so long deserved. His late 1950s recordings on Riverside had done so well that in 1962 he was offered a contract from Columbia. As a performer he was equally successful, commanding, in 1960, $2,000 for week-long engagements with his band and $1,000 for single performances. His December 1963 concert at New York's Philharmonic Hall, a big-band presentation of originals, was for him a personal landmark. As *Keyboard* observed, "the Philharmonic Hall was special: it was within walking distance of his apartment, a part of the neighborhood he had criss-crossed on his long meditative strolls. After years of hassles with local clubs and unsympathetic critics, Monk had finally made it close to home." In 1964 he appeared on the cover of *Time* magazine—an extremely rare honor for jazz artist.

Last Concert at Carnegie Hall

In the early 1970s, Monk made a few solo and trio recordings for Black Lion in London and played a few concerts. Beginning in the mid-1970s he isolated himself from his friends and colleagues, spending his final years at the home of the Baroness Nica de Koenigswarter in Weehawken, New Jersey. In *Keyboard*, Keepnews speculated on his seclusion: "He may just have worn down and stopped caring . . . From an early '60s peak that even saw his picture on the cover of *Time* magazine, this once-obscure pianist had slid back towards obscurity. To someone who had never really cared all that much about communicating with the public, it couldn't have seemed worth the effort to start climbing again. Towards the end he reportedly had ignored or rejected some very fancy offers from would-be promoters of comeback concerts. I hope those reports are accurate; I would like to think that he simply felt he had said all he cared to say to any of us." In fact, after playing a concert at Carnegie Hall in March, 1976, Monk was too weak physically to make further appearances. He died on February 17, 1982, in Englewood Hospital, after suffering a massive stroke.

There was "a Monk fever in the jazz world" for at least two years before his death, as Stanley Crouch observed in the *Village Voice*. "Everywhere musicians were buying Monk records, transcribing them, learning the chords and the rhythms, talking about him and his contribution, almost unconsciously making him into a patron saint while he lived." But as Keepnews observed In *Keyboard*, performing Monk's music is no easy feat. His "material can be basically divided into two categories: difficult and impossible. . . . In the difficult category are selections . . . ('I Mean You,' 'Straight, No Chaser') that can be handled by strong musicians willing to give themselves a strenuous workout. Then there are the impossible ones: compositions I sometimes suspect he wrote as a form of nose-thumbing revenge on those who claimed he was devoid of technique, which I have seen drive normally unflappable master players straight up the walls of recording studios. Try your hand at, say, 'Brilliant Corners' or 'Jackie-ing' and you'll wind up feeling even more in awe of this man."

Monk's eccentric piano technique did, in fact, raise eyebrows among music critics. "Holding his fingers almost totally flat, he sacrificed accuracy in arpeggios and runs in order to get the sound he wanted, even playing with his elbows if necessary," *Keyboard* observed. "This elbow maneuver baffled and alienated a lot of critics and musicians, but typically their reaction made little impact on Monk . . . . As he told Valerie Wilmer, 'I hit the piano with my elbow sometimes because of a certain sound I want to hear, certain chords. You can't hit that many notes with your hands. Sometimes people laugh when I'm doing that. Yeah, let 'em laugh! They need something to laugh at.'" Concerning those who criticized his technique, Monk told *Crescendo International*, "I guess these people are surprised when they hear certain things that I've done on records. They must feel awful silly about saying I don't have no technique. Because I know you've heard me make some fast runs. You can dig how stupid the statement is."

Looking back on his career, Monk told *Crescendo International*, "As for the hard times I've had—I've never been jealous of any musician, or anything. Musicians and other people have told lies on me, sure, and it has kept me from jobs for awhile. . . . But it didn't bother me. I kept on making it—recording and doing what I'm doing, and thinking. While they were talking I was thinking music and still trying to play. And I never starved. I always *could* make it. . . . What turned the tide in my favour? The sons took over. A lot of the fathers kicked off, went out of business, or retired. And their sons are in power now, that like different music and take better chances. In other words, it's younger people running things. . . . I take it as it comes—as long as I can make a living, take care of my family and everybody can be comfortable. And if I can do what I want when I feel like doing it—which generally means financially—then everything is all right. If you want to eat, you can buy some food. If you want a suit, you can buy one. If you don't want to walk, you can ride in a cab, or buy a car. That's all you need to do. Sleep when you want, get up when you want— be your own boss. . . . I've never wished for anybody else's job. I enjoy what I do and I'm myself all the time. And I'll continue to be me."

Further Reading

Chilton, John, *Who's Who of Jazz: Storyville to Swing Street*, Chilton, 1972.

Giddons, Gary, *Rhythm-A-Ning: Jazz Tradition and Innovation in the 80s*, 1986.

Hentoff, Nat, *The Jazz Life*, Da Capo, 1975.

Crescendo International, June 1984.

Daily News, February 18, 1982.

Jazz Journal, August 1964.

Jazz Review, November 1958.

Keyboard, July 1982.

New York Post, February 18, 1982; September 30, 1989.

New York Times, September 30, 1989.

Time, February 28, 1964.

Village Voice, March 9, 1982.

Thelonious Monk: Straight, No Chaser, directed by Charlotte Zwerin, Warner Bros., 1989. □

Duke of Monmouth and Buccleugh

James Scott, Duke of Monmouth and Buccleugh (1649-1685), was the natural son of Charles II of England. He was an important political pawn in the reigns of Charles II and James II.

Born to Lucy Walters at The Hague, the result of a liaison between her and Prince Charles (later Charles II), James Scott was not officially recognized until 1663, when he was patented to his dukedom. However, for the first 14 years of his life and through the remainder of Charles's life, he was treated with considerable indulgence by his father. He was constantly forgiven by Charles for a variety of peccadilloes, which in his maturity included treason and at least loose commitment to an attempt on the King's life. Further, he was the center of nearly every conspiracy, from 1670 onward, to supplant his uncle, James, Duke of York, as the heir to the throne.

As a general, Monmouth showed some ability, at least in his youth, and the high point in his military career was the suppression of a Scots rebellion in 1679. This same period furnished Monmouth with his moment of highest political importance. During the exclusion crisis, which accompanied the Popish Plot hysteria, he was generally considered to be the 1st Earl of Shaftesbury's candidate for the succession.

So serious was Monmouth's candidacy taken that Charles exiled both him and the Duke of York. Against the royal wishes Monmouth returned to England during the crisis. Charles at this point deprived Monmouth of all his offices and once more forced him out of the country.

After the exclusion crisis passed, Monmouth became involved in further Whig machinations to change the succession. To what degree either Monmouth or any of the leading Whig figures were involved in the details of the actual plot has never been ascertained. Again forgiven,

Monmouth was exiled to Zealand (Sjaelland), where he was received by the Prince of Orange. After the death of Charles II in 1685, Monmouth was contacted by Robert Ferguson, a plotter, and enlisted to lead an expedition to England to overturn the monarchy. The rebellion, which was mounted in the West Country, drew little support and is principally noted for the savagery of the King following its suppression.

Monmouth pleaded on his knees for his life after his capture, but his uncle, James II, refused to extend him pardon. He was executed in the Tower on July 15, 1685. Monmouth was a man of some military ability but, in part because of birth and in part because of the way he was treated and used, he never reached true maturity or any real understanding of his position.

Further Reading

The best biography of Monmouth is still George Roberts, *Life, Progresses and Rebellion of James, Duke of Monmouth* (2 vols., 1844), although it is more an apologia than a thorough examination. Allan Fea, *King Monmouth* (1902), is a rather sensational approach to Monmouth's career as a potential successor. The general histories of the period only touch on Monmouth in passing, although he is the center of considerable attention in Bryan D. G. Little, *The Monmouth Episode* (1956).

Additional Sources

Watson, J. N. P., *Captain-General and rebel chief: the life of James, Duke of Monmouth*, London; Boston: G. Allen & Unwin, 1979.

Wyndham, Violet, *The Protestant Duke: a life of Monmouth*, London: Weidenfeld and Nicolson, 1976. □

Jean Monnet

The French economist Jean Monnet (1888-1979) was primarily responsible for the introduction of national economic planning in post-1945 France and was an outstanding leader in the postwar movement for the unification of Europe.

The son of an important brandy distiller, Jean Monnet was born at Cognac on Nov. 9, 1888. Highly intelligent, ambitious, and well-connected, while he was still a young man in his 20s he was appointed to represent France on the Interallied Maritime Commission during World War I. He participated in the preliminary meetings for the Versailles Conference and in 1919 was appointed deputy secretary general and financial adviser of the League of Nations.

On the death of his father in 1923, Monnet resigned from the League and took over the declining family business. After reorganizing and modernizing it, he became a free-lance economist and financial adviser to foreign governments. In this capacity he advised the Chinese how to manage their railroads, the Austrians how to reorganize their banking system, and an American investment bank how to place its capital overseas. Following the suicide of the Swedish financier Ivar Kreuger in 1932 he supervised the liquidation of Kreuger and Toll, the great international match trust.

In 1939, with war approaching, Monnet was called back to government service. His first task was to negotiate the purchase of warplanes from the United States. Shortly thereafter he became chairman of the Franco-British Economic Coordination Committee in London. There in June 1940 he played a central role in the abortive attempt to fuse the British and French empires. After the fall of France, Monnet was accredited as a diplomat by the government of Winston Churchill. During much of the war he was headquartered in Washington, D.C., as a member of the British Supply Council.

When he arrived in the United States, Monnet was alarmed at America's unreadiness for war. Convinced that the United States must eventually enter the war against the Germans and Japanese, he persuaded American officials to calculate what would have to be produced to win victory. He supervised this project, and when the United States found itself at war after the Japanese attack on Pearl Harbor in December 1941, a plan for America's economic and military mobilization—the famed "Victory Program"—was in hand. The plan accurately provided targets and guidelines for American production during the years 1942-1945. Had it not been for Monnet's alarm and advice, the American war effort would have followed a far more erratic course.

In 1943 Monnet was sent by the American government to Algiers with the task of arranging a reconciliation between Gen. Charles De Gaulle and Gen. Henri Giraud. Returning to France in 1944, he became minister of commerce in the provisional government of De Gaulle, who distrusted Monnet's "antinational" tendencies and his "everlasting efforts to mix the unmixables." In 1945 Monnet proposed that the government should adopt a "plan for the modernization and equipment of the French economy." His recommendations were accepted, and in January 1947 he was appointed commissioner general for planning, a post he held until 1955. Because of the great influence and prestige that accrued to him as he presided over the postwar "economic miracle" of France, Monnet's critics often portray him unflatteringly as the *éminence grise* of the Fourth Republic.

In 1949 Monnet suggested the fusion of the coal and steel industries of Germany and France as a means of preventing any future war between these two traditional rivals. The idea was quickly taken up by the foreign minister, Robert Schuman, and ratified the following year by the parliaments of both countries. From 1952 to 1955 Monnet served as the first president of the High Authority of the newly created European Coal and Steel Community.

In 1955 Monnet founded the Action Committee for the United States of Europe and became its president in 1956. It was eventually disbanded in 1975. He was a driving force behind the organization of the Common Market, which was established by the Treaty of Rome in 1958. For these and other services to the European cause he was awarded the first Robert Schuman Prize by the University of Bonn in 1966. In his later years Monnet lived in active retirement, while remaining an outspoken advocate of further efforts toward European unity. He died in 1979.

Further Reading

There is no biography of Monnet. His role in postwar French and European affairs can be traced in detail, however, in Herbert Luethy, *France against Herself* (trans. 1955), and in Alexander Werth, *France, 1940-1955* (1956); both authors discuss Monnet with undisguised hostility. □

Jacques Monod

Jacques Monod (1910-1976) was a French biologist who discovered messenger RNA, a crucial factor in the functioning of the cell.

Jacques Lucien Monod was born in Paris, France, on February 10, 1910. He spent most of his youth in Cannes, in the south of France, where he went to high school. He developed an interest in biology from his father, who was an avid reader of Darwin. In 1928 he went to Paris to pursue a college education at the Faculte des Sciences of the University of Paris. He received a Bachelor's degree in natural science in 1931, at which time he obtained a fellowship to work with Edouard Chatton at the University of Strasbourg. He was engaged in research on the evolution of life from 1932 to 1934, when he was appointed assistant professor of zoology at the Faculte des Sciences.

In 1936 he obtained a Rockefeller fellowship to study genetics at the California Institute of Technology. Back in France he received his D.Sc. in 1941 from the University of Paris and was appointed laboratory chief at the Pasteur Institute in 1945. Eight years later he became the head of the institute's department of cellular biochemistry. He was appointed full professor at the Faculte des Sciences in 1959 and director general of the Institute Pasteur in 1971. Jacques Monod died of illness in 1976. He had been married to Odette Bruhl, who died in 1972. They left twin sons, Olivier and Philippe.

Monod shared the Nobel Prize in Physiology/Medicine in 1965 with Andre Lwoff and Francois Jacob for his role in elucidating the nature of messenger RNA (ribonucleic acid) and the operon structure of the gene. At the time he did his work the field of genetics was in a state of turmoil. It had been discovered that DNA (deoxyribonucleic acid) was the primary chemical constituent of the hereditary material—"the genetic code." What was not known, however, was the process by which DNA contained in the nucleus could confer the genetic information it carried to cellular regions outside the nucleus (the cytoplasm). How did the DNA "communicate" with enzymes (biological catalysts) and other structures involved in protein synthesis, all of which were located in the cytoplasm? It was this mystery that Monod set about solving.

Jacques Monod (left)

Biologists had known for some time that RNA differed from DNA in that it is present both inside the cell nucleus and in the cytoplasm, whereas DNA is only present in the nucleus. Mahlon Hoagland and Paul Zimmerick of Harvard University had shown that the carrier of amino acids in the cytoplasm during certain chemical reactions was a type of RNA they dubbed "transfer" RNA. Scientists at the Oak Ridge National Laboratories discovered that, after bacteriophage (a virus composed of a core of DNA surrounded by a layer of protein which infects only bacteria) infection, a kind of RNA was formed that was similar to the DNA originally in the bacteriophage. They named this type "DNA-like RNA." While this substance was subsequently isolated in other laboratories, its role in the formation, or synthesis, of protein remained a mystery.

In the mid-1940s Monod found that the synthesis of an enzyme known as-galactosidase could be prevented by infection by bacteriophage without affecting the actual activity of the enzyme. This was a curious discovery, and it prompted him to look for the relationship between-galactosidase and the gene which coded for its production. After several years of research he found that there was a relationship between the activity of the enzyme and protein synthesis.

Monod carried out more experiments in this area in 1958 with Francois Jacob and Arthur Pardee. The results of these experiments and others led Monod and Jacob to propose the ideas of messenger RNA and the operon. Their idea was that, through a process resembling the one in which DNA reproduces itself within the nucleus, a kind of RNA is formed from the DNA template that contains an exact copy of the genetic information contained in the DNA. This RNA was the "DNA-like RNA" observed earlier; Monod and Jacob named it messenger RNA, due to the communicative role it played between structures located on either side of the nuclear membrane. Upon entering the cytoplasm messenger RNA associates itself with ribosomes, which are small granules composed of ribosomal RNA, essential to protein synthesis. The messenger-ribosomal RNA complexes then combine with transfer RNA to initiate protein synthesis.

The operon is composed of a series of structural genes regulated by a single shared gene known as their operator. If the operator is "open," the genes can generate messenger RNA; when it is "closed," there is no messenger RNA. The idea of the operon helped to explain certain important aspects of enzyme synthesis as well as aspects of phage phenomena. The idea of messenger RNA is extremely important because it explains the previously missing link in how DNA initiates protein synthesis, which is a crucial factor in the ability of cells to function.

Jacques Monod received the Louis Rapkine Medal in London in 1958. Two years later he was designated an honorary member of the American Academy of Arts and Sciences. In 1963 he was awarded the Legion d'Honneur, one of the highest distinctions possible for a Frenchman. He possessed a great love for music, almost accepting an invitation offered him by an American orchestra to be their conductor. He was also extremely interested in literature and spoke fluent English.

Further Reading

An in-depth study of Monod's life and work is presented in *Origins of Molecular Biology: a Tribute to Jacques Monod* (1979), edited by André Lwoff and Agnes Ullmann. A short autobiography by Monod is printed in *Nobel Prizes 1965*, issued by the Nobel Foundation. A detailed explanation of some of the scientific phenomena described in this article can be found in *Biological Science* (1968), an introductory biology text. □

James Monroe

James Monroe (1758-1831), fifth president of the United States, a founder of the Jeffersonian Republican party and a major agent in acquiring Louisiana and Florida, authored the celebrated American foreign policy statement, the Monroe Doctrine.

James Monroe was born in Westmoreland County, Va., on April 28, 1758, on his parents' small plantation. He enrolled in William and Mary College in 1774 but left 2 years later, with the beginning of the American Revolution, to enlist as a lieutenant in the 3d Virginia Regiment. He was

seriously wounded in the action at Trenton, and his heroism earned him the rank of major. In 1777 and 1778 he was aide to Gen. William Alexander (Lord Stirling) with the rank of colonel. Unable to obtain a field command because of the excess of officers, he returned to Virginia and entered the lower house of the legislature in 1782. At this time he formed his friendship with Governor Thomas Jefferson, with whom he began to study law.

In 1783 Monroe was elected to the governor's council; the next year he, Jefferson, and Richard Henry Lee were members of the Virginia delegation to the Confederation Congress. Monroe labored to strengthen the central government, but after failing to secure reform through Congress, he endorsed the recommendation that a special convention be held. He was responsible for the structure of territorial government incorporated in the Ordinance of 1787. In 1786 he led the fight against the proposal of John Jay, Secretary for Foreign Affairs, to negotiate a treaty with Spain closing the Mississippi for 20 years in return for commercial concessions. While a member of Congress he married Elizabeth Kortright, one of the most beautiful women of her generation.

Monroe was not a member of the Constitutional Convention, but as a delegate to the Virginia ratifying convention, he opposed ratification unless the Constitution was amended. After the new government was inaugurated and the amending process under way, he ceased his opposition. At this time he shifted his residence to Albemarle County adjacent to Monticello, Thomas Jefferson's home.

U.S. Senator

After a few years of law practice Monroe entered the U.S. Senate in 1790. He emerged as a leading critic of George Washington's administration, which, he felt, was favoring the commercial class and seeking closer ties with Great Britain. He attributed these policies to the influence of Alexander Hamilton. Monroe joined James Madison and Jefferson in organizing the opposition that developed into the Republican party.

Diplomatic Posts

In 1794 Washington appointed Monroe minister to France. Monroe accepted at the urging of the Republicans, who felt that friendship with France was essential for the preservation of republican government in the United States. Arriving in France immediately after the downfall of Robespierre, Monroe was able to ease recent tensions, but he irritated Washington by publicly voicing enthusiasm for the French Revolution. The ratification of Jay's Treaty led to a worsening of relations between France and the United States, and Monroe was recalled in 1796 in a manner casting doubt on his conduct. He published a vindication, asserting that the administration was seeking to join England in the war against France.

As proof that Monroe's recall had not shaken party confidence, the Republicans elected him governor of Virginia in 1799. He proved an able administrator, acting decisively to suppress the attempted slave rebellion (Gabriel's Rebellion) in 1800. In 1803 President Jefferson sent him to France to assist Robert R. Livingston in seeking a port for America at the mouth of the Mississippi River after Spanish authorities had closed the river to American ships. In France, Monroe learned that Napoleon, who had acquired Louisiana from Spain, had offered to sell all Louisiana. Although empowered to buy only a small tract, Monroe and Livingston purchased the whole region. From 1804 to 1807 Monroe was minister to Great Britain.

In 1806 Monroe and William Pinkney concluded a treaty with Great Britain permitting American ships to carry produce of the French colonies to France if American duties were paid. Jefferson and his secretary of state, James Madison, did not consider this arrangement a sufficient compensation for the omission of impressment, which they deemed the sine qua non for any treaty with England. Consequently, it was not submitted to the Senate. Deeply offended, Monroe allowed dissident Republicans in Virginia to run him against Madison in the 1808 presidential election. Madison won, but Monroe garnered enough votes to indicate wide support. In 1811 President Madison, plagued by factional conflicts within his own party and a resurgence of federalism, appointed Monroe secretary of state.

Secretary of State

Monroe's entry into the Cabinet did not change the policy of commercial warfare with Great Britain, but it did strengthen the administration. Enjoying great popularity among the younger Republican congressmen, Monroe worked with them to implement presidential policies. He collaborated with the ''War Hawks'' in drafting the mea-

sures that culminated in the declaration of war against England in 1812. He continued in the State Department during the war, serving simultaneously as secretary of war after John Armstrong retired in disgrace following the burning of the capital.

Presidential Policies

Monroe was named Republican presidential candidate in 1816. The Federalists offered only token opposition. As president, Monroe was an old-fashioned figure, wearing his hair pulled back in a queue and clad in the black clothes of the Revolutionary days. Tall, dignified, and formal in manner, he was admired for his genuine goodness, warmth, and lack of malice. His face was rather plain with massive features, but his widely set gray eyes and his smile reflected benevolence. He did not reach decisions quickly, for he was inclined to reflect carefully on all aspects of a question. His attention to detail gave him a soundness of judgment often lacking in more original minds. His remarkable awareness of the trends of public opinion contributed to his political success. He introduced into the White House a new, more formal note. Although he received congressmen, state party leaders, and citizens freely, he kept diplomats at a distance.

Monroe's Cabinet consisted of John Quincy Adams (State), William H. Crawford (Treasury), John C. Calhoun (War), William Wirt (Attorney General), and Benjamin Crowninshield, followed by Smith Thompson and Samuel L. Southard (Navy). If Monroe's appearance suggested the past, his policies were distinctly contemporary. A moderate nationalist, he supported the Bank of the United States, sought to maintain a large peacetime army, and approved the protective tariff.

Monroe made the restoration of political harmony (which meant, in effect, the elimination of parties) a major goal. To facilitate this, he toured the Union, journeying to New England in 1817 and to the South and West in 1819. The ''Era of Good Feeling'' that followed was short-lived. In 1820 Monroe, who was unopposed, received all the electoral votes but one.

During Monroe's presidency two major domestic crises occurred. The Panic of 1819 resulted from the overexpansion of credit during and after the War of 1812. The abrupt decline in government revenues forced a drastic reduction in the appropriation for the extensive system of coastal fortifications that Monroe had undertaken. The second crisis took place in 1820, following attempts to make the abolition of slavery a condition for the admission of Missouri to statehood. This conflict so divided the nation that many feared the Union would be destroyed. Monroe opposed any restriction on Missouri, but in the interest of harmony he accepted the compromise admitting Missouri as a slave state but excluding slavery from north of 36°30′ in the Louisiana Territory.

Monroe's most important accomplishments were in foreign affairs. In 1819 he capitalized on Andrew Jackson's invasion of Florida to pressure Spain into ceding Florida and establishing the western and northern boundaries of Louisiana. Jackson's seizure of Spanish military posts precipitated a domestic furor. Many felt he should be reprimanded for exceeding his orders. Monroe, who appreciated the advantage Jackson's action gave him in negotiations with Spain, chose a middle course. He restored the posts and acknowledged that though Jackson had violated his orders, he had acted on reasons that seemed sufficient during the campaign.

Monroe Doctrine

In spite of considerable pressure for recognizing the new Latin American states, Monroe held off until 1822, after ratification of the treaty with Spain. His concern that the European powers might intervene in South America to restore Spanish authority seemed justified in 1823, after France suppressed revolution in Spain. Consequently, in 1823 Monroe was inclined to accept Britain's proposal that the United States and Great Britain jointly declare opposition to European interference in Latin America. However, though Jefferson and Madison urged him to accept, Monroe, desiring the United States to pursue an independent course, decided to act unilaterally. In his annual message of Dec. 2, 1823 (subsequently known as the Monroe Doctrine), he expressed disapproval of European intervention and affirmed America's intention of not interfering in the internal affairs of other nations. The message also contained a statement that the Americas were not to be considered open to further European colonization.

Last Years

Monroe's last years in office were harassed by the intraparty battle for the 1824 presidential nomination. His hope for a general rapprochement with England was frustrated when a treaty to suppress the international slave trade was so amended that England withdrew ratification.

Monroe's retirement was plagued by financial difficulties. He obtained some relief when Congress voted him $30,000 in 1826, and a similar sum in 1831. Until his health failed in 1831, he was a member of the board of visitors of the University of Virginia. In 1829, as a member of the Virginia Constitutional Convention, he joined Madison in an unsuccessful attempt to arrange a compromise between Eastern and Western interests. He died in New York City on July 4, 1831.

Further Reading

The Writings of James Monroe was edited by Stanislaus M. Hamilton (7 vols., 1898-1903). Harry Ammon, *James Monroe: The Quest for National Identity* (1971), concentrates on Monroe's political and public life. Useful older biographies are George Morgan, *The Life of James Monroe* (1921), and William P. Cresson, *James Monroe* (1946). Lucius Wilmerding, *James Monroe: Public Claimant* (1960), is an exhaustive study of a minor aspect of Monroe's career.
The presidential elections of 1816 and 1820 are covered in Arthur M. Schlesinger, Jr., *History of American Presidential Elections* (4 vols., 1971). For Monroe's presidency, George Dangerfield's colorful but overdrawn *The Era of Good Feelings* (1952) and his briefer and more restrained *The Awakening of American Nationalism, 1815-1828* (1965) are important works. There is much material on Monroe in Irving

Brant, *James Madison* (6 vols., 1941-1961), and in Dumas Malone, *Jefferson and His Time* (3 vols., 1948-1962). Among the most important works on Monroe's foreign policy are Bradford Perkins, *The Monroe Doctrine* (1927; rev. ed. 1966); Philip C. Brooks, *Diplomacy and the Borderlands: The Adams-Onis Treaty of 1819* (1939); Arthur P. Whitaker, *The United States and the Independence of Latin America, 1800-1830* (1941); Samuel Flagg Bemis, *John Quincy Adams and the Foundations of American Foreign Policy* (1949); and Bradford Perkins, *Castlereagh and Adams: England and the United States, 1812-1823* (1964). □

Marilyn Monroe

The film actress Marilyn Monroe (1926-1962) epitomized the Hollywood sex symbol with her provocative clothes, champagne blond tresses, and breathless, whisper-voiced manner of speaking.

Norma Jean Baker, better known as Marilyn Monroe, experienced a disrupted, loveless childhood that included two years at an orphanage. When Norma Jean, born on June 1, 1926, was seven years old her mother, Gladys (Monroe) Baker Mortenson, was diagnosed as a paranoid schizophrenic and hospitalized. Norma was left to a series of foster homes and the Los Angeles Orphans' Home Society. She opted for an early marriage on June 19, 1942, and her husband, James Dougherty, joined the U.S. Merchant Marine in 1943.

During the war years Norma Jean worked at the Radio Plane Company in Van Nuys, California, but she was soon discovered by photographers. She enrolled in a 3-month modelling course, and in 1946, aware of her considerable charm and the potential it had for a career in films, Norma obtained a divorce. She headed for Hollywood, where Ben Lyon, head of casting at Twentieth Century Fox, arranged a screen test. On August 26, 1946, she signed a $125 a week, one-year contract with the studio. Ben Lyon was the one who suggested a new name for the fledgling actress—Marilyn Monroe.

During her first year at Fox Monroe did not appear in any films, and her contract was not renewed. In the spring of 1948 Columbia Pictures hired her for a small part in *Ladies of the Chorus*. In 1950 John Huston cast her in *Asphalt Jungle*, a tiny part which landed her a role in *All About Eve*. She was now given a seven-year contract with Twentieth Century Fox and appeared in *The Fireball, Let's Make It Legal, Love Nest,* and *As Young as You Feel.*

In 1952, after an extensive publicity campaign, Monroe appeared in *Don't Bother to Knock, Full House, Clash by Night, We're Not Married, Niagara,* and *Monkey Business.* After this the magazine *Photoplay* termed her the "most promising actress," and she was earning top dollars for Twentieth Century Fox.

On January 14, 1954, she married Yankee baseball player Joe Di Maggio. But the pressures created by her

Marilyn Monroe was found dead in her Los Angeles bungalow on August 5, 1962, an empty bottle of sleeping pills by her side.

Further Reading

As a subject of biographies and Hollywood exposé, Marilyn Monroe had no equal. More than 20 books have been written on her brief life. Some, like *Norma Jean* (1969) by Fred Lawrence Guiles, Edwin P. Hoyt's *Marilyn: The Tragic Venus* (1965, 1973), or Robert F. Slatzer's *The Life and Curious Death of Marilyn Monroe* (1974), investigate her life in detail. Others are memoirs: *Marilyn Monroe: Confidential* (1979) by Lena Pepitone and William Stadiem is one such volume. Norman Mailer's *Marilyn* (1973) includes photographs, and *The Films of Marilyn Monroe* (1964) by Michael Conway and Mark Ricci details her many movies and shows stills as well as review excerpts. A careful overall biography is *Goddess* (1985) by Anthony Summers. Gloria Steinem's *Marilyn* (1986) is an insightful account of a tragic life. □

Luc Montagnier

Luc Montagnier (born 1932), a prominent virologist whose contributions in understanding the nature of viruses lead to a significant advance in cancer research. Montagnier is also known for discovering the HIV virus that causes AIDS.

Luc Montagnier of the Institut Pasteur in Paris has devoted his career to the study of viruses. He is perhaps best known for his 1983 discovery of the human immunodeficiency virus (HIV), which has been identified as the cause of acquired immunodeficiency syndrome (AIDS) . However, in the twenty years before the onset of the AIDS epidemic, Montagnier made many significant discoveries concerning the nature of viruses. He made major contributions to the understanding of how viruses can alter the genetic information of host organisms, and significantly advanced cancer research. His investigation of interferon, one of the body's defenses against viruses, also opened avenues for medical cures for viral diseases. Montagnier's ongoing research focuses on the search for an AIDS vaccine or cure.

Montagnier was born in Chabris (near Tours), France, the only child of Antoine Montagnier and Marianne Rousselet. He became interested in science in his early childhood through his father, an accountant by profession, who carried out experiments on Sundays in a makeshift laboratory in the basement of the family home. At age fourteen, Montagnier himself conducted nitroglycerine experiments in the basement laboratory. His desire to contribute to medical knowledge was also kindled by his grandfather's long illness and death from colon cancer.

Montagnier attended the Collège de Châtellerault, and then the University of Poitiers, where he received the equivalent of a bachelor's degree in the natural sciences in 1953. Continuing his studies at Poitiers and then at the University

billing as a screen sex symbol caused the marriage to founder, and the couple divorced on October 27, 1954.

Continually cast as a dumb blond, Monroe made *Seven Year Itch* in 1954. Growing weary of the stereotyping, she broke her contract with Fox and moved to New York City. There she studied at the Actors Studio with Lee and Paula Strasberg. Gloria Steinem recalls a conversation with Monroe during that time in which Monroe referred to her own opinion of her abilities compared to a group of notables at the Actors Studio. "I admire all these people so much. I'm just not good enough."

In 1955 she formed her own studio, Marilyn Monroe Productions, and re-negotiated a contract with Twentieth Century Fox. She appeared in *Bus Stop* in 1956 and married playwright Arthur Miller on July 1, 1956.

Critics described Monroe in the film *The Prince and the Showgirl,* produced by her own company, as "a sparkling light comedienne." Monroe won the Italian David di Donatello award for "best foreign actress of 1958," and in 1959 she appeared in *Some Like It Hot*. In 1961 she starred in *The Misfits,* for which Arthur Miller did the screenplay.

The couple was divorced on January 24, 1961, and later that year Monroe entered a New York psychiatric clinic. After her brief hospitalization there she returned to the Fox studio to work on a film, but her erratic behavior betrayed severe emotional disturbance, and the studio discharged her in June 1962.

of Paris, he received his *licence ès sciences* in 1955. As an assistant to the science faculty at Paris, he taught physiology at the Sorbonne and in 1960 qualified there for his doctorate in medicine. He was appointed a researcher at the Centre National de la Recherche Scientifique (C.N.R.S.) in 1960, but then went to London for three and a half years to do research at the Medical Research Council at Carshalton.

Viruses are agents which consist of genetic material surrounded by a protective protein shell. They are completely dependent on the cells of a host animal or plant to multiply, a process which begins with the shedding of their own protein shell. The virus research group at Carshalton was investigating ribonucleic acid (RNA), a form of nucleic acid that normally is involved in taking genetic information from deoxyribonucleic acid (DNA) (the main carrier of genetic information) and translating it into proteins. Montagnier and F. K. Sanders, investigating viral RNA (a virus that carries its genetic material in RNA rather than DNA), discovered a double-stranded RNA virus that had been made by the replication of a single-stranded RNA. The double-stranded RNA could transfer its genetic information to DNA, allowing the virus to encode itself in the genetic make-up of the host organism. This discovery represented a significant advance in knowledge concerning viruses.

From 1963 to 1965, Montagnier did research at the Institute of Virology in Glasgow, Scotland. Working with Ian MacPherson , he discovered in 1964 that agar, a gelatinous extractive of a red alga, was an excellent substance for culturing cancer cells. Their technique became standard in laboratories investigating oncogenes (genes that have the potential to make normal cells turn cancerous) and cell transformations. Montagnier himself used the new technique to look for cancer-causing viruses in humans after his return to France in 1965.

From 1965 to 1972, Montagnier worked as laboratory director of the Institut de Radium (later called Institut Curie) at Orsay. In 1972, he founded and became director of the viral oncology unit of the Institut Pasteur. Motivated by his findings at Carshalton and the belief that some cancers are caused by viruses, Montagnier's basic research interest during those years was in retroviruses as a potential cause of cancer. Retroviruses possess an enzyme called reverse transcriptase. Montagnier established that reverse transcriptase translates the genetic instructions of the virus from the viral (RNA) form to DNA, allowing the genes of the virus to become permanently established in the cells of the host organism. Once established, the virus can begin to multiply, but it can do so only by multiplying cells of the host organism, forming malignant tumors. In addition, collaborating with Edward De Mayer and Jacqueline De Mayer , Montagnier isolated the messenger RNA of interferon, the cell's first defense against a virus. Ultimately, this research allowed the cloning of interferon genes in a quantity sufficient for research. However, despite widespread hopes for interferon as a broadly effective anti-cancer drug, it was initially found to be effective in only a few rare kinds of malignancies.

AIDS (acquired immunodeficiency syndrome), a tragic epidemic that emerged in the early 1980s, was first ade-

quately characterized around 1982. Its chief feature is that it disables the immune system by which the body defends itself against numerous diseases. It is eventually fatal. By 1993, more than three million people had developed full-blown AIDS. Montagnier believed that a retrovirus might be responsible for AIDS. Researchers had noted that one pre-AIDS condition involved a persistent enlargement of the lymph nodes, called lymphadenopathy. Obtaining some tissue culture from the lymph nodes of an infected patient in 1983, Montagnier and two colleagues, Françoise Barré-Sinoussi and Jean-Claude Chermann, searched for and found reverse transcriptase, which constitutes evidence of a retrovirus. They isolated a virus they called LAV (lymphadenopathy-associated virus). Later, by international agreement, it was renamed HIV, human immunodeficiency virus. After the virus had been isolated, it was possible to develop a test for antibodies that had developed against it—the HIV test. Montagnier and his group also discovered that HIV attacks T4 cells which are crucial in the immune system. A second similar but not identical HIV virus called HIV–2 was discovered by Montagnier and colleagues in April 1986.

A controversy developed over the patent on the HIV test in the mid–1980s. Robert C. Gallo of the National Cancer Institute in Bethesda, Maryland, announced his own discovery of the HIV virus in April 1984 and received the patent on the test. The Institut Pasteur claimed the patent (and the profits) on the basis of Montagnier's earlier discovery of HIV. Despite the controversy, Montagnier continued research and attended numerous scientific meetings with Gallo to share information. Intense mediation efforts by Jonas Salk (the scientist who developed the first polio vaccine) led to an international agreement signed by the scientists and their respective countries in 1987. Montagnier and Gallo agreed to be recognized as codiscoverers of the virus, and the two governments agreed that the profits of the HIV test be shared (most going to a foundation for AIDS research).

The scientific dispute continued to resurface, however. Most HIV viruses from different patients differ by six to twenty percent because of the remarkable ability of the virus to mutate. However, Gallo's virus was less than two percent different from Montagnier's, leading to the suspicion that both viruses were from the same source. The laboratories had exchanged samples in the early 1980s, which strengthened the suspicion. Charges of scientific misconduct on Gallo's part led to an investigation by the National Institutes of Health in 1991, which initially cleared Gallo. In 1992 the investigation was reviewed by the newly created Office of Research Integrity. The ORI report, issued in March of 1993, confirmed that Gallo had in fact "discovered" the virus sent to him by Montagnier. Whether or not Gallo had been aware of this fact in 1983 could not be established, but it was found that he had been guilty of misrepresentations in reporting his research and that his supervision of his research lab had been desultory. The Institut Pasteur immediately revived its claim to the exclusive right to the patent on the HIV test. Gallo objected to the decision by the ORI, however, and took his case before an appeals board at the Department of Health and Human Services. The board in

December of 1993 cleared Gallo of all charges, and the ORI subsequently withdrew their charges for lack of proof.

Montagnier's continuing work includes investigation of the envelope proteins of the virus that link it to the T-cell . He is also extensively involved in research of possible drugs to combat AIDS. In 1990 Montagnier hypothesized that a second organism, called a mycoplasma, must be present with the HIV virus for the latter to become deadly. This suggestion, which has proved controversial among most AIDS researchers, is the subject of ongoing research.

Montagnier also wrote *The Virus and Man* (Odile Jacob, 1994). This book explains how AIDS has transformed not only his life, but also his scientific orientation. He further explains how AIDS research can help scientists to understand and provide better treatment for other affections.

Montagnier married Dorothea Ackerman in 1961. They have three children, Jean-Luc, Anne-Marie, and Francine. He has described himself as an aggressive researcher who spends much time either in the laboratory or traveling to scientific meetings. He enjoys swimming and classical music, and loves to play the piano, especially Mozart sonatas. □

Michel Eyquem de Montaigne

The French author Michel Eyquem de Montaigne (1533-1592) created a new literary genre, the essay, in which he used self-portrayal as a mirror of humanity in general.

Michel Eyquem de Montaigne was born on Feb. 23, 1533, at the family estate called Montaigne in Périgord near Bordeaux. His father, Pierre Eyquem, was a Bordeaux merchant and municipal official whose grandfather was the first nobleman of the line. His mother, Antoinette de Louppes (Lopez), was descended from a line of Spanish Jews, the Marranos, long converted to Catholicism. Michel, their third son, was privately tutored and spoke only Latin until the age of 6. From 1539 until 1546 he studied at the Collège de Guyenne, in Bordeaux, where the Scottish humanist George Buchanan was one of his teachers, as was the less-known French poet and scholar Marc Antoine Muret. Very little is known of Montaigne's life from age 13 to 24, but he may have spent some time in Paris, probably studied law in Toulouse, and certainly indulged in the pleasures of youth.

In 1557 Montaigne obtained the position of councilor in the Bordeaux Parlement, and it was there that he met his closest friend and strongest influence, Étienne de la Boétie. La Boétie and Montaigne shared many interests, especially in classical antiquity, but this friendship was ended by La Boétie's death from dysentery in August 1563. Montaigne was with him through the 9 days of his illness. The loss of his friend was a serious emotional blow that Montaigne later described in his essay "On Friendship." In 1571 Montaigne published his friend's collected works.

Two years after La Boétie's death, after a number of diversionary affairs, Montaigne married Françoise de la Chassaigne, daughter of a cocouncilor in the Bordeaux Parlement. She bore him six daughters, of whom only one survived to adulthood. The marriage was apparently amiable but sometimes cool—Montaigne believed that marriage was of a somewhat lower order than friendship.

In 1568 the elder Montaigne died, thus making Michel lord of Montaigne. Before his death, Pierre Eyquem had persuaded his son to translate into French the *Book of Creatures or Natural Theology* by the 15th-century Spanish theologian Raymond Sebond. The work was an apologia for the Christian religion based on proofs from the natural world. The translation was published early in 1569 and gave clear indication of Montaigne's ability both as translator and as author in his own right. From his work on this translation Montaigne later developed the longest of his many essays, "The Apology for Raymond Sebond." In this pivotal essay, Montaigne presented his skeptical philosophy of doubt, attacked human knowledge as presumptuous and arrogant, and suggested that self-knowledge could result only from awareness of ignorance.

In April 1570 Montaigne resigned from the Bordeaux Parlement, sold his position to a friend, and as lord of Montaigne formally retired to his country estate, his horses, and his beautiful and isolated third-floor library. He carefully recorded his retirement on his thirty-eighth birthday and soon began work on his *Essais.* Ten years later (1580) the first edition, containing books I and II, was published in Bordeaux.

Late in 1580 Montaigne began a 15-month trip through Germany, Switzerland, Austria, and Italy. He visited many mineral baths and watering spas in hopes of finding relief from a chronic kidney stone condition. His journal of these travels, though not intended for publication, was published in 1774. Toward the end of his trip Montaigne learned of his election in August 1580 to the mayoralty of Bordeaux, an office in which he then spent two 2-year terms. By all accounts he served the city with conscientious distinction during a troubled period, although public service was clearly not his aspiration at that time. He himself obliquely defended his regime in the essay "Of Husbanding Your Will."

At the end of his term of office Montaigne spent the best part of a year revising the first two books of the *Essais* and preparing book III for inclusion in the 1588 Paris edition, the fifth edition of the work. In 1586 both war and plague reached his district, and he fled with his household in search of peace and healthier air, receiving at best reluctant hospitality from his neighboring squires. When he returned 6 months later, he found the castle pillaged but still habitable.

Montaigne's last years were brightened by his friendship and correspondence with his so-called adoptive daughter, Marie de Gournay (1565-1645), an ardent young admirer who edited the expanded 1595 edition of his works (mainly from annotations made by Montaigne) and, in its preface, defended his memory to posterity. (It was from her edition that John Florio produced the 1603 English-language edition, which was a source for Shakespeare's *Tempest* and other playwrights' work.)

After 2 years of illness and decline Montaigne died peacefully in his bed while hearing Mass on Sept. 13, 1592. He died a loyal Catholic, but he was always tolerant of other religious views.

The "Essais"

It is difficult if not impossible to summarize the ideas of Montaigne's *Essais.* He was not a systematic thinker and defied all attempts to be pinned down to any single point of view. He preferred to show the randomness of his own thought as representative of the self-contradiction to which all men are prone. His characteristic motto was "Que sais-je?" ("What do I know?") He was skeptical about the power of human reason, yet argued that each man must first know himself in order to live happily. The *Essais* constitute Montaigne's own attempt at self-knowledge and self-portrayal—in effect, they are autobiography. Since he argued that "each man bears the complete stamp of the human condition" ("chaque homme porte la forme entière de l'humaine condition"), these autobiographical exercises can also be seen as portraits of mankind in all its diversity. Although he constantly attacked man's presumption, arrogance, and pride, he nonetheless held the highest view of the dignity of man, in keeping with the dignity of nature.

As a skeptic, Montaigne opposed intolerance and fanaticism, believing truth never to be one-sided. He champ.

pioned individual freedom but held that even repressive laws should be obeyed. He feared violence and anarchy and was suspicious of any radical proposals that might jeopardize the existing order in hopes of childish panaceas. Acceptance and detachment were for him the keys to happiness. In both the form and content of his *Essais,* Montaigne achieved a remarkable combination of inner tranquility and detachment, together with the independence and freedom of an unfettered mind.

Further Reading

Donald M. Frame wrote the best biography, *Montaigne* (1965), and has to his credit the excellent translation *The Complete Works of Montaigne: Essays, Travel Journal, Letters* (1957). His *Montaigne's Discovery of Man: The Humanization of a Humanist* (1955) is a valuable study of Montaigne's humanism, and he also published *Montaigne's Essais: A Study* (1969). Frieda S. Brown, *Religious and Political Conservatism in the Essais of Montaigne* (1963), is a useful study of his political ideas. For a scholarly analysis of Montaigne's philosophical skepticism see Craig B. Brush, *Montaigne and Bayle: Variations on the Theme of Skepticism* (1966).

Additional Sources

Frame, Donald Murdoch, *Montaigne: a biography,* San Francisco: North Point Press, 1984, 1965.

Leschemelle, Pierre, *Montaigne, or, The anguished soul,* New York: P. Lang, 1994.

Lowndes, M. E. (Mary E.), *Michel de Montaigne: a biographical study,* Philadelphia: R. West, 1978. □

Eugenio Montale

The Italian poet and critic Eugenio Montale (1896-1981) was one of the major representatives of Italian hermetic poetry.

Eugenio Montale was born on Oct. 12, 1896, at Genoa, and his youth was spent between that city and a property his family had in southern Liguria. He studied literature at the University of Genoa and took voice lessons with the baritone Sivori, but he turned exclusively to literary pursuits after World War I, in which he had served as an infantry officer. In 1927 he moved to Florence to work for a publishing house. There he was director of the Gabinetto Vieusseux from 1929 to 1938, when he was removed from the post because of his indifference to the Fascist regime. Throughout this time Montale contributed regularly to literary journals, such as *Solaria,* and, being also a perceptive critic, he was the first to point out, in 1925, Italo Svevo's importance as a writer. In 1928 he became head of the Gabinetto Vieusseux Library in Florence and was let go in 1938 due to his anti-Fascist views. He then spent a decade translating English and American literary works into Italian. In 1948 he became editor of a newspaper in Milan.

Although it has been suggested that the closed and difficult style of hermetic poetry was a direct result of "inner emigration" during fascism, there is no doubt that artistic tenets played a dominant role in shaping it. Montale, who is one of the virtuosos of its contrived technique of obscuration, found in the resulting bare and arid style an apt vehicle for his pessimistic views of life that only in his later work show signs of moderation.

The subject of Montale's poetry is the human condition, considered by and in itself, not this or that historical event. To treat such events would mean for Montale to mistake the essentials for their transitory aspects. Thus, his is the poetry of a man who extricates himself from the accidentals of human existence to perceive its essence. This notion no doubt contributed considerably to the "abstract" and intellectual aspect of his poetry.

In Montale's first collection of verse, *Ossi di seppia* (1925), his desolate and pessimistic picture of life finds its pendant in the austere and arid Ligurian landscape, which forms the backdrop of many of his poems. Although there seems to be no hope of escaping the futility of human existence, in some pieces, such as *In limine,* there appears already a tendency to see a way out of the existential dilemma, if only for others.

The second collection, *Occasioni* (1939), with its terse style and disconnected imagery, represents a further step in the application of hermetic tenets almost beyond any possible understanding; yet some of its poems belong to the best that were written in Italy in the 20th century. *Finisterre* (1943) is a reflective and removed reckoning with World War II. In *La bufera e altro* (1956) there is a noticeable

easing of tension and a more balanced relation between the linguistic means and the message they carry. *Satura* (1971) contains 118 poems written between 1962 and 1970, more than two-thirds of them unpublished until then. The lyrical mode of this collection definitely indicates a departure from Montale's earlier abstraction and a turn toward a more open statement without reticence; it also gives the reader an insight into the poet's own personal sphere.

Montale was awarded the Nobel Prize for literature in 1975. He continued to write up until his death at his home in Milan on September 12, 1981.

Further Reading

The major studies of Montale in English are Arshi Pipa, *Montale and Dante* (1968), and Joseph Cary, *Three Modern Italian Poets: Saba, Ungaretti, Montale* (1969). Also useful are the introductory material to Carlo L. Golino, ed., *Contemporary Italian Poetry: An Anthology* (1962); the sections on Montale in Sergio Pacifici, *A Guide to Contemporary Italian Literature: From Futurism to Neorealism* (1962); and Eugenio Donadoni, *A History of Italian Literature* (2 vols., trans. 1969). □

Comte de Montalembert

The French political writer Charles Forbes, Comte de Montalembert (1810-1870), was a Roman Catholic layman who wrote and spoke widely in favor of democratic government and vigorously opposed the union of church and state.

C harles de Montalembert was born in London on April 15, 1810, while his father, who had left France after the Revolution, was serving in the English army. His father returned to France in 1814, when the monarchy was restored, and was raised to the peerage, but Charles stayed behind in the care of his Protestant English grandfather. From this independent and outspoken gentleman Charles absorbed a religious spirit and a zest for learning that he retained for the rest of his life.

Charles was a liberal and could not support the government of Louis Philippe on religious grounds. As a student in France in the 1820s, he began to see more clearly that the Church should be free and on the side of the people rather than under the control of the kings. Much of France's trouble, he felt, came from the close association of the Roman Catholic Church with the French government. In 1830 he collaborated with Félicité de Lamennais, a liberal priest, and Jean Baptiste Lacordaire, an articulate preacher, in publishing a journal called *L'Avenir,* dedicated to "God and Liberty." The journal argued that the Church ought to cut itself off from the government's support. The opposition to *L'Avenir* from conservative French bishops brought Montalembert, Lamennais, and Lacordaire to Rome in 1831 to argue their case before Pope Gregory XVI—un-successfully, as it turned out. Most of *L'Avenir's* doctrines were condemned in two encyclicals by the Pope: *Mirari vos*

(1832) and *Singulari vobis* (1834). Montalembert sadly submitted.

Montalembert continued to speak and write, however, and he began a newspaper, *Correspondant,* to provide a public forum for his ideas, which were a mixture of Catholic belief and liberal politics. Over the years he consistently taught that the Church should live without special privileges and that it should support democratic movements. He said that slavery should be outlawed and was opposed to the French colonial empire. He also worked hard to establish Catholic schools so that the government would not have a monopoly on education. In 1837 Montalembert was elected to the French Parliament; after the Revolution of 1848 he sat in the Chamber of Deputies; and in 1851 he was honored by being named to the French Academy. He was recognized as a formidable opponent of the empire.

An international congress in Malines, Belgium, in 1863 heard Montalembert's memorable speech calling for Catholics to embrace democracy rather than fear it. But his hopes for his Church were crushed a year later, when Pope Pius IX declared in his *Syllabus of Errors* that it was wrong to say the Pope should "reconcile himself . . . with progress, liberalism, and modern civilization." Montalembert died in Paris on March 13, 1870.

Further Reading

An account by Montalembert's contemporary Margaret Oliphant, *Memoir of Count de Montalembert* (1872), is a somewhat dated but interesting personal study. The best book in English on Montalembert is James C. Finlay, *The Liberal*

Who Failed (1968). Charles S. Phillips, *The Church in France, 1848-1907: A Study in Revival* (1936), contains a helpful assessment of the contributions of Montalembert and his associates. □

Juan María Montalvo

Juan María Montalvo (1832-1889) was an Ecuadorian writer. Perhaps the most outstanding polemicist of Hispanic literature, he had a wide appeal in Latin America for his denunciation of dictatorship.

Juan Montalvo was born on April 13, 1832, in the provincial town of Ambato. His grandfather was a Spanish retail merchant, and his father, Marcos, followed the same trade. His mother, Josefa Fiallos, owned some land. Two elder brothers of Juan moved to Quito and came to occupy high positions in education and government.

Montalvo studied in Quito (1846-1854) but dropped out of the university without earning a degree. The connections of his brothers with Gen. José María Urbina, a Liberal who dominated Ecuadorian politics in the 1850s, resulted in Montalvo's appointment to a minor diplomatic post in Rome (1857). The following year he was promoted to secretary of the Ecuadorian legation in Paris. He returned to Ecuador in 1860. By then the Liberals had been ousted by the Conservatives, led by Gabriel García Moreno, and Montalvo was excluded from public employment.

In January 1866 Montalvo published in Quito the first number of a pamphlet series against García Moreno—then out of power—under the title of *El cosmopolita.* Three years later, on the dictator's return to the presidency, Montalvo fled to Colombia, settling in Ipiales.

Montalvo spent his years in exile, in the words of one of his biographers, "in exasperating moral and economic conditions." He received economic support from another exiled Liberal, living then in Panama, Eloy Alfaro. During this period Montalvo's writing consisted mostly of vitriolic and defamatory attacks on García Moreno. When the latter decided to stay as president for a third term, Montalvo wrote *La dictadura perpetua,* which Alfaro published in Panama (1874). The pamphlet circulated in Ecuador. Though it did not produce the hoped-for revolution, on Aug. 6, 1875, a Colombian former mercenary, backed up by a small group of young drifters who had read *La dictadura,* hacked García Moreno to death with a machete. Although the assassin had acted for personal reasons, on hearing of the President's death, Montalvo exclaimed jubilantly: "My pen killed him!"

Montalvo returned to Quito in May 1876 and started to publish *El regenerador,* a pamphlet series in which he attacked President Antonio Borrero's government. By September he was in Guayaquil, backing a Liberal military revolt led by Gen. Urbina and Gen. Ignacio Veintemilla. The latter, a fellow exile of 1869, soon sent Montalvo to Panama

America: From the Beginnings to the Present (1955; 2d rev. ed. 1968). □

for his opposition to the general's dictatorial ambitions. He was allowed to return after 4 months, thanks to his attacks against Borrero, which also assured his appointment as deputy to the constitutional convention of 1878. But in June he turned his guns on President Veintemilla, deploring that a great man like García Moreno should have such a despicable successor. Before long, Montalvo was back in Ipiales, where he wrote his *Catilinarias*. This attack on Veintemilla is Montalvo's outstanding polemical work.

In 1881 Montalvo returned to Paris. He stayed there for the remainder of his life, except for a trip in 1883 to Spain, where he was very well received by distinguished figures of Spanish letters and politics. This last period was marked by the publication of his best works: *Siete tratados* and *Capítulos que se le olvidaron a Cervantes*. He died on Jan. 17, 1889.

Montalvo's fame rested on the stylistic qualities of his writing—much in vogue until the beginning of the 20th century—and on their political content, for which he was hailed by liberals all over Hispanic America. His name is still venerated in Ecuador, even though his writing has much declined in its appeal because of changes in stylistic preferences and in political outlook.

Further Reading

There are discussions of Montalvo's life and work in Enrique Anderson-Imbert, *Spanish-American Literature: A History* (1954; trans. 1963; 2d ed., 2 vols., 1969), and German Arciniegas, *Latin America: A Cultural History* (1965; trans. 1967). See also Hubert Clinton Herring, *A History of Latin

Joe Montana

Joe Montana (born 1956) has earned a reputation as one of the top quarterbacks in professional football, first rising to fame in the 1980s.

Seventh String

Perhaps it was his only moment of indecision in a career devoted to imposing his will on circumstance. As a high-school senior in Monongahela, Pennsylvania, Joe Montana nearly accepted a basketball scholarship at North Carolina State University. But western Pennsylvania is blue-collar football country, the birthplace of legendary quarterbacks Johnny Lujack, George Blanda, John Unitas, and Joe Namath, and such a tradition ultimately swayed Ringgold High's star quarterback to attend Notre Dame on a football scholarship. However, as a homesick freshman Montana may have had lingering doubts about his decision-making skills when he calculated that he was the Fighting Irish's seventh-string quarterback—barely. Early in his college career Montana made the most of his infrequent appearances: as a sophomore he twice led Notre Dame back from fourth-quarter deficits for improbable wins, including a game against Air Force in which he came off the bench with just twelve minutes remaining to erase the Falcons' twenty-point lead. He inspired two more miraculous rallies as a junior and still two more as a senior. These exploits—what Rick Reilly called the "impossible, get-serious, did-you-hear-what-happened-after-we-left comeback"—quickly became Montana's signature. Still, Montana did not become Notre Dame's first-string quarterback until his senior year; in his very last game, the 1979 Cotton Bowl against Houston, he engineered a rescue of operatic proportions. With his team down 34-12 with only 7:37 left on the clock and suffering from hypothermia so disabling that the trainer spent halftime pumping him full of bouillon to raise his body temperature, Montana completed seven of his last eight passes to win the game 35-34. The game's final points came on a touchdown pass on fourth down with two seconds left—in an ice storm. Yet despite his almost supernatural football instincts and his documented savvy under pressure, Montana was not a highly touted prospect when he entered the 1979 NFL draft.

God or Something

Eighty-one players were selected before the San Francisco 49ers drafted Montana late in the third round. New 49ers coach Bill Walsh ignored the negative scouting reports on his rookie signal caller ("average" arm strength, no touch), and envisioned Montana as the orchestrator of his complex ball-control passing attack: "Joe's . . . . an excellent spontaneous thinker, a keen-witted athlete with a unique field of vision. And he will not choke. Or rather, if he

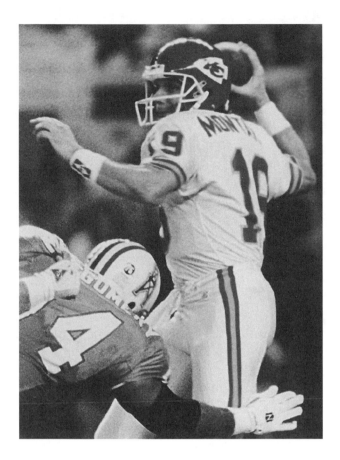

game's Most Valuable Player (MVP). It was to become a familiar scenario during the decade. The 49ers would win four titles by 1990, including consecutive Super Bowls in 1989 and 1990, and Montana was awarded the MVP trophy on three occasions (his favorite receiver, Jerry Rice, won the award in 1989). Not only did Montana complete almost 70 percent of his passes in those four Super Bowl victories—outdueling the likes of Dan Marino, John Elway, and Boomer Esiason in the those title games—but he never threw an interception in 122 attempts. He drove the 49ers 92 yards in the waning moments of Super Bowl XXIII to beat Cincinnati again, 20-16, finishing the Bengals off with a 10-yard touchdown pass to receiver John Taylor with 34 seconds left. After the game Montana described the final drive and hinted that his mythic composure was susceptible to all-too-human frailties: "It's a blur. I hyperventilated to the point of almost blacking out . . . . I was yelling so loudly in the huddle that I couldn't breathe. Things got blurrier and blurrier." Montana's performance in the clutch nevertheless left teammates grasping for comparisons; "He's like Lazarus," claimed 49er cornerback Tim McKyer. "You roll back the stone, Joe limps out—and throws for 300 yards." In Super Bowl XXIV Montana came back with an even more impressive performance, shredding the Denver Broncos' defense with five touchdown passes in a 55-10 rout. When he retired in 1995 Montana held NFL playoff records for completions, yards, and touchdowns, as well as single-season (1989) and career records for passing efficiency.

Intangibles

But statistics do not adequately measure Joe Montana's worth as a quarterback. Watching a young Montana practice in the early 1980s, coach Bill Walsh commented, "there was something hypnotic about him. That look when he was dropping back; he was poetic in his movements, almost sensuous, everything so fluid, so much under control." At six feet two inches and rather fragile, Montana was never physically imposing, and his career was twice suspended by major surgery (a back operation in 1986 to widen his spinal canal and elbow surgery that forced him to miss all of the 1992 season). He never appeared to be a brash and demonstrative leader, and by his own account he struggled to articulate how he seemed to perform miracles so effortlessly. Joe Montana simply had the ability to impose a quiet order on a raw and disorderly game. With his leadership there was always time enough.

Further Reading

Appleman, Marc, *Joe Montana* (1991).
Montana, Joe and Richard Weiner, *Joe Montana's Art and Magic of Quarterbacking* (1997).
Montana, Joe, *Montana* (1995).
Montana, Joe and Alan Steinberg, *Cool Under Fire* (1990).
Telander, Rick, "Joe Montana," *Sports Illustrated,* 81 (19 September 1994): 106-107;
Weiner, Paul, *Joe Montana*: Football Legends (1995).
Zimmerman, Paul, "Born to Be a Quarterback (Part I of II)," *Sports Illustrated,* 73 (6 August 1990): 62-76;
Zimmerman, Paul, "The Ultimate Winner (Part II of II)," *Sports Illustrated,* 73 (13 August 1990): 72-88. □

ever does, you'll know that everyone else has come apart first." Walsh's "system" depended on a nimble quarterback with an accurate arm who could adjust quickly to each defensive sequence as it unfolded. By the 1981 season Montana and the 49ers had become a sophisticated and virtually unstoppable offensive machine, but they met an old nemesis in the National Football Conference championship game, the Dallas Cowboys. The Cowboys had eliminated the 49ers from their last three playoff appearances, and after six San Francisco turnovers had led to a 6-point Dallas lead, it looked as if history would repeat itself. But Montana drove the 49ers 89 yards in the game's final minutes, and with 51 seconds left connected with flanker Dwight Clark for the winning touchdown on what was one of the most heralded plays of the decade. Known simply as "The Catch," the play began with Montana scrambling desperately to his right with three Cowboys in pursuit. Just before he was about to be thrown for a loss, Montana, throwing off his back foot, lofted a pass that appeared to be uncatchable. He later said he never saw Clark get open but knew his receiver would be sprinting across the back of the endzone as a safety valve on the play. Clark went high to catch the pass, landing just inside the boundary: afterward he marveled at the feat, "It was over my head. I thought, 'Oh, oh, I can't go that high.' Something got me up there. It must have been God or something."

Super Bowl Hero

San Francisco went on to win Super Bowl XVI over the Cincinnati Bengals 26-21, and Montana was named the

Montanus

The early Christian prophet Montanus (active 2nd century) was the leader of a group of people who were convinced that their ability to speak in mysterious languages was a gift of the Holy Spirit. Montanism was later condemned as a heresy.

Very little is known about the life of Montanus He was probably an adult convert to Christianity, enthusiastic about his newly found salvation. About 156 he made a strong impression on the town of Ardabau in Asia Minor when he was overcome by a seizure of some kind and began speaking rapidly and forcefully about religion. He said that he was under the influence of the Holy Spirit and that he was prophesying. This happened a number of times over a period of months. Sometimes speaking clearly, sometimes babbling in what seemed to be foreign tongues, he succeeded in convincing several other men and women that the Holy Spirit was really present, to the point that they also would fall into a trance and prophesy. The group began to attract other followers, especially when the similarity between Montanus's actions and some of the events described in the Bible was pointed out. Many people saw his followers as an elite Christian group calling the rest of mankind to a new spirit of religious fervor. They seemed to be inspired.

The movement spread rapidly throughout Asia Minor. Wherever Montanus and his followers went, they stirred the people into a state of ecstatic madness. Crowds screamed with joy, whirling, dancing, singing, convinced that the Holy Spirit was being poured into them. In moments of relative calm Montanus preached. He urged the people to pray and fast and punish themselves. The human body was troublesome, he said. Sex was evil, and marriage should be no more than tolerated. Christians must return to the original fervor of biblical times and give up worldly pleasures. The Holy Spirit, he said, was once again tangibly present in the world, acting through Montanus and his followers.

At one point Montanus preached that the world was about to come to an end. The heavenly Jerusalem, he declared, was soon to come down and be established on a plain between two towns in nearby Phrygia. From all over Asia Minor the followers of Montanus streamed to the appointed place. They were disappointed when the end of the world did not come about as Montanus had predicted. They kept faith in their prophet, however, and his movement continued to spread. It swept through North Africa and Greece, despite the excommunication imposed on its followers by a bishop in Phrygia. Two centuries later it died out, disappearing as quickly as it had arisen.

Further Reading

A helpful analysis of Montanism's basic religious content is in Ronald A. Knox's articulate study, *Enthusiasm* (1950). Henry B. Swete, *The Holy Spirit in the Ancient Church* (1912), describes some of the controversies stirred up by the Montanists. A useful discussion of Montanus and Montanism is in Philip

Carrington, *The Early Christian Church* (2 vols., 1957). See also Newman C. Eberhardt, *A Summary of Catholic History* (2 vols., 1961-1962). ☐

Marquis de Montcalm de Saint-Véran

The French general Louis Joseph, Marquis de Montcalm de Saint-Véran (1712-1759), commanded the French troops in Canada during the French and Indian War and died a hero on the battlefield of Quebec.

Born in Nîmes on Feb. 29, 1712, Louis Joseph Montcalm received a solid classical education. He entered the army at the age of 15 and fought bravely during the War of the Polish Succession. He reached the rank of colonel in the War of the Austrian Succession, and at the battle at Piacenza in 1746 he distinguished himself, was wounded five times, and was taken prisoner. In the following year he became a brigadier general.

Ten years later, as a major general, Montcalm was sent to be commander of the regular military forces in Canada. Specifically subordinated to the civilian governor, the Marquis de Vaudreuil, Montcalm was hampered by a lack of cooperation on the part of the civil authorities. Personal animosity and dissension between Montcalm and Vaudreuil marked their relationship. The dishonesty of certain members of the provincial administration, a general shortage of food throughout New France, and governmental apathy at home also handicapped Montcalm.

In August 1756 Montcalm crossed Lake Ontario, took the British fort at Oswego, destroyed the settlement, and restored French control to the area. In August 1757 he took and destroyed Ft. William Henry at the head of Lake George with a force of 4,000 French troops and 1,000 Indians. When the British garrison surrendered and marched out, Montcalm's Indian allies massacred many soldiers before Montcalm could stop them. In the following year he occupied Ticonderoga (Ft. Carillon) and held it with 3,600 men against a British attacking force of 15,000.

The British sent strong reinforcements to Canada in 1759 to take Quebec, a virtually impregnable fortress high above the St. Lawrence River. Coming from Louisbourg, Gen. James Wolfe landed at the Island of Orleans, just downstream from Quebec. Montcalm concentrated about 14,000 troops, plus some Indians, along the Montmorency River to oppose Wolfe's assault. The first British attack on July 31 was repulsed. But on September 13, through a stratagem—and there is evidence of bribery involved—Wolfe landed about 4,800 men above Quebec and mounted an unguarded path to the Plains of Abraham on the bluff above the river. Montcalm assembled about 4,500 men and attacked at once, but he lacked artillery, which was withheld by Vaudreuil. In the ensuing battle, both

Wolfe and Montcalm led their forces personally. Both were fatally wounded, Montcalm dying the next morning, September 14, in Quebec. The French defeat was the major turning point that broke French power and led to the eventual British conquest of Canada.

Montcalm was a fastidious person who dressed fashionably in the dandified manner of the times. His fine appearance, his gentlemanly behavior, his charm and integrity, his personal bravery, and his concern for his troops made him immensely popular.

Further Reading

The classic account of Montcalm is still Francis Parkman, *Montcalm and Wolfe* (2 vols., 1884; with new introduction, 1962). See also William C. H. Wood, *The Passing of New France: A Chronicle of Montcalm* (1914), and Meriwether L. Lewis, *Montcalm: The Marvelous Marquis* (1961). ☐

Montesquieu

The French jurist, satirist, and political and social philosopher Charles Louis de Secondat, Baron de Montesquieu (1689-1755), was the first of the great French men of letters associated with the Enlightenment.

n order to understand the Baron de Montesquieu, one must look back to the age of Louis XIV. During his long reign, Louis XIV had attempted to assert the absolute authority of the Crown over all aspects of French life and to make France supreme in Europe. Although the Grand Monarch achieved success in many of his endeavors, both his attempt to impose cultural and religious unity and his unsuccessful wars provoked sharp reactions that continued throughout the 18th century. It is within this milieu that Montesquieu must be understood.

Charles Louis de Secondat was born on Jan. 18, 1689, at the castle of La Brède near Bordeaux. His father, Jacques de Secondat, was a soldier with a long noble ancestry, and his mother, Marie Françoise de Pesnel, who died when Charles Louis was 7, was an heiress who eventually brought the barony of La Brède to the Secondat family. As was customary, the young Montesquieu spent the early years of his life among the peasants in the village of La Brède. The influence of this period remained with Charles Louis, showing itself in his deep attachment to the soil and in his rustic Gascon accent.

In 1700 Charles Louis was sent to the Oratorian Collège de Juilly, at Meaux, where he received a progressive education. Returning to Bordeaux in 1705 to study law, he was admitted to practice before the Bordeaux Parlement in 1708. The next 5 years were spent in Paris, continuing his studies. During this period he developed an intense dislike for the style of life of the capital, which he later expressed in his *Persian Letters*. In 1715 he married Jeanne de Lartigue, a Protestant, who brought him a large dowry. He was also

elected to the Academy of Bordeaux. The following year, on the death of his uncle, Jean Baptiste, he inherited the barony of Montesquieu and the presidency of the Bordeaux Parlement.

Scholarly and Literary Career

Montesquieu had no great enthusiasm for law as a profession. He was much more interested in the spirit that lay behind law, that is, the meaning, development, and variations of established laws and their relationship to customs and history. It is from this interest that his greatest work, *The Spirit of the Laws,* developed. To free himself in order to continue his scholarly interests, Montesquieu took little concern in the routine of the Bordeaux Parlement and eventually sold his office as president in 1721.

Montesquieu's early works were concerned with what would now be termed biological investigations. From these studies emerged Montesquieu's interest in the effect of environment on men. During this same period Montesquieu devoted a good deal of time to reading highly popular travel literature, including the newly translated *Arabian Nights* and Morana's *Spy of the Great Mogul in the Courts of the Christian Prince.* The combination of this reading and Montesquieu's own critical attitude toward contemporary manners led him to write the first of his great works, *The Persian Letters.*

The Persian Letters (1721) sparkled with wit and satirical irony, but hidden beneath its deft irreverence was a fierce and bitingly critical view of European civilization and manners. The work takes the form of letters to families and friends at home from three Persians traveling in Europe. Their letters are commentaries on what they see in the West. Montesquieu endowed his travelers with the foreign, commonsense understanding necessary to effectively criticize European (French) customs and institutions, yet he also gave to his Persians the foibles and weaknesses necessary to make his readers recognize in them their own weaknesses. All facets of European life were criticized. Louis XIV was "a great magician"; the Pope "an old idol worshiped out of habit"; great nobles achieved their status by sitting on chairs and possessing ancestors, debts, and pensions. Beneath the wit was the message that society endures only on the basis of virtue and justice, which is rooted in the necessity of human cooperation and tolerance.

Although the *Letters* was published anonymously, it was quickly recognized as the work of Montesquieu and won for him the acclaim of the public and the displeasure of the regent, Cardinal André Fleury, who held up Montesquieu's induction into the French Academy until 1728. In the same year Montesquieu began the first of his extensive tours of Europe, which brought him from Italy to Holland to England (in the last country he was elected to the Royal Society). After his return to Bordeaux in 1731, Montesquieu began his study of the history of Rome. By 1734 he had finished his *Considerations on the Causes of the Grandeur of Rome and Its Decline.* Though less well received than *The Persian Letters*—Voltaire referred to it as less a book than an ingenious table of contents—the work

was less a history than an attempt to get behind history to the general secular causes of events.

According to Montesquieu, Rome achieved greatness because of the martial virtues of its citizens and the flexibility of its institutions, which could be modified to correct political and social abuses. Rome's failure to maintain these characteristics once it acquired an empire marked the beginning of its decline. The development of imperial despotism, epicurean tastes, and the rejection of commerce only hastened the decline of Roman grandeur. Montesquieu's history may not have been scientific in the modern sense, but despite the criticism leveled against it, it was his search for general causal factors that helped to lay the basis for the secularization of historical studies.

The Spirit of the Laws

Fourteen years after his study of Rome, Montesquieu brought his search for the general laws active in society and history to its completion in his greatest work. Published in 1748, *The Spirit of the Laws* was not an analysis of law but an investigation of the environmental and social relationships that lie behind the laws of civilized society. Combining the traditions of customary law with those of the modern theories of natural law, Montesquieu redefined law as "the necessary relationships which derive from the nature of things." Laws, and their most basic political expression, government, thus became a relative relationship between a people's physical environment and their social needs and traditions. Although the basic substance of laws—"reason in action"—remained generally the same under all circumstances, their concrete expression varies according to time and place. Laws "must be adapted to each peoples."

Montesquieu's work was an attempt to study the process of adaptation. Thus, the diversity of laws was viewed as natural and desirable. The best legislator was one who pragmatically adjusted law to the physical and social conditions confronting him. Within this framework Montesquieu defined the basic types of government, identified the dominant virtues associated with each, and stated his most widely known concept of the balance of powers as the best means of establishing and preserving liberty.

An aspect of *The Spirit of the Laws* that has often been overlooked by its commentators is its role in the controversy over the legal rights of the autonomous groups in France following the death of Louis XIV. The last five books are an analysis of medieval French history, designed to prove that, to protect the liberties of the nation and the inviolability of the law, autonomous judicial bodies—the *parlements* of France—possessed independent or "intermediary" powers to thwart the natural despotic tendencies of an absolute monarchy. This aspect of the work helped to lay the basis of the 18th-century movement for constitutionalism, which culminated in the Revolution of 1789. In this sense, Montesquieu's most fundamental thesis may be viewed as an attempt to indicate the necessity of judicial review. *The Spirit of the Laws* was immediately acclaimed as one of the great works of French literature.

Following the completion of his work, Montesquieu, who was going blind, went into semiretirement at La Brède. He died on Feb. 10, 1755, during a trip to Paris.

Further Reading

The best biography is Robert Shackleton, *Montesquieu: A Critical Biography* (1961). Montesquieu's thought is discussed in Ernst Cassirer, *The Philosophy of the Enlightenment* (1951); John P. Plamenatz, *Man and Society: Political and Social Theory*, vol. 2 (1963); and W. G. Runciman, *Social Science and Political Theory* (1963). □

Maria Montessori

The Italian educator and physician Maria Montessori (1870-1952) was the originator of the Montessori method of education for children.

On Aug. 31, 1870, Maria Montessori was born in Chiaravalle. Her father, a tradition-bound army officer, discouraged her interest in a professional career; however, with the encouragement and support of her mother, she prepared herself for her later career. When she was 12, the family moved to Rome to take advantage of the better educational facilities. An interest in engineering technology and mathematics led her to enroll in classes at a technical institute at the age of 14. Later an interest in biology led to her decision to study medicine. This decision required some courage and tenacity, as it was in utter defiance of the customs of a society which excluded women from such endeavors.

In 1894 Maria Montessori became the first woman to receive a medical degree in Italy. Her experiences in the pursuit of this degree reinforced her already well-developed feminist ideas. Throughout her life she was a frequent participant in international feminist congresses.

Maria Montessori's first appointment was as an assistant doctor in the psychiatric clinic of the University of Rome, where she had her first prolonged contact with mentally challanged children. She became convinced that the problem of handling these defectives was as much one of instructional method as of medical treatment. In 1898 she was appointed director of the State Orthophrenic School in Rome, whose function was to care for the "hopelessly deficient" and "idiot" children of the city. She enjoyed tremendous success in teaching the children herself, while refining and applying her innovative methods and training other teachers to work with the children.

In 1901 Dr. Montessori left the school to pursue further studies and research. At the same time she was holding the chair of hygiene at the Scuola di Magistero Femminile in Rome, where she was also a permanent external examiner in the faculty of pedagogy. In 1904 she became a full professor at the University of Rome and from 1904 to 1908 held the chair of anthropology there. She was also a government inspector of schools, a lecturer, and a practicing physician.

In 1906 the Italian government put Dr. Montessori in charge of a state-supported slum school in the San Lorenzo quarter of Rome which had 60 children aged 3 to 6 from poverty-stricken families. By this time her early successes with mentally challanged children suggested to her the idea of trying the same educational methods with normal children. Dealing with culturally deprived children, she used what she termed a "prepared environment" to provide an atmosphere for learning, that is, small chairs and tables instead of rows of desks. The basic features of the method are development of the child's initiative through responsible individual freedom of behavior, improvement of sense perception through training, and development of bodily coordination through games and exercise. The function of the teacher is to provide didactic material, such as counting beads or geometric puzzles, and act as an adviser and guide, staying as much as possible in the background.

Dr. Montessori's view of the nature of the child, on which the Montessori method is based, is that children go through a series of "sensitive periods" with "creative moments," when they show spontaneous interest in learning. It is then that the children have the greatest ability to learn, and these periods should be utilized to the fullest so that the children learn as much as possible; and they should not be held back by nonnatural curricula or classes. Work, she believed, is its own reward to the child, and there is no necessity for other rewards. Self-discipline emerges out of the independence of the atmosphere of learning. Influenced by astrology, she saw self-discipline as something that emerges as a result of a natural law, if all restraints are removed, and as a continuation of the cosmic discipline that governs the movements of the stars.

Dr. Montessori's method was basically at odds with behaviorism, Freudianism, and other major 20th-century trends. Thus it was used only by a relatively few private schools. Since the early 1950s, however, her system has enjoyed a revival, related to curricula reforms and a renewed interest in handicapped children. Her works have been translated into at least 20 languages, and training schools for Montessori teachers have been established in several nations.

Further Reading

Maria Montessori's *Spontaneous Activity in Education,* translated by F. Simmonds (1917; repr. 1965), is particularly useful for beginning students. A recent biography of her life is Edward M. Standing, *Maria Montessori: Her Life and Work* (1957). Among the works on her system are Nancy McCormick Rambusch, *Learning How to Learn: An American Approach to Montessori* (1962), and Edward M. Standing, *The Montessori Method: A Revolution in Education* (1962). For other works see Gilbert E. Donahue, *Dr. Maria Montessori and the Montessori Movement: A General Bibliography of Materials in the English Language* (1962). □

Claudio Giovanni Antonio Monteverdi

Claudio Giovanni Antonio Monteverdi (1567-1643) was an Italian composer who, in addition to being the first great operatic writer, reflected in his works, especially the madrigals, the change in style from late Renaissance to early baroque.

Claudio Monteverdi was undoubtedly one of the more progressive composers between 1590 and 1625. During these years he infused the rather dry *stile rappresentativo of* the early monodists with a lyricism that foreshadowed the later aria, and he introduced a more intensely expressive and dramatic element into music, notably through what he called the *stile concitato* (agitated style). As early as 1600 Giovanni Maria Artusi, a well-known theorist, criticized Monteverdi for some harsh "modernisms."

Monteverdi's influence, both before and after his death, was not commensurate with the high esteem in which he was held by the discerning few; thus he left no "school," and the only significant composer who can be called his pupil was Heinrich Schütz. The reason for this comparative lack of influence was probably Monteverdi's serious cast of mind and a strong tinge of conservatism that mitigated his continuing in the vanguard throughout a period which was, perhaps, the most dichotomous in the history of music and during which taste and fashion changed rapidly. Today he is regarded less as a revolutionary than as one of the outstanding composers of all time,

who combined the old with the new and who forged a style that for dramatic range, emotional expression, and sensuous lyricism had never been equaled before.

Monteverdi was born in Cremona and baptized on May 15, 1567. His mother, Maddalena, and father, Baldassare, a doctor, were probably musical, for both Claudio and his brother Giulio Cesare became professional musicians. It is most likely that Monteverdi became a choirboy at the local Cathedral and received his first musical training there. He was certainly a pupil of the noted composer M. A. Ingegneri, the Cathedral's music director, for in 1582 Monteverdi claims as much on the title page of a collection of three-voiced motets, *Sacrae cantiunculae,* published in Venice.

We know little about the next 10 years, apart from Monteverdi's unsuccessful attempt to get a job in Milan in 1589, but they were certainly productive, for he published a book of *Madrigali spirituali* (1583), one of *Canzonette* (1584), and the first two books of madrigals (1587, 1590). Perhaps in 1590 or the year after, he became a string player at the court of Vincenzo Gonzaga I, Duke of Mantua; he definitely held this position in 1592, the same year that he published his third madrigal book.

Employment at the Court of Mantua

Monteverdi remained at Mantua for about 20 years. During this period he accompanied the duke on two visits to foreign countries, the first (1595) a military expedition to Hungary to fight the Turks (an experience that made a deep impression on him), the second (1599) a journey to Liège,

Antwerp, and Brussels. Shortly before the second visit he married Claudia Cattaneo, who in their brief marriage (she died in 1607) bore him three children, Francesco in 1601, Leonora in 1603, and Massimiliano in 1604. In 1602 Monteverdi was promoted to *maestro della musica;* he published his fourth madrigal book a year later, his fifth in 1605, and the first set of *Scherzi musicali* in 1607.

The *Scherzi* were edited by Monteverdi's brother Giulio Cesare, who had been appointed to the Mantuan court sometime previously and who added an appendix to the volume in which he expounded Claudio's views on music, in particular the elucidation of what Claudio called the *prima prattica,* that is, the old polyphonic style of the late Renaissance, and the *seconda prattica,* that is, the new style in which the poetic text dictated the character and form of the music. This latter style is already apparent to some extent in a few of the pieces in the fourth madrigal book and more obviously so in the last six pieces of the fifth book, which, like the rest of his output in this genre, use a continuo accompaniment and are better described as vocal chamber music than as madrigals.

The Opera *Orfeo*

The year 1607 also saw the production, in Mantua, of Monteverdi's first opera, *La favola d'Orfeo.* This was followed a year later by *L'Arianna;* the Prologue, no longer extant, to a comedy by Giovanni Battista Guarini, *L'idropica;* and *Il ballo dell'ingrate. Orfeo* is perhaps the most remarkable first essay in any musical genre by any composer. The libretto (by Alessandro Striggio) keeps to the original story more closely than the two earlier operas on the same subject by Jacopo Peri and Giulio Caccini (and most later ones), in that Orpheus loses Euridice on the journey back from Hades, though they are reunited in heaven.

The music represents a virtual cross section of contemporary practice, including choruses in imitative polyphony and chordal harmony, solo ensembles, *da capo* arias, dances and other independent instrumental pieces, and the new monodic recitativelike style, to which most of the text is set. The orchestra consists of over 40 instruments, including harpsichords, chamber organs, strings, woodwind, and brass; which of these played when was largely left to the music director, though in certain instances Monteverdi specifies the instrumentation. For example, the spirits of Hades are accompanied by regal (reed) and positive organs, five trombones, two bass gambas, and a violone, which produce a strikingly dark timbre; trombones, indeed, later became traditionally associated with anything "infernal."

Perhaps the most remarkable feature of *Orfeo* is the clearly deliberate attempt at some kind of overall design. This is particularly evident in Act I, where the arrangement of solos, ensembles, choruses, and instrumental ritornelli form two ABA structures, the first large and complex, the second small and simple, and followed by a coda.

Orfeo was revived several times during Monteverdi's lifetime, as was *Arianna,* which if anything was even more popular, especially the celebrated lament *Lasciatemi morire,* the only fragment to have survived. Not only was

this piece arranged for five voices and included in the sixth madrigal book, and adapted to sacred words in the *Selva morale e spirituale,* but it also set a fashion that affected virtually every opera for the next 150 years or so, a well-known example being Dido's lament, "When I am laid in earth," in Henry Purcell's *Dido and Aeneas.*

The *Vespers*

In 1610 Monteverdi published one of his finest works, the *Vespers,* comprising a Mass, 2 Magnificats, 11 "motets," and an orchestral sonata. In it he combines solos, ensembles, choral writing for one and two choirs of up to five voices each, orchestral ritornelli (some in six real parts), in addition to a sonata, and obbligati for various instruments. The style ranges from the old to the new, from richly imitative seven-part polyphony to highly affective monody, from rhythmically clear-cut, ear-catching melodies to complex highly virtuosic melismas. As Denis Arnold (1963) said, "Passion and magnificence—these two are inseparable words when describing this volume."

The *Vespers* may have resulted from Monteverdi's desire to write a large-scale, widely expressive sacred work that complemented, to some extent, his operatic output. It almost certainly was a result of his wish to find another post, a wish that arose from the growing dissatisfaction with conditions, particularly his salary, at the Mantuan court. His situation became aggravated in 1612, when Vincenzo I died, for shortly afterward he was dismissed by Vincenzo's successor, Ferdinand. For over a year Monteverdi sought employment that was commensurate with his now considerable reputation, and finally, in August 1613, he was appointed to one of the most prestigious musical positions in Italy, that of *maestro di cappella* at the famous basilica of St. Mark's in Venice.

Years in Venice

Monteverdi spent the rest of his life in Venice, dying there on Nov. 29, 1643. The only domestic events of note during this period were the arrest in 1627 of his son Massimiliano by the Inquisition and his acquittal the following year, and Monteverdi's entry into the priesthood about 1632. Musically his 30 years in the service of St. Mark's were richly productive. In addition to completely reorganizing the whole musical setup and raising to a new excellence the standards of the singers and instrumentalists, he composed a quantity of music, both sacred and secular. Most of the sacred music was published in *Selva morale e spirituale* (1640), which includes a Mass, two Magnificats, and over 30 other pieces, and in a collection published posthumously in 1650, which contains a Mass, a litany, and over a dozen psalm settings.

The secular music can be divided into chamber and dramatic. The chamber category includes the sixth, seventh, and eighth madrigal books (1614, 1619, 1638) and the second set of *Scherzi musicali* (1632). The dramatic category comprises nine operas, three ballets, incidental music, an intermezzo, a masque, and the dramatic cantata *Il combattimento di Tancredi e Clorinda* (1624). *Il combattimento,* notable for its demonstration of the *stile concitato* via such unusual (at that time) instrumental effects as pizzicato and tremolando, has survived, as have the ballets *Tirsi e Clori* (1616) and *Volgendo il ciel* (1637) and Monteverdi's last two operas, *Il ritorno d'Ulisse in patria* (1641) and *L'incoronazione di Poppea* (1642). *Poppea* is the first opera on a historical subject (as opposed to mythological, biblical, or poetical subjects) and a masterpiece by any standard.

The Operas *Ulisse* and *Poppea*

Monteverdi's two last operas show profound differences compared with *Orfeo*. Both were first produced in Venice, but *Ulisse* is more typically Venetian than *Poppea* in the rapid succession of scenes—comic, serious, and spectacular—the quick patter of its recitative, often broken up by short songlike passages, the infrequency of instrumental numbers, the varied and heightened emotional range, and the reduction of the orchestra to a basic string group, which was first used in *Il combattimento* and has formed the foundation of the orchestra ever since.

In *Poppea* Monteverdi largely rejected the purely spectacular and the restless succession of scenic contrasts, relying more on the vivid and subtle characterization of the leading figures of the drama and maintaining a well-nigh perfect balance between music and drama, the music seeming to spring directly from the drama and not, as happened in most later baroque operas, being an end in itself. Not until Christoph Willibald Gluck, in fact, was such a conception of opera again realized. The music in *Poppea* is seldom less than attractive, and at times it reaches an emotional intensity and a melodic beauty that make an immediate impact today.

The works from Monteverdi's Venetian period that have not survived are the operas *La favola di Peleo e di Tetide* (1617), *Andromeda* (1617), *La finta pazza Licori* (1627), *La Delia e l'Ulisse* (1630), *Proserpina rapita* (1630), *Adone* (1639), and *Le nozze d'Enea con Lavinia* (1641); the Prologue to a sacred play, *La Maddalena* (1617); a Prologue and five "Intermedia" (1627); the ballet *La vittoria d'amore* (1641); the intermezzo *Gli amori di Diana e di Endimione* (1628); and the masque *Mercurio e Marte* (1628). The disappearance of these works, and in particular of all but two of the last nine operas composed in Venice, must be counted the most tragic loss in the history of music, when one considers the exceptional significance of any opera written during the first half of the 17th century, Monteverdi's own stature as a composer, and the high quality of those examples that have come down to us.

Further Reading

Full-length studies of Monteverdi include Henri Prunières, *Monteverdi: His Life and Work* (trans. 1926); Leo Schrade, *Monteverdi: Creator of Modern Music* (1950); Hans F. Redlich, *Claudio Monteverdi: Life and Works* (trans. 1952); and Denis Arnold, *Monteverdi* (1963). For background material see Donald J. Grout, *A Short History of Opera* (1947; 2d ed. 1965); Manfred F. Bukofzer, *Music in the Baroque Era, from Monteverdi to Bach* (1947); and Simon T. Worsthorne, *Venetian Opera in the Seventeenth Century* (1954).

Additional Sources

Fabbri, Paolo, *Monteverdi*, Cambridge; New York, NY, USA: Cambridge University Press, 1994.
Horton, John, *Monteverdi*, Sevenoaks Eng.: Novello, 1975.
Schrade, Leo, *Monteverdi: creator of modern music*, New York: Da Capo Press, 1979, 1950. □

Montezuma II

The ninth ruler of the Aztec empire, Montezuma II (1466-1520) was seized by the Spanish conquistadores, who used him to control and rule the empire.

Montezuma was born in Tenochtitlán, capital of the Aztec empire, and the present site of Mexico City. He received a thorough education in religion, science, and art and was especially devoted to his religion, becoming a priest in the temple of the war god Huitzilopochtli. He also distinguished himself in the numerous Aztec wars.

In 1502 Montezuma succeeded his uncle Ahuitzotl to the throne and became known for his pride and superstition. He lacked the harsh realism of his predecessors and was very much influenced by omens and prophecies. He dismissed all plebeians from his court and increased taxation of the merchants. Although his advisers warned him that his measures would weaken the empire, he requested heavier tribute from conquered tribes and launched numerous expeditions to obtain sacrificial victims. His actions led to revolts and to wars between Tenochtitlán and several tribes.

Under these circumstances Montezuma learned of the arrival of the Spaniards in 1519. Fearing that they were emissaries of the Aztec god Quetzalcoatl, whose return was believed to be imminent, and following the decisions of the Supreme Council of the Indian Confederation, Montezuma tried to appease the conquistadores by sending gifts and offering homage. This only whetted the appetite of the Spaniards. Their leader, Hernán Cortés, allied himself with the Tlaxcalan Indians, who had remained independent from the Aztecs, and marched toward Tenochtitlán.

Conquest of Tenochtitlán

Many Indians welcomed Cortés as a deliverer from Aztec control. Montezuma himself refused to fight Quetzalcoatl emissaries and invited Cortés into the capital. Fearful that the Aztecs might rebel against the Spanish presence, Cortés seized Montezuma, thus becoming the master of the Aztec empire without a struggle. Using Montezuma as his mouthpiece, he governed from behind the throne. Montezuma summoned all his *caciques* (chiefs), ordering them to obey the Spaniards and to collect tribute and gold for the Spanish monarch.

Cortés and his men remained in Tenochtitlán for several months. By then a new Spanish expedition from Cuba had reached the Mexican shores with orders to limit Cortés's power. Leaving one of his lieutenants in command,

Cortés marched to the coast and persuaded his compatriots to join him.

In the meantime an Indian uprising occurred in Tenochtitlán as a result of the ruthless policies followed by Cortés's lieutenants. Cortés hastened back only to find his men barricaded in the palace and threatened by starvation. He ordered Montezuma to arrange for supplies, but the Emperor refused. Cortés then released one of the Aztec chiefs, Cuitlahuac, with orders to open the markets and bring back food. Instead, Cuitlahuac assumed the leadership of the revolt. There was furious fighting in the capital.

Cortés finally convinced Montezuma to address his people and to order them to obey the Spaniards. The angry Indians, however, refused to listen to their captive emperor and showered him with stones. Montezuma died several days later, in June 1520, either from wounds inflicted by the mob or at the hands of the Spaniards.

Further Reading

Much valuable information on Montezuma can be found in George C. Vaillant, *Aztecs of Mexico* (1941; rev. ed. 1962); Frederick A. Peterson, *Ancient Mexico* (1959); and R. C. Padden, *The Hummingbird and the Hawk: Conquest and Sovereignty in the Valley of Mexico, 1503-1541* (1967). □

Carlos Montezuma

Carlos Montezuma (ca. 1865-1923), was a Yavapai (Mohave-Apache) university-educated medical doctor and political leader, who bridged both cultures.

Sometime in the mid-1860s, perhaps as early as 1865 or as late as 1867, Carlos Montezuma was born as Wassaja to Yavapai parents in a band in central or southern Arizona. As that period was quite turbulent, given Anglo-mining expansion and settlement and warfare among the southern Arizona tribes, Wassaja's childhood was far from uninterrupted play. Indeed in 1871, the Yavapai's longtime enemies, the Pimas, attacked Wassaja's band and carried him off, along with his two sisters. A man bound for Mexico soon purchased his sisters, and the boy never saw any of his family again.

Later that same year, an Italian immigrant photographer/artist named Carlos Gentile took pity on the boy, purchased him for $30, and had him baptized as "Carlos Montezuma" on November 17 in Florence, Arizona. Soon Gentile moved to Chicago, where the child attended public school for the next three years, moving on next to Galesburg, Illinois, where Carlos attended a country school for his health for the next two years. The next stop was New York, where the lad went to school in Brooklyn. Gentile's business suffered a reversal, however, due to a fire, and he was unable to care for the child any longer. After a short time under the care of a Mrs. Baldwin, Carlos found himself the ward of a Baptist minister, William H. Steadman, of Urbana, Illinois.

Once in Illinois, Montezuma prepared himself for college and enrolled at the University of Illinois. There he pursued a B.S. degree in chemistry, obtaining grades ranging from middle C's to low A's. He authored a thesis entitled "Valuation of Opiums and Their Products" and received his degree by the mid-1880s. After a brief period of indecision in Chicago, Montezuma resolved to go on to medical school. With the help of a Dr. Hollister at the Chicago Medical College, he entered that program, working at a job cleaning a local drugstore. In 1889, after some setbacks with the faculty, he finally completed medical training and contemplated where best to apply his new skills. Contact with the "Friends of the Indian" reformer group soon propelled him in the direction of becoming an Indian doctor.

Captain Richard Henry Pratt, the founder and director of the Carlisle School in Pennsylvania, was Montezuma's first backer. As early as 1887, Montezuma had been corresponding with the energetic reformer. Pratt was a staunch believer in immersing Indian children in white culture and erasing indigenous traits. For Pratt, and increasingly for Montezuma at this time, no matter how glorious was the Indian's past, the present and future realities dictated that tribal peoples modernize according to the whites' model. At his school, Pratt often brought in reluctant charges for this social experiment. Although Montezuma was too old for Pratt's curriculum, he became an adult example of what the whites' education could accomplish for indigenous people. In 1887, Montezuma thus addressed audiences in New York and Philadelphia on this topic.

Such a bright specimen of the white man's handiwork caught the attention of Commissioner of Indian Affairs Thomas Jefferson Morgan. After an exchange of letters, Morgan appointed Montezuma to be a clerk and physician at Fort Stevenson in Dakota Territory in 1889. Montezuma embarked on the mission with great zeal:

> While there is life in me I shall teach my race the values of life from savagery to civilization. I will lead them to the Father that watched over their forefathers when they fell into the hands of their enemies, to the God who permitted the nation to which they belonged to be nearly wiped out of existence.

Once in Dakota Territory, however, Montezuma found reservation conditions much worse than he had expected. Soon he was in conflict with Office of Indian Affairs policies and personnel. Handling the medical problems of the Arikara, Gros Ventre, and Mandan tribal peoples on the Fort Berthold reservation, Montezuma became convinced that physical problems stemmed from the inadequate supervision of the reservation facilities. Within the year, he and Superintendent George Gerowe were trading accusations. Commissioner Morgan stepped in and transferred Montezuma to the Western Shoshone Agency in Nevada in 1890, where he remained until January 1893. Although Montezuma's service there was less choppy, the lack of medical and other supplies, clashes with tribal shamans and

customs, and rivalry between Catholic and Protestant missionaries frustrated his attempts to make progress. Commissioner Morgan granted his request for another transfer, this time assigning Montezuma to the Colville Agency in Washington state. That move was no better, however; the Colville Agency, too, lacked the necessary supplies and facilities for a doctor to carry out his tasks. Quickly Montezuma secured another transfer to what would be his last Indian Service position, physician at Pratt's Carlisle School. In July 1893, he began his tenure at Carlisle, a position he kept until January 8, 1896.

Montezuma's stay at Carlisle was far happier than his other Indian Service positions. Back with his friend Pratt, he threw himself into the spirit of the school, praising the education, football team, and band. Although critics pointed to discrepancies in Carlisle's mission and its accomplishments—few students graduated or stayed in the East—Montezuma believed in the potential of the school. One of the musicians, a Dakota named Gertrude Simmons or Zitkala-sa, would figure importantly in Montezuma's life. Being in the East also allowed him greater contact with the white reformers. In 1893 and 1895, he attended the annual Lake Mohonk conferences of the "Friends of the Indian." By 1896, despite his positive connections with Carlisle, Montezuma decided to venture back into private practice.

At first back in Chicago, Montezuma had few patients. Then he chanced to meet up with Dr. Fenton Turck, an eminent internalist, who invited Montezuma to assist at his clinic. Montezuma's career prospects improved, although he never became an excellent doctor nor a rich one. Around this time, he and Zitkala-sa reactivated their acquaintance. Friendship blossomed for a time into engagement in 1901, but in August of that year, she broke off the relationship. Within the year, she married Raymond Bonnin, a Sioux. Montezuma was bitter at first, but later the two resumed a friendship and alliance in favor of Indian causes. Probably her biggest impact on him was to reawaken some interest in the Indian past. Montezuma never became an enthusiast for indigenous culture, preferring the path out of what he and most whites considered savagery, but in 1901 he revisited the places of his boyhood. On a trip to Arizona with the Carlisle football team the previous year, Montezuma had returned to his native region for the first time. Now he came back on his own and tracked down some of his distant relatives, especially Mike Burns and Charles Dickens. With them and Charles's brother George, Montezuma was instrumental in the creation of the Fort McDowell Yavapai or Mohave-Apache Reservation by late 1903.

Starting in 1905, Carlos Montezuma attracted national attention as an Indian leader. Much of his energies over the next six years focused on establishing a national organization of Indians, one the indigenous leaders would control themselves, unlike the reformer groups such as the Indian Rights Association. Montezuma joined in this Pan-Indian movement with Zitkala-sa and other prominent native leaders, such as the Sioux Charles Eastman and Henry Standing Bear, the Seneca Arthur Parker, the Oneida Laura Cornelius, the Omaha Thomas Sloan and Rosa LaFlesche, the Ojibwa Marie Baldwin, the Winnebago Henry Roe Cloud, the Arapahoe Sherman Coolidge, and the Peoria Charles Daganett. On Columbus Day, 1911, in Columbus, Ohio, with the help of Ohio State University economics and sociology professor Fayette McKenzie, the Society of American Indians held its first meeting. Montezuma, however, in spite of pleas from Sloan, Eastman, Cornelius, Daganett, and Standing Bear, did not attend. Despite his obvious credentials for leadership in such a movement and his ongoing disputes with Commissioner of Indian Affairs Francis Leupp, Montezuma had become disappointed with the agenda of the society. He suspected that the group had simply become a tool for the Bureau of Indian Affairs, and, as he and Pratt asserted, did not concentrate on the real needs of indigenous peoples. Instead of contributing to what he saw as a charade, Montezuma returned to southern Arizona to resume his efforts on behalf of his Yavapai tribe.

Since the establishment of the Fort McDowell Reservation in 1903, the Bureau of Indian Affairs personnel and the Yavapi themselves had been trying, with some success, to develop a thriving agriculture on the land. Their success, however, depended on the water supply from the Verde River, which cut across the reservation. The time period was a confusing one for water rights in the West as a whole. Although the Newlands Reclamation Act of 1902 projected a bright future for western irrigation, the legal definitions of ownership became murky. The 1908 *Winters v. U.S.* Supreme Court decision ruled that Indians had prior water rights, but it was ambiguous whether the indigenous people themselves or their "guardian" governmental agencies owned the water. Competition with nearby Phoenix and attempts to consolidate the Yavapai with other Arizona tribes clouded the future for Montezuma's people. Problems with setting up or repairing irrigation ditches further complicated matters. So in 1911, Montezuma, now signing his letters Wassajah, joined in with the Dickens brothers to ward off Bureau of Indian Affairs plans to relocate the Yavapai. After a drawn-out struggle, the Yavapai won their case and the right to stay at Fort McDowell. For Montezuma, this victory had repercussions, as the federal government saw him more as an obstacle to bureau plans rather than a cooperative, educated Indian.

The next year, 1912, Montezuma returned to the Society of American Indians. He became a crucial and controversial force within the group, never completely at ease with the society's agendas. He attended the 1912 meeting, again in Columbus, Ohio, but declined to go to the 1913 meeting in Denver, when it became clear that local promoters were using the gathering as publicity for an upcoming Buffalo Bill Cody Wild West show. Instead, he redirected his energies to Yavapai issues and also to an extremely personal one, marriage to a Rumanian-American woman named Marie Keller on September 19, 1913. The following day, Montezuma left for Arizona. (Marie, who lacked her husband's reformer zeal, preferred to stay in the background of his life.) The next February, however, he returned to the Society of American Indians to plan the 1914 meeting in Madison, Wisconsin. Despite arguments with moderates in the organization, such as Arthur Parker, and continuing conflict with the Bureau of Indian Affairs, Montezuma went to the Madison gathering, as well as the 1915 one at Lawrence, Kansas. At the Law-

rence meeting, Montezuma sharpened his attack on the bureau with a talk called "Let My People Go," in which he urged abolition of the federal agency.

Clearly, Montezuma was at an ideological watershed in his opinions, deciding that personal commitment was more important than organizational cooperation with the "enemy." The next April, he published the first number of his personal newsletter, *Wassaja*, an "obsession" that he carried on until shortly before his death. For six and a half years, Montezuma waged an unrelenting war of words with the Bureau of Indian Affairs. That October, even though he was in hot dispute with Arthur Parker, Montezuma attended the sixth annual Society of American Indians convention, held that year at Coe College in Cedar Rapids, Iowa. There matters deteriorated to a shouting match between Montezuma and Sherman Coolidge over the notion of Indians in the employ of the Indian Service. "I am an Apache," Montezuma screamed at Coolidge, "and you are an Arapahoe. I can lick you. My tribe has licked your tribe before." Obviously, with tempers so frayed, the conference accomplished little, and Montezuma was ever more the lone wolf. His editorials in *Wassaja* turned more sarcastic and clever. His main antagonist was the Bureau, but he also attacked churches and schools for what he considered complicity in the scheme to defraud Indians. Indeed, although his primary concern was for his people in Arizona, Montezuma expanded his focus to cover Indian calamities in Montana.

When the United States entered World War I, the Yavapai doctor looked at the war effort with ambiguity. The U.S. should not be able to commandeer indigenous males to fight, he thought, but if any wished to fight, they should be able to do so. His editorials also pointed out the ironies of native peoples fighting for rights abroad that they didn't enjoy at home. When war needs justified the closing of Carlisle School in 1918, Montezuma responded angrily. The bureau became, in his eyes, the "Kaiser of America." He urged the Society of American Indians to meet again—it had canceled the 1917 convocation—and lead the fight against the bureau. At the Pierre, South Dakota, meeting that September, Montezuma delivered an impassioned speech on Carlisle. Better yet, from his perspective, the society voted for abolition of the Indian Bureau. The society also named Gertrude Simmons Bonnin to replace Parker as editor of *American Indian Magazine*. Emotionally elated, Montezuma praised the society lavishly in the pages of *Wassaja*.

Throughout those years of infighting within the society, Montezuma was also busy defending the rights of his beloved Yavapai and other tribes back in Arizona. In 1912, he responded to requests from the Salt River Pimas to become their representative. Washington officials did not look favorably on that match, but in that year Montezuma and the Yavapai received confirmation of their homeland status on the Fort McDowell Reservation. Arguments over ceremonial dancing on the reservation, however, soon plunged Montezuma into conflict with bureau officials Charles Coe, Frank Thackery, C.T. Coggeshall, and Byron Sharp, as well as Indian Rights Association agent Samuel Brosius. Although Montezuma had no intention of reinvigorating tribal customs of the past, he did support the dances as harmless. Mostly the dispute was over the power of Indian agents over the tribal peoples, so any issue would have triggered the physician's anger. The clash over dancing carried on until 1918. Water problems also continued to plague the Arizona Indians. The Yavapai, particularly, wished for a dam and irrigation system, but Indian Bureau officials maintained that the project was too costly. Instead, the bureau recommended the Yavapai accept allotments on the Salt River. Whether or not this was a thinly disguised attempt to relocate the Yavapai, Montezuma and the Dickens brothers led the resistance to the plan. By 1918, even though the water situation was as tenuous as ever, Montezuma had won the battle over keeping Fort McDowell intact.

In what turned out to be the last four years of his life, Carlos Montezuma continued his efforts in national Indian affairs, tried to enroll as a member of the San Carlos Apache, and kept up his interest in southern Arizona concerns. He pressed once again for abolition of the Bureau of Indian Affairs and for citizenship for all Indians (not granted completely until 1924). The Society of American Indians continued to meet, and Gertrude Bonnin still held the editorship of the society magazine, but by the early 1920s, that group was losing its clout and luster. Successive meetings at Minneapolis, St. Louis, Detroit, and Kansas City all witnessed decreases in attendance. By 1922, Montezuma was disillusioned once more with the society. Back in Arizona, however, he launched a more ambitious effort to enroll at the San Carlos Apache agency, because some genealogical tracing had convinced him that his family had ended up on that reservation in 1871. The Indian Bureau, already at odds with the aggressive Yavapai physician, put him through many hoops, requiring sworn statements and proof which Montezuma could not obtain. In the end, the bureau's 1922 denial of his enrollment request was as much a punishment of Montezuma as a bureaucratic technical decision.

Controversies over water rights once again surfaced in 1919. Bureau officials tried yet again to persuade the Yavapai to relocate to the Salt River reservation, and once again Montezuma, the Dickens brothers, and Mike Burns headed off that campaign. In 1920, Montezuma and agent Byron Sharp nearly came to blows on the reservation, an incident that involved some rough handling of Montezuma's wife Marie. Next plans to pipe water to Phoenix across the Fort McDowell lands aggravated Montezuma even further, reinforcing his fears of a gigantic conspiracy between city politicians and the bureau lackeys. Montezuma kept protesting this turn of events, but with the arrival of the new Harding administration and its probusiness secretary of the interior, Albert Fall, Montezuma made little headway. A new Salt River agency superintendent, Frank Virtue, proved as hostile to Montezuma as his predecessors had been. A new generation of Indian leaders would have to pick up the fight for him.

In the summer of 1922, Montezuma noticed that his health was failing. At first, he thought he had influenza, but being the physician he was, he soon diagnosed his condition correctly as tuberculosis, the major Indian-killing disease of the day. Throughout the autumn of 1922, he continued to publish *Wassaja,* but in December, he chose to prepare for his death. He left Chicago for Arizona, had the Dickens family build him a *wickiup* rush shelter near their home, and resisted the medical advice of a Tempe physician to commit himself to a sanatorium. Montezuma lingered for nearly a month, writing letters of encouragement to his wife back in Chicago. On January 23, 1923, he finally succumbed, home at last among his people. Several newspapers and native leaders, including the Society of American Indians, eulogized him, but his overall legacy was uncertain. His crusading passions carried over to other native leaders for a few years after his death, but then his memory faded, outside of the Fort McDowell Reservation. Not until the late 1960s and early 1970s, when a reawakening of interest in native American resistance occurred, did scholars and indigenous leaders rediscover Carlos Montezuma.

Further Reading

American Indian Magazine. 1912-1923.
Papers, Carlos Montezuma at Arizona State University, Chicago Historical Society, University of Arizona, University of Illinois, and Wisconsin State Historical Society.
Wassaja. 1916—1922.
Hertzberg, Hazel W. *The Search for an American Indian Identity; Modern Pan-Indian Movements.* Syracuse University Press, 1971.
Iverson, Peter. *Carlos Montezuma and the Changing World of American Indians.* University of New Mexico Press, 1982.
Olson, James and Robert Wilson. *The Native American in the Twentieth Century.* University of Illinois Press, 1984.
Prucha, Paul Francis, ed. *Americanizing the American Indian: Writings of the "Friends of the Indians,"* 1880-1900. University of Nebraska Press, 1982.
Spicer, Edward H. *Cycles of Conquest: The Impact of Spain, Mexico, and the United States on the Indians of the Southwest, 1533—1960.* University of Arizona Press, 1962. □

Simon de Montfort

The English statesman and soldier Simon de Montfort, 6th Earl of Leicester (1208-1265), led the opposition to Henry III and played a major role in constitutional development.

Simon de Montfort, born in Normandy, was the fourth and youngest son of Simon de Montfort IV and Alice de Montmorency. After spending his first years in Normandy, where in 1210 his father had been deprived of his English estates, Simon decided in 1229 to go to England with his elder and sole brother, Almeric, to claim the earldom of Leicester by right of his English grandmother. He soon became a royal favorite, made friends with such important people as Robert Grosseteste, and on Aug. 13, 1231, was given livery of the estates. In 1236 Simon was seneschal at the coronation of the Queen, and 2 years later he married

Eleanor, the sister of Henry III and widow of William Marshall, Earl of Pembroke.

Simon was formally invested with the earldom on April 11, 1239, and after a quarrel with the King over money matters, he decided to go on crusade. He was so effective that the barons of Jerusalem asked that he remain there as governor. Returning to France in 1242 to help in holding Poitou, he then retired to his English estates for the next years and was called by Henry III in 1248 to govern Gascony. A hard ruler, he was able to force those in opposition to the English to submit. Although charged for his repressive activities, Simon was acquitted, and he resigned in 1252 at the King's request.

Simon hoped to go back into retirement, but the King called upon him to serve on several diplomatic missions to Scotland, France, and Italy. At the "Mad Parliament" of 1258 he served as one of the leaders appointed for effecting administrative reforms, which resulted in the Provisions of Oxford, and Simon moved to join the reformers against the King. Many of the reformers were native English who resented the foreign-born favorites at court, and soon Simon, though foreign-born himself, became their leader.

After being attacked by the King in council in 1260, Simon left the country, but he was called back in 1263 by the leaders of Parliament to head their opposition to the King and his foreign favorites. Claiming that the King had violated his oath and the Provisions, the barons referred the dispute to the arbitration of King Louis IX of France, who sided with the English king in the Mise of Amiens of 1264.

As a result of this defeat, Simon and the barons resorted to civil warfare and in the battle of Lewes on May 14, 1264, defeated the royalist forces and captured the King. To counteract the Mise of Amiens, the barons issued the Mise of Lewes, which placed the King and country under the control of Simon and the barons with a program of reform.

To solidify his position, Simon on December 10 called for a meeting of Parliament in January at London that would be fully representative not only of the traditional members but also of every borough in England. This Parliament, later called the "Model Parliament," established a precedent for greater representation in the Commons.

Simon quarreled with Gilbert de Clare, Earl of Gloucester, who left to join the King's forces led by Prince Edward. Further war resulted, ending in the battle of Evesham on Aug. 4, 1265, at which the opponents of the King were defeated, and Simon was killed. His body was dismembered, and his followers were deprived of their estates. His remains were buried near the high altar at Evesham Abbey, and his tomb became a rallying point for later generations that opposed the powers of the monarchy. Simon's contributions to English constitutional development were not so much in the actions of his life as in their symbolism for later reformers. He stands as a hero for justice rather than as a parliamentary statesman.

Further Reading

There are many studies of Simon de Montfort and his period. Recommended biographies are Charles Bemont, *Simon de Montfort* (trans. 1930); Margaret Wade Labarge, *Simon de Montfort* (1962); and C. H. Knowles, *Simon de Montfort* (1965). For the historical period see Ernest F. Jacob, *Studies in the Period of Baronial Reform and Rebellion, 1258-67* (1925); Reginald F. Treharne, *The Baronial Plan of Reform, 1258-63* (1932); and Sir Frederick Maurice Powicke, *The Thirteenth Century, 1216-1307* (1953).

Additional Sources

Bemont, Charles, *Simon de Montfort, Earl of Leicester, 1208-126,* Westport, Conn., Greenwood Press 1974.

Labarge, Margaret Wade, *Simon de Montfort,* Westport, Conn.: Greenwood Press, 1975, 1962.

Maddicott, John Robert, *Simon De Montfort,* Cambridge; New York: Cambridge University Press, 1994. □

Joseph and Jacques Michel Étienne Montgolfier

The French inventors and industrialists Joseph Michel (1740-1810) and Jacques Étienne (1745-1799) Montgolfier were brothers who invented the hot-air balloon, an important step in the development of aeronautics.

Both Montgolfier brothers were born at Annonay, Joseph in 1740, Étienne on Jan. 7, 1745. Their father owned a large paper mill and gave them a good education. Joseph was placed in a private school, but he left to start a chemical business by himself. Paris, with its famous scientists, attracted him, but after a short stay he was called back to Annonay to help his father run the paper mill. He promptly tried to introduce new techniques into the business, which resulted in his father's giving him funds to establish a business of his own. However, Joseph's inexperience soon led to considerable financial losses.

Étienne's youth was a more conservative one. He received training as an architect, which included some scientific education. When he was 30, his father retired and placed him at the head of the business. Étienne soon earned a name in the paper industry through his careful and profitable improvements in papermaking.

Whatever brought the attention of the brothers to using hot air for a balloon, and whether they even, at first, understood why smoke rose, is not clearly known. But it is known that they rapidly passed from a toy-sized balloon to a large one, and they soon learned that the best fuel was straw mixed with carded wool. The first public experiment, on June 5, 1783, demonstrated to an assembly of the local nobility of Annonay how a balloon some 35 feet in diameter could rise in 10 minutes to a height of well over a mile.

News of the experiment spread rapidly. The central scientific institution in France, the Academy of Sciences, invited the Montgolfier brothers to Paris to repeat their experiment. Bad weather destroyed the first balloon, but a second attempt was made, at Versailles on Sept. 19, 1783, in the presence of the King and his court. The balloon, as was proper for the royal occasion, was elegantly decorated. This time it carried a sheep, a rooster, and a duck. It rose to over 1,000 feet and then floated down.

The successful exhibition before royalty made the Montgolfier brothers national figures. A gold medal was struck in their honor. Étienne received the ribbon of St. Michael; Joseph obtained a pension of 1,000 livres; and their father obtained a patent of nobility. Balloons caught the attention of the public, and the term *montgolfière* was even applied to hair fashions and dresses.

In January 1784 at Lyons, to test whether balloons could carry passengers, Joseph made a mammoth 130-foot-diameter balloon, probably the largest hot-air balloon ever made. After freezing rain and a fire made Joseph's first effort unsuccessful, a second attempt was made on January 19. After a 15-minute flight with Joseph and two other passengers, the balloon made a rather rapid descent but landed without injury. The successful aeronauts were carried in triumph into Lyons. But the Montgolfier brothers soon saw themselves superseded by the exploits of others: long-distance flights, even Channel flights, were soon being attempted. Their real hope, that of creating aerial navigation, was dashed when they found they could not devise any means of controlling the flight of the balloons.

Étienne returned to his paper mill; he died at Neuchâtel, Switzerland, on Aug. 2, 1799. Joseph also returned to the paper industry. His inventive mind turned to other devices; he invented the hydraulic ram and devised an apparatus to distill liquids at reduced temperature and pressure and an apparatus to dry fruit under such conditions. Among many additional honors bestowed on him were membership in the Legion of Honor and appointment to the Institute of France. He died at Balaruc-les-Bains on June 26, 1810.

Further Reading

A short account of the achievements of the Montgolfier brothers is in Shelby Thomas McCloy, *French Inventions of the 18th Century* (1952), and in Charles Singer and others, eds., *A History of Technology* (5 vols., 1954-1958).

Additional Sources

Gillispie, Charles Coulston, *The Montgolfier brothers and the invention of aviation, 1783-1784: with a word on the importance of ballooning for the science of heat and the art of building railroads,* Princeton, N.J.: Princeton University Press, 1983. □

Jacques and Joseph Montgolfier

Bernard Law Montgomery

The English field marshal Bernard Law Montgomery, 1st Viscount Montgomery of Alamein (1887-1976), was an outstanding commander and hero of the British people during World War II.

Bernard Montgomery was born on Nov. 17, 1887. He went to St. Paul's School in London and entered the army in 1908. He fought in France during World War I and was mentioned in dispatches for gallantry in action.

After the usual staff and command assignments, Montgomery was a major general in command of the 3d Division in 1939. The division moved to France with the British Expeditionary Force in that year for the so-called Phony War. Montgomery participated in the withdrawal to Dunkirk in the spring of 1940. In England he became head of the 5th Corps in 1940, of the 12th Corps in 1941, and of the South East Command in 1942. In July 1942 he was appointed commander of the British 8th Army in Egypt, a position that marked the beginning of his rise to fame.

Northern Africa and Italy

Now a lieutenant general, Montgomery reorganized the 8th Army, gave the officers and men confidence in themselves and in eventual victory, and set about to defeat his opponent, German Field Marshal Erwin Rommel. When

Rommel attacked at Alam Halfa on August 31, Montgomery won a defensive battle. On October 23 at the Battle of El Alamein, Montgomery gained an offensive victory. His defeat of the Italo-German army prompted an Axis retreat out of Egypt to the Mareth Line positions in southern Tunisia, 1,500 miles away. Although Montgomery pursued Rommel, he was unable to trap him.

Montgomery was a full general before the end of 1942 and was knighted on November 10 of that year. In February 1943 his 8th Army came under Gen. Dwight D. Eisenhower's Supreme Allied Command and directly under Gen. Sir Harold Alexander, the Allied ground force commander. In March, Montgomery took part in the final Anglo-American offensive in Tunisia, which swept the Axis forces entirely out of North Africa by May.

It was largely Montgomery's plan, one of concentrated rather than dispersed landings, that dictated the invasion of Sicily on July 10, 1943. While Gen. George Patton's U.S. 7th Army landed on the southern coast of Sicily, Montgomery put his 8th Army ashore on the eastern face. Montgomery then tried to drive up the eastern coast to Messina, but his army was blocked at Catania, and American forces reached Messina first.

Montgomery led his army across the Strait of Messina on Sept. 3, 1943, to the Italian mainland. He moved to the Taranto and Bari areas of the eastern coast, where his forces captured the Foggia airfields by October 1.

The 8th Army moved across the Biferno River and captured Termoli after a complicated and brilliant operation that utilized an amphibious landing together with a direct pressure force. But bad weather and difficult terrain, plus obstinate German resistance, prevented rapid progress, and by the end of 1943 Montgomery's army was immobile at the Sangro River.

Invasion of Normandy

At that time Montgomery was assigned to the United Kingdom, where he took command of the British and Canadian forces scheduled to participate in the cross-Channel attack. In addition to being 21st Army Group commander, he was named the Allied ground forces commander for the invasion of Normandy. On June 6, 1944, D-day, he directed the British 2d Army and the U.S. 1st Army, which crossed the Channel.

Montgomery's generalship came under criticism during the first 2 months of the European campaign because of his alleged caution and slowness. He was to have captured Caen on D-day, but he took it only on the forty-second day of the campaign. His Goodwood attack also became the subject of much controversy. Yet Montgomery virtually destroyed two German field armies in the Argentan-Falaise pocket, closed on August 19, and he propelled the four Allied armies across the Seine River in a pursuit that came to an end only at the Siegfried Line.

Montgomery relinquished his command of the Allied ground forces to Eisenhower on Sept. 1, 1944, a change contemplated long before the invasion. He was promoted to field marshal on the same day. He started the discussion now known as the broad-front versus narrow-front strategy. Finally, Eisenhower gave Montgomery permission to launch Operation Market-Garden, a combined air-ground attack planned to get British forces across the lower Rhine River in Holland. The airborne drop was successful, but the ground attack failed, and the hope of driving directly to Berlin and bringing the war to a quick end vanished.

The winter fighting was bitter. It came to a climax on Dec. 16, 1944, when the Germans launched their Ardennes counteroffensive and created the Battle of the Bulge. Eisenhower put Montgomery in command of all the troops on the northern shoulder of the Bulge.

Montgomery crossed the Rhine River late in March 1945, helped encircle and reduce the industrial Ruhr, and swept across the northern German plain to the Elbe River. He commanded the British occupation forces and the Army of the Rhine (1945-1946), then was chief of the imperial general staff (1946-1948). He was chairman of the Western Europe Commanders in Chief Committee (1948-1951) and deputy supreme Allied commander, Europe (1951-1958). He retired in 1958 and wrote his memoirs. He died on March 24, 1976, in Alton, Hampshire.

Further Reading

Montgomery's own books include *El Alamein to the River Sangro* (1948), *Normandy to the Baltic* (1948), *Memoirs* (1958), *The Path to Leadership* (1961), and *A History of Warfare* (1968). A life study of Montgomery is Alan Moorehead, *Montgomery: A Biography* (1967). The best histories of Montgomery's campaigns are in Sir Francis de Guingand, *Operation Victory* (1947); Winston Churchill, *Closing the Ring* (1951); Chester Wilmot, *The Struggle for Europe* (1952); Sir Arthur Bryant, *The Turn of the Tide* (1957); and Alan Moorehead, *The March to Tunis: The North African War, 1940-1943* (1967). A view of Montgomery less favorable than the popular one is offered by Reginald William Thompson in *Churchill and the Montgomery Myth* (1968) and *Montgomery, the Field Marshal: The Campaign in Northwest Europe, 1944/45* (1970). See also Martin Blumenson, *Breakout and Pursuit* (1961) and *Salerno to Cassino* (1969). □

Lucy Maud Montgomery

A popular and financially successful writer, Lucy Maud Montgomery MacDonald (1874-1942) is considered one of Canada's best known and most enduring authors.

Lucy Maud Montgomery was born on November 30, 1874, in Clifton, Prince Edward Island. Her parents, Hugh Montgomery, a former sea captain turned merchant, and Clara Macneill Montgomery, came from large, long-established, and eminent Prince Edward Island families. Clara Montgomery died before her daughter, always known as Maud, was two years old, and her grief-stricken father sent her to live with her elderly, strictly Presbyterian maternal grandparents at their isolated farmhouse in Cavendish, Prince Edward Island.

Young Maud was a solitary child, sensitive, imaginative, and rather out of place in her grandparents' household. She found respite in books, notably Dickens, Scott, Byron, and Longfellow, and in writing stories and poems of her own, a talent which she developed at a very early age. She also enjoyed the company of her many cousins and later school friends.

In 1890 her father, now remarried and with a new family, asked Maud to join him in Prince Albert, Saskatchewan, and she spent the next year in the Canadian West. She found her stepmother uncongenial (she was expected to serve as an unpaid maid and nanny and was kept home from school for months) and her father too busy with a variety of enterprises—business, political, and social—to be much of a companion. However, she soon made several close friends. Although she was thrilled in November 1890 when her first published work, a poem, appeared in the Charlottetown, Prince Edward Island, *Daily Patriot,* she was equally excited to return to Prince Edward Island in August 1891.

In 1893 Maud went to Prince of Wales College in Charlottetown to prepare for a teaching career. She taught in rural schools for three years, finding the work rather taxing and less rewarding than she had hoped, but she was able to devote several hours a day to writing. By the mid-1890s she had achieved moderate success as a writer, having had many stories and poems published for money.

Gives Up Teaching for Writing

Intelligent, energetic, ambitious, and strong-willed, Maud was also very feminine. She loved fashionable clothes, was grateful for her slim good looks, and enjoyed the company and admiration of men. Like most young women of her era, Maud believed that marriage was the highest occupation for women, and she looked forward to her own marriage and children. However, she had high standards—her husband would have to meet certain social and educational criteria—and she had a romantic nature. In 1897 she became engaged to a suitable young man, but she quickly became disillusioned with him. While engaged she met and became involved with another wholly unsuitable young man, whom she thought she loved but knew she could never marry. Within a few months she had broken with both men and henceforth ceased to look for or expect romantic love.

Maud's grandfather died in 1898, and for the next 13 years, with the exception of a brief stint as a reporter for a Halifax newspaper in 1901, she lived with and cared for her aging grandmother in Cavendish. Her life there was very constrained, but she found enjoyment in writing and produced poems and stories which, by the early 1900s, provided considerable income. During this time she also began what were to become two of her most important long-term friendships, based almost entirely on correspondence, with Canadian teacher Ephraim Weber and Scottish journalist G.B. MacMillan. In her long letters to these sympathetic friends she was able to express her hopes and fears as a writer.

In 1907 Maud's previously rejected first novel was accepted by a publisher. *Anne of Green Gables,* the appealing story of an imaginative, irrepressible, red-headed orphan girl who was adopted by two elderly Prince Edward Islanders was published by the L.C. Page Company of Boston in 1908. It was an immediate and tremendous success with readers of all ages and both sexes. With some surprise Maud wrote a friend, "Anne seems to have hit the public taste." Among the thousands of fan letters Maud received was one from Mark Twain, who described her heroine as "the dearest and most lovable child in fiction since the immortal Alice." A sequel, *Anne of Avonlea,* followed in 1909 (there eventually were eight Anne books) and, despite not having received very favorable royalty terms from her publisher, Maud's professional and financial success was assured.

Maud's grandmother died in March 1911, and four months later she married Ewan MacDonald, an attractive, amiable, conscientious Presbyterian minister to whom she had been secretly engaged for five years. After a honeymoon in the British Isles, the MacDonalds returned to Canada, where Ewan resumed his pastoral duties in Leaskdale, Ontario. Maud found that being a minister's wife involved endless rounds of meetings, sewing bees, Sunday school classes, choir practice, and visits. Although she did not enjoy these activities and found herself temperamentally unsuited to them, Maud, with her keen sense of duty, performed them with skill and grace. To these responsibilities she soon added those of a mother (she had two sons: Chester, in 1912, and Stuart, in 1915), and she continued to write. Her busy and full life required very careful organization, and she often felt strained and exhausted.

Growing Appreciation of Her Work

World War I was a source of great concern to Maud, and her relief over the end of the war was soon overwhelmed by a series of travails. In January 1919 her cousin and closest friend, Frederica Campbell, died. Later in the same year her husband suffered an attack of what was termed "religious melancholia," a feeling of hopeless certainty of eternal damnation. Worried for her children (mental illness was believed to be hereditary), Maud also was horrified that others would learn of Ewan's illness. She sought medical help in Toronto and in Boston, but little was forthcoming. After several months Ewan recovered, but he remained subject to attacks at irregular and unpredictable intervals for the rest of his life. Henceforth Ewan became a source of chronic anxiety for Maud. In addition, in 1920 she became engaged in a series of acrimonious, expensive, and very trying lawsuits with publisher L.C. Page, which dragged on until Maud finally won in 1929.

Maud did find consolations in the 1920s, however. Her growing sons were always a source of delight and pride to her. In 1926 the family moved to Norval, Ontario, where Ewan became the minister of a smaller and friendlier congregation. In the early 1920s Maud created a new, highly autobiographical heroine, *Emily of New Moon,* who proved nearly as popular as Anne. Her achievements were recognized when in 1923 she became the first Canadian woman

to be named a fellow of the Royal Society of Arts in England. She was further honored in August 1927 when she was asked to meet the visiting Prince of Wales (the future Edward VIII) and the British prime minister and *Anne of Green Gables* fan, Stanley Baldwin.

The 1930s continued Maud's successes and anxieties. Several new juvenile books were well received. She was invested with the Order of the British Empire in 1935, and in 1936 the Canadian government created a national park on Prince Edward Island in and around Cavendish because of the renown Maud's books had brought the area. Ewan's health, however, was her primary concern. In 1935, after a series of physical ailments, he had a complete breakdown and was institutionalized for months. He slowly improved, but, overwhelmed by stress, Maud had a brief breakdown of her own. In 1935 Ewan retired, and the MacDonalds moved to Toronto, where their sons were at college. Ewan and Maud both had breakdowns again in 1937, but both recovered, and by the spring of 1939 Maud wrote that she was feeling better than she had in years.

Her recovery was of short duration, however. The outbreak of World War II depressed her greatly. Ewan's health declined, and, after a bad fall in 1940, Maud herself became very ill. Her condition worsened in 1941, and she died on April 24, 1942.

The author of over 20 books and hundreds of short stories and poems, Maud never felt she had achieved what she had aimed for—her "great" book. She was appreciative of her financial and popular successes and felt that her work was well-done as far as it went, but she recognized and regretted her limitations. Serious critics agreed with her, and for years she was dismissed as a hack writer of children's books. In the last quarter of the 20th century, however, as part of their search for a unique Canadian identity, Canadian scholars devoted a great deal of attention to L.M. Montgomery and the continued popularity of her works.

Further Reading

The Selected Journals of L. M. Montgomery, so far in three volumes to 1929, edited by Mary Rubio and Elizabeth Waterston (Volume 1, 1985; Volume II, 1987; Volume III, 1992), provide an unparalleled source of information about Montgomery. Engagingly written and ably edited, they present a fascinating, revealing, and honest record of an intelligent, talented, busy, and troubled woman. Montgomery's *The Alpine Path: The Story of My Career,* originally published as a magazine serial in 1917 and reprinted in book form in 1990, is a good-humored look at her childhood and development as a writer. Her long and interesting letters to her friends are published in Wilfred Eggleston's edition of *The Green Gables Letters; From L. M. Montgomery to Ephriam Weber* (1960) and in Francis W.P. Bolger and Elizabeth R. Epperly's edition of *My Dear Mr. M: Letters to G.B. MacMillan from L.M. Montgomery* (1980).

Montgomery has been the subject of several biographies, including Hilda M. Ridley's *The Story of L.M. Montgomery* (1956), a short book with a surprisingly feminist slant; Francis W.P. Bolger's *The Years Before Anne* (1974), which deals with Montgomery's life to 1908; and Hanna Schwarz-Eisler's *L.M. Montgomery: A Popular Canadian Writer for Children* (1991), a study by a German scholar. The most valuable biography is Mollie Gillen's *The Wheel of Things* (1975), which is well-researched and sympathetic. Gillen's later short volume, *L.M. Montgomery* (1978), has a similar outlook, is intended for a youthful audience, and contains many relevant photographs. Montgomery's books have been extensively examined by scholars including Elizabeth Waterston, whose essay "L.M. Montgomery, 1874-1942" (in Mary Quayle Innis, editor, *The Clear Spirit: Twenty Canadian Women and Their Times,* 1966), provides penetrating analyses of Montgomery's works. John Robert Sorfleet, editor of *L.M. Montgomery: An Assessment* (1975), presents seven articles with differing and very serious critical approaches to the L.M. Montgomery opus; Mavis Reimer has edited a similar volume, *Such a Simple Tale: Critical Responses to L.M. Montgomery's Anne of Green Gables* (1992). And *L.M. Montgomery: A Preliminary Bibliography,* by Ruth Weber Russell, D.W. Russell, and Rea Wilmshurst (1986) provides an excellent bibliography of works by and about Montgomery.

Additional Sources

Bolger, Francis W. P. (Francis William Pius), 1925-, *The years before "Anne,"* Halifax, Nova Scotia: Nimbus Pub., 1991.

Gillen, Mollie, *Lucy Maud Montgomery,* Don Mills, Ont.: Fitzhenry & Whiteside, 1978.

Gillen, Mollie, *The wheel of things: a biography of L. M. Montgomery, author of Anne of Green Gables,* London: Harrap, 1976.

Rubio, Mary, *Writing a life: L.M. Montgomery,* Toronto: ECW Press; East Haven, Conn.: Distributed to the trade in the U.S. exclusively by InBook, 1995. □

Richard Montgomery

Richard Montgomery (1736-1775), a colonial general in the American Revolutionary War, was known for his leadership of the attack upon Canada.

Richard Montgomery was born in Dublin, Ireland, on Dec. 2, 1736. He was educated at Trinity College, Dublin, and retained throughout his life "a studious habit, preferring the library . . . to the camp and the field." In 1756 he entered the British army as an ensign and went with his regiment to America to fight in the French and Indian War. He saw action in several major engagements. He returned to England in 1765. Seven years later he left the service and emigrated to America. He married Janet Livingston, daughter of a wealthy and socially prominent landowner in New York, and settled down on his wife's estate in Rhinebeck on the Hudson River.

By the time Montgomery arrived in America, the difficulties between England and the Colonies were brewing; Montgomery quickly adopted the colonists' cause. When hostilities broke out, he offered his services and was appointed by the Continental Congress in June 1775 as one of eight brigadier generals. He was sent to join Gen. Philip Schuyler as second-in-command of the expedition against Canada. He arrived at Ticonderoga, Schuyler's headquarters, to find Schuyler busily gathering troops and supplies, but soon Montgomery became impatient to move. Information from scouts indicated that the time to strike had come.

Taking advantage of Schuyler's absence in Albany, Montgomery started the army on the way to Canada on August 28 without his chief's permission. When Schuyler received the news, he not only gave his approval but joined the advancing army.

In a superbly executed operation, Montgomery first took two forts on the Richelieu River. Next, he turned on Montreal, which he captured on November 13. The final objective was Quebec, where he was to be joined by Gen. Benedict Arnold, who had come up by way of the Maine woods. On December 3 the two forces met a few miles up the St. Lawrence River and began the siege of Quebec. Several factors, however, caused the two generals to decide in favor of storming the city rather than waiting for it to surrender. On December 31 they attacked in two columns in a blinding snowstorm. As Montgomery advanced at the head of his force, he was met by artillery fire, and in the first discharge he was killed. The British found his body in the snow and buried it on the spot. In 1818 it was removed to St. Paul's Church in New York.

Further Reading

A recent study with extensive material on Montgomery is Harrison Bird, *Attack on Quebec: The American Invasion of Canada, 1775* (1968). Also useful is Donald B. Chidsey, *The War in the North: An Informal History of the American Revolution in and near Canada* (1967). See also Justin H. Smith, *Our Struggle for the Fourteenth Colony: Canada and the American Revolution* (2 vols., 1907), and John R. Alden, *A History of the American Revolution* (1969).

Additional Sources

Shelton, Hal T. (Hal Terry), *General Richard Montgomery and the American Revolution: from redcoat to rebel,* New York: New York University Press, 1994. □

Pierre de Montreuil

The French architect Pierre de Montreuil (active ca. 1231-1266/1267) was a great exponent of the Rayonnant Gothic style of architecture.

The exact relationship of Pierre de Montreuil, or Montereau, with Eudes de Montreuil, Gerbert de Montreuil, and other notable figures of the 13th century bearing the name of Montreuil is not certain, especially as references to Pierre de Montereau seem to apply to this same architect. He was a pupil of Jean de Chelles, a leading Parisian master of Rayonnant Gothic architecture.

Montreuil and his nephew, Raoul de Montreuil, probably attracted the attention of King Louis IX through their rebuilding of the upper choir (1231-1239), the transept, and the nave (completed in 1281 after Montreuil's death) of the Basilica at Saint-Denis near Paris. The King must then have commissioned Montreuil to build his private and splendid Cistercian abbey at Royaumont (Oise), founded in 1228 and consecrated in 1238. Here Louis, inclined to ancestor worship nearly as ardently as to Christian piety, had set up under Montreuil's direction a magnificent series of funerary statues representing his royal predecessors, most of which are now at Saint-Denis. All these sculptured works reveal the royal, beatific ideal of serenely smiling countenances and simply draped figures.

The King paid a signal tribute to Montreuil by assigning the construction of the Ste-Chapelle in Paris to him; it was begun in January 1246 and consecrated on April 25, 1248. In 1239 Louis had purchased, at an enormous price, from Baldwin II, the last Latin emperor of Constantinople, the precious relic of the Crown of Thorns and in 1241 several other relics of the Passion. Louis was ready to lavish on a private chapel to house these sacred relics all the splendor that he, as an ascetic, denied himself. Ste-Chapelle was built, like most royal castle chapels, on two floors; its upper level is a veritable casket of jewel-like light passing through great lancet windows, each set with medallions illustrating Bible stories; the window of Moses is composed of 121 parts. All the supporting graceful stonework is brightly polychromed.

Louis was fond of bestowing some of the sacred relics he collected as gifts to stimulate the propagation of the Catholic faith, and the Benedictine abbey at Saint-Germer, attributed to Montreuil, inspired by the Ste-Chapelle and built soon after it, was erected to house such a gift. The Ste-Chapelle is also thought to have inspired the Chapel of the Virgin at the Parisian abbey of St-Germain-des-Près, which Montreuil built between 1245 and 1255 and where he is buried. The last work he is known to have executed was the completion about 1260 of the south transept of Notre Dame in Paris, begun by Jean de Chelles on Feb. 12, 1258.

Further Reading

Other than Erwin Panofsky's *Gothic Architecture and Scholasticism* (1951), in which he treats with brilliance a vastly complex subject, little exists to elucidate the life of Louis's architect, Montreuil. □

Manuel Montt Torres

Manuel Montt Torres (1809-1880) was a Chilean statesman and public servant. One of the ablest and most active of Chile's presidents, he continued the work begun by Diego Portales of organizing his country along orderly, efficient, centralized Conservative lines.

Manuel Montt was born in Petorca of a distinguished family of Catalan descent. After training for the law and entering government service, he played an active part in bringing to justice the assassins of the great Conservative minister Diego Portales, whose spiritual heir he became. Montt was twice appointed minister of the interior, held a succession of other high posts, and completed two terms (1851-1861) as president of Chile.

Montt displayed great energy in promoting reforms in almost every branch of national life. He expanded and remodeled the civil service, founded savings banks, and reorganized the taxation system in order to finance (with the help of a large loan raised in England) his ambitious public works program, which included the construction of key railway lines and telegraphs. His educational reforms were particularly far-reaching. He founded many primary, secondary, technical, and specialized schools, reformed their curricula, and expanded higher education. He encouraged scientific research and endowed Chile with an astronomical observatory.

Under Montt's administration, commerce and industry advanced rapidly, and agricultural production increased, thanks in part to the immigration schemes by which farmers were brought from Europe, particularly Germany, and settled on state lands in southern Chile; the city of Puerto Montt bears witness to his initiative in this field.

Though he was a convinced Conservative himself, Montt's reforms brought him into conflict with the Church, which believed its privileges to be threatened, and with the large landowners angered by his abolition of the colonial system of estates, which Montt believed would encourage a more equitable pattern of landownership. The Liberals had launched an armed rising in an unsuccessful protest against Montt's advent to power in 1851, and toward the end of his second term they renewed their agitation, this time in an unnatural alliance with the extreme Conservatives and with the unruly Araucanians in the south of the country. This created economic and political difficulties for Montt's ad-

S
usanna Strickland was born in Bungay, Suffolk, England. She married J. W. D. Moodie, an English army officer, and in 1832 they emigrated to Upper Canada (now Ontario) and settled first on a farm near Cobourg. In 1834 they moved to a backwoods area in Douro Township and cleared a farm from the wilderness. Capt. Moodie took part in suppressing the abortive Rebellion of 1837, led by William Lyon Mackenzie, and was shortly thereafter appointed sheriff of Hastings County. From that time on, the family lived in Belleville, where Mrs. Moodie did most of her writing. She died in Toronto.

Mrs. Moodie, several of whose sisters were also writers, had begun to write in England. Between 1839 and 1851 she contributed many poems, serial novels, short stories, and prose sketches to the chief Canadian literary magazine of the period, the *Literary Garland*. In 1847 she helped to establish in Belleville the *Victoria Magazine* and was its editor and leading contributor during the year and a half that it survived.

Mrs. Moodie's masterpiece, *Roughing It in the Bush*, appeared in 1852, and its slightly less successful sequel, *Life in the Clearings versus the Bush*, a year later. Since most of the sketches in the former book had been written much earlier and published as sketches in the *Literary Garland*, there is a marked difference in the author's attitudes in the two books. In *Roughing It* she is rather snobbish in her attitude toward less highly educated immigrants and settlers; in *Life in the Clearings* she has adapted herself more fully to the pioneer environment and become more appreciative of the virtues of her neighbors and acquaintances.

ministration, which was succeeded by a Liberal government in 1861.

On leaving presidential office, Montt served on the Supreme Court (where an attempt was made to impeach him) and then as senator, counselor of state, and Chilean envoy to Peru. His severe and inflexible character made him many enemies, but in Chilean history he has seldom been equaled for his probity and many-sided devotion in the public service.

Further Reading

There are no full-length studies of Montt in English. Luis Galdames, *History of Chile* (trans. 1941), contains a useful chapter on Montt's personality and achievements. Hubert Clinton Herring, *A History of Latin America* (1955; 3d rev. ed. 1968), has a discussion of Montt's place in Chilean history. □

Susanna Moodie

Susanna Moodie (1803-1885), a Canadian poet, novelist, and essayist, is chiefly remembered for her classic account of the lives of early settlers in what is now the province of Ontario: "Roughing It in the Bush."

In both books Mrs. Moodie's best qualities are her accurate observations of the people and processes of pioneer life, her dry humor, her gift for striking portraiture of eccentric characters, and her sturdy common sense. She can make even the most commonplace event memorable by the honesty and shrewd wit with which she describes it.

Mrs. Moodie's poems and romantic novels—the latter include *Mark Hurdlestone* (1853), *Flora Lyndsay* (1853), *Matrimonial Speculations* (1854), and *Geoffrey Moncton* (1856)—are much more conventional in their form and content and are typical expressions of Victorian sentimentality, didacticism, and romantic idealization. Her reputation rests firmly on the two books of autobiographical sketches, which together give us the most convincing picture we have of how life in pioneer Ontario struck a sensitive and intelligent woman.

Further Reading

There is no book on Susanna Moodie. The best essays on her are in G. H. Needler, *Otonabee Pioneers* (1953), and Carl F. Klinck's "Introduction" to the new Canadian Library edition of *Roughing It in the Bush* (1962). See also Desmond Pacey, *Creative Writing in Canada: A Short History of English-Canadian Literature* (1952; rev. ed. 1961), and Carl F. Klinck and others, eds., *Literary History of Canada: Canadian Literature in English* (1965).

Additional Sources

Moodie, Susanna, *Roughing it in the bush, or, Life in Canada*, Boston: Beacon Press, 1987. □

Dwight L. Moody

Dwight L. Moody (1837-1899), American evangelist, was an outstanding representative of popular 19th-century Protestant revivalism.

Dwight L. Moody was born on Feb. 5, 1837, in Northfield, Mass. At the age of 17 he went to Boston and entered the retail boot and shoe trade. In 1856 he moved to Chicago to enhance his business opportunities. While in Boston he had come in contact with evangelical Protestants, chiefly through the Young Men's Christian Association (YMCA) and a local Congregational church. He expanded these associations in Chicago, where he soon became a leader in religious circles, chiefly through his work for the local YMCA.

In 1860 Moody abandoned his business career to work full time for the YMCA. He served as president of the Chicago branch from 1865 to 1868. He also ran a large "independent" Sunday school for slum families, which was supported chiefly by local members of the YMCA. This experience was essential in preparing him for his eventual work as a revivalist.

In 1867 Moody visited England, immediately establishing contacts with important English evangelists. In 1872 he launched his formal career as a revivalist in Great Britain,

accompanied by Ira D. Sankey, his famous "singing partner" in all his subsequent major revivals. They first attracted widespread popular support in Scotland; then they moved south into England for a long series of campaigns, climaxed by a 4-month visit in London in 1875.

That year Moody returned to America, a national figure, and immediately launched a series of revivals. In huge revival meetings in New York, Philadelphia, Chicago, and Boston he created the basic machinery of urban mass revivalism. It was chiefly a feat of organization which sought to adapt the traditional theological and institutional practices of evangelical Protestantism to the new urban environment created by industrialism.

Although Moody never abandoned his work as a revivalist, after 1880 he developed other interests. He founded three schools: two private secondary academies in Northfield, Mass., and the Chicago (later Moody) Bible Institute, a training school for urban lay evangelists. He aided national officials of the YMCA in inaugurating the Student Volunteer movement in 1886—a major expression of the American Protestant missionary impulse. At the Northfield schools he also held numerous summer adult and youth conferences offering informal Christian education.

A theological conservative, Moody was bewildered by the rapidly changing intellectual climate of the late 19th century. He found it difficult to deal effectively with the splits between liberals and conservatives in the American churches. His career as a revivalist had noticeably declined by the time he died in December 1899.

Further Reading

The only scholarly biography of Moody is James Findlay, *Dwight L. Moody: American Evangelist* (1969). Briefer analyses of Moody's public career are in Bernard Weisberger, *They Gathered at the River* (1958), and William McLoughlin, *Modern Revivalism* (1959). A revealing sketch of the revivalist by his son is Paul Moody, *My Father: An Intimate Portrait of Dwight Moody* (1938).

Additional Sources

Bennett, David, *D.L. Moody*, Minneapolis, Minn.: Bethany House Publishers, 1994.

Gericke, Paul, *Crucial experiences in the life of D. L. Moody*, New Orleans: Insight Press, 1978.

Moody, William R. (William Revell), *D.L. Moody*, New York: Garland Pub., 1988, c1930.

Pollock, John Charles, *Moody*, Chicago: Moody Press, 1983. □

Sun Myung Moon

Sun Myung Moon (born 1920) was the founder of the Unification Church, a movement combining Christian and Oriental religious traditions which focused on "God-centered marriages" as a way of saving the world. Enormous controversy surrounding the group erupted in America in the 1970s, leading to many kidnappings, deprogrammings, and much inflamed rhetoric.

Sun Myung Moon was born on January 6, 1920, in Jeong-ju in what is now North Korea, then under Japanese occupation. His family converted to Presbyterianism when Moon was ten years old. He entered college at age 19 in Seoul, studying electrical engineering, and graduated in that field from Waseda University in Japan in 1943. He then returned to Korea to pursue his engineering career. However, his work soon became more religious than secular.

On Easter Sunday, 1936, Moon had a vision of Jesus, he reported, in which he was told that he had been assigned to the mission of completing Jesus' unfinished task of saving the human race. For some years afterwards he formulated his religious and theological ideas, which he began teaching seriously at the end of World War II. In 1946 he went to North Korea, but stories soon spread that Moon was preaching heresy and spying for South Korea, and he landed in prison. He was freed, rearrested, and finally freed during the Korean War in 1950. The beginning of the Unification Church as a distinct organization is usually dated at 1951, by which time Moon was back in South Korea at Pusan. He began to attract followers and to put his ideas into written form. Those writings have since become scripture to the movement; in book form they are called *Divine Principle*.

Moon moved from Pusan to Seoul in 1954 and there established his movement under the name of The Holy Spirit Association for the Unification of World Christianity.

By 1958 a mission to Japan was established, and in 1959 a disciple, Young Oon Kim, left for the United States, where she established the first American outpost of Unificationism at Eugene, Oregon. The movement at the time had only a modest success in the United States, but it was growing rapidly in Korea and Japan. Within a few years Japan had outstripped Korea as the country with the largest number of Unification Church members. Meanwhile, in 1960, after at least one earlier marriage, Moon married Hak Ja Han, an event viewed by the movement as extremely important, since marriage and family were seen as essential to the plan of salvation. The first of their many children was born at the end of that year.

In 1972 Moon moved to the United States. In that year and the following three years he undertook extensive speaking tours, and the movement grew, most of the new converts being college-age youth. They actively recruited people in public parks, shopping malls, libraries, city streets, bus and train stations, and centers of countercultural activity, such as college campuses. But opposition also grew. Although Moon's political conservatism and militant anti-Communism appealed to some persons, others began to cast him as a sinister abuser of his largely youthful followers. Tales of sleep deprivation, inadequate diet, and the exercise of sophisticated forms of mind control at the Unification camps and communal living units began to emerge with some frequency. Some opposition also arose to the group's fundraising, done through begging or sales of merchandise on the streets and at airports.

Meanwhile, a Methodist layman named Ted Patrick had, in 1971, developed a strategy called "deprogramming" for use against members of some religious movements seen as extreme. In this process members of such movements were kidnapped and subjected to intensive and prolonged sessions of psychological bombardment in order to persuade them to abandon their new faith. By the mid-1970s Patrick and other deprogrammers had expanded their efforts to oppose a wide range of new religions, among them the Unification Church. The Unificationists resisted the attack, and charges and counter charges flew. By the early 1980s, however, deprogramming seemed to be abating, partly because of legal problems the deprogrammers had experienced (some targets of the deprogrammers had filed civil and criminal suits against their captors) and partly because Unificationism seemed to be drawing fewer new members.

Moon's doctrine, as summarized in *Divine Principle*, states that the human race fell from grace when Adam and Eve sinned in the Garden of Eden, and the history of the human race since then has involved many attempts to return to godliness. The most important such attempt was that of Jesus, but it, like others, failed, because Jesus was executed before he had a chance to complete his work. Moon believed he had the opportunity to complete the work of Jesus. Salvation, he taught, will be accomplished through the creation of God-centered families: husband, wife, and children, with the whole family devoted to the will of God. Moon even required each member of the church to remain celibate for a minimum of three years and often longer after joining the movement. Members openly spoke of problems coping with sexual desires and quenching them through a combination of frequent prayers and cold showers. Thus marriage became the most important part of Unification life; Moon personally selected mates for his followers (many of the matchings were interracial) and united them in marriage at mass ceremonies with thousands of participants. One mass wedding was held in New York in Madison Square Garden.

When enough God-centered families have been created, Moon taught, the world will be ready for the emergence of the Lord of the Second Advent, the equivalent of Christ in the Second Coming. That Lord must come from Korea; although the movement officially teaches that he hasn't been identified, the consensus is that it will be Moon himself.

Since the world must be prepared for the coming of the Lord of the Second Advent, Unificationists strive to make the world a better place. To that end they worked on antipoverty and relief programs, sponsored conferences for scholars and ministers, and undertook an enormous publishing enterprise, including the founding of several daily newspapers, the most prominent of which was the *Washington Times*. The funding for these enterprises came mainly from the movement's prosperous Japanese branch.

In 1981 Moon was accused of criminal tax evasion and eventually served several months in prison for the offense following a spirited defense which included supportive statements from a wide array of religious groups. Following his release in 1985 he returned to active leadership of the movement in New York, where he continues to write papers and deliver speeches on behalf of the Unification Church.

Further Reading

The definitive version of Moon's teaching is *Divine Principle* (several editions; the most important one, 1973). Moon's other works in book form are typically collections of his talks, such as *New Hope* (1973). Much more numerous are works by Moon's followers. One important one is Young Oon Kim, *Unification Theology* (1980). A sympathetic historical and philosophical study of the movement, published by Unificationism's own press, is Sebastian Matczak, *Unificationism* (1982). The most important secondary work on Moon and Unificationism is David G. Bromley and Anson D. Shupe, Jr., *"Moonies" in America: Cult, Church, and Crusade* (1979). Another fairly comprehensive work is Frederick Sontag, *Sun Myung Moon and the Unification Church* (1977). The earliest major study was John Lofland, *Doomsday Cult* (1966). □

Charles Willard Moore

American postmodern architect and educator Charles Willard Moore (1925-1993) is noted for his eclectic range of historicist buildings, each of which represents a unique response to the context of its site and culture—whether in the form of vernacular shed-roof wooden houses, Palladian-inspired stuc-

coed villas, or Federal-style college buildings. All are done as serious comments on current architectural theory and at the same time evoking a sense of gaiety or irony.

Charles Willard Moore was born in 1925 in Benton Harbor, Michigan. Throughout much of his grade school and high school years his parents traveled during the winter months from their home in Michigan either to Florida or California, spending several weeks in such cities as St. Petersburg and Hollywood. As a result of these extensive cross-country travels, Moore gained an inherent understanding of the American city and a rich knowledge of the history of American architecture.

Moore's university training was divided between his undergraduate years at the University of Michigan, where he entered at 16 and received a Bachelor of Architecture degree in 1947; and Princeton University, where he received a Master of Fine Arts degree in 1956 and a Ph.D. in architecture in 1957. At Princeton he studied with Ecole-trained Jean Labatut, the Milanese architect Enrico Peressutti, and American architect Louis Kahn. Throughout this period of Moore's education and early professional career he shunned the purity of the prevailing International Style and focused instead on an architecture that was both historicist and contextual. Likewise, he did not subscribe to the Modernist approach to urban redevelopment which called for wholesale clearance, but rather sought to work within the existing context or urban fabric and to enhance its essential character. His doctoral dissertation, "Water in Architecture," represented another of his consuming interests, the role of fountains and water in public space, an all-encompassing study that traced the history of fountains from Europe and the United States to China and Japan.

After two years of teaching at Princeton in the late 1950s, Moore moved to California to take a teaching position at the University of California at Berkeley. He became chair of the program in 1962. Shortly afterward he designed for himself a house in Orinda, California, which brought him early acclaim because of its evocation of a vernacular tradition and its unique articulation of interior space. In 1963 he formed a partnership with Donlyn Lyndon, William Turnbull, and Richard Whitaker. Their wooden shed-roof designs for the Sea Ranch Condominiums on the coast north of San Francisco brought recognition and feature stories in the leading architectural magazines. A vacation resort built along a ten-mile stretch of the Pacific coast, Sea Ranch garnered acclaim for its pitched-roof, redwood-clad houses set into dramatic cliffsides. The development became a prototype for many suburban communities across the country. Other significant buildings produced by the Moore, Lyndon, Turnbull, and Whitaker partnership include Kresge College of the University of California at Santa Cruz and the Faculty Club of the University of California at Santa Barbara, both of which are informal stucco-clad compositions with irregular plans and picturesque profiles.

In 1965 Moore was appointed chair of the Department of Architecture at Yale University, a position he held until

1969. Upon moving to the East Coast he established a new partnership in Essex, Connecticut, with William Grover and Robert Harper. Projects of the firm include an addition to the Williams College Art Museum and the Hood Museum at Dartmouth University. The Williams College project, completed in 1983, required an addition to a significant 1840s octagonal Federal-style building that once served as the college library. Located on a steeply sloping angular site at the back of the original building, the new structure is built around a triangular court with a cascading stairway that provides a new entrance to the museum and a link to the new galleries. In a similar manner, the Hood Museum at Dartmouth presented Moore with the problem of joining new gallery space to already existing buildings, one Modern, the other Romanesque. Here he linked the two buildings with a connecting corridor and a concrete and brick gateway that gives access to an entrance courtyard. Inside, the building features a polygonal vestibule and a high main gallery with an exaggerated overhead bridge truss and clerestory windows.

Other buildings from this period include Whitman Village in Huntington, New York, and the Jones Laboratory and Sammis Hall at Cold Spring Harbor, New York. As with all of Moore's buildings, they do not represent any single style or dogma, but rather are the result of Moore's response to their setting, their cultural context, and their individual clients. They tend to be playful, full of drama and surprise, expressing cultural aspirations and translating architectural precedents into something new and relevant to the present age.

During the 1970s, Moore and his staff became noted for their "Take Part" design workshops which brought together the architects and their clients, especially when the client was a committee or a church congregation, to discuss and argue over the details of the building program. Significant projects that were done in this method include the Dayton, Ohio, Riverfront and St. Matthew's Episcopal Church in Pacific Palisades, California.

After 1974 Moore worked mostly in Los Angeles with the Urban Innovations Group of the University of California at Los Angeles' School of Architecture and Perez Associates, with whom he designed his best-known project, the Piazza d'Italia in New Orleans, Louisiana. An urban square dedicated to the city's Italian community, it provides a place to play in the water in the setting of a theatrical spectacle akin to Rome's Trevi Fountain. He did it by creating a map of Italy out of marble and concrete paving stones, framed with a backdrop of playful curved walls in the form of abstracted colonnades and triumphal arches, all made of metal panels, stucco, and neon lights. It creates a magical sense of place, the goal being to provide a dream of Italy. Like much of his architecture, including his design for the Wonderwall of the New Orleans Worlds Fair, it combines references to ancient architecture with modern-day kitsch and expresses interest in the contrast between seriousness and functionality and the gayer possibilities of parody and irony.

Moore's numerous houses of the 1980s are characterized by similar concerns, particularly the Frederick Rudolph House in Williamstown, Massachusetts, which is a Pal-

ladian derivative with a pyramidal roof, corner pavilions, and a curved entrance colonnade. Other houses from this period include the Kwee House in Singapore and the Hoffman House in Dallas, Texas.

One of Moore's most challenging commissions was the Beverly Hills Civic Center, in which he linked a series of new and existing buildings with a sequence of elliptical and round spaces lined upon a diagonal axis through the middle of the complex. These geometrically composed spaces are ingeniously defined by a mixture of wall surfaces, pavement patterns, fountains, and screens of palm trees. Stylistically the new buildings of the complex are derived in a typical Moore fashion from the Art Deco style of the existing structures on the site. *TIME* magazine called it one of the best designs of 1990.

In the late 1980s Moore accepted a professorship at the University of Texas at Austin, where he was supported in his wide-ranging travel through numerous field trips with students and had ample opportunity to continue with his selected commissions, which included the Tegel Harbor Library and Housing development in Berlin, West Germany, a project he began in 1980 in partnership with John Ruble and Robert Yudell. Wherever Moore's teaching profession led him, he set up small architectural offices that grew into substantial firms even after Moore moved on. Part of his legacy includes Centerbrook Architects in Essex, Connecticut; Moore Ruble Yudell in Santa Monica, California; and Moore Andersson Architects in Austin, Texas. In 1991 Moore received the Gold Medal of the American Institute of Architects (AIA) for his "outstanding contributions to the profession," an award which is known to be the profesion's highest honor. He also won four honor awards from the AIA.

Known for his teaching style, which *Architectural Record* said had an immense influence on students and other architects, Moore was also a provocative, fairly prolific writer. He wrote or co-authored eleven books, in which he emphasized his opinion that buildings should reflect the particular circumstances of place and use. His projects exhibited his sense of pop, historical, and modern motifs. In a 1965 essay, "You Have to Pay for the Public Life," Moore penned one of the first academic papers that dealt with the social and architectural aspects of theme parks.

Charles Willard Moore died on December 16, 1993 as a result of a heart attack in Austin, Texas. At the time of his death, he was the O'Neil Ford Chair in Architecture at the University of Texas. Vincent Scully said that Moore's technique as an architect was "not of individual invention but of humane community, and of context rather than style, of healing rather than spectacular oppression."

Further Reading

The most comprehensive monograph on Charles Moore is Eugene Johnson's *Charles Moore: Buildings and Projects: 1949-1986* (1986), which was prepared in conjunction with a retrospective exhibition of his work at the Williams College Art Museum, Williamstown, Massachusetts. Also useful are David Littlejohn's *Architect: The Life and Work of Charles W. Moore* (1984), Donlyn Lyndon's *Houses by MLTW, Moore, Lyndon, Turnbull, and Whitaker, vol. I, 1959-75* (1975), Gerald Allen's *Charles Moore* (1980), *Special Issue: Charles*

Moore and Company: Global Architecture (1980), and *The Work of Charles W. Moore; A + U Architecture and Urbanism* (1984). Moore's theoretical ideas are best expressed in his own books, *The Place of Houses* (1974), written with Gerald Allen and Donlyn Lyndon; *Dimensions: Space, Shape and Scale in Architecture* (1976) with Gerald Allen; *Body, Memory and Architecture* (1977) with Kent Bloomer; and *The City Observed, Los Angeles: A Guide to its Architecture and Landscapes* (1984). Information on Moore's death obtained from the *New York Times* (December 17, 1993); *Architectural Record* (January, 1994); and *Art in America* (August 1994). □

Charlotte E. Moore

Charlotte E. Moore (1898-1990), a physicist who gained international acclaim for her analysis of solar and atomic spectra, worked in the atomic physics division of the National Bureau of Standards for over twenty years. In this capacity, she supervised the compilation of numerous solar spectroscopic tables containing analytic information about the chemical and physical properties of the elemental gases comprising the sun and the solar atmosphere.

Moore received worldwide recognition for her analytic interpretations and compilations of solar and stellar spectra, including the honor of being among six women to receive the first Federal Woman's Award from the United States Government in 1961 for her outstanding contributions in a federal career. She was also the first woman scientist elected as a foreign associate, in 1949, into the Royal Astronomical Society of London.

Moore was born on September 24, 1898, in Ercildoun, Pennsylvania, to George Winfield Moore, superintendent of the Chester County Schools, and Elizabeth Palmer (Walton) Moore, a school teacher. Her parents, through their occupations and Quaker following, instilled a disciplined appreciation for learning that Moore maintained throughout her life. Upon graduating from high school in 1916, she entered Swarthmore College, graduating in 1920 with a bachelor's degree in mathematics and membership in Phi Beta Kappa. John A. Miller, Moore's physics professor at Swarthmore, was influential in her decision to pursue a career in physics.

Moore's mathematical inclinations landed her a position in mathematical computation at the Princeton University Observatory in 1920. There, she worked with the astrophysicist Henry Norris Russell, whose research had resulted in a theory of stellar evolution. Typical of most astrophysicists, Moore and Russell used spectroscopy to measure certain cosmological objects' spectra or distribution of radiation at particular wavelengths of light. By determining the wavelength at which certain spectral lines appeared, they identified the elements making up the object under investigation. Russell guided Moore's initial research into atomic spectra, and in 1928 they collaborated on the publication of a monograph on the solar spectrum of elemental iron.

Although Moore's academic astrophysics career began and would later end at Princeton, she spent eight years researching in California. For five years she worked with Dr. Charles E. St. John at the renowned Mt. Wilson Observatory in Pasadena. Their spectroscopical researches resulted in a 1928 revision of Henry Rowland's classic *Preliminary Table of Solar Spectrum Wavelengths* published between 1893 and 1896. This work, together with her previous research, earned Moore the Lick fellowship as she pursued doctoral studies at the University of California at Berkeley. She wrote her dissertation on the atomic lines in the sunspot spectrum and received her degree in 1931.

Upon completing her doctorate, Moore returned to the Princeton University Observatory as a researcher and remained until 1945. While at Princeton, she met astronomer and physicist Bancroft Walker Sitterly; they were married on May 30, 1937. Moore had established her scientific career and received recognition under her maiden name, so she continued publishing many journal articles under that name throughout her life, although a few publications appear under the name Sitterly or Moore-Sitterly.

Moore left the academic surrounds of Princeton and joined the National Bureau of Standards (now the National Institute of Standards and Technology) in Washington, D.C., in 1945. Joining William F. Meggers's section on spectroscopy, Moore was soon placed in charge of a project involving the compilation of data on atomic energy levels. According to her colleague William C. Martin, who authored her obituary for *Physics Today*, Moore regarded her position as much more than the gatherer of previously published data. She scrutinized the data and sought to correct any shortcomings by persuading spectroscopists to provide new analyses. The voluminous amount of unpublished data Moore received attested, Martin claimed, to the spectroscopists' great confidence in Moore's competence. The chief result of her stringent and persistent efforts in collecting data was the publication in 1949, 1952, and 1958 of the three-volume reference source *Atomic Energy Levels as Derived from the Analyses of Optical Spectra* containing an organized representation of the atomic energy information for 485 atomic species and described by Martin as "one of the most highly respected and frequently cited sources of basic atomic data ever published." While at the Bureau of Standards, Moore published other valuable reference sources including *The Masses of the Stars* in 1940 with Russell, her previous Princeton colleague, and *The Solar Spectrum* in 1947 with Harold D. Babcock. In the following decade, Moore began collaborations with Richard Tousey at the Naval Research Laboratory which were to continue until her death, using data gathered from V−2 rockets to analyze ultraviolet solar spectra. Also among Moore's accomplishments was her discovery of the existence of technetium in the sun; technetium is a highly unstable element which naturally occurs only at trace levels on earth.

In 1968, Moore officially retired from the Bureau of Standards. Her career, however, was hardly finished. She spent the next three years working at the Office of Standard Reference Data, then joined Tousey's group working at the

Space Science Division of the Naval Research Laboratory from 1971 to 1978. Throughout this time, Moore retained strong working relationships with her previous colleagues at the National Bureau of Standards. She also increased her involvement in professional astronomical societies. Among those in which she held leadership positions were the American Association for the Advancement of Science, American Astronomical Society, and International Astronomical Union. Moore was the recipient of the Annie Jump Cannon prize of the American Astronomical Society in 1937 and the William F. Meggers award of the Optical Society of America in 1972; her alma mater, Swarthmore College, recognized Moore with an honorary doctorate degree in 1962, as did Germany's University of Kiel in 1968 and the University of Michigan in 1971. Moore died of heart failure in her Washington, D.C., home on March 3, 1990.

Further Reading

Minnaert, M., "Forty Years of Solar Spectroscopy," in *The Solar Spectrum,* edited by C. de Jager, D. Reidel, 1966, pp. 3–25.
Martin, William C., "Charlotte Moore Sitterly," in *Physics Today,* April, 1991, pp. 128, 130. □

George Edward Moore

The English philosopher George Edward Moore (1873-1958) was one of the originators of conceptual and linguistic analysis, the dominant trend in modern English philosophy.

Born on Nov. 4, 1873, in Upper Norwood, a suburb of London, G. E. Moore was the fifth of eight children in a cultivated family. After initial tutoring at home by his father, Moore was sent to a nearby day school, Dulwich College. There he pursued classical studies and music and formed the basis for his fine prose style. Excellence in these studies won him a scholarship to Trinity College, Cambridge, which he entered in 1892.

At Cambridge, Moore discovered philosophy and a wide circle of friends, Bertrand Russell introducing him to both. After completing his degree with a first, Moore won the annual fellowship prize with an essay on Immanuel Kant's ethics. The 6 years of leisure provided by the fellowship enabled Moore to break away from the idealism of J. M. E. McTaggart and F. H. Bradley and to begin to work out his own philosophical views. At the end of this period his first mature work, *Principia Ethica* (1903), was finished.

After a period of independent scholarship, supported by a comfortable inheritance, Moore was invited back to Cambridge in 1911 as a lecturer in psychology. In 1925 he became professor of philosophy there and held this post until his retirement in 1939. The extraordinary impact Moore had upon his students may be gathered from J. M. Keynes's delightful account in *Two Memoirs* (1949). After 1929 Moore attended Ludwig Wittgenstein's lectures and Wittgenstein attended Moore's; between them the two phi-

losophers fundamentally altered the character of English philosophy.

Moore's work is essentially one of analysis and criticism. He has aptly characterized his interest in philosophy as follows: "I do not think that the world or the sciences would ever have suggested to me any philosophical problems. What has suggested philosophical problems to me is things which other philosophers have said about the world or the sciences." He is thus a philosopher's philosopher. He taught his pupils patient and painstaking analysis of concepts, of claims, and, in particular, of their linguistic expression. Moore had a passion for clarity and propriety of usage; he also insisted on the rights of common sense, not as the ultimate norm but as one important basis for criticism, not to be lightly dismissed.

After retirement Moore lectured widely in the United States until 1944. He died on Oct. 24, 1958, in Cambridge, England. His principal works include *Philosophical Studies* (1922), *Some Main Problems of Philosophy* (1953), and *Philosophical Papers* (1959).

Further Reading

Paul A. Schilpp, ed., *The Philosophy of G. E. Moore* (1942; 2d ed. 1952), contains a brief but charming "Autobiography" by Moore, numerous critical essays on his philosophy together with a long "Reply to My Critics," and a detailed bibliography. A major systematic presentation and critique of Moore's work is Alan R. White, *G. E. Moore: A Critical Exposition* (1958), which also includes a bibliography of Moore's work after 1942.

Additional Sources

Levy, Paul, *Moore: G.E. Moore and the Cambridge Apostles,* New York: Holt, Rinehart and Winston, 1980, 1979. □

Henry Moore

The English sculptor Henry Moore (1898-1986) brought about a renewed interest in direct carving and enriched the formal vocabulary of the medium by his continuous examination of figurative motifs and abstract shapes derived from natural phenomena.

Henry Moore was born in Castleford, Yorkshire, on July 30, 1898. He served in the British army (1916-1917). He studied at the Leeds School of Art (1919-1921), where he read Roger Fry's *Vision and Design* (1920), which emphasized the expressiveness and formal power of non-Western art.

In 1921 Moore won a scholarship to the Royal College of Art in London. He spent considerable time at the British Museum, where he admired the Sumerian, Egyptian, and pre-Columbian artifacts. He also became acquainted with the work of the sculptors Jacob Epstein, John Skeaping, Frank Dobson, and Eric Gill, who had also been inspired by non-Western sources. Moore's trips to Paris, beginning in 1923, enabled him to become familiar with the work of Constantin Brancusi. In 1925 Moore went to Italy, where he was particularly drawn to the volumetric painting of Giotto and Masaccio.

Works of the 1920s

In the early phase of Moore's sculpture, about 1922 to 1930, two themes emerged which occupied him for the rest of his career: one, the mother and child, and the other, the reclining figure. In such works as *Mother and Child* (1924-1925, Manchester) and *Reclining Figure* (1929, Leeds) the strong pre-Columbian treatment is overwhelming. Similarly, the numerous masks he executed, such as the concrete *Mask* (1929, collection of Philip Hendy), rely on Aztec and Tolmec prototypes. These early works show his mastery of carving techniques and his use of varied materials such as concrete, alabaster, Hornton stone, verde di Prado, and ebony.

Works of the Early 1930s

Moore became less dependent on non-Western sources in the early 1930s, and the full expression of his imagery developed during the next eight years. In part this was due to his interest in cubism and its variants at this time. He was elected to the Seven and Five Society, a group of English avant-garde artists who were also aware of the possibilities of cubism. Between 1930 and 1933 Moore reworked the reclining figure theme, placing the emphasis on a smooth, flowing transition from part to part, as in *Reclin-*

ing Woman (1930, Ottawa); and he began to develop a nonfigurative biomorphic vocabulary similar to that of Brancusi and Jean Arp, for example, the African wonderstone *Composition* (1932, collection of Mrs. Irina Moore). Moore's tendency toward abstraction became more pronounced in the mid-1930s, and this explains in part why he joined the constructionist-oriented Unit One group.

Two works reflect Moore's refinement of form and composition at this time: the standing ironstone *Two Forms* (1934, collection of R. H. M. Ody), with carefully incised lines carved lightly over the surface, and the wood *Two Forms* (1934, New York). Both seemingly allude to the mother and child theme but remain open, even polyvalent, in their meaning.

Works of the Late 1930s and the War

By the mid-1930s Moore returned to the reclining figure, now treated more abstractly, such as *Reclining Figure Fourpieces* (1934, collection of Mrs. Martha Jackson). The elm-wood *Reclining Figure* (1935-1936, Buffalo) and its counterpart (1936, Wakefield City) reveal a new sensitivity to, even exploitation of, the material. The shapes seem to emerge from the natural configurations of the wood and its inherent structure. Toward the end of the 1930s the reclining figure was again transformed, gradually opened up, and finally eviscerated, as in the lead *Reclining Figure* (1938, New York) and *Recumbent Figure* (1938, London). Moore developed two other motifs at the same time: the interior-exterior image found in *The Helmet* (1939-1940, collection of Roland Penrose) and the abstract pieces with stretched string or wire, a technique borrowed from mathematical models. Of this series the most successful are the *Bird Basket* (1939, collection of Mrs. Irina Moore) and *The Bride* (1940, New York), both playing off mass against volume.

At the outbreak of World War II Moore as Official War Artist entered his most realistic phase, seen in the exceptional set of drawings known as the Shelter Drawings. His major sculptural work was the equally realistic *Madonna and Child* for the church of St. Matthew, Northampton (1943).

Postwar Works

After 1946 Moore moved in a variety of directions. He returned to the reclining figure motif, continually altering the image. The *Reclining Figure* for UNESCO in Paris (1957-1958), while executed in a conventional material, marble, is ingeniously displayed on a tilted platform. The *Reclining Figure* (1963-1964) for Lincoln Center, New York City, is partially submerged in a reflecting pool, the form now broken into two segments. The solution to the composition of the latter commission seems to have been worked out in a series of two-piece figures begun in 1959 and carried out in a number of variations, for example, *Two-piece Reclining Figure No. 4* (1962, Amsterdam). The treatment of the recumbent figure became more abstract and was even broken into three parts, as in *Three-piece Reclining Figure No. 2 Bridge Prop* (1963, Leeds).

Moore also reworked the mother and child image, now translated into the *Family Group* (1946, Washington), and restated in several pieces of 1950-1952 known as the *Rocking Chair*. Similarly, the helmet-head theme and related problems of internal and external relationships also reappeared in the early 1950s, now assuming a more impressive scale and vertical orientation, as in the elm-wood *Internal External Forms* (1953-1954, Buffalo). In addition to these reappearing motifs, Moore developed a much more extensive set of formal images in the postwar period.

The abstract reliefs commissioned from Moore take several forms. The *Time Life Screen* (1952-1953) of the Time Life Building, London, only casually refers to the angular treatment of the abstract carvings of the 1930s, while the unusual *Wall Relief* (1955) for the Bouwcentrum, Rotterdam, literally grows out of the brick wall from which the forms emerge, molded of the same material. The degree of abstraction is carried still further in the large nonfigurative composition known as *Relief No. 1* (1959) for the Opera House, West Berlin. Yet the figure in some form is retained in an unusual set of images, such as the *King and Queen* (1952-1953) placed in an outdoor setting on the grounds of W. J. Keswick, Scotland. Executed in metal, the figures have a skeletal rendering reminiscent of the lead reclining figures. Other figurative concerns are expressed in the full-bodied but fragmented torsos with their archaic references of the *Warrior with Shield* (1953-1954, Minneapolis) and the related *Falling Warrior* (1956-1957, collection of Joseph H. Hirschorn). Finally, although less specifically figural yet retaining a human orientation, are the upright motif series, of which the *Glenkiln Cross* (*Upright Motive No. 1; 1955*, collection of W. J. Keswick) is the most successful.

The late work of Moore was his most powerful, drawing on the theme of interlocking parts, whether based on skeletal structures or stone forms. The scale of his later sculpture increased considerably and, like so much of his larger work, is best viewed out of doors. Most characteristic of this last phase are the *Knife Edge in Two Pieces* (1962, London), the impressive *Locking Piece* (1963, Brussels), and the *Double Oval* (1966, London). Moore died on August 31, 1986 in Much Hadham, England.

Further Reading

The literature on Moore is extensive. Essential to any serious study of the sculptor are the three volumes devoted to the sculpture and drawings that form a continuing *catalogue raisonné: Henry Moore, Sculpture and Drawings, Volume 1, 1921-1948,* edited by David Sylvester with an introduction by Herbert Read (4th ed. 1957); *Volume II, 1949-1955* (1965), also edited by Sylvester with contributions by Read; and *Volume III, 1955-1964* (1965), edited by Alan Bowess with remarks by Read. In addition to these documents, statements by Moore have been collected into one volume, *Henry Moore on Sculpture,* edited by Philip James (1967). John Hedgecol, *Henry Spencer Moore* (1968), is a volume of photographs by Hedgecol and commentary by Moore.

Of the numerous biographical studies of Moore the most illuminating and satisfactory accounts are by Donald Hall, *Henry Moore: The Life and Work of a Great Sculptor* (1966), which is organized around the great "masterpieces" of Moore's career, and John Russell, *Henry Moore* (1968), which is more detailed. An essentially psychoanalytic study is Erich Neumann, *The Archetypal World of Henry Moore* (1959), in which many of Jung's theses are sensibly worked out. □

Marianne Moore

Marianne Moore (1887-1972) was an American poet, editor, reviewer, and translator. Her poetry is an innovative mixture of common and exotic things and creatures, forthright and imaginatively playful.

Marianne Moore was one of the most interesting poets writing in English in the 20th century. It is impossible to compare her with other poets, because she was so special—a fabler whose animals remain animals, a baseball fan, and a praiser of museum rarities, office furniture, scientists, and biblical characters. Her poetry embodies precise observation and language, syllabic meter and light rhyme, the flow of cultivated American talk, and unique forms. Her experimental method, however, served traditional values, for Moore was a moralist, aware herself that she was sometimes too didactic.

Marianne Moore was born near St. Louis, Mo., on Nov. 15, 1887, in her maternal grandfather's Presbyterian parsonage. Her mother was living there with her brother, after her father's nervous breakdown. When Moore's grandfather died in 1894, her mother and the two children stayed temporarily with relatives. In 1896 they moved to Carlisle, Pa., where Moore's mother taught at Metzger Institute. Moore studied there and for recreation sketched, bicycled, and played tennis. At Bryn Mawr College she majored in social sciences and contributed to the literary magazine. Upon graduation in 1909, she studied typing at Carlisle Commercial College with an eye to journalism, but instead, after a summer in Europe, taught commercial subjects at Carlisle Indian School (1911-1915).

Marianne Moore's poems first appeared publicly in 1915. The following year she and her mother joined her brother in Chatham, N.J., where he had begun his Presbyterian ministry. Meanwhile Moore's poems appeared in a variety of "little" magazines. They were usually short lyrics or appreciations of admired writers and biblical characters. "George Moore" is characteristic in its subject, angular visual form, syllabic meter, and rhyme. It is symmetrical, containing 13 lines, 6 lines leading up to a central 7th, and 6 leading away, duplicating the syllable count and rhymes of the first 6, but in reverse.

In 1918 Moore and her mother moved to Greenwich Village in New York City, where Moore worked at the New York Public Library. She began to acquire literary friends, such as William Carlos Williams, Alfred Kreymborg, and Wallace Stevens. She had also become a contributor to the *Dial,* then the most discriminating literary magazine in America.

In 1921 Winifred Ellerman (known as Bryher), an aspiring English novelist, and Hilda Doolittle (H.D.), an expatri-

a Play" is a three-panel poem treating a steeplejack, an aspiring student, and the hero Washington and a dignified Negro guide at Mount Vernon. "The Jereboa" uses an Egyptian desert mouse to contrast defensiveness and the plenty of frugality with luxury and excess. "No Swan So Fine" points an allied moral by means of an art object.

The title poem of *The Pangolin and Other Poems* (1936) gets at values through an anteater. A cluster of poems about Virginia finds virtues and vices in natural and man-made phenomena; these and some uncollected poems make up *What Are Years?* (1941). The title poem alludes to World War I, and the volume ends with "The Paper Nautilus," which asserts that love is life's best hope.

Nevertheless (1944) contains "In Distrust of Merit," an eloquent comment on the war and Moore's shame that "I inwardly did nothing." "The Mind Is an Enchanting Thing" is a delightful cascade of imagery and thought in which subject and manner are one.

In 1946 Moore began her long labor of translating La Fontaine's *Fables.* Her *Collected Poems* appeared in 1951, and the following year she won a Pulitzer Prize, the National Book Award, and the Bollingen Prize. She published her translation of *The Fables of La Fontaine* in 1954. Like all creative translators, she had entered into the original, and at times one is conscious not so much of La Fontaine as of her wit, language, and imagery.

Predilections (1955), a selection of Moore's reviews and essays, demonstrates that she was one of the best informal critics of her age. As in her verse, her urge is to affirm. Other volumes continued to appear, each introducing or recalling rewarding pieces, in 1956, 1959, 1961, and 1966. *The Complete Poems of Marianne Moore* appeared in 1967. Marianne Moore died on Feb. 5, 1972, in New York.

ate American poet, printed Moore's *Poems* in London as a friendly surprise. The title of "The Fish" interestingly runs into the first sentence of the poem. "The Fish" also continues her eccentric couplets and hyphenated line ends, light rhyme, and rhymed, syllabic meter. But the volume shows an advancing skill in sustaining a conversational tone and greater confidence in her own taste and experience, as in "When I Buy Pictures," "Picking and Choosing," and "Poetry." In "Poetry" she states her dislike for "all this fiddle" about poetry, referring to poets as "literalists of the imagination."

Marriage (1923), a blank-verse monologue of nearly 300 lines, blends quotations, allusions, and ironies. *Observations* (1924), which won the annual *Dial* Award, shows a marked increase in free verse among the new poems, for instance, in "Silence," "Bowls," and "An Octopus." The last, an extended commentary, is set in a glacier-dominated national park rich in lessons of adaptation by native forms of life as well as pinto ponies gone native: "the cavalcade of calico competing/ with the original American menagerie of styles."

In 1925 Moore became acting editor of the *Dial* and was editor from 1926 until it ceased publication in 1929. That year she resumed her career as poet and reviewer and moved with her mother to Brooklyn to be near her brother, who had been transferred to the navy yard there.

In *Selected Poems* (1935), Moore renounced free verse. All the new poems in the collection employ rhyme and syllable-count lines. "Part of a Novel, Part of a Poem, Part of

Further Reading

Most of Marianne Moore's work is listed in Eugene P. Sheehy and Kenneth A. Lohf, *The Achievement of Marianne Moore: A Bibliography, 1907-1957* (1958). The only full-length study of her is Bernard F. Engel, *Marianne Moore* (1964), but she is discussed in most books about 20th-century poetry. A chapter in Lloyd Frankenberg, *Pleasure Dome* (1949), demonstrates how Moore transforms facts into enchanting free-form poems. Some of her personal and literary concerns touch those of Pound in *The Letters of Ezra Pound, 1907-1941* (1950). In *The Autobiography of William Carlos Williams* (1951) she appears frequently as friend and fellow craftsman. Roy Harvey Pierce places her historically in *The Continuity of American Poetry* (1961).

Several generations of poets and critics have responded to Moore's work, and their comments are found in collections of their essays: Yvor Winters, *Primitivism and Decadence* (1937); Morton D. Zebel, ed., *Literary Opinion in America* (1951); Wallace Stevens, *The Necessary Angel* (1951); Richard P. Blackmur, *Language as Gesture* (1952); and Randall Jarrell, *Poetry and the Age* (1953). Critical opinion is contained in Charles Tomlinson, ed., *Marianne Moore: A Collection of Critical Essays* (1970). □

Luis de Morales

Luis de Morales (ca. 1519-1586) is known as "El Divino" (the divine) in Spain because of the intensely religious nature of his paintings, which reflect the almost fanatical piety of the Counter Reformation in his native land.

L uis de Morales was born presumably at Badajoz in the province of Estremadura. He may have studied at Évora, Portugal, but it is more likely that he received his training as a painter in Seville. Flemish Renaissance artists at work there were the major influence in his development. Pedro de Campaña (Pieter de Kampeneer), a native of Brussels, had lived and worked in Bologna and Rome previous to his 25-year sojourn in Seville, and his style combined Italian High Renaissance elements with a native Flemish bent for precise objective rendering.

The dark shadows throughout Morales's pictures, particularly in the modeling, contribute greatly to the establishment of a sense of drama, a technical device which is derived at a considerable distance from the dark shadows (*sfumato*) that characterize the work of Leonardo da Vinci, and particularly that of his followers in both Italy and Spain. A number of Morales's paintings of the Madonna and Child have this feature, as well as the profoundly tragic rendering which forecasts the later sacrifice of the Infant Christ.

Most celebrated are Morales's cult images of the Passion of Christ, in which emotion is expressed with searing intensity. The *Pietà* (Madrid), one of his masterpieces, shows the Madonna grasping the bruised body of her dead son in despairing anguish; the elongated figures are placed in the foreground with only the lower part of a vertical cross visible in the background. Scenes of the Flagellation, Christ Carrying the Cross, and the Ecce Homo abound in his work. One of the most eerie and imaginative in its almost surrealistic expressiveness is *Christ Meditating on the Passion* (Minneapolis).

Morales painted in oil, frequently on panel (wood) but sometimes on canvas. His activity was concentrated in Estremadura, where he provided altars for the churches of Badajoz, Plasencia, Arroyo de la Luz, and Higuera la Real, and in Évora. Legend holds that he was called to the court at Madrid about 1560 but failed to please and remained a very short time. There he would have seen the Italian Renaissance masterpieces in the royal collection, and thus would be explained the increased idealism which characterizes pictures such as the *Holy Family* (Roncevaux) and the *Madonna and Child with the Infant Baptist* (Salamanca).

Morales passed the last years of his life at Badajoz, apparently in a declining state of health, which did not prevent him, however, from continuing to paint altarpieces for the conventual churches at Alcántara and devotional works for the Cathedral of Badajoz. Legends of an impoverished old age in a state of approaching blindness are doubtless exaggerated.

Further Reading

The most complete account of Morales in English is Inajald Bäcksbacka, *Luis de Morales* (1962), which includes a catalog of all his known works, a complete bibliography in all languages, and 170 illustrations. The only other study in English is a brief work by Elizabeth Du Gué Trapier, *Luis de Morales and Leonardesque Influences in Spain* (1953). □

Francisco Morales-Bermúdez Cerruti

Francisco Morales-Bermúdez Cerruti (born 1921) was president of Peru during the second half of the "Military Revolution" (1968-1980). He dramatically slowed the pace of reform, later returning the country to civilian rule.

F rancisco Morales-Bermúdez Cerruti was born in Lima on October 4, 1921. His grandfather, Gen. Remigio Morales Bermúdez, was president of Peru from 1890 to 1894, while his father, Segundo Regimio Morales Bermúdez, was a career military officer who was assassinated by political extremists in 1939.

Morales-Bermúdez finished his secondary education in the Jesuit Colegio de La Inmaculada in Lima. In 1939 he entered the Chorrillos Military Academy and graduated in 1943 as a second lieutenant in the Engineering Corps, thereby beginning a long and distinguished career in the Peruvian army.

In 1961 he was promoted to lieutenant colonel, and during the short-lived military government of 1962-1963 he was charged with preparing for new elections, which were held in 1963. Over the next five years Morales-Bermúdez emerged as the foremost economist in the army. He taught courses at the superior War College and at the Army School of Engineering in Lima, as well as at the War College in Argentina, and served concurrently as director of the Office of Army Economics and as the official delegate of the Joint Chiefs of Staff on the board of directors of the Mantaro Corporation.

Promoted to colonel in 1967, Morales-Bermúdez attended the prestigious and selective Center for High Military Studies (CAEM), which since its founding in 1950 had emphasized socio-economic, political, and developmental themes—that is, the role of the military in the process of modernization—instead of purely military topics. It was at CAEM that Morales-Bermúdez prepared himself for national leadership.

He was promoted to brigadier general in 1968 and, while still on active duty, assumed the portfolio of minister of finance and commerce in the civilian government of Fernando Belaúnde Terry (1963-1968). Following the military coup d'etat of October 1968, Morales-Bermúdez was named minister of economy and finances in the "Revolutionary Government of the Armed Forces" and quickly undertook a thorough reorganization of the ministry and of the national economy. He succeeded in refinancing Peru's foreign debt, introduced sweeping reforms in the nation's tax structure, and stabilized the Peruvian currency, the sol.

Between 1969 and 1975 Morales-Bermúdez played a key role in the military government's efforts to restructure Peruvian society. The government nationalized the fish-meal industry; most mining and metal refining; petroleum exploration, marketing, and refining; the railroads; telephone and telegraph companies; the national airline; 51 percent of all television channels; 25 percent of the radio stations; a majority of the banks and insurance companies; and all exports of cotton, sugar, tobacco, and minerals. Moreover, it implemented one of the most far-reaching land reform laws in Latin American history; approved the Industrial Reform Law, which gave workers partial ownership of their companies; and, in general, increased the state's share of the economy from 11 to 26 percent.

Promoted to major general in 1973, Morales-Bermúdez was named prime minister and minister of war in 1975 and became president of Peru in August of that year following the coup d'etat against Juan Velasco Alvarado. His primary tasks as president were to rebuild the badly deteriorated economy and to pave the way for a return to constitutional democracy. The first proved by far the most difficult.

A combination of poor planning, bad administration, natural disasters such as droughts and flooding, and exaggerated promises, particularly in the agrarian sector, had resulted in economic chaos. The rate of inflation rose from 17 percent in 1974 to an alarming 74 percent by 1978. The Peruvian sol was devalued from 55 to the dollar in 1976 to 289 by 1980, and the real income of Lima's urban masses fell over 50 percent in that same period. Concomitantly, the foreign indebtedness of the nation increased at a staggering rate.

Forced to accept the draconian austerity and stabilization measures of the International Monetary Fund (IMF), Morales-Bermúdez demonstrably slowed the pace of reform and even moved to reverse the Industrial Reform Law and to divest the state of certain industries. This was the so-called "Second Phase" (Segundo Fase) of the "Military Revolution," a period which bore the personal stamp of Morales-Bermúdez even more than the "First Phase" had borne that of Velasco Alvarado.

Politically, Morales-Bermúdez enjoyed greater success. Although he imposed a state of emergency in 1976-1977, he later relaxed press censorship, allowed previously banned magazines to reappear, and held elections in 1978 for a constituent assembly which wrote a new constitution incorporating many of the reforms and changes implemented during the military regime. In 1980 general elections were held, and the man whom the military had overthrown 12 years earlier, Fernando Belaúnde Terry, emerged victorious. Nevertheless, on July 28, 1980, Morales-Bermúdez fulfilled his promise and handed over power to the new president, thereby ending the longest period of military rule

in 20th-century Peru and certainly one of the most unique regimes in Latin American history.

Upon retiring from office and active military service, Morales-Bermúdez dedicated himself to writing, lecturing, and politics. In 1985 he formed a new political party, El Frente (The Front), and ran for president. He finished a poor fifth in a field of eight, a clear indication of the degree to which the Peruvian people blamed him personally for the severe economic measures of his presidency and for the subsequent collapse of the Peruvian economy in the early 1980s. He subsequently avoided public appearances.

Further Reading

There is no biography of Morales-Bermúdez, but a good biographical sketch in Spanish is in Alberto Tauro, *Diccionario Enciclopédico del Perú, Apendice* (1975). The best source for Morales-Bermúdez' political and economic ideas is his own book *El Proyecto Nacional* (2nd ed., 1984). An excellent overall analysis of the military regime is Cynthia McClintock and Abraham F. Lowenthal, editors, *The Peruvian Experiment Reconsidered* (1983?). Important background information is in Abraham F. Lowenthal, editor, *The Peruvian Experiment: Continuity and Change Under Military Rule* (1975); Fredrick B. Pike, *The United States and the Andean Republics: Peru, Bolivia and Ecuador* (1977); Rosemary Thorp and Geoffrey Bertram, *Peru, 1890-1977: Growth and Policy in an Open Economy* (1978); and Brian Loveman and Thomas M. Davies, Jr., editors, *The Politics of Antipolitics: The Military in Latin America* (1978), which contains an English translation of a Morales-Bermúdez speech. □

Thomas Moran

Thomas Moran (1837-1926), American painter and graphic artist, specialized in landscape painting. His gigantic canvases depict the grandeur and immensity of the Far West.

B orn in Bolton, Lancashire, England, on Jan. 12, 1837, Thomas Moran was taken to the United States at the age of 7. He was educated in Philadelphia public schools. He early became familiar with the work of Washington Allston, Rembrandt Peale, John Neagle, and other American artists. Three of Moran's brothers were artists, and he learned to paint from his brother Edward.

In 1853 Moran was apprenticed to a wood engraver and illustrator in Philadelphia. In his spare time he did watercolor drawings, and in 1856 he painted his first oil, *Among the Ruins There He Lingered.*

In 1861 Moran went to London to study firsthand the paintings of Claude Lorrain and J. M. W. Turner. Moran returned to America the next year and married. He found that he was increasingly fascinated by the grandiose and vast in nature. In 1860 he had visited the Lake Superior region in northern Michigan. In 1871, serving as a guest artist with the Geological Survey of the Territories, he traveled into the Yellowstone country. The following year he toured the Yosemite Valley in California. In 1873, accompanying a party of the U.S. Geographical and Geological Survey, he explored the mountains of Utah to the north rim of the Grand Canyon of the Colorado River.

Moran sought to suggest the vastness and sweep of the West through huge landscapes that lacked a focal point. His paintings, more than those of any other artist, made the western wilderness familiar to people on the eastern seaboard. At the end of the 19th century few Americans had seen the Rockies, and largely because of this Moran gained great fame. His enormous *Grand Canyon of the Yellowstone* (1893-1901) and his subsequent *Chasm of the Colorado* were purchased by the U.S. Congress. Although his grandiose paintings were executed with considerable skill, he seems best in his smaller paintings and in his drawings.

Moran made some 1,500 illustrations, mostly woodcuts, for *Scribner's Monthly Magazine* and other periodicals, for school texts, travel books, and special editions of American poets. He also did many etchings, especially between 1878 and 1888. He died in Santa Barbara, Calif., on Aug. 26, 1926. Mt. Moran in the Teton Range is named after him.

Further Reading

Fritiof Melvin Fryxell, ed., *Thomas Moran: Explorer in Search of Beauty* (1958), is a biographical account containing excerpts from memoirs of people who knew Moran, including his daughter Ruth, his companion during the western treks, and the photographer and author William Henry Jackson. It contains some illustrations, with reproductions of etchings and oil sketches. A lengthier and more carefully documented work is

Thurman Wilkins, *Thomas Moran: Artist of the Mountains* (1966), with an extensive bibliography. □

Giorgio Morandi

Giorgio Morandi (1890-1964), widely acknowledged as a major Italian painter of the 20th century, built a reputation based especially on his sensitive still-life subjects.

Giorgio Morandi attained stature as one of the most prominent Italian painters of the 20th century, though he lived humbly and developed his art outside the mainstream of Modernism. Born in Bologna on July 20, 1890, he remained closely attached to that city for his entire life. In 1907, after having spent nearly a year working in his father's export office, the teenaged Morandi enrolled at the *Accademia di Belle Arti* in Bologna, where he studied until 1913.

While at the academy Morandi became interested in 19th-century artists as well as Renaissance masters, showing particular respect for Paul Cezanne and Piero della Francesca. Unfortunately he destroyed most of his youthful work. His earliest extant picture, a landscape in part influenced by Macchiaioli painting, an Italian version of Impressionism, dates from 1910. In 1914 he was appointed a drawing teacher in the Bolognese elementary schools. In the same year Morandi found himself swayed by the Futurists, a group of Italian artists, including Filippo Tommaso Marinetti, Umberto Boccioni, and Giacomo Balla, who exalted the dynamism of the machine in their radical ideas on art. Morandi's interest in the Futurists was fleeting, and though he showed at the *Espozione Libera Futurista Internazionale* (1914) his pictures at this time displayed the controlled brushstrokes of Cezanne, as well as the angular forms and cool palette of Cubism.

Morandi's artistic seclusion did not prevent him from joining stylistic trends, yet he arrived at his solutions independently. This was the case with his connection to the "scuola metafisica" (metaphysical school) founded by Giorgio de Chirico and Carlo Carrá (formerly a Futurist) at Ferrara in 1917. Metaphysical painting encompassed stylistic affinities rather than spawning a school in the literal sense. It concerned itself with the symbolic role of objects set within "unreal" arrangements. In 1915 Morandi served briefly in the military until he was discharged as a result of a serious illness. He developed a taste in the following year for still-life and landscape, often presented in a spare, geometric language. Morandi didn't meet de Chirico until 1919 in Rome, yet his paintings anticipated de Chirico's mysterious lyrical qualities.

Morandi's art was most aligned with de Chirico's shortly after their first encounter. His *Still Life* (1919) has a hard-edged quality that departs from his usual painterliness in its depiction of an odd assortment of objects, including the ambiguous silhouette of a table-clock. In 1918 he had his first work reproduced—a 1915 etching which appeared in *La Racolta,* a modest arts journal that promoted the development of the metaphysical school. Even more important for Morandi was the support he received in 1919 from Mario Broglio, editor of *Valori Plastici,* an influential publication devoted to the international arts scene. Broglio arranged for Morandi's first one-man exhibition, in Rome, and bought nearly all the paintings.

The *scuola metafisica* was a short-lived movement, and when its practitioners went their separate ways in the early 1920s Morandi created still-lifes with a poetry and luminosity to rival the 18th-century French master Jean-Baptiste-Siméon Chardin. Although Morandi showed with the "Novecento" (20th century) in 1926, he didn't subscribe to that group's reactionary tenets, and his modest pictures did not reflect its grand pictorial rhetoric. The same year he was appointed schools inspector in Reggio Emilia and Modena.

A brief flirtation with the rustic outlook cultivated by the *"strapaese"* artists led Morandi to evoke 19th-century rural values in scenes of the Bolognese landscape. However, by 1929 he discarded such nostalgic associations and embarked on a series of still-lifes whose formal rigor—often bordering on pure abstraction—would establish his reputation for posterity. Figure painting occupied only a minute portion of his work, and of his 1,300 paintings fewer than a dozen were portraits. Even in the face of Fascism he resisted propagandistic pressure and pursued his own course.

In 1930 Morandi was named professor of Intaglio at the Bolognese academy, a post he held until 1956, though curiously he produced few etchings of his own after 1933. Morandi's etchings complement his paintings and are equally exquisite. He worked carefully, experimenting with technique, and often employed antique papers for their subtle texture. Though he worked in black and white his forceful use of cross-hatching created a colorism that enhances his tranquil still-life compositions. The etchings received early critical acclaim, and several made during the 1940s were planned for use as illustrations in monographs on the artist. Morandi's craftsmanship in this medium may have played a part in the widespread revival of print workshops at mid-century in Italy and elsewhere.

In his late years, as Morandi honed his "cast of characters"—the bottles and crockery of his still-lifes—his work defied aesthetic categorization. His pictures wavered between reverence for objects and dilution of their forms. The soft pastel colors recall Piero della Francesca, and he composed with the intellectual rigor of a classicist. Though he was fond of early Renaissance masters, Morandi's subtle formal manipulations and steady individualism set him apart as modern. His efforts were rewarded in 1948 with the first prize for Italian painting at the Venice Biennial and membership in the Accademia di San Luca. He also won the top award for international painting at the Sao Paolo Biennial in 1957. An exhibition of his work in Winterthur, Switzerland, as well as a Cezanne exhibition in Zurich, lured Morandi from his homeland in 1956, the only occasion on which he left Italy. In 1963 Morandi was given the gold medal of Bologna, and on June 18, 1964, he died in the city of his birth. Often referred to as a "painter's painter,"

Morandi had proceeded with a self-discipline that brought him lasting respect.

Further Reading

Morandi's place in Italian art is discussed in James Thrall Soby and Alfred Barr, *Twentieth Century Italian Art* (1949). A fine recent exhibition catalogue is *Giorgio Morandi,* the Des Moines Art Center, with a preface by James T. Demetrion and essays by Luigi Magnani, Joan M. Lukach, Kenneth Baker, and Amy Namowitz Worthen (1981). This catalogue includes historical and critical analyses of his paintings and etchings. Lamberto Vitali published a general catalogue raisonné of Morandi's work in Italian in 1977. □

Alberto Moravia

Alberto Moravia (1907-1990) was one of the most important, and certainly the most prolific, of modern Italian authors. His keen moralistic approach focuses mainly on the iniquities of bourgeois society.

Alberto Moravia was born Alberto Pincherle on November 28, 1907, in Rome, the son of a well-to-do architect. Stricken with osteomyelitis at the age of nine, he was in a hospital in Cortina d'Ampezzo until 1925. During these years he studied French, English, and German, became a voracious reader, and started writing fiction at the age of 11.

Moravia's first published novel, *Gli indifferenti* (1929; *The Time of Indifference*), was an immediate success. The following year he went abroad as a journalist for various newspapers, an activity which thereafter always accompanied his creative writing. He lived in Paris and London and visited the United States and Mexico (1935), China (1937), and Greece (1938). In the early 1940s he lived on Capri with his wife, the novelist Elsa Morante. Since his relations with the Fascist regime had more and more deteriorated over the years, Moravia went into hiding after Mussolini's return to power in July 1943, and he spent some nine months among peasants and shepherds near Fondi. After the war he returned to Rome.

Moravia held several literary awards, including the Strega (1952) and Viareggio (1961) prizes. In 1952, the year his collected works began to appear, the Roman Catholic Church put all his writings on the Index. Moravia's works have been translated into 27 languages.

His Works

After the appearance of his first novel, Moravia worked toward broadening the spectrum of his moralistic canvas without any discernible evolution, and his works may be called variations on one theme, the caustic portrayal of the disintegration of middle-class mores as revealed through the prism of sex. His critics called him to task for being a novelist who not only believes in simply representing a given reality without any pretense of modifying it but also does not entertain the slightest thought of an interpretation.

For Moravia, ''an intellectual is nothing else than a witness of his time.''

At the root of the modern malaise of alienation, Moravia sees a complete lack of rapport with reality. Of the two possible approaches to objectify this crisis of rapport, critical realism and experimentalism, as he calls them, he opts for the former and its ''objective and in a sense scientific representation of the phenomena of the crisis in all its psychological and social aspects.''

Gli indifferenti is characteristic of his approach, recording with impassibility two days in the life of a Roman family. As a rather candid and unfavorable picture of certain strata of Roman society, it originated a social polemic, albeit unintended by its author, and after a fifth edition the publisher was advised not to undertake a sixth.

The long novel *Le ambizioni sbagliate* (1935; *The Wheel of Fortune*) in a sense depicts the same subject matter within the framework of a precise structure. The story is divided into three parts, each representing a single day in the life of its characters seen at intervals of one month. Against the desolate background of accepted defeat, ambition is analyzed as one of the basic and destructive drives behind human egoism.

L'imbroglio (1937), a collection of five long stories, centers on the familiar theme of man's incapacity to achieve love. *La mascherata* (1941; *The Garden Party*), written in the satirical and surrealist vein of the stories contained in *I sogni del pigro* (1940), and *L'epidemia* (1944) satirize dictatorial government.

The short novel *Agostino* (1944) belongs to the best of Moravia's fiction. Its subject matter being the discovery of evil and sex, the novel minutely analyzes the feelings of a young boy who discovers sex in his mother. *La romana* (1947; *The Woman of Rome*), a novel in first person narrative that established Moravia's fame abroad, is an absorbing inquiry into the psyche of Adriana, a Roman prostitute. At the center of the plot stands the existentialist issue of choice. *La disubbidienza* (1948), treating the discovery of sex by a 15-year-old, pursues the issues raised in *Agostino* on a higher level (these two novels were published in English as *Two Adolescents*).

Il conformista (1951; *The Conformist*), which some critics consider Moravia's worst novel, is on the surface the story of a man who embraces fascism to become ''normal.'' In a deeper sense, however, it should be seen as a comment on the modern tendency to abandon rationalistic and individual positions and to seek the protection of great collective myths. *L'amore conjugale* (1951; *Conjugal Love*) and *Il disprezzo* (1954; *A Ghost at Noon*) portray a relationship between husband and wife that falters because of the husband's excessive concern with his profession. The short-story collections *Racconti romani* (1954; *Roman Tales*) and *Nuovi racconti romani* (1959; *More Roman Tales*) represent a specific aspect of Moravia's approach to reality. *La ciociara* (1957; *Two Women*), considered his contribution to neorealism, depicts the violence of war as he experienced it during the time of his hiding.

La noia (1960; *The Empty Canvas*) is a tightly constructed work that harks back to the topic of Moravia's first book. It is a tribute to the existential malaise as well as a sum total of his other fiction. *L'attenzione* (1965) is perhaps his most differentiated and intricately constructed novel. Besides being concerned with the problem of ''authenticity'' of man's being and his actions, it is a novel about the inability to write a novel which—in the end—is written nevertheless in the form of a diary.

Moravia's plays include *Il mondo è quello che è* (1966), in which a professor divulges his language therapy during a holiday in a country villa that ends with the death of one of his ''pupils''; *L'intervista* (1966), representing an interview between an envoy from the moon and the minister of propaganda of an imaginary state on earth; and *Il dio Kurt* (1968), laid in a German concentration camp in Poland in 1944. Throughout his career Moravia also wrote travel literature, such as *Un'idea dell'India* (1961), and criticism, the most important of which was collected in *L'uomo come fine* (1964; *Man as an End*).

Despite the negative criticism Moravia received in his later years, he continued to write. He wrote *1934* (1982), a story set in the middle of the Fascist era. The novel *La Cosa* (released in Italy in 1983), was released in the United States a few years later under the title *Erotic Tales*. Two of his better known works were *Time of Desecration* (1980) and *The Voyeur* (1987). He died in Rome at the age of 82, on September 26, 1990.

Further Reading

Discussions in English of Moravia's work are Dego Giuliano, *Moravia* (1966), and Donald W. Heiney, *Three Italian Novelists: Moravia, Pavese, Vittorini* (1968). Recommended for general background is Sergio Pacifici, *A Guide to Contemporary Italian Literature from Futurism to Neorealism* (1962). His obituary appeared in the September 27, 1990 edition of the *New York Times*. □

José Francisco Morazán

José Francisco Morazán (1792-1842) was a Central American general and statesman. He was the last president of the Central American Federation and its best-known defender.

Francisco Morazán was born presumably in or near Tegucigalpa, Honduras, on Oct. 3, 1792. The environment afforded scant opportunity for education or employment; hence, Morazán was largely self-taught and his early experience limited.

After Central America won independence, Morazán aligned himself with Liberals and became their most successful military commander in armed conflicts with Conservatives. A succession of local victories in Honduras brought him to San Salvador, capital of neighboring El Salvador, in support of Liberal exiles organized to repossess the governments of the federal republic and the state of Guatemala. At the head of the Liberal forces, in April 1829 Morazán took Guatemala City, capital of the state and of the federation. He exiled Conservative functionaries and their principal collaborators, installed Liberals in both governments, and backed the program of reforms they initiated. In 1830 he was elected president of the federation and was reelected 4 years later.

Conditions, in part of his own making, limited Morazán's opportunity for constructive statesmanship. Expecting to stimulate development in the federated states, he introduced reforms alien to Central American experience, the anticlerical elements of the reforms awakening Conservative opposition. This disaffection led to many of the military threats which almost constantly menaced his regime. In addition, he had to contend with pressures from foreign governments, domestic personal rivalries, regional jealousies, a political system that many contemporaries believed was unworkable in Central America, and a perennially empty treasury that forced frequent resort to the hazardous expedient of exacting forced loans. Moreover, the appearance that office holding was reserved to a narrow circle of Morazán's relatives and intimate friends, and the questionable ethics said to characterize certain of his business transactions and personal relations, gave critics basis to question his disinterestedness and attack his probity.

Increasingly, especially during his second term, Morazán had to confront dissidents who gained control of state governments or generated popular uprisings. A particularly formidable insurrection headed by Rafael Carrera arose in Guatemala in 1837. Neither state nor federal forces could control the insurgents, who overthrew the Liberal government of Guatemala in 1838. Their success encouraged imitators elsewhere. By the end of Morazán's term imminent disintegration threatened the federation; no presidential election was held; and the incumbent's waning moral authority virtually disappeared. In a final effort to defeat Carrera and avert dissolution of the union, Morazán seized Guatemala City in March 1840. After momentary success his army was routed, and shortly thereafter he and his closest associates went into exile.

Morazán returned to Central America in 1842 to attempt to restore the federation. He landed in Costa Rica, overthrew the government of Braulio Carrillo, and was consolidating his position before moving to force the other states into a union, but he was betrayed and captured. He was executed in San José, Costa Rica, on September 15, ironically the anniversary of Central American independence.

Further Reading

The best work on Morazán in English is the brief biography by Robert S. Chamberlain, *Francisco Morazán: Champion of Central American Federation* (1950). It is a synthesis of research available only in Spanish. □

Sir Thomas More

The life of the English humanist and statesman Sir Thomas More (1478-1535) exemplifies the political and spiritual upheaval of the Reformation. The author of "Utopia," he was beheaded for opposing the religious policy of Henry VIII.

Thomas More was born in London on Feb. 6, 1478, to parents whose families were connected with the city's legal community. His education began at a prominent London school, St. Anthony's. In 1490 Thomas entered the household of Archbishop John Morton, Henry VII's closest adviser. Service to Morton brought experience of the world, then preferment in 1492 to Oxford, where More first encountered Greek studies. Two years later he returned to London, where legal and political careers were forged. By 1498 More had gained membership in Lincoln's Inn, an influential lawyers' fraternity.

Christian Humanism

A broader perspective then opened. The impact of humanism in England was greatly intensified about 1500, partly by Erasmus's first visit. His biblical interests spurred the work of Englishmen recently back from Italy; they had studied Greek intensively and thus were eager for fresh scrutiny of the Gospel texts and the writings of the early Church Fathers. John Colet's Oxford lectures on the Pauline epistles, and his move in 1504 to London as dean of St. Paul's Cathedral and founder of its famous humanist school, epitomized this reformist, educational activity among English churchmen. Lay patronage of the movement quickly made Cambridge, where Erasmus periodically taught, a focus of biblical scholarship and made London a favored meeting ground for Europe's men of letters.

England thus shed its cultural provincialism, and More, while pursuing his legal career and entering Parliament in 1504, was drawn to the Christian humanist circle. He spent his mid-20s in close touch with London's austere Carthusian monks and almost adopted their vocation. His thinking at this stage is represented by his interest in the Italian philosopher Giovanni Pico della Mirandola, who had also become increasingly pious when approaching the age of 30 a decade before; More's 1505 translation of Pico's first biography stressed that development.

But More then decided that he could fulfill a Christian vocation while remaining a layman. Both his subsequent family life and public career document the humanist persuasion that Christian service could be done, indeed should be pursued, in the world at large. He first married Jane Colt, who bore three sons and a daughter before dying in 1511, and then Alice Middleton. His household at Bucklersbury, London, until 1524 and then at Chelsea teemed with visitors, such as his great friend Erasmus, and formed a model educational community for the children and servants; More corresponded with his daughters in Latin. His legal career flourished and led to appointment as London's undersheriff

in 1511. This meant additional work and revenue as civic counsel at Henry VIII's court and as negotiator with foreign merchants.

More's first official trip abroad, on embassy at Antwerp in 1515, gave him leisure time in which he began his greatest work, *Utopia.* Modeled on Plato's *Republic,* written in Latin, finished and published in 1516, it describes an imaginary land, purged of the ostentation, greed, and violence of the English and European scenes that More surveyed. Interpretations of *Utopia* vary greatly. The dialogue form of book I and *Utopia*'s continual irony suggest More's deliberate ambiguity about his intent. Whatever vision More really professed, *Utopia* persists and delights as the model for an important literary genre.

Service under Henry VIII

Utopia book I and More's history of Richard III, written during the same period, contain reflections about politics and the problems of counseling princes. They represent More's uncertainty about how to handle frequent invitations to serve Henry VIII, whose policies included many facets distasteful to the humanists. More had written in *Utopia*: "So it is in the deliberations of monarchs. If you cannot pluck up wrongheaded opinions by the root . . . yet you must not on that account desert the commonwealth. You must not abandon the ship in a storm because you cannot control the winds." He finally accepted Henry's fee late in 1517 and fashioned a solid career in diplomacy, legal service, and finance, crowned in 1529 by succession to Cardinal Wolsey as chancellor of England.

More's early doubts, however, proved justified. Under Wolsey's direction More as Speaker of the House of Commons in 1523 promoted a war levy so unpopular that its collection was discontinued. In European negotiations Henry's belligerence and Wolsey's ambition frustrated More's desire to stop the wars of Christendom so that its faith and culture could be preserved.

By the time that Wolsey's inability to obtain the annulment of Henry's marriage to Catherine of Aragon had raised More to highest office and placed him in the increasingly distressing role of Henry's chief agent in the maneuvering that began to sever England from Rome, More was deeply engaged in writings against Lutherans, defending the fundamental tenets of the Church whose serious flaws he knew. More cannot justly be held responsible for the increased number of Protestants burned during his last months in office, but this was the gloomiest phase of his career. The polemics, in English after 1528, including the *Dialogue Concernynge Heresyes* (1529) and *Apologye* (1533), were his bulkiest works but not his best, for they were defensive in nature and required detailed rebuttal of specific charges, not the light and allusive touch of the humanist imagination. He continued writing until a year after his resignation from office, tendered May 16, 1532, and caused by illness and distress over England's course of separation from the Catholic Church.

Break with the King

More recognized the dangers that his Catholic apologetics entailed in the upside-down world of Henry's break with Rome and tried to avoid political controversy. But Henry pressed him for a public acknowledgment of the succession to the throne established in 1534. More refused the accompanying oath that repudiated papal jurisdiction in England, and the Christian unity thereby manifest, in favor of royal supremacy.

More's last dramatic year—from the first summons for interrogation on April 12, 1534, through imprisonment, trial for treason, defiance of his perjured accusers, and finally execution on July 6, 1535—should not be allowed to overshadow his entire life's experience. Its significance extends beyond the realm of English history. For many of Europe's most critical years, More worked to revitalize Christendom. He attacked those who most clearly threatened its unity; once convinced that Henry VIII was among their number, More withdrew his service and resisted to his death the effort to extract his allegiance. His life, like *Utopia,* offers fundamental insights about private virtues and their relationship to the politics of human community.

Further Reading

Preeminent More scholars are now contributing to the Yale Edition of his complete works under the direction of Louis Martz. Thus far published are *The History of King Richard III,* edited by Richard S. Sylvister (1963), and *Utopia,* edited by Edward Surtz and Jack H. Hexter (1965). A convenient edition of *Utopia,* with critical appraisals, is by Ligeia Gallagher, *More's Utopia and Its Critics* (1964); and a recent study is by R. Schoeck, *Utopia and Humanism* (1969).

The classic biography is by More's son-in-law, William Roper, *The Life of Sir Thomas More,* translated by Ralph Robynson and edited with introduction, notes, glossary, and index of names by J. Rawson Lumby (1952). Other good biographies are the Reverend Thomas E. Bridgett, *The Life and Writings of Blessed Thomas More* (1913), and Raymond Wilson Chambers, *Thomas More* (1935). For historical background see Stanley T. Bindoff, *Tudor England* (1954), and Myron Piper Gilmore, *The World of Humanism, 1453-1517* (1962). ☐

José María Morelos

José María Morelos (1765-1815) was a Mexican parish priest who joined the forces seeking to liberate Mexico from Spanish rule. He became the greatest of the insurgent military commanders, and as a statesman he advocated far-reaching political and social reforms.

The struggle for independence began with the celebrated revolt initiated by Miguel Hidalgo, the parish priest of Dolores, on Sept. 16, 1810, now one of Mexico's great national holidays. Although the effort achieved some initial successes, Hidalgo failed to clarify the aims of the revolt or to provide effective leadership. With his capture, trial, and execution in 1811, the movement was suppressed. By that time, however, another figure had emerged to assume leadership—José María Morelos

Morelos was born in Valladolid (now Morelia, the capital of the state of Michoacán) on Sept. 30, 1765. A mestizo (of mixed Spanish and Indian blood), he was thus a member of the lower classes in the Spanish colonial social system. His parents were respectable though poor, and young Morelos went to work at an early age as a mule driver in the *tierra caliente* of southern Mexico.

Schooling and Priesthood

In 1790 Morelos, with money he had saved and the barest rudiments of an education, enrolled at San Nicolás College in Valladolid to begin training for a career in the Church. Hidalgo was rector of the college during Morelos's 2 years of residence there. After further study at the Seminario Tridentino in Valladolid, Morelos in 1795 journeyed to the Royal and Pontifical University of Mexico to take his final examinations and receive a bachelor of arts degree. In 1797 he was ordained a priest and 2 years later was assigned to the parish of Carácuaro, in the heart of the *tierra caliente,* where he remained until 1810.

Carácuaro, with its nearly 2,000 Indian parishioners, was one of the most remote and poverty-stricken curacies in all Mexico, and the work of the priest was extremely demanding and burdensome. Although Morelos performed manifold duties diligently, he became increasingly frustrated about the future of his ministry and irritated with his ecclesiastical superiors, who ignored or rejected his petitions. Yet he probably would have remained in Carácuaro for the rest of his life, outside the stream of history, had he not received news in 1810 of the revolt led by Hidalgo.

In a conference between the two men, Hidalgo convinced Morelos that the revolt was in defense of country and religion, inasmuch as the Spanish officials in Mexico were about to surrender the country to Napoleon Bonaparte and the French. When Morelos responded sympathetically and agreed to join the cause, Hidalgo gave him a military commission and directed him to capture the port of Acapulco and spread the revolution southward.

Revolutionary Leader

During the next 3 years Morelos displayed the kind of leadership and ability for which he became famous in Mexican history. He raised and trained armies, instilled discipline and morale, planned campaigns, selected his commanders, and brought under his control an area south of Mexico City which stretched from the Isthmus of Tehuantepec on the east to Valladolid on the west. His most brilliant achievements were the conquest of the province of Oaxaca and his gallant defense of Cuautla, where he withstood a siege for 2 1/2 months.

Morelos captured Acapulco in 1813 after a long siege, giving Spanish forces elsewhere, however, an opportunity to reorganize and seize the initiative. Thus, the taking of Acapulco, in compliance with Hidalgo's orders, marked the beginning of Morelos's decline.

Political and Social Programs

While Morelos was engaged in the conquest of southern Mexico, he was also formulating a revolutionary political and social program and laying plans for the establishment of an insurgent government. In September 1813 Morelos—the "Servant of the Nation," as he liked to style himself—called the Congress of Chilpancingo, composed of representatives of the provinces under his control, to consider a program which he outlined in a document entitled "Sentiments of the Nation."

In it, Morelos called for the independence of Mexico and for the abolition of all class distinctions, such as Indian, mulatto, and mestizo, in favor of the designation "American" for all native-born persons. Sovereignty, he declared, was vested in the people and should be exercised by a representative congress. He also recommended republican institutions, a strong executive authority, respect for property, voluntary Church contributions, and the abolition of slavery, torture, and the tribute. The cornerstone of a Mexican nation had been laid at Chilpancingo, but the completion of the structure would require military victories during 1814. Such, however, was not to be; Morelos's congress, other than declaring independence and naming him generalissimo, did little.

Military Reverses

A succession of military disasters beginning at Valladolid late in 1813 brought a decline in Morelos's prestige and power, and the congress became an itinerant body relentlessly pursued by the viceroy's forces. In an attempt to salvage something from a dying cause, the congress completed a constitution at Apatzingán in October 1814 which featured a weak executive and a powerful legislature. Morelos voiced his disapproval of the document but conceded that it was the best that could have been framed under the circumstances. His authority by this time was reduced to protecting the new insurgent congress, which had been installed in accordance with the constitution; and when, in November 1815, Morelos attempted to escort that body to a location near the east coast of Mexico, he was captured and brought to Mexico City in chains.

Morelos stood trial before three separate tribunals. A joint civil-ecclesiastical tribunal sentenced him to be degraded from the priesthood for heresy; the Inquisition, in a painful ceremony, carried out the act of degradation; and a civil court sentenced him to be executed for treason. On Dec. 22, 1815, at the village of San Cristóbal Ecatépec, a short distance from Mexico City, the sentence was carried out.

Further Reading

Most of the writing on Morelos is in Spanish. The only full-length treatment in English is Wilbert H. Timmons, *Morelos: Priest, Soldier, Statesman of Mexico* (rev. ed. 1970). A useful biographical sketch of him is in James Aloysius Magner, *Men of Mexico* (1942), and John Anthony Caruso, *The Liberators of Mexico* (1954). Recommended for historical background are Hubert Howe Bancroft, *History of Mexico*, vol. 4 (rev. ed. 1914); Henry Bamford Parkes, *A History of Mexico* (3d rev. ed. 1960); Hugh M. Hamill, Jr., *The Hidalgo Revolt* (1966); and Lesley Byrd Simpson, *Many Mexicos* (4th ed. rev. 1966). □

Giovanni Battista Morgagni

The Italian anatomist Giovanni Battista Morgagni (1682-1771) was the founder of pathological anatomy and the first to demonstrate the relation between disease symptoms and pathological changes in organs.

Giovanni Battista Morgagni was born on Feb. 25, 1682, in Forli. At 15 Giambattista, as he often signed his name, entered the University of Bologna to study medicine and received a degree in 1701. For a short time he continued studying and teaching at Bologna but soon entered medical practice in his native Forli.

In 1706 Morgagni published the first volume of *Adversaria anatomica,* a collection of medical essays communicated to the Academia Inquietorum which established Morgagni in the scientific community. Later contributions were published from 1717 to 1719. In 1711 he was offered the assistant professorship of theoretical medicine at the University of Padua, a school noted for its brilliant achievements in anatomy for 2 centuries. Morgagni accepted the post in 1712 and in 1715 was elevated to the rank of professor of anatomy. He remained at Padua as a popular teacher, anatomist, and clinical consultant until his death on Dec. 6, 1771.

In 1761, at the age of 79, Morgagni published his great work *De sedibus et causis morborum per anatomen indagatis libri quinque* (*On the Seats and Causes of Disease, Anatomically Studied*). For centuries physicians had been guided by the conviction that disease was always generalized throughout the whole body. Although pathological changes in organs had been noted before and although 17th- and early-18th-century anatomists recognized that such changes were sometimes related to the symptoms of specific diseases, *De sedibus* proved conclusively that this relationship was a valid one and demonstrated its full meaning.

Morgagni's work was based on years of careful observation and experiment, including over 600 postmortem examinations, in which he pinpointed pathological changes leading to death and showed the relationship with the symptoms of the illness preceding death. He also recognized the role of the nervous system in making symptoms felt at a point distant from the seat of the disease and the possible influence of such external factors as weather, age, and occupation in causing pathological changes. These achievements, plus his brilliant descriptions of pathological conditions, make Morgagni the founder of pathological anatomy, both as a distinct part of anatomical study and as a critical basis for understanding the cause of illness.

Further Reading

Morgagni's *De sedibus* is readily available, since an English translation made in 1769 by Benjamin Alexander was reprinted in 1960. There is no adequate biographical study of Morgagni. However, his work is discussed in almost all general histories of medicine, many of which contain some biographical data. Of particular help is the chapter on Morgagni in Henry Sigerist, *The Great Doctors: A Biographical History of Medicine* (1933). His life and work are discussed against a background of developments in pathology in Esmond R. Long, *A History of Pathology* (rev. ed. 1965). □

Conway Lloyd Morgan

The English comparative psychologist and social evolutionist Conway Lloyd Morgan (1852-1936) was one of the first to consistently apply the experimental method in observing animal behavior. To interpret animal behavior he formulated his "law of parsimony."

On Feb. 6, 1852, C. Lloyd Morgan was born in London. He attended the Royal School of Mines in London, the Royal College of Science, and the University of Bristol, receiving doctorates in science and in law. He taught for five years at the Diocesan College in Rondesbosch, South Africa. On his return to England in 1884 he joined the University of Bristol as professor of geology and zoology, and three years later he became

principal. In 1910 he assumed the chair of psychology and ethics.

One of the major problems raised by Charles Darwin's theory of evolution was that of animal psychology. There was need for a continuity based on similarities between different animal forms, including similarities between man and the animals. At that time workers dealing with animal behavior ascribed complex and complicated humanlike motivations to the behavior of the nonhuman animals they observed, tending to "read" animal behavior motivations that were in the workers' minds but not necessarily in the minds of the animals they observed. This was called the anthropomorphic or anthropopsychic interpretation of animal behavior.

These early workers also relied on reports of animal behavior from untrained and uncritical observers. Imagination and superstition distorted their accounts. This careless way of collecting information, relying on stories instead of establishing criteria to distinguish fact from fancy, was called the anecdotal method.

It was to these two offenses against scientific accuracy and integrity that Morgan addressed himself. Somewhat unjustly he singled out George John Romanes, a friend of Darwin, as a primary target. Romanes, who coined the phrase "comparative psychology," attributed to animals as much intelligence as their acts would justify. His *Animal Intelligence* (1882) was the first comparative psychology ever written. Morgan reacted against Romanes in *Animal Life and Intelligence* (1890-1891), later revised and retitled

Animal Behavior (1900); he held that "one should, in such a situation, attribute as little intelligence as their acts would justify."

In his best-known work, *Introduction to Comparative Psychology* (1894), Morgan sought to counteract the errors inherent in the anecdotal method, particularly the error of anthropopsychic interpretation. In this book is his famous canon of interpretation: "In no case may we interpret an action as the outcome of the exercise of a higher psychical faculty, if it can be interpreted as the outcome of the exercise of one which stands lower in the psychological scale." He derived this "law of parsimony" from William of Ockham's razor. Considered by some to be of little value as a scientific tool, Morgan's canon had some validity in offsetting a bias of interpretation. He used it as a corrective to the inaccuracies resulting from the twin evils of anthropopsychic interpretation and the anecdotal method, as exemplified in Romanes's works.

In 1920 Morgan became emeritus professor of psychology at the University of Bristol. He was the first person honored by the Royal Society for scientific work in psychology. In his *Gifford Lectures* he expounded his philosophy of emergent evolution, basing the books *Emergent Evolution* (1923) and *Life, Mind and Spirit* (1926) on them. *Mind at the Crossroads* (1929) and *The Emergence of Novelty* (1933) followed.

As a philosopher or social evolutionist, Morgan was interested in the relation of science to philosophic issues. He felt that it was essential to create a metaphysical system within which the naturalistic demonstration of evolution might be placed. He believed that there was one continuous process called evolution, which at irregular intervals was interrupted by discontinuities or critical turning points. These points are distinguished by the abrupt appearance of "emergents." Successive emergents progress evolutionarily as a "pyramidal scheme." This evolution is jumpy rather than uniformly continuous. The emergence of consciousness, he believed, came about not by design or plan but by chance.

On March 6, 1936, Morgan died at Hastings, England.

Further Reading

Excerpts from Morgan's *Introduction to Comparative Psychology* are in William S. Sahakian, *Psychology: A Source Book in Systematic Psychology* (1968). His autobiography is in *History of Psychology in Autobiography,* vol. 2, edited by Carl Murchison (1932). For Morgan's place in psychology see Edwin G. Boring, *History of Experimental Psychology* (1929), and Boring's "The Influence of Evolutionary Theory upon American Psychological Thought" in Stow Persons, ed., *Evolutionary Thought in America* (1950). □

Daniel Morgan

Daniel Morgan (ca. 1735-1802), American soldier, was an excellent battlefield tactician and guerrilla fighter who distinguished himself in major Revolutionary War battles.

Daniel Morgan typified the differences between British and American military practices in the Revolution. Whereas his opponents stressed bulky linear formations and volley fire—commanders manipulating their men like pawns on a chessboard—Morgan, with a tradition of frontier combat behind him, emphasized the thin skirmish line and individual marksmanship.

Almost nothing is known of Morgan's first years, except that his parents, Welsh immigrants, were living in New Jersey at the time of his birth. A restless and high-spirited youth, he left home in his teens and, in 1753, settled in western Virginia. The tall, muscular young man was frequently in trouble with the law for brawling in taverns and not paying his liquor and card debts. As a teamster, he accompanied the ill-fated expedition of British general Edward Braddock against Ft. Duquesne in 1755. Later, he fought in the militia during Lord Dunmore's War.

Morgan's life became more stable after he formed a common-law union with 16-year-old Abigail Curry, with whom he had two daughters. He purchased a farm and earned the respect of his community, gaining a captaincy in the militia and appointment to several minor county offices.

Revolutionary Service in the North

By 1775 Morgan was a tested and tempered back-country soldier. He was proficient in Indian fighting methods and knew how to use the Pennsylvania rifle, a long, slender weapon of great range and accuracy. Not surprisingly, when the Continental Congress authorized the raising of 10 companies of frontier riflemen to serve as light infantry, he was chosen to form one of them and was given the rank of captain.

Morgan's first important assignment came in the fall of 1775, when he served in Benedict Arnold's expedition that invaded Canada. Morgan, stripped to the waist and attired in Indian leggings and breechclout, led the advance. Outside the city of Quebec, Arnold's column united with an American force from Montreal under Gen. Richard Montgomery. During the attack Morgan took temporary command after Montgomery was killed and Arnold was wounded. He fought heroically against the enemy until finally overwhelmed by superior numbers and compelled to surrender.

Although Morgan spent 8 months in a British prison before being exchanged, his performance at Quebec brought him deserved recognition. He was promoted to colonel and given a special corps of light infantry composed of 500 picked backwoodsmen.

Morgan's light corps had its finest hours in the Saratoga campaign of 1777, when Morgan rushed to assist the American northern army, then opposing the southward drive from Canada of British general John Burgoyne. Even before Morgan's arrival, Burgoyne had seen his two supporting columns repulsed at Oswego and Bennington and his supplies run dangerously thin in upper New York. In the two Saratoga battles (Sept. 19 and Oct. 7, 1777), American general Horatio Gates left the bulk of his command in its entrenchments and allowed Burgoyne to wear himself down in fruitless probes. Gates used Morgan's corps to delay and annoy the enemy. The riflemen, using their woodland skills effectively, took a heavy toll of Redcoats. Soon surrounded by Gates's army and swarms of militiamen, Burgoyne laid down his arms at Saratoga. In his report to Congress, Gates declared that "too much praise cannot be given the Corps commanded by Col. Morgan."

A sensitive man, Morgan felt slighted when a particular light infantry assignment went to Anthony Wayne and not himself. Consequently he returned home for nearly a year, until he answered an appeal to join the American southern army, which was endeavoring to halt the forces of Lord Cornwallis.

Revolutionary Service in the South

After discouraging months of inactivity, the American cause in the South brightened with a new commander, Nathanael Greene, who sent Morgan into western South Carolina to sit on the flank and rear of Cornwallis. Determined to rid himself of the pesky Morgan before invading the upper South, Cornwallis sent Banastre Tarleton's famed Tory Legion in pursuit. Morgan, who had long been eager for "a stroke at Tarleton," selected a site near Cowpens to

meet the British forces. Placing his militia in front of his regulars, Morgan had them fire two blasts and then withdraw behind his Continentals. Taking the retirement for flight, the unsuspecting Tory Legion charged into the face of a volley from the regulars. In the confusion Morgan threw his cavalry and reformed militia against the British flanks; this ended the battle. "A more compleat victory never was obtained," exclaimed the colorful Morgan, whose men affectionately called him the "Old Wagoner."

Cowpens, the tactical masterpiece of the war, was Morgan's last major action; he soon retired because of a severe back ailment. Returning to the "sweets of domestic life," Morgan twice emerged for public service: he aided in suppressing the Whiskey Rebellion as a Virginia militia general (1794-1795), and he served a term as a Federalist in the U.S. House of Representatives. He died on July 6, 1802.

Further Reading

There are two recent biographies of Morgan. North Callahan, *Daniel Morgan: Ranger of the Revolution* (1961), takes a life-and-times approach. Don Higginbotham, *Daniel Morgan: Revolutionary Rifleman* (1961), concentrates on the man. A shorter treatment that stresses the relationship between Morgan's fighting methods and the irregular war methods of the 20th century is Don Higginbotham's "Daniel Morgan: Guerrilla Fighter" in George A. Billias, ed., *George Washington's Generals* (1964). Recommended for general historical background are Willard M. Wallace, *An Appeal to Arms: A Military History of the American Revolution* (1951), and Christopher Ward, *The War of the Revolution* (2 vols., 1952).

Additional Sources

Graham, James, of New Orleans, *The life of General Daniel Morgan of the Virginia line of the Army of the United States: with portions of his correspondence,* Bloomingburg, NY: Zebrowski Historical Services Pub. Co., 1993. □

Garrett A. Morgan

A pioneer inventor, Garrett A. Morgan (1877-1963) was responsible for the creation of such life-saving inventions as the gas mask and traffic lights.

In a long and productive career that spanned over forty years, Garret A. Morgan worked diligently to create new products and services to enhance safety in modern-day living. His creations, for many of whom he held patents, brought him much fame and prosperity in his lifetime, and he was nationally honored by many organizations, including the Emancipation Centennial in 1963.

Garrett Augustus Morgan was born in Paris, Kentucky, on March 4, 1877. He was the seventh of eleven children born to Sydney Morgan, a former slave who was freed in 1863, and Elizabeth (Reed) Morgan. Leaving home at age fourteen with only an elementary school education, Morgan eventually settled in Cleveland. He taught himself to repair sewing machines, working with a number of companies before opening his own business specializing in sewing machine sales and repair in 1907. The venture was successful, enabling Morgan to set up house in Cleveland, and in 1908, he married Mary Anne Hassek. Together they had three sons.

Eventually, Morgan opened his own tailoring shop, and it was here that he developed his first unique product. Like other people in the clothing industry, Morgan was trying to solve a prevalent problem inherent in sewing woolen material: the sewing machine needle operated at such high speed that it often scorched the material. Morgan, who was working with a chemical solution to reduce this friction, noticed that the solution he was developing caused hairs on a pony-fur cloth to straighten instead. Intrigued, he tried it on a neighbor's dog, and when it straightened the hair on the dog's coat, Morgan finally tried the new solution on his own hair. The success of the solution led Morgan to form G. A. Morgan Refining Company, the first producers of hair refining cream.

During his lifetime, Morgan continued to experiment with new products, inventing such things as hat and belt fasteners and a friction drive clutch. His most significant invention, however, came in 1912, when he developed the "safety hood," the precursor to the modern-day gas mask. Morgan's patent application for the contraption referred to it as a "Breathing Device." Granted a patent in 1914, the device, which consisted of a hood with an inlet for fresh air and an outlet for exhaled air, drew a number of awards, including the First Grand Prize from the Second International Exposition of Safety and Sanitation in New York City.

Although Morgan tested and demonstrated the use of the safety hood over the next few years, its most critical test occurred on July 24, 1916, during a tunnel explosion at the Cleveland Waterworks. The whole area was filled with noxious fumes and smoke, trapping workers in a tunnel under Lake Erie. Aided by his Breathing Device, Morgan went into the tunnel and carried workers out on his back, saving a number of men from an underground death. For this act of heroism, Morgan received the Carnegie Medal and a Medal of Bravery from the city, and the International Association of Fire Engineers made Morgan an honorary member. Not much later, Morgan established a company to manufacture and sell the Breathing Device in response to numerous orders from fire and police departments and mining industries. Fire fighters came to rely upon the gas mask in rescue attempts, and the invention helped save thousands from chlorine gas and other noxious fumes during World War I.

Next Morgan created the three-way traffic signal, a device responsible for saving thousands of lives over the years. The idea to build the warning and regulatory signal system came to him after he witnessed a carriage accident at a four-way street crossing. Once again, Morgan made sure to acquire a patent for his product, this time in Britain as well as the United States and Canada. Eventually, Morgan sold the rights to his invention to the General Electric Company for $40,000.

In addition to inventing new and unique products Morgan was actively involved in promoting the welfare of African Americans. In 1920, therefore, he began publishing the *Cleveland Call,* a newspaper devoted to publishing local and national black news. Additionally, Morgan served as an officer of the Cleveland Association of Colored Men, remaining an active member after it merged with the National Association for the Advancement of Colored People (NAACP). He developed glaucoma in 1943, losing most of his sight, and died in 1963.

Further Reading

Haber, Louis, *Black Pioneers of Science and Invention,* Harcourt, 1970, pp. 61–72.
Sammons, Vivian Ovelton, *Blacks in Science and Medicine,* Hemisphere Publishing, 1990, p. 176. □

John Morgan

The American physician John Morgan (1735-1789) established the first medical department at a colonial college and was medical director of the Continental Army.

John Morgan, third son of a Welsh merchant, Evan Morgan, and Joanna Biles Morgan, was born in Philadelphia, Pa., on Oct. 16, 1735. Orphaned at 13, John attended West Nottingham School, became a medical apprentice to John Redman, and later became apothecary of the Pennsylvania Hospital. After completing requirements for the bachelor's degree in 1756 at the College of Philadelphia, he participated in frontier warfare as surgeon for the Pennsylvania troops.

Between 1760 and 1763 Morgan studied with eminent physicians in London and completed his medical degree at the University of Edinburgh. He was elected to the Académie Royale de Chirurgie de Paris, to the Royal Society of London, and to the Royal College of Physicians in London and in Edinburgh.

To improve standards of medical training in America, Morgan proposed establishing a medical school at the College of Philadelphia. Chosen professor of the theory and practice of medicine, he expounded his reforms in *A Discourse upon the Institution of Medical Schools in America* (1765). He advocated rigorous training and the separation of the professions of physician, surgeon, and apothecary. Too idealistic and egocentric to work harmoniously with others, he became an archrival of William Shippen, Jr., professor of anatomy and surgery at the college. Morgan won acclaim for his medical lectures but gave up research. After his marriage to Mary Hopkinson in 1765, he encouraged science, philosophy, and fine arts as a member of the American Society for Promoting Useful Knowledge and of the American Philosophical Society.

Morgan reluctantly supported the patriot cause during the Revolution and accepted the directorship of hospitals for the Continental Army in 1775. Faced with overwhelming problems of insufficiently trained medical personnel, scarce supplies, and congressional indifference, he became em-

broiled in acrimonious disputes with Dr. Shippen. Unable to prevent the collapse of the medical service, Morgan was summarily dismissed by Congress in 1777 and did not win vindication until 2 years later.

In postwar Philadelphia Morgan resumed his medical practice but was only belatedly reelected to his professorship after the reorganization of the college as the University of Pennsylvania. Shattered by his wife's death, prematurely old at 50, he withdrew from public life, reappearing briefly to participate in the founding of the College of Physicians. He died on Oct. 15, 1789.

Further Reading

The definitive biography of Morgan is Whitfield J. Bell, Jr., *John Morgan: Continental Doctor* (1965). Further information on him may be found in Lyman H. Butterfield, ed., *The Letters of Benjamin Rush* (1951). Morgan's relationship to the University of Pennsylvania is brought out in Edward P. Cheyney, *History of the University of Pennsylvania, 1740-1940* (1940). Recommended for background reading are Francis R. Packard, *History of Medicine in the United States* (1931); Carl and Jessica Bridenbaugh, *Rebels and Gentlemen: Philadelphia in the Age of Franklin* (1942); and Brooke Hindle, *The Pursuit of Science in Revolutionary America, 1735-1789* (1956; repr. 1967). □

John Pierpont Morgan

John Pierpont Morgan (1837-1913), the most powerful American banker of his time, helped build a credit bridge between Europe and America and financially rescued the United States government twice.

On April 17, 1837, J. P. Morgan was born in Harford, Conn. After 2 years at the University of Göttingen in Germany, he entered the world of banking and commerce in 1857. In 1895 his firm, a private bank engaging in commercial as well as investment banking, adopted its final name of J. P. Morgan & Company.

Early in the Civil War, Morgan lent money to a man who bought rifles from the Federal government and resold them to it; this is the notorious Hall carbine affair, but there is no evidence that Morgan was other than a creditor. Less than 2 decades later Morgan became instrumental in the periodic reorganization of American railroads, emerging as a decisive factor in railroading. He refinanced bankrupt railroads, acted to stabilize rates, and consolidated competing lines. In addition, to protect individuals who purchased railroad securities from his firm, Morgan placed his own representatives on the railroads' boards of directors.

Financial Rescue of the Government

In 1893 America experienced a major economic downturn which, in conjunction with questionable monetary policies (resulting from pressure from the silver inflationists), put an impossible burden on the U.S. Treasury's

gold reserve. President Grover Cleveland's attempts to replenish the gold reserve were ineffective. In 1895 Morgan played the role of central banker, sold government bonds for gold (half obtained abroad through his foreign affiliates), and guaranteed to protect the gold reserve. Though Morgan was charged with profiting exorbitantly and taking advantage of the dire straits of the government, he never revealed the precise amount of his profits, so the validity of such allegations is impossible to assess. His syndicate succeeded temporarily in its objectives; public and private ends harmonized at a price which was probably not excessive, considering the service rendered to the nation.

In 1901 a tremendous conflict opened between James J. Hill and Edward H. Harriman for domination of the railroads west of the Mississippi and in the northern half of the country. Morgan was allied with Hill, and in the course of this contest the price of Northern Pacific stock shares jumped to astronomical heights. The compromise reached was based on pooling all interests in the Northern Securities Company. When this company was dissolved in 1904 as a consequence of successful prosecution under the Sherman Antitrust Act, modern antitrust enforcement had been inaugurated.

Morgan founded the U.S. Steel Corporation in 1901. The culmination of a wave of similar consolidations, it was the largest industrial concern of the time. U.S. Steel never controlled the entire steel industry, and its share of the market has declined steadily.

Solving the Panic of 1907 represents Morgan's highest achievement; never again would private power be vested with so large a public responsibility. When the panic hit, the financial community of New York rallied around Morgan, and the Federal government entrusted its funds to his disposition. He recruited brilliant lieutenants to investigate the resources of the various New York banks and trust companies, determine which were solvent, and act to save them. (There was no central bank, as the Federal Reserve System was created only in 1913 as an after-math to the panic.) Morgan and his cohorts were, for all practical purposes, the central bank.

An Assessment

Morgan was preeminently suited to the world in which he lived. During the years of his power the American economy grew at a prodigious rate. Morgan was one of the "vital few" who made it happen. He was a superb organizer in an economy that was replacing competition with concentration. He chose extremely able associates but reserved the crucial decisions for himself. He earned his economic reward by linking those who needed capital with those who had it to invest, whether in Europe or America. The success of his endeavor actually lessened the investment banker's significance, as enterprises became internally financed and less dependent on external financing.

As an art collector, Morgan avidly sought paintings, sculpture, and tapestries. He made the Metropolitan Museum of Art in New York the equal of any museum in the world, although he contributed to others, too. "The Morgan collections represent the most grandiose gesture of *noblesse oblige* the world has ever known," wrote Aline B. Saarinen (1957). He was a man of genuine taste. His death in Rome on March 31, 1913, left a void, for his was a personal, not an institutional, power and hence not readily transferable.

Further Reading

Since the primary sources are unavailable, there is no definitive biography of Morgan. The best is Frederick Lewis Allen, *The Great Pierpont Morgan* (1949). Of considerably less value are John Kennedy Winkler, *Morgan the Magnificent: The Life of J. Pierpont Morgan* (1930), and Herbert Livingston Satterlee, *J. Pierpont Morgan: An Intimate Portrait* (1939).
Many books deal with a history of Morgan's firm or with particular episodes in which Morgan was prominent: Henry Meyer Balthasar, *A History of the Northern Securities Case* (1906); Abraham Berglund, *The United States Steel Corporation: A Study of the Growth and Influence of Combination in the Iron and Steel Industry* (1907); Stuart Daggett, *Railroad Reorganization* (1908); Alexander D. Noyes, *Forty Years of American Finance* (1909); Lewis Corey, *The House of Morgan* (1930); Allan Nevins, *Grover Cleveland* (1944); Paul Studenski and Herman E. Krooss, *Financial History of the United States* (1952); and Edwin P. Hoyt, Jr., *The House of Morgan* (1966). Excellent selections are in N. S. B. Gras and Henrietta M. Larson, *Casebook in American Business History* (1939), and Jonathan R. Hughes, *The Vital Few: American Economic Progress and Its Protagonists* (1966). Robert Gordon Wasson, *The Hall Carbine Affair: A Study in Contemporary Folklore* (1948), is a historiographical exercise concerning Morgan's complicity in an event used to attack his integrity.

For background see John Moody, *The Masters of Capital: A Chronicle of Wall Street* (1919), and Frederick L. Allen, *The Lords of Creation* (1935). The biographies of two of Morgan's partners are worthy of mention: Thomas Williams Lamont, *Henry P. Davison* (1933), and especially John A. Garraty, *Right-hand Man: The Life of George W. Perkins* (1960). Morgan's role as art patron is treated in Francis Henry Taylor, *Pierpont Morgan as Collector and Patron* (1957), and Aline B. Saarinen, *The Proud Possessors: The Lives, Times, and Tastes of Some Adventurous American Art Collectors* (1957). □

John Pierpont Morgan II

John Pierpont Morgan II (1867-1943), American banker, headed J. P. Morgan & Company, one of the most prestigious private banking firms in the world.

Born in Irvington, N.Y., on Sept. 7, 1867, J. P. Morgan II was the only son of the powerful financier. After he graduated from Harvard University in 1889, he joined the family firm.

On the death of his father in 1913, Morgan became the head of J. P. Morgan & Company and inherited more than $50 million. However, he never had the power or the personal magnetism of his father. His most important accomplishment was to secure the firm's appointment as American fiscal and purchasing agent for the Allied powers prior to United States entry into World War I. The role played by the Morgan bank led to repercussions during the 1930s, when Americans had become disillusioned about the war. A Senate committee investigated the bankers and the munitions makers and their influence on American entry into World War I. Morgan was charged with having profited excessively as agent for the Allies.

During the 1920s Morgan's role was hardly central to the American economy. Investment bankers were not as important as they once had been. Industrial corporations had earned substantial profits during World War I and, then and later, retained enough of their earnings to reduce their dependence on outside financing.

But the stock market crash of October 1929 brought Morgan to the fore once again. His firm organized a money pool to stabilize stock prices. But, in contrast to the elder Morgan's success in stemming the Panic of 1907, this effort, although it succeeded temporarily, ultimately failed.

During the Depression, the Senate Committee on Banking and Currency, investigating the causes of the stock market crash, used Morgan as a conspicuous witness. The committee disclosed that J. P. Morgan & Company employed "preferred lists," which enabled influential persons to buy securities at less than the market price. Morgan never fully grasped the significance of the attack on big business that characterized his years as head of the house of Morgan.

Morgan died on March 13, 1943. He had carried on his father's work in banking and also in philanthropy and the arts.

Further Reading

There is no biography of the younger Morgan. The most extensive treatment of him is in Edwin P. Hoyt, Jr., *The House of Morgan* (1966), although only one-sixth of the book is devoted to him and the emphasis is social rather than economic. Scattered references to him are in Lewis Corey, *The House of Morgan* (1930); a biography written by one Morgan partner about another, Thomas W. Lamont's *Henry P. Davison* (1931); Frederick Lewis Allen's biography, *The Great Pierpont Morgan* (1949); and the autobiography of Thomas W. Lamont, *Across World Frontiers* (1951). □

Julia Morgan

Julia Morgan (1872-1957), California's first licensed female architect, designed both institutional buildings and private homes in the San Francisco area. She preferred to use indigenous materials and carefully designed for often topographically difficult sites.

Julia Morgan was born on January 20, 1872, in San Francisco, California, and died there in 1957. Her career as an architect was shaped by two principal facts: her residence in California, with its distinctive architectural traditions and practical possibilities, and her gender—at the beginning of the 20th century she was a woman attempting to break into a field judged by most of her contemporaries to be the exclusive province of men. In fact, she became California's first licensed female architect.

After graduating with a degree in engineering from the University of California, Berkeley, in 1894, Morgan planned to continue her education at the world's most prestigious architectural school, the École des Beaux-Arts in Paris. In applying there, she was following a pattern established by such well-respected American architects as Henry Hobson Richardson, Louis Sullivan, and her own California mentor, Bernard Maybeck; and while her initial attempts to enroll were rebuffed because she was female, ultimately she was permitted to attend classes there.

Upon her return from Europe in 1902, Morgan began her architectural career in the San Francisco area working for the designer John Galen Howard on buildings for her alma mater; she also collaborated with Maybeck, with whom she was continuing to develop a strong professional relationship. Maybeck's personal style, a product of Beaux-Arts discipline and individual fancy, was one which appealed to her enormously and which had a lasting effect on her own style.

Among Julia Morgan's most important early projects as an independent architect were designs (begun in 1904) for several buildings on the campus of Mills College, a four-year institution for women in Oakland, California. Following the San Francisco earthquake of 1906, Morgan was able to obtain a large number of commissions in the Bay Area, many of them for private homes. Like Maybeck, Morgan took an eclectic approach to design and refused to limit herself to the popular, conservative, turn-of-the-century revival styles sweeping the country and dominating the domestic market. The house that best exemplifies this attitude is also her most famous work "La Casa Grande," William Randolph Hearst's home at San Simeon, California (begun in 1919), one of several commissions executed for the Hearst family. It is actually a complex of domestic buildings, eclectic in style, made comprehensible through Beaux-Arts organization. The commission was a difficult one as Hearst constantly changed his mind about details relating to the design; yet Morgan's patience and resolve carried her through the project.

Morgan's career was financially successful in part because she seemed to be able to deliver the kind of design that would appeal to the Hearsts and others of their economic class. Yet Morgan's works were by no means limited to lavish domestic structures. She designed several centers for the Young Women's Christian Association, as well as private clubs, churches, and commercial establishments.

Further, she created many moderate-sized homes for middle-class families. She specialized in indigenous materials, particularly in her designs for these smaller, less-expensive houses; in this way, her works can be seen to be in keeping with other, more famous California progressive architects, such as her contemporaries Charles and Henry Greene and her mentor Maybeck. The Williams and Mitchell House (1915-1918) is one of several redwood-shingled cottages that are perched astride the Berkeley Hills in the

vicinity of San Francisco. Here, several of her solutions to the problem of the small house placed on a difficult site are in evidence: by eliminating unnecessary rooms and opening up areas of the walls with very large windows, she made the limited space feel open and airy. She also changed scale in an attempt to accommodate the building to the uneven topography. In short, whether designing for a millionaire or a schoolteacher, Morgan gave her client a carefully considered solution.

One of the hallmarks of Julia Morgan's career is that she realized so many of her projects: more than seven hundred buildings were constructed over a career that spanned nearly fifty years. One of the few unbuilt designs was a museum in the medieval style for Golden Gate Park in San Francisco, and the fact that it remained unbuilt saddened the architect in her last years. Morgan ended her career on a dramatic and mysterious note when she ordered virtually all her professional records destroyed a few years before her death in 1957.

Further Reading

An interesting treatment of the life and work of Julia Morgan is Sara Boutelle's *Julia Morgan, Architect* (1988). A modest-sized publication with an excellent text is *Julia Morgan—Architect* by Richard Longstreth (1977). There have been several articles published on Morgan since the centennial of her birth. These include two by Boutelle: "The Woman Who Built San Simeon," in the *California Monthly* (1976), and "Women's Networks: Julia Morgan and her Clients," in *Heresies* of 1981. Nancy Loe's *San Simeon Revisited* (1987) is a collection of the correspondence between the architect and William Randolph Hearst. The University of California at Berkeley has assembled a valuable trove of information on Morgan as part of their regional oral history series. The two volumes are entitled "The Julia Morgan Architectural History Project."

Additional Sources

Boutelle, Sara Holmes, *Julia Morgan, architect,* New York: Abbeville Press, 1988.
James, Cary, *Julia Morgan,* New York: Chelsea House, 1990. □

Junius Spencer Morgan

The American banker Junius Spencer Morgan (1813-1890) was a key participant in the credit bridge between America and Britain in the mid-19th century.

Junius Spencer Morgan was born on April 14, 1813, in West Springfield, Mass. He grew up in Hartford, Conn., where his father was a prosperous merchant with diverse business interests. Morgan entered the business world as an apprentice merchant at the age of 16 before going to New York to learn banking. He then became a partner in various mercantile firms.

A trip to Europe in 1853 decisively altered Morgan's business career and life. He met George Peabody, an American in London, and was invited to become a partner in his merchant-banking firm, founded in 1852, which facilitated the flow of British capital to America.

Morgan moved to London in 1854 to take up his duties as junior partner. Peabody retired a decade later, and Morgan became director of the firm, whose name was changed to J. S. Morgan and Company. He also inherited the high standing of Peabody in England, an asset of incalculable value. That and his abilities enabled him to build the firm into the most important American banking company in Europe. Morgan himself became the most influential American banker in that part of the world.

Morgan met Andrew Carnegie in 1869 and in business dealings with him in 1873 was able to be helpful. He also headed a syndicate which lent France money in 1870 to aid in the continuation of the Franco-Prussian War after a decisive French defeat. One writer has speculated that this was "possibly the greatest single coup organized by Junius Morgan . . . and the whole operation was a sensation in the financial world."

Morgan, with his son as the manager, in 1879 sold in London a sizable block of the New York Central Railroad stock owned by William H. Vanderbilt. He financed Cecil Rhodes in the 1880s in his contest for control of the diamond market against Barney Barnato, who was supported by the banking family, the Rothschilds. Morgan died in Monte Carlo, where he usually wintered, on April 8, 1890. He can justifiably be regarded as the initiator of the house of Morgan, which was made so powerful and famous by his son, John Pierpont Morgan.

Further Reading

There is no single source devoted exclusively to Morgan. Lewis Corey, *The House of Morgan* (1930), and Edwin P. Hoyt, Jr., *The House of Morgan* (1966), although different in many ways, are similar in their emphasis on the son rather than the father. The biographical material on the son contains references to the activities of the father in these useful works: *J. Pierpont Morgan: An Intimate Portrait* (1939) by Morgan's son-in-law, Herbert Livingston Satterlee; Frederick Lewis Allen, *The Great Pierpont Morgan* (1949); and the essays included in Jonathan Hughes, *The Vital Few* (1966).

Additional Sources

Carosso, Vincent P., *The Morgans: private international bankers, 1854-1913,* Cambridge, Mass.: Harvard University Press, 1987. □

Lewis Henry Morgan

The American anthropologist Lewis Henry Morgan (1818-1881) wrote one of the first ethnographies, invented the study of kinship terminology, and made an early attempt to grapple with the idea of universal principles of cultural evolution.

Lewis Henry Morgan was born on Nov. 21, 1818, near Aurora, N.Y. He graduated from Union College in Schenectady in 1840. He then returned to Aurora, where he read law. In 1844 he opened a law office in Rochester.

Morgan became interested in the Iroquois of western New York State and undertook a field study of the Iroquois Confederation, especially the Seneca tribe. His *League of the Ho-dé-no-sau-nee, or Iroquois* (1851) is considered one of the earliest objective ethnographic works.

In the 1850s Morgan concentrated on his law practice. He invested in railroad and mining ventures and accumulated a small fortune. After attending a meeting of the American Association for the Advancement of Science in 1856, he resolved to pursue his anthropological interests scientifically.

Morgan noticed that the Seneca designate their consanguineous kin in a manner different from that of civilized peoples. They merge collateral relatives, such as uncles, cousins, and nephews, into the direct line, classifying those relatives as fathers, brothers, and sons. While the kinship terminologies of civilized peoples recognize a distinction between kin in one's direct line of descent, Seneca kinship terminology does not recognize that distinction.

In 1858, on a business trip to Michigan, Morgan discovered that the Ojibwa have a "classificatory" system like that of the Seneca. He suspected that this system was characteristic of Indians. He believed that if he could find evidence for the system in Asia the Asiatic origin of the American Indians would be proved. He sent a questionnaire to likely informants. Finding evidence for the classificatory

cultural evolution of man: savagery, barbarism, and civilization. Savagery and barbarism are divided into lower, middle, and upper stages. These stages are defined in terms of means of subsistance or technological inventions. Thus, savagery was preagricultural, barbarism was marked by pottery and agriculture, and civilization arose with the invention of writing.

Morgan also traced the growth of ideas of government, the family, and property. Stages in the development of these ideas are associated with stages of savagery, barbarism, and civilization. He saw the evolution of human culture as essentially a single development from the most primitive stage to civilization. Karl Marx and Friedrich Engels viewed Morgan's *Ancient Society* as complementing their own work, and the book is regarded by Marxists as a classic.

Morgan was elected president of the American Association for the Advancement of Science in 1879, the first anthropologist so honored. He died on Dec. 17, 1881, in Rochester.

Further Reading

An excellent biography of Morgan is Carl Resek, *Lewis Henry Morgan: American Scholar* (1960). See also Bernhard Joseph Stern, *Lewis Henry Morgan: Social Evolutionist* (1931).

Morgan's work has undergone several reevaluations. Franz Boas and his students devalued Morgan's *Ancient Society* in their opposition to the idea of cultural evolution. A resurgence of interest in the concept of cultural evolution, begun by Leslie White, has tended to restore Morgan's reputation. Thus the historical writings on him by anthropologists are often mutually contradictory and polemical. For example, Robert Lowie, a student of Boas, paints an unfavorable picture of Morgan in a chapter of *The History of Ethnological Theory* (1937), while a chapter by White in *An Introduction to the History of Sociology* (1948), edited by Harry Elmer Barnes, attributes to Morgan achievements that were not his.

Meyer Fortes describes Morgan's lasting contributions to social anthropology in the first part of *Kinship and the Social Order: The Legacy of Lewis Henry Morgan* (1969). See also the chapter on Morgan and kinship by Frederick Russell Eggon in *Essays in the Science of Culture in Honor of Leslie A. White,* edited by Gertrude Evelyn Dole and Robert L. Carneiro (1960). □

system in India, he circulated an expanded questionnaire. Morgan went on four field trips (1859-1862) to the West, traveling up the Missouri River as far as western Montana, to gather information on kinship terminology and other aspects of culture.

In Morgan's monumental *Systems of Consanguinity and Affinity of the Human Family* (1871) he presented kinship terminologies, showing the widespread occurrence of the classificatory system in both the New and Old Worlds. This work was the first in the important field of kinship terminology, and it represents his most lasting contribution.

Morgan believed that the classificatory system represented a survival from a time of promiscuity when it was impossible to tell fathers from uncles, brothers from cousins, and sons from nephews. Society subsequently developed marriage rules, but the older terminology persisted. Later, according to Morgan, with the rise of civilization and private property, a distinction was made between one's own family line and one's collateral relatives for purposes of establishing inheritence. The "descriptive" system of kinship terminology developed out of the classificatory system. Today anthropologists do not believe that there was a promiscuous stage in the development of the family, at least not in recent human history. Also, Morgan's scheme is a simplification of what is actually a complicated matter.

His interest in the development, or evolution, of social institutions culminated in Morgan's most famous work, *Ancient Society* (1877). He recognized three stages in the

Robin Morgan

Robin Morgan (born 1941), writer, editor, poet, and political activist, was one of the leading feminists in the United States.

R obin Morgan was born on January 29, 1941, in Lake Worth, Florida, the daughter of Faith Berkley Morgan. She grew up in Mount Vernon, New York, and at an early age wanted to be a doctor and a poet. "The male-supremacist society destroyed the first ambition," she once wrote, "but couldn't dent the second."

In the late 1950s she attended Columbia University in New York. On September 19, 1962, she married Kenneth

Pitchford, a poet. They had one child, Blake Ariel Morgan-Pitchford.

During the early 1960s, while working as a literary agent and free-lance editor in New York City, Morgan began publishing poetry. A collection of her poems from the 1960s appeared in 1972 under the title *Monster*. Through the 1960s Morgan engaged in leftist political activities centered around opposition to the U.S. engagement in Vietnam. She contributed articles and poetry to such left-wing journals as *Liberation, Rat, Win,* and *The Guardian.* By the late 1960s, however, Morgan's primary interest and commitment became feminism, the cause with which her best known writings are concerned. That her transition to feminism involved difficult personal change is suggested in her "Letters from a Marriage," which were written mainly to her husband (but with an eye to eventual publication) from 1962 to 1973. They were published in *Going Too Far: The Personal Chronicle of a Feminist* (1977).

By the late 1960s Morgan had become active in New York Radical Women, one branch of which—the Redstockings and later the Radical Feminists—developed much of the theoretical ground for the contemporary women's movement. In particular, these women, many of whom had been active in the peace and civil rights movements, rebelled against the male-dominated "new left" in which they had been accorded second-class treatment. Morgan's article "Goodbye to All That," which appeared in 1970, was later considered a classic expression of the feminists' rejection of the male left.

The "radical feminists" came to believe that all social oppression lay in the domination of women by men. By the early 1970s Morgan called herself a radical feminist and summed up her position (in 1977) by explaining the etymology of the word "radical" as meaning "going to the root": "I believe that sexism is the root oppression, the one which, until and unless we *uproot* it, will continue to put forth the branches of racism, class hatred, ageism, competition, ecological disaster, and economic exploitation."

Morgan, however, remained apart from the theoretical wing of the movement and participated instead in an action-oriented group, WITCH (Women's International Terrorist Conspiracy from Hell). These women engaged in "guerrilla-theater" tactics, such as demonstrating before the Miss America Pageant on September 7, 1968; protesting the New York Bridal Fair on February 15, 1969; and "hexing" Wall Street. *Going Too Far* (1977) includes a selection of articles Morgan wrote during this period which chronicle her feminist transitions.

In 1970 Morgan co-edited (with Charlotte Bunch and Joanne Cooke) a collection entitled *The New Woman.* That same year she put forth the work for which she is perhaps best known, *Sisterhood Is Powerful,* a massive anthology of over 50 articles and numerous manifestoes and documents written in the early years of the contemporary feminist movement. It became one of the most important sources by which feminist ideas were disseminated across the country in the early 1970s. During the rest of the decade Morgan lectured extensively both nationally and internationally, and in 1977 she became a contributing editor to *Ms. Magazine.* She also published another book of poems, *Lady of the Beasts,* in 1976.

In the 1980s Morgan put forth two important works. One, *The Anatomy of Freedom: Feminism, Physics, and Global Politics,* appeared in 1982. The second, *Sisterhood Is Global: The International Women's Movement Anthology,* was published in 1984.

The Anatomy of Freedom is a formally innovative work that combines personal narrative, fable, allegorical drama, and feminist theorizing. In it Morgan presents feminism not just as a struggle for equal rights but as a "vision" that is "crucial to the continuation of sentient life on this planet." Its most intriguing aspect is Morgan's attempt to merge the feminist vision, which she sees as integrative and holistic, with the view proposed in the new physics (quantum theory and relativity), which also, Morgan argues, mandates a holistic, contextual approach to reality. Morgan's position in this work may be labelled "cultural feminism," a view that considers women as heirs to a humane, ecologically holistic value-system, which can be a font of regeneration in a world dominated by a destructive, masculine ethic.

Sisterhood Is Global is in a sense a continuation of *Sisterhood Is Powerful,* but expanded to an international scope. This anthology of over 800 pages includes articles that detail the condition of women in more than 70 countries. In her introduction Morgan continues her cultural feminist perspective by noting the significance of 1984 as a publishing date. Referring to George Orwell's dystopian novel of that title, Morgan asserts that only women working together and in accordance with their historically humane and pacifist ethic can overcome the forces of Big Brother, which she sees operating globally.

Morgan's many awards include the Wonder Woman award for peace and understanding (1982), the Front Page award for distinguished journalism (1982), and the Feminist of the Year award (1990). She is a member of the Feminist Writers' Guild, Media Women, the North American Feminist Coalition, the Pan Arab Feminist Solidarity Association, and the Israeli Feminists Against Occupation.

Further Reading

In addition to the works identified earlier, Morgan put forth *Depth Perception: New Poems and a Masque* (1982). Other important articles by Morgan appear in the following issues of *Ms. Magazine:* August 1978, November 1978, March 1980, and December 1981. A useful history of the contemporary women's movement is Sara Evans, *Personal Politics* (1979). The theoretical background for Morgan's thought is provided in Josephine Donovan, *Feminist Theory: The Intellectual Traditions of American Feminism* (1985). Further information on Morgan can also be found in *The Writer's Dictionary* 1994 edition. □

Thomas Hunt Morgan

The American zoologist and geneticist Thomas Hunt Morgan (1866-1945) established the theory of the gene which helped clarify the process of evolution and formed the modern basis of heredity.

Thomas Hunt Morgan, born on Sept. 25, 1866, in Lexington, Ky., was the son of Charlton and Ellen Morgan. He was descended on both sides from English Cavalier stock. In 1886 he entered the State College of Kentucky and later studied at Johns Hopkins University, where he divided his time between morphology and physiology. In 1890 he received his doctorate for a paper on the embryology and phylogeny of sea spiders. In 1891 he served as professor of biology at Bryn Mawr College, after which he went to Europe for further study, first in Germany and then at the famous zoological station at Naples, Italy. There he met Hans Driesch, the philosopher-scientist who believed in "vitalism." Morgan, however, favored a mechanistic approach to the solution of biological problems.

Upon his return to the United States in 1904, Morgan accepted a professorship at Columbia University which lasted until 1928. While there he undertook a series of breeding experiments to assess the reality of genes as the particles of heredity. Morgan chose the fruit fly (*Drosophila melanogaster*) for his experiments because it was a short-lived organism that could easily be bred in the laboratory under changing condition and could complete its life cycle in about 10 days, supplying as many as 30 generations a year.

Morgan's experiments were so successful that by 1914 he had proved the chromosome theory of heredity as a result of breeding and cytological examination. In 1910 he found his first mutant and proceeded to cross this fly with a normal one. The percentages of normal and mutant offspring were in accordance with Mendel's law of inheritance. Morgan found many mutant characters and soon discovered that certain characteristics not only were sex-linked but also tended to appear together in certain flies. From this he postulated that all sex-linked characters tended to be inherited together because they were associated as a unit on a single chromosome in the nucleus of the original cell. Morgan called these characters linkage groups. By the summer of 1914 three linkage groups had been discovered. He used the word "gene" to represent each character unit, and the exact positions of these genes in the chromosomes was worked out by Alfred Henry Sturtevant, one of Morgan's former students and a member of his research staff. In 1915 Morgan and his assistants published *The Mechanism of Mendelian Heredity* to describe the system of genes. Later he published *The Theory of the Gene* (1926), his culminating work on the subject which discussed at length the chromosome theory of heredity.

In 1928 Morgan established the Kerckhoff Laboratories of Biological Sciences at the California Institute of Technology in Pasadena, which became the leading center for research genetics. In 1933 he received the Nobel Prize in physiology or medicine in recognition of the significance of his theory of heredity for physiology and for the part that the new genetics was destined to play in the future of medicine.

In 1941 Morgan retired as active head of his department at Cal Tech. However, he continued to work on problems in embryology which he had first approached in 1903—trying to find out why the spermatozoon of the common hermaphroditic sea squirt almost never fertilizes the egg of the same individual (self-sterilization) but does fertilize eggs of all other sea squirts. On Dec. 4, 1945, the grand old man of genetics passed away.

Further Reading

No full-length biography or autobiography of Morgan has been published. A detailed account of his life and work is in Bernard Jaffe, *Men of Science in America* (1944; rev. ed. 1958). A biography also appears in National Academy of Sciences, *Biographical Memoirs,* vol. 33 (1959). Short studies of Morgan are in Theodore L. Sourkes, *Nobel Prize Winners in Medicine and Physiology, 1901-1965* (1953; rev. ed. 1967); Katherine Binney Shippen, *Men, Microscopes and Living Things* (1955); Jay E. Greene, ed., *100 Great Scientists* (1964); and Nobel Foundation, *Physiology or Medicine: Nobel Lectures, including Presentation Speeches and Laureates' Biographies* (3 vols., 1964-1967). ☐

Hans J. Morgenthau

Hans J. Morgenthau (1904-1979) was an American political scientist who taught at the University of Chicago and at the Graduate Center at the City University of New York. His classic text, *Politics Among Nations,* was the leading work for students of international politics for over a quarter century.

Hans J. Morgenthau was born on February 17, 1904, in Coburg, a small town in central Germany which is now part of northern Bavaria. His father was a doctor who discouraged his son from attending the University of Berlin, saying: "You are out of your mind. You'll never get in. Go to a lesser school instead." His father's attitude created in the son an inferiority complex, a fear of being rejected, and an undisguised shyness that persisted throughout his life. If his father was tyrannical and authoritarian, his mother was warm and supportive. He remembered being ridiculed when, having graduated first in his class, he spoke at a founder's day ceremony celebrating the crowning of the duke of Coburg. When he made his presentation, the duke and other nobility displayed their anti-Semitism by holding their noses, thus suggesting that all Jews smelled bad.

As a schoolboy during World War I and its aftermath, the young Morgenthau witnessed the defeat of a powerful and confident German army and the flight of that government's leaders. The Weimar regime which followed lacked an understanding of power and a broadly representative political base. The former ruling class, who were dominant in communities like Coburg, propounded the "stab in the back" thesis—that is, the fighting ended with no foreign troops on German soil; therefore, the nation had not been defeated in war, but was brought down by traitors within—socialists, trade unionists, Jews, Catholics, liberals, and

Freemasons. The Weimar regime was destroyed by its inability to govern and to use power and by forces of irrationalism in politics such as blaming military defeat and rampant inflation primarily on the Jews. Morgenthau recalled his mother going to market with a basketful of paper money and his physician father accepting butter, eggs, chickens, or textiles rather than worthless money for his services.

For his advanced studies the young Morgenthau first enrolled in 1923 at the University of Frankfort but later transferred to the University of Munich. He never studied at the University of Berlin. His earliest intellectual interests were philosophy and literature, a harbinger of his determination to see the general in the particular in his approach to history. At first his goal was to become either a writer, a professor, or a poet. In choosing his vocation he was propelled by a deeper concern. In September 1923 he wrote: "My hopes for the future move in two directions. I hope for the lifting of the pressure to which I am exposed by the social environment, and I hope to find a direction and purpose for my future activities. The latter cannot be realized before the former is fulfilled." He explained that his relationship with the environment was determined by three facts: he was a German, a Jew, and had matured following World War I. He vowed to resist the immorality of anti-Semitism and to place service to some higher cause ahead of amassing riches.

In his studies philosophy, with its minute epistemological destructions, left Morgenthau dissatisfied, so at the University of Munich he turned to the study of law. Diplomatic history was a companion interest, and Bismarck's *Realpolitik* offered him a framework that confirmed certain "isolated and impressionistic judgments on . . . foreign policy." He also found in Max Weber's thought the model for an approach to political science. He pursued postgraduate work at the Graduate Institute of International Studies in Geneva, was admitted to the bar, and became acting president of the labor law court in Frankfurt. From 1932 to 1935 he taught public law at the University of Geneva and then in Madrid from 1935 to 1936. He came to the United States in 1937 without sponsors or friends. Subsequently he held faculty appointments at Brooklyn College (1937-1939), the University of Kansas City (1939-1943), the University of Chicago (1943-1971), the City College of New York (1968-1975), and the New School for Social Research (1975 to his death).

His first major work, *Scientific Man vs. Power Politics,* challenged the prevailing "belief in the power of science to solve all problems and, more particularly, all political problems." Drawing on Reinhold Niebuhr, he called for a renewal of faith in "those intellectual and moral faculties of man to which alone the problems of the social world will yield." He also challenged the scientific approach to politics which was dominant in the Charles E. Merriam era of political science at Chicago. However, the university's leadership, and especially its president, Robert M. Hutchins, encouraged Morgenthau while differing with him on such questions as the prospect for world government.

With *Politics Among Nations,* his classic text published in 1948, Morgenthau sought to define the core principles of politics and international politics. He wrote: "Whatever the ultimate aims of international politics, power is always the immediate aim. The struggle for power is universal in time and space and is an undeniable fact of experience." With this work Morgenthau declared war on legalistic and moralistic interpretations and sought to provide a theory of international politics. He also argued, however, that international morality and law were constraints on the struggle for power.

In Defense of the National Interest (1951) he contended that moral principles must be linked with national interest and called for a reconsideration of the approach of the founding fathers. General moral principles must be filtered through the national interest if an effective political morality is to be attained, he argued.

In *The Purpose of American Politics* (1960) he reviewed the influence of transcendent purpose on American foreign policy from the beginnings of the Republic. By the mid-1960s he had emerged as the foremost early critic of the Vietnam War, warning that nations must never place themselves in a position from which they cannot retreat without a loss of face and from which they cannot advance without unacceptable risk.

Morgenthau's main contribution was in providing a framework for understanding foreign policy. He translated a European understanding of politics and foreign policy to fit the American experience. He defended the uniqueness of American democracy while emphasizing its enduring moral and political foundations. He applied his realist philosophy to problems such as human rights, stressing the need for prudence and practical morality. He tried to explain the interconnection and tensions between abstract moral principles and political necessities in world politics.

Further Reading

The most recent Morgenthau books are his classic text, *Politics Among Nations,* revised by Kenneth W. Thompson (sixth edition, 1985). Other Morgenthau books include *In Defense of the National Interest* (revised edition, 1982), which sets forth his framework for analyzing foreign policy; *The Purpose of American Politics* (1982); and Morgenthau and Thompson, *Principles and Problems of International Politics* (1981), which presents text and readings of classic writings in international politics. □

Henry Morgenthau Jr.

Henry Morgenthau, Jr. (1891-1967), was secretary of the U.S. Treasury and a longtime confidant and adviser to President Franklin Roosevelt.

Henry Morgenthau, Jr., was born in New York City on May 11, 1891, into a prosperous family of German-Jewish ancestry. The senior Morgenthau, who had become wealthy through real estate investments, was active in Democratic party affairs and in sponsoring various social welfare projects in the city. Henry Morgenthau, Jr., attended Phillips Exeter Academy and then Sachs Collegiate Institute in New York City before entering Cornell University. Morgenthau left Cornell after three semesters to recuperate from typhoid fever. He again enrolled in Cornell, this time to study agriculture. But he soon left on a trip to the Pacific Coast to investigate different kinds of farming at firsthand. When he returned more excited than ever about a career in farming, his father bought several hundred acres for him in Dutchess County in upstate New York, which in succeeding decades became a highly successful and apple-growing farm.

Morgenthau and Roosevelt

Morgenthau's friendship with Franklin Roosevelt began in 1915, when Roosevelt, hosting Morgenthau at his neighboring Dutchess County estate at Hyde Park, tried unsuccessfully to persuade the young agriculturalist to run for sheriff. The next year Morgenthau married Elinor Fatman, whom he had known since childhood. The Morgenthaus had two sons and a daughter—Henry III, Robert, and Joan—all of whom became well known in their own right.

Morgenthau's first involvement in public service came during World War I, when he helped organize agricultural production in Dutchess County and persuaded U.S. Food Administrator Herbert Hoover to transfer 1,500 tractors to France. After the war Morgenthau became increasingly active in county and state Democratic party affairs and undertook publication of an agricultural weekly in which he

championed such causes as soil conservation, rural electrification, and aid to rural education.

Morgenthau worked hard to elect Roosevelt governor of New York State. In 1929, after Roosevelt's victory, he went to Albany as a member of the state agricultural commission. Following Roosevelt's reelection in 1930, Morgenthau became conservation commissioner. With Harry Hopkins, Morgenthau devised a plan for combining reforestation projects with work relief for the jobless. This became a model of its kind as unemployment skyrocketed during the early years of the Great Depression. In 1932 Morgenthau again helped Roosevelt get elected, this time to the presidency, and again Roosevelt brought Morgenthau with him to the seat of government.

New Dealer

Morgenthau wanted very much to become secretary of agriculture, but he accepted appointment as head of the Farm Credit Administration, which handled most of the New Deal's efforts to aid debt-ridden farmers. During the year and a half he remained at Farm Credit, Federal loans to farmers increased more than 10-fold.

By November 1934, when Morgenthau became secretary of the treasury, the Roosevelt administration had shifted control of money and credit from New York and private financial combines to Washington and the federal government. Always close to Roosevelt, Morgenthau now became an even more central figure in the New Deal. Basically a fiscal conservative, Morgenthau nevertheless went along

with mounting federal deficits as the Roosevelt administration struggled to meet the nation's relief needs and to revive the economy. In 1937, however, Morgenthau finally persuaded Roosevelt to make substantial reductions in federal spending, a move that helped trigger the "Roosevelt recession" of the late 1930s.

Wartime Spender

Morgenthau was an early and vigorous champion of collective security arrangements to resist the growing aggressiveness of Nazi Germany. After the outbreak of World War II in Europe in the fall of 1939, Morgenthau battled within the Roosevelt administration against neutralists and "America First" military strategists to clear British and French purchases of American-made war *matériel* and to step up military production, especially of airplanes. Until the establishment of the Lend-Lease Program in 1941, Morgenthau managed the bulk of American aid to Great Britain.

After Pearl Harbor and America's entrance into the war, Morgenthau administered the biggest and most rapid expansion of federal expenditures in the nation's history. By 1945 total federal outlays, which had been $7.1 billion during Morgenthau's first year at the Treasury, had reached $93.7 billion. Morgenthau's main contribution to the intensifying postwar planning debate within the Roosevelt administration was the much-criticized "Morgenthau Plan," which envisioned not only the disarmament of Germany but its deindustrialization as well. It was largely President Harry Truman's disapproval of the Morgenthau Plan that prompted Morgenthau's angry resignation in July 1945.

In retirement Morgenthau devoted much of his time to philanthropic projects. He was chairman of the United Jewish Appeal (1947-1950), and in the early 1950s he was chairman of the board of the American Financial and Development Corporation for Israel, which handled a $500 million Israeli bond issue. On Feb. 6, 1967, following a succession of heart attacks, Morgenthau died at Poughkeepsie, N.Y.

Further Reading

There is no full-scale biography of Morgenthau. The standard account of his public career is the massive, officially authorized narrative based on Morgenthau's papers by John Morton Blum, *From the Morgenthau Diaries* (3 vols., 1959-1965), which covers the period 1928-1945. Additional treatments of Morgenthau's role in the New Deal are in G. Griffith Johnson, Jr., *The Treasury and Monetary Policy, 1933-1938* (1939); Allan S. Everest, *Morgenthau, the New Deal, and Silver* (1950); James MacGregor Burns, *Roosevelt: The Lion and the Fox* (1956); Arthur M. Schlesinger, Jr., *The Age of Roosevelt* (3 vols., 1957-1960); and Rexford Guy Tugwell, *The Democratic Roosevelt* (1957). Morgenthau's role in the formulation of the Lend-Lease Program is treated at length in Warren F. Kimball, *The Most Unsordid Act: Lend-Lease, 1939-1941* (1969).

Additional Sources

Morgenthau, Henry, *Mostly Morgenthaus: a family history*, New York: Ticknor & Fields, 1991. □

Paul Morin

Paul Morin (1889-1963) was a French-Canadian poet. Erudite, polished, and widely traveled, he was a brilliant exponent of art for art's sake and gave a sense of perfection to French-Canadian literature, which he raised from its then largely parochial level.

Paul Morin d'Équilly was born in Montreal into a family of professional men. His grandfather had come to Canada as a government geographer. His parents, though French Canadians, sent him first to an English-speaking Protestant school, and then to Jesuit colleges in Montreal and Paris. He went on to study law in Montreal and literature in Paris, where he defended a thesis on Longfellow (1912, published 1913). Meanwhile, he had been traveling in France, Italy, Greece, and Turkey, cultivating his taste for exotic visual beauty. This and the prevailing Parnassian fashion in poetry were the predominant influences in his first volume of poems, *Le Paon d'émail* (1911; The Enamel Peacock).

The poems earned him the admiration of Anna de Noailles, whose salon remained the center of Morin's literary world. His Canadian readers acknowledged Morin's artistic perfection and hailed him as their first real master of French language and verse. But his "paganism" aroused enthusiasm in some, hostility and public censure in others. The cult of sensuous beauty, the complete absence of political or moral purpose, and the poet's frequent references to his French soul amounted to a complete rejection of the French-Canadian bucolic tradition. (The importance of the earlier poet, Émile Nelligan, was not yet recognized.) Morin answered criticism of his non-Canadianism with false promises in the poem *A ceux de mon pays* (To Those of My Country), with high seriousness in "Thalatta" (The Sea), or with irony in "Mississippi."

Morin went on to teach French language and literature in various universities, edited a review, and opened a translation agency. In 1922 he published his second collection, *Poèmes de cendre et d'or* (Poems of Ashes and Gold), which shows an increase in virtuosity and incisiveness but not in Canadian content or moralizing. He received various honors in the following years but did not publish his third collection, *Géronte et son miroir* (The Old Man and His Mirror), until 1960. He died in 1963, having lived long enough to see a revival of interest in his work.

Morin does not entirely escape the charge of dilettantism, but his best poems have more than technical brilliance, and his stand for artistic values was a great advance in French-Canadian cultural life.

Further Reading

Morin is discussed in Ian Forbes Fraser, *The Spirit of French Canada* (1939). □

Higinio Morínigo

Higinio Morínigo (1897-1985) was president of Paraguay from 1940 to 1948. He was considered one of the more important figures in Paraguay's modern political evolution.

Higinio Morínigo was born on January 11, 1897, in the small city of Paraguarí, in east-central Paraguay, 40 miles from Asunción. His father, Juan Alberto Moriñigo, had participated in the battle of Acosta-Ñú, during the 1869 War of the Triple Alliance, and his mother, Pabla Martínez, was a native of Villeta, a river port south of Asunción.

Selecting the military for his professional career, Higinio Morínigo was educated in Paraguay and graduated from the military college as a second lieutenant in 1922. A stolid, serious, and dedicated professional, he built a record which reflected steady promotions to the rank of general and continuous active duty including service throughout the Chaco War with Bolivia.

Following the Febrerista revolt of 1936 and the collapse of the short-lived Febrerista administration in 1937, Morínigo was named war minister in the Cabinet of President José Félix Estigarribia. Upon the latter's death in an airplane accident on September 7, 1940, an army high command council nominated Morínigo to assume the presidency for Estigarribia's unexpired term. He became president the following day. Reelected in a general election of 1943 in which he was the unopposed sole candidate, he remained president through the period of World War II and the postwar period until June 1948, when he was deposed by a coup d'etat.

As Paraguay's wartime president, Morínigo decreed the suspension of internal political activity, clamped strict censorship on newspapers, and pursued a neutrality policy which was regarded by some observers as being pro-Axis in its innuendos. In 1943, at the invitation of President Franklin Roosevelt, he traveled to Washington, becoming the first Paraguayan president to visit the United States. The tour featured his prodemocracy address before Congress; he subsequently made a series of official visits to other American republics.

In Paraguay, Morínigo's administrations were marked by his efforts to form a new nationalist revolutionary state, based on the principles of order, discipline, and hierarchy, which would supplant the two traditional parties, the Liberals and Colorados, as well as the new Febrerista party. Failure to generate enthusiasm for this program was followed by renewed rivalry among the three regular parties; in March 1947 this rivalry erupted into full-scale civil revolt.

The revitalized Colorado faction supported Morínigo and the government against a largely Febrerista uprising backed by heavy sectors of the army. By August the 1947 revolution collapsed before the combined efforts of loyal government troops and peasant volunteers recruited by the Colorado party. Now in full control, the Colorados secured their position with the exiling of thousands of Febrerista and Liberal opponents and the subsequent deposing of President Morínigo in June 1948.

Higinio Morínigo went into exile with his wife and sons in a suburb of Buenos Aires. He withdrew from participation in politics but visited Asunción frequently. His major contributions to Paraguay are the eight years of stability which marked his administrations—a term of relative order in sharp contrast to the nation's previously troubled past—and his stout defense in the 1947 revolution, which presaged the modern era of Colorado party hegemony. He died in 1985.

Further Reading

George Pendle, *Paraguay: A Riverside Nation* (1954; 3d ed. 1967), has a solid biographical study of Morínigo. A discussion of Morínigo's role in Paraguayan history is contained in Harris Gaylord Warren, *Paraguay: An Informal History* (1949), and in Philip Raine, *Paraguay* (1956). See also Hubert Clinton Herring, *A History of Latin America: From the Beginnings to the Present* (1955; 3d rev. ed. 1968). □

Samuel Eliot Morison

Samuel Eliot Morison (1887-1976) was a leading American naval historian, biographer, and historian of Puritanism.

Samuel Eliot Morison was born in Boston on July 9, 1887, into a prominent family with deep roots in the Massachusetts past. He attended Harvard, obtaining his doctorate in 1912. There he derived the precept of history as a literary art. His dissertation, concerning Harrison Gray Otis, an ancestor whose papers were in Morison's attic, was sympathetic to the old Federalist.

In 1915 Morison joined the faculty at Harvard. His *Maritime History of Massachusetts, 1783-1860* (1921) earned him considerable fame. The book traced broad social and economic trends in Massachusetts up to the Civil War. While at Harvard he also served on the American Commission to Negotiate Peace between 1918 and 1919 and was one of the key individuals responsible for drafting the Versailles Treaty. Morison became the first Harmsworth professor of American history at Oxford in 1922, a position he held until his return to Harvard in 1925 to become Trumbull professor of American history. He retired from Harvard in 1955.

Morison's interest in textbooks was evident in 1927, when his *Oxford History of the United States* appeared. This book became part of the base for *The Growth of the American Republic,* written in collaboration with Henry Steele Commager, which first appeared in 1930. It also served to point the way to *The Oxford History of the American People* (1964).

In the 1930s Morison's attention moved toward the Puritans. *Builders of the Bay Colony* (1930), a collection of biographies, depicted the Puritans as human and fallible with primary religious motivation. He continued his defense of Puritanism with *The Puritan Pronaos* (1936) and in his institutional history of Harvard. In these works Morison claimed that Puritan thought was rich and sophisticated, that the Puritan had strong ties to England, and that Harvard reflected the social values of Puritan society.

Morison retraced Columbus's voyages as commodore of the "Harvard Columbus Expedition" and turned this experience into *Admiral of the Ocean Sea* (2 vols., 1942). This work won him a Pulitzer Prize. Morison then joined the Navy as historian and with his staff produced the monumental *History of the United States Naval Operations in World War II* (15 vols., 1947-1962).

After the war Morison wrote biographies of John Paul Jones, which also earned him a Pulitzer Prize, and Commodore Perry, as well as essays in which he attacked historical relativism. His *H.G. Otis: Urbane Federalist* (1969) marked a return to the subject of his doctoral dissertation. In *The European Discovery of America: The Northern Voyages* (1971) he describes the voyages up to the early 17th century.

In 1964 Morison received the U.S. Presidential Medal of Freedom and was also elected to the American Academy of Arts and Letters. He remained an active proponent of history until his death in 1976.

Further Reading

Morison's own writings provide insights into his life and professional career. His *One Boy's Boston, 1887-1901* (1962) tells as much about Morison as about Boston, and in *Vistas of History* (1964) he discusses his professional experiences. This work also contains a comprehensive bibliography of Morison's writings to 1964. His historical work is discussed in Michael Kraus, *A History of American History* (1937) and *The Writing of American History* (1953). See also John Higham and others, *History* (1965), and Robert Allen Skotheim, *American Intellectual Histories and Historians* (1966). □

Akio Morita

Akio Morita (born 1921), along with a few other entrepreneurs, embodied the postwar recovery and growth of Japanese industry. Morita and Sony Corporation, which he cofounded with Masaru Ibuka, challenge conventional notions about Japan's "economic miracle." The energy and inventiveness of small, independent companies like Sony, not *keiretsu* (industrial conglomerate arrangements) or the Ministry of International Trade and Industry (MITI), were the impetus for Japan's postwar economic development; their dependable high technology products changed the image of Japanese exports abroad.

Akio Morita was born January 26, 1921, the first son and fifteenth-generation heir to a sake-brewing family in Kosugaya village near Nagoya. Influenced as a boy by his mother's love of classical music (his family was one of the first to own an RCA Victrola in Japan), Morita developed a keen interest in electronics and sound reproduction. He became so engrossed in his electronic experiments, even building his own ham radio, that he almost flunked out of school; but after concentrating on his studies for a year, he entered the prestigious Eighth Higher School as a physics major. At Osaka Imperial University he assisted his professor in research for the Imperial Japanese Navy. Rather than be drafted, he signed up with the navy to continue his studies. After his graduation in 1944, Lieutenant Morita supervised a special project group of the Aviation Technology Center on thermal guidance weapons and night-vision gunsights. There he met Masaru Ibuka, an electronics engineer 13 years his senior. The two became close friends and eventually cofounded Sony Corporation. After World War II, Morita became a physics professor while working part time in Ibuka's new telecommunications lab.

In March 1946 Morita and Ibuka established Tokyo Tsushin Kogyo, or Totsuko, with only $500 capital and roughly 20 employees, in a rented office in a burned-out department store in Tokyo.

To find a niche in a market that would be highly competitive when large prewar electronics manufacturers returned, Ibuka decided to produce completely new consumer products. Sony's most significant development was a high frequency transistor radio that not only established the company's reputation but also revolutionized the consumer

electronics industry. The project, however, was launched following a drawn-out approval by the Ministry of International Trade and Industry (MITI). After Morita reached agreement with Western Electric on the transistor technology in 1953, MITI officials dallied six months before finally remitting the foreign exchange for the licensing fee. Although the relationship between government and industry is one of trust, Morita observed, government often impedes innovative change and developments by excessive intervention and obsolete regulations. By investing six to ten percent of its annual sales in research and development, Sony took the lead in developing new consumer products independently of government help or *keiretsu* support. A pioneer of products ranging from transistorized radios to solid-state television sets to the Walkman and Discman to VCRs, by 1990 Sony employed more than 100,000 workers and was the world's leading maker of consumer, nonconsumer, industrial, and professional electronics and entertainment software.

Morita was a pioneer in marketing as well. His initial failure to sell tape recorders developed in 1950 convinced him that market creation must accompany product development. On his first trip to Europe in 1953, he was deeply impressed and encouraged by the success of N.V. Philips, which had grown from a small light bulb maker in a rural Dutch town into the world's leading electronics maker. Morita then decided to target the world market, particularly the affluent U.S. market, rather than the poor and congested Japanese domestic market. Recognizing the importance of establishing company identity in the world market, Morita adopted "Sony" (finding a Western root from the Latin *sonus,* meaning "sound," and combining it with the English nickname "Sonny"), a name that foreign customers could easily remember, as his company's trademark in 1955. Totsuko became Sony Corporation in 1958.

In the mid 1950s most Japanese producers relied on giant Japanese trading companies to export their goods, but Morita decided to build his own distribution route in which the message of the new technology and its benefits could be directly passed on to the consumer. In 1960 Morita established Sony Corporation of America and Sony Overseas S.A. (Switzerland) as its sales arms. In 1961 Sony became the first Japanese company to offer its stock in the United States in the form of ADRs (American Depositary Receipts). In February 1960, Sony established the Sony Corporation of America; and in less than two years, they became the first Japanese company to offer its stock in the United States. Sony felt that moving much of its manufacturing and sales to the United States and Europe would only improve its business, something other Japanese companies had yet to discover. Sony subsequently expanded its sales force and production facilities into an international network, with a few hundred subsidiaries and affiliated companies worldwide. Sony acquired CBS Records in 1988 and Columbia Pictures and Tri-Star film studios in 1990 (now Sony Pictures Entertainment) to expand its business in entertainment. Beginning in 1986, in response to changing world market conditions, Sony expanded into the nonconsumer sector, such as broadcasting equipment, semiconductors, video communications, and computers. In 1987, Morita wrote *Made In Japan,* a historical biography detailing his rise to success that, according to *Inc.,* Stanford graduate school professor Jim Collins recommends to students for best learning from those who have forged the trails.

Morita was often a spokesman for Japanese management. In articulating his own ideas, he emphasized the importance of teamwork and of motivating people by providing challenging work in a family-like environment; engineers in industrial companies particularly need targets for their creativity. Above all, management must treat workers not as tools but as fellow human beings. Morita argued that manufacturing determines the strength of the economy and blamed excessive financial dealings to create paper profits for undermining this base. Morita praised familialism and loyalty to the company as facilitating long-range planning and investment. He often criticized American management's preoccupation with quarterly profits and dividends and its tendency to postpone investment in equipment.

Morita was also outspoken on U.S.-Japanese relations. He warned, for example, against "hollowing out" the economy in the United States by moving manufacturing plants overseas to exploit cheap labor. In 1989 an unauthorized translation of *A Japan That Can Say "No",* a book based on conversations between Morita and Shintaro Ishihara, Liberal Democratic Party member of the House of Representatives in Japan, caused a stir in the United States. Although most of the controversial statements were credited to Ishihara, some critics blamed Morita for his arrogance. Morita, however, praised the openness of American markets

and, in his efforts to reciprocate it, established in 1972 the Sony Trading Company, whose mission is to promote U.S. exports to Japan.

Morita became executive vice-president of Sony Corporation in 1959, president in 1971, chairman and chief executive officer in 1976. In 1972, Sony was awarded an Emmy by the National Academy of Television Arts and Sciences for the development of Trinitron—the first time an Emmy had been given for a product. In 1976, with Morita as CEO, Sony received another Emmy for the U-Matic video tape recording system. Sony's third Emmy was awarded for their one-inch helical-scan videotape recording; and it's fourth came in 1984, for a new video recorder with mass image storage capability specially suited for computer graphics. In 1985, *Billboard* gave Sony its Trendsetter Award for their revolutionary small D-5 compact disc player. Morita, himself, received the Albert Medal of the Royal Society of Arts "for outstanding contributions to technological and industrial innovation and management, industrial design, industrial relations and video systems, and the growth of trade relations." Morita became chairman of the board in 1989. As vice-chairman of Keidanren (Japan Federation of Economic Organizations) and chairman of the Council for Better Corporate Citizenship within Keidanren, Morita was active in educating Japanese companies abroad to become good citizens of local communities. He addressed a letter to the G-7 leaders meeting in Tokyo—the Presidents and Prime Ministers of the United States, Japan, Germany, France, Britain, Italy, and Canada—encouraging them to seek ways to lower all economic barriers between North America, Europe, and Japan to forge a new world economic order.

On November 30, 1993 at the age of 72, Morita suffered a cerebral hemorrhage. Sony, struggling at that time due to a decrease in profits, now had to worry about whether Noria Ohga, Morita's handpicked successor and president/chief executive officer as well as the chair of Sony Software Corporation and Sony Corporation of America, would be able to fill Morita's shoes. Ohga has been blamed for a $3.2 billion loss in Sony Pictures Entertainment's performance. Besides the Sony Corporation's concerns, much of Japan worried about what the loss of Morita from the helm would mean for the country. Jolie Solomon and Peter McKillop wrote in *Newsweek* that Morita is seen as "the epitome of the transnational executive," or, as General Electric chairman Jack Welch calls him, "spiritually global." After years as a maverick who was more beloved abroad than at home, Morita has lately been acknowledged even in Japan as the country's "most powerful and persuasive voice"

In recognition of "his distinguished corporate leadership and for a lifetime of innovative contributions in bringing advanced technologies to consumer electronics products," The Institute of Electrical and Electronics Engineers (IEEE) presented Akio Morita with its Founders Medal less than a year after his stroke. The award was accepted by his wife and one of his sons, as Morita was still in recovery stages. On November 25, 1994, three months after being honored by IEEE and almost exactly a year after his stroke,

Morita decided it was time to step down as chair of Sony, still debilitated from his brain hemorrhage. His resignation secured the Sony position for Noria Ohga, who still intended to retain his other Sony responsibilities.

Morita took over from Masaru Ubuka as honorary chair of Sony, *Billboard* reported, as well as being formally recognized as founder of the corporation. Ibuka was named founder in 1990 and will continue in that role and has also been named chief advisor. Steve McClure noted in his *Billboard* article that in Japan, such titles (which indicate the friends' joint role in starting Sony) are often awarded to executives who have essentially retired from their companies.

Morita's 1993 stroke left him partially paralyzed. He left for his Hawaii condominium in the fall of 1994 to recuperate. *Fortune* magazine reported that although his spirits were good and his mind lucid, he often had trouble speaking and moving. Part of his therapy involved his speaking in Japanese and English on alternate days. Morita gave up his honorary chair position, but is still considered "Sony's patriarch," Brent Schlender and Cindy Kano said in *Fortune,* still maintaining contact with his Japanese protegés by phone and fax. Sony executives make stops in Hawaii to see Morita on trips between Japan and the United States. His power and influence are still prominent factors in Sony's efforts. When Ohga reached his 65th birthday, an age at which he and Morita had previously decided was when one should relinquish the presidency of Sony, he met with Morita to get approval for appointing Nobuyuki Idei— someone with no engineering experience, unlike the usually Sony régime—as the next commander-in-chief. Idei, who began work with Sony in 1960, caught Morita's attention early on. He spent over ten years in Europe where he founded Sony's French subsidiary. When he returned to Japan, he was made general manager of Sony's audio division in 1979, where he was in charge of marketing such products as the Walkman and helped Ohga promote the audio CD. In the 80s, he ran Sony's home-stereo component group, and the video group when he helped with the promotion of the 8mm camcorder. By 1990, Idei had secured Ohga's former position of director of Sony's Design Center and was responsible for Sony's merchandising and product promotion. In 1993, he took over corporate communications, making Idei Sony's most visible senior executive. In many ways, Schlender and Kano reported, Idei had more direct involvement in much of Sony's business than anyone else with the company. Believing that Idei's marketing experience, his resourcefulness, and his enthusiasm for technological advancement, Morita agreed that Ohga's selection was appropriate.

Akio Morita was awarded an honorary Doctor of Law degrees from the University of Pennsylvania and Williams College and various medals of honor in Japan, Great Britain, France, West Germany, Austria, and Brazil, among others. In 1995, he was presented with the Japan Society Award for outstanding contributions to better United States-Japan understanding.

Throughout his career Morita remained an avid sportsman. He played golf for over 40 years. At age 55 he took up tennis; at 60, downhill skiing; at 64 he resumed water skiing; and at 68, scuba diving. Morita and his wife, Yoshiko, have two sons and a daughter.

Further Reading

The most comprehensive biographical account is Akio Morita, Edwin M. Reingold, and Mitsuko Shomomura, *Made in Japan: Akio Morita and Sony* (1986). For information about his life and thoughts, see Akio Morita, *Gakureki muyo-ron* (Never Mind School Records) (Tokyo: 1987); Akio Morita and Shintaro Ishihara, *No to ieru Nippon* (A Japan That Can Say "No") (Tokyo: 1989); Akio Morita, "When Sony Was an Up-and-Comer," *Forbes* (October 6, 1986); Akio Morita, "Technological Management Will Be the Key to Success," *Research Management* (March/April 1987). On history of the Sony Corporation, see *Genryu: Sony 40th Anniversary* (Tokyo: 1986) and its English translation, *Genryu: Sony Challenges 1946-1986.* Also see: Larry Armstrong, "Sony's Challenge," *Business Week* (Industrial/Technology Edition) (June 1, 1987); and Yoko Konaga, "Sony Corp.: New Fields, New Strategies," *Tokyo Business Today* (June 1989); "What am I in for?" *Inc.* (July 1992); Akito Morita, "Toward a New World Economic Order," *Atlantic Monthly* (June 1993); Jolie Solomon and Peter McKillop," We Have Lost a Very Important Player,'" *Newsweek* (December 13, 1993); William Livingstone and Bob Ankosko, "Awards and Prizes," *Stereo Review* (August 1994); "Akio Morita," *US News and World Report* (December 5, 1994); Steve McClure, "Ohga Now Stands Alone Atop Sony Corp.," *Billboard* (December 17, 1994); Brent Schlender and Cindy Kano, "Sony On the Brink," *Fortune* (June 12, 1995); and Bob Ankosko and William Livingstone, "Morita Honored," *Stereo Review* (January 1996). Online information may be obtained via http://www.digitalcentury.com/encyclo/update/sony. □

John Morley

The English statesman and author John Morley, Viscount Morley of Blackburn (1838-1923), was one of the principal Victorian expositors of the ideas of the Enlightenment. He was a leader of the Liberal party, which drew nourishment from those ideas.

John Morley was born at Blackburn on Dec. 24, 1838. He left Lincoln College, Oxford, in 1859 to pursue a literary career in London. He was editor of several periodicals and was known as an incisive reviewer with radical sympathies. His major achievement in journalism was his conduct of the *Fortnightly Review,* which he edited with great distinction from 1867 to 1883. He was also editor of *Macmillan's Magazine* for a short time. For Macmillan's, Morley also edited the "English Men of Letters Series," starting in 1878. To it he contributed the volume on Edmund Burke (1879), one of the best of the series.

Morley's career as a critic generally either preceded his election to Parliament in 1883 or filled up the intervals between office thereafter. His chief works were the books *Voltaire* (1872), *Rousseau* (1873), *Diderot and the Encyclopaedists* (1878), and *Walpole* (1889). His *Life of*

Cobden (1881) was primarily a defense of the ideas of that radical politician. After the death of William Gladstone, Morley undertook to write his biography. The *Life,* which appeared in 1903, drew on a vast collection of materials and presented the life of the eminent Liberal prime minister with sympathy and perceptiveness. The book is Morley's major work.

His career in politics overshadowed Morley's literary life. He entered Parliament at a by-election in Newcastle-on-Tyne in 1883, and his capacities soon earned him a prominent position in the Commons. He became secretary for Ireland in Gladstone's governments of 1886 and 1892 and was an ardent supporter of Irish home rule. He also sided with the Liberals in their anti-imperialist policies. In 1895 he lost his Newcastle seat but found another in Scotland for the Montrose Burghs.

Morley became secretary of state for India in Henry Campbell-Bannerman's Cabinet of 1905. He was firm in his handling of seditious tendencies in India but was a sympathetic advocate of Indian participation in government administration and he helped to decentralize the operations of the government. He retained his post in Herbert Asquith's Cabinet of 1908, and then, in 1911, he became lord president of the council. From 1908 he sat in the upper house as Viscount Morley of Blackburn. In the Lords he was active in persuading the house, much against its will, to pass the budget of November 1909.

At the outbreak of World War I Morley, who was a well-known pacifist, resigned his office. During his retirement he wrote his *Recollections* (1917), a valuable late defense of Victorian liberalism. At the time of his death on Sept. 23, 1923, he was accounted one of the venerables of English letters.

Further Reading

Useful biographical and critical works are Francis Wrigley Hirst, *Early Life and Letters of John Morley* (2 vols., 1927, 1978), and Frances Wentworth Knickerbocker, *Free Minds: John Morley and His Friends* (1943). See also the chapter on Morley in Basil Willey, *More Nineteenth Century Studies: A Group of Honest Doubters* (1956). Two studies of Morley's period in India are Manmath Nath Das, *India under Morley and Minto: Politics behind Revolution, Repression and Reforms* (1965), and Stanley A. Wolpert, *Morley and India, 1906-1910* (1967). Recommended for general historical background are George Macaulay Trevelyan, *British History in the Nineteenth Century, and After, 1782-1919* (1937; new ed. 1962), and Walter Houghton, *The Victorian Frame of Mind, 1830-1870* (1959). □

Thomas Morley

The composer, organist, and theorist Thomas Morley (ca. 1557-ca. 1602) was the chief English exponent of the Italian madrigal tradition.

Thomas Morley was born about 1557 and, sometime between 1602 and 1608, died after a long illness. During his early years he studied composition with William Byrd and organ under Sebastian Westcote. In 1588 Morley received a bachelor of music degree from Oxford and took the position of organist at St. Giles, Cripplegate. In 1591 he became organist at St. Paul's, joining the Chapel Royal the following year. About this time Morley married; he and his wife, Susan, had three children between 1596 and 1600.

During this period Morley, like Byrd a Roman Catholic, encountered trouble as a recusant. Charles Paget, an agent, had intercepted letters which held enough incriminating evidence for him to have had Morley hanged. He repented so abjectly, however, that Paget let him off.

In 1598 Morley applied successfully for the license to print music. But by then his health had begun to fail, and the new outlet proved more burdensome than productive. He had already published his *Canzonets to Three Voices* (1593), *Madrigals to Four Voices* (1594), *Ballets to Five Voices,* and *Canzonets to Two Voices* (both 1595), and his *Canzonets ... Selected out of ... Italian Authors, Canzonets to Five and Six Voices,* and his treatise *A Plain and Easy Introduction to Practical Music* (all 1597). Between 1598 and 1601 he produced and published a new collection each year and also reedited a great many of his earlier publications. He also left a great quantity of unpublished music, including ten motets, four services, five anthems, keyboard music, and viol consorts.

Morley has been called the father of the English madrigal. He was the earliest and the chief figure in the wholesale transplantation of the Italian madrigal tradition to England, and the quick assimilation of Italian styles and forms into a burgeoning English tradition was largely of his doing. Single-handedly he translated the Italian canzonet into a native form, the English short ayre, in his *Canzonets* of 1593 and 1595. In the latter collection he also included nine two-part instrumental fantasias, which, though bearing fanciful Italian titles, are marvelous examples of a new and sprightly English counterpoint. In these canzonets, as in the *Madrigals to Four Voices and Ballets to Five Voices,* Morley obviously patterned his works after Italian models, even paraphrasing a few, but he surpassed these models in harmonic variety and tonal sophistication.

Morley's sacred music is more deeply serious and moving than the canzonets and madrigals. But these sacred works show no greater contrapuntal skill, no more elegant finish in the new English style than the hundredodd secular pieces he had composed on models straight from late Renaissance Italy.

Further Reading

Morley's *A Plain and Easy Introduction to Practical Music* was edited by R. Alec Harman and contains a brilliant foreword by Thurston Dart (1952). In the absence of a monograph on Morley, the following readings are suggested: Peter Warlock, *The English Ayre* (1926); Edmund Horace Fellowes, *English Cathedral Music* (1941; rev. ed. 1970), and *The English Madrigal Composers* (1948); and Joseph Kerman, *The Elizabethan Madrigal: A Comparative Study* (1962). □

Aldo Moro

Aldo Moro (1916-1978) was a prominent leader of Italy's Christian Democratic Party. He was a major proponent of the "Centro-Sinistra"—the center-left government coalitions in the 1960s—and in the early 1970s of the compromise between the Christian Democrats and the Communists. In 1978 he was kidnapped and then murdered by the Red Brigades, a left-wing terrorist organization opposed to his "historic compromise" policies.

Aldo Moro was born in Maglie (in the southeastern province of Lecce) on September 23, 1916. His parents were both educators. His father was an inspector for the ministry of public instruction, and his mother was an elementary school teacher. Moro attended school in Taranto. His obesity often made him a target of teasing by his school mates, but he studied hard and ranked at the top of his class.

Moro's background was strongly Catholic, and he was active in church-sponsored youth groups both in the Gioventù Cattolica Italiana at the high school and in the Federazione Universitaria Cattolica Italiana (FUCI) at the

University of Bari. At the university he studied law and was president of the local Catholic student chapter. In 1939 he transferred to Rome. There he became the national president of FUCI and followed Pope Pius XII's line on behalf of peace in Europe and neutrality in Italy for World War II. In 1942 he resigned his position after being drafted for military service.

In 1945 Moro, then a professor of law at the University of Bari, was elected to the Constituent Assembly on the Christian Democratic list and began a distinguished political career. He was the youngest of the 18 members of the coordination committee that drew up the Italian republic's constitution. He was subsequently elected to the Chamber of Deputies in 1948 and was appointed by Alcide De Gasperi to serve as undersecretary to the foreign minister, a post he retained until 1950. In 1954 Moro accepted his first cabinet post, minister of justice, under Antonio Segni. As minister of justice Moro was in charge of all prisons in Italy. He enacted a series of sweeping reforms after inspecting every prison in the country and talking with thousands of prisoners, something no predecessor had done in more than 100 years.

Subsequently he served as minister of public instruction in the government of Adone Zoli before becoming secretary of the Christian Democrats in 1959. Although the Christian Democrats were badly divided and in danger of splitting, Moro managed to rally the party around him. He was always a staunch anti-Communist and told the Christian Democrats' seventh congress in October 1959 that for Christian Democracy, "the first duty is to resist Communism

in every sector: human, moral, political and social." Nevertheless, he was uneasy that his party, in order to form a governing coalition, was so heavily dependent on right wing parties with pro-Fascist sympathies. His goal was to form coalitions that were both anti-Communist and anti-Fascist. After a period of initial reluctance, he began talks with the Socialists of Pietro Nenni, who claimed to have broken with the Communists. The negotiations resulted in the parliamentary coalition of the Center-Left, the "apertura a sinistra" (opening to the left). Eventually this led to the formation of Moro's first government in 1963. He headed three governments between 1963 and June 1968 and two more in the mid-1970s.

After a series of electoral gains by the Italian Communist Party in the early 1970s, Moro began to urge Christian Democrats toward the "Compromesso Storico" or "Historic Compromise." According to this informal agreement, which lasted from 1976 to 1979, the Communists refrained from voting against the Christian Democrats in return for an informal voice in governmental policy.

As a politician Moro was not a brilliant speaker, but he was able to bring political antagonists together. He built a reputation as a master of ambiguous political formulas, subtle maneuvers, and compromises between seemingly irreconcilable positions. In describing a deal between the Christian Democrats and left-wing groups in a shaky government coalition, he spoke of "parallel convergencies." The phrase, a contradiction in terms, became famous as an example of the Moro style of politics.

Moro was married and the father of three daughters and a son. He lived quietly with his family in a modest apartment in Rome.

In March 1978 Moro became the most sensational victim of the Red Brigades, a left-wing terrorist organization bitterly opposed to Moro's "historic compromise." In a daring maneuver outside his home in Rome the kidnappers killed Moro's five police guards and abducted him. In letters to the government, newspapers, and Moro's family the kidnappers demanded the release from jail of 13 terrorist leaders awaiting trial or sentencing.

The government faced a terrible dilemma. To give in to the terrorists would expose politicians to future kidnappings. To give in would also admit that the life of a political leader was worth saving, but not the lives of policemen, judges, journalists, or businessmen—all past victims of terrorist attacks. The government and the political parties rejected the kidnappers' demands. After a fruitless 54-day search by security forces, Moro's body was found in May in the trunk of a car in the center of Rome. Symbolically, the car was parked half way between the national headquarters of the Christian Democratic and Communist parties.

Further Reading

Frank J. Coppa, editor, "Moro," in *Dictionary of Modern Italian History* (1985), and Corrado Pizzinelli's, *Moro* (Milan, 1969) provide additional information on Moro. □

James Wilson Morrice

James Wilson Morrice (1865-1924), the first Canadian painter to win an international reputation, was a pioneer of "pure" painting as opposed to the painting of local scenery.

James Wilson Morrice was born in Montreal on Aug. 10, 1865, the son of David Morrice, a textile merchant. From 1882 to 1886 James attended the University of Toronto, and from there he went on to study law at Osgoode Hall. As a student, he began to paint landscapes in the Adirondacks and at Lake Champlain, and in 1888, while articled to a law firm, he exhibited a painting with the Royal Canadian Academy.

In 1889, with the encouragement of Sir William Van Horne, president of the Canadian Pacific Railway and a perceptive art collector, Morrice abandoned the practice of law for good and set sail for Europe. After a brief period of study at the Académie Julian in Paris, he pursued his own course with the advice of the veteran landscape painter Henri Joseph Harpignies. His associates at this time included the Americans Maurice Prendergast, Robert Henri, and William Glackens. Morrice first visited Venice about 1896, and Saint-Malo about 1900.

Every year or so Morrice returned to Canada and sketched in Quebec and Montreal, sometimes with the Canadian impressionists Maurice Cullen and William Brymner. In 1904 the French government bought Morrice's *Quai des Grands Augustins, Paris* and the Pennsylvania Museum of Art his *The Beach, Paramé*. The National Gallery began to purchase his paintings in 1909.

During this period Morrice became a familiar figure in the international group of artists and writers who met at the Chat Blanc, a small restaurant in Paris. Among the group were Somerset Maugham and Arnold Bennett; the former's character Cranshaw in *Of Human Bondage* and the latter's Farll in *Buried Alive* are based in part on Morrice. In 1908 he met Henri Matisse, and they traveled in Morocco in 1911-1912 and 1912-1913, although they did not paint together.

Characteristically, Morrice made small pencil drawings or oil sketches on wooden panels no larger than 5 by 6 inches while seated in a café from which he could observe the passing show, a glass of whiskey at his elbow. He painted all his large pictures in his studio on the Quai des Grands Augustins, in broad areas of harmonious color and with detail kept to the minimum.

Morrice remained in France for much of World War I and was commissioned to paint the Canadian troops in action in Picardy in 1918. From 1919 on, his health began to decline, and he spent more time in warmer climates, visiting the West Indies in 1920-1921. He died while on a visit to Tunis on Jan. 23, 1924.

Further Reading

Morrice's chief biographer was Donald W. Buchanan, who wrote *James Wilson Morrice: A Biography* (1936).

Additional Sources

Laing, G. Blair, *Morrice: a great Canadian artist rediscovered,* Toronto: McClelland and Stewart, 1984. □

Justin Smith Morrill

Justin Smith Morrill (1810-1898), an American legislator, is best known for his educational legislation providing Federal land grants to the states to set up agricultural and mechanic arts colleges.

Justin Smith Morrill was born in Strafford, Vt., on April 14, 1810, to the family of a blacksmith of modest means. His formal education ended at 14, when he became a general-store clerk. He gained more experience later as a tradesman in Portland, Maine, and then returned to Strafford as a partner and manager of a country store. After 15 years as an active businessman, he went into farming.

In an age when the country store was the local gathering spot for social information and political discussion, Morrill's work made him well known. He also participated in politics, serving on local and state committees for the Whig party. In 1854 he first won a seat in Congress. Thus began continual congressional service which lasted until his death—12 years as a representative and 32 years as a senator.

Morrill's interest in educational legislation started early. There were then no colleges for agriculture and few offering advanced engineering training. At first Morrill promoted an unsuccessful resolution for a national agricultural school on the model of West Point. In 1857 he introduced his first bill providing for use of public land to form a common fund shared by all the states for the advancement of scientific and industrial education. The measure proved premature and received President James Buchanan's veto. However, by July 1862 Morrill had introduced the plan again and won both congressional approval and President Abraham Lincoln's signature.

The idea for the use of public lands may not have originated with Morrill, but his move charted a new course for Federal aid to higher education which directly affected public educational life in every state. His measure provided each state with public land (on the basis of 30,000 acres per each national representative and senator) for the establishment of schools of applied science. The Morrill legislation of 1890 provided further Federal funds for the land-grant colleges.

Education was not his only concern. In Congress, Morrill was well regarded for his knowledge of finance, and he is credited with shaping the protective tariff legislation of 1861. In the House he served as chairman of the Ways and Means Committee, and in the Senate he was chairman of the Finance Committee. He took an active interest in Washington, D.C., leading moves to complete the Washington Monument and to construct buildings for the Library of Congress and the Supreme Court, among others. He died in Washington on Dec. 28, 1898.

Further Reading

The standard biography is William Belmont Parker, *The Life and Public Services of Justin Smith Morrill* (1924). Also informative is Earle Dudley Ross, *Democracy's College: The Land-grant Movement in the Formative Stage* (1942). □

Gouverneur Morris

Gouverneur Morris (1752-1816), American statesman and diplomat, was one of the important authors of the U.S. Constitution.

Gouverneur Morris was born on Jan. 31, 1752, in his family's manor house at Morrisania, N.Y. After graduating from King's College, New York City, in 1768, he studied law under the chief justice of New York and in October 1771 was licensed as an attorney.

Although some members of his family remained loyal to the British crown, Morris supported the rebel cause during the American Revolution. In 1775 he served as a member of New York's provincial congress and in the following year sat in its constitutional convention. With John Jay and Robert R. Livingston, he drafted New York's first constitution. In 1778 he was elected a delegate to the Continental Congress, where he served as chairman of some of the Congress's most important standing committees. His authorship of a number of essays on public finance brought him to the attention of Robert Morris, the Congress's superintendent of finance, who appointed Gouverneur Morris his assistant, a post he held until 1785. As a delegate to the Constitutional Convention in 1787, he played a leading role, speaking more often than any other delegate and contributing substantially to the writing of the U.S. Constitution.

In 1788 Gouverneur Morris sailed for Europe to attend to Robert Morris's extensive business affairs. In Paris he branched out into speculative enterprises of his own and over the next decade amassed a considerable fortune. His wit, charm, and fluent command of French soon made him the most popular American in Paris. Among his acquaintances were leading members of the Parisian nobility and influential crown officials. His diary gives a lively account of his social life and is one of the best sources on the early stages of the French Revolution.

Early in 1792 Morris was appointed U.S. minister to France. He served until 1794, when the French government demanded his recall, but he traveled in Europe instead and returned to the United States in 1799. The following year he accepted an interim appointment of 3 years as U.S. senator from New York. An extreme Federalist partisan, he was one of President Thomas Jefferson's most severe critics.

Morris was not elected to a new term, and during his retirement, after 1803, he supervised his numerous business activities and carried on an active correspondence with acquaintances abroad and at home. In his correspondence he was sharply critical of the foreign policy pursued by Jefferson and James Madison, particularly their alleged hostility to Great Britain. Believing the War of 1812 to be "unjust, unwise, mismanaged," he supported the disastrous Hartford Convention of 1814. He died at Morrisania on Nov. 6, 1816.

Further Reading

Morris's diary was edited by Beatrix Cary Davenport, A *Diary of the French Revolution* (2 vols., 1939). The standard life is still Jared Sparks, *The Life of Gouverneur Morris with Selections from His Correspondence* (3 vols., 1832). Theodore Roosevelt, *Gouverneur Morris* (1888; repr. 1917, 1980), remains useful. The best popular biography is Howard Swiggett, *The Extraordinary Mr. Morris* (1952).

Additional Sources

Kline, Mary-Jo, *Gouverneur Morris and the new nation, 1775-1788,* New York: Arno Press, 1978, 1971. □

Lewis Morris

Lewis Morris (1671-1746) was an American colonial official. Chief justice of New York, he later became royal governor of New Jersey.

The son of a Barbadian merchant, Lewis Morris was born on Oct. 15, 1671, on the 500-acre estate his father and uncle had purchased in New York. His parents died the following year, and the uncle became Morris's guardian, trying to raise his ward with Quaker discipline. A headstrong boy, Lewis improved sufficiently so that, when his guardian died in 1691, he inherited the quadrupled Bronx estate and 3,500 acres in Monmouth County, N.J.

Morris married Isabella Graham, daughter of New York's attorney general, on Nov. 3, 1691, establishing his home in Monmouth County. Quickly he became a lesser judge in East Jersey and member of Governor Andrew Hamilton's council. Morris visited England in 1702 to promote transfer of the colony from the proprietors to the Crown, hoping to be appointed first royal governor. The ministry, however, named Lord Cornbury executive for both New York and New Jersey. Disappointed, Morris returned home, where he again became a member of the council, but his outspoken criticism of the corrupt Cornbury resulted in his dismissal. Elected to the Assembly in 1707, he collaborated in New Jersey's formal protest against Cornbury's conduct, which brought the governor's removal the next year.

Endorsing the able administration of the new governor, Morris spent more time in New York, particularly after Governor Hunter made Morris chief justice of that colony (1715). Nevertheless, he continued serving on New Jersey's

council under succeeding governors. When William Cosby took over, Morris fell out with the royal representative, ruling one of Cosby's proceedings illegal. Removed from the bench (1733), Morris was elected to the New York Assembly, where he battled Cosby's "court party." In 1734 he carried the Assembly's case to London, failing to get the new chief justice removed but winning vindication of his own judicial conduct.

When New Jersey became a separate province in 1738, Morris was named governor. In office he was a strong executive, hostile to any questioning of his authority. He engaged in wordy controversies with the legislature over taxation, the militia, land titles, and bills of credit. Morris frequently upbraided the Assembly over its duties, protesting to England that the Assembly claimed as much power as the British Commons. An Anglican vestryman, he actively supported the Church's missionary and educational activities. Although he was vain and contentious, Morris gave New Jersey an honest administration. He died near Trenton on May 21, 1746.

Further Reading

Information on Morris's life is relatively scant. The best account is in Elizabeth Morris Waring Lefferts, *Descendants of Lewis Morris of Morrisania* (1907). Also helpful are Edgar Jacob Fisher, *New Jersey as a Royal Province* (1911), and Alexander C. Flick, ed., *History of the State of New York*, vol. 3 (1933).

Additional Sources

Sheridan, Eugene R., *Lewis Morris, 1671-1746: a study in early American politics*, Syracuse, N.Y.: Syracuse University Press, 1981. □

Mark Morris

Mark Morris (born 1956) was probably the most versatile choreographer of the second half of the 20th century. His musicality was the basis of his work. He used his compositional skills on all types of music. His movement vocabulary was eclectic.

Mark Morris was born in 1956 in Seattle, Washington. He grew up in a family full of music and dance. His father taught him how to read music. His mother introduced him to flamenco (her favorite dance) at age nine, then to Balkan folk dance and ballet. As a child he created dances for musicals. As a teenager dancing in the Koleda Balkan Folkdance Ensemble, he was already determined to do his own work. His father died when he was in high school, strengthening the bond with his mother. After graduation from high school he spent almost a year in Europe, part of it in Spain, where he continued to study flamenco. Back in Seattle he studied with Verla Flowers and Perry Brunson.

Two years later he showed up in New York. He performed with a diverse assortment of companies over the years, including the Lar Lubovitch Dance Company, Hannah Kahn Dance Company, Laura Dean Dancers and Musicians, and Eliot Fields Ballet. He started creating dances in a rented studio space at the Merce Cunningham Studio in 1980 and then formed the Mark Morris Dance Group, giving concerts. The beginning years were hard, and the dancers had to take on part-time jobs to pay for food and rent. Reactions to his work were strong. Critics called him the "enfant terrible," and he developed a reputation of being an angry young man with his provocative choreographies. The Mark Morris Dance Group was cohesive. He selected his dancers very carefully, choosing individuals of every color and physical description. He cast without regard to race, rank, or sex. He was enormously proud of his dancers' achievements, and they were a constant source of his inspiration.

On a European tour he was "discovered" by the Belgian Mortier, director of the Theatre Royal de la Monnaie in Brussels, who offered Morris the position of director of dance, vacated by Maurice Bejart. Morris accepted, and from 1988 until 1991 he and his dancers worked on regular salaries and in spacious studios. Morris was thrilled to use the resident orchestra and choir for his productions. The three years turned out to be very challenging, as Morris had to content with anti-American sentiment and discrimation because he was homosexual. Although he was very productive, his unhappiness does shine through in a few dark

pieces created at the time. (Two examples are "Behemoth", which is performed in silence and "Going Away Party".)

The company was later based in New York, but residencies, such as Dance Umbrella in Boston, required him to live a traveler's life. In 1990 he and Mikhail Baryshnikov founded White Oak Dance Project. This special touring company consisted of dancers from leading ballet and modern dance companies performing many works by Morris.

Morris was tall with a steady frame, copious long curls, and bright blue eyes. He was direct, refreshingly honest, and worked hard and expected the same from his dancers, collaborators, and observers. He was a diverse choreographer and a gifted dancer. His work could be hilarious, shocking, lyrical, raw, beautiful, and satirical, without being vulgar. His choices ranged from popular music of all decades and cultures to religious classical, Vivaldi, and country/western. While choreographing, he held the sheet music, absorbed in the music yet aware of the world outside. He prepared the choreography alone, and in the studio he translated and adjusted his ideas for the dancers. While creating a new dance he sought to perfect the slightest detail, until a dancer felt the emotion, musicality, and rhythm of the movement. The technique he used for his choreographies was eclectic, using different dance styles along with gestures of daily life, performed in a unique and meaningful way. He taught classical ballet in its simplest form. Although he acknowledged that ballet dancers want to defy gravity, as a modern dancer he was constantly challenged by this concept.

In addition to creating over 70 works for his own dance company, beginning in 1980 he also created dances for the Boston Ballet, the Joffrey Ballet, American Ballet Theatre, the Paris Opera Ballet, the White Oak Dance Project, and Les Grands Ballets Canadiens, among others. He also worked extensively in opera, for instance on a new production of "Le Nozze di Figaro." One of his two masterpieces, created while in residence in Brussels, was "L'Allegro, Il Penseroso ed Il Moderato." It was his first full-length work to Handel's music of the same name and based on poems by John Milton. Twenty-four dancers weave movement, music, and text together with tenderness and ingenuity. This piece was considered Morris' transition from "enfant terrible" to "true artiste". The second masterpiece was "The Hard Nut," a modern mockery of the conventional Christmas Ballet, "The Nutcracker," with the Tchaikovsky score. Morris' version was placed in the 1960s, breaking through cliches by letting all his dancers, men and women alike, wear tutus in the famous snowflake scene. The costumes and the set were elaborate and done in cartoon character. This ballet was televised and enjoyed by millions. In another choreography, "Dido and Aenas," Morris mixed subtlety and humor. The movements and gestures are drawn from modern and Indian dance, European folk dance, and sign language for the deaf. The diversity of Mark Morris was nearly legendary.

Morris was proclaimed by critics and audiences as "his generation's one and only." He was often mentioned in the same breath with Balanchine. Granted a Bessie Award for choreographic achievement in 1984, he received a Guggenheim fellowship in 1986 and was named a fellow of the MacArthur Foundation in 1991. He recieved the Capezio Dance award in April 1997. By 1995, the Mark Morris Group was the fourth largest modern dance troupe in the United States, with an annual budget of two million dollars.

Further Reading

In Joan Acocella's biography *Mark Morris* (1993) you will find an overview of the works he created in dance and opera. In "Dance as a Theatre" (1992) you can find an edited transcript of a 1990 British television documentary. Articles appear frequently in many magazines, such as in *Rolling Stone, Dance Magazine* and *People Weekly*. □

Robert Morris

An American merchant, financial expert, land speculator, and banker, Robert Morris (1734-1806) performed a valuable service for the new republic as superintendent of finance for the Continental Congress.

Robert Morris was born on Jan. 31, 1734, in Liverpool, England. At the age of 13 he was taken to America by his father, a tobacco agent who settled in Maryland. Several years later Morris was sent to Philadelphia as an apprentice to the merchant Charles Willing. Morris proved adept, and eventually he became a full partner in Willing and Morris, a firm with important connections abroad. With Thomas Willing, Morris invested in ships and land on a large scale and conducted far-flung operations that began to yield high profits. His magnificent Philadelphia town house was a social center run by his wife, Mary White, whom he had married in 1769.

Entry into Politics

Essentially a political conservative, Morris crept toward an open break with England while more headstrong Americans were running. On the Pennsylvania delegation to the Continental Congress, Morris opposed independence but later signed the Declaration of Independence. He served in Congress from 1775 to 1778 and sat intermittently in the Pennsylvania Assembly from 1775 to 1781. His capacity for work, attention to detail, and commitment to the American cause were impressive.

At the same time, Morris used his political power for personal gain. As chairman of the secret congressional Committee of Trade, he diverted large sums for his own firm's use, and at least $80,000 was never accounted for. His agents transported private cargoes in naval vessels and traded on their own account for profits while their zeal for public business often lagged.

Morris's attitude in these ventures was explained in a letter to one partner, Silas Deane: "I shall continue to discharge my duty faithfully to the Public and pursue my

Private Fortune by all such honorable and fair means as the time will admit of." Public criticism of these activities led to a congressional investigation in 1779. Morris's integrity was upheld by the committee's report.

Morris therefore suffered little inconvenience from the war. His abilities so impressed other congressmen that in May 1781 they despairingly dumped the chaotic and penniless Treasury Office in Morris's lap. His firmness and bold measures as superintendent of finance restored confidence, and aided mainly by foreign loans and the American victory at Yorktown, Va., Morris was able to effect much-needed reforms in the tottering bureaucratic structure. His improved system encompassed naval supplies, public credit, military contracts, and army garrisons. Morris founded the Bank of North America, partly with public money, and issued bank notes to maintain cash payments on government business.

Unquestionably, Morris managed public finances superbly and under the most trying conditions. When he left office in 1784, the Treasury had $20,000. Morris was convinced that the new nation could survive only with a centralized financial system. He urged the sound-money faction to press for a Federal revenue program and a consolidated national debt that would undergird the total economy. Assumption of the wartime debt by the national government was a key part of his program.

Return to Business

Morris returned to the business world, signed a tobacco-supply contract with the French monopoly, ventured into the growing China trade, and began reckless purchases of land. He was elected a delegate to the Constitutional Convention, where he apparently never entered the debates but probably spoke out in private sessions. He must have supported plans to build a strong navy and create a powerful central government. After ratification of the Constitution, Morris was elected a senator from Pennsylvania. He worked with Treasury Secretary Alexander Hamilton on details of the first revenue act and the bill for assumption of state debts.

Morris retired from the Senate in 1795, but his enemies sniped away at his failure to settle wartime accounts with the government. In 1796 Morris gave bonds for $93,312 to clear his ledger of these debts. At that time he was widely regarded as the richest American alive. Behind the facade of immense land holdings, however, there was a dwindling supply of cash.

Imprudently, Morris joined with James Greenleaf and John Nicholson in grandiose schemes for developing the newly designated capital at Washington, buying over 7,000 lots. They also acquired millions of acres beyond the Ohio River, in western New York, and in several southern states. With his partners, Morris combined all his holdings so that more than 6 million acres of land seemed sufficient collateral for all his ventures. But rumors of his impending ruin grew, and after a London bank failure Morris was drained of £124,000. He was never able to recover his financial equilibrium. A joint-stock company scheme failed; Morris was land-rich but headed for bankruptcy. Hounded by bill collectors and process servers, he retreated to a country home.

In February 1798 Morris was taken to a Philadelphia debtors' prison and jailed until a reform bankruptcy act permitted his release in August 1801. Court records showed that he owed $3 million. A thoroughly humbled man, Morris lived thereafter on the charity of friends and died on May 8, 1806.

Further Reading

A project to gather and publish Morris's papers is under way, guided by E. James Ferguson. The standard biographies are William Graham Sumner, *The Financier and the Finances of the American Revolution* (1891), and Ellis P. Oberholtzer, *Robert Morris, Patriot and Financier* (1903). Clarence L. Ver Steeg, *Robert Morris* (1954), and E. James Ferguson, *The Power of the Purse: A History of American Public Finance, 1776-1790* (1961), are analytical works of unusual merit. The sketch of Morris in Howard Swiggett, *The Forgotten Leaders of the Revolution* (1955), challenges some past assumptions.

Additional Sources

Chernow, Barbara Ann, *Robert Morris, land speculator, 1790-1801,* New York: Arno Press, 1978, 1974.

Wagner, Frederick, *Robert Morris, audacious patriot,* New York: Dodd, Mead, c 1976. □

William Morris

William Morris (1834-1896), one of the most versatile and influential men of his age, was the last of the major English romantics and a leading champion and promoter of revolutionary ideas as poet, critic, artist, designer, manufacturer, and socialist.

B orn at Walthamstow, Essex, on March 24, 1834, William Morris was the eldest son of a bill and discount broker with wealth and status approaching those of a private banker. Nature and reading were the passions of William's childhood, and the novels of Walter Scott inspired him with an abiding love of the Middle Ages. Morris was educated at Marlborough and Exeter College, Oxford, where he formed a close friendship with Edward Burne-Jones.

Originally intended for holy orders, Morris decided to take up the "useful trade" of architect after reading Thomas Carlyle and John Ruskin, and he was apprenticed to G.E. Street, who had a considerable ecclesiastical practice, in 1856. But Burne-Jones introduced him to the group of artists known as the Pre-Raphaelite Brotherhood, and by the end of the year Dante Gabriel Rossetti had advised him to become a painter, which he did.

In 1859 Morris married Jane Burden, a Rossetti-type beauty; they had two daughters, Jane and Mary (May). In 1861 he founded the firm of Morris, Marshall, Faulkner and Company to carry out in furniture, decoration, and the applied arts the artistic concepts of his friends. In 1875 Morris reorganized the firm and became sole owner. He himself designed furniture (the Morris chair has become a classic), wallpaper, and textiles.

Literary Career

Morris's literary career had commenced at Oxford, where he wrote prose romances for the *Oxford and Cambridge Magazine.* His fame was confined to a small circle of admirers until *The Earthy Paradise* (3 vols., 1868-1870) established him as a major romantic poet. He chose the device of legendary poems from classical and medieval sources recited by Norwegian seamen who had sailed westward to find the earthly paradise.

In 1868 Morris took up the study of Icelandic, published a translation of the *Grettis Saga* with the assistance of Eiríkr Magnússon (1869), and visited Iceland in 1871 and 1873. Morris also translated *The Aeneids* (sic; 1875), the *Odyssey* (1887), *Beowulf* (1895), and *Old French Romances* (1896). He regarded as his finest literary achievement *Sigurd the Volsung, and Fall of the Niblungs* (1876), his own retelling in verse of the Icelandic prose Volsunga saga, a version J. W. Mackail (1899) described as "the most Homeric poem which has been written since Homer."

His Politics

Morris first entered the arena of politics in 1876 to attack Disraeli's Tory government and call for British intervention against the Turks for savagely suppressing a nationalist revolt of oppressed Bulgarians. In his appeal *To the Working Men of England* (1877) he denounced capitalist selfishness on grounds that appealed to both Liberals and Communists. The debate on Morris as a Socialist has given rise to a considerable literature, for the nobility of his utterances led almost every political camp to claim him, including orthodox Marxists. In 1886 Friedrich Engels described him scornfully as "a settled sentimental Socialist." A year later, in ignorance of this criticism, Morris wrote to a friend that he had an Englishman's horror of government interference and centralization, "which some of our friends who are built in the German pattern are not quite enough afraid of I think."

Arts and Crafts Movement

From a series of notable homes—the Red House, Upton, Kent; Kelmscott Manor on the upper Thames; and Kelmscott House, Morris's London house from 1878—he carried on a prodigious activity as a public speaker, member of committees and radical organizations, and leader of the Arts and Craft movement. He founded the Society for the Protection of Ancient Buildings in 1877 and the Kelmscott press in 1890. He died at Kelmscott House on Oct. 3, 1896.

Morris's plea for an integrated society in which everything made by man should be beautiful radically distinguishes him from other social theorists. His insistence on beauty as a central goal makes most modern approaches to a welfare society seem lacking in an essential nobility. For him art was the very highest of realities, the spontaneous expression of the pleasure of life innate in the whole people. An esthetic doctrine underlies his most political writings, like *The Dream of John Ball* (1888). Paradoxically, the designer-manufacturer who failed to grasp the esthetic possibilities of the machine was the father of modern industrial design, which aims to create a beautiful environment for mankind freed from poverty. A notable advance on his theory was made by the Bauhaus, the famed school of architecture and applied art in Germany, where Walter Gropius and his colleagues applied Morris's principles to the machine and scientific technology.

Further Reading

The Collected Works of William Morris (24 vols., 1910-1915) was edited by his daughter May, and *The Letters of William Morris to His Family and Friends* (1950) was edited by Philip Henderson. The classic work on Morris is J. W. Mackail, *The Life of William Morris* (2 vols., 1899; repr. 1968, 1995). A readable narrative biography with excellent illustrations is Philip Henderson, *William Morris: His Life, Work and Friends* (1967). An outstanding, comprehensive study is Edward P. Thompson, *William Morris: Romantic to Revolutionary* (1955). Paul Thompson, *The Work of William Morris* (1967), deals especially with Morris's art in relation to its Victorian background and discusses his writings and social theory in the light of recent research. R. Page Arnot, *William Morris: The Man and His Myth* (1964), is an ingenious attempt to claim Morris as an orthodox Marxist.

Additional Sources

Bloomfield, Paul, *William Morris*, Philadelphia: R. West, 1978.
Bradley, Ian C., *William Morris and his world,* London: Thames and Hudson, 1978.

Cary, Elisabeth Luther, *William Morris, poet, craftsman, socialist,* Philadelphia: R. West, 1978, 1902.
Faulkner, Peter, *Against the age: an introduction to William Morris,* London; Boston: Allen & Unwin, 1980.
Harvey, Charles, *William Morris: design and enterprise in Victorian Britain,* Manchester England; New York: Manchester University Press; New York, NY, USA: Distributed exclusively in the USA and Canada by St. Martin's Press, 1991.
Lindsay, Jack, *William Morris: his life and work,* New York: Taplinger Pub. Co., 1979, 1975.
MacCarthy, Fiona, *William Morris: a life for our time,* New York: Knopf, 1995.
Vallance, Aymer, *William Morris, his art, his writings, and his public life: a record,* Boston: Longwood Press, 1977. □

Toni Morrison

Toni Morrison (born 1931) was best known for her intricately woven novels, which focused on intimate relationships, especially between men and women, set against the backdrop of African American culture. She won the 1988 Pulitzer Prize for her fifth novel *Beloved* and the 1993 Nobel Prize for literature.

Chloe Anthony Wofford, better known in the literary world as Toni Morrison, was born in Lorain, Ohio, in 1931 to Ramah and George Wofford. Her maternal grandparents, Ardelia and John Solomon Willis, had left Greenville, Alabama, around 1910 after they lost their farm. Morrison's paternal family left Georgia and headed north to escape sharecropping and racial violence. Both families settled in the steel-mill town of Lorain on Lake Erie.

Morrison's childhood was filled with the African American folklore, music, rituals, and myths which were later to characterize her prose. Her mother sang constantly, much like the character "Sing" in *Song of Solomon*, while her Grandmother Willis (reminiscent of Eva Peace in *Sula* and Pilate Dead in *Song of Solomon*) kept a "dream book," in which she tried to decode dream symbols into winning numbers. Her family was, as Morrison says, "intimate with the supernatural" and frequently used visions and signs to predict the future. Her real life world, therefore, was often reflected later in her novels. Morrison attributes the breadth of her vision to the precision of her focus. She sees her literature as functioning much as did the oral storytelling tradition of the past that reminded members of the community of their heritage and defining their roles.

Choosing a Literary Career

Morrison cited the difficulty people at Howard University had in pronouncing "Chloe" as the reason for changing her name to Toni. While at Howard she was a member of the Howard University Players, a repertory company that presented plays about the lives of African American people in the South during the 1940s and 1950s. This experience brought into focus her own family's history of lost land and

racial violence. Years later this theme would appear time and time again in her fiction.

After receiving the B.A. in English from Howard and the M.A. from Cornell, also in English, Morrison returned to Howard to teach. In 1958 she married Harold Morrison, a young architect from Jamaica who also taught at Howard. The marriage, which ended in divorce in 1964, produced two sons, Harold (also known as Ford) and Slade. A year and half later she was in Syracuse, New York, working as a textbook editor for a subsidiary of Random House, with two small children, and with lots of free time in the evenings. This environment helped her turn to writing novels.

For several years Morrison continued as a senior editor at Random House, where she became a force in getting other African-American writers published, including Toni Cade Bambara, Gayl Jones, and June Jordan. She not only held down this job, but taught part-time and lectured across the country, while at the same time writing novels: *The Bluest Eye* (1970); *Sula* (1974), which was nominated for a National Book Award; *Song of Solomon* (1977), which won a National Book Critics Circle Award in 1977 and an American Academy of Arts and Letters Award and was chosen as the second novel by an African American to be a Book-of-the-Month selection (the first was Richard Wright's *Native Son* in 1940); *Tar Baby* (1981); and *Beloved* (1987) a novel of recovering power out of the devastation of slavery. Meanwhile she served as writer-in-residence at New York State University, first at Stony Brook and later at Albany, before moving to Princeton.

Morrison's novels were characterized by carefully crafted prose, in which ordinary words were placed in relief so as to produce lyrical phrases and to elicit sharp emotional responses from her readers. Her extraordinary, mythic characters were driven by their own moral visions to struggle in order to understand truths which are larger than those held by the individual self. Her subjects were large: good and evil, love and hate, friendship, beauty and ugliness, and death.

Making Her Point Through Fiction

The Bluest Eye depicted the tragic life of a young black girl, Pecola Breedlove, who wanted nothing more than to have her family love her and to be liked by school friends. These rather ordinary ambitions, however, were beyond Pecola's reach. She surmised that the reason she was abused at home and ridiculed at school was her black skin, which was equated with ugliness. She imagined that everything would be all right if she had blue eyes and blond hair; in short, if she were cute like Shirley Temple. Unable to withstand the assaults on her frail self-image, Pecola goes quietly insane and withdraws into a fantasy world in which she was a beloved little girl because she has the bluest eye of all.

Against the backdrop of Pecola's story was that of Claudia and Frieda MacTeer, who managed to grow up whole despite the social forces which pressured African-Americans and females. For them, childhood was much like it was for Morrison herself in Lorain; their egos were comforted and nurtured by family members, whose love did not fail them.

Sula was about a marvelously unconventional woman, Sula Peace, who becomes a pariah in her hometown of Medallion, Ohio, which was much like Lorain. With the discovery at the age of 12 that she and her friend Nel Wright ''were neither white nor male, and that all freedom and triumph was forbidden to them, they set about creating something else to be.'' Nel married and her life follows convention, while Sula's life evolved into an unlimited experiment. Not bound by any social codes, Sula was first thought to be unusual, then outrageous, and eventually evil. In becoming a pariah in her community, she was the measure for evil and, ironically, inspired goodness in those around her. At her death both the community and Nel learned that Sula was their life force; she was the other half of the equation. Without Sula, Nel felt incomplete.

The female vantage point shifted to an African-American male perspective in *Song of Solomon,* which traced the process of self-discovery for Macon Dead III. Macon, or ''Milkman'' as he was called by his friends, set out on a series of journeys to recover a lost treasure in his family's past, but instead of discovering economic wealth, he uncovered something more valuable. He gathered together the details of his ancestry, which he thought had been lost to him forever. In a larger context Milkman's odyssey became a kind of cultural epic for all African-American people; it mapped in symbolic fashion the heritage of a people, from a mythic African past, through a heritage obscured by slavery, to a present built upon questioned values.

Tar Baby, Morrison's fourth novel, moved beyond the small Midwestern town setting to an island in the Caribbean. As the title suggested, the story employed a folktale about how a farmer used a tar baby to catch a troublesome rabbit. When the tar baby doesn't return the rabbit's greeting, he hits the tar baby and gets stuck. He begs the farmer to skin him alive, to do anything but throw him into the briar patch. The farmer throws him in the briar patch, where the rabbit escapes.

As the story opens, Jadine (also called Jade) has left Paris, where she was a fashion model, to visit Valerian and Margaret Street in the Caribbean. Jade, who was orphaned at an early age, has been cut off from her black heritage. She was raised and educated by Valerian Street, a rich, white, retired candy magnate and employer for her aunt and uncle, Sydney and Ondine. Valerian has paid for Jade's French education, and she has substituted Valerian's cultural heritage of wealth and status for her black heritage of struggle and survival. Therefore, Jade was an orphan in the literal sense of the word, with no personal attachments.

On Christmas Eve a young black vagrant, Son, jumped ship and intruded on their lives. His presence brings to the surface years of their locked up secrets and forced them to give expression to their violent racial, sexual, and familial conflicts. Jade and Son became passionately entangled with one another. Because she had no racial past, no tribe, to cling to—no briar patch, as it were—she cannot share his life with him, but he does not want to live without her. She flees from him, and he searches for her.

Beloved, Morrison's fifth novel, has been called her most technically sophisticated work to date. Using flashbacks, fragmented narration and shifting viewpoints, Morrison explored the story of the events that have led to the protagonist Sethe's crime. Sethe lived with her surviving daughter, Denver, on the outskirts of Cincinnati in a farmhouse haunted by the tyrannical ghost of her murdered baby daughter. Paul D., fellow slave from Kentucky comes to live with them. He violently casts out the baby spirit or so they think, until one day a beautiful young stranger with no memory arrived, calling herself 'Beloved'. The stranger was the embodiment of Sethe's murdered daughter and the collective anguish and rage of sixty million and more who have suffered the tortures of slavery. She eventually takes over the household, feeding on Sethe's memories and explanations to gain strength. Beloved nearly destroyed her mother until the community of former slave women who have ostracized Sethe and Denver since the murder join together to exorcise Beloved at last.

Although the work was considered Morrison's masterpiece, she failed to win either the National Book Award or the National Book Critic's Award. Forty-eight prominent African-American writers and critics who were outraged and appalled at the lack of recognition for the novel, signed a tribute to her achievement that was published in the New York Times in January 1988. Later that year Morrison won the Pulitzer Prize for Fiction for *Beloved.* She won the Nobel Prize for literature based upon the quality of her work in 1993. In 1996, the National Book Awards presented her with its NBF Medal for Distinguished Contribution to Ameri-

can Letters. During her acceptance speech Morrison said "writing is a craft that seems solitary but needs another for its completion, that requires a whole industry for its dissemination. At its best, it offers the fruits of one person imaginative intelligence to another without restraints."

Further Reading

For biographical information see the following periodical pieces: Colette Dowling, ''The Song of Toni Morrison,'' *The New York Times Magazine* (May 20, 1979); Charles Ruas, ''Toni Morrison's Triumph,'' *The Soho News* (March 11, 1981); and Jeane Strouse, ''Black Magic,'' *Newsweek* (March 30, 1981). For critical information see the following books: Barbara Christian, *Black Women Novelists* (1981); Barbara Christian, *Black Feminist Criticism* (1985); Mari Evans, ''Toni Morrison'' in *Black Women Writers, 1950-1980* (1983); and Claudia Tate, *Black Women Writers at Work. The Bluest Eye, Sula, The Black Book, Song of Solomon, Tar Baby, Dreaming Emmett, Beloved, Jazz,* and *Playing in the Dark: Whiteness and the Literary Imagination* are a few of Morrison's works. □

Dwight Whitney Morrow

Dwight Whitney Morrow (1873-1931) was an American lawyer, a banker, and an unconventional but highly successful diplomat.

Dwight Morrow was born in Huntington, W.Va., on Jan. 11, 1873. He was one of eight children, and his family, though of intellectual bent, was in modest circumstances. He attended Amherst College in Massachusetts, where he was a classmate of Calvin Coolidge, and he conceived a strong admiration for the silent New Englander, an admiration that tells something of Morrow's political philosophy. In 1896 he entered the Columbia Law School; he graduated in 1899.

Morrow then entered the firm of Reed, Simpson, Thacher, and Varbum in New York and was made a member of the firm in 1905. Often his work was concerned with the organization of important businesses, and this brought him into contact with many leading figures in the world of industry. In 1914 he was made a member of J. P. Morgan & Company and continued in the banking business until 1927. During World War I he performed important services in connection with the Morgan loans to the Allied powers and made a significant study of the vital problem of war transport. He was an ardent partisan of Coolidge for president and lobbied pertinaciously for him at the convention of 1920.

In 1927, as president, Coolidge appointed Morrow as ambassador to Mexico. At this time relations between Washington and Mexico City were tense because of Mexican attacks on the American oil industry and land-holders there. American opinion was also stirred by the attacks of the regime of President Plutarco Elías Calles upon the Church. Morrow's diplomacy was unconventional. He dealt firsthand with the President, breakfasting with him at his private ranch and accompanying him on a trip in which

nation of geographical knowledge about the American continent.

Jedidiah Morse was born in Woodstock, Conn., on Aug. 23, 1761, the son of a Congregationalist minister. Early training at home and in the local academy provided his education before he went to Yale, from which he graduated in 1783. While in college Morse decided to become a clergyman, and in order to help support his studies he served as a schoolmaster. As a teacher, he was dissatisfied with the deficient, inaccurate geographic information about America contained in the only available textbooks, which were European.

Morse compiled materials on American geography and published them as *Geography Made Easy* (1784). This work, the first geography by an American, launched his fame as a geographer. It had reached 22 editions by 1820. His subsequent efforts in gathering authentic, accurate, up-to-date information, particularly about American geography, provided material for more detailed compilations. These included information not only about the geography of the new country but also about the general and natural histories of all its regions. By revising his works periodically, he kept them current with the nation's expansion.

American Geography appeared in 1789. This was followed by *The American Universal Geography* (1793), *The American Gazetteer* (1797), and *The New Gazetteer* (1802). Because his works were widely adopted in schools, colleges, and libraries and were used in thousands of households, Morse remained foremost in the field for several decades.

Meanwhile Morse had completed his preparation for the ministry, and he had accepted a permanent post with the First Congregational Church in Charlestown, Mass., in 1789. About the same time, he married Elizabeth Ann Breese of New Jersey. As a clergyman, Morse was very active in defending orthodox religious tenets against the theses of Unitarianism. He participated in founding a seminary at Andover, Mass., so that orthodox Congregational theology would continue to flourish. Religious controversy caused him to leave the ministry in 1819.

For the next three years Morse attended to the plight of the American Indian as a U.S. War Department agent investigating their conditions. His report, including a plan for remedying Indian problems, was presented to President James Monroe and to Congress in 1822. It was subsequently published at the author's own expense. The last years of Morse's life were spent preparing further publications in American history and geography. After several years of ill health he died on June 9, 1826, in New Haven. The inventor Samuel F. B. Morse was his eldest son.

the two men inspected the impressive irrigation schemes under way in Mexico. Building up goodwill, the ambassador was able to secure an important modification of the Mexican oil laws and to soften the attack upon the Church. His success was dramatized by the visit of Charles Lindbergh to Mexico, which helped to produce a new attitude toward the United States.

In 1930 Morrow was a delegate to the London Naval Conference, and in the same year he was elected to the U.S. Senate. He died in Englewood, N.J., on Oct. 5, 1931.

In politics Morrow was a temperate conservative and a regular Republican, but he had a knack for understanding views other than his own. His diplomatic methods emphasized reason and goodwill rather than the use of force, and, though the results he achieved were not lasting, his mission marked an important step in what became the good-neighbor policy.

Further Reading

A fine biography of Morrow is Harold Nicholson, *Dwight Morrow* (1935). ☐

Jedidiah Morse

Jedidiah Morse (1761-1826), American geographer and clergyman, was most influential for his dissemi-

Further Reading

The standard biography of Morse is William Buell Sprague, *The Life of Jedidiah Morse, D.D.* (1874). A fairly clear account of his life as a clergyman and his participation in the New England religious controversy is in James King Morse, *Jedidiah Morse: A Champion of New England Orthodoxy* (1939).

Additional Sources

Moss, Richard J., *The life of Jedidiah Morse: a station of peculiar exposure*, Knoxville: University of Tennessee Press, 1995. □

Samuel Finley Breese Morse

Samuel Finley Breese Morse (1791-1872), American artist and inventor, designed and developed the first successful electromagnetic telegraph system.

Samuel F. B. Morse was born in Charlestown, Mass., on April 27, 1791; he was the son of Jedidiah Morse, a clergyman. Samuel graduated from Yale College in 1810. At college he had painted miniatures on ivory and wished to pursue a career in art, but his father was opposed to this. Samuel took a job as a clerk in a Charlestown bookstore. During this time he continued to paint, and his work soon came to the attention of two of America's most respected artists, Gilbert Stuart and Washington Allston, both of whom spoke highly of his abilities. His father reversed his decision and in 1811 allowed Morse to travel to England with Allston. He studied with Allston for 4 years in London. During this time Morse also worked at the Royal Academy with the venerable American artist Benjamin West.

In 1815 Morse returned to America and set up a studio in Boston. He soon discovered that his large canvases attracted favorable comment but few customers. In those days Americans looked to painters primarily for portraits, and Morse found that even these commissions were difficult to secure. He traveled extensively in search of work, finally settling in New York City in 1823. Perhaps his two best-known canvases are his portraits of the Marquis de Lafayette, which he painted in Washington, D.C., in 1825.

In 1826 Morse helped found, and became the first president of, the National Academy of Design, an organization which was intended to help secure commissions for artists and to raise the taste of the public. The previous year Morse's wife had died; in 1826 his father died. The death of his mother in 1828 dealt another severe blow, and the following year Morse left for Europe to recover.

In October 1832 Morse returned to the United States aboard the packet *Sully*. On the voyage he met Charles Thomas Jackson, an eccentric doctor and inventor, with whom he discussed electromagnetism. Jackson assured Morse that an electric inpulse could be carried along even a very long wire. Morse later recalled that he reacted to this news with the thought that "if this be so, and the presence of electricity can be made visible in any desired part of the circuit, I see no reason why intelligence might not be instantaneously transmitted by electricity to any distance." He immediately made some sketches of a device to accomplish this purpose.

Morse again returned to his artistic career, becoming a professor of painting and sculpture at the University of the City of New York. At the same time he entered politics. Like many Americans, he was intolerant of both immigrants and Catholics, and he became a candidate for mayor of New York on a "nativist" platform. In later life his prejudices softened, and he was better able to tolerate the ethnic diversity of the growing country.

The telegraph was never far from Morse's mind during these years. He had long been interested in gadgetry and had even taken out a patent. He had also attended public lectures on electricity. His knowledge of the subject was rudimentary, however, and outdated by the rapid developments in the field during this period. His shipboard sketches of 1832 had clearly laid out the three major parts of the telegraph: a sender which opened and closed an electric circuit, a receiver which used an electromagnet to record the signal, and a code which translated the signal into letters and numbers. By January 1836 he had a working model of the device which he showed to Leonard Gale, a colleague at the university. Gale advised him of recent developments in the field of electromagnetism and especially of the work of the American physicist Joseph Henry. As a result, Morse was able to greatly improve the efficiency of his device.

In September 1837 Morse formed a partnership with Alfred Vail, who contributed both money and mechanical skill. They applied for a patent, and Morse went to Europe seeking patents there as well. He was rejected in England, where a similar device had already been developed. The American patent remained in doubt until 1843, when Congress voted $30,000 to finance the building of an experimental telegraph line between the national capital and Baltimore, Md. It was over this line, on May 24, 1844, that

Morse tapped out his famous message, "What hath God wrought!"

Morse was willing to sell all his rights to the invention to the Federal government for $100,000, but a combination of congressional indifference and private greed frustrated the plan. Instead he turned his business affairs over to Amos Kendall. Morse then settled down to a life of acclaim and wealth. He was generous in his philanthropies and was one of the founders of Vassar College in 1861. His last years were marred, however, by controversies over the priority of his invention and questions as to how much he had been helped by others, especially Joseph Henry. Morse died in New York City on April 2, 1872.

Further Reading

The standard biography of Morse is Carleton Mabee, *The American Leonardo: A Life of Samuel F. B. Morse* (1943). A shorter study is Oliver W. Larkin, *Samuel F. B. Morse and American Democratic Art* (1954). The development of the telegraph network is described in Robert L. Thompson, *Wiring a Continent* (1947). □

Wayne L. Morse

During his two dozen years as U.S. senator from Oregon, Wayne L. Morse (1900-1974) was an independent critic of many federal policies, especially the Vietnam War.

Wunderkind Senator Wayne Lyman Morse left his impression on the nation by his intractable commitment to principle. In a Senate career of 24 years, he built a reputation as an outspoken maverick of whom *The Nation* editorialized: "He said what he thought, he had a sharp intelligence, and he never minced words."

Born on a Wisconsin farm on October 20, 1900, Morse was the son of farmer-rancher Wilbur Morse and his wife Jessie (White) Morse. His father exercised a strong influence on his life, inculcating values of thrift and stressing the necessity of a good education. All his life Morse loved the land, took a keen interest in farm problems, and raised livestock professionally as a hobby.

At the University of Wisconsin Morse studied economics and labor problems as well as devoting a substantial amount of time to debate and argumentation. He earned Bachelor's and Master's degrees in 1923 and 1924 respectively. For four years he taught at the University of Minnesota, earning an L.L.B. there during the same period. A year's fellowship at Columbia University advanced his career greatly; his published study of grand juries brought him national attention and the coveted J.D. degree from Columbia. By the age of 31 Morse was a full professor and dean of the University of Oregon's School of Law.

Oregon became his home, and he devoted all his talents to it, studying crime in the state, serving as a legal education official for the state government, and earning a

nationwide reputation for his school. His life-long interest in labor problems also made Morse a natural choice as a labor arbitrator.

His reputation as tough, knowledgeable, and even-handed earned him respect from labor and management alike and brought him to the attention of the Roosevelt administration during the New Deal. Morse's negotiating skills became more valuable as the United States moved toward World War II. Through his efforts several crucial labor disputes were settled in 1941.

When war came, President Roosevelt appointed Morse to the 12-member National War Labor Board, a move which brought the 41-year-old into greater public focus than he had ever enjoyed before. He waged a fierce battle against anyone he believed to be impeding the war effort, even if he was alone in his dissent. Within a short time the nation—and the citizens of Oregon in particular—began to recognize him as a different sort of public figure, and the terms "maverick," "courageous," and "incorruptible" became associated with his name.

Until the 1940s Morse had hoped for a career as an appointed official, perhaps a federal judge. After one such hope fell through he embarked on an elective career, running for the Senate on the Republican ticket in 1944. A liberal Republican, Wayne Morse had little in common with many of his fellow party members—but he was alienated from many Democrats, too. Practical politics, including the ratio of Republicans over Democrats in Oregon, also dictated his ballot line. He defeated the incumbent Republican senator in the primary and overwhelmed his Democratic opponent on election day.

In the Senate Morse lived up to his maverick reputation by challenging the leadership of both parties, crossing swords with such legendary figures as Senators Robert A. Taft of Ohio and Lyndon B. Johnson of Texas. In 1950 he overwhelmed his Democratic opponent with more than 75 percent of the vote to gain re-election.

Never popular with his colleagues, he was respected and feared for his outspoken candor. He fought his party's Taft-Hartley Labor Act of 1947 and opposed its presidential nominee in 1952. Morse's opposition did not stem from antipathy to Dwight D. Eisenhower so much as from the Republican platform and Ike's choice of Sen. Richard M. Nixon of California as his running-mate. After the Republican ticket defeated Adlai Stevenson Morse dropped his Republican Party allegiance and served his second Senate term as an Independent, converting to the Democratic Party before running for a third term in 1956. Following a spirited primary, Morse faced former Gov. Douglas McKay in November and defeated him decisively, setting a vote-getting record for Oregon. In 1962 he won a fourth term.

As a Democrat Morse was no more popular with his colleagues than he had been as a Republican. He was particularly out of step with his party during the early days of the Vietnam War. In the summer of 1964 Congress voted approval of the Tonkin Gulf Resolution, granting wide powers to President Johnson to defend South Vietnam. The vote was 414 to 0 in the House and 88 to 2 in the Senate, Morse joining Alaska senator Ernest Gruening in dissent.

The 1968 presidential election put Richard Nixon in the White House and Wayne Morse in retirement, being replaced by youthful Republican Robert W. Packwood. Thus ended a career filled with fierce feuds and strongly expressed feelings. Morse was never at a loss for words, one of his Senate speeches setting a one man filibuster record of 22 hours 26 minutes in 1953.

An avid husbandman, Morse raised horses and cattle on his Oregon ranch. Kicked by one of the horses, he was hospitalized in 1951, thereby laying the groundwork for a famous national confrontation with Clare Booth Luce, wife of publisher Henry Luce. When in 1959 Clare Luce's nomination as American ambassador to Brazil was being defeated, Morse vigorously opposed Eisenhower's choice. She injudiciously ascribed Morse's conduct to his having been "kicked in the head by a horse." Morse won a victory when Luce resigned without serving in the post. The Morse-Luce feud was one of several which made headlines during his career and helped—along with his substantive measures—to earn him the reputation "Tiger of the Senate."

The United States has been enriched in different ways at different times by the widely diffused family of British emigrant John Morse, who came to Connecticut in 1639. In the 19th century the family gave the nation Samuel F. B. Morse and the telegraph; in the 20th, another communicator named Wayne Lyman Morse brought his message of uncompromising idealism and lonely commitment to his land.

Further Reading

Wayne Morse's life and career are the subject of A. Robert Smith's *The Tiger of the Senate: The Biography of Wayne Morse* (1962). Morse co-authored *The Two Americas* (1965), an account of U.S.-Latin American relations. ☐

John Clifford Mortimer

Best known for his *Rumpole of the Bailey* television series, John Clifford Mortimer (born 1923) was a noted and prolific writer of novels, stories, and plays for radio, stage, television, and film, as well as a translator, interviewer, critic, editor, and lawyer.

John Clifford Mortimer was born to Clifford Mortimer, a barrister, and Kathleen May (Smith) Mortimer in London, England, on April 21, 1923. As an only child he grew up in an isolated, adult-centered environment. By the time Mortimer was 13 his father was totally blind and his mother devoted herself to leading him about London's law courts and their own Oxfordshire garden. Mortimer read novels and poetry to his father, who in turn told him stories and took him to the theater.

At his progressive prep school at Harrow and eventually at Brasenose College, Oxford, Mortimer mingled with England's upper classes and was encouraged to indulge his love of theater and acting. While at Harrow he had his first story published in the school literary magazine and began writing his first novel. Realizing that his dream of being an actor was impractical, he decided to be a writer. His father sent him to Oxford to study law so that he would "have something to fall back on," but Mortimer continued to write.

After graduating from Oxford in 1942, Mortimer, who was declared unfit for active army service because of vision problems, got a job as fourth assistant director and screen writer for the Crown Film Unit and spent the war years making propaganda documentaries for the government. *Charade* (1947), his first published novel, is based on these film unit experiences. *Charade* was followed by five more novels in the next decade. *Rumming Park* (1948), *Answer Yes or No* (1950), *Like Men Betrayed* (1953), *The Narrowing Stream* (1954), and *Three Winters* (1956) established Mortimer's reputation as a competent if somewhat derivative writer.

Called to the bar in 1948, Mortimer handled divorces and then practiced criminal law to support the children of his first wife, Penelope Ruth Fletcher Dimont, whom he married in 1949. Her four daughters from a previous marriage and their own two children, Sally (1950) and Jeremy (1955), provided an antidote to the isolation of his youth.

Mortimer had already done radio adaptations of his fiction, and in 1957 he wrote his first radio play for the BBC Third Program. *The Dock Brief* was well received and established Mortimer's gift for ironic comedy as well as his

tendency to use autobiographical material as the basis for his writing. During the next 20 years Mortimer wrote nearly twenty more original one act and full-length plays, many of which were adapted for radio, stage, and television. He also made frequent trips to Hollywood to work on screen plays. As a playwright, Mortimer was compared to Chekhov and Gogol, Ionesco, Tennessee Williams, and Edward Albee. While often grouped with Britain's "Angry Young Men" of the late 1950s (Osborne, Wesker, and Pinter), his main interest was charting the decline of the middle class rather than the rise of the working class.

The *menage a trois,* the failure to communicate, and the unhappy marriage are themes to which he returned time and time again. *I Spy* (1957), *What Shall We Tell Caroline?* (1958), *Call Me a Liar* (1958), *The Wrong Side of the Park* (1960), *Lunch Hour* (1960), *Collect Your Hand Baggage* (1962), four one acts in *Come as You Are* (1970), *Collaborators* (1973), and *The Bells of Hell* (1977) are all bitingly comic plays which sympathetically explore relationships between men and women and the various accommodations they make, for the most part, to maintain the status quo. Not surprisingly, it was during this period that Mortimer's own first marriage was floundering; he was divorced in 1972 and married Penelope Gollop the same year.

In addition to the autobiographical probing of male-female relationships, Mortimer's writing drew heavily on his childhood experiences and professional expertise, first as a barrister and then as queen's council. His plays *Two Stars for Comfort* (1962) and *The Judge* (1967) introduce characters who view the law as a repressive force. The law is also a

focus in the widely praised, highly autobiographical *A Voyage Round My Father* (stage play 1970 and television adaptation 1980), which explores the relationship between Mortimer and his blind father. Much of this material reappears in his autobiography, *Clinging to the Wreckage: A Part of Life* (1982), which wittily and lovingly details Mortimer's life through 1970. Another installation of his memoirs was *Murderers and Other Friends* in 1994.

The late 1970s and early 1980s were particularly prolific years. In addition to his autobiographical works, he also adapted numerous Graham Greene stories (1976) and Evelyn Waugh's novel *Brideshead Revisited* (1981) for television. The first *Rumpole of the Bailey* series was produced for the BBC in 1975; five more followed. These programs feature a seedy, aging barrister, Horace Rumpole, played by Leo McKern, who bears an uncanny resemblance to Mortimer. Elements of Mortimer's father and Mortimer himself are evident in the composite Rumpole who, plain spoken, irascible, and definitely anti-establishment, often has more sympathy for his clients than his peers. Ten collections of Rumpole stories have been published to date, most recently *Rumpole on Trial* (1992), *The Best of Rumpole* (1993), *and Rumpole and the Angel of Death* (1996).

Mortimer's versatility continued unabated. He was known as a translator, primarily of Feydeau farces, as a skilled interviewer for *In Character* (1983) and *Character Parts* (1986), and as an editor for *Famous Trials* (1984), *Great Law and Order Stories* (1991), and *The Oxford Book of Villains* (1992). But it was his return to the novel after an absence of nearly 30 years that was perhaps most noteworthy. *Summer's Lease* was published in 1988. *Paradise Postponed* (1985) and its sequel, *Titmuss Regained* (1990), explore politics and power in the post World War II England of Margaret Thatcher. Mortimer's later novel, *Dunster* (1992), peopled with Dickensian eccentrics and figures from his past, expanded his reputation as a teller of wryly humorous stories. His *Felix in the Underworld* was published in 1997.

Further Reading

A Voyage Round My Father (1970), *Clinging to the Wreckage: A Part of Life* (1982) and *Murderers and Other Friends* (1994) are autobiographical. No book-length critical study of Mortimer's work yet exists, but chapters discussing his plays have appeared in John Russell Taylor's *Anger and After: A Guide to the New British Drama* (1969), George E. Wellwarth's *Theater of Protest and Paradox: Developments in Avant-Garde Drama* (1971), and Ronald Hayman's *British Theater Since 1955: A Reassessment* (1979). Good portraits of Mortimer appeared in the *New Yorker.* (March 20, 1995) and in *The New York Times* (April 12, 1995). □

Nelle Katherine Morton

Nelle Katherine Morton (1905-1987) was a church activist for racial justice, a teacher of Christian educators, and, later in her life, one of the leading influ-

ences on the powerful and growing movement of women's spirituality and feminist theology.

Nelle Morton began her journey in 1905, when she was born in the hill country of east Tennessee. Her circumstances were humble, but her heritage was proud. As she would later write, "I did not have to start at the beginning." One historian has referred to her grandmother's people as a little band of Presbyterians from the Scottish Highlands seeking freedom and justice. Morton's mother, whom she referred to as "a strong Appalachian Amazon," remained a powerful influence all of Morton's days, entering even into a vision reported in one of her final essays. Her mother was a schoolteacher, a faithful church woman, and a social activist who had written in her youth a prize-winning speech entitled "The Woman I Want To Be." In Morton's teens her mother gave her the speech to use in an oration contest. She won the prize with it. Morton noted that the speech expressed sentiments we would now call feminist and wrote that in many ways she gave her mother "back her own pages."

Morton's long career as a teacher began during her summers off from her studies at Flora MacDonald College. She taught in vacation church schools. She then became the sixth grade teacher in a Kingsport, Tennessee, public school. During these years she developed an extraordinary attunement to the imaginative gifts of children which would shape her pedagogy and her theology.

Morton then made the great leap from Appalachia to New York City, where she graduated from Biblical Seminary and moved on to direct the educational programs of Plymouth Congregational Church in Brooklyn. At the same time she led advanced seminars for Christian educators at Union Theological Seminary. The urban experience began to refocus her ministry in terms of social justice as she began to confront a poverty that degrades and entraps, a poverty unlike that with which she had been well acquainted among the hill people. During the 1930s she directed the youth programs for her own denomination, the Presbyterian Church in the United States, based in Richmond. She consistently challenged the racial segregation laws of the South as a board member for the denomination's board of education.

During her seven years in Virginia she challenged the racial laws and customs of the South by organizing interracial youth camps and conferences. Then in 1943 Morton accepted the call to become the general secretary of the Fellowship of Christian Churchmen (one source called it the Fellowship of Southern Churchmen), a prophetic network of African American and white southern leaders committed to racial justice, equality, and integration. This is the group in which Martin Luther King, Jr., would rise to prominence, a group which did indispensable preparatory work for the later civil rights movement. Morton was instrumental in changing the Fellowship's annual conference into an (illegally) interracial family camping week in a secluded mountain cove. On one occasion she and her campers hid all night between the rows in a cornfield to elude a local group

threatening to take the law into their own hands. In 1947 she took part in the first Freedom Ride, a key historic event designed to challenge the racist laws inhibiting interstate travel for African Americans.

A bout with cancer caused her to resign the Fellowship post and return to the family home in Tennessee. During her ultimately successful convalescence she occupied herself teaching mentally handicapped children for whom she pioneered camping programs. Morton made a prize-winning film on the subject for the Virginia State Department of Education. During this period she was also writing, publishing two books on her perspectives on Christian and theological education.

In 1956 Drew Theological School in Madison, New Jersey, then a Methodist seminary with a strong international flavor due to its involvement in German existential theology, called her to join its faculty. She came as an instructor in Christian education, the only field then open to women in seminary education. She became the first, and for many years only, woman on the faculty. Drew invited her to use her commitments and experiences to broaden its understanding of the church's educational ministries. And indeed she never relented in her willingness to challenge colleagues at Drew and in the churches as to the multidimensional scope of their accountabilities, urging them to become more active in the church's mission of the time. In her teaching and writing she drew not just on the dimensions of social and global justice but also on the avant garde theater and art museums of New York.

In 1962 she took a sabbatical leave to study in Switzerland with Jean Piaget. Here she learned the requisite tools for her critique of the theological tradition of the Word and its hyperabstractions of transcendence. It was in the late 1960s that Morton began to make the connections between image, word, and the newly emerging feminist movement. At this point, she wrote, "My whole life just fell open." In 1969 she taught what seems to be the first course anywhere on women, language, and the Bible. For the two remarkably creative decades remaining to her, she would focus attention on what she called "the woman question."

After her retirement from Drew in 1971, Morton was free to embark on a period of intense intellectual activity, including writing, teaching, and speaking at events around the world. She became involved in the formative discussions, behind the scenes and on the forefront of the new set of theories and practices known as feminine theology. From her new home in Claremont, California, she participated in the newly created Commission on Women formed by the National Council of Churches by examining women's roles in articulating theology. Morton also led and participated in feminist spirituality groups, forming an academic group on women and religion called Thiasos.

From papers written during this decade she edited her book *The Journey Is Home*. This book reveals why Christian feminists such as Rosemary Ruether, and post-Christian feminists, such as Mary Daly, consider her a great foremother.

In its pages her earthy Appalachian roots underlie a project which finally embraced every dimension of spiritual and political consciousness. Her way was not to pontificate. The essays are concise explorations rather than conclusive treatises. Her famous phrase, ''hearing each other to speech,'' suggests her own method. For Morton even the act of divine creation is no longer to be imagined as the ultimate speech-act; rather, ''in the beginning was the hearing.''

This open, liberating concept of hearing is linked to consciousness, whence metaphors arise. Following the power of metaphor to both break the deadlock of old images and liberate our energies with new ones, she challenges the sociocultural icons of patriarchy. Instead of the old revelation of the Word from above, she evokes a movement which carries the aspirations for wholeness of all persons who have been kept down, whether by race, class, or gender. And it carries the bodily, emotive, relational energies which wait to come forth as sacred in each of us. Finally, her work centered on the idea of the Goddess as metaphor. Her work reports not just the history and the theory supportive of a Goddess-spirituality, but also her own imaginative visionary experiences. Yet her message remained unmistakable; the ''Goddess,'' or God as woman, is a metaphor. Its purpose is iconoclastic and epiphanic—to break the exclusivistic hold of masculine images of the divine and to disclose new possibilities. If the Goddess ceases to be a live metaphor, perhaps when sexism itself has been overcome, then ''she'' must also shatter or else become a dull and dogmatic idol like the usual uses of ''God the Father.''

A respected critic said her thoughts of Morton were of ''a pucker of dissatisfaction, of systematic suspicion, knitting her brow; or of her radiant burst of innocent wonder, unconditionally affirmative; or her continuum of undiluted curiosity. Her passion to know what was going on, especially but not exclusively with women and minorities, kept her reading immense piles of books and journals and kept her in touch with an endless network of friends.'' Despite a review in a journal that indicated Morton had moved to the margin of the Presbyterian faith in her later years, Morton believed herself to be even more faithful to her challenge of church assumptions about women. Even in her 80s, Morton was an advocate for religion and theology to be ''an embodied, communal process, an evolving politics of the imagination in which we are, in her famous idiom, heard to our own speech.''

Morton's full life of over eight decades never ceased to be a journey. It ended on July 14, 1987. In her view, the journey does not arrive eventually at a final destination called ''home.'' Rather, ''home is a movement, a quality of relationship, a state where people seek to be 'their own,' and increasingly responsible for the world.'' In this sense, ''the journey is home.'' She was one whose immeasurable influence will long continue to come home to those concerned with justice and gender in the churches.

Further Reading

The best introduction to Nelle Morton is her own book *The Journey Is Home* (1985). See also Catherine Keller, ''Ear, Goddess and Metaphor on the Journey of Nelle Morton'' in *Feminist Studies in Religion,* and ''Nelle Morton: Hearing to Speech'' in *The Christian Century* (February 7-14, 1990); and ''Nelle Morton: Journeying Home'' in *The Christian Century* (August 26-September 2, 1987). □

Oliver Hazard Perry Throck Morton

The American politician Oliver Hazard Perry Throck Morton (1823-1877), as governor of Indiana during the Civil War, ably organized support for the Union.

Oliver Perry Morton was born on Aug. 4, 1823, in Salisbury, Ind., but grew up in Ohio. After 2 years at Miami University in Ohio, he left in 1845 to read law in Centreville, Ind. He served briefly as a circuit judge in 1852. Although a strongly partisan Democrat, Morton broke with his party over the Kansas-Nebraska Act in 1854, which allowed the further extension of slavery into new territories, and he was expelled for disloyalty. Finding reconciliation impossible, he helped found the Indiana Republican party. In 1860 he was elected lieutenant governor and became governor when the incumbent went to the Senate.

Morton zealously favored the Civil War and energetically threw the resources of his state behind the national government. He quickly and effectively raised troops, money, and supplies. But the political situation in Indiana was touchy because the potent Democratic opposition believed the Republicans had provoked an unnecessary sectional conflict for their own partisan advantage. Morton assiduously worked to divide and intimidate the Democrats. He denounced them as traitors and Copperheads intent on destroying the Union, and he worked with military and judicial authorities to harass, weaken, and imprison the Democratic leadership.

Nevertheless, the Democrats secured control of the Indiana Legislature in 1862, primarily by playing on white racial fears aroused by President Abraham Lincoln's Emancipation Proclamation. The new legislative majority determined to limit Indiana's war activities as a means of appealing to the South to return to the Union. They tried to weaken Morton's authority over military matters, demanded a 6 months' armistice in the war, and threatened to withhold all state appropriations. Morton bitterly resisted. The Republican members withdrew from the legislature, leaving the body without a quorum and legally unable to transact business. Then Morton borrowed money from individuals and the national government to finance state operations and continued as before. The crisis ended when Morton was reelected with a Republican legislature in 1864.

Morton suffered a stroke in 1865. In 1866 he joined other Republicans in denouncing President Andrew Johnson's conservative Reconstruction policies. Morton was elected to the Senate in 1867, where he generally supported the Radical Republicans. He backed military reconstruction, the 14th and 15th Amendments, and Johnson's impeachment in 1868. He served as a member of the electoral

commission to decide the Hayes-Tilden election controversy in 1876. He died in Indianapolis on Nov. 1, 1877, of another stroke.

Further Reading

William Dudley Foulke, *Life of Oliver P. Morton* (2 vols., 1899, 1974), is a complete, albeit partisan, biography. The Indiana political situation is well described in Kenneth M. Stampp, *Indiana Politics during the Civil War* (1949). Frank L. Klement, *The Copperheads in the Middle West* (1960), is an excellent analysis of Morton's opponents. Also useful is William Best Hesseltine, *Lincoln and the War Governors* (1948). □

William Thomas Green Morton

The American dentist William Thomas Green Morton (1819-1868) was an early experimenter with anesthesia.

William Morton was born on Aug. 9, 1819, in Charlton, Mass. He went to Boston at the age of 17 to try a career in business, but after several years he took up the study of dentistry at the Baltimore College of Dental Surgery.

In 1842 Morton began his practice in Farmington, Conn., where he met Horace Wells, a dentist who was interested in anesthesia and who was to experiment later with nitrous oxide gas. They set up a practice together in Boston, but it was dissolved after a few months. Morton then entered Harvard in 1844 to study for a medical degree but left because of financial pressures and his marriage that year to Elizabeth Whitman.

Morton resumed his dental practice and began to concentrate on manufacturing and fitting artificial teeth, work which led him to consider using anesthesia. Before a patient could be fitted with artificial teeth, the roots of his old teeth had to be extracted—a tedious and painful operation. Morton had observed experiments with ether in his chemistry classes at Harvard, and his professor Charles T. Jackson encouraged him to try it on his patients. Morton first tested ether on animals and then upon himself to measure the possible aftereffects. When he was convinced of its safety, he decided to put it to use on a patient.

On Sept. 1, 1846, in a demonstration attended by witnesses, he put a patient to sleep by ether inhalation and painlessly extracted an infected tooth. The success of this operation was reported in the newspapers and attracted wide attention, particularly among Boston doctors, who were interested in the use of ether for surgery.

Morton was jealous of his discovery, however, and refused to divulge the formula for his sleep inducer, which he called "letheon." He was issued a patent for letheon in 1846 and insisted on personally issuing licenses for the use

of his discovery. When the French Academy of Medicine awarded Jackson and Morton a joint prize of 5,000 francs, Morton turned it down on the grounds that it rightfully belonged to him alone. In 1849 he petitioned Congress for a reward for the discovery of anesthesia, and two bills advocating the payment of $100,000 to Morton were introduced at separate sessions. But the lengthy debates which took place between the warring factions left the issue hopelessly deadlocked.

Morton's legal expenses and the neglect of his practice in the pursuit of financial gain for his discovery reduced him to poverty in his later years. On July 15, 1868, he died in New York City.

Further Reading

Two recent accounts of Morton are Grace Steele Woodward, *The Man Who Conquered Pain: A Biography of William Thomas Green Morton* (1962), and Betty MacQuitty, *The Battle for Oblivion: The Discovery of Anaesthesia* (1970). There are a number of older works on Morton: P. B. Poore, *Historical Materials for the Biography of W. T. G. Morton* (1856); Nathan P. Rice, *Trials of a Public Benefactor, as Illustrated in the Discovery of Etherization* (1859); James M. Sims, *History of the Discovery of Anaesthesia* (1877); and René Fülöp-Miller, *Triumph over Pain* (trans. 1938). □

Carol Mosely-Braun

Carol Mosely-Braun (born 1947), Democrat from Chicago, Illinois, became the fourth African American and the first African American woman elected to the U.S. Senate when she defeated Republican Rich Williamson on November 3, 1992.

Carol Mosely-Braun was born August 16, 1947, and began life in a middle-class Chicago neighborhood. Her father, a policeman, and her mother, a medical technician, divorced when Mosely-Braun was in her teens, and she moved in with her grandmother in an African American Chicago neighborhood. One of four children, her childhood was marred by a sometimes abusive father and the responsibilities of caring for her younger siblings. But her parents also imbued her with a sense of social responsibility that helps explain her political activism in high school. As a teenager she staged a one-person sit-in at a restaurant that refused to serve her, integrated a previously all-white beach, and marched with Martin Luther King, Jr., in a local civil rights demonstration.

Mosely-Braun attended Chicago public schools and earned a B.A. in political science from the University of Illinois, Chicago. Upon graduation she took a law degree from the University of Chicago Law School in 1972 and then worked for the federal government for three years as an assistant U.S. attorney under Jim Thompson. She married Michael Braun, a lawyer, in 1973. Four years later she gave birth to her only child, Matthew. In 1978 Mosely-Braun ran for and won election to the state legislature. She served for

ten years and after two terms became the fist woman and the first African American ever elected to serve as assistant majority leader. She also became Chicago Mayor Harold Washington's legislative floor leader and sponsored bills to reform education and to ban discrimination in housing and private clubs. In addition, she introduced the bill that barred the State of Illinois from investing funds in South Africa until the apartheid system was abolished. Finally, Mosely-Braun filed, and won, the reapportionment case that affirmed the "one man-one vote" principle in Illinois. While in the state legislature, she gained a reputation as a superb debater and coalition builder.

Near the end of her service in the state legislature Mosely-Braun suffered some personal losses, including divorce from her husband, a stroke to her mother, and the death of her younger brother, Johnny. Despite these personal misfortunes, she agreed to join Harold Washington's multi-ethnic, multi-racial, and gender-balanced "Dream Ticket" in 1987 and ran for the office of recorder of deeds. Her victory made her the first African American woman to hold executive office in Cook County. As recorder she managed an $8 million budget and 300 employees. In that position she modernized the recorder of deeds office and saved the city significant sums of money. It was while serving as recorder that she decided to run for the U.S. Senate.

Angered by the Senate's handling of the sexual harassment case involving Supreme Court nominee Clarence Thomas and the University of Oklahoma law professor Anita Hill, Mosely-Braun decided to run in the Democratic primaries against incumbent Senator Alan Dixon, who had voted to confirm Thomas. Although virtually a political unknown, she launched a grassroots campaign to win the nomination from Dixon (who had never before lost an election) and a third candidate, Albert Hofeld, a personal injury lawyer with a $5 million campaign chest. Despite being outspent in the campaign by more than 10-to-1, and having a campaign described as underfunded, disorganized, and understaffed, Mosely-Braun won the three-way Senate primary with 38.9 percent of the vote. According to Mosely-Braun, the turning point came when she hired Kgosie Matthews to run her campaign, although the English educated South African himself became a controversial figure during the campaign. He also became her fiancée. The victory made her the first African American woman ever nominated to the U.S. Senate by a major political party.

In the general election she ran against Richard Williamson, a former official in President Ronald Reagan's administration. Mosely-Braun's victory in that election made her only the fourth African American to win a U.S. Senate seat. She was also the first African American woman ever elected to the Senate and one of seven women to win congressional races in the November elections.

Shortly after taking office on January 5, 1993, Mosely-Braun was named to the Judiciary Committee, the Banking, Housing and Urban Affairs Committee, and the Small Business Committee. Her first year in office was marked by controversy over her handling of several personal financial dealings and praise for her stand against the renewal of the patenting for the Confederate flag as the insignia of the United Daughters of the Confederacy. She single-handedly reversed the Senate's vote on the matter and cajoled the Senate to defeat Senator Jesse A. Helm's (Republican, North Carolina) amendment to renew the patent. Such action demonstrates the importance of having a more inclusive U.S. Senate.

Mosley-Braun continued to make headlines in Washington. In 1994, she sponsored the education Infrastructure Act, which was designed to repair and restructure public schools with federal money. In 1995 she was appointed to the Senate Finance Committee thus making her the first woman to ever hold such a position. Moseley-Braun will be up for re-election in 1998.

Further Reading

No full-length biography exists for Mosely-Braun, but good biographical material can be found in Karima A. Haynes, "Campaigning for History" in *Ebony* (June 1, 1992), and in Jill Nelson, "Carol Mosely-Braun: Power Beneath Her Wings" in *Essence* (October 1, 1992). □

Moses

The Old Testament prophet Moses (ca. 1392-ca. 1272 B.C.) was the emancipator of Israel. He created Israel's nationhood and founded its religion.

Moses was the son of Amram and Yochebed of the tribe of Levi. He was born in Egypt during the period in which the Pharaoh had ordered that all newborn male Hebrew children be cast into the Nile. Rescued by the daughter of the Pharaoh, he was brought up in the splendor of the Egyptian court as her adopted son. Grown to manhood, aware of his Hebraic origin, and with deep compassion for his enslaved brethren, he became enraged while witnessing an Egyptian taskmaster brutally beating a Hebrew slave. Impulsively he killed the Egyptian. Fearing the Pharaoh's wrath and punishment, he fled into the desert of Midian, becoming a shepherd for Jethro, a Midianite priest whose daughter Zipporah he later married. While tending the flocks on Mt. Horeb far in the wilderness, he beheld a bush burning that was not consumed. In the revelation that followed, he was informed that he had been chosen to serve as the liberator of the children of Israel. He was also told to proclaim the unity of God to his entire people, which doctrine heretofore had been known only to certain individuals.

The tremendous responsibility of his task, his innate humility, and his own feeling of unworthiness evoked a hesitancy and lack of confidence in Moses. He was assured, however, that Aaron, his more fluent brother, would serve as his spokesman both to the children of Israel and to the Pharaoh.

Moses returned to Egypt and persuaded the Hebrews to organize for a hasty departure from the land of bondage. Together with Aaron, he informed the Pharaoh that the God of the Hebrews demanded that he free His people. The Pharaoh refused to obey, bringing upon himself and his people nine terrible plagues that Moses wrought upon Egypt by using the miraculous staff he had received as a sign of his authority. The tenth plague, the killing of the firstborn sons of the Egyptians, broke the Pharaoh's resistance and compelled him to grant the Hebrews permission to depart immediately. Moses thus found himself the leader of an undisciplined collection of slaves, Hebrew as well as non-Hebrew, escaping from Egyptian territory to freedom.

Moses' immediate goal was Mt. Horeb, called Mt. Sinai, where God had first revealed Himself to him. The Hebrews came to the sacred mountain fired by the inspiration of their prophetic leader. Summoned by God, Moses ascended the mountain and received the tablets of stone while the children of Israel heard the thundering forth of the Ten Commandments. Inspired, the people agreed to the conditions of the Covenant.

Through 40 years in the wilderness of Sinai, overcoming tremendous obstacles, Moses led the horde of former slaves, shaping them into a nation. He selected and set them apart for a divine purpose and consecrated them to the highest ethical and moral laws. Only a man with tremendous will, patience, compassion, humility, and great faith could have forged the bickering and scheming factions who constantly challenged his wisdom and authority into an entity.

Moses supplemented the Ten Commandments by a code of law regulating the social and religious life of the people. This collection of instructions, read to and ratified by the people, was called the Book of the Covenant.

Under his leadership, most of the land east of the Jordan was conquered and given to the tribes of Reuben and Gad and to half of the tribe of Menashe. Moses, however, was not permitted to lead the children of Israel into Canaan, the Promised Land, because he had been disobedient to God during the period of wandering in the desert. When the people were in need of water, God told Moses to speak to a rock and water would spring from it. Instead he had struck the rock with his staff. From the heights of Nebo he surveyed the land promised to his forefathers, which would be given to their children. Moses, 120 years old, died in the land of Moab and was buried opposite Bet Peor.

Further Reading

No single work on Moses is satisfactory. One full study is Martin Buber, *Moses* (1946; new ed. 1958). Mordecai Roshwald and Miriam Roshwald, *Moses: Leader, Prophet, Man* (1969), draws from legend, fiction, drama, and poetry as well as from the Bible. The best short essays on Moses are in Rudolph Kittel, *Great Men and Movements in Israel* (1929), and Fleming James, *Personalities of the Old Testament* (1939). For archeological and historical background consult Max L. Margolis and Alexander Marx, *A History of the Jewish People* (1927); Robert H. Pfeiffer, *Introduction to the Old Testament* (1941; rev. ed. 1948); William F. Albright, *The Archaeology of Palestine* (1949; rev. ed. 1956); Harry M. Orlinsky, *Ancient Israel* (1954); and Martin Noth, *The History of Israel* (1958; rev. ed. 1960). □

Grandma Moses

Anna Mary Robertson Moses (1860-1961) was probably America's best-known primitive painter.

Anna Mary Robertson was born in Greenwich, N.Y., on Sept. 7, 1860, one of 10 children of a farmer. At 12 she began earning her living as a hired girl. In 1887 she married a farm worker, Thomas S. Moses, and the couple settled on a farm in Virginia. They had 10 children, 5 of whom died at birth. In 1907 the family moved to Eagle Bridge, N.Y., where Grandma Moses spent the rest of her life. She died on Dec. 13, 1961.

While living on the farm, Grandma Moses had embroidered pictures in yarn. At the age of 76, because of arthritis, she gave up embroidery and began to paint. Her early work was usually based on scenes she found in illustrated books and on Currier and Ives prints. Her first one-woman show was held in New York City in 1940 and immediately catapulted her to fame. Her second one-woman show, also in New York, came 2 years later, and in the intervening time her colors had become more discreet and her handling of space more assured. By 1943 there was an overwhelming demand for her pictures, partially because her homespun, country scenes evoked much nostalgia.

Most of Grandma Moses' paintings were done on pieces of strong cardboard, 24 by 30 inches or less. She

habitually portrayed happy bucolic scenes, sometimes depicting herself as a child. She also painted a number of history pictures, usually dealing with her ancestors, one of whom built the first wagon to run on the Cambridge Pike. In some works figures are dressed in 18th-century costumes, as people might have dressed in the country. Certain color schemes correspond to the various seasons: white for winter, light green for spring, deep green for summer, and brown for autumn. Among her most popular paintings are *The Old Oaken Bucket, Over the River to Grandma's House, Sugaring Off,* and *Catching the Turkey.*

Grandma Moses worked from memory, portraying a way of life she knew intimately. The people in her paintings are actively engaged in farm tasks, and, although individualized, are part of the established order of seasonal patterns. In most paintings the landscape is shown in a panoramic sweep and was completed before the tiny figures were put in.

Technically the work of primitive painters is distinguished by a conceptual rather than a visual approach to painting. This involves, too, a naiveté of handling based on a totally linear format, with atmospheric perspective, cast shadows, and, frequently, modeling eliminated. The strength of primitive painting lies in the feeling for pattern and the charm of the mood that is projected. In Grandma Moses' paintings the spectator comes to feel a joyous acceptance of existence. In *McDonnel's Farm* (1943), for example, a group of children are shown in a circular dance at the right, while all the other figures are busily engaged in farm tasks: one man loads the haywagon, another harvests, an-

other cuts the grass with a scythe. In her paintings there is no despair, unhappiness, or aging, yet this unrealistic view of existence is presented with remarkable conviction.

Further Reading

Grandma Moses' *My Life's History* (1952), edited by Otto Kallir, who tape-recorded her account of her life in 1949, is dull and prosaic, and the quality of the illustrations is poor. *Grandma Moses, American Primitive* (1946), edited by Kallir, contains biographical extracts and facsimiles of Grandma Moses' handwritten notes used as commentaries for the illustrations; it contains little analysis of the paintings. □

Robert Moses

Robert Moses (1888-1981), New York City's controversial impressario of public works, did more to reshape his city and, by example, to influence the course of American urban development than did any other figure of the mid-20th century. Moses, who by training was neither planner, architect, nor engineer, attained unprecedented power without ever being elected to public office.

Born December 18, 1888, in New Haven, Connecticut, Robert Moses was the second of three children of Emanuel and Bella Choen Moses. The elder Moses, a Jew of German extraction, retired in 1897 from the department store business which made him a millionaire and moved with his family to New York City. Young Robert was sent to private preparatory schools and graduated from Yale University in 1909. He received a Master's degree in political science from Oxford University in 1911 and a Ph.D. from Columbia University in 1914, with a dissertation on the British civil service system.

Moses promptly went to work for the Bureau of Municipal Research, a business-dominated New York political reform body which stressed the importance of the application of business management principles to the conduct of municipal affairs. Here Moses met Mary Louise Sims, whom he married in 1915. The couple had two daughters, Barbara and Jane.

Upon the election of reform mayor John Puroy Mitchell in 1914, Moses was appointed technical adviser to the Mayor's Civil Service Commission. Moses and his staff produced a report calling for the complete revision of the city's civil service system along what may be described as meritorcratic lines. The report occasioned much controversy and was not implemented. Moses was removed from office when Mitchell lost his bid for re-election.

Learning to Use Political Power

After working briefly again with the Bureau of Municipal Research and with the United States Food Commission, Moses became chief of staff to Belle Moskowitz, who had been appointed by newly-elected New York governor Al-

fred Smith to head a commission charged with reorganizing the state's administrative structure. Moses became a key adviser to Smith, and during Smith's first two terms (1918-1920 and 1922-1924) he gained essential experience in practical politics. This, combined with his expertise in the theory of government, prepared Moses for his role as New York's "Master Builder."

In 1924 Smith appointed Moses to the presidency of the newly-created Long Island State Park Commission, a body whose enabling legislation Moses himself had drawn up. Together with the State Parks Council, of which Moses became chairman, this body had unprecedented power to appropriate land and build park highways. Special purpose non-elective governments such as these were a well-worn progressive device for removing public works and services from the direct control of politicians and from what many considered an unthinking electorate. Moses' contribution, aside from the extraordinary powers given the bodies he helped to create, was his ability to build a public, political, and special interest constituency for such bodies. This made them, and him, truly independent forces in state and local administration.

During the remainder of the 1920s Moses used this power to fight for automobile highways and recreational facilities on Long Island, and each success increased his power. The Northern and Southern State parkways on Long Island embroiled Moses and Smith in a bitter contest with the island's wealthier residents, who feared an influx of what one described as "rabble." This, along with the multi-million dollar development of the island's Jones Beach for public recreation, helped cast Moses, as well as Smith, as a promoter of public works for the masses.

In 1928 Smith left office to run for the U.S. presidency and was succeeded in the governorship by Franklin Delano Roosevelt, who had come into conflict with Moses during Smith's administration. Roosevelt could not, however, remove Moses from his positions in the park system. As popular with the press and with some reformers as he was disliked by many state politicians, Moses had begun to build a power base independent of electoral outcomes.

The Great Depression and the New Deal brought Moses fully into his own. His mastery of the details of legislation and of public works planning made Moses invaluable to New York City's activist mayor, Fiorello LaGuardia, and Moses' growing network of connections made him increasingly invulnerable to political change. After Moses' disastrous defeat as Republican candidate for the governorship of New York in 1934, LaGuardia appointed him commissioner of the newly-created New York City Park Department, with power to "coordinate" all city parks and "related developments." In effect this gave Moses an important voice in transportation and public facilities policy throughout much of the city. Within a few months of his appointment, 1,700 projects large and small had been completed.

The "Master Builder" at Work

Even more important, Moses was the dominant member and, from 1936, chairman of the Triborough Bridge Authority, charged with creating a 22-lane auto-sorter between three New York boroughs. As later modified, this authority had the power to construct tributary roads and became effectively self-perpetuating because it could begin new projects with revenues from the original bridge. Even Roosevelt, now president of the United States, was unable to have Moses removed from the chairmanship of this powerful body, whose first project called for $44 million in federal funds. When Roosevelt, through his secretary of the interior, attempted to make Moses' removal a condition of federal assistance, Moses took the matter to the press and forced the administration to back down.

By the end of World War II Moses had accumulated posts which gave him the most important single voice in park, bridge, and road construction in the New York area. Appointed New York City construction coordinator in 1946, Moses also presided over public housing and urban renewal policies, which increasingly emphasized austere high rise housing for the poor and expanded use of renewal land for private development. He had a controlling hand in many other public works of the 1945-1965 period, including the building of the United Nations Headquarters, Lincoln Center, the New York Coliseum, and the 1964-1965 World's Fair facilities.

Moses encountered increasing opposition beginning in the late 1950s, when massive "cut and burn" urban renewal tactics began to lose favor nationally. Community opposition to his Cross Bronx Expressway (which displaced 1,500 families in a single one-mile stretch) was followed by revelations of scandals involving the use of urban renewal

land in which some of Moses' associates were implicated. Moses' press support had waned by the early 1960s as, for the first time, his vision of the urban future seemed badly out of step with contemporary values. When Moses threatened to resign his park posts in a dispute with New York governor Nelson Rockefeller, the governor accepted. Having been required to relinquish his New York City posts in order to accept the presidency of the World's Fair, Moses retained only one important part of his power base, the Triborough Bridge Authority. He was phased out of this post as well when the authority was merged into a new Metropolitan Transportation Authority in 1968.

Moses spent the remaining 13 years of his life promoting projects which he favored and defending himself and his policies against the opponents of large-scale autocratic planning who held public attention during the 1970s. Robert Caro's massive 1974 biography of Moses, *The Power Broker,* helped fix the reputation of Moses as an anti-democratic policymaker who fostered the auto-mobilization of American cities and the piecemeal destruction of the urban environment he proported to improve. In fact, Moses' legacy was mixed.

Robert Moses left behind 2.5 million acres of state parks, 416 miles of parkways, a dozen bridges, two dams, 568 playgrounds, and numerous important public buildings. He spent the equivalent of $27 billion and displaced at least a quarter of a million people. He spread his approach to urban public works through consultancies in seven other cities and, by example, nationwide. Yet while Moses' power and impact were unique, his aims were not. He promoted parks in the age in which parks were widely seen as a cure for urban ills. He fostered automobile use during the half-century in which middle-class Americans seem to have seen the private car as an unmitigated good. His ruthless approach to urban renewal and apparent disregard for the traditions and opinions of poor city dwellers were not untypical of the 1940s and 1950s. Moses accentuated, but did not create, the approach to urban public works with which he is identified.

Further Reading

The classic work on Moses is Robert A. Caro, *The Power Broker: Robert Moses and the Fall of New York* (1974). Moses' own story is in Robert Moses, *Public Works: A Dangerous Trade* (1970). Alternative views of Moses may be found in Eugene Lewis, *Public Entrepreneurship: Toward a Theory of Bureaucratic Political Power* (1980), and Cleveland Rodgers, *Robert Moses, Builder for Democracy* (1952), a pangyric which contains some priceless Moses quotations. For the period after 1974 see *New York Times,* March 8, 1978; April 29, 1978; and July 30, 1981. □

Moshweshwe

Moshweshwe (ca. 1787-1868) was a South African king and founder of the Basotho nation. He is generally regarded as the doyen of southern Africa's diplomatic geniuses of the 19th century.

Moshweshwe was born in Menkwaneng during the famine of 1787. His father, Mokhachane, was head of the Bamokoteli, a Sotho-speaking subclan, which paid tribute to its more powerful neighbors, the Basekake. Moshweshwe was given the name Lepoqo (disasters) because of the misfortunes in which he was born.

As was the custom among the princely families, Mokhachane took his son to Mohlomi, a famous seer and philosopher, to study law and acquire wisdom. Mohlomi, whose renown had spread all over southern Africa, taught him that the practice of virtue and discipline was the first prerequisite for the successful governance of men. The wise ruler sought to live in peaceful coexistence with his neighbors and encouraged habits of thrift and industry among his people.

Mohlomi also added that he was concerned about the future of the Sotho-speaking peoples of the plateau above the Drakensberg Mountains. He could see clouds of red dust rising from the east, blowing over the lands of the Sotho and leaving desolation in their wake. The philosopher's teachings made an impression on Lepoqo which was to last all his life. The reference to the red dust made him anxious about the future; he thought the seer had the white people in mind. This fear combined with his hatred of the Basekake tyranny to give him a strong sense of political direction, while the military weakness of his subclan made him a realist who would go to the limits of conciliation and fight with determination when left with no choice.

His African Neighbors

As future leader of the Bamokoteli, Lepoqo was encouraged to participate in the assembly debates, where he made it clear that he wanted to temper justice with mercy. Makara, a notorious cattle rustler and chieftain, had in 1808 fled to Mokhachane for sanctuary. Mokhachane arrested him, and the Bamokoteli clamored for the rustler's execution. Lepoqo intervened, and the assembly spared Makara's life, but the military commanders were angered.

Knowing the effects the military's anger could have on his career and wanting to forestall it, Lepoqo organized a raid on the Khilibileng cattle post of Chief Moeletsi and returned with hundreds of cattle. For this he was said to have "shaved Moeletsi's beard," that is, he had humiliated him. From then he took on the name of Moshweshwe (the shaver).

Cattle raiding was an accepted norm of life in southern Africa at the time. Clans, tribes, and nations built their names and wealth by seizing cattle from their wealthy or weak neighbors. The Basekake planned a raid on the Bafokeng and demanded reinforcements from the Bamokoteli. Moshweshwe feigned illness; his men refused to march without him. When the Basekake left, Moshweshwe marched to Bafokeng territory and captured their livestock for his people. Infuriated, the Basekake warlords seized Moshweshwe's booty. Moshweshwe retaliated by massacring them in their capital and scattering the survivors. Returning home a hero and liberator, he found his father estranged. Mokhachane saw a threat in his son's popularity. Moshweshwe protested that he had no

designs on his father's position. He withdrew from Menkwaneng and settled near Butha-Buthe mountain. There he built himself a kraal and called it Qhobosheane.

In 1821 Shaka, the Zulu king, had decided to bring an end to the feuding, the cattle raiding, and the prevalent insecurity and had used the spear to weld the various Zulu-speaking peoples on the eastern side of the Drakensberg into a single, disciplined nation. Many tribes and clans perished resisting him; others fled to the caves of the Drakensberg, where threatening starvation forced them to become cannibals. Moshweshwe reinforced Butha-Buthe mountain and stored grain and water in the caves for the event of an invasion by the Zulu. In 1822 Queen Mantatisi marched on Qhobosheane and in a seesaw battle put Moshweshwe's forces to flight.

The Mantatisi invasion made it clear to Moshweshwe that Butha-Buthe would be difficult to defend against a protracted siege. He slipped out of his mountain fortress and trekked with his people to Qilwane mountain near Qhobosheane. But his grandfather Peete, his sister Mamila, two of his wives, and nearly a dozen babies were cut off from the main body of Bamokoteli by the cannibals and taken to Sefikeng, the cannibal stronghold. Moshweshwe dispatched armed scouts who rescued the three women but reported that Peete and the babies had been eaten. Moshweshwe vowed that he would solve the cannibal problem. He continued the march until late one night he reached the top of Qilwane mountain, which he renamed Thaba Bosiu (mountain ascended in the darkness).

From Thaba Bosiu he sent a mission under Poho to Shaka to arrange a truce with the Zulu and offer to pay tribute. That kept the Zulu out of his lands. In 1826 Moshweshwe sent an army to round up the cannibals and bring them to Thaba Bosiu. The army returned with Rakotswane, their chief, and some of his people. Moshweshwe addressed them on the evils of cannibalism and added that he understood the reasons for their depravity. He ordered them into the cattle enclosure where his medicine men put them through the purification process.

To their surprise, Moshweshwe sent them back home with cattle, grain, and seed and asked them to start a normal life again. Some of the cannibals refused to leave Butha-Buthe, saying no ruler had understood their tragic situation or treated them in the way Moshweshwe had done. Bands of them started coming to Thaba Bosiu to ask for Bamokoteli citizenship. Refugees from all over southern Africa converged on the mountain capital. Before long, Moshweshwe could command a force of 5,000 men. The Basotho nation had been born.

Boers and Britons

Up to 1826 Moshweshwe had dealt largely with African adversaries who used the spear. After 1830 he was to deal with people who carried and used the guns: the Korannas, bandits of mixed blood from the Orange area; the Boers trekking from the Cape Colony; and the British trying to impose their rule on the Boers.

About this time Adam Krotz, a Griqua hunter who was deacon of the church at Philippolis, visited Lesotho. When

Moshweshwe asked him for help in procuring the guns, Krotz said he knew of white missionaries who could offer him something better than arms. Moshweshwe asked Krotz to do all in his power to bring them to Lesotho. Three Frenchmen from the French Evangelical Society arrived in Lesotho in 1833, led by Eugene Casalis, who was to be Moshweshwe's friend to the end of the King's days.

From 1835 onward bands of Boer settlers crossed the Orange River and occupied lands belonging to the Sotho peoples. In 1843 the British sent an army to bring the Boers under the Queen's authority. The British governor at the Cape, Sir George Napier, sent an emissary to Moshweshwe to enter a treaty with the British in which he would undertake to keep law and order in Trans-orange, deliver fugitives to the Cape Colony, and keep the Cape government informed on subversion against it. In return the British would pay him an annual grant of £75 or its equivalent in arms and ammunition. They would recognize the junction of the Orange and Caledon rivers as his western boundaries, while his country would stretch to Butha-Buthe on the east, the Orange River in the south, and an imaginary line about 30 miles to the north of Caledon. Moshweshwe signed the treaty.

The Boer incursions continued, and Moshweshwe appealed in vain to the British for help. In the end he insisted that all whites, with the exception of the missionaries, should leave Lesotho territory. The British replied by proclaiming the lands to the north the Orange River Sovereignty and continued to shorten Moshweshwe's boundaries. When he resisted, they sent a motley force against him in the winter of 1850. Moshweshwe sent it to flight at the battle of Viervoet mountain.

In the meantime Moshweshwe was keeping his missionary friends in London briefed on developments in his country. They exerted enough pressure on Sir George Grey, the secretary of state for the colonies, to persuade him to discourage warlike policies against the Basotho. Impressed by this triumph of Sotho diplomacy, the Boers undertook to be neutral in the event of war between Moshweshwe and the British.

In 1852 the British restored to Lesotho some of the lands previously incorporated in the Orange River Sovereignty. But the new governor at the Cape, Sir George Cathcart, distrusted Moshweshwe and he believed there could be no peace in the north unless Moshweshwe's power was broken. Cathcart marched to the sovereignty at the head of an armed force and sent an ultimatum to Moshweshwe, demanding 10,000 head of cattle and 1,000 horses for Basotho attacks on the Boers in the sovereignty. He gave the Basotho 3 days in which to deliver the animals. Moshweshwe met Cathcart at Platberg and asked for an extension of time. Cathcart insisted on the deadline and threatened forcible collection.

Three days later Moshweshwe sent about 3,000 cattle and some horses, but war followed. After the first day of fighting Moshweshwe declared himself a British subject, forcing Cathcart to withdraw. The Basotho were jubilant with this triumph of Moshweshwe's diplomacy. Although the request for British protection had been refused previously, Lesotho was proclaimed a protectorate on April 15, 1868.

Moshweshwe's health had been failing for many years. He had gone to church regularly but had not embraced Christianity. Like Constantine the Great, he announced his conversion on his deathbed. He died on March 11, 1868.

Further Reading

In *Hill of Destiny: The Life and Times of Moshesh, Founder of the Basotho* (1969) Peter Becker gives a sympathetic and informative picture of Moshweshwe and his times and problems. For a better understanding of the Basotho, D. Fred. Ellenberger and J. C. Macgregor, *History of the Basuto: Ancient and Modern* (1912; repr. 1969), in spite of weaknesses can be recommended. Further background can be found in G. Tylden, *The Rise of the Basuto* (Cape Town, 1950); John G. Williams, *Moshesh: The Man on the Mountain* (1950; 2d ed. 1959); and Eric A. Walker, *A History of Southern Africa* (3d ed. 1957; originally published in 1928 as *A History of South Africa*). □

Tomás Cipriano de Mosquera

Tomás Cipriano de Mosquera (1798-1878) was a Colombian statesman. Four times his country's president, he headed Colombia's most productive administration in the 19th century and through the expropriation of Church property put its economy on a capitalistic basis.

Tomás Cipriano de Mosquera was born in Popayán on Sept. 26, 1798, to the leading family of southern Colombia. From 1820, when he became a captain in the patriot army, to 1830, by which year he was a general, Mosquera rose rapidly in military and administrative rank. An enthusiastic partisan of Simón Bolivar's dictatorship (1828-1830), at its fall he went on an extended tour of Europe and the United States (1831-1833).

During 1834-1837 Mosquera was a leader of the congressional opposition to Francisco de Paula Santander's regime. Mosquera became secretary of war under President José Ignacio de Márquez in 1838. Mosquera's success as a battlefield commander in the civil war of 1839-1842, although marred by acts of cruelty, firmly established his military and political reputation.

The Presidency

After diplomatic missions to Chile and Peru (1842-1845), Mosquera returned to win the presidency. His first administration (1845-1849) was the most constructive in 19th-century Colombia. It sponsored substantive developments in transportation (steamboats, railroads, highways, and canals), education (technical and classical), and scientific research and marked a dramatic shift from a colonial-style fiscal system toward one based on free trade.

In business in the United States from 1850 to 1854, Mosquera returned in 1854 to participate in the Liberal-Conservative military effort against the dictatorship of Gen. José María. Mosquera failed to create a third party and lost his bid for the presidency in 1856. He did win the presidency of his native Cauca State in 1858 and, using its resources (it included almost half of Colombia), led a victorious Liberal revolution in 1860-1861.

Mosquera endorsed a massive assault on the Church which destroyed its wealth, much of which had maintained social welfare services for the masses. This measure, by ending mortmain, freed large tracts of property from a number of peculiarly binding mortgages and brought capitalism fully into being in Colombia.

After ruling as provisional president from 1861 to 1863, he was elected president for a year (May 1863-April 1864). His fourth presidency was to have lasted from 1866 to 1868, but with his arbitrary closure of Congress, he was arrested on May 23, 1867, tried, and exiled to Peru (until 1870). He never recovered his national stature, though he did retain his political base, serving again as president of Cauca State (1871-1873), his last major political office. He died, close to Popayán, on Oct. 7, 1878.

In addition to a number of polemics, Gen. Mosquera was the author of a biography of Bolivar (1853) and of three important works on Colombian geography. These, plus his abiding support of the natural sciences, won him election to many learned societies in Europe and the United States. Not only the Colombian best known to his contemporaries abroad, Mosquera was also the only military man in his country's history to achieve (for his brilliant destruction of an Ecuadorian invasion in December 1863) field marshal rank.

Mosquera was headstrong, ruthless, and vain to a fault; but his driving ambition and superior intelligence combined to make him the modernizer of Colombia.

Further Reading

Major biographical and critical work on Mosquera is in Spanish. For an appraisal of his historical role see J. León Helguera's "The Problem of Liberalism versus Conservatism in Colombia, 1849-85" in Frederick B. Pike, ed., *Latin American History: Select Problems* (1969). A useful general background work is J. M. Heñao y Melguizo and Gerardo Arrubla, *History of Colombia* (1938). □

Mohammad Mossadegh

Mohammad Mossadegh (1882-1967), Iranian nationalist politician and prime minister (1951-1953), led the movement for the nationalization of the Anglo-Iranian Oil Company. His democratically elected government was overthrown as the result of a coup d'état sponsored by Great Britain and the United States.

Mohammad Mossadegh (Musaddiq) was born in Tehran into a prominent family of notables. His father was a senior official of the state treasury and his mother was related to the ruling Qajar dynasty. Mossadegh was in his teens when he assumed the administrative position of his deceased father, as was the custom at the time. In 1901 he married Zia us-Saltaneh, who came from a family of politico-religious dignitaries. They had five children. An active supporter of the Constitutional Revolution of 1906-1907, Mossadegh was elected a deputy to the first Parliament (Majles), but was below the required minimum age for qualification and therefore could not take up his seat. In 1909 he went to Paris to pursue higher education, but illness forced him to return home. He resumed his studies in 1911, this time in Neuchatel in Switzerland, where he gained a doctorate in law. Returning to Iran in August 1914, he taught at the School of Political Science; wrote on legal, financial, and political issues; and engaged in party political activity before his appointment as an under-secretary in the Ministry of Finance.

Mossadegh bitterly opposed the abortive Anglo-Iranian Agreement of 1919, which aimed to formalize British tutelage over Iran. He occupied various ministerial posts and provincial governorships before coming to national prominence as a deputy in both the 5th and 6th Parliaments (1924-1928), establishing himself as a skillful parliamentarian, dedicated to promoting democratic constitutionalism and national sovereignty. In October 1925 he was one of the few deputies to oppose the bill that paved the way for the assumption of the throne by Reza Khan, a leader of the

coup of February 1921. Mossadegh continued to oppose the new regime, but with the consolidation of the Pahlavi autocracy he was excluded from political life, and from 1936 onward was forced to live as a recluse in his country home in Ahmadabad, north of the capital. In June 1940 he was summarily arrested, on the orders of the shah, and imprisoned in a desolate town in southern Khorasan, where he twice tried to commit suicide. Six months later he was allowed to return to his country home as the result of intercession by the crown prince, Mohammad Reza.

Following the British-Russian occupation of Iran in 1941, Mossadegh returned to the political scene as first deputy for Tehran in the 14th Parliament (1944-1946), having received the highest number of votes cast in the capital. He advocated neutralism in foreign policy and, in the wake of American, British, and Soviet demands for oil concessions, sponsored a bill banning the granting of oil or other concessions to foreigners. He also emphatically but unsuccessfully advocated a reform of electoral laws that would render elections less prone to rigging. The government rigging of elections to the 15th Parliament prevented Mossadegh's reelection, but he was elected to the 16th Parliament (1950-1952) as Tehran's first deputy, despite the government's efforts to exclude him and his supporters. The National Front, led by Mossadegh, was formed during the election campaign for the 16th Parliament. The National Front advocated free and fair elections, freedom of the press, and an end to martial law.

In October 1947 the Parliament had rejected a draft agreement to grant oil concessions to the Russians and had empowered the government to redeem Iranian rights over the country's southern oil resources, then controlled by Britain. The much resented British oil concession—granted in 1901 and revised in 1933—was thus formally placed on the agenda of Iranian politics and became an increasingly dominant issue, closely intermingled with Iranian domestic politics. British refusal to concede to Iranian demands eventually provoked the call for nationalization of the oil industry, championed by the National Front, and led in turn to the premiership of Mossadegh in May 1951. The oil issue had served as a rallying cry for a popular movement with nationalist as well as democratic aspirations that linked national self determination, symbolized by the act of nationalization, to popular sovereignty. Mossadegh's premiership constituted not only a challenge to Britain's entrenched position in Iran but also involved forcing the shah to comply with the constitutional principle that the monarch should reign and not rule. Mossadegh's task proved daunting. The British, although ostensibly willing to negotiate with him, were not genuinely prepared to accept the reality of nationalization, which Mossadegh in turn considered irrevocable. They attempted through various tactics, including an embargo on the sale of Iranian oil, to destabilize his government. They also resorted to covert measures to engineer his downfall.

Faced with a relentless opposition from pro-British and royalist elements, Mossadegh felt increasingly incapacitated. British efforts to replace him, together with the refusal of the shah—who had only grudgingly acquiesced in Mossadegh's premiership—to transfer the War Ministry to the prime minister, eventually resulted in Mossadegh's resignation in July 1952. However, he was returned to power a few days later as the result of a popular uprising. He now enjoyed greater authority, but there seemed to be no realistic prospect of settling the oil question.

Meanwhile, the government's economic and financial difficulties were increasing. The Tudeh (Communist) Party, although banned since 1949, not only harassed the government but also enabled Mossadegh's opponents to claim that a communist takeover was likely. The army would not readily accept prime ministerial control, and some of Mossadegh's own supporters joined his opponents. Although the Parliament had granted him extra powers, his position was inherently vulnerable, and toward the end of his term of office relations between the government and the Parliament proved increasingly difficult. Mossadegh resorted to a referendum to dissolve the Parliament and start fresh elections on the basis of a new electoral law. This provided an ideal opportunity for the British and American secret services, aided by his domestic opponents, to engineer his downfall through a coup d'état in August 1953.

The coup, which established royal autocracy, firmly committed Iran to the West and revoked the substance of oil nationalization. Mossadegh and many of his supporters were arrested, accused of violating the constitution. He was tried by a military tribunal and, despite a vigorous self defense, was condemned to three years imprisonment and subsequently confined to his country home until his death on March 5, 1967 at the age of 84. In the aftermath of the coup of 1953 repressive measures prevented the revival of the National Front, but Mossadegh's charisma and the appeal of the ideals and sentiments associated with his name persisted in the collective memory of large numbers of Iranians. He remained a potent source of inspiration for opponents of royal autocracy. His legacy, consisting of civic nationalism and liberal democracy combined with personal integrity, civility, and public spiritedness, remained dominant ingredients in the enduring aspirations of large segments of the Iranian populace.

Further Reading

A thorough biography of Mossadegh remains to be written. For a useful account see Farhad Diba's *Mosaddegh: A Political Biography* (London, 1986). See also Homa Katouzian's *Musaddiq and the Struggle for Power in Iran* (London, 1990). On Mossadegh's career as a parliamentarian and prime minister see Fakhreddin Azimi, *Iran: The Crisis of Democracy, 1941-53* (1989). On Mossadegh and the oil question see James A. Bill and Wm. Roger Louis (eds.), *Musaddiq, Iranian Nationalism, and Oil* (London, 1988), and Musafa Elm, *Oil, Power and Principle: Iran's Oil Nationalization and Its Aftermath* (1992). An English translation of Mossadegh's memoirs, which contains many useful insights into his life, career, and ideas, is available as *Musaddiq's Memoirs,* edited and introduced by Homa Katouzian (London, 1988). □

Rudolf Mössbauer

Nobel Prize-winning physicist Rudolf Mössbauer (born 1929) studied gamma rays and nuclear resonance florescence and discovered methods for exact measurement in several areas of science.

R udolf Mössbauer's study of the recoilless emission of gamma rays and nuclear resonance florescence led to the discovery of methods for making exact measurements in solid-state physics, archeology, biological sciences, and other fields. His measurement method was used to verify Albert Einstein's theory of relativity and is known as the Mössbauer effect. He was honored with a 1961 Nobel Prize in physics for his work.

Rudolf Ludwig Mössbauer was born on January 31, 1929, in Münich, Germany. He was the only son of Ludwig and Erna (Ernst) Mössbauer. Ludwig Mössbauer was a phototechnician who printed color post cards and reproduced photographic materials. Mössbauer grew up during a difficult time in Germany, during the disruptions accompanying the rise of Adolf Hitler's National Socialism (Nazi party) and the onset of World War II. Still, he was able to complete a relatively normal primary and secondary education, graduating from the Münich-Pasing Oberschule in 1948. His plans to attend a university were thwarted because, due to Germany's loss in the war, the number of new enrollments was greatly reduced.

Through the efforts of his father, Mössbauer was able to find a job working as an optical assistant first at the Rodenstock optical firm in Münich and later for the U.S. Army of Occupation. Eventually Mössbauer saved enough money from these jobs to enroll at the Münich Institute for Technical Physics. In 1952 he received his preliminary diploma (the equivalent of a B.S. degree) from the institute, and three years later he was awarded his diploma (the equivalent of an M.S. degree). For one year during this period, 1953–54, he was also an instructor of mathematics at the institute.

After receiving his diploma in 1955, Mössbauer began his doctoral studies at the Münich Institute for Technical Physics. His advisor there was Heinz Maier-Leibnitz, a physicist with a special interest in the field of nuclear resonance fluorescence. As a result of Maier-Leibnitz's influence, Mössbauer undertook his thesis research in that field. His research was not carried out primarily in Münich, however, but at the Max Planck Institute for Medical Research in Heidelberg, where Mössbauer received an appointment as a research assistant.

Nuclear resonance fluorescence is similar to widely-known phenomena such as, for example, the resonance in tuning forks. When one tuning fork is struck, it begins to vibrate with a certain frequency. When a second tuning fork is struck close to the first, it begins vibrating with the same frequency, and is said to be "resonating" with the first tuning fork. Fluorescence is a form of resonance involving visible light. When light is shined on certain materials, the atoms that make up those materials may absorb electromagnetic energy and then re-emit it. The emitted energy has the same frequency as the original light as a result of the resonance within atoms of the material. This principle explains the ability of some materials to glow in the dark after having been exposed to light.

The discovery of fluorescence by R. W. Wood in 1904 suggested some obvious extensions. If light, a form of electromagnetic radiation, can cause fluorescence, scientists asked, can other forms of electromagnetic radiation do the same? In 1929, W. Kuhn predicted that gamma rays, among the most penetrating of all forms of electromagnetic radiation, would also display resonance. Since gamma rays have very short wavelengths, however, that resonance would involve changes in the atomic nucleus. Hence came the term nuclear resonance fluorescence.

For two decades following Kuhn's prediction, relatively little progress was made in the search for nuclear resonance fluorescence. One reason for this delay was that such research requires the use of radioactive materials, which are difficult and dangerous to work with. A second and more important factor was the problem of atomic recoil that typically accompanies the emission of gamma radiation. Gamma rays are emitted by an atomic nucleus when changes take place among the protons and neutrons that make up the nucleus. When a gamma ray is ejected from the nucleus, it carries with it a large amount of energy resulting in a "kick" or recoil, not unlike the recoil experienced when firing a gun. Measurements of gamma ray energy and of nuclear properties become complicated by this recoil energy.

Researchers looked for ways of compensating for the recoil energy that complicated gamma ray emission from radioactive nuclei. Various methods that were developed in the early 1950s had been partially successful but were relatively cumbersome to use. Mössbauer found a solution to this problem. He discovered that a gamma emitter could be fixed within the crystal lattice of a material in such a way that it produced no recoil when it released a gamma ray. Instead, the recoil energy was absorbed by and distributed throughout the total crystal lattice in which the emitter was imbedded. The huge size of the crystal compared to the minute size of the emitter atom essentially "washed out" any recoil effect.

The material used by Mössbauer in these experiments was iridium–191, a radioactive isotope of a platinum-like metal. His original experiments were carried out at very low temperatures, close to those of liquid air, in order to reduce as much as possible the kinetic and thermal effects of the gamma emitter. Mössbauer's first report of these experiments appeared in issues of the German scientific journals *Naturwissenschaften* and *Zeitschrift fur Physic* in early 1958. He described the recoilless release of gamma rays whose wavelength varied by no more than one part in a billion. Later work raised the precision of this effect to one part in 100 trillion.

In the midst of his research on gamma ray emission, Mössbauer was married to Elizabeth Pritz, a fashion designer. The couple later had three children, two daughters and a son. In 1958, Mössbauer was also awarded his Ph.D. in physics by the Technical University in Münich for his study of gamma ray emission.

The initial reactions to the Mössbauer papers on gamma ray emission ranged from disinterest to doubt. According to one widely-repeated story, two physicists at the Los Alamos Scientific Laboratory made a five-cent bet on whether or not the Mössbauer Effect really existed. When one scientist was in fact able to demonstrate the effect, the scientific community gained interest.

Physicists found a number of applications for the Mössbauer Effect using a system in which a gamma ray emitter fixed in a crystal lattice is used to send out a signal, a train of gamma rays. A second crystal containing the same gamma ray emitter set up as an absorber so that the gamma rays travelling from emitter to absorber would cause resonance in the absorber. Therefore, the emission of gamma rays stays resonating and constant until a change, or force such as gravity, electricity, or magnetism enters the field. By noting the changes in the gamma ray field, unprecedented measurements of these forces became available.

One of the first major applications of the Mössbauer Effect was to test Einstein's theory of relativity. In his 1905 theory, Einstein had predicted that photons are affected by a gravitational field, and therefore an electromagnetic wave should experience a change in frequency as it passes near a massive body. Astronomical tests had been previously devised to check this prediction, but these tests tended to be difficult in procedure and imprecise in their results.

In 1959, two Harvard physicists, Robert Pound and Glen A. Rebka, Jr., designed an experiment in which the Mössbauer Effect was used to test the Einstein theory. A gamma ray emitter was placed at the top of a sixty-five-foot tower, and an absorber was placed at the bottom of the tower. When gamma rays were sent from source to absorber, Pound and Rebka were able to detect a variation in wavelength that clearly confirmed Einstein's prediction. Today, similar experimental designs are used for dozens of applications in fields ranging from theoretical physics to the production of synthetic plastics.

Mössbauer's Nobel Prize citation in 1961 mentioned in particular his "researches concerning the resonance absorption of gamma-radiation and his discovery in this connection of the effect which bears his name." The Nobel citation went on to say how Mössbauer's work has made it possible "to examine precisely numerous important phenomena formerly beyond or at the limit of attainable accuracy of measurement." The physics community acknowledged the enormous scientific and technical impact the discovery would eventually make.

After receiving his Ph.D. in 1958, Mössbauer took a position as research fellow at the Institute for Technical Physics in Münich. Two years later he was offered the post of full professor at the Institute, but, according to his entry in *Nobel Prize Winners,* declined the offer because he was "frustrated by what he regarded as the bureaucratic and authoritarian organization of German universities." Instead, he accepted a job as research fellow at the California Institute of Technology and was promoted to full professor a year later, shortly after the announcement of his Nobel award.

In 1964, Mössbauer once more returned to Münich, this time as full professor and with authority to reorganize the physics department there. In 1972, he took an extended leave of absence from his post at Münich to become director of the Institute Max von Laue in Grenoble, France. After five years in France, he returned to his former appointment in Münich. In addition to the Nobel Prize, Mössbauer has received the Science Award of the Research Corporation of America (1960), the Elliott Cresson Medal of the Franklin Institute (1961), the Roentgen Prize of the University of Giessen (1961), the Bavarian Order of Merit (1962), the Guthrie Medal of London's Institute of Physics (1974), the Lomonosov Gold Medal of the Soviet Academy of Sciences (1984), and the Einstein Medal (1986).

Further Reading

Abbott, David, *The Biographical Dictionary of Scientists—Physicists,* P. Bedrich, 1984, p. 118.
Frauenfelder, Hans, *The Mössbauer Effect,* W. A. Benjamin, 1962.
Halacy, D. S., Jr., *They Gave Their Names to Science,* Putnam, 1967, pp. 118-129.
McGraw-Hill Modern Scientists and Engineers, McGraw-Hill, Vol. 2, 1980, pp. 331-332.
Weber, Robert L., *Pioneers of Science: Nobel Prize Winners in Physics,* American Institute of Physics, 1980, pp. 184-185. □

Robert Motherwell

American artist Robert Motherwell (1915-1991) was one of the founders and last surviving members of the path-breaking Abstract Expressionist movement in painting.

Robert Motherwell was born in Aberdeen, Washington, in January 1915. He pursued an extensive liberal arts education before he fully committed himself to painting. He received his bachelor of arts degree in philosophy from Stanford University, where he studied between 1932 and 1937, with a year away at the California School of Fine Arts. He did graduate work in philosophy at Harvard University in 1937-1938; he attended the University of Grenoble in the summer of 1938 and did more graduate work at Columbia University in 1940-1941, this time in art history. His interest in painting persisted through these years. He was largely self-taught.

Motherwell began painting only after completing his academic studies. Early in his career, he was attracted to Surrealist notions of tapping into the unconscious as a source of imagery, a method called "psychic automatism." As he put it, "You don't have to paint a figure to express human feelings. The game is not what things look like. The game is organizing as accurately and with as deep discrimination as one can, states of feeling, and states of feeling . . . become questions of light, color, weight, solidity, airiness, lyricism, whatever." He shared with other founders of Abstract Expressionism (Pollock, de Kooning, Rothko) the conviction that the source of art was in untrammeled inner reality, rather than in observed actuality. Painting was a process of self-discovery and self-revelation, and a picture was evidence of that search. This new movement in art was highly successful, and because of his ease with matters intellectual, Motherwell served as Abstract Expressionism's unofficial spokesman.

While in the 1940's ex-patriate Surrealists in New York took young Motherwell's work seriously, and while he was friends with the Chilean Surrealist Matta, he wasn't interested in the look of Surrealist art. Motherwell's heros were Céezanne, Picasso, Mondrian, and especially Matisse. He regarded these influences as inevitable. "My father had a vineyard in the Napa Valley [in California]. I grew up in a landscape not at all dissimilar to Provence, or to the central plateau of Spain, or to parts of Italy and the Mediterranean basin."

In drawing, Motherwell invented his own elegant calligraphy fluid diagrams of emotional states as well as testimony to a faultless sense of placement. Drawing was primary; color was but a means of carrying content. "Generally, I use few colors," he said, "yellow ochre, vermillion, orange, cadmium green, ultramarine blue. Mainly I use each color as simply symbolic: ochre for the earth, green for the grass, blue for the sky and sea. I guess that black and white, which I use most often, tend to be protagonists."

In his collages there is vivid evidence of his life-long love of things French, and of his delight in anything Mediterranean. They show clearly the basis of his art in French modernism, his enthusiasm for French poetry, food, even for the color of French cigarette wrappers (Gauloise blue). For Motherwell, the collages "are a kind of private diary, not made with an actual autobiographical intention, but one that functions in an associative way for me."

Motherwell enjoyed a long and successful career of national and international exhibitions. His first one-man show took place at Peggy Guggenheim's adventurous "Art of This Century" gallery in New York. He exhibited at the Kootz Gallery during the late 1940's, at the Sidney Janis Gallery through the 1950's and early 1960's, and at the Marlborough-Gerson Gallery in the late 1960's. His work also was featured in important international exhibitions, including the São Paulo and Venice biennials and the Brussels World's Fair. In the 1990's his works were on exhibition in New York galleries, in several other American states, and in other countries.

Motherwell's best known images are probably the *Spanish Elegies,* the first of which appeared in 1948. Originally, he intended them as a tribute to the short-lived Spanish Republic, but they preoccupied him off and on until his death. He said the *Elegies* were "also general metaphors of the contract between life and death, and their interrelation." Most of these works were executed in black and white. Another series of paintings called the *Opens* came from seeing a small canvas in the studio leaning against a larger one; the series is "severely geometric."

Motherwell's rich intellectual background consistently found expression outside the studio. In 1947-1948 he co-edited the cultural magazine *Possibilities.* With William Baziotes, Barnett Newman, and Mark Rothko, he founded an art school, "Subjects of the Artist," in 1948. In 1951 he edited *The Dada Painters and Poets,* a major anthology of the early 20th-century movement, which helped to inspire the revival of Dada during the late 1950's and early 1960's. (Harvard University issued a second edition of this work in 1989.) Between 1951 and 1957 he taught at Hunter College, and in the mid-1960s he served as art director for the *Partisan Review.* He was also a brilliant speaker and lectured at colleges and universities throughout the United States.

In 1961 Motherwell began making limited editions of his work. He was the only one of the original abstract expressionists to take up printmaking. He combined his unique abstract style with the materials and technical requirements of printmaking to create more than 200 editions over the next 30 years. Robert Motherwell died in July, 1991.

Further Reading

For works by Motherwell, see *The Dada Painters and Poets: An Anthology,* which he edited in 1951 (second edition, 1989) and Stephanie Terenzio, ed., *The Collected Writings of Robert Motherwell* (1992). For recent collections of his work, with commentaries, see Stephanie Terenzio, *The Prints of Robert Motherwell,* David Rosand (ed.) *Robert Motherwell on Paper: Drawing, Prints, Collages* (1997), Stephanie Terenzio, *Robert Motherwell and Black* (1980); for critical works, see Robert S. Mattison, *Robert Motherwell: The Formative Years* (1987), Mary Ann Caws, *Robert Motherwell: What Art Holds* (1996).

□

John Lothrop Motley

The American historian and diplomat John Lothrop Motley (1814-1877) is best known for his outstanding history of the Dutch struggle for independence.

John Lothrop Motley was born in Dorchester, Mass., on April 15, 1814, to an old New England merchant family. He studied under historian George Bancroft at the noted Round Hill School in Northampton, Mass., and then went on to Harvard. After graduating in 1831 Motley continued his studies in Germany at Göttingen and Berlin.

After 1840 Motley pursued both a diplomat's and a historian's career. For a few months in 1841 he was secretary of the U.S. legation in St. Petersburg, Russia. In 1847 he settled on his life's work as a writer: the study of the struggle of the Netherlands for independence from Spain. "My subject," he wrote in retrospect, "had taken me up, drawn me on, and absorbed me into itself." Motley served as minister to Austria (1861-1867) and as minister to Great Britain (1869-1870).

Motley's *Rise of the Dutch Republic* (3 vols., 1856), published at his own expense, was an immediate success. Like other romantic historians, he wove his material into a picturesque, dramatic narrative dominated by striking personalities. His hero was William of Orange; his villain, Philip II. Motley's next work was *The History of the United Netherlands* (4 vols., 1860-1867). He hoped to cap his lifework with a history of the Thirty Years War, but it remained undone. Instead, he published *The Life and Death of John of Barneveld, Advocate of Holland* (1874), which included a study of the "causes and movements" of the Thirty Years War.

Motley's work accented political and religious liberty and the threat to it posed by Catholicism and the Spanish monarchy. His Protestant bias was exceedingly strong. His passion for research and the artistry of his composition, however, made him a master historian. Oliver Wendell Holmes (1879) compared Motley's colorful style to Peter Paul Rubens's paintings. A serious flaw in Motley's books was his tendency to contrast the best of Protestant civilization with the worst of Catholicism. Yet the reader cannot withhold praise for the strength of characterization Motley gave historical figures. Later scholars wrote their own versions of the rise of the Dutch Republic, but they paid tribute to the vitality of Motley's narrative. He died at Frampton Court, England, on May 29, 1877.

Further Reading

George W. Curtis edited *The Correspondence of John Lothrop Motley* (2 vols., 1889). Additional material appears in Susan

Stackpole Mildmay and Herbert St. John Mildmay, eds., *John Lothrop Motley and His Family: Further Letters and Records* (1910). Motley's friend Oliver Wendell Holmes wrote *John Lothrop Motley: A Memoir* (1879), an excellent account based on personal knowledge and correspondence. A later study of Motley's life and work, with selections from his writings, is Chester P. Higby and B. T. Schantz, *John Lothrop Motley* (1939). □

John R. Mott

John R. Mott (1865-1955), American ecumenical pioneer and official of the Young Men's Christian Association, was the foremost Protestant layman of his time.

J ohn R. Mott grew up in Iowa in a home warmed by Methodist evangelical piety. He went to Cornell University, where he was caught up in the foreign-missionary enthusiasm among students. Elected president of the Cornell Christian Union, he developed it into the largest and best-organized student religious society in the world.

Mott graduated Phi Beta Kappa in 1888 and accepted a traveling secretary's position with the national student Young Men's Christian Association (YMCA). Welding the associations of the United States and Canada into a strong movement, he emerged as an outstanding organizer and leader. During his chairmanship of the Student Volunteer Movement (until 1920) over 8,000 volunteers were sent abroad.

Mott's most creative achievement was his founding of the World's Student Christian Federation (1895), on whose behalf he journeyed to the Orient and Australasia; in 21 months he organized 70 associations and 5 indigenous national movements. Federation fellowship and conferences realized Mott's dreams of a universal Christian student brotherhood.

The chairmanship of the Edinburgh Missionary Conference in 1910 earned Mott universal recognition as the Protestant world's leading missionary statesman. In 1912-1913 he traveled around the world in behalf of missionary cooperation. From 1915 to 1928 he was general secretary of the American YMCA. During World War I he traveled behind the lines on both sides in the interest of YMCA and church-sponsored work. He was personally responsible for the successful postarmistice campaign that raised the largest sum ever subscribed for war relief.

In the 1920s Mott began to turn his attention more to the worldwide concerns of the International Missionary Council, the World's Alliance of the YMCAs, and the effort to bring Orthodox churches into ecumenical fellowship. His chairmanship of the American committee for a world council of churches was highly influential. In pursuit of a unified Christian world Mott rejected appointments as ambassador or university president to raise millions of dollars and travel almost 2 million miles. He was awarded seven honorary degrees, the Nobel Peace Prize, the Distinguished

Service Medal, and numerous other decorations. In 1948 he was elected the first honorary president of the new World Council of Churches.

Further Reading

Addresses and Papers (6 vols., 1946-1947) was selected by Mott from his papers in the Yale University Divinity School Library. Useful biographies of Mott are Basil Mathews, *John R. Mott* (1934); Galen M. Fisher, *John R. Mott* (1952); and Robert C. Mackie and others, *Layman Extraordinary: John R. Mott, 1865-1955* (1965). Recommended for background reading are Ruth Rouse, *The World's Student Christian Federation* (1948); Charles Howard Hopkins, *History of the Y.M.C.A. in North America* (1951); William Richey Hogg, *Ecumenical Foundations* (1952); and Clarence P. Shedd and others, *History of the World's Alliance of Young Men's Christian Associations* (1955).

Additional Sources

Hopkins, Charles Howard, *John R. Mott, 1865-1955: a biography*, Grand Rapids: Eerdmans, 1979. □

Lucretia Coffin Mott

The American Quaker Lucretia Coffin Mott (1793-1880) was a pioneer feminist leader and radical abolitionist.

L ucretia Coffin was born on Jan. 3, 1793, on the island of Nantucket, Mass. Her father was the master of a whaling ship and her mother a storekeeper. The family became Quakers and in 1804 moved to the mainland. Island women were self-reliant, and Quakers were distinguished for the high place they gave to women. Lucretia's independent views were therefore honestly come by. She was educated in Boston and New York. After working briefly as a schoolteacher, she married James Mott in 1811. He set up business with Lucretia's father in Philadelphia.

At the age of 28 Mott became a Quaker minister, and when the denomination divided over matters of doctrine she supported the liberal, or Hicksite, faction. The Motts were abolitionists, and their home became a station on the Underground Railroad, by which Southern slaves escaped to the North. Mott helped found the first antislavery society for women in 1837, and later, with other militant abolitionist women, helped William Lloyd Garrison take over the American Antislavery Society.

Although Mott was a radical abolitionist, she was not a typical agitator. At a time when the causes of woman's rights and abolition attracted vivid personalities, she was outstanding for her gentle manners and disarmingly soft ways. She was a beloved figure, especially because her sweet character was complemented by unswerving dedication to principle.

In 1840 Mott was one of a band of women who accompanied Garrison to London for a world antislavery convention. The orthodox Quakers and English abolitionists who

Additional Sources

Bacon, Margaret Hope, *Valiant friend: the life of Lucretia Mott,* New York, N.Y.: Walker, 1980. □

William Sidney Mount

William Sidney Mount (1807-1868), one of America's first and best anecdotal painters, portrayed rural life on Long Island.

William Sidney Mount was born on Nov. 26, 1807, at Setauket, Long Island. He worked on the family farm at Stony Brook until 1824, when he was apprenticed to his older brother Henry, a sign and ornamental painter in New York City. About the same time, another older brother became a fellow apprentice. All three brothers soon became painters. William, who had begun drawing on his own in 1825, studied for a short time with Henry Inman, a leading portrait painter, but lack of funds, ill health, and his desire to be original made him return home in 1827. The following year he painted his first likeness, a stiff, naive painting of himself holding a flute. Next he executed his first figure painting on a religious theme, which was greatly influenced by Benjamin West.

In 1829 Mount moved back to New York and resumed his studies. The following year he painted his first genre subject, the *Rustic Dance,* which was exhibited at the National Academy of Design and praised for its novelty, realism, and humor. In 1832 he was elected to the academy and for 33 years exhibited there regularly.

From 1829 to 1836 Mount spent most of his time painting portraits in New York City. He made remarkable progress as an artist. In 1836 he painted two canvases for the famous early collector Luman Reed. One of these, *Bargaining for a Horse,* is among Mount's finest works. Finely composed and deftly painted, it combines humor, warmth, and keen observation.

In 1837 Mount returned home, leaving only for brief trips to New York City. Unlike many American artists of his time, he did not travel to Europe, and unlike his brothers, he never married. He preferred life at Stony Brook, where he could paint familiar scenes and people. His paintings show a fondness for African Americans, music, and children. Through numerous engravings and color lithographs made in America and France, his work reached a wide audience.

In spite of the popularity of his genre subjects, Mount's main source of income was his portraits, which usually lack the warmth and vitality of his narrative paintings. Although he devoted more than 30 years to painting, his output was relatively small—no more than 200 canvases. This is because he developed an idea of a painting very slowly, was painstaking in each detail, and sometimes did not paint for several months.

About 1860 Mount designed a portable studio and home on wheels which was drawn by horses. He spent

dominated the meeting refused to seat them, fearing the convention would seem ridiculous if females participated. Garrison, who sat with the rejected women in the gallery, noted the contradiction in having a convention to abolish slavery "and at its threshold depriving half the world of their liberty." Like most of the American women, Mott found the experience wounding.

At the convention Mott met the young Elizabeth Cady Stanton, who attended it with her husband. Their friendship developed, although both were busy wives and mothers, and Mott was involved in promoting peace, temperance, and abolition along with woman's rights. Mott inspired her young protégé, who in time grew more radical than her mentor. This became apparent at the Woman's Rights Convention in Seneca Falls, N.Y., called by Stanton—the first such convention. Mott thought its resolution asking for woman's suffrage to be too far in advance of public opinion.

During the Civil War, Mott spoke on behalf of the 13th Amendment to the Constitution. She was deeply distressed by the split in the woman's-rights movement that developed in the late 1860s. She worked to heal it until her death on Nov. 11, 1880.

Further Reading

Otelia Cromwell, *Lucretia Mott* (1958), is fine scholarly biography. Anna D. Hallowell, ed., *James and Lucretia Mott: Life and Letters* (1884), is helpful, and so are volumes 1 (1881), 2 (1882), and 3 (1888) of the *History of Woman Suffrage,* edited by Elizabeth Cady Stanton, Susan B. Anthony, and Matilda Joslyn Gage.

much time during his last years in this unique conveyance, but he painted very little because of declining health. He died on Nov. 19, 1868, at Setauket.

Further Reading

Bartlett Cowdrey and Hermann W. Williams, Jr., *William Sidney Mount* (1944), contains a life of the artist, a catalog of his genre and landscape paintings, and valuable research material. Since 1944 additional paintings have been located, many of which are included in an exhibition catalog of Mount's work by Alfred Frankenstein, *Painter of Rural America: William Sidney Mount, 1807-1868* (1968). This catalog also contains passages from Mount's own writings, most of which have not been published before. □

Bill Moyers

Television journalist and author Billy Don (Bill) Moyers (born 1934) served as special assistant, speechwriter, chief of staff, and press secretary to President Lyndon B. Johnson.

Billy Don Moyers was born June 5, 1934, in Hugo, Oklahoma, and grew up in Marshall, Texas. By the age of 15, Moyers was working as a reporter on his local paper, the Marshall *News Messenger*. He started college at North Texas State College, where he became class

president. In 1954 he worked on Lyndon B. Johnson's Senate campaign and then, at Johnson's urging, transferred to the University of Texas at Austin, where he majored in journalism and worked at KTBC, the Johnson's television station. He graduated from the University of Texas in 1956, then spent a year studying church history at the University of Edinburgh, Scotland, before returning to study for a bachelor of divinity degree at Southwestern Baptist Theological Seminary, which he completed in 1959. Meanwhile, he married Judith Davidson in 1954. They had three children.

In 1960 Moyers abandoned plans to pursue graduate work in American studies in order to join the campaign staff of Lyndon Johnson as a personal assistant, then a special assistant, during the Kennedy-Johnson presidential campaign. In 1961 Moyers became associate director of public affairs, in effect the chief lobbyist and public relations director of the Peace Corps, working under R. Sargent Shriver. He became deputy director of the Peace Corps in 1963.

On the day that John F. Kennedy was assassinated in Dallas, Texas, Moyers was in Austin helping with the presidential trip to Texas. When he heard that Kennedy had been shot, Moyers flew to Dallas to offer his services to Lyndon Johnson, sending a handwritten note, "I'm here if you need me." From that moment until the end of 1966, Moyers served Johnson in a variety of important roles under the traditional and ambiguous title of "special assistant to the President." Moyers coordinated the work of the 14 task forces that produced the legislative foundation for Johnson's "Great Society" programs in a sweeping series of bills designed to implement the "War on Poverty." These domestic

programs were the most ambitious and progressive social welfare measures to be enacted since the New Deal of Franklin Delano Roosevelt, though their impact was blunted by the burdens imposed by the war in Vietnam.

Moyers helped to write the Democratic party platform of 1964, which had a strong commitment to civil rights. As Johnson's liaison with the advertising firm that was preparing television advertising for the campaign, Moyers ordered a strong attack on Barry Goldwater. Moreover, he approved of the famous "Daisy" ad, which showed a young girl counting the petals on a daisy, then cut to a countdown to a nuclear explosion with a voiceover of Johnson speaking of the importance of peace. The ad evoked protests from the Goldwater campaign and was aired only once. Though it never explicitly mentioned Goldwater or the Republicans, the ad was a highly effective evocation of Goldwater's reputation for nuclear bellicosity.

As a special assistant, Moyers acted as an adviser, as chief speech writer, as chief of staff, and from July 1965 until he resigned in December 1966, as White House press secretary, where he was highly regarded by the working press. As the Vietnam War deepened, Moyers became one of the most visible doves in the White House, and he became increasingly isolated from Johnson. Moyers resigned in December 1966, with considerable bitterness on Johnson's part, to become publisher of *Newsday,* a large circulation daily paper on Long Island with a reputation for conservative political views. Moyers hired star writers such as Pete Hamill and, for special reports, Daniel Patrick Moynihan and Saul Bellow. He led the paper in a progressive direction and to a series of journalistic awards. But the conservative Harry Guggenheim, who owned a controlling interest in the paper, withdrew his support of Moyers and sold out to the Times-Mirror company. Moyers left the paper in 1970.

Moyers took time out to write *Listening to America* (1971), based on interviews conducted on a tour across America. He then turned to a successful career as a television journalist for CBS and the Public Broadcasting Service (PBS). At PBS, Moyers found he had the freedom to examine and tell stories that interested him in whatever way he wanted to present them. Moyers was editor-in-chief of "Bill Moyers Journal" on PBS from 1971 to 1976 and again from 1978 to 1981. He was editor and chief correspondent of the "CBS Reports" series from 1976 to 1978 and senior news analyst for CBS News, 1981-1986. Beginning in 1987 he was executive editor of Public Affairs TV, Inc., an independent production company making documentary and public affairs series for public television. His television work won virtually every major broadcasting award.

Moyers' television style was a traditional mix of news and documentary formats, in which he acted as narrator and interviewer. His series were distinguished not for innovations in form so much as for their combination of deep seriousness, earnest curiosity, attentiveness, and respect to his subjects (without, however, giving up his own views). Moyers held a consistent and clear set of values that were progressive and humane, and he possessed an ability to aim his material in such a way as to be both popular and intellectually lively.

As part of his series "A Walk Through the Twentieth Century with Bill Moyers," Moyers tackled such subjects as the arms race, labor history, and the influence of television on political campaigns. The most noted show of the series was "Marshall Texas, Marshall Texas," a description of the town in which he grew up, containing interviews of friends, residents, and former teachers. The series included a long interview with James Farmer, a civil rights leader who also grew up in Marshall, but whom Moyers had not known at the time he lived there because of the culture of segregation (hence the image of Marshall as two towns, and the repetition of the name in the title of the show).

In 1988 Moyers released the six-part series "Joseph Campbell and the Power of Myth." Campbell, for many years a professor of comparative religion at Sarah Lawrence College and author of a number of influential works on world mythology, talked with Moyers about myth as a way of coming to an experience of "the rapture of being alive" as Moyers, trained as a Baptist minister, engaged with him in a search for the cosmic truth behind religious doctrines and mythical tales.

In a five-part PBS series that premiered in 1993, Moyers examined the connection between emotions and physical response. *Healing and the Mind* took viewers first to China and the ancient medical traditions of "qi" (pronounced "chee"), which emphasizes the mental-physical energy that herbalists, acupuncturists, and massage therapists have insisted is the basis of good health. Moyers also paid visits to hospitals in the United States where nontraditional therapies are being used: a hospital in Massachusetts uses Buddhist meditation to aid patients with unyielding pain; and a Boston hospital showed how "the relaxation response" has been beneficial in the treatment of insomnia, hypertension, and infertility. Georgetown was slated to be the first medical school with a thorough course of study in mind-body techniques. Dr. David Eisenberg, who developed an "unconventional medicine" course at Harvard, reported that 34 percent of the people they surveyed had tried at least one unconventional therapy in the past year for primarily chronic conditions, such as back pain, insomnia, and headaches, a percentage that converts to about 61 million people. Moyers' series reinforced a growing popularity of alternative medicine. The companion book soared to the top of the best-seller lists, and PBS scored ratings with *Healing and the Mind* double what they usually earned at that time of the year.

Moyers was not as fortunate with his 1995 series, *The Language of Life,* in which he spent eight installments celebrating poetry readings and workshops which were flourishing after decades of relative disappearance. Although he did point out that the publication of poetic tomes had been abandoned by many trade publishers, Moyers showed how enlightened and unified poets are after what Brad Leithauser described as "the poetry reading as a blend of A. A. Meeting and encounter-group therapy," in his article for *Time.* Leithauser criticized Moyers' lack of probing questions about what the public needs to understand about the contemporary poet, not just the joy of sharing one's work. Most poets, for example, still have to teach to earn a living.

Furthermore, he questions why we continue to refer to poetry as Postmodernist after 75 years. "Moyers makes virtually no attempt to place the poet in a larger social context—to view poetry as a profession (or, perhaps more to the point, to analyze what it means that ours is a culture where it's all but impossible to be a professional poet)," Leithauser wrote.

The next issues Moyers tackled were ones more close to home for the ordained Southern Baptist minister. *Newsweek* called his Spring 1996, five-part series, *The Wisdom of Faith* "disappointing." The show was to center around religious guru Houston Smith, one of the foremost scholars of world religions; yet Kenneth Woodward said it lacked focus. Moyers, he said, was unable to decide if the programs were about Smith and his experiences or about the six "wisdom traditions" of Hinduism, Buddhism, Confucianism, Christianity, Judaism, and Islam. The fall of 1996 brought better reception of his probe of the first book of the Bible. *Genesis: A Living Conversation* was a ten-part "outreach," bringing together small groups of scholars, writers, and other intellectuals for hour-long discussions. PBS widely promoted the programs, distributing more than 100,000 copies of a 177-page accompanying guide. Moyers' intention was to promote study groups around the country like the one broadcasted into living rooms, anticipating "that this series will become part of the resurgence of democratic conversation." Hoping to capture the same success as *Healing and the Mind,* Moyers recycled some of his journalistic techniques to find contemporary meaning out of the ancient text. Believing the Baptist conviction that everyone is equipped to interpret the Bible for him or herself, Moyers brought together a diverse group, consisting of a psychotherapist, poet, author, evangelicals, and even nonbelievers to reveal the meaning of the stories of Genesis. Moyers wanted people to "listen and understand," not to change their beliefs, and "to talk to each other without that kind of false protocol and superficial tact we sometimes pretend we have." Kenneth Woodward and Anne Underwood of *Newsweek* commended Moyers for performing "a public service by discussing Genesis in extended conversation." However, they recognized that the series did little to explain why the stories found their literary forms or how they influence the Biblical material and message. Moyers told *Christianity Today* that he perceives himself more as a student than as an adversarial journalist. Because he finds himself drawn to learn what others have to offer, *Genesis: A Living Conversation* became what Woodward and Underwood called "too much free association and self-confession for a series that wants us to be serious about the Bible."

Nevertheless, during the decades in which television news evolved into a form of entertainment and public television sometimes seemed to play it safe by hiding behind nature documentaries, Moyers was one of the most consistent champions for the democratic potential of public affairs television, exercising a special blend of historical awareness, moral imagination, and intellectual integrity.

Further Reading

For additional information see especially works by Bill Moyers: *Listening to America* (1971); *A World of Ideas* (1989); *The Secret Government* (1988); and *The Power of Myth,* with Joseph Campbell (1988). Video tapes of Moyers' television series are available in many university libraries. For biographical accounts of Moyers, see Patrick Anderson, *The President's Men* (1968); Martha Gross, *The Possible Dream* (1970); and Mimi Swartz, "The Mythic Rise of Billy Don Moyers," in *Texas Monthly* (November 1989). Periodical sources cited are "Mind Over Malady," *Time* (March 1, 1993); "Helping Docs Mind the Body," *Newsweek* (March 8, 1993); "Prince of PBS," *Modern Maturity* (October-November 1993); "I'm Ed, and I'm a Poet," *Time* (July 3, 1995); "The Spiritual Surfer," and "In the Beginning," *Newsweek* (April 1, 1996 and October 21, 1996, respectively); and "Bill Moyers' National Bible Study," *Christianity Today* (October 28, 1996). □

Daniel Patrick Moynihan

Daniel Patrick Moynihan (born 1927), United States senator from New York, was a politician and scholar whose career marked him as one of America's most influential public figures in the second half of the 20th century.

Daniel Patrick Moynihan was an academician, presidential adviser, diplomat, legislator, and author. He was renowned for his willingness to confront diverse issues ranging from race to social security to disarmament to international order. Yet the enigma of "Pat" Moynihan is that, despite his varied careers and numerous achievements, he never seemed identified with any one of them. He could not exclusively be called scholar, although he wrote 16 books (he's written more books, columnist George Will said, than most politicians have read); nor politician, despite many years as New York State's senior senator; nor statesman, even with unique service as ambassador to India and to the United Nations. Neither could he be called bartender, newspaper hawker, shoeshine boy, dockworker, or naval officer, although he was all of those. There exists a rather Chaucerian quality about this personality which made him master of the trades he undertook.

Moynihan was at home on both sides of Manhattan's 1940s: the steamy tenements of Hell's Kitchen on the west and the rarified air of the U.N. General Assembly on the east. Yet this self-proclaimed "Yorker," who lived in Delaware County's Pindars Corners and boasted a deep love of the Empire State, was born in Tulsa, Oklahoma, on March 16, 1927. He was the firstborn of John Henry Moynihan and Margaret Ann Phipps. A brother named Michael arrived the following year and a sister Ellen was born in 1931. The family lived an itinerant life, much of it in New York, following his father's indifferent career in journalism and advertising. In 1937 his father deserted the family, leaving the fate of the children in his mother's hands.

Moynihan's father, an advertising copywriter for RKO Pictures, left home never to see his family again. Used to a middle-class existence, his mother and her three children disappeared from their life in the New York City suburbs and into shabby apartments, including one above a bar in the rough Hell's Kitchen area of New York. Moynihan's mother supported the family through welfare until she was able to get back on her feet. She married again briefly to an older man who provided temporary financial security and a move back to the suburbs. Nevertheless, Moynihan's adolescence was far from stable, moving around each time his mother took a new job.

A strong-willed, pragmatic woman, Moynihan's mother poured her life into her children's educations. Moynihan attended New York City Catholic and public schools and graduated first in his class from Benjamin Franklin High School. His yearbook predicted that he would grow up to be "cussing out the labor unions and durn radicals." He started City College in 1943. Moynihan insisted college was a fluke for him, taking the entrance exam only to prove he was "as smart as I thought I was." After a year of college, he joined the Naval Reserve with Vermont's Middlebury College V-12 program to train for an officer position. The Navy sent Moynihan to continue his education at Tufts in Medford, Massachusetts, where he earned a bachelor's and master's degree.

His interests were extremely broad, including urban politics, international labor, auto safety, and race relations. Although he started doctoral work at Tufts' Fletcher School of Law and Diplomacy soon after earning his master's de-

gree in 1949, he did not graduate until 1961. But the 1950s were well spent. Three years in England, including a one-year Fulbright at the London School of Economics at age 33, broadened him greatly, as did campaigns for New York's mayoral and gubernatorial candidates. He also chose a career in academe which took him to Syracuse, Wesleyan, and finally Harvard. When Moynihan returned to the U.S. after his stay in London, he began to make his way through the New York political arena. As a volunteer in Robert Wagner's 1953 mayoral campaign, he learned he was enjoying politics and went on to work on Averell Harriman's race for governor. It was here where he met Elizabeth Brennan, bursting into her room one night soon after they met and declaring, "You are going to marry me," before passing out on her floor. They married in 1955. She became her husband's chief advisor and handler, running his Senate campaigns. They had three children: Tim, a papier-mâché sculptor; Maura, a singer, actress, and writer; and John, a cartoonist.

By the time of the Kennedy-Nixon campaign of 1960, Moynihan had wide contacts and held iconoclastic but insightful opinions on many subjects. His association with urban politics and strong sympathies for the poor, whose plight he knew first hand, impressed Kennedy's advisers and brought him appointment as assistant to Labor Secretary Arthur Goldberg.

Far removed from President Kennedy's inner circle, Moynihan was nevertheless "New Frontier" material. He soon made powerful friends among the dynamic men who surrounded the young president. He moved to assistant secretary of labor in 1963.

Kennedy's assassination that November affected him deeply, diverting his loyalties to Attorney-General Robert Kennedy, who won a Senate seat from New York in 1964. Moynihan served President Lyndon Johnson's Great Society administration loyally and effectively but did not enjoy the fullest confidence of Johnson's inner circle.

In 1965 as an assistant secretary in the Labor Department of President Johnson's cabinet, Moynihan wrote a report entitled *The Negro Family: The Case for National Action,* which careened him to the lowest point in his career. In the report he warned that rising illegitimacy rates and a "tangle of pathology" threatened the stability of African American families and put at risk the income and equality gains African Americans had achieved through the Civil Rights Movement. Instead of receiving recognition for his perceived keen insight, he was widely criticized by African Americans and liberals as a racist.

In the 1960s Moynihan began his association with Harvard University and the Harvard-MIT Joint Center for Urban Studies. A popular work of scholarship called *Beyond the Melting Pot* brought him national attention even though his co-author, Nathan Glazer, wrote most of the work. Moynihan's principal (but not sole) contribution was the chapter on New York's Irish. He moved in and out of government, and unsuccessfully sought the New York City Council presidential nomination.

Moynihan's commitment to the Democratic party was deeply rooted in his family. Yet it did not prevent him from serving the Nixon administration in an unusual and extremely influential way. President-elect Nixon, finding Moynihan's thinking "refreshing and stimulating" (as he later recounted in his *Memoirs*), named him head of the newly created Urban Affairs Council.

Moreover, Moynihan became a presidential mentor who could always be relied upon to speak his mind candidly. He even provided reading lists for Nixon's edification. The president accepted his advice on many matters, but was especially sympathetic to him as a fellow "outsider" whose humble origins he shared. One major incident that proved embarrassing to the administration consisted of an observation made by Moynihan that African American families might benefit from being left alone a bit to work out their own destinies. This apparently innocent possibility was described by Moynihan as "benign neglect," and the press and some segments of the public inferred from it a diminished ardor for civil rights, which the administration—rightly or wrongly—had never been noted for previously. Notwithstanding this flap, Nixon retained complete confidence in Moynihan, viewing his chief domestic adviser as an invaluable public servant.

After his reelection, Nixon offered Moynihan the post of ambassador to India, a selection demonstrating Moynihan's Chaucerian adaptability and Nixon's perspicacity in recognizing it. He served for two years under both the Nixon and Ford administrations, receiving an appointment in 1975 by President Ford as the nation's permanent representative to the United Nations. In this latter capacity he became a powerful voice of post-Vietnam American moralism, condemning Soviet obstructionism and imperialism and excoriating the venality of many Third World countries. He refused, as he once put it, to apologize for his fallible nation, challenging his listeners to "find its equal."

In 1976 he was elected to the United States Senate and served New York in this capacity for the next decade and a half, being reelected in 1982 and 1988. Although he can put his Johnson report and Nixon memo behind him, his past follows him. During a recent campaign the Reverend Al Sharpton, an African American protestor, made his own run for Senate and tried to remind voters of the latter incidents.

Known for his quirkiness (Elise O'Shaughnessy's profile of him in *Vanity Fair* described his gestures and speech patterns as belonging to someone with "intellectual Tourette's syndrome"), Moynihan's oddity, nevertheless, has worked for him. Recognized for his ability to recall and process voluminous amounts of information and popularize the ideas of others than for facilitating his own scholarship or original thinking, Moynihan has significantly contributed to the Senate. His popularity among voters (he's been elected for four terms and served in the cabinets or subcabinets of four presidents) and his firm belief that a government's purpose is to promote goodness in society earned him the chair of the Finance Committee when Lloyd Bentsen left to become head of the Treasury Department. Although he also has a reputation for making his own government nervous (he criticized President Clinton's health-care bills; battled for better welfare reform—his pet

issue—calling Clinton's ideas "boob bait for the Bubbas;" and suggested that a special prosecutor ought to look into the controversial Whitewater affair), most people realize that his candid personality contributes to the forward motion of government. "Pat Moynihan does a very simple thing that at the end of the 20th century has become the most inexplicable trait a politician can have: he says what he thinks," Laurence O'Donnell, Jr., the director of Moynihan's Finance Committee said.

Wherever he traveled in government or academic life, Moynihan brought his wit and capacity for innovative thinking. His brief assignment to the United Nations produced *A Dangerous Place,* a zesty account of America's rendezvous with world government. *On the Law of Nations* briefly but trenchantly continues the subject of the nation's efforts to carve its place in world history. *Counting our Blessings,* dedicated to his colleague Nathan Glazer, ranges far and wide, but never very far from his first loves: the family, the needy, and those deprived of participating in the dream by racial or ethnic factors. He is, as *Time* reporter Hugh Sidey stated, "the Senate's most eccentric, brilliant and fearless purveyor of uncomfortable truth. He has probably shaped as much national, social, and economic policy . . . as any other person."

Further Reading

Douglas Schoen's *Pat* (1979) is a clear and sympathetic account of the senator's life and career. Richard Nixon's *R.N.: The Memoirs* gives full credit to Moynihan for domestic accomplishments in his administration. Moynihan's many books give insight into his ideas and hopes for America and its society. *A Dangerous Place,* written with Suzanne Weaver (1975), *Counting Our Blessings* (1974), and *On the Law of Nations* (1990) provide a good source for evaluating his ideas and accomplishments. Periodical references can be located in "The Professor and the 400-Lb. Gorilla," *Time,* (June 21, 1993); "Is Independent Agency Status In Social Security's Future?" and "Moynihan Prevails: Senate Grants Independence," *Congressional Quarterly Weekly Report,* (October 9, 1993 and March 5, 1994, respectively); "The Moynihan Mystique," *Vanity Fair,* (May 1994); "Moynihan Rules," *New York,* (May 2, 1994); "The Newest Moynihan," *New York Times Magazine,* (August 7, 1994); and "Social Insecurity," *Newsweek,* (January 20, 1997). □

Wolfgang Amadeus Mozart

Wolfgang Amadeus Mozart (1756-1791) was an Austrian composer whose mastery of the whole range of contemporary instrumental and vocal forms—including the symphony, concerto, chamber music, and especially the opera—was unrivaled in his own time and perhaps in any other.

Wolfgang Amadeus Mozart was born on Jan. 27, 1756, in Salzburg. His father, Leopold Mozart, a noted composer and pedagogue and the author of a famous treatise on violin playing, was then in the service of the archbishop of Salzburg. Together with his sister, Nannerl, Wolfgang received such intensive musical training that by the age of 6 he was a budding composer and an accomplished keyboard performer. In 1762 Leopold presented his son as performer at the imperial court in Vienna, and from 1763 to 1766 he escorted both children on a continuous musical tour across Europe, which included long stays in Paris and London as well as visits to many other cities, with appearances before the French and English royal families.

Mozart was the most celebrated child prodigy of this time as a keyboard performer and made a great impression, too, as composer and improviser. In London he won the admiration of so eminent a musician as Johann Christian Bach, and he was exposed from an early age to an unusual variety of musical styles and tastes across the Continent.

Salzburg and Italy, 1766-1773

From his tenth to his seventeenth year Mozart grew in stature as a composer to a degree of maturity equal to that of his most eminent older contemporaries; as he continued to expand his conquest of current musical styles, he outstripped them. He spent the years 1766-1769 at Salzburg writing instrumental works and music for school dramas in German and Latin, and in 1768 he produced his first real operas: the German *Singspiel* (that is, with spoken dialogue) *Bastien und Bastienne* and the opera buffa *La finta semplice.* Artless and naive as *La finta semplice* is when compared to his later Italian operas, it nevertheless shows a latent sense of character portrayal and fine accuracy of Italian text set-

ting. Despite his reputation as a prodigy, Mozart found no suitable post open to him; and with his father once more as escort Mozart at age 14 (1769) set off for Italy to try to make his way as an opera composer, the field in which he openly declared his ambition to succeed and which offered higher financial rewards than other forms of composition at this time.

In Italy, Mozart was well received: at Milan he obtained a commission for an opera; at Rome he was made a member of an honorary knightly order by the Pope; and at Bologna the Accademia Filarmonica awarded him membership despite a rule normally requiring candidates to be 20 years old. During these years of travel in Italy and returns to Salzburg between journeys, he produced his first large-scale settings of opera seria (that is, court opera on serious subjects): *Mitridate* (1770), *Ascanio in Alba* (1771), and *Lucio Silla* (1772), as well as his first String Quartets. At Salzburg in late 1771 he renewed his writing of Symphonies (Nos. 14-21).

In these operatic works Mozart displays a complete mastery of the varied styles of aria required for the great virtuoso singers of the day (especially large-scale da capo arias), this being the sole authentic requirement of this type of opera. The strong leaning of these works toward the singers' virtuosity rather than toward dramatic content made the opera seria a rapidly dying form by Mozart's time, but in *Lucio Silla* he nonetheless shows clear evidence of his power of dramatic expression within individual scenes.

Salzburg, 1773-1777

In this period Mozart remained primarily in Salzburg, employed as concertmaster of the archbishop's court musicians. In 1773 a new archbishop took office, Hieronymus Colloredo, who was a newcomer to Salzburg and its provincial ways. Unwilling to countenance the frequent absences of the Mozarts, he declined to promote Leopold to the post of chapel master that he had long coveted. The archbishop showed equally little understanding of young Mozart's special gifts. In turn Mozart abhorred Salzburg, but he could find no better post. In 1775 he went off to Munich, where he produced the opera buffa *La finta giardiniera* with great success but without tangible consequences. In this period at Salzburg he wrote nine Symphonies (Nos. 22-30), including the excellent No. 29 in A Major; a large number of divertimenti, including the *Haffner Serenade;* all of his six Concertos for violin, several other concertos, and church music for use at Salzburg.

Mannheim and Paris, 1777-1779

Despite his continued productivity, Mozart was wholly dissatisfied with provincial Austria, and in 1777 he set off for new destinations: Munich, Augsburg, and prolonged stays in Mannheim and Paris. Mannheim was the seat of a famous court orchestra, along with a fine opera house. He wrote a number of attractive works while there (including his three Flute Quartets and five of his Violin Sonatas), but he was not offered a post.

Paris was a vastly larger theater for Mozart's talents (his father urged him to go there, for ''from Paris the fame of a man of great talent echoes through the whole world," he wrote his son). But after 9 difficult months in Paris, from March 1778 to January 1779, Mozart returned once more to Salzburg, having been unable to secure a foot-hold and depressed by the entire experience, which had included the death of his mother in the midst of his stay in Paris. Unable to get a commission for an opera (still his chief ambition), he wrote music to order in Paris, again mainly for wind instruments: the Sinfonia Concertante for four solo wind instruments and orchestra, the Concerto for flute and harp, other chamber music, and the ballet music *Les Petits riens* . In addition, he was compelled to give lessons to make money. In his poignant letters from Paris, Mozart described his life in detail, but he also told his father (letter of July 31, 1778), "You know that I am, so to speak, soaked in music, that I am immersed in it all day long, and that I love to plan works, study, and meditate." This was the way in which the real Mozart saw himself; it far better reflects the actualities of his life than the fictional image of the carefree spirit who dashed off his works without premeditation, an image that was largely invented in the 19th century.

Salzburg, 1779-1781

Returning to Salzburg once more, Mozart took up a post as court conductor and violinist. He chafed again at the constraints of local life and his menial role under the archbishop. In Salzburg, as he wrote in a letter, "one hears nothing, there is no theater, no opera." During these years he concentrated on instrumental music (Symphony Nos. 32-34), the Symphonie Concertante for violin and viola, several orchestral divertimenti, and (despite the lack of a theater) an unfinished German opera, later called *Zaide* .

In 1780 Mozart received a long-awaited commission from Munich for the opera seria *Idomeneo,* musically one of the greatest of his works despite its unwieldy libretto and one of the great turning points in his musical development as he moved from his peregrinations of the 1770s to his Vienna sojourn in the 1780s. *Idomeneo* is, effectively, the last and greatest work in the entire tradition of dynastic opera seria, an art form that was decaying at the same time that the great European courts, which had for decades spent their substance on it as entertainment, were themselves beginning to sense the winds of social and political revolution. Mozart's only other work in this genre, the opera seria *La clemenza di Tito* (1791), was a hurriedly written work composed on demand for a coronation at Prague—and it is significantly not cast in the traditional large dimensions of old-fashioned opera seria, with its long arias, but is cut to two acts like an opera buffa and has many features of the new operatic design Mozart evolved after *Idomeneo.*

Vienna, 1781-1791

Mozart's years in Vienna, from age 25 to his death at 35, encompass one of the most prodigious developments in so short a span in the history of music. While up to now he had demonstrated a complete and fertile grasp of the techniques of his time, his music had been largely within the range of the higher levels of the common language of the time. But in these 10 years Mozart's music grew rapidly

beyond the comprehension of many of his contemporaries; it exhibited both ideas and methods of elaboration that few could follow, and to many the late Mozart seemed a difficult composer. Franz Joseph Haydn's constant praise of him came from his only true peer, and Haydn harped again and again on the problem of Mozart's obtaining a good and secure position, a problem no doubt compounded by the jealousy of Viennese rivals.

Mozart disparaged many of his less gifted contemporaries in scathing terms; Leopold often entreated him to write in a simple and pleasing style ("What is slight can still be great"). Replying to such a plea, Mozart (letter of Dec. 28, 1782, from Vienna) wrote of his own work in a way that might apply to much of his music: "These concertos [K. 413-415] are a happy medium between what is too easy and what is too difficult . . . there are passages here and there from which only connoisseurs can derive satisfaction; but these passages are written in such a way that the less learned cannot fail to be pleased, though without knowing why."

The major instrumental works of this period encompass all the fields of Mozart's earlier activity and some new ones: six symphonies, including the famous last three: No. 39 in E-flat Major, No. 40 in G Minor, and No. 41 in C Major (the *Jupiter* -a title unknown to Mozart). He finished these three works within 6 weeks during the summer of 1788, a remarkable feat even for him.

In the field of the string quartet Mozart produced two important groups of works that completely overshadowed any he had written before 1780: in 1785 he published the six Quartets dedicated to Haydn (K. 387, 421, 428, 458, 464, and 465) and in 1786 added the single *Hoffmeister* Quartet (K. 499). In 1789 he wrote the last three Quartets (K. 575, 589, and 590), dedicated to King Frederick William of Prussia, a noted cellist. The six Quartets dedicated to Haydn undoubtedly owe something to Mozart's study of the earlier work of Haydn, perhaps most to the self-asserted "new and special manner" of Haydn's Op. 33 of 1781, a phrase that may refer to the complete participation in these works of all four instruments in the motivic development. Mozart's works entirely meet the standards set by Haydn up to now, and surpass it.

Other chamber music on the highest level of imagination and craftsmanship from Mozart's Vienna years includes the two Piano Quartets, seven late Violin Sonatas, the last Piano Trios, and the Piano Quintet with winds; and in the last five years of his life, the last String Quintets and the Clarinet Quintet. This decade also saw the composition of the last 17 of Mozart's Piano Concertos, almost all written for his own performance. They represent the high point in the literature of the classical concerto, and in the following generation only Ludwig van Beethoven was able to match them.

A considerable influence upon Mozart's music during this decade was his increasing acquaintance with the music of Johann Sebastian Bach and George Frederick Handel, which in Vienna of the 1780s was scarcely known or appreciated. Through the private intermediacy of an enthusiast for Bach and Handel, Baron Gottfried van Swieten, Mozart came to know Bach's *Well-tempered Clavier,* from which he made arrangements of several fugues for strings with new preludes of his own. He also made arrangements of works by Handel, including *Acis and Galatea,* the *Messiah,* and *Alexander's Feast.*

In a number of late works—especially the *Jupiter* Symphony, *Die Zauberflöte* (*The Magic Flute*), and the *Requiem*—one sees an overt use of contrapuntal procedures, which reflects Mozart's awakened interest in contrapuntal techniques at this period. But in a more subtle sense much of his late work, even where it does not make direct use of fugal textures, reveals a subtlety of contrapuntal organization that doubtless owed something to his deepened experience of the music of Bach and Handel.

Operas of the Vienna Years

Mozart's evolution as an opera composer between 1781 and his death is even more remarkable, perhaps, since the problems of opera were more far-ranging than those of the larger instrumental forms and provided less adequate models. In opera Mozart instinctively set about raising the perfunctory dramatic and musical conventions of his time to the status of genuine art forms. A reform of opera from triviality had been successfully achieved by Christoph Willibald Gluck, but Gluck cannot stand comparison with Mozart in pure musical invention. Although *Idomeneo* may indeed owe a good deal to Gluck, Mozart was immediately thereafter to turn away entirely from opera seria. Instead he sought German or Italian librettos that would provide stage material adequate to stimulate his powers of dramatic expression and dramatic timing through music.

The first important result was the German *Singspiel* entitled *Die Entführung aus dem Serail* (1782; Abduction from the Seraglio). Not only does it have an immense variety of expressive portrayals through its arias, but what is new in the work are its moments of authentic dramatic interaction between characters in ensembles. Following this bent, Mozart turned to Italian opera, and he was fortunate enough to find a librettist of genuine ability, a true literary craftsman, Lorenzo da Ponte. Working with Da Ponte, Mozart produced his three greatest Italian operas: *Le nozze di Figaro* (1786; The Marriage of Figaro), *Don Giovanni* (1787, for Prague), and *Cosi fan tutte* (1790).

Figaro is based on a play by Pierre Caron de Beaumarchais, adapted skillfully by Da Ponte to the requirements of opera. In *Figaro* the ensembles become even more important than the arias, and the considerable profusion of action in the plot is managed with a skill beyond even the best of Mozart's competitors. Not only is every character convincingly portrayed, but the work shows a blending of dramatic action and musical articulation that is probably unprecedented in opera, at least of these dimensions. In *Figaro* and other late Mozart operas the singers cannot help enacting the roles conceived by the composer, since the means of characterization and dramatic expression have been built into the arias and ensembles. This principle, grasped by only a few composers in the history of music, was evolved by Mozart in these years, and, like everything he touched, totally mastered as a technique. It is this that

gives these works the quality of perfection that opera audiences have attributed to them, together with their absolute mastery of musical design.

In *Don Giovanni* elements of wit and pathos are blended with the representation of the supernatural onstage, a rare occurrence at this time. In *Cosi fan tutte* the very idea of "operatic" expression—including the exaggerated venting of sentiment—is itself made the subject of an ironic comedy on fidelity between two pairs of lovers, aided by two manipulators.

In his last opera, *The Magic Flute* (1791), Mozart turned back to German opera, and he produced a work combining many strands of popular theater but with means of musical expression ranging from quasi-folk song to Italianate coloratura. The plot, put together by the actor and impresario Emanuel Schikaneder, is partly based on a fairy tale but is heavily impregnated with elements of Freemasonry and possibly with contemporary political overtones.

On concluding *The Magic Flute,* Mozart turned to work on what was to be his last project, the *Requiem.* This Mass had been commissioned by a benefactor said to have been unknown to Mozart, and he is supposed to have become obsessed with the belief that he was, in effect, writing it for himself. Ill and exhausted, he managed to finish the first two movements and sketches for several more, but the last three sections were entirely lacking when he died. It was completed by his pupil Franz Süssmayer after his death, which came on Dec. 5, 1791. He was given a third-class funeral.

Further Reading

The most important source materials on Mozart available in English are *The Letters of Mozart and His Family, Chronologically Arranged,* edited by Emily Anderson (3 vols., 1938; 2d ed. 1966); and Otto Erich Deutsch, *Mozart: A Documentary Biography* (1964). The most comprehensive study in English of Mozart is Alfred Einstein, *Mozart: His Character, His Work* (1945).
Studies of individual works or groups of works include Edward J. Dent, *Mozart's Operas: A Critical Study* (1913; 2d ed. 1947); Georges de Saint-Foix, *The Symphonies of Mozart* (1947); C. M. Girdlestone, *Mozart's Piano Concertos* (1948); Siegmund Levarie, *Mozart's Le Nozze de Figaro: A Critical Analysis* (1952); and *The Mozart Companion,* edited by H. O. Robbins Landon and Donald Mitchell (1956). A wide variety of analysis is in the special Mozart issue of the *Musical Quarterly* (1956), reprinted as *The Creative World of Mozart,* edited by Paul Henry Lang (1956). For analyses of his works see Felix Salzer, *Structural Hearing* (2 vols., 1952; rev. ed. 1962). □

Ezekiel Mphahlele

Ezekiel Mphahlele (born 1919) is an acknowledged scholar on African literature. His works have been regarded as the most balanced of African literature.

"A writer who has been regarded as the most balanced literary critic of African literature," Ezekiel Mphahlele can also "be acknowledged as one of its most significant creators," writes Emile Snyder in the *Saturday Review*. Mphahlele's transition from life in the slums of South Africa to life as one of Africa's foremost writers was an odyssey of struggle both intellectually and politically. He trained as a teacher in South Africa but was banned from the classroom in 1952 as a result of his protest of the segregationist Bantu Education Act. Although he later returned to teaching, Mphahlele first turned to journalism, criticism, fiction, and essay writing. Mphahlele is acknowledged as one of the leading scholars on African literature.

During an exile that took him to France and the United States, Mphahlele was away from Africa from over a decade. Nevertheless, "no other author has ever earned the right to so much of Africa as has Ezekiel Mphahlele," says John Thompson in the *New York Review of Books*. "In the English language, he established the strength of African literature in our time." Some critics, however, feel that Mphahlele's absence from his homeland has harmed his work by separating him from its subject. Ursula A. Barnett, writing in the conclusion of her 1976 biography *Ezekiel Mphahlele,* asserts that Mphahlele's "creative talent can probably gain its full potential only if he returns to South Africa and resumes his function of teaching his discipline in his own setting, and of encouraging the different elements in South Africa to combine and interchange in producing a modern indigenous literature."

Mphahlele himself has agreed with this assessment, for after being officially silenced by the government of his homeland and living in self-imposed exile for twenty years, Mphahlele returned to South Africa in 1977. "I want to be part of the renaissance that is happening in the thinking of my people," he commented. "I see education as playing a vital role in personal growth and in institutionalizing a way of life that a people chooses as its highest ideal. For the older people, it is a way of reestablishing the values they had to suspend along the way because of the force of political conditions. Another reason for returning, connected with the first, is that this is my ancestral home. An African cares very much where he dies and is buried. But I have not come to die. I want to reconnect with my ancestors while I am still active. I am also a captive of place, of setting. As long as I was abroad I continued to write on the South African scene. There is a force I call the tyranny of place; the kind of unrelenting hold a place has on a person that gives him the motivation to write and a style. The American setting in which I lived for nine years was too fragmented to give me these. I could only identify emotionally and intellectually with the African-American segment, which was not enough. Here I can feel the ancestral Presence. I know now what Vinoba Bhave of India meant when he said: 'Though action rages without, the heart can be tuned to produce unbroken music,' at this very hour when pain is raging and throbbing everywhere in African communities living in this country."

His 1988 publication *Renewal Time,* contains stories he published previously as well as an autobiographical afterword on his return to South Africa and a section from *Afrika My Music,* his 1984 autobiography. Stories like "Mrs. Plum" and "The Living and the Dead" have received praise by critics reviewing Mphahlele's work. Charles R. Larson, reviewing the work in the *Washington Post Book World,* says that the stories in the book present "almost ironic images of racial tension under apartheid." He cites "Mrs. Plum" as "the gem of this volume." The story is a first-person narrative by a black South African servant girl, and through her words, says Larson, "Mphahlele creates the most devastating picture of a liberal South African white."

Chirundu, Mphahlele's first novel since his return to South Africa, "tells with quiet assurance this story of a man divided," says Rose Moss in a *World Literature Today* review. The novel "is clearly this writer's major work of fiction and, I suppose, in one sense, an oblique commentary on his own years of exile," observes Larson in an article for *World Literature Today.* Moss finds that in his story of a man torn between African tradition and English law, "the timbre of Mphahlele's own vision is not always clear"; nevertheless, the critic admits that "in the main his story presents the confused and wordless heart of his charcter with unpretentious mastery." "*Chirundu* is that rare breed of fiction—a novel of ideas, and a moving one at that," says Larson. "It has the capacity to involve the reader both intellectually and emotionally." The critic concludes by calling the work "the most satisfying African novel of the past several years."

On the subject of writing, Mphahlele commented: "In Southern Africa, the black writer talks best about the ghetto life he knows; the white writer about his own ghetto life. We see each other, black and white, as it were through a keyhole. Race relations are a major experience and concern for the writer. They are his constant beat. It is unfortunate no one can ever think it is healthy both mentally and physically to keep hacking at the social structure in overcharged language. A language that burns and brands, scorches and scalds. Language that is a machete with a double edge—the one sharp, the other blunt, the one cutting, the other breaking. And yet there are levels of specifically black drama in the ghettoes that I cannot afford to ignore. I have got to stay with it. I bleed inside. My people bleed. But I must stay with it."

Further Reading

Two biographies on Mphahlele are available. They are Ursula A. Barnett, *Ezekiel Mphahlele* (1976) and N. Chabani Manganyi, *Exiles and Homecomings: A Biography of Es'kia Mphahlele* (1983). Gerald Moore also wrote two books of interest: *South African Writers* (1962) and *The Chosen Tongue* (1969). Books of relevance that the subject, himself, wrote include *Afrika My Music: An Autobiography, 1957-1983* (1984) and *Down Second Avenue* (1959). See also *Twentieth Century Caribbean and Black African Writers* (1993); *African Writers Talking* (edited by Dennis Durden, 1972); Donald E. Herdeck, *African Writers: A Companion to Black African Writing*, 1300-1973 (1973); and *South African Voices* (edited by Bernth Lindfors, 1975). □

Samuel Edward Krune Mqhayi

Samuel Edward Krune Mqhayi (1875-1945) was a South African novelist and poet who excelled in the Xhosa praise-poem.

Samuel Mqhayi was born on Dec. 1, 1875, among the Xhosa of Cape Province (South Africa). He was trained as a teacher at the Lovedale institution, but he soon became famous as a traditional poet. He began his writing career by contributing to various Xhosa newspapers and by writing a story entitled *Ityala lama-wele* (1914; The Lawsuit of the Twins). Dealing with a trial in a tribal court, it was mainly designed to extol customary judicial procedure, which was threatened by the growing implantation of European courts.

Mqhayi's deep concern with the lore and history of his people prevented him from teaching at Lovedale, for he could not agree with the official version of South African history in the textbooks. He therefore devoted himself more and more to writing. His major imaginative work, *U-Don Jadu* (part 1, 1929), is a utopian projection of an ideal, multiracial, South African society under the leadership of the title character, Don Jadu: it is a forward-looking society which places a high premium on education and intellectual progress; and it is a tolerant society which integrates into a Christian framework many of the beliefs and customs dear

to African hearts. In 1935 Mqhayi was awarded a prize in the first May Esther Bedford Competition for the part 3 of *U-Don Jadu,* and in 1936 he took part in the First Conference of Bantu Authors, convened in Transvaal.

Mqhayi's keen interest in the past and the future of Africa is apparent in the dual nature of his inspiration. While writing biographical accounts of such modern Negroes as Dr. J.E.K. Aggrey or the Reverend John Knox Bokwe (1925), he also published a collection of cantos in the traditional manner on the reign of 19th-century Xhosa paramount chief Hintza. Mqhayi's autobiography documents the writer's formative years.

Yet it was as a poet that Mqhayi was chiefly valued by his Xhosa audience, not least because he had fully mastered the form and the spirit of the traditional praise-poem (*izibongo*) while adapting it to modern circumstances and topics. His volume *Inzuzo* (1942; Reward) exhibits considerable variety, some aspects of may be unfamiliar to the Western reader. Side by side with praise poems about prominent Africans, it contains, for example, a poem in appreciation of an agricultural journal published in the Transkei.

While Mqhayi's nature poems may be dull, and his moralizing pieces about such subjects as truth, hope, and love are apt to be mere oratorical exercises, he excelled in poetry of the traditional type. This is often heroic but also at times satirical: in a praise-poem written on the occasion of the Prince of Wales's visit to South Africa in 1925, Mqhayi expatiated with overt irony on the ambiguity of Britain's contribution to the "enlightenment" of Africans: "She sent us the preacher, she sent us the bottle; she sent us the Bible and barrels of brandy."

In thus bridging the gap between tradition and novelty, Mqhayi deserved to be called the father of Xhosa poetry by Zulu critic B. W. Vilakazi. Mqhayi died on July 29, 1945.

Further Reading

The fullest account of Mqhayi is to be found in Albert S. Gérard, *Four African Literatures* (1971). Further background is in Jahnheinz Jahn, *Neo-African Literature: A History of Black Writing* (1966; trans. 1968), and Robert H.W. Shepherd's two works, *Lovedale and Literature for the Bantu: A Brief History and a Forecast* (1945) and *Bantu Literature and Life* (Lovedale, 1955).

Additional Sources

Mqhayi in translation, Grahamstown: Department of African Languages, Rhodes University, 1976. □

Muawiya ibn Abu Sufyan

Muawiya ibn Abu Sufyan (died 680) was the founder of the Umayyad dynasty of caliphs. His clan, which had resisted Mohammed and his message longest and most vehemently, eventually won political control over the Islamic community.

As son of Abu Sufyan, one of the leaders of the Meccan opposition to Mohammed, Muawiya did not adopt Islam until the conquest of Mecca in 630. Muawiya at this time was made secretary to the Prophet, but it was as a warrior in the army sent by the caliph Abu Bakr to conquer Syria that Muawiya first distinguished himself in the Moslem community.

Building a Power Base

As a result of his military exploits, Muawiya was awarded the governorship of Damascus and, under the caliph Omar, became governor over all Syria, in which capacity he served for 20 years. He built the province into a base of support on which he was able to draw during his contest with Ali for the caliphate.

Muawiya appeased the native Christian population of Syria by his tolerance, which included the employment of Christians at his court; and he cultivated the Syrian tribesmen of southern Arabian origin by a marriage alliance, when he took a woman of the Kalb tribe as wife. In addition, Muawiya built Syria into a powerful military and naval base from which he launched raids by land into Byzantine Asia Minor and naval expeditions against Cyprus, Rhodes, and the coast of Lycia.

Struggle for the Caliphate

The second significant phase of Muawiya's career began in 655 with the murder of the caliph Othman by rebels from Egypt and Iraq who resented the favoritism shown by Othman toward his Umayyad kinsmen. When Othman was assassinated, the duty of avenging his death devolved upon Muawiya as the strongest member of the clan. The issue which pitted Muawiya against Ali ibn Abu Talib, the new caliph, was the punishment of the regicides.

Although Ali had not himself participated in the murder, he neglected to take any action against the assassins and, in fact, adopted certain anti-Umayyad measures that the rebels had advocated, such as removing Othman's governmental appointees. This Muawiya regarded as proof of Ali's complicity in the murder; accordingly, he refused to pay homage to Ali as caliph.

Ali marched against Syria and was met by Muawiya at the famous battle of Siffin. Muawiya was able to avoid defeat by adopting the clever ruse of placing pages of the Koran on his soldiers' lances, which signified that his quarrel with Ali should be settled not through fighting but by consulting the book of God. Both sides subsequently chose arbitrators who agreed that since Othman had committed no crime his murder was not justified. Muawiya's stand being thereby vindicated, his Syrian supporters declared him the rightful caliph (658).

To strengthen his military position, Muawiya conquered Egypt in the same year and later launched attacks against Arabia, Iraq, and Yemen, but the conflict between the two claimants to the caliphate ended only by Ali's murder in 661 at the hands of zealots who claimed that neither of the two was entitled to the caliphate.

Once Muawiya had persuaded Ali's son, Hasan, to renounce his claim to the caliphate, Muawiya's own position was secure, and he set about restoring the unity and renewing the expansion of the Moslem state. His strength continued to come from two quarters—the Syrian tribesmen and his Umayyad kinsmen. To consolidate the support of the former, he transferred the center of Moslem government from Iraq to Damascus, and the loyalty of the latter he ensured by appointing them as provincial officials.

Lacking the support of the influential religious circles, Muawiya transformed the Islamic government from a theocracy (which had in practice ended with the murder of Othman) into an Arab tribal aristocracy served by a bureaucracy. He ruled with the advice of a council of Arab elders, along with delegations from various tribes, and strengthened the bureaucracy, a holdover from Byzantine rule, by creating a postal service and a bureau of registry. A tolerant policy toward Christians and the distribution of bribes to dissident tribes contributed to the maintenance of internal stability.

Further Conquests

Having restored peace and unity within Moslem territory, Muawiya was free to assume the religious obligation of military expansion incumbent upon a caliph. The Arab invasions, which had come to a halt during the period of civil strife in the caliphates of Othman and Ali, were renewed by Muawiya on land and sea, to the north, east, and west, with such spectacular success that a new era of Moslem Arab conquest was established.

To the east, Muawiya sent an expedition into the northeastern province of Persia—Khurasan—which, once conquered, was used as a base for raids across the Oxus River into Transoxiana. To the west, Muawiya's governor in Egypt sent an expedition under the famous conqueror Uqba ibn Nafi against North Africa which penetrated Byzantine defenses as far west as Algeria. It is significant, however, that these advances into Algeria and Transoxiana, at the eastern and western extremities of Muawiya's campaign, were not consolidated by Moslem occupation and were not finally conquered for Islam until later in the Umayyad dynasty.

To the north, in addition to annual raids against Byzantine frontier holdings in Asia Minor, which served to keep the tribal armies in fighting trim, Muawiya launched two unsuccessful attacks against Constantinople itself; the first was led by his son Yazid, and the second took the form of a naval campaign fought intermittently over a period of seven years (674-680).

Further Reading

In the absence of a full-length biography of Muawiya in a Western language see Sir William Muir, *The Caliphate: Its Rise, Decline and Fall* (1898). A full account of his reign is in Philip K. Hitti, *History of the Arabs, from the Earliest Times to the Present* (1937; 10th ed. 1970). See also Joel Carmichael, *The Shaping of the Arabs* (1967). □

Hosni Mubarak

Hosni Mubarak (born 1928) led Egypt after the assassination of Anwar Sadat in 1981. He continued the policy of peace with Israel and also won back diplomatic relations with Arab Sates that had cut themselves off from Egypt when Sadat decided to recognize Israel's right to exist.

Hosni Mubarak came from the same Nile delta province, Minufiya, as his predecessor and patron, Anwar Sadat. Mubarak's village of Kafr-El Moseilha had a reputation for stressing education and had produced four cabinet ministers. His father was a minor official in the Ministry of Justice. After primary schooling in his village and secondary studies in the near-by provincial capital of Shibin El-Kom, Mubarak attended Egypt's Military Academy and its Air Academy, graduating from the latter in 1950. He completed the military training in only two years, opting to continue studying instead of taking his summer leave. He became a pilot and spent part of his training in the then Soviet Union.

Mubarak spent the next 25 years in the Air Force. He taught at the Air Academy and commanded Egypt's bomber force in the Yemen civil war in the 1960s. He visited the Soviet Union on several occasions and spent a year at the Soviet's Frunze military academy. He spoke Russian and English in addition to Arabic.

President Gamal Abdel Nasser named Mubarak director of the Air Academy in 1967, giving him the crucial task of rebuilding the air force, which the Israelis had destroyed on the ground in the Six Day War of June 1967. Mubarak moved up to Air Force chief-of-staff in 1969, and in 1972 he became its commander-in-chief. He helped plan the successful surprise attack on the Israeli forces occupying the east bank of the Suez Canal on October 6, 1973, launching the Yom Kippur War.

President Sadat rewarded Mubarak's patient competence in 1975 by naming him vice president. Sadat disliked routine administration and enjoyed the international limelight, so Mubarak quietly took over the day-to-day running of the government. Mubarak presided over cabinet meetings, controlled the security apparatus, and became vice president of the ruling National Democratic party. Diplomatic assignments abroad gave him experience with foreign affairs. He was sent to Syria, Iraq, the United States, and China. His expertise was integral to the negotiations for the 1978 Camp David Accords which Egypt and Israel signed, ending decades of conflict.

Mubarak escaped with a minor hand wound when Islamic fundamentalists gunned down Sadat at a military review on October 6, 1981. Moving quickly to restore order and consolidate his position, Mubarak crushed an Islamic uprising in Asyut and jailed over 2,500 members of militant Islamic groups. He executed a handful, had others sentenced to prison terms, and gradually released the rest. He also released the more secular political figures whom Sadat had indiscriminately jailed in the September crackdown that helped provoke his assassination.

Mubarak only slightly modulated the main lines of Sadat's foreign and domestic policies. He kept the 1979 Camp David treaty with Israel and Sadat's close ties to the United States. Egypt regained the Sinai peninsula when the Israelis withdrew in 1982. Egypt remained cool to Israel, however, because of a minor border dispute, the Israeli invasion of Lebanon in 1982, and Israeli policies toward the Palestinians in the West Bank. In 1986, however, he agreed to return the Egyptian ambassador to Tel Aviv.

Throughout the 1980s Mubarak combated Egypt's most pressing problems, unemployment and a struggling economy. He increased the production of affordable housing, clothing, furniture, and medicine. He also kept a tight rein on his officials, firing ministers at the first hint of scandal and fining parliamentary legislators for unnecessary absences.

Egypt's heavy dependence on U.S. military and economic aid and her hopes for U.S. pressure on Israel for a Palestinian settlement continued under Mubarak. He carefully offered the Americans only military "facilities" and not bases, however, and quietly improved relations with the Soviet Union, whose ambassador returned to Cairo in 1984.

All the Arab states but three had broken relations with Egypt to protest the treaty with Israel. Without renouncing the treaty, Mubarak patiently rebuilt bridges to Jordan, Iraq, Saudi Arabia, and Yasser Arafat of the Palestine Liberation Organization. It was Mubarak who prodded Arafat to recognize Israel's right to exist and moderate his extremist stance.

Internally, the military, the swollen government bureaucracy, the consumer-oriented upper middle class, and the rural power structure were still the mainstays of Mubarak's regime. The scattered opposition included Muslim idealists who longed for a theocracy, Nasserists and leftist who looked back to the populist redistributive policies of the early 1960s, and the New Wafd rightists who wanted further economic and political liberalization. Egypt's Christians, the Copts, remained nervous about the political resurgence of Islam. Mubarak's National Democratic party won a comfortable majority in the May 1984 elections. He told U.S. News and World Report that in Egypt "no religious political parties are allowed, and I am not going to change the laws . . . I don't want headaches. I would like to build a country and not cause reasonable people to fight one another."

Sadat's "open-door" economic policies—which encouraged foreign and local private investment—continued, although Mubarak tried to shift the emphasis from imported luxuries to productive enterprises. Mubarak did not dare to discontinue the costly government subsidies which reduced the prices of basic foods to consumers.

Mubarak dismissed several cabinet ministers from the Sadat days for corruption, prosecuted Sadat's brother (who had amassed a fortune overnight), and sternly warned his own relatives to avoid such temptations. He razed the luxury weekend retreats on the pyramids' plateau at Giza. Like Nasser, but unlike Sadat, Mubarak followed local mores in separating his public from his private life. His wife Suzanne, who had a master's degree in sociology, did not try to play the highly visible "first lady" role which had attracted Westerners to Jihan Sadat but had offended many Egyptians. In 1987 Mubarak won election to a second six-year term.

Mubarak was shocked and angered over the 1990 Iraqi invasion of Kuwait. He thought the Gulf War could have been avoided, but placed that responsibility on Saddam Hussein. He felt that the Saudi Arabians were justified in inviting assistance from the West to protect their sovereignty. He sent 45,000 troops to the allied coalition, with the unanimous approval of the Egyptian people. After the war Mubarak's prompt actions and support boosted Egypt to the forefront in leading the Arab world.

In 1993 Mubarak was elected for a sixth term with 96.3 percent of the vote. Many felt that the vote reflected the Egyptian's approval and confidence in Mubarak's stand against Islamic fundamentalists. Plots to assassinate Mubarak had surfaced in 1992 and 1993 but had failed. In 1995 however after two policemen and assailants were killed in another attack against the president, Mubarak continued his hard-line stance against the extremists. Not only were they plotting to overthrow the government, but their actions had damaged Egypt's already unsteady economy. His crackdown brought his government accusations of torture, summary execution intimidation of the press, and other human-rights violations.

In 1997, Mubarak embarked on the New Valley Canal project which many called his "great pyramid" or lasting legacy to Egypt. In effect Mubarak planned to "make the desert bloom" by creating a new canal through one of the hottest and driest places on earth, turning arid desert into arable farm land.

Further Reading

No book-length biography of Mubarak in either Arabic or English has yet appeared. He refused to discuss his private life, so articles on him and interviews with him necessarily concentrate on his public policies. See, for example, J. G. Merriam, "Egypt under Mubarak," *Current History,* 82 (1983); William E. Farrell, "Mubarak's Time of Testing," *New York Times Magazine,* 131 (January 31, 1982); and Hamied Ansari, "Mubarak's Egypt," *Current History,* 84 (1985). Also, *U.S. News and World Report,* May 19, 1997; April 10, 1989; April 16, 1990, *Barrons,* Jan 21, 1991, *Facts on File,* Oct 10, 1993; June 29, 1995, and *Time,* October 19, 1981; Sept 10, 1990; February 25, 1991; July 10 1995. □

Otto Mueller

Otto Mueller (1874-1930), frequently called the "Gypsy-Mueller" due to his preference of gypsy-type figures in his work, was the most lyrical of German expressionist painters.

Otto Mueller was born on October 16, 1874, in Liebau, German Silesia. His mother had been adopted as a young girl, giving rise to the story that he was the son of a gypsy—a story he never denied. He was a cousin to the famous German writers and dramatists Gerhart and Carl Hauptmann (the latter's novel "Einhart der Lächler" is an imaginary portrait of the painter). After four years of apprenticeship with a lithographer, Mueller entered the Academy of Fine Arts in Dresden in 1894. He was dissatisfied with the conservative instructions and left after two years. The next several years he lived close to his influential cousins, and for a short while he went to Munich to study with the famous painter Franz von Stuck. Information about his life and work until 1908—when he settled in Berlin—is sketchy, especially since the artist destroyed many of his earlier works.

In Berlin Mueller met the expressionist sculptor Wilhelm Lehmbruck, whose concept of the human form had a decisive influence on his own perception. When in 1910 his entries to the exhibition of the Berlin Secession were rejected he joined the members of the artist group "Die Brücke" (The Bridge) and exhibited with the New Secession and thus met Ernst Ludwig Kirchner, Ernst Heckel, and Karl Schmidt-Rottluff. He became their lifelong friend, and, while only slightly influenced by their woodcut techniques, he contributed in return his experience in lithography and especially his techniques of distemper painting (colors bound by glue or size). This technique permits the quick coverage of large areas of the very rough canvas (burlap) which he preferred and adds a subdued luminosity. Since overpainting in distemper is not possible, the artist has to have a clear conception of his work before he begins. The technical devices strengthened the Brücke painters' desire to "flatten" the image on the canvas—following the examples of Paul Gauguin and even Edvard Munch and rejecting the academic preference for an emphasis on three-dimensionality of the subject.

In his graphic works Mueller experimented with mixtures of woodcut and lithography, the rubbing of the printer's ink, frequently adding color in the form of watercolor or colored chalk, until he had the technical means of the Breslau Academy available to make true color lithographs. His "Gypsy-Portfolio" (nine color lithographs in a portfolio of 1927), which used as many as five stones, is one of his great achievements as a graphic artist.

From 1916 to 1918 he served as a soldier in World War I, an experience which left no impact on his work. Shortly after his return he was appointed professor at the Breslau Academy of Art, where he taught until his death. Mueller's work shows only three motifs: landscapes, gypsies, and primarily nudes in landscapes. The last motif dominated his work. The earthen color of his mostly young, subtle but angular nude girls forms with the subdued and delicate greens of the landscape backgrounds a vision of a lost past. There is a frequently melancholic nostalgia in his works, presenting a harmony between nature and the human form which is not only opposite to the academic approach but also to that of the other Expressionists. While the latter also "flattened" the human figure in their works, Mueller saw the simplicity and directness of Egyptian painting as his ideal. The compositions of his works are simply built by careful overlapping of the forms which require no intrusion of perspective, thus adding to the "other-worldliness" of the otherwise so natural scenes. Mueller's love for the gypsies prompted a number of trips to Hungary, Romania, and Bulgaria. He did not idealize these migratory groups—the poverty and harshness of their lives is quite visible in Mueller's works—but he presented them in a simple directness which made them blood-relatives of his young girls in the idyllic landscapes.

Mueller married three times, the last time to Elfriede Timm shortly before his death on September 24, 1930, in Breslau. In his choice of subject matter, in his technique of distemper painting, and in his approach to a nostalgic vision of harmony of the human form within nature, Mueller was a unique artist who—regardless of his friendship with and close relations to the Expressionists—retained his own style with his continuously varying compositions of his three main motifs. His friends of the "Brücke" referred to what Ernst Ludwig Kirchner stated in his chronology of the artist group: Mueller exemplified a "sensual harmony of life and his work."

Further Reading

The first important article on Otto Mueller was written by Paul Westheim and published in *Das Kunstblatt* N.5 of 1918. The most comprehensive monograph on the artist was published by Lothar-Günther Buckhein—*Leben und Werk* (*Life and Work*) in 1963 (Feldafing) with an oeuvre catalogue for the graphic works by Florian Karsch. For the 100th birthday of the artist, Florian Karsch published a corrected oeuvre catalogue of the graphics (Berlin, 1975). Eberhard Troeger published a short monograph (1949), but more information about the artist can be found in the standard texts on Expressionism: Bernard S. Myers, *The German Expressionists, a Generation in Revolt* (n.d.) and Peter Selz, *German Expressionist Painting* (1974). A concise small paperback by John Willett (1978) is a general introduction to this period. □

Robert Gabriel Mugabe

Robert Gabriel Mugabe (born 1924) was in the forefront of the liberation struggle in Zimbabwe (formerly Southern Rhodesia) for nearly two decades. Despite detention and harassment from the white settler regime, Mugabe resisted attempts to break him and maintained a fierce commitment to the principles of racial equality and democracy. In 1980 he was rewarded by becoming Zimbabwe's first elected black prime minister.

Robert Mugabe was born on February 21, 1924, at Kutama Mission in Zvimba, Southern Rhodesia (now Zimbabwe) four months after it became a British Crown colony. Mugabe was the son of a peasant farmer and carpenter. He began his education at a nearby Jesuit mission and soon proved an able student under the guidance of Father O'Hea. For nine years he taught in various schools while also continuing to study privately for his matriculation certificate before going on to the University of Fort Hare in South Africa, where he received a bachelor of arts in English and history in 1951. He returned to teach in Southern Rhodesia, obtaining his bachelor of education by correspondence in 1953. Two years later he moved to Chalimbana Training College in Northern Rhodesia (now Zambia), where he taught for nearly four years while also studying for a bachelor of science in economics by correspondence from the University of London. In 1958 he completed that degree in Ghana, where he taught at St. Mary's Teacher Training College and also met his future wife, Sarah "Sally" Heyfron. In Ghana he found a society that was recently independent and proudly Marxist, with a government intent on bringing universal education and opportunity to even those formerly on the lowest levels of society. The Ghanaians cheerful public spirit and their wholehearted way of seizing the chance to better themselves made a profound impression on Mugabe.

In 1960 Mugabe returned to Zimbabwe on home leave and became caught up in the African nationalist struggle against Great Britain and the settler regime. He resigned his job in Ghana, remained in Zimbabwe, and joined the National Democratic party (NDP) as secretary for publicity. Mugabe proved a capable organizer, and he quickly built the youth wing of the party into a powerful force. His determination to achieve racial and social justice in Zimbabwe soon made him a respected and important voice in the party. He was one of the principal opponents of the 1961 constitutional compromise offering black Africans token representation in a still white-dominated government. This document offered no specific target date for adopting majority rule and it proposed a two tier electoral system whose upper level was available only to voters who had completed secondary school, thereby eliminating a majority of the black African population, giving blacks only half the voting power of whites. Such was the vociferous opposition of the 450,000 blacks that the United Nations called upon Britain to suspend the new constitution and begin discussions about true majority rule.

That same year the government banned NDP, but Mugabe retained his position in the successor party, the Zimbabwe African People's Union (ZAPU). When ZAPU was banned in 1962, Mugabe was restricted for three months, but he eluded imprisonment and fled to Dar es Salaam, Tanzania, which had become the party's operational headquarters in exile. He organized regular broadcasts to Zimbabwe from Radio Tanzania.

Dissension over tactics split the ZAPU leadership, and Mugabe and other ZAPU dissidents returned home to form a new nationalist party, the Zimbabwe African National Union (ZANU), in August 1963. This party opposed another group led by Joshua Nkomo, who was preoccupied with gaining external support against the Rhodesian government. The ZANU called for a firmer policy of confrontation with the settlers. Ndabaningi Sithole became president and Mugabe the secretary-general. In response, ZAPU established the People's Caretaker Council (PCC) to act for the banned ZAPU.

Clashes between the two parties weakened the movement, and white conservative settlers gained power through the election of the Rhodesian Front's Ian Smith in 1964. Smith quickly banned the two parties and a year later declared unilateral independence from Britain. The United Nations imposed sanctions that severely damaged the economy and left Smith to struggle without support of his longtime ally Mozambique. The former Portuguese colony had become a Marxist state, and as such, no longer a staunch friend to Rhodesia.

Meanwhile, Mugabe, Nkomo, and other nationalist leaders spent the next ten years in prison, during which time various lieutenants directed the still weak armed struggle. Mugabe used his imprisonment to further his studies, obtaining a bachelor of law and a bachelor of administration from the University of London. He also tutored fellow inmates, and at the time of his escape he was studying for a master of law degree. In 1974 Smith allowed Mugabe out of prison to attend a conference in Lusaka. Mugabe seized this opportunity to escape across the border to Mozambique, gathering young troops of guerrillas along the way.

The guerrilla war intensified during this period as ZANU's military wing, the Zimbabwe African National Liberation Army (ZANLA), gained experience in the field and training abroad (especially in China). On April 28, 1968, ZANLA guerrillas clashed with Rhodesian forces—since commemorated as Chimurenga Day, the start of the armed struggle. The war expanded dramatically in 1972 when the Mozambique border became available as a base for guerrilla forces.

In response to the escalating guerrilla war, the Rhodesian government began extending its military call-up, while also searching for an acceptable compromise with moderate African leaders. Following long talks with representatives from Zambia, South Africa, and elsewhere, a detente scenario was drafted in Lusaka in October 1974. Smith released detained nationalist leaders for preliminary talks. Several of these leaders signed a declaration of unity in Lusaka, and Smith declared a ceasefire. Mugabe and ZANU refused to sign and ignored the ceasefire, which consequently failed to take place.

Mugabe and Nkomo left Zimbabwe in order to direct their respective military forces. ZANU leaders had become disenchanted with Sithole's willingness to compromise with Smith and in 1975 appointed Mugabe the leader of ZANU. That same year a ZANU leader, Herbert Chitepo, was assassinated in the Zambian capital of Lusaka and the Zambian government arrested most of the Zambian-based ZANU leaders. As a result, Mugabe moved to Mozambique, which became ZANU's main headquarters and staging ground for guerrilla attacks. B.J. Vorster of South Africa and Kenneth Kaunda of Zambia tried to get Smith to negotiate with the nationalists, but talks broke off within a few hours. The war resumed on three fronts: Tete, Manica, and Gaza. In 1976 ZANU and ZAPU formed the Patriot Front to establish a united front to better prosecute the war. The new army was called the Zimbabwe People's Army (ZIPA), which included cadres from ZANLA and ZAPU's Zimbabwe People's Revolutionary Army (ZIPRA).

Military and political pressures gradually pushed Smith towards an internal settlement. In 1977 Smith rejected peace proposals put forward by the United States and Britain, and instead opened negotiations with three moderate African leaders: Bishop Abel Muzorewa, Chief Chirau, and Sithole. In 1978 these leaders agreed to form a transitional government which would proceed to majority rule, and a year later a white referendum approved the new Zimbabwe-Rhodesia constitution. Muzorewa won the subsequent national election.

Both the international community and the Patriotic Front rejected this compromise, and guerrilla activity continued despite amnesty proposals. Britain, the United States, and the Front-Line States (the African countries bordering Zimbabwe) stepped up pressure on Smith and Muzorewa to hold another constitutional conference which included the Patriotic Front. In 1979 at the Commonwealth summit in Lusaka, Britain's Prime Minister Margaret Thatcher agreed to convene a constitutional conference. The resulting Lancaster House conference established a new constitution, and a ceasefire took effect. In 1980 Mugabe won British-supervised elections in an independent Zimbabwe and became the first black prime minister and minister of defense in Zimbabwe. After the election Mugabe presided over Zimbabwe's difficult transition from a racialist settler regime to a multi-racial socialist government. He brought his moral force, personal discipline, and commitment to social justice to this difficult task, although not always receiving full cooperation from Nkomo's Matebele people.

Mugabe ignored the departure of the white population, concetrating his efforts on improving the lot of the black African peoples. By Jan 1, 1981, Zimbabwe boasted free primary education for all students, guaranteed admission to secondary school for all who qualified, free medical care for those with low incomes and a new housing law granting freehold ownership to home renters of 30 year's standing.

Many problems remained between Mugabe's forces and those of Nkomo's. Resentment smoldered when Mugabe was once again reelected over Nkomo, spilling over into fighting and murder until finally the two leaders agreed to settle their differences. In December 1987 the two rival factions merged with Mugabe as President and Nkomo as a senior minister. With the friction eased, attention could be turned to bettering the economy.

By 1989 a five year plan was created to restructure the government, relaxing price controls and giving farmers the right to set their own prices. By 1994 the structural adjustment had produced some improvements with slight growth showing in agriculture, manufacturing, and mining. In 1996 Mugabe took the controversial stance of supporting the seizure of white-owned land without compensation in order to reverse the economic imbalances that disadvantaged the majority blacks. He also refused to revise the constitution that is tailored to a one party state, or release his hold on the media.

In 1991 Mugabe's wife Sally died. He then married his long-time mistress (and mother of his two children) Grace Marufu. While the wedding was lavish and almost regal (Marufu invited 20,000 guests to attend the ceremony), it sparked anger among the Zimbabwean people, causing them a disillusionment with the president who led them to independence. Other signs of unrest were that 60,000 civil servants went on strike over a 6 percent pay raise when inflation was at 22 percent. Moreover, the government revoked their traditional Christmas bonus, while awarding themselves a 130 percent pay increase. Although the Mugabe government negotiated a settlement to the strike, it signaled a breakdown of the relationship between Mugabe and his people.

Further Reading

Mugabe's *Our War of Liberation* (1983) discusses his part in the armed struggle in Zimbabwe. His career is discussed in David Martin and Phyllis Johnson, *The Struggle for Zimbabwe* (1981) and in Diana Mitchell, *African Nationalist Leaders in Zimbabwe: Who's Who 1980* (1980, revised 1983). Also see: *Zimbabwe: A Country Study* (1983), "End of the affair: Zimbabwe," *Economist,* August 31, 1996. □

Muhammad bin Tughluq

Muhammad bin Tughluq (reigned 1325-1351) was a medieval Indian ruler whose reign saw the beginning of the disintegration of the empire of Delhi.

The son and successor of the Turk Ghiyas-ud-din (reigned 1321-1325), the founder of the Tughluq dynasty that replaced Khilji rule in Delhi, Muhammad bin Tughluq displayed an extraordinary capacity for classical learning and military leadership. He was formally crowned in 1325, when his father met an accidental death in which Muhammad was implicated.

In spite of a wealth of information on Muhammad's reign from contemporaries—such as Zia-ud-din Barani, the well-known chronicler of medieval India, and the Moorish traveler Ibn Battuta, who was in India during 1333-1346—there is a great deal of confusion about the sequence of events in his reign and their precise nature. Muhammad's regime of 26 years seems to have largely been occupied with fighting rebellions (some 22 are listed), planning ambitious projects of conquest of farflung areas, and making administrative innovations that brought disgrace to the ruler and suffering for his subjects.

The most serious of these rebellions were in the Deccan (1326, 1347), Mâbar (tip of the Indian peninsula, 1334), Bengal (1338), Gujarat (1345), and Sind (1350). These rebellions led to Delhi's loss of control over the south and the Deccan, Bengal, Gujarat, and Sind. The rebellions in Gujarat and Sind exhausted Muhammad, for it was in the course of his expedition in Sind that he died near Thatta in 1351.

Among Muhammad's ambitious military projects was his plan to invade Khurasan in Persia in 1329; a large army was raised and paid for, all of which was a wasted effort because the Sultan realized its impracticality. During 1337-1338 he attacked the kingdom of Nagarkot in the Punjab and secured a limited success.

Muhammad's administrative innovations also smacked of the spectacular. In 1327 he ordered that the imperial capital be shifted from Delhi in the north to Daulatabad in the Deccan, a distance of over 750 miles. After moving by force a part of the Delhi population, Muhammad realized that his move was ill-advised, and the capital was moved back to Delhi.

In 1328-1329 Muhammad ordered an enhancement of agricultural taxes in the Doab (area watered by the Ganges and the Jamuna rivers), and the impost was collected with such severity that it bred rebellions and led to devastation of large tracts. In 1330-1332 Muhammad conceived the idea of introducing a token copper currency without taking the necessary precautions against private minting of copper coins. The result was the flooding of the market with spurious coins which were then withdrawn in exchange for gold and silver coins.

In his religious views Muhammad was a liberal, though he requested recognition from the Caliph in Egypt in 1340. He loved holding discussions with philosophers and men of learning and was undoubtedly an extraordinary man who combined within himself numerous contradictions.

Further Reading

Agha Mahdi Husain, *Tughluq Dynasty* (Calcutta, 1963), is largely devoted to a detailed discussion of the career of Muhammad bin Tughluq. Wolsley Haig, ed., *The Cambridge History of India* (Delhi, 1958), and R. C. Majumdar, ed., *The History and Culture of the Indian People,* vol. 6: *The Delhi Sultanate* (Bombay, 1960), also have substantial sections dealing with the reign of Muhammad. □

Elijah Muhammad

Elijah Muhammad (1897-1975) was the leader of the Nation of Islam ("Black Muslims") during their period of greatest growth in the mid-20th century. He was a major advocate of independent, black-operated businesses, institutions, and religion.

Elijah Muhammad was born Elijah (or Robert) Poole on October 7, 1897, near Sandersville, Georgia. His parents were ex-slaves who worked as sharecroppers on a cotton plantation; his father was also a Baptist preacher. As a youngster Elijah worked in the fields and on the railroad, but he left home at age 16 to travel and work at odd jobs. He settled in Detroit in 1923, working on a Chevrolet assembly line.

Poole and his two brothers became early disciples of W.D. Fard, the founder of the Nation of Islam. Fard, of mysterious background, appeared in Detroit in 1930, selling silk goods and telling his customers in Detroit's African American ghetto of their ancestral "homeland" across the seas. Soon Fard began holding meetings in homes, and then in rented halls, telling his listeners tales purporting to describe their nonwhite kin in other lands and urging them to emulate these brothers and sisters in such matters as dress and diet. Fard proclaimed Islam the one correct religion for African Americans, denouncing Christianity as the religion of the slavemasters. His meetings became dominated by his bitter denunciations of the white race. Soon Fard announced the opening of the Temple of Islam. It featured much antiwhite invective and embodied an unorthodox form of Islam, but the movement also emphasized African American self-help and education.

Fard disappeared, as mysteriously as he had arrived, in the summer of 1934. The movement he had founded quickly developed several factions, the most important of which was led by Poole, who had become a top lieutenant to Fard and whose name along the way had been changed to Elijah Muhammad. The movement had long had a policy of requiring members to drop their "slave" names.

Settling in Chicago, away from hostile Muslim factions in Detroit, Muhammad built what quickly became the most important center of the movement. Chicago soon featured not only a Temple of Islam, but a newspaper called *Muhammad Speaks,* a University of Islam (actually a private elementary and high school), and several movement-owned apartment houses, grocery stores, and restaurants. Temples were opened in other cities, and farms were purchased so that ritually pure food could be made available to members. The movement was a sharply disciplined one. Members had strict rules to follow regarding eating (various foods, such as pork, were forbidden), smoking and drinking (both banned), dress and appearance (conservative, neat clothing and good grooming were required), and all kinds of personal behavior (drugs, the use of profanity, gambling, listening to music, and dancing were all outlawed).

Muhammad also revised the theology of the movement. Under his system, Fard was proclaimed the earthly incarnation of Allah, the Muslim name for God; (Elijah) Muhammad was his divinely-appointed prophet. Muhammad also taught that blacks constituted the original human beings, but that a mad black scientist named Yakub had created a white beast through genetic manipulation and that whites had been given a temporary dispensation to govern the world. That period, however, was due to end soon; now the time was at hand for blacks to resume their former dominant role. It was understood that violent war would be likely before the transition could be completed. In the meantime, Muhammad advocated an independent nation for African Americans.

In 1942 Muhammad was one of a group of militant African American leaders arrested on charges of sedition, conspiracy, and violation of the draft laws. He was accused of sympathizing with the Japanese during World War II and of encouraging his members to resist the military draft. He had, indeed, argued that all nonwhites are oppressed by whites, and that it made no sense for African Americans to fight those who were victims of white racism as much as they themselves were. Muhammad was certainly no pacifist, but he argued that the only war in which African Americans should participate would be the coming "Battle of Armageddon," in which blacks would reassert their rightful superiority. For his words and actions Muhammad spent four years, from 1942 to 1946, in federal prison at Milan, Michigan.

Factions occasionally withdrew from Muhammad's movement. In the early 1960s Muhammad came to be over-shadowed by the charismatic Malcolm X, leader of the New York Temple. Tensions between Malcolm X and Muham-mad's leadership grew; finally, after Malcolm X commented that John F. Kennedy's assassination was a case of "the chickens coming home to roost," Muhammad suspended him. Shortly thereafter, in 1964, Malcolm X founded his own movement, which moved toward a more orthodox form of Islam. However, Malcolm X was assassinated on February 21, 1965.

Elijah Muhammad died on February 25, 1975. After his death the leadership of his movement passed to his son, Wallace (now Warith) Deen Muhammad. The younger Muhammad renamed the movement the World Community of Al-Islam in the West, and then the American Muslim Mission; he also began to call blacks "Bilalians," after Bilal, who was said to have been an African follower of the prophet Muhammad. Warith Muhammad relaxed the strict dress code, abandoned resistance to military service, en-couraged members to vote and to salute the flag, and even opened the movement to whites. In general, he made the movement much more conventionally Islamic.

Many members were disturbed at the movement's new, moderate direction and withdrew to form more tradi-tionalist splinter groups. The most important of them re-tained the old name, the Nation of Islam, and was led by Louis Farrakhan (born Louis Eugene Walcott of British West Indian parents in 1934). Farrakhan generally retained Elijah Muhammad's ideas and practices, including the strict be-havioral rules. He achieved prominence when he became a major adviser to Jesse Jackson during the latter's presidential campaign in 1984. At that time Farrakhan aroused contro-versy, particularly for his reported death threats directed at Jackson's Jewish critics.

Further Reading

The life and role of Elijah Muhammad are prominently discussed in the first thorough study of the Nation of Islam, C. Eric Lincoln, *The Black Muslims in America* (1961). His own principal work is *Message to the Blackman in America* (1965). Basic information can also be found in Malcolm X and Alex Haley, *The Autobiography of Malcolm X* (1965). Information on Muhammad's life and ideas can be found in a number of books and articles on Black religion in America. See, for example, Henry J. Young, "Elijah Muhammad (1897-1975): Messenger of Allah," *Major Black Religious Leaders Since 1940* (1979). For an interesting interpretation of the role of Fard, see Wallace D. Muhammad, "Self-Government in the New World," in Milton C. Sernett, editor, *Afro-American Religious History: A Documentary Witness* (1985). □

Askia Muhammad Ture

Askia Muhammad Ture (ca. 1443-1538) founded the Askia dynasty of the West African Songhay empire. He extended the conquests of Sunni Ali, promoted **commerce, and increased the political influence of Islam in his state.**

Muhammad's father was a Soninke from the Futa Toro region of modern Senegal. Although his mother was a Songhay, who may have been the sister of Sunni Ali himself, Muhammad was later to be thought of as a "foreign" usurper because of his father's ancestry. Little is known about his early life before his career as a general in Ali's army, but his reign is one of the best-documented in early West African history.

Accession to the Throne

Sunni Ali died in November 1492 and was succeeded by his son, Sunni Baru. Baru, unlike his father, tried com-pletely to ignore Moslem interests when he came to power and thus committed a mistake which threw Moslem support behind Muhammad, then a popular general. Muhammad coalesced his support and met and defeated Baru in April 1493. He declared himself king and took the title of Askia. During the next decade he vigorously eliminated all the survivors of the Sunni line and of its predecessor, the Za. Muhammad was aware of his equivocal position as a usurper, and he sought a new basis of legitimacy in Islam. He assiduously cultivated Moslem support, and within 2 years his throne was so secure that he felt he could risk a long absence from the Sudan.

Muhammad knew that by undertaking a holy pilgrim-age to Mecca he would make a clean break with the "magician-king" tradition of the past and thus further but-tress his support among the growing number of Songhay Moslems. He used the accumulated wealth of Ali's reign to put together an entourage which surely rivaled that of the famous 14th-century Mali king, Mansa Musa. By the time of Muhammad's hajj, however, his arrival in the Near East was not such a novelty, and he failed to make a similar sensa-tion, although he spent and gave out 300,000 pieces of gold.

Completion of the pilgrimage automatically gave Muhammad the honored title of al-Hajj, but he succeeded in obtaining an additional title from the sharif of Mecca, who named him the Caliph of the Western Sudan. This was strictly an honorific title, but it further added to his authority in Songhay.

Political Consolidation

Upon his return to Gao in 1497, the main task facing Muhammad was that of consolidating the vast but tenuous empire left by Sunni Ali. He in fact had to renew many of Ali's conquests militarily. In 1498 he led a force to the west, annexing portions of the Mali empire, and he eventually expanded almost to the Atlantic coast. In the east he started by gaining control of the important trade route to Air in 1501 and finished by conquering for the first time much of Hausaland by 1512. Songhay control of the most distant areas was not, however, longlived. Nevertheless, by about 1516 Muhammad had imposed permanent control over much of what is now the Republic of Mali and the western portion of the Republic of Niger.

During these 2 decades of military campaigns he advanced the professionalization of the army that had been started by Ali and built a stronger navy. The loss of great numbers of men in the campaigns against Mali encouraged him to incorporate even more conquered peoples into his armies in order to reduce the need for levies on his own people, thus allowing agriculture to develop.

Despite his military prowess Muhammad's most important achievements were political. He gave the empire an administration based upon a pyramidal ranking of territories.

Gao was administered directly, but most of the rest of the empire was ruled under four great provinces, each governed by members, or favorites, of the ruling family. Few vassal kings remained in power as they had under Ali, and unity was achieved through the royal family itself. The widely respected military lent stability to this system. Muhammad also introduced a unified system of weights and measures and appointed commerce inspectors, which led to a new era of prosperity within the empire.

Even though Muhammad may have closely embraced Islam for political reasons, he was genuinely interested in Islamic theology, and he generously supported Moslem scholars. He frequently corresponded with North African scholars for legal advice. Nevertheless, he made no attempt to model his government on purely Islamic lines and did not promote any mass conversions. He continued to retain many non-Islamic elements in his court practices, and the mass of rural Songhay people remained non-Moslem.

His Last Years

A general weakness of the Songhay state, as well as many other African states, was the absence of an orderly system of political succession. Muhammad himself was deposed by three of his sons in 1528, when he was old and blind. The eldest of these sons, Musa, took the throne and tried to secure his position by killing his brothers. Muhammad was probably too infirm by this time to pose any threat himself because he was allowed to stay on in his Gao palace. The other brothers were unhappy with the new turn of events, and they deposed Musa in 1531 in favor of a nephew of Muhammad, Muhammad Bengan. This new king promptly exiled his uncle to an island on the Niger River, where he remained until 1537, when another son, Ismail, gained the throne and recalled him. By then Askia Muhammad was ill, and he died the next year. The solid foundations which he had laid for the empire allowed it to survive numerous dynastic struggles for the remainder of the century, only to fall finally to a Moroccan invasion in 1591, which saw the introduction of firearms to the Western Sudan.

Further Reading

There is no full-length biography of Muhammad, but short sketches may be found in Sir Rex Niven, *Nine Great Africans* (1964); Lavinia Dobler and William A. Brown, *Great Rulers of the African Past* (1965); and A.A. Boahen, *Topics in West African History* (1966). Among the general sources are E.W. Bovill, *The Golden Trade of the Moors* (1958; 2d ed. 1968); J. Spencer Trimingham, *A History of Islam in West Africa* (1962); K.M. Panikkar, *The Serpent and the Crescent: A History of the Negro Empires of Western Africa* (1963); and J. O. Hunwick, "Religion and State in the Songhay Empire, 1464-1591," in I. M. Lewis, ed., *Islam in Tropical Africa* (1966). □

Heinrich Melchior Mühlenberg

Heinrich Melchior Mühlenberg (1711-1787) was the German-born clergyman who organized the scattered Lutheran congregations in America into an independent sect.

Heinrich Melchior Mühlenberg was born in Einbech, Germany, on Sept. 6, 1711. He was a Pietist to whom religion was a way of life, not belief in a creed. This concept of religion was brought to America early in the 18th century by groups of German immigrants. Accustomed to a state church in the homeland, these people were at a loss in America, where there were neither ministers nor schoolmasters enough for their small settlements.

Mühlenberg, trained at the University of Halle, was sent to America in 1742 by the Pietist center to minister to the Lutherans in three Pennsylvania congregations. He was 31, energetic, dedicated to the ideals of Pietism, and possessed executive ability and a high degree of common sense. Fortunately, he could preach in three languages, English, German, and Dutch. His three congregations were widely scattered, requiring a hundred miles of traveling each week to serve them, and he even discovered a fourth group. He also discovered that two young impostors, pretending to be ministers, had laid claim to two of these congregations.

In a month's time, Mühlenberg had gotten rid of the impostors and had arranged to teach the children for a full week in each of his four parishes by turn, as there was no schoolmaster in any of these settlements. He had also collected members for a fifth congregation in New Jersey. A long and difficult visit to Georgia, another to groups along the Hudson River, and a missionary trip through Maryland filled many months. His reports back to the Pietist center in Halle brought helpers and funds, as many calls for ministers and schoolmasters continued to come in. He built churches and a schoolhouse, arbitrated church quarrels, and restored order in tangled situations.

After 6 years of energetic and imaginative labors, Mühlenberg felt the time had come to unite all the churches he served into a representative body with power to license and install their own preachers and to handle their common problems. With this in mind, he called a synod in 1748 of pastors and representative laymen from each parish. A common liturgy was adopted and reports given of each church

and parochial school. Thus the Lutherans of America became a sect independent of Old World control.

Meanwhile Mühlenberg had become a permanent resident of America. He had married Anna Marie Weiser, daughter of Johann Conrad Weiser, an intermediary between colonial governors and the Indians, and had founded a distinguished American family. He died in New Providence (now Trappe), Pa., on Oct. 7, 1787.

Further Reading

Biographies of Mühlenberg include William J. Mann, *Life and Times of Henry Melchior Mühlenberg* (1887); Reverend William K. Frick, *Henry Melchior Mühlenberg: "Patriarch of the Lutheran Church in America"* (1902); and Paul A. W. Wallace, *The Muhlenbergs of Pennsylvania* (1950).

Additional Sources

Riforgiato, Leonard R., *Missionary of moderation: Henry Melchior Muhlenberg and the Lutheran Church in English America,* Lewisburg Pa.: Bucknell University Press; London: Associated University Presses, 1980. □

William Augustus Muhlenberg

William Augustus Muhlenberg (1796-1877), American clergyman, was the principal representative in the Protestant Episcopal Church of the reform enthusiasm that swept America during the early 1800s.

Born on Sept. 16, 1796, into a prominent Pennsylvania family, William Augustus Muhlenberg received both secondary and college education at the University of Pennsylvania. Although his ancestors were leaders among Pennsylvania Lutherans, his mother permitted him his preference for the Protestant Episcopal Church. In 1820 he became a priest and assumed a pastorate in Lancaster, Pa.

For the next several years Muhlenberg busied himself with writing hymns and helping found a public school system, but the community was uncongenial. At the age of 30, while visiting relatives at Flushing, N.Y., he agreed to serve for 6 months as minister to their parish. Subsequently he joined with local businessmen to found the first Episcopal church school and became its headmaster. His emphasis on educating the "whole child" foreshadowed progressive education in the 20th century.

Muhlenberg's energies, however, soon sought a new outlet. In 1846, distressed by the fact that only the upper socioeconomic groups appeared in Episcopal congregations, he organized the Church of the Holy Communion in New York City, where both rich and poor could worship. It was a "free" church in the sense that pews were not rented or bought. With its service programs—medical care for the indigent, needlework for unemployed women, and holiday

dinners for the poor—the Church of the Holy Communion was a prototype of the "institutional church" characteristic of the later Social Gospel movement.

The spirit of Muhlenberg's ecumenical ministry was reflected in his journal, the *Evangelical Catholic,* in which he argued the universality of the Church's mission. In 1853 he sought to spread that spirit to his whole denomination by presenting a "Memorial" asking for reform at that year's general convention. Many of his demands were too radical for his day, but his efforts did lead to changes in the prescribed order of service.

While at the Church of the Holy Communion, Muhlenberg launched a drive to fund a charity hospital, St. Luke's. He also sponsored the first Protestant sisterhood, composed of women devoted to nursing. In 1859 he left his congregation to take up duties as full-time pastor of St. Luke's.

After the Civil War, Muhlenberg undertook one last project, the establishment of a Christian socialist community on Long Island. Intended as a refuge for poor families from New York, the community languished until the emphasis shifted to providing a home for elderly men and physically challenged children. There Muhlenberg lived out his last years.

Further Reading

There is little modern scholarship on Muhlenberg's life. The only biography, a brief account marred by tedious digressions on the nature of religious virtue, is William W. Newton, *Dr. Muhlenberg* (1890). William T. Addison's discussion of Muhlenberg in *The Episcopal Church in the United States, 1789-1931* (1951) reflects the faults of its source—Newton. □

John Muir

The writings of John Muir (1838-1914), American naturalist and explorer, are important for their scientific observations and their contributions to the cause of conservation.

John Muir was born in Dunbar, Scotland, on April 21, 1838. If his recollections in *The Story of My Boyhood and Youth* (1913) can be credited, his father was harsh and tyrannical, enforcing piety and industry by frequent whippings. In 1849 the Muirs moved to America, establishing a homestead near Portage, Wis. When Muir's father forbade him to waste daylight hours on reading, he asked and received permission to rise early in order to study. He invented "an early-rising machine" that dumped him out of bed at one o'clock each morning. In 1860 he displayed this and other inventions at the Wisconsin State Fair.

In 1861 Muir entered the University of Wisconsin to study science. Subsequently he tried studying medicine but soon gave it up for various jobs that challenged his inventive skills. In 1867 he made the career decision he never regretted: to give up his own inventions "to study the inventions of God." He set out on the tour described in *A*

Thousand Mile Walk to the Gulf (1916). Actually he went as far as Cuba. In 1868 he traveled to San Francisco and worked on a sheep ranch. Exploring Yosemite Valley occupied much of the next 6 years. On all explorations he kept a journal of scientific and personal observations and also pencil sketches.

In 1880, returning from exploring in Alaska, Muir married Louie Wanda Strentzel. In 1881, after another trip to Alaska, he settled on a fruit ranch near Martinez, Calif. He worked 10 years to make the ranch pay enough to enable him to give it up. Having thus provided permanently for his wife, two daughters, and himself, he turned his full attention to the study of nature. Glaciation particularly interested him, and his work contributed to its explanation.

In 1889 Muir argued in *Century Magazine* that Yosemite Valley should become a national park. The passage of legislation for that in 1890 owed much to his influence. *The Mountains of California* (1893), *Our National Parks* (1901), and his many articles in popular magazines greatly advanced the conservation movement.

Muir's wife died in 1905. During the 10 years Muir survived her, he published four books, including *Stickeen* (1909), which was a much-admired dog story, and *My First Summer in the Sierra* (1911). He died in Los Angeles on Dec. 24, 1914. *John of the Mountain,* drawn from Muir's journal of his 1899 Alaskan expedition, appeared in 1938.

Further Reading

Linnie M. Wolfe, *Son of the Wilderness: The Life of John Muir* (1945), is an admiring biography. Edwin Way Teale, *The Wilderness World of John Muir* (1954), provides an introduction to Muir and a selection of his writings. The development of Muir's ideas and character is surveyed in Herbert F. Smith, *John Muir* (1965). Muir is discussed at length in Norman Foerster, *Nature in American Literature* (1923). □

Sheik Mujibur Rahman

Sheik Mujibur Rahman (1920-1975) was a charismatic leader who organized dissent and rebellion against the British in India, led the Bengalis of East Pakistan in their resistance to the unjust actions of the post-colonial Pakistani government, and finally helped found the independent nation of Bangladesh in 1972.

Sheik Mujibur Rahman (Mujib) was born on March 17, 1920, in Tongipara village in the Gopalganj subdivision of the Faridpur district in the eastern part of the province of Bengal in British India. An extroverted, sports-loving young man, Mujib was well liked by his teachers and friends, but never distinguished himself in his studies. To the dismay of his father, a small landholder (sheik is one of the titles often assumed by the landed gentry) and a government official, Mujib showed the first sign of his future revolutionary leadership by distributing rice from his father's stockpile to the famine-stricken peasantry of his area.

A charismatic leader, Sheik Mujib epitomized anticolonial leadership in the Third World. He organized dissent and rebellion against the British and rose against the injustice and exploitation by the power-wielders in West Pakistan against the Bengali population of East Pakistan. For Sheik Mujib the battle for freedom from exploitation was never-ending. Even after winning independence for Bangladesh from Pakistan, an exploitation-free Bengali society eluded him. When he seemed to be having some success in tiding over the most difficult period of post-liberation history, he was assassinated and his family massacred in a fluke coup staged by a handful of junior officers of the fledgling Bangladesh army.

Seeking Justice for Bengal

Joining the Awami Muslim League Party in 1949 with his mentor, Hussain Shahid Suhrawardy, and later elected its general secretary (1953), Mujib formed a coalition of a number of East-Bengali-based political parties. In the provincial election of 1954 the coalition (Jukta Front) inflicted a landslide defeat on the Muslim League Party, which had been responsible for the creation of Pakistan and was often equated with Pakistan itself. He served in the cabinet of Fazlul Huq until the election was voided and Huq put under house arrest by the central government of Pakistan.

Earlier, in 1952, Mujib had played a leading role in the student movement demanding that Bengali, the language of the majority of the people of the country, be made an official language. The Karachi government of Pakistan subsequently conceded the demand under public pressure, but not before a number of Bengali students had been killed by the police. The 1954 incident reiterated what Mujib had suspected before—that Bengalis were not going to receive their rights without a fight.

In 1957 Mujib became the undisputed leader of the Awami League, defeating Ataur Rahman in the struggle for the party presidency after Maulana Abdul Hamid Khan Bhashani, the founder-president of the party, resigned over foreign policy disagreements with fellow party leader Prime Minister H. S. Suhrawardy. Mujib's stand on the language issue and his later open challenge to certain orders of the martial law projected him as an undaunted fighter for human rights. Sensing that Mujib was organizing another mass movement, the central government ordered his arrest on a trumped up charge of corruption in 1958 when he refused to comply with the new law (Elective Bodies Disqualifications Order of 1958) requiring all Pakistani politicians to refrain from political activity for six years. By now Dhaka jail had become a second home to Mujib; he spent a number of years during the pre-and post-independence periods there.

His extensive grass-roots tour of East Pakistan between 1960 and 1962, defying the martial law ban against political activities, made Bengali appreciate Mujib for his uncompromising commitment to equality and justice. For his increased visibility as a Bengali nationalist and for his defiance of the military, Mujib was again jailed in 1962 for six months. After the promulgation of the second constitution by Ayub Khan the same year, Mujib came out of prison, began preparations for a mass movement against the Ayub regime, and waited for the opportune moment to start it.

A Drive for Bengali Autonomy

The opportunity came after the 1965 Indo-Pakistan war in which East Pakistan, with its Bengali majority, was practically left defenseless by the central government. In November 1965 Mujib worked out a six-point program for enabling his party to secure political and economic justice in a federal system. The scheme involved setting up a federal system in which the power of the central government would be dramatically curtailed; only foreign affairs and defense were to be left as central subjects. The provinces were to have jurisdiction over currencies and fiscal policy, with the stipulation that the federal government was to be provided with requisite revenues for meeting only the requirements of defense and foreign affairs. Mujib's six-point program also demanded that a constitutional provision was to be made providing that separate accounts for foreign exchange earnings and foreign trade could be maintained under the provincial governments. A last point emphasized that a separate military for East Pakistan was to be raised and maintained in order to contribute to national security.

Mujib's program was rejected by the leaders of the Pakistan Democratic Movement (composed of the leaders of the combined opposition party who had unsuccessfully challenged Ayub in the election of 1964) at an all-party meeting in Lahore in February 1966. Undiscouraged, Mujib quickly decided to start a mass movement based on his program. In 1966 he was once more arrested, and in 1967 the central government brought a charge of treason against him for his alleged conspiracy with Indian leaders to make East Pakistan secede from Pakistan. Pressured by a nation-wide mass movement, the Ayub regime withdrew the conspiracy charge against him and others and Mujib was set free unconditionally on March 2, 1969.

Under the Legal Framework Order of Yahya Khan, who took over power from Ayub in 1969, the dates for national and provincial elections were set for December 5 and 17, 1970, respectively. Perhaps the November cyclone which claimed half a million lives and rendered 3 million homeless and the apparent lack of concern for the victims by the Yahya junta changed the course of Pakistan's political history. Mujib's Awami League won a landslide victory—167 seats out of a possible 313—thereby securing an absolute majority in the Assembly. This was unacceptable to West Pakistan's military and political elites. As a result, the Assembly was indefinitely postponed by President Khan on March 1, 1971, two days before the first session was to convene. This infuriated the Bengalis, and a spontaneous mass movement against the military erupted. Mujib tried to turn the rising public anger into a non-violent, civil disobedience movement.

During the three week long movement Mujib ruled East Pakistan as the de facto head of government. A last effort to negotiate a peaceful settlement failed on March 23. On midnight of March 25, 1971, the military crackdown on the Bengali autonomy movement began, resulting in the arrest of Mujib, the round-up of suspected nationalists, and a general disarming of the Bengali police and Bengali members of Pakistan's armed forces. The crackdown, accompanied by senseless killing of Bengali police, soldiers, and civilians, served to harden Bengali resolve to fight the Pakistan military to the last. Although Mujib remained in a West Pakistan prison waiting execution for alleged treason, his name became a symbol of inspiration and strength for Bengalis everywhere.

From Jail to the Presidency

After India's defeat of the Pakistani army in East Pakistan on December 16, 1971, and the transfer of power in Pakistan from the military junta to civilian leaders headed by Zulfikar Bhutto, Mujib was freed. On January 10, 1972, he returned to Bangladesh as a hero. Promptly he took charge of the new nation and inspired the people to rebuild their war-torn country. His initial success as inspirer, as integrator, and as consensus-builder was reflected in the first general election of the new nation in 1973, when his Awami League Party secured another landslide victory.

Earlier in 1972 Mujib, popularly called *Bangabandhu* (friend of Bengal), had given the new nation of Bangladesh its first constitution. It incorporated four basic principles of state policy: democracy, socialism, secularism, and nationalism; together they were called Mujibism. The first step

which Mujib took in order to ensure quick economic recovery was to nationalize all banks and major industries, most of which were owned by West Pakistanis. After the landslide electoral victory in 1973, Mujib became overconfident and complacent about the future, and, to the neglect of national priorities, he began to concentrate on building grass roots bases of his party. This necessitated a drastic redistribution of resources, which segments of the Bengali elite—particularly within the civil and military bureaucracy—found difficult to accept. The consecutive droughts in 1973 and 1974 also created an unmanageable situation for Mujib and his regime, which lacked both the experience of crisis management and the support of the largest food donor of the world—the United States.

The worsening situation was used as the chief justification by Mujib to declare a state of emergency on December 28, 1974, and to amend the constitution in early 1975, transforming Bangladesh's parliamentary system into a presidential one, giving Mujib unlimited power as the new president of the Republic, and establishing a one party system. Armed with this amended constitution Mujib forced the leaders of the opposition parties to join his newly created party—Bangladesh Krishak Sramic Awami League—popularly known as BAKSAL.

Using his new power, Mujib tried to bring fundamental changes to Bangladesh's political, economic, and administrative structure through political centralization and administrative decentralization. But before he could see his dream of ''golden Bengal'' come true, he and most members of his family were assassinated in a pre-dawn coup staged by a handful of junior officers of the Bangladesh army of August 15, 1975, the anniversary of the day India won independence from the British in 1947. The coup leader, Khondar Kar Mushtaque Ahmed, took over the presidency. Two more coups in rapid order brought to power Ziaur Rahman.

Further Reading

Additional information can be found in Zillur R. Khan, *Leadership in the Least Developed Nation: Bangladesh* (1983); *International Who's Who 1972-1973*; and *TIME* 99 (January 17, 1972).

Additional Sources

Sheikh Mujib: a commemorative anthology, London: Radical Asia Books, 1977.
Tribute to Sheikh Mujib: fifth death anniversary, 17 March 1920-15 August 1975, London: Bangabandhu Society, 1980. □

Shirley Muldowney

Drag racer Shirley Muldowney (born ca. 1940) was the first woman to break through in that sport, making her virtually a household name in the 1970s on par with daredevil motorcycle-jumper Evil Knievel.

Shirley Muldowney was the first woman of drag racing, a certifiably macho sport that entails placing a driver inside a specially constructed 20-plus-foot four-wheeled cage with an engine underneath. Speeds can reach 250 miles an hour. Within the National Hot Rod Association's Top Fuel classification in which Muldowney achieved most of her wins, the car's engine is powered by nitromethane and is geared to burn out after a quarter-mile strip, the distance of a match. Her male competitors liked to assert the woman driver had an unfair advantage because of her weight, which hovered just above 100. Buying and maintaining such vehicles is both expensive and risky, but more dangerous are the physical hazards that drag racing presents, and Muldowney came close to becoming a martyr for the sport in 1984 when she endured a horrible accident. Undaunted, she returned to the sport two years later.

Diminutive But Determined

Muldowney inherited her challenging nature from her father, a former prizefighter. She was born around 1940 to Belgium "Tex Rock" Benedict Roque, a cab driver; her mother Mae worked in a laundry in Schenectady, New York, where she and her older sister grew up. When Muldowney, who was small for her age, became the victim of schoolyard bullies, her father instructed her: "Here's what you do: You pick up a board, you pick up a pipe, you pick up a brick, and you part their hair with it," Mae Muldowney recalled in an interview with *Sports Illustrated*'s Sam Moses. The toughness ingrained in Shirley by her father turned to rebelliousness in her teenage years; she would

regularly sneak out of the house in her pajamas to attend informal drag racing heats with her boyfriend, Jack Muldowney.

At the age of sixteen—the year she started to drive as well—Muldowney married her boyfriend and quit school. A son, John, followed two years later. During this period she began drag racing herself in a 1940 Ford her husband had fitted with a Cadillac engine. "I'd say the first time I ever took my life in my own hands and got away with it was when I really appreciated what I thought I was capable of," she told Moses. She and her husband entered drag racing competitions for fun, first with stock cars and later the Funny Car, another classification in the NHRA denoting a fiberglass body. "I went racing because I didn't dig having the cleanest wash on the block," she told Bruce Newman in *Sports Illustrated*. "After a few years, Jack couldn't bring himself to tour anymore. So one night I just put my Funny Car on the trailer and left."

Began Winning Top Fuel Heats

In 1971, Muldowney met Connie Kalitta, a racer and race-car builder. It was the start of a tempestuous seven-year relationship which culminated in Muldowney winning the 1977 National Hot Rod Association Top Fuel championship after her last competitor of the day couldn't start his car; by then she had switched over to the more risky Top Fuel division. Muldowney and Kalitta would also race together, and she was billed as "Cha Cha" Muldowney, which she quickly dropped after the romantic and professional partnership ended, admitting later that she always hated the nickname. During this decade she became one of the most popular drivers on the circuit—with the fans. Her hot pink car, pink cowboy boots, and diminutive stature attracted mostly positive attention, but her son John (who became a member of her crew when he was in his early teens) did assault a male heckler once; the police took John and Muldowney's mechanic, Rahn Tobler, away in handcuffs. "Shirley, crying, had to use volunteers to rebuild her motor for the semifinal," recalled Moses in *Sports Illustrated*. She won the race. "I do not rattle on the line," she said of that day. "I simply *do not rattle.*"

Her son had joined her team in part because Muldowney had a difficult time putting together a crew. "I always got the mechanics that nobody else wanted, because it was 'degrading to work for the broad,'" she told Moses. Eventually Rahn Tobler, who had been named Mechanic of the Year by one of the race-sponsoring companies, joined her crew and became her head mechanic. Chauvinistic attitudes prevailed in other areas as well. Muldowney found it nearly impossible to attract a sponsor for a time, until she began taking home first-place trophies, and her fellow drivers both respected and derided her. "That's why I paint that racecar pink," she explained to *Sports Illustrated* in 1981. "It isn't *just* to rub them, but if it does, fine. That's the way I feel."

Hollywood Interested in Life Story

By 1983 Muldowney had won three National Hot Rod Association championships and 17 other national competitions. That same year, *Heart Like a Wheel,* a film biography of her life through 1977, debuted. Actress Bonnie Bedelia received an Academy Award nomination for her performance; Beau Bridges played Connie Kalitta. Her rivals on the Top Fuel circuit were Richard Tharp and Don "Big Daddy" Garlits, a veteran who broke the 200-mile-per-hour barrier in the 1960s. Until that point, Muldowney's most serious brush with danger was the 1973 incident in which her car caught fire after the motor exploded, and 14-year-old John was witness to the accident. Fortunately, she was wearing protective goggles and a helmet, but when she climbed out of the car, her helmet was aflame, her eyelids singed together, and the goggles had seared circles around her eyes.

Muldowney's most terrifying brush with death came at the Sanair Speedway near Montreal, Canada, in the summer of 1984. As she completed a run, her front tire tube snapped, locked the wheels, and sent both car and driver into a spinout and tumble. The crash resulted in shattered bones in her legs, a fractured pelvis, two broken hands, and three broken fingers. She had been in a roll cage, saving her from death by ejection, but the car had rolled 600 feet and it took doctors six hours with wire brushes to clean the dirt and grease out of her skin before they could operate. Muldowney remained in Montreal two months, then returned home to suburban Detroit, where she was then living. Her system could not tolerate most painkillers, even morphine, and after several tries doctors were finally able to prescribe something that could alleviate her misery. More pain and challenge came with the long process of rehabilitation, and she needed five more operations, including a skin graft. Tobler, now her boyfriend as well as her mechanic, became her round-the-clock nurse too.

Only six months after the crash, Muldowney had already come to grips with her career and what had happened in Montreal—and decided she wanted to race again. By early 1986, she was back on the Top Fuel circuit, and at a press conference before her first meet, the initial question from reporters was "Why?" *Sports Illustrated* reported that Muldowney answered simply, "A lot of reasons. I missed my friends, I missed my job, I missed the life-style, I needed the money, it was what I did best." She admitted one of the most difficult consequences of the crash was having to give away 60 pairs of high heels, a particular passion of hers, but impractical now since one leg was slightly shorter than the other. She answered almost 5,000 get-well letters, and was touched that archrival Garlits offered sympathy as well as financial help.

Excited as a New Era Entered

That press conference marked the return of Muldowney to the sport at the Firebird International Speedway near Phoenix, Arizona. Her near-disaster had ushered a new, more safety-conscious era in drag racing with a new tire design. Her new car, like all dragsters, now had a retaining groove on the front wheels. This vehicle, which was designed by Tobler and John Muldowney, also had a larger-than-usual clutch pedal that Muldowney could operate even with a disabled ankle that could not bend.

Finally, she also changed her trademark color, replacing the hot pink with a vivid purple.

Sadly, her career failed to take off again. Mechanical problems plagued her vehicle, and even enlisting the help of archrival Don Garlits as a consultant did not help. Losing races meant a loss of sponsorship, and without that a racer could not come up with the $1 million needed to maintain the car. By 1989, wrote *Sports Illustrated's* J. E. Vader, "the most important piece of equipment on the dragster isn't the engine or the supercharger—or even the driver—but the computer." The end result was that drivers became symbolic personalities associated with "their" winning car; it also made it easier for telegenic women to break into the sport. Muldowney reflected on this change in the interview with Vader in *Sports Illustrated.* "I'm a bit of a toughie, and I had to be in the early days or I would not have survived. I like to think I made it easier for other ladies, but maybe I made it too easy, because now they license people who simply did not earn it."

Further Reading

New York Times, April 1, 1976, p. 38.
Newsweek, February 17, 1986, p. 8.
Sports Illustrated, July 18, 1977, p. 26; June 22, 1981, p. 71; February 10, 1986, p. 90; September 4, 1989, p. 22. □

Hermann Joseph Muller

The American geneticist Hermann Joseph Muller (1890-1967) was the first to induce mutations in an organism by severe x-ray treatment.

Hermann J. Muller was born in New York City on Dec. 21, 1890. His father died before Hermann was 10 years old, but he had already been imbued by his father with a sense of the grandeur of evolution and a sympathy for oppressed people. After graduation from Morris High School in the Bronx, he entered Columbia University. After receiving a master's degree there in 1911, he continued his studies at the Medical School of Cornell University for a year, returning to Columbia University for his doctorate, which he received in 1916.

At Columbia University Muller came under the influence of Thomas Hunt Morgan, who had gathered together a group of young researchers to study genetic inheritance in fruit flies (*Drosophila melanogaster*). Muller worked with this group in 1910 and discovered a fly mutant which established the reality of the "M," or fourth, chromosome of the fruit fly. In 1915 Muller joined the biology department of Rice Institute, but 3 years later he returned to Columbia for 2 years of research and teaching. In 1920 he went to the University of Texas.

In 1926 Muller reported at the Sixth International Congress of Genetics in Berlin that he had succeeded in jolting the genes in the chromosomes of the fruit fly; that is, his x-rays had broken them apart and rearranged them, resulting

in an increase in the mutation rate 150-fold. He had thus artificially accelerated the evolutionary process. Controlled mutation was now a fact, and overnight, at the age of 36, Muller became famous. For this classic experiment he was awarded the Nobel Prize in medicine in 1946. In 1945 Muller was called to Indiana University in Bloomington to become distinguished service professor of zoology. He remained there until his death.

Muller had a strong social awareness and believed that his own researches and the work of other scientists should be used to improve the genetic composition of mankind as well as the general living conditions of all people. He held that the ultimate objective of his own work was "the control of the evolution of man by man himself." After the severe depression that struck the United States in 1929, Muller, who had become sympathetic with some form of socialism, left Texas to work in Germany. But having seen the rise of Nazism, he went on to the Soviet Union in 1933. He was given a laboratory in the Institute of Genetics in Moscow, where he worked as senior geneticist for almost 4 years. However, Trofim Lysenko, who was violently opposed to the Morgan theory of the gene and preached the Lamarckian view of the inheritance of acquired characters, was able to win the political favor of Stalin, and his theory became the official doctrine of heredity in Russia. Those who taught and did research along the lines of Morgan's school of genetics were dismissed or harassed. Muller became disillusioned, left the country, and denounced Russian communism.

In 1955, together with Albert Einstein and other famous scientists, he signed an appeal to all countries to forswear war in view of the danger that the hydrogen bomb would threaten the health of future generations and even the existence of mankind. He campaigned vigorously against the use of nuclear bomb tests because of the harmful mutations that would result. Muller was also interested in the quality of man's life in the future and went so far as to urge the freezing of sperm of gifted men for use after their death in artificial insemination. He fought for the promotion of sperm banks, an idea that provoked bitter criticism.

Between 1955 and 1959 Muller served as president of the American Humanist Association and was president also of the newly launched American Society of Human Genetics. He was a member of many scientific societies as well as of the American Philosophical Society. Muller died of a heart ailment on April 5, 1967.

Further Reading

Muller's unpublished autobiographical notes, written in 1936, are now in the Lilly Rare Books Library of Indiana University. A popular account of his life and achievements is in Bernard Jaffe, *Men of Science in America* (1944; rev. ed. 1958). ☐

Johannes Peter Müller

The German medical scientist Johannes Peter Müller (1801-1858) made important contributions to several branches of medicine, including anatomy, physiology, embryology, and pathology.

Johannes Müller the son of a shoemaker, was born in Coblenz, Rhineland-Palatinate, on July 14, 1801. He went to school in Coblenz before studying medicine at the University of Bonn from 1819 until 1822. At Bonn he was influenced by *Naturphilosophie,* including the belief that the smallest part of nature reflected grand themes running through the whole of creation. After taking his degree at Bonn, he spent 18 months in Berlin studying for the state medical examination. Although he never gave up his belief in a purposeful universe and the large generalizations of *Naturphilosophie,* he increasingly taught that experimental research was the way forward in medicine.

From 1824 until 1833 Müller taught medicine at Bonn, reaching the rank of professor in 1830. There his main achievements were in embryology and physiology. In 1825 he discovered the duct named after him and went on to make a pioneer study of the development of the genital glands in the embryo. He put forward a theory of color vision based on the study of a variety of animals and also investigated the way in which different nerves functioned.

In 1833 Müller became professor of anatomy and physiology and director of the Museum of Comparative Anatomy at the University of Berlin. He built up a famous school, and his students dominated German medical science in the second half of the 19th century. In 1833 Müller published the

their superconducting properties in the early 1980s, which led to the discovery that these compounds superconduct at record high temperatures.

K. Alex Müller was born on April 20, 1927, in Basle, Switzerland. His family was fairly wealthy (his grandfather founded a chocolate company) and could afford to entertain Müller's teen-aged interests in radio and electronics. The first years of his life were spent with his parents in Salzburg, Austria, where his father studied music. He and his mother later moved to Dornach, near his birthplace, to the home of his grandparents; and from there they moved to Lugano, the Italian-speaking part of Switzerland. Müller soon became bilingual. When his mother, Irma, died in 1938, Müller was only eleven. He and his father, Paul, lived in the eastern part of Switzerland, in Schiers, where he earned his secondary education at the Evangelical College. He arrived just before the start of World War II and left just after it ended. He assumed he would study electrical engineering after high school, but a high school physics teacher at Evangelical College recognized his talents and encouraged him to pursue physics instead. After completing his military service in the Swiss Army, he entered the Physics and Mathematics Department of the Swiss Federal Institute of Technology (ETH) in Zurich. He seriously considered changing to electrical engineering but was talked out of it. He received his doctorate in 1958.

From 1959 to 1963 Müller worked for the Battelle Memorial Institute in Geneva and was a lecturer at the University of Geneva where he was given the title of professor in 1970. In 1963 he became a research staff member at the IBM Zurich Research Laboratory, Ruschlikon. He spent the next 15 years investigating the properties of perovskites—compounds consisting of two different metal atoms and three oxygen atoms. His work enhanced his reputation and he took over as head of the laboratory's physics department in 1972. He was appointed an IBM fellow in 1982, allowing him the freedom to work on whatever projects he wished. During an 18-month sabbatical in the United States ending in 1980, Müller started working in the field in which he was to become famous, solid-state physics and superconductivity. He became particularly interested in a class of compounds known as ceramics: glass-like compounds of oxygen and at least one metallic element.

Some metals, as well as a fair number of compounds, show a dramatic change in the way they conduct electricity when they are cooled to very low temperatures. These materials in fact lose all resistance to the flow of electricity if they are cooled to a low enough temperature. Discovered in 1911, the phenomena of superconductivity had occupied the labors of physicists for decades. However, little progress was made in discovering a material that would superconduct at a temperature above 23 K (23 degrees above absolute zero, or 250 degrees below zero on the Centigrade scale). Such cold temperatures make practical applications of superconductivity difficult to implement.

Müller was convinced that higher temperature superconductors could be discovered but the trick was to figure

first part of his *Manual of Human Physiology*. It became the leading textbook on its subject and was revised and republished many times. At Berlin he continued his research on nerve physiology but also undertook extensive investigations in comparative anatomy, writing large works on fishes and echinoderms. He was one of the first to make extensive use of the microscope in pathology, and in 1838 he published a volume on the pathology of tumors. In 1834 he had founded the journal known as *Müller's Archiv*.

Müller was rector of the University of Berlin during the revolutionary year of 1848, and the strain caused by the political upheavals impaired his health. In 1855 he was rescued from a sinking ship on a return voyage from Norway. He died in Berlin on March 28, 1858, without ever fully recovering from the shock of these two events.

Further Reading

A short account of Müller's life is in Henry E. Sigerist, *The Great Doctors: A Biographical History of Medicine* (1932). □

Karl Alexander Müller

The Swiss-born solid-state physicist Karl Alexander Müller (born 1927) spent years at the IBM Zurich Research Laboratory studying the properties of a class of compounds called perovskites. In collaboration with J. Georg Bednorz, he began to examine

out which materials to test. Although the perovskites that he had been working with for years normally did not conduct electricity well, he reasoned that they could be induced to superconduct by varying the composition of the perovskites. In addition, a few other similar compounds had demonstrated superconductivity, but all these compounds began to superconduct at temperatures far below the record high of 23 K. Müller thought that perovskites containing the element nickel might superconduct at higher temperatures. In mid-summer 1983 he enlisted the aid of J. Georg Bednorz, a former student and now his colleague at IBM, in preparing samples of the compounds. The relationship Müller and Bednorz had was one of opposites attracting. Müller, called "a visionary theoretician, a bright, irascible Swiss physicist who liked to work alone at home," complemented his German counterpart, who was a skilled researcher and enjoyed spending long hours at the laboratory. Bednorz worked in his spare time and in the evenings making sample after sample, slightly altering the ratios of the elements in each sample. No sign of superconductivity was found in any of the samples. The project almost ended, partly because the equipment used for the measurements of conductivity was borrowed from another team, which meant that Bednorz could test for superconductivity only in the evening. The equipment was also out of date. In late 1985 colleagues at IBM agreed to let Bednorz use new automatic equipment during normal working hours.

At this time they switched from nickel-containing samples to ones that contained copper. Soon after, Bednorz read about the work of a team of French physicists who reported that a perovskite-type compound consisting of barium (Ba), lanthanum (La), copper (Cu), and Oxygen (O) showed metallic-like electrical conductivity at room temperature. In January 1986 Bednorz began preparing samples of the Ba-La-Cu oxide, altering the ratios of the various elements in each sample. The samples showed superconductivity occurring at 35 K, shattering the old record by contemporary standards.

Müller knew that there had been many unsupported claims for superconductivity at "high" temperatures (35 K is high in this context). Many more tests were done to make sure that the results were correct. By the spring of 1986 they were confident of their result, but they did not have the equipment necessary to test the magnetic properties of their sample, which would demonstrate beyond question that their compound was superconducting. They decided to publish their results anyway using the cautionary title "Possible High [Transition Temperature] Superconductivity in the Ba-La-Cu-O System." Their article appeared in September 1986, the same month they were able to confirm the sample's magnetic properties. By November two teams of physicists confirmed that their sample became superconducting at 35 K. After presenting these findings at the Materials Research Society meeting in Boston on December 5, 1986, the world was aware that the Müller-Bednorz 2-1-4 structure (so called due to the arrangement of the perovskite-like crystal arrangement) was the superconductor. Müller and Bednorz had also begun work on a 1-2-3 compound of yttrium, barium, and copper oxide, which also proved to be a superconductor.

Their discovery, while at first met with skepticism, ignited a flurry of research into similar compounds. Physicists realized that this new class of superconducting compounds brought them a step closer to large-scale practical applications, which had been their dream since 1911. With such impressive developments, a special session on the new superconductors took place in March of 1987 at the meeting of the American Physical Society in New York. The session became historic because of the unprecedented numbers of those attending. Therefore, it has often been referred to as the "Woodstock of physics." Their findings of superconductivity at higher temperatures were phenomenal and their achievement spread rapidly among physicists and the world. Other experiments continued to confirm their results. Müller and Bednorz were awarded the Nobel Prize in October 1987 for their discovery of new superconducting materials.

After his Nobel Prize, Müller continued to work on superconductivity ceramics at his IBM lab. In addition to his Nobel Prize, Müller was also awarded the Marcel-Benoist Prize (1986), the Thirteenth Fritz London Memorial Award, the Dannie Heineman Prize, the Robert Wichard Pohl Prize of the German Physical Society (1987), the Hewlett-Packard Europhysics Prize, the American Physical Society International Prize for New Materials Research, the Minnie Rosen Award (1988), and the Special Tsukuba Award (1989). He earned honorary degrees from the University of Geneva, Switzerland, the Technical University of Munich, Germany, and Universita degli Studi di Pavia, Italy (1987); University of Leuven, Belgium, Boston University, USA, Tel Aviv, University, Israel, and the Technical University of Darmstadt, Germany (1988); University of Nice, France, and Universida Politecnica, Madrid, Spain (1989); and the University of Bochum, Germany and Universita degli Studi di Roma, Italy (1990). He was elected as a Foreign Associate Member of the Academy of Sciences in the United States in 1989. Müller married Ingeborg Marie Louise Winkler in 1956. They have two children: Eric, a dentist, and Silvia, a kindergarten teacher.

Further Reading

Biographical works on Müller include profiles in *Notable Twentieth-Century Scientist,* Volume 3 (1995), *Physics 1981-90 Nobel Lectures](1993),* and *The Nobel Prize Winners: Physics,* Volume 3, 1968-1988 (1989). Works that include a discussion of Müller include Randy Simon and Andrew Smith's *Superconductors: Conquering Technology's New Frontier* (1988), Robert Hazen's *The Breakthrough: The Race for the Superconductor* (1988), and John Langone's *Superconductivity: The New Alchemy* (1989). See also *Science* (October 23, 1987), *Physics Today* (December 1987), and Müller's Nobel lecture (1987). □

Paul Hermann Müller

The Swiss chemist Paul Hermann Müller (1899-1965) is noted for his discovery of the insecticidal powers of DDT.

Paul Müller was born on Jan. 12, 1899, at Olten, Switzerland, the son of an official of the Swiss Federal Railways. The family soon moved to Basel. Encouraged by his father, Müller performed experiments at home with chemicals bought at a local pharmacy. After a brief spell as a laboratory technician Müller entered Basel University. In 1925 he was awarded a doctorate for a thesis on the chemical and electrochemical oxidation of a substance known as asymmetrical *m-xylidine* and some of its derivatives. That year he joined the firm of J.R. Geigy as research chemist.

Müller's first research interest at Geigy was in the field of leather tanning, and he was able to develop several synthetic tans with good fastness to light. He also developed an interest in the conservation of hides and in the associated problem of rendering wool resistant to attack by moths. Although the firm had by this time considerable expertise in mothproofing textiles on an industrial scale, Müller believed that an alternative approach to the problem was necessary. Hitherto the insecticides used had been oral poisons. Müller proposed a search for insecticides that could act by mere contact, and for this he did his own biological testing, which was unusual for a chemist. Realizing that compounds with a—CCl_3 group (for example, chloroform) were often lethal to insects, he examined several of these until, in 1939, he came to DDT (dichlorodiphenyltrichloroethane), which, although known since 1873, was now revealed as a far more effective contact insecticide than any other and was easily manufactured.

This discovery came at a crucial moment in history. DDT, with its lethal action on malaria-carrying mosquitoes, played a vital role in maintaining the health of the Allied armies in the Far East. As a routine precaution, the shirts of British and United States troops were impregnated with DDT. Its first use on a large scale was at Naples in 1943, when a typhus epidemic was brought under control within 3 weeks. Today, discovery of pesticide residues in animal bodies has revealed a toxic hazard unsuspected in Müller's day, and controls in the use of DDT and other pesticides are being demanded.

For his discovery Müller received the Nobel Prize for physiology or medicine in 1948. In 1962 he was given an honorary doctorate at Thessalonica (Salonika) in recognition of the valuable effects of DDT in the Mediterranean area.

Müller became deputy chairman of Geigy and assistant research director of its pesticides division. He died in October, 1965.

Further Reading

A brief biographical sketch of Müller is in H. Schück and others, *Nobel: The Man and His Prizes* (trans. 1951; 2d rev. ed. 1962), and Eduard Farber, *Great Chemists* (1961). □

Martin Brian Mulroney

Martin Brian Mulroney (born 1939) revolutionized Canadian politics, leading his Conservative party to its first consecutive election victories (1984, 1988) since early in the 20th century and breaking the Liberal stranglehold on the province of Quebec. As prime minister of Canada, he was responsible for a major Canada-U.S. free trade agreement and for sweeping proposals to change the national constitution.

Martin Brian Mulroney was born March 20, 1939, at Baie Comeau, Quebec, a town created by Colonel Robert McCormick of the *Chicago Tribune* to supply his papers with newsprint. Mulroney's father, Ben an electrician and later a foreman in the McCormick paper mill, was one of the town's pioneers in the 1930s. Ben Mulroney and his wife, Irene, were descended from Irish immigrants to Canada. Brian was the eldest son of their six children and the third child born. Ben had big dreams for his family, and Brian had all of his father's drive, ambition, determination, and intense loyalty to family and friends.

Mulroney grew up excelling as a public speaker in both French and English. Receiving his education at Catholic schools in Baie Comeau until the tenth grade, Mulroney

then left home to attend St. Thomas High School in Chatham, New Brunswick. Mulroney was a good student and talented athlete. He had a gift for singing as well, and was often asked by Robert McCormick to perform at the company's social affairs. From there, at the age of 16, he moved farther east to St. Francis Xavier University in Antigonish, Nova Scotia. He was not only a student of political science, but a student of politics as well. He was an active member of the Conservative party both on the campus and at the national student level. In 1956, he volunteered to help in the successful provincial campaign of Robert Stanfield, the conservative Nova Scotia premier who eventually replaced John Diefenbaker as Canada's national leader. Mulroney was only 17 at the time, but made quite an impact on the older campaign workers for Stanfield. Said Finlay MacDonald in *Maclean's,* "One word described my first impression of Brian Mulroney—irrepressible. He was enthusiastic, charming and dogged—a doggedness he could always back up with performance. If you told him, for example, to tie a pink ribbon to a dog's tail, it was tied—and in the right spot." Mulroney was soon given such responsibilities as making speeches and writing radio commercials, duties not normally assigned to teenagers. When asked why he became a Tory, he recalled that the other party, the Liberals, were just no fun. They took themselves too seriously. Even as a child, recalled a boyhood friend, Wilbur Touchie, Mulroney had political aspirations, always saying he wanted to be a Prime Minister one day. He was well on his way.

By 1961 Mulroney was back in Quebec as a law student at Laval University after a year at Dalhousie University in Halifax, Nova Scotia. In 1964 he went to work at Montreal's largest law firm, specializing in labor matters. Still very thin (his nickname was "Bones"), eager to please, obviously effective at bringing people together, he was quickly well-connected in Quebec business and political circles. Mulroney was also becoming one of the key Conservative political organizers and fund-raisers in the province. He was on the rise.

Mulroney also served as the vice-chair of "Youth for Dief" in Diefenbaker's 1956 campaign. When Diefenbaker won the Prime Minister spot in 1957, the two remained in touch, with Diefenbaker calling and visiting Mulroney on campus. Students who weren't sure whether to believe the relationship between the two was indeed real, changed their minds quickly when Diefenbaker was spotted eating lunch with Mulroney in the cafeteria.

Mulroney always believed in the value and strength of friendships, perhaps as a result of his alliance with Diefenbaker, relying on them for support. He maintained his connections from St. Francis Xavier and expanded his circle of contacts once he reached Laval. Many of the people he met along his political journey were rewarded with positions in his government when he reached power.

Continuing to build friendships and influence people, Mulroney's performance with Montreal's Howard Cate Ogilvy law firm propelled him into the labor lawyer spotlight; and it was here where his affinity for late-night deal-making started to put down the groundwork for his future

political career. After fighting imposing cases in 1966, Mulroney was getting noticed by political leaders who wanted to work with him.

First Try for Party Leadership

The 1970s brought public attention. Mulroney was a tough-minded and articulate member of the Cliche Commission on violence and corruption in the construction industry in 1974-1975. In 1976, building on that experience, he declared for the vacant leadership of the national Conservative party. It was too soon. His conscious efforts to imitate the appeal and oratory of fellow Irishman John F. Kennedy fell flat, and both the delegates and political professionals doubted that he had sufficient substance. For all that, "the boy from Baie Comeau" finished in a solid third place behind the eventual winner, Joe Clark. All the characteristics that made him likable among his friends—loyalty, industry, generosity—didn't help his politics. He was instead perceived as too well-packaged, slick, manipulative, free-spending, thin-skinned, and of course, inexperienced.

It was not easy for Mulroney to accept defeat. He was frequently depressed in the years that followed, drinking often and putting a strain on his marriage. Furthermore, he was not above undermining Clark's leadership from his still powerful position within the party. He became vice-president of the Iron Ore Company of Canada in 1976, and president in 1977. Iron Ore was an American branch plant not unlike Colonel McCormick's operation in Baie Comeau, and Mulroney had the diplomatic and labor relations talents to run it skillfully. He demonstrated that skill in deftly closing down the company's operations in Schefferville, Quebec, in 1983.

Mulroney had his eye on more than Schefferville. Clark had decided to put his position as party chief on the line in another leadership contest. Mulroney could not believe his good luck; Clark would almost certainly have won the next election, despite widespread criticism from within his own ranks. Learning from his 1976 defeat, Mulroney operated a careful, low-key campaign. On the final ballot, June 11, 1983, there were only two candidates left; Mulroney defeated Clark by a narrow but clear margin. Mulroney now made his first bid for electoral office, becoming the member for Central Nova (Nova Scotia) in August 1983 and assuming the role of leader of the opposition in Parliament. He made a measured case against the controversial policies of longtime prime minister Pierre Elliott Trudeau, which he said had needlessly divided Canadians and brought Canadian-American relations to their lowest state in decades. Along the way, he took a brave stand for minority French language rights in the province of Manitoba. That was his finest hour.

Role as Prime Minister

Trudeau retired in 1984. His successor, John Turner, promptly called an election after only nine days in office, ensuring that he would be one of the shortest-lived leaders in Canadian history. Mulroney proved a brilliant campaigner, capitalizing on Trudeau's unpopularity and pinning Turner down on the Liberals' record of handing out the best jobs to their friends. The Conservatives took the most seats in Canadian parliamentary history, 211 out of a total of 282. Mulroney, moreover, seized Quebec from the Liberals, beating his rival 28,208 votes to 9,640. He had, since a young man, been arguing that the Conservatives must succeed in his mostly French-speaking and traditionally Liberal home province if they were to achieve lasting power. He took what seemed like a big chance by running in Manicouagan, the riding (election district) that contained Baie Comeau; his Conservatives won not only there but in 58 of Quebec's 75 constituencies. Mulroney was elected as Canada's Prime Minister on September 4, 1984.

It was easier to get power than to govern. Within days, Mulroney was in President Ronald Reagan's Washington, promising to dismantle Trudeau's controversial policies on energy and investment. Canadians wanted better relations with the Americans, but they soon were criticizing Mulroney for being in Reagan's "hip pocket." In a similar vein, the new prime minister took strong action to sweeten the poisoned atmosphere between the federal government in Ottawa and the provinces, signing important agreements with the energy-producing regions in 1985. That helped to ease the tension, but critics wondered if Mulroney had simply opened up a federal candy store to dispense power to the provinces. As part of an effort to reduce the federal government's huge deficit, Mulroney announced the partial de-indexing of old age pensions and family allowances. The outcry was so great, however, that he had to back down. It was a crucial early mistake. He appeared weak and indecisive to many. Others would never forgive him for his betrayal of what he had once called a sacred trust. Canadians, indeed, were finding that they did not like or have respect for their leader, whose high living and high sounding platitudes had begun to grate already. By the end of 1985, his first full year in power, 60 percent of Canadians thought Mulroney had not kept his promises. After two years in office, the same number wanted another prime minister.

Mulroney persevered in the face of growing unpopularity, demonstrating a particular ability to keep his own members of Parliament on his side. One of his goals had been to win Quebec over to the 1982 Canadian constitution, and in 1987 that apparently was accomplished with the Meech Lake Accord, which proposed new powers for all the provinces. This was naturally popular in provincial capitals, and it seemed accepted throughout the country, and it certainly was in Quebec. Mulroney was the only prime minister able to get all premiers to sign a constitutional accord—three times—but was still unable to pass it through. In 1987, too, an important agreement was reached between Canada and the United States; the Free Trade Agreement was signed by Mulroney and Reagan on January 2, 1988. The prime minister made the agreement the centerpiece of a campaign for reelection. On November 21, 1988, he was returned to power, having made a magical comeback from disastrously low personal and party popularity ratings, outdoing his Liberal party opponent 33,730 votes to 5,994. Free trade, getting ever closer to the United States, was a deeply divisive issue, but Mulroney was able to convince enough Canadians of his case to win a solid par-

liamentary majority. No one doubted that 1988 was his victory.

Mulroney did not have much time to savour it. Support plummeted again, this time to historic new lows. He introduced a detested new goods and services tax, indulged shamelessly in the patronage he had so criticized, and aligned his government unquestioningly with the foreign policy aims of the United States. The Meech Lake Accord, still unratified by two provinces, blew up in an angry round of meetings in the summer of 1990, leading Quebec to make louder noises than ever before about separation from the rest of Canada. There were failures enough to go around—of policy, of vision, of generosity—but Canadians kept returning to the man himself, a man seen as too obsessed by power and its exercise to be interested in anything else.

In 1992 the Charlottetown accord was presented to the polls, touting "something for everyone," *The Economist* reported. Instead of asking voters if Canada should remain unified or break off into self-governing units, it asked that they approve of a constitutional deal devised by Mulroney. In it, he tried to appease the smaller issues in order to get voters to believe that their interests and concerns were being addressed. Each group wanted its individual claims recognized. As a result, the new constitutional order wasn't particularly concerned with larger issues, such as freedom as speech. Since Mulroney's popularity had sunk to extremely low levels, instead of a pact that could make everyone happy, most everyone hated it because they weren't happy with their leader in the first place. Voters turned it down, and Mulroney's campaign for the accord got him twice as many no votes as yes votes in a popularity survey conducted soon after the vote.

Mulroney Steps Down

Signing the first trade agreement with President Reagan and the United States led to larger agenda in 1992. On December 17 Mulroney signed NAFTA, the North American Free Trade Agreement, with the United States and Mexico. Presidents Bush and Salinas, along with Prime Minister Mulroney, felt that the agreement would eliminate most trade and investment barriers among the three countries for the next 15 years. When George Bush signed NAFTA, he was in the last days of his presidency, having lost the 1992 election to Bill Clinton. Clinton assured Mulroney he would not renegotiate any part of the agreement without him during Clinton's scheduled trip to Mexico. Mulroney, who was fishing buddies with Bush, hoped for little change in the generally warm rapport between the neighboring countries and governments.

Mulroney took much heat from Canadians for his attraction to controversial, unpopular issues and his attempts to persuade the people that his policies would be for their own good. Few were pleased when following the Free Trade Agreement, statistics indicated a loss of 130,000 jobs and consistently rising unemployment rates. His Goods and Services Tax, which replaced a hidden manufacturers' sales tax was deemed "political suicide" by Diane Francis in *Maclean's*. Not since 1990 had Mulroney's approval ratings passed 20 percent, and on February 24, 1993, Brian Mulroney announced that he would be stepping down as Canada's 18th prime minister after his party chose a successor in mid-June of that year. The party settled on Kim Campbell, a former litigation lawyer and political philosophy teacher who was Canada's first female defense minister.

A commentary by Hershell Erzin published in *Maclean's* soon after Mulroney's announcement said that he "gave good ideas a bad name." While Mulroney acted earnestly to help Canada change for the better and keep up with the rest of the world, the issues he took on were not satisfactorily addressed and the people could not successfully adapt to the changes. In addition, Erzin noted, he wavered on policy issues, often contradicting himself. Still, Mulroney maintained that he was pleased with his life and with what he tried to do for his country. He felt that even when he stepped down that the Conservative party was in good shape and the country was improving. He took on quarrelsome causes and essentially reinvented Canada while doing so. His reasons for leaving, he told *Maclean's*, were simply that his priorities had changed. "I don't know what comes over you, but all of a sudden the kinds of things that were important when you were 23 aren't important when your [sic] 53. I don't know if it is called perspective or if it's called growth or if it's called what. But it's just there."

Controversy Continues

When Mulroney and his family left their Ottawa prime ministerial residence for the last time in June of 1993, they returned to Quebec where Mulroney went back to practicing law in Montreal. He was unable to entirely leave controversy behind him, however, when Stevie Cameron's 1994 book *On The Take* portrayed Mulroney as a prime minister who obtained a fortune well above that of most leaders by curious means. She alleged that the Tory party supplemented the family income to help support their lavish lifestyle. She charged that Mulroney, as Prime Minister, was involved in "flagrant kickback schemes, bid-rigging of government contracts, misappropriation of parliamentary budgets, favors to corporate supporters of the party, and an unprecedented orgy of patronage appointments that didn't end until the day Mulroney left office." Cameron was also sure to mention the generous consulting feels and directorship payments he earned after leaving his post from the boards on which he sat: Horsham Corporation, American Barrick Resources Corporation, and the food-processing giant Archer-Daniels-Midland Company, in addition to his hefty salary from his job as a partner with the Ogilvy Renault law firm.

A second book that poked at Mulroney was Marci McDonald's *Yankee Doodle Dandy: Brian Mulroney and the American Agenda,* released in 1995. In it, she points out how Mulroney's decisions in regards to the Persian Gulf War were influenced by President Bush's. Canadians were not happy when Mulroney's judgment to send troops into battle without passing it through Parliament and his zeal for committing more power didn't win him much respect.

Even more distressing controversy reached an extreme personal level when Mulroney was mentioned in an investi-

gation of the 1988 purchase of 34 Airbus A-320 passenger planes from a European firm for $1.8 billion. The Royal Canadian Mounted Police (RCMP) and Swiss authorities alleged that Mulroney was directly involved in conspiracy to defraud taxpayers and that he had accepted a $5 million kickback as a result of the airbus purchase. In addition, Swiss bank accounts records appeared, indicating that one account was for Mulroney. Mulroney flatly and fiercely denied all allegations by filing a $50 million action suit for libelous damage to his character, accusing the government and the RCMP of making "false and reckless" accusations against him—$25 million in actual damages to Mulroney's reputation and $25 million in punitive damages, which he planned to donate to charity if he won the case.

To prepare for the case, Federal lawyers sent Mulroney's attorneys some 40 pages of questions for which they said they needed answers to defend their clients. Mulroney's lawyers said the request for such detailed information was unnecessary and they won an appeal in Quebec to deny the attorneys access to such material. At pretrial hearings held in April 1996 Mulroney called the Canadian government and the RCMP Kafka-esque fascists, saying he was set up and accused without proof. His appearance at the hearings was intended to be for the government to assail him with questions to use as ammunition in the actual trial. Instead, a strong, composed Mulroney lashed out at the government, presenting his own case, banking on his skill for exploiting questions to deliver a speech.

A January 6, 1997 date was set in Quebec Superior Court for Brian Mulroney to take his suit to trial, where his lawyers tried to blame the department of justice for maligning Mulroney and accuse them of witch-hunting. Instead of walking away with the $50 million he wanted from the case that was initially estimated to last no less than three months, Mulroney agreed to settle for an decisive apology and a promise that the government would pay his $1 million in legal fees. *The Economist* reported that although both sides claimed victory, it was Mulroney's testimony that was more convincing. His reputation was at least somewhat restored and the government just appeared to be vindictive and sloppy.

When asked what he hoped the history books would say about him, Mulroney told *Maclean's* that he wants people to remember that he had never been elected anywhere, but made it to the House of Commons as leader of the Opposition and led his party to the greatest victory in Canadian history. His back-to-back triumphs were the first accomplishment by a Conservative in 100 years. He kept his party together and won a majority in the Senate for the first time in 50 years. Mulroney believes that he made a "profound and fundamental" difference and hopes that the future will prove that they were beneficial.

Brian Mulroney is married to the former Mila Pirnicki. They were wed in 1972 and had four children: Caroline, Nicolas, Mark, and Ben.

Further Reading

L. Ian MacDonald, *Mulroney: The Making of the Prime Minister* (Toronto: 1984) admiringly takes the story to the election of

1984. Mulroney's early years in power are critically examined in David Bercuson, J. L. Granatstein, and W. R. Young, *Sacred Trust? Brian Mulroney and the Conservative Party in Power* (Toronto: 1986) and in Michael Gratton, *"So, What Are the Boys Saying?" An Inside Look at Brian Mulroney in Power* (Toronto: 1987). A fine book on the 1988 election is Graham Fraser, *Playing for Keeps: The Making of the Prime Minister, 1988* (Toronto: 1989). See also articles in the following periodical sources: *Business Week,* June 28, 1993, p. 49; *Chinatown News,* April 15, 1995, p.2; *Congressional Quarterly Report,* December 19, 1992, p. 3883; *The Economist,* October 17, 1992, p. 18; January 11, 1997, p. 43; *Maclean's,* January 18, 1993, p. 12 and p. 19; February 1, 1993, p. 16 and p. 46; March 8, 1993, pp. 9, 10-13, 22-3, 24-9, 30-3, 34-5, 36-40; March 15, 1993, p. 37; October 31, 1994, p. 20; September 25, 1995, p. 46; November 27, 1995, p. 20; January 29, 1996, p. 17; February 26, 1996, p. 27; April 29, 1996, p. 24; September 9, 1996, p. 19; December 30, 1996/January 6, 1997, pp. 74-5, 79-81; *Newsweek,* June 14, 1993, p. 43; *Time,* November 9, 1992, p. 21; March 8, 1993, p. 18. □

Lewis Mumford

Lewis Mumford (1895-1990), American social philosopher and architectural critic, analyzed civilizations for their capacity to nurture humane environment. He emphasized the importance of environmental planning.

Lewis Mumford was born in Flushing, Long Island, New York, on October 19, 1895. He attended Stuyvesant High School until 1912. He studied evenings at the City College of New York for five years but did not receive a degree. Instead he became a student of the cities, beginning with New York City, whose libraries, theaters, and museums were his academy. Later, he wrote a series of "Skyline" essays for the *New Yorker* magazine which were intimate visits to buildings and quarters of the city that illustrated New Yorkers' aspirations and failures in their continuing act of building and rebuilding.

In 1915 Mumford read Patrick Geddes's essays expressing an organic view of society and claimed Geddes as his mentor in the years after 1923 when they met. In 1916 Mumford gained experience in the labor movement by serving as investigator of the dress and waist industry. Briefly in 1917 he worked for the Bureau of Standards in Pittsburgh, testing cement. He served as a radio operator in the U.S. Navy in 1918. The following year he became an editor of *Dial* magazine and then went to London in 1920 to serve as acting editor of the *Sociological Review.* Returning to New York City, he wrote *The Story of Utopias* (1922).

The English utopian planner and advocate of garden cities, Ebenezer Howard, inspired Mumford toward an active role in city and regional planning. He helped organize the Regional Planning Association of America (1923) and served as special investigator for the New York Housing and Regional Planning Commission, beginning in 1924. He edited the pioneering regional planning issue of *Survey Graph-*

ic (1925) and helped edit five volumes of *The American Caravan* (1927-1936). In city planning, he advocated the conservation of "green belts," with self-contained cities supporting residence, work, markets, education, and recreation. The new cities were to be constructed on a pedestrian's scale with organic coherence among the urban functions. As a city planning consultant, he forcefully urged such ideas throughout the world.

In his writing, Mumford tried to define the American conscience: its traditions and allegiances and the forces that periodically betrayed it. Louis Sullivan is the hero of *Sticks and Stones;* Henry Hobson Richardson is the hero of *The Brown Decades* and *The South in Architecture;* both men were gargantuan talents who wedded art and technology to give a distinctively indigenous form to American architecture. In his pioneering study *Herman Melville* (1929), Mumford disclosed his tragic sense of art and life. Art, he affirmed, is man's declaration against a universe that is "inscrutable, unfathomable, malicious . . . Not tame and gentle bliss, but disaster, heroically encountered, is man's true happy ending."

In *Technics and Civilization* (1934) and *The Culture of Cities* (1938) Mumford tried to show that artifacts are instruments of a civilization's cultural and social process and to examine architecture and machines in terms of the social conditions that nurture them. His thesis was that contemporary civilization must undergo a moral reformation to have the quality of life known to many earlier societies.

Between 1935 and 1951 Mumford wrote a series of books (the "Renewal of Life series," he labeled them) concluding with *The Conduct of Life.* They are long, sometimes tedious pleas for an understanding of the moral problems of public policies. Preoccupied with the rising threat of fascism, Mumford departed from his earlier pacifism and urged in 1935 that the United States declare its intention to defend against the totalitarian states. *Men Must Act* (1939) called for American intervention in World War II. The 1950's were very prosperous for Mumford's literary works. His early books including *Sticks and Stones, The Brown Decades,* and *The Golden Day* were all republished in 1995.

After the war Mumford worried about the ruin of cities through wholesale urban renewal, the growing dominance of highways, and the military mind's domination of foreign and nuclear policies. In *Faith for Living,* he wrote that "in a world in which violence becomes normalized as part of the daily routine, the popular mind becomes softly inured to human degeneracy." He held visiting professorships at North Carolina State College, the University of Pennsylvania, and the Massachusetts Institute of Technology. In his most searching book, *The City In History* (1961), he wrote, "We need a new image of order, which shall include the organic and personal, and eventually embrace all the offices and functions of man." *The City In History* was honored the National Book Award for nonfiction in 1962. In 1964, Mumford made six twenty-eight minute films based on *The City In History.*

In his much later work *The Myth of the Machine* (1970) he looks down upon technology, labeling the megamachine as the "guilty party." Mumford died in 1990.

Further Reading

The major source for information on Mumford's life is Van Wyck Brooks, *The Van Wyck Brooks-Lewis Mumford Letters: The Record of a Literary Friendship, 1921-1963,* edited by Robert E. Spiller (1970); it is virtually a social history of the era. Mumford's early career is detailed in Roy Lubove, *Community Planning in the 1920's: The Contribution of the Regional Planning Association of America* (1964). Mumford's views on urban life are analyzed in Morton and Lucia White, *The Intellectual versus the City: From Thomas Jefferson to Frank Lloyd Wright* (1962); W. Warren Wagar, *The City of Man: Prophecies of a World Civilization in Twentieth-century Thought* (1963); and Alan A. Altshuler, *The City Planning Process: A Political Analysis* (1965). Other sources include *Lewis Mumford and American Modernism: Eutopian Theories for Architecture and Urban Planning* written by Robert Wojtowioz (1996), *Coping with the Past: Patrick Geddes, Lewis Mumford, and the Regional Museum* by John L. Thomas (1997). ☐

Edvard Munch

The Norwegian painter and graphic artist Edvard Munch (1863-1944), working in an antinaturalistic expressionist style, illustrated man's emotional life in

love and death. His art was a major antecedent of the expressionist movement.

Born on Dec. 12, 1863, in Loieten near Kristiania (now Oslo), Edvard Munch was the son of a military doctor. Childhood experiences with death and sickness—both his mother and sister died of tuberculosis—greatly influenced his emotional and intellectual development. This and his father's fanatic Christianity led Munch to view his life as dominated by the "twin black angels of insanity and disease."

In 1880 Munch began to study art and joined the realist painters and writers of the Kristiania bohemian circle. His ideas were strongly influenced at this time by the anarchist writer Hans Jaeger, who sought to establish an ideal society based on materialist atheism and free love. Jaeger's hopeless love affair with the wife of Christian Krohg, dean of the bohemian painters, and Munch's own brief affairs caused him to intensify the identity he saw between women, love, and death.

Munch's paintings during the 1880s were dominated by his desire to use the artistic vocabulary of realism to render subjective content. His depiction of the *Sick Child* (1885-1886), which employed a motif popular among Norwegian realist artists, coloristically rendered a mood of melancholy depression serving as a pictorial memorial to his dead sister. Because of universal critical rejection, Munch turned briefly to a more conservative style and through the large painting *Spring* (1889), a more academic version of the *Sick Child,* he obtained state support for study in France.

After studying briefly at a Parisian art school, Munch began to explore the possibilities made available by the French postimpressionists. The death of his father in 1889 caused a major spiritual crisis, culminating in his rejection of Jaeger's philosophy. Munch's *Night in St. Cloud* (1890) embodied a renewed interest in spiritual content; this painting served as a memorial to his father by presenting the artist's dejected state of mind. He summarized his intentions, ''I paint not what I see, but what I saw,'' and identified his paintings as ''symbolism: nature viewed through a temperament.'' Both statements accent the transformation of nature as the artist experienced it.

In 1892 the Berlin Artists' Association, an official organization consisting primarily of German academic artists, invited Munch to exhibit there. His paintings provoked a major scandal in Germany's artistically provincial capital, and the exhibition was forcibly closed. But Munch used the publicity to arrange other exhibitions and sell paintings; his art prospered and he decided to stay in Germany. He also began work on a series of paintings later entitled the *Frieze of Life,* which concentrated on the themes of love, anxiety, and death. Incorporating many of his best-known works, the *Frieze* was essentially completed in 1893 but not exhibited as a unit until 1902.

To make his work accessible to a larger public, Munch began making prints in 1894. Motifs for his prints were usually derived from his paintings, particularly the *Frieze.* The *Frieze* also served as the inspiration for the paintings he made for Max Linde (1904), Max Reinhardt's Kammerspielhaus (1907), and the Freia Chocolate Factory in Oslo (1922).

Following a nervous breakdown, Munch entered a sanatorium in Copenhagen in 1908. In the lithograph series *Alpha* and *Omega* he allegorically depicted his love affairs and his relationship to friends and enemies. In 1909 he returned to Norway to lead an isolated life. He sought new artistic motifs in the Norwegian landscape and in the activities of farmers and laborers. A more optimistic view of life briefly replaced his former existential anxiety, and this new life view attained monumental expression in the murals of the Oslo University Aula (1911-1914).

During World War I Munch returned to his earlier motifs of love and death; his own increasing age combined with the tensions of world affairs to arouse a new pessimism in him. Symbolic paintings and prints appeared side by side with stylized studies of landscapes and nudes during the 1920s; as a major project, never completed, he began to illustrate Henrik Ibsen's plays. During his last years, plagued by partial blindness, Munch edited the diaries written in his youth and painted harsh self-portraits and memories of his earlier life. He died in Ekely outside Oslo on Jan. 23, 1944.

Further Reading

Some of Munch's own writings are contained in Johan H. Langaard and Reidar Revold, *Edvard Munch* (1963; trans. 1964). Reinhold Heller, *Edvard Munch: The Scream* (1972), is the first book in English to make use of Munch's unpublished

writings and of his drawings; although it concentrates on a single drawing, it serves as an introduction to his art in general. □

George William Mundelein

George William Mundelein (1872-1939) was an outstanding American Roman Catholic prelate and an outspoken foe of totalitarianism in the 1930s.

B orn in New York City on July 2, 1872, of American-born parents of German descent, George Mundelein was raised by his maternal grandmother. After graduating from Manhattan College in 1889 he spent 3 years at St. Vincent's Seminary in Beatty, Pa. He completed his studies at the Urban College of the Propagation of the Faith in Rome, receiving a doctor of divinity degree, and was ordained in 1895. He returned to his diocese of Brooklyn to serve as secretary to Bishop Charles E. McDonnell, becoming chancellor and auxiliary bishop in 1909. Mundelein succeeded James Edward Quigley as archbishop of Chicago in 1915.

Mundelein was noted as an administrator and fund raiser. He built hundreds of schools, churches, hospitals, and charitable institutions to keep pace with the needs of his rapidly growing archdiocese. He founded Quigley Preparatory Seminary in 1918, and it was soon the largest in the nation. In 1921 he established a seminary, St. Mary of the Lake, which he regarded as the major achievement of his career. When he was elevated to the College of Cardinals in 1924, his supporters donated $1 million for the seminary. Two years later he presided over the Eucharistic Congress in Chicago, one of the largest religious meetings in history. In 1918 he launched the Associated Catholic Charities of Chicago; he supported the work of Big Brothers, in which Holy Name Society men served as friends and advisers of needy young men. He sponsored the first diocesan council of the Legion of Decency. After the onset of the Great Depression in 1929, diocesan agencies worked closely with governmental programs aimed at relief and reform.

Always aware of the existence of social injustice, Mundelein warned against the exploitation of labor and warmly supported the New Deal administration of Franklin Roosevelt. A close friend of the President, he defended Roosevelt's program against Catholic critics, notably the radio orator Father Charles Coughlin. In 1937 Mundelein warned against isolationism and vigorously denounced Nazism and Adolf Hitler. His diocese was a center of social action programs, with Catholic priests and other leaders supporting the unionizing drives of the new Committee for Industrial Organization and participating in efforts at civic improvement and social reform. Mundelein died in Chicago on Oct. 2, 1939, on the eve of a planned radio address supporting a more vigorous American policy of resistance to totalitarianism.

Further Reading

Mundelein wrote two books, *Two Crowded Years* (1918) and *Letters of a Bishop to His Flock* (1927). The only biography of him is Paul R. Martin, comp., *The First Cardinal of the West* (1934), a laudatory testimonial.

Additional Sources

Kantowicz, Edward R., *Corporation sole: Cardinal Mundelein and Chicago Catholicism,* Notre Dame, Ind.: University of Notre Dame Press, 1983. □

José Luís Alberto Muñoz Marín

José Luís Alberto Muñoz Marín (1898-1980), Puerto Rican political leader, was instrumental in gaining self-rule and, later, commonwealth status for his country.

Luis Muñoz Marín was born on February 18, 1898, the son of Luís Muñoz Rivera and Amalia Marín. In 1910, his father was elected resident commissioner, and the family moved to Washington, D.C., where Muñoz was sent to boarding school. He later attended Georgetown University. After the death of his father in 1916, Muñoz returned to Puerto Rico. Muñoz was soon back in Washington as secre-tary to the new resident commissioner and briefly attended Georgetown Law School.

Muñoz then moved to New York City, where he began to make his living as a writer. He married a Mississippian poet, Muna Lee, in 1919. Shortly afterward, they went to Puerto Rico, where Muñoz joined the Socialist party for a brief period. At the age of 24, *A Ninety-eight Percent American in Puerto Rico* (1922) was published in *The New Republic.* On his return to New York City, Muñoz wrote an article about the intense poverty in Puerto Rico which was published in the *Nation* in 1925 titled *Puerto Rico: The American Colony.* In another article for *The American Mercury* (February 1929), he again wrote about the inequity of American denomination of Puerto Rico.

In 1931 Muñoz went back to Puerto Rico, this time to stay. He worked for *La Democracia,* the newspaper his father had founded. Muñoz joined the Liberal party and in 1932 was elected to the Puerto Rico Senate. During this period he and Carlos Chardón, the chancellor of the University of Puerto Rico, formulated a long-term economic plan, known as the Chardón Plan, which formed the basis for the Puerto Rican Reconstruction Administration started in 1935. In 1938, Muñoz formed the Popular Democratic party. During this time, Muñoz divorced his wife and married Inés María Mendoza de Palacios.

Running for the Senate under his new party affiliation, Muñoz began to campaign vigorously throughout the island with the slogan "Bread, Land, and Liberty." It was customary that plantation owners and politicians buy the peasant

vote at $2 each, a large sum to the poor. Muñoz asked each person not to sell his vote but to lend it to him."Remember this," he said, "You can have justice, or you can have two dollars. But you can't have both." He won the election and was senator from 1940 to 1948. Among his promises was self-government for Puerto Rico. In 1947 the U.S. Congress consented to self-government, and the first elections for governor were held in 1948. Muñoz easily won because of his outstanding Senate record.

As governor, Muñoz pressed for commonwealth status, and in 1952 Puerto Rico was declared an associated free state. Operation Bootstrap, the continuation of the Chardón Plan, was an economic success story, and Puerto Rico, under Muñoz's leadership, became the showcase for under-developed countries. In 1964 he declined the nomination for governor after serving four terms; instead he ran for the Senate and won. Muñoz passed away in 1980. His daughter, Victoria "Melo" Muñoz followed her father's footsteps, also running for the senate and winning.

Further Reading

The best book currently available in English on Muñoz Marín is Thomas Aitken, Jr., *Poet in the Fortress* (1964). □

Luís Muñoz Rivera

Luís Muñoz Rivera (1859-1916), Puerto Rican political leader, was instrumental in securing autonomy for his country from Spain in 1897.

Luís Muñoz Rivera was born in Barranquitas on July 17, 1859, the eldest son of Luís Ramon Muñoz Barrios, a leader of the Conservative party, and Monserrate Rivera Vasquez. After attending the elementary school in his town, he was largely self-educated. He wrote a number of patriotic poems and later became interested in editorial writing.

In 1887 Muñoz participated in the assembly that demanded autonomy for Puerto Rico from Spain. In 1890 he founded *La Democracia,* a newspaper expounding the Autonomist party's platforms. His editorials aroused the Spanish administration and led to lawsuits, but they also aroused the support of the Liberal party. Muñoz was soon a major leader and force within the party. In 1893 he married Amalia Marín. In 1896 he reached an agreement with the Spanish premier, Praxedes Sagasta, that, on his Liberal party's return to power, Spain would grant autonomy to Puerto Rico. The following year the Liberals returned to power; a royal decree of November 25 then granted autonomy to Puerto Rico and Cuba.

In the first Cabinet, formed on Feb. 8, 1898, Muñoz was secretary of grace, justice, and government, the highest post. War between the United States and Spain broke out 7 days later, and on July 25 the United States invaded Puerto Rico. The island was placed under United States military law. On October 18 the transfer of sovereignty to the United States took place, and the Cabinet members resigned, but Gen. Brooks, the first military governor, refused to accept their resignations. The Cabinet continued until 1899, when a second United States general succeeded to the governorship. Muñoz then resigned, organized the Federal party, and founded *El Diario de Puerto Rico* in 1900. In 1901 he went to New York City and began the English-language newspaper *Puerto Rico Herald* to call attention to the problems of Puerto Rico.

In 1902 the Unionist party, a fusion of the Federal and Republican parties, was formed, and Muñoz returned to Puerto Rico to campaign for its candidates. In 1906 he was elected to the Puerto Rican House of Delegates. In 1910 he was elected resident commissioner for Puerto Rico to the United States. He then proceeded to learn English, at the age of 50, in order to present his country's needs and desires to Congress. He worked hard on the Jones bill to grant U.S. citizenship to Puerto Ricans and delivered his most important speech in Congress in favor of it in 1916. That year, on November 15, he died in a suburb of San Juan.

Further Reading

One of the best books on Muñoz Rivera in English is Marianna Norris, *Father and Son for Freedom* (1967). See also the essays in Philip Sterling and Maria Brau, *The Quiet Rebels* (1968), and Jay Nelson Tuck and Norma C. Vergara, *Heroes of Puerto Rico* (1970). □

Frank Andrew Munsey

Frank Andrew Munsey (1854-1925), American publisher, built a newspaper and magazine empire in the early 20th century.

Frank Munsey was born in Mercer, Maine, on Aug. 21, 1854, the son of poor but hardworking parents. A sober industrious boy, he went to work for the Western Union Telegraph Company. Steady and ambitious, he soon became manager of its office in Augusta, Maine. For obscure reasons, he settled upon publishing as his means to reach fortune, and in 1882 he went to New York City to publish *Golden Argosy,* a juvenile magazine. He helped *Argosy* by writing Horatio Alger-type tales, while buying, merging, and closing down other publishing properties, some distinguished, like *Godey's* and *Peterson's.*

Munsey struggled to succeed. He did not marry and did not develop any striking or individual side interests. He was dedicated to business during a period that witnessed the emergence of the popular magazine. In 1891, with *Argosy* producing less revenue than his plans permitted, he began *Munsey's,* aimed at a broad, general audience to which his competitors were selling magazines at 25 cents or more. *Munsey's* was less distinguished than most of these, but in 1893 Munsey made the magazine more salable by cutting his price to 10 cents.

When Munsey was refused distribution privileges by the American News Company, which feared the effect of his price on its control of the field, Munsey struck back by setting up his own distribution system. His brief, courageous battle broke the monopoly and established the popular magazine, making it available to a new and wider readership.

With his income now assured, Munsey began a drive that affected many journalistic careers. He turned his attention to newspapers—buying, consolidating, or closing numerous publications, including the *New York Sun,* the *Baltimore Star,* and the *Philadelphia Times.* Though many of his transactions were resented, Munsey insisted that unprofitable newspapers deserved to be killed and that consolidation was the one answer to this problem. However, his mounting power as a journalistic overlord gave no evidence of distinguished policies or technical innovations.

Munsey expanded his interests, assuming ownership of a chain of grocery stores and speculating in the stock market. His support of Theodore Roosevelt and the Progressive party in 1912 surprised some observers, who were of Munsey's generally conservative politics. However, Munsey's position only indicated his awareness that large industry had more to gain from government regulation than from freebooting enterprise, which could embarrass financiers through panics or recessions. More typical of Munsey's thought was his opposition to the League of Nations. He died on Dec. 22, 1925, leaving only his controversial empire.

Further Reading

An account of Munsey is in George Britt, *Forty Years—Forty Millions* (1935). Louis Filler, *Crusaders for American Liberalism* (1939), treats Munsey as a pioneer in the creation of the popular magazine. See also Oswald G. Villard, *Some Newspapers and Newspaper-men* (1923). □

Thomas Münzer

The German Protestant reformer Thomas Münzer (1489-1525) was associated with the "radical" Reformation, in the early stages of which his revolutionary social views placed him at the head of the Peasants' Rebellion.

Thomas Münzer was born at Stolberg in Saxony. He read widely and became a secular priest, first in Frohse and later in a convent in Beuditz. After meeting Martin Luther at Leipzig in 1519, Münzer experienced a religious crisis in which his doubt as to God's existence was resolved into a concept of the decline of the Church, the spiritual unity of all true believers, and his own conviction that he was an especially chosen instrument of God to purge the world of ecclesiastical abuses. His appointment to the town of Zwickau in 1520 brought him into contact with the socially radical Zwickau prophets, and Münzer began proclaiming his vision of a purified Christianity, devoid of ecclesiastical and social hierarchies and dependent upon personal revelation and the immediacy of the Day of Judgment.

Forced to leave Zwickau in 1521, Münzer went to Prague, where he further preached his visionary theology and vociferously denounced the social oppression of the poor which had been a result of ecclesiastical distortion of true Christian doctrine. In 1522 Münzer was appointed provisional pastor at Allstedt, where he married, carried out liturgical reforms (including services in the vernacular), and further developed his concept of the three stages in the true Christian life: utter despair, fear inspired by God, and finally personal illumination by the Holy Spirit. His increasingly radical position was made clear in his famous sermon to the princes of Saxony in 1524, in which Münzer urged the temporal rulers to lead God's chosen people against the "forces of antichrist." Forced to leave Allstedt later in the same year, Münzer joined the Peasants' Rebellion, which had broken out in June 1524.

The rebellion was the result of a complex series of social, legal, and theological disputes, and it soon swept up many peasants in what is now southwestern Germany. Demanding considerable social and religious reforms, the peasants practiced an apocalyptic Christianity and, with Münzer's influence, came to regard themselves as God's purifying army and Münzer as the "sword of Gideon." Münzer, from his base in Mühlhausen, issued broadsides proclaiming his completely radicalized theological and social views. He urged the destruction of all religious images, the sharing of property in common, and the immediate

establishment of God's kingdom on earth. Vilifying Luther as "Doctor Liar, the Wittenberg Pope," Münzer was in turn denounced by Luther: "Anyone who has seen Münzer can say that he has seen the devil at his worst." After the defeat of the peasants at Frankenhausen in 1525, Münzer was forced to recant his "errors" before being beheaded.

Further Reading

Some English translations of Münzer's writings are in George Huntston Williams and Angel M. Mergal, eds., *Spiritual and Anabaptist Writers* (1957). The best account of Münzer's life and thought is in George Huntston Williams, *The Radical Reformation* (1962). On Münzer and the millenarian tradition see Norman Cohn, *The Pursuit of the Millennium* (1957), and Gordon Rupp, *Patterns of Reformation* (1969).

Additional Sources

Friesen, Abraham, *Thomas Muentzer, a destroyer of the godless: the making of a sixteenth-century religious revolutionary,* Berkeley: University of California Press, 1990.
Gritsch, Eric W., *Thomas Muentzer: a tragedy of errors,* Minneapolis: Fortress Press, 1989. □

Murasaki Shikibu

Murasaki Shikibu (ca. 976-ca. 1031) was a Japanese writer of the late Heian period. Her "The Tale of Genji," the world's first psychological novel, is one of the longest and most distinguished masterpieces of Japanese literature.

The exact dates of the life of Lady Murasaki are not known, nor is her name. Shikibu, a title, may refer to her father, who served in the Ministry of Ceremonial, or of Rites (Shikibu Shō). The name Murasaki, literally "Violet," could refer to one of the heroines of *The Tale of Genji* or to the first element of her maiden name, Fujiwara, one of the greatest names in Japanese history. Murasaki was born into a lesser but distinguished and cultured branch of this family in the last quarter of the 10th century. Her father, Fujiwara Tamatoki, an official and poet, was at one time a provincial governor; his grandfather was a poet.

Murasaki records in her diary her lessons in Chinese with her brother. She was so quick to learn that her father regretted that she was not a boy. Presumably Murasaki was educated in the usual Chinese and Buddhist classics as well as in Japanese literature, though this kind of learning was not stressed for young women in those days. Murasaki was married at about the age of 20, but her husband died soon after, in 1001, leaving her with a daughter. After her husband's death, Murasaki lived in retirement for some years.

In 1004 Murasaki's father was appointed governor of the province of Echizen, 80 miles from the capital, a great distance in the 11th century. Arrangements were made for Murasaki to enter the service of Akiko, the young consort of Emperor Ichijo, as lady-in-waiting. Murasaki's diary, begun in 1008 and continued for 2 years thereafter, recounts her

life at court. At the death of Emperor Ichijo in 1011, the Empress, with her suite of ladies, went into retirement. At this time Murasaki's father was appointed governor of the province of Echigo; in 1016 he retired from the world to take holy orders. Little or nothing of Murasaki's life is positively known from the time she entered the service of Empress Akiko. Murasaki is thought to have died about 1031.

Her Writings

Murasaki's knowledge of the great world is amply exhibited in *The Tale of Genji* (*Genji monogatari*) as well as in her *Diary,* and it may be assumed that she chronicled something resembling her own life, however idealized. Murasaki may have begun her novel about 1003 and continued writing it, with interruptions, until her death, at which time it might or might not have been finished.

The size and scope of *The Tale of Genji* are enormous. Divided into 54 books or episodes, the novel is twice as long as *War and Peace.* The action, covering the better part of a century, with over 400 characters and four generations, is meticulously and consistently elaborated by Murasaki. The hero, Hikaru Genji, the Shining One, pursues love and happiness impelled always by the haunting image of his dead mother, Kiritsubo, the consort of an emperor. Her early death overshadows Genji's youth. By virtue of his exuberant personality Genji becomes supremely popular at court, indulges in a series of amorous encounters, and wins the admiration of his peers when he dances the "Waves of the Blue Sea."

The character of Genji may be based in part on the personality of Fujiwara Korechika (975-1010), a nephew of Fujiwara Michinaga (966-1027), a great statesman and distant relative of Lady Murasaki. Genji, as a result of his numerous love affairs, incurs the jealousy and wrath of powerful rivals who bring about his disgrace and exile. But this ill luck is of short duration, and Genji is pardoned, is recalled to the capital, and regains his prominence. An encounter with the girl Murasaki Ue had led Genji to undertake her education so that she could be molded into the perfect wife. He builds his sumptuous villa in the capital and installs his several wives in their apartments with Murasaki in the place of honor. But excess of passion takes its toll, and Genji suffers emotional agony because of unhappiness in love. Murasaki, his favorite wife, dies childless, leaving Genji in a world of memories.

Soon, Genji too passes from the Realm of Maya, and the center of attention is turned to his descendants, Kaoru, his supposed son, and Niou, his grandson. Both have aspects of Genji's personality but cannot take his place. This portion of the novel, called the "Uji Chapters" because much of the action takes place at the small village of Uji, depicts the confrontation of Kaoru and Niou for the affections of the girl Ukifune. Kaoru, sensitive, retiring, obsessed by the mystery of his paternity, would sacrifice his high position for Ukifune. But she is confused by her feelings for him and for the high-spirited and charming Niou, who in so many ways resembles Genji.

Having yielded to Niou's blandishments, Ukifune can resolve her dilemma only by an attempt at suicide and, when that fails, by retirement from the world to live out her life as a nun. Kaoru is left in grief, bewilderment, and uncertainty, for although he comes to suspect that Ukifune may still be alive, he is never able to learn the truth. Thus, the lengthy novel, which began with the enchanting atmosphere of a fairy tale, ends in the most complex psychological analysis of unhappy people shrouded in blackest gloom.

Further Reading

Lady Murasaki's *The Tale of Genji* was translated by Arthur Waley in 1926. Useful background studies are George B. Sansom, *Japan: A Short Cultural History* (1938; rev. ed. 1962); Annie Shepley Omori, trans., *Diaries of Court Ladies of Old Japan,* with an introduction by Amy Lowell (1961); and Ivan Morris, *The World of the Shining Prince* (1964).

Additional Sources

Murasaki Shikibu, *Murasaki Shikibu, her diary and poetic memoirs: a translation and study,* Princeton, N.J.: Princeton University Press, 1982. □

Joachim Murat

The French marshal Joachim Murat (1767-1815), brother-in-law of Napoleon I, served in the wars of the French Revolution and Empire. He was king of Naples from 1808 to 1815.

Joachim Murat was born at La Bastide-Fortumière (Lot) on March 25, 1767. He was the second son of an innkeeper who intended the boy to make his career in the Church. He was educated first at Cahors and then studied canon law at Toulouse. Realizing that he had no calling to the religious life, Joachim left his studies and enlisted in a cavalry regiment. He remained in military service until 1790, at which time he was discharged for disciplinary reasons. Shortly thereafter, he reentered the army (1791).

Capt. Murat was in Paris in 1795, and he was employed by Napoleon Bonaparte on 13 Vendémiaire to aid him in putting down the rising against the Directory. Bonaparte then took him to Italy in 1796 as his first aide-de-camp, where he served during the first Italian campaign. In 1798 he sailed with the Army of Egypt to the banks of the Nile, where he commanded the cavalry during the Battle of the Pyramids. The following year he took part in the Syrian expedition. In the summer of 1799, when Bonaparte returned to France with only a small group of favored officers, Murat was among them. He was promoted to the rank of general of division in October 1799. On the 18th of Brumaire (Nov. 10, 1799) Murat commanded the grenadiers who evicted the Council of Five Hundred from their meeting hall at Saint-Cloud, thus assuring the overthrow of the Directory and the establishment of the Consulate. Napoleon, the new first consul, appointed him commandant of the consular guard and gave him his sister, Caroline Bonaparte, in marriage (Jan. 20, 1800). The second Italian campaign saw Murat at the head of the cavalry, and he took part

in the Battle of Marengo. During the next 4 years of peace on the Continent he was governor of the Cisalpine Republic and governor of Paris. With the creation of the Empire in 1804, he was named marshal and invested with the grand eagle of the Legion of Honor.

The renewal of hostilities in 1805 found Murat once again at the head of the cavalry. He took an active part in the campaigns of 1806 and 1807 and fought with distinction at Jena, Eylau, and Friedland. In 1808 he was named general in chief of the French Army of Spain. He had high hopes of being named king of Spain, but the Emperor placed his own older brother Joseph on the throne. As a conciliation, Murat was given the throne of Naples (Aug. 1, 1808).

Styling himself King Joachim Napoleon, Murat established an extravagant court at Naples and continued the reforms that Joseph Bonaparte had begun. His principal problem was his relationship with his all-powerful brother-in-law. It was Napoleon's intention that the kingdom of Naples should be governed in the best interests of France. Murat balked but remained in line.

In 1812 the King of Naples again headed the cavalry of the Grand Army. Throughout the Russian campaign and the retreat, he distinguished himself by his bravery in the face of enemy fire. When the French retreated beyond the Rhine after the defeat at Leipzig (Oct. 16-18, 1813), Murat retired to Italy. He now realized that the Napoleonic Empire would not survive. He therefore opened negotiations with Austria in an effort to save his throne. On Jan. 11, 1814, he signed a treaty with Austria that guaranteed him the throne of Naples

in return for his renunciation of Napoleon and active military support against France. But Austria was the only great power supporting him, and at the Congress of Vienna the other Allied nations wished to return the deposed King Ferdinand to Naples. Thus, in coordination with Napoleon's return to France in March 1815, but without the returning Emperor's approval, Murat went to war with Austria in the name of Italian unification.

The Neapolitan army was defeated in its first engagement with the Austrians, and Murat was forced to flee from his kingdom to France. Napoleon, still furious with his former lieutenant, refused to give him service in the French army or even to allow him to remain on French soil. In early October he made one last bid to reestablish himself in Italy. Landing at Pizzo on October 8 with a handful of men, he was at once captured. On Oct. 13, 1815, he was condemned to death by a court-martial and shot.

Further Reading

Neither of the two biographies of Murat in English can be considered definitive: A. H. Atteridge, *Joachim Murat, Marshal of France* (1911), however, is better than A. Berlam, *King of Naples* (1922). A. Espitalier, *Napoleon and King Murat* (1912), is a good account of the relationship between the two men. Useful background works include R. M. Johnston, *The Napoleonic Empire in Southern Italy* (2 vols., 1904); Piers G. Mackesy, *The War in the Mediterranean* (1957); and Owen Connelly, *Napoleon's Satellite Kingdoms* (1965). □

Lodovico Antonio Muratori

The Italian historian and antiquary Lodovico Antonio Muratori (1672-1750) is known for his publication of historical documents. He has been called the father of Italian history.

Lodovico Antonio Muratori was born at Vignola in the duchy of Modena on Oct. 21, 1672. He took minor orders in 1688 and had become a doctor of Roman and canon laws by 1694. Immediately after his ordination in 1695, Muratori was appointed to a post at the Ambrosian library in Milan. While a young man, his interest in philological studies and antiquarian scholarship had been awakened by the director of the library of the dukes of Modena, Father Benedetto Bacchini. At Milan he completed the first volumes of his first major work, the *Anecdota* (Milan, 1697-1698; Padua, 1713), a collection of documents drawn from the Ambrosian collections. In 1700, on Bacchini's retirement, he returned to Modena to take over the directorship. From this point on, his life story is the story of his publications.

Italian historical scholarship in the 17th century had been dominated by the spirit of the Counter Reformation. All events were viewed in the light of theological truths; moral fervor and religious orthodoxy were more important than historical accuracy. Muratori brought to Italy the exacting standards of the Benedictines of St. Maur, a French monastic group who had applied to historical studies the philological techniques first developed by 15th- and 16th-century humanists. Rigorous correction of texts through careful comparison of manuscripts, precise dating through philological and historical analysis, and elaborate historical erudition were the hallmarks of their work. All these Muratori introduced to 18th-century Italian historical scholarship.

Of Muratori's many works the most important were the *Return italicarum scriptores* (28 vols., 1723-1751; Writers of Italian History), the *Antiquitates italicae medii aevi* (6 vols., 1738-1743; Italian Antiquities of the Middle Ages), and the *Annali d'Italia* (12 vols., 1744-1749; Annals of Italy). *The Rerum* is an anthology of Italian chronicles from A.D. 500 to the 16th century. It includes the histories of Jordanus, Procopius, and Paul the Deacon; the Lombard Laws; the *Liber pontificalis;* the major monastic chronicles of the Middle Ages; and the most important regional chronicles of the Renaissance. Muratori's edition served Italian scholarship until the late 19th and 20th centuries, when most of the texts were given modern editions.

The *Antiquitates* is a collection of 75 dissertations on a variety of historical subjects, such as ordeals, heresies, the development of commerce, and the etymologies of words. In volume 3 Muratori published the earliest known list of the books of the New Testament, a text dating from before A.D. 200 that he had found in an 8th-century codex. It is still known as the Muratorian Canon. The *Annali,* a history of Italy from the time of Christ to the 18th century, is really a series of notes in which historical events are listed year by year. Muratori died on Jan. 23, 1750.

Further Reading

There is no study of Muratori in English. Background information on historiography is in Benedetto Croce, *History: Its Theory and Practice* (trans. 1923), and in Fritz Stern, ed., *The Varieties of History* (1956). □

Sir Roderick Impey Murchison

The British geologist Sir Roderick Impey Murchison (1792-1871) established the Silurian as a new geological system and cofounded the Devonian system.

Roderick Murchison, descended from an old Highland family, was born in Scotland on Feb. 19, 1792. After a time in the army in the Peninsular War, he married and, having ample means, took up fox hunting and an interest in art and antiquities. Influential friends, aided by his wife, persuaded him to pursue a scientific career, and from the age of 32 he devoted himself to geology.

In 1831 Murchison began his great research into the mass of hitherto geologically unknown graywacke rocks, that is, Lower Paleozoic, underlying the Old Red Sandstone

in South Wales and the Welsh Borderland. His monumental work *The Silurian System* (1839) contained a description of the sequence of the graywacke rocks and their fossils. In the same year he and Adam Sedgwick established the Devonian system. In 1841, after explorations in Russia with French colleagues, he proposed the name Permian for yet another worldwide geological system, the uppermost of the Paleozoic. *The Geology of Russia in Europe and the Ural Mountains* was published in 1845. The book *Siluria* (1854 and subsequent editions) surveyed those ever-widening regions which he was incorporating in his Silurian domain.

Murchison was involved in the two most important geological controversies of the 19th century. The first was the unfortunate and bitter argument over the Cambrian and Silurian systems, in which the other protagonist was Sedgwick. Here Murchison's case was undoubtedly the stronger. The other was the crucial question of the geological structure of the Highlands of Scotland. Here Murchison was only involved retrospectively, and it turned out that his interpretation was wrong.

In 1855 Murchison became director general of the Geological Survey of Great Britain. Meanwhile he had presided over the Geological Society, the Geographical Society, and the British Association for the Advancement of Science. He was knighted in 1846 and was made a baronet in 1866. Among his many honors from British and foreign institutions was the Wollaston Medal, the highest award of the Geological Society.

Murchison was one of the most distinguished geologists of the 19th century. His liberality and social position plus the pride he took in his science were of immense value in furthering the cause of learning in Britain. He died in London on Oct. 22, 1871.

Further Reading

The standard biography of Murchison is Sir Archibald Geikie, *Life of Sir Roderick I. Murchison* (2 vols., 1875). Murchison's connection with the Geological Society of London is narrated in Horace Bolingbroke Woodward, *History of the Geological Society of London* (1908), in which there is also an impartial discussion of the Cambrian-Silurian controversy. Sir John Smith Flett, *The First Hundred Years of the Geological Survey of Great Britain* (1937), and Sir Edward Bailey, *Geological Survey of Great Britain* (1952), give detailed accounts of Murchison and his tenure as director general.

Additional Sources

Stafford, Robert A., *Scientist of empire: Sir Roderick Murchison, scientific exploration and Victorian imperialism,* Cambridge; New York: Cambridge University Press, 1989. □

Iris Murdoch

The works of the novelist and philosopher Jean Iris Murdoch (born 1919) portray characters whose warped and often dreamlike perceptions of reality create suffering among those whose lives they attempt to dominate.

Jean Iris Murdoch was born in Dublin, Ireland, on July 15, 1919. In 1942, she obtained her Bachelor of Arts degree with first-class honors in the Classical Greats from Oxford University in England. From 1942 to 1944, she worked as assistant principal in the British treasury and from 1944 to 1946, with the UN Relief and Rehabilitation Center. In 1947, she returned to her education and obtained a studentship in Philosophy at Cambridge University, also in England. In 1948, she became a tutor at St. Anne's College in Oxford, England; a position she held for the next 20 years.

Murdoch published several philosophical studies during the early 1950s, including one of Jean Paul Sartre, a philosopher to whom she has been compared. She has also written over 50 novels. The first novel was *Under the Net* (1954), about a man who fails in his personal relationships because he sees the world as a hostile place and people are not completely real to him. In 1956, Murdoch married John Bayley, a novelist and lecturer. Her second novel, *The Flight from the Enchanter* (1956), is about a rich and powerful man who sees all human relationships as power struggles and uses his power to draw the other characters into his grasp. Murdoch's third novel, *The Sandcastle* (1957), deals with a man who attempts to free himself from what he considers the death of him; his marriage. *The Bell* (1958) has a similar theme, except that a young woman decides not to go back to her mate so that she may find herself.

Many of Murdoch's later novels contain themes that are rewritten from her earlier works. For example, *A Severed Head* (1961) returns to the theme of *Flight from the Enchanter:* the extent to which human relationships—in this case, sexual ones—are damaged when they are seen as ways to overpower others. *An Unofficial Rose* (1962), like *The Sandcastle,* features a hero who feels enslaved by his marriage; while *The Unicorn* (1963), the study of a passive, guilt-ridden woman who poisons all her relationships by holding to one view of herself is repeated in *The Bell. The Italian Girl* (1964), *The Read and the Green* (1965), *The Time of the Angels* (1966), *The Nice and the Good* (1968), *Bruno's Dream* (1969), and *A Fairly Honourable Defeat* (1970). Murdoch often writes novels that involve the fantasy of freedom—often sexual—versus conventional responsibility and the difficulty of establishing loving relationships between equals. Also characteristic of much of her late work are the brooding, dreamlike landscapes and the bizarre turns of plot which have prompted many critics to refer to her as a Gothic novelist.

Even in her later years, Murdoch continues to write rather lengthy, complex, and mind grabbing novels. Her latest titles are *Metaphysics as a Guide to Morals* (1982), *The Good Apprentice* (1986), and *The Green Knight* (1993). Murdoch has published over 50 titles.

Further Reading

Two useful studies of Iris Murdoch's work are Antonia S. Byatt's *Degrees of Freedom: The Novels of Iris Murdoch* (1965), and Peter Wolff's *The Disciplined Heart: Iris Murdoch and Her*

Novels (1966); *First Things* written by Alan Jacobs (February 1995) discusses Murdoch's later novels. *Iris Murdoch and the Search for Human* edited by Maria Antonaccio and William Schweiker is a collection of essays that examine Murdoch's thoughts on human goodness. □

Rupert Murdoch

Starting out as a newspaper publisher in his native Australia, Rupert Murdoch (born 1931) became a powerful media entrepreneur with wide holdings in England and the United States. His style of journalism evoked criticism from serious readers but served the entertainment needs of a broad audience.

orn March 11, 1931, in Melbourne, Australia, (Keith) Rupert Murdoch was the son of a distinguished journalist. His father, Sir Keith Murdoch, was a celebrated World War I reporter who later became chief executive of the leading Melbourne *Herald* newspaper group. From the beginning in 1955 with the tiny Adelaide *News* inherited from his father (who died in 1952), Murdoch created an international communications empire which eventually published over 80 papers and magazines on three continents.

In the process of expanding his $1.4 billion a year News Corp. Ltd., Murdoch acquired critics as fast as properties for his sensationalistic brand of journalism. Appealing to the prurient interests of readers, Murdoch was compared to such yellow journalism tycoons of the past as William Randolph Hearst. Yet his business philosophy of offering readers what they were willing to buy most closely resembled the outlook of entertainer P. T. Barnum.

After studying at Oxford, Murdoch entered journalism as a reporter for the Birmingham *Gazette* and served an apprenticeship on the London *Daily Express,* where he learned the secrets of building circulation from the press baron Lord Beaverbrook. Returning to Australia to begin his publishing career, Murdoch revived the Adelaide *News.* In 1956 bought and built up the Perth Sunday *Times.* In 1960 he purchased the dying Sydney Daily and Sunday *Paper,* which he turned into the largest selling newspaper in Australia by employing aggressive·promotion and a racy tabloid style. In 1964 he started *The Australian,* a national paper aimed at a more serious audience.

In early 1969 Murdoch debuted as a London publisher when he gained control of the Sunday paper *News of the World,* the largest-circulation English-language paper in the world. Later in 1969 he bought cheaply a tired liberal paper, the *Sun,* which he radically transformed into a sensationalistic tabloid featuring daily displays of a topless girl on page three. The *Sun* became the most profitable paper in his empire. In 1983, with circulation around four million, it earned $50 million, over 40 percent of News Corp.'s annual profits. In 1981 Murdoch bought the failing but prestigious London *Times.*

Murdoch expanded into the American market in 1973 when he acquired the San Antonio (Texas) *Express* and *News.* In early 1974 he started the weekly tabloid the *National Star* (later renamed *Star*) to compete with the popular *Enquirer.* Initially a weak imitation of the *Sun,* it adopted a format based on celebrity gossip, health tips, and self-help advice which boosted its circulation to almost four million.

In his quest for a big-city audience, Murdoch surprised the publishing world in 1976 when he bought the *New York Post,* a highly regarded liberal paper. By transforming its image he nearly doubled the circulation. In 1977 he took control from Clay Felker of the New York Magazine Corp., which included the trendy *New York* magazine, *New West,* and the radical weekly the *Village Voice.* Focusing on the struggling paper in competitive urban markets, Murdoch extended his holdings by buying the ailing *Boston Herald* in 1982 and the modestly-profitable *Chicago Sun-Times* in 1983.

From his first involvement in publishing, Murdoch applied a recognizable formula to most of his papers. His trademark operations included rigid cost controls, circulation gimmicks, flashy headlines, and a steady emphasis on sex, crime, and scandal stories. Reminiscent of the personalized style of the fictional Citizen Kane, Murdoch's uninhibited sensationalism was scorned as vulgar and irresponsible by his peers. One critic charged that what Murdoch did "just isn't journalism—it's a different art form."

On the other hand, Murdoch was seen as an astute and effective popular journalist who catered to the interests of his audiences, a view he espoused. Ignoring his critics, he regarded most papers as too elitist in their approach and too bland in appearance. He preferred a bright and entertaining product which would attract the largest body of readers. While he didn't think papers should be in the business of preaching to the public, he used his news columns to promote personal causes. With regard to a Labor government in Australia, he stated, "I elected them. And incidentally I'm not too happy with them. I may remove them."

Murdoch's newspaper style, though, did not fare as well in the United States as in Britain. The *New York Post* was a steady financial drain despite its increased circulation. Murdoch's formula did not attract advertisers. Collectively, led by the more subdued *Star,* Murdoch's American papers did not show a profit until 1983.

In 1983 Murdoch purchased a controlling interest in Satellite Television, a London company supplying entertainment programming to cable-television operators in Europe. His plan for beaming programs from satellites directly to homes equipped with small receivers did not progress, and his attempt to gain control of Warner Communications and its extensive film library did not succeed. However, in 1985 he did purchase the film company Twentieth Century Fox. A year later he bought six (Metromedia) television stations and sought to create a fourth major network called Fox Television. Since foreign nationals were not permitted by the United States to own a broadcast station, Murdoch became a naturalized citizen of the U.S. in 1985, in order to maintain his control of Fox Television. In 1987 he bought the U.S. publishing house Harper and Row.

Other than publishing, Murdoch's business interests included two television stations in Australia, half ownership in the country's largest private airlines, book publishing, records, films (he co-produced Gallipoli), ranching, gas and oil exploration, and a share in the British wire service Reuters News Corp. Ltd. which earned almost $70 million in 1983. His holdings rivaled such U.S. giants as Time, Inc. and the Times Mirror (now Time Warner) Company. In 1988, in connection with his television network, he bought Triangle publications—with holdings that included TV Guide, the leading television program listing publication—from Walter Annenberg for $3 billion. In 1995 he underwrote the *Weekly Standard,* a political magazine that generally supports Republican politics. In 1997, he tried to buy the Los Angeles Dodgers baseball team, which many see as another dig at his long time media competitor and rival Ted Turner, owner of the Atlanta Braves and numerous cable and broadcast networks such as CNN. Murdoch's ambitions caused him to seek out new ventures in cable broadcasting such as a Fox News service, and an all-sport network.

Murdoch's personal wealth was estimated at over $340 million. Seen as ruthless in his business dealings, Murdoch was known as being shy in his personal life. Living primarily in New York, he guarded his privacy with his wife Anna (a former Sydney *Daily Mirror* reporter) and their four children, one by a previous marriage.

Further Reading

Good Times, Bad Times (1984) by Harold Evans a former London *Times* editor; *Arrogant Aussie: The Rupert Murdoch Story* (1985; *Citizen Murdoch* (1987). □

Bartolomé Esteban Murillo

Bartolomé Esteban Murillo (1617-1682) was a Spanish painter whose baroque style was adulated for close to 200 years, condemned for almost 100, and, since the 1950s, has been reevaluated with hedging enthusiasm.

B artolomé Esteban Murillo was born and died in Seville; he led an uneventful life of professional activity and success within the context of personal goodness and contentment. G. Kubler and M. Soria (1959) call him the "Fra Angelico of Spanish painting." The difficulty is that the primitivism of Fra Angelico's art allows the sweetness of his artistic expressions an autonomous existence beyond the pale of human experience, whereas the realism of Murillo's art causes the same gentleness to mock the psychic torment and spiritual alienation of present-day humanity.

If Murillo had conceived his saints of the Old and New Testaments as heroic, their excellence of soul would be more palatable today, but he presented them as middleclass benefactors who perform their acts as though they were commonplaces and look like God-oriented, good men: *Moses' Miracle of the Waters* (1670-1674) and *St. Thomas of Villanueva Giving Alms to the Poor* (1668). Murillo's sacroprofanity, or failure to separate the sacred from the merely human, was as natural as breathing to him and as unquestionably sincere.

Murillo was born of well-to-do parents, Gaspar Esteban, a barber-surgeon, and Maria Murillo, and was baptized on Jan. 1, 1618. Orphaned at 11, he became the ward of an uncle who placed him a year later as an apprentice to another relative, the painter Juan del Castillo. The allegation that Murillo visited Madrid and studied with Diego Velázquez is most probably false. At 17 Murillo was working independently, painting small, religious compositions for the Latin American market.

In 1645 Murillo married Beatriz de Cabrera y Sotomayor; in the same year he achieved fame owing to his series of 11 paintings for the Franciscan monastery in Seville. Of his nine children, five entered religious life. He founded an art academy in 1660 and served as its first president. He became enrolled in the Brotherhood of Charity in 1665. Murillo sustained mortal injuries when he fell from a scaffold in the Capuchin church of Cadiz in 1681; he died on April 3, 1682, in Seville.

Murillo's *Self-portrait* (ca. 1678; National Gallery, London) is an excellent example to justify why recent reevaluation of his art stresses his portraiture. In addition, his

masterly handling of landscape is cited as most praiseworthy. The fact is that the life and art of Murillo are in desperate need of research. Apparently the adverse judgments made so sweepingly against his art have intimidated scholarship. Since he rarely signed or dated his works, much of the chronology must be reviewed. Jusepé de Ribera, Alonso Cano, Peter Paul Rubens, Anthony Van Dyck, Correggio, and the Venetian school, particularly Titian, are cited as his influences, but too seldom is it known exactly which originals, copies, or prints Murillo saw. Arbitrary assignations of anonymous works have caused his rightful fame to suffer from the inferiority of his disciples and other imitators. Finally, the proved stylistic range and thematic variety of his art compound the difficulties of scholarly analysis: *The Family* (ca. 1660), *Grape and Melon Eaters, St. Leander* (1655), the *Santiago Madonna* (ca. 1670-1675), the Leningrad *Immaculate Conception,* and the *Miracle of the Loaves and Fishes.*

If the art of El Greco may be cited as the supreme expression of Spain's anguish during the Reformation, Murillo's art is undoubtedly the major manifestation of his country's best Counter Reformational response: a way of life in a Franciscan sacroprofanity and fragrance.

Although Murillo had disciples, they did not assist him in executing his works. It seems clear he preferred to be solely responsible for his commissions.

Further Reading

Two sources in English on Murillo's art are recommended because they represent divergent, scholarly points of view: George Kubler and Martin Soria in *Art and Architecture in Spain and Portugal and Their American Dominions, 1500-1800* (1959) claim for Murillo accurate and facile draftsmanship, harmony of composition, and unity of conception and execution; Juan Antonio Gaya Nuño in the article on Murillo in the *Encyclopedia of World Art,* vol. 10 (1965), suggests poor drawing, awkward composition, and a dichotomy between form and content. A highly respected third source is C. B. Curtis, *Velázquez and Murillo* (1883). □

Charles Francis Murphy

The American politician Charles Francis Murphy (1858-1924) was a Democratic boss who controlled Tammany Hall in New York City from 1902 to 1924.

Charles Francis Murphy, the son of Irish immigrants, was born on June 20, 1858, in New York City and raised there. He quit school at the age of 14 and held a succession of unskilled jobs. Hardworking and frugal, he saved enough money by 1880 to buy a small saloon. He made "Charlie's Place" into a popular hangout and the base of his political power in the rough East Side tenement region known as the Gas House District. In the early 1880s Murphy opened three more saloons and aligned himself with Tammany Hall in city politics.

A shrewd judge of men, a good listener, and a charitable, churchgoing Catholic, Murphy was elected Democratic leader of the Gas House District in 1892. Five years later the mayor appointed him dock commissioner, the only official public post Murphy ever held. Although he never broke the law, he stretched it by granting favored companies leases and contracts without competitive bidding. When he left office in 1901, he was close to being a millionaire.

In 1901 Tammany was without a leader, and a power struggle ensued from which Murphy emerged as Tammany Hall's new boss in 1902. In the 1903 municipal election he engineered a victory over Seth Low's reform administration, and his Tammany Democratic slates dominated city elections for the next decade. Murphy's success in a period of heightened reform feeling was in large part due to his choice of reform-minded Democrats to head the Tammany ticket and his sponsorship of such outstanding young Democrats as Robert Wagner and Alfred E. (Al) Smith.

At times Murphy's methods backfired. By 1910 he had extended his power to the state level, and in 1912 he backed William Sulzner for governor. When Sulzner proved too independent and turned against the machine, Murphy had Sulzner impeached by the Tammany-dominated state legislature in 1913. But 4 years of public disapproval followed. However, in 1917 Tammany was returned to power in the city elections.

Murphy ruled more by accommodation than autocratic direction. He was flexible enough to satisfy his constituents

Frank Murphy was born in Harbor Beach, Mich., on April 13, 1890. He developed an enduring hatred against "industrial slavery" as a boy worker in a local starch factory. With his mother's teaching of racial equality and Christian love, Murphy evolved into a dynamic defender of the underprivileged. He worked his way through the University of Michigan. After receiving his law degree in 1914, he worked as a law clerk in Detroit and taught in a night school.

At the outbreak of World War I Murphy enlisted and served in France. After the war he studied law in Trinity College, Dublin, and in Lincoln's Inn, London. He was chief assistant to the U.S. attorney of Eastern Michigan District (1919-1920) and was reputed never to have lost a case. After private practice (1920-1923) he was appointed judge of Recorder's Court in Detroit (1923-1930) and handled criminal cases. He was mayor of Detroit from 1930 to 1933.

In 1932 Murphy was appointed governor general of the Philippines. He demonstrated his generous sympathy for the plight of the Filipino masses, especially for the land-hungry and oppressed tenant farmers, and emphasized the need for social justice. He was high commissioner of the islands in 1935-1936. In an interview in 1947 he expressed his belief that a revolution by the workers and peasants against the prevailing inequality in the Philippines was inevitable and bound to win.

When Murphy became governor of Michigan in 1936, he was faced with a sitdown strike by General Motors workers. The corporation obtained a court order to compel

with patronage, while giving the public respectable mayors and better municipal services. He responded to growing progressive sentiment by endorsing labor legislation, woman's suffrage, and the direct primary. When he died in New York City on April 25, 1924, he was at the peak of his power, working for the presidential nomination of his protégé, Al Smith.

Further Reading

Nancy Joan Weiss, *Charles Francis Murphy, 1858-1924; Respectability and Responsibility in Tammany Politics* (1968), is a solid, full-length biography. Shorter scholarly sketches of Murphy are in Harold Zink, *City Bosses in the United States* (1930), and Alfred Connable and Edward Silberfarb, *Tigers of Tammany: Nine Men Who Ran New York* (1967). The standard histories of Tammany are somewhat dated: Gustavus Myers, *The History of Tammany Hall* (1901; 2d ed. rev. 1917), and M. R. Werner, *Tammany Hall* (1928). □

Frank Murphy

Frank Murphy (1890-1949), American jurist and diplomat, campaigned against municipal corruption and crime as U.S. attorney general. He was a liberal sympathizer of the Filipino independence movement when he was governor general and high commissioner of the Philippine Islands.

the workers to quit striking, but Murphy refused to enforce it by calling the troops; for this he was severely criticized by the establishment. Although acclaimed by liberals, he lost the support of politicians and workers and was defeated for reelection in 1938. Appointed in 1939 as U.S. attorney general, he waged a relentless crusade against crime syndicates, notably against Thomas Pendergast in Kansas City, and political racketeers. His indictment of 16 alleged Communists and fellow travelers in Detroit for having recruited volunteers for Loyalist Spain earned him the censure of liberals throughout the country.

President Franklin Roosevelt appointed Murphy associate justice of the Supreme Court in 1940 in recognition of his support of the New Deal program. As a member of the five-man liberal majority on the Court, Murphy fought all forms of racketeering and safeguarded the rights of minorities. In April he wrote the decision invalidating antipicket laws and thus won general praise for his firm stand against antistrike measures.

After 15 years of service in the Justice Department, Murphy died in Detroit on July 19, 1949. Quiet in manner, courteous, somewhat ascetic and pious, Murphy followed his motto, "Speak softly and hit hard," in his work. He expressed the ruling principle of his life thus: "I should like to belong to that small company of public servants and others who are content to do some of the homely and modest task of perfecting integrity in government and making government more efficient and orderly."

Further Reading

Harold Norris, ed., *Mr. Justice Murphy and the Bill of Rights* (1965), has a biography of Murphy along with some of his Supreme Court opinions. The best source for Murphy's life is Richard D. Lunt, *The High Ministry of Government: The Political Career of Frank Murphy* (1965). A useful biography of Murphy by J. P. Rodie is in Allison Dunham and Philip B. Kurland, eds., *Mr. Justice* (1956; rev. ed. 1964). The Philippine background is given in Theodore Friend, *Between Two Empires: The Ordeal of the Philippines, 1929-1946* (1965).

Additional Sources

Fine, Sidney, *Frank Murphy*. Ann Arbor: University of Michigan Press, 1975-c1984. □

James Murray

The British general James Murray (1721-1794) came to prominence during the campaigns against the French in North America. After the fall of Quebec, he became its first English military governor and then its first civil governor.

James Murray was born on Jan. 21, 1721, at Ballencrief, Scotland. He was the fifth son of Alexander, the 4th Lord Elibank. In 1740 Murray was appointed a second lieutenant in Wynyard's Marines and served subsequently in the West Indies, Flanders, and Brittany and at the defense of

Ostend in 1745. He took part in the Rochfort expedition of 1757 and commanded a brigade during the successful siege of Louisbourg, Cape Breton, in 1758.

At the decisive battle of the Plains of Abraham near old Quebec on Sept. 13, 1759, Murray commanded the left wing of the British army. After the death of James Wolfe and the French surrender of the garrison, he was put in charge with 4,000 troops under his command.

After a winter filled with hardships both for the British forces and for the French inhabitants of Quebec, Murray was faced in the spring of 1760 with a French force greatly superior in numbers. On April 28, 1760, he met the French at Saint-Foy but was forced to retreat to the citadel. The French forces, led by Levis, laid siege to Quebec but were forced to retire when, on May 15, a British naval squadron arrived. Murray then reorganized his forces and proceeded to Montreal. He was there with his troops when Vaudreuil surrendered Montreal and New France to the British on Sept. 13, 1760.

In October 1760 Murray was appointed military governor, and, after the signing of peace between England and France in 1763, he became the first civil governor of Quebec. He got on well with many of the leading French Canadians in the colony and ignored the imperial authorities' wishes for the summoning of an elected assembly. The English merchants demanded not only an elected assembly but the introduction of English civil law, and when these demands were not met, they forced Murray's recall.

In 1774 Murray was appointed governor of Minorca off Spain. In August 1781 a force of 16,000 French and Spanish troops laid siege to Fort St. Philip on Minorca. Murray held out for some months but finally was forced to surrender on Feb. 5, 1782. He was subsequently tried by a general court-martial, but he was acquitted early in 1783 of all charges except two minor ones. He was made a full general in February 1783 and subsequently served for a time as governor of Hull in Yorkshire. He died at his residence, Beauport House, near Battle, Sussex, on June 18, 1794.

Further Reading

There is no recent biography of Murray. An early study is R. H. Mahon, *Life of General the Hon. James Murray, a Builder of Canada* (1921). Hilda Neatby, *Quebec: The Revolutionary Age, 1760-1791* (1966), offers a fresh view of Murray and places his career within the context of the period. □

Leslie Allan Murray

The Australian Leslie Allan Murray (born 1938) was an outstanding poet of his generation and one of his country's most influential literary critics. A nationalist and republican, he saw his writing as helping to define, in cultural and spiritual terms, what it means to be Australian.

Leslie Allan Murray was born in 1938 in Nabiac, a village on the north coast of New South Wales, Australia, and spent his childhood and youth on his father's dairy farm nearby. The area is sparsely populated, hilly, and forested, and the beauty of this rural landscape forms a backdrop to many of Murray's best poems, such as "Spring Hail":

> . . . Fresh-minted hills
> smoked, and the heavens swirled and blew away.
> The paddocks were endless again, and all around
> leaves lay beneath their trees, and cakes of moss.

His parents were poor and their weatherboard house almost bare of comforts; Murray remarked that it was not until he went to the university that he first met the middle class. His identification was with the underprivileged, especially the rural poor, and it was this that gave him his strong sense of unity with Aborigines and with 'common folk.' The title he chose for his Selected Poems, *The Vernacular Republic,* indicates both this sense of unity and his Wordsworthian belief that through the use of "language really spoken by men" poets can speak to and for the people.

Many of the Scottish settlers on the New South Wales coast had been forced out of Scotland by the Highland clearances of the 19th century, and they in turn were among those who dispossessed the Aboriginal Kattang tribe around the Manning valley; in later years Murray's own father was forced off the land by family chicanery. The theme of usurpation, whether of land or of culture, as well as the influence of Murray's Celtic background, are often present in his work, as one sees in poems such as "A Walk with O'Connor," in which the two Australian Celts try in vain to understand Gaelic on a tombstone, the grave becoming symbolic of the death of Celtic culture:

> . . . reading the Gaelic, constrained and
> shamefaced, we tried
> to guess what it meant
> then, drifting away,
> translated Italian off opulent tombstones nearby
> in our discontent.

Religion in his Poetry

In 1957 Murray went to the University of Sydney to study modern languages. While there he worked on the editorial boards of three student publications. At Sydney he was converted from the Free Kirk Presbyterianism of his parents to Roman Catholicism, "the spirit in which the poems are bathed," according to Murray, quoted in *Commonweal.* "What a poem is at its best," said Murray, "is a quiet little removal of death from ordinary circumstances. It's been placed one small, decisive step beyond the mortal. It's something that's been made immortal but is quite ordinary at the same time."

The influence of passionately held Christian convictions can be seen everywhere in his verse, though seldom overtly except in his dedication of his books "to the glory of God;" instead it shows itself, in poems such as "Blood" or "The Broad Bean Sermon," in a strong sense of the power of ritual in everyday life and of the sacramental quality of existence. "Almost everything they say is ritual," he remarked of rural Australians in one of his best-known poems, "The Mitchells."

He left Sydney University in 1960 without a degree, and in 1963, on the strength of his studies in modern languages, became a translator of foreign scholarly material at the Australian National University in Canberra. His first volume of poems, *The Ilex Tree* (written with Geoffrey Lehmann), won the Grace Leven Prize for poetry on its publication in 1965, and in the same year Murray made his first trip out of Australia, to attend the British Commonwealth Arts Festival Poetry Conference in Cardiff. His appetite whetted by this visit, he gave up his translator's post in 1967 and spent over a year traveling in Britain and Europe. Travel had the effect of cementing his Australian nationalism; he was a republican who believed that Australia should throw off the shackles of political and cultural dependence, and he saw his work as helping to achieve that end.

A Writing Career

On his return to Australia he resumed his studies, graduating from Sydney University in 1969. After that he earned his living as a full-time poet and writer. He was one of Australia's most influential literary critics and a prolific contributor of book reviews and literary articles to newspapers and journals, acted as poetry reader for the publisher

Angus & Robertson from 1976 to 1991, edited the magazine *Poetry Australia* from 1973 to 1979, and became literary editor of the journal *Quadrant* in 1990. Three selections of his prose pieces appeared in volume form: *The Peasant Mandarin* (1978), *Persistence in Folly* (1984), and *Blocks and Tackles* (1990).

However, it was his steady output of volumes of poetry that gave Murray his position of unchallenged eminence. In addition to *The Ilex Tree,* these include *The Weatherboard Cathedral* (1969), *Poems Against Economics* (1972), *Selected Poems: The Vernacular Republic* (1976), *Ethnic Radio* (1977), *The Boys Who Stole the Funeral* (1980), *Equanimities* (1982), *The Vernacular Republic: Poems 1961-1981* (1982), *The People's Otherworld* (1983), *The Daylight Moon* (1987), *The Idyll Wheel* (1989), *Dog Fox Field* (1990), *The Rabbiter's Bounty: Collected Poems* (1992), *Translations from the Natural World* (1992), and *Subhuman Redneck Poems* (1996), for which he was honored with the T.S. Eliot Prize of poetry in January 1997.

Murray's poems cover a great diversity and range, but a number of themes run through them from start to finish. Chief among these are his celebration of life and nature in all their diversity; his sense of the sanctity of human existence, and yet of its pathos as well; his association with 'the people,' particularly common country folk, and a concomitant distrust of elites; and his strong sense of what it means to be an Australian, paradoxically combined with a deep-rooted cosmopolitanism resulting from his reading in a wide range of languages.

His poetry is remarkable for its energy and for the bounding Elizabethan fecundity of its images. In the manner of the 17th-century poets too, it is often intellectually demanding, while never surrendering its claim to be popular. Its emotional range is very wide: Murray is a master of lightly humorous verse and of brilliant description, but he can also be deeply moving or bitingly satirical, as in the fine series of 'Police' poems he published in *Lunch and Counter Lunch.* He seldom plays with words merely for the sake of the play; his poetry has a passionately felt message to convey. It draws attention also by its variety of poetic forms: Murray is able to use free verse or the most difficult of traditional stanzaic forms with equal ease, and his work showed this flexibility from the very start of his career.

Perhaps the most impressive demonstration of his technical skill came in *The Boys Who Stole the Funeral,* in which he produced a verse novel consisting of 140 sonnets. Since the volume makes a plea for the maintenance of order and traditional values, the formality of its structure can be seen as contributing directly to its meaning. This unity of form and content is evident in many of Murray's best poems.

The Boys Who Stole the Funeral also further developed an element which had shown itself early on in Murray's work: a deep interest in Aboriginal poetry, and an ability to use the conventions and concerns of Aboriginal oral culture in poetry that is distinctively and maturely Australian, yet has a very wide appeal. His focus on the poor and dispossessed, his love of the land and his sense of its spiritual value, the importance of the clan in his writing (some of his best poems are about his family), all these are elements which link his work with Aboriginal culture.

He was widely recognized as the outstanding poet of his generation in Australia, and he was the recipient of numerous awards and prizes. Murray also became an arbiter of Australian poetry in 1996 with the publication of *The New Oxford Book of Australian Verse,* which he edited. Murray was both praised and criticized for his democratizing of Australian poetry through his choice of entries.

Until 1986 Murray lived chiefly in Sydney; afterwards he made his home on a small farm in Bunya, just a few miles from where he spent his boyhood, with his wife Valerie and the youngest of his five children. His volume of poems *The Idyll Wheel* reflects his sense of joyful renewal at this return to his rural roots.

Subject of an ABC documentary in 1991 and short-listed for the T.S. Eliot prize in 1992, then winner of the European Petrarch Award in 1995 for his life's work of over 30 books, many translated in multiple foreign languages, Murray was gripped by diabetes and a "Black Dog" depression. He collapsed in 1996 and was hospitalized with a liver infection from which he emerged only after two operations, the last rites of the church, and 20 days in intensive care. Murray quipped that his doctors cut out not only part of his liver, but also his depression (with help from well-wishers worldwide), but his brush with death left him too weak to travel to England the next year when the T.S. Eliot prize finally became his.

Prolific as he is, nearly as much has been written and spoken about Murray as by him. Among his admirers is Derek Walcott, who said, quoted in a 1992 issue of *Commonweal,* "There is no poetry in the English language now so rooted in its sacredness, so broad-leafed in its pleasures, and yet so intimate and so conversational."

Further Reading

Leslie Murray writes on his own work in "The Human Hair Thread," reprinted in his volume *Persistence in Folly* (1984). His other volumes of prose pieces *The Peasant Mandarin* (1978) and *Blocks and Tackles* (1990), are also illuminating in this way.

Murray gave interviews to Robert Gray in *Quadrant* (1976); and Missy Daniel in *Commonweal* (May 22, 1992), as well as a talk he gave about the writer's craft in *Australian Literary Studies* (1984). There is a biographical sketch by Graeme Kinross Smith in *Westerly* (1980). The many article-length discussions of Murray's work include those by Peter Alexander in *The Australasian Catholic Record* (1981); Lawrence Bourke in *Southerly* (1987) and in *Australian Literary Studies* (1988); James Tulip in *Poetry Australia* (1989); Kevin Hart in *Australian Literary Studies* (1989), Susan Wyndham in the *Sydney Morning Herald* (Oct. 19, 1996); and Stephen Burt in *Poetry Review* (vol. 87, No. 1, Spring 1997).

Biographical information may be found on the Internet at www.magna.com, a site maintained by Murray's publisher, Duffy & Snellgrove. □

Philip Murray

Philip Murray (1886-1952), American labor leader, helped organize America's mass-production workers into industrial unions through the establishment of the Congress of Industrial Organizations.

Philip Murray, John L. Lewis, Sidney Hillman, and David Dubinsky built the American labor movement as it now functions. During the Great Depression and the New Deal of the 1930s, they brought trade unionism out of the doldrums and, through the creation of industrial unions, into a position of power whereby labor influenced big business and national politics.

Murray was born on May 25, 1886, in Lanarkshire, Scotland, to Irish immigrant parents. His father was a coal miner active in the Scottish trade union movement. When Philip entered the mines at the age of 10, he was already a novice trade unionist knowledgable about strikes. In 1902 the Murray family emigrated to America. They settled in the western Pennsylvania mining district of Westmoreland County, where they had relatives.

Early Union Career

Within 2 years Murray had become a union militant, leading a strike against the coal company for which he worked. As a result, the Murray family was evicted from a company house and Philip was banished from the county.

From that moment he decided to devote his life to the labor movement.

Murray rose rapidly within the ranks of the United Mine Workers of America (UMWA). By 1912 he was a member of the international executive board, and in 1916 he won election as president of District 5, the powerful Pittsburgh bituminous region. In 1920 John L. Lewis, the UMWA president, appointed Murray vice-president.

Throughout the 1920s and early 1930s, when the UMWA was racked with factionalism and suffered a sharp membership decline, Murray remained unshakably loyal to Lewis. Because Murray proved so knowledgable about the economics of coal and other major industries and because of his proven negotiating ability, when Lewis formed the Steel Workers Organizing Committee (SWOC) in 1936 he appointed Murray chairman.

Ideas and Programs

By then Murray had firm ideas about the place of the labor movement in American society. Devout Catholicism and the family tradition of unionism combined to form his own vision of social justice. Unionism led him to espouse the workers' case against employers; Catholicism caused him to oppose all so-called revolutionary "isms" and, in accord with the papal encyclicals on labor-management relations, to see the employers' as well as the workers' rights in the industrial and social systems. He expounded these ideas in a book he coauthored with industrial engineer Morris Llewellyn Cooke, *Organized Labor and Production*. The book asserted that if employers recognized trade unions and engaged in productive collective bargaining, the result would be justice for the worker, harmonious industrial relations, security for private ownership of property, increased productivity, and higher profits and wages.

Congress of Industrial Organizations

As chairman of SWOC, Murray sought to put his ideas into action. Financed by Lewis and the UMWA, SWOC succeeded in February 1937 in winning a collective bargaining agreement from United States Steel and from many smaller companies. But later that year the "Little Steel companies" defeated SWOC in a brutal and bloody strike.

Murray's patience, warmth, and negotiating skills kept SWOC alive and vital until conditions once again favored union growth. When World War II erupted and America moved into defense and war production, Murray succeeded in 1942 in breaking down Little Steel's barriers to trade unionism. That same year he transformed SWOC into the United Steelworkers of America (USA) and became its first president.

As president, Murray demonstrated what he had learned as Lewis's loyal lieutenant. Other industrial unions that emerged during the 1930s had democratic union constitutions and rank-and-file participation, but the USA was controlled from the top down. At the 1942 founding convention Murray demanded and won a constitution that vested almost complete power in the leadership, meaning in this case Murray, who was also president of the Congress of

Industrial Organizations (CIO) as well as a vice president of the UMWA.

Relations with Lewis

Despite his debt to Lewis, Murray could not avert a break. When Lewis repudiated Franklin Roosevelt in 1940, Murray remained committed to the President and the New Deal. As a result, Lewis retired as president of the CIO and was replaced by Murray. Lewis called Murray before the UMWA executive board in 1942, charged him with disloyalty, and stripped him of his union vice presidency. Murray, however, retained his presidencies of the CIO and the USA until his death.

Always a moderate attuned to the climate of the times and eager to make the labor movement more respectable, Murray rode the tide of anticommunism after the war. At the 1949 CIO convention he declared that, while there was room within the organization for all varieties of thought, there was no room for communism. He then led the convention delegates to expel 11 allegedly Communist-dominated unions from the CIO. He died in San Francisco on Nov. 9, 1952.

Further Reading

There is no substantial biography of Murray. The best place to find information on him is in two long and detailed histories of labor by Irving Bernstein, *The Lean Years: A History of the American Worker, 1920-1933* (1960) and *The Turbulent Years: A History of the American Worker, 1933-1941* (1970). For Murray's part in the struggle for industrial unionism with the American Federation of Labor see the dry, objective account by Philip Taft, *The A.F. of L. from the Death of Gompers to the Merger* (1959). The best study of Murray's role in the SWOC and CIO organizing drives in the mass-production industries is Walter Galenson, *The C.I.O. Challenge to the A.F. of L.* (1960). □

Edward Roscoe Murrow

Edward Roscoe Murrow (1908-1965), American radio and television news broadcaster, pioneered in developing journalism and political and social commentary for the mass media.

Edward R. Murrow was born Egbert R. Murrow on Polecat Creek near Greensboro, N.C., on April 25, 1908. The family moved in 1913, and Murrow grew up in Washington state. He worked in logging camps during vacations from Washington State College, changing his first name in the process.

Murrow began his career in international student exchange, but after his marriage to Janet Huntington Brewster he joined the Columbia Broadcasting System (CBS) in 1935 as director of talks. In 1937 he went to London to arrange speeches and concerts for the American radio network. However, in 1938, he was plunged into news broadcasting when Adolf Hitler annexed Austria to Germany, and he

continued to broadcast throughout World War II. The German "blitz" against London in 1940 made Murrow's the best-known American radio voice from overseas, identified by his incisive personal reporting from rooftops and airfields and his social and political probing behind the wartime headlines. After America entered the war, Murrow won renown for his broadcasts describing a bombing raid against Berlin, the liberation of the Buchenwald concentration camp, and the American capture of Leipzig.

Returning to the United States after the war, Murrow inaugurated television journalism-in-depth in 1951 with the weekly program "See It Now." It examined political and social issues and in 1954 challenged the nation's most feared demagogue at that time, Senator Joseph McCarthy. "See It Now" stirred controversy as it explored various national concerns, and Murrow ranged the world to film news and interview political figures. With his good looks and forceful personality, he became a well-known public figure in his own right, especially after starting another television program, "Person to Person," which brought him electronically into the homes of celebrities.

But the widening mass nature of television with its increasing commercialism and costs put the emphasis on entertainment programs that won audience ratings. Murrow's brand of purposeful news broadcasting found less and less time on the air. A notable speech to the broadcasting industry in 1958 appealing for better programs found little response. Murrow left broadcasting in 1961 to become director of the U.S. Information Agency (USIA). He restored the USIA's morale and effectiveness, damaged in the Mc-

Carthy years, but found conflict between his role as government propagandist and his independent journalistic past. Ill health compelled his resignation, and he died on April 27, 1965.

Further Reading

A collection of Murrow's wartime broadcasts is his *This Is London* (1941). A much wider range of his radio and television broadcasts is provided by Edward Bliss, Jr., ed., *In Search of Light* (1967). Murrow's associate Fred W. Friendly wrote about him in *Due to Circumstances beyond Our Control* (1967). Alexander Kendrick, *Prime Time* (1969), is a full biography. □

Musa Mansa

Mansa Musa (died 1337), king of the Mali empire in West Africa, is known mostly for his fabulous pilgrimage to Mecca and for his promotion of unity and prosperity within Mali.

Very little is known about the life of Mansa Musa before 1312. In that year he succeeded his father, Abu Bakr II, to the throne and thus gained the hereditary title of mansa. After this point he is fairly well covered in the *tarikhs* (Moslem chronicles) of North Africa and the western Sudan, which tell of his reign as a golden age. In contrast to his famous 13th-century predecessor Sundiata, Musa is practically forgotten in Malinke oral traditions.

Many modern writers feel that Musa's importance in West African history is exaggerated because of the fame he obtained during his truly impressive pilgrimage to Mecca in 1324-1325. Other Sudanese monarchs had undertaken the pious journey in previous centuries, but the very scale and opulence of Musa's caravan made an impact on Cairo and Mecca which was remembered for years. He is said to have been accompanied by 500 slaves, each carrying a 4-pound staff of gold, and 80 camels with 300 pounds of gold each. All of this wealth was spent or given out as alms in the Arab cities.

The effect of this sudden glut of gold on Egypt was an inflation still observable 12 years later when al-Umari visited Cairo and recorded much of what we now know about Musa and Mali. The reputation which Musa established in Egypt soon spread to Europe, where as early as 1339 Mali appeared on a world map along with Musa's name. For the next 6 centuries the name of Mali was associated with fabulous wealth by Europeans.

Completion of his pilgrimage earned for Musa the coveted title of *al-hajj*, but this experience also taught him a great deal about orthodox Islam, and he returned to Mali with a strong desire to reform Islam there. He brought with him North African architects and scholars to carry out this task, but Islam remained, as before, the religion of the towns. The majority of the people lived in the country, and they continued to follow Malinke religious beliefs.

Musa developed diplomatic ties with the North African states and thereby facilitated an unprecedented growth of trans-Saharan trade, which in turn further enriched and strengthened the imperial government. Internal commerce and agriculture flourished, and the order and prosperity found in Mali in 1352-1353 by the famous Arab traveler Ibn Battuta were largely attributable to Musa's enlightened leadership earlier in the century.

On his death in 1337 Musa was succeeded by his son, Mansa Maghan (reigned 1337-1341), who had ruled during Musa's visit to Mecca and Cairo.

Further Reading

There is no book-length biography of Musa, but short biographical sketches are in Lavinia Dobler and William A. Brown, *Great Rulers of the African Past* (1965), and A. Adu Boahen, *Topics in West African History* (1966). More general books on West Africa should also be consulted, including E. W. Bovill, *The Golden Trade of the Moors* (1958; rev. ed. 1968), and J. S. Trimingham, *A History of Islam in West Africa* (1962). □

Thea Musgrave

Thea Musgrave (born 1928) was a prominent Scottish-born composer whose works include operas, ballet scores, orchestral pieces, chamber music, and vocal and choral works. Her music was performed in Great Britain, Europe, and the United States.

Thea Musgrave was highly regarded for her talent in a wide variety of musical forms. Her compositional techniques included serial writing and electronically generated sound, but her personal style was not confined to one school of composition. She described the form of some of her music as "dramatic-abstract" and said,

Music goes from moment to moment, and I'm very conscious of voice-leading. I'm also conscious of the big gesture, the route the music will follow, and that is where tonality comes in, creating the feeling of home. The feeling of home can be established by a chord or a color or a rhythm. Or when you arrive at E-flat. It's not E-flat major, but you know it's E-flat. I do compose in long lines, long gestures, and I know where I'm going. At the same time, I compose each moment as beautifully, as perfectly as I can.

Musgrave was born in Edinburgh in 1928, attending Edinburgh University, where she studied harmony and analysis under Mary Grierson and counterpoint and history of music under Hans Gal, from 1947 to 1950. She attended the Paris Conservatory (1952-1954), and she studied composition privately with Nadia Boulanger from 1950 to 1954. She lectured on music at London University (1959-1965) and later was a visiting professor at the University of California at Santa Barbara. In the mid-1980s she lived in Norfolk, Virginia, with her husband, Peter Mark, who was conductor and general director of the Virginia Opera Association.

Musgrave received many commissions and awards, among them the Donald Francis Tovey prize and the Lili Boulanger Memorial prize, which she won while she was a student. In 1974 she received the Serge Koussevitsky Music Foundation award, for which she composed *Space Play,* a chamber piece for nine instruments. The piece was given its premiere performance in the United States by the Chamber Music Society of Lincoln Center. Musgrave was also awarded two Guggenheim Fellowships.

The BBC awarded her commissions for the composition of *The Phoenix and the Turtle* (1962), a work for small choir and orchestra; *Night Music* (1969) for chamber orchestra; and the *Viola Concerto* (1973). The Royal Philharmonic Society commissioned her to write the *Concerto for Clarinet and Orchestra* (1968). Other commissions came from the Gulbenkian Foundation, for which she wrote the full-length ballet *Beauty and the Beast* (1968-1969), and from the Virginia Opera Association, for which she wrote *A Christmas Carol* (1978-1979). The association performed the work in 1979. The many other commissions she received included a wide variety of music, from songs such as *Sir Patrick Spens* (1961), which was commissioned by Peter Pears, to the *Trio for Flute, Oboe and Piano* (1960), which was commissioned by the Mabillon Trio. Her versatility as a composer contributed to her success. Musgrave wrote for orchestra, chamber groups, and voice with the same assurance that she wrote for the opera, a medium in which she was particularly interested. Of the operas she wrote one of the best known is *Mary, Queen of Scots.*

Mary, Queen of Scots

Mary, Queen of Scots was composed between 1975 and 1977 and was first performed at the Edinburgh International Festival in 1977. Musgrave wrote the libretto of the opera herself, although it is based on an unfinished play by Amalia Elguera entitled *Moray.* The libretto focuses on the period in Mary's life when, as a widow of 19 and a Catholic, she returned to Scotland as queen. The opera covers the seven years she stayed in Scotland before fleeing to England to escape the consequences of her personal and political intrigues.

Andrew Porter wrote in a review of the American debut of the opera in 1978, "There is a sure congruence between musical and theatrical proportions. Each episode has just enough words and just enough action to allow a full yet economical musical development. Nothing goes on too long."

Other Operas

Musgrave wrote four other operas before completing *Mary, Queen of Scots.* The first was *The Abbot of Drimock* (1955), a chamber opera based on Wilson's *Tales of the Border.* Her second opera, *The Decision* (1964-1965), was first performed by the New Opera Company at Sadler's Wells in 1967. Another chamber opera, *The Voice of Ariadne* (1977), was performed by the New York City Opera in 1977. The libretto was written by Amalia Elguera and was inspired by a Henry James story, *The Last of the Valerii.* The libretto recounts the story of an Italian count whose infat-

uation with the voice of a ruined statue of Ariadne produces a reaction of jealousy from his American wife. The plot serves as a setting for the conflict between the two cultures represented by the count and his wife, as well as a depiction of a romantic triangle.

Following the completion of *Mary, Queen of Scots,* Musgrave wrote *A Christmas Carol,* given its first American performance by the Virginia Opera Association in 1979. Musgrave wrote of the opera, "One of my earliest decisions was to cast the Spirit of Christmas in all its manifestations as a dancer and that Marley's ghost should be an actor, thus putting these supernatural characters on a quite different level to the other singers. The musical style of this opera is melodic, and, I hope, accessible, as befits the subject."

In March of 1985 the first performance of Musgrave's opera *Harriet: A Woman Called Moses* was given by the Virginia Opera Association, which had commissioned the work along with the Royal Opera of Covent Garden. Musgrave wrote her own libretto for the opera, which she based on the life of Harriet Tubman, the African-American woman who enabled slaves to escape to the north via the "underground railroad." Bernard Holland wrote of the opera, "*Harriet* . . . offers terribly effective music for the stage. . . . If there are dull spots, they involve Miss Musgrave's whites interacting among themselves. Black culture, on the other hand, sharpens her inspiration."

Orchestral Works

The dramatic sensibility evident in her operas is also present in many of her orchestral and chamber works. In *Concerto for Orchestra* (1967) the various sections of the orchestra are the center of the musical focus. In the climax of the piece individual soloists stand and perform music which is notated, but whose rhythm is freely interpreted by the performer. In *Concerto for Clarinet* (1968) the soloist moves around the orchestra, a device which Musgrave said "grows out of the musical demand" because "the soloist plays with different small groups and they can't hear him unless he joins them."

Musgrave wrote *Night Music* in 1969. Stanley Sadie wrote about the piece that it "avowedly has no programme, but [the] vivid graphic writing invites description in emotive adjectives. Music in fact underlaid by strong feelings and also lucidly laid out." Following *Night Music* Musgrave wrote *Memento Vitae (Concerto Homage to Beethoven)* (1969-1970), *Concerto for Horn and Orchestra* (1971), *Viola Concerto* (1973), *Orfeo II* (1975) for solo flute and 15 strings, and *From One to Another* (1980) for solo viola and 15 strings. Continuing the practice of placing orchestra members about the stage and theater for dramatic effect, Musgrave, in the closing part of the *Concerto for Horn and Orchestra,* had the orchestral horn section play from different positions behind the audience and, in the *Viola Concerto,* the viola section at one point rises and plays as if taking instruction from the soloist.

Peripeteia was completed in 1981 and was performed in 1984 by the New York Philharmonic under Leonard Slatkin. The title means "a sudden change, especially that on which the plot of a tragedy hinges." In the piece an initial opening section is followed by an "event," after which the original music can never fully reassert itself. Musgrave called the piece "a kind of opera without words or specific plot."

Chamber Music and Choral Works

Musgrave wrote three chamber concertos (1962, 1966, and 1966), the second of which is a tribute to Burl Ives in which she, like Ives, inserted a popular American song into her music. Following these concertos Musgrave wrote *Impromptu for Flute and Oboe* (1967), *Impromptu No. 2 for Flute, Oboe and Clarinet* (1967), *Music for Horn and Piano* (1969), *Elegy for Viola and Cello* (1970), *From One to Another* for viola and tape (1970), *Space Play* (1974), and *Orfeo I* (1975) for flute. *Space Play* is a humorous and lyric piece which involves special placement of nine performers around the stage. Wit and lyricism, as well as a sophisticated use of instrumental timbres, characterize her writing for both chamber and orchestral combinations.

Her choral works employ a wide variety of texts. They are taken from Hesiod *The Five Ages of Man* (1963); from Shakespeare *The Phoenix and the Turtle* (1962); from D. H. Lawrence *The Last Twilight* (1980); from Chaucer *Triptych* (1962); from Michelangelo *Caro m'e il sonno* (1978); and from John Donne *Memento Creatoris* (1967), among many others. In *Triptych,* which is written for solo tenor and orchestra, three songs convey three different moods, one lyric, another insistent, and the last, gay. The dramatic techniques evident in her other musical form are also present in *The Phoenix and the Turtle* (1962), *The Five Ages of Man* (1963), and the *Last Twilight* (1980), which is labelled a theater piece for chorus and instruments.

Recent works include *The Voice of Ariadne* (1989), *Piccolo Play* (1991), a multimedia piece *Echoes Through Time* (1989), *Pierrot* (1994), and *Simon Bolivar* (1995). She also wrote a book *The Choral Music of 21st Century Women Composers* (1997), with Elizabeth Lutyens and Elizabeth Merconchy.

Thea Musgrave wrote, in addition to the pieces already mentioned, many others including songs, ballet music, and incidental pieces. She forged an individual style of composition that explored the dramatic possibilities of music and the ways in which that drama can assist in creating large musical structures within the framework of the 20th-century musical language.

Further Reading

Thea Musgrave: A Bio-bibliography (1984) by Donald Hixon contains a biography and a complete list of works, a discography, and a bibliography of writings by and about Musgrave and her music. In addition, her works are listed in the *International Encyclopedia of Women Composers* published by R. R. Bowker in 1981. □

Robert Edler Von Musil

The Austrian novelist, dramatist, and essayist Robert Edler von Musil (1880-1942) gained a largely posthumous fame for his monumental and unfinished novel "The Man without Qualities."

Robert Musil was born on Nov. 6, 1880, in Klagenfurt, Carinthia, Austria. The son of a professor of engineering, Musil received his elementary education at military schools from 1892 to 1897. After serving for a period as an officer in the Austrian army, he began engineering studies, later changing to philosophy, logic, and experimental psychology. In 1908 he obtained a doctorate for his work on Ernst Mach from the University of Berlin. Between 1911 and 1914 Musil served as librarian at the Technische Hochschule in Vienna. During this time he also was briefly an editor of *Die neue Rundschau,* a review. During World War I Musil was an officer in the Austrian army, and in the postwar period he was employed in the War Office and in various other government ministries.

Between 1922 and 1938 Musil lived in Berlin and Vienna, supporting himself as a writer and through systematic contributions from interested friends. After the Anschluss, Musil went voluntarily into exile, living in Switzerland until his death. He died in Geneva on April 15, 1942, in poverty and almost completely unknown.

Stories and Dramas

Musil published his first novel, *Die Verwirrungen des Zöglings Törless* (*Young Törless*), in 1906. It is a story of troubled adolescence set in a military school modeled upon the one attended by both Musil and Rainer Maria Rilke. Musil's chief problem in the book was achieving an emotional equilibrium both within his characters and in their relationships to their fellow human beings. The book was immediately successful, and Musil next published *Vereinigungen,* two short stories, in 1911. In both of them— *Die Vollendung der Liebe* and *Die Versuchung der stillen Veronika*—unbearable reality is transformed by excessive imagination. The resulting heightening of the emotions brings about a spiritual, nonphysical union with the loved one.

Both of Musil's dramas, *Die Schwärmer* (1921) and *Vinzenz und die Freundin bedeutender Männer* (1924), represent stepping-stones toward achievement of a more tangible equilibrium. In times of great emotional intensity, says Musil, limits vanish, and man can achieve identification and union with one's fellowman. The three short stories of *Drei Frauen* (1921-1924) posit and resolve the problems caused by logical, rational, and emotionally limited men in relationship to emotionally more complicated women.

Monumental Achievement

In a sense all of Musil's early work was a preparation for his great novel and masterpiece, *Der Mann ohne Eigenschaften* (*The Man without Qualities*), which he began in the early 1920s. The first volume was issued in German in 1930, the second in 1933, and the third in 1942. He was working on the fourth at the time of his death. About 365 pages of this novel were published in English translation in 1953. They represent about one half of volume 1. Volumes 2 and 3 were also published in English translation.

Musil's *magnum opus* is a novel of the life and history of pre-World War I Austria. Ulrich, the hero of the novel, is the man without qualities, that is to say, a man with unimpaired potential. Like his creator, he has been an officer, engineer, and mathematician. He is the secretary of a celebration, whose planning begins in 1913, for the 1918 anniversary of the Austro-Hungarian Empire. The ironical implication is that the empire will have collapsed before the celebration is held.

Ulrich takes a year's leave from his duties to attempt to discover the meaning of life. His scientific training enables him to look at life as a laboratory, and he regards emotional intensity as the only meaningful morality. He achieves balance and equilibrium after he meets his sister Agathe. As they analyze their emotional lives, they experience a state of mystical intensity based upon a rational interpretation, the highest degree of feeling.

Further Reading

The most valuable study of Musil in English is Burton Pike, *Robert Musil: An Introduction to His Work* (1961), the preface of which includes biographical information. A discussion of *Young Törless* appears in Frank Kermode, *Puzzles and Epiphanies: Essays and Reviews, 1958-1961* (1962). Musil figures in general surveys of modern German literature, such as Harry T. Moore, *Twentieth-century German Literature* (1967); August Closs, *20th Century German Literature* (1969); and Henry Hatfield, *Crisis and Continuity in Modern German Fiction* (1969).

Additional Sources

Hickman, Hannah, *Robert Musil & the culture of Vienna*. La Salle, Ill.: Open Court Pub. Co., 1984. □

Edmund Sixtus Muskie

United States Senator Edmund Sixtus Muskie (1914-1996), the 1968 Democratic vice-presidential nominee and briefly a presidential candidate in 1972, was one of the key congressional leaders in formulating national policy on urban affairs and the environment during the 1960s and 1970s.

Edmund S. Muskie was born on March 28, 1914, to Stephen and Josephine Muskie in Rumford, Maine. Stephen Muskie was born Stepen Marciszewski in Poland in 1882, then a province of the Russian Empire. Because young Poles were frequently conscripted into Czarist armies, Stephen's parents arranged for him to be apprenticed to a tailor when he was 12 years old and for his emigration from Poland when he was 17 years old.

After three years in England Stephen Marciszewski arrived in the United States in 1903, settled in Dickson City, Pennsylvania, and changed his name to Muskie. He married Josephine Czarnecka of Buffalo in 1911. While on their honeymoon in Maine, the couple decided to settle in Rumford. Edmund, the second of six children, was born there three years later.

The Muskies were one of only three Polish families in the western Maine paper mill town of Rumford, and young Edmund was frequently the subject of schoolyard taunts for his ancestry, his religion, and, he found later, his father's politics, as the elder Muskie was one of the few Democrats in the town. Nevertheless, Muskie excelled in high school and earned a small scholarship at nearby Bates College. He graduated with a B.A. from Bates in 1936 and a law degree from Cornell University in 1939.

Winning as a Democrat in Maine

Muskie began practicing law in 1940 in Waterville, Maine, but his career was interrupted by naval service during World War II. When he returned home he decided to run for the Maine legislature in 1946 as a Democrat. Muskie's political affiliation was not particularly surprising; Franklin Roosevelt's New Deal greatly influenced Muskie politically. New Deal legislation helped provide funds for his education and promoted the causes he supported.

His political allegiance, however sensible personally, nevertheless seemed to be a liability in an overwhelmingly Republican state. But Muskie accepted the challenge.

When asked by a reporter during the campaign why he was a Democrat in Maine, he wryly replied, "Well if I lived down South I'd probably be a Republican. Somebody has to do it."

Muskie was the surprise winner in the 1946 legislative race, served three terms in the state legislature, and in 1954 became Maine's first Democratic governor in 20 years and only the second in the century. Muskie's personal popularity helped reestablish the Democratic Party as a force in Maine politics. His promotion of economic development, fiscal conservatism, and cooperation with the Republican-dominated state legislature appealed to the state's voters, many of whom split their tickets to become "Muskie Republicans." In 1958, when Muskie became the state's first Democrat elected to the U.S. Senate in nearly a century, other Democrats were elected governor and to the U.S. Congress in two of Maine's three congressional districts. Muskie was reelected to the Senate in 1964, 1970, and 1976.

A Liberal, Hard-Working Senator

Senator Muskie soon developed a reputation as an expert in writing and enacting legislation. His willingness to modify proposals to gain bipartisan support, a skill acquired during his years as Maine's governor, made Muskie one of the most effective and respected members of the Senate. As chairman of the Housing Subcommittee of the Senate Banking and Currency Committee, Muskie was responsible for much of the national legislation associated with urban affairs, including creation of the Department of Housing and Urban Development in 1965 and the Model Cities Act of 1966.

Muskie was an ardent defender of the environment, a concern reflected in ten major bills he sponsored between 1963 and 1976. Those measures included the 1965 Water Quality Act, the 1967 Air Quality Act, and the 1970 National Air Quality Act which required pollution-free automobiles by 1975. Muskie was a key supporter of the Environmental Protection Agency, established in 1970.

Muskie's legislative successes also included the 1970 Securities Investor Protection Act, which insured investors against brokerage house failures, and the 1972 Truth-in-Government Act, which created an independent board authorized to make available to the public government documents which did not compromise national security. In 1973 he was Senate floor manager of the War Powers Act, which passed over President Richard Nixon's veto. The act clearly defined presidential and congressional authority in war-making decisions. Muskie-supported increases in social security benefits, continued federal aid to education, civil rights measures, a national draft lottery, and the vote for 18-year-olds. Although an early supporter of American involvement in the Vietnam War, by 1969 he had become one of its leading critics.

Campaigns for Vice President and President

Although Edmund Muskie officially campaigned for the presidency only once—in 1972—the Maine senator was promoted for national office as early as 1960. Muskie was already known among Democratic Party activists outside Maine because of his election victories through the 1950s in an overwhelmingly Republican state. His Polish ancestry, once considered a liability in Maine, made him a popular lecture circuit speaker among ethnic groups and with Democratic candidates in large, vote-rich, Northeastern states such as New York, Pennsylvania, Ohio, and Massachusetts. In 1960 Muskie was briefly mentioned as a possible vice-presidential candidate. In 1964 President Lyndon Johnson fueled speculation that Muskie might be his vice-presidential choice until he selected Minnesota Senator Hubert Humphrey. Finally, in 1968, Vice-President Humphrey, the Democratic presidential nominee, selected Muskie as his running mate. Although the GOP nominees, former Vice-President Richard Nixon and Maryland Governor Spiro Agnew, easily defeated the Democrats, Muskie's impressive campaign performance propelled him into national prominence. Muskie was famous for this response during the campaign: "In Maine, we have a saying that you don't say anything that doesn't improve on silence."

On January 4, 1972, Edmund S. Muskie officially announced his candidacy for the presidency. After winning the New Hampshire and Illinois primaries but losing in Florida, Wisconsin, Pennsylvania, and Massachusetts, Muskie withdrew from the race in April 1972. As the party's acknowledged frontrunner, his staff had become overconfident and conducted a vague and cautious campaign. But Muskie was also the victim of the Nixon administration's "dirty tricks" campaign which attempted to discredit his presidential bid by distributing phony Muskie press releases and campaign literature, heckling the senator's speeches, and disrupting campaign communications.

Muskie did not react well to Nixon's "dirty tricks." In response to printed accusations that his wife had behaved in a drunken and unladylike manner, and that he had used a derogatory word "canuck" to describe French Canadians, Muskie became very emotional. Reporters on the scene maintained that Muskie was crying, although he always denied this—claiming that snowflakes gave the appearance of tears. He was out of the race by April. Muskie later said that that incident "changed people's minds about me, about what kind of guy I was. They were looking for a strong, steady man, and there I was, weak."

Muskie did not again campaign for national office. However, he remained one of the Democratic Party spokesmen and in 1976 was considered a possible vice-presidential running mate for Democratic presidential nominee Jimmy Carter. In 1980 Edmund S. Muskie resigned his U.S. Senate seat to become secretary of state in the Carter administration, where he worked to negotiate the release of 52 American hostages held 14 months in Teheran, Iran. Muskie retired from public life in 1981 and returned to Maine. He was called back to public service in 1986 by President Reagan to serve on a three-man committee charged with investigating the role of the Reagan administration in the Iran-Contra scandal. When the report came out in 1987, it was highly critical of President Reagan.

After he retired from political life, Muskie practiced law, dividing his time between Washington D.C. and

Maine. On March 26, 1996, Edward Muskie died of a heart attack. In reaction, President Clinton said that Muskie was "a dedicated legislator and a caring public servant."

Further Reading

Muskie (1971) by Theo Lippman, Jr. and Donald C. Hansen; *Muskie of Maine* (1972) by David Nevin; Muskie also wrote an autobiography, *Journeys* (1972); also, Theodore H. White's, *The Making of the President, 1968* (1969) and *The Making of the President, 1972* (1973); for a discussion of Muskie as a target of the Nixon White House see Theodore White, *Breach of Faith* (1975); Bob Woodward and Carl Bernstein, *All the President's Men* (1974); and John W. Dean, *Blind Ambition: The White House Years* (1976); Muskie's legislative achievements are discussed in *U.S. Congress, Senate, Biographical Directory of the American Congress, 1774-1971* (1971), Robert Sobel, ed.; and his brief term as secretary of state is outlined in Hamilton Jordan's, *Crisis: The Last Year of the Carter Presidency* (1982). □

Louis Charles Alfred de Musset

The French poet, dramatist, and fiction writer Louis Charles Alfred de Musset (1810-1857), a major romantic poet, is remembered for his lyric poems, elegant comedies, and the powerful drama "Lorenzaccio," perhaps the finest French play of the 19th century.

Alfred de Musset was born in Paris on Dec. 11, 1810. He was a brilliant student at the Lycée Henri IV and early frequented the important romantic circles. In 1828 he published his first book, *L'Anglais mangeur d'opium,* an adaptation of Thomas De Quincey's *Confessions of an English Opium Eater.* His first volume of verse, *Contes d'Espagne et d'Italie,* appeared in 1830. The same year his one-act comedy *La Nuit vénitienne* failed on the stage, and he decided to write no more for the theater.

In June 1833 Musset met the French writer George Sand. Their ensuing love affair, passionate and somber, was one of the most famous of the romantic period. After a winter together in Venice and infidelity on both sides, the lovers quarreled and separated. Musset returned to Paris ill and broken in spirit. His affair with George Sand inspired his finest poems; but his life thereafter was one of dissipation and sorrow. Musset continued to write and was elected to membership in the French Academy in 1852. He died in Paris on May 2, 1857.

Musset's poems are collected in two volumes: *Premières poésies* (to 1835) and *Poésies nouvelles* (1835-1852). In the first volume the *Contes d'Espagne et d'Italie,* the poem *Ballade à la lune,* and *Le Spectacle dans un fauteuil* remain of interest. Musset's finest poetry is in the *Poésies nouvelles,* which contains the famous poems inspired by his love for George Sand: *La Nuit de mai, La Nuit de décembre, La Nuit d'août,* and *La Nuit d'octobre.* It also contains *Lettre à Lamartine, Souvenir, À la Malibran, Tristesse, Rappelle-toi,* and *Une Soirée perdue.* The four *Nuits,* or "Nights," and their lovely pendant, *Souvenir,* trace the poet's gradual recovery from his bitter disillusionment after his affair with George Sand. Musset wrote *Souvenir* after he had passed once more through the forest of Fontainebleau, where he had been with George Sand 7 years earlier. It concludes on the immortal quality of love.

Musset's theater pieces in verse comprise *Les Marrons du feu* (in the *Contes d'Espagne et d'Italie,* 1830); *La Coupe et les lèvres* and *À quoi rêvent les jeunes filles* (in *Le Spectacle dans un fauteuil,* 1832); a two-act comedy, *Louison* (1849); and an incomplete tragedy, *La Servante du roi.*

After the failure of *La Nuit vénitienne* on the stage in 1830, most of Musset's later prose comedies were written for the *Revue des deux mondes* and were published in volume form in 1840. They include *Les Caprices de Marianne* (1833), *Fantasio* (1834), *On ne badine pas avec l'amour* (1834), *Barberine* (1835), *Le Chandelier* (1835), *Il ne faut jurer de rien* (1836), and *Un Caprice* (1837). In 1845 Musset published *Il faut qu'une porte soit ouverte ou fermée.* His delightful comedies were not played in France until the late 1840s. Popular recognition led to Musset's writing once again for the stage. He then published *On ne saurait penser à tout* (1849), *Carmosine* (1850), and *Betine* (1851). Musset's comedies, which have kept much of their freshness, are characterized by their elegance, sophistication, irony, and sentiment.

Musset wrote the serious dramas *André del Sarto* (1833) and *Lorenzaccio* (1834). The latter has as its protagonist a fascinatingly ambiguous "stranger" or "outsider" with very modern qualities of mind.

Musset's brief tales include such stories as *Emmeline* (1837), *Frédéric et Bernerette* (1838), *Croisilles* (1839), *Histoire d'un merle blanc* (1842), *Mimi Pinson* (1843), and *Pierre et Camille* (1844). *La Confession d'un enfant du siècle* (1836) was Musset's famous autobiographical attempt to analyze the causes of the *mal du siècle* that affected the youth of France after the close of the Napoleonic Wars.

Further Reading

There is a translation of *The Complete Writings of Alfred de Musset* by Andrew Lang and others (10 vols., 1907). In 1962 Peter Meyer published a translation of *Seven Plays of Musset*, containing *Marianne, Fantasio, Camille and Perdican, The Candlestick, A Diversion, A Door Must be Kept Open or Shut, and Journey to Gotha*. Biographies of Musset are Paul Edeme de Musset, *The Biography of Alfred de Musset* (trans. 1877); Henry Dwight Sedgwick, *Alfred de Musset, 1810-1857: A Biography* (1931); and Charlotte Haldane, *Alfred: The Passionate Life of Alfred de Musset* (1960). For Musset's drama see Herbert S. Gochberg, *Stage of Dreams: The Dramatic Art of Alfred de Musset, 1828-1834* (1967). □

Benito Mussolini

The Italian dictator Benito Mussolini (1883-1945) was head of the Italian government from 1922 to 1943. A Fascist dictator, he led Italy into three successive wars, the last of which overturned his regime.

Benito Mussolini (top, center)

B enito Mussolini was born at Dovia di Predappio in Forlì province on July 29, 1883. His father was a blacksmith and an ardent Socialist; his mother taught elementary school. His family belonged to the impoverished middle classes. Benito, with a sharp and lively intelligence, early demonstrated a powerful ego. Violent and undisciplined, he learned little at school. In 1901, at the age of 18, he took his *diploma di maestro* and then taught secondary school briefly. Voluntarily exiling himself to Switzerland (1902-1904), he formed a dilettante's culture notable only for its philistinism. Not surprisingly, Mussolini based it on Friedrich Nietzsche, Georges Sorel, and Max Stirner, on the advocates of force, will, and the superego. Culturally armed, Mussolini returned to Italy in 1904, rendered military service, and engaged in politics full time thereafter.

Early Career and Politics

Mussolini became a member of the Socialist party in 1900, and his politics, like his culture, were exquisitely bohemian. He crossed anarchism with syndicalism, matched Peter Kropotkin and Louis Blanqui with Karl Marx and Friedrich Engels. More Nietzschean than Marxist,

Mussolini's socialism was *sui generis,* a concoction created entirely by himself. In Socialist circles, nonetheless, he first attracted attention, then applause, and soon widespread admiration. He "specialized" in attacking clericalism, militarism, and reformism. Mussolini urged revolution at any cost. In each attack he was extremist and violent. But he was also eloquent and forceful.

Mussolini occupied several provincial posts as editor and labor leader until he suddenly emerged in the 1912 Socialist Party Congress. Shattering all precedent, he became editor of the party's daily paper, *Avanti,* at a youthful 29. His editorial tenure during 1913-1914 abundantly confirmed his promise. He wrote a new journalism, pungent and polemical, hammered his readership, and injected a new excitement into Socialist ranks. On the Socialist platform, he spoke sharply and well, deft in phrase and savage in irony.

The young Mussolini proved a formidable opponent. In a party long inert, bureaucratic, and burdened with mediocrity, he capitalized on his youth, offered modernity with dynamism, and decried the need for revolution in a moment when revolutionary ferment was sweeping the country. An opportunist to his bones, Mussolini early mastered the direction of the winds and learned quickly to turn full sail into them.

From Socialist to Fascist

This much-envied talent led Mussolini to desert the Socialist party in 1914 and to cross over to the enemy camp, the Italian bourgeoisie. He rightly understood that World War I would bury the old Europe. Upheaval would follow its wake. He determined to prepare for "the unknown." In late 1914 he founded an independent newspaper, *Popolo d'Italia,* and backed it up with his own independent movement (Autonomous Fascists). He drew close to the new forces in Italian politics, the radicalized middle-class youth, and made himself their national spokesman.

Mussolini developed a new program, substituting nationalism for internationalism, militarism for antimilitarism, and the aggressive restoration of the bourgeois state instead of its revolutionary destruction. He had thus completely reversed himself. The Italian working classes called him "Judas" and "traitor." Drafted into the trenches in 1915, Mussolini was wounded during training exercises in 1917, but he managed to return to active politics that same year. His newspaper, which he now reinforced with a second political movement (Revolutionary Fascists), was his main card; his talents and his reputation guaranteed him a hand in the game.

After the end of the war, Mussolini's career, so promising at the outset, slumped badly. He organized his third movement (Constituent Fascists) in 1918, but it was stillborn. Mussolini ran for office in the 1919 parliamentary elections but was defeated. Nonetheless, he persisted.

Head of the Government

In March 1919 Mussolini founded another movement (Fighting Fascists), courted the militant Italian youth, and waited for events to favor him. The tide turned in 1921. The elections that year sent him victoriously to Parliament at the head of 35 Fascist deputies; the third assembly of his fledgling movement gave birth to a national party, the National Fascist party (PNF), with more than 250,000 followers and Mussolini as its uncontested leader, its *duce.*

The following year, in October 1922, Mussolini successfully "marched" on Rome. But, in fact, the back door to power had been opened by key ruling groups (industry try and agriculture, military, monarchy, and Church), whose support Mussolini now enjoyed. These groups, economically desperate and politically threatened, accepted Mussolini's solution to their crisis: mobilize middle-class youth, repress the workers violently, and set up a tough central government to restore "law and order." Accordingly, with the youth as his "flying wedge," Mussolini attacked the workers, spilled their blood liberally over the Italian peninsula, and completed triumphantly the betrayal of his early socialism. Without scruple or remorse, Mussolini now showed the extent to which ambition, opportunism, and utter amorality constituted his very core. He was in fact eminently a product of a particular crisis, World War I, and a special social class, the petty bourgeoisie. Mussolini's capture of power was classic: he was the right national leader at the right historical moment.

Fascist State

Once in power, Mussolini attacked the problem of survival. With accomplished tact, he set general elections, violated their constitutional norms freely, and concluded them in 1924 with an absolute majority in Parliament. But the assassination immediately thereafter of the Socialist leader Giacomo Matteotti, a noted opponent, by Fascist hirelings suddenly reversed his fortunes, threw his regime into crisis, and nearly toppled him. Mussolini, however, recouped and with his pivotal speech of Jan. 3, 1925, took the offensive. He suppressed civil liberties, annihilated the opposition, and imposed open dictatorship. Between 1926 and 1929 Mussolini moved to consolidate his regime through the enactment of "the most Fascist laws" (*le leggi fascistissime*). He concluded the decade on a high note: his Concordat with the Vatican in 1929 settled the historic differences between the Italian state and the Roman Catholic Church. Awed by a generosity that multiplied his annual income fourfold, Pope Pius XI confirmed to the world that Mussolini had been sent "by Divine Providence."

As the 1930s opened, Mussolini, seated safely in power and enjoying wide support from the middle classes, undertook to shape his regime and fix its image. Italy, he announced, had commenced the epoch of the "Third Rome." The "Fascist Revolution," after the French original, would itself date civilized progress anew: 1922 became "Year I of the New Era"; 1932, Year X. The regime called itself the "Corporate State" and offered Italy a bewildering brood of institutions, all splendidly titled but sparsely endowed. For if the rhetoric impressed, the reality denied.

The strongest economic groups remained entrenched. They had put Mussolini into power, and they now reaped their fruits. While they accumulated unprecedented economic control and vast personal fortunes, while a class of nouveau riche attached itself to the regime and parasitically sucked the nation's blood, the living standard of the working majority fell to subsistence. The daily consumption of calories per capita placed Italy near the bottom among European nations; the average Italian worker's income amounted to onehalf his French counterpart's, one-third his English, and one-fourth his American. As national leader, Mussolini offered neither solutions nor analyses for Italy's fundamental problems, preferring slogans to facts and propaganda to hard results. The face of the state he indeed refashioned; its substance he left intact. The "new order" was coating only.

Il Duce ruled from the top of this hollow pyramid. A consummate poseur, he approached government as a drama to be enacted, every scene an opportunity to display ample but superficial talents. Cynical and arrogant, he despised men in the same measure that he manipulated them. Without inspired or noble sentiments himself, he instinctively sought the defects in others, their weaknesses, and mastered the craft of corrupting them. He surrounded himself with ambitious opportunists and allowed full rein to their greed and to their other, unnameable vices while his secret agents compiled incriminating dossiers. Count Galeatto Ciano, his son-in-law and successor-designate, defined Mussolini's entourage as "that coterie of old prostitutes." Such was Mussolini's "new governing class."

Mussolini's Three Wars

In 1930 the worldwide economic depression arrived in Italy. The middle classes succumbed to discontent; the working people suffered aggravated misery. Mussolini initially reacted with a public works program but soon shifted to foreign adventure. The 1935 Ethiopian War, a classic diversionary exercise, was planned to direct attention away from internal discontent and to the myth of imperial grandeur. The "Italian Empire," Mussolini's creation, was announced in 1936. It pushed his star to new heights. But it also exacted its price. The man of destiny lost his balance, and with it that elementary talent that measures real against acclaimed success. No ruler confuses the two and remains in power long. Mussolini thus began his precipitous slide.

The 1936 Spanish intervention, in which Mussolini aided Francisco Franco in the Civil War, followed hard on Ethiopia but returned none of its anticipated gains. Mussolini compounded this error with a headlong rush into Adolf Hitler's embrace. The Rome-Berlin Axis in 1936 and the Tripartite Pact in 1937 were succeeded by the ill-fated Steel Pact in 1939. Meanwhile, Mussolini's pro-Hitlerism struck internally. Having declared earlier that the racial problem did not exist for Italy, Mussolini in 1938 unleashed his own anti-Semitic blows against Italian Jewry. As the 1930s closed, Mussolini had nearly exhausted all toleration for himself and his regime within Italy.

World War II's surprise outbreak in 1939 left Mussolini standing on the margins of world politics, and he saw Hitler redrawing the map of Europe without him. Impelled by the prospect of easy victory, Mussolini determined "to make war at any cost." The cost was clear: modern industry, modern armies, and popular support. Mussolini unfortunately lacked all of these. Nonetheless, in 1940 he pushed a reluctant Italy into war on Hitler's side. He thus ignored the only meaningful lesson of World War I: the United States alone had decided that conflict, and consequently America, not Germany, was the key hegemonic power.

Disaster and Death

In 1940-1941 Mussolini's armies, badly supplied and impossibly led, strung their defeats from Europe across the Mediterranean to the African continent. These defeats constituted the full measure of Mussolini's bankruptcy. Italy lost its war in 1942; Mussolini collapsed 6 months later. Restored as Hitler's puppet in northern Italy in 1943, he drove Italy deeper into the tragedy of invasion, occupation, and civil war during 1944-1945. The end approached, but Mussolini struggled vainly to survive, unwilling to pay the price for folly. The debt was discharged by a partisan firing squad on April 28, 1945, at Dongo in Como province.

In the end Mussolini failed where he had believed himself most successful: he was not a *modern* statesman. His politics and culture had been formed before World War I, and they had remained rooted there. After that war, though land empire had become ossified and increasingly superfluous, Mussolini had embarked on territorial expansion in the grand manner. In a moment when the European nation-state had passed its apogee and entered decline (the economic depression had underscored it), Mussolini had pursued ultranationalism abroad and an iron state within. He had never grasped the lines of the new world already emerging. He had gone to war for more territory and greater influence when he needed new markets and more capital. Tied to a decaying world about to disappear forever, Mussolini was anachronistic, a man of the past, not the future. His Fascist slogan served as his own epitaph: *Non si torna indietro* (There is no turning back). A 19th-century statesman could not survive long in the 20th-century world, and history swept him brutally but rightly aside.

Further Reading

Mussolini wrote *My Autobiography* (1928; rev. ed. 1939) and *The Fall of Mussolini: His Own Story,* edited with a preface by Max Ascoli (trans. 1948). Most of the studies of Mussolini in English are either archaic and sterile or anecdotal and useless. A comprehensive, objective, and well-written biography is Ivone Kirkpatrick, *Mussolini: A Study in Power* (1964). Frederick W. Deakin, *The Brutal Friendship* (1962; rev. ed. 1966), offers valid, original scholarship but unfortunately treats only Mussolini's last years. Alan Cassels, *Mussolini's Early Diplomacy* (1970), is a well-documented study of Mussolini during the 1920s. Works on the history of fascism in Italy include Frederico Chabod, *A History of Italian Fascism* (1961; trans. 1963), and Elizabeth Wiskemann, *Fascism in Italy: Its Development and Influence* (1969). Ernst Nolte, *Three Faces of Fascism* (1963; trans. 1965), discusses the theory and the history of the movement in Italy, France, and Germany. For pertinent documents of the Fascist era in Italy and a brief study of the period see S. William Halperin, *Mussolini and Italian Fascism* (1964). For general background see Denis Mack Smith, *Italy: A Modern History* (1959). □

Modest Petrovich Mussorgsky

Modest Petrovich Mussorgsky (1839-1881) is generally acclaimed the finest of the group of Russian composers known as the Mighty Five.

Without Modest Mussorgsky the notion of the Russian 19th century as one of musical realism would be unsupportable. In his operas, especially *Boris Godunov,* he successfully explored human emotions and failings individually and collectively in a new and forthright manner singularly bereft of the pretensions and emotional excess of the 19th century. His operatic work marks a crossroads in the understanding and use of the form in music history.

Mussorgsky was born on March 9, 1839, in the village of Karevo in the Pskov district. His family was of the middle landed gentry, which placed them high above the serfs, although Mussorgsky had some serf blood. His cultured mother gave him piano lessons and encouraged his clumsy but early efforts at composition. At 10 he went to St. Petersburg to study piano with Anton Herke, to prepare for cadet school, and to be tutored in the ways of a young urban gentleman. He entered the Imperial Guards Cadet School in 1852 and, in the course of the year, published (at his family's expense) *Porte Enseigne Polka* for his classmates. His lessons with Herke continued until 1854. Mussorgsky joined the glittering Preobrazhensky Imperial Guards Regiment in 1856.

As a teen-age officer, Mussorgsky met, while on duty, Aleksandr Borodin, a medical officer. The two were not to come together as members of the Mighty Five for some few years, but Borodin remembered Mussorgsky as a smart, dapper, well-mannered, slightly French and slightly foppish youth who played the piano coquettishly at parties, eliciting cries of "charmant!" and "delicieux!" from the assembled young women.

The years brought considerable change in that image. In 1859 Mussorgsky met Aleksandr Dargomyzhsky, who introduced him to César Cui, also a military officer, and to Mily Balakirev, later the leader of the Mighty Five. In late 1857 and 1858 Mussorgsky went through the first of several emotional crises and resigned from the Guards in 1859. That same year he spoke to Balakirev of having been "reborn," not only in the sense of recovery from his nervous disorder but in his conversion, he said, from cosmopolitan to patriot. The thinking of the music and art critic Vladimir Stasov is reflected here, but more particularly that of the Russian social critics Chernyshevsky and Dobroliubov. Among these new friends, Mussorgsky was writing music with some seriousness. In 1860 his Scherzo in B-flat for

orchestra was performed in St. Petersburg. In 1861 Mussorgsky's financial base was destroyed: the emancipation of the serfs led to the liquidation, over a 2-year period, of the family estate.

In the early 1860s Mussorgsky felt musically dependent on, but fretted under, Balakirev and was close to Dargomyzhsky. Mussorgsky had established certain work patterns: he started something new with great enthusiasm only to bog down in self-doubt, insecure in his technical abilities. Three projected operas were among such works. Mussorgsky did not associate with the other members of the Balakirev circle but with "proletarian" friends in a communal setting. In 1863 he began work on the opera *Salammbo* (from Gustave Flaubert's novel). Although he did not finish it, music from this opera figured in later work, most importantly in *Boris Godunov*. He left another opera, *The Marriage* (1864-1868), unfinished; Cherepnin completed the work in 1909.

By 1869 Mussorgsky had abandoned his communal style of living and reentered government service, in the Forestry Department. He was already a serious alcoholic with epileptic tendencies. Though he was a nominal member of the Mighty Five (the term, literally the "Mighty Fist," was used by Stasov in 1867), his life style set him apart from the others. Indeed, he often denied vehemently his belonging, creatively, to any group.

From a suggestion by Stasov, but developing his own ideas and preparing his own libretto from texts by Aleksandr Pushkin and Nicolai Karamzin, Mussorgsky set to work on *Boris Godunov* in 1868. The first version was finished in 1869; that date was but the beginning of a fitful series of redrawings of music and scenario by Mussorgsky and others which has probably not even yet ended. He returned to it in 1871 and again in 1872 but was lured away by, among other things, the joint effort at an opera, *Mlada*, by himself, Borodin, Nicolai Rimsky-Korsakov, and Cui. The collective effort was abortive, but all used music from it for other works. In 1872 Mussorgsky also started *Khovanshchina,* an opera based on another Russian historical episode. This, too, was unfinished, but enough was done to establish it as one of his major works. He worked on *Khovanshchina* and another opera, *Sorochinsk Fair* (finished by Liadov and Karatygin), until 1880. The period 1871-1881 also saw the piano tribute to artist-architect Viktor Hartmann, *Pictures at an Exhibition* (1874; orchestrated by various composers, including Maurice Ravel in 1922), *The Songs and Dances of Death* (1875), and a number of other works, making this, though his last, his most productive decade.

The Mighty Five had begun to disintegrate as a circle after 1872, and Mussorgsky's health was worsening. Near the end of his life he toured with the singer Daria Leonova. He died, more or less in her care, on March 16, 1881, in St. Petersburg.

"Boris Godunov"

Musically one turns again and again to *Boris Godunov* to reveal what Mussorgsky was and what he wanted. The work is intensely, intimately vocal. And, although he wrote effectively for orchestra, the voice was the instrument he trusted and understood (he had given voice lessons). He had a lyric quality that was curiously enhanced by laconic punctuation; and it was just such anomalies that disturbed the doctrinaire Rimsky-Korsakov, who complained of the "absurdity, ugliness, and illogic" of so much of Mussorgsky's music. Made vulnerable by his technical lapses, Mussorgsky thus suffered, too, for his originality.

There is a relentless, inevitable movement forward in Mussorgsky's style, in significant measure related to his understanding of the folk process in music, which provides him with the deftness of the caricaturist's hand: his vignettes of a drunken priest, a clown, an idiot, a vain princess, or a mad czar are sure and convincing. The crowd scenes in *Boris Godunov* are particularly telling; they range from groups of worshipers through coronation crowds to peasants and soldiers. It is not sufficient to point out the approximations to human speech and sounds; Mussorgsky believed that speech itself followed strict musical rules and that music, like all art, is a means of communicating with people. He not only dealt in living scenes of real people but drew out of such situations certain principles and truths. And it is in the latter rather than the former that realism lies. That Czar Boris is the tortured product of forces of both good and evil is nowhere stated; but in depicting his inchoate rage at his enemies on the one hand and the beauty of his tenderness to his daughter on the other, Mussorgsky focuses effectively on the conflict.

Further Reading

Jay Leyda and Sergei Bertenson edited *The Mussorgsky Reader* (1947), a selection of Mussorgsky's letters and other memorabilia mostly taken from a collection of Andrei Rimsky-Korsakov published in Moscow in 1932. The most important study of Mussorgsky is Michel D. Calvocoressi, *Modest Mussorgsky: His Life and Works,* edited by Gerald Abraham (1956). Earlier, less complete works by Calvocoressi are *Mussorgsky: The Russian Musical Nationalist* (1919) and *Mussorgsky* (1946). Less scholarly is Victor Seroff, *Modeste Mussorgsky* (1968). For background on Mussorgsky's milieu see Gerald Abraham and Michel D. Calvocoressi, *Masters of Russian Music* (1936). □

Abraham Johannes Muste

Abraham Johannes Muste (1885-1967), American pacifist, led the movement for world peace and pioneered in developing nonviolent resistance as a means of securing social change.

On Jan. 8, 1885, A. J. Muste was born in Zierikzee, the Netherlands. His family emigrated to America 6 years later. He was raised in Grand Rapids, Mich., and attended Hope College, a church-affiliated school. In 1906 he entered the Theological Seminary of the Dutch Reformed Church in New Brunswick, N.J., and was ordained in 1909. That same year he married Anna Huizenga.

While first minister of Fort Washington Collegiate Church in New York City, Muste attended Union Theological Seminary, where he received a bachelor of divinity degree *magna cum laude* in 1913. Strongly influenced by liberal theological doctrines and shocked by the wretchedness of the urban poor, he became increasingly socially committed. In 1914 he gave up his conservative parish to become minister of the Central Congregational Church in Newtonville, Mass. Muste also became a pacifist, joining the Fellowship of Reconciliation (FOR) in 1916. With America's entry into World War I, he found this church post, too, untenable.

In early 1919 Muste was catapulted into the leadership of 30,000 striking textile workers in Lawrence, Mass. He became the general secretary of the Amalgamated Textile Workers of America that same year. In 1921 he was named educational director of Brookwood Labor College, which provided advanced education for potential union leaders and organizers. But Muste was increasingly drawn toward organization of the mass-production industries and actively participated in the labor struggles of the Conference for Progressive Labor Action (CPLA), formed in 1929. In 1933 he left Brookwood to devote his energies to the newly formed American Workers party (which absorbed the CPLA), to an alliance with the American followers of Leon Trotsky, and to radical agitation. In 1936 he returned to the FOR and to Christian pacifism, convinced that "he who denies love betrays justice."

Muste now began his efforts to combine radicalism and pacifism in a direct action movement. Appointed industrial

secretary of the FOR in 1936, he became director of the Presbyterian Labor Temple in New York in 1937 and national secretary of the FOR in 1940. During World War II, he championed the rights of conscientious objectors, helped found the Congress of Racial Equality, and sought to encourage adoption of Gandhian resistance tactics by pacifists. In the postwar era Muste sponsored draft resistance, tax resistance, and organizations seeking to promote massive civil disobedience.

In the late 1950s and early 1960s, as chairman of the Committee for Non-Violent Action (CNVA), Muste fostered a series of dramatic acts of civil disobedience outside missile bases, inside thermonuclear testing zones, and during civil defense drills. Under his leadership the peace movement became increasingly dynamic. The civil rights movement's adoption of nonviolent resistance owed much to his example and influence. In 1965 and 1966 Muste coordinated the first massive public demonstrations against the Vietnam War, and in 1966 he went to Saigon with a group of CNVA activists. He died on Feb. 11, 1967.

Further Reading

Muste's works include *Non-Violence in an Aggressive World* (1940), *War Is the Enemy* (1942), *Wage Peace Now* (1942), *Not by Might* (1947), and *The Camp of Liberation* (1954). A good sampling of his shorter writings from 1905 to 1966 is provided in *The Essays of A. J. Muste,* edited by Nat Hentoff (1967). The only biography is Hentoff's extremely sympathetic *Peace Agitator: The Story of A. J. Muste* (1963). See also Lawrence S. Wither, *Rebels against War: The American Peace Movement, 1941-1960* (1969).

Additional Sources

Robinson, Jo Ann, *A.J. Muste, pacifist & prophet: his relation to the Society of Friends,* Wallingford, Pa.: Pendle Hill Publications, 1981.

Robinson, Jo Ann, *Abraham went out: a biography of A.J. Muste,* Philadelphia: Temple University Press, 1981. □

Mutesa I

Mutesa I (ca. 1838-1884) was a kabaka, or monarch, of Buganda and one of the outstanding African rulers of the 19th century. Under his dynamic leadership Buganda became one of the most powerful and influential kingdoms of East Africa.

Mutesa Walugembe Mukabya was the son of the reigning kabaka, Suna II; his mother's identity is in dispute. Since Buganda had no fixed system of succession, Mutesa was one of many eligible for the position of kabaka. Backed by powerful members of Ganda society, he rose from obscurity to that office in 1856. The first years of his reign were troubled, but by a ruthless exercise of authority he eliminated all opposition, in the

process greatly strengthening the powers of his office. By the end of his reign, Buganda was regarded as possessing one of the most centralized ruling structures in all of Africa.

Mutesa ruled Buganda during the period when foreign, non-African forces entered the kingdom to begin a fundamental alteration of the internal composition of Ganda society. Arab and African Moslems from Zanzibar had been visiting Buganda since the 1840s to trade firearms, gunpowder, and cloth for ivory and slaves. By the mid-1860s Mutesa had outwardly adopted the tenets of Islam, favoring its acceptance by his subjects for a 10-year period.

But before Islam had the opportunity to win wide acceptance among the Ganda, representatives of Christian Europe reached Buganda, beginning in 1862 with the arrival of the explorers John Speke and James Grant. They were greatly impressed with the flourishing state of Buganda, and their reports attracted visitors. In 1875 Henry Stanley reached Mutesa's court. The wily African ruler, then threatened by an Egyptian thrust southward from the Sudan, expressed his willingness to receive Christian missionaries, effectively concealing the political motives for his decision from Stanley.

The British Church Missionary Society, a Protestant group, answered Stanley's call; their first expedition reached Buganda in 1877. Roman Catholic White Fathers followed in 1879. The Ganda system kept the newcomers at Mutesa's court; here they found a receptive audience among the youths sent from all parts of the kingdom to serve as pages for the newcomers' teaching, and during Mutesa's lifetime a profound transformation began to take place within the state as new concepts of belief replaced traditional values among an elite which would later dominate the kingdom's evolution.

Mutesa, however, never fully accepted any of the new beliefs. He attempted to manipulate them in the interests of his state, largely succeeding in using the Moslem and Christian outsiders to increase the already substantial dominance of the Ganda over their African neighbors. He died in 1884, leaving a deserved reputation as the greatest of all rulers of Buganda.

Further Reading

A sensible biography by a Ganda scholar is M. S. M. Kiwanuka, *Muteesa of Uganda* (1967). The best account of the life and times of Mutesa is in Roland Oliver and Gervase Mathew, eds., *History of East Africa,* vol. 1 (1963). □

Mutesa II

Mutesa II (1924-1969), a monarch of Buganda, was the last traditional ruler of the Ganda people in Uganda. He was a firm defender of his right to control the destinies of his kingdom in opposition to the rising tide for democratic principles of government within Uganda.

Edward Frederick William Walugembe Mutebi Luwangula Mutesa was born on Nov. 19, 1924, the son of the reigning kabaka, or monarch, Sir Daudi Chwa II. Mutesa's early education was conducted under private auspices and then at King's College, Budo. When his father died in 1939, he was selected to succeed him as kabaka; the state remained under the control of three regents until Mutesa's coming of age in 1942. From 1943 to 1945 Mutesa studied at Makerere University College, Kampala, and from 1945 to 1948 he read history, economics, and law at Magdalene College, Cambridge University.

Mutesa II attained international prominence in 1953. In that year the British secretary of state for colonies delivered a speech in England referring to a possible federation of the British colonies in East Africa. Many Africans were justly fearful of any such move due to the recent example of the British-imposed union of the Federation of Rhodesia and Nyasaland, a step which allowed local European domination of Africans. Mutesa, looking back to Britain's original agreements with Buganda, demanded that his state be given separate independence within a fixed time. In the meantime he refused any Ganda cooperation with British plans to develop Uganda as a unitary state.

First Exile

When the British proved unable to end Mutesa's opposition, Governor Andrew Cohen had him exiled to Britain on Oct. 30, 1953. This harsh step did not end the crisis, however, since almost all Ganda rallied to support their traditional ruler. The British attempted to run Buganda through a regency, but faced with general non-cooperation plus disturbances which twice led to the imposition of a state of emergency, they had to reconsider the exile. Mutesa was allowed to return to his country on Oct. 7, 1955, by a compromise agreement which fixed Buganda as a province of Uganda and which made the kabaka ruling Buganda a constitutional monarch with no executive powers.

The continuing resistance of Mutesa and his supporters to the British and non-Ganda African schemes for a unified Uganda came to a head in June 1960, when the kabaka called once more for an end to British protection for Buganda; he also announced that Buganda would not participate with the rest of Uganda in the scheduled national elections unless a constitutional decision agreeable to Buganda was decided upon in advance. But elections were held despite Mutesa's stand, allowing Benedicto Kiwanuka and his Democratic party to secure victory; Kiwanuka became the first chief minister of the new internally independent government of Uganda.

And the process leading to a unitary state continued. In 1961 a British commission recommended that Uganda become a unitary democratic state with a strong central government; Buganda was to be allowed a federal relationship under its kabaka within the new state. After hard negotiations on the details, Mutesa bowed to pressure and accepted the agreement in October. A political party under Mutesa's control was founded in Buganda, Kabaka Yekka (Kabaka Alone). It allied with the Uganda Peoples' party of Milton Obote, and the coalition won the election of 1962; Obote

was then chosen prime minister, with Uganda receiving its independence from Britain in October 1962.

The Uganda Peoples' party, however, was a modern African political organization opposed to the traditional practices represented by Mutesa. Its alliance with Kabaka Yekka was merely an expedient until Obote was able to command enough support to rule Uganda without Mutesa's participation. By 1964 the trend to Obote's position seemed clear, with members of the Democratic party and Kabaka Yekka increasingly crossing over to join the Uganda Peoples' party. In the meantime Obote circumspectly appointed Mutesa to the ceremonial position of president of Uganda in 1963.

Second Exile

The final crisis came in 1966, when a member of the opposition charged the government with complicity in the illegal passage of gold from the Congo. Obote reacted by suspending the constitution, arresting four ministers, and relieving Mutesa of the presidency. Later in the year he announced a new constitution which abolished the federal status of Buganda. In an unclear interval of charges and countercharges, tenseness grew, leading to hostilities that culminated in the successful storming on May 24, 1966, of the kabaka's palace by central government troops. Mutesa escaped the defeat, eventually reaching safety in the neighboring state of Burundi. He later was granted asylum in Britain and lived in London until his death in November 1969.

Further Reading

Mutesa tells his story in *Desecration of My Kingdom* (1967). B.A. Ogot and J.A. Kieran, *Zamani* (1968), places his career in perspective. □

José Celestino Mutis

José Celestino Mutis (1732-1808) was a Spanish-Colombian naturalist, physician, and mathematician. He assembled one of the richest botanical collections in the world of his time.

During the middle and later decades of the 18th century the Spanish government subsidized scientific expeditions and encouraged individuals to determine the natural wealth of its American colonies by the systematic study of their flora and fauna. One of these investigators who won world renown was José Celestino Mutis, a descendant of a Majorcan family in the Balearic Islands. He was born in Cadiz, Spain, on April 6, 1732, and spent the last 48 years of his life in Bogotá, the capital of viceregal New Granada and the later Republic of Colombia.

After studying medicine and philosophy at the University of Seville and continuing work in the natural sciences and mathematics while teaching anatomy at the University of Madrid, Mutis visited European centers of learning at government expense. These included Stockholm, where he came under the influence of the great Swedish botanist Carolus Linnaeus, who was to pay high tribute to the achievements of his disciple at Bogotá.

Appointed the personal physician of the viceroy of New Granada, Pedro Mesia de la Cerda, in 1760, Mutis accompanied this official to Bogotá, where for nearly half a century he actively furthered research and the teaching of botany, entomology, medicine, mineralogy, mathematics, and astronomy. He was the first to explain Newton's theories in that part of America, and he successfully defended the doctrine of Copernicus before the Inquisition. He advised viceroys on educational and economic matters while carrying on extensive correspondence with European scholars which brought him membership in the Academy of Science of Paris and of Stockholm.

From 1760 to 1790 Mutis kept a diary of observations on the natural sciences and made contributions in these fields both by original discoveries and by applying new knowledge to the rudimentary economy and medicine practiced in the Spanish American colonies, where he also introduced vaccination. Especially renowned were his studies of quinine (cinchona) and the establishment of its various pharmacological classifications.

Probably Mutis's most remarkable accomplishment was the creation of the Botanical Mission in 1783, a center for collecting and mapping the distribution of every kind of flora and fauna of Colombia; a corps of draftsmen and artists was employed to prepare thousands of colored drawings

and large plates of the many species. So beautifully executed were the paintings of this large collection that it excited the unqualified admiration of the great German scientist Alexander von Humboldt, whose years of travel in colonial Spanish America resulted in comprehensive and well-documented works in many volumes that remain indispensable to this day. The herbaria of Mutis's collection are prudently estimated at from 20,000 to 24,000 specimens representing some 5,000 distinct species.

Mutis was ordained a priest in 1774. He died in Bogotá on Sept. 11, 1808.

Further Reading

For background and further information on Mutis see Bernard Moses, *Spanish Colonial Literature in South America* (1922; 2d ed. repr. 1961), and Germán Arciniegas, *Latin America: A Cultural History* (1967).

Additional Sources

Amaya, Jose Antonio, *Mutis,* Madrid: Editorial Debate: Itaca, 1986.
Martin Ferrero, Paz, *Celestino Mutis,* Madrid: Historia 16: Quorum, 1987?. □

Mutsuhito

Mutsuhito (also known as Meiji Tenno; 1852–1912) was a Japanese emperor, who became the symbol for, and encouraged, the dramatic transformation of Japan from a feudal closed society into one of the great powers of the modern world.

The transformation of Japan's political and social structure in the late 19th century was an incredible phenomenon, unmatched in the long history of the expansion of Western civilization. From 1600, Japan was divided into several hundred feudal domains, ruled by largely autonomous regional lords. The power of the central government was nominally in the hands of the imperial family and the emperor, who claimed descent from the Sun Goddess Amaterasu. From the 12th century, the real power and influence, however, was wielded by a succession of warrior families appointed as military deputies to the emperor. Titled *shoguns,* they used their military power to administer the country, granting land and bestowing titles on supporters and followers and playing rivals off one against the other. The early 17th century saw the ascension of the Tokugawa house to the *shogunate,* a position borne by successive Tokugawas until 1867.

Under the *shogun* lordship, Japan was rigidly regulated to ensure control. A strict hierarchy of hereditary economic and social positions and harshly enforced regulations ensured continuity and minimized change. Foreign contact was forbidden for most of the population after 1640 to minimize potentially negative influences. In addition, the country was divided by strong regional loyalties which were

was treated accordingly. Mutsuhito's education, however, was far more liberal than his predecessor's had been. He was exposed to the customs and history of the outside world, acquiring a knowledge which tempered the traditional Japanese distrust of foreign influences. He was also taught theories of government and sovereignty which, in the words of the turn of the century British historian John Morris, "thoroughly fitted [him] for the duties of active sovereignty over his people." At the same time, Mutsuhito's early training was characterized by a strict discipline and rigor which produced a hardy and athletic youth, dedicated to his nation and people. Indeed, the future emperor had a love for horses and physical activity, as well as competitive sports. His training and education resulted in a disciplined servant of the people.

Mutsuhito's "progressive" and broad-minded education complemented the social and political changes occurring in Japan concurrent with his succession. The *shogun's* weakness produced a succession of crisis and groups determined to restore the predominance of the imperial court. Imperial advocates believed that a centralized government and administration was the only means of preventing further encroachments by foreign nations. Encouraged by regional enemies of the *shogun,* the emperor Komei and his court maneuvered the *shogun* into open rebellion and defeated his armies. The Tokugawa forces were successfully repelled in 1866, the year that Komei died. Young Mutsuhito ascended to the throne the next year after the proper period of mourning, and his coronation in 1868 coincided with the restoration of imperial rule and the final defeat of the supporters of the *shogun.* The impressionable young emperor was undoubtedly dominated by the victorious military and political leaders of the rebellion against the Tokugawa *shogun,* many of whom obtained prominent positions at court, but the co-operation of the emperor was essential if a centralized government was to be successful. Mutsuhito adopted the name Meiji and gave his name to the rebellion, the Meiji Restoration, and the period.

The Meiji emperor established the tone for his rule in his coronation oath, the "Charter Oath of Five Principles" that is believed to have been at least partially spontaneous and genuine. He observed that a representative legislative assembly would be created as soon as was practicable, that feudal customs would be abolished, and that the new government, economic and defense systems would be based on the examples of the Western powers. By so recreating Japan, he hoped that it would be able to resist foreign intervention and take a place among the great imperial powers of the day. This was certainly the wish of the men who dominated the government in the first years of the restoration. Mutsuhito's support of the growing popular consensus on the need for modernization along Western lines became ever more invaluable, however, as the emperor's position as supreme executive authority was expanded by those around him.

Mutsuhito was not the initiator of the policies that were implemented to modernize the Japanese nation. Shortly after the emperor's marriage in 1869, the government leaders took steps to abolish the feudal land system and establish

encouraged by the *shoguns* as a means of control. The *shogun's* control, however, depended on their military strength and influence. Through the 19th century, strong social and political reactions were increasingly perceived as a threat to the *shogunate* predominance. The undercurrent of dissatisfaction with the administration of the *shogun* was brought to the surface by the unwelcome appearance of Matthew Perry's American warships in 1853 and the subsequent treaties which, under threat of force, opened Japan to Western "barbarians." The *shogun's* inability to resist the foreign intervention became the issue which led to its ultimate demise.

The rallying point for the forces opposed to the *shogunate* was the long-moribund imperial court and emperor. "It was not an office of state," explains Herschel Webb, "but one of the state's adornments." The imbalance between the imperial court and the government, however, had slowly begun to evolve in the 19th century due to a number of aggressive court figures. Several notes of displeasure were sent by the Emperor Komei to the *shogun* and, while they were not initiated by the emperor himself, the increased political involvement had an impact. Only 15 when he succeeded to the throne, Komei kept abreast of the domestic and international developments of the day, and he made a conscious effort to educate his son about the evils of Western civilization. Komei's conclusions regarding European influences, however, were not absorbed by the crown prince, Mutsuhito.

Born in 1852, Mutsuhito was the second son of Emperor Komei. He was declared crown prince in 1860 and a new school system. Further initiatives organized government departments and the military along the pattern of European states. The promise of constitutional government, however, remained unfulfilled, sparking protests and prompting charges that a new authoritarian government was in the making. The unrest was exacerbated by the social and economic changes that were being wrought. Not all Japanese were pleased with the modernization, particularly the European model, that their country was adopting. In the 1870s, the unrest became increasingly violent.

Mutsuhito's role during this period was largely symbolic. "In the first years after the Restoration," wrote Carol Gluck, "the new government invoked the imperial institution as the symbolic center of the unified nation and displayed the young Meiji emperor as the personal manifestation of the recently wrought political unity." Nevertheless, the emperor was not simply a passive observer. He strongly believed in the changes that were taking place and supported the direction the nation was taking. Only by his own prerogative could the Meiji become a highly visible symbol of the new Japan, and the young emperor enthusiastically responded to the call. His proximity to the people increased dramatically. He appeared in public on carefully selected and important occasions such as the completion of the nations first rail line, a cleverly orchestrated illustration of the link between the emperor and modernization. His public appearances, limited though they were, were considered acts of extreme concession and were symbolic of the new relationship between the people and their rulers at the imperial court.

Mutsuhito's personal lifestyle further endeared him to the population, setting as he did an example of frugality and disciplined hard work that the people sought to emulate. His retinue was not ostentatious and horses were his only visible leisure activity. He took an active interest in the business of the state, arriving punctually at his desk at 8 a.m. and departing only when the day's agenda was completed. Under the Japanese system, the emperor's approval was a requirement for the enactment of any legislation or policy initiative. Laws were promulgated in his name, officials appointed "as though by him," and he spoke to the people on matters of significance. Mutsuhito's abilities and dedication thus took on a great importance. His pronouncements legitimized the changes and, despite several threats to his life by disgruntled Nationalists, the emperor continued to support modernization. He also helped to make it more palatable through his personal cultivation of a balance between traditional Japanese customs and Western ideas. Mutsuhito wore Western-style clothes, ate Western-style food, and his stature became closer to that of a Western-style monarch. Nevertheless, the Meiji Emperor composed poems in the traditional Japanese style and retained the Confucian philosophy of personal relations which characterized Japanese society.

Mutsuhito's role as a symbol of national unity underwent a change in the 1880s and 1890s as the imperial institution was legally defined in the constitutional discussions of the period. The conservative Satsuma-Choshu oligarchy that dominated the imperial court had gradually come to the conclusion that constitutional government and its accompanying representative institutions were necessary for Japan to truly complete its modernization. Slowly, they implemented the necessary changes—a cabinet system was adopted in 1885, a constitution promulgated in 1889, and the Japanese Diet was officially opened in 1890. Simultaneously, government leaders reflected on the necessity of centering, as Jansen and Rozman observe, all institutions around the Imperial House "in the absence of a vital tradition of national religion comparable to the ties that bound western nations together." There was much debate as to exactly how to define the emperor in a constitution, but the role as it emerged after 1889 proved to be far different than the preceding decade.

Carol Gluck asserts that "the late 1880s and 1890s saw the emperor become the manifestation of the elements associated with national progress . . . and the symbol of national unity, not of a political and legal, but of a patriotic and civic kind." The emperor, in short, became the embodiment of the state and as such was raised above politics, returned "above the clouds" as the son of heaven. Mutsuhito was placed in the ironic situation of being removed from the actual practice of governing but concurrently being the nominal last court of appeal. His financial and administrative independence was enshrined in the constitution; his public appearances were reduced to a bare minimum and his contacts were limited to the state élite. After his "bestowal" of the Constitution of 1889, the emperor's political role became largely ceremonial—he opened the Diet, held ministerial meetings, and issued proclamations of the "government's will." In reality, his influence in policy was kept to a minimum.

The emperor, however, maintained an active interest in state affairs. He kept abreast of all policy initiatives through a constant reading of cabinet documents and was a voracious reader of national as well as provincial newspapers. Unfortunately, no record exists of Mutsuhito's personal feelings on his gradual estrangement from the very people he was supposed to personify. His reaction to some of the elements of "national progress," however, provide some gauge to his personal dedication. One measure of Japan's westernization and progress was her adoption of the expansionist tendencies of the imperial powers of the late 19th century. An over-crowded island nation lacking in resources, Japan looked to the Asian mainland, particularly the Korean peninsula, for that which it did not have. This brought Japan into conflict with China and Russia, and in two separate wars the Japanese proved how well they had adopted Western military techniques and technology. The Sino-Japanese War erupted in 1894 and the emperor played an active role as commander-in-chief of the armed forces. Mutsuhito moved with the imperial headquarters in Tokyo to the campaign debarkation headquarters at Hiroshima. For eight months, he devoted himself to the business of war, overseeing the naval and military plans for the prosecution of the campaigns to the minutest details.

When the war was over, he returned to the reclusive routines of peace-time imperial life, but a decade later the emperor again vigorously supported and took an active, if somewhat different role, in the prosecution of the Russo-Japanese War, 1904-05. Unlike the first war, the emperor did not move and suffer with the troops, but remained in Tokyo overseeing policy. His removal from direct planning allowed him to be credited with victories but shielded him from the blunders of the war. More than ever, Mutsuhito became a sympathetic father figure, bemoaning the fate of his war-torn people. It was this role of social benefactor that he was increasingly called on to play towards the end of his rule. Social activism was not, however, a responsibility that he avoided. The learned Meiji had, for example, been instrumental in establishing imperial support for education, and some of his few public appearances were those at the convocations of the Imperial University in Tokyo. While the government leaders actively strived to use education and the imperial image to present Japan's new modernity to the young, Mutsuhito's belief in the value of education was unquestioned. Writes Carol Gluck, "Summoning the minister of education at the time of the Russo-Japanese War, [Mutsuhito] issued a rescript urging that 'education should not be neglected even in times of military crisis.' Despite the emperor's support of Japan's expansion, he was concerned lest it interfere with the advancement of the people as a whole.

The heavy casualties of the Russo-Japanese War, and an unsatisfactory peace settlement, triggered sporadic eruptions of a social unrest that was simmering below the surface prior to the war. Mutsuhito and the imperial court became ever more involved in the government's attempts to quell the unrest. He took a direct role through an increase in assistance to the needy and social causes. More importantly, the emperor's image was evoked to ease the antagonisms between the people and the state. In the long run, this damaged the government's prestige. The military, for example, perceived itself as directly responsible, and answerable, to the emperor and the state. They gradually became the civil power's equal with tragic consequences for the future. Mutsuhito, however, was largely oblivious to such machinations, shielded by the deification process that was underway. When he died in 1912, the modernization process that he had done so much to encourage was largely completed, but the imperial institution had been removed from the practical governing of the country—placed above such mundane concerns. His name was evoked to justify many policies he had little to do with. Nevertheless, his implicit support of the expansionist policies that characterized the modern westernized Japan he helped create was a crucial factor in their implementation and would, ironically, bring about an even more far reaching transformation in the near future.

Further Reading

There is no English-language biography of Meiji. Background information is in Nobutaka Ike, *The Beginnings of Political Democracy in Japan* (1950); Hugh Borton, *Japan's Modern Century* (1955); Ryusaka Tsunoda, William Theodore de Bary, and Donald Keene, *Sources of the Japanese Tradition* (1958); Marius B. Jansen, *Sakamoto Ryoma and the Meiji Restoration* (1961); George M. Beckmann, *The Modernization of China and Japan* (1962); John K. Fairbank, Edwin O.

Reischauer, and Albert M. Craig, *East Asia: The Modern Transformation* (1965); and Robert E. Ward, ed., *Political Development in Modern Japan* (1968).

Additional Sources

Gluck, Carol. *Japan's Modern Myths: Ideology in the Late Meiji Period.* Princeton University Press, 1985.
Jansen, Marius B. and Gilbert Rozman, eds. *Japan in Transition: From Tokugawa to Meiji.* Princeton University Press, 1986.
Morris, John. *Makers of Japan.* London: Methuen, 1906.
Webb, Herschel. *The Japanese Imperial Institution in the Tokugawa Period.* Columbia University Press, 1968.
Beasley, William G. *The Meiji Restoration.* Stanford University Press, 1972.
Hunter, Janet E. *The Emergence of Modern Japan.* London: Longman House, 1989. □

Mwanga

Mwanga (ca. 1866-1901) was a monarch of Buganda and the last independent ruler of that important East African kingdom.

When the great kabaka, or monarch, of Buganda, Mutesa I, died in 1884, his state was a major force in the Lake Victoria region. During his seminal reign, contacts with the worlds of Europe and the East African coast had introduced new forces into Ganda society which would complicate the rule of his son Mwanga Mwanga became kabaka in October 1884 with the general support of his people, but it was soon apparent that he lacked the talents to master the difficult problems confronting his administration. Internal political life in Buganda was troubled by conflict between factions grouped around Protestant, Roman Catholic, Moslem, and African traditional leaders. Externally, East Africa was just facing the beginning of its partition by Britain and Germany.

Mwanga, faced with these difficult conditions, soon weakened his position by removing from office the older chiefs who had served his father. He also began persecuting Christian and Moslem Ganda, but this was done in sporadic fashion, and Mwanga eventually gave the young men of these factions increasing influence within his administration. Under such leaders as Henry Nyonyintono and Apolo Kaggwa, they emerged as a major power block, and Mwanga reacted to their position too late. He prepared a surprise action at a time when he had few supporters left among his people because of the harshness and indecision of his rule. The result was a joining of the Christian and Moslem elite to depose their powerless ruler in 1888, replacing him with his elder brother, Kiwewa. The uneasy alliance between Christians and Moslems soon collapsed, however, and a Moslems coup gave them control of the state with a new kabaka, Kalema (Mwanga's younger brother).

Mwanga had been allowed to flee the country, living in hardship until the Christian refugees accepted him again as their leader. Their forces ousted Kalema and the Moslems in a series of conflicts lasting to February 1890. Mwanga was restored as kabaka, but his position was much curtailed since the new Christian ruling group strengthened its position within Ganda politics.

Meantime Britain had been given control over Buganda in 1890; the first officers arrived at the end of the year to administer the country by means of a private chartered company. The Protestant Ganda supported the company, under its representative Frederick Lugard, while the Catholic Ganda were generally mistrustful of their British rulers. After a period of intense intrigue, in which Mwanga played a serious role, the Protestants and Lugard broke the Catholic strength in a battle on January 1892.

Mwanga, who had joined the Catholics, once more fled his country. He was allowed to return, with even more reduced authority, a situation he endured until a public humiliation led him to revolt against the British in 1897. Securing little Ganda support, Mwanga was defeated and deposed for his infant son, Daudi Chwa. Mwanga escaped capture until 1899; then he was sent into exile and died in 1901.

Further Reading

Mwanga's life may best be followed in Roland Oliver and Gervase Mathew, eds., *History of East Africa*, vol. 1 (1963). ☐

Carl Mydans

Carl Mydans (born 1907) was an American photojournalist. He worked briefly for the Farm Security Administration during the 1930s documenting rural American life. In 1936 he joined the newly formed *LIFE* magazine where he became well known for his photographic coverage of World War II. He continued as a war photographer through the early 1970s.

Carl Mydans was born in Boston on May 20, 1907. The family moved to Medford, Massachusetts, on the Mystic River where Carl went to high school and worked in the local boatyards after school and on weekends. He later became interested in journalism and worked as a free-lance reporter for several local newspapers. In 1930 he graduated from the Boston University School of Journalism.

Mydans then moved to New York and, while working as a reporter for the "American Banker," began to study photography at the Brooklyn Institute of Arts and Sciences. In July 1935 his skill with the new 35mm "miniature" camera landed him a job with the Department of the Interior's Resettlement Administration, which soon merged into the Farm Security Administration (FSA). Mydans joined Walker Evans and Arthur Rothstein as the core of the remarkable team of photographers assembled by Roy Stryker to document rural America.

While travelling through the southern states photographing everything that had to do with cotton, Mydans developed the shooting style he would use throughout his career. He concentrated on people, and he photographed them in a respectful and straightforward manner. As he had been taught to do as a reporter, he kept careful notes on every shot.

When Mydans joined the staff of *Life* in 1936 he joined a group of photojournalists who were changing the way press photography was done. Photojournalists had traditionally used 4x5 Speed Graphic cameras with flashguns and reflector pans, and their pictures of people tended to look much the same: overlit foregrounds fell off to dark backdrops that had no detail. But Mydans and his colleagues at *Life* relied on 35mm cameras that allowed them to work with available light, capturing a new kind of excitement and activity in their photographs. Their success with the small camera revolutionized the practice of photojournalism.

In 1938 Mydans went overseas with his wife, *Life* reporter Shelley Mydans, and began his long career as a war photographer. During the next 30 years he covered conflicts in Europe, the Far East, and Southeast Asia. In World War II he was a prisoner of the Japanese for 21 months. Always, he focussed his camera on the small human drama that revealed the larger story. He retired from *Life* in 1972 but continued to work for *Time* and other magazines.

Carl Mydan's work has been displayed in various galleries throughout the United States. The *New York Times*

Magazine featured his work, along with Alfred Eisenstaedt's and Joe Rosenthal's in May of 1995.

Mydans called himself a "story-teller with pictures" and always maintained that he did not photograph war because he liked it, but because he thought it was important to make an historic record of his times. "Long after I am gone," he said, "I want people to be able to see and especially feel what I have seen and felt."

Further Reading

Mydan's autobiography, *More Than Meets the Eye* (1959; *Carl Mydans: Photojournalist* (1985). □

Karl Gunnar Myrdal

The Swedish economist and sociologist Karl Gunnar Myrdal (1898-1987) helped shape social and economic planning in Sweden, focused attention on the problems of the African American, and worked on the problems of the underdeveloped nations.

Gunnar Myrdal was born in Gustafs on Dec. 6, 1898. He graduated from the University of Stockholm Law School in 1923 and received a doctorate of laws in economics in 1927. From 1927 to 1950, he taught economics and, in the 1960s, international economics at the University of Stockholm.

In 1934, Myrdal and his wife, Alva, a sociologist, wrote *Crisis in the Population Question,* which studied the excessively decreasing Swedish birthrate. Their analysis stressed the need for social planning in order to raise the birthrate without lowering the high standard of living. Their work greatly influenced Scandinavian social planning in the 1930's and opened the way for general social reforms in Sweden. Myrdal served on the new government commissions which were instrumental in bringing about "social engineering," and as a member of the Swedish Senate (1936-1938) and the board of the National Bank of Sweden, he also helped in the rational planning of the economy.

Myrdal directed a study of the African American for the Carnegie Corporation published as *An American Dilemma: The Negro and Modern Democracy* (1944). Now regarded as a classic of legal, sociological, and anthropological scholarship, it helped focus attention on America's race problem. He believed that the African American plight was a focal point of the general moral dilemma of America: the conflict between the just American goals and ideals and the actual practices of the individual members of society. His work has been cited in U.S. Supreme Court decisions.

Myrdal served as minister of commerce in Sweden (1945-1947). He used his neutrality and objectivity as an international civil servant and as director of the United Nations Economic Commission for Europe (1947-1957). In the 1950s and 1960s, he wrote prolifically on international economics, the problems of underdevelopment, and value biases in Western economic thought.

In 1968, Myrdal completed another major study, *Asian Drama: An Inquiry into the Poverty of Nations* (3 vols.), which pessimistically analyzes the difficulties of development in southern Asia. Myrdal feels that the disparity between rich and poor nations cannot be bridged until old myths about development are rejected. He argues that the crucial factor is not the amount of foreign aid or the kind of economic system used but the social discipline of the masses. Without more native self-help, without the rousing of the masses and their real participation in nation building, without strong programs of birth control, and without the rooting out of corruption in government, Myrdal concludes that the Asian drama could become a tragedy. His later work includes *The Challenge of Affluence* (1963). In 1974, he won the Nobel Laureate in Economics, principally for his work on the critical application of economic theory of Third World countries. He passed away in 1987 in Sweden.

Further Reading

Information on Myrdal's economics can be found in Ben B. Seligman's, *Main Currents in Modern Economics: Economic Thought since 1870* (1962); and G. L. S. Shackle's, *The Years of High Theory: Invention and Tradition in Economic Thought, 1926-1939* (1967). Herbert Aptheker's, *The Negro People in America* (1946), is a critique of Myrdal's *An American Dilemma* (2 vols., 1944). John H. Madge, *The Origins of Scientific Sociology* (1964), has a detailed chapter examining *An American Dilemma.* □

Myron

The Greek sculptor Myron (active ca. 470-450 B.C.) was one of the most renowned sculptors of the early classical period.

Myron was born at Eleutherai on the Attic side of Mt. Kithairon, probably before 500 B.C. We do not know his father's name; his teacher is said by Pliny the Elder to have been Hageladas, the principal caster of monumental bronze statues at Argos about 500. Myron established no school, his only known pupil being his son Lykios. His period of major activity seems to have been during the quarter century following the decisive Greek victories over the Persians in 480-479.

Our knowledge of Myron's work comes from ancient literary sources, among the most important of which is Pliny. Pausanias, who traveled through Greece during the third quarter of the 2d century A.D., contributes additional important information about works of Myron still visible. Although Myron made at least one cult statue, an image of Hekate on Aegina, most of his recorded works, at least 21 of which are mentioned by classical authors, were votive in nature: dedications of victorious athletes and worshipers at sanctuaries. His statues are said to have been scattered in sanctuaries throughout the Greek world, from Sicily to Ionia, with a concentration on the Athenian Acropolis. As far as is known, Myron worked exclusively in bronze, with the exception of the *Hekate,* done in wood. He also fashioned vessels in metal, following a pattern of involvement in the minor arts common to sculptors in the 5th and 4th centuries B.C.

Of Myron's recorded works, there are two for which little or no doubt remains for identification through copies. The first is the famous *Diskobolos, or Discus Thrower.* Lucian's description of the statue, which depicts the midpoint of the youthful athlete's windup for the throw, is almost unanimously considered to refer to a statue of which several large-scale marble copies exist (for example, the Lancelotti statue and the copy from Castel Porziano, both in the Museo Nazionale Romano, Rome), as well as statuettes and depictions on gems. The composition, highly rhythmical as well as seemingly unstable, reflects an "experimental" spirit that runs through many other works of early classical sculpture, which explored many variations in poses of violent action and arrested movement. The *Diskobolos* is widely admired for its particular resolution of the exertion and instability of an instant of motion into a composition of unified balance and harmony. The statue is designed within a single plane, apparently meant to be seen from the sides only. Its date must be very near 450 B.C.; its subject and occasion for execution, most likely an athletic victory, remain unknown.

Also identified beyond reasonable doubt is a group of Athena and the satyr Marsyas, which stood on the Athenian Acropolis. Athena has thrown down the flutes, and Marsyas is about to pick them up. The principal copy of the *Marsyas* is in the Vatican Museums, Rome. The *Athena* has been recognized in a Roman statue in the Städtische Galerie, Frankfurt am Main. Details missing from the two copies can be seen on Athenian bronze coins struck under emperor Hadrian (A.D. 117-138) and an Attic red-figured oinochoe of the third quarter of the 5th century B.C. The composition, in which both figures move away from each other and the central element, the fateful flutes, is tense with drama and foreshadows the centripetal arrangement given to the contest of Athena and Poseidon in the west pediment of the Parthenon.

Myron's statues of athletes elicited much admiration in antiquity; among these, the statue of Ladas, an Olympic victor in the footrace, seems to have captured the fleetness of the runner, poised on tiptoe at the start of the race. No copies of this statue have been identified. Numerous scholarly efforts to attribute male heads of early classical style to Myron must remain tentative. Among his more ambitious compositions is the over-life-size group of three figures that stood in the Heraion at Samos; in Franz Willemsen's view (1965), it may represent the introduction of Herakles to Olympos.

Myron also was famous as a sculptor of animals; his *Heifer* on the Acropolis was particularly well known. That this statue, an appropriate votive offering, had widespread influence among his contemporaries and successors cannot be doubted; again, scholarly attempts to identify individual marble sculptures or bronze statuettes as copies of the *Heifer* cannot be definitely proved.

Ancient critical opinion held that Myron fell short of full classical perfection. Most modern scholars consider him to be the great experimental innovator of the early classical period ("Severe style").

Further Reading

For a discussion of the ancient sources on Myron see Jerome J. Pollitt, *The Art of Greece, 1400-31 B.C.* (1965). Scholarly discussions of Myron are found in Franz Willemsen's article "Myron" in the *Encyclopedia of World Art,* vol. 10 (1965); G.M.A. Richter, *The Sculpture and Sculptors of the Greeks* (4th ed. 1970); and B. S. Ridgway, *The Severe Style in Greek Sculpture* (1970). □

Mzilikazi

Mzilikazi (ca. 1795-1868) was a southern African warrior leader who, after being driven out of his homeland, created the Ndebele, or Matabele, kingdom.

A younger son of the Kumalo chieftain Mashobane, Mzilikazi spent his early life in the north of what was later to become the Zulu kingdom. During his young manhood, the Kumalo were victims of a power struggle between the Zulu chief, Shaka, and the Ndwandwe chief, Zwide. The latter, Mzilikazi's maternal grandfather, had Mashobane killed, but Mzilikazi, who was elevated to the vacant Kumalo chieftainship, identified his interests with the rising star of Shaka.

Although Shaka's program of conquest and expansion commonly involved the elimination of members of former chiefly houses, Mzilikazi received specially favored treatment and seems to have been left, after the destruction of the Ndwandwe (ca. 1818), with the authority of a territorial subchief on the northern marches of the new Zulu kingdom.

In 1823, after endangering his position by refusing to surrender to Shaka certain cattle captured in a raid, Mzilikazi fled Zululand. With a few hundred warriors he began a career of conquest that contributed to the Difaqane, a violent upheaval among the South African chiefdoms of the interior, which produced political consolidation in certain areas but left much of the central plateau practically uninhabited.

Shifting westward, in stages, across the Transvaal, Mzilikazi eventually settled at Mosega on the Marico River. These moves gave him greater geographical security and enhanced his power. By piecemeal conquest and absorption of Transvaal Sotho groups and by incorporating Nguni refugees from Zululand, his Ndebele state became the dominant power on the "highveld," with an army trained and regimented on the Zulu pattern.

In 1836 Mzilikazi was faced by Trekkers (immigrant Boers, or Afrikaners, from the Cape) seeking lands beyond the area of British control. Although he was by no means ill-disposed toward whites and developed a close friendship with the missionary Robert Moffat, Mzilikazi determined to repulse these uninvited intruders. However, firearms gave the Trekkers and their black supporters an advantage that was ultimately decisive. In January 1837 Mosega was sacked, and in a 9-day battle in November Mzilikazi's warriors were defeated.

An epic journey followed in which the Ndebele made their way northward in two contingents and at last established a new "Matabeleland" beyond the Limpopo. Here, in a portion of the former Rozwi empire, Mzilikazi's Nguni followers and their Sotho adherents superimposed themselves on Shona people and built a military monarchy based on a caste system that only slowly lost its definition.

Mzilikazi is commonly remembered as a marauder who left a trail of devastation in his wake, but his achievement was also a constructive one. Although the Ndebele state collapsed less than 30 years after his death under the tide of white advance, one of the praise-names by which the "Matabele" of Rhodesia remember him is Umdabuli we Sizwe, the Maker of the Nation.

Further Reading

Peter Becker, *Path of Blood* (1962), is a popular account of the rise and conquests of Mzilikazi, based on oral tradition and written sources. It should be supplemented by A.T. Bryant, *Olden Times in Zululand and Natal* (1929), and J.D. Omer-Cooper, *The Zulu Aftermath* (1966). Also helpful is Monica Wilson and Leonard Thompson, eds., *The Oxford History of South Africa* (1969).

Additional Sources

Knight, Ian, *Warrior chiefs of Southern Africa: Shaka of the Zulu, Moshoeshoe of the BaSotho, Mzilikazi of the Matabele, Maqoma of the Xhosa,* Poole, Dorset: Firebird Books; New York, NY: Distributed in the United States by Sterling Pub. Co., 1994.
Rasmussen, R. Kent., *Migrant kingdom: Mzilikazi's Ndebele in South Africa,* London: Collings, 1978.
Rasmussen, R. Kent., *Mzilikazi of the Ndebele,* London: Heinemann Educational, 1977. □

N

Vladimir Nabokov

The Russian-born American poet, fiction writer, critic, and butterfly expert Vladimir Nabokov (1899-1977), one of the most highly acclaimed novelists of his time, was noted for his sensuous and lyrical descriptions, verbal games and experimental narrative style, and his carefully structured and intricate plots.

Best known as the author of *Lolita,* the scandalous 1950s novel about an underage temptress, Vladimir Nabokov was much more than a chronicler of lecherous professors. He was one of the most productive and creative writers of his era. His novels, short stories, essays, poems, and memoirs all share his cosmopolitan wit, his love of wordplay, his passion for satire, and his complex social commentary. Nabokov's work appeals to the senses, imagination, intellect, and emotions. His themes are universal: the role of the artist in society; the myth of journey, adventure, and return; and humanity's concepts of memory and time, which he called a tightrope walk across the "watery abyss of the past and the aerial abyss of the future."

Child Prodigy

Nabokov was born in St. Petersburg, Russia, as one of five children of a wealthy noble couple. Nabokov's parents encouraged the gifted youth to follow his mind and imagination. He played with language and linguistics, mathematics, puzzles and games including chess, and soccer, boxing and tennis. He read English before he read Russian. Interested in butterflies, he became a recognized entomological authority while still young and remained a noted lepidopertist his entire life. Nabokov began to write poems when he was 13 and, as he described it, "the numb fury of verse making first came over me." His first book of poetry was published in 1914, and a second appeared in 1917. He called his early writing an attempt "to express one's position in regard to the universe."

Nabokov's father, a lawyer who edited St. Petersburg's only liberal newspaper, rebelled against first the czarist regime, then against the Communists. Bereft of land and fortune after the Russian Revolution, the family fled Russia for London in 1919, where Nabokov entered Cambridge University. He graduated with honors in 1922 and rejoined his family in Berlin, where Nabokov's father was gunned down by a monarchist. Nabokov married Vera Slonim in 1925 and they had a son, Dmitri, who later became an opera singer. In Berlin, Nabokov taught boxing, tennis and languages and constructed crossword puzzles. He began writing under the pseudonym "V. Sirin," selling stories, poems and essays to Russian-language newspapers in Berlin and then, after fleeing the Nazis in 1938, in Paris. His work included translations as diverse as *Alice in Wonderland* and the poem *La Belle dame sans merci* into Russian, literary criticism, short stories, plays, and novels. He began writing in English and in 1940 moved to the United States.

Early Days in America

In 1940, Nabokov taught Slavic languages at Stanford University. From 1941 to 1948 he taught at Wellesley College and became a professor of literature. He also was a research fellow in entomology at the Museum of Comparative Zoology at Harvard University from 1942 to 1948, and later discovered several butterfly species and subspecies, including "Nabokov's wood nymph." While teaching, he

wrote *The Real Life of Sebastian Knight* (1941), a parody of the mystery-story genre, whose hero is derived from the author's own life. A Guggenheim fellowship in 1943 resulted in his scholarly 1944 biographical study of Russian author Nicolai Gogol. Nabokov became an American citizen in 1945 and by then was a regular contributor to popular magazines.

Nabokov's 1947 novel *Bend Sinister* is about an intellectual's battle with a totalitarian police state. It is considered a parody of the utopia genre. In 1949 Nabokov was appointed professor of Russian and European literature at Cornell University, where he taught until 1959. His memoir of his early life in Russia, *Speak, Memory* (1951), is a charming autobiography. Several short sketches published in the *New Yorker,* were incorporated into *Pnin* (1957), his novel about a Russian emigre teaching at an American university.

Lolita Brings Notoriety

Despite Nabokov's vast productivity, scholarly status, and high standing in literary circles, he remained relatively unknown to the general public until *Lolita,* a sadly hilarious account of Humbert Humbert, a pompous middle-aged professor who is seduced by a 12-year-old schoolgirl. It was first published in Paris in 1955. After its first American edition came out in 1958, some U.S. libraries banned it. The scandal helped the book become immensely popular. Critical reaction ran the gamut from outrage to high praise. Nabokov sold the film rights and wrote the screenplay for the 1962 movie directed by Stanley Kubrick. With royalties from the novel and the film, Nabokov was able to quit

teaching and devote himself entirely to his writing and to butterfly hunting.

In 1959 Nabokov published *Invitation to a Beheading,* a story of a man awaiting execution, which he had first written in Russian in 1938. In 1960 he and his family moved to Montreux, Switzerland. Nabokov received critical acclaim for *Pale Fire* (1962), a strange, multidimensional exercise in the techniques of parable and parody, written as a 999-line poem with a lengthy commentary by a demented New England scholar who is actually an exiled mythical king.

Playing with Time

In 1963 Nabokov's English translation of Alexander Pushkin's romantic verse novel *Eugene Onegin* was published; the four-volume scholarly work was, Nabokov said, his "labor of love." Several translations of earlier Russian works followed, including *The Defense,* a novel about chess. Nabokov's *Ada* (1969), an "autumnal fairy tale" whose principal characters are imprisoned by time, is subject to many levels of interpretation, with its intricate construction, complex allusions, word games, staggering erudition, chronological ambiguities and literary parody. Time in this novel is blended into a totally free-ranging and distorting present, what Nabokov called "the essential spirality of all things in their relationship to time." The novel is the fulfillment of Nabokov's theme from *Speak, Memory:* "I confess I do not believe in time. I like to fold my magic carpet, after use, in such a way as to superimpose one part of the pattern upon another. Let visitors trip."

Nabokov constructed his novels like puzzles, rather than working from beginning to end. In 1964, he told *Life* magazine: "Writing has always been for me a blend of dejection and high spirits, a torture and a pastime." Nabokov died July 2, 1977, at the Palace Hotel in Montreux, Switzerland, where he had lived since 1959.

Further Reading

See *Nabokov: The Man and His Work,* edited by L.S. Dumbo (1967); Andrew Field's, *VN, The Life and Art of Vladimir Nabokov* (1986); *Vladimir Nabokov: The American Years* and *Vladimir Nabokov: The British Years* (both 1991) by Brian Boyd's; *Escape into Aesthetics: The Art of Vladimir Nabokov* (1966) and his introduction to *Nabokov's Congeries* (1968) by Page Stegners). □

Joaquim Aurelio Nabuco de Araujo

Joaquim Aurelio Nabuco de Araujo (1849-1910) was a Brazilian abolitionist, statesman, and author. Best remembered as the outstanding leader of the Brazilian abolitionist movement, he was also an ardent supporter of Pan-Americanism.

Joaquim Nabuco was born on Aug. 19, 1849, into the plantation aristocracy of Recife, Pernambuco. During 1865-1870 he studied at the law academies of São Paulo and Recife. During his years in São Paulo (1865-1869) he was stirred by the currents of liberalism, romanticism, and humanitarianism which permeated the southern city, and he joined the abolitionist movement.

After graduation Nabuco seemed content to lead the life of a comfortable dilettante. Yet the years from 1870 to 1878 merely served as a period of apprenticeship. He casually engaged in his law practice and contributed to various literary journals. In 1872 he published his first book, a literary study entitled *Camöens and the Lusiads*. In 1876-1877 he served as legation attaché in Washington and London.

In 1878, following the death of his father, Nabuco returned to Recife to continue the family political tradition. He soon won a seat in the national Chamber of Deputies. With the philosophy of Walter Bagehot as his political guide, the English humanitarians his inspiration, and abolition his constant goal, Nabuco hoped to gain complete abolition by legal processes based on humanitarianism and social justice without resort to the terrible civil war experienced by the United States.

In 1880 Nabuco promoted the foundation of the Brazilian Antislavery Society, which gave a loose organization to disparate abolitionist groups. A 2-year self-imposed exile in London, following an unsuccessful reelection campaign in 1881 because of his position on slavery, resulted in *O Abolicionismo* (Abolitionism), a polemical indictment of Brazilian slavery. Of transitory importance, as is most polemical literature, *O Abolicionismo* was the most learned and forceful study presented against slavery during the abolitionist campaign. In 1886, disheartened by reverses in the antislavery movement, Nabuco wrote *O Eclypse do abolicionismo* (The Eclipse of Abolitionism) but 2 years later exalted in the proclamation of total, uncompensated abolition.

Nabuco, a stout proponent of parliamentary monarchy, unsuccessfully led a campaign to federalize the empire—a longtime goal of the Liberal party. But when the monarchy fell and a republic was established in November 1889, Nabuco began a 10-year retirement from public life.

During this respite, Nabuco produced his most important literary work. *Um estadista do imperio* (1889; A Statesman of the Empire), a study of the life and times of his father, Senator José Thomaz Nabuco, and his own episodic autobiography, *Minha formacão* (1900; My Formation), were his best efforts.

Although not completely reconciled to the new regime, in 1898 Nabuco agreed to present Brazil's case in the boundary dispute with British Guiana. Soon after Nabuco arrived in London, the Brazilian minister died, and Nabuco reluctantly agreed to fill the vacancy. He served in that capacity until 1905, when he became Brazil's first ambassador, the Washington legation having been elevated to the rank of an embassy. At a time when United States—Latin American relations were at an all-time low, Nabuco remained a staunch supporter of hemispheric unity. In 1906

he served as president of the Third Pan-American Conference in Rio.

In the United States Nabuco was a popular ambassador and able representative of his country. But his health, racked by a combination of heart difficulties and migraine headaches, deteriorated in mid-1909. He died in Washington, D.C., on Jan. 17, 1910.

Further Reading

The major work on Nabuco is a biography by his daughter, Carolina Nabuco, *The Life of Joaquim Nabuco* (1950). It is a detailed account of Nabuco's life and is greatly enriched by extensive quotations from his speeches, books, articles, and letters. □

Elie Nadelman

Elie Nadelman (1882-1946), the Polish-American sculptor and graphic artist, evolved a highly distinctive sculptural style by abstracting human forms and stressing the curvilinear interplay of contours.

Elie Nadelman, born in Warsaw, was the seventh child of cultivated parents who encouraged their children to take an interest in the arts and philosophy. His studies at the Art Academy in Warsaw were interrupted by a year of military service. He returned to Warsaw in 1901 and then went to Cracow, but he realized that art in his native land was provincial and that he must leave to learn.

The following year Nadelman went to Munich, where he saw the drawings of the English Art Nouveau illustrator Aubrey Beardsley. These highly stylized works undoubtedly influenced Nadelman. He responded to Beardsley's elegant patterning and curvilinear invention but rejected his eroticism and *fin-de-siècle* posturing. Nadelman was deeply impressed by the archaic Greek sculpture in the museums; it was the first original ancient classical art he had seen, and its impact was lasting. He also took delight in German folk sculpture and Meissen figurines. It was as if these early influences merged in forming a style for Nadelman that was classical in spirit but not heroic, playful but never trivial.

After spending 6 months in Munich, Nadelman went to Paris. His first sculptures suggest those of Auguste Rodin, but by 1905 he had steered away from the French master's impressionistic concepts and toward forms defined by sweeping contours that assumed a detached, coolly geometric aspect. Nadelman began his research by making many drawings. In them, and later in his sculptures, he attempted to reduce the human figure to a complex of arcs. The titles he gave all his sculptures executed between 1905 and 1915 best characterize the spirit and nature of the work: *Research in Volume* and *Accord of Forms*.

Nadelman's one-man show of 1909 in Paris was a great success, critically and financially, although the swaggering, svelte nudes and neoclassicistic marble heads, which seemed so novel then, appeared mannered and dated later. In 1910 Nadelman wrote that true form is abstract, that is, composed of geometrical elements. "Here is how I realize it," he volunteered. "I employ no other line than the curve, which possesses freshness and force. I compose these curves so as to bring them in accord or opposition to one another. In that way I obtain the life of form, i.e. harmony."

In 1911 Nadelman had a one-man show in London. Helena Rubinstein, the cosmetician, bought everything in it. Reportedly at her invitation, Nadelman went to America in 1914. The following year he had a one-man show at Alfred Stieglitz's "291" gallery. *Man in the Open Air,* shown at this time, is, like most of the work that followed, severely stylized, with the elegance of a superior store mannikin.

Nadelman made spirited animal pieces and employed color in his figures in wood, terra-cotta, and papiermâché. He did a series of plaster figures during the 1930s and 1940s in the manner of Tanagra figures. Two sets of his papiermâché figures were enlarged and placed in the New York State Theater at Lincoln Center, New York City.

Further Reading

Lincoln Kirstein, *The Sculpture of Elie Nadelman* (1948), is the catalog of his 1948 exhibition at the Museum of Modern Art. It is scholarly and well illustrated, but it tends to be effusive. □

Ralph Nader

The American social crusader and lawyer Ralph Nader (born 1934) became a symbol of the public's concern over corporate ethics and consumer interests. He inspired investigations that were intended to improve the operations of industries and government bureaus.

Ralph Nader was born on February 27, 1934, in Winsted, Connecticut, to Lebanese immigrants. He graduated *magna cum laude* from Princeton University's Woodrow Wilson School of Public and International Affairs in 1955 and then went to Harvard Law School, receiving his degree in 1958. Nader served briefly in the U.S. Army, traveled, then opened a law office in Hartford, Connecticut. He also lectured in history and government at the University of Hartford.

Nader was one among many concerned for safety in auto design, but most writers and members of safety and auto associations saw the problem as one in engineering and individual preference in a consumers' market. Nader, while still at Harvard, had studied auto injury cases and was persuaded that faulty design, rather than driver incompetence, was responsible for the staggering accident statistics. He testified before state legislative committees on the subject and wrote articles for magazines.

In 1964 Nader was appointed a consultant to the Department of Labor and undertook to study auto safety in depth. He also worked with Senator Abraham A. Ribicoff's Government Operations Subcommittee, providing it with data on auto accidents. In 1965 he left the department to prepare a book on the subject.

Nader's *Unsafe at Any Speed: The Designed-in Dangers of the American Automobile* (1965) appeared while Ribicoff's committee was holding hearings on the subject. Nader, a tall, attractive figure, testifying before the committee, became a target of auto manufacturers then coping with lawsuits by victims of auto accidents who were charging faulty car design. Although new safety laws were inevitable, their character was given new facets by Nader's revelations that he had been personally harassed and his private life investigated by detectives. The admission in March 1966 by General Motors president James M. Roche that his firm had indeed had Nader under surveillance received national television coverage and made Nader a public figure. *Unsafe at Any Speed* became a best seller and a factor in the legislation which in September became law.

Nader enlarged his investigations of the auto industry and the National Traffic Safety Agency, which was responsible for administering the new law. In November he sued General Motors for $26 million, alleging invasion of privacy. He also began a series of studies in various fields intended to upgrade responsible industrial production and human relations. These included safety in mines, control of oil and gas pipes dangerous to people and the environment, and justice for Native Americans. One cause which harked back to Upton Sinclair's 1905-1906 crusade was Nader's activity in behalf of what became the 1967 Wholesome Meat Act.

Living austerely, working with swiftness and economy, and supplementing with foundation grants his income from royalties, article writing, and lectures, Nader attracted over a hundred young people—soon known as "Nader's Raiders"—from law schools and elsewhere. They helped him gather data about industries and government bureaus. In 1969 he organized his Center for the Study of Responsive Law. Its work resulted in such publications as *"The Nader Report"* on the *Federal Trade Commission* (1969) and *The Interstate Commerce Commission* [sic]: *The Public Interest and the ICC* (1970), with more publications promised in all social fields. In August 1970 Nader was once more in the headlines, having been awarded $425,000 from General Motors, funds promptly put into his expanded crusade.

From the late 1970s through the early 1990s, Nader's public image faded from his *Unsafe at Any Speed* heyday. But by 1988, he successfully campaigned to roll back California car insurance rates, then ignited public opinion to block a proposed 50 percent pay hike for members of Congress.

He gained notoriety in 1990 when a *Forbes* magazine story accused him of working together with trial lawyers for supporting Americans' right to sue. The criticism didn't deter him from other investigations, including safety flaws in the airline industry because of financial instability following deregulation. But his book, *Collision Course: The Truth About Airline Safety,* with Wesley J. Smith, was panned by some for questionable use of statistics.

After failing to stop the North American Free Trade Agreement (1993), he was nominated as 1996 Green Party candidate for President, winning some support in popular polls. Nader himself had summed up his philosophy: "You've got to keep the pressure on, even if you lose. The essence of the citizens' movement is persistence."

Nader and his coworkers were patently in the Progressive tradition. However, their precise relation to public wants and preferences remained controversial. His critics held that he sought to impose his own standards of production rather than to help determine public interest. Nevertheless, he appeared to the public as a dedicated and valuable citizen whose full achievement was yet to be determined.

Further Reading

Nader and his crusades are treated in G.S. McClellan, ed., *The Consuming Public* (1968); G. De Bell, ed., *The Voter's Guide to Environmental Politics* (1970); J.G. Mitchell and C.L. Stallings, ed., *Ecotactics* (1970), with an introduction by Nader; J. Ridgeway, *The Politics of Ecology* (1970); A. A. Aaker and G. S. Day, eds., *Consumerism* (1971); and L. J. White, *The Automobile Industry since 1945* (1971). Articles on Nader have appeared in the *Ann Arbor News* (March 31, 1996); the *Nation* (January 8, 1996); *Business Week* (March 6, 1989); and *Fortune* (May 22, 1989). □

Ernest Nagel

A leading American philosopher of science, Ernest Nagel (1901-1985) developed a logical empirical theory of science within the framework of pragmatic naturalism.

Ernest Nagel was born in Czechoslovakia on Nov. 16, 1901. His family emigrated to the United States when Ernest was 10 years old. He became an American citizen in 1919. While teaching for a decade in New York City public schools, he earned a bachelor of science degree from the City College of New York in 1923 and his doctorate from Columbia University in 1930. Except for a year at City College at the beginning of his teaching career and a year (1966-1967) at Rockefeller University, he was a professor of philosophy at Columbia University. In 1967, he became a University Professor at Columbia, the most distinguished academic rank. In addition, he served as an editor of the *Journal of Philosophy* (1939-1956) and of the *Journal of Symbolic Logic* (1940-1946).

Pioneer in Scientific Logic

At City College, Nagel studied under Morris Cohen, who emphasized the role of reason in science. Nagel's association with Cohen led to the publication of *An Introduction to Logic and Scientific Method* (1934), one of the first and most successful textbooks in the field. Cohen and Nagel claimed to have found "a place for the realistic formalism of Aristotle, the scientific pragmatism of [Charles S.] Peirce, the pedagogical soundness of [John] Dewey, and the mathematical rigor of [Bertrand] Russell." They interpreted empirical science experimentally, stressing the role of hypotheses in conducting research.

Trained as a logician, Nagel wrote his earliest books on logic. In the 1930s, Nagel wrote two textbooks, *Principles of the Theory of Probability* and *The Logic of Measurement*. He married Edith Haggstrom in 1935; they had two children, Alexander and Sidney.

Introduced Wittgenstein to Americans

After a year of study in Europe, Nagel published a historic report, "Impressions and Appraisals of Analytic Philosophy in Europe," in the *Journal of Philosophy* (1936). This essay introduced Americans to the philosophical work of the European philosophers Ludwig Wittgenstein and Rudolf Carnap. Nagel sought to adapt the teachings of the logical positivists to the more comprehensive framework of American pragmatic naturalism. The influence of logical positivism on his thought resulted in his concepts of logic and mathematics in linguistic terms. This conclusion was developed in his 1944 paper "Logic without Ontology."

Most of Nagel's writings took the form of journal articles and book reviews. Two of his books *Sovereign Reason* (1954) and *Logic without Metaphysics* (1957) consist wholly of previously published articles. These showed him to be one of the most analytic and critical thinkers in American philosophy. They also expressed and illustrated Nagel's method of contextualistic analysis, by which he interpreted "the meanings of theoretical constructions in terms of their manifest functions in identifiable contexts."

Proponent of Naturalism

Nagel expounded his naturalism in 1954, in his presidential address before the annual meeting of the Eastern Division of the American Philosophical Association. He defined naturalism as "a generalized account of the cosmic scheme and of man's place in it, as well as a logic of inquiry." Naturalism, to Nagel, was "the executive and causal primacy of matter in the executive order of nature" and "the manifest plurality and variety of things, of their qualities and their functions, . . . [as] an irreducible feature of the universe."

The Structure of Science (1961), heralded as one of the best works in the philosophy of science, examined the logical structure of scientific concepts and evaluated the claims of knowledge in various sciences. Nagel tried to show that the same logic of scientific explanation was valid in all sciences. He viewed the controversy between the descriptive, the realist, and the instrumentalist views of scientific concepts to be simply conflicts over "preferred modes of speech."

Nagel became a University Professor Emeritus in 1970 and remained a special lecturer at Columbia until 1973. In 1980, while receiving Columbia's Nicholas Murray Butler Medal in Gold, he explained his view of philosophy: "Philosophy is in general not a primary inquiry into the nature of things. It is a reflection on the conclusion of those inquiries that may sometimes terminate, as it did in the case of Spinoza, in a clarified vision of man's place in the scheme of things." Nagel died of pneumonia at Columbia-Presbyterian Medical Center in New York City on Sept. 22, 1985.

Further Reading

The New American Philosophers (1968) by Andrew J. Reck; *Thinkers of the Twentieth Century* (1987) and *The Encyclopedia of Unbelief* (1985). □

Imre Nagy

Imre Nagy (1896-1958), Hungarian politician, served as prime minister of Hungary between 1953 and 1955, then again in 1956 during the revolution. He was tried and executed in 1958.

Imre Nagy was born into a peasant family at Kaposvār on July 6, 1896. As a young man he was an engineering apprentice, then a worker in Budapest. He was sent to the Russian front during World War I. Taken prisoner, he joined the Red Army in 1917 and the Bolshevik Party in 1918. He returned to Hungary in the early 1920s and joined the then illegal Communist Party. He organized the peasants in a movement calling for agrarian reform. He was in charge of Communist Party work in the countryside, concentrating on agrarian questions. Politically very active, he was tried and sentenced several times by the Hungarian government.

In 1928 Nagy left the country and settled in Vienna. In March 1930 he joined the staff of the International Agronomy Institute in Moscow. He published several articles in the Hungarian emigre journal *Sarló es Kalapács* (Sickle and Hammer). In 1932, commissioned by the Comintern, he drafted the Communist program of action on agrarian problems. He never joined any of the emigre Hungarian Communist factions, which may be one of the reasons why he escaped the Stalinist purges of the 1930s.

In 1941 he became assistant editor, then editor-in-chief, of Radio Kossuth, which broadcast programs directed to Hungary. In 1944 Nagy drew up a plan for Hungarian agrarian reform. At the end of the year he returned to Hungary and was appointed minister for agriculture in the provisional government at Debrecen. In April 1945, following the World War II liberation of the country by the Red Army, the government moved to Budapest, where life began to resume its normal course. The agrarian reform implemented in Hungary was based on Nagy's plan and carried out under his direction. This made him very popular among the peasants.

In the elections held on November 4, 1945, the conservative Smallholders Party won 57.7 percent of the votes, the Social Democratic Party 17.4 percent, the Communist Party 17 percent, and the National Peasant Party 8 percent. These parties formed a coalition government. Imre Nagy became minister of the interior. On March 12, 1946, the Communist, Social Democrat, and National Peasant parties formed a "left block" inside the government coalition and organized demonstrations against the deputies from the right wing of the Smallholders Party. Under pressure, the Smallholders Party expelled 23 deputies. Later in March 1946 the Communist Party charged Imre Nagy with "lack of vigor" and relieved him of his post. It appointed Laszlo Rajk as his successor.

In order to force further nationalization, the Communist Party in February 1947 launched fresh attacks on the Smallholders Party. The secretary general of the party was arrested by the Soviet Control Commission and charged with anti-Soviet activities. He was tried and condemned to death, together with other party leaders.

In May the three largest banks were nationalized. New elections were held in August, in which 60 percent of the votes were won by the government coalition. Imre Nagy was elected president of the Parliament, a largely ceremonial office.

In March 1948, under pressure from the Communist Party, which was seeking a merger with the Social Democrats, the latter expelled some of its leading members who were opposed to such a union. Later that month businesses with more than 100 employees were nationalized. In June the Communist and Social Democratic parties decided to unite; for all practical purposes, the Social Democratic Party was absorbed by the Communists. A large-scale purge began in September, leading to the expulsion of some 100,000 members from the Communist Party: "former Social Democrats or unreliable elements."

Nagy had serious disputes with Matyas Rákosi, the Communist Party leader, from 1948. Nagy disagreed with the "personality cult" and the forced pace of collectivization, pointing out the dangers of this policy. In 1949 he was forced to withdraw from political life, having been removed from the politboro. He became director of the University of Agronomy and devoted himself to the study of agrarian questions.

A show trial of Rajk took place in September 1949; it was designed to justify the attacks on Yugoslavia. Rajk was sentenced to death. By December the nationalization of industry was completed. In the beginning of 1950 the first Five Year Plan took effect. It concentrated on the development of heavy industry and on intensified collectivization.

In 1951 Nagy was allowed to return to political life. He was again elected to the politboro and was made a member of the secretariat. In 1952 he was made minister for farm deliveries, and later, when Rákosi became president of the council, he was appointed as his second deputy.

In 1953, three months after Stalin's death, the new leaders of the Soviet Communist Party made a vigorous attack on the Hungarian party leaders and forced them to adopt a new line and to appoint Imre Nagy as prime minister. In his new post he introduced a series of measures. In addition to a reorganization of the economy, he announced measures of political liberalization. The peasants were allowed to withdraw from the cooperatives and were promised tax relief. Agricultural credit was eased. The deportations were ended. A new Patriotic People's Front was formed. In October 1954 Nagy announced intensified democratization. In December Rákosi attacked the line of policy adopted by Nagy. New instructions from Moscow strengthened Rákosi's position. In March 1955 the Central Committee condemned Imre Nagy's course, and in April he was expelled from the Central Committee and relieved of all his offices. At the end of 1955 he was expelled from the party.

After the 20th Congress of the Soviet Communist Party in 1956 it was important to rehabilitate Nagy's policy. In July Rákosi was removed; in October Nagy was re-admitted to the party. On October 23 and 24 workers went on strike; there were demonstrations in the streets against occupying Soviet troops; and the demand was raised for the return to power of Nagy. Nagy delivered a radio address calling for an end to the fighting. On October 26 delegations from all over the country urged Nagy to take new measures to liberate the country. During the following days a new government was formed and discussions began concerning the complete withdrawal of the Soviet troops. But more Soviet troops entered the country. The Hungarian government denounced the Warsaw Pact and declared the country neutral. Soviet forces launched a general offensive against Hungary, crushing the uprising. Nagy took refuge at the Yugoslav embassy (some 200,000 Hungarians fled the country).

Nagy remained under the protection of the embassy until November 22, when he was duped into leaving it. On his way home he was captured. He was tried, sentenced to death, and executed in 1958.

Further Reading

Selected speeches on policies adopted by Nagy are in Imre Nagy, *On communism, in defense of the new course* (1957). Speeches made at the session of the National Assembly in January 1954 are in Imre Nagy, *The activity of the government during the past six months and the tasks for 1954. The plan of national economy for 1954* (Budapest, *Hungarian Bulletin,* 1954), edited by Bela Szalai. The story of the 1956 revolution in Hungary can be found in Tibor Merai, *Thirteen Days That Shook the Kremlin* (1959). □

Nahmanides

The Spanish-born Jewish scholar Nahmanides (1194-1270), also called Moses ben Nahman, was the first outstanding rabbi to declare that resettlement in the land of Israel was a biblical precept binding upon all Jews.

Nahmanides was born in Gerona and educated in Spanish rabbinic schools. He became the leader of Spanish Jewry, which was centered at Gerona. His studies and his natural frame of mind inclined him toward a mystical interpretation of the Bible and toward the philosophic doctrines of the Cabalists.

Nahmanides's chief achievements lay in two directions. First, he reorganized and revivified the study of the Talmud in Spain. He produced a series of short works, each of which consisted of a selected passage from the Talmud that he analyzed and commented upon. In fact, Nahmanides inaugurated this form of rabbinic literature. Second, Nahmanides profoundly influenced Jewish biblical theology through his exegetical work. It was in this area that his mystical leanings and Cabalistic traits appeared. Nahmanides believed that the ultimate and complete meaning of the Bible was a mystical one to be penetrated through enlightened faith and through the science of the Cabalistic masters. Respecting reason within its limits, Nahmanides nevertheless opposed the rationalizations and philosophizings of Maimonides. He denied that human reason could answer all questions, and as a result his exegetical work, a commentary on the Pentateuch, was heavily loaded with mystical references. Nahmanides employed both literal meanings and Haggadic and Halakic interpretations; but he usually pointed to the mystic meaning as most significant.

The rabbi's circle of students and followers issued a wide range of scholarly works. *Sefer Temuna* (Book of Image) describes each of the 22 letters of the Hebrew alphabet as an image of God. Nahmanides also explained the various periods of world history in the light of these images.

Nahmanides formed part of the Spanish school of Cabalists, which also included Judah ben Yaqar, Ezra ben

Solomon, Azriel, and Jacob ben Sheshet. They were all steeped in Neoplatonic speculation, which intruded into the Gnostic type of mysticism that had hitherto reigned in Jewish mysticism. This Gnostic mysticism had originated in a rabbinic gnosis of the 1st and 2d centuries A.D. It had centered on the throne (*Merkabha*) of God as described in Ezekiel I. The Neoplatonic trend of Nahmanides's mysticism centered on the *sefirot,* or "soul" or "inner life," of the hidden transcendent God. On this basis Nahmanides formed his mystical theory of history and thus became a forerunner of the mystical historical doctrines of the 18th and 19th centuries.

Nahmanides was the outstanding Jewish protagonist in the famous Barcelona Disputation of 1263, in which his adversary was the anti-Jewish agitator Pablo Christiani. The Christian hierarchies commonly organized disputations of this sort as a form of public entertainment in the Middle Ages. Generally, they involved a converted Jew who challenged one of his former coreligionists. In the Barcelona Disputation, Nahmanides won the victory and received as a reward a purse of money from King James I of Aragon, in whose presence the disputation had taken place. In 1267 Nahmanides moved to Palestine. He died in Acre 3 years later.

Further Reading

Information on Nahmanides is in Gershom G. Scholom, *Major Trends in Jewish Mysticism* (1946; 3d rev. ed. 1954). □

Sarojini Naidu

The Indian poet and nationalist leader Sarojini Naidu (1879-1949) became famous in India after her three small volumes of verse, published between 1905 and 1917, won critical acclaim in England.

Sarojini Chattopadhyay, later Naidu belonged to a Bengali family of Kulin Brahmins. But her father, Agorenath Chattopadhyay, after receiving a doctor of science degree from Edinburgh University, settled in Hyderabad State, where he founded and administered the Hyderabad College, which later became the Nizam's College.

Sarojini was the eldest of eight children and learned English at an early age. At 16 she was sent to England, where she studied at King's College, London, and at Girton College, Cambridge, without getting a degree. On her return to India in 1898, she married Govindarajulu Naidu, a medical doctor who belonged to a low caste. The marriage caused some consternation in orthodox Hindu society, but it was a happy marriage. Sarojini Naidu gave birth to two sons and two daughters.

Naidu's birth in a state which was ruled by the Moslem nizam and where the elite culture was strongly Islamic not only gave her some of the themes of her poetry but, in her political life, made her useful to Mohandas Gandhi in his efforts to heal Hindu-Moslem hostilities.

Her Poetry

As a girl in England, Naidu became acquainted with two eminent English critics, Arthur Symons and Edmund Gosse. Gosse read some of her early poems, and although he found them "skillful in form, correct in grammar, and blameless in sentiment," he also felt they were Western in feeling and in imagery. He advised her "to set her poems firmly among the mountains, the gardens, the temples, to introduce to us the vivid populations of her own voluptuous provinces."

There is no doubt that Sarojini Naidu made these changes in her work, but the tone of a bright, tenderhearted, Victorian girl, influenced by Tennyson, Shelley, and Elizabeth Barrett Browning, seems to linger in her work. In any event, she received serious recognition and much acclaim and was spoken of as the "nightingale of India" long after she had ceased to sing.

Naidu's poetry is lyrical and musical, using many types of meter and rhyme and filled with rich imagery. It deals with love and death, separation and longing, and the mystery of life, all important themes for poetry. There is much rhetorical gesturing, much longing for an ideal past or an ideal love. In the end the poetry tends to become monotonous and repetitive.

Naidu's claim to lasting fame will likely rest upon her distinguished career as a leader of the Indian nationalist movement. Her poetry was transmuted into oratory. She swayed audiences both in India and abroad with her speeches about India's struggle. In 1914 she met Gandhi in London and became one of his most trusted followers. She was one of the founders of the Women's India Association, in which she worked closely with Margaret E. Cousins and Annie Besant.

At the same time Naidu was active in the work of the Indian National Congress, of which she was named president in 1925. She was imprisoned five times during the independence movement. Gandhi sent her as his envoy to South Africa to help the Indians there against the oppressive acts of the South African government. She also was sent to the United States to refute, it is said, the bad publicity created by Katherine Mayo's sensational book *Mother India.*

In the frequently difficult relations with the Indian Moslem League, Naidu was deputed often to try to ease tensions, and she remained always a friend of Mohammad Ali Jinnah, the founder of Pakistan. In 1947, after the independence of India, she became the first governor of the state of Uttar Pradesh. She died on March 2, 1949, in the capital of the state, Lucknow.

Further Reading

Sarojini Naidu's three volumes of verse—*The Golden Threshold,* written in 1905; *The Bird of Time,* 1912; and *The Broken Wing,* 1917—were published in 1916 and 1917. The three books were combined in *The Sceptred Flute* (1928). Some later poems are included in *The Feather of the Dawn* (1961).

The most detailed biography of Sarojini Naidu is Padmini Sengupta, *Sarojini Naidu: A Biography* (1966). □

V. S. Naipaul

V. S. Naipaul (born 1932) was one of the foremost spokespersons in English prose of the post-colonial Third World.

Vidiadhar Surajprasad Naipaul was born August 17, 1932, in Trinidad, where his grandfather, an indentured worker, had come from India. An agnostic, Naipaul very early experienced a profound alienation, both from the close-knit family life of his Brahmin ancestors and from the social and political life of his native Trinidad: "It was a place where the stories were never stories of success but of failure: brilliant men, scholarship winners, who had died young, gone mad, or taken to drink." A scholarship winner himself out of the Queens Royal College, he used the award to escape to England in 1950, where he attended University College in Oxford. England, more than Trinidad, became his home beginning in the 1950s.

The first fruit of Naipaul's escape from the colony was a series of gently satiric short novels set in Trinidad. In *The Mystic Masseur* (1957) a semiliterate medicine man makes good as therapist to his village community because of the ignorance and gullibility of the local people. In *The Suffrage of Elvira* (1958), Naipaul turned a wry critical eye on the first general election held in a town where possibilities for democratic reform abort because of longstanding petty group enmities: Hindu-Moslem, black-white, Indian-Spaniard. *Miguel Street* (1959) is a "Winesburg, Ohio" collection of vivid character portraits drawn from the author's neighborhood. It closes in the Sherwood Anderson manner: the young narrator leaves his neighbors to continue his education in life abroad, but will immortalize them in his future role of writer.

Next came a big generational novel one of two Naipaul masterpieces *A House for Mr. Biswas* (1961). Set also in Trinidad, it echoes in some passages the light tone and fun of the earlier, shorter pieces, but achieves the stature of only a few other 20th-century novels largely through the detailed, compassionate picture of Biswas the fictional representative of the author's own father defeated in the struggle for a place of his own, alien both in a matriarchal Indian family and in the larger colonial society still not open to non-Europeans of talent in the 1940s.

Using London as a permanent return base, Naipaul began to travel extensively after 1960. His prolific writing continued, alternating between autobiographical fiction and reportorial non-fiction based on these travels. The unifying persona is that of an alienated ex-colonial, cut off temperamentally both from his native roots and from the European culture upon which he attempts to graft himself. In the novel *The Mimic Men* (1967) the action shifts between England and Trinidad. The protagonist, Ralph Singh, is out of place in both worlds as a scholarship student in London, and later as a deposed political minister and real estate speculator on his native island; his marriage to a liberal white English woman ends miserably. At the end of the novel, Singh, a disillusioned London recluse, is left writing his memoirs: "We pretended to be real, to be learning, to be preparing ourselves for life, we mimic men of the New World."

In two fine subsequent novels of the 1970s there is little trace of the earlier comic tone. *In a Free State* (1971) is set in a sub-Saharan African state in uneasy transition between incompetent post-colonial governments. Powerful descriptive passages juxtapose hauntingly beautiful natural settings with the detritus of European technology. New themes of sadistic violence and homosexuality link this work with the longer *Guerillas* (1975). In both novels the focus of alienation is on a liberal white couple whose pretensions political and sexual are ruthlessly exposed by the "Heart of Darkness" context. Naipaul himself explicitly pointed out his lineage to that earlier writer in quoting Joseph Conrad on authorial purpose: "To awaken the sense of true wonder. That is perhaps a fair definition of the novelist's purpose in all ages."

Perhaps Naipaul's finest sustained writing is to be found in the 1979 novel *A Bend in the River*. Here, in a small village in "New Africa," the writer explores all of his important themes, treated separately elsewhere: the disorder left in the wake of imperialism; the problems of emergent but underdeveloped third world peoples caught between old tribal ways and the new technology of dangerous arms and tinsel consumer materialism; and the liberal white woman as sexual symbol of Third World political trust and ultimate despair. Here, fortunes are made and lost overnight in gold, copper, and ivory; a Hindu couple from Africa's East Coast, poor shopkeepers one day, strike it rich the next when they are awarded proprietorship of the sole Bigburger franchise of the region. Instability and alienation are indigenous; the Moslem narrator of the novel, back from a short trip abroad, finds his small store nationalized by the Big Man, president-dictator of the Progressive State. After a brief stint in a concentration-camp-like prison, he is lucky to escape with his life. But to what place? He has no "home": "There could be no going back; there was nothing to go back to. We had become what the world outside had made us; we had to live in the world as it existed." Many felt the village was based on Kisangani, Zaire, and in 1997 as the city crumbled, some even hailed his 1979 work as prophetic.

A 1987 work, *The Enigma of Arrival,* was classified as fiction, although much of the material is indistinguishable from Naipaul's own life.

The variety of Naipaul's interests as a traveller-observer is suggested by the following survey of some of his nonfiction. His two personal roots are explored in the fusions of history with contemporary political analysis which make up *The Loss of El Dorado* (1969), about Trinidad, and *India: A Wounded Civilization* (1977). *Among the Believers* (1981) records impressions of the author's visits to several important Moslem nations, including Iran and Pakistan. *Finding the Center* (1984) includes an essay on his stay in the relatively stable and prosperous West African Ivory Coast. Here the observer analyzes sympathetically the balance of power between competing tribal and European values. In 1996 Naipaul released *The World's Great Places An Area of Darkness* to favorable reviews.

Naipaul published several new works in the late 1980s and early 1990s, including *A Turn in the South* (1989), *India: A Million Mutinies Now* (1990), and *Way in the World: A Sequence* (1994).

Further Reading

The first section of *Finding the Center* (1984) is an autobiographical essay; *A Flag on the Island* (1967) is a collection of short stories; *The Overcrowded Barracoon* (1972), is a selection of essays; William Walsh's *V. S. Naipaul* (1973) is a brief but comprehensive introduction to the writer's life and work; Robert K. Morris's *Paradoxes of Order* (1975) focuses critically on Naipaul's fiction. A good general analysis of Naipaul's work is to be found in Anthony Boxill's *V. S. Naipaul Fiction: In Quest of the Enemy* (1983). □

Mohammad Najibullah

Mohammad Najibullah (1947-1996) ruled the Republic of Afghanistan from May 4, 1986, until April 15, 1992, spanning a period during which control of the country by the former Soviet Union waned and

one of the cold war's final proxy conflicts became, once again, a civil war. As the country dissolved into fighting between rebel factions, Najibullah survived four more years under the protection of the United Nations before he was captured and killed.

Origins

Najibullah (meaning "Honored of God") was born in August 1947 to a moderately prosperous family belonging to the Pushtun Ahmadzai sub-tribe of the Ghilzai. Though his ancestral village was located between the towns of Said Karam and Gardez, capital of Pakhtya Province, Najibullah was born in Afghanistan's capital city, Kabul.

Najibullah's father, Akhtar Mohammad Khan, who died in 1983, served during the 1960s as the Afghani trade commissioner and consul in Peshawar, Pakistan, where he established friendly ties with prominent Pakistani Pushtun tribal leaders. These included Abdul Ghaffar Khan, who, with his son Wali Khan, consistently supported leftist Kabul regimes in opposition to official Pakistani policy. A frequent holiday visitor to Peshawar during his father's tenure, Najibullah maintained these contacts to good advantage.

After graduating from Kabul's Habibiya Lycee in 1964, Najibullah entered the Faculty of Medicine of Kabul University in 1965 and received a medical degree in 1975. His academic career was plagued by interruptions, including

two stays in prison (1969, 1970), because of his political activities during this period of liberal political experimentation in Afghanistan. Najibullah married a descendant of the royal line of King Amanullah (1919-1929). He and his wife, Fatanah, a headmistress, had three daughters.

The leftist Peoples Democratic Party of Afghanistan (PDPA) was launched on January 1, 1965. The same year, three PDPA candidates won seats in the Lower House of Parliament during the first elections held under the 1964 constitution. Among them was Babrak Karmal, who broke away in 1967 to form the Parcham faction in opposition to his Khalq rivals within the party. This continuing and widening split had more to do with conflicting personalities, family relationships, and urban-rural origins than ideology. Parcham, however, emphasized party unity and dialogue with national forces rather than the Marxist class struggle promoted by Khalq.

Najibullah, who joined the PDPA shortly after its creation, became a devoted follower and preeminent disciple of Babrak. He acted as a trusted bodyguard, writer for the newspaper *Parcham,* and principal organizer of the largely Parcham-inspired radical student demonstrations and strikes which beset Kabul during the late 1960s. Hard-working, self-assertive, and intensely involved, the imposingly tall and burly Najibullah acquired the pejorative nickname of Najib the Bull. Yet numbers of his classmates in exile today attribute their survival to the bonds of friendship established during these student days.

The disputes between Parcham and Khalq were bitter, but these were set aside ten years later when the two factions reunited in July 1977 to oppose the government of Mohammad Daud. The new ruler had accepted Parcham's participation in staging a coup on July 17, 1973, only to remove them from his administration over the following years. Najibullah was appointed an ordinary member of the PDPA Central Committee at the time of the 1977 reunion.

Rise to Power

Less than a year later, on April 27, 1978, the PDPA staged a successful coup of its own, and with their assumption of power Najibullah's ambitious climb to the pinnacle began. He was promoted to the Revolutionary Council (1978); became secretary of the Central Committee and director-general for the State Information Service, KHAD (1980-1985); Politburo member (1981); general-secretary of the PDPA (1985); and president (1986).

The path to the summit, however, was far from smooth, for deep rifts within the party resurfaced almost immediately after the coup. In July 1978 when most of the Parcham leadership was exiled as diplomats by Khalq, Najibullah was sent as ambassador to Iran. He held this post only until October when he was dismissed and subsequently expelled from the party for alleged complicity in an attempt to overthrow the Khalqis in Kabul. Remaining at large, reportedly in Eastern Europe and the U.S.S.R., he was brought back to Afghanistan in the wake of the December 1979 Soviet invasion when Babrak Karmal was elevated to prime minister and general-secretary of the PDPA.

The Soviet invasion was largely occasioned by the inability of the PDPA to put down the burgeoning armed resistance which threatened to collapse the Khalqi government. The identification of dissidents and the need to undermine and divide the resistance became key priorities and were undertaken by the Soviet KGB through its reorganization of the Afghan intelligence services into KHAD (Khedmati Etal'ati Daulati), the State Information Service. KHAD became the state's most effective and dreaded control institution, and as director-general Najibullah possessed great power, managing an enormous budget, up to 30,000 employees, 100,000 paid informers, and an army division complete with helicopters and tanks. KHAD was, as it was described by an Afghan, a state within the state.

Neither the harsh methods of KHAD nor the massive war efforts of the Soviet Union were able to diminish the success of the resistance, which was bolstered by foreign military assistance, including aid from the United States. Babrak's faction-rent government proving entirely ineffective, the Soviets selected Najibullah as his replacement on May 4, 1986. This led the pro-Babrak forces within Parcham to further splinter the leadership and Najibullah was unable to stabilize the situation despite efforts to legitimize and popularize his regime. He renewed calls for reconciliation and concessions regarding Islam, economic liberalism, and political pluralism, and constructed many ploys to turn resistance leaders and win over tribal groups, minorities, and religious leaders.

Hold on the Presidency Slips

Growing Soviet disillusionment with the Kabul leadership, added to numerous other factors including changes taking place in the former Soviet Union, ultimately led to the withdrawal of Soviet troops from Afghanistan in February 1989. It was generally predicted that Najibullah would quickly fall. However, enormous Soviet military and economic aid estimated at $300 million a month continued to flow into Afghanistan. Although Parcham-Khalq infighting still raged, Najibullah retained his position with his usual outward air of self-assured confidence. Far from popular, he adroitly maneuvered his political opponents inside and outside Afghanistan.

As support of Najibullah's regime became more of an economic burden and an embarrassment to a fast-changing Soviet leadership, the superpowers negotiated an agreement to cut off arms to both sides of the conflict in 1991, thus sealing the fate of Afghanistan's president. Najibullah's political skills proved no match for discontent in the capital as supplies of arms, food, and money dwindled. Though he attempted to negotiate with the leaders of the rebel *mujahedin,* his political opponents were in no mood to compromise with a figure who purportedly engineered the torture and execution of tens of thousands of their comrades, stamping to death many of them personally, according to reports of former political prisoners.

With guerrilla factions closing in on the capital, Najibullah relinquished his power in mid-April 1992 and attempted to flee to India. His plan was thwarted, however, by troops of a former supporter and he was forced to seek protection from U.N. officials in Kabul.

In Hiding

With Najibullah no longer in power, rebel factions turned on each other in a conflict which would continue another four years, destroying areas surrounding Kabul which had survived years of *mujahedin* attacks on Soviet-controlled regimes, and killing another 30,000 people.

The guerrilla leader whose ascendancy had led to his election as interim president, Burhanuddin Rabbani, fell to an invasion in 1996 of the Taliban, a fundamentalist Islamic extremist movement which had formed two years earlier among refugees in Pakistan and had gained control over three quarters of the country. The Taliban entered the U.N. compound where Najibullah had been hiding with his brother, former security chief Shahpur Ahmedzi, and aides. Kabul awoke on September 27, 1996 to find the brothers' battered bodies hanging from a tower in an intersection outside the presidential palace. Crowds gathered to jeer the remains of the "Butcher of Kabul." Najibullah's personal secretary and bodyguard were hanged the following day.

After Najibullah's bloody death, the Taliban consolidated their hold on Afghanistan, putting an end to the fighting between warring guerrilla factions following the Soviet withdrawal in 1989, but introducing their own brand of state-sponsored brutality.

Further Reading

For more information on the period and the man, see J. Bruce Amstuz's, *Afghanistan: The First Five Years of Soviet Occupation* (1986); Raja Anwar's, *The Tragedy of Afghanistan* (1988); Amin Saikal and William Maley's, (editors), *The Soviet Withdrawal from Afghanistan* (1989); and Artyom Borovik's, *The Hidden War* (1990).

Nijibullah's loss of power, resignation, and eventual death are chronicled in many articles in the *New York Times Magazine* (December 29, 1991; page 14); *Newsweek Magazine* (April 27, 1992; page 35); *The National Review* (May 11, 1992; page 16); *Time International Magazine* (October 7, 1996); and *Time Magazine* (April 27, 1992); as well as in stories distributed worldwide on the Internet by the Associated Press, dated September 27, 1996 and May 26, 1997. □

Yasuhiro Nakasone

Nakasone Yasuhiro (born 1918) was a Japanese politician who helped rebuild pride in the nation and in Japan's world role. He was active in the Liberal Democratic Party for over 30 years before becoming prime minister in 1982. He served an unprecedented five years, retiring in 1987.

During the American occupation of Japan after World War II, the young politician Nakasone Yasuhiro warned that American idealism had a dark side. Yes, the Americans wanted to create a new Japan,

a democratic Japan. But in return, they expected subservience, and subservience was not an attitude from which the Japanese could draw the strength necessary to rebuilding their nation. Many critics saw in Nakasone's warning an attempt to resurrect a power-oriented world, an attempt to reassert the pre-war values that had plunged Japan into war and brought defeat, values that had been discredited. In short, Nakasone made enemies, more enemies than friends. Yet it was Nakasone who became prime minister during the delicate period when Japan was re-asserting its ability to self-govern and the United States was re-thinking its involvement with Japan a reordering that continued into the late 1980s.

Early Entrance into Politics

Nakasone Yasuhiro was born on May 27, 1918, the second son of a lumber merchant in Takasaki, a city on the northwestern approach to Tokyo. He attended the prestigious Shizuoka High School, then went on to Tokyo University, where he studied political science in the law division. In 1941 he passed the higher civil service examination and became an official in the Ministry of the Interior. Later in the same year he joined the navy, from which he was discharged in 1945 as a lieutenant commander. In February 1945 he married Tsutako, the third daughter of Kobayashi Giichiro; in November, they had their first son, Hirofumi, who became a councillor in the Diet, the national assembly. In 1947 they had their first daughter, Michiko, and in 1949 they had their second daughter, Mieko.

After he was demobilized, Nakasone returned to the Interior Ministry. Under Japan's first constitution, the emperor assigned the right to rule to his appointed officials. In December 1946 Japan's new constitution proclaimed "that sovereign power resides with the people." In Nakasone's words, "This made me realize that I was wasting my time in Tokyo. . . . I resigned from the ministry and returned home. . . . I decided to run for a seat in the House of Representatives."

That opportunity came in April 1947. The election was hard-fought. "The communists came with their red flags held high. I went bearing the Japanese flag, even though the Occupation authorities had forbidden its display. In their eyes, that made me a rightist." He won. He was 28 years of age.

He joined the Japan Democratic Party, a conservative opposition party. In 1955 that party allied with the Japan Liberal Party to form the Liberal Democratic Party, which became the majority party with the power to choose the prime minister, who then could choose a cabinet. The LDP held this power to form a government through the mid-1980s. Political battles between the parties became less important than the political battles between the factions within the LDP, as the faction leaders contested the right to be prime minister. Nakasone joined the faction of Kono Ichiro, who died in 1965 after losing a battle with Sato Eisaku for the prime minister's seat. Several Kono lieutenants stepped forward to claim the Kono mantle: Nakasone was one of them. Three years were to pass before Nakasone prevailed and the Kono faction became the Nakasone faction.

In theory, Nakasone was now in position to vie for the prime minister's chair. But Nakasone had lost faction members during the succession struggle. He had no money to support the faction. Finally, he had not demonstrated the ability to rule. To correct these deficiencies, he allied himself with Sato Eisaku, still prime minister. To the charge that he was a political weathercock, he answered, "A weathercock stays set but moves his body. That's the essence of politics." Under Sato's aegis, Nakasone served as transportation minister, director general of the defense agency, chairman of the LDP executive council, and minister of international trade and industry (MITI). When Sato stepped down, Nakasone allied with Tanaka Eisaku, who then became the prime minister. This alliance brought him the MITI post again. Under the next prime minister, Nakasone became the secretary general of the LDP, a post which all prime ministers had held before they became prime ministers. Finally, in 1982, Nakasone became the prime minister.

A Prime Minister Becomes a World Leader

Japan had 44 prime ministers from the time when the post was created in the late 19th century until the mid-1980s. The average length of time in office has been a little over two years. Nakasone is one of only several prime ministers who have served more than five years. That fact alone distinguishes him.

What accounts for Nakasone's extended tenure? There are several reasons for his success, including favorable economic conditions during his tenure and his ability to pass his domestic program through the Diet. But, unlike his predecessors who had often assumed office with only 30 percent approval from the public because the prime minister is chosen by his peers rather than by popular vote Nakasone cultivated his popularity with the people. In the early 1960s Nakasone argued that the prime minister should be popularly elected. That reform did not get enacted, but Nakasone never considered a political move without preparing his public. Other politicians criticized Nakasone for playing to the grandstand, but their voices were stilled by the immense popularity of Nakasone's party and cabinet popularity so great that in the 1986 elections the party won more seats in the Diet than it had ever won before.

Nakasone's greatest contribution was in foreign affairs. The quickest to industrialize in spite of the fact that it began its technological development later than most industrialized nations, Japan had great troubles accommodating itself to the international order. Before World War II, it was perceived as being too aggressive; after World War II, this opinion was reversed and Japan was seen as being too passive. Other nations have looked at Japan's business activity and concluded that Japan is an economic animal, though these same nations have said they hope to emulate Japan in building a prosperous and stable nation.

Nakasone is seen as having changed these circumstances. He brought Japan into the colloquy of nations and was responsible for propagating a better understanding of Japan among the nations. Most of all, Nakasone instilled a national pride in the Japanese people in their new-found world identity.

In 1947, to help win his first election, Nakasone created the Purple Cloud Society (Seiun Juku) among the young men in his Gumma electoral district. In its charter are listed these three goals: to restore pride and independence to Japan; to foster Asian democracy; to change for the better the world and Japan's position in it. Those goals still form a sturdy tripod on which to base an understanding of Nakasone.

By the mid-1980s Japan had developed a strong balance of trade in its favor (money from its exports far exceeded the money spent on imports). This strained relations with the United States, which was suffering an unfavorable trade balance, in large measure because Japanese goods found a ready market in the United States while far fewer U.S. goods were sold in Japan. Nakasone, who had become a personal friend of President Ronald Reagan, worked hard to avoid a serious trade war between the two nations. (The media dubbed the two leader's friendly meetings "The Ron and Yasu show.")

Sales Tax Trouble

While Nakasone was known as a charismatic leader, even he couldn't avoid political trouble. In what he termed his "last and greatest reform," Nakasone called for a comprehensive reform of Japan's tax system in 1986. *Time* magazine called this "a supreme test of Nakasone's political will, skill and power,'' as Nakasone introduced a plan to drastically cut income tax. In addition, he proposed to add a ''value added'' or sales tax. This would pay for the income tax cut, and Nakasone hoped, it would also help correct the trade imbalance with the United States. (The sales tax would not apply to imported goods, making them more attractive.) It was this last provision that proved unpopular, especially since Nakasone had made a campaign promise not to introduce ''a large scale levy (tax).''

Party rules required that Nakasone step down from office in 1987. He became the only postwar prime minister to name his successor, Takeshita Noboru. Nakasone took his place in the Diet, but his political career was far from over.

Scandal

For the next several years, scandal rocked the Japanese political system, and Nakasone was caught up in the storm. In 1989 Nakasone fell under suspicion in what became known as the Recruit Cosmos Share Scandal. Prime Minister Takeshita Noboru resigned as a result. The scandal was very complicated, but basically amounted to accusations that the Liberal Democratic Party accepted shares and other kinds of bribes in exchange for political favors.

At first, Nakasone refused to testify under oath. He also refused to leave his position in the Diet. He later relented, and agreed to testify. He also agreed to vacate his leadership position of his faction, but not to leave the Diet. Nakasone was never charged officially with any crime, but he left the party and active politics as a result of the scandal.

Return to Plitics

In the early 1990s, Nakasone quietly returned to politics. He became head of the Takeshita faction, replacing Shin Kanemaru, who left in disgrace. Nakasone's political influence again grew stronger when he was named as one of the senior advisers to the LDP in 1991. Despite his alleged connection in the Recruit scandal, Nakasone will be remembered as a good leader for Japan. In 1987 *Time* Magazine said ''Nakasone put Japan on the world map and the rest of the world on Japan's map.''

Further Reading

There is not as yet a biography of Nakasone. An insightful description of Japanese politics can be found in Gerald L. Curtis', *The Japanese Way of Politics* (scheduled for 1998 publication). A broad description of the Japanese and their nation can be found in Edwin O. Reischauer's, *The Japanese* (1977). Nakasone is also profiled and interviewed in numerous periodicals. □

Albert Namatjira

Albert Namatjira (1902-1959) was the first Australian Aboriginal artist to receive national acclaim from the white community.

Albert Namatjira was born in 1902 in the Central Australian desert, which is one of the harshest environments in the world. His parents were Namatjira and Ljukuta of the Aranda people, and in accordance with their customs the child would normally remain unnamed until old enough to appreciate the significance of his given names and to be initiated into the group's complex social structure.

Australia had been invaded by Europeans little more than a century before Namatjira's birth, and the story of that occupation was similar throughout the country. The indigenous peoples, whose history spanned at least 40,000 years, were seen as a nuisance and were slaughtered in great numbers or else gathered and moved from their hunting grounds, where sheep and cattle soon replaced the native game. The bases of Aboriginal economic, social, and cultural life were almost destroyed, and, like many others, Namatjira and Ljukuta became part of a settled community—in their case at the Lutheran mission at Hermannsburg near Alice Springs. The young couple received religious instruction and were baptized on Christmas Eve 1905. Accepting Christian customs, they forsook their tribal names for ''Christian'' ones. Namatjira became Jonathan, Ljukuta became Emelia, and their son was baptized Albert. At the mission Aboriginal children were given only one name and ''Namatjira,'' his father's totemic name, meaning ''Flying White Ant,'' was dropped for many years.

Finding a Vocation

Though superficially Aboriginal people complied with the demands of the Europeans, traditional practices were continued more-or-less covertly, and at the age of 13 Albert disappeared, not be seen at the mission again for months. He was taken by the elders of his tribal group to distant ceremonial grounds, where he received instruction and was initiated into manhood. When he was 18 he disappeared again, but this time to elope with Ilkalita, an attractive, intelligent young woman forbidden to him on the grounds of their traditional kinship incompatability. They stayed away for three years until word reached them that they had been forgiven, and, with their three children, they were able to return to the mission, where Ilkalita was baptized and renamed Rubina and their children were named Enos, Oscar, and Maisie. Namatjira found work with an Afghan camel team as a shearer, stockman, carpenter, and handyman and as a carver of Aboriginal souvenirs.

In 1934 Namatjira saw an exhibition of water colors by visiting artists Rex Battarbee and John Gardner at the mission. The impact on him was immediate and lasting. He revealed later than it gave him a perception of his own country, for the first time, in terms of its visual beauty, color, light, and atmosphere. Previously he had understood the land in terms of its mythology and as a source of economic survival. He watched Battarbee at work and determined that he, too, would paint in that manner. The people of the Central Australian desert had been artists from time immemorial, and art had always been an integral part of their ceremonial life. Their songs and dances of the corroboree, storytelling, body ornamentation, rock carvings, and abstract ground patterns were as significant to the desert people as were the great religious works of medieval times to Europeans. Traditional desert art was symbolic, and much of it sacred and secret, its meaning revealed on a graduated scale only to initiated men. It could not be reproduced without causing anger or possibly even death.

Having a reverence for the art forms of his people's mythology, Namatjira had no intention of reproducing them for commercial purposes. Battarbee's method and subject matter promised an alternative artistic outlet, and, as the artist had offered to give him lessons, Namatjira planned an itinerary for Battarbee's next visit which would take them by camel to the most beautiful places in the region. In 1936 the two had an eight-week painting tour.

With his power of concentration, his keen perception, and his fine craftsmanship, Namatjira was an adept pupil, and, at an exhibition of his own work in the following year, Battarbee showed three of Namatjira's paintings, which were well-received. This led, in 1938, to Namatjira's first one-man-show at Melbourne's Fine Art Gallery. These paintings were the first to bear the signature "Albert Namatjira," and within three days all were sold. Most critics were loud in their praise, but this was not unanimous. Some suggested that Namatjira was only of curiosity value and that his paintings were mere imitations of his teacher. This mixed reception became the pattern for later shows. His second exhibition, however, was another sell-out, and this time the Adelaide Art Gallery bought one, making it the first state gallery to buy a watercolor by an Aboriginal artist. A great future was forecast for Namatjira.

Success as Painter Is Mixed Blessing

World War II brought security investigations for all German people and organizations in Australia, including the Hermannsburg Mission. Because of his World War I service and his long association with Hermannsburg, Rex Battarbee was appointed as its security officer. Namatjira's paintings were selling as quickly as he could produce them to Australian and American servicemen stationed in Central Australia. Battarbee formed the Aranda Art Group to promote other Aranda artists, and he was chairman of an advisory group formed to help manage Namatjira's affairs. It was decided that in order to keep his standards (and prices) high, Namatjira should restrict his production to about 50 paintings a year.

His exposition of 1944 made Namatjira a national figure; he became the first Aboriginal person ever included in "Who's Who in Australia," and the first book about him appeared. The 1945 exhibition was his first in Sydney. It was rushed, and within minutes of the opening the entire collection was purchased. Buyers included American servicemen and representatives from American, British, and New Zealand galleries.

Reproductions of his work became popular and appeared on Christmas cards and calendars. He toured the capital cities; his portrait was hung in the Art Gallery of New South Wales; he met the Queen of England and other royalty—he was feted. In 1957 he was granted citizenship. Until then, like other Aboriginal people at that time,

Namatjira had, in law, been a "ward of the state" denied the normal rights of a citizen.

The change in status gave him the legal right to drink alcohol but not to share it with other Aborigines. To an Aboriginal person this was unthinkable, as everything must be shared with kin. His camp became the scene of regular drunkenness and brawling, which climaxed in the death of a young woman. Namatjira was not involved in the brawl that resulted in the girl's death, but he was charged with supplying liquor to fellow Aborigines, which at that time was a criminal offense.

Namatjira was convicted and sentenced to six month's hard labor. An appeal, fought to the high court, reduced the sentence to three months, which Namatjira served, a bewildered and broken man. He gave up painting and died in 1959, within four months of his release.

A shocked nation fell into mourning, and an examination of the national conscience on its treatment of Aboriginal Australians followed. Institutionalized racism had kept most Aborigines from claiming a prominent place in the dominant society and had successfully cut down the first who had achieved it. Albert Namatjira is remembered as an artist of significance and as a person whose treatment highlighted the inequalities of Australian society, thus helping to pave the way towards citizenship rights for Aboriginal people.

Further Reading

C. P. Mountford's book *The Art of Albert Namatjira* (Melbourne, 1949) was one of the early books about this artist. It was based on a visit made by the author to Namatjira in his own country. After the artist's death a flood of articles and a number of books appeared. Notable among these were Joyce Batty's *Namatjira . . . Wanderer Between Two Worlds* (1963) and "Albert Namatjira, Feted and Forgotten," *Origin* (September 1969). Rex Battarbee kept a public silence on his former pupil for 12 years after Namatjira's death, but in an article in *Walkabout* in October 1971 entitled "Namatjira . . . The Man Behind the Myth" by Virginia Freeman, Battarbee revealed his perceptions. In the same year a book co-authored by Rex Battarbee and his wife Bernice, entitled *Modern Aboriginal Painters* (Sydney, Australia, 1971), was published. It dealt with the work of Albert Namatjira and the other artists of the Aranda Group. A more recent assessment of Namatjira's work was provided by P. McCaughey in an article entitled "Namatjira in His Own Landscape" which was published in *The Age*, a Melbourne newspaper, on July 11, 1984, after a retrospective exhibition of Namatjira's work opened the Araluen Arts Centre in Alice Springs.

Additional Sources

Albert Namatjira: the life and work of an Australian painter, South Melbourne: Macmillan, 1986. □

Sir Lewis Bernstein Namier

The English historian Sir Lewis Bernstein Namier (1888-1960) was a major force in introducing

stronger empirical methods and social analysis into the study of 18th-century politics.

Lewis Namier was born Ludvik Bernstein near Warsaw on June 22, 1888. He studied briefly at Lausanne and the London School of Economics before entering Balliol College, Oxford. The Oxford years, from 1908 to 1912, were crucial in his development. There he acquired a British self-identity, changing his name to Namier (derived from his family's older name, Niemirowski); there he also acquired a deep and permanent interest in British history of the 18th century.

Throughout his life Namier was strongly attracted to the world of power and policy making. At the start of World War I, he enlisted in the British army but was discharged in 1915 because of poor eyesight. As a civilian, he served in the Propaganda Department (1915-1917), the Department of Information (1917-1918), and the Political Intelligence Department of the Foreign Office (1918-1920). He attended the Versailles Peace Conference as a technical expert on eastern European affairs.

Namier started his serious work on the "imperial problem during the American Revolution" while a postgraduate student at Oxford in 1912 and continued these researches while in business in New York in 1913-1914. In 1920 he returned to academic life at Balliol College. Finding that this did not allow him sufficient time for research, he resigned to go into business during 1921-1923, hoping to save enough

to support his serious studies. Without any regular income, living on grants, loans, and savings, he devoted the years 1924 through 1929 entirely to research and writing. From these fruitful years came his two great works on 18th-century politics.

During the 1920s Namier became active in the Zionist movement and in 1929 accepted the position of political secretary of the Jewish Agency for Palestine. Finding that he lacked the personal political skills necessary for such a delicate job, he resigned after 2 years. From 1931 until his retirement in 1953, Namier was professor of modern history at Manchester University. He was knighted in 1952 and received many academic honors during the 1950s. Sir Lewis died in London Aug. 19, 1960.

Historical Work: 18th Century

Namier's scholarly reputation is based primarily on his two related works on 18th-century politics. In *The Structure of Politics at the Accession of George III* (1929), he attempted a static analysis of political society and the political process as it existed from 1754 until 1762, during the ascendancy of the Duke of Newcastle. In this great work he broke forever the remnants of the "Whig myth," deriving ultimately from Horace Walpole and Edmund Burke, which saw the politics of the first 2 decades of the reign of George III as adhering to the two-party model of the 19th century. He showed parliamentary politics to be based not upon coherent parties but, rather, on a congeries of familial-personal factions and interests, with a significant element supporting the government of the day regardless of its composition and another congenitally but unstably "independent." In most constituencies, family favor and personal dependency best explained voting patterns.

In *England in the Age of the American Revolution* (1930), Namier moved from static analysis to narrative history, in which he was less masterful. He intended to follow volume 1, which covered only 1760-1762, with other volumes but was deflected by teaching, other scholarly interests and international events.

In his work on 18th-century parliaments, Namier collected data on hundreds of members of Parliament. He realized that the work of all scholars doing such work would be immensely aided by the compilation of a biographical dictionary of all members of the House of Commons, with collective analysis where possible. As early as 1928 he helped publicize the project for such a history of Parliament, and after World War II, when the reorganized project obtained government support, Namier joined the new editorial board and devoted the years after his retirement in 1953 to editing the volumes on the period 1754-1790. His *History of Parliament* (3 vols., 1964) is a tool of inestimable value for students of pre-Victorian politics.

Historical Work: 19th and 20th Centuries

Namier was deeply interested in European history, particularly central and east-central Europe, in the years since 1815. Starting with a propaganda piece, *Germany and Eastern Europe* (1915), he published a number of short interpretive essays (many republished in *Vanished Supremacies,*

1962) rich in insight and fresh interpretation. On a somewhat larger scale was his *1848: Revolution of the Intellectuals* (1946), which measured the formal liberal ideology of the central European revolutionaries against their class and national prejudices.

After 1940 Namier became involved in the problem of the diplomatic origins of World War II. Using government publications, early memoirs, and interviews with exiled officials in London, he published a series of articles, starting in 1943, on the diplomatic origins of the war. These were republished in 1948 as *Diplomatic Prelude 1938-1939*. He continued to publish articles and review essays in this area, subsequently republished in *Europe in Decay* (1950) and *In the Nazi Era* (1952). These were important for the rigorous scrutiny he gave to the dubious evidence and arguments advanced by some self-or national apologists.

Though he did not produce a major work on the 19th century, Namier had considerable influence on A. J. P. Taylor and others working since 1945 on central European history. His work on the diplomatic origins of World War II has stood up well and is still the starting point for all students in the field. The influence of his 18th-century studies is likely to last, for it has given us a whole new way of approaching the historical study of political behavior.

Further Reading

For Namier's life see Julia Namier, *Lewis Namier: A Biography* (1971). His work is discussed by Catherine Sims in Herman Ausubel and others, eds., *Some Modern Historians of Britain* (1951), and Herbert Butterfield, *George III and the Historians* (1957; rev. ed. 1959).

Additional Sources

Colley, Linda, *Lewis Namier,* New York: St. Martin's Press, 1989.
Rose, Norman, *Lewis Namier and Zionism,* Oxford: Clarendon Press; New York: Oxford University Press, 1980. □

Nanak

Nanak (1469-1538) was an Indian religious reformer and founder of the Sikh religion. He combined elements of both the Moslem and the Hindu traditions in his teachings.

N anak was born into an upper-caste Hindu family near Lahore. His environment was richly immersed in Hindu and Moslem religious culture, especially their mystical and devotional forms. The religious life of the times was marked by a syncretic vitality which saw the emergence of a number of ecstatic devotional movements combining aspects of both religious traditions. He married and fathered several children and worked as a storekeeper and clerk for the Moslem governor of the province.

But Nanak's sensibilities moved him more and more to feel a deep, if at first ill-defined, religious calling. He finally

underwent a decisive religious experience in which—according to Sikh tradition—he had a vision of God's presence summoning him to a prophetic mission for the "one God whose 'Name is True' (*Sat Nam*), the Creator, devoid of fear and enmity, immortal, unborn, self-existent, great and bountiful."

The universal thrust of Nanak's mission was signified by his insistent affirmation that "there is no Hindu and no Moslem"—only those who are the disciples (Sikh means disciple) of the one God. He left his family and began a long period of wandering and preaching in the company of a Moslem minstrel who provided musical accompaniment for the evangelistic hymns in which Nanak's prophetic message was expounded. His teachings were unsystematic but imbued with a profoundly self-consistent devotionalism which combined Islamic monotheism with pervasive aspects of Hindu mysticism.

Nanak deliberately attired himself in a costume which represented the garb and symbols of both religious traditions, and he visited the major holy places, where he preached and sang, frequently in criticism of the archaic traditional rites. And he preached against caste and other traditional hierarchies: "What power has caste? It is the reality (of faith) that is tested. He who obeys God's order shall become a noble in his court." At first he was often rebuffed, treated with hostility, and occasionally imprisoned. His moods of despair are reflected in some of his sayings: "The Age is a knife. Kings are butchers. . . . Justice hath taken wings and fled. . . . In this dark night of falsehood the moon of Truth is never seen to rise."

But slowly Nanak acquired a wide following. By the time of his death the movement was securely instituted and was maintained by his designated successors—the gurus (teachers).

The little sect was at first rigorously pacifist. Nanak's sayings were collected in the principal Sikh holy book—the *Adi Granth* (Original Book), and the life of the community was centered on the famous place of worship at Amritsar. However, as the community grew in strength and economic power, it encountered increasing hostility from both Moslem and Hindu orthodoxy. Eventually, it assumed the role of an aggressive, often warlike, socio-political sect which, ironically, provided the British colonial armies with some of their best fighting men.

Further Reading

For material on Nanak see Ernst Trumpp, *The Adi Granth* (1877); Max A. Macauliffe, *The Sikh Religion: Its Gurus, Sacred Writings and Authors* (6 vols., 1909); Hari Ram Gupta, *A History of the Sikhs from Nadir Shah's Invasion to the Rise of Ranjit Singh, 1739-1799* (3 vols., 1944-1952); and John C. Archer, *The Sikhs in Relation to Hindus, Moslems, Christians, and Ahmadiyyas* (1946). □

Fridtjof Nansen

The Norwegian polar explorer, scientist, and statesman Fridtjof Nansen (1861-1930) was a pioneer of oceanography and achieved world stature as a vital force in the League of Nations.

Fridtjof Nansen was born on Oct. 10, 1861, on an estate near Christiania (Oslo), the son of Baldur Nansen, a lawyer, and Adelaide Wedel-Jarlsberg Nansen. In 1880 Nansen entered Christiania University. A promising student of zoology, he was encouraged to do research aboard an Arctic sealer, and in 1882 he sailed for Greenland waters, where his first interest in the Arctic was probably awakened. Returning to Norway, he became curator of the zoological collection at the Bergen Museum and continued his research there and in Italy. In 1888 Nansen received his doctorate in zoology from Christiania University.

Explorer and Scientist

As early as 1884 Nansen conceived the idea of crossing Greenland on skis from the rugged, uninhabited east coast to the west, but it was not until 1887 that he felt able to proceed with his plan. The Norwegian government refused funds for his expedition, but a wealthy Danish citizen agreed to finance him. Having built the necessary equipment in the spring, he left Norway with five companions in

May 1888. After great difficulty and delay in landing because of ice conditions, they began the trek across the ice cap on August 16. In early October the six men reached the village of Godthaab on the west coast. The last ship of the season had already sailed, forcing the expedition to winter at Godthaab, where Nansen used the time to study Eskimo life and survival skills. Back in Norway in May 1889, Nansen found himself a national hero and, although the public acclaimed the exploit itself, the expedition also made a solid contribution to the understanding of the Greenland interior. Perhaps more important, it confirmed Nansen's theories on Arctic exploration techniques.

After the Greenland success, Nansen had comparatively less difficulty attracting support for a long-standing and more ambitious project, an attempt to reach the North Pole. While elaborating his plans for a polar expedition, he married Eva Sars, wrote two books on Greenland, and lectured in several large European cities. In February 1890 he presented his plan publically for the first time to the Norwegian Geographical Society. He again outlined his plan in 1892 and, although many were skeptical, he found support in the government and in the Norwegian people, who subscribed nearly $125,000 to defray his expenses. Together with the naval architect Colin Archer, Nansen designed and built the *Fram* ("Forward"). The specially strengthened hull was constructed in such a way that the pressure exerted on the sides of the hull by the ice would force the ship upward, thus preventing it from being crushed. The *Fram* was launched in late 1892, and on June 24, 1893, Nansen and a crew of 12 departed.

Northeast of Cape Chelyuskin at 77° 43'N, 134°E, the *Fram* was made fast to an ice floe, and on Sept. 22, 1893, the 3-year voyage began. In the summer of 1894 Nansen's impatience and the fact that the *Fram's* drift seemed unlikely to take them as near to the pole as they had first calculated led to his decision to strike out for the pole on skis. Nansen left the ship with a single companion in the following spring. Ice conditions made the march impossibly difficult, and on April 8, having reached 86° 14'N, they were forced to turn back. The return trek across the ice covered nearly 700 miles; it was late August before the men reached the western islands of Franz Josef Land, where they decided to spend the winter of 1895-1896. In 1896 they encountered a British expedition, and by August they were back in Norway.

Nansen planned other explorations, particularly to the South Pole, but these were never brought to fruition. From this point on, his commitment to scientific research and writing, his involvement in the crisis of Norwegian independence, and, later, his engagement in the problems of World War I and its aftermath occupied all of his time.

International Statesman and Humanitarian

In 1917 Norway, dependent on American food supplies, was in danger of severe shortages, for when the United States entered World War I it had placed an embargo on the export of foodstuffs. Nansen was appointed head of a commission to negotiate with the United States for the release of supplies. In May 1918 he obtained an agreement which also served as a model for treaties with other neutral countries. When he returned from America, he became embroiled in domestic politics and was approached on several occasions to lead a coalition government of the bourgeois parties. In the mid-1920s he supported a new patriotic society to unite the Norwegian people in the face of postwar dangers. Paradoxically, though Nansen was committed to peace, he also led an organization to promote Norwegian military preparedness. The Defense League was necessary, he felt, because peace was threatened by the Great Powers' designs on the small nations, not by the arms of the small nations themselves.

Once the war was over, Nansen undertook his most significant work. In 1919 he presided over the Norwegian Union for the League of Nations; in 1920 he served as a delegate to the League itself. Then he was offered the post of director of prisoner-of-war repatriation. Reluctantly, he accepted, even though he realized that it meant sacrificing much of his scientific research. But he understood the work of repatriation as being vital, not only as a humanitarian duty but also as a means of strengthening the League of Nations and of reconciling former enemies. The League, to Nansen, was the best hope of ensuring the small nations security and of guaranteeing future peace. The relief and rehabilitation of refugees occupied Nansen's attention throughout the remainder of his life, and he served as League high commissioner for refugees from 1921 until his death. However, he was concerned not only with displaced persons but also with the effects of war on resident populations.

In December 1922 Nansen was awarded the Nobel Peace Prize. In acknowledging the honor, he stated: "The soul of the world is sick unto death, courage has failed, ideals have grown dim, the desire to live is destroyed. . . . To whom shall we turn for a remedy?" His answer was to turn to the people rather than the "political speculators," to the cooperation and goodwill of nations as a whole. He died at his home in Norway, Polhögda, on May 13, 1930.

Further Reading

Many of Nansen's books are available in English. A primary source is Hjalmar Johansen, *With Nansen to the North* (1899), an eyewitness account by Nansen's companion in the attempt to reach the pole on skis. Most of the recent books on Nansen are not in English. One of the best in English is Jon Sörensen, *The Saga of Fridtjof Nansen*, translated by J. B. C. Watkins (1932), which is perhaps uncritical of Nansen but is sensitively written and draws upon numerous sources not readily available. Of less value and more limited in scope is Edward Shackleton, *Nansen the Explorer* (1959). □

Dadabhai Naoroji

Dadabhai Naoroji (1825-1917) was an Indian political leader and one of the founders of the Indian National Congress. A leading nationalist author and spokesman, he was the first Indian to be elected to membership in the British Parliament.

Dadabhai Naoroji was born into a leading Parsi family in Bombay. After an outstanding career at Elphinstone College, Naoroji served briefly as professor of mathematics at Elphinstone. In 1855 Naoroji became a partner in an important Parsi commercial firm in London, and in 1862 he set up his own commercial house there. In the same year he founded the influential East Indian Association to educate the English public on Indian affairs.

In 1873 Naoroji accepted the difficult post of Divan, or chief minister, of the prominent Indian princely state of Baroda but left it fairly soon for an elected seat in the Bombay Municipal Corporation. It was here that his public service career truly began. After several busy years in the public life of the province, Naoroji published his famous indictment of British exploitation of India, *Poverty and Un-British Rule in India*. This book guaranteed his position in the very front rank of the Indian nationalist movement.

In 1885 Lord Reay, the governor of Bombay, appointed him to the Legislative Council, and in the same year Naoroji played a leading role in the creation of the Indian National Congress, the major organization promoting Indian nationalism. A year later he was elected president of the Indian National Congress at its second session. During the same year he was one of a very few prominent Indians chosen to testify before the Royal Commission on the Public Services in India.

In 1892 Naoroji was elected to the British Parliament on the Liberal ticket from Central Finsbury. He was the first Indian to win a seat in the House of Commons. A year later he was, for the second time, elected to the presidency of the Indian National Congress. In 1895 Naoroji lost his seat in Parliament, but in 1896 he was appointed to the influential Royal Commission on Indian Expenditures, to whose labors he made a significant contribution. The report of the commission was important in shaping Indian fiscal practices. In 1906 Naoroji's public service was given special mark when he was elected to a third term as president of the National Congress. Naoroji's probity, care in the use of evidence, painstaking research in Indian economic conditions, and persistent advocacy of the Indian cause were the hallmarks of his active and impressive career.

Further Reading

A convenient one-volume edition of Naoroji's writings and speeches is *Essays, Speeches, Addresses and Writings,* edited by C. L. Parekh (1887). The best study in English of Naoroji is Rustom P. Masani, *Dadabhai Naoroji* (1939). See also Vidya Dhor Mahajan, *The Nationalist Movement in India and Its Leaders* (1962).

Additional Sources

Rawal, Munni, *Dadabhai Naoroji, a prophet of Indian nationalism, 1855-1900,* New Delhi: Anmol Publications, 1989. □

John Napier

The Scottish mathematician John Napier (1550-1617) discovered logarithms and effectively introduced the modern notation of decimal fractions.

J ohn Napier, or Neper, the son of Sir Archibald Napier, was born at Merchiston Castle near Edinburgh. At the age of 13 he entered the University of St. Andrews. He might also have studied at universities in the Low Countries, France, and Italy. What is known with certainty is that by 1571 Napier was back home and the next year married Elizabeth Stirling. His life at the newly built castle at Gartnes left him with ample time for such varied interests as mathematics, agriculture, and religious politics.

A Calvinist resolved to keep Catholicism out of Scotland at any price, Napier rallied against the conspiracy known as the Spanish Blanks with a book, *A Plaine Discovery of the Whole Revelation of St. John* (1594). To make the resistance more effective, he devised four new weapons: two kinds of burning mirrors, a piece of artillery, and a battle vehicle covered with metal plates having small holes for emission of offensive firepower and moved and directed by men inside.

Since the danger of the Catholic, or rather, Spanish, take-over soon evaporated, Napier resumed his other avocations. In agriculture he advocated the use of manure and common salt for the improvement of the soil. In mathematics his efforts were not only epoch-making but also met with immediate and universal approval. His method of calculating with logarithms was published in *Mirifici logarithmorum canonis descriptio* (1614). During the next 16 years more than 20 accounts, excerpts, and translations of its contents were printed, a clear evidence of the extent to which the new invention reduced the labors of trigonometrical calculations present in navigational and astronomical work. Napier's *Mirifici logarithmorum canonis constructio* (1620), on the art of computing logarithms, was published posthumously.

Napier sent a copy of his 1614 work to Henry Briggs, professor at Gresham College. While Briggs was explaining it to his students, the idea occurred to him that Napier's logarithms could be made easier to handle if the logarithm of 1 was set at 0. Briggs's proposal met with Napier's full approval, but Napier left it to Briggs to prepare a new logarithmic table based on that proposition; it is known as the table of common logarithms and was first published in 1624.

For over 2 decades Napier worked on a problem the solution of which was of crucial importance for physical science. The device, known as Napier's bones or rods, evidences the creativity of his mind in practical mathematics. With that device one could perform multiplication and division by mechanical means, and thus it was a distant forerunner of slide rules and analog computers. Its details were disclosed in a two-volume work, *Rabdologiae; seu Numerationes per Virgulas libri duo* (1617), published the year he died.

Further Reading

The most important modern source of information on Napier's life, writings, and activities is the work edited by Cargill G. Knott, *Napier Tercentenary Memorial Volume* (1915). E. W. Hobson, *John Napier* (1914), is a biography of his life and achievements. For broad background see Charles Singer, *A Short History of Science to the Nineteenth Century* (1941). □

Napoleon I

Napoleon I (1769-1821), emperor of the French, ranks as one of the greatest military conquerors in history. Through his conquests he remade the map of Europe, and through his valuable administrative and legal reforms he promoted the growth of liberalism.

N apoleon Bonaparte was born Napoleon Buonaparte (the spelling change was made after 1796) on Aug. 15, 1769, in the Corsican city of Ajaccio. He was the fourth of 11 children of Carlo Buonaparte and Letizia Romolino. His father derived from the lesser Corsican nobility. Following the annexation of Corsica by France in 1769, Carlo was granted the same rights and privileges as the French nobility. After an elementary education at a boys' school in Ajaccio, young Napoleon was sent in January 1779 with his older brother Joseph to the College of Autun in the duchy of Burgundy. In May of the same year he was transferred to the more fashionable College of Brienne, another military school, while his brother remained at Autun. Here Napoleon's small stature earned him the nickname of the "Little Corporal."

At Brienne, Napoleon received an excellent military and academic education, and in October 1784 he earned an appointment to the École Militaire of Paris. The royal military school of Paris was the finest in Europe in the years before the Revolution, and Napoleon entered the service of Louis XVI in 1785 with a formal education that had prepared him for his future role in French history. Napoleon joined an artillery unit at Valence, where he again received superior training.

First Military Assignments

Now a second lieutenant, Napoleon continued his education on his own, but he was distracted by Corsica. Until 1793 his thoughts, desires, and ambitions centered on the island of his birth. Following the death of his father, he received an extended leave (1786) to return to Corsica to settle his family's affairs. After rejoining his regiment at Auxonne, he again spent more than a year on his native island (1789-1790), during which time he was influential in introducing the changes brought about by the Revolution. Returning to France, Napoleon was transferred to Valence in June 1791. But by October he had returned to Corsica, where he remained for 7 months. He spent the critical summer of 1792 in Paris and then returned to Corsica for

one last episode in October. On this visit he took part in the power struggle between the forces supporting Pasquale Paoli and those supported by the French Republic. After Paoli was victorious, Napoleon and the Bonaparte family were forced to flee to the mainland, and the young officer then turned his attention to a career in the French army.

The Revolution of 1789 did not have a major effect upon Bonaparte in its early years. He did not sympathize with the royalists. Nor did he take an active part in French politics, as his thoughts were still taken up with affairs in Corsica. Napoleon was in Paris when the monarchy was overthrown in August 1792, but no evidence indicates that he was a republican. Upon his return from Corsica in the spring of 1793, Capt. Bonaparte was given a command with the republican army that was attempting to regain control of southern France from the proroyalist forces. He took part in the siege of Avignon, and then while on his way to join the French Army of Italy Napoleon was offered command of the artillery besieging the port of Toulon.

National Acclaim

The siege of Toulon provided Napoleon with his first opportunity to display his ability as an artillery officer and brought him national recognition. France had gone to war with Prussia and Austria in 1792. England, having joined the struggle in 1793, had gained control of Toulon. After his distinguished part in dislodging the British, Napoleon was promoted to the rank of brigadier general. He also made the acquaintance of Augustin Robespierre, the younger brother of the powerful Maximilien, and though Napoleon was not politically a Jacobin, he derived benefits from his association with influential party members. The overthrow of the Jacobin regime on 9 Thermidor (July 1794) led to Napoleon's imprisonment in Fort Carré on August 9. When no evidence could be found linking him to the British, Napoleon was released after 10 days of confinement.

Throughout the winter of 1794-1795 Napoleon was employed in the defense of the Mediterranean coast. Then, in April 1795, he was ordered to Paris, and in June he was assigned to the Army of the West. He refused this position, pleading poor health. This refusal almost brought an end to his military career, and he was assigned to the Bureau of Topography of the Committee of Public Safety. While serving in this capacity, he sought unsuccessfully to have himself transferred to Constantinople. Thus Napoleon was in Paris when the royalists attempted to overthrow the Directory on Oct. 5, 1795.

Gen. Paul Barras had been placed in command of the defense of Paris by the government, and he called upon Gen. Bonaparte to defend the Tuileries. Napoleon put down the uprising of 13 Vendémiaire by unhesitatingly turning his artillery on the attackers, dispersing the mob with what he called "a whiff of grapeshot." In gratitude he was appointed commander of the Army of the Interior and instructed to disarm Paris.

Marriage and Italian Campaign

In the winter of 1795 Napoleon met Josephine de Beauharnais, the former Mademoiselle Tascher de La

Pagerie. Born on the island of Martinique, she had been married to Alexandre de Beauharnais at the age of 16 and had borne him two children, Eugène and Hortense, before separating from him. Alexandre, a nobleman from Orléans, was executed in the last days of the Terror in 1794, leaving Josephine free to marry Napoleon. Their civil ceremony took place on March 9, 1796. Within a few days Napoleon left his bride behind in Paris and took up his new command at the head of the Army of Italy.

On March 26 Napoleon reached his headquarters at Nice, and on March 31 he issued the first orders for the invasion of Italy. The campaign opened on April 12, and within several weeks he had forced Piedmont out of the war. In May, Napoleon marched across northern Italy, reaching Verona on June 3. The campaign was then bogged down by the Austrian defense of Mantua, which lasted 18 months. During this period Napoleon beat back Austrian attempts to relieve the fortified city at Castiglione, Arcole, and Rivoli. Finally, in the spring of 1797, Napoleon advanced on Vienna and forced the Austrians to sign the Treaty of Campoformio (Oct. 17, 1797). The treaty gave France the territory west of the Rhine and control of Italy.

After spending the summer and fall at the palace of Monbello, where he established with Josephine what in reality was the court of Italy, Napoleon returned to Paris the hero of the hour. He was the man who could make war and peace. Napoleon was given command of the Army of England after drawing up a plan to invade that island. However, after a brief visit to the English Channel he abandoned any hope of crossing that turbulent body of water with the available French fleet. Returning to Paris, he gave up his command.

Egyptian Campaign

Napoleon did not wish to remain idle in Paris; nor did the government wish to see a popular general in the capital without a command to occupy him. Thus, when an expedition to Egypt was proposed, probably by Charles Maurice de Talleyrand, both the general and his government gave it their support. Strategically, the expedition would extend French influence into the Mediterranean and threaten British control in India. Napoleon sailed from Toulon on May 19, 1798, with an army of 35,000 men. On June 11-12 he captured Malta, and on June 30 the task force reached Alexandria, Egypt. The city was taken, and Napoleon's army marched up the west branch of the Nile to Cairo. In sight of the city and of the Pyramids, the first major battle took place. With minimal losses the French drove the Mamluks back into the desert in the Battle of the Pyramids, and all of lower Egypt came under Napoleon's control.

Napoleon reorganized the government, the postal service, and the system for collecting taxes; introduced the first printing presses; created a health department; built new hospitals for the poor in Cairo; and founded the Institut d'Egypte. During the French occupation the Rosetta Stone was discovered, and the Nile was explored as far south as Aswan. But the military aspect of Napoleon's Egyptian venture was not so rewarding. On Aug. 1, 1798, Horatio Nelson destroyed the French fleet in Aboukir Bay, leaving the

French army cut off from France. Then Napoleon's Syrian campaign ended in the unsuccessful siege of Acre (April 1799) and a return to the Nile. After throwing a Turkish army back into the sea at Aboukir (July 1799), Napoleon left the army under the command of Gen. Jean Baptiste Kléber and returned to France with a handful of officers.

The Consulate

Landing at Fréjus on Oct. 9, 1799, Napoleon went directly to Paris, where the political situation was ripe for a coup d'etat. France had become weary of the Directory, and in collaboration with Emmanuel Joseph Sieyès, Joseph Fouché, and Talleyrand, Napoleon overthrew the government on 18 Brumaire (Nov. 9-10, 1799). The Constitution of the Year VIII provided for the Consulate. Napoleon was named first consul and given virtually dictatorial powers. The trappings of the republic remained—there were two legislative bodies, the Tribunate and the Corps Legislatif—but real power rested in the hands of the first consul.

Napoleon began at once to solve the problems that faced France at the turn of the century. With mailed fist and velvet glove he ended the civil war in the Vendée. He then personally led an army over the Grand-Saint-Bernard Pass into Italy and defeated the Austrians, who had declared war on France while Napoleon was in Egypt, at the Battle of Marengo (June 14, 1800). This victory, which Napoleon always considered one of his greatest, again brought Italy under French control. After a truce that lasted into December, French armies forced Austria out of the war for the second time. The Treaty of Lunéville (Feb. 9, 1801) reconfirmed the Treaty of Campoformio. It was followed on March 25, 1802, by the Treaty of Amiens, which ended, or at least interrupted, the war with England. The Concordat that Napoleon signed with Pope Pius VII in 1801 restored harmony between Rome and Paris, and it ended the internal religious split that had originated in the Revolution. Napoleon also reformed France's legal system with the Code Napoleon.

The Empire

By 1802 Napoleon was the most popular dictator France had ever known, and he was given the position of first consul for life with the right to name his successor. The establishment of the Empire on May 18, 1804, thus changed little except the name of the government. The Constitution of the Year VIII was altered only to provide for an imperial government; its spirit was not changed. The Emperor of the French created a new nobility, set up a court, and changed the titles of government officials; but the average Frenchman noticed little difference.

The Treaty of Amiens proved to be no more than a truce, and in May 1803 the war with England was renewed. The Emperor planned to invade the island kingdom in the summer of 1805, but his naval operations went amiss. In September, Napoleon turned his back on the Channel and marched against Austria, who together with Russia had formed the Third Coalition. At Ulm (October 14) and Austerlitz (December 2) Napoleon inflicted disastrous defeats upon the Allies, forcing Alexander I of Russia to retreat behind the Neman and compelling Austria to make peace. At the Battle of Austerlitz, Napoleon reached the height of his military career. The Treaty of Pressburg (Dec. 27, 1805) deprived Austria of additional lands and further humiliated the once mighty Hapsburg state.

Victory throughout the Continent

The year 1806 was marked by war with Prussia over increased French influence in Germany. The overconfident Prussian army sang as it marched to total destruction at the battles of Jena and Auerstädt (Oct. 14, 1806), and Napoleon entered Berlin in triumph. Prussia was reduced to a second-rate power, and the fighting moved eastward into Poland as the Russians belatedly came to the aid of their defeated ally. Although at the Battle of Eylau (Feb. 8, 1807) the French were brought to a standstill, on June 14 at Friedland the Emperor drove the Russian army from the field. Alexander I made peace at Tilsit on June 25, 1807. This understanding between the two emperors divided Europe. Alexander was to have a free hand in the east to take Finland and Bessarabia, while Napoleon was free to reshape western and central Europe as he pleased. The most significant result was the creation of the grand duchy of Warsaw (1807). Sweden was defeated in 1808 with Russia's help. Napoleon was now master of the Continent. Only England remained in the field.

Problems with England and Spain

On Oct. 21, 1805, Adm. Horatio Nelson had destroyed the combined Franco-Spanish fleet off Cape Trafalgar, Spain. This loss made it virtually impossible for Napoleon to invade England. He, therefore, introduced the Continental system, or blockade, designed to exclude all British goods from Europe. In this manner he hoped to ruin the British economy and to force the "nation of shopkeepers" to make peace on French terms. His plan did not work, and it led Napoleon into conflicts with Spain, the papacy, and Russia, and it undoubtedly formed a major cause for the downfall of the Empire.

In Spain in 1808 French interference led to the removal of the Bourbon dynasty and to the placement of Joseph Bonaparte as king. But the Spanish people refused to accept this Napoleonic dictate and, with aid from Great Britain, kept 250,000 French troops occupied in the Peninsular War (1808-1814). The refusal of Pope Pius VII to cooperate with Napoleon and the blockade led to the Pope's imprisonment and a French take-over of the Papal States. In the case of Russia refusal proved even more serious. Alexander's refusal to close Russian ports to British ships led to Napoleon's Russian campaign of 1812, which was highlighted by the Battle of Borodino (September 7) and the occupation of Moscow (September 14-October 19). However, the ultimate result of this Russian campaign was the destruction of the Grand Army of 500,000 troops.

Fall from Glory

The Napoleonic system now began to break up rapidly. At its height three of the Emperor's brothers and his brother-in-law sat on European thrones. Napoleon had also secured an annulment of his marriage to Josephine and then married Marie Louise, the daughter of Emperor Francis II of Austria, in March 1810. Despite this union, Napoleon's father-in-law declared war on him in 1813. Napoleon's defeat at the Battle of the Nations at Leipzig (Oct. 16-18, 1813) forced him behind the Rhine, where he waged a brilliant, but futile, campaign during the first 3 months of 1814. Paris fell to the Allies on March 31, 1814, and the hopelessness of the military situation led the Emperor to abdicate at Fontainebleau (April 4, 1814) in favor of his son Napoleon II. However, the Allies refused to recogize the 3-year-old boy, and Louis XVIII was placed on the French throne.

Napoleon was exiled to the island of Elba, where he was sovereign ruler for 10 months. But as the alliance of the Great Powers broke down during the Congress of Vienna and the French people became dissatisfied with the restored royalists, Napoleon made plans to return to power. Sailing from Elba on Feb. 26, 1815, with 1,050 soldiers, Napoleon landed in southern France and marched unopposed to Paris, where he reinstated himself on March 21. Louis XVIII fled, and thus began Napoleon's new reign: the Hundred Days. The French did not wish to renew their struggle against Europe. Nevertheless, as the Allies closed ranks, Napoleon was forced to renew the war if he was to remain on the throne of France.

The Waterloo campaign (June 12-18) was short and decisive. After a victory over the Prussian army at Ligny, Napoleon was defeated by the combined British and Prussian armies under the Duke of Wellington and Gebhard von Blücher at Waterloo on June 18, 1815. He returned to Paris and abdicated for a second time, on June 22. Napoleon at first hoped to reach America; however, he surrendered to the commander of the British blockade at Rochefort on July 3, hoping to obtain asylum in England. Instead, he was sent into exile on the island of St. Helena. There he spent his remaining years, quarreling with the British governor, Sir Hudson Lowe, and dictating his memoirs. He died on St. Helena, after long suffering from cancer, on May 5, 1821.

Further Reading

The best one-volume work on Napoleon in English is James M. Thompson's slightly pro-British account, *Napoleon Bonaparte* (1952). Also excellent are Felix Markham, *Napoleon* (1964), and André Castelot, *Napoleon* (1971). The two-volume work of Georges Lefebvre, *Napoleon* (1936; trans. 1969), is a masterful account of the period 1799-1815; primarily a political history, it includes all aspects of the Napoleonic era.

A number of books deal with Napoleon's period of exile: Gilbert Martineau, *Napoleon's St. Helena* (1966; trans. 1969), which includes illustrations and a good bibliography; Michael John Thornton, *Napoleon after Waterloo: England and the St. Helena Decision* (1968), detailing the weeks in July and August 1815 during which Napoleon waited his fate on a British warship; and an account based on the diary of the secretary to the governor of St. Helena, Gideon Gorrequer, *St. Helena, during Napoleon's Exile: Gorrequer's Diary*, edited by James Kemble (1969). One of the best of the many biographies of Josephine is André Castelot, *Josephine*, translated by D. Folliot (1967), which provides many insights into Napoleon as husband and lover.

Three fine works on Napoleonic military history are Vincent J. Esposito and John R. Elting, *A Military History and Atlas of the Napoleonic Wars* (1964); David G. Chandler, *The Campaigns of Napoleon* (1966); and Sir James Marshall-Cornwall, *Napoleon as Military Commander* (1967). A useful account for the general reader of Napoleon's invasion of Russia is in Leonard Cooper, *Many Roads to Moscow; Three Historic Invasions* (1968). Claude Manceron, *Napoleon Recaptures Paris,* translated by George Unwin (1969), is a lively account of Napoleon's take-over of Paris in March 1815. □

Napoleon III

Napoleon III (1808-1873) was emperor of France from 1852 to 1870. Elected president of the Second French Republic in 1848, he staged a coup d'etat in 1851 and reestablished the Empire.

Between 1848 and 1870 France underwent rapid economic growth as a result of the industrial revolution, and Napoleon III's government fostered this development. These years were also the period of the Crimean War and the unifications of Italy and Germany, and France played a pivotal role in these affairs.

Napoleon was born in Paris on April 20, 1808, the youngest son of Louis Bonaparte, the king of Holland and brother of Napoleon, I, and of Hortense de Beauharnais, daughter of Josephine. His full name was Charles Louis Napoleon Bonaparte, but he was generally known as Louis Napoleon. After 1815 Louis Napoleon lived with his mother in exile in Augsburg, Bavaria, where he attended the Augsburg gymnasium, and at Arenburg Castle in Switzerland. In 1831 he and his brother joined rebels against papal rule in Romagna.

The Pretender

The death of his brother during this rebellion, followed by the death of Napoleon I's son, made Louis Napoleon the Bonaparte pretender. He took this position seriously, beginning his career as propagandist and pamphleteer in 1832 with *Rêveries politiques*. He also joined the Swiss militia, becoming an artillery captain in 1834 and publishing an artillery manual in 1836. Louis Napoleon attempted a military coup d'etat at Strasbourg on Oct. 30, 1836, but the ludicrous venture failed. Louis Philippe deported him to America, but Louis Napoleon returned to Arenburg to attend his mother, who died in October 1837.

France threatened invasion when the Swiss government refused to expel him, but Louis Napoleon withdrew voluntarily to England. There he produced his most famous pamphlet, *Des Idées napoléoniennes* (Napoleonic Ideas), effectively stating his political program, which combined the ideas of liberty and authority, social reform and order, and glory and peace. Louis Napoleon attempted a second coup d'etat on Aug. 6, 1840, at Boulogne-sur-Mer, but failed again. He was tried by the Chamber of Peers, condemned to perpetual imprisonment, and interned in the

fortress of Ham (Somme). There he studied, and he wrote, among other things, *L'Extinction du paupérisme,* which increased his reputation as a social reformer. In 1846 he escaped to England.

Second Republic

Louis Napoleon hastened to Paris when he received news of the Revolution of 1848, but he withdrew on request of the provisional government. He declined to be a candidate in the April elections and resigned his seat when elected in four constituencies in June. In September 1848 he was again chosen by five districts and took his seat in the Assembly.

Louis Napoleon was of middle height with a long torso and short legs. He had gray eyes, pale immobile features, a prominent nose, and a thick auburn mustache. He was not a particularly impressive figure. Nonetheless, the appeal of the Bonaparte name, strengthened by the spread of the Napoleonic legend, and a general demand for order following the workers' uprising of June 1848 won him overwhelming election as president of the Second French Republic on Dec. 10, 1848.

Louis Napoleon used a French expeditionary force to restore, and then to protect, papal supremacy in Rome, thus winning Roman Catholic support at home. In 1850 the legislature established residence requirements that disenfranchised nearly 3 million workers. The next year it rejected a constitutional amendment permitting re-election to the presidency. Louis Napoleon used these actions to justify his overthrow of the republic by a coup d'etat on Dec. 2, 1851. His action was endorsed by nearly 7,500,000 votes, with fewer than 650,000 negative votes. A year later more than 7,800,000 Frenchmen approved reestablishment of the Empire, which was inaugurated on Dec. 2, 1852.

Domestic Policies of the Emperor

Napoleon III governed by the principle of direct, or Caesarean, democracy, through which power was transferred directly from the people to an absolute ruler who was responsible to them and whose acts were confirmed by plebiscite. Although he established a senate and a legislative assembly chosen by universal suffrage, they had little power. Elections were carefully manipulated, and political activities and the press were closely controlled. The Emperor's ideal was to serve as representative of the whole nation, and hence he never organized a true Bonapartist party. In 1853 he married the Spanish beauty Eugénie de Montijo, and in 1856 she bore him an heir, thus providing for the succession.

In economic affairs Napoleon III considered himself a socialist, and he believed that government should control and increase national wealth. His ideals resembled those of the Saint-Simonians, emphasizing communications, public works, and credit. The imperial government built canals, promoted railroad development, and fostered the extension of banking and credit institutions. The Emperor inaugurated great public works programs in Paris and in leading provincial cities, sponsored trade expositions, and in 1860 introduced free trade, which was unpopular with industrial leaders but ultimately strengthened French industry.

Foreign Policy

In policy statements Napoleon III consistently asserted that the Empire stood for peace, but in practice Bonapartism demanded glory. Napoleon III believed in national self-determination, and he wished to assume leadership in redrawing European frontiers in accordance with his "principle of nationalities." Thus he hoped to restore France to the position of arbiter of Europe that it had enjoyed under Napoleon I. In practice, Napoleon III vacillated between his principles and promotion of France's self-interest, and he involved France in three European wars and several colonial expeditions.

The first European conflict, the Crimean War (1854-1856), brought little material gain, but Napoleon III defended France's protectorate of the holy places and joined the British to avenge Russia's defeat of Napoleon I. In the Congress of Paris, Napoleon III came close to his ideal of serving as arbiter of Europe. Among other things, he championed Romanian nationalism, gaining autonomy for Moldavia and Walachia and later aiding those provinces to achieve unification.

Napoleon III's second war was fought in 1859 for the Italian nationalist cause. Shortly after Felice Orsini's attempt to assassinate him in 1858, Napoleon III planned the liberation of Italy with Camillo di Cavour at Plombières. He envisaged the creation of a federation of four states under the presidency of the pope. Although French battles against Austria were successful, Napoleon III was unable to control the Italian nationalist movement, was threatened on the Rhine by Prussia, and lost support from proclerical elements in France, who saw Italian unification as a threat to the papacy. Napoleon III therefore made peace at Villafranca di Verona without freeing Venetia, thus disappointing the Italians and alienating French liberals. Although he had not fully honored his commitment, Napoleon III later received Nice and Savoy, and this brought an end to the British alliance that had been a cornerstone of his early diplomacy.

In 1862 Napoleon III became involved in an attempt to establish a friendly, pro-Catholic regime in Mexico under the Austrian prince Maximilian. Mexican resistance proved stronger than expected; the United States concluded its Civil War and exerted pressure; and Napoleon III withdrew his forces in 1866-1867. This fiasco provoked powerful criticism in France, which was intensified by the subsequent execution of Maximilian in Mexico. Meanwhile, the Emperor had also failed in his attempt to gain compensation for France in the Austro-Prussian War of 1866.

Liberal Empire

Growing opposition after 1859 encouraged Napoleon III to make concessions to liberalism. In 1860-1861 he gave the legislature additional freedom and authority, and in 1868 he granted freedom of press and assembly. The elections of 1869, fought with virulence, brought more than 3 million votes for opposition deputies. The results induced Napoleon III to appoint the former Republican Émile Ollivier to form a responsible ministry. After further turbulence following a Bonaparte scandal, the Emperor resorted to plebiscite, and on May 8, 1870, more than 7,300,000 Frenchmen voted to accept all liberal reforms introduced by Napoleon III since 1860.

Franco-Prussian War

In 1870, when the Spanish invited Leopold of Hohenzollern-Sigmaringen to become their king, French protests induced Prussia's William I to have the candidacy withdrawn. The ambassador to Prussia was then instructed to demand a Prussian promise that no Hohenzollern would ever become king of Spain. William's refusal to consider this enabled Otto von Bismarck to provoke war by publishing William's dispatch from Ems in slightly altered form, making it appear that insults had been exchanged. France declared war on July 19, 1870, and Napoleon III took command of his troops although he was so ill from bladder stones, which had long troubled him, that he could scarcely ride his horse. The Emperor's troops were surrounded at Sedan, and Napoleon III surrendered with 80,000 men on Sept. 2, 1870. Two days later the Third Republic was proclaimed in Paris.

When the Germans released him in 1871, Napoleon III joined his wife and son at Chislehurst in England. He still hoped to regain the throne for his son, but he died on Jan. 9, 1873, following a series of bladder operations. His son was killed in South Africa in 1879 while serving in the British army.

Further Reading

The best studies of Napoleon III's youth and early career are the two works of Frederick A. Simpson: *The Rise of Louis Napoleon* (1909; new ed. 1925) and *Louis Napoleon and the Recovery of France* (1923; 3d ed. 1951), but Simpson does not continue beyond 1856. An up-to-date one-volume biography that presents a balanced interpretation is James M. Thompson, *Louis Napoleon and the Second Empire* (1958). Albert Léon Guérard, *Napoleon III* (1943), is a more generous attempt to rehabilitate the Emperor and portrays him as an idealist and a Saint-Simon on horseback. T. A. B. Corley, *Democratic Despot: A Life of Napoleon III* (1961), also gives a generally favorable interpretation of Napoleon III, and it contains an excellent bibliography.

Important studies of specific aspects of Napoleon III's policies include Lynn M. Case, *French Opinion on War and Diplomacy during the Second Empire* (1954); David H. Pinkney, *Napoleon III and the Rebuilding of Paris* (1958); Theodore Zeldin, *The Political System of Napoleon III* (1958); Howard C. Payne, *The Police State of Louis Napoleon Bonaparte, 1851-1860* (1966); and E. Ann Pottinger, *Napoleon III and the German Crisis, 1865-1866* (1966). □

Jayaprakash Narayan

Jayaprakash Narayan (1902-1979), Indian nationalist and social reform leader, was India's leading indigenous critic after Mohandas Gandhi.

A disciple of Mohandas Gandhi and leader of India's independence movement, Jayaprakash Narayan remained a rebel in his native land until the end of his life. Born of middle-caste Hindu parents in a small village in Bihar on Oct. 11, 1902, he became politically active in high school. Just before his graduation, he followed the call of Indian nationalists to quit British-assisted institutions. In 1922, he went to the United States, where he studied political science and economics at the universities of California, Iowa, Wisconsin and Ohio State.

Socialist and Resistance Leader

During his seven years in the United States, Narayan paid his tuition by working as a fruit picker, jam packer, waiter, mechanic and salesman. His nationalist and anti-imperialist convictions developed into Marxist beliefs and participation in Communist activities. But Narayan was opposed to policies of the Soviet Union and rejected organized communism upon returning to India in 1929.

Narayan became secretary of the Congress party, whose leader was Jawaharlal Nehru, later to become the first independent Indian prime minister. When all other party leaders were arrested, Narayan carried on the campaign against the British; then he, too, was arrested. In 1934, Narayan led other Marxists in the formation of a Socialist group in the Congress party.

During World War II, Narayan became a national hero by leading violent opposition to the British. Embracing the resistance movement led by Mohandas Gandhi, Narayan repudiated its commitment to nonviolence, engineering strikes, train wrecks and riots. He was repeatedly jailed by the British, and his escapes and heroic activities captured the public's imagination.

Advocate of "Saintly Politics"

After India gained independence, violence and Marxism waned in Narayan. He led his socialist group out of the Congress party in 1948 and later merged it with a Gandhian-oriented party to form the People's Socialist party. Narayan was considered Nehru's heir apparent, but in 1954 he renounced party politics to follow the teachings of Vinoba Bhave, an ascetic who called for voluntary redistribution of land. He embraced a Gandhian type of revolutionary action in which he sought to change the minds and hearts of people. An advocate of "saintly politics," he urged Nehru and other leaders to resign and live with the impoverished masses.

Narayan never held a formal position in the government, but remained a leading political personality operating outside party politics. Late in his life, he regained prominence as an active critic of the increasingly authoritarian policies of Prime Minister Indira Gandhi, Mohandas Gandhi's daughter. His reform movement called for "partyless democracy," decentralization of power, village autonomy and a more representative legislature.

Toppled Indira Gandhi's Government

Despite ill health, Narayan led student agitators in Bihar in a fight against government corruption, and under his leadership, a People's Front took power in western Gujarat state. Indira Gandhi responded by branding Narayan a reactionary fascist. In 1975, when Gandhi was convicted of corrupt practices, Narayan called for her resignation and a massive movement of pacifist noncooperation with the government. Gandhi declared a national emergency, jailed Narayan and 600 other opposition leaders and imposed censorship of the press. In prison, Narayan's health collapsed. After five months, he was released. In 1977, thanks largely to Narayan's uniting of opposition forces, Gandhi was defeated in an election.

Narayan died at his home in Patna on Oct. 8, 1979, from the effects of diabetes and a heart ailment. Fifty thousand mourners gathered outside his home, and thousands followed as his casket was carried through the streets. Calling Narayan "the conscience of the nation," Prime Minister Charan Singh declared seven days of mourning. Narayan was remembered as the last of Mohandas Gandhi's colleagues in the independence movement.

Further Reading

The most useful book on Narayan is *Socialism, Sarvodaya, and Democracy: Selected Works of Jayaprakash Narayan,* edited by Bimla Prasad (1964). Two different assessments of Narayan are in Margaret W. Fisher and Joan V. Bondurant's, *Indian Approaches to a Socialist Society* (1956), and Welles Hangen''s, *After Nehru, Who?* (1963). Narayan is profiled in the *Biographical Dictionary of Modern Peace Leaders* (1985).

☐

R. K. Narayan

R. K. Narayan (born 1906) is one of the best-known of the Indo-English writers. He created the imaginary town of Malgudi, where realistic characters in a typically Indian setting lived amid unpredictable events.

Rasipuram Krishnaswami Narayanswami, who preferred the shortened name R.K. Narayan, was born in Madras, India, on Oct. 10, 1906. His father, an educator, travelled frequently, and his mother was frail, so Narayan was raised in Madras by his grandmother and an uncle. His grandmother inspired in young Narayan a passion for language and for people. He attended the Christian Mission School, where, he said, he learned to love the Hindu gods simply because the Christian chaplain ridiculed them. Narayan graduated from Maharaja's College in Mysore in 1930. In 1934 he was married, but his wife, Rajam, died of typhoid in 1939. He had one daughter, Hema. He never remarried.

Creating a Small-Town World

Narayan wrote his first novel, *Swami and Friends,* in 1935, after short, uninspiring stints as a teacher, an editorial assistant, and a newspaperman. In it, he invented the small south Indian city of Malgudi, a literary microcosm that critics later compared to William Faulkner's Yoknapatawpha County. More than a dozen novels and many short stories that followed were set in Malgudi.

Narayan's second novel, *Bachelor of Arts* (1939), marked the beginning of his reputation in England, where the novelist Graham Greene was largely responsible for getting it published. Greene has called Narayan "the novelist I most admire in the English language." His fourth novel, *The English Teacher,* published in 1945, was partly autobiographical, concerning a teacher's struggle to cope with the death of his wife. In 1953, Michigan State University published it under the title *Grateful to Life and Death,* along with his novel *The Financial Expert;* they were Narayan's first books published in the United States.

Subsequent publications of his novels, especially *Mr. Sampath, Waiting for the Mahatma, The Guide, The Man-eater of Malgudi,* and *The Vendor of Sweets,* established Narayan's reputation in the West. Many critics consider *The Guide* (1958) to be Narayan's masterpiece. Told in a complex series of flashbacks, it concerns a tourist guide who seduces the wife of a client, prospers, and ends up in jail. The novel won India's highest literary honor, and it was adapted for the off-Broadway stage in 1968.

At least two of Narayan's novels, *Mr. Sampath* (1949) and *The Guide* (1958), were adapted for the movies. Narayan usually wrote for an hour or two a day, composing fast, often writing as many as 2,000 words and seldom correcting or rewriting.

Making the Mundane Extraordinary

Narayan's stories begin with realistic settings and everyday happenings in the lives of a cross-section of Indian society, with characters of all classes. Gradually fate or chance, oversight or blunder, transforms mundane events to preposterous happenings. Unexpected disasters befall the hero as easily as unforeseen good fortune. The characters accept their fates with an equanimity that suggests the faith that things will somehow turn out happily, whatever their own motivations or actions. Progress, in the form of Western-imported goods and attitudes, combined with bureaucratic institutions, meets in Malgudi with long-held conventions, beliefs, and ways of doing things. The modern world can never win a clear-cut victory because Malgudi accepts only what it wants, according to its own private logic.

Reviewing Narayan's 1976 novel *The Painter of Signs,* Anthony Thwaite of the *New York Times* said Narayan created "a world as richly human and volatile as that of Dickens." His next novel, *A Tiger for Malgudi* (1983), is narrated by a tiger whose holy master is trying to lead him to enlightenment. It and his fourteenth novel *Talkative Man* (1987) received mixed reviews.

In his 80s, Narayan continued to have books published. He returned to his original inspiration, his grandmother, with the 1994 book *Grandmother's Tale and Other Stories,* which *Publishers Weekly* called "an exemplary collection from one of India's most distinguished men of letters." Donna Seaman of *Booklist* hailed the collection of short stories that spanned over 50 years of Narayan's writing as "an excellent sampling of his short fiction, generally considered his best work" from "one of the world's finest storytellers." Narayan once noted: "Novels may bore me, but never people."

Further Reading

Harish Raizada's, *R. K. Narayan: A Critical Study of His Works* (New Delhi, 1969), provides a detailed description and evaluation of his work. Discussions of his work are in K. R. Srinivasa Lyengar, *Indian Writing in English* (1962); David McCutchin's, *Indian Writing in English: Critical Essays* (1969); and Marion Wynne-Davies', (editor), *Bloomsbury Guide to English Literature* (1990). □

Antonio Nariño

Antonio Nariño (1765-1823) was a Colombian patriot and champion of human rights in Latin America. Colombia named one of its provinces in his honor.

Born in Bogotá on April 9, 1765, of a well-to-do family, Antonio Nariño was educated at a renowned school where he studied philosophy and law. During these years Bogotá, then capital of the viceroyalty of New Granada, was strongly influenced by European culture, especially in the fields of natural science, literature, and political thought. Nariño, an avid reader, gathered around him a group of congenial friends who shared his ideas. He occupied several positions of public trust and engaged in the exportation of cacao, tobacco, and quinine, a lucrative trade which furnished him a comfortable living.

The outbreak of the French Revolution set Nariño's mind on fire. He translated the Declaration of the Rights of Man and had the document printed in his own house (1794). He might as well have handled dynamite. He was accused of sedition, convicted by the highest court of the land, and sentenced to 10 years of imprisonment in Africa, permanent exile, and the confiscation of his property (1795).

Nariño escaped his captors in Cadiz and fled to Paris, where he began to study the new laws of Revolutionary France. Converted to a belief in centralized government, he went to England in the hope that he might interest the British in the liberation of his native country. He was unsuccessful and finally made his way back to Bogotá. He was permitted to reside in the country and to administer his personal holdings.

The outbreak of the Latin American revolution led once more to Nariño's arrest (1809-1810). He was held in the notorious prison of Cartagena and treated as a common criminal. Freed during the progress of the revolution, he stepped into the forefront of the fight that was shaking New Granada to its foundations. At least three "sovereign states" had emerged, and one of them chose Nariño as its president.

Civil war soon erupted between the various factions, the strife centering on the question of federalism versus centralism, a characteristic problem of South America. Nariño, a staunch centralist, failed in his attempt to subjugate the rebellious southern provinces by force. He met with the opposition of the federalists and also the resistance of the royalists, who had remained faithful to Spain. In 1814 he was again a prisoner in Cadiz, held in solitary confinement for 4 years.

Nariño's incarceration may have been a blessing in disguise. In Bogotá he would probably have been shot by the Spaniards when they reconquered the city in 1816. The revolt against Ferdinand VII in 1820 afforded Nariño his freedom, and in 1821 he returned home. This was the year of Simón Bolívar's attempt to create a republic of the Andes, to be called Colombia. It was also the year when a constituent assembly met in Cúcuta to draft a constitution for the new state. Nariño joined the deputies and was elected interim vice president but soon renounced his office for reasons of health. His enemies were determined that he not be elected senator from his native province of Cundinamarca and accused him of malfeasance of public funds, cowardice, and even treason. He made a brilliant defense, but the accumulation of ingratitude proved the deathblow to an already weakened constitution. He died in Leiva on Dec. 13, 1823.

Like so many others of his generation, Nariño was a twilight figure, standing between sunshine and shadow. And like many another, he was made to suffer what Bolivar called the "thanklessness of things American."

Further Reading

A study of Nariño in English is Thomas Blossom, *Nariño: Hero of Colombian Independence* (1967). Nariño is discussed in E. Taylor Parks, *Colombia and the United States, 1765-1934* (1935), and Salvador de Madariaga, *Fall of the Spanish Empire* (1948). □

Pánfilo de Narváez

The Spanish soldier and explorer Pánfilo de Narváez (1478?-1528) participated in the conquests of Jamaica and Cuba and led an ill-fated expedition to colonize Florida.

Pánfilo de Narváez was born in Valladolid. Seeking his fortune as a soldier, he migrated to the island of Hispaniola (modern Dominican Republic and Haiti). In 1509 he accompanied Juan de Esquirel in the conquest of Jamaica. Two years later, as a commander of 30 crossbowmen, he joined Diego de Velázquez in the conquest of Cuba.

The tall, red-bearded Narváez, with a resonant voice "as if it came from a cave," emerged from the conquest with a reputation of being "brave against Indians." But as a commander of expeditions, he was both blundering and unlucky. His misfortunes began when Governor Velázquez appointed him in 1520 to lead an expedition to Mexico, where he was to arrest Hernán Cortés and replace him as commander in the conquest of Mexico. Cortés outwitted Narváez, won over most of his men, and defeated the few who resisted. Narváez, who lost an eye during the skirmish, was imprisoned by Cortés for 2 years.

Narváez returned to Spain, where he secured a royal grant to conquer and settle Florida. When the company reached Hispaniola in 1527, nearly a fourth of the men deserted. With his reduced forces he landed in the vicinity of Tampa Bay on Good Friday in April 1528. The Indians told him of a land to the north, called Appalachen, which was teeming with gold.

Narváez's decision to separate his forces from the sustaining ships sealed the doom of the expedition. After a year of futile effort to make contact with the land forces, the ships sailed to Mexico. Meanwhile, the land forces, consisting of 300 men, struck out into the interior and northward until they reached Appalachen, near the present site of Tallahassee. "Golden" Appalachen turned out to be a town of clay huts, and Narváez decided to return to Cuba. Upon reaching the coast, they built their own vessels. Iron from their stirrups and crossbows was fashioned into nails; pitch pine

was used for caulking; shirts became sails; and the frames of the boats were covered with horsehide.

On Sept. 22, 1528, the 240 survivors embarked in five overloaded and unseaworthy boats. As they passed the mouth of the Mississippi River, a storm and strong currents separated the boats. By November 6 only the boat commanded by Narváez remained afloat. While the boat was anchored along the Texas coast at night, a strong north wind swept Narváez and two others, who had remained aboard, out to sea. They were never heard from again.

Of the original company, only four survived. Led by Álvar Núñez Cabeza de Vaca, they began their epic 8-year journey across the southwestern United States, southward into Mexico, reaching Mexico City in 1536.

Further Reading

The most detailed and reliable account of Narváez's career is in Woodbury Lowery, *The Spanish Settlements within the Present Limits of the United States, 1513-1561* (1901). Other useful works which refer to his career are William H. Prescott's classic *History of the Conquest of Mexico* (1873; rev. ed. 1879); Bernal Diaz del Castillo, *The True Story of the Conquest of New Spain* (trans. 1916); Herbert E. Bolton, *The Spanish Borderlands: A Chronicle of Old Florida and the Southwest* (1921); and Cleve Hallenbeck, *Alvar Núñez Cabeza de Vaca: The Journey and Route of the First European to Cross the Continent of North America* (1940). □

John Nash

John Nash (1752-1835), English architect and town planner, was one of the principal architects of the Regency period.

John Nash was born in London in September 1752. He began his career in the office of Sir Robert Taylor. In 1777 Nash established his own practice, but he went bankrupt in 1783 and moved to Wales, where he built country houses, cottages, and various minor public works. By 1791 he had achieved considerable success.

In 1796 Nash returned to London and entered into a partnership with the landscape gardener Humphrey Repton (dissolved in 1802). In 1798 Nash designed a conservatory at Brighton for the Prince of Wales (later King George IV), and he became an intimate member of the prince's circle. During the next 15 years Nash designed a number of remarkable country houses in the form of picturesque pseudomedieval castles, such as East Cowes Castle, Isle of Wright, for himself (1798); Luscombe, South Devon (1800-1804); West Grinstead and Knepp Castles, Sussex (ca. 1806); Ravensworth, County Durham, and Caerhayes, Cornwall (ca. 1808); and Cronkhill, Shropshire (ca. 1802), the first neo-Italian villa in England, from which sprang the Italianate revival of the late Regency and early Victorian eras. He also built the picturesque cottages and dairy at Blaise Hamlet near Bristol (1805-1811) and the most important of all *cottages ornées,* the Royal Lodge at Windsor (1812).

Nash became architect to the Department of Woods and Forests in 1806 and prepared plans for developing Marylebone Park. His scheme provided for the laying out of Regent's Park with villas and surrounding terraces of grand houses and for the creation of a processional thoroughfare (Regent Street) from Marylebone to the seat of government in Whitehall. This gigantic program, known as the Metropolitan Improvements, was a masterpiece of early town planning and transformed London's West End. In these works Nash expressed his genius for grand spectacular effects, but he was much criticized for the carelessness and incorrectness of his classical details.

In 1813 Nash was appointed one of the three "attached architects" to the Board of Works. Tow years later he began the transformation of the Royal Pavilion at Brighton, then a simple classical villa, into an Oriental dream palace with an Indian exterior and a richly fantastic chinoiserie interior, which became the most magnificent expression of Chinese taste in Europe. For the building of Buckingham Palace (1825-1830), when his creative powers were failing, Nash incurred severe official criticism. After the death of George VI in 1830, he was dismissed from the Board of Works and retired to East Cowes Castle, where he died on May 13, 1835.

Further Reading

The pioneer biography of Nash is John N. Summerson, *John Nash: Architect to King George IV* (1935). Complementary to Summerson's work is Terence Davis, *The Architecture of John Nash* (1960), which consists of a comprehensive collection of over 200 photographs and engravings of Nash's works, descriptive notes on each illustration, and a long historical introduction by Summerson. This book was followed by Davis's admirable *John Nash: The Prince Regent's Architect* (1966), which embodies a great deal of new material and provides a reassessment of Nash's place in British architecture. Nash is discussed in two other works by Summerson: *Georgian London* (1945; rev. ed. 1970) and *Architecture in Britain, 1530-1830* (1954; 4th rev. ed. 1963).

Additional Sources

Summerson, John Newenham, Sir, *The life and work of John Nash, architect,* Cambridge, Mass.: MIT Press, 1980. □

James Nasmyth

James Nasmyth (1808–1890) was an inventor and contributed greatly to the inventions of power tools, most notably the steam hammer.

James Nasmyth invented the steam hammer, one of the integral contributions to the industrial revolution in Europe. Nasmyth was born in Edinburgh, Scotland, on August 19, 1808, the son of an artist. He left school at age twelve to make model engines and other mechanical devices. At nineteen he built a full-size steam carriage which performed with acclaim. When he was twenty-one, Nasmyth accompanied his father on a trip to London, England, where he met machinist and engineer Henry Maudslay. During the next two years, Nasmyth studied and worked under Maudslay, learning from him as well as making valuable contributions, such as designing hexagonal-headed nuts and a flexible shaft of coiled spring steel for drilling holes in awkward places. In 1834, Nasmyth opened his own shop in Manchester, England, later moving to a foundry at Patricraft, England, where he became known for his craftsmanship and steam-powered tools. It was also here, in 1839, that he invented the steam hammer, a device that allowed large materials to be forged with great accuracy. The concept of the steam hammer was simple, even though the idea was totally new. A hammering block was hoisted by steam power to a vertical position above a piece of metal. Once the hammer reached an appropriate height, steam in the piston was released and the block fell. The pistons could be regulated not only in strength of blow, but also in frequency of strokes. At the time, Nasmyth decided to postpone patenting, building, and marketing the new steam hammer. Two-and-a-half years later, however, while visiting a fellow machinist in France, Nasmyth was shown a steam hammer that had been built from his own rough sketches. Nasmyth quickly returned to England, patented his work, and manufactured hammers for an eager market. Soon he was making hammers with four-and five-ton blocks, and by 1843 he had improved on them by injecting steam above the piston to add force to the downward blow.

The steam hammer allowed larger forgings with heavier metals, tightened bonds, and made metals stronger and more dense. Not surprisingly, Nasmyth soon revived a previous interest and became involved in manufacturing steam locomotives for various railway companies. In fourteen years, he built 109 high-pressure steam engines, pumps, and hydraulic presses. His steam hammer was exhibited at the Great Exhibition of 1851 alongside his prize-winning maps of the moon. Nasmyth retired in 1856 and dedicated his last thirty years to astronomy, a life-long interest and hobby. He built a number of telescopes and charted sunspots as well as the surface of the moon. Besides his steam hammer, a direct predecessor of the pile driver, Nasmyth also devised a vertical cylinder-boring machine and milling machines. He died a financially successful inventor, unlike many of his peers, on May 7, 1890. □

Gamal Abdel Nasser

Gamal Abdel Nasser (1918-1970) was an Egyptian political leader and hero of much of the Arab world. His devotion to Arab unity and a strongly anti-imperialist ideology came to be called "Nasserism."

The family of Gamal Abdel Nasser were well-to-do Moslem peasants who lived in Beni Morr near Asyût (Upper Egypt). His father was a post-office employee. Gamal was born on Jan. 15, 1918, in Alexandria. As early as his grammar school years, he participated in demonstrations against the English occupation of Egypt. In 1937 he entered the military academy at Cairo; he left the following year with the rank of second lieutenant.

In 1943, after several years of service in Upper Egypt and the Sudan, he became an instructor at the military academy and then at the army staff college. During 1948-1949 he took part in the unsuccessful campaign against the new state of Israel. In this conflict he commanded a position from the "pocket of Faludja," south-west of Jerusalem, where three Egyptian battalions were surrounded for more than 2 months by Israeli forces. Nasser resisted gallantly with his troops until the cease-fire was declared. This was the only comparatively successful Arab exploit of the war.

Overthrow of King Farouk

For many years Nasser had been in contact with some of the army officers who were indignant over the corruption in the royal Egyptian government. These young radicals were strongly nationalistic, but they could not agree on an ideology or on an alliance with other forces. However, under the impact of the defeat by Israel in Palestine, the secret "movement of free officers" was organized (1949), with Nasser as one of the principal founders. This group overthrew King Farouk on July 23, 1952.

Behind the new government, nominally headed by Gen. Mohamed Neguib, Nasser was chairman of the Revolution Command Council (which held the actual power), headed the new "Liberation Rally," and then was deputy premier and minister of the interior. Meanwhile, Neguib had begun to alienate most of the officers by his involvement in efforts to reestablish parliamentary rule. Early in 1954 Nasser displaced Neguib, taking the title of prime minister in April (and in 1956 he was elected first president of the Egyptian republic).

The regime was at first pro-Western and respected the free-enterprise system. It obtained an agreement for the English to surrender control of the Suez Canal in July 1954. However, the Nasser government reacted strongly to the West's attempting to organize Egypt into an anti-Soviet bloc and yet refusing to support Egypt against Israel (Israeli troops raided into Gaza in February 1955). Then, in the face of the West's refusal to supply arms unless Egypt entered into a coalition under the direction of Turkey and Iraq (Baghdad Pact, February-April 1955), Nasser moved toward neutralism.

Nasser became friends with Prime Minister Jawaharlal Nehru of India and President Tito of Yugoslavia, participated in the "Third World" Conference at Bandoeng in Java (April 1955), and purchased arms from Czechoslovakia. America's unwillingness to finance the High Dam of Aswan, a project essential for the development of Egypt, led Nasser to nationalize the Suez Canal in July 1956. A combined Anglo-Franco-Israeli expedition (October-November 1956) tried to reestablish control over the canal, but it failed, thanks largely to American and Soviet pressures to withdraw.

United Arab Republic

Nasser then began to strengthen his neutralist position. Under request from the Syrian Baath party, which was fearful of a Communist seizure, he presided over the incorporation of Egypt and Syria into the United Arab Republic (Feb. 1, 1958). But on Sept. 28, 1961, Syria seceded from the union. Nasser, convinced that this was a reactionary move, instituted several socialistic measures in Egypt, free enterprise being deemed unable to promote a self-directed development.

The accomplishments of the Nasser regime (agrarian reform, mobilization of the people, industrialization, vast social measures) were carried out despite both internal and external opposition. The leftist elements were integrated into the regime; the rightists were put under control. Abroad, support was obtained from the Soviet bloc of nations without breaking all ties with the West. The crisis of the third war with Israel, in June 1967, reaffirmed Nasser's popular support and led to a certain amount of internal liberalization.

Nasser was a pragmatic politician, faithful above all to Egyptian patriotism. He disliked violence and extreme revolutionary activities. Although he was attracted for a time by the dream of political hegemony over the Arab world, his desires were nevertheless tempered by the needs and circumstances of the moment. His primary goal was always the development of Egypt into a modern nation with no sacrifice of complete independence. He died on Sept. 28, 1970.

Further Reading

Nasser's political views are presented in his own work, *The Philosophy of the Revolution* (1959). Joachim Joesten, *Nasser: The Rise to Power* (1960), contains useful details but has many errors and is incomplete. A fine book is Robert Stephens, *Nasser: A Political Biography* (1971). Miles Copland, *The Game of Nations* (1969), is very useful.

Solid studies of Nasser's Egypt are available. They include Jean and Simonne Lacouture, *Egypt in Transition* (1956; trans. 1958), an excellent account of the early phases of the revolution; Tom Little, *Modern Egypt* (1967; originally published as *Egypt* in 1958); and P. J. Vatikiotis, *The Modern History of Egypt* (1969), with a useful bibliography. Anouar Abdel-Malek, *Egypt, Military Society: The Army Regime, the Left and Social Change under Nasser* (1962; trans. 1968), is a notable sociohistorical analysis. Peter Mansfield, *Nasser's Egypt* (1966), is a readable general survey. For background on foreign affairs, particularly Arab affairs, see Malcolm H. Kerr, *The Arab Cold War, 1958-1964: A Study of Ideology in Politics* (1965), and Maxime Rodinson, *Israel and the Arabs* (1967; trans. 1968). For further background see P. J. Vatikiotis, ed., *Egypt since the Revolution* (1968), and the chapter in Jean Lacouture, *The Demigods: Charismatic Leadership in the Third World* (1969; trans. 1970). □

Thomas Nast

The American caricaturist and painter Thomas Nast (1840-1902) is noted for his political cartoons attacking corruption in New York City government and supporting Radical Reconstruction in the South.

Thomas Nast was born on Sept. 27, 1840, in Ludwig, Bavaria. The family emigrated to the United States in 1846, and Thomas was raised and schooled in New York City. He displayed an early talent for drawing. At the age of 15 he took some drawings to *Leslie's Weekly,* one of the popular magazines of the day, and was hired as an illustrator. In 1862 he joined *Harper's Weekly.* Throughout the Civil War he turned out patriotic drawings exhorting Northern readers to help crush the Rebels. Abraham Lincoln called him "our best recruiting sergeant."

By the end of the war Nast and *Harper's Weekly* had become virtually inseparable, and Nast turned his hand toward attacking President Andrew Johnson's attempts to subvert the Radical Republican Reconstruction program. He hammered away at those who tried to undermine Negro political rights in the South with the same zeal and venom he had used earlier on Rebels.

In attacking Johnson's policies, Nast began to depart from conventional representational illustration by distorting and exaggerating the physical traits of his subjects. Because of the technical skill and the self-righteous fervor he brought to the task, it was often said that the art of political caricature

reached a new peak of sophistication and importance in his work.

The heights were probably reached in Nast's unrelenting attack against political corruption in New York City in the early 1870s. Nast's caricatures of William "Boss" Tweed and his henchmen in Tammany Hall (the New York County Democratic political machine) played a major role in defeating the machine and imprisoning Tweed. Nast demonstrated his own incorruptibility by refusing to accept a $200,000 bribe to stop his attacks.

During the political crusades Nast also made what have become his most famous, if not his most important, contributions to American politics: he invented and popularized the Democratic donkey, the Republican elephant, and the Tammany tiger. Nast reached his peak of fame, influence, and wealth in the 1870s. Thereafter he began a long, frustrating decline. Technical changes in magazine reproduction led to the obsolescence of the wood-carved plates at which he excelled. In addition, his continued attempts to reopen the wounds of the Civil War made many people uneasy. Tweed's death in 1878 deprived Nast of another favorite target. Nast tried his hand at attacking various other groups who aroused his ire, such as labor unionists (whom he portrayed as vicious, foreign, bomb-throwing anarchists) and the Catholic Church, but the public failed to respond with the same enthusiasm. His contract with *Harper's Weekly* terminated in 1884, and his work appeared with decreasing frequency.

In 1902 Nast was rescued from an impecunious end by an admirer, President Theodore Roosevelt, who arranged for his appointment as U.S. consul in Guayaquil, Ecuador. Nast did not really want to go to Guayaquil. However, he was in no position to turn down a steady source of income. He died there of yellow fever on Dec. 7, 1902.

Further Reading

The standard work on Nast is Albert Bigelow Paine, *Th. Nast: His Period and His Pictures* (1904). Although uncritical and dated in its historical interpretations, Paine's work contains a wealth of information on Nast and examples of much of his work. Morton Keller, *The Art and Politics of Thomas Nast* (1968), is very good and more balanced in interpretation. The short text in John Chalmers Vinson, *Thomas Nast: Political Cartoonist* (1967), tends toward the same laudatory tone as Paine but contains 120 pages of large reproductions of Nast's work.

Additional Sources

Paine, Albert Bigelow, *Thomas Nast, his period and his pictures*, New York: Chelsea House, 1980. □

George Jean Nathan

George Jean Nathan (1882-1958) was the leading American drama critic of his time. Active from 1905 to 1958, he zealously practiced what he called "destructive" theater criticism. Nathan wrote during the most important period of U.S. theater's history and set critical standards that are still being followed.

George Jean Nathan was born in Fort Wayne, Indiana, on February 14, 1882. He grew up in Cleveland, Ohio, where he graduated from that city's high school. On his mother's side, the German Nirdlingers, there were rugged pioneers who literally crossed the country in a covered wagon from Chambersburg, Pennsylvania, to settle Fort Wayne. Nathan's maternal grandfather was one of the founders of this frontier trading post.

Two of Nathan's maternal uncles were to influence his career as a drama critic. Charles Frederic Nirdlinger was a playwright and drama critic who encouraged Nathan's entrance into journalism. Uncle Samuel Nixon-Nirdlinger was an important theater manager who secured free tickets for Nathan's family; loyalty to this uncle also may have engendered Nathan's rather benevolent attitude toward the Theatrical Syndicate. (The Syndicate was a nearly omnipotent group of theater managers who controlled the American theater in the late 19th and early 20th centuries.) Nathan's mother, Ella Nirdlinger Nathan, was a devout Catholic who attended the same convent school, St. Mary's in South Bend, Indiana, as playwright Eugene O'Neill's mother. The two became lifelong friends, as would their sons.

On his father's side Nathan was French; his father, Charles Naret Nathan, was the son of a Parisian attorney. He

was one of the owners of the Eugene Peret vineyards in France and of a coffee plantation in Brazil. Nathan's father spoke eight languages fluently and took frequent business trips to Europe. All through Nathan's childhood the family spent alternate summers in Europe. Young George was thus brought up in an aristocratic and cosmopolitan atmosphere.

Nathan attended Cornell University where he was a champion fencer. He also edited the *Sun,* the college newspaper, and the *Widow,* Cornell's humor magazine. After being graduated in 1904, Nathan took a cub reporter's job at the *New York Herald.* Two years later Nathan managed to secure a third-string reviewer's post, and with his review of *Bedford's Hope* (January 29, 1906) the most important career in 20th-century American dramatic criticism was launched.

Nathan's personal life proceeded into a routine. He settled into a bachelor's apartment at New York's Royalton Hotel. He remained there for 45 years, the rooms gradually filling with books and manuscripts. Romantically linked with numerous actresses throughout his career (including a long relationship with Lillian Gish), Nathan finally married Julie Haydon, after a 14-year courtship, in 1956. More than the most feared first-nighter in New York, Nathan was a renowned man-about-town (and the model for the acerbic critic Addison De Witt in the film *All About Eve*).

Dissatisfied with the daily grind at the *Herald,* Nathan left the newspaper and began writing for magazines. It was here that he began to make his mark as critic. In 1908 he joined *The Smart Set* as its dramatic critic and met H.L.

Mencken, its book reviewer. The two became friends and in 1914 assumed joint editorship of *The Smart Set.* Here was one of the great partnerships in American letters, for Mencken and Nathan were the arbiters, if not dictators, for what the "flaming youth" of 1920s America deemed worthwhile reading. Nathan and Mencken were much more than trend selectors though; in the pages of their magazine appeared the most influential and artistically promising writing of the era. A satirical poem of the day, "Mencken, Nathan and God," summed up their particular hold on the literate public of the 1920s.

Nathan was most important as a drama critic though, and his crusades against the buncombe of the Broadway show-shop and his avowedly "destructive" methods earned him the hatred of those whose work he scorned; and since he worked hard to live up to his own personal credo, "be indifferent," he made few friends. Among the chosen few, however, were Eugene O'Neill and another playwright, Sean O'Casey. Another writer of Irish background, George Bernard Shaw, considered him "intelligent playgoer number one."

Nathan liked very little, but when he decided to champion a playwright—or a performer—there was nothing he would not do. He never hesitated to use his influence with producers to get plays put on, nor did he hesitate to give suggestions to authors or directors about revisions or casting before plays went into rehearsal. Nathan knew of O'Neill's early experimental plays that were being performed in Greenwich Village, and he campaigned relentlessly to get the playwright produced on Broadway. In 1920 O'Neill's *Beyond the Horizon* was mounted on the Great White Way by John Williams, due in part to Nathan's influence. For the rest of his career Nathan was O'Neill's champion. He wrote in 1932: "O'Neill alone and single-handed waded through the dismal swamplands of American drama, bleak, squashy, and oozing sticky goo, and alone and single-handed bore out of them the water lily that no American had found there before him."

Nathan said he chose the theater as his sphere because it was a place for "the intelligent exercise of the emotions." In his books Nathan did not so much expound a particular theory or methodology as reveal his own criteria for theatrical excellence. He was an impressionistic critic who argued that personal taste is the ultimate critical arbiter. Nathan established the standards to which all responsible drama critics adhere: the critic owes allegiance to his or her own principles, not to the theater as an institution.

Nonetheless, Nathan's critical hauteur was often at odds with the cap-and-bells style in which he wrote. He was also part of a tradition in American theater criticism. He followed in the wake of Irving, Poe, and Whitman, all of whom fought against contemporary critical trends. Nathan demanded a new and more serious American theater, a theater that responded to artistic needs rather than box office appeal. He deplored the pretensions of David Belasco's productions and the all-American banality of Augustus Thomas. (He was no bluenose, though. He reveled in the Ziegfeld Follies.) Not the least of his contributions to the theater was his unflinching critical independence. Nathan's courage forced the puffsters and pseudo-academic hacks of criticism to flee the field.

Finally, Nathan was able to wield his influence by explaining the differences between the theater that he saw and the theater that he wanted to see. He did so with a singular, if sometimes antic, style that reached a tremendous audience. Nathan's erudition mingled with a zany and breathtaking wit that made him the most famous, highest paid, and most widely read and translated theater critic in the world. He created modern American drama criticism and was crucial to the development of the modern American theater and its drama. In his will he established the annual George Jean Nathan Award for drama criticism. He died in New York City on April 8, 1958.

Further Reading

Nathan wrote over 40 books, almost all of them collections of his criticism. The most important are: *The Critic and the Drama* (1922), in which he explained some principles behind his criticism; *The Autobiography of an Attitude* (1925) and *The Intimate Notebooks of George Jean Nathan* (1932), which reveal critical insights and show the reader something of Nathan's compelling theatrical persona; *The Theatre, The Drama, The Girls* (1921), probably his best book; and his brilliant *Theatre Book of the Year* series, which is much more than a theatrical annual—here he intersperses essays about the nature of drama, of comedy or tragedy, of the decline of burlesque, and so forth with reviews of each season's shows (1942-1943 to 1950-1951).

Thomas Quinn Curtiss' *The Magic Mirror* is the best of the Nathan anthologies. It contains an especially good introduction. There are also outstanding collections of correspondence: Nancy and Arthur Roberts' *"As Ever, Gene": The Letters of Eugene O'Neill to George Jean Nathan* (1987); and Robert Lowery and Patricia Angelin's *"My Very Dear Sean": George Jean Nathan to Sean O'Casey. Letters and Articles* (1985). As for books about Nathan, Isaac Goldberg's *The Theatre of George Jean Nathan* (1926) is a good account of his career up to that time. It also reprints his play "The Eternal Mystery" and a cynical essay on love that Nathan authored at age 16. Constance Frick's *The Dramatic Criticism of George Jean Nathan* (1943) is rather superficial, but contains additional material on Nathan's later years. ☐

Carry Amelia Moore Nation

The actions of Carry Amelia Moore Nation (1846-1911), American temperance reformer and moral agitator, helped bring on the prohibition era.

Carry Amelia Moore was born in Garrard County, Ky., on Nov. 25, 1846, into a well-to-do slave-holding household. She was raised in an intensely religious atmosphere. On her mother's side there was evidence of eccentricity and insanity, and Carry's youth mixed emotionalism with stern suppression. The Moores moved a number of times, and during the Civil War her father lost his fortune. In 1865 the family settled in Belton, Mo. Carry earned a teaching certificate at the state normal school.

In 1867 Carry married Dr. Charles Gloyd. He soon proved an irresponsible alcoholic, and though she loved him and was pregnant, she returned home. He died shortly after. Her child, born weak of mind, was an expense and trouble for years. After teaching school for a few years, Carry married David Nation, a lawyer, minister, and journalist, in 1877.

The Nations moved to Medicine Lodge, Kans. In 1889 a great fire stopped short of Nation's hotel, convincing her that she was divinely shielded. Her religious fervor increasingly took the form of hallucinations and public displays. She found an outlet in the work of the Women's Christian Temperance Union (WCTU) throughout the 1890s. This group became very active because the Kansas law prohibiting the sale of liquor was not being enforced.

In 1899 and into 1900 Nation and other WCTU women developed a campaign of prayer and religious song outside local saloons. A tall, powerful, determined woman, Nation was first treated roughly and with contempt. She then began an offensive which made her internationally famous. She and her friends returned to the "joints" and in violent confrontations and challenges to the law, which she held remiss for not enforcing prohibition, they succeeded in closing the saloons.

The tumult Nation had stirred up inspired her to broaden her campaign. In Wichita and Topeka, Kans., and other cities, wearing her famous black dress and bonnet and carrying a Bible and an iron rod, she roused citizens and

officials. On Jan. 21, 1901, at Wichita, she first used the hatchet that became her trademark.

Strongly convinced of divine guidance—she thought her name (Carry A. Nation) had been predestined—Nation extended her activities, though on occasion she stood trial and served time in jail. The WCTU was not in wholehearted support of her. Her husband divorced her on grounds of desertion. Her lectures and publications (*The Smasher's Mail, The Hatchet*) earned money that she spent freely on such reforms as a home for wives of alcoholics in Kansas City, Kans.

A trip to New York City was picturesque but ineffective, and increasingly, during raids in major cities from San Francisco, Calif., to Washington, D.C., Nation became a symbol of aggression rather than of temperance reform. Her distaste for tobacco and contemporary women's clothes accentuated her conservative character. By the time of her death in Leavenworth, Kans., on June 2, 1911, it was clear that she had outlived her time.

Further Reading

Carry Nation's autobiography, *The Use and Need of the Life of Carry A. Nation* (1904), is vivid and informative. Her major biographers have been remarkably judicious and understanding, though philosophically opposed to her on most counts. See Herbert Asbury, *Carry Nation* (1929); Carleton Beals, *Cyclone Carry: The Story of Carry Nation* (1962); and Robert Lewis Taylor, *Vessel of Wrath: The Life and Times of Carry Nation* (1966).

Additional Sources

Madison, Arnold., *Carry Nation,* Nashville: T. Nelson, 1977. □

Irene Natividad

Irene Natividad (born 1948), who served as the head of the National Women's Political Caucus, is an educator and ardent activist for women's rights in both economic and political spheres.

When the phone rings in Irene Natividad's Washington, D.C., office, one thing is certain—the caller is a person with political power and influence. Natividad is simultaneously at the center of activity in many arenas as chair of the National Commission on Working Women, which works to improve the economic status of working women in the United States; as director of the Global Forum of Women, a biannual international gathering of women leaders that convenes to explore leadership issues for women worldwide; as executive director of the Philippine American Foundation, which implements programs to foster grassroots rural development to alleviate poverty in the Philippines; and as principal of Natividad and Associates, which provides consulting services for groups wishing to reach specific segments of the voting constituency. Natividad continues to rise to top executive positions in every activity she pursues.

Born in Manila, Philippines, on September 14, 1948, Irene Natividad is the eldest of four children. Her father's work as a chemical engineer took the family from the Philippines to Okinawa, Iran, Greece, and India. Irene's ability to quickly master new languages was the key to adjusting to the ever-changing schools and communities she encountered while growing up. Partly because of her family's frequent moves, Natividad speaks Spanish, French, Italian, Tagalog, Farsi, and Greek fluently, and is adept at working with people from other countries and cultures.

But if Natividad's international upbringing broadened her understanding of other cultures, it also made her aware of the limited options available to women. In a 1985 interview with the *Bergen* (New Jersey) *Record,* Natividad described how her mother's experience during the family's frequent moves helped to shape her own perspective on women's roles: "My father had his job, we kids had our schools, and she had nothing," Natividad said. "In all those countries, a woman was not allowed to work . . . I think I have a very intelligent, outspoken, articulate mother, and she had no outlet."

Her parents had high expectations for their three daughters and one son. In Greece, Natividad completed her high school education as valedictorian of her class. A few years later, when her mother indicated that she would not attend Natividad's 1971 graduation from Long Island University unless her daughter was valedictorian, Irene made sure her mother was there by earning the number one spot in her class. In 1973, she received a master's degree in American literature and a masters in philosophy in 1976,

both from Columbia University in New York; she has only to complete her dissertation to earn her doctorate. She has been awarded honorary doctorates from Long Island University (1989) and Marymount College (1994).

Natividad's first forays into the working world were during the 1970s, when she held faculty and administrative positions in higher education. She was an adjunct instructor in English at Lehman College of the City University of New York in 1974; an instructor in English at Columbia University from 1974 to 1976; and director of continuing education at both Long Island University and William Paterson College in New Jersey from 1978 until 1985. In continuing education, she relished the opportunity to support and guide women seeking to return to the work force or to upgrade their skills.

While working as a waitress, Natividad launched her career as an activist by organizing the other waiters and waitresses to demand higher pay. Although she was fired as a result, Natividad thereafter remained a committed activist employing organizational and political means to achieve a goal. In 1980, Natividad served as founder and president of Asian American Professional Women and as founding director of the National Network of Asian-Pacific American Women and the Child Care Action Campaign.

It wasn't long before Natividad turned her formidable leadership talents toward the political arena. Natividad's first taste of politics came in 1968 when she distributed campaign leaflets for Eugene J. McCarthy's presidential bid. Her appetite for organizing and constituency building had been whetted, and she went on to serve as chair of the New York State Asian Pacific Caucus from 1982 to 1984, and as deputy vice-chair of the Asian Pacific Caucus of the Democratic National Committee. By 1984, when Geraldine Ferraro made history by becoming the first woman from a major party to run for vice-president of the United States, Natividad was tapped by the Democratic party organization to serve as Asian American liaison for Ferraro's campaign. Ferraro joined Walter Mondale on the Democratic ticket, and although the Mondale/Ferraro team lost the election to Republicans Ronald Reagan and George Bush, Natividad viewed the campaign as a significant turning point for women in politics. In 1985, Natividad told the *Honolulu Star-Bulletin,* "[Ferraro's] legacy is she broke the credibility gap for all women candidates, from presidential down to the local level. I don't consider '84 a loss. I consider it a win."

By 1985 Natividad's career as a political activist was in full swing. She was elected to chair the National Women's Political Caucus, becoming the first Asian American woman to head a national women's organization. Commenting about her election to head the caucus, Natividad told *USA Today* in 1985, "A minority group [Asian Americans] perceived as invisible now has a very visible spokeswoman."

The National Women's Political Caucus, headquartered in Washington, D.C., was founded in 1971 by a small group of feminists (including former congresswomen Bella Abzug, Shirley Chisolm, and Patsy Mink) to focus on putting women in public office. The caucus is bipartisan as a registered Democrat, Natividad succeeded a Republican as leader of the group. But as a very pragmatic political insider,

Natividad acknowledged the need to look to both political parties for support. Natividad described the caucus in the *Bergen* (New Jersey) *Record* as including "friends on both sides of the aisle [in the U.S. Congress]. I'd like to think [the National Women's Political Caucus] is party blind."

Throughout her career Natividad has focused on using organizations to achieve her goals. Her election to head the 77,000-member Caucus was a logical step on her mission to help women gain power and influence through the political system. In a 1985 interview with the *New York Times,* Natividad laid out her goals for the caucus: "One of our missions [at the National Women's Political Caucus] is to transfer the political experience we have developed on a national level to the state and local level. We want to train women to run for local offices because if we don't feed that pipeline we won't have state winners. We have to insure that we have more wins at the local level, for that is where it all starts." During her tenure, the caucus trained candidates and their staffs throughout the United States on the basics of campaigning. The workshops covered topics key to running a successful campaign, such as polling techniques, fundraising, grassroots organization, and strategies for dealing with the news media.

Under Natividad's leadership, the caucus gathered hard data to analyze factors influencing women's congressional races and compiled an annual Survey of Governors' Appointments of Women to state cabinets. The caucus also established the first-ever Minority Women Candidates' Training Program and created the Good Guy Award honoring men who further the cause of women's rights. As a result of their activities, the caucus gained real clout. Through the work of the caucus' Coalition for Women's Appointments in 1988, Natividad was invited to meet with President George Bush to promote women candidates for administration posts. An estimated one-third of all women appointed to high-level positions in the Bush administration had been recommended by the coalition led by Natividad.

In 1989, Natividad stepped down as chair of the National Women's Political Caucus to pursue other interests and to make way for fresh leadership. Her interest in and commitment to women's issues has not waned, but has rather taken on an international dimension.

Natividad's interests are truly global in scope. She has frequently written and spoken on topics ranging from the struggle for democracy in Czechoslovakia and her native Philippines, to proposals for changes in the workplace culture that will benefit both women and men. Reflecting on her commitment to work at the grassroots level, Natividad is editor of a reference book for public and school libraries, the *Asian American Almanac,* published in 1995.

In 1992, Natividad served as a director of the Global Forum of Women, a gathering in Dublin, Ireland, of 400 women leaders from fifty-eight countries to develop strategies for addressing issues facing women worldwide. This international summit was followed in 1994 by a Forum in Taiwan (attended by representatives from eighty countries), for which Natividad developed a program that focused on political empowerment. The basic premise of the Taiwan gathering was that no real change can take place regarding women's lives unless women themselves are the policy-makers. Natividad's program featured practical "nuts-and-bolts" techniques of running for public office and skills-building workshops for policymakers. Natividad develops and leads political training workshops at locations around the world, from Barcelona to Bangkok. Natividad contributed to planning for a conference that ran in conjunction with the 1995 U.N. Fourth World Conference on Women.

In 1996, Natividad returned to domestic issues by joining several other activists and politicians to develop "Project Vote Smart." The founders of this program sought to increase voter education and registration in the U.S. Furthermore, Natividad became the Chair of "Women's Vote '96." Although women are more concerned today about the economy, education, crime, and health, she believes that women are becoming more alienated from government. According to Natividad, "Voting provides an answer, a way for women to gain more control over their lives and futures. At this critical juncture, an unprecedented coalition has created a voter outreach campaign designed to make the suffragists' dream a reality."

Natividad's accomplishments have been frequently recognized. In 1994, *A. Magazine: The Asian American Quarterly,* named her to their list of "Power Brokers: The Twenty-five Most Influential People in Asian America." In 1993, she was named as one of the "Seventy-four Women Who Are Changing American Politics" by *Campaigns and Elections* magazine. The National Conference for College Women Student Leaders awarded Natividad its Woman of Distinction Award in 1989, the same year in which she received an honorary doctorate in humane letters from Long Island University. In 1988, *Ladies' Home Journal* included her in their list of "100 Most Powerful Women in America." In 1987, she received the Innovator for Women$hare Award from the Women's Funding Coalition. Americans by Choice presented the 1986 Honored American Award to Natividad, and the Women's Congressional Caucus presented her the Women Making History Award in 1985.

Natividad is married to Andreas Cortese, director of Digital Communications Services for the Communications Satellite Corporation. They have one son, Carlo Natividad-Cortese, whose birth in 1984 coincided with Natividad's becoming leader of the National Women's Political Caucus. She remarked to *Ladies' Home Journal* on the demanding life of a political activist, "It is satisfying knowing that for a brief point in time you made a difference."

Further Reading

Women's Vote Will Decide the '96 Election: "http://www.feminist.com/vote.html," p. 1. □

Soseki Natsume

The Japanese novelist and essayist Soseki Natsume (1867-1916) was one of the greatest Japanese novelists of the modern period. In his fiction and essays he displays keen psychological insight into the person-ality of man undergoing the transition from traditional to modern.

Soseki Natsume was born Kinnosuke Natsume in Tokyo; he is known in Japanese literature by his pen name of Soseki. His parents were rather well-to-do townspeople, whose fortunes, however, declined after the Meiji restoration of 1868. An unhappy childhood, including a period spent with foster parents, and the realization that he was an unwanted child, left an indelible mark on Soseki's imagination which he was to carry to the grave.

Of a studious disposition, Soseki early learned classical Chinese, with much enthusiasm, and English. Entering the university in 1884, he specialized in English literature. During his formative years Soseki was exposed to the growing conflict between excessive Westernization and Japanese nationalism, which no doubt resulted in his being at once very modern and very Japanese. Soseki mastered English to the extent of being able to read and write it with great fluency. At the time of his death his library included hundreds of English-language books on all subjects, many of them containing his marginal annotations in English.

Graduating from the university in 1893, Soseki took a post at Tokyo Normal College and in 1895 went to Matsuyama, where he found a position in the high school. In 1896 he moved to Kumamoto to the Fifth National College. Later that year a marriage was arranged for him with a young woman from Tokyo. In 1900 a government scholarship made it possible for Soseki to go to England for 2 years of study. Unfortunately, his stipend was not adequate for him to lead the life he would have liked. His loneliness in a foreign city, his concern for money, and his arduous studies all contributed to nervous disorders which were to haunt him for the rest of his life. It was even rumored that he had a mental breakdown.

After his return to Japan in 1903, Soseki was confronted with the flood tide of nationalism which was leading to the Japanese attack on Russia. Although he firmly admired the literature of the West, he did not indulge in excessive admiration or slavish imitation of all things foreign but, rather, sought to create something of lasting value based on the traditions of his own country.

Soseki resided in Tokyo, where he was given a lectureship at the Imperial University. During the 4 years that he remained there teaching, a chore for which he had little liking, Soseki began writing novels and acquiring a literary reputation. It was in 1907 that he abandoned the security and prestige of a university professorship to work for the *Asahi Newspaper* with the understanding that his novels would be published serially in that distinguished publication. From that time until the end of his life he devoted himself to writing, spurning official honors.

Career as a Novelist

Wagahai wa Neko de Aru (I Am a Cat) appeared in 1905. An immediate success, it is a series of loosely connected episodes having as their narrator a cat, his master a shy, ineffectual schoolteacher with a delicate digestion.

With delightful irony Soseki depicts an assortment of contemporary types caught in the struggle of daily life and torn between idealism and materialism. *Botchan* (1906; *Young Master*) tells of the adventures of a youth who leaves Tokyo to teach in a provincial high school in the south of Japan. It was perhaps partly inspired by Soseki's own experiences in Matsuyama. The young master learns a bit about life, leaves the school, and returns to Tokyo, where he finds a satisfactory job. *Kusamakura* (*Pillow of Grass*), written in the same year in a poetic style, was described by Soseki as "a novel in the manner of a haiku." It is an intensely impressionistic account of a painter from the city wandering in a mountain village. *Nowaki* (1907; *Autumn Wind*), written in rather a more serious vein, portrays modern people struggling with ideals and suffering intensely in the illusion of this world.

Soseki's next three novels form a trilogy. *Sanshiro* (1908) tells of a youth's disillusionment in first love and disappointment in life. *Sorekara* (1909; *And Then*) describes the plight of an educated young Japanese in early-20th-century society suffering from hypochondria and boredom. In *Mon* (1910; *The Gate*) Soseki deals with the quest for happiness and understanding of a middle-aged, childless couple.

The theme of loneliness is taken up in great depth in *Kojin* (1912; *The Wayfarer*) and *Kokoro* (1914; *The Heart*). The hero of *The Wayfarer* is driven to a state of near madness by the realization of his loneliness. In *The Heart* , Soseki's most pessimistic novel, suicide is presented as the solution to man's inevitable solitude. The Sensei (teacher), having suffered great mental anguish in life, at last finds the courage to be the master of his own destiny by removing himself from this earthly existence. *Michikusa* (1915; *Grass on the Wayside*), frankly autobiographical, sums up much of Soseki's own resentment toward life. Its hero, his personality disintegrating, needs love but cruelly, rejects it and feels betrayed by those whose affection and loyalty he should have enjoyed.

Soseki's health was deteriorating rapidly because of stomach ulcers by 1915. His last novel, *Meian* (1916; *Light and Darkness*), a most complex analysis of egocentric personalities of the modern age, was left unfinished at his death.

Further Reading

A study of Soseki is in Edwin McClellan, *Two Japanese Novelists: Soseki and Toson* (1969). □

Martina Navratilova

Martina Navrotilova (born 1956) was ranked number one in female tennis. She has won 17 grand slam titles and broken the record for total victories.

The clouds gathered, the sky darkened, and the summer rain fell on the grass, center court in the suburbs of London, England. This was early in the summer of 1988, late in the fortnight at Wimbledon, the most prestigious tennis tournament in the world. In progress: the championship match of the women's competition between Martina Navratilova and Steffi Graf. Navratilova, 31, was the defending champion. A native of Czechoslovakia who is now an American citizen, she was seeking her seventh straight English crown and ninth there in the past 11 years. On the other side of the net was Graf, 19, a West German who had lost the previous year's title match to Navratilova but seemed on her way to her first victory here.

When the rains came, each woman had won one set of the best-of-three finale. Navratilova had won the first, 7-5, but Graf had rebounded with an impressive 6-2 victory in the second set and had taken a 3-1 lead in the third. At one point, Graf had won nine straight games and had broken Navratilova's service five straight times. To borrow a cliche from another individualist sport, boxing, Graf had Navratilova on the ropes. "No one had treated Navratilova so rudely in years," wrote Paul Attner of the *Sporting News*. Would Navratilova, queen of this court through most of the 1980s, use the unplanned rest to gather her strength, adjust her strategy, prepare a dramatic comeback, and keep her title? With time on her hands, would Graf dwell on the enormity of her opportunity, lose her momentum, and squander what seemed in reach?

Perhaps it would happen in dreams, in fairy tales, or in movie scripts, but not on the lawn at Wimbledon in 1988.

"In truth," wrote Curry Kirkpatrick of *Sports Illustrated,* " it was a reign stoppage." When they returned to the court, Graf quickly won the next three games to take the final set, 6-1, and leave with the silver plate that is presented to the champion by the Duchess of Kent. "It wound up being a sad scene for [Navratilova]," Graf said, "but a special one for me." Admitted Navratilova: "I got blown out. This is definitely the end of a chapter. . . . Pass the torch, I guess."

Although the defeat at Wimbledon meant the end of a chapter, it certainly didn't close the book on the career of Navratilova, one of the world's most successful, colorful, and controversial athletes of her generation. Top female players in the past have excelled well into their late thirties, and Navratilova intends to join that list. "Retirement is still a ways off," Navratilova wrote in her autobiography, *Martina,* co-authored by George Vecsey, in 1985. "People say I can play until I'm forty, and I don't see any reason why I can't. . . . Robert Haas used to claim that with all the work I was doing on myself, I could be winning Wimbledon at the age of forty. People scoffed, but that's really not unreasonable when you look at Billie Jean King, who reached the 1982 and 1983 semifinals at Wimbledon at age thirty-nine and forty. Barring an injury or lack of motivation, I can see myself doing it."

Certainly, she always has shown determination, motivation, and a- willingness to shape her future for herself. Even if she hadn't been a tennis champion, Navratilova would have been an unusual and interesting person for at least two reasons. First, she is a political defector from Czechoslovakia, a communist country of the Soviet Eastern Bloc, who was outspoken about her desire to become a citizen of the United States; and second, she says she is a bisexual and has often discussed the sometimes taboo subject of lesbian love in interviews and in her autobiography.

Even in terms of tennis, she has been unique in that she has shown more willingness than others of her generation to seek technical, physical, and emotional coaching from other persons inside and outside her sport. While Navratilova isn't the first to do such things, some experts feel her dedication to coaching and training has influenced the approach of other tennis players for the next generation. "I'm not saying she's the first to do it," said Mary Carillo, a former player who is now a television commentator, in an interview for *Newsmakers.* " Margaret Court did it and Billie Jean King did it. But when Martina did it, everybody followed her lead. A lot of players now go to sports psychologists. Martina soared so far beyond everybody else, the only thing to do was to follow her lead. She did more than dominate the early 1980s. She set a whole new standard. She changed her diet and her fitness status. She made it scientific. She made it specific."

Navratilova was born on October 18, 1956, in Prague, Czechoslovakia and was raised in the suburb of Revnice by her mother and her stepfather. (Her real father committed suicide after the divorce.) As a lean, small child, Navratilova excelled in many sports, including hockey and skiing. She often competed against boys. "I'm not very psychologically oriented and I have no idea how I was affected by my real father's abandonment, the secrets and the suicide, or my feeling about being a misfit, a skinny little tomboy with short hair," she wrote in her autobiography. "In Czechoslovakia, nobody ever put me down for running around with boys, playing ice hockey and soccer. From what I've been told, people in the States used to think that if girls were good at sports, their sexuality would be affected."

As a teenager, Navratilova's tennis skills allowed her to tour foreign countries, including the United States. She felt stifled in Czechoslovakia and defected at the U.S. Open in 1975, shortly before her 19th birthday. At the time, she said it was strictly a matter of tennis. "Politics had nothing to do with my decision," she said in an Associated Press story. "It was strictly a tennis matter." In Prague, a reporter told her grandfather, who was quoted as replying, "Oh, the little idiot, why did she do that?" The defection was prompted in part, she said, by an incident early in 1975 when she was playing in a tournament at Amelia Island off the coast of Florida. She received a telegram from the officials of the Czech Sports Federation demanding that she return home. "I was in the middle of the tournament," she said. "I had to call upon the U.S. Tennis Association to help get me permission to play. That was when I really decided that I should leave Czechoslovakia."

Life in a capitalist country brought wealth-and problems. "I didn't do it for the money, but it's nice to have," she told the *Detroit Free Press* more than two years after the defection. She began to buy cars and houses, often owning several of each at the same time. She maintains a home in Fort Worth, Tex., and a townhouse in Aspen, Colo. Among the problems were loneliness and a fondness for the fattening foods sold in fast-food restaurants in the United States. "I miss my family badly," she told Bud Collins of the *New York Times Magazine.* " I worried for awhile that there would be retaliation against them, but there wasn't much." Her weight grew to 167 pounds shortly after her defection. She is five feet, seven and one-half inches tall. A decade later, after undergoing her physical conditioning program, she was 145 pounds of lean muscle.

Her physique stood in contrast to that of many American female athletes of the past who tried to maintain the-unlikely combination of round, soft, "feminine" curves and the athletic ability that comes with muscle tone and conditioning. Her appearance and personal behavior quickly led to public discussions of her sexual preference. "I never thought there was anything strange about being gay," she wrote in her book. "Even when I thought about it, I never panicked and thought, Oh, I'm strange, I'm weird, what do I do now?"

The book details many of Navratilova's relationships and living arrangements with women and how some soured and ended in bitterness. She tells of her professional relationship with Renee Richards, a female tennis player and coach who at one time was a man but had undergone a sex-change operation. Another one of her professional aides was Nancy Lieberman, a basketball player who Navratilova used for training and motivational purposes. At times, her many coaches and associates didn't get along. "Things got worse at Wimbledon when Renee was not invited to a surprise birthday party for Nancy, planned by some friends of Nancy's," Navratilova wrote in her book. "Renee thought it was Nancy's idea, but that was ridiculous. I knew the party was being planned, but I had other things on my mind." Navratilova's break-up with girlfriend Judy Nelson sparked considerable media attention when Nelson sued for half of Navratilova's earnings. A settlement was eventually reached between the two women.

The political side of her life story came to the fore in the summer of 1986, when she returned for the first time to Czechoslovakia. As an American citizen, she represented the United States in the Federation Cup in Prague. The return was a major media event as soon as she stepped off the plane. "Lights. Shouts. Rudeness. Pushing. Shoving," wrote Frank Deford in *Sports Illustrated*. " How Kafka must have chuckled in his nearby grave as Navratilova beat a retreat." As she played well and won, she became a favorite of the fans, if not of Czech tennis officials. "Every day the lady from Revnice was winning more hearts," Deford wrote. "Young men dashed on the court to give her roses. The crowds began to acclaim her, and she grew more responsive—first waving shyly, then giving the thumbs-up sign and, last, blowing kisses. Why, it almost seemed as if the Statue of Liberty had gone on tour, turning in her torch for a Yonex racket. Czech officials grew so enraged that on Friday they ordered the umpire not to introduce Navratilova by name. She became 'On my left the woman player from the United States.'"

Although her personal life is interesting, there are other persons who are defectors from Czechoslovakia and others who overcame obesity and others who are bisexual. What makes Navratilova a famous person is her ability to play tennis consistently with the best in the world. She holds the racket in her left hand and plays aggressively. "The pattern of attack is a vital factor in Martina's supremacy," Shirley Brasher wrote in *Weekend Magazine of Canada*. " She gives her opponents no time to find their own rhythm, no time to play at a safe speed. Instead, she rushes them and pushes them around the court, hitting out for the lines and blanketing the next with her reach, power and speed."

As the years went by and her victory totals grew, Navratilova became a favorite subject of sports writers who watched her grow from an emotional teenager to a more self-assured adult. "She has evolved in the eyes of many," John Ed Bradley wrote in the *Washington Post*," into a strong-armed automaton with a mean top spin forehand . . . and a tough, insensitive attitude that has wiped clean the memory of her emotional loss to Tracy Austin in the 1981 U.S. Open. Has the world forgotten that she wept violently at center court after dropping the third-set tie breaker?" As her career peaked, late in 1986, Peter Alfano wrote in the *New York Times:* " For the fifth consecutive year, Ms. Navratilova will finish as the No. 1 player in the world in the computer rankings. Her hold is so strong that a rare defeat is celebrated like a holiday on the tour, her victorious opponent treated like a conquering hero. Then come the whispers: Is Martina slowing down?"

Two years later, the whispers were common conversation. Her computer ranking fell to No. 2 and held there for 1988. Going into competition in 1988, she had won 17

Grand Slam titles. (A Grand Slam event is one of the four major tournaments: Wimbledon, the U.S. Open, the French Open and the Australian Open.) Only three women had won more: Margaret Court (26), Helen Wills Moody (19), and Chris Evert (18). Prior to 1988, Navratilova had won at least one Grand Slam singles title in seven consecutive years. But the year 1988 was difficult for her with no Grand Slam titles. After being upset by Zina Garrison in the U.S. Open in suburban New York, Navratilova said, "If this year were a fish, I would throw it back."

Navratilova continued to play singles tennis despite constant retirement rumors. In 1992 she won her one hundred and fifty-eighth professional tennis title. With this win, Navratilova broke the record for more tennis titles than any other man or woman. Playing with Jonathan Stark, the pair won the mixed doubles title at Wimbledon in 1995. A second attempt at a mixed doubles title at Wimbledon was squelched by a loss to Lindsay Davenport and Grant Connell in 1996. Reporters continue to ask Navratilova what her plans are and if she will return for another match. Her answer remains that she does not know when she will retire from the professional tennis tour.

Navratilova has devoted some of her time off of the tennis court to writing. Her autobiography *Martina* chronicles her life from growing up in the former Czechoslovakia to her defection to the United States and subsequent rise to greatness and reveals much about trials and triumphs she has experienced along the way. Her mystery novels *The Total Zone* and *Breaking Point* were released in 1994 and 1996

Further Reading

Associated Press, September 8, 1975.
Boston Globe, November 5, 1988.
Chicago Tribune, November 16, 1987.
Christian Science Monitor, August 25, 1986; September 8, 1986; September 9, 1986.
Detroit Free Press, February 19, 1975; August 12, 1985; July 6, 1986; June 28, 1987; July 5, 1987.
Los Angeles Times, September 15, 1985; September 22, 1985; July 27, 1986; August 25, 1986; September 7, 1986; September 8, 1986; November 24, 1986.
New York Times, December 7, 1975; August 25, 1986; September 8, 1986; September 10, 1986.
New York Times Magazine, June 19, 1977.
Orlando Sentinel, April 25, 1985.
People, September 22, 1986.
Sport, March, 1976.
Sporting News, July 11, 1988.
Sports Illustrated, February 24, 1975; April 4, 1983; September 19, 1983; May 26, 1986; August 4, 1986; September 12, 1986; July 11, 1988.
Tennis, December, 1974.
Time, July 11, 1983; July 16, 1984.
Washington Post, January 9, 1985; September 8, 1986.
Weekend Magazine of Canada, June, 1979.
Women's Sports, August, 1985.
Women's Sports Fitness, November, 1986.
World Tennis, May, 1975; March, 1983; October, 1983; December, 1983; May, 1985. □

Gloria Naylor

The author Gloria Naylor (born 1950) wrote novels that emphasized the strengths of women, especially African American women, and the effects on the lives of people of racism, sexism, and the drive for material gain at any expense.

Gloria Naylor was born in Harlem on January 25, 1950, a month after her parents, Alberta and Roosevelt Naylor, arrived in New York City. Her parents were sharecroppers from Robinsonville, Mississippi, and her mother was especially determined that her children, Gloria and two younger sisters, receive the best education that could be provided for them. Even as a farm worker Alberta Naylor had used some of her meager wages to buy books that the segregated libraries of Mississippi denied her. When Gloria was old enough to sign her name, her mother began to take her to the library. Naylor became a fervent reader and began to write poems and stories as a child.

Alberta Naylor worked as a telephone operator, and Roosevelt Naylor was a motorman for the New York Transit. The family eventually moved to Queens. A good student, Naylor attended classes for the gifted and talented. After graduating from high school, she decided to postpone college in order to serve as a Jehovah Witness missionary. This decision was greatly influenced by the assassination of Martin Luther King, Jr. Naylor felt that she needed to work to change the world, and the Witnesses' notion of a theocratic government seemed a viable solution to her. From 1968 to 1975 she proselytized in New York, North Carolina, and Florida.

Troubled by the restrictions of the religion and spurred by the need to develop her talents, she matriculated at the Medgar Evers campus of Brooklyn College. Working as a telephone operator in New York City hotels, she pursued a degree in nursing. However, when it became clear that she preferred her literature classes, she transferred to a major in English. As an avid reader from childhood, she already admired such writers as Austen, Dickens, the Brontes, Faulkner, Ellison, and Baldwin. She soon recognized that all of these writers were either "male or white."

Fortunately, a creative writing class introduced her to Toni Morrison. It was an inspirational discovery. Although Naylor considered herself a poet then, Morrison became a model for rendering one's own reality and for crafting beautiful language. Naylor began to attend readings by Morrison and to hone her own skills as a fiction writer.

In 1980 Naylor entered into a marriage that lasted for ten days. That same year she published her first story in Essence magazine. The secretary to the president of Viking publishing company, who was a friend of a friend, circulated four of Naylor's stories among the editors in January 1981. Two weeks later Naylor had a contract for the book that eventually became *The Women of Brewster Place: A Novel in Seven Stories* (1982). The novel is actually a cycle of interconnected stories about seven women of different

backgrounds who live in a decrepit building on Brewster Place, a dreary street cut off from the rest of the city by a wall. Despite their differences, all of them are united by their inability to fulfill dreams deferred by racism and sexism. *The Women of Brewster Place* won the American Book Award for the best first novel in 1983.

In 1981 Naylor received her B.A. from Brooklyn College and, using an advance from *The Women of Brewster Place,* set off for Spain in a brief sojourn patterned after the expatriate adventures of Hemingway and Baldwin. As a single woman traveling alone, she found herself approached often by men and began to resent the fact that she did not have the freedom to explore enjoyed by male writers, white and black. She shut herself up in a boarding house in Cadiz and began to write *Linden Hills* (1985).

The initial idea for this novel was influenced by her reading of *The Inferno* in a Great Literature course at Brooklyn. Linden Hills is an African American middle-class neighborhood patterned after the circular geography of Dante's hell. Two younger poets, outsiders in Linden Hills who are looking for work the week before Christmas, discover the neuroses and crimes of the bourgeois inhabitants, who have relinquished culture and values for material gain.

In 1981 Naylor had enrolled in the graduate program in African American studies at Yale. She thought it important to study works that "were reflections of me and my existence and experience" (Goldstein). She received her M.A. in 1983.

Naylor's third novel, *Mama Day,* was published in 1988. Its settings are New York City and Willow Springs, a sea island off the coasts of Georgia and South Carolina whose most powerful inhabitant is Miranda (Mama) Day, healer and magician. When Mama Day's beloved niece, Cocoa, brings her husband George to visit, they all become involved in a plot to save Cocoa from a deadly curse. Naylor examined the conflicts between men and women, portraying the woman as the repository of the sensual and emotional and the male as the essence of rationality. Like Naylor's other novels, this one reverberates with the influences of traditional literature, this time Shakespeare's *The Tempest.*

Naylor has penned two other works *Bailey's Cafe* (1992) and a dramatic version of the story for the stage in 1994. In *Bailey's Cafe* published in 1992, Naylor focused on the interesting lives of the proprietors of a diner and it's various patrons. In this novel, Naylor demonstrates her ability to find heroism in the lives of everyday people, while at the same time showing their frustration at not being able to escape their position in life. Naylor is also the sole founder of One Way Productions, an independent film company.

Gloria Naylor was the recipient of a fellowship from the National Endowment of the Arts (1985) and a Guggenheim fellowship (1988), Naylor was one of only a few African American women ever to receive this honor. She was a cultural exchange lecturer for the United States Information Agency in India in 1985. She served as the writer-in-residence of the Cummington Community of Arts (Summer 1983); and as a visiting professor at George Washington University (1983-1984), University of Pennsylvania (1986), New York University (Spring 1986), Princeton (1986-1987), Boston University (1987), Brandeis University (1988), and Cornell (1988).

Further Reading

For more biographical information on Gloria Naylor see Naylor and Toni Morrison's, ''A Conversation,'' in *The Southern Review* (Summer 1985) and W. Goldstein's, ''Talk with Gloria Naylor,'' in *Publishers Weekly* (September 9, 1983). For critical information, see Michael Awkward's *Inspiriting Influences* (1989) and Catherine Ward's, ''Gloria Naylor's *Linden Hills* A Modern *Inferno*,'' in *Contemporary Literature* (Spring 1987). □

Ibrahim ibn Sayyar al-Nazzam

The Moslem thinker and theologian Ibrahim ibn Sayyar al-Nazzam (died ca. 840) was one of the major figures of the school of thought in Islam known as the Mutazila.

A l-Nazzam was educated in Basra and spent most of his active life (apparently a short one) in the Abbasid capital, Baghdad. Although his main impact was to be upon orthodox Moslem theology, he also engaged in polemics against the Manichaeans, whose ideas were filtering into the Islamic milieu even as they had into Christendom. His writings have come down to us only in fragmentary quotations in later Moslem writers.

Although a knowledge of Greek rationalist thought must be attributed to al-Nazzam, he, along with the rest of the Mutazila, should not be really classified as a philosopher. The main preoccupation of the Mutazilites was theology, and they used philosophical tools to bolster their dogmatism. Moslem thinkers had taken most enthusiastically to Greek methods as soon as philosophical works— mostly Aristotle and Neoplatonic works—became available in Arabic in the generation just before al-Nazzam. It was assumed rather too easily that the genius of these Greek minds would of course harmonize with the revelations transmitted by the prophet Mohammed and with the Traditions of the early Moslem community.

For al-Nazzam, the Koran is the only possible foundation for his intellectual system; it is worth noting, moreover, that his approach to religion is almost completely an intellectual one. The intellectual vigor which al-Nazzam and the other Mutazilites brought to theological discussion was largely channeled into polemics, both against other religions and against other shades of thought within Islam, such as the more extreme sectarians of the Shiis.

The Mutazilites insisted, as good Moslems, upon the absolute oneness of God and upon His justice. The first of these ideas led them logically to insist also that the Koran is created, rather than coeternal with God, as the more traditional Moslems believed. A similar zeal for absolute monotheism led al-Nazzam, in particular, to deny the power of God over evil: God is Absolute Justice and Absolute Good and is All-Wise. Since these statements are true, God cannot be the author of evil, since this would imply that He is either ignorant or in need of the creation of something evil; therefore the source of evil must be sought elsewhere.

The method of thought employed in this example is characteristic of al-Nazzam's approach; another example of his logic is a theory of creation which posits a single act on the part of God, with future events and things latent: all mankind was created at the same instant as Adam but only became manifest later.

The importance of al-Nazzam and other Mutazilites for Islamic thought is in their sharpening of the rationalistic tools which, ironically, were to be turned by later orthodox Moslems against excessive reliance upon rationalism in theology.

Further Reading

In English, a brief account of al-Nazzam's ideas is in Mian Mohammad Sharif, *A History of Muslim Philosophy,* vol. 1 (1963). □

Nebuchadnezzar

Nebuchadnezzar (reigned 605-562 B.C.) was a king of Babylon during whose long and eventful reign the Neo-Babylonian Empire attained its peak and the city of Babylon its greatest glory.

Nebuchadnezzar—more properly Nebucha-drezzar—is the biblical form of the name Nabu-kudur-utsur (Nabu has set the boundary). He was the son of Nabopolassar, a Chaldean chief who in 626 B.C. led a revolt against Assyrian rule, proclaimed himself king of Babylon, and, in alliance with the Medes and Scythians, succeeded in overthrowing the vast Assyrian Empire and destroying Nineveh in 612 B.C. Nebuchadnezzar, as crown prince, was given command of the Babylonian army harrying the remainder of the Assyrians in northern Syria. Early in 605 B.C. he met Necho, the king of Egypt, in battle and defeated him at Carchemish. A few months later Nabopolassar died, and Nebuchadnezzar hastened home to claim his throne. He soon returned to the west in order to secure the loyalty of Syria and Palestine and to collect tribute; among those who submitted were the rulers of Damascus, Tyre, Sidon, and Judah.

Nebuchadnezzar's Conquests

In 601 B.C. Nebuchadnezzar attempted the invasion of Egypt but was repulsed with heavy losses. Judah rebelled, but Jerusalem fell in March 597 B.C., and the ruler, Jehoiakim, and his court were deported to Babylon. Eight years later another Jewish rebellion broke out; this time Jerusalem was razed and the population carried into captivity. Expeditions against the Arabs in 582 B.C. and another attempt at invading Egypt in 568 B.C. receive brief mention in Nebuchadnezzar's later records.

Nebuchadnezzar built temples in many of the cities of his kingdom, but the main achievement of his reign was the rebuilding of Babylon, on a scale and with a magnificence never before envisaged. The city covered some 500 acres and was protected by massive double fortifications. The Euphrates River, which bisected it, was spanned by a bridge. In the great palace, built to replace Nabopolassar's, he created the terraced cloister known to the Greeks as the Hanging Gardens and reckoned among the Seven Wonders of the World. It was said that he built it to please his mountain-born wife, Amytis, daughter of Cyaxares, the Median king.

The last years of Nebuchadnezzar's life were clouded by family strife, and he left no strong successor: his son was overthrown by a usurper after reigning only 2 years. Babylon, however, survived and was seen by the Greek historian Herodotus, who described its marvels.

Further Reading

Tablets containing new information about Nebuchadnezzar's military activities were translated by D. J. Wiseman in *Chronicles of Chaldaean Kings* (1956). These texts supplement the account of R. Campbell Thompson in J. B. Bury and others,

eds., *The Cambridge Ancient History* (12 vols., 1923-1939). For a description of Babylon in Nebuchadnezzar's time see James G. Macqueen, *Babylon* (1964), based on Robert Koldewey's excavations before World War I. □

Jacques Necker

The French financier and statesman Jacques Necker (1732-1804) served King Louis XVI as director general of finances. His efforts to reform French institutions prior to 1789 and to compromise with the Estates General after the start of the Revolution failed.

Jacques Necker was born in Geneva, Switzerland, where his father, of Prussian origin, taught at the university. At the age of 18 Necker moved to Paris to work in a bank. He rose rapidly in the world of finance and accumulated a considerable fortune, partly as the result of speculation in the French East India Company, of which he became a director, and in the grain trade.

In 1765 Necker founded his own bank. A year earlier he had married Suzanne Curchod, the gifted daughter of a Swiss pastor, whose salon was soon frequented by leading literary and diplomatic figures. As a result of his wife's influence, Necker abandoned his bank to his brother in 1772 and decided to embark upon a political career. In order to enhance his reputation as a financial expert, he wrote a number of works, the most important being *Éloge de Colbert* (1773) and *Essai sur la législation et le commerce des grains* (1775). In the latter he attacked A.R.J. Turgot's policy of free trade in grains. Necker also provided financial services for a number of writers and high nobles.

On June 29, 1777, Louis XVI named Necker director general of finances, and Necker soon became a virtual prime minister. Because he was a foreigner and a Protestant he could not receive the official title of controller general. Scholars differ about Necker's first ministry, some accusing him of excessive caution in introducing necessary reforms. Necker sought to reduce public expenditures by such measures as abolishing unnecessary positions and by demanding larger payments from the private companies that had purchased the right to collect indirect taxes. He also attempted to introduce some reforms in the inequitable system of taxation.

Because Necker financed French aid to the American colonies in their war of independence against England without raising taxes, he was regarded as a financial genius. As a result of Necker's loans, however, the public debt greatly increased. Necker anticipated one goal of the French Revolution by founding a number of provincial assemblies in which the three estates sat and voted together. These efforts aroused opposition from the privileged classes, who urged Louis XVI to dismiss his minister. In 1781 Necker published a response to his critics, his famous *Compte rendu au roi,* a report on the fiscal condition of France. However, he was dismissed from office on May 19, 1781. Necker retired to

his Swiss estate, Coppet, where he wrote *Traité de l'administration des finances de la France* in 1784.

Necker's second ministry began in August 1788, when Louis XVI recalled him to office after agreeing to convoke the Estates General to deal with France's fiscal crisis. On Necker's advice, Louis XVI agreed to the doubling of the number of delegates from the Third Estate, but after some hesitation he rejected the vote by head demanded by the Third Estate, and he also rejected Necker's suggestion for a compromise. Influenced by the most conservative nobles, the King, who now planned to use force against the Estates General, dismissed Necker on July 11, 1789, because he regarded him as too sympathetic to the Third Estate. Necker's departure from office contributed to the unrest in Paris that culminated in the storming of the Bastille on July 14, 1789. A few days later popular pressure forced Louis XVI to recall Necker.

Necker, however, distrusted by the nobles and soon by the deputies to the legislature, could not cope with the fiscal crisis and the demands for radical reforms. In September 1790 he retired from public office for the last time and returned to Switzerland. There he lived with his famous daughter Madame Germaine de Staël and wrote a number of works defending his policies. Necker died on April 4, 1804.

Further Reading

The most scholarly biographies of Necker are in French. In English, Mark Gambier-Parry, *Madame Necker, Her Family and Her Friends* (1913), offers some information on Necker's administrations. Useful background works include Hippolyte A. Taine, *The French Revolution* (3 vols., 1878), and Alfred Cobban, *A History of Modern France* (1957).

Additional Sources

Harris, Robert D., *Necker and the revolution of 1789,* Lanham, MD: University Press of America, 1986. □

Nefertiti

Nefertiti (1390 B.C.-ca. 1360 B.C.) was an Egyptian quenn who still remains a mystery to scholars today.

One of the most famous women in antiquity, Nefertiti remains somewhat of a puzzlement to scholars because of her mysterious ancestry and her disappearance from the record during the last years of Akhenaten's reign. Some believe that she was of Egyptian blood, others that she was a foreign princess. Her name, which translates to "The Beautiful One is Come," is an Egyptian birthname—thus not indicative of a foreign birth—and evidence indicates that she had an Egyptian wet-nurse or governess of noble rank, strong support for a birth within the circle of the Egyptian royal court. She may have been a niece of Ay, who ascended to the throne after Tutankhamen.

Her role, if any, late in Akhenaten's rule remains equally unclear. During the first five years of his reign, Nefertiti enjoyed a high profile, and the large number of carved scenes in which she is shown accompanying him during the ceremonial acts he performed is evidence of her political importance. She is depicted taking part in the daily worship and making offerings similar to those of the king— acts quite unlike those relegated to the generally subservient status of previous chief queens. But after the 14th year of Akhenaten's rule, Nefertiti disappears from view. Some have hypothesized that she was the power behind the throne and thus responsible for the innovations during his rule until being dismissed from her position and banished to the North Palace at Amarna. Her banishment would there-fore reflect within the royal family an ideological rift, with Nefertiti favoring the continued worship of Aten while Akhenaten and Tutankhamen supported a return to the wor-ship of Amen-Re. Most scholars, however, now suppose that Nefertiti simply died soon after Akhenaten's 14th regnal year, after which first Meritaten and then Ankhesenpaten took her place at the pharaoh's side. A more dramatic, if less accepted, theory holds that she assumed a new, masculine, identity toward the end of Akhenaten's rule—that Nefertiti and the young pharaoh Smenkhkare were, in fact, the same person. ☐

Jawaharlal Nehru

Jawaharlal Nehru (1889-1964) was a great Indian nationalist leader who worked for independence and social reform. He became first prime minister of in-dependent India, a position he retained until his death. He initiated India's nonalignment policy in foreign affairs.

Jawaharlal Nehru was born on Nov. 14, 1889, in Al-lahabad into a proud, learned Kashmiri Brahmin family. His father, Motilal Nehru, was a wealthy barrister and influential politician. Jawaharlal was an only child until the age of 11, after which two sisters were born. The atmo-sphere in the Nehru home was more English than Indian; English was spoken. It was also a luxurious home, with an impressive stable and two swimming pools. Jawaharlal was educated at home by tutors, most of them English or Scot-tish. Under the influence of a tutor Nehru joined the Theosophical Society at 13.

At the age of 15 Nehru left for England, where he studied at Harrow and Cambridge and then for the bar in London. He was called to the bar in 1912. His English experience reinforced his elegant and cosmopolitan tastes. As Nehru said of himself at Cambridge, "In my likes and dislikes I was perhaps more an Englishman than an Indian." In London he was attracted by Fabian ideas; nationalism and socialism from this time on provided his intellectual motive force.

Early Political Moves

Back in India, Nehru began to practice law with his father. It was not until 1917 that Nehru was stirred by a political issue, the imprisonment of Annie Besant, an Irish theosophist devoted to Indian freedom. As a result, Nehru became active in the Home Rule League. His involvement in the nationalist movement gradually replaced his legal practice. In 1916 Nehru was married to Kamala Kaul, of an orthodox Kashmiri Brahmin family. They had one daughter (later Indira Gandhi, third prime minister of independent India).

Apart from his father and Besant, the greatest influence on Nehru politically was Mohandas Gandhi. Gandhi had been educated much like Nehru but, unlike him, remained basically untouched, essentially Indian. A second issue which fired Nehru's nationalism and led him to join Gandhi was the Amritsar massacre of 1919, in which some 400 Indians were shot on orders of a British officer.

The year 1920 marked Nehru's first contact with the Indian *kisan,* the peasant majority. Nehru was "filled with shame and sorrow . . . at the degradation and overwhelming poverty of India." This experience aroused a sympathy for the underdog which characterized many of Nehru's later political moves. The plight of the peasant was a challenge to his socialist convictions, and he attempted to persuade the peasants to organize. From this time on Nehru's concerns were Indian. He began to read the *Bhagavad Gita* and practiced vegetarianism briefly. Most of his life he practiced yoga daily.

In 1921 Nehru followed Gandhi in sympathy with the Khilafat cause of the Moslems. Nehru was drawn into the first civil disobedience campaign as general secretary of the United Provinces Congress Committee. Nehru remarked, "I took to the crowd, and the crowd took to me, and yet I never lost myself in it." Nehru here articulated two of his most distinctive traits throughout his career: his involvement with the people and his aloof and lonely detachment. The year 1921 also witnessed the first of Nehru's many imprisonments. In prison his political philosophy matured, and he said that he learned patience and adaptability. Imprisonment was also a criterion of political success.

International Influences

In 1926-1927 Nehru took his wife to Europe for her health. This experience became a turning point for Nehru. It was an intellectual sojourn, highlighted by an antiimperialist conference in Brussels. Here Nehru first encountered Communists, Socialists, and radical nationalists from Asia and Africa. The goals of independence and social reform became firmly linked in Nehru's mind. Nehru spoke eloquently against imperialism and became convinced of the need for a socialist structure of society. He was impressed with the Soviet example during a visit to Moscow.

Back in India Nehru was immediately engrossed in party conferences and was elected president of the All-India Trades Union Congress. In speeches he linked the goals of independence and socialism. In 1928 he joined the radical opposition to proposals for dominion status by his father and Gandhi. In 1930 Gandhi threw his weight to Nehru as Congress president, attempting to divert radicalism from communism to the Congress.

In 1930 Nehru was arrested and imprisoned for violation of the Salt Law, which Gandhi also protested in his famous "salt march." Nehru's wife was also arrested. From the end of 1931 to September 1935 Nehru was free only 6 months.

During the 1937 elections the Moslem League offered to cooperate with the All-India Congress Committee in forming a coalition government in the United Provinces. Nehru refused, and the struggle between the Congress and the Moslem League was under way. Nehru also established the precedent for economic planning in a suggestion that the Congress form a national planning committee. In 1938 Nehru paid a brief visit to Europe. On his return he was sent briefly as envoy to China until war intervened and made it necessary for him to return.

War in Europe drew India in, together with England. For Indian leaders the question was how an honorable settlement could be reached with England and still allow India to participate on the Allied side. Negotiations toward this end culminated in the Cripps mission and offer of dominion status in March 1942. Nehru refused to accept dominion status, as did the rest of Congress leadership. There followed the Congress "Quit India" resolution and the imprisonment of Nehru, Gandhi, and other Congress leaders until June 1945. There were nationwide protests, a mass demand for independence.

Prime Minister

In 1945, as Congress president, Nehru was pressed into negotiations with the Moslem League and the viceroy. Congress-Moslem League negotiations were marked by communal killings in Calcutta, followed by sympathetic outbreaks throughout India. Final decisions were reached in conversations between the last British viceroy, Lord Mountbatten, and Nehru, Gandhi, and Mohammad Ali Jinnah. According to the Mountbatten Plan, two separate dominions were created. Nehru became prime minister and minister of external affairs of independent India in 1947.

Following Gandhi's assassination in January 1948, Nehru felt very much alone facing economic problems and the possibility of the Balkanization of India. In 1949 he made his first visit to the United States in search of a solution to India's pressing food shortage.

Free India's first elections in 1951-1952 resulted in an overwhelming Congress victory. Economic planning and welfare were the first claims on Nehru's attention. He inaugurated a diluted version of socialist planning: concentration of public investment in areas of the economy that were free from private interests. The Planning Commission was created in 1950 and launched the First Five-Year Plan in 1951, stressing an increase in agricultural output. Nehru also took pride in the Community Development Program, established to raise the standard of living in the villages. He saw the Third Five-Year Plan operative before his death on May 27, 1964, in New Delhi.

Nehru was the architect of nonalignment in foreign policy. Economic weakness and the Indian tradition were powerful factors in formulating the policy. The other influence on Nehru's foreign policy was his controversial minister of defense, Krishna Menon. Nehru sought closer relations with nonaligned Asian states, with India in the role of leader.

Nehru's nonalignment policy was criticized by many Westerners and some Indians as giving preference to totalitarian countries rather than to democracies. Some critics believed that nonalignment left India no effective means to deal with China, national defense, the Great Powers, or the underdeveloped community. On the other hand, nonalignment had many Indian defenders, even in the face of the Chinese invasion of Indian border territory in 1962. Some held that nonalignment was a strategy for deterrence and peace, a force for protecting Indian independence and preservation of the international community on ethical grounds. Nevertheless, nonalignment as implemented by Nehru did not prevent the government from resorting to force in Hyderabad, Kashmir, and Goa.

Nehru the man and politician made such a powerful imprint on India that his death on May 27, 1964, left India with no political heir to his leadership. Indians repeated Nehru's own words of the time of Gandhi's assassination: "The light has gone out of our lives and there is darkness everywhere."

Further Reading

A useful collection of Nehru's speeches and writings is *Nehru: The First Sixty Years,* selected and edited by Dorothy Norman (2 vols., 1965). Major biographies are Frank Moraes, *Jawaharlal Nehru* (1956); Donald E. Smith, *Nehru and Democracy: The Political Thought of an Asian Democrat* (1958); Michael Brecher, *Nehru: A Political Biography* (1960); and M. N. Das, *The Political Philosophy of Jawaharlal Nehru* (1961). A journalistic account, written by an intimate of the Nehru household, is Marie Seton, *Panditiji: A Portrait of Jawaharlal Nehru* (1967), a valuable book for students of Indian politics and history. A somewhat simplified biography, particularly suitable for young adults and casual readers, is Bani Shorter, *Nehru: A Voice for Mankind* (1970).

Works that assess Nehru's achievements and evaluate his place in history include K. Natwar-Singh, ed., *The Legacy of Nehru: A Memorial Tribute* (1965); *The Emerging World: Jawaharlal Nehru Memorial Volume* (1965); and G. S. Jolly, ed., *The Image of Nehru* (1969), all of which are laudatory and should be balanced by more critical appraisals, such as that in Brecher's biography. Walter Crocker, an intimate friend, yet sometimes a critic, of Nehru, wrote *Nehru: A Contemporary's Estimate* (1966), which is a more balanced appraisal. Paul F. Power and Columbia University Committee on Oriental Studies, eds., *India's Nonalignment Policy* (1967), deals with various Indian and foreign views of Nehru's foreign policy and contains a good bibliography on the subject. Another work by Michael Brecher, *Nehru's Mantle: The Politics of Succession in India* (1966), analyzes the parliamentary system in India that made possible a peaceful succession. □

Motilal Nehru

Motilal Nehru (1861-1931) was an Indian lawyer and statesman who influenced the fate of the Indian nation not only by direct political action but also through his offspring, whom he educated.

Motilal Nehru was born in Allahabad on May 6, 1861, into the Kashmiri Brahmin community, most aristocratic of Hindu subcastes. His father, serving as a police officer in Delhi, had lost his job and property in the mutiny of 1857. A posthumous son, Nehru got his early education at home in Persian and Arabic and spoke Urdu as his mother tongue, reflecting the fusion of Hindu and Moslem cultures in the United Provinces. He attended the government high school in Cawnpore and matriculated at Muir Central College in Allahabad. Though he did not complete his degree, he passed the examinations as a lawyer. Following an apprenticeship in Cawnpore, he began practice at the High Court in Allahabad in 1886.

Nehru was twice married but while still in his teens lost his first wife and a child. Jawaharlal Nehru, Vijaya Lakshmi Pandit, and Krishna Hutheesing were children of his second marriage. Nehru was a strong-willed, imperious man who lived the life of an English gentleman, traveled in Europe, and imported to India one of the first automobiles.

Motilal Nehru was too independent to acquiesce in orthodox caste strictures. Returning to India from a trip to London, he explained: "My mind is made up. I will not indulge in the tomfoolery of the *prayshchit* [purification ceremony]." He developed advanced social ideas and wielded a powerful influence in forging the secular outlook of the Congress party organization. When Mohandas Gandhi appeared on the political scene, he attracted a large following of young nationalists, including Jawaharlal.

The relationship between Motilal Nehru and his son was very close and significant in the leadership of the nationalist movement. Motilal Nehru and Gandhi by 1920 were also close allies as leaders in the Congress Working Committee, Nehru representing the Congress party Old Guard and Gandhi the new power of the masses. Through Gandhi's influence Nehru gave up his practice and devoted himself wholly to the nationalist cause. Gandhi hesitated to make important decisions without consulting both Nehrus.

Known as a moderate realist early in his career, Motilal Nehru became increasingly revolutionary with age. To a group of several thousand people he proclaimed in 1917: "The Government has openly declared a crusade against our national aims . . . Are we going to succumb to these official frowns?" He was imprisoned together with his son in 1921. With Chitta Ranjan Das, Nehru formed the Swaraj (Freedom) party in 1922, which generaly followed Congress party policies. He served several times as president and secretary of the Congress party. One of his chief concerns was the problem of Hindu-Moslem unity, reflecting the blend of influences in his background. His son, Jawaharlal, and granddaughter, Indira Gandhi, both prime ministers of

India, gained experience and a taste and aptitude for politics through his guidance. He died on Feb. 6, 1931.

Further Reading

Books on Nehru include S.P. Chablani, ed., *Motilal Nehru: Essays and Reflections on His Life and Times* (1961); Bal Ram Nanda, *The Nehrus: Motilal and Jawaharlal Motilal Nehru* (1962); and Beatrice Lamb, *The Nehrus of India: Three Generations of Leadership* (1967).

Additional Sources

Bhattacharyya, Upendra Chandra, *Pandit Motilal Nehru: his life and work,* Delhi: B.R. Pub. Corp.; New Delhi: Distributed by D.K. Publishers' Distributors, 1985. □

Alexander Sutherland Neill

The Scottish psychologist Alexander Sutherland Neill (1883- 1973) is most famous as the founder of Summerhill School and as the developer of its radical child-centered theory of education.

A Failure at School

Born in Forfar, Scotland, on Oct. 18, 1883, Alexander S. Neill received his early education in his father's one-room, five-class village school. Because of his inability to progress very far in education, he was the only child in the family who was not sent on to Forfar Academy.

At the age of 14, Neill went to work as an office boy in an Edinburgh factory, but he became so lonely and homesick that his parents allowed him to return home. He then worked as an assistant in a dry-goods shop. Shortly thereafter, he became a pupil-teacher in his father's school, where he remained for four years. He then spent what he described as three wretched years as a teacher in a school in Fife, received his teaching certification, and moved on to a school where discipline was easier and his life was somewhat happier for two years.

At the age of 25 Neill enrolled as a student of agriculture at Edinburgh University. Although he passed his first year's program, he said he understood little of the lectures. Changing his major to English, he came under the influence of the scholar and prose stylist George Saintsbury and received his master's degree in 1912. He then worked briefly in journalism and did editorial work for an encyclopedia.

Progressive Influences

At the beginning of World War I, Neill became headmaster of a coeducational school in Scotland which pre-

pared its students for work on farms and in domestic service. It was at this time that he first became convinced that conventional education was oppressive and futile.

Neill voluntarily left the school for a brief sojourn as an artillery cadet. There he met Homer Lane, one of the early advocates of "progressive education," who introduced him to Freudian psychology and convinced him that the best way to deal with a recalcitrant or delinquent child is to allow the child to govern himself. Following the war Neill had a brief appointment at the King Alfred School in Hampstead, where he tried to implement his theory of self-government for children. He was forced to resign in 1920.

Creating Child-Centered Education

After a short stint as coeditor of the *New Era* (the organ of the New Education Fellowship), Neill and several others founded Summerhill, an international school near Dresden, Germany, in 1921. Political turmoil in Dresden caused him to move the school to the Austrian Tirol. However, the peasants in that area and the Austrian government became upset with his unorthodox curriculum and methods, and after seven months of harassment, he removed the school to England in 1924, establishing it in the town of Leiston in Suffix.

In his influential 1960 book *Summerhill: A Radical Approach to Child Rearing,* one of 21 books he wrote, Neill recalled that he and his first wife, Ada, wanted "to make the school fit the child instead of making the child fit the school." To do so, he wrote, the founders renounced "all discipline, all direction, all suggestion, all moral training, all religious training." Ada died in 1944, and Neill remarried the next year, to Edna May Wood. They had one daughter .

Neill founded Summerhill as a small, coeducational, self-governing boarding school. Class attendance and extracurricular activities were optional. There was no teaching method, leaving children free to learn by their own impulse. Rules were decided in a weekly general assembly, at which each student and teacher had one vote. The children were segregated in housing by age groups, with a house mother for each age.

Neill believed many of children's problems resulted from poor sex education. He tried to demonstrated how the family created hates and jealousies. Neill denied that the atmosphere at Summerhill was "permissive." He did not believe in giving children everything they wanted nor in allowing them to violate another's rights, but he cautioned against moral judgments. He argued that other systems of education did nothing more than coerce children into the neurotic image of their elders.

The Summerhill Legacy

In the 1960s and 1970s, Summerhill became a model for child-centered schools in the United States and elsewhere. Neill became the center of controversy over traditional versus alternative education. Unwavering, Neill noted: "People so often fail to understand that freedom for children does not mean being a fool about children." He titled his 1972 autobiography *Neill! Neill! Orange Peel!* after a child's taunt that he turned into a comic tradition at Summerhill. Christopher Lehmann-Haupt, reviewing the book in the *New York Times,* noted Neill's "practical good sense about the worthlessness of most education, and his passionate desire to connect life with learning, thinking with feeling" as well as "his patiently reasonable, flawlessly logical, but always witty arguments against repression and punishment" and "his careful distinction between freedom and license." Neill once said that "the absence of fear is the finest thing that can happen to a child" and said his role at Summerhill was to "sit still and approve of all the things that a child disapproves of in himself."

Further Reading

Works by Neill include, *A Domine's Log* (1916); *A Domine Dismissed* (1917); *Summerhill: A Radical Approach to Child Rearing* (1960); *The Booming of a Bunkie: A History* (1919); *A Domine in Doubt* (1922); *A Domine Abroad* (1923); *The Problem Child* (1927); *The Problem Parent* (1932); *That Dreadful School* (1937); *The Free Child* (1953); and *Neill! Neill! Orange Peel!"* (1972). Studies of Neill and his career include Leslie R. Perry, ed., *Bertrand Russell, A. S. Neill, Homer Lane, W. H. Kilpatrick: Four Progressive Educators* (1967) and *Summerhill: For and Against* (1970). □

Horatio Nelson

The English admiral and naval hero Horatio Nelson, Viscount Nelson (1758-1805), was noted for his bravery and for his victories, including the decisive Battle of Trafalgar. He ranks as the last great naval hero of a proud seafaring nation.

Horatio Nelson was born at Burnham Thorpe on Sept. 29, 1758. He entered the Royal Navy at the age of 12, and by 20 he had risen from midshipman to commander. In 1780 Nelson took a convoy to America and the West Indies, but the Admiralty placed him on half pay the next year after the American Revolution ended. Nelson then went to France to learn the language.

In 1784 Nelson was given command of the *Boreas* and sent again to the West Indies. There he gained considerable ill will by seizing five American merchantmen who were violating the Navigation Acts through irregular trading. He also met a young widow, Mrs. Frances Nisbet, whom he married in 1787. Nelson was then ordered home. For nearly 6 years, somewhat in disfavor at the Admiralty, he was unemployed. But when England entered the French Revolutionary Wars in 1793, Nelson was given command of the *Agamemnon* and sent to the Mediterranean Sea. In August he arrived at Naples, where he met Sir William Hamilton, the English ambassador, and his charming young wife, Emma. Nelson's romantic and naval careers both began to blossom.

Rising Hero

In 1794 Lord (Samuel) Hood sent Nelson, in command of seamen and marines, to build and arm batteries about

Basti during the English attack on Corsica. He was successful in this assignment and also at Calvi, where he lost the sight of his right eye as the result of a stone-splinter wound during a cannonade against one of his batteries. Nelson's eye patch soon became a symbol. In 1796 Nelson was made commodore and sent to harass the French coastal trade. Then, as commander of the *Captain,* he joined Sir John Jervis's fleet.

On Feb. 13, 1797, while on a southerly course off Portugal, the British sighted the Spanish fleet in loose formation heading north. Jervis steered between the two halves of the enemy, but he misjudged his course reversal. Nelson perceived the problem, boldly broke away from the line, and headed for the Spaniards. Jervis, seeing Nelson's intention, ordered Cuthbert Collingwood to aid him. The result was that Nelson and Collingwood hit the Spanish fleet and threw it into confusion, enabling the rest of Jervis's ships to come up and to achieve a victory. Fortunately for Nelson, Jervis was not a stickler about rules. Nelson was praised for his action rather than court-martialed as he feared. As a result of the victory off Cape Saint Vincent, Nelson received promotion to rear admiral.

Victorious Admiral

Returning once again to the inshore squadron off France, Nelson lost his right arm in an attempt to cut out a treasure ship at Santa Cruz de Tenerife. In April 1798 he rejoined the fleet and was sent to watch the French fleet at Toulon. Eventually, the French evaded Nelson. He pursued them to Alexandria, Egypt, and found the French fleet an-

chored in Aboukir Bay. Now Nelson's careful training of his captains paid dividends when he discovered that the French were prepared only for attack from the sea. As dusk fell, his ships approached the French line from the west, splitting as they reached the anchored vessels so that they doubled up, one on each side of the enemy. The result was the complete annihilation of all the French ships except two frigates that escaped. Napoleon I and the entire French army were left stranded in Egypt. As soon as the news reached Britain, Nelson was created Baron Nelson of the Nile. His name became known throughout Europe.

Nelson then returned to Naples, which, having declared war on Napoleon, had been overcome by French troops and fifth columnists while Nelson was at Leghorn. Hastily recalled, Nelson insisted on the annulment of the capitulation agreed to by the Neapolitan general Fabrifio Ruffo and on the absolute surrender of the Neapolitan Jacobins. He court-martialed and hanged the Neapolitan commodore Francesco Caracciolo, who had deserted, and he restored civil power. For these acts the grateful king of the Two Sicilies made him Duke of Bronte.

During this period Nelson became infatuated with Emma, Lady Hamilton. While living with her, he conducted the blockades of Egypt and Malta. In 1800 he was permitted to return home because of ill health, and he traveled across Europe with the Hamiltons. In London he met his wife and separated amicably from her. That same year, 1801, Lady Hamilton bore Nelson a daughter, Horatia.

In 1801 Nelson was promoted to vice-admiral and sent as second-in-command to Sir Hyde Parker on an expedition to break up the armed Northern Neutrality League. His first act upon joining was characteristically direct and insubordinate—he wrote to the Admiralty that Sir Hyde stayed abed late with his young wife. The expedition sailed shortly. The Danes refused the British ultimatum, and Nelson was given the job of attacking the anchored Danish fleet and hulks in Copenhagen harbor. He skillfully moved his fleet through shoals after rebuoying the channel, and then on the morning of April 2, 1801, he fought a bitter 4-hour action that resulted in eventual victory. The battle was ended by an armistice called for by Nelson in order to save the lives of Danish sailors. Though his ships were badly battered and he had ignored an optional recall signal flown by Sir Hyde Parker, Nelson achieved a diplomatic success and was created a viscount.

Nelson returned to England, where in order to impress the French he was put in command off Dover. This command was not a great success, and Nelson's expedition against Boulogne became an expensive failure because the French were prepared. As soon as the armistice that led to the Peace of Amiens in 1801 was signed, Nelson came ashore and settled with the Hamiltons on his new estate at Merton, Surrey, about an hour's drive from the Admiralty. Sir William Hamilton died in April 1803, and thereafter Nelson and Lady Hamilton were together exclusively.

Battle of Trafalgar

Upon the outbreak of war again in 1803, Nelson was dispatched to command the fleet in the Mediterranean.

There he watched the French under adverse circumstances, blockading the French fleet at Toulon for 22 months. In January 1805 Napoleon decided that the way to conquer the whole of Europe was to combine the French and Spanish fleets in the West Indies, lure the English away from the Channel, and seize the British Isles. With this in mind, the French commander, Pierre de Villeneuve, gave Nelson the slip and headed west while Nelson chased east to Egypt in vain. Dogged by poor intelligence reports and foul winds, Nelson pursued the French to Martinique and back to Europe but could not overtake them. Meanwhile, the returning French fleet had been met off Cape Finisterre by Sir Robert Calder.

On Oct. 9, 1805, Nelson arrived once more off the European coast. He resumed command off Cadiz and issued his famous order for the fleet to attack in two columns. On October 21 Nelson came upon the combined French and Spanish fleets, under Villeneuve, sailing north in a long crescent column off Cape Trafalgar, Spain. Hoisting a signal that became immortal, "England expects every man to do his duty," Nelson led the northern column to cut off and hold the Allied van while Collingwood annihilated the center and rear. Nelson, in spite of advice, insisted upon wearing his full uniform into battle, and at the height of the encounter he was badly wounded by a musket shot from the fighting top of the French ship *Redoubtable*, which his flagship *Victory* had fouled. He died 3 hours later as the victory, one of the most significant in history, was completed. Twenty enemy ships were captured, and one was blown up. The English lost no ships. This decisive English victory ended Napoleon's power on the sea.

Nelson's body was placed in a cask of brandy and carried home for burial in St. Paul's Cathedral, London. The celebrated Nelson Column in Trafalgar Square, London, commemorates Nelson's victory.

Nelson the Man

No one, perhaps, better symbolized the British hero than Nelson—dashing naval commander, viscount, and lover. More than this, Nelson ranks high as a leader of men not only for the bravery and dash he displayed at Cape Saint Vincent, but also for his coolness under fire, his joy in battle, and the humanity he displayed at Copenhagen. Nelson was a beloved leader because he knew his officers and men. His captains knew what he wanted to do and how he thought it should be done. The whole combination was called the Nelson touch.

Further Reading

The best accounts of Nelson are by English naval historian Oliver Warner, *A Portrait of Lord Nelson* (1958; American title, *Victory*) and *Nelson's Battles* (1964), which updates the previous work and includes many portraits and illustrations of the battles. A worthwhile book is Sir William M. James, *The Durable Monument* (1948). Other studies include Robert Southey, *Southey's Life of Nelson*, edited by Kenneth Fenwich (1813; new ed. 1956), and Alfred T. Mahan, *The Life of Nelson: The Embodiment of the Sea Power of Great Britain* (1968). An excellent account of the Battle of Trafalgar is by a distinguished chronicler of the Napoleonic Wars, David Ho-

warth, *Trafalgar: The Nelson Touch* (1969), which makes good use of the most recent studies by naval historians and is interspersed with first-rate illustrations. See also Jack Russell, *Nelson and the Hamiltons* (1969). For more on Nelson and his navy in general see Robin Higham, ed., *A Guide to the Sources of British Military History* (1971), and G. J. Marcus, *The Age of Nelson* (1972).

Additional Sources

Bradford, Ernle Dusgate Selby., *Nelson: the essential hero,* New York: Harcourt Brace Jovanovich, 1977.

Delaforce, Patrick., *Nelson's first Love: Fanny's story,* London: Bishopsgate Press, 1988.

Grenfell, Russell., *Horatio Nelson: a short biography,* Westport, Conn.: Greenwood Press, 1978.

Hattersley, Roy., *Nelson,* New York, Saturday Review Press 1974.

Hibbert, Christopher, *Nelson: a personal history,* Reading, Mass.: Addison-Wesley, 1994.

Howarth, David Armine, *Lord Nelson: the immortal memory,* New York: Viking, 1989, 1988.

The Nelson companion, Annapolis, MD: Naval Institute Press, 1995.

Pocock, Tom., *Horatio Nelson,* New York: Knopf, 1988.

Pocock, Tom., *The young Nelson in the Americas,* London: Collins, 1980.

Walder, David., *Nelson,* London: Hamilton, 1978.

Walder, David., *Nelson, a biography,* New York: Dial Press/J. Wade, 1978.

Warner, Oliver, *A portrait of Lord Nelson,* Harmondsworth, Middlesex, England; New York, N.Y., U.S.A.: Penguin Books in association with Chatto & Windus, 1987, 1958. □

Howard Nemerov

The American writer Howard Nemerov (1920-1991) was recognized for his novels, short stories, criticism, nonfiction, drama, and satiric poetry, as well as for being the third poet laureate of the United States.

Howard Nemerov was born on March 1, 1920, in New York City. His parents were David and Gertrude (Russek) Nemerov. David, his father, served as president and chairman of the board of Russeks, a now defunct but once prestigious retail store, where he earned the reputation of "Merchant Prince." The elder Nemerov's talents and interests extended to art connoisseurship, painting, and philanthropy—talents and interests undoubtedly influential upon his son.

Young Howard was raised in a sophisticated New York City environment where he attended the Society for Ethical Culture's Fieldstone School. Graduated in 1937 as an outstanding student and second string team football fullback, he commenced studies at Harvard University where, in 1940, he was Bowdoin Essayist and, in 1941, earned the Bachelor of Arts degree.

Upon graduation at the age of 21 he joined a Royal Canadian unit of the U.S. Army Airforce, serving as a pilot throughout World War II. After training in both Canada and England, he flew coastal command missions over the North Sea and was discharged in 1945 at the rank of first lieutenant. Prior to discharge he married Margaret Russel, on January 26, 1944.

Returning from the war, he and his wife spent a year in New York where he finished work on his first book of poetry. Nemerov then turned to college teaching—a profession he found compatible with his writing career. He served on the faculties of Hamilton College in Clinton, New York (1946-1948); Bennington College in Bennington, Vermont (1948-1966); Brandeis University in Waltham, Massachusetts (1966-1969); and in 1969 joined the faculty of Washington University in St. Louis, Missouri. During this time Howard and Margaret parented three sons: David, Alexander, and Jeremy.

During the years 1963 and 1964, Nemerov served as consultant in poetry to the Library of Congress, where later he held the post of poet laureate of the United States (1988-1990). Nemerov became a member of the American Academy of Arts and Letters in 1977. In 1978 he was recipient of both the Pulitzer Prize in Arts and Letters and the National Book Award for his *Collected Poems*.

The early promise of Nemerov's first book of verse, *The Image and the Law* (1947), was satisfyingly fulfilled in his later publication of poems, *War Stories* (1987), which provides a kindly light on the bleak landscape of contemporary American poetry. Nemerov persisted in a gentle irony which satirizes as much through self-deprecation as indict-

ment of others, a kind of collective guilt and redemption exquisitely expressed in his 1980 poem "The Historical Judas," whose name" . . . shall surely live/To make our meanness look like justice in/All histories commissioned by the winners."

Transcending mere polemic, Nemerov's poetic argument with history captivates, by virtue of his humor and humanism. Composing in narrative, meditative, lyrical, satirical, and a variety of other forms, Nemerov's poems are profoundly concerned with the individual perception of nature, and human history as a part of nature—a concern which might be intellectually ponderous were it not for the comic relief provided by his native wit. But Nemerov is a poet, not a philosopher, and his poetic wit disperses accusations of academic philosophical waxing with a whip woven of puns, slang, and irony.

Nemerov's quarrel with the world resounds with the lesson that humanity does not learn from history, but is seemingly doomed to repeat mistakes of the past. The importance of hope itself becomes ironic at the hands of the poet, as notice is made of the contradictions between the facts of history and the fictions of human aspiration. Sharing the collective guilt of the humorist, Nemerov's irony is sometimes too light an instrument for the dispatch of the sorrows of the human condition. Nemerov was perhaps a bit too accepting of man's inevitable fate; but neither is he a Pangloss (incurable optimist) nor a rager against the night.

Nemerov's poetic vision, his perceptual struggle with illusion and reality through a mysterious roseate but dark glass, never descended from poetic flight to epistemological speculation—not even on that most dangerous killing ground of political poetry. In versatile blank verse, Nemerov was at his best, conjuring the poetic experience out of a sense elusive world.

In spite of his other endeavors as editor, critic, and nonfiction writer, Nemerov was a master at throwing the magic switch between the prose and poetic modes of composition. Facile accusations of academicality, intellectuality, and ideationality against his poetry pale in confrontation with the poetic imagery of his 1967 poem "The May Dancing." Another 1967 poem, "Learning by Doing," mildly reminiscent of Frost's "Birches," is fraught with imagery, as is his 1989 publication "Landscape With Self Portrait."

If, in both his earlier and later works, his historical imagery is mistaken for history per se, the fault is not his. Nemerov pointed out clearly that: "The reason we do not learn from history is/Because we are not the people who learned the last time." Knowledge is not inherited, but must be earned by each new generation. Today's history lesson derives from yesterday's characters; events and ideas become image and metaphor in poetic time; time mellows metaphor into symbol and myth.

All too lazy an age has wrongfully castigated Nemerov for his technical knowledge of poetry, his use of form, and his foundation in tradition. In essence, his versification virtues are mistakenly deemed vices; his own historical poetic derivation is unrecognized by those ignorant of that poetic history; his artistic order is minimized as mere orderliness by the disorderly—and still, a well turned scherzo refreshes, and craft and art are still the best of friends.

On July 5, 1991, Howard Nemerov died of cancer at his home in University City, Missouri.

Further Reading

Additional information on Howard Nemerov and his work can be found in Edward Hungerford, editor, *Poets in Progress* (1962); Howard Nemerov, *Poetry and Fiction: Essays.* New Brunswick, N 43. *Reflexions on Poetry & Poetics* (1972); and Raymond Smith, ''Nemerov and Nature: 'The Stillness in Moving Things,'' *SoR* (January 1974). Selections from Nemerov's poetry, short fiction, and essays were published by the University of Missouri Press in *A Howard Nemerov Reader* (1991).

Additional Sources

Nemerov, Howard., *Journal of the fictive life,* Chicago: University of Chicago Press, 1981. □

St. Philip Neri

The Italian reformer St. Philip Neri (1515-1595) is known as the Apostle of Rome. With his distinctly joyous and personal manner, he was one of the influential figures of the Catholic Reformation. His special contribution was the creation of the Congregation of the Oratory.

Philip Neri was born in Florence on July 21, 1515, the son of a lawyer. As a boy, Philip befriended the Dominicans at the convent of S. Marco. In 1532 or 1533 he went to San Germano (Cassino) to learn business under the tutelage of an uncle, but, repelled by commercial affairs and feeling a pronounced desire for a life of close union with God, he left San Germano after a few months and went to Rome. There he studied philosophy and theology at Sapienza University and Sant'Agostino. He made friends easily and met regularly with some of them at the church of S. Girolamo della Carità for discussion, prayer, and the reception of Holy Communion. S. Girolamo became his home for 32 years. On May 23, 1551, after 18 years in Rome, Philip was ordained a priest. His room, the center for the intimate and prayerful meetings, became known about 1554 as the ''Oratory.''

Philip, who dreaded formalism and loved spontaneity, gave his little groups a definite character. Scripture readings, short commentaries, brief prayers, and hymns were the usual program. Giovanni Palestrina wrote much of the musical setting for the scriptural texts, the motets, and the *laudi spirituali,* which gave rise to the term ''oratorio.'' This kind of apostolate suffered under the stern pontificates of Paul IV and Pius V. But Philip numbered among his friends some of the great saints of the age: Charles Borromeo, Francis de Sales, Felix of Cantalice, Camillus de Lellis, and Ignatius of Loyola. As more priests became his followers, Philip, who

did not wish a tightly organized group united by religious vows, created a congregation of secular priests living in community. In 1575 Pope Gregory XIII approved the Congregation of the Oratory.

Philip's famous walks especially won him the title Apostle of Rome. Surrounded by a laughing and joking group, he penetrated all corners of the city, radiating gaiety by his simple friendship and playful wit. Beneath his external life were the deep foundations of an intense spirit of prayer and love for the priestly offices of hearing confessions and offering the Mass. For hours at a time, he received an abundance of unusual supernatural gifts when he was wrapped in ecstasy. In 1575 S. Maria in. Vallicella became the Oratorians' church. Philip moved there in 1583, and there he died on May 26, 1595.

Further Reading

A most readable and scholarly biography is Louis Ponnelle and Louis Bordet, *St. Philip Neri and the Roman Society of His Times, 1515-1595,* translated by Ralph F. Kerr (1932). Louis Bouyer wrote a beautifully sensitive appreciation of St. Philip in *The Roman Socrates,* translated by Michael Day (1958). □

Walther Nernst

Walther Nernst (1864-1941) made a significant breakthrough with his statement of the Third Law of Thermodynamics, which holds that it should be im-

possible to attain the temperature of absolute zero in any real experiment. For this accomplishment, he was awarded the 1920 Nobel Prize for chemistry.

In addition to his important work with thermodynamics, Walther Nernst made contributions to the field of physical chemistry. While still in his twenties, he devised a mathematical expression showing how electromotive force is dependent upon temperature and concentration in a galvanic, or electricity-producing, cell. He later developed a theory to explain how ionic, or charged, compounds break down in water, a problem that had troubled chemists since the theory of ionization was proposed by Svante A. Arrhenius .

Born Hermann Walther Nernst in Briesen, West Prussia (in what is now part of Poland) on June 25, 1864, he was the third child of Gustav Nernst, a judge, and Ottilie (Nerger) Nernst. He attended the gymnasium at Graudenz (now Grudziadz), Poland, where he developed an interest in poetry, literature, and drama. For a brief time, he considered becoming a poet. After graduation in 1883, Nernst attended the universities of Zurich, Berlin, Graz, and Würzburg, majoring in physics at each institution. He was awarded his Ph.D. summa cum laude in 1887 by Würzburg. His doctoral thesis dealt with the effects of magnetism and heat on electrical conductivity.

Nernst's first academic appointment came in 1887 when he was chosen as an assistant to professor Friedrich

Wilhelm Ostwald at the University of Leipzig. Ostwald had been introduced to Nernst earlier in Graz by Svante Arrhenius. These three, Ostwald, Arrhenius, and Nernst, were to become among the most influential men involved in the founding of the new discipline of physical chemistry, the application of physical laws to chemical phenomena.

The first problem Nernst addressed at Leipzig was the diffusion of two kinds of ions across a semipermeable membrane. He wrote a mathematical equation describing the process, now known as the Nernst equation, which relates the electric potential of the ions to various properties of the cell.

In the early 1890s, Nernst accepted a teaching position appointment at the University of Göttingen in Leipzig, and soon after married Emma Lohmeyer, the daughter of a surgeon. The Nernsts had five children, three daughters and two sons. In 1894, Nernst was promoted to full professor at Göttingen. At the same time, he also received approval for the creation of a new Institute for Physical Chemistry and Electrochemistry at the university.

At Göttingen, Nernst wrote a textbook on physical chemistry, *Theoretische Chemie vom Standpunkte der Avogadroschen Regel und der Thermodynamik* (*Theoretical Chemistry from the Standpoint of Avogadro's Rule and Thermodynamics*). Published in 1893, it had an almost missionary objective: to lay out the principles and procedures of a new approach to the study of chemistry. The book became widely popular, going through a total of fifteen editions over the next thirty-three years.

During his tenure at Göttingen, Nernst investigated a wide variety of topics in the field of solution chemistry . In 1893, for example, he developed a theory for the breakdown of ionic compounds in water, a fundamental issue in the Arrhenius theory of ionization. According to Nernst, dissociation, or the dissolving of a compound into its elements, occurs because the presence of nonconducting water molecules causes positive and negative ions in a crystal to lose contact with each other. The ions become hydrated by water molecules, making it possible for them to move about freely and to conduct an electric current through the solution. In later work, Nernst developed techniques for measuring the degree of hydration of ions in solutions. By 1903, Nernst had also devised methods for determining the pH value of a solution, an expression relating the solution's hydrogen-ion concentration (acidity or alkalinity).

In 1889, Nernst addressed another fundamental problem in solution chemistry: precipitation. He constructed a mathematical expression showing how the concentration of ions in a slightly soluble compound could result in the formation of an insoluble product. That mathematical expression is now known as the solubility product, a special case of the ionization constant for slightly soluble substances. Four years later, Nernst also developed the concept of buffer solutions —solutions made of bases, rather than acids—and showed how they could be used in various theoretical and practical situations.

Around 1905, Nernst was offered a position as professor of physical chemistry at the University of Berlin. This move was significant for both the institution and the man.

Chemists at Berlin had been resistant to many of the changes going on in their field, and theoretical physicist and eventual Nobel Prize winner Max Planck had recommended the selection of Nernst to revitalize the Berlin chemists. The move also proved to be a stimulus to Nernst's own work. Until he left Göttingen, he had concentrated on the reworking of older, existing problems developed by his predecessors in physical chemistry. At Berlin, he began to search out, define, and explore new questions. Certainly the most important of these questions involved the thermodynamics of chemical reactions at very low temperatures.

Attempting to extend the Gibbs-Helmholtz equation and the Thomsen-Berthelot principle of maximum work to temperatures close to absolute zero—the temperature at which there is no heat—Nernst eventually concluded that it would be possible to reach absolute zero only by a series of infinite steps. In the real world, that conclusion means that an experimenter can get closer and closer to absolute zero, but can never actually reach that point. Nernst first presented his "Heat Theorem," as he called it, to the Göttingen Academy of Sciences in December of 1905. It was published a year later in the *Nachrichten von der Gesellschaft der Wissenschaften zu Göttingen*. The theory is now more widely known as the Third Law of Thermodynamics. In 1920, Nernst was awarded the Nobel Prize in chemistry in recognition of his work on this law.

The statement of the Heat Theorem proved to be an enormous stimulus for Nernst's colleagues in Berlin's chemistry department. For at least a decade, the focus of nearly all research among physical chemists there was experimental confirmation of Nernst's hypothesis. In order to accomplish this objective, new equipment and new techniques had to be developed. Nernst's Heat Theorem was eventually integrated into the revolution taking place in physics, the development of quantum theory. At the time he first proposed the theory, Nernst had ignored any possible role of quantum mechanics. A few years later, however, that had all changed. In working on his own theory of specific heats, for example, Albert Einstein had quite independently come to the same conclusions as had Nernst. He later wrote that Nernst's experiments at Berlin had confirmed his own theory of specific heats. In turn, Nernst eventually realized that his Heat Theorem was consistent with the dramatic changes being brought about in physics by quantum theory. Even as his work on the Heat Theorem went forward, Nernst turned to new topics. One of these involved the formation of hydrogen chloride by photolysis, or chemical breakdown by light energy. Chemists had long known that a mixture of hydrogen and chlorine gases will explode when exposed to light. In 1918, Nernst developed an explanation for that reaction. When exposed to light, Nernst hypothesized, a molecule of chlorine (Cl_2) will absorb light energy and break down into two chlorine atoms ($2Cl$). A single chlorine atom will then react with a molecule of hydrogen (H_2), forming a molecule of hydrogen chloride and an atom of hydrogen ($HCl + H$). The atom of hydrogen will then react with a molecule of chlorine, forming a second molecule of hydrogen chloride and another atom of chlorine. The process is a chain reaction because the remaining atom of chlorine allows it to repeat.

In 1922, Nernst resigned his post at Berlin in order to become president of the Physikalisch-technische Reichsanstalt. He hoped to reorganize the institute and make it a leader in German science, but since the nation was suffering from severe inflation at the time, there were not enough funds to achieve this goal. As a result, Nernst returned to Berlin in 1924 to teach physics and direct the Institute of Experimental Physics there until he retired in 1934.

In addition to his scientific research, Nernst was an avid inventor. Around the turn of the century, for example, he developed an incandescent lamp that used rare-earth oxide rather than a metal as the filament. Although he sold the lamp patent outright for a million marks, the device was never able to compete commercially with the conventional model invented by Thomas Alva Edison . Nernst also invented an electric piano that was never successfully marketed.

The rise of the Nazi party in 1933 brought an end to Nernst's professional career. He was personally opposed to the political and scientific policies promoted by Adolf Hitler and his followers and was not reluctant to express his views publicly. In addition, two of his daughters had married Jews, which contributed to his becoming an outcast in the severely anti-Semitic climate of Germany at that time.

Walther Nernst was one of the geniuses of early twentieth-century German chemistry, a man with a prodigious curiosity about every new development in the physical sciences. He was a close colleague of Einstein, and was a great contributor to the organization of German science—he was largely responsible for the first Solvay Conference in 1911, for example. In his free time, he was especially fond of travel, hunting, and fishing. Nernst also loved automobiles and owned one of the first to be seen in Göttingen. Little is known about his years after his retirement. Nernst died of a heart attack on November 18, 1941, at his home at Zibelle, Oberlausitz, near the German-Polish border.

Further Reading

Concise Dictionary of Scientific Biography, Macmillan, 1981, pp. 499–501.

Farber, Eduard, editor, *Great Chemists,* Interscience, 1961, pp. 1203–1208.

Gillispie, Charles Coulson, editor, *Dictionary of Scientific Biography,* Volume 15, Scribner, 1975, pp. 432–453.

Mendelsohn, Kurt, *The World of Walther Nernst: The Rise and Fall of German Science, 1864–1941,* Pittsburgh, 1973.

Einstein, Albert, ''The Work and Personality of Walther Nernst,'' in *Scientific Monthly,* February, 1942, pp. 195–196.

Partington, James R., ''The Nernst Memorial Lecture,'' in *Journal of the American Chemical Society,* 1953, pp. 2853–2872. □

Nero Claudius Caesar

Nero Claudius Caesar (37-68) was the last of the Julio-Claudian line of Roman emperors. His erratic personal and public life caused numerous revolts

and uprisings and set the scene for the ascension of the military emperors.

Born in Latium a few months after the death of the emperor Tiberius, Nero was the son of Domitius Ahenobarbus and Agrippina. Agrippina was the daughter of Germanicus and therefore the great-granddaughter of Augustus; and after the death of Ahenobarbus and a brief second marriage, she wedded the emperor Claudius. A powerful and clever woman, she persuaded her new husband to disown his own son, Britannicus, name Nero as his successor and heir, and give his daughter, Octavia, in marriage to her son in A.D. 50.

The future emperor was given an excellent education in the classical tradition; under the tutelage of the philosopher Seneca, Nero was schooled in Greek, philosophy, and rhetoric. When Claudius died in 54 (some say he was poisoned by Agrippina), the 17-year-old Nero appeared before the Senate, delivered a panegyric in honor of the dead emperor, and was proclaimed by the Senate as the new ruler of Rome.

Nero and His Mother

In the beginning, Nero's rule was relatively peaceful; Agrippina's desire to control the empire through her son was tempered by the advice and counsel which Seneca and Burrus, commander of the Praetorian Guard, gave the young emperor. Agrippina became angered as she saw her

influence over Nero wane, and the estrangement between them grew when Nero became involved with Acte, a freedwoman, and threatened to divorce Octavia. Although divorce was averted, Nero, in spite of his mother's objections, began living openly with Acte as his wife.

Meanwhile, the Senate, to which Nero had promised on his accession a full restoration of the republic, was governing, but poorly without any powerful leader to guide it. Agrippina, who saw her son increasingly neglect the imperial duties and devote himself to the imperial pleasures, turned to Britannicus and threatened Nero by supporting the former's claims to the throne. However, Britannicus died suddenly (perhaps murdered by Nero) toward the end of 55. Agrippina then began to stir up opposition to Nero, and the Emperor retaliated by banishing her. In 58 the final and disastrous breach between mother and son came. Nero, who had by this time abandoned Acte, became enamored of Poppaea Sabina, a young woman of noble birth who was married to Otho, a noted member of the Roman aristocracy.

The Emperor now proposed to marry Poppaea, but two things stood in his way: adverse public opinion over a divorce of Octavia, and his mother, Agrippina. Agrippina's opposition was removed by her murder in 59, and public horror at the crime was diverted by a successful campaign against the Parthians and the conquest of Armenia, as well as the quelling of revolt in Britain.

Decline into Hedonism

With Agrippina now out of the way, Nero's dissipated and profligate nature began to reveal itself. Partly to satisfy his own desire and partly to win the support of the Roman people, the Emperor spent money freely on spectacles and circuses and initiated great public works in Rome. He encouraged competitions in music, singing, dance, and poetry, in which the himself took part. In 62 Burrus died, and the final restrictions on the Emperor were removed. Seneca retired from the court, and Tigellinus took Burrus's place. Nero divorced Octavia on grounds of adultery, exiled her, and later had her killed. Shortly after, he married Poppaea.

Nero now seemed to take increasing delight in flaunting the traditions and ideals of Rome. In 64 he appeared on the public stage as a singer, but the scandal that this act might have caused was averted by a great calamity: the fire which burned for 10 days in July of 64, thoroughly destroying three-quarters of the city. Although Nero seemingly did everything he could to mitigate the effect of the disaster—opening public buildings to the homeless, building temporary shelters, providing food against the possibility of famine—rumors quickly spread as to the cause of the fire. Suetonius and Dio Cassius positively assert that Nero himself started the conflagration, but Tacitus admits that he was not able to prove the truth of this accusation. Although in all probability the fire was an accidental catastrophe, rumors that the fire was purposely set were so rife that it was necessary to find a guilty party. The blame was laid at the door of the Christians, and the first large-scale persecution against this new and secret sect began.

Destruction of most of the city gave Nero an opportunity to fulfill his ambition of building a more glorious Rome.

This project, however, required capital, and in order to gain it Nero reinstituted condemnations and confiscations on grounds of treason; he took money from the temples, sold public offices and contracts, raised taxes, and devalued the currency.

The reaction to this policy was a conspiracy led by Gaius Calpurnius Piso, a Roman aristocrat. Among the members of the plot were a number of knights and senators, the poet Lucan, and Nero's old tutor, Seneca. Its purpose was to kill Nero and apparently then make Piso emperor. The plan was discovered quite by accident, and the leading conspirators, as well as many other noted Romans (especially those with money and property), were condemned and killed. It was during that same year that the Emperor's pregnant wife died, after having been kicked in the stomach by her husband.

Last of the Julio-Claudian Emperors

The following year Nero went to Greece, and while he entertained himself with dramas, circuses, and contests, the affairs of the empire worsened. The revolt which was to lead to the destruction of the Temple in Jerusalem broke out in Judea. In Gaul the governor of the province himself led an insurrection against Rome. Although this revolt was quickly crushed, the man who crushed it, the governor of Germania Superior, was proclaimed emperor on the battlefield. Soon after, Galba, commander of the Spanish legions, joined the revolt.

Galba was now declared a public enemy, but Nero was lacking the support of the Senate and the army; the Senate pronounced the sentence of death against him, and Galba was proclaimed the new emperor of Rome. In June 68, when he learned of the events in Rome, Nero committed suicide. The last of the Julio-Claudian emperors, the line which had in effect created the concept of the Roman Empire, was dead.

Further Reading

Ancient sources for Nero are Dio Cassius and Suetonius. Modern treatments of the Emperor are Bernard William Henderson, *The Life and Principate of the Emperor Nero* (1903), and the relevant chapters in Guglielmo Ferrero and Corrado Barbagallo, *A Short History of Rome: The Empire* (1919).

Additional Sources

Bradley, K. R., *Suetonius' Life of Nero: an historical commentary,* Bruxelles: Latomus, 1978.

Griffin, Miriam T. (Miriam Tamara), *Nero: the end of a dynasty,* New Haven: Yale University Press, 1985, 1984.

Reflections of Nero: culture, history, & representation, Chapel Hill: University of North Carolina Press, 1994.

Shotter, D. C. A. (David Colin Arthur), *Nero,* London; New York: Routledge, 1996.

Walter, Gerard, *Nero,* Westport, Conn.: Greenwood Press, 1976, 1957. □

Pablo Neruda

Pablo Neruda (1904-1973) was perhaps the greatest Spanish poet of the 20th century.

The poet known as Pablo Neruda was named Neftalí Ricardo Reyes Basoalto at his birth in 1904. He signed his work ''Pablo Neruda'' (although he did not legally adopt that name until 1946) because his father, a railroad worker, disapproved of the son's poetic interests.

Neruda grew up in southern Chile and in 1921 moved to Santiago and enrolled in college with the intention of preparing himself for a career as an instructor of French. He left soon after, however, in order to devote more time to poetry, which had already become his central interest. His first book, *Crepusculario* (*Twilight Book*), was published in 1923, and the following year he published *Veinte poemas de amor y una canción desesperada* (*Twenty Love Poems and a Song of Despair*), a book of intensely romantic and erotic poems. This became his most popular work, more than a million and a half copies of which were published in Spanish alone before his death.

Between 1927 and 1935 Neruda was a Chilean diplomat in, successively, Burma, Ceylon, Java, Singapore, Argentina, and Spain. In 1930 he married for the first time, but the marriage was unhappy, and a few years later he left his wife to live with Delia del Carril, with whom he stayed until 1955. In the late 1920s and early 1930s he completed the first two volumes of *Residencia en la tierra* (*Residence on Earth*) (1933, 1935), universally considered the finest surrealist poetry in Spanish. He claimed, however, that when he wrote these works he knew nothing of surrealism; he had simply responded to the same currents in the air which led to the formation of the surrealist movement elsewhere.

Neruda's horror at the civil and military barbarities (including the assassination of his friend the poet Federico García Lorca) which accompanied Franco's invasion of Spain transformed him into a deeply committed political poet and led to his eventual alignment with the Communist Party. The third volume of *Residencia en la tierra* (1947) and his subsequent poetry, particularly *Canto general* (General Song, 1950), are marked by this commitment. In place of the introspection and surrealist complexities of the first two volumes of *Residencia,* he produced a poetry that is open and direct, written not for academics and other sophisticated readers of poetry but rather, as Neruda repeatedly emphasized, workers and the politically oppressed.

Neruda also insisted that he was specifically a Latin American poet. *Canto general,* which he considered his principal work, celebrates his Latin American heritage. That volume includes "Alturas de Macchu Picchu" ("The Heights of Macchu Picchu"), possibly Neruda's greatest poem.

Canto general was written largely in the late 1940s while Neruda was in hiding in Chile to avoid arrest for statements he had made against the government. He escaped from Chile in 1949 and did not return until 1952 when a new regime came to power. He married Matilde Urrutia three years later and spent most of the rest of his life with her at his homes in Santiago and at Isla Negra on the Chilean coast. Isla Negra provided him with the subject or inspiration for many later poems, including his verse autobiography, *Memorial de Isla Negra* (*Black Island Memorial,* 1964). During these years he also wrote his *Odas Elementales* (Elemental Odes, 1954-1957), in which he developed a clear, simple, and at times humorous poetic style.

Neruda was awarded the International Peace Prize in 1950, the Stalin Peace Prize in 1953, a Doctorate in Literature from Oxford in 1965, and the Nobel Prize in 1971. In 1969 he was nominated by the Chilean Communist Party for president, but he stepped aside in favor of his friend Salvador Allende. When Allende was murdered four years later Neruda was very sick from cancer, but that event undoubtedly hastened his own death a few days later. At his death, he left 34 books of poems, essays, and drama in print as well as eight more volumes of poetry and a memoir which he had hoped to publish on his 70th birthday.

Neruda was clearly a prolific writer. His major works include *Veinte poemas de amor y una canción desesperada,* the three volumes of *Residencia en la tierra, Canto general,* and *Odas elementales,* but there are few Neruda books which do not contain works or passages of a high order.

Neruda cannot be categorized by a single poetic style. No sooner had he mastered one poetic form or mood than he moved to another. The sensual, erotic poems of *Veinte poemas* are quite distant from the hermetic, surrealist poems of *Residencia,* and the political, epical *Canto general* is

entirely unlike the conversational, colloquial, occasionally whimsical *Odas elementales*. His poems range from painfully intense introspection to fiery political rhetoric, yet a clarity of poetic vision and emotional conviction is found throughout his work. There have been few poets as prolific as Neruda and few who have sought after, and achieved, such high and diverse standards of excellence. The least that can be said of Neruda is that he was the greatest Spanish poet of the century.

Further Reading

Neruda has been fortunate in his translators. His chief translator has been Ben Belitt, whose anthology *Five Decades: A Selection* (*Poems 1925-1970*) provides an excellent introduction to the range of Neruda's achievement. Belitt talks about the problems and pleasures of translating (and reading) Neruda in *Adam's Dream* (1978). An outstanding translation of "The Heights of Macchu Picchu" was made by Nicholas Tarn (1966). Excellent translations of various works have been made by Robert Bly, Angel Flores, Alastair Reid, Donald Walsh, and many others. Neruda has been the subject of a vast amount of critical work, but most of it is available only in Spanish. English readers might begin with René de Costa's *The Poetry of Pablo Neruda* (1979), but Robert Pring-Mill's introduction to his *Pablo Neruda: A Basic Anthology* (1975) also provides a concise and valuable survey of Neruda's life and work. Valuable insights into the poetry are provided by Neruda himself in his *Memoirs,* translated by Hardie St. Martin (1976). □

Gérard de Nerval

The French poet and writer Gérard de Nerval (1808-1855) was an early romantic. His prose and poetry mark him as a precursor of the many movements, from symbolism to surrealism, that shaped modern French literature.

Gérard de Nerval was born Gérard Labrunie on May 22, 1808, in Paris. Because of his parents' immediate departure for Silesia, where his mother died, Nerval was taken to the home of maternal relatives in the Valois. This region played a prominent part in many of his works. The fact that his early years were bereft of parental care probably contributed to his subsequent lack of mental equilibrium.

Upon his father's return from the Napoleonic Wars in 1814, Nerval returned to Paris. As a day pupil at the Lycée Charlemagne, he distinguished himself by his precocious literary gifts and made the acquaintance of a lifelong friend, the poet Théophile Gautier.

Nerval's translation in 1827 of J. W. von Goethe's *Faust* (*Part I*) earned him the praise of Goethe and opened influential Parisian literary circles to him. His admiration for Victor Hugo converted him to the romantic movement. In the 1830s Nerval belonged to the *petit cénacle,* a group of minor artistic figures that gravitated around Gautier.

In 1834 Nerval received an inheritance from his maternal grandparents that enabled him to pursue exclusively the literary career of which his father disapproved. Nerval gave up his nominal study of medicine and made a brief trip to Italy, a tour that had a powerful and lasting effect on his imagination.

Meanwhile, Nerval fell in love with Jenny Colon, an actress, for whom he founded a theatrical review, *Le Monde dramatique*. It failed after 2 years. The brilliant and gay life that Nerval led during this brief period of prosperity was succeeded by a lifetime of financial difficulties and personal sadness. The poet lost both his small patrimony and Jenny Colon, who married another. During this period Nerval centered his main literary efforts on the theater, a genre basically uncongenial to his talents. In spite of an occasional success, such as *Piquillo* (1837), his efforts in the theater generally met with failure.

The years 1839-1841 were ones of growing eccentricities and depression for Nerval. His translation of *Faust* (*Part II*), which appeared in 1840, culminated in a mental breakdown that caused him to be hospitalized in 1841. His mental stability thus shattered, Nerval's life became more precarious and difficult because he depended upon his pen for his living. In order to mend his health, Nerval made a trip to the Orient in 1843. His health regained, he published articles dealing with his travels in serial form in various periodicals. During these years of remission from mental breakdown, he also published chronicles, essays, poems, and novellas in many magazines, all the time trying unsuccessfully to establish himself in the theater. He also traveled in foreign countries and in the Valois. Wandering had become a temperamental necessity, and it is an important theme in his major works.

In 1848 Nerval published his translation of Heinrich Heine's poetry. In 1851 *Le Voyage en Orient* appeared. Under the guise of a travelog, it concerned itself with the pilgrimage of a soul, being more revealing of the inner geography of Nerval than of Egypt, Lebanon, or Turkey.

Nerval's major works were all written in the last few years of his life under the threat of incurable insanity. A serious relapse in 1851 marked him irrevocably. In 1852 he published *Les Illuminés,* a series of biographical sketches of unorthodox and original figures. In 1853 *Les Petits châteaux de Bohême* appeared. It was a nostalgic recounting of his happy years. It also contained the *Odelettes,* early poems in the manner of Pierre de Ronsard. Nerval then published his best and most famous story, *Sylvie,* in the *Revue des deux mondes.* In this tale he explored the sources of memory and transfigured the Valois of his childhood. It was included in *Les Filles du feu* in 1854. That same year *Les Chimères,* a series of 12 hermetic sonnets, also appeared.

During this period Nerval was also writing an autobiographical work, *Les Nuits d'Octobre,* and *Aurélia,* his last and most occult work. In *Aurélia* Nerval described the experience of madness and his attempt to overcome it by means of the written word.

In January 1855, destitute and desperate, Nerval committed suicide by hanging himself in a Parisian alley.

Further Reading

Two full-length studies of Nerval are Solomon A. Rhodes, *Gérard de Nerval, 1808-1855: Poet, Traveler, Dreamer* (1951), and Alfred Dubruck, *Gérard de Nerval and the German Heritage* (1965). □

Pier Luigi Nervi

The Italian architect, engineer, and builder Pier Luigi Nervi (1891-1979) was one of the most inventive exploiters of reinforced-concrete construction of the 20th century.

R einforced concrete, a material combining the monolithic compressive strength of concrete with the tensile strength of steel reinforcing rods, entered the history of architecture at the end of the 19th century in France. The earlier patented processes of Joseph Monier, François Coignet, and others were applied by François Hennebique at the Charles VI Mill at Tourcoing (1895) and by Anatole de Baudot in the church of St-Jean-de-Montmartre in Paris (1894-1897). Those were the first significant uses of reinforced concrete for large-scale architectural problems. Some later builders used reinforced concrete in traditional, linear ways; others recognized that the material could accommodate an experimental approach using continuous curving systems. Pier Luigi Nervi was a leader in the latter approach.

Born on June 21, 1891, in Sondrio, Italy, a town in the Alps, Nervi, the son of a postmaster, graduated from the School of Civil Engineering in Bologna in 1913. He gained practical training with building firms specializing in concrete construction, in Bologna before World War I and in Florence afterward.

Early Work

In 1923 Nervi established his own firm in Rome. His first all-concrete building was a small cinema in Naples, built in 1927. He recalled later how skeptical architects were "sure my building would cave in for lack of proper support." In 1929 he produced a work of remarkable significance: the Municipal Stadium in Florence. An economical design, with a grandstand roof cantilevering some 55 feet and exterior stairs of cantilevered spirals, the stadium established Nervi's reputation.

In 1932, he formed a new firm, Nervi and Bartoli, and that company in 1936 developed a series of airplane hangars using reinforced concrete that was poured in place. Two hangars were built, but the difficulties of poured-in-place concrete construction led in 1939 to a second hangar design using precast concrete sections, a system Nervi used with great success after World War II. Six hangars of the second type were erected; Paul Goldberger of the *New York Times* described them as "graceful, flying forms of con-

crete." All eight hangars were dynamited by retreating German forces in 1944, and Nervi was so upset, one of his sons recalled, that "he wanted to crawl under those hangars and die with them."

Visions in Concrete

Nervi designed and built an exhibition hall, the Salone Agnelli, in Turin (1947-1949) using a system of prefabrication he developed. The structure is composed of precast sections of what Nervi called *ferrocemento,* a material made of a fine mesh of steel wire filled and covered by a thin layer of cement. The use of precast sections eliminates costly and time-consuming wooden formwork, creates a system of mass production that can begin even while the foundations are being dug, speeds construction, and is economical. At Turin the hall is covered by precast sections 1 1/2 inches thick forming undulating ribs that carry the structural load across the 328-foot-wide room to fan-shaped piers at the sides. It took just seven months to erect. One critic likened the hall to a suspension bridge, "for it has the sense of materials being pushed to their utmost, yet without ever appearing to strain," as Goldberger noted.

In 1946 Nervi began lecturing on architectural engineering at Rome University. He collaborated with other architects on a series of internationally important buildings in the 1950s. The UNESCO Building in Paris (with Marcel Breuer and others, 1952-1957) has a reinforced-concrete structure, the most interesting part of which is the continuous folded slab of the walls and roof of the General Assembly. The 32-story Pirelli Office Building in Milan (with Gio Ponti and others, 1955-1956) has a more traditional load-bearing structural system. Nervi also designed two sports arenas erected for the Roman Olympics of 1960. The 5,000-seat "little palace" (with Annibale Vitelozzi, 1957) has prefabricated diamond-shaped sections descending from an overhead compression ring to exposed, prefabricated, Y-shaped piers sloped to receive their diagonal thrusts. The 16,000-seat "palace" (with M. Piacentini, 1958-1960), has piers covered on the exterior by a glass skirt.

For the Palace of Labor in Turin (1960-1961) Nervi combined reinforced concrete with steel (designed by G. Covre) to create a large rectangular hall filled with a forest of treelike structures forming ceiling and support. At the Burgo Paper Mill outside Mantua (1961-1962) he used steel cables (also by Covre) suspended between concrete piers to create a clear span of 525 feet.

International Reputation

Nervi collaborated on projects as far afield as Australia and the United States. The Bus Station at the George Washington Bridge in New York City, famous for the butterfly-like wings of exposed concrete that make up its roof, and the Field House for Dartmouth College in New Hampshire (both 1961-1962) were erected at the same time that he was delivering the Charles Eliot Norton Lectures at Harvard University. In 1964 he received the Gold Medal of the American Institute of Architects, the highest honor in American architecture. Nervi's bus station design helped him win fame in the United States, but its design was altered later because open spaces between the concrete wings, left to allow bus fumes to escape, let cold winds off the Hudson River intrude.

His Theory

The delicacy of the lacy coverings for large-span halls such as that at Chianciano (1952) and the Roman sports palaces might lead one to forget how essentially businesslike was Nervi's approach to structure. He looked and thought exactly like what he was: the head of a firm engaged in the cutthroat business of building. In his writings, Nervi constantly reminded readers that 90 percent of his contracts were awarded in competitions where the governing factors were economy and speed of construction. He thrived on these limitations and, indeed, "never found this relentless search for economy an obstacle to achieving the expressiveness of form" desired.

Architecture, for Nervi, was "a synthesis of technology and art." To find the logical solution to a limiting set of factors within a highly competitive situation was, for him, "to build correctly." His mastery of concrete bespoke a love for its adaptability. "Concrete is a living creature which can adapt itself to any form, any need, any stress," he once said.

Further Reading

Structures (1956); *Buildings, Projects, Structures, 1953-1963* (trans. 1963), which contains many illustrations of his works, and *Aesthetics and Technology in Building* (1965) by Nervi are in English; *Pier Luigi Nervi* (1960), by Ada Louise Huxtable, is well illustrated; sketches on Nervi are also available in Muriel Emanuel, ed., *Contemporary Architects* (1994); and in Randall J. Van Vynckt, ed., *International Dictionary of Architects and Architecture* (1993). □

Count Karl Robert Nesselrode

The Russian diplomat Count Karl Robert Nesselrode (1780-1862) served as minister of foreign affairs from 1814 to 1856.

Karl Robert Nesselrode was born on Dec. 14, 1780, in Lisbon, Portugal, where his father was Russian ambassador. Young Karl received his education in Berlin, Germany. At the age of 16 he entered the Russian navy, where he became naval aide-de-camp to Paul I. He then went into the army, received another court appointment, and at last entered the diplomatic service.

Count Nesselrode served at Russian embassies in The Hague and Berlin. In 1806 he went on a mission to southern Germany. His assignment was to report on French troops to Alexander I, who was turning away from Napoleon in his foreign policy. Nesselrode assisted Alexander I at the Peace of Tilsit in 1811, which, according to Mikhail Speranski, contained practically all the ingredients for a future war between Russia and France.

On June 24, 1812, the French army, without a declaration of war, crossed the Neman River and entered Russian territory. During the Franco-Russian War, Nesselrode served as diplomatic secretary to generals Mikhail Kamenski, Friedrich von Buxhowden, and Levin August Bennigsen. During the negotiations at the Congress of Vienna, Nesselrode succeeded Count N. P. Rumiantsev in August 1814 as Russian minister of foreign affairs.

Russia's design on Poland met with opposition from other powers, especially England and Austria. Nesselrode played a subordinate role and was seldom consulted by Alexander I on major issues. By the end of 1814, the discussions of the Polish and Saxon problems having reached an impasse, England and Austria made preparations for war against Russia. A compromise, however, averted another war. By the Final Act of the Congress of Vienna (June 1816), the greater part of the former duchy of Warsaw was given to Russia.

In November 1831 Mohammed Ali, Pasha of Egypt, revolted against Sultan Mahmud II, and by the following year Ibrahim Pasha, commander of the insurgent army, had conquered Syria and was threatening Constantinople. The Sultan asked the Western powers for help but met with indifference. Russia, however, was eager to provide Turkey with military assistance because the Turko-Egyptian War offered a golden opportunity for the consolidation of Russia's hold over Turkey. Nicholas I and Nesselrode, moreover, saw in Mehemet Ali a rebel against his suzerain (Mahmud) and a puppet in the hands of revolutionary France. Sultan Mahmud accepted Russia's military aid,

which alarmed France and England. Peace was achieved between Mohammed Ali and Mahmud at the Convention of Kintayah, negotiated in April and May 1833.

Several months later Russia signed the Treaty of Unkiar Skellesi with Turkey on July 8, 1833. The importance of the treaty was the provision by which the two monarchs "promise to come to agreement without reserve on all matters concerning their respective tranquility and safety and for this purpose, mutually to lend each other material aid and most effective assistance." Nesselrode then wrote that "our intervention in the affairs of Turkey has acquired a basis of legality."

Nesselrode tried unsuccessfully to avert the Crimean War (1853-1856). After he concluded the Treaty of Paris, he retired as foreign minister but continued as chancellor, a post he had held since 1844. He died on March 23, 1862, in St. Petersburg.

Further Reading

For background on Count Nesselrode see Andrei Lobanov-Rostovsky, *Russia and Europe, 1789-1825* (1947) and *Russia and Europe, 1825-1878* (1954); A. J. P. Taylor, *The Struggle for Mastery in Europe, 1848-1918* (1954); Barbara Jelavich, *A Century of Russian Foreign Policy, 1814-1914* (1964); and Patricia Kennedy Grimsted, *The Foreign Ministers of Alexander I* (1969). □

Nestorius

The heresiarch Nestorius (ca. 389-ca. 453) was patriarch of Constantinople from 428 to 431. He was the "founder" of the Nestorian Church.

Nestorius was probably born about 389 in Germanicia in the province of Cilicia. During his youth he moved to Syrian Antioch, where he received the major portion of his education. He is first seen with historical certainty as a monk in the monastery of Eupreprius near Antioch. He seems to have been a popular and learned preacher—fiercely orthodox—and a writer of considerable theological acumen.

In 428 Nestorius was called to be patriarch of Constantinople. The imperial city had for years been in the throes of theological strife, so it seemed best to the emperor, Theodosius II, to call someone in from outside. Upon his arrival in Constantinople, Nestorius immediately exhibited his zeal by his attacks upon heresy and paganism. He moved about as befits a bishop, little realizing that his role as protector of the faith would soon be radically altered.

By virtue of his Antiochene training and background, Nestorius was bound to differ theologically with the tenor of thought common to Alexandria; and because of his present position, he was bound to be in conflict politically with that same city. Both of these feuds had existed for some time, and Nestorius's episcopate fanned the flames of the controversy. The difficulty began when one of the monks that Nestorius had brought with him from Antioch—a certain Anastasius—preached a sermon on the Virgin Mary denying that she should be referred to as *theotokos,* or God-bearer. The sermon offended many pious Christians and caused such a stir that Nestorius embarked upon a series of sermons himself, supporting Anastasius' views and developing them theologically.

World of these events soon reached Cyril, the patriarch of Alexandria, whose latent anti-Constantinopolitan sentiments were immediately aroused. The controversy between the two patriarchs began with a relatively cordial exchange of letters, but soon the words became heated and bitter, with charge answered by countercharge. Nestorius's Antiochene position vis-à-vis the Person of Christ was that "Mary did not give birth to the divinity, but to man, the instrument of divinity." Thus, for him, the two natures of Christ—divine and human—were in intimate harmony, but each functioned according to its own attributes. Cyril, on the other hand, inherited from his Alexandrian tradition the strong emphasis on the essential unity of Christ, so much so that the attributes of one nature could be ascribed to the other. Therefore, *theotokos* was not just pious; it was a theologically necessary title for the Virgin Mary. In the course of the controversy Nestorius sought and obtained the support of John, the bishop of Antioch, while Cyril astutely won the ear and confidence of Celestine, the bishop of Rome.

The issue was brought to a head at the Council (third ecumenical) of Ephesus, called by Theodosius II in 431. Actually there were two councils, since Cyril and his supporters, without waiting for the delegation from Antioch, met first (June 22) and condemned Nestorius. A week later John of Antioch arrived and, meeting with his supporters, condemned Cyril. On July 10 the Roman envoys arrived, and they joined their voices to the condemnation of Nestorius. Subsequent sessions proved fruitless, so finally imperial pressure was brought to bear. Both patriarchs were declared to be in error, Cyril was imprisoned, and Nestorius was sent back to Antioch. But Cyril's political acumen soon won him freedom and a supposed victory, and, on the orders of the Emperor, Nestorius was exiled to Oasis in Upper Egypt, where some 20 years later he died.

During his exile Nestorius wrote his famous *Bazaar of Heraclides,* explaining his position in such a way as to lead many scholars to conclude that he was not, as charged, guilty of Nestorianism. The definitive Formula of Chalcedon, promulgated in 451, combined the positions of Cyril and Nestorius in a compromising fashion, with the result that today Christological "orthodoxy" borrows from each. Theological support for Nestorius's views survived his condemnation and exile, expressing itself both in the establishment of Nestorian churches in the East and in the persistent development of his views in the Latin Church.

Further Reading

The most comprehensive and sympathetic monograph on Nestorius is James Franklin Bethune-Baker, *Nestorius and His Teaching: A Fresh Examination of the Evidence* (1908). A survey of the issues relating to Nestorius's theological position is in George L. Prestige, *Fathers and Heretics: Six Studies in*

Dogmatic Faith with Prologue and Epilogue (1940), and Alois Grillmeier, *Christ in Christian Tradition* (1965). □

Binyamin Netanyahu

Former Israel ambassador to the United Nations, Binyamin Netanyahu (born 1949) became party head of the Likud opposition in 1993. He was then elected to the position of Prime Minister in 1996.

On March 24, 1993, Binyamin Netanyahu—better known to the Israeli public as "Bibi"—was elected leader of the right-of-center, nationalist Likud Party, at the age of 43 replacing the 77-year-old former prime minister, Yitzchak Shamir. Netanyahu's rapid, dramatic rise to high political office and surprise selection was likely to have a profound dual impact on Israeli national politics. First, in receiving 52.1 percent of the votes from the Likud rank-and-file membership in U.S.-style primaries he out-maneuvered three more senior Likud candidates. They were former foreign minister David Levy, the formidable Ariel Sharon, and Benny Begin, son of the former respected party leader and premier Menachem Begin. In this sense Netanyahu opened a new era in Likud Party politics. Second, by his youth and engaging media style, Bibi at the same time signaled a change at the national level of politics. The first of the younger Israeli-born generation of politicians to head a major party, his choice hastened a similar process among the other parties, especially in the rival Labor alignment, of passing over the "old guard" and promoting newer faces appealing to younger Israeli voters.

Netanyahu was born in Jerusalem on October 2, 1949, to Ben-Zion Netanyahu, a professor of history, and his wife Tsilla. At the age of 18 he began his military training. He served as a soldier and officer in an elite unit of the Israel Defense Forces from 1967 to 1972. In this he followed his brother, Yonatan ("Yoni") Netanyahu, the celebrated hero of the 1976 Entebbe rescue operation who was killed in action freeing a planeload of Israelis held hostage in Uganda. Another brother, Iddo Netanyahu, was a physician.

Bibi attended Cheltenham High School in Philadelphia and graduated from the Massachusetts Institute of Technology in 1976. After graduating, he held several industrial consulting and managerial positions in the United States. In 1976 he returned to Israel to become director of the Jonathan Institute, founded to study ways for democratic governments to combat terrorism. With his wife Sarah, he had one son, Yasir.

In 1982 he began a diplomatic career when appointed deputy chief of mission to the United States, where he served until 1984, already then impressing people in Jerusalem with his television "persona" and ability to defend Israeli hard-line policies. In 1984 Netanyahu shifted from Washington to New York, serving for the next four years as

Israel's ambassador to the United Nations, again proving extremely effective.

Regarded as the protégé of Yitzchak Shamir, Netanyahu was recalled to Israel, where he acted as deputy foreign minister (1988 to 1991) and deputy minister for information in the prime minister's office (1991 to 1992), participating as a member of the Israeli delegation in the 1991 Madrid Middle East peace conference and subsequent early peace talks in Washington. All this time he involved himself increasingly in internal Likud Party politics, being elected in 1988 to the Knesset, where he was a strong advocate of electoral reform and helped to pass legislation establishing direct election of the prime minister.

Netanyahu gained control of the Likud Party in March 1993. His upset victory unquestionably constituted a tremendous personal triumph and overnight regained for him the world press attention he had enjoyed during the 1991 Persian Gulf war when he appeared regularly as a principal spokesman for Israel on CNN and other network commentary programs. However, he also faced the immediate challenge of reorganizing a party demoralized and in disarray following its defeat in the June 1992 general elections at the hands of Labor, led by Yitzchak Rabin and Shimon Peres. No less of a challenge was the need for Netanyahu to orchestrate efforts at redefining the Likud Party's strategy and platform to reflect both changing global and Middle Eastern circumstances as well as national priorities. Nor would his task be made any easier by the lingering resentment of those party veterans who had lost out to Netanyahu, and who, each in his own way, continued to question Netanyahu's's leadership capabilities.

David Levy, thinking himself the logical successor to Begin and Shamir and having his source of power among the large numbers of working-class Sephardim (Israelis of oriental origin) from the development towns, openly criticized Netanyahu's early decisions and kept aloof from party activities. Israeli political experts similarly forecast that former general Sharon would work behind the scenes to undermine Netanyahu's authority and to be positioned to put forward his own candidacy should the new party leader lose popularity or commit a serious political misstep. One further complicating factor was the opposition Labor government's foreign policy initiative of September 1993 aimed at a territorial compromise with the Palestinians and paving the way for an eventual Palestinian state—a prospect to which the Likud had always taken the strongest opposition. To consolidate his position and to assert his leadership, Netanyahu was compelled to steer a middle-of-the-road course between ideology and pragmatism in trying to present to an Israeli public anxious for peace a viable Likud alternative peace strategy that stopped short of major territorial concessions.

After the November 1995 assassination of Prime Minister Yitzchak Rabin, elections were scheduled for May of the following year. During the campaign, Netanyahu and the Likud Party ran on a "Peace Through Security" platform, which on some points asserted that the peace process was rushed and thus doomed to fail. During the ugly campaign, Netanyahu was not seen as the front runner.

For the first time in Israeli history, voters could choose the prime minister and the Knesset representatives separately. On May 29, 1996, Netanyahu was elected prime minister, winning by a less than one percent margin to the surprise of many. He was the youngest man to ever hold the position. His election stunned the international community, who now feared that the hard-won Oslo agreements of 1992 and 1993, which Netanyahu inherited but did not like, would be railroaded by Israeli conservatives.

In September 1997 Netanyahu met with U.S. Secretary of State Madeleine Albright, during her first mission to the Middle East. They discussed Israeli-Palestinian relations, and there appeared to be a wide gap between the philosophies of the Clinton administration and those of the Israeli government. Although Albright condemned terrorist activities, she urged Netanyahu to make concessions. Netanyahu responded that no progress would be made "until Arafat arrests terror suspects and increases cooperation with Israeli security forces . . . If they fight terrorism, there will be progress."

Further Reading

Binyamin Netanyahu edited *Terrorism: How the West Can Win* (1986); and authored *A Place Among the Nations: Israel and the World* (1993), an analysis of Israel's situation in relation to the Arab world and to the West. See also *Time*, Sept. 15, 1997. □

António Agostinho Neto

António Agostinho Neto (1922-1979) was a leading African intellectual and nationalist in the three decades following the close of World War II. A doctor and poet, he was also the president of the Popular Movement for the Liberation of Angola, directing the armed struggle within Angola against the Portuguese colonial rule, and the first president of the People's Republic of Angola.

António Agostinho Neto was born near the town of Catete, a short distance inland from Luanda, the Angolan capital, on September 17, 1922. As a boy his family lived in Luanda where his father was the pastor of a large Methodist church and his mother was a kindergarten teacher. He was one of the few Africans who received a secondary school education at the famous Silva Correia High School. Neto was quiet, reserved, competent, and a good student. He bought his school books and supplies by working part-time as a secretary for the Methodist bishop. Unable to study medicine as he wanted, Neto went to work for the government health services in Luanda from 1944 to 1947. He participated in the formation of cultural associations which were an expression of African nationalism at a time when political organizations were forbidden by the Portuguese authorities.

In 1947 Agostinho Neto received a scholarship from the Methodist church for medical studies, first at the University of Lisbon and then at Coimbra. Together with other African students, he took an active part in opposing the Salazar dictatorship in Portugal. He was arrested and imprisoned on three occasions for organizing petitions, joining in demonstrations, and writing poetry. (His poems mirrored the harsh conditions of African life under Portuguese colonialism and the longing of his people for freedom and justice.) Neto was now well-known as a leading African intellectual and nationalist, and some of the most famous international writers, artists, and liberal politicians petitioned for and secured his release. In 1958 he completed his medical studies, which had been interrupted by his imprisonment, and the next year returned to Angola with his Portuguese wife, Maria Eugenia.

Doctor, Writer, and Liberation Leader

Agostinho Neto was one of the few Angolans who had the education that would have allowed him to live a life of privilege and security. Instead, on his return to Luanda he started a medical practice where he welcomed all patients, however poor and whatever their background. At the same time he continued writing. One line of a poem expressed his belief in the inevitability of the victory of African nationalism with the words "No one can stop the rain."

He had hardly begun his work as a doctor when he was again arrested, in his consulting room. This action sparked off a demonstration in his home village. Thirty people were killed and many injured as Portuguese soldiers fired on the

his people and country motivated him as it had done in his years as a student, as a doctor, and as a leader in exile. His own inclination was more to intellectual pursuits and a private life, but he continued to give Angola the strong leadership that it needed. He acted as a moderating influence within his government while remaining fully committed to building a socialist state. Agostinho Neto has deservedly been called "the father of modern Angola." His work was cut short by his death from cancer on September 10, 1979.

Further Reading

Some of Agostinho Neto's poems have been translated into English and published under the title *Sacred Hope* (1974). On general background, see Lawrence W. Henderson *Angola: Five Centuries of Conflict* (1979). Recommended on the role of Neto and MPLA in the liberation struggle is John Marcum, *The Angolan Revolution,* two volumes (1969 and 1978), and on events since independence see Michael Wolfers and Jane Bergerol, *Angola in the Front Line* (1983). □

Elizabeth F. Neufeld

Elizabeth F. Neufeld (born 1928) is best known as an authority on human genetic diseases . Her research at the National Institutes of Health (NIH) and at University of California, Los Angeles (UCLA), provided new insights into mucopolysaccharide storage disorders (the absence of certain enzymes preventing the body from properly storing certain substances).

Neufeld's research opened the way for prenatal diagnosis of such life-threatening fetal disorders as Hurler syndrome. Because of this research, she was awarded the Lasker Award in 1982 and the Wolf Prize in Medicine in 1988.

She was born Elizabeth Fondal in Paris, on September 27, 1928. Her parents, Jacques and Elvire Fondal, were Russian refugees who had settled in France after the Russian revolution. The impending occupation of France by the Germans brought the Fondal family to New York in June 1940. Her parents' experience led them to instill in Neufeld a strong commitment to the importance of education "They believed that education was the one thing no one could take from you," she told George Milite in a 1993 interview.

Neufeld first became interested in science while a high school student, her interest sparked by her biology teacher. She attended Queens College in New York, receiving her bachelor of science degree in 1948. She worked briefly as a research assistant to Elizabeth Russell at the Jackson Memorial Laboratory in Bar Harbor, Maine. From 1949 to 1950 she studied at the University of Rochester's department of physiology. In 1951 she moved to Maryland, where she served as a research assistant to Nathan Kaplan and Sidney Colowick at the McCollum-Pratt Institute at Johns Hopkins

crowd. The Portuguese exiled Neto to the Cape Verde Islands and later sent him to Portugal, where he was first imprisoned and then kept under house arrest. In 1962 he and his wife and two small children escaped to Morocco and from there travelled to Léopoldville (now Kinshasa, Zaire).

Neto was now the most famous of the Angolan nationalist leaders, and in the same year he was elected as the president of the liberation movement, MPLA (Popular Movement for the Liberation of Angola). For the next 12 years Neto directed the armed struggle of MPLA within Angola against Portuguese colonial rule. He travelled to Europe, the Soviet Union, and other African countries to rally support for his organization. During the 1960s several volumes of his poetry were published. Some were translated and published in other languages, including English. In 1974 a coup in Portugal toppled the Salazar dictatorship. Neto, as the head of MPLA, opened the negotiations with Portugal and with other Angolan liberation movements which led to the independence of Angola.

First Angolan President

On November 11, 1975, Neto was sworn in as the first president of the People's Republic of Angola. The problems of building a modern nation state on the ruins of an old colonial empire were immense. For example, illiteracy was about 85 percent; many trained Portuguese had left the country; and rival liberation movements supported by foreign powers refused to recognize the MPLA government and continued the war. Neto's compelling sense of duty to

University. In 1952 Neufeld moved again, this time to the West Coast. From 1952 to 1956 she studied under W. Z. Hassid at the University of California, Berkeley. She received her Ph.D. in comparative biochemistry from Berkeley in 1956 and remained there for her postdoctoral training. She first studied cell division in sea urchins. Later, as a junior research biochemist (working again with Hassid) she studied the biosynthesis of plant cell wall polymers—which would prove significant when she began studying Hurler syndrome and related diseases.

Neufeld began her scientific studies at a time when few women chose science as a career. The historical bias against women in science, compounded with an influx of men coming back from the Second World War and going to college, made positions for women rare; few women could be found in the science faculties of colleges and universities. Despite the "overt discrimination" Neufeld often witnessed, she decided nonetheless to pursue her interests. "Some people looked at women who wanted a career in science as a little eccentric," she told Milite, "but I enjoyed what I was doing and I decided I would persevere."

After spending several years at Berkeley, Neufeld moved on to NIH in 1963, where she began as research biochemist at the National Institute of Arthritis Metabolism and Digestive Diseases. It was during her time at NIH that Neufeld began her research on mucopolysaccharidoses (MPS), disorders in which a complex series of sugars known as mucopolysaccharides cannot be stored or metabolized properly. Hurler syndrome is a form of MPS. Other forms of MPS include Hunter's Syndrome, Scheie Syndrome, Sanfillipo, and Morquio. These are all inherited disorders. Defectively metabolized sugars accumulate in fetal cells of victims. The disorders can cause stunted physical and mental growth, vision and hearing problems, and a short life span.

Because some plant cell wall polymers contain uronic acids (a component of mucopolysaccharides), Neufeld, from her work with plants, could surmise how the complex sugars worked in humans. When she first began working on Hurler syndrome in 1967, she initially thought the problem might stem from faulty regulation of the sugars, but experiments showed the problem was in fact the abnormally slow rate at which the sugars were broken down.

Working with fellow scientist Joseph Fratantoni, Neufeld attempted to isolate the problem by tagging mucopolysaccharides with radioactive sulfate, as well as mixing normal cells with MPS patient cells. Fratantoni inadvertently mixed cells from a Hurler patient and a Hunter patient—and the result was a nearly normal cell culture. The two cultures had essentially "cured" each other. Additional work showed that the cells could cross-correct by transferring a corrective factor through the culture medium. The goal now was to determine the makeup of the corrective factor or factors.

Through a combination of biological and molecular techniques, Neufeld was able to identify the corrective factors as a series of enzymes. Normally, the enzymes would serve as catalysts for the reactions needed for cells to metabolize the sugars. In Hurler and other MPS patients, enzyme deficiency makes this difficult. A further complication is that often the enzymes that do exist lack the proper chemical markers needed to enter cells and do their work. Neufeld's subsequent research with diseases similar to MPS, including I-Cell disease, showed how enzymes needed markers to match with cell receptors to team with the right cells.

This research paved the way for successful prenatal diagnosis of the MPS and related disorders, as well as genetic counseling. Although no cure has been found, researchers are experimenting with such techniques as gene replacement therapy and bone marrow transplants.

In 1973 Neufeld was named chief of NIH's Section of Human Biochemical Genetics, and in 1979 she was named chief of the Genetics and Biochemistry Branch of the National Institute of Arthritis, Diabetes, and Digestive and Kidney Diseases (NIADDK). She served as deputy director in NIADDK's Division of Intramural Research from 1981 to 1983.

In 1984 Neufeld went back to the University of California, this time the Los Angeles campus, as chair of the biological chemistry department, where she continues her research. In addition to MPS, she has done research on similar disorders such as Tay-Sachs disease. But her concerns go beyond research. She strongly believes that young scientists just starting out need support and encouragement from the scientific community, because these scientists can bring new and innovative perspectives to difficult questions and issues. At the same time, young scientists can learn much from the experience of established scientists. In her capacity as department chair, Neufeld encourages interaction among established scientists, young scientists, and students.

Neufeld has chaired the Scientific Advisory Board of the National MPS Society since 1988 and was president of the American Society for Biochemistry and Molecular Biology from 1992 to 1993. She was elected to both the National Academy of Sciences (USA) and the American Academy of Arts and Sciences in 1977 and named a fellow of the American Association for Advancement in Science in 1988. In 1990 she was named California Scientist of the Year.

Married to Benjamin Neufeld (a former official with the U.S. Public Health Service) since 1951, she is the mother of two children. Although her work takes up a great deal of her time, she enjoys hiking when she gets the chance, and travel "when it's for pleasure and not business."

Further Reading

O'Neill, Lois Decker, editor, *The Women's Book of World Records and Achievements,* Anchor Press, 1979.

Neufeld, Elizabeth F., *Interview with George Milite conducted December 17,* 1993.

UCLA Medical School, "http://www.mednet.ucla.edu/acadprog/som/ddo/biochem/labs/neufeld.htm," July 22, 1997. □

Balthasar Neumann

The German architect Balthasar Neumann (1687-1753) created some of the finest baroque buildings of the 18th century for the Schönborn family in central Germany, notably the Residenz in Würzburg and the church of Vierzehnheiligen.

In the great flowering of the arts which took place in central Europe during the early decades of the 18th century, it was largely in the field of architecture that the most famous achievements were made. The greatest architect of the time, it is acknowledged, was Johann Bernhard Fischer von Erlach of Vienna. His spiritual heir was Balthasar Neumann, who, working for the powerful Schönborn family, key figures at the imperial court and rulers of several important principalities within the Holy Roman Empire and passionate builders all, was provided with almost limitless possibilities to display his talents.

Neumann was born in January 1687 at Eger (Erlau) in Bohemia, the son of a clothier. He was trained as a cannon and bell founder but apparently showed such promise that he was sent to Würzburg to study civil and military engineering, as well as to continue his work in the foundries. In 1714 he enlisted in the palace guards at Würzburg as a lieutenant of artillery; he served in the imperial forces in the Belgrade campaign of 1717 as a military engineer.

After 3 years of travel Neumann returned to Würzburg, where, with the architect Johann Dientzenhofer, he shared responsibility for planning the future episcopal palace, which the Prince-Bishop Philip Franz von Schönborn had decided to build in place of his residence in the fortress of Marienburg overlooking the city. This enterprise occupied Neumann for most of his life and was the crowning achievement of his career.

The Residenz

Although Neumann's control over the planning of the episcopal palace was anything but absolute at the beginning, for the prince-bishop sought advice about it everywhere—from his relatives, from other German architects like Maximilian von Welsch and Johann Lucas von Hildebrandt, and even from the French architects Robert de Cotte and Gabriel Germain Boffrand—Neumann gradually won the confidence of his patron and served as the stabilizing influence and coordinator of all their suggestions and alterations, adding his own ideas as well to the general scheme. It is chiefly Hildebrandt's influence, particularly in the treatment of surfaces, that predominates over all the others. The result of this collaboration was a huge building complex, with a *cour d'honneur* surrounded on three sides by blocks with inner courts, the central block accentuated by the large octagonal dome over the main hall, and the exterior facades enlivened by pavilionlike projections. The palace chapel, designed by Neumann and decorated by Hildebrandt (begun in 1730), has a basic plan of intersecting ovals, and its almost bewilderingly rich interior decoration is in marked contrast to the relatively plain exterior of the building.

In the great stairway, which Neumann began in 1737, he revealed his special talent, the manipulation of dynamic space. A single flight of stairs leads from the ground floor to the landing, where two flights then lead up and back to the main floor. In this huge space, for the ceiling is unsupported by arcades or columns, the visitor only gradually becomes aware of the size of the stairway hall and of the vastness and complexity of the fresco decoration executed by Giovanni Battista Tiepolo (1752-1753). In his representation of the four continents he created his finest fresco. On the cornice before the personification of Europe, he portrayed Neumann in his military uniform, seated on a cannon, one of the more appealing portraits of the period. The stairway lacks the elaborate balustrade which Hildebrandt certainly planned for it, and the rich effects he had intended have been diminished. This is not the case in the Marble Hall, which serves as the climax for the whole stairway, where the huge enclosed oval space is enriched with splendid stucco ornament and with frescoes by Tiepolo (1750-1752).

At Schloss Bruchsal (destroyed), where Neumann was called to work in 1728 after much of the palace had been done, he was able to continue his work on stairways. Here he constructed (1731-1732) an oval landing joining the staterooms, with the stairways encircling it as they ascend, presenting a rather enclosed feeling until one arrives at the spacious and elaborate landing on the main floor. He was able to resolve, again, the problem of the stairway (1740) at Schloss Brühl by lightening the supporting walls of the upper flights with arches, thus giving a spacious effect to the whole lower level of the stairwell. The stairs seem to float in the air as they rise upward to the richly decorated upper level, topped with an oval dome pierced with windows.

Church Architecture

During the 1740s Neumann began his two greatest churches: the pilgrimage church of Vierzehnheiligen near Bamberg, and the abbey church at Neresheim in Swabia. The church at Vierzehnheiligen (1743-1772) was to have, as its central element, an altar built over the spot where the 14 saints known as the Helpers in Need had appeared in a miraculous vision. At first it was thought that the church should be built on a central plan, but Neumann's design for a longitudinal-plan church with the altar under the dome over the crossing was accepted. The builder entrusted with the construction began the chancel incorrectly, and Neumann had to step in and alter his plan, so that the altar was now in what would have been the nave. He skillfully resolved this unfortunate situation by breaking the nave up into ovals; in the center of the largest oval was the altar, thus giving the impression that it is, indeed, in the center of the whole edifice.

This concern with blending a central-plan church with a longitudinal nave, so fortuitously worked out at Vierzehnheiligen, found its fullest expression at Neresheim, Neumann's last great church (1747-1792). Here the longitudinal oval of the crossing grows out of the ovals of the transepts and the two ovals which make up the nave and the two of the deep chancel, yet the whole is broken up in such a way that one sees only a vast and intricate articulated space over which the dome seems to float. Although altered somewhat after Neumann's death, it still is the purest expression of his architectural ideas.

Other Activities

Throughout his life Neumann remained an officer in the bishop's military and continued to concern himself with problems of military engineering. He also developed a freshwater supply for the city of Würzburg (1730), built a glass factory and a mirror factory (1733), and taught military and civil engineering at the University of Würzburg.

Neumann was fairly prosperous, the owner of vineyards and a fine country house. Although under the less splendid successors of the Schönborn bishops he was not always able to build as he would have wished, he continued to concern himself until his death with plans for great palaces, complete with vast and complex stairways, such as his designs for the Hofburg in Vienna (1747) and the palaces at Stuttgart (1747, 1749, 1750) and Karlsruhe (1749), none of which were executed. He died, a colonel, in Würzburg on July 18, 1753.

Further Reading

The only literature on Neumann in English is contained in Nicolas Powell, *From Baroque to Rococo* (1959); John Bourke, *Baroque Churches of Central Europe* (1962); Eberhard Hempel, *Baroque Art and Architecture in Central Europe* (1965); and Henry-Russell Hitchcock, *Rococo Architecture in Southern Germany* (1968). ☐

Richard Joseph Neutra

The lifework of the Austrian-born American architect Richard Joseph Neutra (1892-1970) was an attempt to combine the technical precision of the International Style with other elements more organic to American architectural traditions.

Richard Neutra was born in Vienna on April 8, 1892. He trained at the Technische Hochschule, receiving his diploma in 1917. While there he was greatly influenced by the buildings and writings of a contemporary Viennese architect, Adolf Loos, one of the pioneers of the modern movement in Europe. Loos introduced Neutra to innovations occurring in American architecture, particularly the experiments of Louis Sullivan and the Chicago school. Neutra's interest in American architecture grew when he became familiar with the work of Frank Lloyd Wright.

In 1918 Neutra went to Switzerland, working as a landscape architect and city planner. In 1921 he moved to Lukenwalde, Germany, to serve in the Municipal Building Office. The next year he became associated with Erich Mendelsohn in the design of the Business Center in Haifa,

Palestine. Neutra emigrated to the United States in 1923, joining the Chicago firm of Holabird and Roche. At the same time he met Frank Lloyd Wright and began working at Wright's Wisconsin home, "Taliesin." Three years later Neutra moved to Los Angeles, setting up a partnership with another Vienna-born architect, Rudolph Schindler.

As his first major American commission, Neutra designed a home for Richard Lovell (1927-1929) in Los Angeles. Its clear-cut lines and planar surfaces are suggestive of the International Style, but the placement of the building on its mountain site echoes Wright's concept of organic setting. The house is constructed of thin steel elements cantilevered over a ravine; the entire structure is supported from above by steel cables. Interestingly, the smooth white treatment of the walls and the use of broad areas of glass may have influenced Wright himself in his design for the kaufmann House (1936) in Bear Run, Pa.

During the 1930s Neutra continued to express the boxlike forms of the International Style in his own personal idiom. For example, in both the Josef von Sternberg House (1936) in the San Fernando Valley and the Corona School (1934-1935) in Bell, Calif., he combined many of the technical approaches associated with the International Style with the use of unusual building materials such as native stone and redwood.

The most significant of Neutra's projects in the early 1940s was Channel Heights, a government-sponsored housing development in San Pedro, Calif. Neutra was responsible for the entire project, from the overall plan to the

specific details such as redwood trim. Although the units were identical, he succeeded in individualizing them by varying the placement of each house in accordance with its particular terrain. Neutra designed a number of private homes in southern California. Among them was the Kaufmann (now Lisk) House in Palm Springs; here by brilliantly integrating the house with its desert site, Neutra reached a high point in his domestic style.

In 1949 an expanding practice prompted Neutra to form a partnership with Robert E. Alexander. Although the firm continued to design domestic structures, it concentrated on larger, public commissions, designing, for example, office buildings and university libraries. A motel complex at Malibu Beach, Calif. (1955), which overlooks the Pacific, is characteristic of Neutra's ambition to express as vividly and simply as possible the relationship between a structure and its natural surroundings. By successfully maintaining structural clarity while relating a building to its site, Neutra achieved a uniquely personal style. He died on April 16, 1970, in Wuppertal, West Germany.

Further Reading

Useful for an understanding of Neutra's work is his early theoretical essay, *Survival through Design* (1954). The best work on him is Esther McCoy, *Richard Neutra* (1960). Bruno Zevi, *Richard Neutra* (1954), is a good, secondary biography and critique. A résumé of Neutra's projects and designs through the 1950s is in Willy Boesiger, ed., *Richard Neutra: Buildings and Projects* (3 vols., 1966). □

Louise Nevelson

Louise Nevelson (1900-1988) was an American abstract sculptor who explored both the density and transparency of materials. Her imagery was based on surrealist and cubist models.

Born in Kiev, Russia, Louise Nevelson emigrated with her family to the United States in 1905. She studied painting at the Art Students League, New York City, from 1929 through1930 and traveled to Munich in 1931 to study with Hans Hofmann. In the mid-1930s, she turned to sculpture. In 1944, a piece designed an abstract sculpture composed of wood was shown to the public for the first time. In her early work she uses traditional materials and processes, and the images are almost exclusively figures, as in *Mountain Woman* (1949-1950).

By the mid-1950s Nevelson had emerged as a significant force in American sculpture. She constructed freestanding and relief pieces in wood that was finished in a monochromatic hue. *Black Majesty* (1955) is a series of totemic events vertically projecting from a horizontal pedestal. At the same time, the presentation of her pieces became environmental in scope, and she often exhibited them under a common title or theme, for example, *The Royal Voyage* (1956) with jagged forms sprawled on the floor as

well as mounted on pedestals, *The Forest* (1957), and *Moon Garden plus One* (1958).

Some comparisons have been made between Nevelson's work of the 1950s and concurrent attitudes in American painting, such as abstract expressionism. However, her compositions—while at first glance open-ended and freely handled in their assembled state—exhibit greater control, both formally and in their mythopoetic intent. Like some contemporary sculptors, she used cast-off materials; but her ingenious framing and pedestal devices, such as the relief, the box, and the column, in addition to her painterly concerns with light and dark, set her apart.

By the end of the 1950s Nevelson had moved from black and natural surfaces to overall white in the memorable series *Dawn's Wedding Feast*. The scale of this exhibition seemed to forecast her large single wall reliefs *Homage to 6,000,000 I* (1964) and *Homage to the World* (1966). She, again returned to wood painted black (triangular) in *Silent Music I* (1964).

In the mid-1960s Nevelson came to prefer compositions with fewer elements, more rigidly controlling the relief space. She turned to such new materials as black lucite, aluminum, and magnesium, as in *Atmosphere* and *Environment*. In *Environment* she achieved open, freestanding structures that are as concerned with volume as with mass. In her work of the late 1960s she used welded vertical shapes; however, she also continued to execute wood constructions.

Nevelson's artwork of the mid-1970s, she utilized cast paper in *Dawn's Presence* (1976). The early 1980s and mid-1980s, she worked with detailed PHSColograms in *Keeping Time with Fashion* (1983) and painted wood in *Mirror Shadow XI* (1985). Remembered for her natural abstract sculptures, her death in 1988 marked a significant loss to the world of art.

Further Reading

The most comprehensive work on Nevelson is John Gordon's, *Louise Nevelson* (1967), published on the occasion of the Whitney Museum retrospective exhibition of her sculpture; *Louise Nevelson* (1970), by Mary Hancock Buxton is valuable for the artist's later work; *Louise Nevelson: Prints and Drawings, 1953-1966,* by Una E. Johnson (1967); and *Louise Nevelson* (1969), exhibition catalog of the Museum of Fine Arts, Houston, and College of Fine Arts, University of Texas; useful for general background is a work by the editors of *Art in America,* entitled *The Artist in America* (1967); Nevelson's updated artwork can be located in *Imaging Incorporated* (1995-96); *Early Nevelson* (1997); and *Pace Editions Inc.* (1976); www.Artincontext.com. ☐

John Williamson Nevin

John Williamson Nevin (1803-1886) was a conservative opponent of the enthusiastic revivalism that characterized 19th-century American Protestantism.

Born in Franklin Country, Pa., on Feb. 20, 1803, John Williamson Nevin grew up on his parents' farm, imbibing their strict Presbyterianism. He graduated at the age of 19 from Union College in Schenectady, N.Y., and then attended Princeton Theological Seminary in New Jersey, although uncertain of his call to the ministry. After completing studies at Princeton, he accepted appointment as professor of biblical literature at Western Theological Seminary in Allegheny, Pa. Finally, in 1835, he received ordination as a minister in the Presbyterian Church.

A scholar by temperament, Nevin learned the German language and studied the German theologians of the day. His newspaper articles on temperance and abolition spread his reputation; in 1840 the trustees of the German Reformed Church's seminary at Mercersburg, Pa., offered him a professorship in theology. It was a big step for an innately cautious man, but he decided to accept the call and converted to the German Reformed Church.

Dignified in appearance and somewhat preoccupied in manner, Nevin inclined to a conservative approach on all questions, including those then agitating American Protestantism. The revivalistic fervor sweeping many denominations found no friend in Nevin, although in his youth he had experienced a mild "awakening." He published a series of lectures, *The Anxious Bench: A Tract for the Times* (1843), which criticized the "new measures" and angered their proponents. The absence of emotionalism from the Lu-

theran and German Reformed Churches of that day was partly due to Nevin.

Nevin and his colleagues went on to develop a conservative doctrinal position eventually labeled the "Mercersburg Theology." His *Mystical Presence: A Vindication of the Reformed or Calvinistic Doctrine of the Holy Eucharist* (1846) drew much public criticism for its alleged sympathy with Roman Catholic belief.

In 1841, in addition to his seminary duties, Nevin became the temporary president of Marshall College, the seminary's undergraduate division. Bedeviled by the school's financial problems, he helped engineer a merger with Franklin College in Lancaster, Pa. In 1851 he gave up teaching for reasons of health and because his controversial opinions made him the target of public attack. In retirement, he worked on a new liturgy for his adopted church, but in 1866 he accepted the "provisional" presidency of Franklin and Marshall College. He served for 10 years, resigning again in 1876 in order to relieve the college of the financial burden of his salary. He died on June 6, 1886.

Further Reading

There is no modern biography of Nevin. Aside from his own incomplete autobiographical sketches in the German Reformed Church's *Messenger,* the only authority is Theodore Appel's filiopietistic *The Life and Work of John Williamson Nevin* (1889; repr. 1969). James Hastings Nichols, *Romanticism in American Theology: Nevin and Schaff at Mercersburg* (1961), contains an extended account of Nevin's theology. ☐

Allan Nevins

Allan Nevins (1890-1971) began life as a journalist but ended it with a reputation as one of the best popular American historians of the day. Although he wrote a number of books on a variety of topics, he is most famous for his eight-volume study of the Civil War.

Allan Nevins was born on a farm near Camp Point, Illinois, on May 20, 1890, the son of Joseph and Emma (Stahl) Nevins. According to Nevins, his father, who was a stern Presbyterian, enjoined him to work hard, an injunction he followed faithfully all of his life.

Nevins received his academic training at the University of Illinois, earning an A.B. in 1912 and an A.M. the following year. His first academic appointment was as a graduate instructor in English while working on his master's degree. While still a student at Illinois he began writing two books, one on Robert Rogers, which was published in 1914, and a second on the history of the University of Illinois, which was published in 1917. Both books are now forgotten, but their very existence demonstrates Nevins' energetic and workaholic ways.

After graduating from Illinois in 1913, Nevins became an editorial writer for both the *New York Evening Post* and

The Nation. Not only did he fill both these positions, but he also continued to do research in the New York Public Library and to write at home in the evenings. His busy schedule continued even after his marriage to Mary Fleming Richardson on December 30, 1916, and the birth of their two children, Anne Elizabeth and Meredith. He did sever his relationship with *The Nation,* however, in 1918.

The 1920s were a particularly productive time for Nevins. He published a history of the *New York Evening Post—The Evening Post: A Century of Journalism*—in 1922, a year before he left the paper. His next book was *American Social History as Recorded by British Travellers* (1923), a collection of eye-witness accounts of American society. The book was highly regarded and was re-issued 25 years later under the title *America Through British Eyes.*

Nevins became literary editor for the *New York Sun* in 1924, but left the position after a year to become an editorial writer for the *New York World.* In 1927 he published *The American States During and After the Revolution, 1775-1789.* The book, which was a study of conditions in each of the states during the Revolutionary period, became one of the standard works on that era. The same year Nevins took a year's leave from his newspaper duties to teach American history at Cornell University. The trial year convinced Nevins that he should continue to teach, so after he returned to New York City, and to the *New York World,* he became an associate professor of history at Columbia University. This position entailed teaching two classes each term. Nevins continued, however, as a fulltime editorial writer.

In 1931 Nevins cut his ties to the newspaper world and became, for the first time, a full-fledged academic as professor of history at Columbia. A year after his appointment Nevins published *Grover Cleveland: A Study in Courage* (1932), the first of two biographies of his to win Pulitzer prizes. The book combines careful historical research with literary charm and added considerably to Nevin's reputation. Two years later he wrote a *History of the Bank of New York and Trust Company, 1784-1934,* which was done at the behest of the company and which demonstrated an interest in business history which was to continue. In 1936 he won a second Pulitzer Prize for *Hamilton Fish: The Inner Story of the Grant Administration.* A fourth book in that decade, *The Gateway to History* (1938), was an exercise in historiography, another interest of Nevins.

During the 1930s Nevins began to collect honorary degrees and to accept invitations for visiting professorships at other universities. He held the Sir George Watson Chair of American History, Literature, and Institutions in England in 1934-1935; was visiting professor of history at the California Institute of Technology in 1937-1938, as well as a visiting scholar at Huntington Library; and in 1940-1941 he was Harmsworth Professor at Oxford University, a post he was to fill again in 1964-1965.

During World War II Nevins worked in several capacities to further the war effort. He collaborated with Henry Steele Commager, his Columbia colleague, to write *America: The Story of a Free People* (1942), an effort to argue that the United States had a valuable historic heritage. He then served as a special representative of the Office of War Information in Australia and New Zealand in 1943-1944 and was chief public affairs officer at the American embassy in London in 1945-1946.

Following his return to Columbia Nevins began his most ambitious project, which was to become an eight-volume series on the Civil War. The first to be published was *The Ordeal of Union* (1947), which won the Bancroft Prize and the $10,000 Scribners' Literary prize. In 1948 he began the Oral History Project, a pioneer effort at collecting the memories of living individuals at Columbia University.

In the 1950s Nevins continued his work on the Civil War, publishing *The Emergence of Lincoln,* 2 volumes (1952), and *The War for the Union,* 2 volumes (1959). Two further volumes with the same title were published in 1961. He also began to write the biographies of important American business leaders, believing that these giants had built America's industrial strength and deserved more favorable treatment than that accorded them by the muckrakers. In 1953 he published *John D. Rockefeller: A Study in Power,* which presented a much more favorable view of the oil magnate than had earlier biographies. The next year he, along with Frank E. Hill, co-authored the first of a three-volume book on Henry Ford called *Ford: The Times, the Man, and the Company.* The remaining two volumes appeared in 1957 and 1963.

Nevins retired from Columbia in 1958 after an exhausting career in which he had not only taught and published books and articles, but had also supervised over 100 doctoral dissertations. He did not stop working, however, but instead moved to California to become senior research associate at the Huntington Library. There he continued to write. Among the books produced there were *Herbert H. Lehman and His Era* (1963) and *James Trustlow Adams: Historian of the American Dream* (1968).

When he died in San Marino, California, on March 5, 1971, Nevins had accumulated a distinguished career of service as well. He had been president of the American Historical Association, the Society of American Historians, and the American Academy of Arts and Letters. Only he knew exactly how much he had written. Ray Allan Billington has estimated that he wrote over 50 books and 1,000 articles and edited another 75 books, but was unsure of the actual total.

Further Reading

The best evaluation of Nevins is the essay entitled "Allan Nevins, Historian: A Personal Reminiscence," written by Ray Allan Billington in his compilation on *Allan Nevins on History* (1975). The book contains essays by Nevins on a variety of topics and is an excellent introduction to his work. There are several short passages on Nevins' attempts to write history that was at once scholarly and popular in John Higham's *History* (1965). □

Alexander Nevsky

The Russian leader Alexander Nevsky (1219-1263) was prince of Novgorod and then grand prince of Vladimir. An outstanding military leader and statesman, he earned his surname from a victory over the Swedes at the Neva River.

Alexander Nevsky was the son of Iaroslav Vsevolodovich, Prince of Pereiaslavl and Novgorod. When his father moved to Kiev in 1236, Alexander succeeded him as prince of Novgorod. In 1237 Mongols began to invade Russia from the east, while in the west the Swedes and the Germanic Sword Knights of Livonia pressed against Novgorod under the pretense of a crusade.

His father, who had become grand prince of Vladimir, entrusted Alexander with the defense of the western frontiers. Although greatly outnumbered, Alexander decisively defeated the Swedes on July 15, 1240, at the mouth of the Neva River. Because of a conflict with Novgorod nobility, he had to leave the city shortly afterward but was recalled when the Sword Knights attacked the land. He trapped them on the ice of Lake Peipus on April 5, 1242, and destroyed most of their force.

Seeing the impossibility of waging a successful war with the Mongols, in 1242 Iaroslav recognized their sovereignty over Russia and pledged his allegiance to the Mongol Khan. When Iaroslav died in 1246, Alexander succeeded him in Kiev, and Alexander's brother Adrei ascended the throne of Vladimir. In 1252, when Adrei refused to pledge allegiance to the new great Khan, he was driven out of Russia, and the title of grand prince of Vladimir was passed to Alexander.

In spite of strong opposition among the Russian people, Alexander remained faithful to his father's policy of cooperation with the Mongols. He had the full support of the Russian Orthodox Church, which enjoyed considerable freedom and influence under the Mongols. Slowly, he won the people too, for in return for his cooperation Alexander received major concessions from the Mongol khans. Most importantly, they agreed to reduce, and later abandon, their demands for Russian troops and to withdraw their tax collectors from Russian lands.

Alexander died in 1263. His people greatly admired him for his incessant efforts to alleviate the Mongol yoke, his heroic defense of Russia and Orthodoxy in the west, and his deeply felt Christianity. After his death, Alexander came to be venerated as one of the most popular rulers in Russian history, a savior of Russia, and a saint. Bowing to popular pressure, the Russian Church canonized him locally in Vladimir in 1380 and generally in 1547.

Further Reading

A popular sketch of Alexander's life is in Constantin de Grunwald, *Saints of Russia* (trans. 1960). He has also received considerable attention in two works on Russia: Vasilii O. Kliuchevskii, *A History of Russia*, vol. 1 (trans. 1911), and George Vernadsky, *A History of Russia,* vol. 3 (1953). □

John Newbery

English publisher John Newbery (1713-1767) was the first person to create books specifically for children. His work reflected the changes in attitudes about children during the eighteenth century and aimed to present entertaining and educational materials designed for a child's reading level and interests.

The eighteenth-century publisher John Newbery was the first person to focus on the creation and marketing of books for children. The success of his work was due in part to the rise of the British middle class during this period and the increased amount of money and leisure time they were able to spend on their children. Another factor was a changing philosophy about the role and nature of children; rather than being looked upon as miniature adults, children were beginning to be recognized as having interests, energies, and attention spans that were greatly different from those of adults. Newbery's accomplishments in catering to these new trends in society and the foundations he laid for the ongoing practice of children's publishing are recognized today in the Newbery Awards—the annual honors bestowed upon outstanding works of children's literature by the American Library Association.

Newbery was born in 1713 in Waltham, Berkshire, England. He was the son of a farmer, Robert Newbery, but other members of his family were active in the publishing business. Newbery received a modest education in his home district, learning only the basics traditionally thought necessary for a farmer. But the boy also had a great love of reading and was drawn to a career that would indulge his appreciation of books. At the age of 16, he was apprenticed to a printer in the town of Reading, nine miles from his home. There he learned the skills of the printing trade from William Carnan and assisted in the production of Carnan's newspaper, the *Reading Mercury.* Eventually, Newbery was promoted to the position of assistant to the printer.

Built Successful Newspaper Business

When Carnan died in 1737, the 24-year-old Newbery inherited half of his printing business, sharing the company with Carnan's brother. The publisher soon gained more control over the business by marrying Carnan's widow. Newbery took responsibility for Carnan's children, and eventually had three of his own. The *Reading Mercury* thrived under his supervision; by 1743 it was sold in nearly 50 markets and was one of the top provincial papers of the day. The paper's success may have been in part due to Newbery's active interest in promoting his paper and investigating new markets and business possibilities. In 1740 he had undertaken a tour of England for these purposes, gaining information that may have guided him in his later book publishing ventures. It was in 1740 that Newbery published his first book, beginning the career for which he would be best remembered. For much of his life, however, a large part

of his income was not from his publishing activities but from his side business ventures. One of these enterprises involved the sale of about thirty different patent medicines, including Dr. James' Fever Powder; advertisements for these products often appeared in Newbery's publications.

In his ongoing search for new opportunities, Newbery moved to London, opening the Bible and Sun publishing company in 1745 at St. Paul's Churchyard. This marked the beginning of Newbery's most productive years as a publisher. In London, he began the writing and selling of children's books, a market in which there was a growing demand for materials, particularly during the Christmas holidays. The books he produced were aimed both at the amusement and education of children. His first success in this area was the 1744 book *A Pretty Little Pocket Book,* a high-quality work that featured an entertaining and colorful style, including expensive copperplate engravings and a gilt cover. The book contrasted sharply with the dull and cheap appearance of earlier chapbooks, and the public eagerly snatched up copies; at least 10,000 copies were distributed between its initial publication and the end of the century.

Created High-Quality Children's Books

In 1746, Newbery published two more books directed at the education of children, *Circle of the Sciences: Writing* and *Circle of the Sciences: Arithmetic.* An introduction to the ideas of the English physicist and mathematician Isaac Newton were presented in the 1761 work, *The Newtonian System of Philosophy Adapted to the Capacities of Young Gentlemen and Ladies . . . By Tom Telescope,* popularly known as simply *Tom Telescope.* The book's author is a subject of debate; some believe that the author Oliver Goldsmith wrote the book, while others suggest that Newbery himself was the creator. This was another great success for Newbery, going through at least ten printings for a total of around 30,000 books by 1800. Newbery was cautious in business though, and his first printings were usually very small; only once he was able to gauge the interest of the market would he undertake further printings.

Children's literature was only one aspect of Newbery's role in literature and publishing in his day. He was an associate of a number of leading English writers, including Samuel Johnson, Oliver Goldsmith, and Christopher Smart. These authors and others contributed to Newbery's numerous newspapers in London and the provinces. One such paper was *The Universal Chronicle or Weekly Gazette,* which he founded in 1758; the paper published a number of famous works by Johnson, including "The Idler," "The Rambler," and "The Lives of the Poets." *The Public Ledger,* initiated in 1760, featured Goldsmith's "A Citizen of the World" in its first issue. Newbery also published Goldsmith's book *The Vicar of Wakefield* in 1766.

Memorialized in Book Awards

Newbery died on December 22, 1767, in London at the age of 54. His publishing business was carried on by his son, Francis Newbery, and later by one of Newbery's nephews, then the nephew's wife. Although the business lasted until 1801, it never again reached the remarkable level of success that Newbery had accomplished with his varied publishing projects. His contributions to the promotion of children's literature resulted in similar ventures by other companies, however, insuring a continuing commitment to the field. More than 150 years after the publisher's death, the Newbery Award for children's literature was established in 1922 by the American Library Association, honoring Newbery's pioneering work in presenting the first materials specifically designed for the amusement and entertainment of children.

Further Reading

For more information, see Darton, F. J. Harvey, *Children's Books in England,* Cambridge University Press, 1932; Meigs, Cornelia, *A Critical History of Children's Literature,* Macmillan, 1953; Noblett, William, "John Newbery: Publisher Extraordinary," *History Today,* April, 1972, pp. 265-71; and Welsh, Charles, *A Bookseller of the Last Century, Being Some Account of the Life of John Newbery,* Griffith, Farran, Okeden and Welsh (London), 1885. □

Simon Newcomb

The American astronomer Simon Newcomb (1835-1909) was important in government scientific circles during the late 19th century. Primarily a mathematical astronomer, he studied the motion of the moon and the planets and redetermined various astronomical values.

Simon Newcomb was born on March 12, 1835, at Wallace, Nova Scotia, the son of an itinerant New England schoolteacher. Apprenticed at the age of 16 to a herbalist doctor, Newcomb ran away 2 years later to the United States. He taught at country schools in Maryland for several years and in 1857 was appointed a computer in the Nautical Almanac Office, then located at Harvard University, although the *Almanac* was published by the Federal government. He took advantage of his stay at Harvard by attending the Lawrence Scientific School, from which he received a bachelor of science degree in 1858. He married Mary Caroline Hassler in 1863.

Newcomb's government service continued from 1857 until his retirement in 1897. In 1861 he was commissioned professor of mathematics in the U.S. Navy and shortly thereafter was assigned to the Naval Observatory and Nautical Almanac Office. At the observatory he began his mathematical investigations of such fundamental questions as the orbits of Neptune and Uranus, the motion of the moon, and the right ascensions of the equatorial fundamental stars. His revision of the value of the solar parallax published in 1867 remained standard until 1895, when it was superseded by his own revision.

In 1877 Newcomb was appointed superintendent of the American Ephemeris and Nautical Almanac Office. He immediately began a reorganization of the office and a program to reform the entire basis of fundamental data involved in the computation of the ephemeris. Most of this reformation, a monumental task involving virtually a recomputation of all known astronomical measures, was completed during his lifetime.

As early as 1867 Newcomb had suggested the desirability of accurately determining the velocity of light as a means of obtaining a reliable value for the radius of the earth's orbit. In 1878 he began the experiments, for a while collaborating with Albert Michelson, whose later works far overshadowed Newcomb's efforts in this line.

In addition to a large number of papers on almost every branch of astronomy, Newcomb published a number of mathematical textbooks and several astronomical books for a popular audience, including *Popular Astronomy* (1878), *The Stars* (1901), *Astronomy for Everybody* (1902), and his autobiographical *Reminiscences of an Astronomer* (1903). He also wrote a novel, *His Wisdom, the Defender* (1900), and three books and a large number of articles on economics, a subject on which he was considered a great authority in his day. He died in Washington, D.C., on July 11, 1909.

Further Reading

Except for William W. Campbell's *Biographical Memoir: Simon Newcomb, 1835-1909* (1924), the only source for Newcomb's life is his own *Reminiscences of an Astronomer* (1903).

Additional Sources

Moyer, Albert E., *A scientist's voice in American culture: Simon Newcomb and the rhetoric of scientific method,* Berkeley: University of California Press, 1992. □

Thomas Newcomen

The English inventor and engineer Thomas Newcomen (1663-1729) developed the first practical steam engine, an important feature of the industrial revolution.

Thomas Newcomen was born on Feb. 24, 1663, at Dartmouth, Devonshire. It seems probable that as a youth he was apprenticed to learn the blacksmith trade and later became an itinerant ironmonger, a craftsman who made tools, nails, and other hardware, which he sold throughout the mining areas about Dartmouth.

Many mines at that time had been dug so deep that they were constantly flooded, and to continue them in operation the operators had to find a better means to pump out the water. It was this omnipresent problem which led Newcomen to attempt to devise a machine which could drive a water pump. As to how Newcomen might have achieved this, 18th- and 19th-century writers usually pointed to earlier attempts to use steam as a motive force. However, no evidence has been found of any borrowing on the part of Newcomen. On the other hand, he never took out a patent of monopoly on his engine, as Thomas Savery did in 1698, because Savery's patent covered all means utilized to raise water by fire. This is probably why Newcomen found it necessary to purchase, from the proprietors of the Savery patent, the right to build a steam engine—a transaction which probably occurred about 1705. Thus it is doubtful whether Newcomen benefited financially from his invention, since it had to be exploited under another's patent. The first Newcomen engine which can be documented dates from 1712. It has been estimated that it required at least 10 to 15 years of development. Both the Newcomen and Savery engines were based upon the use of condensed steam; however, they also differed in important fundamentals.

The basic principle of Newcomen's engine was simple. Steam was injected into a cylinder, forcing a piston to move out. Cold water was then sprayed into the piston, the steam condensed, and a partial vacuum was formed. Atmospheric pressure then returned the piston to its original position, so that the process could be repeated. The piston's reciprocating motion was finally transferred to a water pump by a beam which rocked about its center. That this to-and-fro motion might somehow be transformed into the more useful rotary motion was a problem which had not as yet been recognized.

Newcomen's steam engine spread throughout the mining area of England and rescued many mines from bankruptcy. It was not until John Smeaton's and, more important,

James Watt's versions of the steam engine were developed, almost three-quarters of a century later, that Newcomen's machine was superseded. Newcomen died in London on Aug. 5, 1729.

Further Reading

A biography of Newcomen is L. T. C. Rolt, *Thomas Newcomen* (1963). Some material on him is in H. W. Dickinson, *A Short History of the Steam Engine* (1939). □

Samuel Irving Newhouse

Samuel Irving Newhouse (1895-1979) built a multimillion-dollar newspaper, magazine, and radio/television/cable empire—which his sons Samuel Jr. and Donald continued—by following the trend away from a largely political, crusading press and toward a commercial, profit-oriented media of great enterprises.

Born on May 24, 1895, in New York's Lower East Side, Samuel Irving (usually called S.I.) Newhouse followed a Horatio Alger pattern of rags-to-riches by combining remarkable drive, memory for figures, and talent for picking subordinates with a grass-roots sense of pleasing advertisers and the public.

Newhouse grew up in Bayonne, New Jersey. The oldest of eight children in a Russian immigrant family whose father failed at business, he left school at 13 to become the principal breadwinner. Soon he became involved in nursing the troubled Bayonne *Times* newspaper to health, learning lessons that he applied in later life.

The key was raising revenue by gaining retail advertising through aggressive salesmanship, attractive formats, and various discounts. He fostered readership loyalty with home delivery and emphasized features, comics, and brisk, local human interest stories. Vigorous in cutting labor and other costs, Newhouse opposed unionization in the 1930s, rationalized and consolidated operations, and saved substantially through merging with opposing papers. He founded only one paper; instead, he bought and revived declining papers whose location in potentially prosperous areas made them good risks. He plowed profits back into his family-owned enterprises rather than paying dividends, thus gaining the capital to buy additional papers without requiring large bank loans.

While helping to run the Bayonne *Times,* Newhouse earned a high school equivalency diploma and then attended law school at night, graduating at age 21, in 1916. Never a courtroom lawyer, he combined the management of a local law office with that of the *Times,* observing its operations, receiving a share of the profits, and reaching out for his first paper in a partnership to buy the Fitchburg, Massachusetts, *News* in 1920. This venture failed due to local resentment, but Newhouse profited when selling the

property and succeeded in another partnership to buy the *Staten Island Advance* in 1922; he gained majority control in 1924.

Shunning the 1920s stock market boom, Newhouse easily survived the crash and the Great Depression. He was attracted to growing, often suburban, neighborhoods. He bought the *Long Island Press* (1932) and the *Newark Ledger* (1935), and merged two other papers into the *Long Island Star Journal* (1938). In 1939 another merger turned the *Newark Star-Eagle* and the *Ledger* into the *Newark Star-Ledger*. Newhouse controlled key issues personally, never went public, and kept labor and other costs low.

In 1939 Newhouse began branching out, paying fully $1.9 million for two upstate New York papers that he merged into the *Syracuse Herald-Journal*. Discreetly acquiring the *Syracuse Post-Standard* in 1942, he had a city-wide monopoly, but editorial outlook did not change. His focus was revenue. In 1945 he bought Jersey City's *Jersey Journal*, strengthening his presence in that heavily populated region. In 1947 he acquired the Harrisburg, Pennsylvania *Patriot* and *Evening News* for $2.5 million. Newhouse, fearing local objections to an outsider, kept his own involvement secret. He achieved a local monopoly in 1948 by buying and closing the *Harrisburg Telegraph*.

Newhouse focused on raising profits, not on news content or editorials, with which he rarely interfered, in part to counter fears in the mid-sized, middle American cities whose papers were bought by this New York, Jewish outsider. So Newhouse, who generally relied only on his family

and a few old subordinates, kept a low public profile until well into his sixties, avoiding interviews, keeping to generalities, and successfully opposing efforts to write his biography.

Newhouse and his family grew wealthy, especially as America boomed after 1945, but he maintained a low profile, finally going national in 1955, when he paid a record-setting $5.6 million for the prestigious Portland *Oregonian*. That year he bought the *St. Louis Globe-Democrat* for $6.5 million and two Alabama newspapers—the *Birmingham News* and the *Huntsville Times* —plus a television station and three radio stations for $18.7 million. Newhouse's career was changing, shifting to a drive for national prominence and distinction.

By the late 1950s Newhouse, with assets of some $200 million, stood behind only Scripps-Howard and Hearst as America's third largest media owner. In 1959 he diversified into women's magazines by acquiring for $5 million the famous but financially troubled Conde Nast Publications: *Vogue, Glamour, Young Brides,* and *House and Garden* . Then Newhouse bought Street & Smith, the country's oldest magazine firm, merging some of its women's magazines with those from Conde Nast, thus taking virtual control of the rich market in women's magazines.

As he aged in the 1960s and 1970s, Newhouse's appetite for empire grew. He had bought many papers where the heirs chose not to continue the founder's work, but his sons—Samuel Jr. and Donald—were happy to carry on. By 1967 Newhouse owned 22 papers, having bought the *Cleveland Plain-Dealer* and the New Orleans *Times-Picayune* and *States-Item*. In 1976 he added eight small Michigan papers and *Parade,* a Sunday supplement giant. Newhouse reached the peak of recognition in 1964 with millions in gifts to the S.I. Newhouse School of Public Communications at Syracuse University. President Lyndon Johnson spoke at the dedication.

Newhouse gradually withdrew from business in the mid-1970s. His sons took over and, after his death on August 29, 1979, continued one of the largest private ventures in the nation, while buying or reviving such famous media enterprises as Random House publishing, the *New Yorker,* and *Vanity Fair.*

Further Reading

Newhouse consciously discouraged accounts of his life. An unauthorized, highly critical biography is Richard Meeker, *Newspaperman: S.I. Newhouse and the Business of News* (1983). A. J. Liebling, *The Press* (1960) offers general background. *TIME* (July 27, 1962) and *Business Week* (January 26, 1976) contain cover stories. *Esquire* (August 1959) and the *Saturday Review* (October 8, 1960) have short profiles. There were lengthy obituaries on August 30, 1979, in *The New York Times* and *The Washington Post*. The *Wall Street Journal* (February 12, 1982) surveys policy since Newhouse's death.

Additional Sources

Maier, Thomas, *Newhouse: all the glitter, power, and glory of America's richest media empire and the secretive man behind it,* New York: St. Martin's Press, 1994.

Meeker, Richard H., *Newspaperman: S.I. Newhouse and the business of news,* New Haven: Ticknor & Fields, 1983.
Newhouse, Samuel I., *A memo for the children,* New York: s.n., 1980. □

Ne Win

Ne Win (born 1911) was a Burmese general and political leader who twice seized power from elected premier U Nu and ruled Burma (now Myanmar) as a repressive and isolationist socialist government until he resigned in 1988.

Born in Prome, Burma (now Myanmar), Ne Win was named Shu Maung by his parents. An ardent but little-known nationalist agitator in the 1930s, he failed to complete his degree at the University of Rangoon. In the 1930s, as Thakin (Master) Shu Maung, he was a member of the Dobama Asiayone (We Burmans Association), which became the most extreme and energetic nationalist group fighting British colonial rule.

"Bright Sun"

In 1941 Ne Win, then still known as Thakin Shu Maung, was selected by Aung San, the de facto leader of the younger wing of the Burmese nationalist movement, to go to Japan for training and to return with the Japanese the next year to oust the British from Burma. Aung San and the 29 young men who went to Japan with him became known in Burma as the legendary "Thirty Comrades." Shu Maung, one of the oldest of the Thirty Comrades, adopted a new name that served both as disguise and symbolism, Ne Win, meaning "bright sun."

Returning to Burma with the Japanese, Aung San, and the Burma Independence Army in 1942, Ne Win became commander of the renamed Burma Defense Army under Japan in 1943. Its original commander, Aung San, accepted the position of war minister in Ba Maw's newly proclaimed "independent" government. Ne Win remained in the titular role of commander when Aung San led this force, now called the patriot Burmese Forces, into armed opposition against the Japanese in 1945.

Rise in the Military

Distinguishing himself in his military service, Ne Win was taken into the regular army after World War II as a major. He became second-in-command of the 4th Burma Rifles and rose quickly to commanding officer. Elected in 1947 to the Constituent Assembly to frame a constitution for an independent Burma, he soon spurned representative politics and turned all his attention to his military responsibilities.

Promoted to brigadier general in 1948, the year Burma attained its independence, Ne Win in February 1949 became commander of the armed forces, with a rank of major general. As various ethnic minorities and communists

Ne Win (far left)

launched rebellions against the government in 1949-1950, Gen. Ne Win served as minister for defense and for home affairs under Premier U Nu. Together with U Nu, Ne Win made the Burmese armed forces powerful enough to reduce the size of the various insurgent groups by the mid-1950s.

Repressive Leader

In 1958, pressed by key subordinates who saw an increase in the insurgent threat following a split in U Nu's government party, Ne Win ousted the popular elected leader in a bloodless coup. Ne Win permitted the holding of elections in February 1960, however, and U Nu won. Ne Win left his post of caretaker premier in April 1960.

On March 2, 1962, Gen. Ne Win deposed U Nu a second time. This time, he abolished Parliament and the constitution, jailed most of the civilian politicians for four to six years, and embarked on a crash course of socialist development. Known as the "Burmese Way to Socialism," Ne Win's isolationist policies were opposed both by U Nu and the Communists. His policies brought the country's export economy to a virtual standstill and necessitated food rationing to avoid famine in a country once rich in rice.

By 1971, Ne Win had transformed Burma into a one-party police state run by his Burma Socialist Programme Party. Under a new constitution in 1974, he installed himself as president and kept that title until 1981. He continued to rule until July 1988, when massive demonstrations against his repressive regime forced him to resign. Under his rule Myanmar went from one of Southeast Asia's most developed nations to one of its poorest. The once- wealthy nation was granted least developed country status by the United Nations in 1987.

Even after his resignation, Ne Win played a major role in a violent September 1988 coup led by his crony Gen. Saw Maung that returned the army to power and shut down the pro-democracy movement, shooting, torturing and jailing thousands of its followers. Even into his 80s, Ne Win was widely assumed to be steering the new regime, the State Law and Order Restoration Council (SLORC), which, in the assessment of Susan Blaustein in the *Nation,* "may have outdone its mentor [Ne Win] in alienating Burma's population, isolating the country and savaging its economy." Foreign journalists were banned from visiting, and a 1990 election was assumed to be rigged. Myanmar's government was repeatedly cited for human rights violations. As Ne Win recedes from view, his repressive legacy remains strong.

Further Reading

Frank N. Trager, *Burma, from Kingdom to Republic* (1966); Richard Butwell, *U Nu of Burma* (1969); Willard A. Hanna, *Eight Nation Makers: Southeast Asia's Charismatic Statesmen* (1964); Maung Maung, *Burma's Constitution* (1959); F.M. Bunge, *Burma: A Country Study* (1983). □

Barnett Newman

The American painter Barnett Newman (1905-1970) was a central figure among color-field abstractionists between 1950 and 1970.

Barnett Newman was born in New York City on Jan. 29, 1905. Between 1922 and 1926 he studied with Duncan Smith, John Sloan, and William von Schlegell at the Art Students League and at the same time attended the City College of New York, where he received a bachelor of arts degree in 1927. He did graduate work at Cornell University. In 1936 he married Annalee Greenhouse, and in 1948 he and William Baziotes, Robert Motherwell, and Mark Rothko founded a school of art in New York called "Subjects of the Artist." Throughout his life Newman traveled extensively in the United States, Canada, and Europe. He also taught occasionally: at the University of Saskatchewan in 1959 and at the University of Pennsylvania in 1962-1964. He died in New York City on July 3, 1970.

During most of his career Newman shunned one-man exhibitions, preferring to have his work seen by a small group of friends, patrons, and fellow artists. His list of one-man shows is therefore limited to five. By the 1960s Newman's stature in the field of contemporary painting became increasingly apparent to a wider audience. His work was included in a number of national and international group shows, including the Seattle World's Fair (1962), the São Paulo Bienal (1965), and the Metropolitan Museum of Art's

"New York Painting and Sculpture, 1940 to 1970" (1969-1970).

Criticism of Newman's work has shifted recently. During the 1950s he was generally regarded as an abstract expressionist and was linked with artists as diverse as Jackson Pollock, Willem de Kooning, Mark Rothko, Franz Kline, and Robert Motherwell. This link was in part justifiable: in addition to being a member of the abstract expressionist generation, Newman was that group's spiritual ally in its struggle to gain recognition for its new and often radical work.

More recently, Newman's art has been associated with a younger generation of painters, including Jules Olitski and Kenneth Noland. In this case the association is based on the fact that Newman's work consistently eschewed the painterly expressiveness of artists such as De Kooning or Kline. Like his younger counterparts, Newman seems to have been most concerned with generating pictorial space through color alone rather than through violent or explosive brushwork.

In Newman's best paintings, such as *Cathedra* (1950-1951) and *Vir heroicus sublimis* (1950-1951), the imagery consists of a single field of color that is inflected by one or two thin vertical bands. But the paint is applied with light, feathery brushstrokes that blend softly into one another and nowhere permit the barest sensation of tactile pigmentation. His rich pictorial space is created through varying densities of a particular color rather than through lines or discrete shapes. In this sense, his paintings are purely optical and eschew the perceptual values of objects or spaces in the world outside of painting.

Further Reading

For Newman's position within contemporary art see Michael Fried, *Three American Painters* (1965), and Thomas B. Hess, *Barnett Newman* (1969). An essay by one of Newman's early champions is "Barnett Newman: The Living Rectangle" in Harold Rosenberg, *The Anxious Object: Art Today and Its Audience* (1964).

Additional Sources

Newman, Barnett, *Barnett Newman,* New York: Abrams, 1978. □

John Henry Newman

The English cardinal and theologian John Henry Newman (1801-1890) was a leading figure in the Oxford movement. After his conversion to Rome, his qualities of mind and literary style won him a position of respect among English intellectuals and theologians.

John Henry Newman was born in London on Feb. 21, 1801. His father was a banker of Evangelical religious beliefs. At the age of 15 Newman experienced a religious "conversion" that was the foundation of his lifelong intense faith in God. In 1816 he matriculated at Trinity College, Oxford, from which he graduated in 1821. Having determined upon taking Holy Orders, he applied for a fellowship at Oriel College, to which he was elected in 1822. There Newman came under the influence of Richard Whately and the "Oriel Noetics," who taught a strict logical approach to religious faith. To them he was indebted for his skill in analysis and argument. In 1824 he was ordained and became curate of St. Clement's, Oxford. In 1826 Newman was appointed public tutor of Oriel and 2 years later became vicar of St. Mary's, Oxford. During this time he had separated from the Noetics in matters of doctrine and had come under the Anglo-Catholic influence of Hurrell Froude and John Keble. He had also begun his studies in the history and doctrine of the early Church. In 1832 Newman resigned his office and went on a tour of the Mediterranean with Froude. During the trip he wrote most of the *Lyra apostolica* and the hymn "Lead, Kindly Light."

Oxford Movement

Newman returned to England in July 1833. On July 14 Keble preached at Oxford his famous sermon "National Apostasy" against the Whigs who were seeking to disestablish the Church. This sermon is regarded as the inauguration of the Oxford movement. Its organization dates from a meeting later that month of Froude and others at the

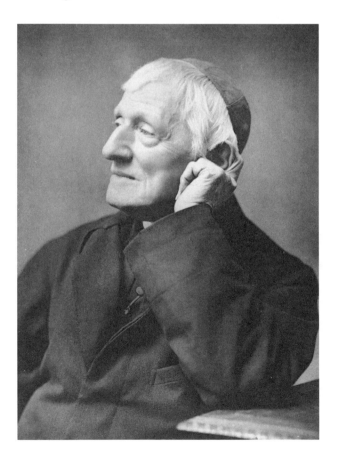

Hadleigh vicarage of H.J. Rose, editor of the *British Magazine.* They determined to initiate a fight for the doctrine of apostolic succession and for the integrity of the Prayer Book. Several weeks later Newman independently began to publish his *Tracts for the Times,* which gave to the movement the alternate name of tractarianism.

The aims of the Oxford movement were to combat the influence of the state over the Church and to establish a foundation of doctrine for the Church of England by teaching its descent from the early Church and its Catholic traditions. Newman complemented the tracts with his celebrated Sunday afternoon sermons delivered in St. Mary's, which attracted many followers and admirers.

Newman's influence was at its height by the end of the 1830s, though opposition was gathering to the "Romish" tendencies of the movement. However, he himself was at first firmly committed to the notion of the Anglican Church as a *via media*—in the positive sense of keeping a path of truth between erroneous extremes. But, gradually, by 1839 he had begun to doubt the strength of the Anglican position, noting a resemblance between Anglicanism and certain heresies of the early Church. Newman's *Tract XC,* published in 1841, showed the tide of his feelings. In order to "test the tenability of all Catholic doctrine within the Church of England," he examined the Thirty-nine Articles to show that they had been directed not against the Roman Catholic position but only against popular errors and exaggeration. The tract aroused a storm of controversy and the bishop of Oxford ordered the series suspended.

Conversion to Rome

In 1842 Newman retired to his dependent chapel at Littlemore and spent the following 3 years in prayer and study. During this time he wrote his *Essay on the Development of Christian Doctrine,* which expounded the principle by which he reconciled himself to later accretions in the Roman creed. In 1843 he formally recanted all his criticism of the Roman Catholic Church and resigned the living of St. Mary's. Two years later he was received into the Roman Catholic Church.

In 1846 Newman went to Rome and was ordained a priest. He joined the Oratorian order, and he returned to England to found the Oratory at Edgbaston near Birmingham, and later the London Oratory. The next years were difficult for him as he could find no secure position, being distrusted by English Protestants and Roman Catholics alike. He delivered a brilliant series of lectures, *The Idea of a University,* setting forth his humane ideas of education.

The "Apologia"

In 1864 Newman's opportunity for self-justification arrived. His veracity had been incidentally slighted in an article by Charles Kingsley in *Macmillan's Magazine.* In reply Newman wrote the *Apologia pro vita sua,* an autobiographical account of his religious development and opinions. The directness and honesty of the work vindicated the author's integrity and restored him to public favor. In 1870 he published *The Grammar of Assent,* in which he argued the psychological validity of faith against the rational approach to religious truth. In 1878 Newman was made an honorary fellow of Trinity College, Oxford, and the following year he was created a cardinal. He died, much loved and revered, on Aug. 11, 1890.

Further Reading

The standard biographical works are Anne Mozely, ed., *Letters and Correspondence of John Henry Newman during His Life in the English Church, with a Brief Autobiography* (2 vols., 1891), and Wilfrid Ward, *The Life of John Henry, Cardinal Newman* (2 vols., 1912). To these may be added Meriol Trevor, Newman: *Light in Winter* (1962) and *Newman: The Pillar of the Cloud* (1962). The best introduction to Newman's work as a whole is Charles F. Harrold, *John Henry Newman: An Expository and Critical Study of His Mind, Thought, and Art* (1945). An excellent introduction to Newman's theory of education is A. Dwight Culler, *The Imperial Intellect* (1955).

On the Oxford movement the standard account is R. W. Church, *The Oxford Movement: Twelve Years, 1833-1845* (1891). Another helpful study is Geoffrey Faber, *Oxford Apostles* (1933; repr. 1954). For the period's intellectual background see Walter Houghton, *The Victorian Frame of Mind 1830-1870* (1957; repr. 1963), and Basil Willey, *Nineteenth Century Studies* (1949; repr. 1964).

Additional Sources

Dessain, Charles Stephen., *John Henry Newman*, Oxford; New York: Oxford University Press, 1980.

Elwood, J. Murray., *Kindly light: the spiritual vision of John Henry Newman*, Notre Dame, Ind.: Ave Maria Press, 1979.

Giese, Vincent J., *John Henry Newman: heart to heart*, New Rochelle, NY: New City Press, 1993.

Gilley, Sheridan., *Newman and his age*, Westminster, Md.: Christian Classics, 1991.

Henderson, Heather, *The Victorian self: autobiography and Biblical narrative*, Ithaca: Cornell University Press, 1989.

Hutton, Richard Holt, *Cardinal Newman*, New York: AMS Press, 1977.

Ker, I. T. (Ian Turnbull), *John Henry Newman: a biography*, Oxford: Clarendon Press; New York: Oxford University Press, 1988.

Martin, Brian., *John Henry Newman, his life and work*, London: Chatto & Windus, 1982.

Sugg, Joyce., *A saint for Birmingham?*, London: Catholic Truth Society, 1978.

Trevor, Meriol., *Newman's journey*, Huntington, Ind.: Our Sunday Visitor, 1985.

John Henry, Cardinal Newman, Norwood, Pa.: Norwood Editions, 1976. □

Huey P. Newton

Huey P. Newton (1942-1989) founded the Afro-American Society and was a co-founder of the Black Panther Party, serving as its minister of defense during much of the 1960s. Later he turned to community service for the poor.

Huey P. Newton was born February 17, 1942, in Monroe, Louisiana. The youngest of seven children, Huey was named for former Louisiana governor Huey Pierce Long. The Newton family moved to Oakland, California, in 1945 to take advantage of the job opportunities created by World War II wartime industries. In Oakland the family moved often, and in one house Huey was compelled to sleep in the kitchen. Even though the Newtons were poor and victims of discrimination and segregation, Huey contends that he never felt deprived as a child and that he never went hungry.

Huey attended the Oakland public schools where, he claimed, he was made to feel "uncomfortable and ashamed of being black." He responded by constantly and consistently defying authority, which resulted in frequent suspensions. At the age of 14, he was arrested for gun possession and vandalism. In his autobiography, *Revolutionary Suicide*, Newton wrote, "during those long years in the Oakland public schools, I did not have one teacher who taught me anything relevant to my own life or experience. Not one instructor ever awoke in me a desire to learn more or to question or explore the worlds of literature, science, and history. All they did was try to rob me of the sense of my own uniqueness and worth, and in the process they nearly killed my urge to inquire."

According to Newton, he did not learn to read well until he had finished high school. "I actually learned to read—really read more than just 'dog' and 'cat,' which was about all I could do when I left high school—by listening to records of Vincent Price reading great poetry, and then

looking up the poems to see how the words looked." In order to prove that high school counselors were wrong in saying he was not college material, Newton attended Merritt College intermittently, eventually earning an Associate of Arts degree. He also studied law at Oakland City College and at San Francisco Law School.

Newton claimed he studied law to become a better burglar. He was arrested several times for minor offenses while still a teenager and he supported himself in college by burglarizing homes in the Oakland and Berkeley Hills area and running the "short change" game. In 1964, at age 22, he was convicted of assault with a deadly weapon and sentenced to six months in the Alameda County jail. Newton spent most of this sentence in solitary confinement, including the "soul breaker"—extreme solitary confinement.

While at Oakland City College, Newton had become politically oriented and socially conscious. He joined the Afro-American Association and played a role in getting the first black history course adopted as part of the college's curriculum. He read the works of Frantz Fanon, Malcolm X, Chairman Mao Tse-tung, and Che Guevara. A child of the ghetto and a victim of discrimination and the "system," Newton was very much aware of the plight of Oakland's African-American community. Realizing that there were few organizations to speak for or represent lower class African-Americans, Newton along with Bobby Seale organized the Black Panther Party for Self Defense in October 1966, with Seale as chairman and Newton as minister of defense. Like a wary panther that would not attack unless attacked, so too was the organization regarded.

Cop-haters since childhood, Newton and Seale decided the police must be stopped from harassing Oakland's African-Americans; in other words, to "defend the community against the aggression of the power structure, including the military and the armed might of the police." Newton was familiar with the California penal code and the state's law regarding weapons and was thus able to convince a number of African-Americans of their right to bear arms. Members of the Black Panther Party for Self Defense began patrolling the Oakland police. Guns were the essential ingredient on these patrols. Newton and other Black Panther members observed police procedure, ensured that African-American citizens were not abused, advised African-Americans of their rights, and posted bail for those arrested. In addition to patrolling the police, Newton and Seale were responsible for writing the *Black Panther Party Platform and Program,* which called for freedom, full employment, decent housing, education, and military exemption for African-Americans. But there was a darker side to the group, described in Former Panther Earl Anthony's book, *Spitting in the Wind* as a party created with the goal to organize America for armed revolution. Moreover, Washington, D.C., intelligence spent many years trying to bring down what they believed to be "the most violence-prone of all the extremist groups."

Huey Newton proved to be as violent as the party he helped to create when he was thrust into the national limelight in October 1967; accused of murdering Oakland police officer John Frey. In September 1968 Newton was convicted of voluntary manslaughter and was sentenced to two to 15 years in prison. In May 1970 the California Appellate Court reversed Newton's conviction and ordered a new trial. After two more trials the State of California dropped its case against Newton, citing technicalities including the judge's failure to relay proper instructions to the jury.

After his release from prison Newton overhauled the Black Panther Party, revised its program, and changed its rhetoric. While he had been imprisoned, party membership had decreased significantly in several cities, and the FBI had started a campaign to disrupt and eventually bring down the Black Panthers. Abandoning its Marxist-Leninist ideology, Newton now concentrated on community survival programs. The Black Panthers sponsored a free breakfast program for children, sickle-cell anemia tests, free food and shoes, and a school, the Samuel Napier Intercommunal Youth Institute. However, as before, the Black Panthers were not without controversy. Funding for several of their programs were raised as the result of the co-operation of drug dealers and prostitution rings.

Newton tried to shed his image as a firebreathing revolutionary, but he continued to have difficulty with the police. In 1974 several assault charges were filed against him, and he was also accused of murdering a 17-year-old prostitute, Kathleen Smith. Newton failed to make his court appearance. His bail was revoked, a bench warrant issued, and his name added to the Federal Bureau of Investigation's most wanted list. Newton had jumped bail and escaped to Cuba, where he spent three years in exile. In Cuba he worked as a machinist and teacher. He returned home in 1977 to face murder charges because, he said, the climate in the United States had changed and he believed he could get a fair trial. He was acquitted of the murder of Kathleen Smith after two juries were deadlocked.

In addition to organizing the Black Panther Party and serving as its minister of defense, Newton unsuccessfully ran for Congress as a candidate of the Peace and Freedom Party in 1968. In 1971, between his second and third trials for the murder of John Frey, he visited China for ten days, where he met with Premier Chou En-lai and Chiang Ch'ing, the wife of Chairman Mao Tse-tung. While there he was offered political asylum. Newton studied for a Ph.D. in the history of social consciousness at the University of California in 1978. In 1985 the 43-year-old Newton was arrested for embezzling state and federal funds from the Black Panthers' community education and nutrition programs. In 1989 he was convicted of embezzling funds from a school run by the Black Panthers, supposedly to support his alcohol and drug addictions. By this time the Panthers had turned to less violent activism. On August 22, 1989, Newton was gunned down by a drug dealer, ironically in the same city streets of Oakland that saw the rise of the Black Panthers 23 years ago. Bill Turque in *Newsweek* described a sad but appropriate farewell: "A small florist's card, resting with bouquets of red gladiolus's and white dahlias on a chain-link fence near the shooting scene, summed it up: 'Huey: for the early years.'"

Further Reading

Huey P. Newton's *Revolutionary Suicide* (1973) and *To Die for the People: The Writings of Huey P. Newton* (1972) provide information on Newton's political philosophies; Gene Marine, *The Black Panthers* (1969); Gilbert Moore, *A Special Rage* (1971); and Bobby Seale, *Seize the Time: The Story of the Black Panther Party and Huey P. Newton* (1968) also provide information on the philosophies and tactics of the Black Panther Party and background information on the setting in which Newton operated; *Spitting in the Wind,* by Former Panther Earl Anthony takes an inside look into the Black Panther Party itself, describing the many facets of the organization's operations. □

Sir Isaac Newton

Sir Isaac Newton (1642-1727) was an English scientist and mathematician. He made major contributions in mathematics and theoretical and experimental physics and achieved a remarkable synthesis of the work of his predecessors on the laws of motion, especially the law of universal gravitation.

Isaac Newton was born on Christmas Day, 1642, at Woolsthorpe, a hamlet in southwestern Lincolnshire. In his early years Lincolnshire was a battle-ground of the civil wars, in which the challenging of authority in government and religion was dividing England's population. Also of significance for his early development were circumstances within his family. He was born after the death of his father, and in his third year his mother married the rector of a neighboring parish, leaving Isaac at Woolsthorpe in the care of his grandmother.

After a rudimentary education in local schools, he was sent at the age of 12 to the King's School in Grantham, where he lived in the home of an apothecary named Clark. It was from Clark's stepdaughter that Newton's biographer William Stukeley learned many years later of the boy's interest in her father's chemical library and laboratory and of the windmill run by a live mouse, the floating lanterns, sundials, and other mechanical contrivances Newton built to amuse her. Although she married someone else and he never married, she was the one person for whom Newton seems to have had a romantic attachment.

At birth Newton was heir to the modest estate which, when he came of age, he was expected to manage. But during a trial period midway in his course at King's School, it became apparent that farming was not his métier. In 1661, at the age of 19, he entered Trinity College, Cambridge. There the questioning of long-accepted beliefs was beginning to be apparent in new attitudes toward man's environment, expressed in the attention given to mathematics and science.

After receiving his bachelor's degree in 1665, apparently without special distinction, Newton stayed on for

his master's; but an epidemic of the plague caused the university to close. Newton was back at Woolsthorpe for 18 months in 1666 and 1667. During this brief period he performed the basic experiments and apparently did the fundamental thinking for all his subsequent work on gravitation and optics and developed for his own use his system of calculus. The story that the idea of universal gravitation was suggested to him by the falling of an apple seems to be authentic: Stukeley reports that he heard it from Newton himself.

Returning to Cambridge in 1667, Newton quickly completed the requirements for his master's degree and then entered upon a period of elaboration of the work begun at Woolsthorpe. His mathematics professor, Isaac Barrow, was the first to recognize Newton's unusual ability, and when, in 1669, Barrow resigned to devote himself to theology, he recommended Newton as his successor. Newton became Lucasian professor of mathematics at 27 and stayed at Trinity in that capacity for 27 years.

Experiments in Optics

Newton's main interest at the time of his appointment was optics, and for several years the lectures required of him by the professorship were devoted to this subject. In a letter of 1672 to the secretary of the Royal Society, he says that in 1666 he had bought a prism "to try therewith the celebrated phenomena of colours." He continues, "In order thereto having darkened the room and made a small hole in my window-shuts to let in a convenient quantity of the Suns light, I placed my prism at its entrance, that it might be thereby refracted to the opposite wall." He had been surprised to see the various colors appear on the wall in an oblong arrangement (the vertical being the greater dimension), "which according to the received laws of refraction should have been circular." Proceeding from this experiment through several stages to the "crucial" one, in which he had isolated a single ray and found it unchanging in color and refrangibility, he had drawn the revolutionary conclusion that "Light itself is a heterogeneous mixture of differently refrangible rays."

These experiments had grown out of Newton's interest in improving the effectiveness of telescopes, and his discoveries about the nature and composition of light had led him to believe that greater accuracy could not be achieved in instruments based on the refractive principle. He had turned, consequently, to suggestions for a reflecting telescope made by earlier investigators but never tested in an actual instrument. Being manually dexterous, he built several models in which the image was viewed in a concave mirror through an eyepiece in the side of the tube. In 1672 he sent one of these to the Royal Society.

Newton felt honored when the members were favorably impressed by the efficiency of his small reflecting telescope and when on the basis of it they elected him to their membership. But when this warm reception induced him to send the society a paper describing his experiments on light and his conclusions drawn from them, the results were almost disastrous for him and for posterity. The paper was published in the society's *Philosophical Transactions,* and the reactions of English and Continental scientists, led by Robert Hooke and Christiaan Huygens, ranged from skepticism to bitter opposition to conclusions which seemed to invalidate the prevalent wave theory of light.

At first Newton patiently answered objections with further explanations, but when these produced only more negative responses, he finally became irritated and vowed he would never publish again, even threatening to give up scientific investigation altogether. Several years later, and only through the tireless efforts of the astronomer Edmund Halley, Newton was persuaded to put together the results of his work on the laws of motion, which became the great *Principia.*

His Major Work

Newton's *magnum opus, Philosophiae naturalis principia mathematica,* to give it its full title, was completed in 18 months—a prodigious accomplishment. It was first published in Latin in 1687, when Newton was 45. Its appearance established him as the leading scientist of his time, not only in England but in the entire Western world.

In the *Principia* Newton demonstrated for the first time that celestial bodies follow the laws of dynamics and, formulating the law of universal gravitation, gave mathematical solutions to most of the problems concerning motion which had engaged the attention of earlier and contemporary scientists. Book 1 treats the motion of bodies in purely mathematical terms. Book 2 deals with motion in resistant mediums, that is, in physical reality. In Book 3, Newton describes a cosmos based on the laws he has established.

He demonstrates the use of these laws in determining the density of the earth, the masses of the sun and of planets having satellites, and the trajectory of a comet; and he explains the variations in the moon's motion, the precession of the equinoxes, the variation in gravitational acceleration with latitude, and the motion of the tides. What seems to have been an early version of book 3, published posthumously as *The System of the World,* contains Newton's calculation, with illustrative diagram, of the manner in which, according to the law of centripetal force, a projectile could be made to go into orbit around the earth.

In the years after Newton's election to the Royal Society, the thinking of his colleagues and of scholars generally had been developing along lines similar to those which his had taken, and they were more receptive to his explanations of the behavior of bodies moving according to the laws of motion than they had been to his theories about the nature of light. Yet the *Principia* presented a stumbling block: its extremely condensed mathematical form made it difficult for even the most acute minds to follow. Those who did understand it saw that it needed simplification and interpretation. As a result, in the 40 years from 1687 to Newton's death the *Principia* was the basis of numerous books and articles. These included a few peevish attacks, but by far the greater number were explanations and elaborations of what had subtly evolved in the minds of his contemporaries from "Mr. Newton's theories" to the "Newtonian philosophy."

London Years

The publication of the *Principia* was the climax of Newton's professional life. It was followed by a period of depression and lack of interest in scientific matters. He became interested in university politics and was elected a representative of the university in Parliament. Later he asked friends in London to help him obtain a government appointment. The result was that in 1696, at the age of 54, he left Cambridge to become warden and then master of the Mint. The position was intended to be something of a sinecure, but he took it just as seriously as he had his scientific pursuits and made changes in the English monetary system that were effective for 150 years.

Newton's London life lasted as long as his Lucasian professorship. During that time he received many honors, including the first knighthood conferred for scientific achievement and election to life presidency of the Royal Society. In 1704, when Huygens and Hooke were no longer living, he published the *Opticks,* mainly a compilation of earlier research, and subsequently revised it three times; he supervised the two revisions of the *Principia;* he engaged in the regrettable controversy with G. W. von Leibniz over the invention of the calculus; he carried on a correspondence with scientists all over Great Britain and Europe; he continued his study and investigation in various fields; and, until his very last years, he conscientiously performed his duties at the Mint.

His "Opticks"

In the interval between publication of the *Principia* in 1687 and the appearance of the *Opticks* in 1704, the trend was away from the use of Latin for all scholarly writing. The *Opticks* was written and originally published in English (a Latin translation appeared 2 years later) and was consequently accessible to a wide range of readers in England. The reputation which the *Principia* had established for its author of course prepared the way for acceptance of his second published work. Furthermore, its content and manner of presentation made the *Opticks* more approachable. It was essentially an account of experiments performed by Newton himself and his conclusions drawn from them, and it had greater appeal for the experimental temper of the educated public of the time than the more theoretical and mathematical *Principia*.

Of great interest for scientists generally were the queries with which Newton concluded the text of the *Opticks*—for example, "Do not Bodies act upon Light at a distance, and by their action bend its rays?" These queries (16 in the first edition, subsequently increased to 31) constitute a unique expression of Newton's philosophy; posing them as negative questions made it possible for him to suggest ideas which he could not support by experimental evidence or mathematical proof but which gave stimulus and direction to further research for many generations of scientists. "Of the Species and Magnitude of Curvilinear Figures," two treatises included with the original edition of the *Opticks,* was the first purely mathematical work Newton had published.

Mathematical Works

Newton's mathematical genius had been stimulated in his early years at Cambridge by his work under Barrow, which included a thorough grounding in Greek mathematics as well as in the recent work of René Descartes and of John Wallis. During his undergraduate years Newton had discovered what is known as the binomial theorem; invention of the calculus had followed; mathematical questions had been treated at length in correspondence with scientists in England and abroad; and his contributions to optics and celestial mechanics could be said to be his mathematical formulation of their principles.

But it was not until the controversy over the discovery of the calculus that Newton published mathematical work as such. The controversy, begun in 1699, when Fatio de Duillier made the first accusation of plagiarism against Leibniz, continued sporadically for nearly 20 years, not completely subsiding even with Leibniz's death in 1716.

The inclusion of the two tracts in the first edition of the *Opticks* was certainly related to the controversy, then in progress, and the appearance of other tracts in 1707 and 1711 under the editorship of younger colleagues suggests Newton's release of this material under pressure from his supporters. These tracts were for the most part revisions of the results of early research long since incorporated in Newton's working equipment. In the second edition of the *Principia,* of 1713, the four "Regulae Philosophandi" and the four-page "Scholium Generale" added to book 3 were apparently also designed to answer critics on the Continent who were expressing their partisanship for Leibniz by attacking any statement of Newton's that could not be con-

firmed by mathematical proof; the "Scholium" is of special interest in that it gives an insight into Newton's way of thought which the more austere style of the main text precludes.

Other Writings and Research

Two other areas to which Newton devoted much attention were chronology and theology. A shortened form of his *Chronology of Ancient Kingdoms* appeared without his consent in 1725, inducing him to prepare the longer work for publication; it did not actually appear until after his death. In it Newton attempted to correlate Egyptian, Greek, and Hebrew history and mythology and for the first time made use of astronomical references in ancient texts to establish dates of historical events. In his *Observations upon the Prophecies of Daniel and the Apocalypse of St. John,* also posthumously published, his aim was to show that the prophecies of the Old and New Testaments had so far been fulfilled.

Another of Newton's continuing interests was the area in which alchemy was evolving into chemistry. His laboratory assistant during his years at Cambridge wrote of his chemical experiments as being a major occupation of these years, and Newton's manuscripts reflect the importance he attached to this phase of his research. His Mint papers show that he made use of chemical knowledge in connection with the metallic composition of the coinage. Among the vast body of his manuscripts are notes indicating that his *Chronology* and *Prophecy* and also his alchemical work were parts of a larger design that would embrace cosmology, history, and theology in a single synthesis.

The mass of Newton's papers, manuscripts, and correspondence which survives reveals a person with qualities of mind, physique, and personality extraordinarily favorable for the making of a great scientist: tremendous powers of concentration, ability to stand long periods of intense mental exertion, and objectivity uncomplicated by frivolous interests. The many portraits of Newton (he was painted by nearly all the leading artists of his time) range from the fashionable, somewhat idealized, treatment to a more convincing realism. All present the natural dignity, the serious mien, and the large searching eyes mentioned by his contemporaries.

When Newton came to maturity, circumstances were auspiciously combined to make possible a major change in men's ways of thought and endeavor. The uniqueness of Newton's achievement could be said to lie in his exploitation of these unusual circumstances. He alone among his gifted contemporaries fully recognized the implications of recent scientific discoveries. With these as a point of departure, he developed a unified mathematical interpretation of the cosmos, in the expounding of which he demonstrated method and direction for future elaboration. In shifting the emphasis from quality to quantity, from pursuit of answers to the question "Why?" to focus upon "What?" and "How?" he effectively prepared the way for the age of technology. He died on March 20, 1727.

Further Reading

Newton's writings are available in many editions, several of which contain scholarly introductions and notes of great value. Louis T. More, *Isaac Newton* (1934), is the major biography written in this century, but it lacks the benefit of recent scholarship. Two good newer accounts are Herbert D. Anthony, *Sir Isaac Newton* (1960), a short but comprehensive and interestingly presented biography, and Frank Manuel, *Isaac Newton* (1968), an illuminating psychological study of Newton.

A convenient biographical introduction in John David North's brief study, *Isaac Newton* (1968), which relates the highlights of Newton's life and work. A psychologically oriented essay on Newton is in Dunkwart A. Rustow, ed., *Philosophers and Kings: Studies in Leadership* (1970). Among the older works, William Stukeley's *Memoirs of Sir Isaac Newton's Life,* for which he collected material during Newton's last years but which was not published until 1936, is an interesting compilation of anecdotes and observations. Sir David Brewster, *Memoirs of the Life, Writings and Discoveries of Sir Isaac Newton* (1855; repr. 1965), is still a useful biographical source.

Useful evaluations of Newton's work include Edward N. da C. Andrade, *Isaac Newton* (1954), available in paperback; the chapter on Newton in James G. Crowther, *Founders of British Science* (1960); Arthur E. Bell, *Newtonian Science* (1961); and Alexandre Koyré, *Newtonian Studies* (1965). □

Martin Anderson Nexø

The novels and stories of the Danish author Martin Andersen Nexø (1869-1954) evoke the life of the proletariat in a manner that transcends politics and nationality.

Martin Andersen Nexø was one of 11 children of an impoverished stonecutter. After spending 6 years as a shoemaker's apprentice, he attended a folk high school where he made his first acquaintance with literature. Supporters of the school sent him abroad to recover his health after a serious illness, and, while living in Spain, he discovered that the plight of the working class was international. His first book, a collection of stories, appeared after his return to Denmark, where he worked as a teacher. After 1901 he lived exclusively by his pen.

Nexø's first novels are in the decadent, pessimistic manner common around the turn of the century. His mature authorship began with the four-volume *Pelle the Conqueror* (1906-1910), and from this time on Nexø devoted his writing to the awakening proletariat, the existence of which had gone virtually unnoticed in Danish literature.

Pelle is the story of a boy who grows up in extreme poverty, awakens to the injustice of his class's suffering, and develops into a leader in the workers' struggle for political power. The first two volumes constitute one of the finest stories of childhood in European literature. The novel as a whole is peopled by a large number of memorable characters, such as Pelle's father, Lasse, and the occupants of the fabulous slum tenement appropriately called the "Ark."

The title figure of Nexø's other masterpiece, the five-volume *Ditte, Child of Man* (1917-1921), is Pelle's female counterpart, who symbolizes the situation of the proletarian woman. While this novel gives a darker picture of proletarian life than *Pelle,* Nexø's optimism is seen in Ditte's lifelong vitality and in the miraculous kindness and love that she and many other characters exhibit in spite of their crushing poverty.

After World War I Nexø broke with the Social Democratic party, became a Communist, and remained for the rest of his life a supporter of the Soviet Union. His politics often made him an unpopular figure in Denmark between the two world wars. In this period he lived for 7 years in Germany and made extended visits to the Soviet Union. After World War II he lived in Denmark, the Soviet Union, and East Germany; he died in Dresden, East Germany, where he had made his home since 1951.

Today Nexø is acknowledged as one of Denmark's finest realistic storytellers, the only modern Danish writer who has an undisputed place in world literature.

Further Reading

The only critical treatment of Nexø work in English in book form is "Socialist Humanism: Martin Andersen Nexø Pelle the Conqueror" in Harry Slochower, *Three Ways of Modern Man* (1937). □

Michel Ney

The French soldier Michel Ney (1769-1815) rose from humble origins to become one of the principal military figures of the Napoleonic era. He was named Duke of Elchingen, Prince of the Moskowa, and Marshal of the Empire.

Michel Ney was born at Saarlouis on Jan. 10, 1769. He received a very elementary education and at the age of 19 enlisted in the army. When the Revolution swept over France, he embraced the new political and social ideas and in 1792 was elected lieutenant. During the Revolutionary Wars he rose to the rank of general (1799). The advent of Napoleon Bonaparte at the turn of the century led to a change in Ney's political views. He put aside his republicanism and became a staunch Bonapartist. His marriage to Eglé Auguié on Aug. 5, 1802, was the handwork of Josephine Bonaparte. With the establishment of the empire, Ney was named among the original 16 marshals.

As commander of the VI Corps of the Grand Army, Ney played a major role in the campaign of 1805. His victory at Elchingen led to the surrender of the Austrian army at Ulm and opened the road to Vienna. In recognition of this service and of the significant part he played in the Prussian and Polish campaigns of 1806-1807, Napoleon named him Duke of Elchingen in 1808.

Ney spent the next 3 years with the Army of Spain in the unfortunate struggle that provided neither glory nor victory. When the new Grand Army was assembled in the spring of 1812 for the invasion of Russia, he was given command of the III Corps. At the Battle of Borodino he commanded the center with distinction and entered Moscow with the victorious army. As the withdrawal from Moscow became first a rout and then a complete disaster, Ney commanded the rear guard. As the frozen remnants of the once proud army fled westward across the Neman River, Ney was the last to leave Russian soil. In recognition of his services Napoleon bestowed upon him the title Prince of the Moskowa.

The campaign of 1813 found Ney again at the head of a corps. He took part in the battles of Dresden and Leipzig, retreating with the army to France after the latter defeat. He also fought in the short but decisive campaign of 1814 and was at Fontainebleau when Napoleon signed his abdication.

When Louis XVIII ascended the throne of France, Ney was among the first of the Napoleonic marshals to pledge his loyalty. Although employed, he was not accepted by the returning royalists. Nevertheless, when Napoleon returned to France from Elba in March 1815, Ney denounced the former emperor and reaffirmed his support of the King.

No sooner had Ney taken up his command at Besançon than he deserted the Bourbon cause. Returning to Paris after Napoleon had reinstated himself, he sought employment in the army that was preparing once more to defend the empire against Europe. Napoleon refused his request. When hostilities began in June, the Emperor, hard-pressed for experienced corps commanders, placed Ney at the head of the left wing of the army (June 13). Ney played an important role in the week of fighting that followed. At Waterloo he led the last desperate charge against the English line. When all was lost, he returned to Paris in a state of complete despair.

Ney declared in favor of a second restoration of Louis XVIII even before Napoleon had decided upon his second abdication. When the list of proscribed officers was published in the last week of July 1815, Ney's name was among those at the top. He was taken into custody on August 5. The ultraroyalists, with the support of Europe, demanded retaliation. After considerable delay, Ney was condemned to death. On Dec. 7, 1815, he was shot in the gardens of the Luxembourg in Paris.

Further Reading

The best record of Ney's life is *The Memoirs of Marshal Ney* (2 vols., 1833), which carries the story to 1805; Ney did not live to finish the work. More than any other Napoleonic marshal Ney has caught the imagination of historians throughout the Western world. Three reliable biographies in English are Andrew H. Atteridge, *The Bravest of the Brave* (1912); James E. Smoot, comp., *Marshal Ney: Before and after Execution* (1929); and Piers Compton, *Marshal Ney* (1937). Harold Kurtz, *The Trial of Marshal Ney* (1957), is very good on the last months of Ney's life. Among the books written to show that Ney was not shot in 1815 but escaped to the United States, two good studies are James A. Weston, *Historic Doubts as to the Execution of Marshal Ney* (1895), and LeGette Blythe, *Marshal Ney: A Dual Life* (1937).

Additional Sources

Horricks, Raymond, *Marshal Ney, the romance and the real*, London: Archway, 1988.

Horricks, Raymond, *Military politics from Bonaparte to the Bourbons: the life and death of Michel Ney, 1769-1815*, New Brunswick, N.J., U.S.A.: Transaction Publishers, 1995. □

Ronald Gideon Ngala

Ronald Gideon Ngala (1923-1972) was a Kenyan politician. His career was marked by a realistic approach to politics and by a devotion to Kenya which allowed him to place his country's stability over his own political ambition.

Ronald Ngala was born in the coastal town of Kilifi in the British colony of Kenya. He was educated at Alliance High School and at Makerere University College, where he received a diploma in teaching. He then began a teaching career (1949-1954), rising to the positions of headmaster of the Buxton School (1955-1956) and of supervisor of schools (1957-1958).

During the 1950s, national political parties were banned in the British colony, but regional parties were allowed in some areas. African and non-African groups were competing for the chance to influence Kenya's future. Ngala began his national career by being elected to the Legislative Council in 1957. In 1959, the Kenya National party, a multiracial grouping, was formed with Ngala its secretary. The party was generally opposed by the more radical members of the African community.

At the Lancaster House Conference of February 1960, the Africans sent a united delegation under the compromise leadership of Ngala. The conference was an attempt by the British to control Kenya's evolution to independence. But rivalries among African politicians remained. The leaders in the legislative council split into two parties, the Kenya African National Union (KANU) and the Kenya African Democratic Union (KADU). Ngala was chosen as treasurer of KANU, but he was dissatisfied with that minor post and went over to KADU, and was elected its president.

In the elections of 1961 KANU, under the leadership of Oginga Odinga, won the popular vote and elected the most legislators. Most Kenyans still regarded the independence movement leader Jomo Kenyatta as their leader even though the British held him in detention. After secret negotiations the British gave KADU the opportunity to form a government with the promise that Kenyatta would be released in four months. Ngala was appointed leader of "government business." But with the release of Kenyatta, Ngala soon was relegated to the background. Both KANU and KADU sought to win Kenyatta's approval. Ngala attempted to compromise

to preserve African unity, but he proved unable to control his party, and Kenyatta became president of KANU.

A new constitution in 1962 led to elections, won by KANU, and in May 1963 Kenyatta became prime minister of Kenya. Ngala was leader of the opposition, but when KADU members began crossing to KANU out of loyalty to Kenyatta, it became clear that KADU had no future. In 1964, Ngala dissolved the party and joined KANU in what became a one-party state. Ngala became minister of cooperatives and social services in Kenyatta's government. He never again played a major role in the political life of Kenya, but he was remembered as one of its leaders in the fight for independence.

Further Reading

A. J. Hughes's, *East Africa* (1963). □

Sir Apirana Turupa Ngata

Sir Apirana Turupa Ngata (1874-1950) was a Maori leader, politician, and scholar who inspired improvements in official policy toward the Maori people in New Zealand between 1905 and 1934.

Apirana Ngata was born on July 3, 1874, at Kawaka, the eldest son in a family of 15 children. He was educated at the Waiomatatini Maori School and Te Auta College, an Anglican school for Maori at Hawke's Bay. A scholarship took him to Canterbury University College, where he specialized in political science, and in 1893 he became the first Maori to graduate from the University of New Zealand. He received his master's degree the following year, and 2 years later he took his bachelor of laws degree and was admitted to the bar.

Ngata practiced for a few years as a lawyer, but having resolved to devote himself to improving the position of his people, he became travelling and organizing secretary of the Young Maori party, formed by former pupils of Te Aute College with the aim of securing legislation that would directly benefit the Maori people. In 1905 he was elected to Parliament as a Liberal and retained a seat for 38 years. He represented the Maori in Sir Joseph Ward's government (1909-1912) and was minister of native affairs in Ward's next government (1928-1930) and in George Forbes's government (1930-1934).

Ngata was a significant influence on the thinking of the European population about Maori affairs. He was a good speaker, and his personality helped to make him a remarkably successful raiser of money for community welfare. He was a powerful exponent of Maori language, culture, and traditions, and he stimulated popular interest in Maori history and problems. He campaigned for equal opportunity for the Maori in education and sports, but his greatest effort was given to land settlement and development and the attempt to assist Maori farmers to be more efficient without affecting detrimentally Maori communal life or customs.

The Native Land Settlement Bill of 1929 was in large measure a personal triumph for Ngata, though its effectiveness was limited by the onset of the worldwide economic depression and the financial difficulties that went with it. Ngata was perhaps inclined to favor his own tribe, the Ngatiporou on the east coast of North Island, and to be somewhat careless as an administrator. He pushed ahead with his schemes without adequate support from government departments, ignored official regulations, and took no precautions in regard to the financial implications.

Irregularities arose, and the auditor general's report in 1934 drew attention to them. A royal commission was appointed to investigate the whole question of native land settlements and reported unfavorably on Ngata's methods, especially his management of public money intended for Maori land development. There was no evidence that Ngata had benefited personally from his administration, but he felt obliged to resign his office, and he finally left Parliament in 1943.

Ngata continued as a member of the senate of the University of New Zealand and served on the Maori recruiting committee in World War II. He was president of the Polynesian Society for 9 years, encouraged ethnological research, wrote extensively about the Maori, and made a collection of Maori songs and chants. One of his last tasks was to supervise the revision of the Maori Bible. He was knighted in 1927 and died on July 14, 1950.

Further Reading

Ngata contributed to the discussion of the Maori situation in I. L. G. Sutherland, ed., *The Maori People Today* (1940). Eric Ramsden, *Sir Apirana Ngata and Maori Culture* (1948), should also be consulted.

Additional Sources

Na to hoa aroha = From your dear friend: the correspondence between Sir Apirana Ngata and Sir Peter Buck, 1925-50, Auckland: Auckland University Press in association with the Alexander Turnbull Library, Endowment Trust, and the Maori Purposes Fund Board; s.l.: Distributed outside New Zealand by Oxford University Press, 1986-1988. □

Ngugi wa Thiong'o

Ngugi wa Thiong'o (born 1938) was Kenya's most famous writer. Best-known as a novelist, he also wrote plays, literary criticism, and essays on cultural and political topics.

Ngugi wa Thiong'o (formerly James Ngugi and known generally as Ngugi) was born in Limuru, Kenya, on January 5, 1938. Educated initially at a mission school and then at a Gikuyu independent school during the Mau Mau insurgency, he went on to attend Alliance High School in 1955-1959 and Makerere University College in Kampala, Uganda, in 1959-1964. After earning a B.A. in English he worked as a journalist for Nairobi's *Daily*

Nation for half a year before leaving to continue his studies in literature at the University of Leeds in England.

He returned to Kenya in 1967 and taught in the English department at Nairobi University College until January 1969, when he resigned in protest during a students' strike. He lectured in African literature at Northwestern University in Illinois from 1970 through 1971, then resumed teaching at Nairobi University College, where he soon was appointed acting head of the English Department. In December 1977 he was arrested by the Kenyan government and detained for a year; no formal charges were ever filed against him, but it is assumed that his involvement in an adult literacy campaign aimed at raising the political consciousness of peasants and workers in his hometown of Limuru led to his imprisonment. When he was released he was unable to regain his position at the university. In 1982 he went to England at the invitation of his publisher (Heinemann Educational Books) to launch a novel he had written while in detention. During his absence there was an attempted coup in Kenya, after which a number of his friends and associates fled the country. Ngugi wa Thiong'o chose to live in exile in London.

Ngugi came to the United States, teaching at Yale University and Amherst College before becoming the Erich Maria Remarque professor of comparative literature and a professor of performance studies at New York University, New York City, New York.

Ngugi's literary works were concerned with major social, cultural, and political problems in Kenya, past and present. His first two novels, *Weep Not, Child* (1964) and *The River Between* (1965), set in the colonial period of his childhood, focussed on the traumatic effects of the Mau Mau uprising on Gikuyu family life and on the impact of the independent schools movement on rural Gikuyu society. His third novel, *A Grain of Wheat* (1967), combined memories of the Mau Mau era with a depiction of Kenya on the eve of independence—a time of great bitterness, Ngugi claimed, "for the peasants who fought the British yet who now see all that they fought for being put on one side." In *Petals of Blood* (1977), his longest and most complex novel, he described in even greater detail the exploitation of Kenya's masses by its own established elite.

Ngugi always sympathized with the oppressed and underprivileged people in his nation. Before independence this included most Kenyans, for the country was being ruled by foreigners; but after independence he showed that the poor, rural, working-class people continued to suffer—this time at the hands of their more fortunately placed fellow countrymen who controlled all the levers of political and economic power. So Ngugi's primary target of criticism shifted from the colonial government to the neo-colonial government.

This was most evident in the works he wrote after *Petals of Blood*. For the adult literacy campaign in Limuru he coauthored in Gikuyu a musical, *Ngaahika Ndeenda* (1980), later translated and published as *I Will Marry When I Want*, (1982), which exposed the hardships of the landless poor and the greed and arrogance of wealthy landowners. In a subsequent Gikuyu novel, *Caitaani Mūtharaba-inī*

(1980), translated and published as *Devil on the Cross* (1982), he turned to allegory and transparent symbolism to indict the evils of capitalism in contemporary Kenya. Another of his Gikuyu musical dramas that stirred controversy in Kenya in 1981, *Maitu Njugira* (Mother, Sing for Me), was immediately published. Ngugi said that it was his imprisonment that persuaded him to persist in writing novels and plays in Gikuyu so that he could convey his message directly to the exploited masses among his people.

However, he continued to write his political and cultural essays in English in order to reach a broad international audience. These miscellaneous pieces have been collected in four volumes: *Homecoming: Essays on African and Caribbean Literature, Culture and Politics* (1971), *Writers in Politics* (1981), *Barrel of a Pen: Resistance to Repression in Neo-Colonial Kenya* (1983), *Decolonizing the Mind: The Politics of Language in African Literature* (1986), and *Moving the Centers: The Struggle for Cultural Freedom* (1993). He also produced an autobiographical work based on his year behind bars: *Detained: A Writer's Prison Diary* (1981). He also wrote two children's books *Njamba Nene and the Flying Bus* and *Njamba Nene's Pistol,* both in 1995.

For his literary accomplishment, Ngugi has received many awards. He received the Distinguished Africanist Award from the New York African Studies Association (1996), the Fonlon-Nichols prize (1996), the Zora Neale Hurston-Paul Robeson Award (1993), the Lotus prize for Afro-Asian literature (1973), UNESCO first prize (1963), and the East Africa Novel Prize (1962).

In all of his writings Ngugi attacked injustice and oppression and championed the cause of the poor and dispossessed in Kenya. He "set out to develop a national literature for Kenya in the immediate wake of that nation's liberation from British rule," wrote Theodore Pelton in the *Humanist* (March-April 1993). He was East Africa's most prolific and most politically engaged author.

Further Reading

There have been three books devoted to Ngugi's works: C. B. Robson, *Ngugi wa Thiong'o* (1979); G. D. Killam, *An Introduction to the Writings of Ngugi* (1980); and David Cook and Michael Okenimpke, *Ngugi wa Thiong'o: An Exploration of His Writings* (1982); a collection of essays entitled *Critical Perspectives on Ngugi wa Thiong'o* (1985), G. D. Killam, ed.
□

Nichiren

The Japanese Buddhist monk Nichiren (1222-1282), also known as Rissho Daishi, was the founder of the Nichiren sect. Different from other Buddhist leaders of his time because of his uncompromising attitude toward religion and state, he intended to purify and unite Buddhism.

N
ichiren was born the son of a humble fisherman in Kominato, Awa Province. He was given the name Zennichimaru, but in 1237 he was ordained under the religious name of Rencho, which he later changed to Nichiren (*nichi,* "sun," standing for the Light of Truth as well as for the Land of the Rising Sun, and *ren,* "lotus," for the Lotus Sutra). He received instruction in Amidist ideas but apparently from the beginning doubted the efficacy of the *nembutsu* (invocation of Amida's name).

From 1243 to 1253 Nichiren studied at the Tendai center on Mt. Hiei. He came to feel that the true teaching lay in Tendai doctrine, not, however, the degenerate one of his own times but that of Saicho, the founder of the sect. Tendai since Saicho, he felt, had degenerated, for it had been largely infiltrated by Esoteric practices. Thus Nichiren's aim was to unify and to purify Japanese Buddhism. In 1253 he left Mt. Hiei and returned to his former monastery at Kiyozumi. There he preached his new doctrine: hope for the present degenerate age lay in the Lotus Sutra.

Views on Religion and State

Concerned about the state of the nation, Nichiren in 1260 presented to the regent a tract entitled *Rissho ankoku ron* (A Treatise on the Establishment of Righteousness and the Peace of the Country). This important work was conceived in the form of a dialogue between a householder (Nichiren, probably) and a visitor with whom he discusses the times. The author claims that religion and national life are one and the same and proposes that his doctrine become a kind of state religion. The intolerance of his tone is striking: killing heretics, he claims, is not murder; and it is the duty of the government to root them out by the sword. He especially censures Honen and his works.

There is definitely an apocalyptic character about this work. Nichiren divided Buddhist history into three millennia since the death of the historical Shakyamuni, which, according to Chinese reckoning, took place in 947 B.C. Thus the world of the 13th century was in the third period, that of disintegration, or *mappo* (End of the Law). The Lotus Sutra tells how the bodhisattva of Superb Action (Vishishtacharita; Japanese, Jogyo) was to preach the doctrine after the Buddha's death. Nichiren considered himself to be the reincarnation of this bodhisattva, and his aim was to fulfill the prediction by specifically preaching the Lotus Sutra. The Sutra, he maintained, was concentrated in the invocation *namu myo ho renge kyo* (Hail to the Scripture of the Lotus of the Good Law). Sakyamuni, as the eternal, omnipresent mind, encompasses all. Every grain of dust can become Buddha, for it exists in the Buddha mind and shares its essence. In the *Rissho ankoku ron* Nichiren was uncompromising in his disdain of other sects, especially Jodo; but elsewhere Zen, Shingon, and Ritsu receive the same treatment. Kukai he called Japan's great liar (*Nihon no dai mogo*), and Zen a doctrine of demons and fiends.

His Banishment

The government was shocked at the *Rissho ankoku ron,* and a mob was incited by his enemies to attack his hermitage. Nichiren escaped, but on his return to Kamakura in

1261 he was banished to Izu Peninsula. For reasons unknown, the banishment was short, and he returned, unrepentant, to Kamakura.

In 1264 Nichiren returned to his native village, for his mother was seriously ill. Her unexpected recovery, he claimed, was due to the intervention of his prayers. Then, from 1264 to 1268, he traveled on missionary work throughout the eastern provinces, where he was successful in making many converts.

As he had predicted in the *Rissho ankoku ron,* Mongol envoys arrived in 1268 to demand tribute; and Nichiren called on the government to adopt his teachings as the national religion, claiming that this was the only way to save the country. For 3 years the government made no move; but in 1271 Nichiren was arrested, tried, and sentenced to banishment. But according to the custom at the time, the authorities had the right to execute if they so wished, and the death penalty was set for Oct. 17, 1271.

There are a number of stories of how the execution was stayed while Nichiren was on the very execution ground, Nichiren himself claiming divine intervention. He was detained in Kamakura until December of that year and then sent to the isle of Sado, off Echigo, where he remained until 1274. There in 1272 he wrote his famous *Kaimokusho* (Eyeopener), in which he vehemently confirmed his intention of continuing his former activities. In it he set forth his three vows: he would be the pillar of Japan, the eyes of Japan, and the great vessel of Japan, by which he doubtless meant that he would be the receptacle that contained the Truth that was to save the country.

In 1274 he was released from Sado and returned to Kamakura, where he found a more conciliatory government despite his continued adamancy. He left Kamakura and with some disciples settled at Minobu near Mt. Fuji. He built temples there and at Ikegami which are still the chief sites of the sect. He died at Ikegami reciting stanzas from the Lotus Sutra. He was accorded the posthumous title of Rissho Daishi.

Nichiren in his aggressiveness corresponded to the rough warrior type of the age. He reacted strongly against what seemed to him the flaccidity of the Amidists. Salvation had to be strived for by positive action; it was not enough to put oneself passively in the hands of a saving divinity like Amida. In this period of warfare, interest turned to Zen on the one hand, with its direct, anti-intellectual apprehension of the Truth, and to the crusading spirit of Nichiren's beliefs.

Further Reading

Translated excerpts from some of Nichiren's writings are in Ryusoku Tsunoda, William Theodore de Bary, and Donald Keene, eds., *Sources of Japanese Tradition* (1958; 2d ed. 1964). Masaharu Anesaki, *Nichiren: The Buddhist Prophet* (1916; repr. 1966), is an informative and readable account of Nichiren and his beliefs. A good short essay on Nichiren by G. B. Sansom is in Sir Charles Eliot, *Japanese Buddhism* (1935).

Additional Sources

Kirimura, Yasuji, *The life of Nichiren Daishonin / EDITION:First ed,* Tokyo: Nichiren Shoshu International Center, 1980. □

Nicholas I

The Russian czar, statesman, and autocrat Nicholas I (1796-1855) reigned from 1825 to 1855. During his reign Russian 19th-century autocracy reached its greatest power.

The third son of Czar Paul I, Nicholas was tutored in political economy, government, constitutional law, jurisprudence, and public finance. He learned to speak Russian, French, German, and English, and he studied Greek and Latin. Nicholas showed great aptitude for the science of warfare, especially military engineering, and became an expert drillmaster. His education ended in the middle of 1813. In 1814 Nicholas joined the army, for which he retained a strong affection throughout his life. On July 1, 1817, he married Charlotte of Prussia, daughter of King Frederick William III. Nicholas took no part in the administration of public affairs during the reign of his brother Alexander I. He was put in charge of a brigade of the guards and was inspector general of army engineers.

Paul I's second son had renounced his right to the throne, and on Alexander's death in 1825 Nicholas became czar. But the confusion over the succession led to the Decembrist Rebellion of 1825. This uprising was a shock to Nicholas, for it involved the army, especially the guards, whom the Czar regarded as the backbone of the throne. Nicholas supervised the investigation of the conspiracy. He labeled the Decembrists "a handful of monsters." In spite of numerous secret committees and proposals, no significant reforms were enacted. The general attitude of Nicholas is pointed out by his remarks on the emancipation of serfs. "There is no doubt that serfdom, in its present form, is a flagrant evil which everyone realizes," Nicholas proclaimed in the state council on March 20, 1842, "yet to attempt to remedy it now would be, of course, an evil even more disastrous."

Nicholas's rigid conservatism, his fear of the masses, and his desire to preserve autocracy and to protect the interests of the nobility hindered reforms. Thus, his regime became a dictatorship.

Nicholas's conservative views determined Russian foreign policy, over which he exercised personal control. His opposition to the principle of national self-determination, which spread throughout Europe, caused him to come into conflict with every democratic and liberal movement in England and on the Continent. His aggressive and unpredictable foreign policy in Asia and the Near East annoyed the European powers and caused suspicion. His bloody suppression of the Polish insurrection of 1830-1831 and the destruction of Polish autonomy enhanced Nicholas's unpopularity.

Under Nicholas I the first railway between St. Petersburg and Tsarskoe Selo (Pushkin), 17 miles long, was opened to the public in 1837. By the end of his reign Russia had 650 miles of railways. Some progress was also made with river shipping.

It is a paradox that during the absolutism of Nicholas I the golden age of Russian literature occurred. Of the authors whose work does not extend beyond the chronological limits of Nicholas's rule, the most prominent were Aleksandr Pushkin, Mikhail Lermentov, Aleksei Koltsov, and Nikolai Gogol. In addition, intellectual movements emerged to debate the destiny and the contributions to civilization of Russia. The two best-known movements were the Westerners and the Slavophiles. The Westerners were primarily Russian humanitarians. They admired European science and wanted constitutional government, freedom of thought and of the press, and emancipation of the serfs.

Slavophilism of the 1840s was a romantic nationalism that praised Russian virtues as superior to those of the decadent West. The Orthodox Church, according to this movement, was the source of strength in the past and Russia's hope for the future. The Slavophiles criticized the Westernization of Peter the Great as an interruption in the harmonious course of Russian history.

Certainly, Nicholas's defeat in the Crimean War exposed the military and technological backwardness of Russia to the world. He was aware of the failure of his reign, and whatever illusions he might have cherished were dispelled by the Crimean War. He died in St. Petersburg on March 2, 1855.

Further Reading

Two histories of the Romanov dynasty, both written for the general reader and based on solid scholarship, offer biograph-

ical information and a discussion of Nicholas I: John Bergamini, *The Tragic Dynasty* (1969), and Ian Grey, *The Romanovs: The Rise and Fall of a Dynasty* (1970). Alexander I. Herzen, *My Past and Thoughts* (6 vols., 1924-1927), is a classic autobiography and an unsurpassed source of information and insight into the life of the Russian intelligentsia in the reign of Nicholas I.

Both Sidney Monas, *The Third Section: Police and Society in Russia under Nicholas I* (1961), and P. S. Squire, *The Third Department: The Establishment and Practices of the Political Police in the Russia of Nicholas I* (1969), are studies of the foundation and development of the organization in which the czarist secret police received its classic embodiment in the first half of the 19th century. An outline of the ideology of the reign of Nicholas I and discussions of the personalities involved are in Nicholas V. Riasanovsky, *Nicholas I and Official Nationality in Russia, 1825-1855* (1959).

Recommended for general historical background are Alexander A. Kornilov, *Modern Russian History from the Age of Catherine the Great to the End of the Nineteenth Century,* translated by Alexander S. Kaun (1943), which gives an excellent picture of internal policies in the 19th century, and Michael T. Florinsky, *Russia: A History and an Interpretation* (1953), the most thorough narrative of prerevolutionary Russian history available in English. □

Nicholas II

Nicholas II (1868-1918), the czar of Russia from 1894 to 1917, was a staunch defender of autocracy. A weak monarch, he was forced to abdicate, thus ending more than 300 years of Romanov rule in Russia.

The son of Alexander III, Nicholas was born on May 6, 1868. He studied under private tutors, was an accomplished linguist, and traveled extensively in Russia and abroad. In 1890-1891 he made a voyage around the world. Nicholas held customary commissions in the guards, rising, while heir apparent, to the rank of colonel. His participation in affairs of state prior to the death of his father was limited to attendance at meetings of the committee of ministers and of the state council.

His Personality

Throughout his life Nicholas kept with remarkable regularity a diary that throws much light on his character and interests. Hardly a day passed without a record of what Nicholas regarded as its most noteworthy events. These entries, comprising merely a few lines each, noted official visits; dwelt with affection on the doings of his wife and children; and listed his recreational activities. In his relations with courtiers and officials, Nicholas was considerate and kind, but his ministers could never be certain that the policies seemingly agreed upon would actually receive his assent or that a gracious audience would not be followed by a curt dismissal from office.

Nicholas became emperor on the death of his father on Oct. 20, 1894. Less than a month after his coronation, he married Princess Alice of Hesse-Darmstadt. It was a marriage of love, and he remained to the end an exemplary husband and devoted father. His son Alexis, born in 1904, suffered from hemophilia. Desperate efforts to save Alexis's life later led to the incredible episode of Rasputin, a monk who employed hypnotic power to stop Alexis's bleeding. In this manner Rasputin became a dominating influence at the royal court. The deeper cause of Rasputin's influence, as well as of many of Nicholas's difficulties, lay in the Czar's refusal to concern himself with political questions and his staunch conviction that he must maintain the autocracy of his father.

Reaction and Oppression

Nicholas carried on his father's nationalism, his curtailment of the rights of minority nationalities, and his restrictions on nonorthodox religious groups. He limited Finnish autonomy, which had been honored by Russian monarchs since 1809. The Czar's manifesto of February 1899 abolished the Finnish constitution and placed the function of making laws for Finland under the Russian imperial council.

Nicholas pursued a strongly anti-Semitic policy. Jews could enroll in higher schools only under quota limits and were excluded from law practice, zemstvos (local district and provincial assemblies), and city councils. Christian dissenters also were persecuted.

The industrial boom of the early 1890s led to Russia's first important strike movement between 1895 and 1897. In 1897 the government passed legislation curtailing the workday to 11 1/2 hours, but it also ordered the capture and punishment of all strike leaders. University students had also begun to organize demonstrations and strikes. The students' confrontations with the officials of St. Petersburg University led to a general strike in Russian higher education. Nicholas unsuccessfully tried both leniency and harshness as methods of alleviating student disturbances.

The Socialist Revolutionary Battle Organization undertook a terrorist campaign with a series of political murders or attempted murders of provincial governors and other officials. The revolutionary movement was spreading widely. Nicholas and his government lacked a policy to deal effectively with the situation.

Imperialism in the Far East

In form, Nicholas's foreign policy was similar to, and shaped after, that of the other eastern European monarchies: Germany and Austria-Hungary. Nor was it so different from the foreign policy of the western European democracies: France and Great Britain. The main effort of all the Great Powers was not so much to win control over new territories as to preserve the European status quo. However, mutual distrust and the suspicion of one power that another sought to change the status quo often provoked a crisis. In the last quarter of the 19th century, most of the European Great Powers were active in extending their influence and possessions into Africa and Asia. As a result, there was much concern as to whether "imperialist gains, losses, or transfers abroad might upset the balance of interests in Europe itself."

Nicholas's Russia began to challenge Japan in Manchuria and in Korea. An adventurer named Bezobrazov convinced Nicholas to finance a timber concession on the Yalu River on the northern border of Korea. When Tokyo concluded that Bezobrazov had won the support of the Czar, the Japanese attacked the Russian fleet at Port Arthur in January 1904 without declaring war.

Russia suffered a series of defeats on land and sea in the war with Japan. The main factors for the Japanese victory over the Russians were the inadequate supply route of the Transsiberian Railway, the outnumbering of the Russian forces in the Far East by Japan, and Russian mismanagement in the field. A peace treaty, negotiated between Russia and Japan on Sept. 5, 1905, called for Russia's recognition of Japanese hegemony in Korea, annexation of southern Sakhalin by Japan, and Japan's lease of the Liaotung Peninsula and the South Manchurian Railway. The war had ended without forcing too excessive a price for peace.

Revolution of 1905

In 1905 Father George Gapon, leader of a workers' group, led a procession of workers to Nicholas II in order to seek relief for their grievances. The procession was fired upon, and the incident—known as "Bloody Sunday"—may be considered the beginning of the Revolution of 1905. Millions of people participated in this mass movement. The primary goal of the rebellion was a "four-tail constituent assembly"—that is, universal, secret, equal, and direct suffrage to decide the country's future form of government. Other demands included civil liberties, especially freedom of speech, press, and assembly, and the enactment of an 8-hour workday.

When the general strike of October materialized, Minister of Finance Sergei Witte advised Nicholas to choose between a constitutional regime and a military dictatorship, but he added that he would participate only in the former. On Oct. 5, 1905, Nicholas promulgated the October Manifesto. It was drafted by Witte, who became Russia's first prime minister. The manifesto promised: "(1) To grant to the population the inviolable right of free citizenship, based on the principles of freedom of person, conscience, speech, assembly, and union. (2) Without postponing the intended elections for the State Duma and insofar as possible . . . to include in the participation of the work of the Duma those classes of the population that have been until now entirely deprived of the right to vote, and to extend in the future, by the newly created legislative way, the principles of the general right of election. (3) To establish as an unbreakable rule that without its confirmation by the State Duma, no law shall go into force and that the persons elected by the people shall have the opportunity for actual participation in supervising the legality of the acts of authorities appointed by it." Nicholas ended with an appeal to "all the true sons of Russia" to help reestablish law and order.

Fall of the Monarchy

At the beginning of February 1917 Nicholas left the capital and went to supreme headquarters at Mogilev. On March 8 demonstrations were held to celebrate International Women's Day, and these throngs merged with rioting crowds protesting the scarcity of bread in Petrograd. As the riots continued, Nicholas could do nothing but prorogue the Duma, which he did on March 11. The next day the Duma gathered in defiance of his order and chose a provisional committee, composed of members of the progressive bloc and two representatives of parties to the left of it. On March 15, 1917, Nicholas decided to abdicate in favor of his brother Michael. A delegation from the provisional committee, which by now had become the provisional government, waited on the Grand Duke Michael, who refused to be crowned czar of Russia. The monarchy "thus perished without a murmur from either the dynasty or its supporters."

Nicholas abdicated his throne peacefully. On his train the next day he wrote in his diary: "I had a long and sound sleep. Woke up beyond Dvinsk. Sunshine and frost . . . I read much of Julius Caesar." Nicholas and the entire imperial family were forced to depart for Siberia in the summer of 1917. They were murdered by the Communists in July 1918.

Further Reading

Biographical information and a discussion of Nicholas II are in two collective biographies and histories of the Romanov dynasty, both written for the general reader and both based on solid scholarship: John Bergamini, *The Tragic Dynasty* (1969), and Ian Grey, *The Romanovs: The Rise and Fall of a Dynasty* (1970). Hugh Seton-Watson, *The Decline of Imperial Russia, 1855-1914* (1952), is a thorough and well-balanced work that surveys both Russian internal and foreign policies. A study of European diplomacy that pays considerable attention to Russian policy and conduct is Benedict H. Sumner, *Tsardom and Imperialism in the Far East and Middle East, 1880-1914* (1954). Michael T. Florinsky, *Russia: A History and an Interpretation* (1953), is the most complete narrative of prerevolutionary Russian history in English. □

Nicholas of Oresme

The French clergyman, scientist, economist, and translator Nicholas of Oresme (ca. 1320-1382) is best known for his treatise on money, "De moneta," and for his services to King Charles V of France.

Nicholas of Oresme was born at Allemagne in Normandy. Little is known of his early years, except that he studied theology. He attended the College of Navarre of the University of Paris in 1348 and served as master of that college from 1356 to 1361. By 1370 he had become royal chaplain to King Charles V, and he had probably been Charles's tutor during the reign of Charles's father, King John II.

Nicholas wrote on a great variety of scientific subjects, but he is best known for his economic theory, his translations of the works of Aristotle, and his opposition to astrology. Charles V, a patron of the early Renaissance in France, collected a library of several thousand volumes. He com-

missioned Nicholas to translate, from Latin into French, Aristotle's *De caelo* (*On the Heavens*), *Ethics, Politics,* and *Economics*. The influence of the King can also perhaps be seen in Nicholas's chief interest, economics. Under the pressure of the economic disruption caused by the Hundred Years War, Charles V reorganized royal finances into a system that was preserved until 1789. In these circumstances, Nicholas wrote his treatise *De moneta* (*On Money*) between 1355 and 1360. In it Nicholas maintained that money is the property of the community, not of the ruler, and that, therefore, the ruler has an obligation to preserve the purity of coinage and may not debase it. *De moneta* is not always a realistic reflection of late medieval economy, but it became very popular in the 17th century.

Astrology was a fad of Nicholas's times, and he wrote in both French and Latin against the notion that the future can be predicted from a study of the stars. For example, borrowing his title and purpose from Cicero, Nicholas wrote *De divinatione* (*On Divination*) in order to attack dream interpreters and horoscopes. In general, Nicholas argued that supposedly magical events can be explained by natural causes. To support his arguments, he studied astronomy; and although he accepted the Ptolemaic system, in which the universe was believed to revolve around the earth, he granted that terrestrial motion cannot be disproved. Nicholas encouraged the study of nature and the use of reason in examining the Christian faith, remarking that "Everything contained in the Gospels is highly reasonable."

Nicholas became bishop of Lisieux in 1377, and he died there on July 11, 1382.

Further Reading

Nicholas's *De Proportionibus, and Ad Pauca Respicientes,* with introduction, translation, and notes by E. Grant (1966), contains a charming biographical sketch. Three works contain both biographical accounts of Nicholas's life and translations of his writings: G. W. Coopland, *Nicole Oresme and the Astrologers: A Study of His "Livre de Divinacion"* (1952); Charles Johnson, ed. and trans., *The "De Moneta" of Nicholas Oresme* (1956); and Marshall Clagett, ed., *Nicole Oresme and the Medieval Geometry of Qualities and Motions* (1968). □

Ben Nicholson

Ben Nicholson (1894-1982) was the first English painter to create geometrical abstract paintings and reliefs that directly contributed to the international abstract movement.

Ben Nicholson was born near Uxbridge, England, on the outskirts of London, on April 10, 1894. His father, William Nicholson, and his uncle, James Pryde, were leading painters of their generation in England, and his mother was also a painter. Nicholson had little formal artistic training, except for one term at the Slade

School of Fine Arts in London in 1911, where he began working with jugs, cups, mugs and bottles, frequent subjects of his later work. Nicholson left the school because he was dissatisfied with the provincial character of painting taught there and wanted to find his own way.

Influenced by Cubism

After traveling in Europe, Nicholson went to Pasadena, California, in 1921. While there, he saw his first Cubist work — a painting by Picasso. He later said that "none of the actual events in one's life have been more real than that, and it still remains a standard by which I judge any reality in my own world."

Nicholson's landscapes and still lifes of the early 1920s are mostly soft and luminous, with delicate colors and fluid, indeterminate forms. In 1922 in London, he had his first one-man show. His landscapes of the later 1920s reveal his poetic feeling for nature which was an important element in his work. There is a remarkable freedom in the treatment of scale and perspective in his work, and the forms often have a playful, toylike character. His almost naive approach has something in common with the work of Christopher Wood, with whom Nicholson was closely associated during the 1920s. Along with Wood, in 1928 he discovered at St. Ives in Cornwall the work of Alfred Wallis, the greatest modern English primitive. The work of Wallis had a profound effect on Nicholson.

Nicholson's still lifes of the late 1920s and early 1930s show a gradually increasing concern with structure under the influence of late Cubism. After his meeting in 1931 with the sculptor Barbara Hepworth, who became his second wife, he made frequent trips to Paris, visiting the studios of Piet Mondrian, Georges Braque, Constantin Brancusi, and other leading artists. These artists prompted Nicholson's conversion in 1933 to abstract art. He joined the group Abstraction-Création in Paris and in the following years became the principal link between the international abstract movement and England. His works of this period, perhaps his finest, consist of geometrical abstract paintings composed of rectangles and circles of clear, uniform colors and of carved white reliefs of extraordinary purity, made from wood and synthetic board. These works are perhaps closest to the neoplasticism of Mondrian, who lived in London from 1938 to 1940 and was in close contact with Nicholson and his wife. During this period in London, Nicholson edited *Circle,* a publication on constructivist art, and joined an avant-garde artists' group called Unit One.

In 1939, shortly after the outbreak of World War II, Nicholson and his family moved from London to St. Ives in Cornwall. There he began to turn away from the severity, purity, and strictly rectilinear structure of his works. He made paintings and drawings of the harbors and landscapes of western Cornwall and still lifes in an abstracted form of late Cubism, in which the objects are indicated by overlapping linear silhouettes, with silvery tones enlivened by small patches of brilliant color.

International Acclaim

It was not until Nicholson was well into his fifties that he began to receive international attention. In 1952, he took first prize at the Carnegie International Art Exhibition in Pittsburgh. In 1954 he won the Ulissi Prize at the Venice Biennale. The next year he won the Governor of Tokyo's Award and was honored by the Belgian Art Critics in Paris. In 1956 he won the Guggenheim International Award. Beginning in the mid-1950s and especially after his move to Switzerland, near Ascona, in 1956, Nicholson's work consisted mainly of reliefs and linear drawings. Unlike his white reliefs of the 1930s, his later ones have contrasting stony textures and the shapes are tilted in different directions; they are usually carved in hardboard with a razor blade in very low relief.

In 1968, Queen Elizabeth II made Nicholson a member of the Order of Merit. London's Tate Gallery has housed scores of his paintings.

Nicholson was married three times. With his first wife, painter and writer Winifred Dacre Roberts, he had two sons and a daughter. With Hepworth, he had triplets, a son and two daughters. His third wife was writer-photographer Felicitas Vogler; they were childless.

Nicholson wanted to make abstract art accessible. In 1941, he wrote that looking at abstract paintings should be easy: "There is no need to concentrate; it becomes a part of living. I think that so far from being a limited expression, understood by a few, abstract art is a powerful, unlimited and universal language."

Further Reading

The most comprehensive monograph on Nicholson, with 298 reproductions and a perceptive introduction, is John Russell's, *Ben Nicholson: Drawings, Paintings and Reliefs, 1911-1968* (1969); Herbert Read's, *Ben Nicholson: Paintings, Reliefs, Drawings* (1948; rev. ed. 1956), also contains many plate; Ian Chilvers and Harold Osborne, *Oxford Dictionary of Art.* □

Sir Francis Nicholson

Sir Francis Nicholson (1655-1728) was colonial governor of a number of colonies: New York, Virginia, Maryland, Nova Scotia, and South Carolina.

Francis Nicholson was born on Nov. 12, 1655, in Yorkshire, England. Entering the army in 1679, he spent several years as courier and aide to the governor of Tangier in West Africa. In 1686 he went to America, where he became a member of the Council of the Dominion of New England. In 1688 he was appointed lieutenant governor of New York.

Nicholson went to Virginia in 1690 to govern in the name of the absentee governor. He industriously studied frontier problems, encouraged postal service, and aided the Reverend James Blair in establishing the College of William and Mary. In 1692 he returned to England.

Returning to the Colonies as governor of Maryland in 1694, Nicholson was so active in church affairs and education that one exaggerated report claimed he was responsible for founding 2 universities and 28 churches. His early popularity waned, and the last years of his administration were marked by bitter personal quarrels.

Nicholson returned to Virginia as governor in 1698. His violent temper and dictatorial methods estranged him from many of the colony's leaders. He was active in suppressing piracy, in moving the capital from Jamestown to Williamsburg, and in improving the efficiency of government operations. His political enemies forced his recall in 1705. In 1706 Nicholson was elected a member of the Royal Society. Now a colonel, he volunteered in 1709 to accompany an attack on Canada. His energetic activities led the northern governors to urge that he command the expedition, but the plan collapsed when troops from England failed to arrive.

At the request of Massachusetts, Nicholson, now a brigadier general, was given command of the expedition that resulted in the bloodless victory at Port Royal, Nova Scotia. Named governor of Nova Scotia in 1713, Nicholson devoted little time to the province but busied himself inquiring into colonial finance, smuggling, prize money, and educational affairs. His blunt methods irritated other officials. After the accession of George I, he returned to England, where he acted as something of an unofficial consultant to the Board of Trade.

In 1720 Nicholson returned to America as governor of the new royal colony South Carolina. His administration had much to recommend it, but he alienated Charleston merchants who petitioned for his recall because he failed to oppose the issuing of paper money. In poor health, he requested his own recall in 1725. He died on March 5, 1728.

Further Reading

There is no full-length biography of Nicholson. For information on his life and for historical background see Charles M. Andrews, *The Colonial Period of American History* (4 vols., 1934-1938), and Wesley Frank Craven, *The Colonies in Transition, 1660-1713* (1968). □

Jack Nicklaus

For most of the past 30 years Jack Nicklaus (born 1940) has been considered golf's greatest. His longevity has proved equal to Arnold Palmer's , and only Ben Hogan and Bobby Jones can be considered players in Nicklaus's league.

In numbers of major tournaments won, golfer Jack Nicklaus stands alone with 20 victories—a remarkable figure that does not include major titles won on the Senior Tour. He has won 70 times on the PGA Tour and had 58 second-place and 36 third place finishes. Nicklaus has

finished top PGA Tour money winner and held the tour's low-score average eight times. He was named the PGA Tour Player of the Year in 1967, 1972, 1973, 1975, and 1976, and *Golf* magazine in 1988 celebrated American golf's centennial by naming Nicklaus the "Player of the Century."

Took Amateur Titles

Nicklaus shot a fifty-one for the first nine holes he ever played. At the age of 13 he broke a 70 and held a three handicap. By then his hero had become the great Jones, who won the 1926 U.S. Open at Nicklaus's home course, the Scioto Country Club. Tutored by club pro Jack Grout, Nicklaus early on realized his potential for tournament play, dominating local and national junior golf events and going on to capture two U.S. Amateur Championships (1959 and 1961). Indeed, by the time he turned pro in November 1961 he had established himself as an the country's greatest amateur golfer while simultaneously giving the professionals a scare as runner-up to Arnold Palmer by only two strokes in the 1960 U.S. Open and as an a fourth-place finisher in the 1961 U.S. Open.

Victory over Palmer

In 1962, at the Oakmont Country Club outside of Pittsburgh, Nicklaus beat Arnold Palmer in a play-off to win the U.S. Open. Palmer's millions of diehard fans—and huge throng of gallery members, called Arnie's Army, that followed their hero from tee to green—were crushed by their hero's loss, and the Nicklaus victory went down as an one of the most unpopular the world of golf had ever known. The

two men could not have been more different in appearance and temperament. Palmer was a handsome, dashing figure whose powerful, lunging swing often knocked his ball into troublesome spots well off the fairway. Nicklaus was round-faced and pudgy—his girth and blond hair giving rise to his nickname, the Golden Bear—and his well-oiled, smoothly tempoed swing rarely failed him. Palmer wore his emotions on his sleeve, often grimacing and chain-smoking his way through a particularly tough round. Nicklaus was often expressionless on the course, and although he smoked—at one time up to two packs a day—he never lit up on the golf course. In explaining his ability to abstain from a nerve-smoothing addiction while playing a nerve-racking game, Nicklaus simply stated, "I don't think about it." Nicklaus's mind, even more than his great natural talent and long-ball swing, was the key to his phenomenal success. He rarely made a poor tactical decision in a tournament; he had an unflappable ego, never second-guessing himself—and his powers of concentration were intense.

In 1963 Nicklaus won the Masters and the PGA. He ran away with the 1965 Masters, winning by nine strokes in what Jones called "the greatest performance in golf history." Nicklaus shattered Hogan's seemingly insurmountable Masters record of 274 by three strokes. Nicklaus successfully defended his Masters title the following year and won his first British Open, becoming one of only four golfers to win all four majors (the others are Gene Sarazen, Hogan, and Gary Player). At the 1967 U.S. Open Nicklaus pulled away from Palmer in the final round to win by four strokes, signaling to even the most obstinate among Arnie's Army that the Golden Bear had forever robbed the king of his throne.

The New Bear

The beginning of the new decade saw a leaner, more fashionable Bear. Nicklaus dropped weight and let his golden hair grow prior to the 1970 season. He adopted more colorful golf course attire, adding color and flair to an image that had suffered from fat jokes and the general perception that Nicklaus was boring and mechanical. When it came to winning consistently, however, Nicklaus was every bit a machine. Between 1970 and 1975 he won several more majors—the only victories "that count," he liked to say. His 1973 PGA title put him one ahead of Jones's 13 major victories, and his 1975 Masters was his fifth win in Augusta, Georgia, and was proclaimed by observers and sportswriters to have been one of the most thrilling golf victories of all time. On Augusta's sixteenth hole the last day of the tournament, Nicklaus sank a 40-foot putt to take a one-stroke lead and held on the last two holes—winning by one over Tom Weiskopf and two over Johnny Miller.

Improved Failing Game

In 1977 Nicklaus was involved in a thrilling duel with Tom Watson, America's new star, at the British Open. He lost what sportswriters later called the "Duel in the Sun" but returned in 1978 to claim the British title. With the emergence of players such as Watson, however, Nicklaus's victories seemed less easy to come by with each passing year,

and by the end of the decade, many in golfing believed that Nicklaus's dominance—at least when it came to the majors—had ended. In 1979 Nicklaus had his worst season to date, having gone winless and finishing seventy-first on the money list. His length off the tee and the long flight and high trajectory of his iron shots had once given him a huge advantage over the rest of the field—and had revolutionized the game. But there was a new generation of golfers who hit the ball as high and as far as their idol could. Nicklaus decided to go back to the drawing board, looking to improve his biggest weakness—the short game—and turn it into a strength. In 1980 he returned to top form, winning the U.S. Open and PGA Tour during the 1980s, and at the 1986 Masters he scored perhaps golf's most emotion-stirring victory. He had by then become the game's elder statesman and had gone from being golf's villain—the fat kid who beat Arnie—to being one of the most popular athletes the world of sports had ever known. □

Harold George Nicolson

Sir Harold George Nicolson (1886-1968) was a British diplomat, historian, biographer, critic and journalist, and diarist of note.

Harold Nicolson was born in Tehran, Persia (now Iran), on November 21, 1886, where his father was British *charge d'affaires.* His father eventually became the first Lord Carnock, and as a child Harold visited the estates of his uncle in Ireland, Lord Dufferin. Harold was an aristocrat through and through.

His early life was spent in diplomatic posts with his father—the Balkans, the Middle East, Morocco, Madrid, and St. Petersburg (Leningrad). He went into the diplomatic service himself, quite naturally, in 1909, after going to Balliol College, Oxford. On leave from his diplomatic post in Constantinople he married Vita Sackville-West in 1913 in the chapel at Knole, Kent. She was the daughter of Lord Sackville, and in his house at Knole there were 365 rooms: it had been a 16th-century present from Queen Elizabeth I to Thomas Sackville, Earl of Dorset.

In 1915 the young couple bought Long Barn, a medieval cottage near Knole, where they lived for 15 years. Vita was a poet, novelist, and gardener. Afterwards they lived in Sissinghurst Castle, also in Kent. Their friends were aristocrats, diplomats, and literary notables, among whom was Virginia Woolf, the famous stream-of-consciousness novelist. Vita was in love with Virginia, as she was in love with several other women in her life. Harold was a homosexual too, and they also loved each other. Vita and Harold had two sons, one of whom has written a book about their marriage: Nigel Nicolson, *Portrait of a Marriage* (1973), which depicts his parents as loving each other until the day they died.

As a diplomat, Nicolson was at the Paris Peace Conference at the end of World War I, and in the 1920s he served in the Middle East and Berlin. He resigned in 1929 to be near his wife and to write. His first book was *Paul Verlaine* (1921), which was the first of six literary biographies: *Tennyson* (1923), *Byron: The Last Journey* (1924), *Swinburne* (1926), *Benjamin Constant* (1949), and *Sainte-Beuve* (1957). He also published a brace of novels—*Sweet Waters* (1921) and *Public Faces* (1932); essays—*Some People* (1927), *The English Sense of Humor* (1947), *Good Behaviour* (1955), *Journey to Java* (1957), *The Age of Reason* (1960), and *Monarchy* (1962); some more biographies—*Curzon, the Last Phase* (1934), *Dwight Morrow* (1935), and *Helen's Tower* (1937); and some historical works, among which were *Peacemaking, 1919* (1933), *Diplomacy* (1939), and the distinguished *The Congress of Vienna* (1946) and *The Evolution of Diplomatic Method* (1954).

And he had time for his *Diaries*. They were published by his son Nigel, in three volumes, in 1966-1968. He was said to have never written a boring line. On reaching 50 he commented: "I am still very promising, and shall continue to be so until the day of my death" (which came 32 years later!).

In politics, he was a member of Parliament for the National Labour Party for West Leicester from 1935 to 1945. He was intensely opposed to Munich—the Munich Pact of 1938, signed by Prime Minister Neville Chamberlain and dictated by Hitler, for German subjugation of the Sudetenland of Czechoslovakia. He was committed, with Winston Churchill, in opposition to all dictators.

But he was not much of a "Labour man." After the war he failed in the election of 1945 as a National Labour Party candidate; he tried again in 1948 in a by-election at North Croydon, this time as a Labour Party contestant. He was unsuccessful. In his own words, he was a "cerebral socialist." He could not sympathize with the point of view of his mainly working-class constituents; they were too far from his own class, socially and intellectually. He was so civilized and so cultured that he seemed the last "gentleman" in politics.

He observed in 1948: "How difficult the proletariat are! . . . They destroy the grass, and there were little ragomuffins sailing cigarette cartons on the two pools. Yes, I fear my socialism is purely cerebral; I do not like the masses in the flesh."

Nicolson's suspicion of the working-classes was paralleled by his snobbishness about Jews, Arabs, Blacks, and Americans. He shared these prejudices with his wife. He knew these feelings were not worthy of him, but he could not seem to do anything about them. For instance, in the first three months of 1933 he and his wife were on a lecture-tour of the United States. Vita said: "with all their kindnesses, these people have very little *imagination*."

Of all the works Nicolson wrote, the history and diplomacy books stand out, and the *Diaries*. He died at Sissinghurst Castle on May 1, 1968, six years after his wife, never having recovered from her death.

Further Reading

Sources of additional information include Nigel Nicolson, *Portrait of a Marriage* (1973); Michael Stevens, *V. Sackville-West* (1973); Sir Harold Nicolson, *Diaries and Letters, 1930-1962* (3 vols., edited by Nigel Nicolson, 1966-1968); and *Newsweek 72* (July 15, 1968).

Additional Sources

Lees-Milne, James., *Harold Nicolson: a biography*, Hamden, Conn.: Archon Books, 1982, 1980-1984. □

Marjorie Hope Nicolson

Marjorie Hope Nicolson (1894-1981), a pioneer investigator of the relationship between literature and science, helped shape the contemporary study of English and the humanities in American higher education as teacher, scholar, and administrator. She was the first woman president of Phi Beta Kappa and later served as president of the Modern Language Association.

Marjorie Hope Nicolson was born February 18, 1894, in Yonkers, New York, and died in White Plains, New York, on March 9, 1981. Her father, Charles Butler Nicolson, was the editor-in-chief of the Detroit *Free Press* during World War I and later became the paper's Washington correspondent. Her mother's maiden name was Lissie Hope Morris.

Nicolson took her B.A. at the University of Michigan in 1914 and her M.A. there in 1918. In 1920 she got her Ph.D. from Yale and did additional graduate work at Johns Hopkins from 1923 to 1926. She worked briefly for her father's paper, first as a drama critic, then in the Washington office during the early 1920s. While her father was sick for three months she ran the office by herself. The need to write compact, coherent copy for general audiences under deadline pressures helped shape her readable scholarly style as well as her direct and compelling classroom manner. Frederick Hard, President of Scripps College, remarked that Nicolson belonged "to that rare company of scholars who speak as lucidly, as readily, and as eloquently as they write. . . ."

Her teaching career began in the public schools of Michigan. It was said that at one point she developed the art of wiggling her ears to keep the attention of her high school students. For college and graduate students of English she lectured without notes in syntactically complicated sentences and elaborately organized paragraphs, producing well-shaped oral essays. She cited large portions of text, poetry, and prose from memory. She could hold audiences spellbound with a mixture of erudition, clear delivery, and a sense of the human interest inherent in her subject. Her book *John Milton: A Reader's Guide to His Poetry* provides a good sense of her classroom manner, reading almost like a transcript of actual lectures.

She began her college teaching at the University of Minnesota in 1920, moving to Goucher College in 1923. In 1927 she joined the Smith College faculty, becoming professor of English in 1928 and dean in 1929. In 1941 she left to assume a professorship in Columbia University's graduate Department of English and Comparative Literature, the first woman to do so. She remained at Columbia until her retirement in 1962, becoming chairwoman of the department in 1954.

Nicolson had begun her scholarly career early, with a Guggenheim fellowship in 1926 and 1927, working in libraries abroad. Her early articles and books covered a wide range of subjects, including a student text of 19th century poets and one in *The Art of Description*. She also published articles and essays on detective fiction, Shakespeare, and college teaching and scholarship.

Her works examining the relationships among science, philosophy, imagination, and literature, however, constitute her most famous body of studies. A selection of her books in this area comprise a virtual outline of the subject: *The Microscope and English Imagination* (1935); *A World in the Moon* (1936); *Newton Demands the Muse* (1946), which received a prize from the British Academy; *Voyages to the Moon* (1948); *The Breaking of the Circle* (1950); *Science and Imagination* (1956); and *Mountain Gloom and Mountain Glory* (1959). She also wrote and lectured on the conflict between humanists and scientists in the 17th and 18th centuries as well as in the 20th century.

Recognition of her contributions to teaching, administration, and critical scholarship was abundant. She received 18 honorary degrees from such prestigious institutions as Princeton, Columbia, University of Michigan, Mt. Holyoke, Yale, Goucher, Rutgers, and Smith College. The American Council of Learned Societies and the American Association of University Women honored her. From 1930 to 1937 she was a member of the Guggenheim Foundation awards committee, and she remained a consultant until 1962.

At various times she was a visiting scholar or professor at Johns Hopkins and Princeton universities, Claremont Graduate School, and the Institute for Advanced Study at Princeton. She served on the editorial boards of *The American Scholar* and of the *Journal of the History of Ideas* and was a consultant to the publications of the Modern Language Association and to *Studies in Philology*.

In 1940 she was elected president of Phi Beta Kappa, the first woman to hold that post and the only person to serve two terms. In 1963 she served as president of the Modern Language Association.

While she influenced the course of study for women while dean at Smith College, her period of greatest influence was at Columbia University, where she became a virtual legend.

Further Reading

Further biographical and bibliographical details may be found in the *Directory of American Scholars* and in *Contemporary Authors*. An extended essay on her time at Columbia may be found in Morris Freedman's "Marjorie Hope Nicolson," *The American Scholar*, 50 (Winter 1980-1981). □

Barthold Georg Niebuhr

Barthold Georg Niebuhr (1776-1831), German historian and statesman, is best known for his original, trailblazing work and lectures in Roman history. He initiated a new method of critical historical scholarship.

Barthold Georg Niebuhr son of Karsten Niebuhr, an explorer and Danish government official, was born in Copenhagen on Aug. 26, 1776. After studying at the University of Kiel (1794-1796), where he became acquainted with the philosophy of Immanuel Kant, Niebuhr accepted a position as private secretary to the Danish minister of finance in Copenhagen. Niebuhr studied agriculture and physical science in London and Edinburgh (1798-1799). On his return to Copenhagen he entered the Danish state service, developed great expertise in financial matters, and was appointed director of the Danish National Bank in 1804.

In 1806 Baron Stein offered Niebuhr an appointment in the Prussian state service. Arriving in Berlin on the eve of the Battle of Jena, which led to the collapse of the Prussian state, he joined the Prussian government in its flight to Königsberg and Riga. In 1810, after Stein's dismissal, Niebuhr resigned because he could not work with Stein's successor.

Niebuhr remained in Berlin, became a member of the Berlin Academy of Sciences, and started his famous lectures on Roman history. Out of these lectures emerged the first two volumes of his *Roman History* (1811-1812). He rejoined the Prussian government service in financial affairs (1813-1816), publishing the semiofficial *Preussischen Korrespondenten* and writing extensively in support of Prussian annexation of Saxony.

Disappointed by the narrowness of the Restoration climate after 1815, Niebuhr accepted an appointment as Prussian ambassador in Rome, where he served until 1823. During this time he continued his studies in Roman history. In the Cathedral library of Verona he discovered the long-lost *Institutes of Gaius* (later edited by Karl von Savigny), which had served as a basis for the "Institutes" of Emperor Justinian's great codification of Roman Law. Niebuhr also discovered and published fragments of Cicero and Livy and participated in the edition of Cicero's *De republica* (1820).

In 1823 Niebuhr became a professor at the University of Bonn. He rewrote and republished *Roman History* (1827-1828) and completed the third volume (published 1832), bringing the story to the end of the First Punic War. He died in Bonn on Jan. 1, 1831.

Niebuhr filled history, which up to that time had been viewed as a grand painting of philosophical or esthetic edification or as a fragmentary pile of individual learned

discoveries, with the life of hard reality. He pioneered the introduction of philological methodology and introduced social history as a new discipline. His impact on his contemporaries is best exemplified by J. W. von Goethe: "It was really Niebuhr and not Roman history which intrigued me. His penetrating mind and his diligent ways were what really edified us. All those agrarian laws did not really interest me; but the manner in which he explained them, the way in which he clarified complicated relations, was of benefit to me, and laid upon me the obligation to proceed in like manner in the performance of my own tasks."

Further Reading

The two major English translations of Niebuhr's works are by Leonhard Schmitz: *Lectures on the History of Rome* (2d ed., 3 vols., 1849-1850) and *Lectures on Ancient History* (3 vols., 1852). The best, although short, English evaluation of Niebuhr's life and work is in George Peabody Gooch, *History and Historians in the Nineteenth Century* (1913; rev. ed. 1965). Niebuhr is discussed in William Ward Fowler, *Roman Essays and Interpretations* (1920), and Sir John E. Sandys, *A History of Classical Scholarship* (1921).

Additional Sources

Tod, Robert James Niebuhr., *Barthold Georg Niebuhr, 1776-1831: an appreciation in honour of the 200th anniversary of his birth,* Cambridge: Printed by Nicholas Smith at the University Library, 1977. □

Helmut Richard Niebuhr

The Protestant theologian Helmut Richard Niebuhr (1894-1962) was one of the most original and perceptive American theologians of the 20th century.

On Sept. 3, 1894, H. Richard Niebuhr was born in Wright City, Mo., the youngest of five children of a German immigrant Protestant minister, Gustav Niebuhr, and his American-born wife, Lydia. Three of the Niebuhr children were to distinguish themselves in theology. Niebuhr graduated from Elmhurst College (1912) and Eden Theological Seminary (1915) and received his master of arts degree from Washington University (1917).

In 1916 Niebuhr was ordained to the ministry of the Evangelical and Reformed Church and served as pastor of a church in St. Louis until 1918. He taught at Eden Seminary from 1919 to 1922. He married Florence Marie Mittendorff in 1920.

In 1922 Niebuhr matriculated at Yale University, receiving his bachelor of divinity degree from Yale Divinity School in 1923 and his doctorate the following year. He returned to Elmhurst College to serve as its president until 1927 and then went to Eden Seminary, where he taught until 1931. Niebuhr's first book, *The Social Sources of Denominationalism* (1929), remains a classic analysis of the social factors in the rise and perpetuation of Protestant denominations and reveals his characteristic use of data and methods from the social sciences.

Niebuhr accepted a post as associate professor of Christian ethics at Yale Divinity School in 1931, where he spent the rest of his career. In 1938 he was promoted to the rank of professor, and in 1954 he became Sterling professor of theology and Christian ethics. His *The Kingdom of God in America* (1937) is a study of the central role played in American Protestant history by the biblical idea of the kingdom of God and how that idea underwent fundamental shifts of emphasis between 17th-century Puritanism and 20th-century Protestantism. In *The Meaning of Revelation* (1941) Niebuhr sought to articulate the Christian understanding of revelation—the self-disclosure of God to man in Christ—in the light of the relativity of human knowledge disclosed by modern investigation, especially in the social sciences. His next book, *Christ and Culture* (1951), distinguished five basic ways of understanding the relationship between the lordship of Christ and human culture which have been used in the history of Christian thought: Christ against culture, the Christ of culture, Christ above culture, Christ and culture in paradox, and Christ the transformer of culture.

In 1954 and 1955 Niebuhr directed a survey of theological education in the United States and Canada. The fruits of this study and evaluation are embodied in *The Ministry in Historical Perspectives* (1956), edited by Niebuhr and Daniel Day Williams, and *The Purpose of the Church and Its Ministry* (1956) and *The Advancement of*

Theological Education (1957), which Niebuhr wrote in collaboration with Williams and James M. Gustafson.

Niebuhr's last book, *Radical Monotheism and Western Culture* (1960), was the most complete presentation of his basic theme: Christianity's anchor and critical principle in the sovereignty of the one God amid the relativities of man's thinking and living. His Robertson Lectures at the University of Glasgow in 1960 were published posthumously as *The Responsible Self* (1963). The book is the fullest statement of his approach to Christian ethics, centering on the notion of Christian responsibility as the "fitting response" to other human beings and society arising out of a biblically grounded interpretation of what God is bringing about in the world of men. For Niebuhr the theological key was to be found in the biblical perception of the transcendence of God over all finite things, including man's knowledge of God.

During his distinguished career Niebuhr was awarded many honorary degrees. He participated in ecumenical work, contributing to major study documents drawn up for World Council of Churches assemblies. He was an architect of the United Church of Christ, formed in 1957 by a merger of the Congregational Christian and the Evangelical and Reformed Churches, and helped draft its Statement of Faith. He died on July 5, 1962, in Greenfield, Mass.

Further Reading

Niebuhr has not been given the widespread and comprehensive attention he deserves as a leading American theologian. There are two full-length books on him: Paul Ramsey, ed., *Faith and Ethics: The Theology of H. Richard Niebuhr* (1957), a symposium of excellent essays on Niebuhr's thought by distinguished students and colleagues, and John D. Godsey, *The Promise of H. Richard Niebuhr* (1970). □

Reinhold Niebuhr

The American theologian Reinhold Niebuhr (1892-1971) was a major figure in the "Neo-Orthodox" movement in Protestant theology, which reoriented the entire thrust of theological and biblical studies from the 1920s on.

Reinhold Niebuhr was born in Wright City, Mo., on June 21, 1892, the son of an immigrant German Evangelical and Reformed minister who served as pastor to German-American communities in small towns. Early deciding to enter the ministry, Niebuhr studied at Elmhurst College and Eden Theological Seminary and then spent 2 years at Yale Divinity School. After receiving his master of arts degree from Yale in 1915, he left the academic world to take his first and only pastorate—a small mission church in Detroit, where he remained until 1928.

At the time Niebuhr arrived there, the automobile industry was just beginning its rapid expansion, and Detroit was developing into one of America's major cities. Many of the employees of the Ford Motor Company lived in his parish. He had the opportunity to observe at firsthand the impact of industrial society upon the factory workers. As Niebuhr said much later, "The resulting facts determined my development more than any books I may have read." He watched the dehumanizing effects of assembly line speedups and irregular job opportunities upon workers unprotected by legal or associational powers. By the end of the 1920s he was questioning seriously the basic assumptions of liberal Protestantism and the Social Gospel, on which he had been nurtured. In public he urged churchmen to examine critically the capitalist social order, and he pressed for greater realism concerning the pervasiveness and subtlety of human pride or sin. His first book, *Does Civilization Need Religion?* (1927), reflected these attitudes.

In 1928 Niebuhr moved to New York City to join the faculty of Union Theological Seminary, where he remained until his retirement in 1960. He reached New York just as the Depression began and found all about him confirmation of his ideas concerning the severe strictures of capitalism. For a time he became a Socialist, influenced strongly by the Marxist critique of a floundering capitalist society; but at the same time his theological perspective was becoming more conservative, and he was reaching back to recover and reassert the classic formulas of Christian doctrine.

Niebuhr was not a systematic theologian. He was pragmatic, stressing a dialectical, problematic approach in his intellectual inquiries. In a series of important books published during the 1930s and early 1940s, his mature reflections on the relationship of the Christian faith to the

industrial, technological world gradually unfolded. *Moral Man in an Immoral Society* (1932) was a full-scale attack upon liberal Protestantism, especially its lack of understanding of the nature and use of power in modern society. In *Interpretation of Christian Ethics* (1935) he replaced his largely critical and destructive polemics against liberalism with an attempt at a constructive restatement of the relation of ethics to politics. In *Beyond Tragedy* (1937), a series of essays that originally had been sermons, Niebuhr reasserted the centrality of human sinfulness in explaining and understanding the human predicament and offered Christ's crucifixion as the most profound means of transcending that human condition. He also stressed the importance of myth as a method for making comprehensible to modern man the biblical world view, which he now so vigorously espoused.

All of Niebuhr's previous work was knitted together in more comprehensive and systematic form with the publication of the Gifford Lectures, which he delivered in Scotland in 1939, under the title *The Nature and Destiny of Man* (2 vols., 1941, 1943). This work was his principal intellectual achievement. Nearly all of his subsequent books sought to expand upon selected aspects of this richly varied material. The central concern of the work was an inquiry into the nature of selfhood. Niebuhr demonstrated that his vision of human existence was, at its core, ambiguous. Man was "both free and bound, both limited and limitless." Moreover, it was the Christian faith, above all other world views, that perceived most clearly this ambiguity and proposed means to cope with, and perhaps even to overcome, the anxiety that was inevitably a product of that ambiguity.

Niebuhr persistently tried to relate his religious insights to the concrete political and social problems of the contemporary world. He involved himself actively in politics, once as a Socialist candidate for local office, later as one of the founders of Americans for Democratic Action, a liberal study group within the Democratic party. He preached often on college campuses throughout the nation, involved himself in the ecumenical movements of national and international church bodies, and produced an endless stream of articles for popular journals, both religious and secular. He also continued to publish more serious studies in theology and politics. Two especially important analyses of democracy, *Children of Light and Children of Darkness* (1944) and *The Irony of American History* (1952), appeared at a time when the Western democracies were facing fundamental ideological and spiritual challenges.

The flirtation with Marxism and support of pacifism characteristic of Niebuhr in the early 1930s gave way to disenchantment with communism and a willingness to support "realistically" the use of force in international politics as the world was engulfed in World War II. Urging the participation of the United States in the power politics of the postwar period, Niebuhr became a major influence on the thinking of high-ranking academicians and government officials. (Consistently enough, the massive extension of American power into Southeast Asia provoked criticism from Niebuhr comparable to that directed against the Communists in the immediate post-World War II period.)

His health seriously impaired by a stroke in 1952, Niebuhr was forced to limit his activities. He died in Stockbridge, Mass., on June 1, 1971. He was one of the major spokesmen for Protestant theology in the 20th century.

Further Reading

An important statement by Niebuhr concerning his intellectual and personal development is included among a series of illuminating essays by many scholars edited by Charles Kegley and Robert Bretall, *Reinhold Niebuhr: His Religious, Social, and Political Thought* (1956). An engaging, perceptive biographical study is June Bingham, *Courage to Change* (1961). Ronald H. Stone, *Reinhold Niebuhr: Prophet to Politician* (1972), emphasizes his political philosophy. A useful, brief pamphlet that analyzes the salient points in Niebuhr's system of ideas is Nathan Scott, *Reinhold Niebuhr* (1963).

Additional Sources

Bingham, June, *Courage to change: an introduction to the life and thought of Reinhold Niebuhr,* Lanham: University Press of America, 1993.

Brown, Charles C. (Charles Calvin), *Niebuhr and his age: Reinhold Niebuhr's prophetic role in the twentieth century,* Philadelphia: Trinity Press International, 1992.

Clark, Henry B. (Henry Balsley), *Serenity, courage, and wisdom: the enduring legacy of Reinhold Niebuhr,* Cleveland, Ohio: Pilgrim Press, 1994.

Fox, Richard Wightman, *Reinhold Niebuhr: a biography,* New York: Pantheon Books, 1985; San Francisco: Harper & Row, 1987, 1985.

Stone, Ronald H., *Professor Reinhold Niebuhr: a mentor to the twentieth century,* Louisville, Ky.: Westminster/John Knox Press, 1992. □

Carl August Nielsen

Carl August Nielsen (1865-1931) was one of the major symphonists of the postromantic epoch and Denmark's most eminent composer. His works are characterized by lyricism, accomplished contrapuntal skill, mastery of form, and a fresh approach to tonality.

C arl Nielsen was born on June 9, 1865, in Nørre-Lyndelse on the island of Fünen, the seventh of 12 children of Niels Jørgensen, a poor house painter and country fiddler. His poor but not unhappy rural youth Nielsen described in a moving memoir, *My Childhood* (1927), a classic of Danish literature. Introduced early to music, though with limited training, he entered a military band at 14. Growing interest in music and composition led to scholarship study at the Copenhagen Conservatory (1884-1886).

Nielsen won his first public success with *Little Suite for Strings,* Opus 1 (1888), and the following year he acquired a steady job as a second violinist of the Royal Orchestra. In Paris he met and married the sculptor Anne Marie Brodersen. Their marriage inspired his First Symphony (premiered 1894) and his choral work on the varieties of love, the *Hymnus amoris* (1896). The next decade witnessed the appearance of two operas, the majestically tragic *Saul and David* (produced 1902) and the deliciously comic *Masquerade* (produced 1906) after Holberg's play, and two of his most appealing orchestral works, the Second Symphony (*The Four Temperaments*, 1901) and the concert overture *Helios* (1903), the latter inspired by the Athenian sun during a visit to Greece.

In 1908 Nielsen became the conductor of the Royal Theater. Though he met with some criticism and public resistance for his continued departure from the traditions of romanticism in such works as his Third Symphony (*Sinfonia espansiva*, 1910-1911) and his Violin Concerto (1911), he was emerging to undeniable predominance in Danish music. He was also perfecting his techniques of what analysts have called "progressive" tonality, a pattern of composing not in but toward a basic key, which allowed new possibilities for exploring the harmonic and structural expression of conflict and resolution in musical terms. This technique he put to particularly telling use in two orchestral reflections of his reactions to World War I and its aftermath: the Fourth Symphony (*The Inextinguishable*, 1915-1916) and the Fifth Symphony (1921-1922), both affirmations in abstract musical terms of positive human values against the forces of negativism and brutality.

The bold *Chaconne*, the *Theme with Variations*, and the *Luciferic Suite* (1919) are among Nielsen's finest original and unconventional contributions to the literature for solo piano. He wrote the richly inventive Wood-wind Quintet

(1922) for five wind-playing friends, for whom he also planned to compose individual solo concertos. However, he completed only two: one for the flute (1926) and the other for the clarinet (1929).

Though Nielsen's prestige mounted at home and brought him at the end of his life the conservatory's directorship, the international fame he desired still eluded him. The first signs of the heart trouble that would kill him seem to have added to the unusual mood that produced his Sixth Symphony (*Sinfonia semplice*, 1924-1925), which enigmatically combines tender poetry with grimly sardonic whimsy. His exploration of new possibilities continued, as exemplified in his austere, Palestrina-like *Three Motets* (1929) and monumental organ work *Commotio* (1931).

Notwithstanding the wide-ranging development of his style, from the romanticism of his youth to the "modernism" of his later years, Nielsen's enduring directness of personality and his patriotism found regular expression in his output of Danish song. His tuneful, folksy choral work *Springtime on Fünen* (1922) is a loving tribute to his home island; and his lifelong production of simple, melodious songs contributed many a popular classic to the Danish heritage.

Further Reading

Nielsen's set of short essays, *Living Music* (1925), and his memoir, *My Childhood* (1927), are available in English translations by Reginald Spink (both 1953). The volume of penetrating analysis by Robert Simpson, *Carl Nielsen: Symphonist, 1865-1931* (1952), includes a biographical essay by Torben Meyer. Johannes Fabricius, *Carl Nielsen: A Pictorial Biography*, in Danish and English (1965), is a vivid evocation of the man. Jürgen Balzer, ed., *Carl Nielsen, 1865-1965: Centenary Essays* (1965), is comprehensive in scope. □

Oscar Niemeyer Soares Filho

The Brazilian architect Oscar Niemeyer Soares Filho (born 1907) was the leading exponent of the International Style in Latin America. He is especially identified with the public buildings of Brasilia, Brazil's new capital.

Oscar Niemeyer Soares Filho was born on Dec. 15, 1907, in Rio de Janeiro, the son of a well-to-do family. He attended the National School of Fine Arts (1930-1934), and for many years he regarded his work more as a sport than a profession. Both his brilliance and his much decried haste can be attributed to this attitude, although after the mid-1950s he began to take himself and his work more seriously.

In 1936 Niemeyer began work with a team of young Brazilians on a project directed by Le Corbusier, the Swiss architect, to design a building to house the Ministry of Education (executed 1937-1942). They experimented with several bold ideas, erecting part of the structure on pillars that straddle a gardened walkway, covering it in decorative tile, and facing one entire wall of the skyscraper with independently movable concrete shades or blinds (*brise-soleils*). From Le Corbusier, Niemeyer and his colleagues also learned the flexibility of reinforced concrete, a quality that made a virtue out of Brazil's steel-short economy.

Before this project was completed, Niemeyer was named chief designer for a group of buildings at Pampulha, a residential suburb near Belo Horizonte. He designed a casino, restaurant, yacht club, and, most important, the church of S. Francisco (executed 1942-1943). The church is a series of concrete parabolic curves, and two of the walls are downward extensions of the roof. He also designed the Brazilian Pavilion at the New York World's Fair of 1939 and participated in the planning of the United Nations headquarters in New York, beginning in 1947.

Although a prolific designer of private homes, business offices, and recreational facilities, Niemeyer is best known for the public buildings in Brasilia that he designed after 1956. There he found room in which to exercise his powerful imagination, keen sense of proportion, and plastic sensibility. The Palácio da Alvorada (official presidential residence) has a simple grandeur. Tiny white supports suggest that the building floats lightly beyond a reflecting pool from which the eye glides smoothly toward the upward curves that frame the glass walls of the main foyer. Other major achievements in Brasilia are the Congress complex, the Palace of the Dawn, and the flowerlike Cathedral (still

being constructed in 1971), which reveal a sculptured quality only reinforced concrete could lend them. On the other hand, his massive apartment buildings are monotonous and monolithic, besides being poorly designed from both an engineering and a social standpoint.

Further Reading

Two works by Stamo Papadaki describe and evaluate the work of the Brazilian architect: *Oscar Niemeyer: Works in Progress* (1956) and *Oscar Niemeyer* (1960). □

Friedrich Nietzsche

The German philosopher Friedrich Nietzsche (1844-1900) foresaw a European collapse into nihilism. In works of powerful and beautiful prose and poetry he struggled to head off the catastrophe.

F riedrich Nietzsche was born on Oct. 15, 1844, in Röcken, a village in Saxony where his father served as a Lutheran pastor. The father's death, when the child was 4 years old, was a shattering blow to which Nietzsche often referred in his later writings. This death left Nietzsche in a household of women: his mother, grandmother, several aunts, and a sister, Elizabeth.

After attending local schools in Naumburg, in 1858 Nietzsche won a scholarship to Pforta, one of the best boarding schools in Germany. Here he received a thorough training in the classics and acquired several lifetime friends. At the end of this period of schooling, Nietzsche, who had earlier fully shared the genuine piety of his family, found that he had ceased to accept Christianity—a view that soon hardened into outright atheism. With the highest recommendations of his Pforta teachers, Nietzsche enrolled in the University of Bonn in 1864.

There he pursued classical studies with Friedrich Ritschl, and when the latter, within the year, moved to Leipzig, Nietzsche followed him. Nietzsche attempted to enter into the social life of the students, even joining a dueling fraternity, but he soon discovered that his sense of his own mission in life had isolated him from the pursuits and interests most students shared. At this time, too, Nietzsche apparently contracted syphilis in a Leipzig brothel. The incurable disease gradually undermined his strong constitution. In middle life he suffered almost constantly from migraine and gastric upsets. Loneliness and physical pain were thus the constant background of his life—though Nietzsche later came to interpret them as the necessary conditions for his work.

Nietzsche's early publications in classical philology so impressed his teacher that when a chair of philology opened up at Basel, Ritschl was able to secure it for Nietzsche, then only 24 years old and still without his degree. This the University of Leipzig gave him on the strength of his writings without requiring an examination, and Nietzsche entered upon a teaching career. Important for Nietzsche's intellec-

Oscar Niemeyer Soares Filho (holding pencil)

tual development was his discovery in these Leipzig years of the philosophy of Arthur Schopenhauer and Friedrich Lange and the music dramas of Richard Wagner.

When Nietzsche took up residence in Basel, Wagner was nearby at Tribschen, and Nietzsche was soon drawn into his circle. Wagner was then at work on the *Ring* cycle and on the great festival at Bayreuth that would be inaugurated for its premiere. The project needed publicity and financial support, and many German intellectuals were backing it. Nietzsche entered into the cause with enthusiasm and for several years was a frequent house-guest at Tribschen. Friendship with the charismatic but egocentric Wagner was, however, incompatible with independence of thought, the quality Nietzsche most valued. Before long he began to reassert his own ideas and plans. This led finally to a break, followed by some bitter polemics.

Prior to the break, Wagner had greatly influenced Nietzsche's first book, *The Birth of Tragedy* (1872), which gave an imaginative account of the forces that led to the rise of Athenian tragedy and to its subsequent decline. Nietzsche's book ends with a rousing advocacy of Wagner's music drama as a revival of Hellenic tragedy. But no sooner had it been published than Nietzsche began to perceive the difference between Wagner's musical genius and the shabby pseudophilosophy of the Wagnerian cult. From then on, though he still felt affection for Wagner's person, Nietzsche attacked ever more vigorously the "decadence" of Wagner's political and philosophical ideas. Two works of his last year of writing deal with the subject: *The Wagner Case* (1888) and *Nietzsche contra Wagner* (1888).

Nietzsche's teaching at Basel was interrupted frequently by prolonged bouts of sickness and by several months of service as a medical orderly during the Franco-Prussian War, which further aggravated his illness. In April 1879 his health had deteriorated so much that he was driven to resign. He was given a small pension, and he now began a 10-year period of wandering in search of a tolerable climate. Though racked by increasing pain from the relentless progress of his disease, Nietzsche managed to produce 10 substantial books before his final collapse. They belong to the first rank of German literature and contain a provocative set of philosophical ideas.

His Philosophy

Nietzsche believed that European man was standing at a critical turning point. The advance of scientific enlightenment, in particular the Darwinian theory, had destroyed the old religious and metaphysical underpinnings for the idea of human dignity. "God is dead," declares Nietzsche's spokesman Zarathustra, and man, no longer "the image of God," is a chance product of a nature indifferent to purpose or value. The great danger is that man will find his existence meaningless. Unless a new grounding for values is provided, Nietzsche predicted a rapid decline into nihilism and barbarity.

Nietzsche aimed in all his work to provide a new meaning for human existence in a meaningless world. In the absence of any transcendent sanction, men must create their own values. Nietzsche's writings are either analyses and criticisms of the old system of values or attempts to formulate a new system. For European man, the Judeo-Christian tradition was the source of the old values. Nietzsche attacked it head on in such works as *A Genealogy of Morals* (1887) and *The Antichrist* (1888).

In his constructive works Nietzsche sought to find in life itself a force that would serve to set human existence apart. He found it in the hypothesis of the will to power—the urge to dominate and master. All creatures desire this, but only man has achieved sufficient power to turn the force back upon himself. Self-mastery, self-overcoming: these are the qualities that give a unique value to human life. The ideal man, the "superman," will achieve a fierce joy in mastering his own existence, ordering his passions, and giving style to his character. The sublimation of passion and of life's circumstances that the ideal man achieves in his self-overcoming will release in him a flood of creative energy. The lives of such men will be the justification of reality; their preferences will constitute the standard of value.

All morality is thus the result of self-overcoming, but Nietzsche discerned a criterion by which to distinguish the morality of the superman from the "decadent" morality of Christianity. The latter undercuts earthly life in favor of an illusory afterlife, condemns self-assertion as pride, and perverts bodily functions with guilt and fear. Its tendency is toward nihilism and the denial of life. The new morality, on the other hand, will affirm life, encourage self-assertion, and eliminate guilt consciousness. In *Thus Spake Zarathustra* (1883) Nietzsche formulated the ultimate test of the superman's affirmations. Confronted with the hypothesis of eternal recurrence, the notion that the world process is cyclical and eternal, the superman still affirms life. Let it be—again and again—with all its joys and sorrows.

On Jan. 3, 1889, Nietzsche collapsed on a street in Turin, Italy. When he regained consciousness, his sanity was gone. He began to send off wild letters to friends and strangers signed "Dionysus—the Crucified." He was taken to his mother's home and lived on in a twilight condition, sinking ever further from the real world until his death on Aug. 25, 1900.

Further Reading

Nietzsche's last work, *Ecce Homo* (trans. 1911), is an autobiographical review of his published works; although fascinating and illuminating, it shows signs of megalomania and incipient madness. The best biography of Nietzsche is R. J. Hollingdale, *Nietzsche: The Man and His Philosophy* (1965). Of the numerous recent critical works on Nietzsche, the best is Walter Kaufmann's provocative *Nietzsche: Philosopher, Psychologist and Antichrist* (1950; 3d rev. ed. 1968). □

Florence Nightingale

The English nurse Florence Nightingale (1820-1910) was the founder of modern nursing and made outstanding contributions to knowledge of public health.

Florence Nightingale was born in Florence, Italy, on May 12, 1820, of wealthy parents. Her father was heir to a Derbyshire estate. Her mother, from solid merchant stock, dedicated herself to the pursuit of social pleasure within the circumscribed life then proper for women of high station. Though Florence was tempted by prospects of a brilliant social life and marriage, she had a stronger strain that demanded independence, dominance in some field of activity, and obedience to God by selfless service to society.

In 1844 Nightingale decided to work in hospitals. Her family furiously resisted her plan, on the ostensible ground that nurses were not "ladies" but menial drudges, usually of questionable morals. Nevertheless, she managed to do some private nursing and then to spend a few months at Kaiserworth, a German school and hospital. In 1853 she became superintendent of the London charity-supported Institution for Sick Gentlewomen in Distressed Circumstances. This opportunity allowed her to achieve effective independence from her family and also to try out novel techniques of institutional organization and management, conducted in a scientific, nonsectarian spirit.

In October 1854 Nightingale organized a party of 38 nurses, mostly from various religious orders, for service in the Crimean War. They arrived at Constantinople in November. Conditions at the British base hospital at Scutari were appalling and grew steadily worse as the flow of sick and wounded soldiers from the Crimea rapidly increased. The medical services of the British army were both insuffi-

cient and inefficient: a supply system of infinite and archaic complexity actually cut off deliveries to the patients; the Barrack Hospital, where Nightingale and her nurses were quartered, sat over a massive cesspool which poisoned the water and even the fabric of the building itself. However, the attitude still prevailed that the common soldier was an uncivilized, drunken brute on whom all comforts and refinements would be wasted.

Nightingale saw that her first task was to convert the military doctors to accept her and her nurses. Her discretion and diplomacy, combined with the influx of new sick and wounded, soon brought this about. She also had a large fund of private money, much of it raised by the *London Times,* with which she could cut through the clogged supply system. By the end of 1854 some order and cleanliness had been created, not only through her efforts but also through the revelations and improvements made by a governmental sanitary commission. The death rate among patients fell by two-thirds. But with improvement came new problems, with the defensiveness and hostility of the officials responsible for conditions now exposed and with the sectarian squabbling among the nurses, which Nightingale called the "Protestant Howl" and the "Roman Catholic Storm."

Florence Nightingale left Scutari in the summer of 1856, soon after the hostilities ended. By now she was idolized by the troops and the public as the "Lady with the Lamp" and the "Nightingale in the East." But this popular image is essentially false. Although she did active nursing in the wards, her real work lay outside the expression of tenderness and compassion. It began with her deliberate refusal to respond to public adulation and with her use of her influence in high places, even to the Queen and Prince Albert, to fight for effective reform of the entire system of military hospitals and medical care. Nightingale planned tactics from behind the scenes. In *Notes on Matters Affecting the Health, Efficiency and Hospital Administration of the British Army* (1857) she used the experiences of the war as a body of data to prove the necessity of a new system. Within 5 years this effort led to the reconstruction of the administrative structure of the War Office.

Nightingale's *Notes on Hospitals* (1859) detailed the proper arrangements for civilian institutions. In the next year she presided over the founding of the Nightingale School for the training of nurses at St. Thomas's Hospital in London. After 1858 she was recognized as the leading expert on military and civilian sanitation in India, in which capacity she advocated irrigation as the solution to the problem of famine.

Nightingale's personality is well documented. Her whole life she rebelled against the idle, sheltered existence of her family. She achieved a dominant position in a masculine world, driving and directing her male allies with the same ruthless force she applied to herself. She frequently complained of women's selfishness, and she ironically had no sympathy with the growing feminist movement. But she also developed a conception of spiritual motherhood and saw herself as the mother of the men of the British army—"my children"—whom she had saved.

Florence Nightingale never really recovered from the physical strain of the Crimea. After 1861 she was housebound and bedridden. She died on Aug. 13, 1910.

Further Reading

There are two substantial standard biographies of Miss Nightingale: Sir Edward Cook, *The Life of Florence Nightingale* (2 vols., 1913), and Cecil Woodham-Smith, *Florence Nightingale* (1951), a most effective and satisfying treatment. Other biographies are Irene Cooper Willis, *Florence Nightingale: A Biography* (1930), and Margaret Goldsmith, *Florence Nightingale, The Woman and the Legend* (1937). Florence Nightingale is the subject of a famous chapter in Lytton Strachey, *Eminent Victorians* (1918); though unduly harsh, it rests on solid insight and has shaped the understanding of her personality. □

Vaslav Nijinsky

The ballet dancer Vaslav Nijinsky (1890-1953) electrified his audiences with a virtuosity directly related to the characterizations he forged by the genius of his imagination. Although his dancing and choreographic career was short, he remains a symbol of human artistic achievement.

aslav Nijinsky was born in Kiev, Ukraine, on March 12, 1890 (some sources say 1888, others 1899). The Nijinsky children accompanied their Polishborn, academy-trained mother and father, Eleonora and Thomas, on the tours that featured their parents' character dances in Russian opera houses, concert halls, summer theaters, and circuses.

Vaslav's sister, Bronislava, younger by three years, had kept notes almost from the time she could write. She worked closely with Vaslav during the years he was the dazzling star of Diaghilev's Ballets Russes and she a member of the company (she was later to choreograph numerous distinguished ballets, among them *Les Noces*—1923—and *Les Biches*—1924). A brother, Stanislas, two years older than Vaslav, succumbed to mental illness in early adolescence.

In her book, *Early Memoirs* (1981), Bronislava describes the young Vaslav as lively, mischievous, and adventurous. He would stand on the knobs of a door and swing side to side with it, and could bounce just as high and forcefully as a rubber ball, and would sneak off to a nearby gypsy camp to enjoy and imitate the action he saw there.

Introduction to the Ballet

At the age of ten Vaslav was brought to the Imperial Ballet School in St. Petersburg by his parents. He was auditioned and accepted for both academic and ballet training. He was soon recognized as "remarkable" by his ballet teacher, N. Legat, although he was considered not very bright academically, except in geometry. Diaghilev's scenic

artist, Alexandre Benois, in his *Reminiscenses of the Russian Ballet* writes of Nijinsky a few years later as being "a short, rather thick-set little fellow with the most ordinary colourless face."

In 1908 Vaslav was graduated from the Imperial School with honors and a few months later was partnering leading ballerinas on the stage of the Imperial Theatre in St. Petersburg. It was at this time that he met Sergei Diaghilev, 18 years his senior, and became his protegé and lover. In the summer of 1909 Diaghilev brought a group of Russian dancers to Paris for a brief season, with Vaslav dancing the lead roles in the Fokine ballets *Pavillon d'Armide, Les Sylphides, Prince Igor,* and *Cleopatre.* The response to the company was spectacular, the success of Nijinsky dazzling. Again on leave for a season in 1910, the troupe brought *Scheherazade* and *Carnaval* to Paris. The company with its brilliant music, decor, and dance was wildly acclaimed, and Nijinsky was adored. Back in St. Petersburg, Nijinsky was dismissed from the Imperial Theatre when he refused to wear trunks over his tights in an appearance with Tamara Karsavina in *Giselle* . Diaghilev then determined to set up a permanent company in the West.

From 1911 through 1913 the Diaghilev Ballets Russes was met with overwhelming enthusiasm throughout Europe. Nijinsky danced *Le Spectre de la Rose* and, encouraged by Diaghilev, made his first attempt at choreography with *L'apres-midi d'un Faune.* In 1913, still as lead dancer, he also choreographed *Le Sacre du Printemps* and *Jeux,* both controversial and breaking the molds of classic ballet. His dancing remained extraordinary. Marie Rambert, who worked with Nijinsky in the Jaques-Dalcroze method, made vital comment about his dancing in *Quicksilver* (1972): " . . . One is often asked whether his jump was really as high as it is always described. To that I answer: I don't know how far from the ground it was, but I know it was near the stars. Who would watch the floor when he danced? He transported you at once into higher spheres with the sheer ecstacy of his flight."

Marriage Brings Dismissal from Ballets Russes

Sergei Diaghilev had a fierce fear of the sea and when later in 1913 the company left for a tour of South America he did not accompany it. On the boat trip Nijinsky became interested in a young Hungarian heiress, Romola, who was in the corps de ballet, and when they landed in Buenos Aires they were married.

Upon receiving the news of the marriage Diaghilev cabled Vaslav Nijinsky to inform him that he was dismissed from the company. Severed from his personal and professional ties with the ballet, the importance of Nijinsky as dancer and choreographer went into decline.

While he was active as a ballet dancer he electrified his audiences with protean performances and a virtuosity that was never exhibitionistic, but always related to the characterizations he forged by the genius of his creative imagination. As choreographer, also briefly, he provided a daring and exotic breakthrough into the 20th century.

His dancing was seen by relatively few audiences during the brief nine years of his professional dance activity, and there are no moving pictures of him. But there are photographs, and they are telling. Is it the same dancer who looks so unreal in *The Spectre of the Rose,* that grovels as the straw puppet in *Petrouchka,* that portrays the patrician Albrecht of *Giselle* and the sensuous harem slave of *Scheherazade,* the earthy Greek sculpture-come-to-life in *Afternoon of a Faun?* Each has a different weight, stance, movement, style.

Edwin Denby conveyed his keen observations of accents, counterforces, and relationships of body parts and assists us in seeing the nuance of the artist's superb gift of communication in his *Notes on Nijinsky Photographs,* which first appeared in an illustrated monograph edited by Paul Magriel (1946).

Mental Illness Ends Professional Life

In the spring of 1914 Nijinsky made an unsuccessful attempt to start his own company, and signs of mental illness began to appear. From 1914 to 1916 he was interred as a civilian prisoner of war in Austro-Hungary, his wife's country. In 1916 he rejoined the Diaghilev company and went with it to the United States with only tepid success. He tried another tour soon after with his own company, choreographing and dancing the lead role of *Til Eulgenspiegel.* There was still another brief tour in South America. Then came the end of his professional life.

He and Romola went to Switzerland, and for the next decade there was constant shifting from one clinic to another in the hope of finding a cure. Attempts to bring back his memory and interest in ballet were also futile. For the more than half of his life that remained—he died at the age of 60—his mind and body were engulfed by a mental disease identified as schizophrenia. There was not a day of respite.

Romola Nijinsky's *Life of Nijinsky,* assisted by Lincoln Kirstein (1933), blames much on Diaghilev. Kirstein, who had never seen Nijinsky dance, was inspired by the photos. It was with Romola Nijinsky's help that he met George Balanchine, who then arranged to bring him to the United States. There was much scandal and controversy over the homosexual relationship with Diaghilev. Was it a Svengali situation? Was it that the artist needed the support of the sponsor? Would there have been no breakdown had there been no break with Diaghilev?

The Diary of Vaslav Nijinsky (1968), edited by Romola Nijinsky, includes drawings made during the years in mental institutions and has painful-to-read recitations of what is called "Reflections on Life, Death, and Feelings" in which Vaslav identifies himself with God and calls out for peace and love.

Vaslav Nijinsky died in 1953 and is buried in Paris. Romola died in 1978. Daughter Kyra Nijinsky, born in 1914, painted many dance portraits of Vaslav, although she never saw her father dance. Daughter Tamara, born in 1920, worked with puppets.

Further Reading

Most of what we know about Nijinsky comes from the vast literature, diverse and often controversial, that perpetuates the legend of his greatness. Some of this was written by those who knew him, much by those who never saw him dance but fell in love with the legend and were inspired to investigate and share their discoveries. *Nijinsky* by Vera Krasovskaya (1974) includes additional background information with emphasis on the Russian elements of the dancer's life and training. *Nijinsky* by Richard Buckle (1971) provides a comprehensive account of casts, dates, descriptions, and details of negotiations based on definitive research and information from those who worked closely with him. The Denby essay is reprinted in the outsize *Nijinsky Dancing,* a compilation of over 100 photographs with brilliant text and commentary by Lincoln Kirstein (1975).

Additional Sources

Buckle, Richard., *Nijinsky,* Harmondsworth etc.: Penguin, 1975.

Nijinsky, New York: Schirmer books, 1979.

Nijinsky, Romola de Pulszky., *Nijinsky and The last years of Nijinsky,* New York: Simon and Schuster, 1980.

Ostwald, Peter F., *Vaslav Nijinsky: a leap into madness,* Secaucus, NJ: Carol Pub. Group, 1996.

Parker, Derek., *Nijinsky: god of the dance,* Wellingborough, Northamptonshire, England: Equation; New York, N.Y.: Distributed by Sterling Pub. Co., 1988. □

Nikita Minov Nikon

Nikita Minov Nikon (1605-1681) was patriarch of the Russian Orthodox Church from 1652 to 1666. He enacted the reforms of Church books and practices which resulted in a split, or schism, in the Russian Orthodox Church.

Nikon was born in the village of Veldemanovo in the province of Nizhni Novgorod (now Gorki) of peasant parents. When he was 12 years old, he ran away from home to escape the ill treatment of his stepmother and entered a monastery. But his parents persuaded him to leave the monastery and to marry.

In 1624 Nikon became a priest in the village of Kolychevo but within 2 years was called to a parish in Moscow. When three of his children died, Nikon sought repentance and solitude. He renounced his wife and family and lived as a monk and hermit from 1634 to 1646. In 1646 Nikon met Czar Alexis, whom he favorably impressed. In the same year Alexis appointed him abbot of Novosparsskii Monastery in Moscow. The strong-willed Nikon exercised a powerful personal influence on the younger and softer monarch. Alexis even gave Nikon the title of Great Sovereign, and his name appeared next to that of the Czar in official documents.

Church reform was among Nikon's main concerns. On his own initiative and without consulting a Church council, he ordered the revision of certain generally accepted Church practices. A Church council in 1654 approved additional reforms in religious texts.

Vigorous opposition to the reforms arose, led by the archpriest Avvakum. The opponents, the Raskolniki, declared that the reforms were a perversion of the faith and that the corrected books were the work of the antichrist. With the enactment of the reforms, the position of Nikon began to deteriorate. His curt and arrogant manner made many enemies. Alexis himself grew tired of the overbearing ways of the patriarch and ceased to invite Nikon to the palace and avoided him at Church ceremonies.

In 1658 a message from the Czar that he was not coming to a Mass that day led to a bitter outburst from Nikon, who left Moscow for a monastery. There he waited to be asked back, but the request did not come. In 1666 Nikon was tried by a Russian Church council for repudiation of patriarchal duties and offense to the Czar. He was convicted, deprived of the patriarchate and the rank of bishop, and exiled to a remote monastery. Alexis' successor, Feodor III, recalled Nikon from exile, but the former patriarch died on his way back to Moscow on Aug. 27, 1681.

Nikon's reforms, however, survived. The Church council that convened in 1666 affirmed the changes. The opponents had to submit or defy the Church openly. Numerous priests and whole monasteries refused to accept them, and the result was a permanent cleavage among the Russian believers.

Further Reading

The best study of Nikon is William Palmer's monumental *The Patriarch and the Tsar* (6 vols., 1871-1876). A general survey of religious dissent in Russia is F.C. Conybeare, *Russian Dissenters* (1921). The position of dissenters is vividly portrayed in *The Life of the Archpriest Avvakum Written by Himself* (1924). □

Chester William Nimitz

Chester William Nimitz (1885-1966), American naval officer, commanded the Pacific Fleet during World War II and played a major role in formulating and executing the strategy which led to the defeat of Japan.

Chester Nimitz was born on Feb. 24, 1885, in Fredericksburg, Tex. He graduated from the U.S. Naval Academy in Annapolis in 1905, seventh in a class of 114. Despite being court-martialed and reprimanded for running aground his second command, the destroyer *Decatur,* he rose relatively rapidly in the Navy. During World War I he was chief of staff to the commander of the Submarine Division, Atlantic Fleet. Later he was appointed the first professor of naval science at the University of California. During the 1930s he served aboard submarines, cruisers, and battleships. In 1939 Rear Adm. Nimitz was appointed chief of the Bureau of Navigation.

The Japanese attack upon Pearl Harbor precipitated a major shake-up in the Navy's command structure. In December 1941 Nimitz was promoted to admiral and made commander in chief of the Pacific Fleet. A few months later he was also named commander in chief of Allied forces in the Pacific Ocean area. This title proved somewhat inaccurate as Gen. Douglas MacArthur exercised an independent command over southwestern Pacific operations.

While realizing that the battered American fleet was in no condition to risk a major confrontation in early 1942, Nimitz knew that some offensive action was necessary to restore the Navy's confidence. He authorized a series of fast carrier strikes upon Japanese positions, culminating with Jimmy Doolittle's raid on Tokyo. While inflicting only limited damage, these helped maintain morale.

Nimitz's skill as a strategist and his ability to delegate authority produced more concrete results later in 1942 when he directed the Navy's actions in May at the Battle of the Coral Sea, which slowed Japan's advance southward, and in June at the Battle of Midway, where Japan's attack across the central Pacific was permanently halted. The United States next moved to occupy the island of Guadalcanal. When the first months of this operation produced heavy American naval losses, pressures began to build for evacuation. Nimitz, while admitting the gravity of the situation, continued to pour all available aid into the area and in October appointed the popular and aggressive Adm. William Halsey its overall commander. The following month Halsey decisively defeated the Japanese fleet, ensuring victory on Guadalcanal.

In 1943, with new units rapidly joining the fleet, the United States began major Pacific offensives. A dual approach was approved, with a force under Nimitz attacking across the central Pacific, while MacArthur's command moved up from New Guinea. Nimitz played a major role in developing the "leapfrogging" tactic of bypassing strongly held enemy positions and then neutralizing them by aerial attack and naval blockade.

Adm. Nimitz contributed major organizational methods to the Pacific war. He devoted considerable effort to creating forward repair stations and maintenance squadrons, without which the war effort might have been seriously hampered. He also devised the separate fleet staff organizations for his single fleet of fast carriers and their supporting vessels. While one staff commanded operations at sea, the other planned the next assaults. This arrangement provided continuous pressure upon the Japanese, leading them to overestimate American naval strength, and created as well improved command procedures.

In 1944 Nimitz was made a five-star fleet admiral. This gave him rank equal to Gen. MacArthur at a time when distinctions between their areas of command were becoming increasingly vague. Despite previous differences, they worked well together during the final stages of the war. In August 1945 Japan surrendered, and the following month, on behalf of the United States, Adm. Nimitz signed its instrument of surrender.

Following the war Nimitz was appointed chief of naval operations. In this position he dealt effectively with the massive problems of demobilization and successfully defended the Navy's continued control over carrier aviation under the proposed unification of the armed services. In December 1947 he retired and moved to San Francisco. From 1949 he devoted much time to serving as a goodwill ambassador for the United Nations. He died in San Francisco on Feb. 20, 1966.

Further Reading

There is no book-length study of Nimitz's career. Many of his ideas on strategy can be gleaned from the volume which he and E. B. Porter coauthored, *Sea Power: A Naval History* (1961). Probably the best one-volume history of the U.S. Navy's role in World War II is Samuel Eliot Morison, *The Two Ocean War* (1963). The development and use of naval air power in the Pacific are well set forth in Clarke G. Reynolds, *The History and Development of the Fast Carrier Task Forces, 1943-45* (1964), and Joseph James Clark and Clark G. Reynolds, *Carrier Admiral* (1967).

Additional Sources

Brink, Randall., *Nimitz: the man and his wars,* New York: D.I. Fine Books/Dutton, 1996.

Driskill, Frank A., *Admiral of the hills: Chester W. Nimitz,* Austin, Tex.: Eakin Press, 1983.

Potter, E. B. (Elmer Belmont), *Nimitz,* Norwalk, Conn.: Easton Press, 1988. □

Anais Nin

Nin (c. 1903-1977) is best known for her erotica and for her seven volumes of diaries published from 1966 to the end of her life.

Nin's other works, which include novels and short stories, are greatly influenced by Surrealism, a movement initiated in the 1920s by artists dedicated to exploring irrationality and the unconscious, and by the formal experiments of such Modernists as D. H. Lawrence and Virginia Woolf, who employed expressionistic and stream-of-consciousness narration. Rather than relying on a chronological ordering of events as in conventional narratives, Nin wrote in a poetic style featuring repetition, omission, and pastiche as organizing principles. Critics favorably note her attention to physical details and the influence of sensory information on the moods, thoughts, and interactions of her characters. Nin's predominant subject is psychological, and her insights into the behavioral and thought patterns of women have been particularly praised as both astute and free of misanthropy.

Nin began her diary as an ongoing letter to her father, Spanish musician and composer Joaquin Nin, who abandoned his family when she was eleven years old. Nin kept a journal throughout her life, recording such experiences as friendships with famous artists and writers, her years in psychotherapy, and, eventually, her worldwide travels on speaking engagements. Because she edited and excerpted her original diaries for publication in seven volumes as *The Diary of Anais Nin,* many commentators assess them for insights they shed upon Nin's literary technique. Nin's diaries relate incidents in the present tense and feature real people who appear as carefully delineated characters in fully-realized settings. The diaries are divided according to theme and share many of the concerns expressed in Nin's fiction, including the life of the creative individual, psychoanalysis, the relation between the inner and the outer world, and the nature of sexuality. The volumes include photographs, conversations presented in dialogue form, and letters from Nin's personal correspondence, completing the impression of a thoughtfully orchestrated work of art rather than a spontaneous outpouring of emotions. Susan Stanford Friedman determined: "The *Diary* records Nin's attempt to create a whole identity in a culture that defines WOMAN in terms of her fragmented roles as mother, daughter, wife, and sister."

Nin's first published work, *The House of Incest,* is often considered a prose poem due to its intensely resonant narrative. This book achieves a dream-like quality through its emphasis on psychological states rather than on surface reality. Nin's next publication, *The Winter of Artifice,* contains three long short stories. The first, "Djuna," concerns a *menage a trois* that closely resembles the relationship Nin depicted in her diary as existing between herself, novelist Henry Miller, and Miller's second wife, June. In "Lilith," Nin portrays the disappointing reunion of a woman with her father, who abandoned her in her childhood, while "The Voice" features an unnamed psychoanalyst and his four female patients who must learn to incorporate the emotions experienced in their dreams into their conscious lives. *Under a Glass Bell,* another collection of Nin's short fiction, contains "Birth," one of her most celebrated pieces. In this story, a woman undergoes excruciating labor only to bear a stillborn child and discover that through this process she has been symbolically freed of her past. *This Hunger . . . ,* Nin's next collection of short fiction, extends her exploration of the female unconscious in psychoanalytic terms.

Cities of the Interior, which Nin described as a "continuous novel," is often considered her most ambitious and critically successful project. Between 1946 and 1961, Nin published the work in five parts; these installments were published as *Ladders to Fire, Children of the Albatross, The Four-Chambered Heart, A Spy in the House of Love,* and *Seduction of the Minotaur. Ladders to Fire* concerns Lillian, a character known for her violent temper, who is as dissatisfied with her extramarital affair as she is with her marriage. Lillian seeks the perfect lover as an antidote to the problems of her life. In *Children of the Albatross,* Djuna, a minor character in *Ladders to Fire,* is emotionally stunted due to her father's abandonment. Djuna prefers playing mother to a series of adolescent lovers rather than becoming involved in a mature relationship with a man. In *The Four-Chambered Heart,* Djuna gains a measure of self-awareness through her relationship with Rango, a Guatemalan musician and political activist. *A Spy in the House of Love,* Nin's most popular novel, features Sabina, a minor character in the earlier volumes. A woman looking for affection through sexual gratification, Sabina discovers she has never experienced love. *Seduction of the Minotaur* reintroduces Lillian, who realizes the preciousness of human life while travelling in Mexico and returns to her husband a more mature woman. *Collages* (1964), an experimental novel that relies upon pastiche unified by a single character, reworks themes from Nin's earlier novels.

Much of Nin's fame is attributable to the short erotic pieces she wrote for a patron while living in Paris during the early 1940s. Collected in *Delta of Venus* and *Little Birds,* these works have garnered much commentary regarding their status as literature. Although many feminist critics object in principle to sexually explicit literature, some have championed Nin's erotica, declaring that these stories advocate mutual respect and consent between the participants in a sexual relationship. Some critics defend Nin's graphic depiction of sexual situations as an exploration of psychological truths, while others emphasize that her artistry removes these pieces from the category of pornography.

Further Reading

Newsweek, January 24, 1977.
New York Times, January 16, 1977.
Time, January 24, 1977.
Washington Post, January 16, 1977.
Anais Nin Observed: From a Film Portrait of a Woman as Artist, Swallow Press, 1976.
Authors in the News, Gale, Volume II, 1976.
Contemporary Literary Criticism , Gale, Volume I, 1973, Volume IV, 1975, Volume VIII, 1978, Volume XI, 1979, Volume XIV, 1980.
Cutting, Rose Marie, *Anais Nin: A Reference Guide,* C. K. Hall, 1978.
Dictionary of Literary Biography , Gale, Volume II: *American Novelists since World War II,* 1978, Volume IV: *American Writers in Paris,* 1980.
Evans, Oliver, *Anais Nin,* Southern Illinois University Press, 1968.
Franklin, Benjamin V, *Anais Nin: A Bibliography,* Kent State University Press, 1973. □

Joaquín María Nin-Culmell

Joaquín María Nin-Culmell (born 1908) became an American composer, pianist, and conductor. NinCulmell combined the features of national Spanish music he learned from his father, Cuban composer and pianist Joaquín Nin, and the neo-classical elements of modernist composition that he learned from Manuel de Falla.

J oaquín Nin-Culmell's father, Joaquín Nin, was taken from Cuba to Barcelona as a child to study music. In 1902 he moved to Paris, where he studied piano with Moszkowski and composition at the Schola Cantorum. In 1905, at the age of 26, Nin became a professor of piano at

this institution, where later his son would also study. When he moved to Berlin in 1908 he retained an honorary professorship at the Schola Cantorum.

Joaquín Nin-Culmell was born in Berlin in 1908. His father moved the family to Cuba in 1910 and there created a concert society and a music magazine. Joaquín Nin toured Europe and South America as a concert pianist and returned to Europe for a long stay in the 1930s. His son, Nin-Culmell, studied at his father's alma mater, the Schola Cantorum, and he also studied composition with Dukas at the Paris Conservatoire in 1934. From 1930 to 1934 he studied piano, as well, with Alfred Cortot and Ricardo Viñes and composition in Granada with Manuel de Falla.

Joaquín Nin left Europe when World War II began in 1939. He was a well-regarded interpreter of Bach and of early Spanish music, and he argued against performing this repertoire on the harpsichord, notably with Wanda Landowska in a public exchange of views. His compositions combined Spanish baroque and French impressionist elements. His scholarly writings were collected and published in Spain, with biographical notes by his son, Joaquín Nin-Culmell.

Joaquín Nin-Culmell, meanwhile, had emigrated to the United States in 1936. He toured regularly as a concert pianist throughout the United States, Europe, and Cuba. He was named professor of music and chairman of the department of music at Williams College in Williamstown, Massachusetts, posts he held until 1950 when he took a position at the University of California at Berkeley. He was chairman of the department of music there from 1950 to 1954, and then professor of music. He conducted the university orchestra from 1950 to 1956. Nin-Culmell was named emeritus professor at Berkeley in 1974.

Joaquín Nin-Culmell's compositions use the Spanish melodies and rhythms of his compositional mentors, his father Joaquín Nin and his teacher Manuel de Falla. However, he combined these elements with modernist harmonies and the abrupt rhythms of neo-classical modernism, just as Igor Stravinsky employed elements of Russian folk music in his modernist style.

Nin-Culmell was soloist in his own *Piano Concerto* in 1946 at a concert with the Rochester Philharmonic in Williamstown. He also composed a *Piano Quintet,* an opera— *La Celestina* — a *Cello Concerto,* four books of *Tonadas* for piano, *Jorge Manrique* for soprano and string quartet, and numerous cycles of songs. He composed the *Dedication Mass* for mixed chorus and organ for the dedication of the Cathedral of St. Mary in San Francisco. A newly composed opera was scheduled to debut in Barcelona in 1999.

Further Reading

Articles on Joaquin María Nin-Culmell are in *The New Grove Dictionary of Music and Musicians* (London, 1980) and *Baker's Biographical Dictionary,* 6th edition (1978); Nin-Culmell wrote the biographical notes for his father's collected writings, *Pro arte e ideas y comentarios* (Barcelona, 1974). □

Marshall Warren Nirenberg

Marshall Warren Nirenberg (born 1927) is best known for deciphering the portion of DNA (deoxyribonucleic acid) that is responsible for the synthesis of the numerous protein molecules which form the basis of living cells. In 1968 he was awarded the Nobel Prize for physiology or medicine.

Nirenberg's research has helped to unravel the DNA genetic code, aiding, for example, in the determination of which genes code for certain hereditary traits. For his contribution to the sciences of genetics and cell biochemistry, Nirenberg was awarded the 1968 Nobel Prize in physiology or medicine with Robert W. Holley and Har Gobind Khorana.

Nirenberg was born in New York City on April 10, 1927, and moved to Florida with his parents, Harry Edward and Minerva (Bykowsky) Nirenberg, when he was ten years old. He earned his B.S. in 1948 and his M.Sc. in biology in 1952 from the University of Florida. Nirenberg's interest in science extended beyond his formal studies. For two of his undergraduate years he worked as a teaching assistant in biology, and he also spent a brief period as a research assistant in the nutrition laboratory. In 1952, Nirenberg continued his graduate studies at the University of Michigan, this time in the field of biochemistry. Obtaining his Ph.D. in 1957, he wrote his dissertation on the uptake of hexose, a sugar molecule, by ascites tumor cells.

Shortly after earning his Ph.D., Nirenberg began his investigation into the inner workings of the genetic code as an American Cancer Society (ACS) fellow at the National Institutes of Health (NIH) in Bethesda, Maryland. Nirenberg continued his research at the NIH after the ACS fellowship ended in 1959, under another fellowship from the Public Health Service (PHS). In 1960, when the PHS fellowship ended, he joined the NIH staff permanently as a research scientist in biochemistry.

After only a brief time conducting research at the NIH, Nirenberg made his mark in genetic research with the most important scientific breakthrough since James D. Watson and Francis Crick discovered the structure of DNA in 1953. Specifically, he discovered the process for unraveling the code of DNA. This process allows scientists to determine the genetic basis of particular hereditary traits. In August of 1961, Nirenberg announced his discovery during a routine presentation of a research paper at a meeting of the International Congress of Biochemistry in Moscow.

Nirenberg's research involved the genetic code sequences for amino acids. Amino acids are the building blocks of protein. They link together to form the numerous protein molecules present in the human body. Nirenberg discovered how to determine which sequences patterns code for which amino acids (there are about 20 known amino acids).

Nirenberg's discovery has led to a better understanding of genetically determined diseases and, more controver-

sially, to further research into the controlling of hereditary traits, or genetic engineering. For his research, Nirenberg was awarded the 1968 Nobel Prize for physiology or medicine. He shared the honor with scientists Har Gobind Khorana and Robert W. Holley. After receiving the Nobel Prize, Nirenberg switched his research focus to other areas of biochemistry, including cellular control mechanisms and the cell differentiation process.

Since first being hired by the NIH in 1960, Nirenberg has served in different capacities. From 1962 until 1966 he was Head of the Section for Biochemical Genetics, National Heart Institute. Since 1966 he has been serving as the Chief of the Laboratory of Biochemical Genetics, National Heart, Lung and Blood Institute. Other honors bestowed upon Nirenberg, in addition to the Nobel Prize, include honorary membership in the Harvey Society, the Molecular Biology Award from the National Academy of Sciences (1962), National Medal of Science presented by President Lyndon B. Johnson (1965), and the Louisa Gross Horwitz Prize for Biochemistry (1968). Nirenberg also received numerous honorary degrees from distinguished universities, including the University of Michigan (1965), University of Chicago (1965), Yale University (1965), University of Windsor (1966), George Washington University (1972), and the Weizmann Institute in Israel (1978). Nirenberg is a member of several professional societies, including the National Academy of Sciences, the Pontifical Academy of Sciences, the American Chemical Society, the Biophysical Society, and the Society for Developmental Biology.

Nirenberg married biochemist Perola Zaltzman in 1961. While described as being a reserved man who engages in little else besides scientific research, Nirenberg has been a strong advocate of government support for scientific research, believing this to be an important factor for the advancement of science.

Further Reading

Wasson, Tyler, editor, *Nobel Prize Winners,* H. W. Wilson, 1987, pp. 767–768.
New York Times, October 12, 1982, p. C3. □

Ni Tsan

The Chinese painter Ni Tsan (1301-1374) was one of the "Four Great Masters" of the Yüan dynasty. He was famous for his poetry and calligraphy and, above all, for his cool, serene landscapes painted in monochrome ink.

Ni Tsan was born in Wu-hsi in Kiangsu Province, the birthplace of many scholarly painters. His family were wealthy merchants, and Ni Tsan never embarked on an official career. Instead, he devoted himself to literature and scholarship, poetry and art. He was an ardent collector and connoisseur, with a passion for cleanliness.

In the middle of the 14th century the alien Yüan (Mongol) government was beginning to lose control over China and resorting to crippling taxation, which fell most heavily on the landed gentry of the Chekiang-Kiangsu region. About 1350, to escape the rapacious tax collectors and the deepening social chaos, Ni Tsan gave his fortune away to his relatives and left home. For the next 20 years he drifted in a houseboat among the lakes, rivers, and canals of Kiangsu, lodging sometimes in temples, while he continued to enjoy the pleasures of painting and connoisseurship. He led a simple life and dressed as a Taoist monk, refusing to sell his paintings but giving them away to anyone who appreciated them.

While Ni Tsan found some inspiration in the masters of the 10th century, such as Li Ch'eng and Tung Yüan, he so transformed their styles as to create landscapes unique in the history of Chinese painting. Again and again he used variations of the same simple composition, in which a group of trees and perhaps an empty hut stand on a rocky spur in the foreground, separated from distant hills by a clear expanse of water. Ni Tsan often wrote a poem or long inscription on the upper part of the picture, thus forming a subtle union of painting and calligraphy. He painted in monochrome ink on paper, very seldom adding any color, and using ink, as his contemporaries said, as sparingly as if it were gold. His brush-work is dry, sensitive, and bland. With these simple means he painted landscapes which captured the inner spirit rather than the outward appearance of nature.

Among Ni Tsan's finest landscapes are *Jung-hsi Studio* and *Mountain Scenery with River Lodge* (both 1372). He also painted rocks and bamboo with the same delicate touch. A typical example is *Bamboo, Rock and Tall Tree* (ca. 1348), painted shortly before Ni Tsan left his home in Wu-hsi.

Many later exponents of the literati painting (*wen-jen hua*) imitated Ni Tsan's deceptively simple composition and technique, but none ever captured the feeling of his landscapes, for, as the 17th-century artist Tao-chi put it, "Their air of supreme refinement and purity is so cold that it overawes men."

With the founding of the Ming dynasty in 1368, China was at last at peace, and Ni Tsan returned to his old home, where he died 6 years later.

Further Reading

There is no full-length study of Ni Tsan in any Western language, but some information about his life and work is found in Osvald Sirén, *Chinese Painting* (7 vols., 1956-1958). A more general treatment of the art of the Yüan period, which gives a good picture of the conditions under which painters such as Ni Tsan lived and worked, is Sherman E. Lee and Wai-kam Ho, *Chinese Art under the Mongols: The Yüan Dynasty, 1279-1368* (1968). □

Nikkyo Niwano

Nikkyo Niwano (born 1906) was president of Rissho Kosei-kai and one of the most important religious leaders of modern Japan.

President Nikkyo Niwano of Rissho Kosei-kai, a Japanese lay Buddhist organization, received two international awards in the late 1970s: the Albert Schweitzer (United States) and the Templeton (England). Both were given in recognition of his leadership in religion, marking him as one of the most important religious leaders in Asia and the world. This was quite an accomplishment for a man who only had a primary school education (but became a lifetime student) and whose sect of Japanese Buddhism was related to Nichiren Buddhism (often noted as the most nationalistic and narrow of Buddhist groups). In addition, his involvement in international concerns did not begin until the late 1960s. His life was a testament to overcoming obstacles to achieve greatness.

Born in the snow country of northern Japan on November 15, 1906, as Shikazo Niwano, he was the son of Jukichi Niwano, a farmer. He learned the special kind of cooperation that was needed to survive the most severe winter climate in Japan. At the age of 17 he left home and went to Tokyo, only to arrive there five days before the great earthquake of 1923. He returned home but again went to Tokyo the following year, working first as a gardener and then in a charcoal shop. In 1926 he entered the Japanese navy and served for three years. Upon discharge he returned to the charcoal shop, got married, and began a family. His interest in the owner's practice of fortunetelling led him into esoteric and traditional folk religion. Serious illness of his first children, both daughters, led him to explore folk spirituality — paranormal phenomena such as faith healing, prophecy, and knowledge of personality traits from physical correspondents such as name interpretation. He joined one of the so-called new religions named Reiyukai.

Young Niwano began to neglect both his family and his newly started pickle business for his religious work, so he opened a milk shop in order to have enough time to continue his religious practices. One of his customers was Masa Naganuma, who was ill, and he interested her in faith healing. Internal dissension within Reiyu-kai led Niwano and some 30 others to start their own religious group. On March 5, 1938, Niwano and Masa Naganuma founded *Rissho* (establishing the teaching of the law in the world) *Ko* (mutual exchange of thought) *Sei* (perfection of the personality and the attainment of Buddhahood) *Kai* (association, society). Niwano changed his first name to Nikkyo and Masa Naganuma to Myoko (she became known as Myoko Sensei, teacher Myoko). Rissho Kosei-kai was classified by the government as a new religion as it brought together folk and Nichiren Buddhist elements. (This misnomer fails to account for religious strains going back centuries in Japan — hardly a new religion. Some scholars have finally noticed this discrepancy.) Because the militarists believed that Nichiren Buddhism was nationalistic, little pressure was brought to bear on Rissho Kosei-kai during its first years. In August of 1941, however, President Niwano and Myoko Sensei were arrested on charges brought by their former religious group — that they were confusing the local people. Because of the arrests, many ceased their membership. This became known as the "first flight of steps."

In 1944 Niwano faced a crisis of a personal nature. Myoko Sensei had a revelation for Niwano to live similarly to a Buddhist monk, so he sent his family to the country. She also revealed to him that he was to do no other reading than the Lotus Sutra. He used the next ten years for study and discipline. But in 1954 he brought his family back, choosing a Buddhism of laity rather than that of the clergy. His harder decision was between revelations from mediumship and knowledge from the Lotus Sutra. He finally opted for the latter when there was any discrepancy between the two. Within three years Myoko Sensei died and the use of mediums ended.

In 1956 the "second flight of steps" occurred when more members left after a newspaper attacked the organization, its business practices, and its leadership for a three month period. Even though the criticisms were refuted, nearly 20 percent of the membership had walked away.

With Myoko Naganuma's death in 1957 President Niwano made Shakyamuni Buddha and the Lotus Sutra the central focus of Rissho Kosei-kai. The postwar years saw phenomenal growth. A practice of meeting together in small groups presided over by a leader conversant in the teachings of the Lotus Sutra may have contributed to this growth more than any other factor. The practice was called Hoza.

Receiving advice to avoid controversies with Sokagakkai over what was the true Buddhism, Niwano began to

involve Rissho Kosei-kai in sharing Buddhism's compassion for suffering and concern for peace beyond his own country. This came at a time when Japanese were not too welcome in most parts of the world. Through cooperation with the International Association for Religious Freedom (IARF) and with the World Conference on Religion and Peace, Niwano began ten years of work and service that would culminate in the two international awards mentioned earlier. Then in 1981 he was elected president of IARF and brought the first IARF Congress to Asian soil.

Niwano built in Rissho Kosei-kai the most international religious organization in Asia as evidenced by the relief campaigns for Southeast Asia and Africa in the 1980s. His Niwano Peace Foundation gave annual recognition to persons whose activities advanced religion and peace. Another measurement of his influence was his work with the United Nations (UN), the Vatican, and the World Council of Churches; there was growing expertise within Rissho Kosei-kai (RKK) in international diplomacy. A stream of dignitaries passed through RKK's headquarters to talk with Niwano or the RKK staff. Niwano's efforts for peace and worldwide cooperation made him one of the most active religious leaders in the world.

Further Reading

Niwano's autobiography has been translated into English as *Lifetime Beginner* (1978); other writings by him include *The Richer Life* (1975), *Buddhism for Today* (1976), and *A Buddhist Approach to Peace* (1977); *Liberal Religious Reformation in Japan* (1984) by George M. Williams. □

Richard Milhous Nixon

Although Richard Milhous Nixon (1913-1994) successfully served as a member of the House of Representatives and of the Senate and was vice president under Dwight Eisenhower, the thirty-seventh president of the United States will probably best be remembered as being the first president who resigned from office.

Richard Nixon was born on his father's lemon farm in Yorba Linda, California, on January 9, 1913. Of the four other sons in the family, two died in childhood. Nixon's ancestors had emigrated from Ireland in the 18th century and settled principally in Pennsylvania and Indiana. His mother's family were Quakers; his Methodist father adopted the Quaker religion after his marriage. As a youth, Nixon regularly attended Quaker services in Whittier, California, where the family moved in 1922 after the farm failed. Nixon's father ran a grocery store in Whittier. Some biographers have noted that Nixon's father was known to kick his sons and that his mother was manipulative. Nixon had a troubled childhood and adopted elements of both his parents' personalities. Some historians have believed that as a result of his childhood, Nixon had a drive to succeed and felt he had to pretend to be "good" while using any tactics necessary to acheive his goals.

At Whittier College, a Quaker institution, Nixon excelled as a student and debater. He was president of his freshman class and, as a senior, president of the student body. Less successful on the football team, he persevered and played doggedly in occasional games. Graduating second in his class in 1934, he won a scholarship to Duke University Law School on the recommendation of Whittier's president, who wrote, "I believe Nixon will become one of America's important, if not great leaders." Nixon maintained his scholarship throughout law school. Though he was a member of the national scholastic law fraternity, he failed to land a job in one of the big New York law firms. This failure, along with the views of his father, left him with a stong dislike of the "eastern establishment."

In Whittier, Nixon joined the law firm of Kroop and Bewley, which within a year became Kroop, Bewley, and Nixon. Active in a variety of business and civic ventures, at the age of 26 he was elected a member of the Whittier College Board of Trustees. Soon after returning to Whittier, Nixon met Thelma Catherine Patricia (Pat) Ryan, a high school teacher. The two were married in 1940; they had two daughters, Patricia and Julie.

Early Public Service

Shortly before the United States entered World War II, Nixon began working for the Federal government in the Office of Emergency Management, the forerunner of the

Office of Price Administration (OPA). His legal work there as a price regulator strongly influenced his political philosophy. "I came out of college more liberal than I am today, more liberal in the sense that I thought it was possible for government to do more than I later found it was practical to do," Nixon later told Earl Mazo, his biographer. "I also saw the mediocrity of so many civil servants. And for the first time when I was in OPA I also saw that there were people in government who were not satisfied merely with interpreting regulations, enforcing the law that Congress passed, but who actually had a passion to *get* business and used their government jobs to that end. These were of course some of the remnants of the old, violent New Deal crowd. They set me to thinking a lot at that point."

Nixon entered the Navy as a lieutenant junior-grade in August 1942. He was sent to a naval air base in Iowa. After 6 months there (which he valued because it helped him know the Midwest, the base of his later political support), he was sent to the Pacific as an operations officer with the South Pacific Combat Air Transport Command. Fourteen months later he returned to the United States to work as a lawyer in uniform. He was a lieutenant commander in Baltimore when, in September 1945, a group of Whittier Republicans asked him to run for Congress. He jumped at the opportunity, was mustered out of the Navy in January 1946, and began his victorious campaign.

Nixon's friends described him as a mild and tolerant human being, basically shy and much influenced by his Quaker upbringing. Yet in all his early campaigns he conducted what he himself has described as "a fighting, rocking, socking campaign." He early infuriated the opposition. Though he called himself a liberal Republican and a progressive Republican, he had strong right-wing support. In his congressional campaign he had attacked his liberal New Deal Democrat and onetime Socialist opponent as a tool of the Congress of Industrial Organizations (CIO) and an enemy of free enterprise.

Congressional Activities and National Fame

As congressman, Nixon was assigned to the House Labor Committee and to the Select Committee on Foreign Aid. In 1947 he and other committee members toured Europe. "We cannot afford to follow a policy of isolation and let the people of Europe down at this point, and therefore allow Russia full sway in Europe," he said shortly after his return. "The sure way to war is for the United States to turn isolationist." Supporting the Marshall Plan, Nixon established himself as an internationalist in foreign policy.

As a member of the House Un-American Activities Committee (HUAC), Nixon became a leading anti-Communist crusader. He collaborated on the bill requiring Communist-front organizations to register with the attorney general. It was on HUAC that he first attracted national attention when he led the suit that resulted in the conviction of Alger Hiss, a former State Department official charged with Communist connections; Hiss was finally convicted for perjury. As Nixon wrote in *Six Crises* (1962), "The Hiss case brought me national fame. But it also left a residue of hatred and hostility toward me—not only among Communists but also among substantial segments of the press and the intellectual community—a hostility which remains even today, ten years after Hiss's conviction was upheld by the United States Supreme Court." Nixon said he also incurred opposition from many apostles of anticommunism because "I would not go along with their extremes." These anti-Communists assailed him for supporting international programs like foreign aid, reciprocal trade, and collective security pacts.

Nixon again aroused the enmity of liberals and intellectuals in his 1950 victorious senatorial campaign. He charged his Democratic opponent with displaying a "soft attitude toward communism" and said that she was part of a small clique that voted "time after time against measures that are for the security of this country."

It was thus as a fiery crusader against communism and a staunch Republican partisan that Nixon was known to the country when Gen. Dwight Eisenhower chose him as his running mate in the presidential election of 1952. Nixon's personality and character became permanent issues in all his political campaigns. He seemed to overuse political hyperbole and oversimplify complex issues. Some critics believed his fascination with political techniques showed lack of principle regarding substantive issues.

Nixon said that he was guided by his Quaker heritage: "The three passions of Quakers are peace, civil rights, and tolerance. That's why, as a Quaker, I can't be an extremist, a racist, or an uncompromising hawk. While all this may seem to be the opposite of what I've stood for, I'm actually consistent." An objective observer who got to know the private Nixon said that he had an able if not overly subtle mind. He listened well, asked probing questions, and nearly always impressed persons with whom he spoke privately.

Two months after becoming Republican vice-presidential candidate, Nixon was charged with being the beneficiary of a fund, totaling $18,235, collected from private citizens. Nixon said the sensational controversy resulted in "the most scarring personal crisis of my life." Nixon fought back. In a television speech that accounted for the money, he convinced his foes that he was artful and tricky, but he rallied Republicans to his banner. While his defense saved his candidacy and made him even better known, this controversy also left a bitter residue.

The Vice Presidency

As vice president, Nixon continued to please his supporters and anger his critics. He was the chief political spokesman in Eisenhower's administration, traveled widely in support of Republican candidates, and was influential in the workings of the administration.

Eisenhower believed that a vice president should have an active role and should be fully informed about all foreign and domestic policies. Chief among Nixon's assignments was foreign travel. In office less than a year, Nixon made an extended trip through Asia, visiting, among other places, Hanoi, North Vietnam, then under French control. He made many useful friends on these trips and impressed critics at home with his seriousness of purpose and knowledge of

foreign affairs. On a trip to Latin America in 1958, he was assailed by mobs but handled himself coolly. In 1959 he visited the Soviet Union and Poland. While in Moscow, his meeting with Soviet premier Nikita Khrushchev prepared the way for Khrushchev's later visit to the United States to confer with Eisenhower.

Running for President

In 1960 Nixon won the Republican presidential nomination and chose Henry Cabot Lodge, ambassador to the United Nations, as his running mate. The campaign against the Democratic team of senators John F. Kennedy and Lyndon Johnson was close from the beginning, although Nixon initially ran ahead in the polls. In the first of four televised debates with Kennedy, Nixon, concerned with projecting an image of reasonableness and nonpartisanship, did not sharply challenge his opponent. He also looked pale and unwell, possibly because of poor lighting. He lost the election by some 100,000 votes out of the 68 million cast.

Nixon returned to Los Angeles to practice law and to write *Six Crises*. In 1962, losing the race for governor of California, he blamed his defeat on the press. "You won't have Nixon to kick around any more," he told newsmen, "because, gentlemen, this is my last press conference."

A few months later, Nixon joined the New York law firm of Mudge, Stern, Baldwin & Todd, which later became Nixon, Mudge, Rose, Guthrie, Alexander & Mitchell. However, in 1964, after the Republican defeat by President Lyndon Johnson, it became clear that Nixon again considered himself a serious presidential contender. In 1968, winning his party's presidential nomination, he picked Governor Spiro T. Agnew of Maryland as his running mate.

Nixon and Agnew ran against the Democratic team of Hubert Humphrey and Edmund Muskie. Third party candidate George Wallace of Alabama, a threat to both tickets, hurt Humphrey more. In the end, though the Republicans had the presidential victory, the Democrats retained control of Congress.

The Presidency

Nixon took the oath of office on Jan. 20, 1969. In his inaugural address he appealed for reconciliation among the elements of American society divided over the issues of the Vietnam War and domestic racial discord. He promised to bring the nation together again.

Nixon's first foreign objective—to negotiate an end of the Vietnam War—was unsuccessful. Despite repeated attempts, negotiations with North Vietnam at the Paris peace talks were unproductive. Meanwhile, in June he began replacing American troops by South Vietnamese troops. After a conference with South Vietnam's president Nguyen Van Thieu, Nixon ordered 25,000 American combat troops brought home. By the end of 1969, having ordered 110,000 troops home, he expressed hope, not realized, that all American combat troops would be out of Vietnam by the end of 1970. Not until the end of 1972, when most American ground troops had been withdrawn from Vietnam, did negotiations suggest that peace might be at hand.

In his second month in office, the President embarked on a tour of Western Europe. In the summer he visited Asia, including a stop in Saigon. His official visit to Romania made him the first American president to visit a Communist country. While on the Asian tour, the President enunciated what became known as the "Nixon Doctrine." The United States will honor its treaty commitments, he said, but it will not bear the brunt of the fighting in another country. He called for cooperative endeavors and promised American material aid but said that Asian countries must defend their freedoms with their own troops. In his first year the President signed the nuclear nonproliferation treaty, negotiated during the previous administration. In addition, negotiations were begun with the Soviet Union toward placing limits on the production of nuclear armaments.

On the domestic front, Nixon waged a major battle against inflation. With Congress pressing for more government spending, the administration fought to curb expenditures and balance the budget. The economy continued to decline while the administration waged its battle against inflation. Finally, to reverse a dangerous trend, the President, in August 1971, completely reversed himself, instituted wage and price controls, imposed a tax on imports, and asked for tax cuts. Early in 1972, after he agreed to devaluation of the dollar, the economy began to improve.

In 1971 Nixon made the dramatic announcements that he would visit Peking and Moscow in the first half of 1972. He also announced progress in the negotiations with the Soviet Union on an arms limitation treaty. The visit to Peking took place in February and he was invited to meet Chairman Mao Zedong, a mark of high respect. In May, he visited Moscow and signed the agreement limiting the nuclear arsenals of the United States and the Soviet Union.

In the presidential election of 1972 Nixon and Agnew ran against Democrats George McGovern and Sargent Shriver. The election was a landslide for Nixon, as the polls had predicted it would be: he won 61 percent of the popular vote and received 521 electoral votes, losing only Massachusetts and the District of Columbia. However, as in the election of 1968, the Democrats retained control of Congress.

The Fall from Grace

During his last election campaign, what first appeared as a minor burglary was to become the beginning of the end of Nixon's political career. A break-in at Democratic national headquarters in Washington, D.C.'s Watergate apartment complex was linked to Republicans.

During the trial of six men charged in the crime, the existence of the cover-up began to emerge, taking government officials down like dominos in its path. Nixon elicited the resignation of two top aides in April, 1973 in an effort to stem the tide. But in October, as the Watergate investigation continued, he lost his vice president, Spiro T. Agnew, who resigned before pleading "nolo contendere" (no contest) in federal charges of income tax evasion related to accusations of accepting bribes.

Nixon's efforts to avoid the taint of those scandals were fruitless when subpoenaed tapes he was ordered to give up

by the U.S. Supreme Court showed he obstructed justice in stopping an FBI probe of the Watergate burglary. On August 9, 1974, in national disgrace, he became the first President of the United States to resign. He boarded a plane with his wife and returned to his his California home, ending his public career. A month later, in a controversial move, President Gerald Ford issued an unconditional pardon for any offenses Nixon might have committed while president.

Private Citizen

After a period of relative anonymity and when some criticism had softened, Nixon emerged in a role of elder statesman, visiting countries in Asia, as well as returning to the Soviet Union and China. He also consulted with the Bush and Clinton Administrations, and wrote his memoirs and other books on international affairs and politics.

The Richard Nixon Library & Birthplace opened in the early 1990s in Yorba Linda, California. On January 20, 1994, in what would be his last public appearance, cermonies honoring him on the 25th anniversary of his first inauguration, were held. He also announced the creation of The Center for Peace and Freedom, a policy center at the Richard M. Nixon Library & Birthplace.

He died of a stroke on April 22, 1994. A State funeral was held five days later in Yorba Linda, California. In 1995, film director Oliver Stone released the contorversial movie "Nixon," staring Academy Award winner Anthony Hopkins in the title role.

Further Reading

The Challenges We Face (1960) is a collection of Nixon's speeches. The most important work is Nixon's *Six Crises* (1962), which records the major events of his life to the early 1960s. The most factually complete biography is Earl Mazo and Stephen Hess, *Nixon: A Political Portrait* (1968). James Keogh, *This Is Nixon* (1956), written as a campaign biography, contains valuable quotations from Nixon's speeches. A perceptive analysis of Nixon's character and politics is Gary Wills, *Nixon Agonistes: The Crisis of the Self-made Man* (1970). A good sketch of Nixon's personality is in Stephen Hess and David S. Broder, *The Republican Establishment* (1968). An excellent portrait is in Stewart Alsop, *Nixon and Rockefeller* (1960). Information on the The Richard M. Nixon Library & Birthplace and a biography of the former President can be accessed on the internet at http://www.chapman.edu/nixon/library/overview.html (August 5, 1997). A brief biography can be also accessed on the internet at the A & E Biography website at http://www.biography.com (August 5, 1997).

Other books deal with aspects of Nixon's career. Mark Harris, *Mark the Glove Boy: Or the Last Days of Richard Nixon* (1964), deals with the gubernatorial race between Pat Brown and Nixon. Nixon figures prominently in works dealing with presidential campaigns: Theodore H. White, *The Making of the President, 1960* (1961) and *The Making of the President, 1968* (1969), and Joe McGinnes, *The Selling of the President, 1968* (1969). Arthur M. Schlesinger, Jr., *History of American Presidential Elections* (4 vols., 1971), covers the 1968 election, won by Nixon. Also useful are Ralph De Toledano, *Man Alone: Richard Nixon* (1969), and John Osborne, *The Nixon Watch* (1970). □

Khaliq Ahmad Nizami

Khaliq Ahmad Nizami (born 1925), an Indian historian, religious scholar, and diplomat, was best known for his work on the history of medieval India and in particular for his studies of the Muslim community of that time.

Khaliq Ahmad Nizami was born in the town of Amroha in the United Provinces of British India on December 5, 1925. He was the son of Aziz Ahmad and Sayyidah Nizami. Khaliq Ahmad received his education in India, and though he travelled extensively and gained much recognition abroad, he also largely pursued his academic career in his native country. He attended the University of Agra, where he completed the M.A. in history in 1945. In the following year he was awarded the LL.B. degree by the same institution. Married to Raziyah Nizami, the couple had five children.

In 1947 Nizami joined the staff of the Aligarh Muslim University in Aligarh, India, in the Department of History. The Aligarh Muslim University was the premier institution of higher education for Muslims in India in both pre-partition and post-partition days. In the period between 1937 and 1947 it was the foremost center of the Muslim political agitation that eventually led to the partition of India and the creation of Pakistan. Nizami was among those Muslim intellectuals who opted for Indian nationalism and the cause of the Indian National Congress. In consequence, he remained in India with his family when the country was divided in 1947.

Nizami's rise in position at Aligarh was both steady and swift. In 1953 he became reader in history, and in 1963 he was promoted to the rank of professor. The latter appointment was accompanied by his being made head of the university's Centre of Advanced Study in History, which has numbered many of the best and most famous twentieth-century historians of India among its personnel. In 1968 he gained the respected title of senior professor of the university. He also played an important part in the administration of the Aligarh Muslim University. He acted as pro-vice-chancellor in 1972-1973 and in 1974 became vice-chancellor, the highest executive officer of the institution. In 1978 he was made the Indian ambassador to Syria, but at the same time between 1978 and 1980 he served as dean of the social sciences at the university. In 1980 he became head of the Department of History at Aligarh.

In addition to his formal duties in the university, Nizami was active in a number of extra-curricular and professional organizations, especially those designed to promote the study of Indian history. He served as secretary of the Islamic Studies Section of the International Congress of Orientalists held in New Delhi in 1963; he was president of the Medieval Indian History Section of the Indian History Congress convened at Allahabad in 1965; similarly, he served as president of the History Section of the Punjab History Congress in 1969. He was a member of the U.P.

Regional Records Survey in Allahabad. He participated in many other congresses and conferences, both in India and elsewhere.

Nizami's principal scholarly concern was the history of medieval Muslim India, and the majority of his publications were in that field. For instance, he wrote extensively on the Sultanate of Delhi, giving particular attention to the religious dimensions of the history. In addition to a general book on the sultans of Delhi (originally in Urdu), he wrote studies on prominent sufis such as Shaykh Farid al-Din Ganj-i Shakir and on the saints of the Chishti order.

One of the more consequential of his efforts was the publication of the political correspondence of the 18th-century Muslim reformer and philosopher Shah Waliullah of Delhi; this correspondence provided the basis for an enlarged understanding of Waliullah's contribution to Indian Muslim history. There is also a group of works devoted to Sayyid Ahmad Khan, the founder of the Aligarh Muslim University and the most important intellectual and political leader of the Indian Muslims in the latter part of the 19th century. In addition to the studies of the life and times of Sayyid Ahmad and the history of the Aligarh movement, these studies include an illustrated album and a collection of poems about Sayyid Ahmad and some of his associates.

Perhaps the most enduringly important of his contributions is his work, together with Muhammad Habib, another Aligarh historian, on *The Comprehensive History of India* and his *Supplement to Elliot and Dowson's History of India* which has been a standard source (in translation) of original source materials for Indian history. In all, by 1984 Nizami had published 20 books dealing with various aspects of medieval Indian history and culture. His articles on these subjects, spread through a variety of publications, were even more numerous.

In addition to these publishing activities relating to works from his own pen, he was general editor of the Crescent-Lotus book series. He also served as director of the Sir Syed Academy, one of whose purposes is publication in the field of its interest.

In view of these activities Nizami must be counted among the select group of the most important contemporary historians of India. His position with respect to the study of Muslim India is one of even greater prominence.

Further Reading

The Indian reference work *Who's Who;* his writings should be available in any library that collects materials concerning India and its history. □

Joshua Mqabuko Nkomo

Joshua Mqabuko Nkomo (born 1917) was a leader in the African nationalist movement in southern Rhodesia during the post-World War II period. President of the Zimbabwe African People's Union, he was active in the first independent African government in

Zimbabwe and was vice president of Zimbabwe from 1990-1996.

Son of a cattle-owning teacher and lay preacher, Nkomo was born June 19, 1917, in the Semokwe reserve of Matebeland in southern Rhodesia. He spent his formative years being educated in South Africa at Adams College in Natal and at the Jan Hofmeyer School in Johannesburg.

Nkomo returned home in 1945 and worked as a welfare officer with Rhodesian Railways while practicing as a lay preacher on most Sundays. In 1951 he completed a correspondence Bachelor of Arts degree in social science from the University of South Africa. That same year Nkomo became general secretary of the Rhodesian Railways African Employees' Association, and he soon built up one of the best organized unions in central Africa.

Trade unionism became a stepping stone for politics. Nkomo joined other young radicals who opposed white settler domination in southern Rhodesia. As chairman of the Bulawayo branch of the otherwise largely dormant African National Congress (ANC) in southern Rhodesia, Nkomo accompanied Premier Sir Godfrey Huggins (later Lord Malvern) to London for a conference about the possible federation of northern and southern Rhodesia and Nyasaland.

The failure of African protestations at the conference galvanized Nkomo's commitment to the African nationalist

cause in southern Rhodesia, and upon return home he abandoned his railway job for insurance work in order to have more time for politics. In 1953 he contested and lost a seat in the first federal election, but soon emerged as the leading African nationalist in southern Rhodesia. He gradually rebuilt the ANC around Bulawayo, and when the African National Youth League (based in Salisbury) and the Bulawayo ANC merged in 1957, Nkomo became the president of the new ANC in southern Rhodesia. The party soon incurred the government's wrath, and in February 1959 it was banned and 500 members were arrested.

Nkomo was in Cairo attending an Afro-Asian conference at the time and so escaped imprisonment. He moved to London, where he became the external affairs director (and later president) of the party established to succeed the banned ANC — the National Democratic party (NDP). Nkomo toured the world trying to arouse public opinion against the Rhodesian government, particularly in Britain and at the United Nations.

For a while Nkomo's strategy seemed reasonable. The British prime minister, Harold Macmillan, made his "winds of change" speech in Cape Town. As the federation plan faltered, Britain agreed to hold separate constitutional conferences for the two Rhodesias. But compromises were too little and too late, and party radicals forced Nkomo to repudiate the conference. Soon afterwards, the NDP was banned, but the nationalists quickly formed a new party — the Zimbabwe African People's Union (ZAPU), with Nkomo as president. Within nine months, this party was also banned. Again outside the country at the time, Nkomo decided to set up ZAPU headquarters in nearby Tanzania where he could continue his quest for international support.

The struggle within Rhodesia waivered as Nkomo concentrated on external ties, and in 1963 dissention within the ZAPU leadership led to the formation of a breakaway nationalist party, the Zimbabwe African National Union (ZANU). The new organization was increasingly committed to a military strategy and sent recruits from its military wing, the Zimbabwe African National Liberation Army (ZANLA), to China for training in guerrilla warfare. Nkomo established the People's Caretaker Council (PCC) to carry out ZAPU's internal struggle.

In 1964 the Rhodesians elected Ian Smith, who supported a unilateral declaration of independence from Britain (accomplished in 1965). Smith promptly banned ZANU and PCC and arrested Nkomo and other nationalist leaders, who began a decade's imprisonment.

Meanwhile, warfare spread as nationalist insurgents from both parties stepped up attacks on the settler regime. In 1972 the Mozambique border opened up, giving ZANLA an opportunity to prosecute the war with renewed vigor. ZANU, now led by Robert Mugabe, called for complete surrender, but some moderate African leaders tried to reach compromise settlements with Smith. Nkomo's attempt to negotiate with Smith in 1975 hurt his reputation as a nationalist leader. Although Nkomo agreed to merge ZAPU and ZANU military forces in the Patriotic Front, Mugabe had eclipsed Nkomo as the leading nationalist in Southern Rhodesia. In 1978 Smith tried to circumvent the Patriotic Front by signing an internal settlement with Bishop Muzorewa. Mugabe and Nkomo rejected the settlement and continued fighting.

International disapproval and continued warfare finally drove Smith to the negotiating table. At the Lancaster House Conference in 1979 Smith agreed to a new constitution, and in 1980 Mugabe became prime minister and minister for defense. Nkomo held positions in the ministry and cabinet for a while, but conflicts with Mugabe erupted in 1982, driving Nkomo into exile. He returned in 1986.

Conflict between Mugabe's party, ZANU-PF, and Nkomo's party ZAPU, caused civil unrest, which often became violent. Talks of merging the two parties surfaced and resurfaced, but it was not until a particularly brutal massacre occurred in Matabeland, in 1987, that a unity agreement was signed. In the same year. Mugabe was elected President, and Nkomo became a minister in his government. With two others, Nkomo oversaw policy, among other responsibilities.

The newly created unified party took on the name ZANU-PF. The agreement between the two parties stated that the party was committed to a one-party state in the Marxist-Leninist tradition. It provided that the party would be headed by Mugabe, but that a constitutional amendment would be passed to create two vice-presidencies — one of which would be filled by Nkomo. It was ratified by both parties in 1988, and this led to more peaceful conditions in Zimbabwe.

In December 1989, ZANU-PF was convened to finish the party merger. Controversy broke out over several of the provisions in the unity agreement, including the creation of the second vice-presidency for Nkomo. Nevertheless, Nkomo was appointed vice-president in 1990.

Mugabe's government proved to be unpopular, student boycotts were suppressed in 1991, and other groups that wished to protest were stifled. Government shortages, inflation, and unemployment were also problematic while Nkomo was vice-president. Although opposition groups formed, they were never strong or organized enough to pose a real threat to Mugabe and Nkomo. In 1996, Nkomo announced his intention to resign his vice presidency, because of ill health.

Further Reading

Joshua Nkomo is listed in *African Biographies* (Zimbabwe, 1); his early career is discussed John Day's *International Nationalism: The Extra-territorial Relations of Southern Rhodesian African Nationalists* (1967); more current description can be found in David Martin's and Phyllis Johnson's *The Struggle for Zimbabwe* (1981). □

Lewis Nkosi

Lewis Nkosi (born 1936) is known chiefly for his scholarly studies of contemporary African literature, and is the author of the novel *Mating Birds* (1986). Critics enthusiastically praised Nkosi's prose style

and narrative structure in *Mating Birds,* and several have compared the work with Albert Camus's *The Stranger.*

Nkosi was born in Natal, South Africa, and attended local schools before enrolling at M. L. Sultan Technical College in Durban. In 1956 he joined the staff of *Drum* magazine, a publication founded in 1951 by and for African writers. In his *Home and Exile and Other Selections* (1965), Nkosi described *Drum*'s young writers as "the new African[s] cut adrift from the tribal reserve— urbanised, eager, fast-talking and brash." According to Neil Lazarus, the description fitted Nkosi as well. "Nkosi's whole bearing as a writer," he wrote, "was decisively shaped by the years in Johannesburg working for the magazine." In 1960 Nkosi left South Africa on a one-way "exit permit" after accepting a fellowship to study at Harvard University. Now living in England, he teaches and writes articles on African literature. In addition to the novel *Mating Birds,* he has also produced several plays and collections of essays, including *The Rhythm of Violence* (1963), *Malcolm* (1972), *The Transplanted Heart: Essays on South Africa* (1975), and *Tasks and Masks: Themes and Styles of African Literature* (1981).

Mating Birds tells the story of Sibiya, who spots a white woman across a fence on a segregated beach in Durban. Although the rules of apartheid keep them from speaking to each other, they begin a wordless flirtation across the fence. Soon Sibiya becomes obsessed with the woman and follows her everywhere. He learns that her name is Veronica and that she is a stripper at the local nightclub. One day Sibiya follows Veronica to her bungalow. Seeing him, she undresses in front of the open door and lies down on the bed. Sibiya enters her bedroom and has sex with her. Shortly after, they are discovered, and Veronica accuses Sibiya of rape. He is then beaten, arrested, and sentenced to death.

Many critics viewed *Mating Birds* as a commentary on South Africa's system of apartheid. George Packer, for example, observed: "*Mating Birds* feels like the work of a superb critic. Heavy with symbolism, analytical rather than dramatic, it attempts nothing less than an allegory of colonialism and apartheid, one that dares to linger in complexity." Other commentators, however, attacked the novel's ambiguous depiction of rape. "Nkosi's handling of the sexual themes complicates the distribution of our sympathies, which he means to be unequivocally with the accused man," noted Rob Nixon in the *Village Voice.* "For in rebutting the prevalent white South African fantasy of the black male as a sex-crazed rapist, Nkosi edges unnecessarily close to reinforcing the myth of the raped woman as someone who deep down was asking for it." For Henry Louis Gates, Jr., even the question of whether Sibiya raped at all remains unclear. This causes problems for the reader, as "we are never certain who did what to whom or why." Sibiya himself is unsure: "But how could I make the judges or anyone else believe me when I no longer *knew* what to believe myself? . . . Had I raped the girl or not?" Gates responded: "We cannot say. Accordingly, this novel's great literary achievement—its vivid depiction of obsession—leads inevitably to its great flaw." Sara Maitland further objected to Nkosi's portrayal of the white woman: "Surely there must be another way for Nkosi's commitment, passion and beautiful writing to describe the violence and injustice of how things are than this stock image of the pale evil seductress, the eternally corrupting female?"

Despite the novel's shortcomings, Michiko Kakutani concluded in the *New York Times, Mating Birds* "nonetheless attests to the emergence of . . . a writer whose vision of South Africa remains fiercely his own." Similarly, Sherman W. Smith lauded: "Lewis Nkosi certainly must be one of the best writers out of Africa in our time."

Exiled after leaving South Africa to study at Harvard University, Lewis Nkosi has written short stories, plays, and criticism from his adopted home in England. Much of his work, however, deals with African literature and social concerns. "As a playwright and short-story writer, he is also the most subtly experimental of the black South African writers, many of whom are caught in the immediacy of the struggle against apartheid," comments Henry Louis Gates, Jr. in the *New York Times Book Review.* According to Alistair Niven in *British Book News* Nkosi is "one of the architects of the contemporary black consciousness in South Africa."

Further Reading

Contemporary Literary Criticism, Volume 45, Gale, 1987.
Best Sellers, July, 1986.
Books and Bookmen, October, 1986.
British Book News, March, 1987.
Choice, June, 1982.
Listener, August 28, 1986.
London Review of Books, August 7, 1986.
Nation, November 22, 1986, pp. 570-574.
New Statesman, August 29, 1986, pp. 25-26; January 22, 1988, p. 32.
New Yorker, May 26, 1986.
New York Times, March 22, 1986.
New York Times Book Review, May 18, 1986, p. 3.
Observer, July 27, 1986.
Southern Review, January, 1987, pp. 106-118.
Spectator, August 16, 1986.
Times Literary Supplement, August 13, 1964, p. 723; February 3, 1966, p. 85; August 27, 1982, p. 928; August 8, 1986, p.863.
Village Voice, July 29, 1986, p. 46.
West Coast Review of Books, September, 1986.
World Literature Today, spring, 1983, pp. 335-337; summer, 1984, p. 462. □

Kwame Nkrumah

Kwame Nkrumah (1909-1972) was the first president of Ghana. Though he effected Ghana's independence and for a decade was Africa's foremost spokesman, his vainglory and dictatorial methods brought about his downfall in 1966, with him a discredited and tragic figure in African nationalism.

The career of Kwame Nkrumah must be seen in the context of the Africa of his period, which sought a dynamic leader but lacked the structures that would make possible the common goal of continental unity. Ghana's and Africa's very inadequacies initially made them insensitive to Nkrumah's failings, conspicuous among which was the ever-widening gap between his rhetoric, which called for a socialist revolution, and his practice, which accommodated itself to the worst aspects of tribal and capitalist traditions.

Preparation for Leadership

Kwame Nkrumah, whose original name was Francis Nwia Nkrumah, was born on Sept. 21, 1909, into the tiny Nzima tribe; his origins, although clouded by controversy, were indisputably humble. His early education was in Catholic mission schools and in a government training college. In 1935, after teaching for several years, with the help of friends and the example of Nnamdi Azikiwe (later Nigeria's first president), Nkrumah left for Lincoln University in the United States.

By this time, Nkrumah was already the most radical of the young "Gold Coasters," resenting deeply the exploitative aspects of colonialism. But it was during the years at Lincoln, and the ensuing ones as a graduate student in philosophy at the University of Pennsylvania, that he was to give substance to his feelings by studying, as he later wrote, "revolutionaries and their methods" (such as Lenin, Napoleon, Gandhi, Hitler, and, most important, Marcus Garvey, the Jamaican whose followers proclaimed him "provisional

president of Africa"). Nkrumah never obtained a thorough grounding in any field and never really demonstrated the intelligence and sensitivity that would have demanded discipline in his thinking. This combination of an inferior schooling and a less than first-rate mind made possible the eclectic and incoherent ideological thought seen in his later writings on "Nkrumaism."

Nkrumah's formal political activity started in America but only began in earnest in London, where he went for further studies in 1945. While in England, he edited a pan-African journal, was vice president of the West African students' union, and helped organize the Fifth Pan-African Conference in Manchester. There, too, George Padmore, the important former-Communist pan-Africanist, became his mentor and was a crucial restraining influence until he died in 1959.

Gold Coast Leader

In 1947 Nkrumah had his chance to return to Africa in a position of leadership. The United Gold Coast Convention (UGCC), a conservative nationalist movement, invited him to be general secretary. He arrived on Nov. 14, 1947. With weak British leadership and the postwar recession, the Gold Coast was ripe for more radical leadership, which Nkrumah ably provided. Riots in early 1948 resulted from economic grievances but were blamed on the UGCC leadership. Nkrumah and others, including Joseph B. Danquah, who later died in one of Nkrumah's political jails, were detained side by side.

After their release later that year, the UGCC leadership demoted Nkrumah, who responded by organizing the Committee on Youth Organization, which (composed of his now numerous admirers) provided the nucleus of Nkrumah's personal support. The inevitable rupture between Nkrumah and the UGCC came in June 1949. At an emotion-packed meeting, the Convention People's party (CPP) was born, with Nkrumah its leader.

The 1948 riots speeded the pace of political reform. Yet Nkrumah, always the radical, rejected proposals for a new Gold Coast constitution. He proposed to precipitate a crisis through "positive action": his followers took the cue and agitated for immediate self-government, leading to a state of emergency and Nkrumah's detention once again by the British. But reform ensued, and the first national elections were held in 1951. The CPP triumphed, thanks to brilliant organization and to the symbol of its incarcerated leader; on Feb. 12, 1951, Nkrumah was released from prison and made "leader of government business." A wholly new period began, in which the principle of ultimate independence was no longer in question.

Power was divided between Nkrumah, who was renamed prime minister in 1952, and the governor. This diarchy symbolized Nkrumah's dilemma of the reconciliation of his image as a revolutionary with his close relationship with the imperial authority. Although this gap was papered over with rhetoric, it always existed in some form. A new enemy of Nkrumah's power appeared in 1954-1956 in the form of a conservative, tribally based political movement derived from the UGCC which even tried to delay

independence. The need to struggle for the "political kingdom" against domestic forces intensified Nkrumah's desire for revenge and for total power. Marxist ideology became his congenial and increasingly convenient justification.

Search for the Political Kingdom

On March 6, 1957, the Gold Coast became independent as Ghana. Although Nkrumah was the prime minister (the governor-general was British) and had the governmental machinery in his hands, watchful British and domestic eyes cautioned him from attempting, for example, to transform the professional civil service into a personal political tool. But in the next 3 years he did much—he called two pan-African conferences, made state tours throughout Africa and to America and Britain, and accelerated educational and social development—and with all of this his power grew. He used a preventive detention act to detain many members of Parliament and supporters of the opposition, and by 1960 it took considerable courage to oppose him.

Debate in Africa and in the West, particularly Britain, over the colonial independence movement and the ability of Africans to govern themselves frequently became a debate over Nkrumah and his professed democratic goals. In 1960 a plebiscite made Ghana a republic with a new constitution, and an election resembling a plebiscite made Nkrumah its first president.

President of the Republic

With the founding of the republic on July 1, 1960, Nkrumah had achieved the political kingdom from which "all else"—in pan-African, domestic, and international policy—was to follow. Pan-African concerns had been laid aside during the struggle for domestic power. Now having established firm control of the republic, Nkrumah could center his activity on the uniting of the continent. But other states with their own leaders and heroes had now emerged, and they resented the constant advice from Accra; nor were they likely to surrender their newly won sovereignty to a great union.

Precisely as the new states consolidated their own positions, and as union became less and less a practicable proposition, Nkrumah's insistence on, and his absorption in, the "Union Government" cause grew. Nkrumah sincerely resented Africa's weakness and sought to prevent its "Latin-Americanization," but his method, his ambition, and the ill-defined nature of his goals doomed the obsession. "Union Government" became a joke in Africa. Thus Ghana's own diplomatic position eroded until, in 1963, it was even denied a position of eminence in the new Organization of African Unity. Yet in the more radical states, Nkrumah himself remained an honored statesman until 1964, when Julius Nyerere, the prestigious president of Tanzania, publicly denounced him in strident terms. After this, nothing sacred was left either of the cause or of the man.

In domestic affairs, the new constitution had been amended by fiat after the plebiscite so as to bestow dictatorial powers on the "Osagyefo" (redeemer—Nkrumah's self-advocated title). In the ensuing years, the remaining opposition within and without his party were detained, driven to exile, or frightened into silence. A small coterie of expatriate and Ghanaian Marxists pressed him to make Ghana Africa's first Communist state and as quid pro quo honored "Nkrumaism." Assassination attempts in 1962 and 1964 made Nkrumah accelerate his timetable for the building of socialism. The first attempt led to a new intimacy in relations with the Communist world and his own public advocacy of "scientific socialism"; the second led to a plebiscite making Ghana a one-party state.

The caution and inconsistency that had always characterized Nkrumah's statecraft remained. Moderates—and rich businessmen—could successfully cloak their sentiments in flattery. The steadily deteriorating financial situation, combined with the reluctance of Nikita Khrushchev's more cautious successors in the Kremlin to bail Nkrumah out, preserved his ultimate dependence on the West. Instinctively opposed to breaking diplomatic relations with Britain over the Rhodesia (now Zimbabwe) question, Nkrumah was forced to do so in order to appear to remain in the vanguard of African radicalism. Actions, not motivations, counted.

Exile and Death

The momentum of Nkrumah's actions, symbolized by the break with Britain, threatened the independence of the army and the police; early on Feb. 24, 1966, three days after Nkrumah had left on a gratuitous peace mission to Vietnam, they toppled the regime, outlawed the party, and announced that "the myth of Kwame Nkrumah is ended forever." The jubilant populace destroyed Nkrumah's statues and renamed the many roads, circles, buildings—even universities—that had borne his name. From a dreary exile in Guinea, Nkrumah ineffectually tried to rally Ghana against the new regime. Though initially proclaimed "copresident of Guinea" on his arrival, a gesture of sentiment, Nkrumah soon found himself watched, isolated, without even his Egyptian wife of 8 years. He died in Conakry, Guinea, on April 27, 1972.

Yet Ghana could no more remove the memory and effects of 15 years of its remarkable first leader than Nkrumah could remove the memories and structures of Ghana's colonial and traditional past. On the negative side were the heavy debts that the country had accrued.

More positively, there were the schools and universities, the Volta Dam, and the aluminum industry which Nkrumah had dreamed of in the 1950s and through persistence had seen through. And, he had given most Ghanaians a sense—and pride—of nationhood in the 1950s and had given people of African blood throughout the world a new pride in their color. Ironically, he had wanted to unite and lead a continent, but he founded a nation; of its small size he was continually embarrassed. Yet it is by his successes and failures as leader of that country that his biographers must ultimately judge him.

Further Reading

Nkrumah's autobiography, *Ghana* (1957), is probably the most revealing picture of him. His subsequent books became increasingly less important as he relied more and more on others to compose them. His *I Speak of Freedom* (1961) is largely a compilation of speeches; *Africa Must Unite* (1963) is a paean to his Ghanaian accomplishments; *Consciencism* (1964), probably written by two African Marxists and launched with fanfare and rapidly abandoned, attempts to give African nationalism a Marxist ideological context; and *Neo-Colonialism: The Last Stage of Imperialism* (1965) was widely thought to have been unread by its purported author. Nkrumah's subsequent books, published in exile, are essentially the tracts of a bitter man, although *Challenge of the Congo* (1967) is useful for some important documentary material.

There is no significant intimate study of Nkrumah. A balanced account of his regime, written by T. Peter Omari, a Ghanaian sociologist on the United Nations staff, is *Kwame Nkrumah: The Anatomy of an African Dictatorship* (1971). A brief study of Nkrumah is in Dankwart A. Rustow, ed., *Philosophers and Kings: Studies in Leadership* (1970). A slender, important specialized work, written by a European who was chief of the defense staff of the Ghanaian army, reveals much about Nkrumah's ambitions: H. T. Alexander, *African Tightrope: My Two Years as Nkrumah's Chief of Staff* (1966).

Nkrumah is best studied in the context of the forces of his time. Dennis Austin, *Politics in Ghana: 1946-1960* (1964), is the standard work. An essential study is George Padmore, *Pan-Africanism or Communism* (1956); and David E. Apter, *The Gold Coast in Transition* (1955; rev. ed. entitled *Ghana in Transition*, 1963), is excellent for the domestic politics of Ghana and the transfer of institutions to the new nationalism. Nkrumah as pan-Africanist and diplomatist is examined in W. Scott Thompson, *Ghana's Foreign Policy, 1957-1966: Diplomacy, Ideology, and the New State* (1969).

Additional Sources

Assensoh, A. B., *Kwame Nkrumah: six years in exile, 1966-1972,* Ilfracombe: Stockwell, 1978.

Donkoh, C. E., *Nkrumah and Busia of Ghana,* S.l.: s.n., 1974 (Accra: New Times Corp..

Kanu, Genoveva., *Nkrumah the man: a friend's testimony,* Enugu, Anambra State, Nigeria: Delta of Nigeria, 1982.

Meyer, Joe-Fio N., *Dr. Nkrumah's last dream: continental government of Africa,* Accra: Advance Pub., 1990.

Rooney, David., *Kwame Nkrumah: the political kingdom in the Third World,* New York: St. Martin's Press, 1989, 1988.

Timothy, Bankole., *Kwame Nkrumah, from cradle to grave,* Dorchester, Dorset: Gavin Press, 1981. □

Alfred Bernhard Nobel

The Swedish chemist Alfred Bernhard Nobel (1833-1896) invented dynamite and other explosives, but he is best remembered for the Nobel Prizes, which he endowed with the bulk of his personal fortune.

Alfred Nobel was born Oct. 21, 1833, in Stockholm. His father, impecunious in the Sweden of the 1830s, was more fortunate in Russia and by 1842 had established himself in a St. Petersburg engineering and armaments concern. From there in 1850 Alfred Nobel set out on a 2-year tour of western Europe and the United States, seeking ideas and contacts in engineering. Cancellation of munitions contracts after the Crimean War crippled the St. Petersburg concern, and Nobel's father was again impoverished.

Alfred Nobel remained in Russia when his father returned to Stockholm in 1858. Both were attempting to tame the violent explosive liquid nitroglycerin. In 1863 Alfred rejoined his father, and in that year he succeeded in exploding nitroglycerin at will by initiating the detonation with a gunpowder charge. In 1865 he introduced the mercury fulminate detonator, the key to all the later high explosives. Nobel patented his invention and set about exploiting it. Works for the manufacture of nitroglycerin were established near Stockholm and Hamburg, and the explosive oil was shipped the world over. In 1866 Nobel visited the United States and erected factories in New York and San Francisco.

Meanwhile, in Europe the Nobel companies faced mounting criticism arising from numerous accidental nitroglycerin explosions in transit or storage. Nobel had foreseen these difficulties and as early as 1864 had tried absorbing the sensitive liquid in porous solids, including kieselguhr. This material reduced the blasting efficiency by a quarter, but the resulting explosive was solid, plastic, and relatively

insensitive to physical or thermal shock. This was dynamite, patented in 1867. The new invention was vigorously exploited and a worldwide industry established. In 1875 came gelignite, a mixture of nitrocellulose and nitroglycerin; and in 1887 ballistite, similar to gelignite, was produced in response to the military demand for a smokeless, slow-burning projectile propellant. This was Nobel's last major invention, but throughout his life he improved on them all in detail, patented them, and left them to his companies, with which he had as little formal contact as possible.

From 1865 to 1873 Nobel lived in Hamburg and then in Paris until 1891, when the Italian military adoption of ballistite made him unpopular there. He moved to San Remo, Italy, where he died on Dec. 10, 1896. He was truly international, traveling ceaselessly. For all his achievements, he was a reserved and shy man who hated personal publicity.

Nobel's will directed that the bulk of his estate, above 33 million kronor, should endow annual prizes for those who, in the preceding year, had most benefited mankind in five specified subjects: physics, chemistry, medicine, literature, or peace. His will was proved within 4 years and the Nobel Foundation created. A Nobel Prize is one of the highest honors that an individual can receive.

Further Reading

The basic biography of Nobel is J. Henrik Schück and R. Sohlman, *The Life of Alfred Nobel* (trans. 1929). Perhaps the best of the many shorter works is E. Bergengren, *Alfred Nobel: The Man and His Work* (1962). Other biographies include Michael Evlanoff, *Nobel-Prize Donor: Inventor of Dynamite, Advocate of Peace* (1943), and Michael and Marjorie Fluor Evlanoff, *Alfred Nobel: The Loneliest Millionaire* (1969). The work of the Nobel Foundation is described in J. Henrik Schück, ed., *Nobel: The Man and His Prizes* (2d rev. ed. 1962). ☐

Umberto Nobile

The Italian explorer and airship designer Umberto Nobile (1885-1978) was a pioneer in Arctic aviation. His dirigible flight over the North Pole encouraged greater use of aircraft in the Arctic.

Umberto Nobile was born in Lauro, Italy, near Naples on Jan. 21, 1885. One of seven children whose father was a government official with limited income, Nobile had to earn his own way at the University of Naples. He graduated with honors in engineering. His early interest in aviation led to a career in dirigible design and construction. Physically unfit for active service in World War I, Nobile was commissioned in the Italian air force and became director of the military factory of aeronautical construction in Rome and eventually a general. His professional skills and long hours of work made him a leading designer of lighter-than-air craft. Convinced of the superior airworthiness of semirigid airships, he designed and built dirigibles for the navies of Italy and other countries.

His 34-ton airship *Roma,* sold to the United States government in 1921, crashed into a high-voltage line near Langley Field, VA, in 1922, killing 34 people. Despite the accident, explorer Roald Amundsen, who won a dogsled race to become the first man to reach the South Pole in 1912, wanted to use Nobile's airship the *Norge* to fly over the North Pole. In 1926, they flew from Spitsbergen, Norway, to Alaska, with Gen. Nobile as pilot and Amundsen and American explorer Lincoln Ellsworth as crew members. They were the second group to fly over the North Pole, beaten by Americans Richard Byrd and Floyd Bennett, who crossed it by airplane three days earlier. The competence and courage Nobile displayed earned him wide acclaim and aroused Amundsen's resentment.

Blamed for Arctic Disaster

Nobile undertook another polar flight in 1928, this time under his own command, using the airship *Italia.* He reached the North Pole on May 24, but on the return flight to Spitsbergen, the dirigible was wrecked in a storm and the survivors stranded on the pack ice. The disaster prompted a massive international rescue operation using, for the first time, large numbers of aircraft. Although severely injured, Nobile set a courageous example for his crew members during the 31 days before help arrived. Nobile was flown off the ice by a Swedish air force ski-plane, and the other survivors were picked up by the Soviet icebreaker *Krassin*

18 days later. Amundsen, who had volunteered for the search and rescue effort, died when his airplane crashed in the sea. Eight of the 16 men that had been aboard the dirigible also died.

Nobile's single-minded interest in aviation and exploration gave him little appreciation of the political implications of his exploits. The popular enthusiasm for his dirigible flights engendered a resentment within certain Fascist circles, especially those connected with the Italian air force. A group of these antagonists, led by Marshal Italo Balbo, exploited the *Italia* tragedy to attack Nobile and his advocacy of lighter-than-air craft. Protesting against the findings of an official inquiry which blamed him for the crash and the deaths, Nobile resigned from the air force in March 1929.

Vindication

After his resignation, Nobile served as an aviation consultant in the Soviet Union and also taught for several years in the United States, becoming head of the aeronautical engineering department of Lewis College of Science and Technology in Lockport, Ill., in 1936. In 1943 he returned to Italy. After the defeat of the Fascists, he wrote a book, *I Can Tell the Truth,* arguing that the inquiry against him was rigged. In 1945, he was cleared of the charges against him and restored to the rank of major general in the air force. Nobile was a delegate to Italy's Constituent Assembly in 1946, but a year later retired from politics to spend the remainder of his life in research, writing, and teaching. He wrote five more books on the voyage and crash of the *Italia,* and the last one, *The Red Tent* (1967), was made into a movie.

Nobile made a significant contribution to polar exploration during his brief period of activity. Not only did he make the first transpolar flight, increasing knowledge of Arctic geography, but he also demonstrated the feasibility of using aircraft in the Arctic for both exploration and transport.

Further Reading

Nobile's published books include *My Polar Flights: An Account of the Voyages of the Airships Italia and Norge* (1959; trans. 1961); *I Can Tell the Truth* (1943); *The Red Tent* (1967); and *With the Italia to the North Pole* (1930; trans. 1930). Accounts of the flights of the *Norge* and the *Italia* are contained in Basil Clarke's, *Polar Flight* (1964). Clarke presents a factual and concise description of Nobile's contribution to Arctic flying, though he does not deal extensively with the rescue of the *Italia* survivors. A more complete examination is found in Wilbur Cross, *Ghost Ship of the Pole: The Incredible Story of the Dirigible Italia* (1960). Cross is highly sympathetic to Nobile and deals fairly well with the attacks made against him by Balbo and others. Other works of interest are *The First Flight across the Polar Sea* (1927) by Roald Amundsen and Lincoln Ellsworth; Einar Lundborg, *The Arctic Rescue: How Nobile Was Saved* (1928; trans. 1929); and Davide Giudici, *The Tragedy of the Italia: With the Rescuers to the Red Tent* (1928). □

Oda Nobunaga

Oda Nobunaga (1534-1582) was a Japanese warrior chieftain who undertook the first stage in the military unification of Japan in the later 16th century after nearly a hundred years of disorder and disunion.

From the time of its founding in 1336 the shogunate (military government) of the Ashikaga family exercised at least theoretical military overlordship of medieval Japan. The first great leader of the Ashikaga, Takauji, established his headquarters in Kyoto near the imperial court and attempted to impose shogunate control over as wide an area as possible extending outward from the central provinces of Honshu.

But, as the result of a great struggle among the vassal barons of the shogunate from 1467 to 1477, this hegemony was completely destroyed. Although the shogunate was not abolished, it exercised little more central governance during the next century than the imperial court, which had been largely deprived of its ruling powers by the rise of the provincial military in the 12th century.

Nobunaga as Unifier

The period from 1477 until 1573, when the Ashikaga shogunate was formally terminated, is known in Japanese history as the Age of Provincial Wars. During this time the country was riven by internecine civil strife as warrior bands everywhere fought with one another to establish territorial bases. From this condition of seemingly endless conflict, however, a new group of barons—known as daimyos—ultimately carved out regional domains which they maintained and defended as autonomous "states." And from about the 1550s the most important of these daimyos began to compete among themselves to reunify the land.

The Oda family held its domain in the region of present-day Nagoya. Oda Nobunaga after succeeding to the family leadership upon the death of his father in 1551, won his first great battle in 1560 against a powerful neighboring daimyo. As a result of this victory, he was able to make alliances that set the stage for a campaign toward Kyoto, the first goal of all would-be unifiers among the daimyos.

Nobunaga entered Kyoto in 1568 after 8 years of hard fighting. He did so with the approval of the Emperor and in the company of an exiled member of the Ashikaga house whom he installed as shogun. But it was, of course, Nobunaga who was now the holder of central military power in the country, and in 1573 he deposed the Shogun, thus bringing about dissolution of the Ashikaga shogunate after some 2 1/2 centuries of tumultuous existence.

Although Nobunaga had established a new hegemony in the central provinces, he still had many enemies to deal with, including both opposing daimyos and the members of certain militant Buddhist sects. In his campaigns against these enemies Nobunaga acted with a ruthlessness that appears to have been considered extreme even in this harsh

age. Accounts reveal that he slaughtered thousands without apparent mercy or remorse. Sir George Sansom, the 20th century's most eminent Western scholar of Japan, labeled Nobunaga a "callous brute" who imposed his control over perhaps a third of Japan "at a terrible cost."

Arrival of Westerners

One unusual factor during the period of Nobunaga's rise to power was the presence of Europeans in Japan for the first time. The Portuguese arrived in the early 1540s, and within a few decades both they and the Spanish were actively engaged in trade and Christian missionary work. Later Japanese leaders were to undertake with increasing vigor the suppression of Christianity, and in the 17th century they proscribed it completely. Yet Nobunaga showed no particular animosity toward the foreign religion; indeed, he even gave his approval to the spread of its proselytizing activities. No doubt one of his reasons for doing this was his hatred of those Buddhist sects that actively opposed both him and the Christians.

The introduction of firearms by the Portuguese did not drastically alter methods of warfare in Japan in the late 16th century. This was chiefly because they remained difficult to obtain in any substantial quantity. Nobunaga in particular won some important battles with muskets, but by the end of the century, when these weapons became widely available, unification had been completed and warfare ceased.

Nobunaga as Ruler

It is difficult to assess Nobunaga's qualities as a ruler, because he died before completing the task of military unification and never really had the opportunity to develop permanent governing offices or procedures. He was obliged to concentrate almost entirely on the pursuit of his campaigns of pacification.

Nobunaga did, however, take the time to build a great fortified castle at Azuchi, a short distance to the northeast of Kyoto, in 1576, which he made his headquarters until his death 6 years later. By obliging many of his warrior followers to take up residence near the castle and by providing favorable inducements to commerce, Nobunaga created a flourishing castle town at Azuchi.

One important result of Nobunaga's campaigns was the abolition of barriers of various kinds which had been erected between the daimyo domains, and the consequent freedom of movement and transport that this made possible, at least in the central provinces. Although the new foreign trade with the Europeans was conducted mainly in the westernmost island of Kyushu, most of the luxury goods brought by the Portuguese and Spanish were sent directly to the central provinces, where they were in greatest demand. In the absence of Nobunaga's new hegemony in this region, distribution of these goods would have been immeasurably more difficult.

Assassination of Nobunaga

After establishing control over the central region, Nobunaga launched a major campaign into the western provinces of Honshu, where several powerful and highly independent daimyos had their domains. Nobunaga commissioned two of his leading generals, Toyotomi Hideyoshi and Akechi Mitsuhide, to lead their forces in a two-pronged invasion of the west. It was during the course of this campaign that Hideyoshi first truly demonstrated the strategic and tactical brilliance that was to make him the greatest general in Japanese history.

In 1582 Hideyoshi undertook the siege of a castle at Takamatsu which was held by forces of the Mori family, and he requested reinforcements from Nobunaga. In the course of arranging to meet this request, Nobunaga left Azuchi with a small retinue and went to Kyoto, where he lodged at a temple called the Honnoji. That night Mitsuhide, who had returned from the fighting in the west, attacked the Honnoji. In the struggle that ensued, the temple was set afire and Nobunaga perished in the flames. His body was never found.

Mitsuhide's precise reason for assassinating his overlord is not known, but one possibility is that he feared he was losing favor with Nobunaga while his chief competitor, Hideyoshi, was rising in Nobunaga's esteem. In any case, Mitsuhide does not appear to have had any carefully considered plan of how to proceed after the assassination. As he hesitated, Hideyoshi concluded a truce with the Takamatsu garrison, marched back at great speed to the central provinces, and destroyed Mitsuhide. In a dramatic sequence of events, Hideyoshi thus emerged as the most powerful figure in the country.

Nobunaga's untimely death at the age of 48 undoubtedly deprived him of a greater place in Japanese history than he actually holds. Hideyoshi and Tokugawa Ieyasu, who took command of the country after Hideyoshi's death in 1598 and established the great Tokugawa shogunate, are rightfully regarded as the two most significant figures of this heroic age of unification. Yet it should not be forgotten that both were the beneficiaries of the outstanding achievements of Nobunaga.

Further Reading

There is no biography of Nobunaga in English, but good accounts of his rise to power are in Sir George Bailey Sansom, *A History of Japan* (3 vols., 1958-1963), and John Whitney Hall, *Government and Local Power in Japan, 500 to 1700* (1966). Two other works that deal specifically with Europeans and Christianity in Japan but are also excellent general sources for the period of unification are Charles R. Boxer, *The Christian Century in Japan, 1549-1650* (1951; rev. ed. 1967), and Michael Cooper, ed., *They Came to Japan* (1965). □

Emmy Noether

Emmy Noether (1882-1935) was a world-renowned mathematician whose innovative approach to modern abstract algebra inspired colleagues and students who emulated her technique.

Dismissed from her university position at the beginning of the Nazi era in Germany—for she was both Jewish and female—Noether emigrated to the United States, where she taught in several universities and colleges. When she died, Albert Einstein eulogized her in a letter to *New York Times* as "the most significant creative mathematical genius thus far produced since the higher education of women began."

Noether was born on March 23, 1882, in the small university town of Erlangen in southern Germany. Her first name was Amalie, but she was known by her middle name of Emmy. Her mother, Ida Amalia Kaufmann Noether, came from a wealthy family in Cologne. Her father, Max Noether, a professor at the University of Erlangen, was an accomplished mathematician who worked on the theory of algebraic functions. Two of her three younger brothers became scientists—Fritz was a mathematician and Alfred earned a doctorate in chemistry.

Noether's childhood was unexceptional, going to school, learning domestic skills, and taking piano lessons. Since girls were not eligible to enroll in the gymnasium (college preparatory school), she attended the Städtischen Höheren Töchterschule, where she studied arithmetic and languages. In 1900 she passed the Bavarian state examinations with evaluations of "very good" in French and English (she received only a "satisfactory" evaluation in practical classroom conduct); this certified her to teach foreign languages at female educational institutions.

Instead of looking for a language teaching position, Noether decided to undertake university studies. However, since she had not graduated from a gymnasium, she first had to pass an entrance examination for which she obtained permission from her instructors. She audited courses at the University of Erlangen from 1900 to 1902. In 1903 she passed the matriculation exam, and entered the University of Göttingen for a semester, where she encountered such notable mathematicians as Hermann Minkowski, Felix Klein, and David Hilbert. She enrolled at the University of Erlangen where women were accepted in 1904. At Erlangen, Noether studied with Paul Gordan, a mathematics professor who was also a family friend. She completed her dissertation entitled "On Complete Systems of Invariants for Ternary Biquadratic Forms," receiving her Ph.D., summa cum laude, on July 2, 1908.

Noether worked without pay at the Mathematical Institute of Erlangen from 1908 until 1915, where her university duties included research, serving as a dissertation adviser for two students, and occasionally delivering lectures for her ailing father. In addition, Noether began to work with Ernst Otto Fischer, an algebraist who directed her toward the broader theoretical style characteristic of Hilbert. Noether not only published her thesis on ternary biquadratics, but she was also elected to membership in the Circolo Matematico di Palermo in 1908. The following year, Noether was invited to join the German Mathematical Society (Deutsche Mathematiker Vereinigung); she addressed the Society's 1909 meeting in Salzburg and its 1913 meeting in Vienna.

In 1915, Klein and Hilbert invited Noether to join them at the Mathematical Institute in Göttingen. They were working on the mathematics of the newly announced general theory of relativity, and they believed Noether's expertise would be helpful. Albert Einstein later wrote an article for the 1955 Grolier Encyclopedia, characterizing the theory of relativity by the basic question, "how must the laws of nature be constituted so that they are valid in the same form relative to arbitrary systems of co-ordinates (postulate of the invariance of the laws of nature relative to an arbitrary transformation of space and time)?" It was precisely this type of invariance under transformation on which Noether focused her mathematical research.

In 1918, Noether proved two theorems that formed a cornerstone for general relativity. These theorems validated certain relationships suspected by physicists of the time. One, now known as Noether's Theorem, established the equivalence between an invariance property and a conservation law. The other involved the relationship between an invariance and the existence of certain integrals of the equations of motion. The eminent German mathematician Hermann Weyl described Noether's contribution in the July 1935 *Scripta Mathematica* following her death: "For two of the most significant sides of the general theory of relativity theory she gave at that time the genuine and universal mathematical formulation."

While Noether was proving these profound and useful results, she was working without pay at Göttingen University, where women were not admitted to the faculty. Hilbert,

in particular, tried to obtain a position for her but could not persuade the historians and philosophers on the faculty to vote in a woman's favor. He was able to arrange for her to teach, however, by announcing a class in mathematical physics under his name and letting her lecture in his place. By 1919, regulations were eased somewhat, and she was designated a Privatdozent (a licensed lecturer who could receive fees from students but not from the university). In 1922, Noether was given the unofficial title of associate professor, and was hired as an adjunct teacher and paid a modest salary without fringe benefits or tenure.

Noether's enthusiasm for mathematics made her an effective teacher, often conducting classroom discussions in which she and her students would jointly explore some topic. In *Emmy Noether at Byrn Mawr,* Noether's only doctoral student at Bryn Mawr, Ruth McKee, recalls, "Miss Noether urged us on, challenging us to get our nails dirty, to really dig into the underlying relationships, to consider the problems from all possible angles."

Brilliant mathematicians often make their greatest contributions early in their careers; Noether was one of the notable exceptions to that rule. She began producing her most powerful and creative work about the age of 40. Her change in style started with a 1920 paper on non-commutative fields (systems in which an operation such as multiplication yields a different answer for a x b than for b x a). During the years that followed, she developed a very abstract and generalized approach to the axiomatic development of algebra. As Weyl attested, "she originated above all a new and epoch-making style of thinking in algebra."

Noether's 1921 paper on the theory of ideals in rings is considered to contain her most important results. It extended the work of Dedekind on solutions of polynomials—algebraic expressions consisting of a constant multiplied by variables raised to a positive power—and laid the foundations for modern abstract algebra. Rather than working with specific operations on sets of numbers, this branch of mathematics looks at general properties of operations. Because of its generality, abstract algebra represents a unifying thread connecting such theoretical fields as logic and number theory with applied mathematics useful in chemistry and physics.

During the winter of 1928–29, Noether was a visiting professor at the University of Moscow and the Communist Academy, and in the summer of 1930, she taught at the University of Frankfurt. Recognized for her continuing contributions in the science of mathematics, the International Mathematical Congress of 1928 chose her to be its principal speaker at one of its section meetings in Bologna. In 1932 she was chosen to address the Congress's general session in Zurich.

Noether was a part of the mathematics faculty of Göttingen University in the 1920s when its reputation for mathematical research and teaching was considered the best in the world. Still, even with the help of the esteemed mathematician Hermann Weyl, Noether was unable to secure a proper teaching position there, which was equivalent to her male counterparts. Weyl once commented: "I was ashamed to occupy such a preferred position beside her whom I knew to be my superior as a mathematician in many respects." Nevertheless, in 1932, on Noether's fiftieth birthday, the university's algebraists held a celebration, and her colleague Helmut Hasse dedicated a paper in her honor, which validated one of her ideas on noncommutative algebra. In that same year, she again was honored by those outside her own university, when she was named cowinner of the Alfred Ackermann-Teubner Memorial Prize for the Advancement of Mathematical Knowledge.

The successful and congenial environment of the University of Göttingen ended in 1933, with the advent of the Nazis in Germany. Within months, anti-Semitic policies spread through the country. On April 7, 1933, Noether was formally notified that she could no longer teach at the university. She was a dedicated pacifist, and Weyl later recalled, "her courage, her frankness, her unconcern about her own fate, her conciliatory spirit were, in the midst of all the hatred and meanness, despair and sorrow surrounding us, a moral solace."

For a while, Noether continued to meet informally with students and colleagues, inviting groups to her apartment. But by summer, the Emergency Committee to Aid Displaced German Scholars was entering into an agreement with Bryn Mawr, a women's college in Pennsylvania, which offered Noether a professorship. Her first year's salary was funded by the Emergency Committee and the Rockefeller Foundation.

In the fall of 1933, Noether was supervising four graduate students at Bryn Mawr. Starting in February 1934, she also delivered weekly lectures at the Institute for Advanced Study at Princeton. She bore no malice toward Germany, and maintained friendly ties with her former colleagues. With her characteristic curiosity and good nature, she settled into her new home in America, acquiring enough English to adequately converse and teach, although she occasionally lapsed into German when concentrating on technical material.

During the summer of 1934, Noether visited Göttingen to arrange shipment of her possessions to the United States. When she returned to Bryn Mawr in the early fall, she had received a two-year renewal on her teaching grant. In the spring of 1935, Noether underwent surgery to remove a uterine tumor. The operation was a success, but four days later, she suddenly developed a very high fever and lost consciousness. She died on April 14th, apparently from a post-operative infection. Her ashes were buried near the library on the Bryn Mawr campus.

Over the course of her career, Noether supervised a dozen graduate students, wrote forty-five technical publications, and inspired countless other research results through her habit of suggesting topics of investigation to students and colleagues. After World War II, the University of Erlangen attempted to show her the honor she had deserved during her lifetime. A conference in 1958 commemorated the fiftieth anniversary of her doctorate; in 1982 the university dedicated a memorial plaque to her in its Mathematics Institute. During the same year, the 100th anniversary year of Noether's birth, the Emmy Noether Gymnasium, a coed-ucational school emphasizing mathematics, the natural sciences, and modern languages, opened in Erlangen.

Further Reading

Brewer, James W., *Emmy Noether: A Tribute to Her Life and Work,* edited by Martha K. Smith, Marcel Dekker, 1981.
Kramer, Edna E., *The Nature and Growth of Modern Mathematics,* Princeton University, 1981, pp. 656–672.
Magill, Frank N., editor, *Great Events from History II,* Books International, 1991, pp. 650–654, 716–719.
Osen, Lynn M., *Women in Mathematics,* Massachusetts Institute of Technology, 1979, pp. 141–152.
Perl, Teri, *Math Equals: Biographies of Women Mathematicians,* Addison-Wesley, 1978, pp. 172–178.
Srinivasan, Bhama and Judith D. Sally, *Emmy Noether in Bryn Mawr: Proceedings of a Symposium,* Springer-Verlag, 1983.
Kimberling, Clark H., "Emmy Noether," in *The American Mathematical Monthly,* February, 1972, pp. 136–149. □

Isamu Noguchi

Isamu Noguchi (1904-1988), American sculptor and designer, was one of the few legitimate heirs to the sculptural tradition begun by Brancusi. His sculptures, fountains and gardens are focal points in many cities in the United States and worldwide.

Isamu Noguchi was born on November 17, 1904, in Los Angeles, California. His father was a Japanese poet and authority on art, his mother an American writer. In 1906 he moved with his family to Japan, where his father married a Japanese woman, and Noguchi remained with his mother until he was 14 years old. In 1918, his mother sent him back to the United States to finish his education. He became an apprentice to Gutzon Borglum, the sculptor of Mount Rushmore, who told Noguchi he was not talented enough to be a sculptor. So Noguchi enrolled as a pre-medical student at Columbia University in 1923.

Prophet of His Age

In 1925, however, Noguchi enrolled at the Leonardo da Vinci Art School in New York City to study sculpture. The school's director, Onorio Ruotolo, proclaimed Noguchi the "new Michelangelo." Noguchi also attended the East Side Art School in New York. In 1927 he won a Guggenheim fellowship and moved to Paris, where he was an apprentice to abstract sculptor Constantin Brancusi. "Brancusi gave me respect for tools and materials," Noguchi later said. He also was a strong influence on Noguchi's art. "It became self-evident to me that in so-called abstraction lay the expression of the age and that I was especially fitted to be one of its prophets," said Noguchi in 1929, the year his first one-man exhibition took place in New York City.

After visits to New York, Paris, and Beijing, Noguchi lived in Japan for six months in 1930, working with clay and studying gardens. There he realized that land could be sculpture and sculpture could be put to public use. In the

1930s he made art reflecting his social concerns, including a sculpture of a lynched man, and a cement mural, 72 feet long, in Mexico City, chronicling Mexican history. In 1935 he began making stage sets for dancer Martha Graham, a collaboration that would continue for 50 years. Throughout his career, Noguchi also worked with other choreographers. In 1938 he made his first sculpture in stainless steel, a symbol of freedom of the press at the entrance to the Associated Press building in Rockefeller Center, New York City.

Power in Stone

Noguchi enjoyed periodic and selective exhibitions throughout the United States, Europe, and the Orient. Among his important group shows was the exhibition of "14 Americans" at the Museum of Modern Art, New York City, in 1946. A return trip to Japan in 1949 prompted Noguchi to begin direct carving in stone. "Stone is the primary medium, and nature is where it is, and nature is where we have to go to experience life," he said. "When I'm with the stone, there is not one second when I'm not working."

Noguchi received a fellowship from the Bollingen Foundation in 1950. He also traveled throughout the world — to Mexico, the U.S.S.R., and Israel, among other countries — and his work was purchased by numerous important museums. His only marriage, to actress Yoshiko Yamaguchi, lasted from 1951 to 1955. In 1968 the Whitney Museum of American Art sponsored a Noguchi retrospective, and in 1978 the Walker Art Center exhibited his show *Imaginary Landscapes.*

Connection with Nature

Much of Noguchi's sculpture incorporates the spirit of Brancusi's reduced and simplified naturalism. Even when he worked with marble, as with *Euripides* (1966), Noguchi's forms seem to suggest natural or human entities that interact with one another or with their surroundings. Like Brancusi, Noguchi invariably retained in his pieces a strong feeling for the integrity of the materials. His penchant was generally for wood or stone, and he had a remarkable ability for dramatizing the textural potential of each, but without sacrificing their inherent identity.

Noguchi's work was also richly inspired by European surrealism and abstraction. His experiences in the Orient endowed him with a unique ability for garden and piazza design. Among his numerous important commissions were the gardens and sculpture for the Connecticut General Life Insurance Company, Hartford, Connecticut; a piazza and sculpture (1960) for the First National Bank, Fort Worth, Texas; a fountain and sculpture for the John Hancock Building, New York City; a garden (1956-1958) for the UNESCO Headquarters, Paris; the Billy Rose Garden of Sculpture (1960-1965) at the Israel National Museum, Jerusalem; a sunken garden at Yale University (1960-1964); and the 1968 *Red Cube,* a steel sculpture on Broadway in New York City.

Prolific to the End

In 1979 a basalt sculpture Noguchi had made in Japan was installed near New York's Metropolitan Museum of Art. The next year the Whitney Museum held an exhibit of his landscape projects and theater sets. In 1982 Noguchi was awarded the Edward MacDowell Medal for outstanding lifetime contribution to the arts. In 1984, Noguchi's memorial to Benjamin Franklin, the *Bolt of Lightning,* a 102-foot stainless steel sculpture, was installed in Philadelphia. In 1985 the Isamu Noguchi Garden Museum, displaying more than 200 of his works, opened in Queens, New York.

In 1986, Noguchi ended his long career with a playful signature as the U.S. representative to the Venice Biennale. His exhibition of sculpture and lamps included the *Slide Mantra,* a religious-looking marble sculpture which visitors could climb up and slide down.

Noguchi was best known for sculpture, but he worked in many other media, including painting, ceramics, interior design, and architecture. His fountains grace several cities, including Detroit. In every work, he remained deeply attuned to his material and sensitive to its connection to nature and to society. According to Michael Brenson of the *New York Times,* he "was marked by an Asian esthetic that believed in a link among all the arts, and he was constantly searching for ways to bring them together." His work bridged East and West and spoke to universal themes. In 1985, Noguchi wrote: "For me it is the direct contact of artist to material which is original, and it is the earth and his contact to it which will free him of the artificiality of the present and his dependence on industrial products."

Further Reading

Noguchi's *A Sculptor's World* (1968); *Isamu Noguchi,* by John Gordon (1968); Noguchi is also featured in Sam Hunter's, *Modern American Painting and Sculpture* (1959); *Legends in Their Own Time* (1994); and Les Krantz's *American Artists* (1985). □

Sidney Robert Nolan

The Australian expressionist painter Sidney Robert Nolan (1917-1992) emerged in the 1940s as a leading figure among the artists then beginning to articulate Australians' newfound awareness of their environment.

Born in Melbourne on April 22, 1917, Sidney Nolan was the son of a tram driver. He attended public schools and at age 14 began studying design at a technical college. His early interest was poetry, and his first job was as a poster painter for a hat company. Nolan began formal training at the National Gallery of Victoria and quickly developed a distinctive figurative manner of painting.

In the late 1930s he began painting outback landscapes and urban scenes, experimenting widely and with great imaginative energy. He exhibited abstract paintings in his first one-man show, in Melbourne in 1940, but soon concentrated on impressionistic renderings of the outback, with outlaws and animals most prominent. Later he moved from this stream-of-consciousness outpouring of personal symbolism to an art in which choice, decision, and will played a larger part.

The Ned Kelly Series

In the late 1940s and into the 1950s, Nolan gained public attention in Melbourne with a series of 25 paintings developed around the story of Ned Kelly, an impenitent "Robin Hood," glorified as one of the nation's heroes from colonial days. Nolan had heard first-hand tales of the Kelly gang's exploits from his grandfather, a policeman. In 1948 he moved to Sydney, joining Russell Drysdale at the head of the Sydney Group, an exhibiting society. Nolan painted landscapes and extended the series on Kelly before moving to London in 1955. For the rest of his life he was based in England but traveled worldwide.

Nolan was represented in the Twelve Australian Artists Exhibition, sponsored by the Arts Council of Great Britain (1953), and at the Venice Biennale in 1954. The Italian government awarded him a scholarship in 1956, and he received a Commonwealth Fund fellowship to the United States in 1958.

By the late 1950s Nolan was credited with having uncovered and enshrined the Australian myth through his works on Ned Kelly. In his poetic and poignant interpretations of the legend, he used a blend of realism and fantasy. Kelly's head was depicted as a black square. His distorted bodies resembled the postwar figurative styles in Europe and America. Critic James Gleeson (1969) underscored Nolan's ability to create "striking and beautiful" visual relationships. While maintaining a simple narrative value, Nolan developed a wide range of style and technique.

Nolan's work showed a continuing concern with the irony of the human situation. In one of the compelling pictures of the Kelly series, *Kelly in Spring,* he invests the outlaw with the face of a dreamer imprisoned within a black iron frame, while surrounded by tree branches releasing their promise of beauty and fruitfulness.

International Acclaim

Absorption with myth gave ambience and reach as well as a personal focus to Nolan. Working in London, he moved on from Australian colonial subjects to timeless and universal themes drawn from mythology, and he gained international recognition for the powerful imagery of his work. He became Australia's most acclaimed modern painter and was considered by art historian Kenneth Clark to be one of the major artists of the 20th century.

Throughout his career Nolan continued to expand the scope of his subjects, while he maintained the primitivism that marked his earlier work. His highly personal manner of executing a series of paintings was demonstrated with great success in his works on Leda and Prometheus and his recreation of the Australians' courageous storming of the Gallipoli heights during World War I. His work grew in scale and included a huge mural in Melbourne, *Paradise Garden* (1968- 1970), that consisted of 1,320 floral designs in crayon and dyes.

Nolan also excelled at printmaking and designed ballet sets for several productions. In the 1970s and 1980s he visited Australia almost annually and returned to the Kelly theme, each time with different techniques. He remained a prolific artist in his later years, painting a series of Chinese landscapes, another on Australian miners, and drawings for poems by Dante, Rimbaud, Shakespeare and others. He died in London on November 28, 1992.

Further Reading

Sidney Nolan: Myth and Imagery (1967), by Elwyn Lynn, a review which includes perceptive and illuminating discussions of the relationship between Nolan's technical innovations and his art as a whole; also by Lynn *Sidney Nolan: Australia* (1979);*Sidney Nolan: Such Is Life,* a Biography (1987) by B. Adams. □

Kenneth Noland

Kenneth Noland (born 1924) became a major American color-field painter. His works, extremely abstract in feeling, are strong in the splendor of the colors and their taut control.

Kenneth Noland was born in Asheville, North Carolina, on April 10, 1924. After serving in the Air Force in World War II, he used the G.I. bill to study at Black Mountain College in North Carolina from 1946 to 1949. There he worked under Ilya Bolotowsky, whose painting, a combination of geometrical design derived from the Dutch abstractionist Piet Mondrian and very personal color choices, had some influence on Noland's later work. Noland also studied sculpture and painting with Ossip Zadkine in Paris in 1948. While in Paris he had his first one-man show, in 1949.

In 1949 Noland moved to Washington, D.C., where he taught at the Institute of Contemporary Art and then at Catholic University (until 1960). He also was an instructor at the Washington Workshop of the Arts, and there, in 1953, he met the painter Morris Louis. The two became friends and often traveled together to New York. On one visit they went to Helen Frankenthaler's studio, where they saw *Mountains and Seas* (1952), which had been influenced by the paintings of Jackson Pollock. This work, with its airy and delicate washes of stained pigment, greatly influenced both painters.

After a period of experimentation, Noland's mature art emerged in 1958, when he began a series of stain paintings (using thin pigment to stain raw canvas) usually showing a "target" made up of concentric circles. Since there was little variety of shape, attention was placed solely on the vivid hues and their relationships. Moreover, the colors seemed disembodied and purely optical, owing to the stunning effect of the staining technique, which eliminated any tactile difference between painted and unpainted areas. The softness, which also resulted from staining, mitigated the potential brittleness of the geometric design. The extreme flatness of the painting created a powerful impact, and color pulses seemed to radiate from the canvas.

Noland tended to work in series, keeping his layouts constant while exploring different color possibilities. In 1962 he changed his format by suspending a series of colored chevrons from the top of the picture. These dramatic paintings, along with his concentric-circle pictures, were shown in the United States Pavilion at the Venice Biennale in 1964. The following year Noland received a retrospective at the Jewish Museum in New York City, where he had moved in 1961. With Louis and other painters in Washington, D.C., Noland became known as the Washington Color Painters.

After 1964 Noland filled the entire surface of his paintings with colored bands, giving them a forceful and compact presence. He employed either a diamond-shaped canvas to accommodate chevrons or diagonal color stripes, or simply placed horizontal bands within a long, horizontally shaped format. The latter layout permitted him the greatest range of expressive color. After 1964, Noland was included among the artists known as the post-painterly abstractionists.

During the late 1960s Noland began to make sculptures, and in the 1970s made sculptures of sheet steel. In the early 1970s, Noland introduced a grid structure into his paintings, reminiscent of Mondrian. In the late 1970s and early 1980s he began working with irregularly shaped canvases, and by the mid-1980s he returned to his earlier chevron designs but with thicker paint. A 1995 exhibition in New York, *Kenneth Noland at Leo Castelli*, covered 35 years of Noland's work, starting with two target paintings from 1960 and ending with paintings from his *Flare* and *Flow* series of the 1990s, multipanel paintings with capricious curved shapes, sometimes separated by strips of colored Plexiglas.

Further Reading

Comprehensive works on Noland include Kenworth Moffett's *Kenneth Noland* (1977); Diane Waldman's *Kenneth Noland: A Retrospective* (1977); and K. Wilkin's *Kenneth Noland* (1990). □

Emil Nolde

Emil Nolde (1867-1956) was one of the major German expressionist painters. His religious scenes, landscapes, and still lifes are distinguished by an intense coloristic richness and primitivistic angularity.

Emil Nolde, born Emil Hansen on a farm in northern Schleswig near the town of Nolde on Aug. 7, 1867, was almost totally self-taught as a painter. Until 1892 he was a wood-carver in furniture factories. He taught drawing at a museum school in St. Gall, Switzerland (1892-1898), and designed postcards with personified images of the Swiss Alps. The money earned permitted him to study painting full time in Munich. In Paris in 1899, he was impressed by Titian, Rembrandt, and Édouard Manet, but he was disappointed by the formal training he received and a year later moved to Copenhagen. His deep despondency and anguished loneliness were only partially relieved by his marriage in 1902, when the artist also changed his name to Nolde.

Up to this time Nolde's paintings had been eclectic symbolic works dependent on his Munich teachers and on Arnold Böcklin. In 1904 he adopted an impressionist manner, but the experience of Vincent Van Gogh and Edvard Munch turned him away from these soft nuances to bright pigments vehemently and freely brushed onto the canvas. Since 1898 Nolde had also been executing etchings, usually grotesques and fantasies.

In 1905 Nolde exhibited in the Berlin Secession. While he was a member of Die Brücke (The Bridge) in Dresden (1906-1907), his colors increased in brilliance and abandoned application, and he also learned woodcut and lithography techniques.

The fantastic imagery of his prints appeared in Nolde's paintings from 1909 to 1912. He expressed his mystical religious views in biblical scenes and lives of saints; the figures are heavy and primitive and have masklike faces. Masterpieces of this period are the *Last Supper* and *Pente-*

cost (both 1909) and the celebrated triptych *Life of St. Mary Aegyptiaca* (1912). Although Nolde made several attempts to donate his religious paintings, none of them was ever permanently installed in a church. Scenes from city life, seascapes, and still lifes complemented these symbolic works with subjective views of contemporary life.

When the Berlin Secession rejected his paintings in 1910, Nolde founded the New Secession and became a rallying point for the German avant-garde. He joined an expedition to New Guinea (1913-1914) to study the life and art of the aborigines, an experience which served as the source for Oriental and primitive motifs in his paintings, as in *South Sea Islander* (1914).

Renown and success came to Nolde in the 1920s, and in 1931 he was appointed to the Prussian Academy of Art. But in 1937 his art was declared "degenerate" by the Nazis, and his works were removed from German museums; in 1941 he was forbidden to paint. The small watercolors called "Unpainted Pictures," made secretly during this time, became known after World War II, when Nolde's significance was recognized in a number of retrospective exhibitions. He died in Seebüll on April 13, 1956.

Further Reading

Two brief monographs on Nolde are Werner Haftmann, *Emil Nolde* (1959), and Peter Selz, *Emil Nolde* (1963). Excellent background studies are Bernard S. Myers, *The German Expressionists* (1957), and Werner Haftmann, *Painting in the Twentieth Century* (rev. ed. 1965).

Additional Sources

Pois, Robert A., *Emil Nolde,* Washington, D.C.: University Press of America, 1982. □

Luigi Nono

The Italian composer Luigi Nono (1924-1990) was one of the most socially engaged of 20th-century composers. His Marxist political views influenced most of his avant-garde compositions.

Luigi Nono was born on January 29, 1924, in Venice, Italy, where his father was a prosperous engineer. He started studying music in 1941 at the Venice Conservatory. He received his doctorate in law in at the University of Padua while studying music with composer Gian Francesco Malipiero. In 1946 he began studies with composer-conductor Bruno Maderna and with German conductor Hermann Scherchen, who both became early proponents of his work. Nono also attended the important Summer Course for New Music in Darmstadt, Germany, where his first compositions, which were strongly influenced by composer Anton Webern, were performed.

Nono was an active member of the Italian Communist Party, and he often used Marxist texts and revolutionary writings as a basis for his compositions. In the mid-1950s,

his highly ideological scores attracted notoriety. "An artist must concern himself with his time," Nono said. "Injustice dominates in our time. As man and musician I must protest." The *Canto sospeso* (1960; "Suspended" or "Interrupted" Song) for soprano, alto, tenor, mixed chorus, and orchestra is one of his most important and characteristic works, showing his concern with the human condition, expressed in a highly sophisticated and complicated musical language. The texts are taken from farewell letters written by young captured resistance fighters awaiting execution by the Nazis. The British critic Reginald Smith Brindle described the work as "so full of tragic emotion, or compassion for the agony of mankind, [that it] is surely the most poetic product of its generation."

Nono's next composition to attract wide attention was his opera *Intolleranza,* first composed in 1960 and revised in 1970. It attacked racial segregation and nuclear weapons. The theme of the work is opposition to all totalitarian systems that restrict individuality and freedom. The protagonist is a miner who seeks the meaning of life. There are three main scenes: a mine cave-in, a political demonstration crushed by the police, and a catastrophic flood. The work employs multimedia techniques. Scenes of injustice are projected on multiple screens, along with the faces of the principal singers. Even the audience sees itself in projected images so it cannot ignore its involvement. The chorus, which plays an important role, is heard from a pre-recorded tape, the sounds emanating from loudspeakers placed throughout the auditorium. At its premiere in Venice in 1961, the audience rioted.

Intolleranza was produced in Boston in 1965. Nono was denied a visitor's visa because of his membership in Italy's Communist party, but after two Boston newspapers and a large group of musicians intervened he was allowed to enter the United States to conduct his work.

Nono's *A floresta e joven e chea de vida* (1967; *The Forest Is Young and Full of Life*) was another multimedia protest work, against United States involvement in Vietnam. It consists of taped sounds and highly amplified live sounds produced by a singer, a clarinetist, reciters, and six percussionists who bang on bronze sheets. The work is characterized by an enormous volume of sound, described as depicting mass panic after the collapse of a metallic bomb shelter. It was probably more successful as political propaganda than as music.

Nono's *Sul Ponte del Hiroshima* (1962) was written in opposition to the atomic bomb. His *Y Entonces Comprendió* (1970) included a tape recording of Cuban premiere Fidel Castro reading letters of Marxist guerilla fighter Che Guevara. His second opera, *Al Gran Sole Carico d'Amore*, written in 1975, focuses on the revolutionary Paris Commune of 1871. Nono also wrote several works inspired by his visits to Nazi concentration camps; a third opera, *Prometeo;* and a work for violin, tape and electronics, *La Nostalgica-Futura.*

Nono's early works were influenced by composer Arnold Schoenberg. In 1955, Nono married Schoenberg's daughter Nuria. They had two daughters, Silvia and Serena. Nono died of a liver ailment on May 6, 1990.

Further Reading

Nono's work is discussed in Paul Henry Lang and Nathan Broder, eds., *Contemporary Music in Europe: A Comprehensive Survey* (1966); and Eric Salzman, *Twentieth-Century Music: An Introduction* (1967); Nono is also discussed in Brian Morton and Pamela Collins, editors, *Contemporary Composers* (1992); and in Stanley Sadie, editor, *New Grove Dictionary of Opera* (1992). □

Baron Nils Adolf Erik Nordenskjöld

The Finnish-Swedish polar explorer and mineralogist Baron Nils Adolf Erik Nordenskjöld (1832-1901) was the first to make a ship voyage from Scandinavia to Alaska through the Northeast Passage.

Adolf Erik Nordenskjöld was born on Nov. 18, 1832, in Helsinki, the third of seven children of Nils Gustaf Nordenskjöld, chief of the Finnish mining department and a member of an old Swedish family that had settled in Finland. The boy took an early interest in natural history and mineralogy. He specialized in mineralogy and geology and collected minerals in parts of Finland and Russia while attending the University of Helsinki, where he obtained his degree in 1855. During his studies at the uni-

versity, Nordenskjöld had developed certain Swedish and Western sympathies which implied criticism of Russian political control in Finland. As a result, he incurred the displeasure of the authorities, and in 1856 he lost his mining office position and was forced to leave the country. He finally settled in Sweden in 1858, where he took employment at the National Museum of Natural History in Stockholm.

Nordenskjöld's first polar experience was in 1858 with the Swedish geologist Otto Torell to Spitsbergen. He followed this with other Spitsbergen trips: in 1861 with Torell, and as leader in 1864, 1868, and 1872-1873. Through these expeditions he made fundamental contributions to the knowledge of geography of the area. On the 1868 expedition, in the iron steamer *Sofia,* he went farther north (82°42′N) in the Eastern Hemisphere than anyone ever had. Two years later, Nordenskjöld led an expedition to the west-central coast of Greenland to collect minerals and fossils and study the inland ice. The visit stimulated his interest in exploring the interior of Greenland, where he believed there might be an ice-free forested area. Such an exploration took place in 1883, when two of Nordenskjöld's Lapp companions reached the central part of the ice cap, but they did not find an ice-free area.

Then Nordenskjöld turned his attentions to what was to become his major polar achievement—the making of the Northeast Passage. In the years before that trip, he had made two preliminary voyages, pioneering the use of ships on the northern sea route for trade with Russia. In 1875-1876 he accomplished passage of the Kara Sea to the mouth of the Yenisei River in Siberia, and this was repeated in 1876-

1877. On June 22, 1878, Nordenskjöld sailed from Karlskrona, Sweden, on the steam vessel Vega, accompanied on part of its voyage by three other ships. The mouth of the Yenisei was reached on August 6, Cape Chelyuskin on August 19, and the Lena River on August 27. The ship was frozen into the sea on September 27 near Kolyuchin Bay, about 100 miles from the Bering Strait, and did not make the passage until July 1879. Before returning to Sweden via Japan, the Suez Canal, and the Mediterranean, Nordenskjöld visited parts of Alaska. He was made a baron by King Oscar on his return to Stockholm in 1880. In 1893 he was elected to the Swedish Academy.

Nordenskjöld's later years were spent studying mineralogy and in gathering together old hand-drawn maps and charts. He had these published in two volumes entitled *Periplus* (trans. 1897). He died at Dalbijo on Aug. 12, 1901, a much-respected scientist and explorer.

Further Reading

A biography of Nordenskjöld in English is in Alexander Leslie, *The Arctic Voyages of Adolf Eric Nordenskiold, 1858-1879* (1879), and in Sten Lindroth, ed., *Swedish Men of Science, 1650-1950* (1952).

Additional Sources

Hèakli, Esko, *A.E. Nordenskjöld, a scientist and his library,* Helsinki: Helsinki University Library, 1980. □

Nils Otto Gustaf Nordenskold

The Swedish polar explorer and geologist Nils Otto Gustaf Nordenskold (1869-1928) is best known as the leader of the Swedish South Polar Expedition of 1901-1903.

On Dec. 6, 1869, Otto Nordenskold was born in Småland. He entered the University of Uppsala in 1886, obtaining a doctor's degree in 1894. Between 1895 and 1897 he began his polar and subpolar travels on an expedition to the Tierra del Fuego and other Magellanic lands. In 1898 he visited the Alaskan Yukon and followed this in 1900 with a summer on Georg Karl Amdrup's expedition to eastern Greenland.

At the turn of the century, mainly through Nordenskold's initiative and with private funds, several nations, including Sweden, sent out Antarctic expeditions. One of the ships sent by the Swedes was the *Antarctic,* a sailing vessel with steam power that was captained by Carl Anton Larsen. Nordenskold's party, which left Sweden on Oct. 16, 1901, was landed by the *Antarctic* in February 1902 at Snowhill Island at 64°22'S, just off the east coast of the Antarctic Peninsula. In September, Nordenskold led a dog-sledge trip to survey parts of the peninsula and complete the mapping of that coastline. Meanwhile, the *Antarc-*

tic had been unable to reach Snowhill because of thick sea ice and landed a party of three in late December at Hope Bay to make the 50-mile trip south by sledge to tell Nordenskold about the ship's problem. In January 1903 the *Antarctic* was caught by sea ice and a month later was crushed and sank. The crew managed to reach Paulet Island some 75 miles north of Snowhill in small boats. In October the three men from Hope Bay reached Snowhill Island. Then, on November 8, Capt. Larsen and some of his men reached Snowhill and reunited the men. The Argentine relief ship *Uruguay* provided for their return to Sweden. The narratives of these South Polar expeditions were published by Nordenskold in *"Antarctic" Tua ar bland Sydpolens isar* (2 vols., 1904-1905).

Nordenskold continued his polar expeditions and went to Greenland in 1906 and 1909. He was planning another Antarctic expedition with the British in 1914, but the war stopped it. His South American interest brought a trip to Chile and Peru in 1920-1921, where Nordenskold explored the Andes. He was the author of many general works on polar matters, some of which were translated into English, including *The Geography of Polar Regions* (1928). Nordenskold died on June 2, 1928, in Göteborg, where he had been professor of geography at the university since 1905.

Further Reading

There is no biography of Nordenskold in English. Information on him appears in William H. Hobbs, *Explorers of the Antarctic*

(1941); E. W. Hunter Christie, *The Antarctic Problem* (1951); and Walker Chapman, *The Loneliest Continent* (1964). □

3d Duke of Norfolk

The English soldier and councilor Thomas Howard, 3d Duke of Norfolk (1473-1554), was a prominent figure in the government under Henry VIII. He led the conservative faction and opposed both Wolsey and Cromwell.

Thomas Howard was born at a time when the Howard family was rising to prominence through his grandfather's attachment to the Yorkist kings. Sir John Howard, 1st Duke of Norfolk, was a favorite of Richard III; he was killed in the battle of Bosworth in 1485. On the accession of Henry VII, John Howard's son Thomas was attainted and imprisoned, but in 1489 he was released and restored to the nobility as Earl of Surrey. After he led the English forces in a crushing defeat of the Scots at Flodden in 1513, he was created 2d Duke of Norfolk, and his eldest son, Thomas, became Earl of Surrey.

This younger Thomas Howard had been betrothed in 1484 to Anne, a daughter of Edward IV. After 1485 Anne became an attendant to her older sister, Elizabeth of York, Henry VII's queen; in 1495 Anne and Thomas Howard were married in Westminster Abbey. She died in 1513, and Thomas then married Elizabeth, daughter of Edward Stafford, Duke of Buckingham, by whom he had two sons (Henry, later Earl of Surrey, the poet; and Thomas, later Viscount Howard of Bindon) and a daughter who married Henry VIII's illegitimate son Henry Fitzroy.

Thomas Howard began his public career as a soldier, first serving under his father at Flodden and then charged with bringing order to Ireland and fighting the French. At his father's death in 1524 he became 3d Duke of Norfolk. Throughout this decade he opposed the policies of Cardinal Thomas Wolsey. When Wolsey failed to secure the annulment of Henry VIII's marriage to Catherine of Aragon, Norfolk helped turn the King against him; and when Wolsey died in 1530, Norfolk hoped to succeed him as chief adviser. He was important for a time but lacked the genius required to solve the dilemma of Henry's divorce, and he was soon displaced by Thomas Cromwell.

Although always a conservative in religion, Norfolk acquiesced in the King's proceedings against the Pope because they made possible Henry's marriage to Anne Boleyn, Norfolk's niece. He gained further wealth from the dissolution of the monasteries and acted ruthlessly in suppressing the Pilgrimage of Grace (1536). But in 1539 he secured the enactment by Parliament of the reactionary Six Articles of Religion, and in 1540 he had the pleasure of arresting Cromwell and seeing him executed as an upstart and a heretic.

When Henry tired of Anne Boleyn, Norfolk presided at her trial and staged her execution. Later, in 1540, he arranged the King's marriage to another niece, Catherine Ho-

ward. For a time Norfolk wielded great influence in the government; but when Catherine was accused of infidelity and executed, Norfolk lost favor, and he retired from court to the battlefields in France and Scotland.

During the last years of his life Henry VIII relied chiefly upon Thomas Seymour, Earl of Hertford and uncle of the heir apparent, Prince Edward. Hertford, in an effort to remove his rivals, accused Norfolk's son, the Earl of Surrey, of illegally using the royal arms and committing other treasonable deeds. Both Surrey and Norfolk were attainted and condemned to death; Surrey was beheaded, and Norfolk was to have been executed on Jan. 28, 1547. But the King died during the preceding night, and Norfolk was spared, the new councilors hesitating to begin their rule with such a spectacle.

Norfolk remained a prisoner in the Tower during the reign of Edward VI. On the accession of Mary I in 1553, he was freed and restored to his dukedom. He died on Aug. 25, 1554.

Further Reading

There is no full-length biography of Norfolk. Information is in John D. Mackie, *The Earlier Tudors* (1952); Geoffrey Rudolph Elton, *England under the Tudors* (1955); and Melvin J. Tucker, *The Life of Thomas Howard, Earl of Surrey, Second Duke of Norfolk* (1964). □

Manuel A. Noriega

First a friend, then an enemy of the United States, Manuel A. Noriega (born 1934), the strongman of Panama, was finally deposed by a U.S. military invasion, captured, and brought to Miami for trial in 1989.

Manuel Antonio Noriega was born the son of an accountant and his maid in a poor barrio of Panama City in 1934. At the age of five he was given up for adoption to a schoolteacher. He attended the National Institute, a well-regarded high school, with the intention of becoming a doctor, but a lack of financial resources prevented fulfillment of this career choice. Instead, Noriega accepted a scholarship to attend the Peruvian Military Academy. He graduated in 1962 with a degree in engineering. Returning to Panama, he was commissioned a sublieutenant in the National Guard and assigned to a unit at Colon, the city lying near the Caribbean terminus of the Panama Canal.

Colonel Omar Torrijos liked Noriega and obtained for him the command of Chiriqui, the country's westernmost province. In October 1968, military conspirators overturned the civilian government of Arnulfo Arias (twice before turned out by coups). Noriega's troops seized radio and telephone stations in David, the provincial capital, and thus severed communications with the capital. Torrijos emerged from the coup as the strongman. In December 1969, when

Torrijos was out of the country, a trio of rebellious officers tried to seize power, but Torrijos flew into David. The airport had no facilities for night landing, but Noriega lined up motorcars alongside the runway and Torrijos made it safely down. With Noriega's troops at his service, Torrijos retook the capital.

From that moment, Noriega's career blossomed. In 1971 he became useful to U.S. intelligence and, at the behest of the Nixon administration, went to Havana to obtain the release of crewmen of two American freighters seized by Fidel Castro's government. He was also already involved in narcotics trafficking. (Panama's National Guard had been implicated in the heroin trade from the late 1940s.) American officials learned that Noriega was the Panama "connection," and a high-ranking drug enforcement officer recommended that the president order his assassination, but Nixon demurred. Noriega was useful to U.S. counterintelligence. As head of G-2, Panama's military intelligence command, Noriega was the second most powerful man in Panama. In 1975 G-2 agents rounded up businessmen critical of Torrijos' dictatorial populist style, confiscated their property, and sent them into exile in Ecuador. Torrijos once said of him, "This is my gangster."

Torrijos died in 1981 in a mysterious plane crash. In the ensuing two-year contest for power between civilian politicians and ambitious military officers, Noriega emerged triumphant. In late 1983, following his promotion to general and commander of the National Guard, the guard was combined with the navy and air force into the Panama Defense Forces (which also included the national police).

The following year Noriega's choice for president, Nicolás Ardito Barletta, won a narrow victory over Arnulfo Arias. But there was widespread fraud in the election. Barletta tried manfully to grapple with the country's growing economic woes, he failed, and Noriega forced him out. (Panama had received no windfall from the canal treaties Torrijos had negotiated with President Jimmy Carter.)

The reason had less to do with Barletta's economic policies than his alleged threat to investigate the brutal slaying of Hugo Spadafora, who had publicly accused Noriega of being a drug trafficker. G-2 agents had taken him from a bus near the Costa Rican border. In September 1985 searchers found his tortured, decapitated body stuffed in a U.S. mailbag on the Costa Rican side of the border. In June 1986 journalist Seymour Hersh reported that U.S. Defense Intelligence agents had evidence implicating Noriega in Spadafora's death and, just as disturbing, that in the mid-1970s Noriega had obtained National Security Agency classified material from a U.S. Army sergeant and had given it to the Cubans. In addition, Hersh wrote, Noriega had used his position to facilitate sale of restricted U.S. technology to Eastern European governments. In the process, he had earned $3 million.

Noriega denounced these and other allegations as a conspiracy of right-wing U.S. politicians looking for a way to undo the Panama Canal treaties before the canal became Panamanian property on December 31, 1999. It was becoming evident that Noriega had outfoxed his U.S. benefactors. During the Reagan administration's covert war against the government of Nicaragua, Noriega helped to supply arms to the Nicaraguan resistance called the Contras (Congress prohibited any expenditures to bring down the Nicaraguan government). At the same time, he received arms from Cuba and sold them to Salvadoran leftist guerrillas and supplied Nicaraguan leaders with intelligence reports. Although Noriega was a gun-runner, money-launderer, drug trafficker, and double agent, he was still useful to the U.S. government.

The furor caused by the Hersh articles diminished but revived in June 1987 when Noriega's former chief of staff, Colonel Roberto Diaz Herrera (forced into retirement), stated that Noriega had fixed the 1984 election and ordered Spadafora's killing. He also implicated Noriega in the death of Torrijos. Middle-class Panamanians organized street demonstrations, demanding his ouster. Noriega responded by declaring a national emergency. He suspended constitutional rights, closed newspapers and radio stations, and drove his political enemies into exile. A special riot squad—nicknamed "the Dobermans"—laid siege to the home of Diaz Herrera, who was captured and compelled to recant. Church leaders, businessmen, and students organized into the National Civil Crusade, dressed in white, and went into the streets banging pots and pans. The riot squads dispersed them. By now Americans were outraged, and in June 1987 the U.S. Senate called for Noriega's removal. Noriega retaliated by removing police protection from the U.S. embassy. A pro-Noriega mob attacked the building and caused $100,000 in damages.

From that day, the administration of President Ronald Reagan began looking for a way to bring Noriega down. U.S. economic aid and military assistance ended. Noriega lamented that his erstwhile friends in Washington were deserting him. Panamanian bankers began withdrawing their support—Torrijos had transformed the country into an international banking center—and Noriega rapidly lost favor everywhere save for the Panama Defense Forces. The American strategy was to induce discontented officers in the PDF to overturn him. In this way the United States would rid itself of Noriega but not be saddled with a leftist successor to him.

Secret negotiations between U.S. officials and Noriega's representatives called for him to resign and leave the country before the 1988 U.S. presidential election, thus saving George Bush, who as director of the Central Intelligence Agency had dealt with Noriega, from embarrassing revelations in the campaign. There were dark rumors that Noriega was prepared to name high U.S. officials also involved in money-laundering and drug smuggling. As matters turned out, the Justice Department filed indictments against Noriega in federal court in early 1988, which was intended as a warning. Assistant Secretary of State Eliot Abrams went to Panama in a futile effort to get President Eric Del Valle to fire Noriega. Instead, Noriega forced out Del Valle and named a puppet president, Manuel Solis Palma.

Democratic nominee Michael Dukakis tried to make an issue of the "Noriega connection" in the 1988 U.S. presidential campaign, but Bush suffered no apparent damage. After assuming office, President Bush increased pressure. Economic sanctions severely hurt Noriega but did not bring him down. In May 1989 Noriega declined to run in the election but chose yet another puppet candidate, Carlos Duque. The opposition Panameñista Party nominated Guillermo Endara. Sensing opportunity, the Bush administration provided Endara with $10 million. Former President Jimmy Carter and other foreign representatives went to Panama to monitor the election. But as soon as Noriega realized that Duque was losing, he ordered the PDF to seize ballot boxes. When the opposition took to the streets in protest, "dignity battalions" of Noriega goons assaulted them. Endara and a vice-presidential candidate, Guillermo Ford, were severely beaten.

Noriega declared the election void, installed another puppet as provisional president, and, in October 1989, survived a coup hatched among discontented PDF officers and openly supported by U.S. forces. In the aftermath, Noriega was vengeful and boastful; President Bush, humiliated. In this despair over the nation's declining international image and concern that Noriega was in a position to name a crony as canal administrator, Bush acted. Using as pretext Noriega's declaration that U.S. actions had created a virtual state of war, fear that Noriega would jeopardize the security of the canal (which was untrue), and the firing on U.S. soldiers passing the PDF headquarters, the United States launched a full-scale attack (Operation Just Cause) with 24,000 troops on December 20, 1989.

Fighting continued for four days, at times heavy, with U.S. casualties running into the hundreds and Panamanian into the thousands. Noriega evaded capture for a few days but ultimately took refuge in the Papal Nunciature. Under pressure from Vatican officials, Noriega surrendered to the Vatican Embassy in Panama City on January 3, 1990. In a deal worked out with the U.S.-created government headed by Guillermo Endara, U.S. authorities brought Noriega to Miami for trial. However, legal obstacles and technicalities delayed the trial into the early 1990s. He was convicted of cocaine trafficking, racketeering and money laundering. He was sentenced to 40 years in a Miami prison, and was ordered to pay $ 44 million to the Panamanian government. The trial was not without controversy, however. In late 1995 charges of bribery were brought about. The Drug Enforcement Administration (DEA) was told that the Cali drug cartel had paid a witness, Ricardo Bilonik, to testify about Noriega's ties to the Medellin cartel, Cali's rival. Federal prosecutors have determined that the bribery charges are not enough to justify a new trial.

Further Reading

For more on Manuel Noriega consult Steven Ropp, *Panamanian Politics: From Guarded Nation to National Guard* (1982); Walter LaFeber, *The Panama Canal* (1978); David Farnsworth and James W. McKenney, *U.S.-Panamanian Relations, 1903-1978* (1983); William C. Jorden, *Panama Odyssey: From Colony to Partner* (1983); Frederick Kempe, *Divorcing the Dictator: America's Bungled Affair with Noriega* (1990); and, especially, John Dinges, *Our Man in Panama: How General Noriega Used the United States—and Made Millions in Drugs and Arms* (1990). □

Jessye Norman

The repertoire of American-born singer Jessye Norman (born 1945) encompassed an uncommonly wide range, from Monteverdi to Boulez. Her rich soprano voice, however, was sometimes plagued by problems of voice production.

Jessye Norman was born on September 15, 1945, in Augusta, Georgia. Her father, an insurance broker, and her mother, a schoolteacher, encouraged her musically, so she was singing in church choirs from the age of four. Apart from her great love of singing, her childhood was by all accounts typical. Her first step toward a singing career, taken at the suggestion of her high school chorus teacher, was to enter the Marion Anderson vocal competition in Philadelphia at age 16. Though she did not win the competition, as a result of her singing she did gain a full scholarship to Howard University in Washington, D.C. There she studied voice with Carolyn Grant. After graduating from Howard she continued her singing studies with Alice Duschak at Peabody Conservatory in Baltimore and with Pierre Bernac and Elizabeth Mannion at the University of Michigan in Ann Arbor.

Norman fell in love with opera the first time she heard a Metropolitan Opera radio broadcast. "I was nine and didn't know what was going on, but I just loved it" she told Charles Michner of *Vanity Fair* magazine. "After that I listened religiously."

To finance her graduate studies, Norman entered the 1968 International Music Competition of the German Broadcasting Corporation in Munich and took first prize. She learned of her honor while on a U.S. State Department musical tour of the Caribbean and Latin America. This prestigious award accorded her immediate wide recognition and engagements throughout Germany leading to a December 1969 debut with the venerable and prestigious Deutsche Oper in Berlin as Elizabeth in Wagner's *Tannhäuser*. She signed a three-year contract shortly thereafter, and enjoyed rapid success in Europe.

From her student days Norman had been selective about her repertoire, heeding her own instincts and interests more than the advice of her teachers or requests of her management. This tendency put her at odds with the Deutsche Opera and compelled her to seek out musical works on her own that she felt were more suitable to her vocal skills. Her search took her to Italy where, in the spring of 1970, she sang in a lesser-known Handel oratorio, *Deborah,* at the Teatro Communale in Florence. In April of 1972 she made her debut at Milan's famous opera house, La Scala, in the title role of Verdi's *Aida*. Her first well-publicized American performance took place that summer in a concert performance of the same role at the Hollywood Bowl. Later in 1972 she further established herself in the United States with an all-Wagner concert at the Tanglewood Festival in Lennox, Massachusetts, and a recital

tour of the country. That September she made her London debut at the Royal Opera House, Covent Garden, as Cassandra in Berlioz's *Les Troyens.*

During the years 1973-1975 she performed throughout the Western world—in Spain, Holland, Germany, Scotland, Italy, England, France, and Argentina, as well as the United States, often performing works outside the standard repertoire, including Franck's oratorio *Les Béatitudes* and Schoenberg's song cycle, *Die Gurrelieder.*

In 1975 Norman moved to London and had no staged opera appearances for the next five years. While she gave as the reason for her withdrawal the need to fully develop her voice, others felt that this was a period of concern for her weight and thus her stage image. She told John Gruen of the *New York Times,* "As for my voice, it cannot be categorized—and I like it that way, because I sing things that would be considered in the dramatic, mezzo or spinto range. I like so many different kinds of music that I've never allowed myself the limitations of one particular range." She remained internationally active as a recitalist and soloist in works such as Mendelssohn's *Elijah.*

In October of 1980 Norman returned to the operatic stage in the title role of Richard Strauss's *Ariadne auf Naxos* at the Hamburger Staatsoper in Hamburg, Germany. In 1982 she appeared in her American stage debut with the Philadelphia Opera as Dido in Purcell's *Dido and Aneas* and as Jocasta in Stravinsky's *Oedipus Rex*. Her belated debut at the Metropolitan Opera took place in September of 1983, the opening night of its 100th anniversary season, again as Cassandra. She was invited to sing at the January 21, 1985, inauguration of President Reagan, an invitation which she debated as an African American, as a Democrat, and as a nuclear disarmament activist. But she did accept and sang the folk song "Simple Gifts."

Although she was concerned about her stage image, Norman often managed to convert her size to a positive advantage by choosing physically more static roles that called for stately and dignified bearing.

Among the numerous honors bestowed upon Norman were the following: *Musical America's* musician of the year, 1982; honorary doctorates from Howard University (1982), Boston Conservatory (1984), and University of the South (1984); and Commandeur de l'Ordre des Arts et des Lettres from the French government, 1984. She also received awards for her recordings of R. Strauss, *Four Last Songs;* R. Schumann, *Frauenlieben und Leben;* Schoenberg, *Die Gurrelieder;* and Negro spirituals.

New York Times writer Allen Hughes wrote that Norman "has one of the most opulent voices before the public today, and, as discriminating listeners are aware, her performances are backed by extraordinary preparation, both musical and otherwise." Her performances sparked endless ovations from audiences all over the world. In 1985 it was reported that a Tokyo audience applauded for 47 minutes, and the next year an audience in Salzburg Austria applauded for 55 minutes. "Ms Norman's voice seems to draw from a vast ocean of sound. . . . Yet . . . what made the soprano's performance particularly remarkable was the effortlessness with which she could hover over long, soft notes. . . . And there is also the quality of sound that she produces: even the loudest passages are cushioned by a velvety seductive timbre," wrote Michael Kimmelman.

Norman's work in the 1990s included singing at the opening of the Metropolitan Opera's production of *Ariadne auf Naxos* in 1993, taking part at a gala for the New York Philharmonic in 1995, and appearing at concerts throughout the world.

Norman once described the reverent approach that she took to her work in the *New York Times:* "To galvanize myself into a performance, I must be left totally alone. I must have solitude in order to concentrate—which I consider a form of prayer. I work very much from the text. The words must be understood, felt and communicated. . .If you look carefully at the words and absorb them you are halfway home already. The rest is honesty—honesty of feeling, honesty of involvement. If a performer is truly committed, then the audience will respond accordingly. Of course, love is the thing that propels us all. It's what carries us along—that's the fuel!"

In March 1997, Jessye Norman was honored by New York's Associated Black Charities at the 11th Annual Black History Makers Awards Dinner for her contributions to the arts and to African American culture.

Further Reading

Little biographical material is available on Jessye Norman in readily accessible publications. Several articles appeared in *Opera News* between 1980 and 1985. Of these, the issue of December 24, 1983, contains a good review by R. Jacobson of her New York debut. The February 18, 1984, issue includes a revealing interview by Martin Mayer; her New York debut was also covered in the *New York Times* by John Gruen, September 25, 1983; *Vanity Fair* did an in-depth study of her in February 1989. She is listed in the *International Encyclopedia of Music and Musicians* (1975); and in the 1988 *The New Penguin Guide to Compact Discs and Casettes.* She was also profiled in the documentary film *Jessye Norman, Singer: Portrait of an Extraordinary Career* Malachite Productions, 1991. □

Benjamin Franklin Norris Jr.

The best work of Benjamin Franklin Norris, Jr. (1870-1902), American novelist and critic, achieves a raw force that has won him an important place in the history of American fiction.

Frank Norris was born in Chicago on Mar. 5, 1870, the son of a wealthy jeweler. When Frank was 14, the family moved into a mansion in San Francisco. This house would be the model for the mansion in Norris's novel *The Pit* (1903), which also presents a portrait of his mother in the character of Laura.

Education and Early Writings

After a short time in high school, Norris left to study at the San Francisco Art Association. His family, even his no-nonsense father, encouraged him; in fact, they moved to London and then to Paris in 1887 so that he could study painting. Norris enjoyed painting, but after 2 years he returned to San Francisco and in 1890 entered the University of California. He remained for 4 years but did not take a degree. Meanwhile, his mother published his first book: *Yvernelle: A Tale of Feudal France* (1892), a verse romance.

In 1894 Norris's parents were divorced. His father continued to provide for the family financially. Frank, his mother, and his brother, Charles, soon traveled east, and Frank enrolled at Harvard in the creative writing class of Lewis Gates. Later, in a critical essay, Norris stated a conviction he had acquired from Gates: "The construction of a novel is as much of an exact science as the construction of a temple or a sonnet." He also learned that it is best for the novelist "to treat but one thing in one chapter, to keep to one time and one place as much as is possible, and to hold to but one theme from cover to cover." Literary critics are divided in assessing how closely Norris actually followed these precepts in his best novels, but another of Gates's lessons—the insistence that fiction plainly state the "facts of daily life"—is unquestionably reflected in Norris's finest work. Under Gates, Norris began work on *McTeague* and *Vandover and the Brute,* two novels many critics consider his most successful.

Journalist and Critic

After a year at Harvard, Norris traveled to Africa to gather material for fiction and to write newspaper stories for the *San Francisco Chronicle.* However, victimized by a tropical fever and in trouble with the Boer authorities in southern Africa, he returned to San Francisco. There, on the magazine staff of the *Wave* (1896-1898), he contributed over 200 pieces: articles on football; reviews of books, plays, and stories; and a serialized novel. His book reviews reveal his deep appreciation of the pioneering naturalist in French fiction, Émile Zola, whose novels gave Norris "an impression of immensity, of vast, illimitable force, of a breadth of view and an enormity of imagination almost too great to be realized." Though Norris also praised America's leading realist writer, William Dean Howells, he clearly preferred Zola's scope and power and sought the same in his own work.

Meanwhile, Norris led a bohemian life among San Francisco artists and writers. In 1896 he finished *McTeague.* He soon met Jeanette Black, then 17; their courtship became the subject of *Blix,* the lightest, most romantic, and trivial of Norris's novels, but not the worst. The self-portrait contained in the chief character, Conde Rivers, is probably very revealing.

In 1898 Norris moved to New York City. He started working for *McClure's Magazine* but soon went off to cover the Spanish-American War. This venture was a fiasco, and his reports were not published. He succeeded in meeting two important literary men—Richard Harding Davis and Stephen Crane—but the former, whom he had long admired, proved unapproachable thereafter, and the latter's personal conduct repelled Norris. Finally, Norris contracted malaria and returned to San Francisco.

His Novels

The early novels were *McTeague* and *Vandover and the Brute.* (Norris never completed *Vandover;* it was prepared for posthumous publication in 1914 by his brother, Charles, himself a novelist.) *Vandover* concerns a San Francisco artist who lets the brute in his nature dominate his actions, slipping steadily from ease to squalor. The novel is confused, but *Moran of the Lady Letty,* the story Norris serialized in the *Wave* in 1898, is even more so. Though this story was a piece of unredeemable brutality, it had won Norris the job at *McClure's.* Meanwhile, a friend introduced Norris to the influential William Dean Howells, who read *McTeague* and encouraged Norris to continue seeking a publisher. The novel finally appeared in 1899.

McTeague is flawed by Norris's inability to write convincing dialogue, but another of Norris's weaknesses became a positive strength in this novel. Norris could not create characters who behave rationally; his people are never fully developed human beings. But this is the philosophic point in *McTeague,* which concerns characters who are incapable of reasonable behavior. In physical strength McTeague is almost superhuman, but in self-understanding and self-control he is less than half a man. McTeague's wife is equally shallow, and her only emotion is greed. Both characters are impelled toward catastrophe by hidden forces; they are objects, not actors, in the human drama. Yet their story is dramatic and vivid: in 1924 Erich von Stroheim demonstrated how much drama the story contains when he adapted it into his silent-screen classic *Greed.*

Blix was published just after *McTeague.* Norris then returned to California to gather new material and to marry Jeanette Black in 1900. The couple settled in New York City, where Norris continued working on his fiction and served as a reader for Doubleday, Page, and Company. In the latter capacity he recommended the publication of *Sister Carrie,* a novel by an unknown writer, Theodore Dreiser which, today, is considered by some to be an American classic. Doubleday contracted to publish it but later attempted to break the contract, and, failing in that, published the book without trying to sell it. Dreiser realized $68.40 from the transaction.

The hero of Norris's *The Octopus* (1901) is a poet who identifies himself with the struggling wheat farmers of California against the octopus-tentacled Southern Pacific Railroad. His efforts to help the farmers go as far as bombing a railroad building, but nothing he or anyone else does can correct the injustice and brutality of the situation. The poet finally concludes that economic laws which men cannot alter determine the conditions under which they must live. Although the novel rises to power at moments, it is a strident, grandiose work, simplistic in its interpretation of human motivations. Norris planned it as the first of a trilogy called "The Epic of the Wheat"; the second novel takes its name, *The Pit,* from the Chicago grain exchange. It focuses on a self-made capitalist, his wife, and an artistic dilettante.

The scale of the action is smaller than in *The Octopus,* but the characters are much more convincing, probably because Norris was now writing of the economic class in which he had grown up. *The Octopus* could be called a bad major novel, *The Pit* a good minor one.

In 1902, shortly after the birth of their only child, a daughter, the Norrises moved to San Francisco. They planned a world cruise during which Norris would gather material for the third volume of his trilogy. However, Norris neglected an abdominal pain that proved to be appendicitis, and he died on Oct. 25, 1902. *The Pit,* serialized in the *Saturday Evening Post,* appeared as a book in 1903, the same year that saw the publication of *A Deal in Wheat and Other Stories* and a collection of his critical essays, *The Responsibilities of a Novelist.*

Further Reading

A reliable biography of Norris is Franklin Walker, *Frank Norris* (1932). Warren French, *Frank Norris* (1962), provides a biographical sketch and an analysis of his works. Donald Pizer, *The Novels of Frank Norris* (1966), is thorough and scholarly, and his edition of *The Literary Criticism of Frank Norris* (1964) presents valuable material not available elsewhere. There are excellent sections on Norris in Warner Berthoff, *The Ferment of Realism* (1965), and Larzer Ziff, *The American 1890s* (1966).

Additional Sources

Norris, Charles Gilman, *Frank Norris, 1870-1902: an intimate sketch of the man who was universally acclaimed the greatest American writer of his generation,* Philadelphia: R. West, 1977. □

George William Norris

George William Norris (1861-1944), U.S. congressman and senator, authored the 20th Amendment to the Constitution and sponsored numerous pieces of Progressive legislation.

George W. Norris was born on July 11, 1861, in Sandusky County, Ohio. He attended Northern Indiana Normal School (now Valparaiso University), where he received his bachelor of arts and law degrees. Returning to the family farm in 1883, he clerked in a local law office and taught school. He settled in Nebraska and in 1899 opened a law office in McCook, which remained his home until his death.

In 1892 Norris was elected Furnas County prosecutor and 3 years later, district judge. He was elected to the U.S. House of Representatives in 1902, where he aligned himself with the Progressive wing of the Republican party. His most noteworthy achievement was his leadership of the 1910 rules fight which clipped the autocratic powers of the reactionary Speaker, Joseph G. Cannon.

In 1913 Norris was elected to the Senate. He voted against most of the Woodrow Wilson administration's domestic legislative program on the grounds that it was not sufficiently Progressive, and he bitterly opposed Wilson's foreign policy, even voting against the declaration of war against Germany. He was against American membership in the League of Nations and later opposed United States adherence to the World Court.

In the 1920s Norris was a leading supporter of farm relief legislation. He successfully blocked the sale to private interests of the hydroelectric facilities at Muscle Shoals, Ala., and in 1928 and 1931 he pushed through Congress legislation providing for government operation of the facilities. Although presidents Calvin Coolidge and Herbert Hoover vetoed the bills, Norris saw his dream realized with the creation of the Tennessee Valley Authority under the New Deal.

Norris was the cosponsor of the Norris-LaGuardia Act (1932), which outlawed labor contracts that made union membership a condition of employment and drastically limited the use of injunctions in labor disputes; and the Norris-Rayburn Act (1936), which made the Rural Electrification Administration permanent. He was the father of the 20th Amendment to the Constitution (which eliminated the "lame-duck" Congress and changed the date for the president's inauguration) and was instrumental in Nebraska's adoption (1934) of a unique non-partisan, unicameral legislature.

Unlike most Progressives, Norris was a loyal supporter of the New Deal. Alarmed by the Nazi threat, he favored limited American intervention in Europe and backed Frank-

lin Roosevelt's third-term bid in 1940. In 1936 he had formally renounced the Republican label and won reelection, with Roosevelt's endorsement, as an independent. In 1942 Norris again ran as an independent but was defeated. He died in McCook on Sept. 2, 1944.

Further Reading

Norris's autobiography is *Fighting Liberal* (1945). Richard Lowitt's *George W. Norris: The Making of a Progressive, 1861-1912* (1963) and *George W. Norris: The Persistence of a Progressive, 1913-1933* (1971) are two volumes of a projected three-volume biography. Norman L. Zucker, *George W. Norris: Gentle Knight of American Democracy* (1966), analyzes Norris's political thought.

Additional Sources

Lief, Alfred, *Democracy's Norris: the biography of a lonely crusade,* New York: Octagon Books, 1977, 1939.

Lowitt, Richard, *George W. Norris: the triumph of a progressive, 1933-1944,* Urbana: University of Illinois Press, 1978.

Norris, George W. (George William), *Fighting liberal: the autobiography of George W. Norris* , Lincoln: University of Nebraska Press, 1992. □

Frederick North

The administration of the English statesman Frederick North, 2d Earl of Guildford and 8th Baron North (1732-1792), is associated with Britain's loss of the American colonies.

Frederick North was born in London on April 13, 1732. He was educated at Eton and Oxford and after leaving the university traveled for 3 years in Europe. In 1756 he married Anne Speke, the daughter of a Somerset squire, by whom he had seven children.

At the first general election (1754) after he came of age, North entered Parliament. Diffidence rather than ambition marked his early career. Between 1759 and 1767 he occupied a series of state offices without making himself particularly conspicuous. In 1768 he became leader of the Commons and quickly won the respect of the House.

Horace Walpole described North about this time: "Nothing could be more coarse or clumsy or ungracious than his outside. Two large prominent eyes that rolled about to no purpose . . . a wide mouth, thick lips, and inflated visage, gave him the air of a blind trumpeter. A deep, untunable voice, which . . . he enforced with unnecessary pomp, a total neglect of his person, and ignorance of every civil attention, disgusted all who judge by appearance." Though not a great orator, North was intelligent and quick-witted, prompt in reply, and unruffled by criticism. "The bitter sarcasms and severe accusations leveled at him seemed to sink into him like a cannon ball into a wool sack," wrote one commentator.

Perhaps it was these qualities that persuaded George III to offer North the office of first minister in January 1770.

North's administration was distinguished by the loss of the American colonies, an event for which his policy was at least partly responsible. On the taxation of America, North was a disciple of R. T. Grenville. He saw the Boston tea riots of 1773 as an open challenge to British supremacy and, inadequately informed of the temper and feelings of the Americans, introduced punitive legislation designed to overawe the Colonies. Next, faced with a revolutionary situation, he reacted with increased severity and an offer of conciliation, an ambivalent attitude that marked British policy throughout the hostilities.

As the war progressed, North abandoned all hope of reconciliation. To secure an American renunciation of independence, at whatever sacrifice of principle, became his aim. Sanguine expectation and utter despair alternated in his attitude toward the war. Defeat at Saratoga reduced him to an agony of indecision and doubt. Repeatedly he implored the King for permission to resign, and as often agreed to remain. Chronic indecision at critical moments was indeed North's greatest defect as a minister.

But despite his anxieties, further setbacks in America, and the outbreak of war with France, North continued in office. The surrender of Yorktown, however, forced him to a fundamental reconsideration of his policy. He came to believe that the war must be ended even if by a renunciation of sovereignty over America. "Peace with America seems necessary," he wrote to the King in January 1782, "even if it can be obtained on no better terms than some federal alliance, or perhaps even in a less eligible mode." But he did not openly challenge George III's reiterated declaration that he

would not acknowledge American independence. It was the Commons, not North, that forced the King to face reality. The passing of the motion against the "further prosecution of offensive warfare on the continent of North America," on Feb. 27, 1782, was a defeat for the King and a relief to North. A month later he resigned.

North remained in active politics, and in April 1783, on the resignation of Lord Shelburne and the refusal of William Pitt the Younger to form an administration, he effected a coalition with Charles James Fox. The dismissal of the coalition in December marked the end of North's consequence as a parliamentary figure. He continued to speak regularly in the Commons until 1786, when he began to go blind. In August 1790 North succeeded his father as 2d Earl of Guildford. He died in London on Aug. 5, 1792.

Further Reading

Alan Valentine, *Lord North* (2 vols., 1967), is an exhaustive biography. I. R. Christie, *The End of North's Ministry, 1780-1782* (1958), is a specialized study. Essential for background reading is L. B. Namier, *England in the Age of the American Revolution* (1930; 2d ed. 1961). Also useful are R. Ritcheson, *British Politics and the American Revolution* (1954), and Bernard Donoughue, *British Politics and the American Revolution: The Path to War, 1773-75* (1964). □

John Howard Northrop

The Nobel Prize-winning American biological chemist John Howard Northrop (1891-1987) established that enzymes are proteins and also showed that a bacterial virus is a nucleic acid-protein complex.

On July 5, 1891, J. H. Northrop was born in Yonkers, NY. He attended Columbia University, majoring in chemistry and earning a bachelor of science degree in 1912 and a masters degree in science in 1913. He studied the nature of phosphorus in starch for his thesis research and received a doctoral degree in chemistry in 1915. Northrop accepted a position with the biologist Jacques Loeb at the Rockefeller Institute for Medical Research in New York City.

Early Research

In his early career, Northrop was concerned with the effect of environmental factors on the hereditary properties of fruit flies (*Drosophila*). He began by growing the flies aseptically, without pathological microorganisms. It was probably the first time animals had been cultivated free of microorganisms. Northrop found that although carbon dioxide output, a measure of energy expended, was greater at 15°C than at 22°C, the flies lived longer at 15°C than at 22°C. This discovery exploded the existing hypothesis that life duration was regulated by an energy limit.

The entrance of the United States into World War I cut short Northrop's fruit fly research. His talents were needed by the Federal government to produce acetone for the war

effort. He was commissioned a captain in the Army's chemical warfare service. In a short time Northrup developed a method of fermentation of potatoes which produced substantial quantities of acetone.

Work on Enzymes

After the war Northrop returned to the Rockefeller Institute and began studying enzymes. He first tried to determine the conditions which affect the action of the digestive enzymes pepsin and trypsin. By 1929 he had obtained crystals of swine pepsin, but it was not until 1931 that his failure of any of his methods to separate the enzymatic activity from the proteinous material finally convinced him that pepsin must be protein—another significant discovery.

Work on Viruses

Throughout his career Northrop had an interest in self-duplicating systems, one of the prime characteristics of living units. This interest led him to examine, in the 1920s, the way in which tobacco mosaic virus and bacterial viruses (bacteriophages) reproduce. These studies prepared him for work in the late 1930s in which he showed that highly purified staphylococcus bacteriophages contained nucleic acid as well as protein. This was one of the earliest demonstrations of the presence of nucleic acid in virus. Later he drew attention to the possibility that the nucleic acid in bacterial viruses might correspond to the free deoxyribonucleic acid (DNA) of the transforming principle, which in the virus is encased in a protein unit that serves to protect the DNA and to introduce it into the susceptible cell.

Recognition of Achievements

Northrop became a full member of the Rockefeller Institute for Medical Research (now Rockefeller University) in 1923, after Loeb's death. He retained that position throughout his life. He was elected to membership in the National Academy of Sciences in 1934. He shared the Nobel Prize in chemistry in 1946 with his Rockefeller colleague Wendell F. Stanley and with Cornell University's James B. Summer for their work on purification and crystallization of enzymes.

After the closing of the Rockefeller Laboratories in Princeton, New Jersey, Northrop moved to Berkeley, California. There he became a professor of bacteriology and biophysics at the University of California at Berkeley, and he continued to work on mechanisms by which viruses arise in apparently healthy cells. He served as a contributing editor of the *Journal of General Physiology,* beginning in 1925.

Northrop died at his home in Wickenberg, Arizona, on May 27, 1987, after a long retirement. His son-in-law, Frederick Robbins, was also a Nobel Prize recipient, capturing the 1954 award in physiology and medicine.

Further Reading

Most of Northrop's research papers were published in the *Journal of General Physiology;* he also wrote a book, *Crystalline Enzymes* (1939; rev. ed. 1948); The Nobel Foundation's *Chemistry* (3 vols., 1964-1966) contains a biography of Northrop; Information on Northrop and his work is also found in Eduard Farber, ed., *Nobel Prize Winners in Chemistry, 1901-1950* (1953); and in Paula McGuire, ed., *Nobel Prize Winners* (1992). □

Duke of Northumberland

The English soldier and statesman John Dudley, Duke of Northumberland (ca. 1502-1553), was the virtual ruler of England from 1549 to 1553. He was executed when his attempt to place Lady Jane Grey on the throne failed.

John Dudley's father, Edmund Dudley, was one of the principal financial administrators serving Henry VII. He was executed in 1510, soon after the accession of Henry VIII, as a scapegoat to clear the royal family of responsibility for its unpopular exactions.

Young John was placed under the guardianship of Edward Guildford, a minor courtier, whose daughter he later married and through whom he gained a place at Henry VIII's court. In 1523 he was knighted while serving in the army at Calais. When Guildford died in 1534, Dudley and his wife obtained most of his lands, perhaps through the influence of Thomas Cromwell. It was probably also Cromwell who had Dudley appointed master of the horse to Anne of Cleves.

Dudley did not suffer from Cromwell's fall and execution but continued to gain favor and offices. In 1542 he was created Viscount Lisle—the title had previously belonged to his mother's second husband—and appointed high admiral. From 1544 to 1546 he was governor of Boulogne, and he acquired military renown in the conflict with France; he led the English delegation which obtained Francis I's signature to the Treaty of Ardres, which ended the war.

Dudley was the second most powerful man in England at the time of Henry VIII's death (1547), and he was one of the 16 executors named in the King's will. Dudley acquiesced in the arrangement whereby Edward Seymour obtained control of the government as Protector Somerset, and he helped Somerset win the great victory over the Scots at Pinkie. But by 1549 Somerset had shown himself unable to deal effectively with the problems of government, especially the uprisings in Cornwall and Norfolk; only Dudley was able to suppress Ket's rebellion, freeing the city of Norwich from the peasants and hanging their leaders.

Dudley and his supporters now forced Somerset to relinquish power, which was assumed by Dudley himself. Somerset was sent to the Tower for a time, then released, but finally executed in 1552. Dudley acquired additional offices, although he never took the title protector, and in 1551 he was created Duke of Northumberland. Although he lacked sincere religious conviction, he supported the increasingly Protestant policies of Archbishop Thomas Cranmer, and he gained wealth for himself from the pillage of the Church.

By the beginning of 1553 it was evident that Edward VI's health was failing, and Northumberland began to concern himself with the succession to the throne. Wishing to retain power and not desiring the accession of a Catholic, he conceived the "device" whereby Edward's sisters Mary and Elizabeth were excluded in favor of Lady Jane Grey, who had married Northumberland's son Lord Guildford Dudley. When the young king died in July, Northumberland proclaimed Jane queen. But he had not reckoned with the general support for Mary, who as Henry VIII's older daughter was regarded by the English people as the proper heir. Although he attempted to lead a force against Mary, Northumberland soon saw that the attempt was futile, and at Cambridge he proclaimed his support for Mary.

Northumberland was then arrested and sent to the Tower. He was executed on Aug. 22, 1553. On the scaffold he denounced Protestantism and abjectly begged for his life, but without avail.

Further Reading

The only biography of Northumberland is a popular work by Philip Lindsay, *The Queenmaker: A Portrait of John Dudley* (1951). There is relevant material in Hester W. Chapman's two works: *The Last Tudor King: A Study of Edward VI* (1958) and *Lady Jane Grey* (1962). Wilbur Kitchener Jordan, *Edward VI: The Threshold of Power: The Dominance of the Duke of Northumberland* (1970), is the standard scholarly account of the period of Northumberland's supremacy. □

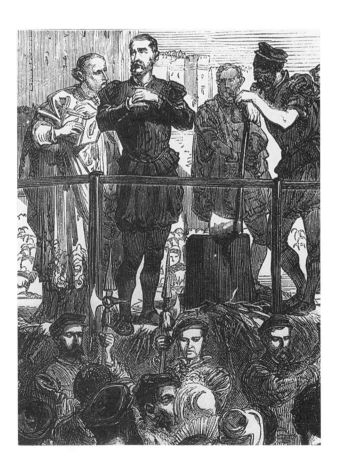

Duke of Northumberland (top row, 2nd from left)

Nostradamus

A physician and astrologer by profession, Nostradamus (1503-1566) is said to have remained awake nights for several years, meditating over a brass bowl filled with water. Through these trances he supposedly could see into the future, and he set his predictions down for posterity in a twelve-volume set he entitled *Centuries*.

Nostradamus is the Latinized name of a sixteenth-century French prophet named Michel de Notredame. Since his death in 1566, scholars and lay people have remained fascinated by Nostradamus's forecasts, in which many future events seem to have been uncannily divined. The French Revolution, the rise of fascism in 1930s Europe, and the explosion of a U.S. space shuttle were supposedly prophesied by the Renaissance scholar.

Questioned Authority

Nostradamus was born in December of 1503 in the south of France; his family was of Jewish heritage but had converted to Catholicism during a period of religious intolerance. Both of his grandfathers were esteemed scholars, one a physician; with the other, he studied classical languages. At the age of 14 Nostradamus left his family to study in Avignon, the ecclesiastical and academic center of Provence. In class, he sometimes voiced dissension with the teachings of the Catholic priests, who dismissed the study of astrology and the assertion of the Polish scientist Copernicus. Copernicus had recently gained fame with his theory that the Earth and other planets revolved around the sun—contrary to the Christian appraisal of the heavens. Nostradamus's family warned him to hold his tongue, since he could be easily singled out for persecution because of his Jewish heritage in the anti-Semitic climate, conversion and baptism or not. Earlier, from his grandfathers he had secretly learned some mystical areas of Jewish wisdom, including the Kabbalah and alchemy.

Nostradamus graduated in 1525 from the University of Montpellier, where he had studied both medicine and astrology, a common professional duality during the era. The first several years of his career as a doctor were spent traveling throughout the many towns and villages in France being decimated by the bubonic plague. Called "Le Charbon" because of the festering black cankers it left on its quickly-dead victim's body, the epidemic had no cure. Doctors commonly "bled" the patient, and knew nothing of how to prevent further infection or how Europe's unsanitary conditions contributed to the spread of the disease. Nostradamus would prescribe fresh air and water for the afflicted, a low-fat diet, new bedding, and often administered an herbal remedy made from rosehips, later discovered to be rich in vitamin C; entire towns recovered.

Nostradamus's herbal remedies were common to the era, but his beliefs about infection control could have resulted in charges of heresy and death.

Devastated by Personal Tragedies

Word of Nostradamus's healing powers made him a celebrated figure in Provence. He wrote a book listing the doctors and pharmacists he had met in southern Europe, translated anatomical texts, developed recipes for gourmet foods, and received his doctorate in 1529 from Montpellier. He also taught at the university for three years, but left when his radical ideas about disease were censured. He chose a wife from among the many offered to him by wealthy and connected families, and settled in the town of Agen. Unfortunately, Le Charbon's recurrence felled his wife and two young children; because the famed physician could not save his own family, citizens suddenly looked upon him with scorn. His in-laws sued for the return of the dowry given to him. His patron, a scholar and philosopher named Julius-Cesar Scalinger, also broke ties with him. A chance remark Nostradamus had once made about a statue of the Virgin Mary landed him in court defending himself against charges of heresy. When told to appear before the feared Church Inquisitors at Toulouse, he became a fugitive.

For the next several years Nostradamus traveled through southern Europe. Scholars have posited that this difficult period probably awakened his powers of clairvoyance. By 1544 torrential rains were again bringing pestilence to southern France, and Nostradamus appeared in Marseilles, then Aix; with his medicinal practices he managed to halt the spread of disease in the latter and was again celebrated for his skills. Moving to the town of Salon, he set up a medical practice, remarried, and began a new family. A devout practicing Catholic outwardly, he spent the night hours ensconced in his study positioned in front of a brass bowl filled with water. Meditation would bring on a trance, and it is also theorized that he may have used herbal means to achieve such a state. In such trances visions would come to him.

Some of these visions for the coming year Nostradamus began writing about when he undertook the first of his *Almanacs,* which appeared annually from 1550 to 1565. Greatly popular with the reading public, the *Almanacs* spoke of astrological phases of the coming year and contained quatrains, or rhymed four-line verse, offering hints of upcoming events. The published works served to spread his fame across France to an even greater degree, and by now his visions were such an integral part of his scholarship that he decided to channel them into one massive opus for posterity. He would call this book *Centuries.* Each of the ten planned volumes would contain 100 predictions in quatrain form. In it, the next two thousand years of humanity would be forecasted.

Prophecies Brought Fame and Fortune

Nostradamus began working on *Centuries* on Good Friday of 1554. The first seven volumes were published in Lyon the following year; although he completed volumes VIII through X by 1558, he would not allow them to be published until after his death. Yet the reception of the initial works made Nostradamus a celebrated figure. "Polite society called Nostradamus a genius," wrote John Hogue in *Nostradamus and the Millennium: Predictions of the Future.* "The peasant Cabans [the superstitious Catholic underclass] called him an instrument of Satan and his dark, cryptic poems the confounded gibberish of Hell. His medical colleagues called him an embarrassment. Philosophers praised and cursed him. Poets either marvelled or scratched their heads at his crabbed and wild verses—a bewildering madness with a method set in riddles and anagrams written in a mixture of French Provencal, Latin, Greek and Italian."

Nostradamus's writings attracted no less than the interest of France's royal family. He was invited to the Paris court of Henry II and his wife, Catharine de Medici. The Medicis were known for their pan-European political ambitions, and the queen hoped that Nostradamus could give her guidance regarding her seven children. Ostensibly, Nostradamus also arrived in Paris in August of 1556 to explain Quatrain 35 of *Centuries I,* assumed to refer to King Henry II. It read: "The young lion will overcome the older one/ On the field of combat in single battle/ He will pierce his eyes through a golden cage/ Two wounds made one, then he dies a cruel death."

Nostradamus told the king that he should avoid any ceremonial jousting during his 41st year, which the regent's own astrologer had also asserted. The physician spent the next few years ensconced in the luxury of the royal court, but received word that Catholic authorities were again becoming suspicious of his soothsaying and were about to investigate him. He returned to his hometown of Salon and his wife and children. Finishing volumes VIII through X, he also began work on two additional volumes of *Centuries,* which were unfinished at the time of his death. On June 28, 1559, in his 41st year, Henry II was injured in a jousting tournament celebrating two marriages in his family. With thousands watching, his opponent's "lance pierced the King's golden visor, entered his head behind the eye, both blinding him and penetrating deep into his brain. He held onto life for ten agonizing days," wrote Hogue in *Nostradamus and the Millennium.*

Spent Later Years Quietly

Already a celebrated persona in France, Nostradamus became a figure inspiring both awe and fright among the populace. His other prophecies regarding France's royal line were consulted, and most seem to predict only death and tragedy. Henry's surviving widow, now Queen Regent Catharine de Medici, visited him in Salon during her royal tour of 1564, and he again told her (as he had when he drew up their astrology charts) that all four of her sons would become kings. Yet all the children came to equally dismal ends: one son became king of Poland, but was murdered by a priest; another died before carrying out a plot to kill another brother; two died young as well; the three daughters also met tragic fates. The family's House of Valois died out with the burial of Queen Margot.

Nostradamus himself died in 1566. He had long suffered from gout, and naturally predicted his own end, although sources say he was off by a year. Many translations of his *Centuries* and treatises on their significance appeared in the generations following his death, and remain popular to the present day. Interpreters claim Nostradamus predicted Adolf Hitler's rise to power as well as the explosion of the U.S. space shuttle *Challenger* in 1986. Biographies of the seer have also appeared periodically. For two centuries the Vatican issued the Index, or a list of forbidden books; *Centuries* was always on it. "No other prophet since Biblical times has held as constant a place in the hearts and minds of the populace as Nostradamus," wrote Dava Sobell in *Omni.* "Whether by dint of the audacity of his future vision or the dreamlike imagery of his verses, he has literally triumphed over time."

Further Reading

Sobell, Dava, "The Resurrection of Nostradamus," in *Omni,* December 1993, p. 42.
Hogue, John, *Nostradamus and the Millennium: Predictions of the Future,* Doubleday, 1987.
Leoni, Edgar, *Nostradamus: Life and Literature,* Nosbooks, 1961.
□

Notker Balbulus

The poet-musician Notker Balbulus (ca. 840-912), a monk in the Swiss monastery of St. Gall, popularized sequences, poems sung during Mass following—as a sequence to—the Alleluia.

B orn not far from St. Gall, Notker, or Notger, Balbulus lost his father in early childhood and was brought up by an old soldier who had served in Charlemagne's army. As a young boy, Notker went to study at St. Gall, then entered the monastery as a monk, and later became its librarian. Always interested in literature, he there found congenial poet friends and like them wrote historical, poetic, and musical works. As a historian, he collected a book of legal deeds and other official documents of his monastery, adding some occasional poems, expanded the existing book of lives of the saints, and chronicled the deeds of Charlemagne. Most of his poetic works were collected in his *Liber hymnorum* (ca. 860-887). Though a larger treatise on music is lost, an *Epistola de musica* survives.

Of these works the book of hymns is by far the most important. It contains 40 sequences for the major feasts of the year, in the order of the calendar. In the foreword Notker tells us that his poems were inspired by a liturgical book containing similar poems that was brought to St. Gall in the 850s by a priest who had fled from the Abbey of Jumièges when it was destroyed during a Norman invasion and taken refuge at St. Gall. Most of Notker's sequences are rather long poems with numerous short stanzas of unequal length. In most of the poems the first and last stanzas were sung by the full choir of monks; the other stanzas, arranged in pairs of equal length, were sung alternately by halves of the choir. In the 11th and 12th centuries all the stanza pairs of a sequence, known as double versicles, were often of similar length and rhymed.

While Notker was working on these poems, his friend Tuotilo, also a monk at St. Gall, expanded the Gregorian chant repertoire by creating shorter songs, called tropes, to be inserted in various other parts of the Mass. Through the next centuries hundreds of sequences and thousands of tropes were created, so that the Mass became increasingly cumbersome. Therefore at the last sessions of the Council of Trent in 1562-1563 the Church decided to eliminate all tropes and all but a few sequences. Thus only five sequences, sung at very special occasions, are still heard today in the Roman Catholic churches: those for Easter, Whitsunday, Corpus Christi, Seven Dolors, and the Mass for the Dead (Requiem Mass)—none of them by Notker.

Further Reading

Information on Notker's life and work is in Gustave Reese, *Music in the Middle Ages* (1940), and Anselm Hughes, ed., *Early Medieval Music up to 1300* (1954). □

Novalis

The German poet and author Novalis (1772-1801) was the most important poet and imaginative writer of the early German romantic movement. Both his poetry and his prose writings express a mystical conviction in the symbolic meaning and unity of life.

Novalis, whose real name was Baron Friedrich Leopold von Hardenberg, was born of an aristocratic family in Wiederstedt, Saxony, on May 2, 1772. While studying philosophy and law at the universities of Jena and Leipzig, he met the philosopher Johann Gottlieb Fichte and the poet Friedrich von Schiller. He also became friends with Friedrich von Schlegel, later the chief theoretician of the romantic school. Novalis also studied at the University of Wittenberg and from 1794 to 1796 worked as an official in Tennstädt.

At Tennstädt, Novalis became engaged to 13-year-old Sophie von Kühn, who died in 1797. Her death affected him deeply, and in the same year he began his *Hymnen an die Nacht* (*Hymns to the Night*), which were published in 1800. In these poems he recounted his experience of Sophie's death and his conversion to a kind of Christian mysticism in which he longed for his own death in order to be reunited with his beloved.

Despite his longings for death, however, Novalis continued his career. He turned to the study of mine engineering, married Julie von Charpentier in 1798 (while maintaining his mystical union with Sophie), and in 1799 became mine inspector in Weissenfels. He had advanced to supervisor by the time of his death.

During these years Novalis also developed his mystical view of the world. In the fragmentary novel *Die Lehrlinge zu Sais* (1798; *The Novices at Sais*) Novalis expressed his belief that the things of the natural world are symbols whose meanings can be discovered by poets. His most important novel, *Heinrich von Ofterdingen,* incomplete at his death, tells of the initiation of a young medieval poet into the mysteries of his calling. Heinrich undertakes a journey, receives poetic instruction, and falls in love. The dominant idea of the novel is the harmony and eternal significance of all life and nature. It also presents the image of the *blaue Blume* (blue flower), which later became the romantics' favorite symbol for any object of mystical aspiration.

Novalis's mystical attitudes also found expression in *Geistliche Lieder* (*Religious Songs*) and in the essay *Die Christenheit oder Europa* (1799; "Christendom or Europe"), which extols the unity of faith and society made possible by medieval Catholicism. Several of Novalis's writings were left unfinished at his death, of tuberculosis, at Weissenfels on March 25, 1801.

Further Reading

For English readers the best general work on Novalis is Frederick Hiebel, *Novalis* (1954; 2d rev. ed. 1959), which provides a detailed study of his life and spiritual development, as well as a careful analysis of each of his major works. For shorter general discussions see Ralph Tymms, *German Romantic Literature* (1955), and Michael Hamburger, *Reason and Energy* (1957). Oskar Walzel, *German Romanticism,* translated by Alma E. Lussky (1932), deals with Novalis's religious attitudes; and August Closs, *Medusa's Mirror* (1957), offers a detailed analysis of the *Hymns to the Night.* □

Robert Noyce

Robert Norton Noyce (1927-1990) coinvented the integrated circuit, an electronic component which is considered to be among the twentieth century's most significant technological developments.

The laptop computer, the ignition control in a modern automobile, the "brain" of a VCR that allows for its programming, and thousands of other computing devices all depend for their operation on the integrated circuit that Robert Noyce coinvented. He was not only a brilliant inventor, credited with more than a dozen patents for semiconductor devices and processes, but a forceful businessman who founded the Fairchild Semiconductor Corporation and the Intel Corporation and who, at the time of his death, was president and CEO of Sematech.

Robert Norton Noyce was born December 12, 1927, in Burlington, Iowa, the third of four boys in the family. His parents were Ralph Noyce, a minister who worked for the Iowa Conference of Congregational Churches, and Harriet Norton Noyce. Growing up in a two-story church-owned house in Grinnell, a small town in central Iowa, Noyce was gifted in many areas, excelling in sports, music, and acting as well as academic work. He exhibited a talent for math and science while in high school and took the Grinnell college freshman physics course in his senior year. Noyce went on to receive his baccalaureate degree in physics from Grinnell, graduating Phi Beta Kappa in 1949. It was at Grinnell that he was introduced to the transistor (an electronic device that allows a small current to control a larger one in another location) by his mentor Grant Gale, head of Grinnell's physics department. Noyce was excited by the invention, seeing it as freeing electronics from the constraints of the bulky and inefficient vacuum tube. After he received his Ph.D. in physics from the Massachusetts Institute of Technology in 1954, Noyce—who had no interest in pure research—started working for Philco in Philadelphia, Pennsylvania, where the company was making semiconductors (materials whose conductivity of an electrical current puts them midway between conductors and insulators).

After three years, Noyce became convinced Philco did not have as much interest in transistors as he did. By chance in 1956 he was asked by William Shockley, Nobel laureate and coinventor of the transistor, to come work for him in California. Excited by the opportunity to develop state-of-the-art transistor technology, Noyce moved to Palo Alto, which is located in an area that came to be known as Silicon Valley (named for the silicon compounds used in the manufacture of computer chips). But Noyce was no happier with Shockley than he had been with Philco; both Shockley's management style and the direction of his work—which ignored transistors—were disappointing. In 1957 Noyce left with seven other Shockley engineers to form a new company, financed by Fairchild Camera and Instrument, to be called Fairchild Semiconductor. At age twenty-nine, Noyce was chosen as the new corporation's leader.

The first important development during the early years at Fairchild was the 1958 invention, by Jean Hoerni (an ex-Shockley scientist), of a process to protect the elements on a transistor from contaminants during manufacturing. This was called the planar process, and involved laying down a layer of silicon oxide over the transistor's elements. In 1959, after prodding from one of his patent attorneys to find more applications for the planar process, Noyce took the next step of putting several electronic components, such as resistors and transistors, on the same chip and layering them over with silicon oxide. Combining components in this fashion eliminated the need to wire individual transistors to each other and made possible tremendous reductions in the size of circuit components with a corresponding increase in the speed of their operation. The integrated circuit, or microchip as it became commonly known, had been born. More than one person, however, was working toward this invention at the same time. Jack Kilby of Texas Instruments had devised an integrated circuit the year before, but it had no commercial application. Nevertheless, both Kilby and Noyce are considered coinventors of the integrated circuit. In 1959 Noyce applied for a semiconductor integrated circuit patent using his process, which was awarded in 1961.

Both technological advances and competition in the new microchip industry increased rapidly. The number of transistors that could be put on a microchip grew from ten in 1964 to one thousand in 1969 to thirty-two thousand in 1975. (By 1993 up to 3.1 million transistors could be put on a 2.15-inch-square microprocessor chip.) The number of manufacturers eventually grew from two (Fairchild and

Shockley) to dozens. During the 1960s Noyce's company was the leading producer of microchips, and by 1968 he was a millionaire. However, Noyce still felt constricted at Fairchild; he wanted more control and so—along with Gordon Moore (also a former Shockley employee)—he formed Intel in Santa Clara, California. Intel went to work making semiconductor memory, or data storage. Subsequently, Ted Hoff, an Intel scientist, invented the microprocessor and propelled Intel into the forefront of the industry. By 1982 Intel could claim to have pioneered three-quarters of the previous decade's advances in microtechnology.

Noyce's management style could be called "roll up your sleeves." He shunned fancy corporate cars, offices, and furnishings in favor of a less-structured, relaxed working environment in which everyone contributed and no one benefited from lavish perquisites. Becoming chairman of the board of Intel in 1974, he left the work of daily operations behind him, founding and later becoming chairman of the Semiconductor Industry Association. In 1980 Noyce was honored with the National Medal of Science and in 1983, the same year that Intel's sales reached one billion dollars, he was made a member of the National Inventor's Hall of Fame. He was dubbed the Mayor of Silicon Valley during the 1980s, not only for his scientific contributions but also for his role as a spokesperson for the industry. Noyce spent much of his later career working to improve the international competitiveness of American industry. Early on he recognized the strengths of foreign competitors in the electronics market and the corresponding weaknesses of domestic companies. In 1988 Noyce took charge of Sematech, a consortium of semiconductor manufacturers working together and with the United States government to increase U.S. competitiveness in the world marketplace.

Noyce was married twice. His first marriage to Elizabeth Bottomley ended in divorce (which he attributed to his intense involvement in his work); the couple had four children together. In 1975 he married Ann Bowers, who was then Intel's personnel director. Noyce enjoyed reading Hemingway, flying his own airplane, hang gliding, and scuba diving. He believed that microelectronics would continue to advance in complexity and sophistication well beyond its current state, leading to the question of what use society would make of the technology. Noyce died on June 3, 1990, of a sudden heart attack.

Further Reading

Bonner, M., W. L. Boyd, and J. A. Allen, *Robert N. Noyce, 1927–1990,* Sematech, 1990.
Encyclopedia of Computer Science, Van Nostrand, 1993, pp. 522–523.
Fifty Who Made the Difference, Villard Books, 1984, pp. 270–303.
Palfreman, Jon, and Doron Swade, *The Dream Machine,* BBC Books, 1991.
Slater, Robert, *Portraits in Silicon,* MIT Press, 1987. □

John Humphrey Noyes

John Humphrey Noyes (1811-1886) was the founder of the Oneida Community, one of the notable experimental societies of his century.

John Humphrey Noyes, born on Sept. 3, 1811, in Brattleboro, Vt., was raised in an individualistic family by a religious mother and a father who became an agnostic, succeeded in business, and served in the U. S. Congress. Noyes graduated from Dartmouth College in 1830 and entered law. Converted by revivals, he attended Andover Theological Seminary and then Yale College. His studies centered on biblical passages which persuaded him that one could be free of sin.

In 1834 Noyes experienced a "second conversion"; his assertion that he had achieved perfection cost him his place at Yale. His essential point, expounded in *The Perfectionist,* was that, being free of sin, he was restricted by man-made laws. Also, God, being composed of man and woman, required both in full relation for salvation from sin. As early as 1834 Noyes expressed dissatisfaction with formal marriage.

This view matured into an article of faith but did not impede Noyes's marriage in 1838 to Harriet A. Holton. In 1846, when his religious followers first engaged in "complex marriage," they created a scandal. Noyes was arrested and faced charges of adultery. He ran off to Oneida,

N.Y., in an area noted for its social and religious experimenters. He was joined by the greater number of his followers in 1848. Noyes's writings of that year, *Bible Communism* and *Male Continence,* along with *The Berean* (1847), summed up his views.

The Oneida community outraged its neighbors and precipitated several scandals, yet its several hundred members settled into an equitable society, living together in a vast house of many chambers, with other establishments for housekeeping and industry. The sales of a steel trap gave the colony economic security. Efforts were made to develop other colonies, and a small one at Wallingford, Conn., succeeded.

"Father" Noyes was absolute dictator of Oneida. Despite defections, the community solidified through such traditions as public confession of egotistical behavior. Noyes pioneered in selective childbearing, expressing his principles in *Scientific Propagation* (ca. 1873). A student of communities, he concluded in his *History of American Socialisms* (1870) that only religiously based communities could flourish. In time, however, elements at Oneida tired of public disapproval. In 1879 Noyes himself prepared plans to dissolve the community, and in 1881 it was reorganized as a corporation. Noyes, to avoid legal suits, moved to Canada. He died at Niagara Falls, Ontario, on April 13, 1886.

Further Reading

Excellent introductions in Noyes's own words are provided in two works edited by George W. Noyes, *Religious Experience of John Humphrey Noyes, Founder of the Oneida Community* (1923) and *John Humphrey Noyes: The Putney Community* (1931). Noyes is sympathetically treated in William A. Hinds, *American Communities* (1878; rev. ed. 1908), and critically treated in Gilbert Seldes, *The Stammering Century* (1928). See also Pierrepont Noyes, *My Father's House: An Oneida Boyhood* (1937).

Additional Sources

Thomas, Robert David, *The man who would be perfect: John Humphrey Noyes and the Utopian impulse,* Philadelphia: University of Pennsylvania Press, 1977. □

Robert Nozick

The American philosopher Robert Nozick (born 1938) established his reputation as a polemical advocate of radical libertarianism, a position arguing for maximum individual rights and a minimal government. He went on to investigate classical issues in philosophy that have often been neglected or dismissed by modern analytic philosophers.

Robert Nozick was born in Brooklyn, New York, on November 16, 1938. His parents were both immigrants, and he referred to himself as just one generation from the *shtetl* (the small-town Jewish communities of Eastern Europe). He earned his B.A. degree in 1959 at Columbia University, where he was a socialist and a member of the left-wing Students for a Democratic Society. He went on to an M.A. (1961) and a Ph.D. (1963) from Princeton University.

After teaching as an instructor and assistant professor of philosophy at Princeton (1962-1965), he went to Harvard as assistant professor (1965-1967), to Rockefeller University as associate professor (1967-1969), then back to Harvard as full professor in 1969. He became a familiar figure in the Harvard Yard, often arriving at his office in athletic togs after running or bicycling from his home.

Nozick won almost instant fame in 1974 with his book *Anarchy, State, and Utopia,* which earned a National Book Award in 1975. The startling effect of the book came from its combination of several qualities. Unlike most books out of academia, it was a manifesto to the public, political world. Its opinions did not quite fit any of the common patterns of scholarly or popular thinking. And its style was a mixing of close philosophical analysis, brash personal assertions, anecdotes, and humor.

The book began with the declaration: "Individuals have rights, and there are things no person or group may do to them (without violating their rights)." That might seem to be a fairly conventional statement in a society nourished in the American Declaration of Independence, but its elaboration quickly struck sparks. Nozick's next paragraph affirmed "that a minimal state, limited to the narrow functions of protection against force, theft, fraud, enforcement of contracts, and so on, is justified; that any more extensive state will violate persons' rights not to be forced to do certain things, and is unjustified."

That position constituted a radical endorsement of freedom of speech, of sexual action, of life styles—pleasing in many ways to the political left, especially the youthful New Left. It implied also a freedom of business enterprise from most forms of government regulation and from much of conventional taxation—pleasing to the political right.

Nozick formulated his position as a two-edged argument. Against anarchism—the position of a very small minority in American society—he argued that a minimal state, enforcing strictly limited laws, is not an undue infringement on personal rights. Against all advocates of a "welfare state" he argued that government has no right to do many of the things that most people today expect government to do.

The basic philosophy is a revision of traditional, political, and economic ideas of John Locke (1632-1704) and Adam Smith (1723-1790). It puts great emphasis on the "entitlement" of people to their own property, including the rights to buy property, sell it, give it away voluntarily, and bequeath it to their heirs. If the Declaration of Independence accents the values of liberty and equality, Nozick puts the emphasis on liberty.

Critics were quick to point out that liberties often conflict. Do employers' rights to hire and fire nullify totally workers' rights to jobs? When does the exercise of freedom become oppressive? Are rights to food, housing, health care, and protection from poverty in old age as important as the right to amass a fortune? Does government have a right to tax citizens to operate public schools and parks or to establish a social security system? What about a military draft in times of national emergency? Since Nozick believed in animal rights—he advocated vegetarianism and for a time listed himself in *Who's Who* as a member of the Jewish Vegetarian Society—what human rights should be restricted for the sake of animal rights?

Nozick did not address all these questions in detail. He candidly acknowledged that his book was an "unfinished" argument. But he was clear on the main point: It is no more the business of the state to distribute wealth than to distribute mates for marriage. All efforts to redistribute wealth (for example, by taxing the rich for the sake of the poor) involve interference in people's lives.

In part, Nozick's argument was a reply to his Harvard colleague, John Rawls. In his famous book *A Theory of Justice* (1971) Rawls gave a high value to equality, justifying functional inequalities only insofar as they benefit the worst off in society. (The poorest player on the team may be better off giving some authority to the quarterback rather than demanding an equal voice in calling the plays.) Nozick acknowledged "no presumption in favor of equality."

Nozick said little about how people acquire the property to which they are "entitled." He referred to Locke's famous theory that individuals are entitled to claim as private property those objects that incorporate their own labor, provided there is "enough and as good left in common for others." Nozick saw problems in that theory, but did not develop an alternative.

One of Nozick's theories might lead to radical consequences, if adopted. He believed that some redistribution of property to rectify past injustices is justifiable. Conceivably that might lead to dismantling some huge corporations and fortunes or to restoration of much of the United States to the Native Americans. But Nozick chose not to "specify the details."

Rather than throw himself into the controversies arising from his first book, Nozick went on to other interests, especially the classical problems of philosophy. He commented that in ten years of teaching at Harvard he never repeated a course. That enabled him to work in a great variety of areas. His second book, *Philosophical Explanations* (1981), is a massive (770-page) study of issues in metaphysics, epistemology, ethics, and "the meaning of life."

These are the problems that philosophers beginning with Socrates have wrestled with. But American philosophy after World War II tended to retreat from them and to concentrate mainly on questions of logic and language. In imitation of scientific disciplines, it sought to work in areas where exactitude is a goal. Nozick argued instead that philosophy is not a branch of science but an "art form." So he re-opened the traditional topics, seeking not proofs but explanations. He even wrote on the question that Martin

Heidegger (1889-1976) made famous: "Why is there something rather than nothing?"—a question that many analytical philosophers had dismissed as nonsensical. Nozick showed an interest in mysticism without committing himself to its beliefs. With his colleague Rawls, despite major disagreements, Nozick restored to philosophical discussion the great issues of ethics in public life.

Recent works by Nozik include *The Examined Life* (1989), which reflects on what is important in life, and *The Nature of Rationality* (1993), which explores rational belief. In 1996, he compiled a collection of essays, *Socratic Puzzles*.

In 1997, Nozik participated in a friend-of-the-court-brief that was submitted to the Supreme Court, in order to outline a philospher's point of view on euthanasia, (the right to die). Nozik was one of a team of philosophers, which included Ronald Dworkin, Thomas Nagel, John Rawls, Thomas Scanlon and Judith Jarvis Thomson. The so called "philosopher's brief" argued in favor of the individual's right to die. The autonomy of the individual, and the neutrality of the state in such matters demanded that freedom in death is as important in freedom in life. Death should come at the indvidual's will and pace, and not by the will and pace of the majority.

Continuing his duties as the Arthur Kingsley Porter professor of philosophy at Harvard, Novik's current work focuses on philosophy that spans many topics, including psychology, neuroscience and metaphysics. He was an important contributor to the evolution of late twentieth century philosophy.

Further Reading

Although Nozick's work attracted wide attention in professional journals and even in the mass media, it is not yet the subject of books. One exception is *Reading Nozick: Essays on Anarchy, State, and Utopia*, edited by Jeffrey Paul (1981). □

U Nu

U Nu (1907-1995) was the first prime minister of independent Burma (now called Myanmar) after freedom was obtained in 1948 from British colonial rule. He was also a leader of the Buddhist revival and a noted writer. After being ousted by the military in 1962, he remained an opposition leader in exile and a proponent of democracy for Myanmar until his death.

Born in the Burmese village of Wakema on May 25, 1907, U Nu was the son of a minor nationalist politician. Educated in Wakema and at Myoma National High School in Rangoon, Nu graduated in 1929 from the University of Rangoon, where one of his friends was U

Thant, later secretary general of the United Nations. Nu spent five years as a teacher and journalist before returning to Rangoon University in 1934 to pursue a law degree.

Nu first came to national attention as a leader of the 1936 students' strike, which was the first mass demonstration of Burmese opposition to British colonial rule. For his revolutionary agitation, he was expelled by the British from the university's law school. A writer and translator of considerable talent, Nu in the late 1930s was the major force behind the Red Dragon Book Club, which published and distributed revolutionary literature. In 1942 he was imprisoned by the British.

Reluctant Leader

Released after the Japanese invaded, U Nu served as foreign minister and information minister in the Japanese-installed government of the nationalist leader Ba Maw. But even while serving in the puppet government, U Nu was organizing an anti-Japanese guerilla force. Nu's perceptive account of these years, *Burma under the Japanese,* was published in the United States in 1954. After the war, Nu, who was a devout Buddhist, attempted to retire to a life of meditation and writing. But when an elected delegate to the constitutional convention died in a drowning accident, Nu was elected in a special by-election in 1947 to succeed him.

Later elected president of the Constituent Assembly, Nu was a secondary figure to Aung San, independent Burma's "founding father." Nu was not even a member of the interim government that was preparing to succeed the

British rulers. But on July 19, 1947, Aung San and most of the other top nationalist leaders were savagely slain by a crazed political rival. The last British governor, Sir Hubert Rance, immediately called on Nu to step into Aung San's shoes as premier-designate of independent Burma. With sorrow and reluctance, Nu became independent Burma's first prime minister when colonial rule ended on January 4, 1948. Nu, who negotiated the final terms of Burmese independence, chose to lead his country out of the British Commonwealth entirely.

Architect of Neutrality

For ten years (1948-1958), with a brief break in 1956 to reorganize the government political party, U Nu was Burma's premier and architect of a foreign policy that avoided commitment to either the American or Soviet sides in the Cold War. Widely acclaimed by the Burmese masses for his devotion to Buddhism, Nu held out successfully against a variety of Communist and ethnic minority rebellions. He also tried, with some success, to modernize his country economically and establish a socialist state.

Known outside Burma primarily for his political career, U Nu was the major force behind the nation's post-colonial Buddhist revival. In 1954-1956, he convened the Sixth Great Buddhist Synod, a major international gathering of Buddhists.

Nu was also a prolific writer of fiction, plays, and political commentary. Probably the best of his works were written before World War II: *Ganda-layit,* based on a 1939 trip to China, and *Modern Plays,* a perceptive series of political parables. In 1952 he wrote *The People Win Through,* subsequently produced as a motion picture, as part of the government's effort to neutralize Communist propaganda. *The Wages of Sin,* staged in 1961, attacked corruption and self-seeking among government officials.

Opposing the Military

In 1958 Nu was toppled from power in a bloodless coup led by Gen. Ne Win, commander in chief of the armed forces. Courageously attacking the new regime, Nu convinced the military to hold elections and return the civilians to office. In February 1960 Nu's party, although harassed by the army, won the most lopsided victory in the country's history.

U Nu was less effective during his second stint as premier, as economic and minority problems worsened. In March 1962, Gen. Ne Win and his army ousted Nu for a second time. From March 1962 to October 1966, Nu was kept in virtual solitary confinement by the very Burmese government he had helped to bring into being. Following his unexplained release by Gen. Ne Win in 1966, Nu slowly returned to public activity. By 1968, Nu was raising funds for the victims of a typhoon.

Deteriorating economic and other circumstances led Ne Win in late 1968 to create a National Unity Advisory Board, and he included U Nu among its 33 members. Nu demanded a return to parliamentary democracy, and by April 1969 he feared he would be again imprisoned or even killed. Feigning illness, he escaped to India.

In August 1969 U Nu set out on a world tour to mobilize international opinion against continued military rule in his country. In London he announced the formation of a new party, the Parliamentary Democracy party, to restore representative government in Burma. A party headquarters and a de facto government-in-exile were established in Bangkok, capital of neighboring Thailand. From there he led the opposition movement until 1973, when he was forced to leave Thailand and move to the United States. In 1988, when a democratic uprising finally ousted Ne Win's regime, U Nu proclaimed himself prime minister of a "parallel government," but the military quickly placed under house arrest Nu and other opposition leaders, including Aung San Suu Kyi, who won the 1991 Nobel Peace Prize. Nu was released in 1992 and spent his last years in seclusion until his death in February 1995.

Further Reading

Nu's *Burma under the Japanese* (translated in 1954) is an excellent account of his formative political years during World War II; the standard biography is Richard A. Butwell, *U Nu of Burma* (1969); Nu's role as the chief architect of independent Burma's foreign policy is described in William C. Johnstone, *Burma's Foreign Policy: A Study in Neutralism* (1963). Economic development during Nu's first premiership is treated by Louis J. Walinsky in *Economic Development of Burma, 1951-1960* (1962); Donald Eugene Smith, *Religion and Politics in Burma* (1965), is perceptive on Nu's dual role as politician and religious leader. Also important is F.M. Bunge's *Burma: A Country Study* (1983). □

Shafiihuna Nujoma

Shafiihuna Nujoma (born 1929) led the Southwest African People's Organization (SWAPO) from exile for almost 30 years. In 1989 he became the first president of independent Namibia.

Shafiihuna (Sam) Nujoma was born May 12, 1929, in the Ongandera area of northwestern Namibia. His name, Shafiihuna, means "a time of trouble," and in fact Nujoma was born during Namibia's period of British rule under a treaty mandate which removed the colony from German control at the end of World War I. Colonial governance was later assumed by an independent South Africa.

The northern part of Namibia in which Nujoma was born and grew up is known as Ovambo(land). He is Ovambo, a member of the largest ethnic group in Namibia, today comprising approximately 60 percent of the population. This relatively fertile and more densely populated land was far from the focus of European interests, which concentrated on Namibia's mineral wealth and ranching lands to the south. Except as a labor reserve, colonial administrations ignored Ovambo, leaving any externally-initiated development efforts to missionaries.

As a child Nujoma attended one of the few schools in the north, which was established by Finnish missionaries.

However, Nujoma's education ended very early, and consequently, he cannot be considered a member of the educated elite. Although Nujoma did eventually receive a standard six certificate, in night school, he never sought a university degree.

Labor Activism

It was while working in the south as a railroad steward that Nujoma became politically active. As had become routine for men living in Ovambo, Nujoma was forced by economic necessity to contract to make his living far from home, separated from his family. During this period of young adulthood, Nujoma became well aware of contract system abuses. He was helpless but to watch as a fellow railroad worker suffered a painful accident and was then sent home by his employer without compensation. This event contributed to Nujoma's decision to pursue the life of an activist, first for workers' rights and later for Namibia's independence.

In 1957 Nujoma was fired from the railroads precisely for such activity, when he attempted to form a union of railroad workers. He and a small group of other Namibians on contract formed the Ovamboland People's Organization (OPO) in the late 1950s to mobilize workers to fight the abuses of the contract system and demand better working and living conditions. Nujoma was elected president of the OPO in 1959 and played an important role in helping to organize various strikes and peaceful demonstrations. However, the South African administration countered any and all dissent with repression.

In 1959 police killed 11 people and wounded over 50 when blacks demonstrated against forced removals from their homes in the "Old Location" section of Windhoek, an incident remembered as "the Windhoek Shootings." This and other acts of repression led to a growing impatience with passive resistance in the nationalist movement. In 1960 the OPO changed its name to the Southwest African People's Organization (SWAPO) and broadened its appeal to attract Namibians from all regions and ethnicities. By the early 1960s SWAPO had also developed into a leading organization calling for Namibia's full independence from foreign domination. As the president of SWAPO, Nujoma was a target for police intimidation. He was arrested and jailed by South African authorities, and upon his release in 1960, Nujoma made the difficult decision to go into exile.

Civil War

Nujoma would spend the next 30 years of his life away from his home, championing the cause of Namibian independence around the world. Nujoma played a particularly active role at the United Nations, which recognized SWAPO as the legitimate representative of the Namibian people. Nujoma became widely known throughout the international community for his fiery speeches and rhetoric, calling not only for an end to South African domination of Namibia, but also an end to all foreign exploitation (particularly by multinational corporations). Concerns over nationalization and varying degrees of alliance with South Africa distanced leading Western powers, including the United States, from Nujoma and SWAPO.

Contributing to this distance was South Africa's portrayal of Nujoma as a communist seeking to drive whites into the sea. As a central figure within SWAPO, Nujoma was instrumental in directing a liberation war against South Africa. After years of peaceful resistance and no reward, and after much of the SWAPO leadership was driven underground through South African crackdowns on all dissent, SWAPO leaders made the decision in 1966 to adopt armed resistance as part of a multifaceted program for independence.

In a guerrilla war that was fought through 1988, SWAPO never posed a conventional military threat to South Africa, but support for independence grew, most notably among newly independent southern African states, Eastern European states, and the Soviet Union. Although the guerrilla movement could not win, it proved remarkably tenacious against the larger and better-equipped South African forces.

Independence

Eventually, a political solution freed Namibia. After years of fruitless negotiations at the United Nations, a breakthrough came in 1988. Through a trilateral agreement involving Cuban withdrawal from Angola, the South Africans finally agreed to give up Namibia and allow a UN-sponsored electoral process to begin April 1, 1989. Free and democratic elections for a constituent assembly were held in November of that year, and the assembly then constructed a constitution and set a date for independence.

Although not specifically a party to the trilateral agreement, SWAPO applauded the process and launched a vigorous campaign, led by Nujoma from exile. Despite a 30-year absence, Nujoma was such a well-known figure in Namibia that his picture alone became a campaign symbol for the party. His return home in September 1989 to register to vote for the first time in national elections was a day of celebration for SWAPO supporters.

Elections proceeded fairly smoothly, and Nujoma's party won a 58 percent majority of the votes. The results disappointed SWAPO, which had hoped to win as much as two-thirds of the vote, but were hardly surprising in light of South Africa's heavy financing of the opposing Democratic Turnhalle Alliance (DTA). The resulting balance of power necessitated a period of coalition building and compromise by all sides, many of whom had been archenemies both before and during the election process. As a leader of the majority party in the parliament, Nujoma fostered a spirit of conciliation. SWAPO made significant concessions, such as limiting the powers of the presidency, while Nujoma facilitated a smooth South African withdrawal.

As the top political figure in Namibia, Nujoma cleared the way for cooperation with the West, calling for investment in Namibia's egalitarian and mixed economy. Completing a life-long dream, Namibia formally became independent on March 21, 1990, and Sam Nujoma became the country's first president.

Namibia's First President

As president, Nujoma continued to polish his skills in reconciliation. Though he asked his newborn country to leave behind memories of the war for independence, many demanded that perpetrators of atrocities on both sides be brought to justice. SWAPO was particularly embarrassed by allegations released in a book in 1996 that the movement tortured comrades accused of spying for South Africa. A civil rights group demanded information on the fate of detainees reportedly held in prison at the end of the war. Nujoma took the unusual step of attacking both the book and its author on national television, prompting charges that he misused that medium in an attempt to trample free speech.

Critics also dogged Nujoma's administration with charges of corruption among high officials, but over 76 percent of the electorate granted the President another term in 1994. Despite opposition warnings that a two-thirds plurality in the National Assembly would permit SWAPO to tinker with the constitution, the party won 53 of 72 seats. (Opposition fears were realized in 1997 when the party proposed that a special congress be convened to consider changes in the constitution, including a provision which would allow Nujoma to stand for election to a third five-year term as president). Analysts attributed some of the party's success to South African President Nelson Mandela's announcement just before the election that he would forgive Namibia's $800 million debt, explaining that South Africa would "no longer saddle Namibia with a burden inherited from an oppressive regime."

While South Africa remained the foremost influence in Namibia's economy, accounting for 80 percent of imports and 35 percent of exports in the mid-1990's, Nujoma took an active role seeking investments and trading partners worldwide. He also repaid debts to those who helped Namibia gain independence. In at least one instance, this put him at odds with other African leaders when he expressed support for an unpopular military regime in Nigeria. Namibia under Nujoma maintained relations with countries estranged from the West, such as Cuba, Libya, Iran, and North Korea. Still, Nujoma recognized the importance of economic ties with the United States and European countries, including Sweden, Germany, Norway, Finland, and France.

Though critics accused Nujoma of heavy-handedness and insensitivity to the fragile rights essential to a healthy democracy, supporters pointed to Namibia's smooth transition under his rule from a colony to a solidly democratic state.

Further Reading

There is no widely published biography of Nujoma. Descriptions of life in colonial Namibia are contained in Ruth First, *South West Africa* (1963); and Robert J. Gordon, *Mines, Masters, and Migrants: Life in a Namibian Compound* (1977); The resistance movement in Namibia is specifically discussed in Peter Katjavivi's *A History of Resistance in Namibia* (1988); and David Soggot's *Namibia: The Violent Heritage* (1986).

Accounts of Nujoma's terms as president can be found in the southern African press, including the South African *Weekly Mail & Guardian* dated December 9 1994, February 3, 1995, March 15, 1996, April 4, 1996, April 26,1996, May 16, 1996, and November 15, 1996; and through *Africa Online,* an Internet service of Prodigy Inc. Company, in releases dated May 8, 1997; and June 2, 1997. ☐

Sam Nunn

An expert on national defense and chairman of the Senate Armed Services Committee in the 100th Congress (1987-1989), Sam Nunn (born 1938) was elected to the United States Senate from Georgia from 1972 until his retirement in 1996.

Sam Nunn's capacity for winning Democratic senatorial elections in Republican years classified him as a "Boy Wonder" of Georgia and the New South. In 1972, when Richard Nixon took nearly 70 percent of the vote in his state, Nunn won his first election to the United States Senate by a comfortable 54 percent against Republican Fletcher Thompson. Again in 1984, when Ronald Reagan captured Georgia by over 60 percent, Sam Nunn won his third election, against Mike Hicks, by a whopping 80 percent. And in the 1984 election he had the support of his Republican senatorial colleague from Georgia, Mack Mattingly.

Born in Perry, Georgia, on September 25, 1938, Sam Nunn was the son of Samuel A. and Elizabeth (Canon) Nunn. Educated in Perry's public school system, where he was a star basketball player, he grew up in a family steeped in learning and politics. His father, a well-known lawyer-farmer, was a dedicated reader and collected an excellent library which Sam Jr. patronized avidly. His uncle, the nationally-known Carl Vinson, set records for congressional service, concentrating on duties as chairman of the House Armed Services Committee.

Sam and his older sister were raised in a strict Protestant atmosphere which brought them to Perry's Methodist Church regularly, under the influence of their mother Elizabeth Nunn, who survived her husband into her 80s, still living in the family home in Perry in 1986.

As a result of his family's political connections, young Sam Nunn had the opportunity to meet many Georgia politicians, including Senator Herman Talmadge, with whom he later served as junior senator during the twilight of Talmadge's career.

Nunn attended Georgia Institute of Technology from 1956 to 1959, then took time out for a stint in the Coast Guard. Returning to civilian life, he graduated with a B.A. from Emory University in 1960 and earned his LL.B. two years later. For a while he practiced law and in 1965 married Colleen O'Brien, with whom he had two children, Mary and Samuel.

In 1968 he won his first election to the Georgia House of Representatives. To him, it was a stepping stone to the

federal House of Representatives, but a planned congressional district which would win him that prize failed to be organized, forcing him to try for the United States Senate in 1972. As a newcomer barely out of his 30s, he had little hope of success—even Carl Vinson felt it was too soon—but Nunn surprised everyone by winning.

From his first days in Washington he concentrated on defense, working with the giants of both parties to learn and develop without regard to ideological factionalism. He disagreed, but without rancorous and divisive rhetoric. When he believed in an issue, he voted for it, whether it was a Carter initiative or one from Reagan. His moderation earned him praise from the more conservative press and political leadership of the nation. His 1981 ratings from Americans for Constitutional Action (conservative) was 71, while Americans for Democratic Action (liberal) gave him a 35. These figures do not explain Nunn's Democratic Party values nearly as much as does his membership in the D.L.C. (Democratic Leadership Council). He founded this organization in 1985 with other moderates such as Charles Robb, Joseph Biden, and Lawton Chiles to restore the South and West, as Nunn put it, to ''. . . the mainstream of American politics''; other goals were a strong national defense, commitment to arms control within reason, and retention of civil rights gains. Among other D.L.C. members, Nunn was perhaps more conservative, as evidenced by his early support for the Strategic Defense Initiative (known popularly as ''Star Wars'') and aid to anti-Communist ''Contra'' forces in Nicaragua.

As a senator, Nunn showed that he was capable of innovation and creativity as well as of the hard work required to master the details surrounding America's national defense. He became expert in defense terminology and had the capacity, tenacity, and wit to see defense issues in the larger context of fiscal integrity and future planning.

The bipartisan ''build down'' proposal, which Nunn co-authored with Republican senator William Cohen of Maine, provided both the United States and the former Soviet Union with the flexibility necessary to replace and modernize their multifarious systems of weapons while at the same time reducing the number of warheads in each arsenal. The purpose was to allay American fears of Russian long-range missiles and Russian fears of American long-range bombers.

Nunn's ideological credentials and his grasp of details made him a formidable foe of Pentagon waste and inefficiency. He was hostile to stretchouts—long periods of funding for weapons development and production—since they tended to bleed the nation of its resources while providing nothing in return. He opposed the controversial new B-1 B bomber on grounds that it could not accomplish its primary mission—namely, to dodge Soviet defenses and strike at internal targets in Russia.

In late 1986, in the wake of the Democratic victory in the Senate, Nunn and his policies were advanced to national stature. By early 1987 he was being selected by four or five percent of Democratic voters as their first choice for presidential candidate in 1988. Regardless of the results of polls and primaries, Sam Nunn, who took over chairmanship of the Senate Armed Services Committee in the 100th Congress (1987-1989) from his Republican friend Barry Goldwater, had become a national figure.

Nunn was known for his unusual consistency in ideals, regardless of party politics. He wasn't happy with the idea of waging war, favoring a strong defense to prevent war instead. As a result, he opposed the sending of troops to Kuwait in 1991, when Republican President George Bush was in office. He also opposed Democratic President Bill Clinton's sending American troops into Haiti and Bosnia. In a controversial move, he opposed Clinton's policy of allowing homosexuals in the military.

Towards the end of his career in the Senate, Nunn became concerned about social issues. In 1995 he backed Empower America, a consumer advocacy group which wanted sensational talk shows to tone down their content.

Retirement from the Senate

In 1996, Nunn decided to retire from the Senate. As one of the last Southern conservative democrats, Nunn's departure was seen as a direct blow to the both the Democrats and to Congress. Since his retirement Nunn has taken on a role of statesman, occasionally giving lectures on matters of foreign policy. *Congressional Quarterly Weekly* (August 17, 1996) called Nunn a potential candidate for the year 2000 presidential elections.

Further Reading

No books and few biographical periodical articles exist on Sam Nunn. His most significant contribution to the disarmament issue, the strategic ''build-down'' concept, is described in Alton Frye, ''Strategic Build-Down: A Context for Restraint,'' *Foreign Affairs,* (Winter 1983); his growing importance in national politics is discussed in R. W. Apple, Jr., ''Delivering the South,'' *New York Times Magazine,* (November 30), 1986. □

Nureddin

Nureddin (1118-1174), or Malik al-Adil Nur-al-Din Mahmud, was a Damascene ruler and one of several Moslem leaders striving to drive the Christian Crusaders out of the Levant.

The father of Nureddin Imad-al-din, son of a Turkish slave of the Seljuk sultan Malik Shah, created a principality based in Mosul and stretching westward to Aleppo. Nureddin was born in Damascus on Feb. 21, 1118. Highly capable, he inherited his father's expansionist proclivities and the western portion of his principality, making Aleppo the capital. Nureddin was a skilled military campaigner who commanded the respect of his men.

In 1144, 2 years before his murder, Nureddin's father had inspired the Second Crusade (1147-1149) by capturing Edessa from its Frankish ruler, Joscelin II; when he died, this important country, which was a fief of Jerusalem and had been the first crusader state, was the first to fall. With its recapture by Nureddin, Moslems again dominated the eastern part of the Baghdad-Mediterranean trade route.

During the Second Crusade, Nureddin captured Damascus and Antioch from fellow Moslems and held them against the crusaders. Damascus and other inland cities never fell to the crusaders, although occasionally they paid tribute. The Damascene payment in 1156 was 8,000 dinars. In a subsequent peace settlement between Nureddin and Baldwin III of Jerusalem, tribute was eliminated. When the Christian rulers of Antioch and Tripoli fell into Nureddin's hands, they were ransomed, Bohemund III after a year and Raymond III after 9.

Saladin, the nephew of Nureddin's lieutenant in Cairo, became vizier and commander in 1169, 5 years after Zangid forces entered Egypt. Saladin resisted Christian attacks and even raided into the kingdom of Jerusalem, but the independence of this young officer curtailed effective cooperation with Damascus against the Franks.

In the north, Nureddin continued his raiding, taking several towns from the Rum sultanate in 1173. While on this campaign he received a diploma of investiture as lord of Mosul, Syria, Egypt, and Konya from the Abbasid caliph in Baghdad. Nureddin died of throat trouble on May 15, 1174.

A pious Sunni, Nureddin was noted for strict adherence to religious dicta in his public and private life. Justice was a paramount feature of his character. He is credited, culturally, with patronizing scholars and with the extensive building of mosques, hospitals, and schools throughout his territories.

Further Reading

Sources on the Seljuks are rare. See Philip K. Hitti, *History of the Arabs* (1937; 10th ed. 1970), and Steven Runciman, *A History of the Crusades* (3 vols., 1951-1954). □

Rudolph Nureyev

The Russian-born dancer and choreographer Rudolph Nureyev (born 1938) captured international acclaim as the greatest male ballet dancer of the 1960s and 1970s. His virtuosity, versatility, and charismatic energy were expressed in countless classical and contemporary roles, on both stage and screen.

Rudolph Hametovich Nureyev, born on a train journey between Lake Baikal and Irkutsk in Russia, was the youngest child of poor parents of Asiatic Mongol stock. Despite early discouragement from his parents, Nureyev began his dancing career with amateur folk dance groups and the Ufa Opera Ballet. At the age of 17 he entered the Leningrad Ballet School to study with the outstanding teacher Alexander Pushkin. After three years of training he

joined the Kirov Ballet as a soloist, dancing full length roles in *Don Quixote, Gayane, Giselle, La Bayadere, The Nutcracker, Swan Lake,* and *The Sleeping Beauty.*

His offstage reputation was equally sensational, bringing him constant trouble with both the Kirov management and the Russian political authorities. In the Kirov's first-ever appearance in Paris in 1961 Nureyev was an outstanding success, yet his defiance of company regulations provoked a command return to Moscow. On June 17, 1961, Nureyev cut his ties with the Soviet Union, seeking political asylum at Le Bourget Airport in Paris.

Within five days, Nureyev embarked on a six-month season with the international Grand Ballet du Marquis de Cuevas, dancing the Prince and the Blue Bird in *The Sleeping Beauty.* As partner to Rosella Hightower, he made his London debut in October 1961 at the Royal Academy of Dancing, where he met the ballerina Margot Fonteyn, who subsequently became his principal partner for many years. He became a regular guest artist with the Royal Ballet from 1962 to the mid-1970s, in addition to performing with Ruth Page's Chicago Opera Ballet, American Ballet Theatre, and on U.S. and French television.

With an inexhaustible stamina, Nureyev continued to perform at a non-stop pace, acquiring over 90 roles and appearances with over 30 major ballet and modern dance companies. Frederick Ashton, the British choreographer, was the first to create a role specifically for Nureyev in *Marguerite and Armand* in March 1963. Nureyev's own first production was the last act of "La Bayadere" for the Royal

Ballet in November 1963, and his first reconstruction the 19th-century three-act classic *Raymonda* for the Royal Ballet in June 1964. His fascination with modern dance, which led to performances with American choreographers Martha Graham, Murray Louis, and Paul Taylor, began with Rudi Van Dantzig's *Monument for a Dead Boy* with the Dutch National Ballet in December 1968. He penetrated the film medium in 1972 with his directing debut of his own production of *Don Quixote* in Melbourne, Australia, and the creation of the film *I Am A Dancer*. The film *Rudolph Valentino,* directed by Ken Russell in 1976, gave Nureyev his debut as a film actor.

Self-reliance and a compulsive drive directed his energy into a performing schedule around the world that only Anna Pavlova could equal. His guest performances were slightly curtailed with his assumption of a three-year directorship of the Paris Opera Ballet in 1983. A mercurial character, shrewd, cunning, charming, and passionate, Nureyev demonstrated a commitment and a savage power equaled by no other dancer in his day. His last stage appearance was for a curtain call at the Palace Garner after the production of his dance *La Bayadere* had been performed. He succumbed to AIDS in Paris, January 6, 1993. He was 54 years old. "Any time you dance," Nureyev once said in an interview in *Entertainment Weekly,* "what you do must be sprayed with your blood."

Further Reading

Nureyev, An Autobiography, edited by A. Bland (London, 1962), was authored by the dancer himself; *The Nureyev Image* by Alexander Bland (1976) offers a comprehensive story, as well as photographs; John Percival's *Rudolph Nureyev, Aspects of the Dancer* (1975) is the product of intensive research and interviews with co-workers. □

Nuri al-Sa'id

Nuri al-Sa'id (1888-1958) was an army officer, a statesman, and an Arab nationalist. He fought with Faisal (who with his father led Arab troops in the revolt against Ottoman rule during World War I) and later became chief of staff, minister of defense, and prime minister when Faisal became king of the newly created Iraq.

Nuri al-Sa'id was born in Baghdad to a poor family in 1888. His father was a minor functionary in the Awqaf department (pious foundation), designed to supervise estates for charitable purposes under the Ottoman administration. After finishing training in a cadet school, Nuri went to study at the Military Academy in Istanbul (Constantinople) in 1903 and was graduated three years later. He returned to Baghdad to serve in an infantry unit whose task was to collect taxes from tribesmen. When the young Turks—a party calling for liberal reform—achieved

power in 1908, Nuri became interested in politics. He went to Istanbul for further training at the Staff College in 1910 and was graduated two years later.

While in Istanbul Nuri, with a few other Arab officers, led by Aziz Ali, an Egyptian officer, formed the Ahd Society (Covenant) and demanded self-government for the Arabs. Nuri, however, disagreed with Aziz Ali on foreign policy. Aziz sought cooperation with the Germans, who supported Ottoman unity, while Nuri was suspicious of their objectives. When Aziz was expelled from Istanbul for his political activities, Nuri left in disguise for Basra seeking protection under its Arab governor. While in Basra World War I broke out, and a British force from India occupied Basra in 1914 to protect the Gulf of Aden from German penetration. As an officer in the Ottoman army, Nuri was sent to India to be interned. From there he escaped to Cairo, where he became engaged with other Arab officers to join Husein ibn Ali (Sharif Husayn) of Mecca, who led the Arab revolt against Ottoman rule.

Nuri's participation in the Arab revolt was the beginning of a life-long association with the Hashemite (Hashimi) house of Husein. He first served in the Hijaz under Husein and later under Faisal, Husayn's son, in Syria and in Iraq. When Faisal's rule over Syria came to an end, since Syrian Nationalists failed to accept the French Mandate, the British assisted Faisal to become king of Iraq. Nuri returned to Iraq early in 1921 to cooperate with other leaders to prepare for Faisal's accession of the throne of Iraq in August 1921 as Faisal I.

For almost a decade, from 1921 to 1930, Iraqi leaders were dissatisfied with the limited independence granted by the British. They demanded complete independence. Nuri preferred to remain in the background of the ensuing struggle for independence. All political leaders had agreed on independence, but they disagreed on the way to achieve it. Some wanted independence at once, others were prepared to wait for it. Nuri saw the need for British assistance and urged rapid development before independence. He concentrated on the building up of a national army and served for almost a decade either as chief of staff or minister of defense.

In 1930, when Britain finally decided to recognize Iraqi independence and replace the mandate with a treaty of alliance, Nuri was the man to deal with Britain. For two years as prime minister he worked to reconcile differences, and a treaty with Britain was signed on June 30, 1930. It provided for an end of British control and recognition of Iraq's independence. For the British promise to protect Iraq from foreign attack, Iraq granted Britain two air bases and the use of all means of communication in time of war. On October 3, 1932, Iraq became a member of the League of Nations as an independent state.

A year after Iraq's independence King Faisal I died in 1933. It devolved on Nuri to lead the country, and he became the principal architect of the country's foreign and domestic policy. From 1930 until his death in 1958 he was prime minister 13 times and many more times foreign minister. The goals of his policy were to assert the country's independence and to make alliances with neighbors as well as with one great power (Britain) in order to protect that independence. He also paid attention to internal development and sought to use the limited resources Iraq had to achieve economic development. This policy proved so successful that Iraq's position in the world seemed quite secure.

After World War II, when almost all Arab countries achieved full independence, Iraq appeared to lag behind them because it was burdened by the treaty with Britain. When Nuri tried to rid his country of the treaty in 1955 he entered into a new defense agreement—the Baghdad Pact—which Britain rejoined as a partner. Iraq not only seemed tied with its former ally, but also committed to the Western bloc as a whole. Since Iraq received Western military and economic assistance, Nuri hoped that other Arab countries might join the Baghdad Pact and become united and strong. He also hoped the Arab countries would influence the Western powers to resolve the Arab-Israeli conflict in their favor.

During the Cold War, most Arab leaders—especially the military leaders of Egypt—did not share Nuri's optimism. There was a widespread suspicion that European powers were not prepared to withdraw their influence from Arab lands, nor were they ready to supply arms in large quantities to strengthen them. As a result, the Arab leaders desired to remain neutral. But neutrality was unacceptable to the West. Nuri's inability to persuade Western and Arab leaders to cooperate weakened his position in the Arab world.

Nuri turned to building up Iraq's internal strength by concentrating on economic development. He created the Development Board for reconstruction and entered into a new oil agreement with the Iraq Petroleum Company on the basis of 50/50 profit sharing, which increased the amount of funds available for development. The board launched ambitious schemes for irrigation and drainage, designed to save the country from the perennial threat of floods and to provide water for agricultural development. But conditions of the poor were hardly touched. Nuri's opponents in Iraq aroused the masses against him, while opponents outside the country concentrated on attacking his foreign policy. Nuri hoped that his development schemes would bring about prosperity and improve conditions of the poor. But time ran short for development. His opponents were able to win over the army against him. The army rose in revolt on July 14, 1958, and overthrew the monarchy and put Nuri to death as well as King Faisal II, who had come to the throne in 1939.

Further Reading

There are two books which cover Nuri's life and policies. The first, Lord Birdwood, Nuri al-Sa'id (London, 1959), is a full biographical study and the second, W. J. Gallman, Iraq Under General Nuri (1964), is a study of Nuri's policy after World War II, with special emphasis on Iraq's relations with the United States. Nuri's political activities are discussed in detail in M. Kadduri's Independent Iraq (London, 2nd edition, 1960) and Republican Iraq (London, 1969). For Nuri's views on foreign policy see Nuri al-Sa'id, Arab Independence and Unity (Baghdad, 1943) and "Last Testament of Iraqi Premier," Life International, Vol. XXV (August 18, 1958). For an evaluation of Nuri's leadership, see M. Khadduri, "The Realistic School: Nuri al-Sa'id," in Arab Contemporaries: The Role of Personalities in Politics (1963). □

Julius Kamberage Nyerere

Julius Kamberage Nyerere (born 1922) was a Tanzanian statesman and political philosopher who became the first president of Tanzania. His carefully reasoned and well-presented policies for the development of Tanzania led to a reputation as Africa's most original thinker.

During the often turbulent era of the 1950s in Africa, as the various colonies worked to gain independence from their European masters, the United Nations Trust Territory of Tanganyika was a significant exception to the norm in its quiet progress to freedom. This was largely because of the leadership of Julius Nyerere. His recognition of the political realities within Tanganyika and his refusal to be associated with any schemes of racial bigotry made him a figure of world interest. His continuing leadership of his country after independence within these lines led to his recognition as one of Africa's most creative politicians.

Julius Nyerere was born in March 1922 at Butiama, the son of Nyerere Burito and his eighteenth wife, Mugaya. Nyerere Burito (1860-1942) was one of the several chiefs of the Zanaki, a small tribal grouping of less than 50,000 individuals. The Zanaki were a poor people, and the chiefs were little richer than their subjects. Julius Nyerere early demonstrated a lively intellect; he was sent to the Native Authority School at Musoma, where he impressed his teachers enough to be encouraged to attempt entry to the important Tanganyika Government School at Tabora. He gained admission in 1937, and again he earned the commendation of his teachers.

In one episode at Tabora, Nyerere acted in a manner that foreshadowed his political course. When appointed prefect of his house, he learned that prefects received special dining privileges, as well as extensive disciplinary powers over fellow students. In the interests of equality, Nyerere successfully agitated to have the special privileges abolished. Nyerere entered Makerere University College in January 1943, where he became one of a group of lively young East Africans discussing the political problems of their countries, which then were all under British rule. He was especially noted for his debating abilities. All during these years Nyerere showed a consistent interest in the Roman Catholic religion; he was baptized in December 1943.

Political Beginnings

Receiving his diploma of education in 1945, Nyerere returned to Tanganyika to teach history and biology at St. Mary's College, Tabora, a Roman Catholic secondary school. He began his political life by joining the Tanganyika

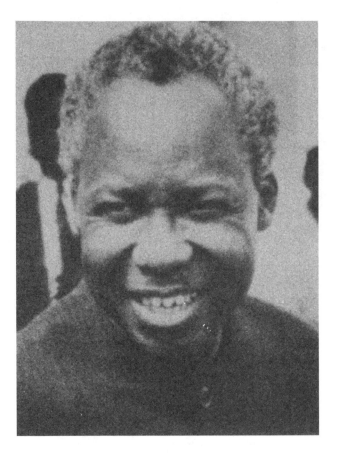

African Association, an organization founded in 1929 by British officials to provide a discussion forum for African opinion. He was elected treasurer of the Tabora branch. The association, however, was not a very vital body, since most educated Africans in Tanganyika were in government service, which by British decision precluded them from any overt political activity.

Nyerere decided that he needed more education; in 1949 he entered Edinburgh University, where he decided against working for an honors degree, instead studying a broad range of subjects. Nyerere later said, "I evolved the whole of my political philosophy while I was there." He received a master's degree in 1952 and returned to Tanganyika, where he was appointed history master at St. Francis' College, Pugu, near the country's capital, Dar es Salaam.

As one of the few Africans with a Western education in Tanganyika, Nyerere was soon caught up in political life. In April 1953 he was elected president of the Tanganyika African Association, devoting his energies to an effort to revitalize that organization into an effective medium for African interests. Perceiving that this was a hopeless task, he organized a new group and on July 7, 1954, announced the formation of the Tanganyika African National Union (TANU). It was the first African political body within Tanganyika; Nyerere was unanimously elected president.

The early years of TANU were difficult ones; Tanganyika's lack of educated Africans free of government restriction and its poor communications system hindered organizational work. But limited progress was made, spearheaded by a group comprising Nyerere, Paul Bomani, Oscar Kambona, and Rashidi Mfaume Kawawa. An opportunity opened for the party because of Tanganyika's relationship to the United Nations. One of the international body's periodic visiting missions went to Tanganyika in 1954. Some of its members were sympathetic to African aspirations; they recommended setting a date for the territory's independence. The British naturally reacted against what they considered ill-informed interference, with one result of the dispute being TANU's decision to send Nyerere to present the party's case before the Trusteeship Council in New York. The reasoned eloquence of his statements about Tanganyika's future drew considerable attention, although no immediate results ensued.

By this period Nyerere was devoting so much time to politics that he found it necessary, in 1955, to resign his teaching post. He did this with considerable regret, for he loved teaching, a fact illustrated by the name most commonly applied to him today within his country, *mwalimu,* the teacher. Without fixed employment, and lacking any personal fortune, Nyerere spent a very difficult period of his life as he traveled widely within Tanganyika to further organize TANU. He also had two additional appearances before the United Nations, in December 1956 and June 1957, where he reinforced the favorable impression made in 1955.

The British could not help but recognize Nyerere's growing influence. In 1957 he was appointed to the Legislative Council, which remained under British control, but when he was unable to make any progress for the policies of TANU, Nyerere resigned in disgust.

In 1958 TANU had to make an important decision. The British had scheduled elections for Tanganyika under a scheme which reserved seats for members of the country's African, Asian, and European communities. Voting, however, was to be by a common, and therefore largely African, electorate. Many members of TANU were against this effort to impose minority representation, but Nyerere carried his point of view for participation in a stormy conference at Tabora. The result was to ensure a peaceful progress to independence. TANU swept the 1958 and 1959 elections.

Toward Independence

This success was matched with an important change in the British leadership of the territory; a new governor, Sir Richard Turnbull, succeeded the more conservative Sir Edward Twining. Turnbull was prepared to support Tanganyika's drive for independence, and he preferred to work in close collaboration with Nyerere so that a stable country would emerge. Their joint efforts culminated in the elections of 1960, when TANU won 70 of 71 seats in the legislature; Nyerere was asked to form the new government, thereby becoming Tanganyika's first elected chief minister. Independence followed quickly on Dec. 9, 1961.

But the success of TANU made obvious many defects in the structure of the party. Nyerere realized that TANU's real work would come with independence; therefore in a dramatic move he resigned as head of the government in

January 1962 to devote his activities to rebuilding the party. His work was successful, and he was overwhelmingly elected in the 1962 elections as the first president of Tanganyika, which became a republic on Dec. 9, 1962.

Political Philosophy

During the years of political struggle, Nyerere had developed the outlines for the policies which his economically poor country should follow. With the motto of *Uhuru na Kazi* (Freedom and Work), he at once mounted a major attack on what he considered the three major enemies of his people—poverty, ignorance, and disease. Nyerere believed that it was unwise for a poor country to depend on the uncertain aid of the richer nations for progress. Instead, Tanganyikans were encouraged to utilize their own strengths, especially their ample manpower, to develop their country themselves.

A series of self-help schemes in road building and other construction projects during 1963-1964 exemplified this approach. In this struggle for human dignity Nyerere found no place for an elite of officeholders, and various schemes were initiated to break down any emerging class barriers within the country. This line of development was most forcefully stated in Nyerere's Arusha Declaration of 1967.

In January 1964 Nyerere had to face the most serious crisis of his political career. The Tanganyikan army mutinied, demanding higher pay and the full Africanization of the officer corps. Nyerere was forced into hiding, and stability was regained only when British forces were called in to restore order. Part of the reason for this unrest was the Zanzibar revolution of January 1964, when revolutionary groups overthrew that island's Arab-led government. The new radical government, with heavy Communist leanings, was subsequently encouraged to unite with Tanganyika. The result was the united country of Tanzania, with Abeid Karume of Zanzibar serving under Nyerere as first vice president.

Looking Back

By 1967, with western nations such as the United States cautious about investing in Nyerere's socialist country, TANU adopted the system of broad government control called the *Arusha Declaration,* designed to regulate economic and social development. This measure called for complete government control of all means of production and distribution, demanded broad development projects, presented a code of ethics for the nation's political leaders, and emphasized the two main themes of egalitarianism and self-reliance along the lines of *Ujamaa.* Nyerere and TANU hoped to break down emerging class barriers and promote universal human dignity.

In the 40th anniversary *Africa Report* published in 1994, Nyerere reminisced about the future of Africa and his country's political path during his 24-year tenure when his people enjoyed more equality, rights, stability, common language (Swahili) and national identity than most other Africans.

He cited the dramatic change from an impoverished nation that had only 12 doctors for nine million people when he took office. By his departure in 1985, he said it was transformed to a country, although still poor, with "thousands" of Tanzanian-trained doctors. All children were receiving seven years of education where before fewer than half received schooling, and nine out of 10 Tanzanians were literate. He told of a people no longer subservient who had learned to stand upright and could look their former colonial rulers straight in the eye.

But by 1992, Nyerere was on the political sidelines, although he had remained head of the ruling party until two years before. By then, the country was moving away from his brand of African socialism embodied in the principle of *Ujamaa* (familyhood) and moving toward privitization.

Nyerere saw many of those previous gains such as schooling for all children slipping away after the country lost control of its economy to the World Bank and International Monetary Fund beginning in the early 1980s.

Looking toward Africa as a whole, Nyerere said its countries needed time to develop their own "people-centered" democratic political systems, able to forge their futures cooperatively across national boundaries, rather than be pressured by rich European countries to adopt those systems.

Further Reading

Nyerere's own writings offered the best guide to his political philosophy: *African Socialism* (1961); *Freedom and Unity* (1967); *Ujamaa: Essays on Socialism* (1968); and *Freedom and Socialism* (1968). William Edgett Smith, *We Must Run While They Walk: A Portrait of Africa's Julius Nyerere* (1971), was a penetrating biographical study. Much information on his life was available in Judith Listowel, *The Making of Tanganyika* (1965). Recommended for general historical background are B. A. Ogot and J. A. Kieran, eds., *Zamani: A Survey of East African History* (1968), and I. N. Kimambo and A. J. Temu, eds., *A History of Tanzania* (1969). Relevant articles can be found in the *Economist* November 2, 1996 and *Africa Report* September/October 1994. An article on the *Arusha Declaration* can be found on the internet at http://www.journalism.wisc.edu/olw/worldnews/Africa/tanzania.html (July 29, 1997). □

Anders Nygren

Anders Nygren (1890-1978) was a leading representative of the so-called Lundensian school of theology. He was professor at the University of Lund, Sweden, then bishop of Lund. An important figure in the ecumenical movement, he served as president of the Lutheran World Federation.

Anders Nygren was born in Gothenburg, Sweden, on November 15, 1890, the third son of Samuel Nygren, then principal of the Elementary Teachers College and inspector of elementary schools in that city, and his wife Anna Maria. The parents were devout church people, yet open to the cultural and intellectual movements of the time. It was in his father's library that Anders found the books that introduced him to philosophy and theology; it was under his father's guidance that he became involved in the church and interested in the theological debates of the time.

At his father's death the family moved to Lund, where young Nygren attended first the cathedral school, then the university. It was philosophy of religion and the methodology of theology that primarily engaged his interest. His primary teacher was Gustaf Aulen, a student of Nathan Soderblom of Uppsala. Through these influences Nygren was led to study Kant and Schleiermacher, Troeltsch and Otto.

Upon graduation in 1912 he was ordained and assigned to a succession of churches in the Gothenburg Diocese. Here he continued his studies, writing a doctoral dissertation on the philosophical issues involved in the theoretical definition of the nature of religion. The book was entitled *The Religious Apriori.*

When Nygren presented his dissertation at the University of Lund in 1921 he was immediately made *docent* (lecturer) in philosophy of religion. Here he was soon joined by Ragnar Bring, a young philosopher of religion who was also a student of Aulen. Together these two young men developed a program to establish theology—especially the discipline of systematic theology—as an acknowledged and respectable academic enterprise within the modern university.

The following decade Nygren produced several important books, one on the scientific foundations of systematic theology, another on philosophical and Christian ethics. In 1924 he became professor of systematic theology, a post which he held until 1948, when he was made bishop of Lund Diocese. Bring became professor in 1933 as Aulen's successor. Aulen, Nygren, and Bring were the three scholars forming the triumvirate called "the Lundensian school of theology."

Nygren's years at the university were filled with teaching, research, and writing. He wanted to do theology in a respectable scientific manner, and to this end he applied the method he had developed—what he called "motif-research"—in a series of historical-critical investigations of basic Christian concepts. His primary focus was *agape*—the Christian concept of love. In seeking out the essence of Christianity, Nygren researched the New Testament, the theology of the early fathers, and the entire history of Christian doctrine to find the unique character of *agape.* He also was interested in the contrasting concept of *eros.*

These studies resulted in a two-volume work, *Agape and Eros,* first published in 1930-1936 and later in four other Swedish editions, two English editions, two Japanese editions, and translations into six other languages. The work is ranked as one of the classics of Christian theology and is certainly one of the most noteworthy theological books of the 20th century. He also wrote a major theological commentary to Paul's Letter to the Romans.

Nygren's influence expanded rapidly when he became an early participant in the ecumenical movement. He repre-sented the Church of Sweden at the Faith and Order Conference at Lausanne in 1927 and at Edinburgh ten years later. He was influential in directing the ecumenical movement to the central points of the Christian message; for Nygren, "the way to unity is the way to the center." He continued to make this point within the World Council of Churches (WCC) at Amsterdam (1948) and Lund (1952), where he served as chairman of the European Section of the Theological Commission on Christ and His Church. This commission was charged with working out the Ecumenical implications of baptism in the struggle for Christian unity. The commission had serious difficulties reaching consensus, until Nygren guided the discussions to the christological foundations for baptism. Many of Nygren's emphases can still be found in the convergence document on "Baptism, Eucharist and Ministry," which was adopted by Faith and Order in 1982 for study and response by the WCC member churches.

Nygren's period as bishop of Lund (1948-1959) was also a productive time. He travelled widely, spoke on many subjects—from philosophy to theology to ethics and Christian practice—and wrote incessantly. He served as president of the Lutheran World Federation and spoke on behalf of his denomination both internally and in ecumenical conversations. A series of lectures on *Christ and His Church* was translated and published in England, Germany, America, and Finland. He received honorary degrees from colleges and universities in Hungary, Germany, Scotland, Canada, and the United States.

In his retirement, from 1959 to his death in 1978, Nygren remained in Lund and returned to his first love, philosophical and theological studies. He found that the newer trends in the analytical study of philosophy could be utilized in the preparation of his own magnum opus, *Meaning and Method, Prolegomena to a Scientific Philosophy of Religion and a Scientific Theology.* The book was published in England and America in 1972 and became recognized as the crowning point of Nygren's theoretical production. The work secured for Nygren a central place in the philosophical and theological debate of his time.

Unfortunately, toward the end of his life Nygren's health failed him. Bedridden and physically dependent, he was still mentally sharp and received a great many visitors who desired to discuss his work. After his death his papers were located in the University Library at Lund.

Anders Nygren was a complex personality, with interests and commitments that spanned scholarship and preaching, the academy and the church, Lutheranism and the ecumenical movement, science and piety, single "motifs" and systematic theology, and philosophical and biblical studies. Nygren was a modern thinker, but he was not a modernist. He was concerned with fundamentals, but he was not a fundamentalist. He was clearly a liberal theologian, but he did not espouse theological liberalism. He was a critical scholar, but he did not subscribe uncritically to philosophical criticism. In some respects he was radical, in others conservative. He had a keen interest in scientific thought, and yet he was committed to the search for the essence of Christian faith.

With all these elements flowing together and being brought into harmony in his own life and thought, it is only "meet and right" that Anders Nygren was honored with the inclusion of his biography in the series "Makers of the Modern Theological Mind."

Further Reading

The biography included in the series "Makers of the Modern Theological Mind," *Anders Nygren,* was written by Thor Hall (1978, 1985). A scholarly survey of Nygren's thought is *The Philosophy and Theology of Anders Nygren,* edited by Charles W. Kegley (1970). Nygren's major works are summarized in "The Nygren Corpus: Annotations to the Major Works of Anders Nygren of Lund," by Thor Hall, in *Journal of the AAR* 47:2. The definitive study of the Lundensian school of theology is Thor Hall's *A Framework for Faith* (1970). Also helpful is Nels F. S. Ferre's *Swedish Contributions to Modern Theology* (1967). Some more negative reviews of Nygren are those by Van A. Harvey in *Religious Studies Review* 1:1 and Gustaf Wingren in *Theology in Conflict* (1958). □

Nzinga Nkuwu

Nzinga Nkuwu (died 1506) was an African ruler also known as João I, the first baptized manikongo, or king of Kongo. The state of Kongo was under Portuguese influence in the late 15th and early 16th centuries.

Nzinga Nkuwu reigned as the divine king of a Bantu African state near the mouth of the Congo River when the Portuguese explorer Diogo Cão discovered it in 1482. Nzinga Nkuwu was fifth in succession of the founding dynasty of Kongo, which had begun in the late 14th century and came to a shadowy end in the late 19th century.

The Kingdom of Kongo was centered in what is today northern Angola, with its capital at Mbanza (later São Salvador), 125 miles from the sea. It exerted authority over a large area bordering the Congo River in the north, the Dande River in the south, the Kwango River in the east, and the Atlantic Ocean in the west. It was divided into six or more provinces under nominally hereditary rulers who more or less acknowledged the supremacy or paramountcy of the manikongo.

The Portuguese equated this polity with their own strongly centralized feudal monarchy. They envisioned its discovery as a great opportunity to secure an African alliance in furtherance of their grand design for a route to the Far East, converts for Christianity, and an anti-Islamic alliance with the semimythical Prester John, Christian king of the Indies. In reality the manikongo's state was rather less stable and less substantial than the Portuguese supposed.

Alliance With Portugal

Two or three years after the first contact, Nzinga Nkuwu welcomed Diogo Cão on a new expedition which brought gifts and emissaries from the Portuguese king, João II. Doubtless he saw in them equally attractive opportunities for an alliance which would strengthen the authority of his own state over its tributaries. Urging the further exchange of gifts, goods, and representatives, he dispatched an African delegation to the Portuguese court, advising João II that he would welcome priests, artisans, and farmers from Portugal to aid his realm.

Consequently, in 1490, Nzinga Nkuwu received another expedition, of three ships under the command of Rui de Sousa, bearing priests, workers, soldiers, and Africans who had been tutored in Portugal. Nzinga Nkuwu was baptized into Christianity within the month (taking the name of his royal Portuguese brother, "João") as João I, first Christian king of Kongo. The connection brought early advantages. Nzinga's power increased, and Portuguese soldiers aided in suppressing a rebellion on the coast north of the Congo's mouth. He sent his first son, Nzinga Mvemba, baptized as Affonso, to Portugal, where he was educated for 10 years, returning more a European prince than an African one.

João I's Portuguese alliance soon soured. By the mid-1490s only a handful of official priestly representatives remained, plus a few soldiers with orders to search overland for Prester John. By 1500 the Kongo "experiment" was at least temporarily abandoned by the Portuguese crown for the sake of the great Indian Ocean discoveries, commencing with Vasco da Gama's historic voyage of 1498. Official relations gave way to a new breed of largely uncontrolled adventurers and renegade traders from the island of São Tomé in the Gulf of Guinea. These operated with different objectives: personal commercial exploitation and the swiftly rising slave trade.

Rejection of European Culture

Meanwhile, the consequences of confrontation between deeply differing cultures and policies were felt in the rise of division and factionalism in the manikongo's court. Traditionalists resisted the imposition of an alien religion coupled with a monogamous social ethic which threatened the structure of politics and the social security of a polygamous society. The parties polarized around rival heirs to João I's throne—his first and second sons, the one the heir presumptive, Affonso, a Europeanized Christian, and the other a traditionalist abetted by the Manikongo's advisers and wives.

The latter son prevailed, and João I, persuaded by the demands of his polygamous court, lapsed from Christianity, exiled his son Affonso to a distant province with his mother and loyal Portuguese advisers, and resumed the original aspect of Nzinga Nkuwu. Nevertheless, upon his death in 1506, the struggle for succession was concluded with the accession of Nzinga Mvemba: Affonso I, the second Christian king of Kongo.

Thus began an extraordinary partnership which remains one of the poignant might-have-beens in the bitter story of Africa's experience with Europe. For what began in the expectation of mutual advantage and development degenerated within two reigns into the rapine of plunder, civil war, and the slave trade.

Further Reading

The important 16th-century account of Kongo is that of merchant-explorer Duarte Lopes and Filippe Pigafetta, translated into English as *Report of the Kingdom of the Congo* (1881). The most useful accounts in English are in James Duffy, *Portuguese Africa* (1959), and Basil Davidson, *Black Mother: The Years of the African Slave Trade* (1961), which also appears in recent editions as *The African Slave Trade*. □

O

Annie Oakley

Annie Oakley (1860-1926), originally Phoebe Anne Oakley Mozee, was known as "The Peerless Lady Wing-Shot," for her marksmanship. She led one of the fabled lives of America's Wild West.

Annie Oakley was born in a Drake Country, Ohio, log cabin on Aug. 13, 1860, the sixth of eight children. After her father died in a blizzard, she began shooting rabbits and quail to provide the family income. Then she went to town, won a shooting match against a vaudeville star named Frank E. Butler, and earned more by shooting glass balls and playing cards at 30 paces.

A few years later she married Butler, and he became her manager. Buffalo Bill hired them for his Wild West Show in 1885. Helped by publicists like Nate Salsbury and her own incredible shooting eye, Oakley remained a star for 17 years, surmounting even a train wreck in 1901 that partially paralyzed her for a time.

Let no one doubt that Oakley could do what she claimed. Thousands of people saw Annie slice a playing card with the thin edge toward her by shooting at 30 paces. Kaiser Wilhelm II had her shoot a cigarette out of his lips. She was death to moving glass balls; one day, by official count, she shot 4,772 out of 5,000.

Oakley charmed everyone with her simplicity and modesty, including Queen Victoria. Dressed in western costume and beating many a man in what was traditionally a masculine world, she intrigued young and old alike. (No wonder that Irving Berlin made her the subject of his Broad-

way musical *Annie Get Your Gun,* which played throughout the 1950s.)

A fundamentalist in religion, Oakley read the Bible throughout her life. She was never involved in the kind of scandal that plagued Buffalo Bill, and at least 18 orphan girls were educated through her generosity.

When Annie Oakley died on Nov. 3, 1926, there was wide mourning and many tributes. By then, any punched complimentary ticket—which looked as if it had holes shot through it—was called an "Annie Oakley." Born at the beginning of the Civil War, she lived through the "classic period" of transition from frontier to 20th-century statehood in the West. Whether or not she was the best lady shot in that epoch, she certainly was thought to be best; fact, fiction, and musical comedy have combined to make "Sharpshooter" an indelible adjunct to her name.

Further Reading

The first creditable biography of Annie Oakley, Courtney Riley Cooper's *Annie Oakley: Woman at Arms* (1927), was surpassed by Annie Fern Swartwout, *Missie: An Historical Biography of Anne Oakley* (1947). See also Stewart H. Holbrook, *Little Annie Oakley and Other Rugged People* (1948), and Walter Havighurst, *Annie Oakley of the Wild West* (1954).

Additional Sources

Havighurst, Walter, *Annie Oakley of the Wild West,* Lincoln: University of Nebraska Press, 1992.

Kasper, Shirl, *Annie Oakley,* Norman: University of Oklahoma Press, 1992.

Riley, Glenda, *The life and legacy of Annie Oakley,* Norman: University of Oklahoma Press, 1994.

Sayers, Isabelle S., *Annie Oakley and Buffalo Bill's wild west,* New York: Dover Publications, 1981. □

year, after beginning work on her doctorate in English, Oates inadvertently encountered one of her own stories in Margaret Foley's anthology *Best American Short Stories.* This discovery prompted Oates to write professionally, and in 1963 she published her first volume of short stories, *By the North Gate* (1963). Oates taught at the University of Detroit between 1961 and 1967. In 1967 she and her husband moved to Canada to teach at the University of Windsor, where together they founded the *Ontario Review.* Since leaving the University of Windsor in 1977, Oates has been writer-in-residence at Princeton University in New Jersey.

Oates's first novel, *With Shuddering Fall* (1964), foreshadows her preoccupation with evil and violence in the story of a destructive romance between a teenage girl and a thirty-year-old stock car driver that ends with his death in an accident. Oates's best-known and critically acclaimed early novels form a trilogy exploring three distinct segments of American society. Critics attribute the naturalistic ambience of these works to the influence of such twentieth-century authors as William Faulkner, Theodore Dreiser, and James T. Farrell. Oates's first installment, *A Garden of Earthly Delights* (1967), is set in rural Eden County and chronicles the life of the daughter of a migrant worker who marries a wealthy farmer in order to provide for her illegitimate son. The woman's idyllic existence is destroyed, however, when the boy murders his stepfather and kills himself. In *Expensive People* (1967), the second work in the series, Oates exposes the superficial world of suburbanites whose preoccupation with material comforts reveals their spiritual pov-

Joyce Carol Oates

One of the United States's most prolific and versatile contemporary writers, Joyce Carol Oates (born 1938) focuses upon the spiritual, sexual, and intellectual decline of modern American society.

Oates was born into a working-class Catholic family outside Lockport, New York, and was raised amid a rural setting on her maternal grandparents' farm. She attended a one-room schoolhouse in Erie County, a parallel community to her fictitious Eden County where many of her works are set, and displayed an early interest in storytelling by drawing picture-tales before she could write. Oates has said that her childhood "was dull, ordinary, nothing people would be interested in," but has admitted that "a great deal frightened me." In 1953 at age fifteen, Oates wrote her first novel, though it was rejected by publishers who found its subject matter, which concerned the rehabilitation of a drug dealer, exceedingly depressing for adolescent audiences.

Oates began her academic career at Syracuse University and graduated from there as class valedictorian in 1960. In 1961 she received a Master of Arts degree in English from the University of Wisconsin, where she met and married Raymond Joseph Smith, an English educator. The following

erty. The final volume in the trilogy, *them* (1969), which won the National Book Award for fiction, depicts the violence and degradation endured by three generations of an urban Detroit family. Critics acknowledge that Oates's experiences as a teacher in Detroit during the early 1960s contributed to her accurate rendering of the city and its social problems. Betty DeRamus stated: "Her days in Detroit did more for Joyce Carol Oates than bring her together with new people—it gave her a tradition to write from, the so-called American Gothic tradition of exaggerated horror and gloom and mysterious and violent incidents."

Oates's novels of the 1970s explore characters involved with various American professional and cultural institutions while interweaving elements of human malevolence and tragedy. *Wonderland* (1971), for example, depicts a brilliant surgeon who is unable to build a satisfying home life, resulting in estrangement from his wife, children, and society. *Do with Me What You Will* (1973) focuses upon a young attorney who is lauded by his peers for his devotion to liberal causes. *The Assassins: A Book of Hours* (1975) is a psychological tale which dramatizes the effects of the murder of a conservative politician on his wife and two brothers. *Son of the Morning* (1978) documents the rise and fall from grace of Nathan Vickery, an evangelist whose spirituality is alternately challenged and affirmed by various events in his life. *Unholy Loves* (1979) revolves around the lives of several faculty members of a small New York college. Considered the least emotionally disturbing of Oates's novels, *Unholy Loves* was praised for its indirect humor and gentle satire.

During the early 1980s, Oates published several novels that parody works by such nineteenth-century authors as Louisa May Alcott, Charles Dickens, Edgar Allan Poe, and Charlotte and Emily Bronte. *Bellefleur* (1980) follows the prescribed formula for a Gothic multigenerational saga, utilizing supernatural occurrences while tracing the lineage of an exploitative American family. Oates included explicit violence in this work; for example, a man deliberately crashes his plane into the Bellefleur mansion, killing himself and his family. *A Bloodsmoor Romance* (1982) displays such elements of Gothic romance as mysterious kidnappings and psychic phenomena in the story of five maiden sisters living in rural Pennsylvania in the late 1800s. In *Mysteries of Winterthurn* (1984), Oates borrowed heavily from the works of Poe as she explored the conventions of the nineteenth-century mystery novel. The protagonist of this work is a brilliant young detective who models his career after the exploits of Sir Arthur Conan Doyle's fictional sleuth, Sherlock Holmes. While some critics viewed these works as whimsical, others, citing Oates's accomplished depiction of evil, maintained that they are significant literary achievements.

Oates's recent novels explore the nature and ramifications of obsession. *Solstice* (1985) revolves around a relationship between a young divorcee and an older woman that evolves into an emotional power struggle. In *Marya: A Life* (1986), a successful writer and academician attempts to locate her alcoholic mother, who had abused and later abandoned her as a child. *Lives of the Twins* (1987), which

Oates wrote under the pseudonym of Rosamond Smith, presents a tale of love and erotic infatuation involving a woman, her lover, and her lover's twin brother. With *You Must Remember This* (1987), Oates returned to a naturalistic portrait of families under emotional and moral distress. Suicide attempts, violent beatings, disfiguring accidents, and incest figure prominently in this novel, which centers on an intense love affair between a former boxer and his adolescent niece. Set in Eden County and containing references to such historical events as Senator Joseph McCarthy's anti-Communist campaign, the executions of Julius and Ethel Rosenberg for conspiracy to commit espionage, and the Korean War, *You Must Remember This* earned high praise for its evocation of American life during the early 1950s. John Updike stated that this work "rallies all [of Oates's] strengths and is exceedingly fine—a storm of experience whose reality we cannot doubt, a fusion of fact and feeling, vision and circumstance which holds together, and holds us to it, through our terror and dismay."

Oates's works in other genres also address darker aspects of the human condition. Most critics contend that Oates's short fiction, for which she has twice received the O. Henry Special Award for Continuing Achievement, is best suited for evoking the urgency and emotional power of her principal themes. Such collections as *By the North Gate; Where Are You Going, Where Have You Been?: Stories of Young America* (1974); *The Lamb of Abyssalia* (1980); and *Raven's Wing* (1986) contain pieces that focus upon violent and abusive relationships between the sexes. One widely anthologized story, "Where Are You Going, Where Have You Been?," a tale of female adolescence and sexual awakening, is considered a classic of modern short fiction and was adapted for film. Oates has also composed several dramas that were produced off-Broadway in New York and has published numerous volumes of poetry. In addition, she is a respected essayist and literary critic whose nonfiction works are praised for the logic and sensibility with which she examines a variety of subjects.

them chronicles three decades, beginning in 1937, in the life of the Wendall family. The novel "is partly made up of 'composite' characters and events, clearly influenced by the disturbances of the long hot summer of 1967," Oates acknowledges. She no longer suggests, as she did in the original author's note, that her protagonist Maureen Wendall was actually her former student. That author's note, later repudiated by Oates as a fiction in itself, describes the book as "a work of history in fictional form," and asserts that Maureen's remembrances shaped the story: "[The book] is based mainly upon Maureen's numerous recollections. . . . It is to her terrible obsession with her personal history that I owe the voluminous details of this novel." Although regarded as a self-contained work, *them* can also be considered the concluding volume in a trilogy that explores different subgroups of American society. The trilogy includes *A Garden of Earthly Delights*, about the migrant poor, and *Expensive People*, about the suburban rich. The goal of all three novels, as Oates explains in the *Saturday Review*, is to present a cross-section of "unusually sensitive—but hopefully representative—young men and women, who confront the puzzle of American life in different ways and come to different ends.''

Further Reading

Allen, Mary, *The Necessary Blankness: Women in Major American Fiction of the Sixties,* University of Illinois Press, 1974.

Authors in the News, Volume 1, Gale, 1976.

Bellamy, Joe David, editor, *The New Fiction: Interviews with Innovative American Writers,* University of Illinois Press, 1974.

Bender, Eileen, *Joyce Carol Oates,* Indiana University Press, 1987.

Bloom, Harold, editor, *Modern Critical Views: Joyce Carol Oates,* Chelsea House, 1987.

Contemporary Literary Criticism, Gale, Volume 1, 1973, Volume 2, 1974, Volume 3, 1975, Volume 6, 1976, Volume 9, 1978, Volume 11, 1979, Volume 15, 1980, Volume 19, 1981, Volume 33, 1985.

Creighton, Joanne V., *Joyce Carol Oates,* G. K. Hall, 1979. □

Titus Oates

The English political and religious demagogue Titus Oates (1649-1705) was the chief fabricator of the Popish Plot, a spurious plan of 1678 supposedly hatched by the Jesuits to assassinate King Charles II and to enthrone his Roman Catholic brother, James.

Titus Oates was born at Oakham. Though he was expelled from the Merchant Tailors' School at the age of 16, he attended Cambridge University, leaving, as his tutor noted, because ''he was a great dunce, ran into debt; and, being sent away for want of money, never took a degree.'' Nevertheless, by 1673 Oates had somehow managed to enter the Anglican clergy. He used his office to defame a local schoolmaster, but he was denounced as a perjurer and jailed; later he escaped. After being expelled from a brief naval chaplaincy, Oates went to London, again posing as a cleric, though it is questionable whether he was ever ordained. In 1676 he joined forces with a vehement anti-Catholic clergyman, Israel Tonge. Together they projected an elaborate plan to discredit Roman Catholicism as a treasonous international conspiracy. The two, taking advantage of the not altogether unfounded rumor that King Charles II planned to sponsor the legalization of the Roman Catholic faith, magnified it into a specific plot to destroy the Protestant Church–state constitution. Oates, feigning conversion to Roman Catholicism for the purpose of gathering evidence, attended two Jesuit missionary schools on the Continent, being quickly expelled from both. He returned to England in 1678 with fictitious evidence that convinced gullible government officials of a plot to kill the king. For 3 years, Oates, through the apparently Catholic-inspired murder of an associate, the inadvertent discovery of seditious letters, confessions wrung from intimidated witnesses, and the timidity of the king himself, was given plenary power by

Parliament and had merely to accuse to convict. He caused the execution of 35 persons, including the Roman Catholic archbishop of Ireland.

Oates's testimony was not discredited until the end of 1681, when it was finally realized that his evidence was hearsay and contradictory. His power and large salary were gradually withdrawn, and when James II came to the throne in 1685, Oates was convicted of perjury, whipped, pilloried, and jailed. Though he was released after the Glorious Revolution of 1688, the rest of Oates's life was marked by lawsuits, debt, and fruitless intrigue and his entrance into, and expulsion from, the Baptist Church. He died in London in July 1705.

Oates exploited the traditional English fear of Roman Catholicism between 1678 and 1681, terrifying the government into giving him complete judicial power. His emotional appeal to large audiences is an early instance of the political manipulation of public opinion.

Further Reading

The only biography of Oates is Elaine Dakers, *Titus Oates* (1949), and a short study of Oates is in Thomas Seccombe, ed., *Lives of Twelve Bad Men* (1894). These inadequate works should be supplemented by Sir John Pollock, *Popish Plot* (1903); David Ogg, *England in the Reign of Charles II* (2 vols., 1934; rev. ed. 1962); and Francis S. Ronald, *The Attempted Whig Revolution of 1678-1681* (1937). □

Apolo Milton Obote

Apolo Milton Obote (born 1925) was a Ugandan political leader who guided his country to independence in 1962. He worked to create a centralized government to replace the divided state left by the British, but his ruthless rule in the 1980s was marked by torture and repression and the killing of more than 100,000 civilians.

Milton Obote was born at Akokoro village in Lango territory in the northern part of the British Uganda Protectorate in 1925. He was the son of a poor local chief in the Lango tribe. He began his education in 1940 at the Lira Protestant Missionary School, continued it at Gulu Junior Secondary School and Busoga College, Mwiri, and finished it at Makerere College (1948-1950). Because the Buganda tribespeople who lived in southern Uganda dominated the economy, Obote went to Kenya to find work. He worked there first for an engineering firm and then for several industrial concerns. While in Kenya, he became interested in politics and was a founding member of the Kenya African Union.

Forging Independence

In 1956 Obote returned to Uganda. He entered politics when he was asked to return to the Lango district to replace a local Uganda National Congress party leader who had been imprisoned. In 1958, a sudden vacancy caused by the resignation of the Lango member of the Legislative Council led to Obote's appointment as a replacement. In Uganda's first direct elections later that year, Obote won the seat by a wide margin, and his rise in Ugandan politics was under way.

Obote soon became president of the Uganda National Congress party, one of many parties trying to forge a unity to bring Uganda independence. In 1960, Obote joined his organization to a rival party, thus founding the Uganda People's Congress; he became its president. When a 1961 conference provided for elections leading to independence, Obote allied his party to the Buganda party under Kabaka (King) Yekka in order to defeat Benedicto Kiwanuka's ruling Democratic party. The coalition gained a majority of the Ugandan votes, and Obote became Uganda's prime minister. He presided over British withdrawal in October 1962.

Failure to Unify Nation

But independence did not solve Uganda's problems. Buganda had been an ancient African kingdom, and British rule had left Buganda autonomous within the Uganda Protectorate. It was the most prosperous part of the country and home to Uganda's most educated elite. In accord with Uganda's constitution, agreed to by the British prior to independence, Obote appointed the ruler of Buganda to the largely ceremonial office of president of Uganda. But Bugandans were not willing to settle for less than a dominant place in the nation's politics, and Obote's alliance with Kabaka Yekka became increasingly unstable as friction grew between Buganda and the central government. The problem erupted into a crisis in 1966. Obote suspended the constitution, declared a state of emergency, and assumed full power. He introduced a new constitution, abolished Buganda and other kingdom-states within Uganda, and assaulted Kampala, the capital of Buganda under the leadership of General Idi Amin. The Bugandan king fled and died in exile in London.

In the late 1960s Obote tried to undermine the Bugandan economic power by moving the nation closer to socialism. In fact, he instituted authoritarian one-party rule but failed to unify the country. On Jan. 25, 1971, while Obote was out of the country on a diplomatic mission, Uganda's army under Amin ousted him from the presidency. Obote fled to Tanzania, and Amin for eight years instituted a bloody regime of terror and repression.

Second Regime of Terror

In 1979, an invasion aided by Tanzania overthrew Amin. After months of unsuccessful sectarian regimes, Obote won an election in 1980 which was widely believed to have been rigged. Obote's second regime continued Amin's terrorist tactics. Obote was opposed by the Bugandas, by the Acholi peoples of the north, and most importantly by a guerilla movement in the west, the National Resistance Army. Under Obote's direction, the Ugandan army tried to crush the guerillas by destroying entire villages and decimating the population. Amnesty International and other groups denounced Obote's police state and torture tactics, and he was charged with directing the killing of more than 100,000 civilians. In 1985, Obote was toppled in a coup and fled to Kenya. He was then granted political asylum in Zambia. His political career was over. Instead of being remembered as the leader of Uganda's independence movement, he left a legacy of totalitarianism and terror.

Further Reading

Obote's early career was chronicled in Ali Mazrui, *Violence and Thought: Essays on Social Tensions in Africa* (1968); A. J. Hughes, *East Africa: Kenya, Uganda, Tanzania* (1969). An earlier work on politics in Uganda was David E. Apter, *The Political Kingdom in Uganda: A Study in Bureaucratic Nationalism* (1961; rev. ed. 1967). A comprehensive history of Ugandan politics since independence and Obote's role is found in David Apter, "Democracy for Uganda: A Case for Comparison," in *Daedalus* (Summer 1995). Also see the A & E Biography website http://www.biography.com (August 13, 1997) for a brief profile. □

Jacob Obrecht

Jacob Obrecht (1450-1505), a Dutch composer, was one of the most important composers in the dominant Netherlandish tradition of the 15th century.

Jacob Obrecht also spelled Hobrecht, was born on St. Cecilia's Day, 1450, in either Bergen op Zoom or Sicily. The information and the uncertainty come from his motet *Mille quingentis*, a lament on the death of his father, Willem, in which he states that he was born on this day when his father was crossing Sicily. Other evidence links the family to Bergen op Zoom and gives the date 1450.

Obrecht spent most of his childhood in the Netherlands, where he must have received his education. As with many of the events of his life, the circumstances of his education are unknown. He may have received a portion of his musical training from his father, who was a city trumpeter in Ghent. He must also have attended a university, since he was a priest by 1480.

The early career of Obrecht is difficult to trace. He may have been in Florence and Ferrara as early as 1474, although evidence for this is not conclusive. In 1479-1480 he held positions in Bergen op Zoom. In 1484 he became chapel master in Cambrai. This would have brought him into close contact with the music of Guillaume Dufay, who had been in residence there for the 30 years preceding his death in 1474. By November 1485 Obrecht was succentor of St-Donatien in Bruges; in 1487 he received a leave to visit Ercole I d'Este in Ferrara. Ercole attempted unsuccessfully to provide a benefice in Ferrara to keep the composer there. Obrecht returned to Bruges, where he remained until 1491. He is listed in the accounts of the Church of Our Lady in Antwerp from 1494 until 1496 and again from 1501 until 1503. He was in Bruges in 1491, 1498, and 1500 and in Bergen op Zoom in 1496 and 1498. In 1504 he went to Ferrara to serve as composer in the D'Este chapel. He died when the plague struck Ferrara in 1505.

Obviously well known in the Low Countries for much of his career, Obrecht also began to be famous in Italy in the 1480s, when Ercole I d'Este was deeply impressed by his music. During his lifetime Obrecht's works were printed in Venice by Ottavio Petrucci, who, in addition to including secular works and motets in a collection, printed a book of five Masses in 1503. Within decades after his death Obrecht had come to be regarded as among the "ancients" (*antichi*) and among those who first made music. This was the result of the important changes in musical style in the first decades of the 16th century.

Obrecht's output includes 8 French chansons, at least 16 settings of Dutch texts, and 1 or 2 settings of Italian texts. The predominance of Dutch texts is significant for a composer of this period and marks the beginning of the regular appearance of secular music in languages other than French. His approximately 25 motets are in some ways conservative in their treatment of *cantus firmus* and lack of pervading imitation, in some cases. His best works are probably his Masses, at least 25 in number, which employ a wide variety of *cantus firmus* techniques.

Although Obrecht is often linked with Johannes Ockeghem, the two composers have rather different styles. The harmonic and rhythmic structure of most of Obrecht's music is quite clear. This results in part from a frequent use of sequence, a device that in some of his weaker works is overemployed. He also has a tendency to have the outer voices move in parallel tenths for considerable stretches of a work. Although one can find relationships between his works and those of his predecessors and successors, in many ways Obrecht stands outside of the main path of development of music in the second half of the 15th century.

Further Reading

Obrecht's life and works are discussed at some length in Gustave Reese, *Music in the Renaissance* (1954; rev. ed. 1959). Also useful is Manfred F. Bukofzer, *Studies in Medieval and Renaissance Music* (1950). Donald Jay Grout, *A History of Western Music* (1960), has a good discussion of Obrecht and is recommended for general background.

Additional Sources

Wegman, Rob C., *Born for the muses: the life and Masses of Jacob Obrecht,* Oxford: Clarendon Press; New York: Oxford University Press, 1994. □

Álvaro Obregón

Álvaro Obregón (1880-1928) was a Mexican revolutionary general and president. His administration marks the beginning of the constructive phase of the Mexican Revolution.

A native of Sonora, born on Feb. 19, 1880, at Siquisava near Álamos, Álvaro Obregón was educated in his home state and was principally a small landholder when he first entered politics in 1911, winning election as municipal president of Huatabampo. The following year he recruited a small force to defend Francisco Madero's government against the Pascual Orozco rebellion. Promoted to the rank of colonel during this campaign, he was named military commander of the state capital, Hermosillo, in 1913.

That year Obregón organized resistance against Victoriano Huerta in Sonora, capturing Nogales on March 13, 1913. Venustiano Carranza designated him head of the war section of the Constitutionalists' Secretariat of the Interior and commander of the Northwest Army. While Pancho Villa moved southward in the central portion of the country, Obregón swept down the west coast, capturing Guadalajara and finally leading the triumphant Constitutionalist army into Mexico City in August 1914.

When a Revolutionary schism developed between Carranza and Villa, Obregón remained with the former in the withdrawal to Veracruz. There he negotiated the Constitutionalist agreement with labor and strongly urged Carranza to issue reform decrees relative to land and labor during the winter of 1914/1915. It was the military leadership of Obregón that gradually recovered the route to the capital and then dealt the *villistas*—a series of military reverses at Celaya and León in the spring of 1915. During one of these engagements Obregón lost an arm. And it was Obregón working behind the scenes who contributed significantly to the triumph of the radical elements in the Constituent Assembly at Querétaro in late 1916 and early 1917.

Reformist President

After briefly serving as secretary of war under Carranza, Obregón returned to private life as a chick-pea farmer until the presidential election of 1920. Together with Plutarco Calles and Adolfo de la Huerta, Obregón successfully revolted under the Plan of Agua Prieta (April 1920) against Carranza's efforts to impose his successor. During De la Huerta's provisional presidency Obregón was elected president for the 1920-1924 period.

It was a period of peace and constructive activity. For the first time the Revolution had a presidential regime committed to carrying out the program of the movement. The basic demands of the *zapatistas* were met and the first wide-scale distribution of land took place. José Vasconcelos directed an imaginative educational program, including volunteer teachers and cultural missions, and a cultural renaissance became dramatically visible with the mural painters. The interests of the favored labor group, led by Luis Morones, were protected.

However, the regime faced difficult times, threatened from without by United States intervention and from within by conservative and dissident Revolutionary elements. In 1923, by the Bucareli Agreement, United States recognition finally was achieved with an apparent settlement of the petroleum and land questions as well as an arrangement on claims. The development came none too soon, as rivalry for the presidential succession brought the De la Huerta rebellion (1923-1924). Support of peasants and workers plus the assistance of the neighbor to the north enabled the regime to triumph.

In 1927 the constitution was reformed to permit Obregón to again seek the presidency. Several abortive military revolts had to be put down, but Obregón was again victorious in the election of 1928. However, on August 17 the president-elect was killed in a restaurant in San Ángel in the Federal District by a religious fanatic, José León Toral. It was ironic since Obregón had been quietly negotiating with Church leaders for a peaceful resolution of the Church-state conflict once he took office.

Further Reading

Although there are many significant writings on the Obregón period in Spanish by participants, English readers should turn first to contributions by two contemporaneous observers: Ernest Henry Grüening, *Mexico and Its Heritage* (1928), and Frank Tannenbaum, *Mexico: The Struggle for Peace and Bread* (1956). A general review of the uprising, which includes a portrait of Obregón, is Ronald Atkin, *Revolution! Mexico, 1910-20* (1970). For specific aspects of the period see Marjorie Ruth Clark, *Organized Labor in Mexico* (1934); Hubert Clinton Herring and Herbert Weinstock eds., *Renascent Mexico* (1935); and Robert E. Quirk, *The Mexican Revolution, 1914-1915: The Convention of Aguascalientes* (1970).

Additional Sources

Hall, Linda B. (Linda Biesele), *Álvaro Obregón: power and revolution in Mexico, 1911-1920,* College Station: Texas A&M University Press, 1981. □

Sean O'Casey

The Irish dramatist Sean O'Casey (1880-1964) is considered the greatest of the Irish playwrights who began writing after World War I.

Sean O'Casey was born John Casey on March 31, 1880, the youngest of a large family living in a Dublin slum. He suffered all his life from painful, ulcerated eyeballs and could not read or write until he was 13, having been forced to begin lessons by an interested Irish clergyman. His later experiences among the laboring class in Dublin, where he worked first as an ironmonger, then as a day laborer despite his frail health, gave him a lifelong interest in the problems of the Irish working people. He was a Marxist and took an active part in proletarian reform movements, such as the transport workers strike of 1913, in which he worked with the labor leader Jim Larkin. Arrested as a political prisoner during the Easter Rebellion (1916), he narrowly escaped execution. However, his later socialist and pacificist convictions, his disenchantment with the results of Irish independence, and his professional disappointment concerning the poor reception of his plays led him to leave Ireland in 1926. He announced that his exile was final in 1928, when the Abbey Theatre's director William Butler Yeats rejected O'Casey's play *The Silver Tassie* (1928) as "unsuitable." Earlier, in announcing his break with the Gaelic League, O'Casey had deplored the preference of contemporary Irish audiences for a "Caithlin ni Houlihan in a respectable dress rather than a Caithlin in the garb of a working woman"—a reference to the romantic and aristocratic treatment of Ireland by Yeats and his circle. In 1928 O'Casey married Eileen Reynolds, an actress, and returned secretly to Dublin (Howth) for the honeymoon. The O'Caseys and their three children then made Devon, England, their permanent home.

Career as a Dramatist

Not until O'Casey had experienced life as a political rebel, poet, laborer, and fighter for Irish independence did he finally discover his true profession as a playwright. His first three attempts at drama were rejected by the Abbey Theatre, but his fourth, *The Shadow of a Gunman* (1923), was an immediate success. His later plays, *Cathleen Listens In* (1923) and the tragicomic masterpiece *Juno and the Paycock* (1924), saved the Abbey from near bankruptcy and placed it on a secure financial footing.

Juno and the Paycock concerns the disintegration of the Boyle family in Dublin in 1922. The main characters are Juno, the long-suffering wife of an unemployed loafer, Jack Boyle (the "peacock"); their daughter, who is engaged to an

Anglo-Irish fortune hunter; and their only son, crippled in the Irish Revolution and suspected of treachery. The comic antics of Boyle and his parasitic friend, Joxer, heighten the stark tragedy of the wife's sufferings, the daughter's seduction and desertion, and the son's murder.

O'Casey's next tragedy, *The Plough and the Stars* (1926), caused riots in Dublin, where audiences objected to what seemed his less than sympathetic portrayal of the heroes of the Easter Rebellion. The action concerns the events of Easter Week and their repercussions on Dublin tenement dwellers, who represent a cross section of political and religious opinion. The chief characters are revealed as a combination of honesty, showy patriotism, shallow opportunism, diehard imperialism, and dedicated communism.

Later Plays

The Silver Tassie (1928), rejected by Yeats and Lady Augusta Gregory as unworthy and produced in 1929 in London, marked a distinct change from the earlier earthy plays with their realistic humor and tragedy. This play progressed from naturalistic farce in the first act to pure expressionism in the second; the remaining two acts combined farce and grim tragedy in the symbolist mode. *The Star Turns Red* (1939) was avowedly communistic, although O'Casey in his autobiography later described himself as "a voluntary and settled exile from every creed, from every party, and from every literary clique." His experimental dramas, *Red Roses for Me* (1942) and *Cock-a-Doodle Dandy* (1949), show his increasing reliance on symbolism and fantasy. *The Bishop's Bonfire,* produced in Dublin in 1955, was described by O'Casey as a play about "the ferocious chastity of the Irish, a lament for the condition of Ireland, which is an apathetic country now."

O'Casey's later plays have been called erratic and formless, especially by American critics; but O'Casey insisted on his right to experiment with new forms "to interpret our times." His juxtaposition of various techniques and genres in one play—farce, realistic comedy, satire, melodrama, expressionism, tragedy—was aimed at breaking down the forms and conventions of dramatic realism. The designed formlessness of his last plays may be seen as a carrying out of his earlier dictum concerning drama, that a play should be "not the commonplace portrayal of the trivial events in the life of this man or that woman, but a commentary on life itself."

O'Casey's autobiography is contained in six volumes: *I Knock at the Door* (1939), *Pictures in the Hallway* (1942), *Drums under the Window* (1945), *Inishfallen, Fare Thee Well* (1949), *Rose and Crown* (1952), and *Sunset and Evening Star* (1954). His attitude toward Ireland seemed to have softened somewhat before his death in England on Sept. 18, 1964.

Further Reading

Although there is no definitive biography of O'Casey, his own six-volume autobiography can be supplemented and corrected by several good studies: David Krause, *Sean O'Casey: The Man and His Work* (1960); Saros Cowasjee, *Sean*

O'Casey: The Man behind the Plays (1963); and Jules Koslow, *Sean O'Casey: The Man and His Plays* (1966), an enlargement and revision of a work which appeared in 1950 as *The Green and the Red.* An extensive treatment of O'Casey's contribution to modern drama is found in Robert G. Hogan, *The Experiments of Sean O'Casey* (1960). Recommended for general background are Ernest A. Boyd, *Ireland's Literary Renaissance* (1916) and *The Contemporary Drama of Ireland* (1917); Dorothy Macardle, *The Irish Republic* (1937; first American ed. 1965); Lennox Robinson, *Ireland's Abbey Theater: A History, 1899-1951* (1951); Estella R. Taylor, *The Modern Irish Writers: Cross Currents of Criticism* (1954); Herbert Howarth, *The Irish Writers, 1880-1940* (1958); Vivian Mercier, *The Irish Comic Tradition* (1962); and Robin Skelton and David R. Clark, eds., *The Irish Renaissance: A Gathering of Essays, Memoirs and Letters from the Massachusetts Review* (1965).

Additional Sources

O'Casey, Sean, *Pictures in the hallway,* London, Pan Books, 1971.

Hunt, Hugh, *Sean O'Casey,* Dublin: Gill and Macmillan, 1980.

Krause, David, *Sean O'Casey and his world,* New York: Scribner, 1976.

O'Connor, Garry, *Sean O'Casey: a life,* New York: Atheneum, 1988. □

Ellen Ochoa

A specialist in optics and optical recognition in robotics, Ellen Ochoa (born 1958) is noted both for her distinguished work in inventions and patents and for her role in American space exploration.

Among Ellen Ochoa's optical systems innovations are a device that detects flaws and image recognition apparatus. In the late 1980s she began working with the National Aeronautics and Space Administration (NASA) as an optical specialist. After leading a project team, Ochoa was selected for NASA's space flight program. She made her first flight on the space shuttle Discovery in April 1993, becoming the first Hispanic woman astronaut.

The third of five children of Rosanne (Deardorff) and Joseph Ochoa, she was born May 10, 1958, in Los Angeles, California. She grew up in La Mesa, California; her father was a manager of a retail store and her mother a homemaker. Ochoa attended Grossmont High School in La Mesa and then studied physics at San Diego State University. She completed her bachelor's degree in 1980 and was named valedictorian of her graduating class; she then moved to the department of electrical engineering at Stanford University. She received her master's degree in 1981 and her doctorate in 1985, working with Joseph W. Goodman and Lambertus Hesselink . The topic of her dissertation was real-time intensity inversion using four-wave mixing in photorefractive crystals. While completing her doctoral research she developed and patented a real-time optical inspection technique for defect detection. In an interview with Marianne Fedunkiw, Ochoa said that she considers this her most important scientific achievement so far.

In 1985 she joined Sandia National Laboratories in Livermore, California, where she became a member of the technical staff in the Imaging Technology Division. Her research centered on developing optical filters for noise removal and optical methods for distortion-invariant object recognition. She was coauthor of two more patents based on her work at Sandia, one for an optical system for nonlinear median filtering of images and another for a distortion-invariant optical pattern recognition system.

It was during her graduate studies that Ochoa began considering a career as an astronaut. She told Fedunkiw that friends were applying who encouraged her to join them; ironically, she was the only one from her group of friends to make it into space. Her career at NASA began in 1988 as a group leader in the Photonic Processing group of the Intelligent Systems Technology Branch, located at the NASA Ames Research Center in Moffett Field, California. She worked as the technical lead for a group of eight people researching optical-image and data-processing techniques for space-based robotics. Six months later she moved on to become chief of the Intelligent Systems Technology Branch. Then in January 1990 she was chosen for the astronaut class, becoming an astronaut in July of 1991.

Her first flight began April 8, 1993, on the orbiter Discovery. She was mission specialist on the STS–56 Atmospheric Research flight, which was carrying the Atmospheric Laboratory for Applications and Science, known as Atlas–2. She was responsible for their primary payload, the Spartan 201 Satellite, and she operated the robotic arm to deploy and retrieve it. This satellite made

forty-eight hours of independent solar observations to measure solar output and determine how the solar wind is produced. Ochoa was the lone female member of the five-person team which made 148 orbits of the earth.

Ochoa's technical assignments have also included flight-software verification in the Shuttle Avionics Integration Laboratory (SAIL), where she was crew representative for robotics development, testing and training, as well as crew representative for flight-software and computer-hardware development. Ochoa was on the STS–66 Atmospheric Laboratory for Applications and Science–3 (ATLAS–3) flight in November 1994. ATLAS–3 continues the Spacelab flight series to study the Sun's energy during an eleven-year solar cycle; the primary purpose of this is to learn how changes in the irradiance of the Sun affect the Earth's environment and climate. On this mission Ochoa was Payload Commander. She is currently based at the Lyndon B. Johnson Space Center in Houston, Texas.

Ochoa is a member of the Optical Society of America and the American Institute of Aeronautics and Astronautics. She has received a number of awards from NASA including the NASA Group Achievement Award for Photonics Technology in 1991 and the NASA Space Flight Medal in 1993. In 1994, she received the Women in Science and Engineering (WISE) Engineering Achievement Award. She has also been recognized many times by the Hispanic community. Ochoa was the 1990 recipient of the National Hispanic Quincentennial Commission Pride Award. She was also given *Hispanic* magazine's 1991 Hispanic Achievement Science Award, and in 1993 she won the Congressional Hispanic Caucus Medallion of Excellence Role Model Award. Ochoa is also a member of the Optical Society of America, the American Institute of Aeronautics ands Astronautics, and Phi Beta Kappa and Sigma Xi honor societies.

Ochoa is married to Coe Fulmer Miles, a computer research engineer. They have no children. Outside of her space research, Ochoa counts music and sports as hobbies. She is an accomplished classical flautist—in 1983 she was the Student Soloist Award Winner in the Stanford Symphony Orchestra. She also has her private pilot's license and in training for space missions flies "back seat" in T–38 aircraft.

Further Reading

NASA Johnson Space Center, *Missions Highlights STS–56,* May 1993.

NASA Johnson Space Center, *Biographical Data—Ellen Ochoa,* August 1993.

NASA Johnson Space Center, *Biographical Data—Ellen Ochoa,,* "http://www.jsc.nasa.gov/Bios/htmlbios/Ochoa.html," July 22, 1997.

Ochoa, Ellen, *Interview with Marianne Fedunkiw,* conducted March 18, 1994. □

Severo Ochoa

Spanish-born biochemist Severo Ochoa (1905-1993) spent his life engaged in research into the workings of the human body. In the 1950s, he was one of the

first scientists to synthesize the newly discovered ribonucleic acid (RNA) in the laboratory.

Severo Ochoa's ability to synthesize RNA in the laboratory marked the first time that scientists managed to combine molecules together in a chain outside a living organism, knowledge that would later prove to be an essential step in enabling scientists to create life in a test tube. For this work, Ochoa received the Nobel Prize in 1959. In addition to his laboratory work, Ochoa, who was trained as a physician in Spain, taught biochemistry and pharmacology to many generations of New York University medical students.

Severo Ochoa was born on September 24, 1905, in Luarca, a small town in the north of Spain. Named after his father, a lawyer, Ochoa was the youngest son in the family. He lived in this mountain town until the age of seven, when his parents decided to move to Málaga, Spain. The move gave young Severo access to a private school education that prepared him for entrance into Málaga College, which is comparable to an American high school. By this time, Ochoa knew that he eventually would enter a career in the sciences; the only question in his mind was in which field he would specialize. Because Ochoa found mathematics at Málaga College very taxing, he decided against pursuing an engineering career, in which such skills would be essential. Instead, he planned to enter biology. After Ochoa received his B.A. from Málaga in 1921, he spent a year studying the prerequisite courses for medical school, at that time physics,

chemistry, biology, and geology. In 1923 he matriculated at the University of Madrid's Medical School.

At Madrid, Ochoa had dreams of studying under the Spanish neurohistologist Santiago Rámon y Cajal, but these were quickly dashed when he discovered that the 70-year-old histology professor had retired from teaching, although he still ran a laboratory in Madrid. Ochoa hesitated to approach Cajal even at the lab, however, because he thought the older man would be too busy to be bothered by an unimportant student. Nonetheless, by the end of his second year in medical school, Ochoa had confirmed his desire to do biological research and jumped at one of his professor's offers of a job in a nearby laboratory.

The Medical School itself housed no research facilities, but Ochoa's physiology teacher ran a small research laboratory under the aegis of the Council for Scientific Research a short distance away. Working with a classmate, Ochoa first mastered the relatively routine laboratory task of isolating creatinine—a white, crystalline compound—from urine. From there he moved to the more demanding task of studying the function and metabolism of creatine, a nitrogenous substance, in muscle. The summer after his fourth year of medical school he spent in a Glasgow laboratory, continuing work on this problem. Ochoa received his medical degree in 1929.

In an attempt to further his scientific education, Ochoa applied for a postdoctoral fellowship working under Otto Meyerhof at the Kaiser-Wilhelm Institute in a suburb of Berlin. Although the Council for Scientific Research had offered him a fellowship to pursue these studies, Ochoa turned down their offer of support because he could afford to pay his own way. He felt the money should be given to someone more needy to himself. Ochoa enjoyed his work under Meyerhof, remaining in Germany for a year.

On July 8, 1931, he married Carmen García Cobian, a daughter of a Spanish lawyer and businessman, and moved with his newlywed wife to England, where he had a fellowship from the University of Madrid to study at London's National Institute for Medical Research. In England Ochoa met Sir Henry Hallett Dale, who would later win the 1936 Nobel in medicine for his discovery of the chemical transmission of nerve impulses. During his first year at the Institute, Ochoa studied the enzyme glyoxalase, and the following year he started working directly under Dale, investigating how the adrenal glands affected the chemistry of muscular contraction. In 1933 he returned to his alma mater, the University of Madrid, where he was appointed a lecturer in physiology and biochemistry.

Within two years, Ochoa accepted a new position. One of the heads of the Department of Medicine was planning to start an Institute for Medical Research with sections on biochemistry, physiology, microbiology, and experimental medicine. The institute would be partially supported by the University of Madrid, which offered it space in one its new medical school buildings, and partially supported by wealthy patrons, who planned to provide a substantial budget for equipment, salaries, and supplies. The director of the new institute offered the young Ochoa the directorship of the section on physiology, which he accepted, and provided him with a staff of three. However, a few months after Ochoa began work, civil war broke out in Spain. In order to continue his work, Ochoa decided to leave the country in September, 1936. He and his wife immigrated to Germany, hardly a stable country itself in late 1936.

When Ochoa arrived, he found that his mentor Meyerhof, who was Jewish, was under considerable political and personal pressure. The German scientist had not allowed this to interfere with his work, though Ochoa did find to his surprise that the type of research Meyerhof conducted had changed dramatically in the six years since he had seen him last. As he wrote of the laboratory in a retrospective piece for the *Annual Review of Biochemistry*: "When I left it in 1930 it was basically a physiology laboratory; one could see muscles twitching everywhere. In 1936 it was a biochemistry laboratory. Glycolysis and fermentation in muscle or yeast extracts or partial reactions of these processes catalyzed by purified enzymes, were the main subjects of study." Meyerhof's change in research emphasis influenced Ochoa's own work, even though he studied in the laboratory for less than a year before Meyerhof fled to France.

Before Meyerhof left, however, he ensured that his protege was not stranded, arranging for Ochoa to receive a six-month fellowship at the Marine Biological Laboratory in Plymouth, England. Although this fellowship lasted only half a year, Ochoa enjoyed his time there, not the least because his wife Carmen started working with him in the laboratory. Their collaboration later led to the publication of a joint paper in *Nature*. At the end of six months, though, Ochoa had to move on, and friends at the lab found him a post as a research assistant at Oxford University. Two years later, when England entered the war, Oxford's Biochemistry Department shifted all its efforts to war research in which Ochoa, an alien, could not take part. So in 1940 the Ochoas picked up stakes again, this time to cross the Atlantic to work in the laboratory of Carl Ferdinand Cori and Gerty T. Cori in St. Louis. Part of the Washington University School of Medicine, the Cori lab was renowned for its cutting edge research on enzymes and work with intermediary metabolism of carbohydrates. This work involved studying the biochemical reactions in which carbohydrates produce energy for cellular operations. Ochoa worked there for a year before New York University persuaded him to move east to take a job as a research associate in medicine at the Bellevue Psychiatric Hospital, where he would for the first time have graduate and postdoctoral students working beneath him.

In 1945, Ochoa was promoted to assistant professor of biochemistry at the medical school. Two years later when the pharmacology chair retired, Ochoa was offered the opportunity to succeed him and, lured by the promise of new laboratory space, he accepted. He remained chairperson for nine years, taking a sabbatical in 1949 to serve as a visiting professor at the University of California. His administrative work did not deter him from pursuing his research interests in biochemistry, however. In the early 1950s, he isolated one of the chemical compounds necessary for photosynthesis to occur, triphosphopyridine nucleotide, known

as TPN. Ochoa continued his interest in intermediary metabolism, expanding the work of Hans Adolf Krebs, who posited the idea of a cycle through which food is metabolized into adenosine triphosphate, or ATP, the molecule that provides energy to the cell. The Spanish scientist discovered that one molecule of glucose when burned with oxygen produced 36 ATP molecules. When the chairman of the biochemistry department resigned in 1954, Ochoa accepted this opportunity to return to the department full-time as chair and full professor.

Once more ensconced in biochemistry research, Ochoa turned his attentions to a new field: the rapidly growing area of deoxyribonucleic acid (DNA) research. Earlier in his career, enzymes had been the hot new molecules for biochemists to study; now, after the critical work of James Watson and Francis Crick in 1953, nucleic acids were fascinating scientists in the field. Ochoa was no exception. Drawing on his earlier work with enzymes, Ochoa began investigating which enzymes played roles in the creation of nucleic acids in the body. Although most enzymes assist in breaking down materials, Ochoa knew that he was looking for an enzyme that helped combine nucleotides into the long chains that were nucleic acids. Once he isolated these molecules, he hoped, he would be able to synthesize RNA and DNA in the lab. In 1955, he found a bacterial enzyme in sewage that appeared to play just such a role. When he added this enzyme to a solution of nucleotides, he discovered that the solution became viscous, like jelly, indicating that RNA had indeed formed in the dish. The following year, Arthur Kornberg, who had studied with Ochoa in 1946, applied these methods to synthesize DNA.

In 1959, five years after he assumed the directorship of the biochemistry department, Ochoa shared the Nobel Prize for Physiology or Medicine with Kornberg, for their work in discovering the enzymes that help produce nucleic acids. While Ochoa was particularly delighted to share the prize with his old colleague, by this time he was no stranger to academic plaudits. The holder of several honorary degrees from both American and foreign universities, including Oxford, Ochoa had also been the recipient of the Carl Neuberg Medal in biochemistry in 1951 and the Charles Leopold Mayer Prize in 1955. Ochoa served as chairperson of NYU's biochemistry department for 20 years, until the summer of 1974, just before his seventieth birthday. When he retired from this post, he rejected the department's offer to make him an emeritus professor, preferring to remain on staff as a full professor. But even that could not keep Ochoa sufficiently occupied. In 1974, he joined the Roche Institute of Molecular Biology in New Jersey.

In 1985 he returned to his native Spain as a professor of biology at the University Autonoma in Madrid to continue his lifelong fascination with biochemical research. At the age of 75 Ochoa wrote a retrospective of his life, which he titled "Pursuit of a Hobby." In the introduction to this piece, he explained his choice of title: at a party given in the forties in honor of two Nobel laureate chemists Ochoa listed his hobby in the guest register as biochemistry, although he was professor of pharmacology at New York University. Sir Henry Dale, one of the party's honorees, joked, "now that he is a pharmacologist, he has biochemistry as a hobby." Ochoa concluded this tale with the statement, "In my life biochemistry has been my only and real hobby."

Severo Ochoa died in Madrid on November 1, 1993.

Further Reading

Nobel Prize Internet Archive, "http://www.almaz.com/nobel/ medicine/1959a.html," Almaz Enterprises, July 22, 1997. *Nobel Prize Winners,* H. W. Wilson, 1987. □

Adolph Simon Ochs

The American publisher and philanthropist Adolph Simon Ochs (1858-1935) rose from a cultured but impoverished background to control the so-called ideal newspaper, the *New York Times*.

Adolph Ochs was born March 2, 1858, in Cincinnati, Ohio. Of German-Jewish stock, he had talent and industry and a disposition that made both productive. He was the eldest of six children and had only a brief exposure to school. However, his father, a teacher fluent in six languages, tutored the boy.

Ochs always referred to the printing office as his high school and college. At the age of 11 he started at the *Knoxville Chronicle* as office boy, and at 13 he became an apprentice. In 1877 Ochs joined in a fruitless effort to establish the *Chattanooga Dispatch.* The owner of the *Chattanooga Times,* victor over the *Dispatch,* was in difficulty and offered to sell to Ochs, then not old enough to vote. On July 2, 1878, with $37.50 working capital, Ochs became a publisher upon handing over $250, which he had borrowed, and assuming $1,500 in debts. He showed a profit the first year. In 1892 Ochs built the Chattanooga Times Building, an outstanding addition to the developing city.

In 1896 Ochs acquired control of the *New York Times.* He mortgaged and risked everything to "conduct a high standard newspaper, clean, dignified and trustworthy." The *New York Times* followed the slogan "All the News That's Fit to Print." From 1896 to 1935 he raised the daily circulation enormously. Ochs started the Sunday book supplement within 10 years after taking over. In 1913 he began publishing the *New York Times Index.* In 1925 Ochs started advancing $50,000 annually for 10 years toward the cost of producing the *Dictionary of American Biography.* He established *Current History* magazine in 1914.

Ochs did not use his papers to express his personality. He "depersonalized" editorship and thought of the *New York Times* as a public institution. His last active year was 1932; he died April 8, 1935. He had set an example of how to conduct a free and responsible press. According to a biographer, Ochs at times failed because he had been deceived or misinformed "but he never lied . . . , the final test of a servant of the truth." He had received honorary degrees from six institutions.

Further Reading

Books about Ochs praise him but show little of his personality. Gerald W. Johnson, *Honorable Titan: A Biographical Study of Adolph S. Ochs* (1946), gives Ochs a glow of glory without humanizing him. Frank Luther Mott, *American Journalism: A History of Newspapers in the United States through 260 Years, 1690-1950* (1950), rather stingily gives Ochs his just due, diminishing the halo only slightly. Other helpful works are Elmer Davis, *History of the New York Times* (1921), Meyer Berger, *Story of the New York Times, 1851-1951* (1951); and Gay Talese, *The Kingdom and the Power* (1969). □

Johannes Ockeghem

Johannes Ockeghem (ca. 1425-1495) was a Netherlandish composer who spent most of his creative life at the French court.

Johannes Ockeghem was born in the Netherlands, possibly in Hainaut. Nothing is known about his early years, although he undoubtedly studied music in one of the cathedral schools for which his homeland was justly famous. The earliest document concerning his activity places him among the more than 50 singers in the choir of the Church of Our Lady in Antwerp in 1443/1444. This is also the only reference to his activity in the Netherlands.

In 1448 Ockeghem appeared on the list of 13 singers employed by Charles, Duke of Bourbon, then residing in Moulin. By 1452 Ockeghem's name was first in the list of singers in the chapel of Charles VII of France. He was to serve the French kings for more than 40 years. By 1454 he was *premier chappelain* and dedicated a book of music, presumably his own, to the king. Records of gifts from the king for this collection and for a single chanson are preserved. References to his activity at court are preserved, unfortunately with little or no mention of particular compositions. Thus, the chronology of his output remains a problem.

The high esteem in which the kings of France held Ockeghem is demonstrated by the positions they secured for him. He became treasurer of the Abbey of St. Martin of Tours, one of the richest abbeys of the time, whose abbots had historically been the kings of France. He was not required to reside there, possibly because of the desire for his musical services at court. In 1465 he also received the title *maistre de la chappelle de chant du roy*. During the remainder of his life he left France only for a short journey to Spain in 1470 and Flanders in 1484.

Ockeghem's fame was not limited to the country of his patrons. Sometime before 1467 his contemporary Antoine Busnois composed the motet *In hydraulis,* which praises Ockeghem. Johannes Tinctoris, leading theorist of the time and active in Naples, dedicated his *Liber de natura et proprietate tonorum* (1476) to Ockeghem and Busnois and named Ockeghem as the most famous musician of his time in the prologue to his *Liber de arte contrapuncti* (1477). Erasmus of Rotterdam wrote a lament on Ockeghem's death.

For a composer of this renown, a surprisingly small number of works have been preserved. These include 20 chansons, 10 complete Mass Ordinaries, 3 incomplete Mass Ordinaries, a Requiem Mass, and no more than 10 motets. Although his works are now seen in a more accurate light, Ockeghem's reputation was formerly based on the knowledge of only a few, atypical works which emphasized complex compositional procedures. The *Missa prolationem,* a series of mensuration canons, and a 36-voice canonic motet were among the first works to come to the attention of scholars. Although each is a tour de force in contrapuntal artifice, they are not typical of his general style.

Ockeghem's output is better characterized by other works, which demonstrate his rhapsodical, asymmetrical melodic style and a general avoidance of pervading imitation. All voices are of equal importance and of similar and eminently vocal character. In contrast to his contemporary Jacob Obrecht, with whom his name is often linked, Ockeghem seemed to consciously avoid clear cadences and their articulating effect. This avoidance of clear phrases and an asymmetrical melodic line have been compared to the mysticism of certain religious movements of the period. Ockeghem also frequently used the lowest part of the vocal range, which resulted in a very dark sound. These are the features that best characterize his work, not the contrapuntal complexity of a few exceptional compositions.

Further Reading

Ernst Krenek, *Johannes Ockeghem* (1953), is a succinct biographical and critical study. A thorough discussion of Ockeghem's life, works, and times is found in Gustave Reese, *Music in the Renaissance* (1954; rev. ed. 1959). Manfred F. Bukofzer, *Studies in Medieval and Renaissance Music* (1950), and Donald Jay Grout, *A History of Western Music* (1960), have good discussions of Ockeghem and are recommended for general background. □

Daniel O'Connell

The Irish statesman Daniel O'Connell (1775-1847) created modern Irish nationalism and served as the most successful champion of democracy in the Europe of his day.

Daniel O'Connell was born on Aug. 6, 1775, at Cahirciveen, County Kerry, a member of the Munster Catholic aristocracy. Following the Celtic traditions of their class, his parents had him brought up as a foster child in a peasant cottage. There he learned the language, values, fears, and frustrations of the Catholic masses. Adopted by his childless uncle, Maurice, head of the clan, O'Connell was sent to the Continent for secondary schooling, attending Saint-Omer and then Douai. In 1793 the spread of the French Revolution forced him to transfer to a London school. The next year, after deciding on a legal career, he enrolled at Lincoln's Inn, moving in 1796 to the King's Inn, Dublin. In 1798 O'Connell was admitted to the Irish bar.

Student reading converted O'Connell to the liberal views of the Enlightenment, including religious skepticism. He admired the ideas of William Godwin, Thomas Paine, and Adam Smith. Later he became a fervent disciple and friend of Jeremy Bentham. O'Connell eventually returned to Catholicism but never ceased to consider himself a radical. In 1798 he was a fringe member of the United Irishmen. At the same time he joined a lawyers' yeoman corps organized to discourage revolution. When revolution came in 1798, O'Connell condemned physical force. He argued that violence would inflame the passions of illiterate peasants, causing them to damage life and property, and lead to their slaughter by trained soldiers. When it was all over, Ireland and Irishmen would be less free than before. O'Connell remained a permanent foe of revolution for Ireland.

In 1800 O'Connell opposed the union with Britain but at the time concentrated his energies on building a successful law practice rather than patriotic causes. In 1802, against the wishes of his uncle, he married a distant cousin, Mary O'Connell, and began to raise a large family. Three years later O'Connell joined the Catholic Committee, quickly becoming its dominant personality. British politicians in 1815 offered Catholic emancipation in exchange for the right of the government to veto papal appointments to the Catholic hierarchy in the United Kingdom. O'Connell opposed the

veto, splitting Catholic forces and delaying emancipation but preserving the Church as a vehicle for Irish nationalism.

Catholic Association

In 1823 O'Connell, Richard Lalor Sheil, and Sir Thomas Wyse organized the Catholic Association. Two years later O'Connell initiated the strategy that made it the most powerful political force in the United Kingdom. Catholic peasants accepted O'Connell's invitation to join the civil-rights movement as associate members paying a shilling a year. Catholic priests, acting as recruiting agents, urged them on. With Catholic Ireland united behind him, O'Connell promised that organized and disciplined public opinion would free the Irish people. Democracy was the wave of the future. After he won an 1828 Clare by-election, Sir Robert Peel and the Duke of Wellington were forced to concede emancipation as a better alternative than possible revolution.

Irish Nationalism

During the early 1830s O'Connell led an Irish nationalist party in the House of Commons. He also spoke for United Kingdom Benthamism. His efforts made possible the 1832 Reform Bill. In 1835 O'Connell entered the Lichfield House Compact with the Whigs: he agreed to stop agitating for repeal of the union in exchange for a promise of significant reform in the administration of Irish affairs. By the end of the decade the Irish leader was disappointed with the meager reform fruits of the Whig alliance. When his old enemy Sir Robert Peel became Tory prime minister in 1841,

O'Connell organized the Loyal National Repeal Association. But he took a virtual sabbatical from agitation to concentrate on his duties as first Catholic lord mayor of Dublin.

In 1843 O'Connell exploited the mistakes of British politicians, Irish grievances (mainly the poor law and the existence of a large and well-organized temperance movement initiated by Father Mathew), and the journalistic talent of Young Ireland and its paper, the *Nation,* to build an agitation equal to the Catholic movement of the 1820s. Again the priests rallied the people, and shillings flowed to Dublin. In a series of monster meetings O'Connell promised freedom before the year was out.

The situation was unlike that in 1828: Peel now had a Parliament united against repeal. He refused to budge, and O'Connell, opposed to violence, had to retreat. In early October 1843 the government banned a monster meeting scheduled for Clontarf. O'Connell obeyed the proclamation. A week later the government arrested him and some of his lieutenants. They were convicted of sedition, fined £2,000, and sentenced to a year in prison. Early in 1844 the Law Lords reversed the verdict of the packed Dublin jury. O'Connell was free, celebrated as a hero and martyr, but he lacked the energy and will to exploit his victory by resuming agitation.

Later Years

The last years of the "Liberator" were a contradiction to former glories. O'Connell's inclination to resume contact with the Whigs, jealousies, bad advice (mainly from his son, John), and a liberal patriot distrust of the narrowness of cultural nationalism led to conflict with Young Ireland and, finally, a split in the repeal movement. O'Connell's health deteriorated, but he lived to witness the onslaught of famine and the refusal of the British Parliament to respond to his final plea for mercy and justice to starving Ireland. He died at Genoa on May 15, 1847, on his way to Rome.

Many 20th-century nationalists condemn O'Connell for his opposition to revolutionary tactics and for his compromise style of politics. But he made possible the final victory of Irish nationalism. He lifted the Irish masses from their knees and began to remove the mental blocks of serfdom. He gave the Irish people dignity, pride, hope, and discipline. O'Connell's tactic of using the pressure of public opinion, backed by the implied threat of reform or revolution, was used by subsequent Irish nationalists and British Radicals in marches toward freedom, social reform, and democracy.

Further Reading

Sean O'Faolain, *King of the Beggars: A Life of Daniel O'Connell, the Irish Liberator* (1938), and William Edward Hartpole Lecky, "Daniel O'Connell," in *The Leaders of Public Opinion in Ireland* (1912), are the two best studies of O'Connell's total career. James A. Reynolds, *The Catholic Emancipation Crisis in Ireland, 1823-1829* (1954), is a valuable investigation of O'Connell's Catholic emancipation victory. Angus MacIntyre, *The Liberator: Daniel O'Connell and the Party, 1830-1847* (1965), discusses O'Connell's important role as parliamentary politician. Keven B. Nowlan, *The Politics of Repeal: A Study in the Relations between Great Britain and*

Ireland, 1841-50 (1965), and Lawrence J. McCaffrey, *Daniel O'Connell and the Repeal Year* (1966), are concerned with the repeal agitation of the 1840s and the contests between O'Connell and Young Ireland and O'Connell and Peel.

Additional Sources

Chenevix Trench, Charles, *The Great Dan: a biography of Daniel O'Connell,* London: J. Cape, 1984.

Daniel O'Connell, portrait of a radical, Belfast: Appletree Press, 1984.

Edwards, R. Dudley (Robert Dudley), *Daniel O'Connell and his world,* London: Thames and Hudson, 1975.

MacDonagh, Oliver, *The emancipist: Daniel O'Connell, 1830-47,* New York: St. Martin's Press, 1989.

MacDonagh, Oliver, *The hereditary bondsman: Daniel O'Connell, 1775-1829,* New York: St. Martin's Press, 1988, 1987.

O'Connell, Maurice R., *Daniel O'Connell: the man and his politics,* Blackrock, Co. Dublin: Irish Academic Press, 1990.

King of the beggars: a life of Daniel O'Connell, the Irish liberator, in a study of the rise of the modern Irish democracy (1775-1847), Westport, Conn.: Greenwood Press, 1975, 1938.

O'Ferrall, Fergus, *Daniel O'Connell,* Dublin: Gill and Macmillan, 1981. □

Flannery O'Connor

Flannery O'Connor (1925-1964) was a writer of short stories and novels in which comedy, grotesquerie, and violence were united with a profound moral and theological vision.

Flannery O'Connor was born in Savannah, Georgia, on March 25, 1925, the only child of Regine Cline and Edwin Francis O'Connor. Both her parents came from Catholic families that had lived in the South for generations. In the late 1930s her father developed disseminated lupus, an immunological disorder that causes the body to make antibodies against its own tissues, and the O'Connors moved to Milledgeville, which had been the home of the Cline family since before the Civil War. At that time lupus was untreatable, and O'Connor's father died in 1941.

O'Connor graduated from Georgia State College for Women in Milledgeville with a degree in social science in 1945. A fellowship enabled her to attend the Writers' Workshop at the State University of Iowa, from which she received a Master of Fine Arts degree in 1947. While at Iowa she published her first short story and won a prize for a novel in progress. After leaving Iowa she continued to work on her novel at Yaddo, the writer's colony at Saratoga Springs, New York; in New York City; and in Connecticut, where she lived in the household of the poet and translator Robert Fitzgerald.

In December 1950, on her way home to Milledgeville for Christmas, she became seriously ill on the train and was hospitalized on her arrival in Atlanta; she was diagnosed as having lupus, the same illness that had killed her father nine years earlier. The recent discovery of cortisone made the disease treatable, but it was still considered incurable. After several months, during which time O'Connor was in and out of the hospital, she and her mother moved to "Andalusia," a dairy farm four miles from Milledgeville that Mrs. O'Connor had recently inherited and that she ran with the help of tenants. Dairy farms, the capable and efficient women who run them, and their tenant help figure largely in O'Connor's later stories. O'Connor spent the remaining 14 years of her life at Andalusia, writing and raising various kinds of fowl, including peacocks.

During the first year after the outbreak of her illness O'Connor continued to work on the final revisions of her first novel, *Wise Blood,* which was published in 1952. Strong, original, drawn with hard outlines and in a peculiarly modern style, at once bizarrely comic and completely serious, it is the story of the ultimately futile attempts of Hazel Motes, the grandson of a Southern fundamentalist preacher, to escape from Jesus.

Following the publication of *Wise Blood* O'Connor returned to writing short fiction. The stories written between the summer of 1952 and 1955 (collected in *A Good Man Is Hard To Find,* 1955) make it obvious that she had come into her own as a short story writer. Wickedly funny, realistic, displaying her sharp eye for the comic and the grotesque and her accurate ear for Southern speech, often ending in unexpected and shocking violence, the best of them—"A Good Man Is Hard To Find," "The Life You Save May Be Your Own," "The Artificial Nigger," "The Displaced Person," "Good Country People"—are classics of the short story form.

O'Connor, who took her Catholicism as seriously as she did her writing, called them stories about original sin. She described her work in general as being about the action of grace in the world, about those moments in which grace, usually in the form of violence, descends on her comically complacent characters, sometimes opening their eyes to an appalling realization, sometimes killing them. Many readers find O'Connor's identification of the transcendent with a violent and disruptive force unpalatable and even more shocking than the stories themselves. O'Connor, however, felt that a violent shock was necessary to bring both her characters and her modern secular audience to an awareness of the powerful reality of the realm of transcendent mystery.

Although a softening of the bone in her hip caused her to have to use crutches, O'Connor frequently accepted invitations to speak at colleges and writers' conferences in the latter half of the 1950s and early 1960s. She took advantage of these opportunities not only to give perceptive talks on the nature of fiction but to clarify her own position as a writer "with Christian concerns." Such a writer, she said, was interested both in the everyday reality seen all around (the level of manners) and in making that everyday reality transparent to the underlying level of mystery, the level of the eternal and the absolute. These talks, together with a number of essays on similar subjects, were edited by Sally and Robert Fitzgerald and published after O'Connor's death under the title *Mystery and Manners* (1969).

O'Connor's second collection of short stories, *Everything That Rises Must Converge,* continued in much the same vein as the first. It was completed just before her death and published posthumously in 1965. Her second novel, *The Violent Bear It Away* (1960), has some thematic similarities with *Wise Blood,* although it is very different in style. As *Wise Blood* follows the protagonist's attempts to escape from his vocation to be a Christian, *The Violent Bear It Away* deals with the efforts of a backwoods Southern boy to escape his calling to be a prophet. In both cases, an act of violence plays a role at the turning points at which the characters embrace their painful vocations.

O'Connor had to have abdominal surgery in the spring of 1964. Her lupus reacted to the stress of the surgery and could not be controlled by drugs. In July she suffered kidney failure, and she died in the Milledgeville Hospital on August 3, 1964. In 1972 she was posthumously awarded the National Book Award for her *Collected Stories.* A collection of her letters, edited by Sally Fitzgerald and titled *The Habit of Being,* was published in 1979.

Further Reading

No biography of Flannery O'Connor has yet been published, but there are more than a dozen critical studies of her fiction. These include Leon Driskell and Joan Brittain, *Eternal Crossroads: The Art of Flannery O'Connor* (1971); David Eggenschwiler, *The Christian Humanism of Flannery O'Connor* (1972); Dorothy Tuck McFarland, *Flannery O'Connor* (1976); and Dorothy Walters, *Flannery O'Connor* (1973), among others. □

Sandra Day O'Connor

In 1981 Sandra Day O'Connor (born 1930) became the first woman to serve as a justice of the United States Supreme Court.

During the final month of the 1980 presidential campaign, candidate Ronald Reagan, whose polls disclosed a lack of support among female voters, announced that, if elected, he would appoint a woman to the Supreme Court. In July 1981 President Reagan kept that promise, nominating Sandra Day O'Connor to become the first female justice in the 191-year history of the court.

Born on August 26, 1930, Sandra Day spent her earliest years on her family's Lazy B Ranch in southeastern Arizona. She was considered a "child of the frontier" as her first home had no electricity or running water. She grew up branding steer, learning to fix whatever was broken and absorbing the influence of her family's vast Arizona cattle ranch built on former Apache land.

Then, because of parental concern that this obviously bright girl could not get an adequate education in rural schools, she went to live with her maternal grandmother in El Paso, Texas. There she attended the private Radford School for girls and Austin High. In 1946 she enrolled at Stanford University, where she studied economics and graduated *magna cum laude* in 1950. A year before receiving her B.A. she entered the law school, from which she received an LL.B. in 1952. A member of the board of editors of the *Stanford Law Review,* Day graduated third in a class of 102, two places behind her future Supreme Court colleague William H. Rehnquist.

Pre-Court Career

Despite her outstanding academic record, she failed in efforts to obtain employment as a lawyer with San Francisco and Los Angeles law firms because she was a woman. The only one willing to hire the future justice at all offered her a job as a legal secretary. Instead, she took a position as a deputy county attorney in San Mateo, California. When her new husband, John O'Connor, who was one class behind her at Stanford, finished law school the couple headed for Germany, where he served as an attorney in the Army, and she worked as a civilian quartermaster corps attorney, specializing in contracts.

Upon their return to the United States the O'Connors settled in the Phoenix, Arizona area. O'Connor and another lawyer opened a law office in suburban Maryvale, but for the next few years she devoted most of her time to rearing the three sons who were born between 1957 and 1962. She also served as a bankruptcy trustee, wrote bar exam questions, set up a lawyer referral service, served on a county zoning appeal board and a governor's committee on marriage and the family, did volunteer work with several civic and charitable organizations, and took an active role in local Republican politics.

In 1965 O'Connor returned to full-time employment as one of Arizona's assistant attorneys general. She remained active in civic affairs, and when the state senator from her district resigned in 1969 Governor Jack Williams appointed her to the seat. She won election to it in 1970 and was easily reelected in 1972. As a state senator O'Connor compiled a moderate to conservative voting record and sufficiently impressed her Republican colleagues that in 1972 they chose her as their majority leader, making her the first woman anywhere in the country to hold that position.

In 1974 O'Connor left the legislature, running successfully for a judgeship in the Maricopa County Superior Court. Although remaining active in Republican politics, she resisted when party leaders tried to persuade her to challenge Democratic Governor Bruce Babbitt in 1978. The following year Babbitt appointed her to the Arizona Court of Appeals. When Reagan selected her for the Supreme Court she became the first appointee in 24 years with prior service on a state court and the first in 32 years with legislative experience.

Supreme Court Justice

It was largely because she was the first woman ever nominated that she was quickly and unanimously confirmed by the Senate. As a justice, her upbringing was expected to keep her solidly conservative and push her into the states-rights camp in court decisions. But her inability to get a job after graduating from law school because she was a woman influenced her as well, and was a point of conten-

tion for right-wing conservatives who objected to her appointment for fear she would not oppose abortion.

There was a certain irony in this, for O'Connor was not part of the organized women's movement. After giving early support to the Equal Rights Amendment, she had backed away from it when the opposition of Arizona's two Republican senators became clear. Although the Moral Majority complained that O'Connor was a proponent of abortion, she had cast votes against as well as for it in the legislature. As a justice she aligned herself with its opponents.

Although not a militant feminist, O'Connor was a founder of both the Arizona Women Lawyers Association and the National Association of Women Judges and had fought to eliminate provisions discriminating against women from her state's bar rules and community property laws. On the Court she quickly established a reputation as a judicial opponent of sex discrimination. Her most famous early opinion was *Mississippi University for Women* v. *Hogan* (1982), in which the Court held it was unconstitutional for a state nursing school to refuse to admit men.

On other issues Justice O'Connor generally aligned herself with the Court's two most conservative members, Chief Justice Warren Burger and Associate Justice Rehnquist. Exhibiting a strong commitment to law and order, she consistently voted against criminal defendants. However, her response to First Amendment claims were lukewarm at best. As her background on the state bench and an article she had written at about the time of her appointment suggested, she opposed further extensions of federal court jurisdiction. Although part of a conservative bloc on most issues, she did break with it occasionally, as on freedom of information matters. Despite his own far more liberal voting record, Justice Harry Blackman quickly concluded O'Connor was a "fine justice, able and articulate."

Second Decade on the Court

During her years following her appointment by Reagan in 1981, O'Connor followed a pattern that has sometimes confounded presidents attempting to solidify political leanings in the Supreme Court. By 1990, following her first decade on the court she, along with fellow Justice Anthony Kennedy, had become an unpredictable swing vote, her opinions courted by both sides in many decisions.

As the 1990s unfolded, O'Connor was influential or determined the direction of a number of key freedom rulings by the Supreme Court. They included an interpretation of Freedom of Speech, censorship, a ruling governing the Internet and cases dealing with freedom of religion where she was instrumental in striking down a state-mandated moment of silence in public schools.

She influenced the court's direction in cases involving discrimination and harassment because of gender, strengthening women's job opportunity rights. However, she was the swing vote in a decision that narrowed the scope of affirmative action in *Adarand* v. *Pena.* And, in 1995, she sided with conservative justices in cases, particularly *Miller* v. *Johnson,* that weakened the Voting Rights Act's congressional district apportionment designed to favor minority representation.

She voted with the majority to strike down the core of the federal *Brady Act* anti-gun legislation requiring background checks of prospective gun purchasers.

In a 1992 challenge to abortion rights, *Planned Parenthood v. Casey,* O'Connor was one of the majority who voted to uphold the provisions of *Roe v. Wade* that made abortion legal for women. In 1997, she ruled against another privacy issue: A terminally ill patient's right to die through physician-assisted suicide.

In a *U.S. News & World Report* story, "The Geography of Justice: Big Decisions by the Supreme Court Turn on the Regional Backgrounds of the Justices," (July, 1997), a former law clerk hinted at the basis for many of O'Connor's decisions. According to the clerk, the justice showed a "great admiration for individual initiative and people taking responsibility for their own actions. . . ." That tendency to discount a need for special protections was called the basis of her voting against every race-based affirmative action issue that came before her.

Throughout many issues before the court, O'Connor stayed true to her roots, joining her fellow conservatives in 123 of 137 decisions by 1997. Although her decisions have not always been popular with feminists, she has served as an excellent role model to women in general. The justice herself became a news item in 1997 when a suspicious-looking package found on her doorstep was suspected of being a bomb. An investigation showed it only contained a pair of tennis shoes the justice had ordered.

Further Reading

Although there was a book-length biography of O'Connor designed for children, adults must look to periodicals for material. Robert E. Riggs, "Justice O'Connor: A First Term Appraisal," *Brigham Young University Law Review* 1983 (1983), provided an excellent analysis of her early performance on the Supreme Court. Vera Glaser, "She's a Lady," *The Washingtonian* 19 (May 1984), was informative on the personal side of O'Connor's life, and Beverly B. Cook, "Women as Supreme Court Candidates: From Florence Allen to Sandra Day O'Connor," *Judicature* 65 (December 1981-January 1982), provided a useful comparative perspective. Sandra Day O'Connor, "Trends in the Relationship Between the Federal and State Courts from the Perspective of a State Judge," *William and Mary Law Review* 22 (Summer 1981), provided limited insights into Justice O'Connor's own thinking. Related articles on Justice O'Connor can be found in *U.S. News & World Report,* July 7, 1997; *Working Woman,* November/December 1996; *Time,* June 17, 1996; and *People,* March 7, 1994. □

Clifford Odets

A playwright, film scenarist, and director, Clifford Odets (1906-1963) was America's outstanding dramatist in the 1930s. His colloquial dialogue, vital ideological protests on behalf of human dignity, and feeling for the family were distinctive.

Clifford Odets was born on July 18, 1906, in Philadelphia, Pa. The family moved in 1912 to New York, where his father became a successful businessman.

In spite of his upbringing with his two sisters in a comfortable, middle-class, Jewish home, Odets was a melancholy child. His formal education ended after 2 years of high school. During most of the 1920s he acted with small theater groups and held various positions in radio stations, joining the Group Theater in 1930. Reportedly, he attempted suicide three times before the age of 25.

The theatrical approach of the Group Theater transformed Odets from a poor actor into a good playwright. While with the Group, he also joined the Communist party. As a result of his sensational writing debut in 1935, he received many offers from Hollywood. In 1937 he married the actress Luise Rainer.

Writings of the Thirties

Waiting for Lefty, Awake and Sing, Till the Day I Die, and *Paradise Lost,* all produced in 1935, quickly established Odets as a powerful dramatist. *Waiting for Lefty,* framed within a union meeting, is a series of indignant vignettes. Although the play has been criticized for simplistic views and characterizations, its raw power and anger are notable. Concerned with a family in the Bronx, *Awake and Sing* pinpoints the impact of the capitalistic economic structure on the people within it and the fraudulency involved in adjusting human lives to economic forces; the characteriza-

tions and use of symbols are well done. *Till the Day I Die* deals with conflict between Nazis and Communists. *Paradise Lost* focuses on the bewilderment of a middle-class family as their values shift in relation to changing social forces. Viewed as a realistic work, it is unsatisfactory; assessed symbolically, it is more convincing.

After *Paradise Lost,* Odets wrote the film adaptation of *The General Died at Dawn.* His next stage play, *Golden Boy* (1937), proved his most popular success. In selecting a career in boxing instead of in music, Joe Bonaparte goes against his nature; he becomes successful but destroys himself. Although *Golden Boy* contains social observations, its orientation is toward individuals rather than politics. (In 1964 it was made into a Broadway musical.) *Rocket to the Moon* (1938) deals with loneliness and the need for love, noting how conditions within and outside man impede attaining love.

Hollywood Years

When the Group Theater dissolved in 1941, it had produced seven of Odets's plays. That year, following his divorce, Odets returned to Hollywood to write and direct films. In quick succession he wrote *Humoresque* (1942), *None but the Lonely Heart* (1943), and *Deadline at Dawn* (1944).

In 1943 Odets married another actress, Betty Grayson; they had two children. In addition to his constant screen obligations (including more than 15 scenarios), he continued to write for the stage. In 1952 he was called before the House Committee on Un-American Activities because of his earlier Communist affiliations; his performance did little to enhance his personal reputation.

Odets's wife died in 1954. He started several plays after that but failed to complete them. His last film, *Wild in the Country* (1961), starred Elvis Presley. At the time of his death in Los Angeles on Aug. 14, 1963, Odets was working on a dramatic series for television.

Later Writings

The burning concern for poor workers that propelled Odets's early success became, ironically, something of an albatross. Though he had changed from his propagandistic style as early as *Golden Boy* and never really returned to extreme political postures in later plays, many critics had trouble accepting him on his new terms. Further, since he had initially championed the poor, his remunerative employment in Hollywood stirred insinuations that he lacked artistic integrity. Thus evaluations of his later writings are occasionally less objective than one might hope.

Night Music (1940), although realistic, has a strong poetic component. Steve Takis's loneliness and frustration have some socioeconomic aspects, but Odets's hand is uncertain. There is confusion in treating the subject and an imperfect development of structure. *Clash by Night* (1941) is a standard treatment of the eternal love triangle to which Odets adds nothing important. Pessimism permeates the work, and there is little hope either by an individual for himself or for understanding between people. Odets felt that his plays were always concerned with "the struggle not to

have life nullified by circumstances, false values, anything.'' *The Big Knife* (1949), showing the annihilation of a Hollywood star, focuses on personal integrity in combat with practical necessity and perhaps displays something of Odets's own dilemma. His increasing craftsmanship, noted in *The Big Knife,* is clearly evident in *The Country Girl* (1950). The portraits of the alcoholic actor Frank Elgin and his confused wife are very effective. A fine piece of theater, the play shows Odets deeply involved in human psychology. *The Flowering Peach* (1954), his last produced play, is Odets at his mature best. His examination of the biblical Noah concentrates on the family, this time with an increased awareness of and tolerance for man's imperfections.

Further Reading

Two works on Odets contain biographical material and criticism of the plays: R. Baird Shuman, *Clifford Odets* (1962), and Edward Murray, *Clifford Odets: The Thirties and After* (1968). Among the many critical studies with material on Odets are Anita Block, *The Changing World in Plays and Theatre* (1939); Harold Clurman, *The Fervent Years: The Story of the Group Theatre and the Thirties* (1945); Eric Bentley, *The Playwright as Thinker: A Study of Drama in Modern Times* (1946); and Daniel Aaron, *Writers on the Left* (1961).

Additional Sources

Brenman-Gibson, Margaret, *Clifford Odets, American playwright: the years from 1906 to 1940,* New York: Atheneum, 1981.

Weales, Gerald Clifford, *Odets, the playwright,* London; New York: Methuen, 1985. □

Ajuma Jaramogi Oginga Odinga

Ajuma Jaramogi Oginga Odinga (1912-1994) was one of the leaders of the African political organizations which secured Kenya's independence. He was a foremost critic of Kenya's ruling party after he resigned as the country's first vice-president in 1966, and he remained a vocal opposition leader until his death.

O ginga Odinga was born in 1912 at Bondo in Nyanza Province, Kenya, a member of the Luo people. His father, a woodworker, selected him as the only child the family could afford to educate. Young Odinga attended Maseno Secondary School and Alliance High School, finishing his formal education with a diploma in education from Makerere University College in 1939. From 1940 to 1942 Odinga taught mathematics at the Church Missionary Society school at Maseno, and from 1943 to 1946 he was headmaster of the Maseno Veterinary

School. In 1947 he moved to the business world, founding the Luo Thrift and Trading Corporation; he served as its managing director until 1962.

Follower of Kenyatta

Odinga entered politics in 1947, when he became a member of Kenya's legislative council. He was a supporter of the Kenya African Union, Kenya's only important African political group. After hearing a speech by the future leader of Kenya, Jomo Kenyatta, Odinga became his devoted follower. In 1953, Kenyatta was jailed by the British, and during Kenyatta's years in detention Odinga became one of the most outspoken resistance leaders calling for his release. In the first African elections for the legislature in 1957, Odinga won election in his home district of central Nyanza.

A major British effort to control Kenya's evolution in peaceful fashion was the Lancaster House Conference of 1960. A unified African delegation attended and accepted the conference's decisions as a step on the path to independence. But when the delegates returned to Kenya, rivalries shattered the unity of the African politicians, with Odinga emerging as one of the leaders of the radical group of dissatisfied Africans. Odinga and other members of the legislative council formed the Kenya African National Union (KANU). The other major African party was the Kenya African Democratic Union (KADU). Odinga's KANU used its strong showing in the 1961 general elections to help gain Kenyatta's release.

Breaking with Leadership

Kenya gained independence in December 1963, and Kenyatta, a member of the Kikuyu, Kenya's largest ethnic group, became president. Odinga, a leader of the second largest ethnic group, the Luo, was appointed minister for home affairs in 1963, and in 1964 he became vice-president. Kenya became a de facto one-party state that year when KADU merged with KANU. Odinga increasingly opposed KANU's direction after the merger, which in his opinion helped turn the government's policies to the right. He openly challenged the government's use of private and foreign investment capital and its close ties with the West.

Within KANU a coalition formed against Odinga. He was left out of decision making, and in 1966 a KANU reorganization conference abolished his post of party vice-president. In April 1966 Odinga resigned from the government and party to form an opposition group, the Kenya People's Union (KPU). The KPU faced government harassment, and some of its leaders were jailed. In October 1969, Odinga was jailed by the government on the charge of organizing a demonstration which turned into a riot. The KPU was banned, and Odinga stayed in prison for 15 months.

Tireless Opposition Leader

Odinga remained an opposition leader throughout the 1970s. After Kenyatta's death in 1978, the new president, Daniel arap Moi, tried to bring Odinga back into KANU. But when Odinga was reinstated into the party in 1980, he attacked Moi and Kenyatta as corrupt and protested U.S. military presence in Kenya. In 1982, the party again banished Odinga and amended the constitution to make Kenya officially a one-party state.

Throughout the 1980s, international criticism of KANU's human rights record grew and Odinga remained vocal in calling for democracy. In 1991, Odinga founded the National Democratic Party, but the government refused to recognize it and briefly jailed Odinga. However, international protests were effective and later that year Odinga and five other opposition leaders formed the Forum for the Restoration of Democracy (FORD), the nucleus of a pro-democracy movement. When other nations cut off aid, KANU was forced to allow opposition activity.

But FORD split in 1992, and a third leader formed another party. The splits allowed Moi to win the presidency in the December 1992 elections with about 35 percent of the vote; Odinga, 81 years old, finished fourth. In 1993, Odinga's reputation suffered when he admitted taking a campaign contribution from a bank accused of bribing government officials. In the months before his death in January 1994, Odinga tried to reconcile his branch of FORD with KANU, but without success. President Moi said at Odinga's death that "Kenya has lost a great son, a nationalist, and a patriotic citizen." In truth, it had lost its strongest opposition leader.

Further Reading

Odinga's account of his life was *Not Yet Uhuru: The Autobiography of Oginga Odinga* (1967). Aspects of his career may be followed in A. J. Hughes, *East Africa* (1963, rev. ed. 1969); George Bennett, *Kenya, A Political History: The Colonial Period* (1963); Richard Cox, *Kenyatta's Country* (1965); and Ali Mazrui, *Violence and Thought* (1969). *Africa Report* magazine, March-April 1994, had an extensive obituary. ☐

Odoacer

The Germanic chieftain Odoacer (433-493), by deposing the Roman emperor Romulus Augustulus, is traditionally credited with ending the Western Roman Empire.

Odoacer was born into a Germanic tribe, the Scirians, and was probably the younger son of Edico, an important person under Attila the Hun. In 470 he and the Scirians entered Italy and, together with many Germanic warriors, took up military service under the Romans. In 472 these German troops, including Odoacer, rebelled and aided the powerful German Ricimer in his bid to make Olybrius emperor. Both Ricimer and Olybrius soon died, and in the ensuing struggle a Roman officer, Orestes, triumphed. In 476 he established his son Romulus Augustulus as emperor, dispossessing the existing Western emperor, Julius Nepos.

However, Orestes failed to satisfy the demands of the Germans, who turned to Odoacer, proclaiming him king on Aug. 23, 476. The Germans then followed him in a rebellion which led to Orestes' death and Romulus's deposition. Significantly Odoacer ceased using shadow emperors and instead claimed himself as the power in the West with whom Zeno, the Eastern emperor, had to deal. Defining the nature of that relationship would concern Zeno and Odoacer as long as Odoacer lived.

An Uneasy Throne

Zeno still claimed to support the deposed Julius Nepos, but he rewarded Odoacer with the title of patrician. In 480 Julius Nepos was murdered, and Odoacer punished his murderers. Zeno had no choice but to recognize Odoacer. Peace lasted until 487, when Odoacer corresponded with a certain Illus, a rebel against Zeno. Although Odoacer had not actually aided the rebel, Zeno regarded his actions as hostile and decided to break his power by sending the Germanic tribe of the Rugians against him (487). Odoacer defeated the Rugians, and Zeno turned for assistance to Theodoric, ruler of the Ostrogoths.

Meanwhile, Odoacer sought to build up his power in Italy. To placate the Germans, he made large grants of land to them. He won the favor of the Roman Senate by awarding high offices to its members. By war and diplomacy, he managed to deal with Italy's two major external threats—

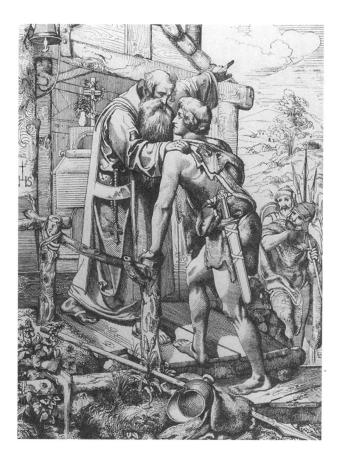

Odoacer (2nd from right)

Euric, King of the Visigoths, and Gaiseric, King of the Vandals. From 477 he even issued coins in his own name.

Theodoric remained the major threat. In 489 he entered Italy. After several major defeats, Odoacer in 490 lost the support of the Roman Senate. He fell back upon the capital at Ravenna, where he endured a siege of 2 years. In 493 a compromise was worked out; Odoacer and Theodoric agreed to rule Italy jointly. However, a few days after entering the city, Theodoric slew Odoacer.

Further Reading

Ancient sources for Odoacer are given in Colin Douglas Gordon, *The Age of Attila* (1960). The best accounts in English are in Thomas Hodgkin, *Italy and Her Invaders* (8 vols., 1880-1889), and J. B. Bury, *A History of the Later Roman Empire* (2 vols., 1889). More recent sources are Stewart Perowne, *The End of the Roman World* (1966), and Arnold H. M. Jones, *The Later Roman Empire, 284-602* (3 vols., 1964) and *The Decline of the Ancient World* (1966). ☐

Manuel Apolinario Odría Amoretti

The Peruvian army officer, dictator-president, and politician Manuel Apolinario Odría Amoretti (1897-

1974) was a war hero who seized the presidency. After eight years of authoritarian rule he surrendered his office, but he continued to influence the affairs of Peru through his personal political party.

Odría was born at Tarma, in the Central Andes, on November 26, 1897, to a middle-class family of Spanish, Italian, and Peruvian Indian ancestry. After graduation from a nearby public high school in 1915 he entered the Chorillos military academy in suburban Lima. Odría graduated four years later at the head of his infantry officers' class. A model, "scientific" soldier in an army striving for increased professionalism, he earned rapid promotion as a military educator and administrator. Odría taught at the military academy, attended the superior war colleges of both the army and the navy, and served as a staff officer with various army commands. During a month-long border war with Ecuador in 1941 Odría's brilliant direction of the army at the decisive Battle of Zarumilla on July 24 won him the laurels of a hero, a promotion to colonel, and a study tour of the United States. He returned to Peru as director of the army war college. Elevated to brigadier general in 1946, Odría was appointed army chief of staff.

At a time of great political unrest in 1947 civilian President José Luis Bustamante y Rivero appointed Odría minister of government and police. But the president and the general quarreled over measures to restrain the disruptive activities of Peru's largest political party, the labor-left American Popular Revolutionary Alliance (APRA) of Víctor Raúl Haya de la Torre, and Odría resigned from the cabinet early the following year. After the failure of a rebellion by a renegade faction of APRA on October 3, 1948, Odría denounced Bustamante for not dealing more firmly with the party and called for his ouster. The general soon gained support from other officers, who installed him as dictator on October 27, 1948.

Odría dismissed the congress and ruled by decree until 1950, when he staged an election. Although he violated the laws pertaining to presidential candidates and permitted only his name to appear on the ballot, Odría "won" a six-year term as "constitutional president." The subservient congress elected with him quickly promoted Odría to division general, the army's highest regular rank. A self-proclaimed "socialist of the right," the general was a short, portly man with bulging eyes who disliked making speeches. "Deeds, Not Words" was his motto.

Odría's eight-year dictatorship, called the "Ochenio," was most notable for political repression and corruption. Employing a vague, sweeping internal security law which circumvented constitutional liberties, Odría harshly suppressed APRA, which he labelled a "Communist front," and stifled all meaningful opposition by his other critics. Official dishonesty pervaded the regime. Odría himself acquired a sumptuous mansion, a fleet of expensive automobiles, and a luxurious wardrobe. The dictator's extravagant lifestyle was scandalously inconsistent with his modest salary. Nevertheless, Odría posted some modest achievements. He purchased modern equipment for the armed forces, improved the social security system, and undertook an ambitious program of public works. Most laudable among the latter projects was the construction of 1,500 schools, many with large, modern auditoriums and playgrounds which doubled as community centers and parks.

Odría ended government economic controls instituted during World War II in favor of orthodox free-market policies. New laws favorable to foreign capital attracted large investments in the oil and copper-mining industries. These measures and, more important, a strong market for Peru's exports during the Korean War (1950-1954) brought a measure of prosperity to the nation's wealthy elite, the small middle class, and some urban workers. But Odría rejected calls for fundamental reforms to improve the condition of poor Peruvians, the vast majority of the population.

When the end to the Korean War brought economic recession, Odría's authoritarian excesses became less tolerable to the nation. Confronted by growing popular discontent and a series of military revolts, he permitted the election of a new president, conservative Manuel Prado y Ugarteche, in 1956. The former dictator now grouped his friends into the National Odriist Union (UNO), a party which appealed to Peru's more traditional conservatives and some urban workers who remembered the general's job-creating public works program. In the presidential election of 1963 Odría polled a poor third behind APRA's Haya de la Torre and Fernando Belaúnde Terry, the victor. Later that year Odría's wife, María Delgado de Odría, unsuccessfully ran for mayor of Lima.

During the Belaúnde administration (1963-1968) Odría's UNO formed a coalition with his former enemy APRA to thwart the president's reforms in congress. In 1968 a clique of radical army officers led by Gen. Juan Velasco Alvarado ousted Belaúnde and instituted a regime of sweeping reform. The military men who dominated the new government viewed Odría and his dictatorship as an embarrassment to the armed forces. Denied influence in the administration, the UNO disintegrated. General Odría died, largely forgotten, on February 18, 1974.

Further Reading

David P. Werlich's *Peru* (1978) traces Odría's career. A chapter on Odría in Tad Szulc, *Twilight of the Tyrants* (1959) is overly generous. David H. Zook's *Zarumilla-Maranon* (1964) treats Odría's service in the war with Ecuador. □

Howard Washington Odum

Howard Washington Odum (1884-1954) was a sociologist, educator, and academic administrator. He was the preeminent sociologist of the American South during the second quarter of the 20th century.

Howard W. Odum was born May 24, 1884, on a small farm near Bethlehem, Georgia. He graduated in 1904 from Emory College in Oxford, Georgia. From there he moved to Mississippi, where he taught in a rural school, earned an M.A. in classics in 1906 from the University of Mississippi, and found time to collect Black folk songs and folklore. He then went north for two Ph.D.'s, one at Clark University in 1909 under the psychologist G. Stanley Hall and one at Columbia in 1910 under the sociologist Franklin H. Giddings. Lasting influences of his doctoral studies included Wilhelm Wundt's folk psychology and William Graham Sumner's concept of the folkways. Odum's breadth of learning was a hallmark of his writings.

Failing to find an academic position in the South, Odum spent two years studying African Americans in the schools for the Philadelphia Bureau of Municipal Research. In 1912 he moved to the University of Georgia as an educational sociologist. Then, as dean of liberal arts at Emory in 1919-1920, he played a major part in the college's move to Atlanta as a university. In 1920 he became Kenan Professor of Sociology at the University of North Carolina at Chapel Hill, a position he held until he retired in 1954. He died November 8, 1954.

Odum was first and foremost a scholar and teacher, but he saw his scholarship as a way to help bring the South into the mainstream of national life. The South of his youth was underdeveloped. Its economy was unbalanced, with too much backward agriculture, a few low-wage industries such as cotton mills, and not much else. It was noted for mistreating its African American citizens and for schools

and prisons that were deplorable by national standards. Yet the region had vibrant folk institutions such as country churches, close-knit families, and deep-rooted ties to home and community. Odum's goal was to help modernize the region while preserving its folk culture—no easy task, and one that made him a complex blend of imaginative reformer and romantic traditionalist. His work was all of a piece in his own mind, but its parts may seem unrelated and almost incompatible when we read them separately.

Odum wrote chiefly about three topics: African American life and culture, folk sociology, and regionalism and social planning. His first book, *Social and Mental Traits of the Negro* (1910), is a mine of facts about the life of Southern rural African Americans of the time. It is marred by views about race differences which were then common among white intellectuals (north and south) and which Odum later outgrew.

He returned to the study of African American culture in *The Negro and His songs* (with Guy B. Johnson, 1925), *Negro Workaday Songs* (with Johnson, 1926), and a partly fictionalized trilogy about the adventures and folk wisdom of a "Black Ulysses," a wandering roustabout whom Odum had come to know in Chapel Hill: *Rainbow Round My Shoulder* (1928), *Wings on My Feet* (1929), and *Cold Blue Moon* (1931). Odum's portrayal of African American culture as seen through the eyes of his picaresque hero was so sympathetic that African American intellectuals criticized him for glamorizing the crudity of a stereotyped African American. Odum's later writings on race were more conventionally scholarly and more explicitly in tune with the integrationist sentiments that had become nearly universal among sociologists by the 1940s. Odum was not an outspoken leader in the fight for racial integration, but he stood up for his student and colleague, Guy B. Johnson, whose liberal views on race brought Johnson and the university under severe attack in the state.

Odum's most nearly systematic theoretical creation was his "folk sociology." Influenced by Sumner, Odum saw folk society and social change as a gradual accumulation of folkways and mores—informal customs that grow from the everyday life of the common people. They are resistant to change, but must change rapidly in a technologically dynamic society. Some of them may be replaced or modified by "technicways"—adaptations of social life to new technologies—and "stateways"—laws that codify and support the technicways. At best, stateways give needed guidance in a world that the old folkways no longer fit. At worst, they are thwarted by deep-rooted folkways or, alternatively, lodge too much power in a central government whose rational planning ignores the feelings of the folk. Odum never laid out folk sociology in any one book, perhaps because his thinking on the subject was incomplete, with loose ends, when he died. For example, he provided no way to predict whether stateways or folkways would prevail when they were irreconcilable.

Odum's regionalism was essentially a call for social planning that would be national in scope while recognizing the special problems of the nation's several regions. His best-known book, *Southern Regions of the United States*

(1936), compiled a massive array of statistics that showed the South trailing the nation in wealth, schooling, indoor toilets, and almost every other quality-of-life indicator. A more analytical though less celebrated work was *American Regionalism* (with Harry Estill Moore, 1938). This book was an imaginative blend of sociocultural analysis and policy advocacy. It delineated six major American regions on the basis of social and cultural differences and argued for using the regions as administrative units for national planning. Odum emphasized the difference between a divisive *sectionalism* and a unifying *regionalism* that would harmonize the regions but preserve their distinctive qualities.

Odum was president of the American Sociological Society in 1930, assistant director of President Hoover's Research Committee on Social Trends from 1929 to 1933, chief of the social science division of the Chicago World's Fair in 1933, president of the Commission on Interracial Cooperation from 1937 to 1944, president of the Southern Regional Council (an organization aimed at bettering race relations) from 1944 to 1946, and president or chairman of several statewide social action and planning organizations in North Carolina. He was visiting professor at Columbia, Yale, and the Universities of Illinois, Southern California, Utah, and Washington.

He did not develop a lasting theoretical perspective or found a school of thought. Most of his 20 books and nearly 200 articles were so focused on the early 20th-century South that they are somewhat time-bound. Nevertheless, he remained influential through the work of his students and their students, many of whom served as presidents of the Southern Sociological Society or the American Sociological Association. Perhaps Odum's most enduring legacies are the institutions he created at the University of North Carolina at Chapel Hill. He founded the university's Department of Sociology (1920), its School of Public Welfare (1920; since renamed the School of Social Work), its sociological journal *Social Forces* (1922), its interdisciplinary Institute for Research in Social Science (1924), and its Department of City and Regional Planning (1946). He was among the small number of faculty members instrumental in founding the University of North Carolina Press in 1922. All of these are widely recognized for the quality of their work. In particular, the Chapel Hill academic departments of sociology and of planning and the journal *Social Forces* have been ranked in national surveys of experts as among the top half dozen in their fields. Through these institutions that survived him, Odum helped bring the South into the national mainstream—but they bear hardly a trace of his concept of regionalism, for there is almost nothing distinctively Southern about them except their location on the map. They recruit faculty and students from all over the world, and their research no longer concentrates on specifically Southern problems. In this sense Odum, a Southerner to the core, may have achieved more than he wanted.

Further Reading

A lucid distillation of Odum's main ideas is Rupert B. Vance, "Odum, Howard W.," in the *International Encyclopedia of the Social Sciences* (1968). Katherine Jocher, Guy B. Johnson, George L. Simpson, and Rupert B. Vance (editors), *Folk, Re-*

gion, and Society (1964) is a collection of Odum's writings chosen to show the broad range of his thought. It contains a biographical sketch and a nearly full bibliography of his publications. Its editors were Odum's former students and its approach is almost wholly sympathetic. A more critical though generally favorable discussion of Odum and his place in American thought appears as Chapter 5 in Daniel Joseph Singal, *The War Within: From Victorian to Modernist Thought in the South, 1919-1945* (1982). Still more critical, and not at all popular with Odum's admirers, is Wayne D. Brazil, "Howard W. Odum: The Building Years, 1884-1930" (Ph.D. dissertation, Harvard University, 1975). Guy Benton Johnson and Guion Griffis Johnson, *Research in Service to Society: Fifty Years of the Institute for Research in Social Science at the University of North Carolina* (1980) gives a thorough and readable account of Odum's role in building a social science center at Chapel Hill.

Additional Sources

Brazil, Wayne D., *Howard W. Odum: the building years, 1884-1930,* New York: Garland Pub., 1988.

Sosna, Morton., *In search of the silent South: southern liberals and the race issue,* New York: Columbia University Press, 1977. □

Hans Christian Oersted

The Danish physicist Hans Christian Oersted (1777-1851) was the first to notice the interaction of electric current and the magnetic needle, thereby initiating the study of electromagnetism.

Hans Oersted was born on Aug. 14, 1777, in Rudköbing on the island of Langeland. Hans received his education from some friendly townspeople, but what was lacking in the way of competent teachers was amply supplemented by Oersted's extraordinary thirst for knowledge. In 1794 he went to Copenhagen and matriculated in science at the university in the fall of that year. The completion of his training in pharmacy came in 1797. Two years later he received his doctorate for a dissertation in which a new and competent theory of alkalies was proposed.

Oersted began his teaching career at the University of Copenhagen as lecturer in pharmacy. In 1801 he went abroad and sought out some of the best philosophic and scientific minds in Germany, the Netherlands, and France, where he spent the winter of 1802/1803. One of the things he immediately realized was the excitement created everywhere by Alessandro Volta's development of the electric battery 2 years earlier. Oersted's attention to this advance was evidence of his ambition to occupy eventually the chair of physics at his university. In 1803 his application was rejected. Clearly he was more of a chemist or pharmacist than physicist. But he kept experimenting and publishing, not only in chemistry but also in physics. His ingenious analysis of Chladni's acoustic figures finally secured for him the position of professor extraordinarius (associate) of physics in 1806. Three years later he published the first volume,

dealing with mechanics, of a longer work planned to cover all areas of natural philosophy (physics).

During 1812 and 1813 Oersted visited in Germany and France. While in Berlin he published in German his *Views of the Chemical Laws of Nature Obtained through the More Recent Discoveries*. It came out the next year in French translation under the revealing title *Researches on the Identity of Chemical and Electrical Forces*. Oersted spoke in his *Researches* about the identity of magnetism and electricity with such assurance that he seemed predisposed to be the discoverer of electromagnetism. In the eighth chapter he noted the close analogies between the properties of magnetic and electric fields, their equally universal presence in nature, and certain reciprocal actions between them such as the loss of magnetism in steel due to rise in temperature and the simultaneous increase of the metal's electrical conductivity. He concluded, "An attempt should therefore be made to see whether electricity, in its most latent stage, has any effect on the magnet as such."

Oersted was also aware of the fact that lightning often resulted in the magnetization of pieces of iron, even to the point of altering the polarity of compass needles. He spent years in search of an elusive goal as he systematically vitiated his work by expecting the magnetic effect to be in the direction of the flow of the current. During those years of search, Oersted blossomed into a most sought-after lecturer both within and outside the university. In recognition of his consummate versatility in scientific matters, he was appointed the leader of a geological survey party charged with the exploration of the island of Bornholm.

In the spring of 1820 Oersted was giving a series of lectures on the interaction between electricity and magnetism before an advanced group of students. The responsiveness of the audience proved to be stimulating, and he was prompted to demonstrate the experimental evidence in support of one of his conjectures. It concerned the possible action of electric discharge on a magnetic needle placed near the circuit. As he expected a discharge through incandescence to be most effective, he inserted in the circuit a very thin platinum wire right above the magnetic compass. "The effect," he wrote, "was certainly unmistakable, but still it seemed to me so confused that I postponed further investigation to a time when I hoped to have more leisure." He resumed the experiments in July, carefully repeating all the steps in the presence of a group of colleagues and students. On July 21 he dispatched to scientists, universities, and learned societies throughout Europe the account of his findings in a four-page essay written in Latin, *Experimenta circa effectum conflictus electrici in acum magneticam* (Experiments about the Effects of an Electrical Conflict [Current] on the Magnetic Needle).

In the essay Oersted noted the dependence of the extent of the needle's motion on the strength of the battery, on the direction of the current in the wire, and on the needle's position with respect to the wire. He found that no effect was noticeable when the wire was perpendicular to the plane of the magnetic meridian. From the dip of the needle, he concluded that the magnetic effect existed in closed circles and not in spirals around the wire. He also found that neither metal plates nor wood nor stoneware would, when interposed between the wire and the needle, screen the effect. This meant that "the transmission of effects through all these matters has never before been observed in electricity and galvanism [current]. The effects, therefore, which take place in the conflict of electricity [current] are very different from the effects of the [static] electricities."

In his account of his discovery given in 1821, Oersted merely cared to correct the belief that the magnetic needle was in its actual position accidentally. It was only 10 years after the event that he emphasized, in the third person, in an article prepared for the *Edinburgh Encyclopedia* that "In composing the lecture, in which he was to treat of the analogy between magnetism and electricity, he conjectured, that if it were possible to produce any magnetical effect by electricity, this could not be in the direction of the current, since this had been so often tried in vain, but that it must be produced by a lateral action." In the same article Oersted also expressed his surprise over the fact that he failed to resume his experiments for 3 months and that those present were not impressed at all as the needle made the historic movement. One of the witnesses later claimed it was by chance that the compass needle was almost under the wire in the desired position.

The impact of Oersted's discovery on the scientific world was enormous. According to Oersted's own count, more than a hundred scientists published their comments and researches on electromagnetism during the first 7 years following its discovery. Oersted was showered with honors and awards. The Royal Society of London gave him the Copley Medal, and the French Academy awarded him a prize of 3,000 gold francs. But his greatest satisfaction was undoubtedly the spectacular growth of a new branch of physics, electromagnetism, which was to have revolutionary impact on modern culture.

Oersted was 43 when he made his great discovery. For the rest of his life he held the position of a leader in science. He had a major role in the establishment of the Royal Polytechnic Institute in 1829, of which he became the first director.

Further Reading

The most authoritative and exhaustive biography of Oersted is the book-length essay by Kirstine Meyer in her edition of *H. C. Oersted: Scientific Papers* (3 vols., 1920). A detailed biography by one of Oersted's contemporaries is in Bessie Zaban Jones, ed., *The Golden Age of Science: Thirty Portraits of the Giants of 19th-Century Science by Their Scientific Contemporaries* (1966). For additional material on Oersted's work and the general historical background see Edmund Taylor Whittaker, *A History of the Theories of Aether and Electricity* (1910; 2 vols., rev. ed. 1951), and Bern Dibner, *Oersted and the Discovery of Electromagnetism* (1961; 2d ed. 1963). □

Jacques Offenbach

The German-French composer Jacques Offenbach (1819-1880) can be considered the father of the operetta because his lighthearted works conquered the world and found imitators everywhere.

Although he created a typically French musical idiom, Jacques, originally Jacob, Offenbach was born in Cologne, the son of a Jewish cantor and itinerant musician from the town of Offenbach. Jacques, one of 10 children, showed precocious musical talent, particularly for the cello. He studied with local teachers and performed in restaurants with a brother and sister. In 1833 the father took Jacques and another son to Paris for further training and for the musical opportunities offered there. The young German was accepted at the conservatory, but he left after a year to enter the professional world of music. His first position was as a cellist at the Opéra Comique, and for the rest of his life he was active in the musical-entertainment world as composer, conductor, and manager.

Offenbach was music director of the Comédie Française for 7 years, but when the International Exposition was held in Paris in 1855, he leased a theater seating only 50 people and presented his own satirical and topical sketches. The project was a sensational success, and he soon moved to a larger theater. In the following years he composed and produced almost 100 operettas. In them, he satirized political figures of the day and pretentious snobbery in the arts. There was nothing sentimental about Offenbach's operettas (this was a later development), only wit and high spirits. The most famous are *Orpheus in the*

Underworld (1858), *La Belle Hélène* (1864), and *La Vie Parisienne* (1866).

During the Paris Universal Exposition in 1867 thousands of visitors, including royalty and nobility as well as commoners, visited Offenbach's theater. In his later years he appeared as guest conductor in London, Vienna, Berlin, and other European centers. In 1875 he visited the United States and conducted special concerts in New York City and Philadelphia. The tour was less than a success, but his memoirs of the trip, *Orpheus in America,* give lively insights into big city life of the time.

Offenbach wrote one serious opera, *The Tales of Hoffmann,* a masterpiece that is frequently performed. It is his operettas, however, with their mixture of social satire with attractive melodies and ebullient dances that gave him his fame. He did not invent the can-can, but his use of this high-spirited, high-kicking dance made it as much a symbol of Paris as the Eiffel Tower.

Further Reading

A translation of Offenbach's account of his trip to the United States was published as *Orpheus in America: Offenbach's Diary of His Journey to the New World* (1957). Siegfried Kracauer, *Orpheus in Paris: Offenbach and the Paris of His Time* (1938), is rich in its treatment of social conditions during the composer's life. For a reasonable estimation of Offenbach's importance as a composer see Harold C. Schonberg, *The Lives of the Great Composers* (1970).

Additional Sources

Faris, Alex., *Jacques Offenbach,* New York: Scribner, 1981, 1980.

Gammond, Peter., *Offenbach,* London; New York: Omnibus Press, 1986 1980.

Gammond, Peter., *Offenbach: his life and times,* Tunbridge Wells, Kent: Midas Books, 1980.

Harding, James., *Jacques Offenbach: a biography,* London: J. Calder; New York: Riverrun Press, 1980. □

Sadako Ogata

International civil servant Sadako Ogata (born in Japan in 1927) was chosen to serve as the United Nations High Commissioner for Refugees in 1991.

On December 21, 1990, Professor Sadako Ogata was called from her post as dean of the Faculty of Foreign Studies at Sophia University in Tokyo and asked to become the United Nations High Commissioner for Refugees (UNHCR). Elected by the full U.N. General Assembly for a three-year term starting January 1, 1991, she assumed office on February 18 at a time when the plight of refugees in many parts of the world thrust the problem to the top of the international agenda.

The High Commissioner's Office, with administrative headquarters in Geneva, was established by General Assembly resolution in 1951 as an integral part of the U.N. system. Governed by an executive committee comprised of representatives from 44 nations meeting annually to set forth UNHCR's guidelines and programs, the High Commissioner is responsible for executing a twofold mandate vis-á-vis refugees, who are defined by statute as "persons who are outside their country of nationality and who, owing to a well-founded fear of persecution for reasons of race, religion, nationality, or political opinion, are unwilling or unable to avail themselves of that country or to return to it." Accordingly, Ogata's primary task was to provide immediate, short-term protection for refugees, such as employment, education, and asylum. This also includes seeking guarantees that neither the life nor liberty of any refugee will be threatened should he or she opt for returning home. A second function is more comprehensive, with UNHCR searching for permanent solutions by facilitating the voluntary repatriation of refugees, their local integration into new national communities, or their resettlement abroad.

High Commissioner Ogata and the Office for Refugees were threatened by an overload of cases, reflected in the statistics. Between 1951 and 1992 UNHCR sought to administer to about 750,000 people a year, whereas beginning in 1992 some 5,000 human beings were forced to abandon their homes each day, or double that total in a single year. By 1993 the spread of violence and ethnic conflict in the post-Cold War world had driven an estimated 44 million people—from Yugoslavia and Burundi to Kuwait—to flee across borders. An additional 24 million refugees were displaced within their own countries, such as Iraq

and Serbia. The sheer magnitude of the escalating global refugee crisis—with displaced persons representing more than one in every 130 inhabitants of the globe—forced Ogata to expand UNHCR'S traditional role and budget. For example, in August of 1994, *The Economist* reported that Ogata upset other UN people by declaring that she would suspend aid to Bosnia if attacks against relief conveys didn't cease. "She had no qualms about defying UN officialdom", the magazine wrote. Ogata was also a fierce advocate for the estimated two million Rwaandan refugees during that crises in the mid-nineties.

Sadako Ogata herself, determined to prove equal to the task, relied on a wealth of experience in international civil administration. Born on September 16, 1927, in Tokyo, most of her first 50 years were directed toward an academic career. After receiving a B.A. from the University of the Sacred Heart in Tokyo, she decided to do graduate study in the United States, where she earned an M.A. in international relations from Georgetown (1953) and a doctorate in political science from the University of California at Berkeley (1963). Returning to her native Japan, Ogata lectured from 1965 to 1974 at the University of the Sacred Heart and also at the International Christian University, serving at the later from 1974 to 1976 as an associate professor of diplomatic history and international relations. In 1980 she moved to Sophia University, where she became a professor and later (1987 to 1988) director of the Institute of International Relations, before promotion in 1989 to dean of the Faculty of Foreign Studies.

Toward the end of the 1970s Ogata had increasingly combined her teaching and research activity with diplomacy. During 1978 and 1979 she was envoy extraordinary and minister plenipotentiary at the permanent mission of Japan to the United Nations, having served there as minister from 1976 to 1978. She was Japan's delegate to the 23rd, 25th, and 30th to 33rd sessions of the General Assembly, and also to the Tenth Special Session, which was devoted to disarmament.

Ambassador Ogata's exposure to the more specialized refugee problem intensified as of 1978-1979 when she acted as chairperson of the executive board of UNICEF, the children's fund. Again, she acquired a first-hand impression of the human dimensions when she was made U.N. special ambassador for Indochinese refugee relief (1979); the representative of Japan to the U.N. Commission on Human Rights (1982 to 1985); and a member of the Independent Commission on International Humanitarian Issues (1983 to 1987). In 1990 she was the independent expert sent by the U.N. Commission on Human Rights to investigate the situation of Cambodian refugees on the Thai-Cambodian border.

Married and the mother of a son and daughter, Ogata became a member of the Trilateral Commission in 1984 and sat on the board of governors of the International Development Research Center beginning in 1986. The busy Ogata also served on many government advisory councils as well as on the boards of academic associations and foundations.

Further Reading

Ogata has published a number of books on diplomatic history and international relations as well as numerous articles. Among her works are: *Defiance in Manchuria—The Making of Japanese Foreign Policy 1931-1932* (1964); *Vantage Point from the United Nations* (*Kokuren kara no shiten*), (Japan, 1980); *Survey of International Organization Studies in Japan* (*Nihon ni okeru kokusal soshiki kenkyu*), (Japan, 1982); and *Normalization with China: A Comparative Study of U.S. and Japanese Processes* (1989). Information on Ogata was also available on the internet, by searching for "Sadako Ogata" (August 13, 1997). □

William Fielding Ogburn

William Fielding Ogburn (1886-1959), American sociologist, statistician, and educator, was concerned with quantitative methods and with the role of technology in social organization.

William Ogburn was born in Butler, Ga., on June 29, 1886. He received his bachelor of science degree at Mercer University and his master of arts degree (1909) and doctorate in sociology (1912) from Columbia University. He was professor of sociology and economics at Reed College (1912-1917) and professor of sociology at the University of Washington (1917-1918). During World War I he was with the National War Labor Board and the U.S. Bureau of Labor Statistics.

Ogburn was professor of sociology at Columbia University (1919-1927) and professor of sociology at the University of Chicago (1927-1951). He was director of research for the President's Research Committee on Social Trends (1930-1933), director of the Consumers Advisory Board of the National Recovery Administration (1933), and research consultant of the Science Committee, National Resources Committee (1935-1943). He was president of the American Statistical Association and the American Sociological Society. From 1953 till his death on April 27, 1959, Ogburn was visiting professor of sociology at Florida State University.

Description and measurement of the tangible aspects of social change were the recurring themes in Ogburn's career. His first major formulation of these problems appeared in *Social Change* (1922), where he traced social evolution through the invention and accumulation of mechanical and scientific forms. He gave special attention to the apparent gap between technical developments and adjustments in values, laws, and customs in contemporary society. This discrepancy, which he named cultural lag, was widely borrowed in later years to explain difficulties and resistances to social change.

During the next 20 years Ogburn encouraged investigators in specifying the effects of technological change in selected social activities. An early and continuing interest in family changes was expressed in several works, particularly *American Marriage and Family Relationships* (1928) and *Technology and the Changing American Family* (1955). As research administrator, he stimulated analyses of varied technological changes in *Recent Social Trends* (2 vols., 1933).

Ogburn's quantitative interests were applied in studies of elections, in many articles on population trends, and in a classic early survey of urban population and economic patterns, *Social Characteristics of Cities* (1937). A particularly ambitious work, *The Social Effects of Aviation* (1946), tried to anticipate the varied consequences of expanded use of air transport for economic, political, recreational, and other aspects of modern society. The widest dissemination of his views has probably developed from *Sociology*, a textbook in collaboration with Meyer Nimkoff, which has been revised several times since 1940.

Further Reading

Otis Dudley Duncan summarized Ogburn's work and provided a number of excerpts from his writings in his edition of Ogburn's *On Culture and Social Change: Selected Papers* (1964). Ogburn's work is also discussed in Llewellyn Gross, ed., *Symposium on Sociological Theory* (1959). □

Peter Skene Ogden

The Canadian fur trader and explorer Peter Skene Ogden (1794-1854) was a leader in the Pacific Northwest fur trade during the mid-19th century.

Peter Ogden, the youngest son of American loyalists Isaac and Sarah Ogden, was born in Quebec. Although his father held a judgeship, young Peter became a clerk for John Jacob Astor's American Fur Company. By the time he was 15 or 16, he had joined the Montreal-based North West Company as a clerk. Between 1810 and 1817 he served in this capacity at several trading posts near Hudson Bay. In 1818 he led several successful trapping expeditions, and his competence brought a promotion. After his company merged into the Hudson's Bay Company, he led six major expeditions between 1824 and 1830.

On the first of these, Ogden met a party of Americans who demanded that the Canadians get out of American territory; Ogden refused. Unfortunately, the Hudson's Bay Company paid Ogden's trappers so little that 23 of his 70 men joined the American party. For the next 5 years the two groups waged a fierce competition to gather furs, and by the 1830s they had denuded the region. In 1835 Ogden was promoted to chief factor, the highest field rank in the company service, and went to Fort St. James on Lake Stuart, where he worked until 1844.

On these expeditions Ogden and his men traveled throughout the mountainous West and up and down the Pacific coast. They brought the first report of the Humboldt River, which was named for Ogden until 1843. Ogden is also credited with naming Mt. Shasta in northern California. Because of his years of trade with and travel among the Indians, Ogden was able to rescue the 47 American prisoners taken by the Cayuse Indians during the Whitman Mission massacre in 1847.

Ogden was married twice, each time to a Native American woman, and he had at least one daughter. Described as a distinguished, short, dark-complexioned man, Ogden was considered a witty and lively conversationalist. He wrote a short book entitled *Traits of American Indian Life and Character,* which he published anonymously in London in 1853. He died on Sept. 27, 1854, in Oregon City, Oregon Territory.

Further Reading

There is no book-length biography of Ogden. The two best sources on his career as a trapper and explorer are his own works: Edwin E. Rich, ed., *Peter Skene Ogden's Snake Country Journals, 1824-25 and 1825-26* (1950), and Kenneth G. Davies, ed., *Snake Country Journal, 1826-27* (1961). For material on the Hudson's Bay Company in the northern Rockies see Frederick Merk, ed., *Fur Trade and Empire: George Simpson's Journal* (1931; rev. ed. 1968); John S. Galbraith, *The Hudson's Bay Company as an Imperial Factor, 1821-1869* (1957); and E. E. Rich, *The History of the Hudson's Bay Company, 1670-1870* (2 vols., 1958-1959).

Additional Sources

Cline, Gloria Griffen, *Peter Skene Ogden and the Hudson's Bay Company,* Norman, Okla.: University of Oklahoma Press, 1974.

Phillips, Fred M., *Desert people and mountain men: exploration of the Great Basin, 1824-1865,* Bishop, Calif.: Chalfant Press, 1977. □

David MacKenzie Ogilvy

David Ogilvy (born 1911), a British-American business executive, was a leader in the post-World War II "creative revolution" in American advertising.

David Mackenzie Ogilvy was born on June 23, 1911, in West Horsley, England. He attended preparatory school in Edinburgh from 1924 to 1929 and won a scholarship in history to Christ Church College, Oxford. By his own admission an indifferent student, Ogilvy left Oxford without a degree in 1931 and spent a year as an apprentice chef in a Parisian hotel. He returned to Great Britain and supported himself by selling cooking stoves door-to-door. He was so successful that his employer asked him to prepare an instructional manual for his fellow salesmen. The manual, together with the intercession of his brother Francis, helped win him a position at the London advertising agency of Mather & Crowther. He remained there until 1939, when he decided to seek new opportunities in the United States, a country that had long intrigued him.

Shortly after his arrival in the United States he was asked by pollster George Gallup to join his Audience Research Institute in Princeton, New Jersey, as associate director. Ogilvy later called this "the luckiest break of [his] life,"

for few other positions could have so quickly educated him to the ways of the American market. While with Gallup Ogilvy conducted over 400 public opinion surveys, many of them for the major Hollywood studios.

In 1942, with the world at war, Ogilvy was recruited by the British intelligence organization in America headed by William Stephenson. Ogilvy's assignment was to collect economic intelligence from Latin America and to prevent the enemy's access to strategic materials there. From 1944 to 1945 he also served as the second secretary to the British embassy in Washington.

In 1948, after a brief stint as a tobacco farmer in Pennsylvania, Ogilvy joined with New York advertising man Anderson Hewitt to form the advertising agency that would eventually become known as Ogilvy & Mather. Although Ogilvy had no previous experience as an advertising copywriter, he directed most of the agency's creative efforts, particularly after Hewitt's departure from the firm in 1953. Ogilvy brought to the task a great flair for language and a visual sense so highly developed that in the early years he usually acted as his own art director.

His talents first came to the attention of a national audience in 1951 when he was approached by Hathaway, a small Maine clothing firm, to promote its line of moderately priced shirts. Ogilvy's copy for the initial ad was effective by itself. But it was the accompanying photograph that propelled the Hathaway campaign into advertising history. At virtually the last moment Ogilvy decided to photograph his male model wearing a Hathaway shirt—and an eyepatch.

''The Man in the Hathaway Shirt'' appeared for the first time in the *New Yorker* of September 22, 1951. It caused a sensation. The eyepatch somehow lent the shirt an air of quality and sophistication. That image was carefully reinforced in a follow-up campaign portraying the Hathaway man as an eyepatched man-about-town. Eventually Hathaway no longer needed to display its name in its advertisements. The ''man with the eyepatch'' was identification enough. The company, meanwhile, could barely keep up with the demand for its shirts.

Ogilvy's reputation as a master of product image was further enhanced in 1953 when he took over the account of Schweppes, a British manufacturer of quinine water then struggling to gain a foothold in America. Ogilvy designed his print campaign around Commander Edward Whitehead, the bearded and ever-so-British director of Schweppes' American operations. In the 1950s a beard was as exotic as the Hathaway man's eyepatch. And it soon proved to be as compelling a sales device. Within five years Schweppes was selling over 30 million bottles a year.

The Schweppes and Hathaway campaigns were primarily tributes to Ogilvy's visual gifts. But he was equally adept at moving consumers through the power of his words. The tag line he composed for the Rolls-Royce automobile company in 1958 (''At sixty miles an hour the loudest noise in this new Rolls-Royce comes from the electric clock'') helped double that firm's American sales in a year.

As the 1960s opened Ogilvy's advertising style was being widely copied on Madison Avenue and his agency had grown to become the 12th-largest in the nation, with such clients as the Shell Oil Company and the Commonwealth of Puerto Rico. But as the number of accounts grew, Ogilvy gradually took a less active role in the creation of the firm's advertising. He continued, however, to oversee operations as chairman of the board until 1975.

Ogilvy served as chairman of the WPP Group in London from 1988-1992. He stepped into the role of consultant in 1992. He was also honored as an officier de L'Ordre des Arts et des Lettres in 1990.

Through best-selling books and widely publicized speeches David Ogilvy emerged as one of advertising's most eloquent spokesmen. Yet he never hesitated to point out the faults of his profession. One of the most creative advertising men of his time, he was scathing in his criticism of those executives so ''creative'' that ''they forget their main mission—to sell the product.'' Certainly no one ever ''sold the product'' better than David Ogilvy.

Further Reading

Ogilvy described his professional career in *Confessions of an Advertising Man* (1963). *Blood, Brains and Beer: The Autobiography of David Ogilvy* (1978) provided the personal details. In *Ogilvy on Advertising* (1983) the master surveyed the contemporary scene. *The Unpublished David Ogilvy* was released in 1988. Ogilvy's achievements were placed in historical perspective in Stephen Fox, *The Mirror Makers: A History of American Advertising and Its Creators* (1984). His most famous advertisements are reproduced and analyzed in Robert Glatzer, *The New Advertising: The Great Campaigns from Avis to Volkswagen* (1970). □

James Edward Oglethorpe

James Edward Oglethorpe (1696-1785), an English soldier, member of Parliament, and humanitarian, was the founder of the colony of Georgia in America.

James Oglethorpe was born in London on Dec. 22, 1696, the third and surviving son of Sir Theophilus and Lady Eleanor Wall Oglethorpe. The family influences which he reflected included sympathy for the claims of the English Stuarts, interest in the military, and a strong personal character inclined to moral causes. He was educated at Eton and attended Oxford before accepting commissions in the British army and on the Continent. Oglethorpe inherited the family estate of Westbrook and settled down in 1719 to the career of a country gentleman.

Member of Parliament

In keeping with family tradition, Oglethorpe was elected to Parliament in 1722; he served for 32 years, despite continued opposition. He became known as a Tory member, opposed to the administration of Robert Walpole, and advocate of an aggressive British posture in the world. More noteworthy were Oglethorpe's humanitarian interests. His initial activities on behalf of penal reform were spurred on by the death of a friend who had been imprisoned for debt. Oglethorpe's attacks on debtors' prisons led to the establishment of a parliamentary committee under his chairmanship in 1729. Subsequent investigations exposed the brutality of penal conditions and questioned the wisdom of imprisonment for debt. His humanitarian impulses were carried further in an antipathy to black slavery, attacks on the practice of impressment, and campaigns against drinking.

Georgia Colony

A continuing theme of the period of colonization was the idea that the new continents might afford a remedy for the ills of Europe. Oglethorpe and others, demanding reform, proposed to establish a colony which might provide a place for the rehabilitation of people imprisoned for debt. For this purpose Oglethorpe and 19 associates received a royal charter in 1732 to found a colony between Spanish Florida and South Carolina; the trustees were to govern Georgia for 21 years, after which the province would revert to royal control. The King accepted the philanthropic aims of Georgia in granting the charter, but he also made clear that the colony was supposed to increase the commerce of Britain and serve as a buffer state for the protection of the southern frontier. The genesis of Georgia arose from this threefold set of motives—philanthropic, commercial, and military.

The trusteeship eventually collapsed, basically because of the incompatibility of the colony's purposes. The size of grants was severely limited, land could not be sold freely, nor could estates be inherited by women. These policies, meant to enhance military security and ensure success, were self-defeating. For example, though immigration was

to be encouraged, restraints on the size of estates and on the right of inheritance repelled new settlers. Of major importance also was the threat of war with Spain. Much of Oglethorpe's life in the colony over a 10-year span was devoted to this problem. In time, the military side of the colonial experiment predominated over everything else.

Given the conflicts that characterized the trusteeship, Oglethorpe's contributions have not always been recognized. Apart from his role in inspiring the colony, his fame in Parliament and military reputation secured the massive public and private funds needed for Georgia's beginnings. Oglethorpe's military leadership was crucial during the periods of war with Spain, although he was unsuccessful in two attempts to conquer St. Augustine in 1740 and 1743.

Road to Oblivion

When Oglethorpe returned to London in 1743, his days of active colonial leadership were coming to an end. Already the trustees were complaining about the cost of defending Georgia, and bitter charges were circulating in England regarding abuses by Oglethorpe and his appointees. Faced with growing discontent among the colonists and insurmountable economic problems, the trustees surrendered their charter to the Crown a year before its expiration in 1752. By this time Oglethorpe had lost much of his authority and had ceased to play a leading part in the life of the colony.

Shortly after his return to London, Oglethorpe married Elizabeth Wright, a wealthy heiress. Called to arms during

the uprising led by the Stuart pretender in 1745, Oglethorpe was later charged with misconduct in the campaign. Although he was cleared and promoted to lieutenant general, his active military career was over. Finally, he lost his seat in Parliament in 1754. His last years were spent in relative obscurity, though he maintained a friendship with Samuel Johnson and others of Johnson's literary circle. Oglethorpe died on June 30, 1785.

Further Reading

Biographies of Oglethorpe are not entirely satisfactory in delineating his character or the complex history of Georgia's beginnings. The best accounts are Leslie F. Church, *Oglethorpe: A Study in Philanthropy in England and Georgia* (1932), and Amos A. Ettinger, *James Edward Oglethorpe: Imperial Idealist* (1936). A recent brief analysis is Trevor Reese, *Colonial Georgia: A Study in British Imperial Policy in the Eighteenth Century* (1963). Indispensable for the background to Georgia's settlement is Verner W. Crane, *The Southern Frontier, 1670-1732* (1928). Of special value for the general history of the Colonies in the 18th century is Lawrence H. Gipson's five-volume *The British Empire before the American Revolution*, especially vol. 2: *The Southern Plantations* (1936; rev. ed. 1960). Useful for the English background is Basil Williams, *The Whig Supremacy, 1714-1760* (1939; 2d ed. rev. 1962).

Additional Sources

Ettinger, Amos Aschbach, *Oglethorpe, a brief biography,* Macon, Ga.: Mercer, 1984.

Garrison, Webb B., *Oglethorpe's folly: the birth of Georgia,* Lakemont, GA.: Copple House Books, 1982.

Oglethorpe in perspective: Georgia's founder after two hundred years, Tuscaloosa: University of Alabama Press, 1989.

Spalding, Phinizy., *James Edward Oglethorpe: a new look at Georgia's founder,* Athens, Ga.: Carl Vinson Institute of Government, University of Georgia, 1988.

Spalding, Phinizy., *Oglethorpe in America,* Athens: University of Georgia Press, 1984, 1977. □

Grace Emily Akinyi Ogot

East Africa's best-known woman author, Grace Emily Akinyi Ogot (born 1930) wrote novels and short stories. She also became an important political figure in modern Kenya.

Grace Emily Akinyi Ogot earned a distinctive position in Kenya's literary and political history. The best known writer in East Africa, and with a varied career background, she became in 1984 one of only a handful of women to serve as a member of Parliament and the only woman assistant minister in the cabinet of President Daniel Arap Moi.

Born in Kenya's Central Nyanza District in 1930, she was the child of pioneering Christian parents in the traditional Luo stronghold of Asembo. Her father, Joseph Nyanduga, was an early convert to the Anglican Church and one of the first men in Asembo to receive a Western education. He later taught at the Church Missionary Society's Ng'iya Girls' School. She remembered him reading her Bible stories, as well as hearing the traditional stories told by her grandmother. Later Ogot's writing reflected this dual background of tradition and modernity and the tensions between them.

Having attended Ng'iya Girls' School and Butere High School, the young woman trained as a nurse in both Uganda and England. Several years working as a nursing sister and midwifery tutor at Maseno Hospital (run by the Church Missionary Society), and later at the Student Health Service at Makerere University College, provided experience in a number of different careers. She worked as a script-writer and broadcaster for the BBC Overseas Service (later having her own popular weekly radio program in Luo), as a community development officer in Kisumu, and as a public relations officer for Air India. In the late 1960s she opened two branches of a clothing boutique known as Lindy's in Nairobi.

She married the historian Bethwell Alan Ogot, a Luo from Gem Location, in 1959 and was the mother of four children. She began to publish short stories both in English and in Luo in the early 1960s and her first novel, *The Promised Land,* was published in 1966. It was concerned with the challenges faced by Luo pioneers who moved across the border into Tanzania in a search of greater opportunity. *Land Without Thunder,* a collection of short stories about traditional life in rural western Kenya, appeared in 1968. Two other short story collections have appeared, *The Other Woman and Other Stories* (Nairobi, 1976) and *The Island of Tears* (Nairobi, 1980), as well as second novel, *The Graduate* (Nairobi, 1980). The novel described the tribulations of a young Kenyan graduate who returns home after study in the United States. Ogot's short stories often weaved old and new material together by presenting traditional curses and mysteries confounding modern Kenyans in new urban settings. A series of historical novels in process went back several centuries to reconstruct Luo history. A number of her stories have been dramatized and performed in Kenya.

In recognition of her blossoming literary career, she was named a delegate to the General Assembly of the United Nations in 1975, and as a member of the Kenya delegation to UNESCO (the United Nations Educational, Scientific, and Cultural Organization) in 1976. Having helped found the Writers' Association of Kenya, she served as its chairman from 1975 to 1980. President Daniel Arap Moi appointed her to the Kenya Parliament in 1985 and as assistant minister for culture. In 1988 she was resoundingly returned to the Parliament from her husband's home in Gem and was reappointed to her ministerial position.

Ogot's family members shared her interest in politics. Her husband, served as head of Kenya Railways and also taught history at Kenyatta University. Her older sister, Rose Orondo, served on the Kisumu County Council for several terms, and her younger brother Robert Jalango was elected to Parliament in 1988, representing their family home in Asembo.

Further Reading

The novels and short stories of Grace Ogot were widely available. Oladele Taiwo devoted a chapter of her *Female Novelists of Modern Africa* (1984) to Ogot's literary development; Bernth Lindfors has published "An Interview with Grace Ogot" in *World Literature Written in English* (1979); O. R. Dathorne included a chapter on "Grace Ogot: Role of the Black Woman" in *African Literature in the Twentieth Century* (1974).

Ogot's book, *The Strange Bride,* was published in 1989; She was one of 570 women writers of the 20th-century chosen to appear in *Modern Women Writers,* a four-volume set including criticism, biographical material, and excerpts from published works, released in 1996. □

Madalyn Murray O'Hair

Madalyn Murry O'Hair (born 1919) was a staunch atheist who court cases brought down rulings from the Supreme Court that prayer is not to be required in public schools.

Madalyn Murray O'Hair called herself "the most hated woman in America." Although *School Board of Abbington Township* v. *Schempp* is usually cited as the case through which the Supreme Court ruled that public schools may not require Bible reading, the second decision on that issue was a case filed in 1959 by O'Hair and her son, William J. Murray (*Murray* v. *Curlett*). The decision was handed down in 1963. As atheists they protested the Baltimore school board's requirement that the public school day begin with prayer or Bible reading. Murray, as she was named then, attracted notoriety by organizing the American Atheist Center (1959), American Atheists, Inc. (1965), and the Society of Separationists (1965). O'Hair's younger son, Jon Garth Murray, and her granddaughter, Robin Murray O'Hair, helped her run the Center. Her American Atheist Radio series was broadcast on over four thousand radio stations. She had a talent for attracting attention as, for example, when she issued statements that she planned to sue to stop governments from giving tax exemptions to places of public worship and other religious organizations. She also announced she would sue to remove the phrase "In God We Trust" from the currency. After being arrested for attacking Baltimore police, she fled to Hawaii and eventually settled in Austin, Texas, where she and her new husband established the American Atheist Center. During the 1960s the American Atheist Press published the first five of O'Hair's more than twenty-five books on the subject of atheism, including *Why I Am an Atheist* (1965).

In August of 1995, at the age of 76, O'Hair mysteriously disappeared along with her son Jon and her adopted daughter Robin. According to a December 1995 issue of the Fort Worth Star-Telegram, the IRS seeks to recover $750,00 in back taxes from her son and daughter. However, the American Atheists news service, which which was started by

O'Hair, continually repudiated all rumors of her reason for disappearing. The organization has failed to release any information leading to her discovery. Then in December 1996 more than $600,000 vanished from the American Atheists Inc. organization, which was controlled by O'Hair. While some believe O'Hair went somewhere secret to die to avoid having "religionists" pray over her body, others question whether she took the missing money. Despite investigations, the answer to these questions, as well as O'Hair's whereabouts, remained a mystery. □

John O'Hara

The American novelist and short-story writer John O'Hara (1905-1970) had an extraordinary ability to reproduce the look and sound of contemporary America.

John O'Hara was born on Jan. 31, 1905, in Pottsville, Pa., the eldest of eight children. He was brought up as a Catholic. Expelled from Fordham Preparatory School and the Keystone State Normal School, he graduated, as class valedictorian, from the Niagara, N.Y., Preparatory School in 1924, but his father's death prevented his entering college.

For the next 10 years O'Hara worked as ship steward, railroad freight clerk, gas meter reader, amusement park guard, soda jerk, and press agent but, more importantly, as a journalist, first in Pottsville and then in New York City. He also wrote magazine pieces for *Time* and the *New Yorker* and worked briefly as a literary secretary and as a press agent.

Appointment in Samarra (1934), O'Hara's first and best novel, is the tragedy of Julian English, who initiates his own downfall by throwing a drink into the face of a social superior. A compelling study of status in Pennsylvania society, it illustrates what critic Lionel Trilling describes as O'Hara's dominant theme: "the imagination of society as some strange sentient organism which acts by laws of its own being which are not to be understood." Upon the success of the novel, O'Hara began work as a Hollywood film writer, his chief occupation until the mid-1940s.

O'Hara's association with the *New Yorker,* dating from 1928, is the source of his story collections. The first, *The Doctor's Son and Other Stories* (1935), was followed by a best-selling novel, *Butterfield 8* (1935), based on a famous murder case and remarkable for its accurate nightclub-underworld argot.

A novel, *Hope of Heaven* (1938), and a story collection, *Files on Parade* (1939), were less significant than O'Hara's series of sketches collected as *Pal Joey* (1940). Adapted by O'Hara in 1941 for the stage, with music and lyrics by Richard Rodgers and Lorenz Hart, it was the season's hit.

In 1944 O'Hara worked as war correspondent for *Liberty* magazine. The following year his only child, his daugh-

ter Wylie, was born. After World War II O'Hara's career remained commercially successful but became critically uncertain. *A Rage to Live* (1949) had huge sales but mixed reviews. *Ten North Frederick* (1955) and *From the Terrace* (1958) were both best-selling novels made into movies, but *Terrace* received especially bad reviews.

O'Hara continued a prodigious output; in addition to two novels, *Elizabeth Appleton* (1963) and *The Lockwood Concern* (1965), seven story and novella collections appeared: *Sermons and Soda Water* (1960), *Assembly* (1961), *The Cape Cod Lighter* (1962), *The Hat on the Bed* (1963), *The Horse Knows the Way* (1964), *And Other Stories* (1968), and *The O'Hara Generation* (1969). He died in Princeton, N.J., on April 11, 1970.

Further Reading

Apart from reviews, O'Hara has received scant critical attention. Sheldon Norman Grebstein, *John O'Hara* (1966), is an excellent short critical biography.

Additional Sources

Bruccoli, Matthew Joseph, *The O'Hara concern: a biography of John O'Hara,* Pittsburgh, Pa.: Universtiy of Pittsburgh Press, 1995.
Long, Robert Emmet, *John O'Hara,* New York: Ungar, 1983.
MacShane, Frank, *The life of John O'Hara,* New York: Dutton, 1980.
O'Hara, John, *A cub tells his story,* Iowa City: Windhover Press; Bloomfield Hills, Mich.: Bruccoli Clark, 1974. □

Bernardo O'Higgins

The Chilean soldier and statesman Bernardo O'Higgins (1778-1842) became a leading figure in the movement for emancipation from Spain and the first head of an independent Chilean Republic.

Bernardo O'Higgins was born in Chillán, the illegitimate son of Isabel Riquelme, daughter of a Chilean landowner. He was known in early life by his mother's name. His father was the Irish-born Ambrosio O'Higgins, later viceroy of Peru. Not openly acknowledged by his father, Bernardo was brought up by foster parents in Chile, then educated at the San Carlos College, Lima, and finally sent to England, where he became imbued with liberal ideas and converted to Francisco de Miranda's projects for the independence of the Spanish colonies. After a couple of years in Spain, where he lived in poverty and the disfavor of his father (who, however, relented on his deathbed and left him an estate near Concepción), he returned to Chile in 1802. He then assumed the name of O'Higgins and made his home with his mother and half sister Rosita.

O'Higgins threw himself into the struggle for emancipation which was then beginning in Chile. Though he lacked outstanding gifts of generalship, he possessed great personal courage, energy, and tenacity. In 1814 he took over command of the patriot forces from the rival independence leader, José Miguel Carrera. Forced to retreat northward before the Spaniards, O'Higgins made a heroic stand at Rancagua and then withdrew with the remnants of the patriot army across the Andes into Argentina. There he joined the forces under the command of Gen. José de San Martín, returning to Chile with him in 1817 to win the battle of Chacabuco and to become the first head (*director supremo*) of an independent Chile.

Liberation of Chile and Peru

For the next 6 years O'Higgins was engaged in campaigns to clear the Spaniards out of Chile and in efforts to build up an expeditionary force and fleet for the invasion of Peru. Though O'Higgins worked hard to organize the country on liberal lines, public discontent increased as a result of the strain of the war, economic prostration, and the increasingly autocratic measures O'Higgins's government felt obliged to take. Realizing that the choice now lay between continuing to rule by force as a dictator or to resign office, O'Higgins chose the latter course and left for exile in Peru (1823). He lived there quietly with his mother and half sister, on the estate given him in recognition of his services for the liberation of Peru, until his death in 1842.

O'Higgins was a man of simple and upright character and liberal principles. Although he devoted his life to the overthrow of the Spanish rule which his father had served with such distinction, he revered his father's memory and strove to continue many of the viceroy's reforms. His valor and patriotism, and his decision to surrender power rather than use it dictatorially, have assured him the foremost place in his country's history.

Further Reading

There is a voluminous literature in Spanish on O'Higgins by Chilean historians and a full study in English by Stephen Clissold, *Bernardo O'Higgins and the Independence of Chile* (1969). For background see Simon Collier, *Ideas and Politics of Chilean Independence, 1808-1833* (1968). □

Georg Simon Ohm

The German physicist Georg Simon Ohm (1789-1854) was the discoverer of the law, named for him, which states the exact relationship of potential and current in electric conduction.

Georg Ohm was born on March 16, 1789, in Erlangen, Bavaria, the eldest of seven children. His father, Johann Wolfgang Ohm, was a master mechanic and an avid reader of books on philosophy and mathematics. He cultivated the obvious mathematical talents of Georg and his younger brother, Martin, and the two soon gained the reputation of being the latter-day version of the famed Bernoulli brothers. Due to financial difficulties, Georg left the University of Erlangen in 1806 after three semesters. For the next year and a half he earned his living as private tutor in Gottstadt, Switzerland, but by 1809 he settled in Neuchâtel to continue privately with his university studies. In 1811 he returned to Erlangen and obtained his doctorate. For the next three semesters Ohm taught mathematics at the University of Erlangen, but the meagerness of his income forced him to take the post of tutor at the realgymnasium in Bamberg.

Following the publication in 1817 of Ohm's first book, a textbook of geometry, he received an appointment as teacher of mathematics and physics at the Royal Prussian Konsistorium in Cologne. The well-equipped laboratory of the local Jesuit gymnasium was put at his disposal, and there he began his epoch-making investigations on the characteristics of electric circuits, a virtually unexplored field at that time.

In 1825 the *Journal für Chemie und Physik* carried Ohm's first communication on the laws of the galvanic (electric) circuit, "Preliminary Notice on the Law according to Which Metals Conduct Contact-electricity." The paper gave an incorrect formula for what later became known as Ohm's law, but within a year Ohm corrected the mistake. The 1826 issue of the *Journal* carried Ohm's "Determination of the Law according to Which Metals Conduct Contact-electricity, Together with the Outlines of a Theory of the Voltaic Apparatus and of the Schweigger Multiplicator [Galvanoscope]." In the introductory part of the paper he noted that the new form of his law was not only in perfect agreement with all experiments but also embodied a unitary explanation of a broad range of phenomena. Consequently, he argued, his law or formula had to be a true law of nature.

These remarks of Ohm are important to note as they hold the key to some of the subsequent misunderstanding of his work. His experimental work was unimpeachable. His data fully justified his conclusion that the ratio of V (the change in electromotive force) and X (the electromotive force) was proportional to the ratio of h (the change in the length of the conducting wire) and x (the wire's original length), or $V/X = h/(b+x)$, where b is a constant.

Ohm was, however, determined to give the law a most general if not an a priori justification. In 1827 he published his most renowned work, *The Galvanic Circuit Mathematically Treated*. It contains the now familiar formula $I = V/R$ written in the notation $S = A/L$, which is followed by the historic statement, "The magnitude of the current in a galvanic circuit is directly proportional to the sum of all tensions [potentials] and indirectly to the total reduced length of the circuit." By "reduced" he meant the appropriate resistances of all parts of the circuit.

Ohm's *Galvanic Circuit* was greeted with some appreciation but largely with indifference and with some hostility. He withdrew from the academic world for 6 years. In 1833 he became professor of physics at the Polytechnic School in Nuremberg. But the real turning point in his life came when the Royal Society of London awarded him the Copley Medal in 1841. Ohm dedicated to the Royal Society the first volume of his *Contribution to Molecular Physics,* a work in which he planned to elucidate the internal constitution of matter with the same success Isaac Newton had achieved in celestial dynamics.

Apart from the gigantic demands of the plan, Ohm's teaching duties stood in the way of its execution. In 1835 he assumed, in addition to his duties in Nuremberg, the chair of higher mathematics at the University of Erlangen. Shortly afterward, he became inspector of scientific education in the state of Bavaria. He achieved his lifelong dream, a position with a major university, in 1849 as professor at the University of Munich. He was working on the manuscript of his textbook on optics when he died on July 6, 1854.

Further Reading

The standard biographies of Ohm are in German. The section on Ohm in Rollo Appleyard, *Pioneers of Electrical Communication* (1930), is informative on the history of electricity in the first half of the 19th century. See also John Munro, *Pioneers of Electricity* (1890), and Bern Dibner, *The Founding Fathers of Electrical Science* (1954). □

Georgia O'Keeffe

The American painter Georgia O'Keeffe (1887-1986) created a distinctive iconography that includes startling details of plant forms, bleached bones, and landscapes of the New Mexico desert—all rendered with pristine clarity.

Born in Sun Prairie, Wisconsin, Georgia O'Keeffe studied at the Art Institute of Chicago (1905) and the Art Students League in New York City (1907-1908). She worked briefly as a commercial artist in Chicago, and in 1912 she became interested in the principles of Oriental design. After working as a public school art supervisor in Amarillo, Texas (1912-1914), she attended art classes conducted by Arthur Wesley Dow at Columbia University. She instituted Dow's system of art education, based on recurring themes in Oriental art, in her teacher-training courses at West Texas State Normal College, where she served as department head (1916-1918).

In 1916 Alfred Stieglitz, the well-known New York photographer and proponent of modernism, exhibited some of Georgia O'Keeffe's abstract drawings. In 1924 O'Keeffe and Stieglitz were married.

Lake George, Coat and Red (1919), a salient example of O'Keeffe's early abstract style, was a roughly brushed composition in which a twisted, enigmatic form looms against a rainbow-hued sky. Early in her career she developed a personal, extremely refined style, favoring inherently abstract subject matter such as flower details and austere architectural themes. Many of her paintings were dramatic, sharp-focus enlargements of botanical details.

Though O'Keeffe insisted that there was no symbolism behind her work, art critics continue to speculate about the sexual imagery in such paintings as *Black Iris* (1926) and *Jack in the Pulpit No. 6* (1930). Indeed, this generative tension underlying her botanical paintings accounts for

much of their force and mystery, and these images exalting life and energy were among her most optimistic and successful.

Between 1926 and 1929 O'Keeffe painted a group of views of New York City. *New York Night* (1929) transformed skyscrapers into patterned, glittering structures that deny their volume. More architecturally characteristic were such paintings as *Lake George Barns* (1926) and *Ranchos Church, Taos* (1929). These simple buildings, further simplified in her painting, were America's anonymous folk architecture; in these forms O'Keeffe found a permanence and tranquility that contrasted with the frenetic urban environment.

In 1929 O'Keeffe began spending time in New Mexico; that region's dramatic mesas, ancient Spanish architecture, vegetation, and desiccated terrain became her constant themes. Total clarity characterizes her elemental vistas, and her subjects existed in self-contained worlds. Even her allegories of death in the desert—a sunbleached skull lying in the sand or affixed to a post (as in *Cow's Skull with Red*, 1936)—were eternalized. She regarded these whitened relics as symbols of the desert, nothing more. ''To me, they are strangely more living than the animals walking around—hair, eyes and all, with their tails switching.'' The dried animal bones and wooden crucifixes of the region which loom in her desert (*Black Cross, New Mexico*, 1929) were disquieting apparitions.

In 1945 O'Keeffe bought an old adobe house in New Mexico; she moved there after her husband's death in 1946. The house served as a frequent subject. In paintings such as *Black Patio Door* (1955) and *Patio with Cloud* (1956) details of doors, windows, and walls were radically reduced to virtually unmodified planes of color.

Many of O'Keeffe's paintings of the 1960s, large-scale patterns of clouds and landscapes seen from the air, reflected a romanticized view of nature evocative of her early themes. *It Was Blue and Green* (1960) used more impressionistic color, and the painting technique was looser, with less reliance on sharp contours. These large paintings culminated in a 24-foot mural on canvas, *Sky above Clouds IV* (1965). Her paintings of the 1970s were intense, powerful renditions of a black cock.

A portrayal of O'Keefe, *In Cahoots with Coyote* from Terry Tempest Williams' 1994 book *An Unspoken Hunger*, painted a vivid narrative of the artist's entrancement with her beloved New Mexico she first visited in 1917.

''I simply paint what I see,'' O'Keefe is quoted as saying, from O'Keefe's own essays published in *Georgia O'Keefe* in 1987.

But, narrated Williams, her search for the ideal color, light, stones, parched bones that contained more life in them than living animals, transformed her forays into desert country into a communion with the perfection around her. Once, in a canyon bottom, she was so enthralled by the sight that she laid her head back Coyote-fashion and howled at the sky, terrifying her companions nearby who feared she was injured. ''I can't help it—it's all so beautiful,'' was her response.

Another, well-known story related by Williams was of O'Keefe purloining a perfectly shaped, totally black stone she coveted from the coffee table of friends. They had found it at a canyon riverbed during a search for stones moments before O'Keefe arrived at the spot, but kept it tantalizingly out of her reach. Obsessed with the stone and seeing it on the table for her to steal if she wanted, she had no doubt she was the rightful possessor of such beauty.

O'Keefe's boldly original American works encompassed a wide vision from taut city towers to desertscapes in such vivid hues and form "as to startle the senses," according to the narrative. O'Keeffe painted until a few weeks before her death. She died on March 6, 1986, less than a year short of turning 100.

Many of her works found a permanent home among the abode buildings of Sante Fe, New Mexico. The Georgia O'Keefe Museum, designed by New York architect Richard Gluckman, opened in 1997 to hold more of her pastels, drawings, paintings and sculpture than any other museum.

Further Reading

The following exhibition catalogs were devoted to the artist: Art Institute of Chicago, *Georgia O'Keeffe* (1943), with an essay by Daniel Catton Rich; Worcester Art Museum, *Georgia O'Keeffe: Forty Years of Her Art* (1960), with an introduction by Rich; Amon Carter Museum of Western Art, *Georgia O'Keeffe* (1966), with quotations from various writers and critics and the artist herself; and Whitney Museum of American Art, *Georgia O'Keeffe* (1970), by Lloyd Goodrich and Doris Bry. Information on the Georgia O'Keeffe museum can be found in *Metropolitan Home* July-August 1997 or be accessed on the internet through Santa Fe, New Mexico's on-line magazine at http://www.rcnews.com/july/realv/realv.html (July 29, 1997). O'Keeffe's obituary appeared in the March 7, 1986 edition of the *New York Times*. □

Toshimichi Okubo

Toshimichi Okubo (1830-1878) was one of the leaders of the Meiji restoration in Japan and perhaps the dominant figure in the new government in its early years. He played a key role in the consolidation of the government.

Toshimichi Okubo was born on Aug. 10, 1830, in Kagoshima, the castle town of Satsuma, a feudal domain in southern Kyushu. He was the eldest son of a lower-ranking samurai family. After attending the domain's academy, he began his career as a minor official. Because he strongly advocated a policy of internal reform and Westernization within Satsuma, he soon became a confidant of its lord, Nariakira Shimazu. As a central figure in the domain government during the early 1860s, Okubo advocated the moderate policy of union between court and shogunate, which stressed the need to share decisions on national policies between the two.

Beginning in 1865, at the time of the shogunate's expedition against the domain of Choshu, Okubo began to work for alliance of his own domain with Choshu. In 1866 he also established close ties with Tomomi Iwakura, a leader of the loyalist faction at the imperial court. In late 1867, after reaching an agreement with representatives from Choshu, Okubo helped plan the coup d'etat which overthrew the power of the shogun and restored the Meiji emperor to full executive authority.

Leader of the Restoration

From the time of the restoration until his death, Okubo was a key leader in the new imperial government. He played an important role in maintaining the alliance between Satsuma and Choshu men and helped bring about the centralization of the government through the abolition of the feudal domains and the establishment of a prefectural system.

In 1873, after returning from the West as a member of the Iwakura mission, he helped to lead the opposition to the expedition against Korea proposed by Takamori Saigo and others. He argued that such a policy was too rash for a weak country like Japan, that it would invite the wrath of the Western powers, and that first priority should be placed on internal reform and consolidation. Although his view prevailed, he did attempt to placate the opposition by the dispatch of an expedition against Taiwanese aborigines in 1874, and he went to China to negotiate a settlement of the affair which gave the Japanese sovereignty over the Ryukyu Islands.

As the minister of home affairs from 1873 to 1878, Okubo steered the government in the direction it was to pursue over the next decade or so. He promoted a policy of rapid, state-sponsored industrialization through the importation of Western technology, the establishment of pilot-plant operations, and government subsidies to key businesses. He also moved vigorously against domestic opposition movements, personally directing the suppression of the Saga revolt in 1874 and the Satsuma rebellion of 1876-1877. At the same time, in 1875 he was careful to maintain the balance of power between men from Satsuma and Choshu within the government and helped initiate efforts toward the establishment of a constitutional system. Equally important was his assiduous effort to recruit bright and talented young men into the government, regardless of their domain origin.

To many, Okubo symbolized the ruthlessness and speed with which the new imperial government had moved. On May 14, 1878, he was assassinated by a disgruntled former samurai from Kaga domain while on his way to the imperial palace. Stern, humorless, and autocratic in temperament, he represented both the best and worst sides of the bureaucratic elite that dominated the formation of modern Japan.

Further Reading

The only English-language biography of Okubo is Masakazu Iwata, *Okubo Toshimichi: The Bismarck of Japan* (1964). It is based on research in Japanese materials and is one of the few scholarly works about a member of the Meiji oligarchy. Further background can be found in Hugh Borton, *Japan's Modern Century* (1955); Ryusaku Tsunoda, William Theodore de Bary, and Donald Keene, *Sources of the Japanese Tradition* (1958); George M. Beckmann, *The Modernization of China and Japan* (1962); John K. Fairbank, Edwin O. Reischauer, and Albert M. Craig, *East Asia: The Modern Transformation* (1965); and Chitoshi Yanaga, *Japan since Perry* (1966). □

Shigenobu Okuma

The Japanese statesman and politician Shigenobu Okuma (1838-1922) was one of the early leaders of the Meiji government. He later broke with it to become one of its most eloquent and respected critics.

Born on Feb. 16, 1838, in Saga, the castle town of the Hizen domain in western Kyushu, Shigenobu Okuma was the son of a middle-rank samurai. In 1855, shortly after his father's death, he abandoned his studies at the domain academy and turned his interest to Dutch (Western) learning. As a member of the imperial loyalist faction within Hizen, he supported the policy of union between court and shogunate. He also studied English, mathematics, international law, and other Western subjects under Guido Verback, a Dutch Reform missionary at Nagasaki.

Although his domain did play a leading role in the restoration, Okuma became an official of the new government by reason of his Western knowledge and his forceful personality. He was an active promoter of speedy Westernization, serving in the Ministry of Finance. He also began to recruit a group of able underlings, many of whom were graduates of Keio Academy. After Toshimichi Okubo's death in 1878, Okuma, along with Hirobumi Ito, emerged as one of the principal younger leaders in the government. His rivalry with Ito, coupled with his bold proposal that Japan adopt an English-style constitution, resulted in his expulsion from the government in October 1881.

Although Okuma returned to serve twice as foreign minister (1888-1889 and 1896-1897) and twice as premier (1898 and 1914-1916), the remainder of his career was primarily spent in moderate opposition to the Meiji oligarchy. Beginning with the Kaishinto, organized in 1882, he led a series of political parties that advocated a moderate Anglophile liberalism and opposed the authoritarian tendencies of the oligarchy.

Okuma also founded a private university, the Tokyo Special Higher School, which later became Waseda University, in the hope that it would foster a spirit of personal and political independence among its students and provide a "forcing ground" for politicians of liberal disposition. Finally, as owner of the *Hochi Shimbun,* and later as editor of *Shin Nippon* and *Taikan,* liberal journals of the late Meiji and early Taisho periods, he commented frequently, and sometimes contradictorily, on public affairs.

Okuma formally retired from politics in 1910 but was called back by the genro to serve as premier in 1914. After serving 2 years, he returned to private life and spent his later years trying to promote mutual understanding of East and West.

When he died on Jan. 10, 1922, Okuma's reputation as a champion of liberalism was somewhat tarnished, but he remained an enormously popular figure.

Further Reading

The only English-language biography of Okuma is Smimasa Idditti, *The Life of Marquis Shigenobu Okuma, a Maker of New Japan* (1940). Prepared for the Okuma family, it is very uncritical and highly eulogistic. Background is in Hugh Borton, *Japan's Modern Century* (1955); Ryusaku Tsunoda, William Theodore de Bary, and Donald Keene, *Sources of the Japanese Tradition* (1958); George M. Beckmann, *The Modernization of China and Japan* (1962); John K. Fairbank, Edwin O. Reischauer, and Albert M. Craig, *East Asia: The Modern Transformation* (1965); Robert E. Ward, ed., *Political Development in Modern Japan* (1968); and Kenneth B. Pyle, *The New Generation in Meiji Japan* (1969). □

Olaf I Tryggvason, King of Norway

Olaf I Tryggrason (968–1000) was a Viking warrior, who acquired wealth and fame by his raids in Britain

and strove to bring national leadership and Christianity to pagan, politically divided tenth-century Norway.

To appreciate King Olaf Tryggvason's role in Norwegian history, it is helpful to provide a brief picture of his time, place, and position. Prior to the tenth century, although most of Western Europe had been Christian for centuries, Norway remained a pagan bastion of politically divided small kingdoms. The warriors of the North, untouched by ecclesiastical and cultural influences, harassed continental Europe from the eighth century on and were considered a major threat to the well-being of their southern neighbors. The ultimate involvement of Norway in the Christian network was due largely to the efforts of an energetic young king, Olaf Tryggvason. His policy of political consolidation and Christianization in Norway—a process which occurred at roughly the same time in Denmark and Sweden—helped to bring about the waning of the viking ("pirate") problem that had plagued Europe for many years.

Harald Fairhair (c. 870-c. 930) is generally recognized as Norway's first true king. By conquering rival *jarls* (earls) and forcing them into subservient positions, he created the precedent of one ruler for the many districts of Norway. During the tenth century, belonging to the family of Harald Fairhair was a political bonus for aspiring kings; in fact, Olaf Tryggvason was Harald's great-grandson. When Harald died around 930, his kingdom passed to his unpopular son Eirik Bloodaxe. But Eirik and his widely detested wife Gunnhild proved unable to retain the throne, and Eirik's younger brother Haakon the Good—who had been raised as a Christian in the court of King Aethelstan of England—overthrew his sibling in 934. Although Haakon was the first Norwegian king who espoused Christianity, he found it politically necessary to revert to pagan ways. When he died in 961, his nephews—the sons of Eirik and Gunnhild—seized power. Among the five sons, the most prominent and politically effective was Harald Greypelt (961-70). During his nine-year reign, he eliminated many of his enemies, including his cousin Tryggve, the father of Olaf.

From 970 until Olaf Tryggvason's rise to power in 995, Norway was ruled by a series of *jarls* who owed allegiance to either the king of Denmark or the king of Sweden. One *jarl* in particular dominated the Norwegian political field: Jarl Haakon, who ruled for King Harald Bluetooth of Denmark and later for the latter's son Svein Forkbeard. Jarl Haakon regarded himself as the sole power in Norway, but his arrogance, violence, and lechery led to his defeat in 995, allowing Olaf Tryggvason to claim the throne as the successor of Harald Fairhair.

Olaf Tryggvason was born in 968, during a critical period in Norwegian history, to the recently widowed noblewoman Astrid. Young Olaf's life was immediately at risk: Gunnhild's sons plotted to kill their newborn cousin. According to the great medieval Icelandic historian Snorri Sturluson, who wrote around 200 years after the event but is considered to have used reliable older sources, Astrid sought refuge in Sweden in 969. By 971, she believed that her son's safety could best be achieved by seeking the assistance of her brother Sigurd in Russia, who enjoyed success as an aide to Duke Valdemar of either Novgorod or Kiev. But during the Baltic crossing, Astrid's party was assaulted by Estonian Vikings, and mother and son were separated and carried off into slavery.

Purchased by a kindly Estonian couple, the three-year-old Olaf Tryggvason was treated well. Six years passed. In 977, Valdemar sent Sigurd to Estonia to collect revenues. Then, according to Snorri:

> In the market place he happened to observe a remarkably handsome boy; and as he could distinguish that he was a foreigner, he asked him his name and family. He answered him, that his name was Olaf; that he was a son of Tryggve Olafsson and Astrid. . . . Then Sigurd knew that the boy was his sister's son.

Impressed by the nine-year-old's adventures and touched to find his nephew still alive, Sigurd took Olaf back to the court of Valdemar. When Olaf's royal background was revealed to the Duke and his queen, the boy was granted every courtesy; indeed, says Snorri, Valdemar "received Olaf into his court, and treated him nobly, and as a king's son."

Remaining in Russia for nine years, Olaf Tryggvason used this time to develop the martial skills so crucial to a Viking career. One of the many poets who praised Olaf claimed that when Olaf was 12 years old, he successfully commanded Russian warships. Generosity toward his men was an essential component of his popularity, but this acclaim proved detrimental to Olaf's security in Russia. Valdemar allowed himself to be persuaded by Olaf's jealous detractors; the young Viking had to leave Russia with the covert assistance of Valdemar's queen. By 986, the 18-year-old Olaf was embarked on a Viking career in the Baltic, obtaining local fame and considerable wealth.

One of Olaf Tryggvason's marauding expeditions took him to Wendland (an area of northern Germany occupied by a fierce Slavic people in the late tenth century). There the king, Burislaf, allowed his daughter Geyra to marry Olaf, but the union proved short, as Geyra died three years later. Olaf's response to her death was to initiate another round of plundering, this time concentrating on areas from Frisia to Flanders.

Several sources attest to Olaf's presence in England by the year 991, including the *Anglo-Saxon Chronicle*:

> In this year came Anlaf with ninety-three ships to Folkestone, and harried outside, and sailed thence to Sandwich, and thence to Ipswich, overrunning all the countryside, and so on to Maldon. Ealdorman Byrhtnoth came to meet them with his levies and fought them, but they slew the ealdorman there and had possession of the place of slaughter.

Snorri Sturluson extends Olaf's British activities to include all of the period 991-94, noting battles waged in Northumberland, Scotland, the Hebrides, and the Isle of Man.

Olaf Tryggvason's acceptance of Christianity most likely occurred in the year 994, during his British campaigns. Snorri attributes his conversion to a legendary hermit who correctly predicted Olaf's future and claimed to have acquired this ability from the Christian God. Olaf was so impressed with the accuracy of the predictions that he and his men were immediately baptized. According to Snorri, Olaf then left the hermit's home in the Scilly Islands and sailed to England, where he "proceeded in a friendly way; for England was Christian and he himself had become Christian." On the other hand, the *Anglo-Saxon Chronicle* attributes no such refined manners to Olaf, stating that in 994 the Christian Olaf was every bit as dangerous as the pagan Olaf had been:

> Anlaf and Svein came to London with ninety-four ships, and kept up an unceasing attack on the city, and they . . . set it on fire. But there, God be thanked, they came off worse than they ever thought possible; so they went away thence, doing as much harm as any host was capable of . . . wherever they went. Then the king and his councillors decided to offer him tribute: this was done and they accepted it.

To seal the efficacy of the bribe, the English king Ethelred the Unready stood as Olaf's sponsor in the sacrament of confirmation.

Having traveled widely, Olaf Tryggvason had firsthand knowledge of the splendor of Christian courts and the ecclesiastical ritual that permeated Christian kingdoms. It is very likely that such observations—combined with the opportunity to topple the unpopular, lecherous Jarl Haakon in Norway—led Olaf to begin his mission to both conquer and Christianize the native land he had scarcely lived in.

By 995, Norwegians were tired of the rule of Jarl Haakon who, apparently lacking in moderation in his libidinal appetites, was subjecting many noble girls to the indignity of becoming short-term concubines. When Olaf learned of the extensive discontent in Norway, he decided to leave England (financed in large part by the bribe paid by Ethelred), return to his native land, and restore the rule of Harald Fairhair's line. Shortly after Olaf Tryggvason's arrival in Norway, Jarl Haakon was treacherously beheaded by his own slave. The Jarl's son Eirik fled to Sweden and nursed his discontent with the sympathetic support of King Olaf of Sweden. Thus, a drawn-out conflict was unnecessary, and in 996 Olaf Tryggvason was proclaimed king of all Norway at a general meeting, called a *thing* in Scandinavia.

Tenth-century Scandinavian kings were constantly in motion: there was no fixed residence (such as a palace), and it was necessary to have the royal presence felt from district to district in order to prevent insurrections. Olaf Tryggvason, only 27 years old in 995, had the energy and charisma to leave his imprint on all of Norway. Perhaps his success may be attributed to his unyielding personality: as Snorri puts it, "He would . . . either bring it to this, that all Norway should be Christian, or die." Certainly Olaf did not hesitate to resort to extreme coercive measures to convert his new realm; Norwegians who refused Christianity were killed, banished, or mutilated. Various sources affirm Olaf's energetic ap-

proach to convert not just Norwegians, but Icelanders and Greenlanders as well. Twelfth-century Icelandic historian Ari the Wise mentions the arrival in Iceland of priests sent by Olaf Tryggvason. It is suggested by Snorri that the great Viking Leif Eriksson adopted Christianity at Olaf's insistence, and in this way Christianity was brought to Greenland.

Olaf Tryggvason spent his five years as king of Norway battling not only pagans, but political enemies as well. For example, the last son of Eirik Bloodaxe and Gunnhild was defeated by Olaf's forces in 999. Despite an earlier alliance with the Danish king Svein Forkbeard during his Viking days in Britain, the political opposition of Olaf's fellow Scandinavian kings remained a constant feature of his five-year reign. Snorri credits Olaf Tryggvason's successful kingship to his Christian zeal and no-nonsense domestic policy:

> King Olaf . . . was distinguished for cruelty when he was enraged, and tortured many of his enemies. Some he burnt in fire; some he had torn in pieces by mad dogs; some he mutilated, or cast down from high precipices. On this account his friends were attached to him warmly, and his enemies feared him greatly; and thus he made such a fortunate advance in his undertakings, for some obeyed his will out of the friendliest zeal, and others out of dread.

During Olaf's brief reign, pagan temples were torn down and churches were erected throughout Norway. Legends tell of the attempts Olaf made to rid his country of pagan spirits, including witches. By demonstrating his superior power over evil spirits, Olaf accomplished two purposes: winning converts to Christianity, and expressing his fitness to rule.

While not all of the sources mention Olaf Tryggvason's four marriages, there seems to be general agreement regarding the major details of his last union. This wedding took place in 999, and the lady was Thyre, a sister of King Svein Forkbeard of Denmark and the ex-wife of Olaf's former father-in-law, King Burislaf. Thyre had fled from Wendland to Norway, appalled at the prospect of married life with an old, pagan king such as Burislaf. Olaf proposed and Thyre considered what "luck it was for her to marry so celebrated a man."

Soon after the wedding, Thyre began to complain to Olaf of her relative poverty. She had left the dowry her brother Svein Forkbeard bestowed on her in Wendland; since Svein disapproved of her flight from old Burislaf, he refused to help her retrieve her dowry. Thyre begged Olaf Tryggvason to go to Burislaf to accomplish this task. Always keen for a foreign adventure, Olaf agreed to gather his warships for an expedition to Wendland. In the summer of 1000, he set out with a large number of warships and men. The reunion with his former father-in-law was a peaceful one, and Olaf was able to obtain Thyre's dowry.

But while Olaf spent the summer in Wendland, the rival Scandinavian kings plotted to ambush him on his way back to Norway. Svein Forkbeard formed an alliance with King Olaf of Sweden and the Norwegian Jarl Eirik, who had gone to Sweden in exile when Olaf Tryggvason came to power in 995. The three leaders met and waited for Olaf Tryggvason's return to Norway, planning to ambush him as he sailed near Svold, an island off of Denmark.

The Battle of Svold is given great attention in Snorri's account, which relates touching anecdotes about Olaf Tryggvason's last fight. Although it is nearly impossible to separate embellishment from fact, there can be no doubt that as a result of the battle, Olaf lost his kingdom. Svein Forkbeard and Olaf of Sweden were successfully repulsed by the Norwegian king, but Olaf Tryggvason was unable to withstand the attack of his fellow Norwegian Jarl Eirik. When the latter's men boarded Olaf's magnificent ship called the *Long Serpent,* Olaf Tryggvason and his few remaining supporters jumped overboard and drowned or disappeared.

Legends immediately sprang up after Svold, claiming that Olaf Tryggvason escaped; some held that he was rescued by one of Burislaf's ships and that he embarked on a long pilgrimage to the Holy Land to atone for his youthful Viking days. "But however this may have been," writes Snorri, "King Olaf Tryggvason never came back again to his kingdom of Norway."

King Olaf Tryggvason was not the first to unite all the districts of Norway, nor was he the first Norwegian ruler to espouse Christianity. His significance stems from the vibrant way he managed to combine both of these accomplishments, firmly turning Norway away from its isolated pagan past and focusing the nation's attention on becoming a settled member of the European Christian community.

Further Reading

The Anglo-Saxon Chronicle. Translated by G. N. Garmonsway, J. M. Dent, 1953.

Sturluson, Snorri. *Heimskringla: The Olaf Sagas.* Vol. 1. Translated by Samuel Laing, J. M. Dent, 1914.

Foote, P. G., and D. M. Wilson. *The Viking Achievement.* Praeger, 1970.

Jones, Gwyn. *A History of the Vikings.* Oxford University Press, 1973.

Larsen, Karen. *A History of Norway.* Princeton University Press, 1948.

Turville-Petre, G. *The Heroic Age of Scandinavia.* Greenwood Press, 1951. □

Olaf II

Olaf II Haroldsson (ca. 990-1030), also called St. Olaf, was king of Norway from 1015 to 1028. The first king of the whole of Norway, he organized its final conversion and its integration into Christian Europe.

Olaf was a son of Harold Graenske, a magnate, or kinglet, in eastern Norway and presumably related to Harold I Fairhair, the first king of Norway. From an early age he partook in Viking expeditions to the Baltic, to England (1009-1011), and to the north of France (1012), where he was baptized at Rouen, having been

converted either in England or in France. He returned to England, supporting Ethelred against Cnut the Great (1014), and was back in Norway in 1015.

Western Norway was ruled by the two Lade jarls. This was the inheritance of King Harold Fairhair. Eastern Norway was ruled by a number of kinglets. After the death of King Olaf Trygvasson in the battle of Svolder (1000), both the jarls and the kinglets seem to have been in some sort of dependence upon the Danish king.

Olaf established himself immediately in eastern Norway as a sort of king of kings, and the next year he defeated the jarls at Nesjar. He then sailed north along the coast and was elected king by the yeomen. Olaf was thus the first king to rule over the whole country, both east and west. During the next years he traveled throughout the country, making this new institution, the national monarchy, physically evident to the chieftains, magnates, and people. He defended the peace, upheld the law, and forcefully converted to the Christian faith those areas that still lived by the old gods.

The general and official introduction of Christianity necessitated a thorough revision of Norwegian law and the addition of new church codes (*kristenretten*) by the yeomen in cooperation with the King and his bishop. Olaf embarked on a national program of church building, establishing and endowing one church in each county (*herred*). Although many of the early missionaries to Norway had come from England, Olaf turned to Germany when he needed more missionaries, and the Norwegian Church was organized as

part of the North German church province of Hamburg-Bremen.

King Olaf's efforts to build a Norwegian Church were no doubt of importance in his work of uniting the Norwegian kingdom. This unification raised the most violent opposition. Olaf wanted to destroy the power of the kinglets, chieftains, and Viking warlords. He was determined to be the sole defender of the law with the right to tax all. His power rested on some regional support, the landed property of the Crown, and his housecarls. The King's wealth derived in a large measure from the alienated property of destroyed magnates. The opposition to him was strongest in the areas controlled by the Lade family-the Trondelag and the North. Cnut the Great of Denmark was their ally, and Olaf led an expedition against Denmark (1026) which was thoroughly defeated.

On Olaf's return to Norway his position became increasingly difficult as large sections of the nation turned against him. He fled the country without battle in 1028, first to Sweden and then to Russia. He returned in 1030 and was defeated by the Lade faction and Trondelag yeomen at the battle of Stiklestad, where Olaf died. The fruits of this victory were Cnut the Great's. He sent his son Svein to rule Norway, together with the boy's mother, Aegifu. It was not a happy choice. Their rule came to be regarded as foreign oppression. Harvests were bad. In 1035 Svein fled in the face of the unresisted advance of Magnus, the son of Olaf.

The dead king was firmly established as the national saint-*Rex perpetuus Norwegiae,* "eternal king of Norway," an extraordinarily powerful symbol for the new monarchy and the new Church which he in many ways had founded. The power of Olaf was evident months after his death, and even his enemies, the group around Svein, seem to have considered him the special guardian of the Norwegian monarchy. Olaf was the most popular of the medieval northern saints. His feast became one of the great turning points of the year; his tomb in the Trondheim Cathedral was the object of countless long pilgrimages; and Norway's traditional law came to be known as the law of St. Olaf.

Further Reading

A modern abridged English-language edition of the sagas, including the saga of St. Olaf, is *From the Sagas of the Norse Kings by Snorri Sturluson* (1967), utilizing the translation of Erling Monsen. For Olaf's place in Norwegian history see Halvdan Koht and Sigmund Skard, *The Voice of Norway* (1944); Wilhelm Keilhau, *Norway in World History* (1944); Karen Larsen, *A History of Norway* (1948); and T.K. Derry, *A Short History of Norway* (1957; 2d ed. 1968). □

Joseph Maria Olbrich

Joseph Maria Olbrich (1867-1908) was a leading architect of the Austrian Art Nouveau and one of the founders of the Vienna Secession.

Joseph Maria Philipp Olbrich was born in Troppau (Opava), then in the Austro-Hungarian Empire, now Czechoslovakia, on December 22, 1867. He attended school there but left without graduating. In 1882 he enrolled at the building department of the Staatsgewerbeschule (State Trade School) in Vienna. In 1886 Olbrich returned to Troppau and worked for the contracting firm of August Bartel, but in 1890 he was back in Vienna studying at the special school of architecture of the Academy of Fine Arts under Carl von Hasenauer. In 1893 he worked for a few months for Otto Wagner, the great Viennese architect who succeeded Hasenauer as professor at the academy.

The following year Olbrich won the Rome Prize and left for Italy, but his trip was cut short when Wagner called him back to Vienna to become his chief draftsman for planning and designing the elevated and underground railroad (*Stadtbahn*) of Vienna. Olbrich assumed considerable design responsibilities and is considered partly accountable for several of the stations that Wagner designed, such as the Hofpavillon in Schönbrunn and Karlsplatz Station.

In April 1897 Olbrich, together with a group of painters, sculptors, and architects, founded the Vienna Secession, an organization of artists opposed to the conservative Künstlerhaus—the official artists' association. Immediately thereafter Olbrich was commissioned to design their headquarters. This building was completed in 1898 and caused a sensation in Vienna. Bold and simple, it consisted of juxtaposed massive blocks and had a distinctly orientalizing effect. However, its cupola of metal openwork with suprabundant floral decoration was unmistakably Art Nouveau in quality.

In 1899 Ernst Ludwig, Grand Duke of Hessen, invited Olbrich, along with Peter Behrens and several other artists, to Darmstadt to form an artistic colony, which was indeed established on a nearby hill called Mathildenhöhe. Olbrich designed all the buildings for the artists' colony, as well as the general layout, the furnishings, the gardens, and the settings for the exhibitions. The architectural focus of the colony was the Ernst Ludwig House built in 1899-1900. This structure had none of the massiveness of his Vienna Secession Building, but consisted of flat surfaces enlivened by an elegant play of the wall planes. The entranceway was dominated by a large Moorish arch. For the 1901 exhibition of the colony titled "Ein Dokument deutscher Kunst" (A Document of German Art"), Olbrich designed several temporary structures, the most interesting of which was the gallery of paintings and sculpture; the dynamic outline of this building was quite striking. Its scheme was repeated again by Olbrich in his competition entry for a railroad station in Basel, Switzerland, which received a prize and was widely imitated subsequently.

In 1904 another exhibition was organized in the artists' colony; for this Olbrich designed the "Three House Group," namely three model workers' dwellings which were rather unsuccessful architecturally. However, the work that he exhibited at the Louisiana Purchase Exposition in St. Louis in the same year was quite remarkable and attracted the attention of many American architects, including Frank Lloyd Wright. Olbrich's work at the Mathildenhöhe culminated in the Exhibition Gallery and the Wedding Tower of 1906-1908. The former was a blocky and rather formal structure with a classicizing flavor. The latter, Darmstadt's wedding present to the Grand Duke, had a remarkable arched and panelled gable of five organ-pipe-like shapes that were still quite Art Nouveau. It also included a new motif, namely bands of windows that carried around the corners—a motif that was destined to be influential in the 1920s.

When Olbrich died of leukemia on August 8, 1908, he was working on two important commissions: the Feinhals House in Cologne-Marienburg built in 1908-1909 and the Tietz Department Store in Dusseldorf, designed in 1906 and completed after his death. The Feinhals House was blocky and symmetrical and had a portico of Doric columns, thus signifying the abandonment of the bold innovative architecture of his earlier years and the return to more conservative modes, a phenomenon that also could be seen elsewhere in Europe and in the United States. The Tietz Department Store emulated the verticalism of Alfred Messel's Wertheim Department Store in Berlin, although Olbrich's detailing was not medievalizing like Messel's but classicizing.

Olbrich assisted in the transformation of the historicist architectural legacy of Central Europe, in which his own education was grounded, into a new formal vocabulary. It was characteristic of the Art Nouveau movement in which he was participating that he was interested in a variety of design problems, including furniture and objects of the minor and the applied arts. His work was of uneven quality, and his buildings occasionally lacked stylistic cohesion; his smaller objects were usually more accomplished. It remains to his credit, however, that decoration was never allowed to obscure the functional aspects of his work. Olbrich was a founding member of the Bund Deutscher Architekten (Association of German Architects) in 1903 and of the Deutscher Werkbund in 1907.

Further Reading

Ian Latham's monograph *Joseph Maria Olbrich* (1980) is profusely illustrated and clearly written. A good article on Olbrich is Robert Judson Clark's "J. M. Olbrich 1867-1908," *Architectural Design* 37 (December 1967). For a concise discussion of the work of Olbrich in the context of European modernism, see Henry-Russell Hitchcock, *Architecture: Nineteenth and Twentieth Centuries* (4th ed., 1977); Leonardo Benevolo's *History of Modern Architecture,* 2 vols. (1977); and Nikolaus Pevsner, *Pioneers of Modern Design: from William Morris to Walter Gropius* (2nd ed., 1975).

Additional Sources

Latham, Ian., *Joseph Maria Olbrich,* New York: Rizzoli, 1980. □

Johan van Oldenbarnevelt

The Dutch statesman Johan van Oldenbarnevelt (1547-1619) was the principal architect of the inde- pendence of the republic of the United Provinces of the Netherlands after the death of William the Silent.

Johan van Oldenbarnevelt was born on Sept. 14, 1547, in the province of Utrecht, in the small city of Amersfoort, into a family of very minor nobility. At the age of 16 he began the study of law in an attorney's office at The Hague, then in 1566 undertook 4 years of formal legal studies in the universities of Louvain, Bourges, Cologne, Heidelberg, and probably Padua. In 1569 he returned to practice law in The Hague and Delft. He chose the party of the Prince of Orange in 1572 and took part in the vain attempt to relieve Haarlem in 1573 and in the successful relief of Leiden in 1574. From 1577 until 1586 he was the pensionary (chief legal officer) of Rotterdam, but his legal duties were subordinated to political tasks, principally representation of the town in the States of Holland, and he acquired increasing importance as a national leader.

Dutch Independence

Oldenbarnevelt did not favor the policy followed by William I (William the Silent) of seeking a foreign sovereign for the Dutch provinces, urging instead until the prince's murder in 1584 that he be named sovereign lord. However, Oldenbarnevelt was a member of the delegation which went to England in 1585 to offer Elizabeth I the sovereignty of the United Provinces. She refused but sent the Earl of Leicester to be governor general.

So Oldenbarnevelt turned to William's son, Maurice of Nassau, as a figure around whom to organize resistance to Leicester's attempts to build a political base in the United Provinces independent of the States General and the provincial States. On Oldenbarnevelt's initiative Maurice was given his father's posts as stadholder of Holland and Zeeland in 1585 and later in other provinces. Meanwhile Leicester was repeatedly thwarted in his political initiatives by Oldenbarnevelt, who became advocate of Holland (a post like that of town pensionary on the provincial level) on May 6, 1586. When Leicester quit his post and went home in 1587, Oldenbarnevelt used the opportunity to shift the primary work of central government in the United Provinces from the Council of State, in which successors of Leicester continued to sit, to the States General. However, he staunchly maintained the principle that the ultimate sovereignty lay in each province.

Oldenbarnevelt supported Maurice in his military campaigns, especially during the 1590s. In 1596 he negotiated a triple alliance with England and France, which constituted the first de facto recognition of the Dutch Republic as an independent state. Although he was unable to prevent Henry IV of France from making a separate peace with Spain in 1598, he did help to persuade Elizabeth to remain at war.

The relations between Maurice and Oldenbarnevelt began to cool after the former's victory at Nieuwpoort in the southern Netherlands in 1600. Maurice began to resent supervision by Oldenbarnevelt, who grew haughty and domineering over the years. Oldenbarnevelt was also looking ahead to peace with Spain, while Maurice was still eager for victories and glory. In 1602 Oldenbarnevelt persuaded the small companies competing in the East Indies trade to join in a single Dutch East India Company. In 1609 he obtained conclusion of a Twelve Years Truce with Spain over bitter opposition from strict Calvinists, refugees from the south, and Maurice.

Later Career

During the truce years the differences between Oldenbarnevelt and Maurice deepened. The advocate of Holland thwarted Maurice's efforts to break the truce in connection with the Jülich succession disputes in 1610 and 1614. However, Oldenbarnevelt's stubborn backing of the Remonstrant or Arminian (moderate Calvinist) side in the religious dissensions gave Maurice a powerful ally in the Contra-Remonstrant or Gomarian (rigorous Calvinist) camp. Under Oldenbarnevelt's prodding and despite the opposition of Amsterdam, the States of Holland decided (1617) to enforce a policy of religious toleration within the Reformed (Calvinist) church and began to recruit provincial soldiers because Maurice would not employ his troops to do so. The States of Utrecht, the only province to follow Holland in refusing a national synod designed to condemn the Remonstrants, also raised a force of provincial soldiers, which Maurice decided to disband on the authority of the States General.

An effort by a delegation from Holland to dissuade his soldiers from this work led to Maurice's decision to have Oldenbarnevelt and three associates (including Hugo Grotius, his successor as pensionary of Rotterdam) arrested (Aug. 29, 1618) and tried for attempted rebellion. The trial was conducted by a special court named by the States General, whose jurisdiction over a servant of the States of Holland Oldenbarnevelt denied to the end. He was found guilty and beheaded on May 13, 1619, in front of the Knights' Hall in The Hague. Maurice had refused to grant a pardon to the 72-year-old statesman unless asked, which the family refused to do as implying admission of guilt.

Modern historians have come to see the trial and execution neither as the straightforward operation of law in a case of manifest guilt nor as an instance of judicial murder, but rather as a tragedy brought on by religious and political passions in a situation where constitutional powers were ill-defined and hotly debated. In the ultimate sense, however, Oldenbarnevelt was a martyr for his political principles.

Further Reading

The classic works of John Lothrop Motley, *History of the United Netherlands, from the Death of William the Silent to the Twelve Years' Truce* (4 vols., 1861-1868) and *The Life and Death of John of Barneveld, Advocate of Holland* (2 vols., 1874), remain, despite their fierce and one-sided advocacy of Oldenbarnevelt's cause and their age, full of information and vivid writing. See also Pieter Geyl, *The Netherlands in the Seventeenth Century,* vol. 1 (1961). □

Claes Oldenburg

American artist Claes Oldenburg (born 1929) created works of art which were a wonderful blend of reality and fantasy. Oldenburg's artistic success was due in part to his irreverent humor and incisive social commentary. He took objects from the everyday world such as typewriters, lipstick, a flashlight; lifted them out of their usual context; and forced viewers to reassess their preconceptions about the objects.

Claes Thure Oldenburg was born January 28, 1929, in Stockholm, Sweden. Because his father was a member of the Swedish foreign service, Claes and his family moved often. From 1930 to 1933 the Oldenburgs resided in New York, and from 1933 to 1936 they lived in Oslo, Norway. In 1936 the family moved to Chicago, where Oldenburg's father served as consul general of Sweden.

Claes Oldenburg graduated from the Latin School in Chicago in 1946 and then enrolled at Yale University, receiving a B.A. degree in 1950. While at Yale, his studies focused on literature and art. In 1950 Oldenburg returned to Chicago, where he remained until 1956. He worked as an apprentice reporter at the City News Bureau and from 1952 to 1954 took classes in painting, figure drawing, and anatomy at the prestigious Art Institute of Chicago. He also attended the Oxbow Summer School of Painting in Saugatuck, Michigan, in 1953.

In 1956 Oldenburg moved to New York City and became an active member of that city's thriving young artistic community. For a time he worked as an assistant in the Cooper Union Museum's library, taking advantage of the opportunity to teach himself more about the history of art. His early years in New York were shaped by his contact with other artists struggling to move beyond the confines of Abstract Expressionism, including Red Grooms, Allan Kaprow, Robert Whitman, Lucas Samaras, George Segal, and Jim Dine. All were interested in art as experience and in pushing to the limit the question "What is art?" They began to stage "happenings" based in part on the European DADA ethos of the 1920s (and a forerunner to the 1980s performance artists). This was the beginning of the Pop Art movement.

Oldenburg's first New York exhibition took place in late 1958, when a selection of his drawings was included in a group show at Red Grooms' City Gallery. In 1959 he had his first public one-man show in New York — an exhibit of drawings and sculpture at the Judson Gallery. In 1962 Oldenburg's work was included in the "New Realists" Exhibition, which defined the Pop Art Movement. That show at the Sidney Janis Gallery largely defined the group of artists with which Oldenburg has since been associated.

Other major exhibitions of Oldenburg's work included a 1964 one-man show at the Sidney Janis Gallery and a 1969 retrospective exhibition at the Museum of Modern Art.

Philosophically, Oldenburg saw himself as a realist, not as an abstract artist. He felt art must relate to the realities of everyday life. Yet he took objects from the real world and placed them out of context, making them soft when they should be hard, large when they should be small. This paradox in his art grew out of his own nature, which was a complex mix of traditional and radical elements. "Reversing the expectations of hard sculpture, these huge collapsing objects rely on gravity and chance for their final form," noted the *Phaidon Dictionary of Twentieth-Century Art*. A writer for *The Economist* pointed out "in the spirit of the surrealists, he has muddled up the usual association of the senses. Things soft, he made hard, or the other way around: a muslin-and plaster roast of beef, a saggy portable typewriter. Things smooth, he has turned furry: ice-cream lollies made of fake-fur and kapok."

Strongly influenced by the writings of Sigmund Freud, Oldenburg underwent an intense period of self-analysis between 1959 and 1961. He carefully recorded his discoveries in notebooks, often including illustrative sketches. This endeavor helped him to shape his approach to art.

Oldenburg's style changed and developed over the years. He worked in a variety of modes, including drawing, painting, film, soft sculpture, and large scale sculpture in steel. After 1959 he was influenced by the theater. His involvement in "happenings" in the early 1960s resulted from his interest in both participatory art and Freudian free association.

Oldenburg often created variations on a theme (for example, *Ray Gun* of 1959 and *Soft Drainpipe* of 1967). He pointed to multiple sources of inspiration and encouraged his viewers to make multiple associations and draw multiple conclusions from the work. Many of his pieces were metaphors for parts of the human body, often having sexual connotations. Both *Ray Gun* and *Soft Drainpipe* may be seen as phallic symbols.

Oldenburg's early work, such as *The Street* (1960) and *The Store* (1961-1962), was rough-edged and primitive looking. It was inspired by tribal art, comics, graffiti, children's drawings, and the artwork of Jean Dubuffet. In 1963 his style changed to one of coolness, precision, and industrial polish. This change marked the beginning of his soft sculpture phase, when the materials of his early years— paper, canvas, plaster, and chicken wire — were replaced by vinyl, formica, and plexiglas. Among the well-known examples of his work in this mode were *Soft Light Switches* (1964) in the collection of the William Rockhill Nelson Gallery of Art, Kansas City, and *Giant Soft Fan* (1966-1967), a piece which was displayed in the American Pavilion at Expo '67 and was later in the Museum of Modern Art. Works such as these take objects of modern technology, which were made of rigid materials, and turned them into flexible floppy forms, which took on a variety of different shapes as they are hung, touched, or moved.

In the mid-1960s Oldenburg also began making projects for giant monuments. An exhibition of these proposals was held at the Museum of Contemporary Art, Chicago, in 1967. Most of these ideas (like a giant teddy bear for Central Park North) were pure fantasy, but the artist viewed some as feasible. Among those executed were the controversial *Lipstick on Caterpillar Tracks* (1969), which created an uproar when first erected at Yale University; *Giant Icebag* (1969-1970), which was motorized and inflates and deflates; and *Flashlight* (1981), a 38-foot steel monument on the campus of the University of Nevada, Las Vegas.

By taking mundane objects and presenting them out of context and in such colossal proportions, Oldenburg forced viewers to reassess their daily lives and values. His work was a social commentary on American popular culture and, by association, on contemporary society's approach to life itself. In 1995, a large traveling show of Oldenburg's works was organized by the National Gallery of Art and the Guggenheim Museum. It made stops in Los Angeles, London and Bonn. One work in it, *From the Entropic Library (1989-90)* consisted of a collection of books whose disoriented pell-mell structure fell upon a base that hosted other sheaves of text. Oldenburg's view of this work which people have termed "a monument to a disintegrating, somehow displaced European culture," was simple: "my single-minded aim is to give existence to fantasy."

Further Reading

Barbara Rose's *Claes Oldenburg* (1970), a comprehensive monograph about Oldenburg was prepared in conjunction with the 1969 retrospective exhibition of Oldenburg's work at the Museum of Modern Art in New York. Also useful are Ellen H. Johnson's *Claes Oldenburg* (1971); and Gene Baro's *Claes Oldenburg, Drawings and Prints* (1969). Among the numerous exhibition catalogues available are Barbara Haskell's *Claes Oldenburg: Object into Monument* (1971) for an exhibit at the Pasadena Art Museum and *Oldenburg: Six Themes* (1975) for an exhibit at the Walker Art Center in Minneapolis. *Large Scale Projects: with Coosje van Bruggen* (1995) is a study of his work with his wife on large projects. Oldenburg's own writings, such as *Injun and Other Histories* (1960) (1966), *Store Days* (1967), and *Claes Oldenburg Notes* (1968), provide insights into his philosophy and approach to art. There are also numerous journal articles dealing with Oldenburg's later work—for example, Jeff Kelly's "Claes Oldenburg's 'Flashlight'," in *Arts Magazine*, 55 (June 1981). □

Patrick Bruce Oliphant

American newspaper editorial cartoonist Patrick Bruce Oliphant (born 1935) was a native of Australia, but came to the United States in 1964 because he saw more opportunity to develop his craft. Using his skill of caricature and satire, he targeted injustice, hypocrisy, and scandal, and skewered hoards of politicians.

Patrick Oliphant was born July 24, 1935, in Adelaide, Australia. Although his parents, Donald Knox and Grace Lillian, nee Price, encouraged him to draw, Oliphant originally set out to be a journalist. He began his newspaper career as a copyboy, first for the *Adelaide News*

and later for the *Adelaide Advertiser*. At the *Advertiser*, though, Oliphant transferred to the art department, and by age 20 had been promoted to editorial cartoonist. Oliphant once said he got his inspiration for political cartooning from his father, "who distrusted parsons and politicians equally." Oliphant's editors liked his work so much that in 1959 they sent him on a world tour to study other cartoonists. On a visit to the United States, Oliphant knew he had found his mecca. In America he saw a bigger audience, plenty of issues, and an opportunity for new approaches to editorial cartooning. Besides, he explained, "Nothing much happens in Australia."

That hardly could have been said of America in 1964, the year Oliphant immigrated to the United States to be editorial cartoonist for the *Denver Post*. The country, still reeling from the assassination of President Kennedy the year before, was embarking on a tumultuous 10-year period Marked by a divisive war, the struggle for racial equality, more assassinations, energy shortages, and finally the resignation of a president in 1974.

The period was perfect for Oliphant. It was packed with issues, plagued by turmoil, and populated by pompous politicians. "If the country was at peace and everything was tranquillity and steadiness, there would be nothing for a cartoonist to do," said Oliphant. In addition, the Australian transplant felt his work required the presence of villains, a commodity never in short supply in American politics. "Cartooning is an inherently negative art form," Oliphant once admitted. "If only good people populated the political scene, I would have nothing to do. Good people make poor targets. I like villains."

Coming to a Boil Every Day

Issues, turmoil, and villains were the ingredients which brought Oliphant to a boil every day. Oliphant thought this agitated condition was necessary for producing strong editorial cartoons. "You've got to be angry," he explained. "The sense of outrage, bringing yourself to a boil once a day, is good for you." Oliphant transformed his anger and outrage into political cartoons that used caricature and satire to deliver their punch. He said, "Without a certain amount of savagery, the cartoonist is really not doing his job."

To Oliphant, the strength of a cartoon came from its immediate visual impact. He felt that a cartoonist should be able to articulate strong ideas without getting bound up in words. In this respect, Oliphant was a pioneer. "The guy's a genius," said his colleague and friend, Paul Rigby, of the *New York Daily News*. "Before Pat, most cartoonists labeled everything and drew figures with little worlds for heads. He's really the revolutionary cartoonist for America."

When Oliphant packed up his bag of cartooning innovations and headed for America, he included his sidekick, Punk, the wisecracking little penguin who was tucked away in a corner of each cartoon, making his own statement. Oliphant had invented Punk when he started as a political cartoonist in Australia as a way of gaining more freedom with his work.

The Watergate Years

Oliphant probably became the most incensed during the Watergate scandal of 1973 and 1974 that ultimately caused the fall of his favorite villain, Richard Nixon. Oliphant once observed that "Watergate was a great time for political cartoonists. I look back on the days of (Richard) Nixon with some nostalgia because there was a new cartoon every day." Political cartooning in the United States, Oliphant believed, lost much of its potency after Watergate and became characterized by gags, imitations, and sameness.

Oliphant, naturally, continued stirring things up even without Watergate and Nixon, although he was bringing himself to a boil for a different newspaper. In 1975 Oliphant left the *Denver Post* for the *Washington Star*. He stayed at the *Star* until it folded in 1981. Rather than join another newspaper, he opted for independence and concentrated on his syndication through Universal Press Syndicate. By 1990 he was the most widely circulated political cartoonist in the world. His cartoons appeared four days a week in more than 500 newspapers in the United States and other countries, including his native Australia. According to Wayne King in a 1990 *New York Times Magazine* profile, Oliphant was "probably the most influential editorial cartoonist . . . working."

Samples of the Oliphant Wit

Some of Oliphant's post-Watergate cartoons that demonstrated the ever-sharp sting of his pen included a cartoon of a rotund Elizabeth Taylor leaping a stone wall with her then-husband, U.S. Senator John Warner, on her back. Another cartoon that stirred things up appeared during the 1980 Democratic primary season. It pitted incumbent President Carter against U.S. Senator Ted Kennedy, showing Kennedy at the wheel of a car, with Carter in the back seat outfitted in scuba gear, thus evoking Kennedy's infamous bridge accident at Chappaquiddick Island. When President Reagan was touting turning government functions over to private enterprise, an Oliphant cartoon depicted how such a scheme might work if applied to Social Security. The cartoon featured Reagan saying, " . . . there's whole bunch of things could be handled a lot better by the private sector! . . . and at a profit, too!" as old people fell from a conveyor belt into a grinder for making fertilizer. "A rather savage view of things," Oliphant admitted.

In early 1987, 50 people picketed the *Syracuse Post-Standard* after it carried an Oliphant cartoon that protesters considered to be anti-Catholic. The drawing satirized a Vatican pronouncement on artificial means of conception. In other cartoons, to underscore the "wimp" image that plagued President Bush, Oliphant depicted him carrying a purse. "I just thought I'd rub it in a little," Oliphant said.

Oliphant did not always resort to his drawings to stir up controversy. In a speech at the Association of American Editorial Cartoonists convention in 1987, for example, he criticized the Pulitzer Prize Board for awarding its editorial cartooning prize to Berke Breathed, creator of the "Bloom County" comic strip. Oliphant said, "The work makes no pretense of being editorial. It is on the funny pages. It does, however, make the pretense of passing off shrill potty jokes and grade-school sight gags as social commentary."

Oliphant, a Pulitzer winner himself in 1967, had been critical of the prize long before it had been awarded to Breathed. After reading a book on past prize-winners, he realized there was a formula that would assure winning. "It was jingoism, flag waving and my country right or wrong," he said. He believed this mindset of Pulitzer judges played a part in his own award. He explained that the 11 cartoons he submitted to the Pulitzer committee included one he drew on Ho Chi Minh while still hawkish on Vietnam. "I wasn't particularly proud of it, and to add insult, some editor changed the meaning of it altogether. Sure enough, I won the Pulitzer and they cited that Ho Chi Minh hack job as typifying my work," Oliphant said.

In addition to the Pulitzer, Oliphant was voted the nation's best editorial cartoonist in 1985 and 1987 by readers of the *Washington Journalism Review*. His other honors include three Reuben awards from the National Cartoonists Society, the Sigma Delta Chi award in 1967, the Distinguished Service Award for Conservation from the National Wildlife Federation in 1969, and an honorary title from Dartmouth College in 1981.

Oliphant the Artist

Although political cartooning was always Oliphant's bread and butter, in the mid-1980s he branched off into sculpture and lithography, which he saw as natural extensions of his drawing. In order to make way for these new interests, Oliphant cut his output; by 1990, he was producing four cartoons each week instead of the five or six he had averaged earlier in his career. That same year, though a collection of his presidential caricatures in cartoons, bronze sculptures, and lithographs was exhibited at the National Portrait Gallery in Washington, D.C. After an eight-month stay at the gallery, the collection traveled to several U.S. cities. A book, *Oliphant's Presidents: Twenty-five Years of Caricature,"* was published to accompany the exhibit.

That book joined a parade of cartoon collections which appeared from Oliphant regularly and were bought eagerly by fans. Recent collections include*Fashions for the New World Order* (1991), *Just Say No!: More Cartoons by Pat Oliphant* (1992), *Why Do I Feel Uneasy?: More Cartoons* (1993), *Oliphant: The New World Order in Drawing and Sculpture, 1983-1993* (1994), *Waiting for the Other Shoe to Drop . . . More Cartoons by Pat Oliphant* (1994), *Off to the Revolution: More Cartoons* (1995), *101 Things to Do With a Conservative* (1996), and *So That's Where They Came from* (1997).

Alan Fern, the director of the National Portrait Gallery, described Oliphant as "a genius. His drawing is the most eloquent and the least labored of any I've ever seen. That quality will cause him to survive in the history of art the way Daumier has." Fern said Oliphant's work was characterized a miniaturist's eye, a director's theatrical sense, and a speed of composition which lent movement to his work without looking labored.

Oliphant's typical work day went a long way toward explaining the qualities of his art. The cartoonist arose by 7 a.m., read two newspapers and watched a television news show to make sure he had not missed an important event. By 9 a.m. he was sitting in front of a blank sheet of paper. By noon, that paper was invariably graced with the lines that Fern characterized as the mark of genius. Before lunch, another completed cartoon was ready to be taken by courier, copied, and sent to 500 newspapers.

Oliphant also took his turn at direct political action. Faced with a newly conservative climate and a Supreme Court edging to the right, Oliphant filed as a friend of the court to defend controversial publisher, Larry Flynt, against charges of libel. The cartoonist explained that a court decision which applied reporters' libel restrictions to editorialists would spell the end of the sort of political cartooning which had made his career.

Further Reading

In addition to the book published in connection with the exhibit, there were a number of books that contain collections of Pat Oliphant's cartoons. These were: *What Those People Need Is a Puppy* (1989); *Nothing Basically Wrong* (1988); *Up to There in Alligators* (1987); *Between Rock and a Hard Place* (1986); *Make My Day* (1985); *Year of Living Perilously* (1984); *But Seriously, Folks* (1983); *Ban This Book* (1982); *The Jellybean Society* (1981); *Oliphant! A Cartoon Collection* (1980); *An Informal Gathering* (1978); *Four More Years* (1973); and *The Oliphant Book* (1969).

Later books included: *Fashions for the New World Order* (1991); *Just Say No!: More Cartoons by Pat Oliphant* (1992); *Why Do I Feel Uneasy? More Cartoons* (1993); *Oliphant: The New World Order in Drawing and Sculpture; 1983-1993* (1994); *Waiting for the Other Shoe to Drop . . . More Cartoons by Pat Oliphant* (1994); *Off to the Revolution: More Cartoons* (1995); *101 Things to Do With a Conservative* (1996); and *So That's Where They Came from* (1997).

There have been a number of magazine and newspaper articles about Oliphant, some of which were in a question and answer format. These included: *The Kansas City Star* (February 19, 1990); *The Washington Post* (July 14, 1985); *Washington Dossier* (January 1985); *USA Today* (March 22, 1983); *New Yorker* (December 31, 1979); *New York Times Magazine* (November 9, 1975 and August 5, 1990); *New Republic* (February 2, 1974); *Newsweek* (June 12, 1972); and *Time* (May 10, 1968, and September 18, 1964). □

James Oliver

The American inventor and manufacturer James Oliver (1823-1908) is noted for the invention of a cast-iron implement known as the Oliver chilled plow.

James Oliver was born in Liddesdale, Roxburghshire, Scotland, on Aug. 28, 1823. The family emigrated to the United States in 1835, settling first in New York and then in Indiana. Oliver's father died in 1837, and the boy held a succession of jobs in the Mishawaka-South Bend area, working on a river barge, in a distillery, as a cooper, and, most importantly for his subsequent career, in a number of

iron foundries. He learned the molder's trade and was employed at the St. Joseph Iron Company in Mishawaka from 1847 until he and two partners went into business for themselves in 1855 in South Bend.

Oliver and his associates determined to produce the best plow in the world and to this end experimented incessantly to turn out a hard-faced plow of chilled iron. In 1869 Oliver made his initial important discovery in the process of chilling. He learned that circulating hot water through the chills (or molds) would prevent the castings from cooling too rapidly or unevenly. He next developed a way to bring the liquid metal into direct contact with the face of the chill, thereby removing all of the soft spots in the cast moldboards and leaving the surface smooth and flawless. He did this by introducing grooves into the chill so as to permit the gases which formed during the pouring to escape. Finally, he developed an improved annealing process so that the strains from shrinkage in the cooling process would not affect the hardness of the chilled faces. By the time all of these basic improvements were patented (1873), Oliver's product was much in demand. The chilled plows were inexpensive, efficient, durable, and adaptable to use in any soil, producing a smooth furrow at a reduced draft.

The Oliver Chilled Plow Works was moved to a new and larger site in South Bend in 1875, where it eventually became the largest plow manufactory in the world. Oliver remained president of his company until his death. He was a civic-minded man, and the development of South Bend was greatly affected by him: he built the Oliver Hotel and the

Oliver Opera House and advanced money to the city for a new city hall. He died in South Bend on March 2, 1908.

Further Reading

There are few published sources on Oliver. The only biography is a popularly written, dated work by Elbert Hubbard, *Little Journeys to the Homes of Great Business Men,* vol. 24 (1909). For background see Robert L. Ardrey, *American Agricultural Implements* (1894), and Waldemar B. Kaempffert, *A Popular History of American Invention* (2 vols., 1924).

Additional Sources

Romine, Joan., *Copshaholm: the Oliver story,* South Bend: Northern Indiana Historical Society, 1978. ☐

Adriano Olivetti

Adriano Olivetti (1901-1960) was known worldwide during his lifetime as the Italian manufacturer of Olivetti typewriters, calculators, and computers.

Olivetti was an entrepreneur and innovator who transformed shop-like operations into a modern factory. In and out of the factory, he both practiced and preached the utopian system of "the community movement," but he was not an astute enough politician to have a mass following.

The Olivetti empire was begun by his father Camillo, an Italian of Spanish origin. His ancestors escaping the Inquisition arrived in Turin around 1600. Initially, the "factory" (30 workers) concentrated on electric measurement devices. By 1908 (25 years after Remington in the United States) Olivetti started to produce typewriters.

Camillo, an engineer and innovator, believed that his children could get a better education at home. Adriano's formative years were spent under the tutelage of his mother, an educated and sober woman. Also, as a socialist, Camillo emphasized the non-differentiation between manual and intellectual work. His children, during their time away from study, worked with and under the same conditions as his workers. The discipline and sobriety Camillo imposed on his family induced rebellion in Adriano's adolescence manifested by a dislike of "his father's" workplace and by his studying at a polytechnic school of subjects other than the mechanical engineering his father wanted.

Nevertheless, after graduation in 1924 he joined the company for a short while. When he became undesirable to Mussolini's Fascist regime, his father sent him to the United States to learn the roots of American industrial power. For the same reasons he later went to England. Upon his return he married Paola Levi, a sister of his good friend, a marriage that produced three children but did not last long.

His visit to the United States at various plants and especially at Remington convinced Adriano that productivity is a function of the organizational system. With the approval of father Camillo, he organized the production system at Olivetti on a quasi-Taylorian mode and transformed the shop into a factory with departments and divisions. Possibly as a result of this reorganization output per man-hour doubled within five years. Olivetti for the first time sold half of the typewriters used in Italy in 1933. Adriano Olivetti shared with his workers the productivity gains by increasing salaries, fringe benefits, and services.

His success in business did not diminish his idealism. In the 1930s he developed an interest in architecture, as well as urban and community planning. He supervised a housing plan for the workers at Ivrea (a suburb of Turin, where the Olivetti plant is still located) and a zoning proposal for the adjacent Valle d'Aosta. Under Fascism, patronizing workers at work and at home was in line with the corporative design of the regime. While Adriano showed distaste for the regime, he joined the Fascist Party and became a Catholic. Yet during World War II he participated in the underground antifascist movement, was jailed, and at the end sought refuge in Switzerland. There he was in close contact with the intellectual emigrees and he was able to develop further his socio-philosophy of the community movement.

During the immediate post-war years the Olivetti empire expanded rapidly, only to be briefly on the verge of bankruptcy after the acquisition of Underwood in the late 1950s. During this period, first calculators and then computers replaced the typewriter as a prime production focus. Adriano shared his time between business pursuits and attempts to practice and spread the utopian ideal of community life. His belief was that people who respect each other and their environment can avoid war and poverty. His utopian idea was similar to that preached by Charles Fourier and Robert Owen during the previous century.

In his enterprises, Adriano Olivetti's attempts at utopia may be translated in practice as actions of an enlightened boss or a form of corporatism. He decreased the hours of work and increased salaries and fringe benefits. By 1957 Olivetti workers were the best paid of all in the metallurgical industry and Olivetti workers showed the highest productivity. His corporatism also succeeded in having his workers accept a company union not tied to the powerful national metallurgical trade unions.

During the 1950s, in a limited way, the community movement succeeded politically in Ivrea. (Camillo was even at one time mayor of Ivrea.) But the utopia at the factory and in Italy at large began withering away even before Adriano's death in 1960.

Adriano Olivetti's era saw great changes in Italian business and in industrial relations. New organizational methods were sought and humanistic idealism spread during the cruel time of World War II as well as during the difficult post-war years. The utopia of Olivetti could not have easily survived, but it helped induce the rapid reconversion of Italy's industry from war to peace-time production.

Further Reading

Most of the biographical sources describing Olivetti are in Italian: Valerio Ochetto, *Adriano Olivetti* (Milan, 1985); M. Fabbri, A. Greco, L. Menozzi, E. Valeriani, editors, *Architetura urbanistica in Italia nel dopoguerra* (Reggio Calabria, 1986); Bruno Caizzi, *Gli Olivetti* (Turin, 1962); and Renzo De Felice, *Storia degli ebrei italiani sotto il fascismo* (Turin, 1961). Adriano Olivetti, "Corrispondenza per gli Stati Uniti" (Milan, 1953) was translated as *Italy, Community versus Communism* (1953). Some of Olivetti's writings were published in English as *Society, State, Community* (London, 1954). □

Laurence Olivier

Internationally acclaimed for his acting and directing, Laurence Olivier (1907-1989) was often regarded as the supreme actor of his generation.

The son of a clergyman, Laurence Olivier was born in Dorking, Surrey, England. His first appearances on the stage were in schoolboy productions of Shakespeare. He was even invited to present a special matinee of *The Taming of the Shrew* at the Shakespeare Memorial Theatre in Stratford-upon-Avon in 1922. Olivier was cast as Katharina.

In preparation for a professional career in acting, Olivier studied at the Central School in London. He found his first paying jobs in the theater during term holidays, working as an assistant stage manager and playing small roles. After a year of experience at various theaters, Olivier joined the Birmingham Repertory Company in 1926, appearing in several parts which included Tony Lumpkin in Goldsmith's

She Stoops to Conquer (1927) and Malcolm in a modern dress production of *Macbeth* (1928). At the age of 20 he also played the title role in Chekhov's *Uncle Vanya* (1927).

He was the first to play Captain Stanhope in R. C. Sherriff's *Journey's End* when it tried out in 1928. To this day *Journey's End* is hailed as one of the greatest plays about the horrors of war. The following year he made his New York debut in Frank Vosper's *Murder on the Second Floor* and appeared in his first film, *The Temporary Widow*. Playing Victor in Noel Coward's *Private Lives* (1930) brought Olivier his first real taste of commercial success, and soon after he made his Hollywood screen debut. However, his early film career was fraught with disappointments, culminating in Greta Garbo's refusal to accept him as her leading man in *Queen Christina*.

Back in England in 1934 Olivier received positive notices for his portrayals of Bothwell in Gordon Daviot's *Queen of Scots* and of Anthony Cavendish in George S. Kaufman's *Theatre Royal*. He next tackled his first major Shakespearean roles on the professional stage, alternating Romeo and Mercutio with John Gielgud at the New Theatre (1935). The following year Olivier starred in his first Shakespearean film as Orlando in *As You Like It*. Although disappointed with the film, he used the actors and composer William Walton for future Shakespeare productions. In 1937 he joined London's Old Vic Company for a season, playing the title roles in *Hamlet* (a production later presented at Elsinore), *Henry V,* and *Macbeth,* and Sir Toby Belch in *Twelfth Night*. The following season he returned to play Iago opposite Ralph Richardson's Othello and Caius

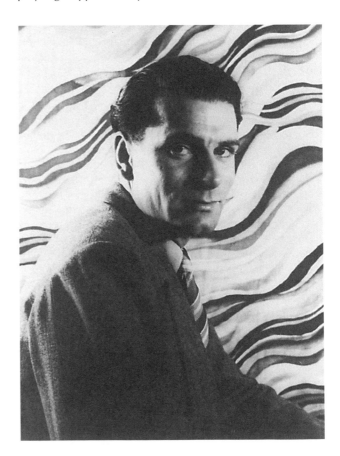

Marcius in *Coriolanus*. Having demonstrated his range, versatility, and interpretative intelligence in Shakespeare's repertoire, Olivier was now recognized as a stage actor of the first rank. Three major screen roles, in *Wuthering Heights* (1939, for which he received his first Academy Award nomination for Best Actor)) and in *Rebecca* (1940, and a second Academy Award nomination) and *Pride and Prejudice* (also 1940), subsequently established his film career. 1940 also saw social successes for Olivier as he and Academy Award-winner, Vivien Leigh, exchanged wedding vows. In 1941 Olivier and Leigh played the tragic lovers in Alexander Korda's *That Hamilton Woman,* regarded as one of the great romantic films of the era.

During World War II Olivier served with the Fleet Air Arm and was released twice to act in British war films. In 1943-1944 he made a film adaptation of *Henry V,* initially conceived as a propaganda project for the war effort. He won a special Academy Award for his triple triumph as director, producer, and star of the film.

Olivier was discharged from the armed service to join the Old Vic's artistic management in rebuilding the company's reputation and solvency after the lean war years. He remained with the company until 1949. Some of his most memorable roles during this time were Sergius in Shaw's *Arms and the Man* (1944), Astrov in *Uncle Vanya* (1945), and the title roles in *Richard III* (1945) and *King Lear* (1946), the latter of which he also directed. Perhaps his most demanding performance was for the double bill in which he appeared in the title role of Sophocles' *Oedipus Rex* and as Mr. Puff in Sheridan's *The Critic* (1945). Returning to film direction in 1948 with his famous black-and-white *Hamlet,* Olivier garnered an Oscar for his portrayal of the title role and the film won the best picture Academy Award. It also earned Olivier a knighthood from King George VI, of England.

In 1951, in London and New York, he appeared opposite Vivien Leigh in *Antony and Cleopatra* and Shaw's *Caesar and Cleopatra,* playing the male title role in both productions. Subsequent stage roles included the Grand Duke in Terence Rattigan's *The Sleeping Prince* (1955), the title roles in *Macbeth* and *Titus Andronicus* during the 1954-1955 season at the Shakespeare Memorial Theatre, and the title role in *Coriolanus* (1959), again at Stratford. He scored his first outstanding success in a modern role as the second-rate music hall comedian Archie Rice in John Osborne's *The Entertainer* (1957), repeating the part in the 1959 film version. He also directed and starred in films of *Richard III* (1955) and *The Prince and the Showgirl* (1957), the latter opposite Marilyn Monroe. He played Berenger in Ionesco's *Rhinoceros* (1960) in London, and in New York played first the title role (1960) and then Henry II (1961) in Anouilh's *Becket.* Later that same year he was appointed the first director of the Chichester Festival Theatre. *Uncle Vanya,* with Olivier as Astrov and his third wife Joan Plowright as Sonya, proved to be a huge success for the company's opening 1962 season.

Olivier was named the first director of the state-subsidized National Theatre. He held the position until 1973. For the National's opening 1963-1964 season Olivier directed

Hamlet and appeared as Astrov in *Uncle Vanya* (which he also directed) and as Brazen in Farquhar's *The Recruiting Officer.* He also offered a controversial but memorable interpretation of Othello. Among his important roles in later seasons were Tattle in Congreve's *Love for Love* (1965), Edgar in Strindberg's *The Dance of Death* (1967), Shylock in a Victorian production of *The Merchant of Venice* (1970), and James Tyrone in O'Neill's *A Long Day's Journey into Night* (1971). His most significant production as director was Chekhov's *The Three Sisters* in 1968. For the 1970 film of the production he again directed and also played Chebutikin. In 1970 Olivier was elevated to the peerage as Lord Olivier of Brighton—becoming the first actor to achieve such a status. During his National tenure he appeared in several other filmed stage productions, and his commercial films included *Nicholas and Alexandra* (1971) and *Sleuth* (1972). After leaving the National, Olivier concentrated on screen work. His films of this later period included Marathon Man (1976), *A Bridge Too Far* (1977), *A Little Romance* (1979), and *The Jazz Singer* (1981).

Until 1987 Olivier was prominent as a film and television virtuoso, making 29 movies in 13 years. During this span he received two more Academy Award nominations, becoming the most nominated actor in history. He also won an Emmy for *Brideshead Revisited.* In 1982 he wrote his autobiography *Confessions of an Actor* and another book, *On Acting* in 1986. In 1987, on his eightieth birthday, he announced to the world his retirement from motion pictures, but promised to remain active in television. On July 11, 1989, Olivier succumbed to complications from a muscle disorder.

Further Reading

Olivier's autobiography is entitled *Confessions of an Actor* (1982). His *On Acting* (1986) provides a tour through his many starring roles. A biography of Olivier's career and life with Vivien Leigh is Felix Barker's *The Oliviers* (1953). Another biography is Foster Hirsch, *Laurence Olivier* (1979), which places particular emphasis on Olivier's early film roles. His involvement with the creation of the Chichester Festival Theatre and with the inception of the National Theatre is charted in Virginia Fairweather, *Olivier: An Informal Portrait* (1969). Interviews with actors, directors, and playwrights who have worked with Olivier are collected in Logan Gourlay, editor, *Olivier* (1973). John Cotrell's *Laurence Olivier* (1975) is another exceptional biography of the actor. *Hamlet,* by Margaret Morley, details Olivier's role in the award-winning production, while Anne Edwards' *Vivien Leigh* provides an excellent biography of the well-known actress, and gives some indication as to what it was like to be a part of Olivier's life. □

Frederick Law Olmsted

Frederick Law Olmsted (1822-1903), American landscape architect, was prominent in promoting and planning recreational parks across the country.

Frederick Law Olmsted was born at Hartford, Conn., on April 26, 1822. He did not matriculate at college because of weak eyes, but he attended lectures at Yale University intermittently and became an honorary member of the class of 1847. He also studied engineering. In 1844 Olmsted decided to become a farmer and, after getting practical experience, settled on Staten Island, where he operated a farm until 1854. In 1859 he married Mary Cleveland Perkins Olmsted, the widow of his brother; the couple had two children.

In 1851 Olmsted visited Andrew Jackson Downing, who with others had conceived the idea of creating a vast park in New York City. Before realizing his dream, Downing died. Olmsted kept the idea alive and in 1857 was appointed superintendent of what became Central Park. He and Calvert Vaux then won the design competition for the park, and in 1858 Olmsted was advanced to chief architect of Central Park. During the Civil War he resigned his appointment over political differences and in 1863 accepted the superintendency of the Frémont Mariposa mining estates in California.

When Olmsted returned to New York in 1865, he and Vaux were reappointed landscape architects for Central Park. The Olmsted firm became the foremost landscape architects in America. Their projects included Prospect Park, Brooklyn (1865); the village of Riverside near Chicago (1868); Mount Royal Park, Montreal (1873-1881); the grounds of the Capitol, Washington, D.C. (1874-1885); the Boston park system (1875-1895); Stanford University, Palo Alto, Calif. (1886-1889); and Jackson Park, Chicago (1895).

Olmsted's most important late work was the design for the World's Columbian Exposition, Chicago (1890-1893).

Restless by nature, Olmsted traveled frequently and often published his diaries and talks. He wrote *Walks and Talks of an American Farmer in England* (1852), *A Journey in the Seaboard Slave States* (1856), *A Journey through Texas* (1857), and *A Journey in the Back Country* (1860).

Always interested in publishing, he and C. S. Sargent founded the journal *Garden and Forest*. Olmsted further encouraged park planning by publishing *Public Parks and the Enlargement of Towns* (1871) and *A Consideration of the Justifying Value of a Public Park* (1881). He died on Aug. 28, 1903, having witnessed the enthusiastic development in American cities of public park systems.

Further Reading

There is no definitive study of Olmsted's work. Important as source material is *Frederick Law Olmsted: Landscape Architect,* edited by F. L. Olmsted, Jr., and Theodora Kimball (2 vols., 1922-1928), which contains many of his papers and emphasizes Central Park. Julius G. Fabos and others, comps., *Frederick Law Olmsted, Sr.: Founder of Landscape Architecture in America* (1968), is a brief, well-illustrated survey of Olmsted's career; it contains illustrations of his projects, an appendix listing his major works, and a chronology of his life. See also Broadus Mitchell, *Frederick Law Olmsted: A Critic of the Old South* (1924). □

Richard Olney

Richard Olney (1835-1917) served as U.S. attorney general and secretary of state under President Grover Cleveland.

Richard Olney, Massachusetts-born, was from an upper-class family. He was educated at Brown University and the Harvard Law School and specialized in corporate law in Boston. Generally unsuccessful in politics and little known to the public, he was considered by many contemporaries to be haughty, temperamental, and stubborn. Grover Cleveland's choice of Olney in 1893 for attorney general was a surprise, but he fitted well into the group of economic conservatives in Cleveland's Cabinet.

As attorney general, Olney made only perfunctory efforts to enforce the Sherman Antitrust Act of 1890 against big business, terming the law "no good." He used the full resources of the Justice Department, however, for a showdown with the American Railway Union. Contending that the Pullman strike of 1894 was a conspiracy in restraint of trade, Olney suggested that the Sherman Antitrust Act be used against labor unions for the first time. At his suggestion Cleveland sent troops to Chicago to deal with the strikers, an act which provoked bloody riots. Workingmen throughout the country turned against the Cleveland administration as well as the Democratic party.

Appointed secretary of state in 1895, Olney turned his talents toward the extension of American influence, particularly in the Western Hemisphere. Olney and Cleveland intervened uninvited in the 1895-1896 boundary dispute between Great Britain and Venezuela. Their actions were in response to jingoist domestic pressures and to demands for the protection of American economic interests in Latin America. The Olney-Cleveland Venezuela policy carried the nation to the brink of war with England, which was averted only when the British agreed to submit the matter to arbitration. Similar concerns with protecting economic interests and American citizens were important in Olney's policy toward a revolt in Cuba and disorders in Turkey and China.

At the end of the Cleveland administration, after his return to private practice, Olney became a vigorous opponent of American expansion by territorial annexation. Still active as a public figure in the first decade of the 20th century, he was associated with efforts by economic conservatives to regain control of the Democratic party from William Jennings Bryan, although he refused all opportunities to return to public service.

Further Reading

Henry James, *Richard Olney and His Public Service* (1923), is a standard source for Olney's public career, based on his papers and addresses. Allan Nevins, *Grover Cleveland: A Study in Courage* (1932), is rich with detail and insight for the period of Olney's governmental service. More specific aspects of his career as attorney general are treated in Almont Lindsey, *The Pullman Strike* (1942), while Walter LaFeber, *The New Empire: An Interpretation of American Expansion, 1860-1898* (1963), analyzes Olney's foreign policy.

Additional Sources

Eggert, Gerald G., *Richard Olney: evolution of a statesman,* University Park, Pennsylvania State University Press 1974. □

Charles Olson

Charles Olson (1910-1970) defined and practiced an open, kinetic poetry which influenced many of the second generation of modern poets.

Charles Olson, born in Worcester, Massachusetts, in 1910, was an energetic giant of a man. In his youth his energy took the form of conspicuous academic success. He was Phi Beta Kappa and a candidate for a Rhodes scholarship at Wesleyan University, where he earned a B.A. in 1932 and an M.A. in 1933 with a thesis on Herman Melville. By 1939 Olson completed course work for a Ph.D. in American civilization at Harvard University, published his essay "Lear and Moby Dick," and received his first Guggenheim fellowship to continue research on Melville. In the 1940s Olson moved away from a traditional academic career, through a disillusioning flirtation with politics, to his lifelong work as a poet. His youthful energy and scholarship came to distinguish his poetry.

Much of the political 1940s were spent in Washington, D.C., but in 1951 Olson joined Black Mountain College in North Carolina as a visiting professor, later becoming rector until financial difficulties forced the close of the college. At Black Mountain Olson found students and staff devoted to the active practice of the arts. In 1957 Olson moved to Gloucester, Massachusetts, where he had spent summers as a boy. He accepted positions as visiting professor at the State University of New York at Buffalo (1963-1965) and at the University of Connecticut (1969). Olson married twice and was the father of two children. He died from cancer in 1970.

The Scholar Poet

Olson's wide reading informed his writings. Prose works, such as *Call Me Ishmael* (1947) and *The Special View of History* (1957), reveal his fascination with 20th-century man's discoveries concerning the dynamic, interactive nature of the world and man's possibilities in such a world. Influenced by Alfred North Whitehead concerning the interaction of the past and the present, Olson believed that each man could select from history what he needed to constitute a rich and useful present. Olson was further influenced by Carl Jung's integration of the world within the mind and the world without: man's lifelong task, Jung argued, was to find in external reality objects and events which can express in symbolic terms the secrets of creation locked in the unconscious. In Olson's poem "The Librarian" (1957) traditional distinctions between the mind and external reality evaporate.

In his influential 1950 essay "Projective Verse" Olson defined poetry in terms of the dynamic world his contemporaries were discovering: "A poem is energy transferred from where the poet got it . . . by way of the poem itself . . . to the reader." The poet's own energy as he writes is among that which is embodied in the poem. The syllable, Olson argued, reveals the poet's act of exploring the possibilities of sound in order to create an oral beauty. The line reveals the poet's breathing, where it begins and ends as he works. Conventional syntax, meter, and rhyme must be abandoned, Olson argued, if their structural requirements slow the swift currents of the poet's thought. The predictable left-hand margin falsifies the spontaneous nature of experience.

In rethinking the possibilities of language, Olson acknowledged his debt to Ezra Pound and William Carlos Williams. Olson also valued the breadth of Pound's historical knowledge, which made available so much of the past necessary to constitute a valuable present. In Williams' attention to the precise nature of individual objects and their relations, however, Olson found an alternative to the prejudices which marred Pound's reading of history. The poem "The Kingfishers" (1949), with its ornithological details and restless search of history, signals Olson's intention to synthesize the best of Pound and Williams.

The Maximus Poems

Olson wrote over 100 shorter poems now collected in *Archaeologist of Morning*. His most sustained effort to practice his poetic theories, however, was the *Maximus Poems,* a 20-year sequence published in three volumes. The poems are set in Gloucester, Massachusetts, and have as their hero the dynamic Maximus, who slowly becomes indistinguishable from Olson himself. The first volume of 39 poems was begun in 1950 and published as *The Maximus Poems* in 1960. Its poems are, in part, an outgrowth of Olson's earlier political interests and his communal experiences at Black Mountain. Maximus labors to found in Gloucester a community devoted to creative pursuits. Its members will be the readers of the poems, to whom Maximus hopes to transfer the same creative energy which motivates him. Finding his efforts sabotaged by capitalism's exploitation of natural and human resources, however, Maximus becomes increasingly enraged and despondent. Nonetheless, he continues to write, developing his own creative powers in order to enhance his creative possibilities in a hostile world.

Maximus Poems IV-V-VI rewards his labor. The history of man's migration west from primeval times reveals an energy to colonize which is precisely what Olson would transfer to his reader. In the tradition of Whitehead, Maximus enacts this history in order to make it a vital contemporary force. He walks through Gloucester, for example, retracing the steps of the colonists who carried western migration across the Atlantic. As the poems accumulate, Maximus pushes farther back into history and myth in order to understand ever more about the dynamics of migration. His efforts earn him a vision of the primal source of the energy which drove man west. For Maximus, this vision, found in "Maximus— from Dogtown IV," expresses in a satisfactory way the secrets of creation which are locked in the unconscious.

In *Maximus Poems: Volume Three* (1975) Maximus explores what he can accomplish now that he is empowered by his knowledge and vision. Because these poems were collected and arranged chronologically by others after Olson's death, the shape he would have given the volume, had he lived, is unknown. In individual poems, however, Olson as Maximus seeks new reconciliations—with his long–dead father, for example—and returns to the unfinished business of the first Maximus poems in an effort to restore Gloucester as a city full of creative possibilities. Yet the death of his wife, the distance of friends, and declining health made him feel more estranged and uncertain than in the first volume. In this, the most personal volume of the Maximus Poems, the empowered Olson and the uncertain Olson contest with one another. As death overtakes him, however, Olson resists despair by recognizing that the life he has lived in his poems may pose a sufficient alternative to the destructive capitalist norm to stand after he falls.

Further Reading

George Butterick provides over 4,000 annotations in his invaluable *A Guide to the Maximus Poems of Charles Olson* (1978). Butterick has also collected the correspondence between Olson and Robert Creeley in *Charles Olson & Robert Creeley: The Complete Correspondence* (6 vols., 1980-1984). Sherman Paul provides a comprehensive study of Olson's intellectual and poetic development in *Olson's Push* (1978). Other titles of important studies are self-explanatory: Donald Byrd, *Charles Olson's Maximus* (1980); Thomas Merrill, *The Poetry*

of Charles Olson: A Primer (1982); and Robert von Hallberg, *Charles Olson: The Scholar's Art* (1979). Finally, there is Paul Christensen's *Charles Olson: Call Him Ishmael* (1979).

Additional Sources

Boer, Charles, *Charles Olson in Connecticut*, Rocky Mount, N.C.: North Carolina Wesleyan College Press, 1991.
Clark, Tom, *Charles Olson: the allegory of a poet's life*, New York: Norton, 1991. □

Sylvanus E. Olympio

Sylvanus E. Olympio (1902-1963), the first president of the Republic of Togo, was distinguished for his pragmatism, brilliance, and moderation. His government was overthrown by the first military coup in tropical Africa, and he was assassinated.

Sylvanus Olympio was born into a very influential Lomé family which had emigrated from Brazil in the mid-19th century. He was educated in Togolese schools, and although a resident of the French area of the Mandated Territory of Togo, he attended the London School of Economics, earning a degree in commerce in 1926. He was immediately employed by the United Africa Company and eventually rose to be its district manager for Togo.

Togolese citizens faced two problems not common to most African territories. In the 1880s Britain, Germany, and France had drawn arbitrary boundaries which divided people of the same tribes. The Ewe were the most affected since they were forced to live in the Gold Coast, Togo, and Dahomey. The mandate system after 1919 further divided Togo between France and Britain. Olympio early associated himself with the Comité de l'Unité (CUT), an association dedicated to Ewe reunification. It also opposed closer links between Togo and the French Empire.

Because of his views, Olympio was interned by the Vichy government in Dahomey during World War II. After his release he resigned from the company and became head of CUT. As president of the Togo Assembly after 1946, and later a deputy to the French Assembly, he was the most articulate spokesman for Ewe unification, appearing a number of times before the United Nations. The Ewe cause was doomed because it was opposed by both Britain and France, and devolution of power to the Gold Coast after 1951 was a further block. In 1956 in a United Nations plebiscite, British Togo voted for union with the Gold Coast.

In 1956 French Togo received limited autonomy, and in the following elections the most cooperative Parti Togolaise du Progrès (PTP) won, and Nicholas Grunitzky became prime minister. Olympio and the CUT protested the election to the United Nations, which refused to recognize the French arrangements until better-supervised elections were completed. The CUT won such an election in 1958, and Olympio became prime minister. Independence was granted Togo in April 1960, and a year later it became a

republic with Olympio its president. The PTP was disqualified by Olympio's government, and thus his party won all 51 seats in the legislature.

Olympio, an economist, realized that Togo, small in size and poor in resources, had to proceed cautiously in its development program. He cooperated with France and instituted stringent controls on expenditure. Economic problems were increased by the actions of Kwame Nkrumah. Angered by his failure to absorb Togo in a federation, he closed the Ghanaian border. Dissatisfaction with Olympio's policies began to develop among the young Togolese who disagreed with his pro-French attitude. Olympio also resisted demands of Togolese veterans of the French army to enlarge the 250-man Togo force. On Jan. 13, 1963, these disgruntled soldiers staged a coup and, although not originally intending to do so, shot Olympio as he was trying to reach the security of the U.S. embassy.

Further Reading

There are no good detailed biographies of Olympio or works on the recent history of Togo available in English. For background see Ruth Shachter Morgenthau, *Political Parties in French Speaking West Africa* (1964; rev. ed. 1967), and John Hatch, *A History of Postwar Africa* (1965). For the history of Togo under international control and the attitudes of Togolese politicians in the period after 1945 see Claude E. Welch, Jr., *Dream of Unity* (1966). Some information on Olympio is in Ronald Segal, *Political Africa* (1961). ☐

Omar al-Mukhtar

Omar al-Mukhtar (about ca. 1860-1931), national hero of Libya and member of the Senusy, a religious organization with administrative and military functions, led the anticolonial resistance in Cirenaica from 1923 to 1931, when he was captured by the Italians and condemned to death.

Little is known of Omar al-Mukhtar until the last decade of his life when he became the undisputed leader of the Senusist resistance in Cirenaica. Even his date of birth is uncertain, somewhere between 1856 and 1862, in el Batwan in oriental Cirenaica. For eight years he studied in the koran school of Giarabub, the Senusy's holy city. He taught in a Senusist *zawiya* but also took part in military operations against the Italians and the allies during World War I.

When the Italians openly attacked Senusy in the spring of 1923 (at the end of April the existing agreements were formally denounced) Omar was among the most competent and active figures in organizing and coordinating the resistance. In his capacity as representative of the Senusy he had assumed command of the guerrilla forces that often baffled and confounded the regular Italian forces.

In the mountainous region of Gebel Akhdar (the Green Mountain) Italian Governor Mombelli succeeded in 1924 in activating a counter-guerrilla force that inflicted a harsh defeat on the rebels in April 1925. Omar then quickly modified his own tactics and was able to count on constant help from Egypt.

In March 1927, notwithstanding the occupation of Giarabub (February 1926) and the reenforcement of the oppression under then Governor Teruzzi, Omar surprised an Italian military force at Raheiba. Following successive clashes in various localities of Gebel, Omar was forced to withdraw. Between 1927 and 1928 Omar fully reorganized the Senusite forces, who were being hunted constantly by the Italians. Even General Teruzzi recognized Omar's qualities of "exceptional perseverance and strong will power."

Pietro Badoglio, the new governor of Libya (January 1929), after extensive negotiations was able to reach a compromise with Omar similar to previous Italo-Senusite accords. Italian sources falsely described the situation as an act of complete submission by Omar. This attitude was confirmed by Italian leaders, including Badoglio (who probably supported the misleading statement hoping to break anti-Italian resistance).

At the end of October 1929 Omar denounced the compromise and reestablished a unity of action among Libyan forces, preparing himself for the ultimate confrontation with General Rodolfo Graziani, the military commander from March 1930. Having failed in a massive offensive in June against Omar's forces, Graziani, in full accord with Badoglio, De Bono (minister of the colonies), and Benito Mussolini, initiated a strong plan to decisively break off the Cirenaica resistance. The plan was to transfer the Gebel population (around 100,000 persons) to concentration camps on the coast and to close the border with Egypt from the coast at Giarabub, thus preventing any foreign help to the fighters and breaking up the solidarity of the population.

From the beginning of 1931 the measures taken by Graziani took their toll on the Senusist resistance. The rebels were deprived of help and reinforcements, spied upon, hit by Italian aircraft, and pursued by the Italian forces aided by local informers. In spite of hardships and increasing risks, Omar courageously continued the fight, but on September 11, 1931, he was ambushed near Zonta. With dignity and calm he faced up to the immediate situation and accepted his death sentence with the words: "From God we came and to God we must return." The execution of the old fighter—carried out in the concentration camp of Solluq on September 16—caused great indignation in the Arab world.

Omar's implacable adversary, General Graziani, has given us this physical and moral description, which is not lacking in admiration: "Of medium height, stout, with white hair, beard and moustache. Omar was endowed with a quick and lively intelligence; was knowledgeable in religious matters, and revealed an energetic and impetuous character, unselfish and uncompromising; ultimately, he remained very religious and poor, even though he had been one of the most important Senusist figures."

In later times author A. Del Boca judged him: "Omar is not only an example of religious faith and a born fighter but also the builder of that perfect military-political organization, which for ten years kept in check troops under four governors."

The memory of Omar remained alive. Libya, independent, monarchic, and revolutionary, declared him its national hero. His life was depicted by Anthony Quinn in the movie "The Lion of the Desert," produced by Siro-American Akkad.

Further Reading

The religious organization that provided the military base of Omar al-Mukhtar is discussed in E.E. Evans Pritchard, *The Senusy of Cirenaica* (Oxford, 1949). Two other relevant books are in Italian: *Omar al-Mukhtar e la riconquista fascista della Libia* (Omar al-Mukhtar and the fascist reconquest of Libia), by various authors (Milan, 1981); and A. Del Boca, *Gli italiani in Libia: Dal fascismo a Gheddafi* (The Italians in Libya: From fascism to Gheddafi), (Bari, 1988). □

Omar ibn al-Khattab

Omar ibn al-Khattab (died 644) was the second caliph of the Moslems and directed the spectacular Arab conquests and organized the Arab Empire.

Because Omar was one of the most adamant opponents of Mohammed's preaching in Mecca, his dramatically sudden conversion to Islam in 615 is often regarded as a turning point in the career of the Prophet. The

fierce loyalty which he gave to Mohammed, both as a warrior in the battles against the Meccans and as an adviser, was reinforced by marriage when his daughter Hafsa married the Prophet.

Nevertheless, in spite of his vigorous support of the Prophet, Omar does not figure prominently in Islamic history until the death of Mohammed in 632, and even then it is as a supporter of Abu Bakr, the first caliph, whose selection Omar imposed on the divided Moslem community by the sheer force of his own personality. Although some modern historians have claimed that Omar was the real power behind the throne during Abu Bakr's short reign (632-634), Omar was careful—if this theory is sound—to stay in the background, perhaps realizing that more vigorous leadership might be resented by the Arab Moslems so soon after the death of their beloved Prophet.

Early Conquests

At any rate, upon Abu Bakr's death in 634, Omar assumed the caliphate in his own right, apparently without opposition. The immediate task confronting him was to direct the two-pronged military campaign (which had been launched in 633 by Abu Bakr) against the Byzantines in Palestine and Syria and the Sassanians in Iraq. In both fields of battle Omar gave new energy to his armies by sending new levies of tribal troops. Thus reinforced, the Syrian army, led by the famous general Khalid ibn al-Walid, captured Damascus in 635 and, in the following year, smashed the

Omar ibn al-Khattab seated on camel

Byzantine army in Syria at the battle of Yarmuk. Further successful campaigns in Syria led to the conquest of Jerusalem in 638. Because Jerusalem was the third holiest city in Islam, after Mecca and Medina, Omar himself visited it as conqueror. Typically, however, he insisted on presenting himself as a simple desert warrior rather than a mighty potentate.

Simultaneously with the conquest of Syria and Palestine, another of Omar's armies was driving the Persian army from Iraq. Here the decisive battle was fought in 636 at Qadisiya, where a Moslem victory left the Sassanian capital of Ctesiphon virtually defenseless and open to plunder by the Arabs. Once the conquest of Syria had been achieved, the Syrian army was free to attack upper Mesopotamia from the west, and it came under the control of the caliphate in 640.

Administrative Reforms

The conquest of such a vast area in such a relatively short time soon created formidable administrative problems for Omar. Since the Arabs had no experience as rulers of an empire, they were forced to rely to a great extent on the bureaucracies created by the Byzantine and Sassanian governments. Nevertheless, Omar is credited with introducing several new administrative practices and institutions which, in conjunction with the customary practice of the conquered lands, gave stability to the Arab occupation and allowed the conquests to maintain their momentum.

Tradition would have it that Omar announced his innovations in a speech made to the Arab military leaders during a lull in the fighting between the battle of Yarmuk and the occupation of Jerusalem. Though this tradition may well be a reconstruction of the gradual evolution of early Moslem policy, it is probable that Omar did lay down guidelines, at least for the solution of pressing problems. Almost all these were related to finances: how to pay the troops and support the Moslem community on a long-term basis without disrupting the economy of the conquered lands.

In general, Omar's solution was to leave the conquered peoples in possession of their lands and their own religion in exchange for the payment of tribute which was to be disbursed in turn by the Moslem government to its armies and citizens. To institutionalize this policy, a divan, or register, was drawn up which regularized the stipends which Moslems were to be paid according to religious and tribal principles. Relations between Moslems and non-Moslems were further stabilized by exempting the latter from military service and guaranteeing them protection in return for the taxes which they paid.

Invasions of Persia and Egypt

Undoubtedly of equal importance to these measures was Omar's decision to establish garrison cities, first in Iraq, and later in Egypt, to administer the newly conquered territory and to serve as bases for the invasion of Persia. In this way, Basra and Kufa were founded by Omar in 635, both of which were to become important centers of Islamic civilization. From these cities Omar launched an invasion of Persia in 640 which was climaxed by the defeat of the Sassanian

army at the battle of Nihawand in 642; the resultant collapse of Sassanian power opened Persia to relatively easy conquest.

At the same time as Omar's armies were achieving victory in Persia, still another army was invading Egypt. Between 639 and 642 the Arabs succeeded in driving the Byzantines from Egypt and establishing a Moslem government there. Again Omar's policy of establishing new garrison cities was followed with the founding of al-Fustât, later to become Cairo.

With astonishing speed, Omar succeeded in spreading Arab Moslem rule from Persia to Egypt under his political and religious leadership. He was also able to establish a remarkable degree of unity in the empire through the appointment of provincial officials loyal to him and his principles and by setting a stern example of piety and morality at the capital. He is celebrated in Arabic historiography for his unaffected, rough manner, coupled with devotion to his religion—the prototype of the unspoiled Arab ruler. A Persian slave, outraged by Omar's refusal to reduce a heavy tax, mortally wounded the Caliph in 644 while Omar was leading the prayers. Refusing to name his successor on his deathbed, he established still another precedent by appointing a council to choose the new caliph.

Further Reading

The only biography in English is Muhammad Shibli Numani, *Omar the Great* (Lahore; trans., vol. 1, 1939; rev. ed. 1943; vol. 2, 1957). Detailed studies can be found in William Muir's dated but still useful study *The Caliphate* (1891; rev. ed. by T. W. Weir, 1915), and in Maulana Muhammad Ali, *Early Caliphate* (Lahore; trans. 1932). For general background see Thomas W. Arnold, *The Caliphate* (1924); S. Khuda Bukhsh, *The Caliphate* (1927); Philip K. Hitti, *History of the Arabs* (1937; 10th ed. rev. 1970); Carl Brockelmann, *History of the Islamic Peoples* (1939; trans. 1949); and Bernard Lewis, *The Arabs in History* (1950; rev. ed. 1958). □

Al-Hajj Omar ibn Said Tal

Al-Hajj Omar ibn Said Tal (ca. 1797-1864) was a West African Moslem leader who started a holy war and established a far-reaching empire on the Upper Niger.

Al-Hajj Omar was born in the Futa Toro near the town of Podar on the Senegal River. His father was a Moslem teacher, and young Omar was educated by prominent Moslem scholars of the Tijaniyya brotherhood, one of whom persuaded him to make the pilgrimage to Mecca in 1826.

The pilgrimage, and Omar's subsequent sojourn in Mecca, was the turning point in his life. While in Mecca he completed his religious studies and was initiated into the leadership of the Tijaniyya order, earning the designation of khalifa of the western Sudan. As a result, Omar had access to the ruling hierarchy throughout the entire Sudan, which was to facilitate his later political career.

On his return journey between 1835 and 1838 Omar visited Bornu and Sokoto, married into the royal families of both states, and learned the tactics of the *jihad,* or holy war. After leaving Sokoto in 1837, he traveled to Macina, where he was given a less friendly welcome by the ruling family, who were members of a rival religious order, the Qadiriyya. Moving on to Ségou, he was imprisoned for a short time before being released and settling finally, in 1838, in the Futa Jallon.

For the next 10 years Omar preached and proselytized in the Futa Jallon, where he acquired a substantial number of loyal supporters. Indeed, his adherents were so numerous, well armed, and well financed that Omar's power became a serious threat to the traditional rulers of the Futa Jallon. In 1849 Omar was forced to move to the town of Dinguiray near the headwaters of the Niger River, from where he launched a series of small wars against the local non-Moslem states.

Holy War

By 1852 Omar believed his forces sufficiently strong to declare holy war against all those who would not accept Islam, and later even against Moslems who would not acknowledge his teachings. During the next decade his troops, the vanguard of which were dedicated Tokolar *talibes* (students of religion) from the Futa Jallon, conquered the lands stretching between the headwaters of the Niger and Timbuktu, creating a unified Tokolar empire which dominated the western Sudan until it was conquered by the French in the last decade of the 19th century.

Omar's objectives during the early years of his empire remain unclear and a subject of controversy. Some scholars believe that he was simply an adventurer and opportunist who desired above all to construct a personal kingdom; others have argued that Omar's primary interests were theological and that he wished only to establish an Islamic state governed by the *Sharia,* or Islamic law, and dedicated to God. Some students believe that his *jihad* was directed primarily at the French who had begun to encroach upon his homeland, the Futa Toro, after 1852, while others argue that he was less interested in the French than he was in conquering the pagan and older Islamic states in the basin of the upper Niger. Omar was probably inspired by all these diverse motives at different times. In any event, before his death in 1864 Omar was able to unite his followers into a formidable military and political force which dominated the western Sudan for another 2 decades before being broken up by the French.

Further Reading

There are solid biographies of al-Hajj Omar in John Spencer Trimingham, *A History of Islam in West Africa* (1962), and Jamil M. Abun-Nasr, *The Tijaniyya: A Sufi Order in the Modern World* (1965). For shorter accounts and background material see Martin A. Klein, *Islam and Imperialism in Senegal: Sine-Saloum, 1847-1914* (1968), and John D. Hargreaves, ed., *France and West Africa: An Anthology of Historical Documents* (1969). □

Omar Khayyam

The Persian astronomer, mathematician, and poet Omar Khayyam (1048-ca. 1132) made important contributions to mathematics, but his chief claim to fame, at least in the last 100 years, has been as the author of a collection of quatrains, the "Rubaiyat."

Omar Khayyam was born in Nishapur in May 1048. His father, Ibrahim, may have been a tentmaker (Khayyam means tentmaker). Omar obtained a thorough education in philosophy and mathematics, and at an early age he attained great fame in the latter field. The Seljuk sultan Jalal-al-Din Malik Shah invited him to collaborate in devising a new calendar, the Jalali or Maliki. Omar spent much of his life teaching philosophy and mathematics, and legends ascribe to him some proficiency in medicine. He died in Nishapur.

Astronomical and Mathematical Works

The product of the efforts of Omar and his two collaborators was a set of astronomical tables entitled *Al-zij al-Malikshahi* after their royal patron. Of this there remains only the table of 100 fixed stars, whose latitude is given for the first year of the Maliki era (1075), and some contradictory descriptions of the Maliki calendar. It is clear that this calendar was intended to retain the basic months of the old Sassanian calendar, in which a year consisted of 12 months of 30 days each plus 5 epagomenal days, with an extra month of 30 days intercalated every 120 years. The intercalation of 30 days in 120 years made the year a Julian year, as in the Julian calendar a day is intercalated every 4 years. The Sassanian and Julian calendars are based on a year of 365.15 days, which is not accurate; Omar and his collaborators devised a modification of the intercalation scheme to overcome this inaccuracy, but the details are obscure.

Omar's work on mathematics is known principally through his commentary on Euclid's *Elements* and through his treatise *On Algebra*. In the commentary he is concerned with the foundations of geometry and, in particular, strives to solve the problems of irrational numbers and their relations to rational numbers, in the process very nearly becoming the first to acknowledge irrationals as real numbers; and he examines Euclid's fifth postulate, the "parallel postulate," which distinguishes Euclidean from non-Euclidean geometry. Omar tried to prove the parallel postulate with only the first four postulates by examining a birectangular quadrilateral. The task was an impossible one, but in the course of his attempted proof Omar recognized the logical results of some forms of non-Euclidean geometry. *On Algebra* is a classification of equations with proofs of each, some algebraic but most geometric. The most original part is found in his classification of cubic equations, which, following Archimedes, he solved by means of intersecting conic sections.

Jacqueline Lee Bouvier Kennedy Onassis

An internationally famous First Lady, Jacqueline Lee Bouvier Kennedy Onassis (1929-1994) raised her two children after the assassination of President John F. Kennedy in 1963. After a seven-year remarriage she turned to a career as a book editor.

Jacqueline Lee Bouvier Kennedy Onassis was born on July 28, 1929. Her mother was Janet Lee Bouvier, and her father, though named John Vernon Bouvier III, was known by all as Black Jack. Her sister Caroline Lee (who was called Lee) was born four years later. Jackie was a headstrong child who was initially a discipline problem at Miss Chapin's, the fashionable school on Manhattan's east side that she attended as a young girl.

Janet and Black Jack had a troubled marriage and they separated in 1936. They reconciled briefly in 1937 but were divorced in 1940. Jackie lived with her mother, though she did see her beloved father frequently. In 1942 Janet married Hugh Dubley Auchincloss, Jr., who was a lawyer from a prestigious old family. The Auchinclosses were much wealthier than the Bouviers, and Jackie and Lee lived with their mother and her new husband. The Auchinclosses had two more children, Janet, Jr., who was born in 1945, and Jamie, who was born in 1947.

The mother's remarriage created a rift in the family. Though Jackie adored her father, she saw less and less of him, particularly since her mother and stepfather moved their family to Washington, D.C. The summers were spent at the Auchincloss home, Hammersmith Farm, in Newport, Rhode Island. In 1944 Jackie was sent to boarding school at Miss Porter's in Farmington, Connecticut.

Jackie was a beautiful and elegant young woman, and when she made her social debut the Hearst newspaper gossip columnist named her Debutante of 1947. Jackie went on to college at Vassar, where she seemed embarrassed by the notoriety attached to her social success. She was a serious student who worked hard and made the dean's list. She spent her junior year abroad in Paris, which she loved.

Career as a Photographer Ends in Marriage

Jackie returned to the United States and finished college at George Washington University in Washington, D.C. She entered a writing contest sponsored by *Vogue* magazine called the "Prix de Paris," which she won. The winner was to receive a year-long position as a trainee at *Vogue,* spending six months in their New York office and six months in the Paris office. Jackie's parents, especially her stepfather, felt that she had spent a long time in Europe already, and they were concerned that if she took the job she would not return to the United States. At their request Jackie turned down the offer and went to work instead at the *Washington Times-Herald* newspaper as a photographer.

The "Rubaiyat"

Shortly after Omar's death, collections of *rubaiyat* circulated under his name. These poems consist of 4 lines of 13 syllables each with the rhyme scheme AABA or AAAA; the rhythm within each line is rather free. *Rubaiyat* had been popular in Persia since the 9th or 10th century as occasional verses extemporaneously recited by all classes of persons; they were used both to express a sort of hedonistic appreciation of life and also Sufi mystical experiences.

Omar's *Rubaiyat* is known in the West largely through the rather inaccurate paraphrase translation of Edward Fitz-Gerald (1859), which in any case seems to contain a number of non-Khayyamian verses. FitzGerald considerably distorted the original to make it conform to Victorian romanticism; these distortions and the non-Khayyamian verses have led some to believe that Omar was himself a Sufi mystic. Recent discoveries of early-13th-century manuscripts of the *Rubaiyat,* however, have shown that Omar's poetry follows the other tradition of this form of poetry and celebrates, with humorous skepticism, wit, and poetic skill, the joys of wine and homosexual love.

Further Reading

A biography of Omar Khayyam is Harold Lamb, *Omar Khayyam: A Life* (1934). The most authoritative treatment of his poetry is Arthur John Arberry, ed. and trans., *Omar Khayyam* (1952). On Omar's contribution to mathematics see Seyyed Hossein Nasr, *Science and Civilization in Islam* (1968). □

In 1951 Jackie met John Fitzgerald Kennedy for the first time. The next year Kennedy was elected senator from Massachusetts and moved to Washington. The two continued to see each other and became engaged in June 1953. On September 12, 1953, Jacqueline Lee Bouvier married John Fitzgerald Kennedy at an enormous wedding that was the social event of the season. There were 1,300 guests at the reception. The only event that marred the wedding for the bride was the fact that her father, who had become an alcoholic, was incapable of escorting her down the aisle or even of attending the wedding.

Jackie Kennedy was a shy, private woman with little experience in politics or knowledge of politicians, but she was a help to her husband in many ways. She worked with him on his public speaking, helping to develop the charismatic style for which he would become so famous. In 1954 Kennedy had surgery to try to alleviate the constant pain he suffered from a back injury. Jackie spent the recovery period by his side.

In 1956 there was speculation that John Kennedy would be the Democratic vice presidential nominee. Many members of the Kennedy family attended the convention, which was an exciting and exhausting one. Jackie was there to lend her support, despite the fact that she was seven months pregnant. Though Jack Kennedy gave a speech nominating Adlai Stevenson as the Democratic candidate for president, Estes Kefauver was selected as the vice presidential candidate.

On August 23, soon after her husband had left for a short vacation, Jackie went into premature labor. The baby was stillborn, and it was Jackie's brother-in-law Bobby Kennedy who consoled her and made the arrangements for the baby's burial.

In 1957 Jackie suffered another loss when her father died. This was also a difficult period in the Kennedy marriage. Much was rumored at the time and has been written subsequently about the various extramarital affairs that John Kennedy had both before and during his presidency, all of which undoubtedly put a strain on his and Jackie's marriage.

On November 27, 1957, Caroline Bouvier Kennedy was born. Just months after Caroline's birth her father was up for reelection as senator from Massachusetts, and Jackie was active in the 1958 senatorial campaign as well.

Jackie Becomes First Lady

Soon after Kennedy was returned to Washington by his constituents he began to seek the presidential nomination. Jackie campaigned vigorously for her husband until she became pregnant in 1960, and even afterwards continued to help as much as she was physically able until the birth of her son John Jr.

As soon as John Kennedy was elected president, Jackie began working to reorganize the White House so that she could turn it into a home for her children and protect their privacy. At the same time she was well aware of the importance of the White House as a public institution. She formed the White House Historical Association to help her with the task of redecorating the building. She also formed a Special Committee for White House Paintings to further advise her. While as a mother Jackie was interested in protecting her children, as First Lady she felt strongly that the White House was a national monument. She wrote the forward to *The White House: A Historical Guide*. She also developed the idea of a filmed tour of the White House that she would conduct. The tour was broadcast on Valentine's Day 1962 and was eventually distributed to 106 countries.

In April of 1963 the Kennedys announced that Jackie was pregnant. On August 7, 1963, Patrick Bouvier Kennedy was born. He died three days later.

In November of 1963 Jackie Kennedy accompanied her husband on a trip to Texas. She was riding by his side when he was assassinated. In the days that followed John Kennedy's death the image of his widow and children, and the dignity with which they conducted themselves, were very much a part of the nation's experience of mourning and loss. Jackie became an icon and a symbol.

After Leaving the White House

In the years immediately after her husband's death Jackie Kennedy was seen very much in the role of his widow, while at the same time there was constant speculation about whether or not she would remarry. Jackie was actively involved in Bobby Kennedy's bid for election as president in 1968. After his assassination in June 1968 she was again a prominent figure at a very public funeral.

In October 1968 Jackie Kennedy married Aristotle Onassis, a Greek shipping magnate. He was 62 and she was 39. Jackie spent large portions of her time in New York to be with her children. As the years went by, the Onassis marriage was rumored to be a difficult one, and the couple began to spend most of their time apart. Aristotle Onassis died in 1975 and, widowed for a second time, Jackie returned permanently to New York.

In 1975 she began working as a book editor at Viking amidst much speculation about whether or not she would be able to get along with her fellow workers, or if her very presence would make it difficult for the office to function. She quickly adapted to her new job and remained at Viking until she resigned in 1977. In 1978 she took a job as an associate editor at Doubleday Publishing where she continued to work into the 1990s. In 1982 she was promoted to full editor and later became a senior editor.

In 1994 Jackie Kennedy made public the information that she was being treated for non-Hodgkin's lymphoma and that her condition was responding well to therapy. However, the disease proved fatal on May 19, 1994. She is buried next to John F. Kennedy in Arlington National Cemetary.

Further Reading

There are several biographies of Jacqueline Kennedy Onassis, including *Jackie* by Illie Frishauer (1976), *Jacqueline Bouvier Kennedy Onassis* by Stephen Birmingham (1978), *Jackie Oh!* by Kitty Kelly (1978), and *A Woman Named Jackie* by C. David Heymann (1989). ☐

Juan de Oñate

The Spanish explorer Juan de Oñate (ca. 1549-ca. 1624), although considered a failure by his monarch, deserves to be called the founder of New Mexico. The colony he established eventually became one of Spain's most important northern outposts.

Juan de Oñate was born in Mexico. His father, Don Cristóbal de Oñate, was one of the discoverers and developers of the rich Zacatecan mines and a wealthy and influential citizen. Little is known of Juan de Oñate's early life, although he claimed to have helped develop the mines in the San Luis Potosi district and to have served with Viceroy Luis de Velasco in wars against the hostile Indians of northern Mexico. He married Doña Isabel de Tolosa, granddaughter of Hernán Cortés and great-granddaughter of the last Aztec ruler, Montezuma II.

In 1583 the combined effects of the voyage of Sir Francis Drake to California and continual pleas of the Church to establish missions among the Pueblo Indians led Philip II of Spain to issue a royal order for the "discovery, pacification and settlement of the province of New Mexico." Revived stories of rich mineral deposits in the north excited great interest, and many applied to lead the expedition, hoping to gain wealth and fame. Finally, in 1595, Oñate received the contract on the provision that he raise a force of 200 men and undertake most of the expenses of colonization. In return the King named Oñate governor and *adelantado* of New Mexico.

After numerous delays, the expedition, consisting of about 400 persons, left Santa Bárbara in January 1598. In May the party crossed the Rio Grande at El Paso and moved north along the trail known as the Jornada del Muerto to a point above present-day Santa Fe where they established San Juan de los Caballeros. During the next few years the tiny colony struggled for existence. Oñate and his captains undertook several expeditions, including one north into Kansas and another west to the Gulf of California, but they discovered no new civilizations, nor were they able to find the elusive mineral wealth of the region.

Meanwhile, the Indians became increasingly hostile. The Ácoma Pueblo rose in a revolt which Oñate suppressed only with great bloodshed. Despite Oñate's best efforts, the colony did not prosper, and the people blamed the governor for all their troubles. In 1607 Oñate, noting that he had already spent 400,000 pesos on New Mexico, asked to be relieved of the governorship. He returned to Mexico about 1609 to answer charges of maladministration. Convicted of disobedience of orders and mistreatment of the Indians and colonists, Oñate appealed the verdict and may have been successful in obtaining a pardon before his death.

Further Reading

The best books on Oñate are George P. Hammond, *Don Juan de Oñate and the Founding of New Mexico* (1927), and *Don Juan de Oñate: Colonizer of New Mexico,* edited and translated by George P. Hammond and Agapito Rey (2 vols., 1953). Gaspar Pérez de Villagrá, *History of New Mexico* (1933), is an interesting contemporary account by one of the New Mexican colonists. See also Paul Horgan, *The Habit of Empire* (1939).

Additional Sources

Simmons, Marc., *The last conquistador: Juan de Oñate and the settling of the far Southwest,* Norman: University of Oklahoma Press, 1991. □

Eugene O'Neill

Eugene O'Neill (1888-1953) was among the foremost dramatists of the America theater. His main concern was with the anguish and turmoil that wrack the spirits of sensitive people.

Eugene O'Neill set out to create meaningful drama in America at a time when the barriers against it were significant. Although outstanding dramatists were getting productions throughout Europe, American dramatists were locked into standard commercial practices by the monopolistic forces controlling the theater. As a result, by the time of O'Neill's first production (1916), the American theater was a quarter century behind European theater. Twenty years later, when O'Neill received the Nobel Prize for literature, America had assumed a leadership position in world drama; O'Neill was preeminent in this rise.

Eugene O'Neill was born on Oct. 16, 1888, in New York City at a hotel on Broadway. His father was James O'Neill, an outstanding romantic actor. Eugene's mother was Ella Quinlan. Eugene had two brothers, James, Jr. (born 1878), and Edmund (born 1883). Edmund's death 2 years later brought deep feelings of guilt into the family.

Eugene spent his first 7 years on tour with his parents. A succession of dreary hotel rooms and a mother addicted to drugs left their impact upon him. He also received a total exposure to theater.

From the age of 7 to 12, Eugene was taught by nuns. His next 2 years were spent under the Christian Brothers. When he rebelled against any further Catholic education, his parents sent him to Betts Academy in Connecticut for high school. He was also learning about life at this time under the guidance of his brother, Jamie, who "made sin easy for him." Eugene's formal education ended with an unfinished year at Princeton University in 1907. By this time his three main interests were evident: books, alcohol, and prostitutes.

O'Neill worked halfheartedly for a mail-order firm until the fall of 1908. In 1909 he secretly married Kathleen Jenkins before leaving on a mining expedition to Honduras, where he contracted malaria. Returning in April 1910, he revealed his marriage because of Kathleen's pregnancy. Eugene O'Neill, Jr., was born the next month.

O'Neill shipped out as a seaman in 1910 and did odd jobs in Buenos Aires, spending almost 6 months as a panhandler on the waterfront before going to sea again. Back in New York in 1911, he spent several weeks drinking in Jimmy the Priest's saloon before shipping out to England. He returned in August to his old hangout. Almost half his published plays show his interest in the sea.

In 1912 O'Neill hit bottom. His marriage was dissolved, his attempt at suicide failed, and he contracted tuberculosis. But he also decided to become a dramatist. He was released from the sanitarium in June 1913.

Early Plays

Tall and thin, dark-eyed and handsome, with a brooding sensitivity, O'Neill was a man of many paradoxical qualities. Though he was ready to work, he was by no means ready to change his way of living completely. During the next year he wrote prolifically. Except for *Bound East for Cardiff,* these early plays are finger exercises. With his father's aid, five of these one-act plays were published in 1914. On the basis of this work and with the assistance of the critic Clayton Hamilton, O'Neill joined George Pierce Baker's playwriting class at Harvard in September 1914.

O'Neill planned to return to Harvard in the fall of 1915 but ended up instead at the "Hell Hole," a combination hotel and saloon in New York City, where he drank heavily and produced nothing. He next joined the Provincetown Players on Cape Cod in Massachusetts. The Players' production of *Bound East for Cardiff* in 1916 signaled a new era in American drama. By the end of 1918, the Players had produced 10 of O'Neill's plays. Such excellent exposure, combined with the support of the critic George Jean Nathan, rocketed O'Neill into prominence. His plays of the sea were most successful, particularly *Bound East for Cardiff* (1916), *In the Zone* (1917), *The Long Voyage Home* (1917), and *The Moon of the Caribbees* (1918), which are sometimes produced together under the title of *S.S. Glencairn*.

In his early writing O'Neill concentrated heavily on the one-act form. His apprenticeship in this form culminated in great success with the production of his full-length *Beyond the Horizon* (1920), for which he won his first Pulitzer Prize. The play is definitely indebted to the one-act form in its structure. Although the drama is essentially naturalistic, O'Neill elevated both characterization and dialogue, and for the first time, by adding a poetic and articulate character, he gave himself the opportunity to reach high dramatic moments.

In 1918 O'Neill married Agnes Boulton. They had a son, Shane, and a daughter, Oona. Meanwhile, O'Neill met his son Eugene, Jr., for the first time in 1922, when the boy was 12 years old. O'Neill's family died in close succession: his father (1920), mother (1922), and brother (1923). Following this tumult, his marriage was troubled; O'Neill had fallen in love with Carlotta Monterey. In 1928 he left Agnes Boulton, divorced in 1929, and soon married Carlotta.

In spite of pressures in his personal life, O'Neill was incredibly productive. In the 15 years following the appearance of *Beyond the Horizon*, 21 plays were produced. Always daring in his conceptions, always willing to experiment, he brought forth both brilliant successes and atrocious failures.

The Successes

O'Neill's successful plays reveal interesting experimentation—apart from *Anna Christie* (1921), a rather standardly organized and realistic play with some romantic overtones which was awarded a Pulitzer Prize, and *Ah, Wilderness!* (1933), a surprisingly nostalgic comedy unique in the O'Neill canon (both were later adapted to the musical stage). *The Emperor Jones* (1920) is a superb theatrical piece in which Brutus Jones moves from reality, to conscious memories of his past, to subconscious roots of his ancient heritage, as he flees for his life. The play ends in the reality of his death. Another expressionistic piece, *The Hairy Ape* (1922), traces the path of a burly stoker shocked into self-awareness by a decadent society woman, as he tries to find out where he belongs in the world.

Two plays deal with the human propensity to hide behind masks. In *The Great God Brown* (1926), masks are actually used. On his death, Dion Anthony wills his mask to William Brown, who then lives under the impact of dual masks. In *Strange Interlude* (1928), a massive treatment of the many roles of women as seen in the life of Nina Leeds, O'Neill used spoken "asides" (interior monologues) to disclose his characters' hidden and normally unspoken thoughts. For this play he received his third Pulitzer Prize.

The final successes stem from O'Neill's desire to reach the essence of tragedy. In *Desire under the Elms* (1924), he probed the tumult of passions burning deep on a New England farm. The peace which Eben and Abby find in their love is decidedly convincing. Ephraim's obdurate persistence also carries the ring of universal truth. *Mourning Becomes Electra* (1931), also set in New England, is O'Neill's version of Aeschylus's *Oresteia*. The ancient guilt of the house of Atreus is converted into Freudian terms in the depiction of the Mannon family. O'Neill's "Electra," Lavinia, is powerfully characterized, and her final expiation is a moving end to a most worthy play.

Mixed Receptions and Disasters

A grim and repulsive drama, *Diff'rent* (1920), a rather psychopathic portrait of a sexually obsessed woman, garnered mixed reviews. *The Straw* (1921), a story of love and selfishness dating back to O'Neill's experiences in the sanitarium, was generally accepted. Though *All God's Chillun Got Wings* (1924) received tremendous publicity before its opening, O'Neill failed to deeply penetrate the realms of myth and bigotry. However, he did achieve a Job-like quality for the black husband. Babbitt and Marco Polo were aligned in a satiric and poetic expression in *Marco Millions* (1928). The play's best aspect is its pageantry; the poetry is somewhat disappointing.

Lazarus Laughed (1928) was not produced commercially in New York. Essentially a religious-philosophical epic, the play has some interesting scenes but a ponderous, turgid style.

Eight plays were disasters: *Chris Christopherson* (1920), *Gold*, (1921), *The First Man* (1922), *Welded* (1924), *The Ancient Mariner* (1924), a dramatization of Coleridge's poem, *The Fountain* (1925), *Dynamo* (1929), and *Days without End* (1934).

Later Life

Carlotta Monterey brought a sense of order to O'Neill's life. His health deteriorated rapidly from 1937 on, but her care helped him remain productive, though their marriage was not without furor.

In addition to the physical and psychological burdens of his poor health, O'Neill was also disturbed by his continued inability to establish relationships with his children. Eugene, Jr., died by suicide in 1950. Shane became addicted to drugs. Oona was ignored by her father after her marriage to actor Charlie Chaplin. The tragic lack of communication for which O'Neill had accused his father was a major flaw in his own relationships with his children. Indeed, he even excluded Shane and Oona from his will. When O'Neill knew that death was near, one of his final actions was to tear up six of his unfinished cycle plays rather than have them rewritten by someone else. These plays, tentatively entitled "A Tale of Possessors Self-dispossessed," were part of a great cycle of 9 to 11 plays which would follow the lives of one family in America. O'Neill's health prevented him from completing them. He died on Nov. 27, 1953.

Last Plays

With the exception of *The Iceman Cometh* (1946), all of O'Neill's late works received their New York production after his death. *The Iceman Cometh,* with its exhibition of pipe dreams in Harry Hope's saloon, fascinated audiences and overcame almost universal complaints about its length. *Long Day's Journey into Night* (1956), autobiographical in its totality, devoid of theatrical effects, utterly scathing in its insistence on truth, showed O'Neill at the height of his dramatic power. It received the Pulitzer Prize.

A Moon for the Misbegotten (1957) and *A Touch of the Poet* (1958), inevitably measured against the brilliance of *Long Day's Journey into Night,* were found to be of a lesser magnitude. In *A Moon for the Misbegotten ,* O'Neill focuses on his brother Jamie. Among all his late plays with their searching realism, *A Touch of the Poet* has the strongest elements of romantic warmth. *Hughie* (1964) offers nothing new in its treatment of illusion. *More Stately Mansions* (1967), a sequel to *A Touch of the Poet,* is not outstanding.

Further Reading

Barbara and Arthur Gelb, *O'Neill* (1962), is the indispensable biography. Doris Alexander, *The Tempering of Eugene O'Neill* (1962), and Louis Sheaffer, *O'Neill, Son and Playwright* (1968), give effective biographical pictures of O'Neill's development period. Agnes Boulton, *Part of a Long Story* (1958), is an account by O'Neill's first wife, and Croswell Bowen, *The Curse of the Misbegotten* (1958), was written with the assistance of O'Neill's son Shane.

Of the numerous critical assessments of his work, particularly valuable are Sophus Keith Winther, *Eugene O'Neill: A Critical Study* (1934; 2d ed. 1961); Edwin A. Engel, *The Haunted Heroes of Eugene O'Neill* (1953); and Doris V. Falk, *Eugene O'Neill and the Tragic Tension* (1958). Interesting criticisms are in Oscar Cargill, N. Bryllion Fagin, and William J. Fisher, *O'Neill and His Plays* (1961), and John Gassner, *O'Neill* (1964). Also worth attention are Barrett H. Clark, *Eugene O'Neill: The Man and His Plays* (1926; rev. ed. 1947); Clifford Leech, *Eugene O'Neill* (1963); and Frederic Carpenter, *Eugene O'Neill* (1964). Jordan Y. Miller, *Eugene O'Neill and the American Critic* (1962), is a most helpful bibliographic work.

For background the following books are recommended: Montrose J. Moses, *The American Dramatist* (1911; rev. ed. 1925); Isaac Goldberg, *The Theatre of George Jean Nathan* (1926); and Joseph Wood Krutch, *The American Drama since 1918* (1939; rev. ed. 1957). □

Terence Marne O'Neill

Prime minister of Northern Ireland from 1963 to 1969, Terence O'Neill (1914-1990) strived to achieve a reconciliation between Catholics and Protestants. However, his efforts proved ineffectual and he resigned from office.

Captain Terence Marne O'Neill, created Lord O'Neill of the Maine in 1970, came from an impeccable Anglo-Irish establishment family which included the ancient O'Neills of Ulster and the English Chichesters, a leading family in the same area since the seventeenth century. Educated privately and at Eton, he served throughout World War II in the Irish Guards, the same regiment as his father, who was killed in December 1914, three months after his son's birth.

His upbringing on the fringes of a great family with the strong influences of private school and army molded his character and outlook, and he was later to find it difficult to relate to the ordinary people of Northern Ireland. Familiar with top Unionist circles from family visits, his first protracted residence in the province was after 1946 when he was nominated—and returned unopposed—to the Northern Ireland Parliament for the constituency of Bannside, County Antrim.

Under the premiership of Sir Basil Brooke (created Lord Brookeborough in 1952), he served as parliamentary secretary to the minister of health (1948-1952), deputy speaker of the House of Commons (1953-1956), and minister of home affairs briefly in 1956. He then became minister for finance in 1956, serving in that office until he succeeded Brookeborough as prime minister in 1963.

Although confirmed as party leader and prime minister by party and Unionist council members in 1963, O'Neill was not the unanimous choice, and his determination to bring political reform to a somewhat backward and conser-

vative area met resistance from the beginning. Northern Ireland was already embarked on a program of economic transformation from old to new industry and was experiencing modernization in almost every sphere of social life, especially in health, education, and welfare. O'Neill realized the need to accompany these changes with matching political progress to heal sectarian differences, to improve the democratic processes, and to remove discriminating practices in such areas as employment, housing, and local government where for historical reasons these still persisted. His vision of economic and social modernization could be widely shared, but his insistence on equal opportunity throughout the political and social system seemed to threaten the Unionist monopoly of power, and to some even the stability of the union of Northern Ireland with Britain. His inability to reassure his own supporters on the one hand or to win over traditional opponents on the other eventually brought his premiership to an end in 1969.

His courageous, if not always sensitive, efforts must be applauded. He inaugurated better relations with the Irish Republic, receiving Prime Minister Sean Lemass in Belfast in January 1965 and soon paying a return visit. He looked, equally, for a better accommodation of the political ambitions of Northern Ireland's own Roman Catholic (and traditionally nationalist) community: a community increasingly better educated and prosperous under the postwar economic and social development of the province. To both trends die-hard Unionists (some within his own cabinet, including Brian Faulkner and William Craig) and more extreme Protestants, especially the Reverend Ian K. Paisley, took increasing exception, while the bane of contemporary Ireland—the persistent celebration of divisive anniversaries—provided ample opportunity to create trouble.

In 1966 the 50th anniversary of Dublin's 1916 uprising gave traditional opponents of Unionism the chance to demonstrate; then in 1967 more modern expression to non-Unionist discontent was given by the founding of the Northern Ireland Civil Rights Association. Annual Orange marches became increasingly the focus of Unionist discontent at concessions to "disloyal" elements of the population, and open conflict grew until violence burst onto the streets in October 1968. Two months later O'Neill announced a reform program: a points system of public housing allocation; an ombudsman; the end of the business vote in local council elections; a review of security legislation; and the establishment of a Londonderry Development Commission.

Amid growing Unionist division O'Neill held an election in February 1969, appealing to voters directly and in many cases supporting his own candidates against hardline official Unionist party nominees. The outcome did not provide a sufficiently strong base from which to proceed with further reforms (the existing package proved quick to anger extreme Protestant Unionists, but slow to confer benefit on moderate Catholic citizens) and on April 28, 1969, O'Neill resigned as premier. He did succeed, as a last achievement on April 23, in reforming the local council franchise to bring it into line with the rest of the United Kingdom ("one man one vote").

O'Neill, with his wife Jean (née Whitaker; they were married in 1944 and had two children), lived largely in England after his retirement from politics. In retrospect it might be fair to say that he was the wrong man with the right ideas: that he lacked the political sensitivity and dexterity to sustain the balancing act of encouraging Catholic hopes while at the same time allaying Protestant fears. He was ill-served by a Unionist Party traditionally based upon the sectarian domination of Protestant over Catholic, backed up by an Orange Order less concerned with constitutional defense than anti-Catholic attack. The Orange Order was sufficiently decentralized in organization for autonomous constituencies to frustrate liberalization from the center. O'Neill was unable to rise above these traditional elements and the religious extremism that accompanied them and in the end became a victim of their combined wrath.

Further Reading

The Autobiography of Terence O'Neill (1972); also the autobiographical *Ulster at the Crossroads* (1969), which has an introduction by John Cole; O'Neill's premiership is covered in F. S. L. Lyons' *Ireland since the Famine* (1971); Patrick Buckland, *A History of Northern Ireland* (1981); and David Harkness, *N. Ireland since 1920* (1983); P. Bew, P. Gibbon, and H. Patterson, *The State in Northern Ireland 1921-72* (1979); an outline of his career is contained in W. D. Flackes, *Northern Ireland: A Political Directory 1968-83* (1983); and in D. J. Hickey and J. E. Doherty, *A Dictionary of Irish History since 1800* (1980); *New York Times,* June 14, 1990. □

Thomas P. O'Neill

After a 16-year career in the Massachusetts legislature, Thomas P. "Tip" O'Neill (1912-1994) won election as a Democrat to the U.S. House of Representatives in 1952. He was easily re-elected thereafter, rising to majority whip, then majority leader, and finally to Speaker of the House, 1977-1987.

Thomas Philip O'Neill, Jr., was born in Cambridge, Massachusetts, on December 9, 1912, the third child of Thomas P. and Rose Ann Tolan O'Neill. His father was a bricklayer and a professional politician, serving on the Cambridge City Council and then as sewer commissioner for that city. Young O'Neill, a rabid baseball fan, acquired the nickname "Tip" after a major league ballplayer also named O'Neill.

His mother having died within nine months of his birth, "Tip" was raised by his father with the help of a housekeeper before his father remarried. A mediocre student at the St. John's parochial school but a social leader, "Tip" dreamed of becoming mayor of Cambridge (a goal befitting his father's oft-repeated maxim, "all politics is local"). At 15 O'Neill worked locally in the presidential campaign of fellow Irish Catholic Al Smith.

After brief experience as a truck driver, O'Neill enrolled in 1933 at Boston College, where he pursued a liberal arts education while continuing to drive a truck and supplementing his income by skillful poker-playing. Following graduation in 1936 he found law school not to his liking and embarked directly on a political career.

Professional Politician

After experiencing the only electoral defeat he would ever suffer (for Cambridge City Council, while a college senior), O'Neill won election to the Massachusetts State House of Representatives as a Democrat in 1936. With his party vastly outnumbered, he could do little but concentrate on patronage—which he did, arranging for the hiring of hundreds of his constituents for public service work. In these early years O'Neill worked between legislative sessions in the Cambridge city treasurer's office.

In June 1941 he married former schoolmate Mildred Anne Miller, with whom he had five children: Rosemary, Thomas P. III (later lieutenant governor of Massachusetts), Susan, Christopher, and Michael. He improved his financial situation in the 1940s when, evicted from his city job by political rivals, he entered into the insurance business—an enterprise he continued for over two decades. He did not serve in the military during World War II, originally receiving exemption to serve in the legislature and then receiving a physical deferment due to mild diabetes.

Popular among party colleagues in the state legislature, in 1946 O'Neill was elected House minority leader. (That same year he unsuccessfully supported a friend against young John F. Kennedy for the Democratic House nomina-

tion in his home congressional district.) As minority leader O'Neill's greatest achievement was helping to organize a successful strategy in 1948 to elect a Democratic majority to the Massachusetts lower house. The Democrats' narrow victory made O'Neill the youngest Speaker in the history of the Massachusetts legislature. He was a highly effective Speaker, proving adept at "headcounting," producing strong party unity, and helping ensure passage of the new Democratic governor's so-called "Little New Deal." Respected for his fairness, the affable O'Neill was willing to apply pressure, when necessary, to keep his troops in line. In 1950 he again masterminded the Democrats' statewide victory. Both he and other Democrats expected he would ultimately become governor.

A Long-time Congressman

In 1952 O'Neill succeeded to John Kennedy's House seat (as Kennedy advanced to the Senate) after winning a hard-fought primary—the last close electoral contest he would face. As a protege of House Majority Leader John McCormack, also of Massachusetts, he rapidly gained access to the inner circle of power in the House. Through the sponsorship of McCormack and powerful Speaker Sam Rayburn, O'Neill was placed in 1955 on the important Rules Committee—as a "loyalist" of the House Democratic leadership. Over the next several years he attained little national visibility but gained a reputation as a shrewd and helpful master of internal House process and a staunch party regular—a "politician's politician."

Democratic control of the White House in the 1960s enabled O'Neill to play a constructive role as he helped to pass the New Frontier and Great Society legislative programs. His only significant rebellion against the Democratic administrations was on the federal school-aid bill, which he opposed.

In 1967 O'Neill revised his image as an unwavering party loyalist by becoming the first "establishment" Democrat to break with President Johnson over the Vietnam War, even backing the anti-war candidacy of Senator Eugene McCarthy for the 1968 presidential nomination. By the early 1970s this stance, combined with his support for a number of House procedural reforms, won him a unique reputation as an old-style politician with reform sympathies. He was thus a popular choice when selected in 1971 by a new Democratic House leadership team to be majority whip.

In less than two years O'Neill rose to the post of majority leader, after the incumbent (Representative Hale Boggs) disappeared and was presumed dead in an airplane crash. As he had done as majority whip, O'Neill brought energy to this new post, eclipsing the indecisive Carl Albert, Speaker of the House during much of the 1970s. Remaining a strong partisan, O'Neill took a cautious line during the Watergate crisis. Still, he was a powerful force in urging his colleagues to prepare for impeachment proceedings against President Nixon in early 1974. After Nixon's resignation O'Neill actively supported legislative initiatives to limit the budget and war-making powers of the presidency. Toward Nixon's successor, his old friend Gerald Ford, O'Neill was personally cordial but politically uncompromising. His deep instinct for the underdog, however, led him to avoid criticizing Ford when the latter gave Nixon a full pardon.

Speaker of the House

When O'Neill succeeded Albert as Speaker in 1977 (without opposition), a new president of his own party moved into the White House: Jimmy Carter. Opposites in personality and divided over the necessity of compromise between Congress and the White House (O'Neill had always thought compromise the essence of politics), O'Neill and Carter nevertheless developed a friendly relationship. The Speaker loyally backed Carter's policies in the House, helping to pass both the president's energy package and a bill creating a Department of Education. O'Neill advised Carter to pay more attention to the domestic problems of inflation and energy shortages and believed, with other traditional liberals, that the president was too conservative in his policies. Yet when Edward Kennedy challenged Carter for the 1980 Democratic nomination, O'Neill remained neutral and eventually served as chairman of the 1980 convention controlled by the president's supporters. During his first years as Speaker one of O'Neill's most notable achievements was passage of a strong code of ethics for House members.

Republican successes in the 1980 elections greatly altered O'Neill's situation. With Ronald Reagan in the White House and the Senate under Republican Party control, the Speaker stood as the top-ranking elected leader of his party. Never a television personality, he made himself very accessible to the press and increasingly spoke out on the major issues. It was as party strategist, however, that he had greatest impact. Unsuccessful in his efforts to block Reagan's sharp reductions in domestic spending and "supply side" tax reductions in 1981, O'Neill kept fellow Democrats from agreeing to a bipartisan compromise on the troubled Social Security System, thereby keeping the subject alive as an issue (along with the 1981 tax measure) for the upcoming congressional elections. The Democrats' strong showing in 1982 vindicated the strategy.

O'Neill enjoyed greater power and prestige in dealing with the Reagan administration after 1982. The president then lacked the working majority of Republicans and conservative Democrats that he had relied on previously and thus had to be more accommodating towards the Speaker and his followers. In early 1984, however, O'Neill announced he would seek only one more House term. Winning re-election easily (as he had for 30 years), he resumed his role as leader of the opposition as Reagan began his second term. Truly a transitional figure between the old politics and the new, he was rated among the strongest House Speakers in history upon his retirement in 1987.

O'Neill's memoirs, *Man of the House* (1987), written with William Novak, became a best-seller. He also wrote *All Politics is Local,* with Gary Hymel. (1994) Tip O'Neill died in Boston, at the age of 82.

Further Reading

The only book-length treatment of O'Neill's life was Paul Clancy and Shirley Elder, *Tip: A Biography of Thomas P. O'Neill,*

Speaker of the House (1980). Jimmy Breslin's *How the Good Guys Finally Won* (1975) discussed at length O'Neill's role in House activities related to Watergate. In 1987 O'Neill with William Novak wrote *Man of the House: The Life and Political Memoirs of Speaker Tip O'Neill.* □

Ong Teng Cheong

Singapore's fifth president, Ong Teng Cheong (born 1936) took office in 1993. It was the climax of Ong's 21-year career as a member of Parliament (MP), cabinet minister, party chairman, and trade union chief.

Ong Teng Cheong was born in Singapore on January 22, 1936. He was educated at the Chinese High School in Singapore and proceeded to the University of Adelaide in Australia, to study architecture. He graduated with a bachelor's degree in architecture in 1961 and worked as an architect in Adelaide for two years before returning to Singapore in 1964. While in Adelaide he married Ling Siew May, also an architect. Ong worked as an architect in the private sector for nearly two years after returning to Singapore. In September 1965 he left for the United Kingdom to pursue a post-graduate degree in town planning at the University of Liverpool on a Colombo Plan scholarship. He obtained his master's degree in civic design (town planning) in 1967.

Ong returned to Singapore in 1967 and joined the planning department of the ministry of national development. However, he was soon sent to the United Nations Development Program (UNDP) special fund for assistance in urban renewal and development project, where he participated in the formulation of a long-term comprehensive concept plan for guiding the future physical development of his country. He had also led teams of planners in designing Telok Blangah new town and in conducting a comprehensive study of central area transportation and land use, with emphasis on the mass rapid transit (MRT). Ong left the civil service in 1971 to work as an architect and town planner in the private sector until June 1975, when he was appointed as senior minister of state for communications.

Ong's interest in community service began in the late 1960s when he assisted Hwang Soo Jin, then member of Parliament (MP) for Jalan Kayu, in his constituency work. However, his political career began after the September 1972 general election, when he was elected MP for Kim Keat constituency after winning 74 percent of the valid votes cast. Ong was among the first batch of ten People's Action Party (PAP) candidates elected into Parliament in 1972 to replace the old guard. After that he was returned as the MP for Kim Keat in 1976, 1980, 1984, and 1988. In 1991 the Kim Keat constituency became part of Toa Payoh Group Representation Constituency (GRC), but Ong succeeded in retaining his parliamentary seat.

After serving three years as senior minister of state for communications, Ong was appointed minister for communications in July 1978. He had been appointed acting minister for culture earlier in September 1977 and continued with this additional portfolio until 1980, when he was made minister for communications and labor. As minister for communications he had been concerned with the need for a mass rapid transit system and initiated detailed feasibility studies and visits to other countries. He succeeded in persuading his cabinet colleagues that Singapore needed the MRT system to improve its public transportation. During the launching of the MRT at Toa Payoh Station in November 1987, Ong said: "For me, this [the MRT] has been a 20-year love affair, from conception to delivery."

In January 1981 Ong was elected chairman of the PAP central executive committee. In May 1983 Ong was made minister without portfolio and was elected secretary-general of the National Trades Union Congress (NTUC), the country's largest trade union. During the 1985 economic recession he was able to convince workers that wage restraint was necessary. In the same year he became chairman of the Singapore Labour Foundation (SLF) and, in that role, was responsible for setting up such social and recreational facilities as the NTUC Club, the NTUC Pasir Ris Resort, and the Orchid Country Club.

In 1985 Ong was appointed second deputy prime minister. In 1990 he became deputy prime minister. Thus, when Ong resigned from the PAP in August 1993 to contest the presidential election, he wore four important hats: deputy prime minister, chairman of the PAP central executive committee, secretary-general of the NTUC, and chairman of the SLF. What greatly interested Ong was amendment number 3 to the constitution, passed by Parliament on January 3, 1991. The new law changed the institution of the presidency from a ceremonial role to an elected position with powers over government budgets and key appointments in the public service.

In endorsing Ong as its choice in the presidential election in August 1993, the *Straits Times,* the major English-language newspaper in Singapore, wrote: "He has what it takes to shape the elected presidency in the nation's best interest."

Further Reading

Most of Ong Teng Cheong's speeches from 1978 onward have been published in *Speeches,* a publication of the information division of the Ministry of Communications and Information in Singapore. However, since December 1990 *Speeches* has been published by the Ministry of Information and the Arts. Ong's most famous speech, "Bridging the perception gap," which was given on July 26, 1992, in his capacity as PAP chairman, can be found in *Petir* (August 1992). For more information on Singapore see Stella R. Quah and Jon S.T. Quah, compilers, *Singapore* (1988), which contains 764 annotated references; and Kernial S. Sandhu and Paul Wheatley, editors, *Management of Success: The Molding of Modern Singapore* (1989), which has over 40 chapters on various aspects of life in Singapore. □

Lars Onsager

Lars Onsager (1903-1976) made significant contributions to chemistry, including his developments in the Debye-Hückel theory of electrolytic dissociation and his work with non-reversable systems. He received the 1968 Nobel Prize in Chemistry.

Born in Norway, Lars Onsager received his early education there before coming to the United States in 1928 to do graduate work at Yale University. After receiving his Ph.D. in theoretical chemistry he stayed on at Yale and ultimately spent nearly all of his academic career at that institution. Onsager's first important contribution to chemical theory came in 1926 when he showed how improvements could be made in the Debye-Hückel theory of electrolytic dissociation. His later (and probably more significant) work involved non-reversible systems —systems in which differences in pressure, temperature, or some other factor are an important consideration. For his contributions in this field, Onsager received a number of important awards including the Rumford Medal of the American Academy of Arts and Sciences, the Lorentz Medal of the Royal Netherlands Academy of Sciences, and the 1968 Nobel Prize in Chemistry.

Lars Onsager was born in Oslo (then known as Christiania), Norway, on November 27, 1903. His parents were Erling Onsager, a barrister before the Norwegian Supreme

Court, and Ingrid Kirkeby Onsager. Onsager's early education was somewhat unorthodox as he was taught by private tutors, by his own mother, and at a somewhat unsatisfactory rural private school. Eventually he entered the Frogner School in Oslo and did so well that he skipped a grade and graduated a year early. Overall, his early schooling provided him with a broad liberal education in philosophy, literature, and the arts. He is said to have become particularly fond of Norwegian epics and continued to read and recite them to friends and family throughout his life.

In 1920, Onsager entered the Norges Tekniski Hoslashgskole in Trondheim where he planned to major in chemical engineering. The fact that he enrolled in a technical high school suggests that he was originally interested in practical rather than theoretical studies. Onsager had not pursued his schooling very long, however, before it became apparent that he wanted to go beyond the everyday applications of science to the theoretical background on which those applications are based. Even as a freshman in high school, he told of making a careful study of the chemical journals, in order to gain background knowledge of chemical theory.

One of the topics that caught his attention concerned the chemistry of solutions. In 1884, Svante Arrhenius had proposed a theory of ionic dissociation that explained a number of observations about the conductivity of solutions and, eventually, a number of other solution phenomena. Over the next half century, chemists worked on refining and extending the Arrhenius theory.

The next great step forward in that search occurred in 1923, when Onsager was still a student at the Tekniski Hoslashgskole. The Dutch chemist Peter Debye and the German chemist Erich Hückel, working at Zurich's Eidgenössische Technische Hochschule, had proposed a revision of the Arrhenius theory that explained some problems not yet resolved—primarily, whether ionic compounds are or are not completely dissociated ("ionized") in solution. After much experimentation, Arrhenius had observed that dissociation was not complete in all instances.

Debye and Hückel realized that ionic compounds, by their very nature, already existed in the ionic state *before* they ever enter a solution. They explained the apparent incomplete level of dissociation on the basis of the interactions among ions of opposite charges and water molecules in a solution. The Debye-Hückel mathematical formulation almost perfectly explained all the anomalies that remained in the Arrhenius theory.

Almost perfectly, but not quite, as Onsager soon observed. The value of the molar conductivity predicted by the Debye-Hückel theory was significantly different from that obtained from experiments. By 1925, Onsager had discovered the reason for this discrepancy. Debye and Hückel had assumed that most—but not all—of the ions in a solution move about randomly in "Brownian" movement . Onsager simply extended that principle to *all* of the ions in the solution. With this correction, he was able to write a new mathematical expression that improved upon the Debye-Hückel formulation.

Onsager had the opportunity in 1925 to present his views to Debye in person. Having arrived in Zurich after traveling through Denmark and Germany with one of his professors, Onsager is reported to have marched into Debye's office in Zurich and declared, "Professor Debye, your theory of electrolytes is incorrect." Debye was sufficiently impressed with the young Norwegian to offer him a research post in Zurich, a position that Onsager accepted and held for the next two years.

In 1928, Onsager emigrated to the United States where he became an associate in chemistry at Johns Hopkins University. The appointment proved to be disastrous: he was assigned to teach the introductory chemistry classes, a task for which he was completely unsuited. One of his associates, Robert H. Cole, is quoted in the *Biographical Memoirs of Fellows of the Royal Society:* "I won't say he was the world's worst lecturer, but he was certainly in contention." As a consequence, Onsager was not asked to return to Johns Hopkins after he had completed his first semester there.

Fortunately, a position was open at Brown University, and Onsager was asked by chemistry department chairman Charles A. Krauss to fill that position. During his 5-year tenure at Brown, Onsager was given a more appropriate teaching assignment, statistical mechanics. His pedagogical techniques apparently did not improve to any great extent, however; he still presented a challenge to students by speaking to the blackboard on topics that were well beyond the comprehension of many in the room.

A far more important feature of the Brown years was the theoretical research that Onsager carried out in the privacy of his own office. In this research, Onsager attempted to generalize his earlier research on the motion of ions in solution when exposed to an electrical field. In order to do so, he went back to some fundamental laws of thermodynamics, including Hermann Helmholtz's "principle of least dissipation." He was eventually able to derive a very general mathematical expression about the behavior of substances in solution, an expression now known as the Law of Reciprocal Relations .

Onsager first published the law in 1929, but continued to work on it for a number of years. In 1931, he announced a more general form of the law that applied to other nonequilibrium situations in which differences in electrical or magnetic force, temperature, pressure, or some other factor exists. The Onsager formulation was so elegant and so general that some scientists now refer to it as the Fourth Law of Thermodynamics .

The Law of Reciprocal Relations was eventually recognized as an enormous advance in theoretical chemistry, earning Onsager the Nobel Prize in 1968. However, its initial announcement provoked almost no response from his colleagues. It is not that they disputed his findings, Onsager said many years later, but just that they totally ignored them. Indeed, Onsager's research had almost no impact on chemists until after World War II had ended, more than a decade after the research was originally published.

The year 1933 was a momentous one for Onsager. It began badly when Brown ended his appointment because of financial pressures brought about by the Great Depression. His situation improved later in the year, however, when he was offered an appointment as Sterling and Gibbs Fellow at Yale. The appointment marked the beginning of an affiliation with Yale that was to continue until 1972.

Prior to assuming his new job at Yale, Onsager spent the summer in Europe. While there, he met the future Mrs. Onsager, Margarethe Arledter, the sister of the Austrian electrochemist H. Falkenhagen. The two apparently fell instantly in love, became engaged a week after meeting, and were married on September 7, 1933. The Onsagers later had three sons, Erling Frederick, Hans Tanberg, and Christian Carl, and one daughter, Inger Marie.

Onsager had no sooner assumed his post at Yale when a small problem arose: the fellowship he had been awarded was for postdoctoral studies, but Onsager had not as yet been granted a Ph.D. He had submitted an outline of his research on reciprocal relations to his alma mater, the Norges Tekniski Hoslashgskole, but the faculty there had decided that, being incomplete, it was not worthy of a doctorate. As a result, Onsager's first task at Yale was to complete a doctoral thesis. For this thesis, he submitted to the chemistry faculty a research paper on an esoteric mathematical topic. Since the thesis was outside the experience of anyone in the chemistry or physics departments, Onsager's degree was nearly awarded by the mathematics department, whose chair understood Onsager's findings quite clearly. Only at the last moment did the chemistry department relent and agree to accept the judgment of its colleagues, awarding Onsager his Ph.D. in 1935.

Onsager continued to teach statistical mechanics at Yale, although with as little success as ever. (Instead of being called "Sadistical Mechanics," as it had been by Brown students, it was now referred to as "Advanced Norwegian" by their Yale counterparts.) As always, it was Onsager's theoretical—and usually independent—research that justified his Yale salary. In his nearly four decades there, he attacked one new problem after another, usually with astounding success. Though his output was by no means prodigious, the quality and thoroughness of his research was impeccable.

During the late 1930s, Onsager worked on another of Debye's ideas, the dipole theory of dielectrics . That theory had, in general, been very successful, but could not explain the special case of liquids with high dielectric constants. By 1936, Onsager had developed a new model of dipoles that could be used to modify Debye's theory and provide accurate predictions for all cases. Onsager was apparently deeply hurt when Debye rejected his paper explaining this model for publication in the *Physikalische Zeitschrift,* which Debye edited. It would be more than a decade before the great Dutch chemist, then an American citizen, could accept Onsager's modifications of his ideas.

In the 1940s, Onsager turned his attention to the very complex issue of phase transitions in solids. He wanted to find out if the mathematical techniques of statistical mechanics could be used to derive the thermodynamic properties of such events. Although some initial progress had been made in this area, resulting in a theory known as

the Ising model, Onsager produced a spectacular breakthrough on the problem. He introduced a "trick or two" (to use his words) that had not yet occurred to (and were probably unknown to) his colleagues—the use of elegant mathematical techniques of elliptical functions and quaternion algebra. His solution to this problem was widely acclaimed.

Though his status as a non-U.S. citizen enabled him to devote his time and effort to his own research during World War II, Onsager was forbidden from contributing his significant talents to the top-secret Manhattan Project, the United State's research toward creating atomic weapons. Onsager and his wife finally did become citizens as the war drew to a close in 1945.

The postwar years saw no diminution of Onsager's energy. He continued his research on low-temperature physics and devised a theoretical explanation for the superfluidity of helium II (liquid helium). The idea, originally proposed in 1949, was arrived at independently two years later by Princeton University's Richard Feynman. Onsager also worked out original theories for the statistical properties of liquid crystals and for the electrical properties of ice. In 1951 he was given a Fulbright scholarship to work at the Cavendish Laboratory in Cambridge; there, he perfected his theory of diamagnetism in metals.

During his last years at Yale, Onsager continued to receive numerous accolades for his newly appreciated discoveries. He was awarded honorary doctorates by such noble universities as Harvard (1954), Brown (1962), Chicago (1968), Cambridge (1970), and Oxford (1971), among others. He was inducted to the National Academy of Sciences in 1947. In addition to his Nobel Prize, Onsager garnered the American Academy of Arts and Sciences' Rumford Medal in 1953 and the Lorentz Medal in 1958, as well as several medals from the American Chemical Society and the President's National Medal of Science. Upon reaching retirement age in 1972, Onsager was offered the title of emeritus professor, but without an office. Disappointed by this apparent slight, Onsager decided instead to accept an appointment as Distinguished University Professor at the University of Miami's Center for Theoretical Studies. At Miami, Onsager found two new subjects to interest him, biophysics and radiation chemistry. In neither field did he have an opportunity to make any significant contributions, however, as he died on October 5, 1976, apparently the victim of a heart attack.

Given his shortcomings as a teacher, Onsager still seems to have been universally admired and liked as a person. Though modest and self-effacing, he possessed a wry sense of humor. In *Biographical Memoirs,* he is quoted as saying of research, "There's a time to soar like an eagle, and a time to burrow like a worm. It takes a pretty sharp cookie to know when to shed the feathers and . . . to begin munching the humus." In a memorial some months after Onsager's death, Behram Kursunoglu, the director of the University of Miami's Center for Theoretical Studies, described him as a "very great man of science—with profound humanitarian and scientific qualities."

Further Reading

Biographical Memoirs of Fellows of the Royal Society, Volume 24, Royal Society (London), 1978.
Current Biography 1958, H. W. Wilson, 1958.
Nobel Lectures in Chemistry, 1963–1970, [Amsterdam], 1972.

☐

Jan Hendrik Oort

The Dutch astronomer Jan Hendrik Oort (1900-1992) overturned the idea that our sun is at the center of the Milky Way galaxy. He contributed greatly to knowledge about the structure and evolution of our galaxy, and also discovered the place of origin of most comets, the Oort Cloud.

Jan Oort was born on April 28, 1900, in the farming village of Franeker in Holland. At the age of 17 he entered the University of Groningen and earned his doctoral degree in 1926. He received the Bachiene Foundation Prize (1920), undertook research at the Leiden Observatory (1924), and lived abroad as a research associate at the Yale University Observatory (1924-1926).

In 1926 Oort became an instructor at the University of Leiden, and the following year he married Johanna M. Graadt van Roggen. They had three children, sons Coenraad and Abraham and a daughter, Marijke. Oort became a professor of astronomy (1935) and director of the observatory (1945) at the University of Leiden. In his career he was elected leader of several international astronomical groups. He received numerous awards, including the important Vetlesen Prize in 1966 from Columbia University.

Oort's early studies, under his teacher Jacobus Kapteyn, made him familiar with Kapteyn's celestial model, which placed the sun at the center of a relatively small galaxy. In 1917, however, Harlow Shapley challenged Kapteyn's model, proposing a far bigger one. Oort's first major scientific achievement was to provide observational evidence that confirmed the main features of Shapley's model. Shortly after he joined the Leiden faculty in 1926, Oort found that stars with velocities greater than about 65 kilometers per second move predominantly toward one hemisphere of the night sky. That is consistent with the theory that our solar system rotates around the distant center of our galaxy and that other solar systems move around the same center. It was the first direct evidence of the Milky Way's rotation.

From his observations and calculations, Oort was able to show that our galaxy was much bigger than previously thought and that it contained many more stars. Oort also determined that the sun was not even close to the galaxy's center. "Like a modern Copernicus, Oort showed that our position in nature's grand scheme was not so special," said Seth Shostak, a U.S. astronomer.

After World War II Oort and his associates at Leiden built a huge radio telescope to detect radio waves in hydrogen and made far-reaching discoveries on the evolution and structure of our galaxy. They found evidence that supported the hypothesis that stars are formed out of hydrogen and dust clouds; they proved the spiral structure of our galaxy and found its period of rotation to be over 200 million years; and they located and investigated the processes occurring in the galactic core and the vast corona of hydrogen encircling the galaxy. They also investigated the origin of radio signal sources, including the group of stars known as the Crab Nebula, which they demonstrated to be a remnant of the supernova that appeared in 1054. Oort was credited with promoting radio astronomy in its early years and with putting the Netherlands in the forefront of postwar astronomy.

Oort's observations showed that there is much more mass in the universe than can be detected visually. This was a pioneering recognition of the undetected "missing mass" or "dark matter" that is believed to make up more than 90 percent of the universe.

Oort is best known to casual students of astronomy for his discoveries in what to him was a sideline, the study of comets. By plotting their trajectories, Oort traced comets back to a region on the outskirts of the solar system. He theorized that in the distant past a planet that occupied a position between Mars and Jupiter exploded, sending most of its material into interstellar space, but a small percentage of the material became trapped in a region roughly 4,000 times as far away from our sun as Pluto. Fragments of this material are occasionally pulled by the gravity of the outer planets or a passing star into an orbit around the sun. The region that is the birthplace of comets became known as the Oort Cloud.

Further Reading

For a general account of Oort's work in a broader context see Otto Struve and Velta Zebergs, *Astronomy of the 20th Century* (1962). An appreciation of Oort by B. Strömgren is in Lodewijk Woltjer, ed., *Galaxies and the Universe* (1968). He is profiled in *Asimov's Biographical Encyclopedia of Science and Technology* (1976). □

Meret Oppenheim

Meret Oppenheim (1913-1985) was most known for her Surrealist objects, most notably her *Furlined Teacup*, which she created when she was only 22 years old.

Meret Oppenheim was born in 1913 near Basel, Switzerland. Perhaps her parents knew that she was to lead a creative and unorthodox life as they named her after Meretlein, the "little Meret" of a book by the Swiss-German novelist and poet Gottfried Keller. In this book Keller wrote of a little girl who was thought to bewitch all by her unconventional habits. Like her namesake, Oppenheim was also a free spirit who never felt confined by social norms.

Oppenheim grew up in Switzerland and in South Germany. Her family was quite accustomed to creative and artistic activities: her aunt, Ruth Werner, was at one time married to Hermann Hesse and her grandmother, Lise Wenger, was a writer and painter. Always receptive to new ideas, Grandmother Wenger stimulated young Meret's imagination with her drawings and stories and later encouraged and supported her choice of an artistic career.

Begins Career in Paris

Although she was an avid reader, Oppenheim felt stifled by the routine and never finished high school. In 1932, when she was nearly 18, she moved to Paris. There she enrolled in the Académie de la Grande Chaumière and lived in Montparnasse. In this famed artist's quarter of Paris Oppenheim met Alberto Giacometti, Kurt Seligmann, Sophie Taeuber, Hans Arp, Marcel Duchamp, and Max Ernst and became a model for the photographer Man Ray. Max Ernst, who shared similar artistic views, soon became a close friend.

In the fall of 1933 Arp and Giacometti asked her to exhibit with them at the Surrealist exhibition at the Salon des Indépendants. She consented and exhibited paintings for the first three years. In 1936 Oppenheim began making sculpture, producing at this time the object for which she is perhaps most known, *Fur-lined Teacup, Saucer, and Spoon* (*Déjeuner en fourure*—Lunch in fur), now at the Museum of Modern Art in New York City.

Although this work has since come to symbolize for many the Surrealist concept of "fortuitous juxtaposition," it was created by Oppenheim as the result of a conversation she had with Picasso and Dora Maar. One day, over a cup of tea at the Café de Flore, Picasso, observing the bracelet she had fashioned by wrapping wire with fur, joked that practically anything could be covered with fur. This observation led all three to point to objects that could be wrapped and Oppenheim pointed to her teacup. Several weeks later, Andre Breton asked her to contribute to the forthcoming Surrealist exhibition and, after a trip to the local discount supermarket, Oppenheim produced her now famous object.

Yet the strangely juxtaposed fur and cup was not the only object created by Oppenheim to cause a furor at this Surrealist show. *Ma Gouvernante, My Nurse, mein Kindermadchen,* was also on view. Again, Oppenheim joined images that led to new and unexpected associations. In this work, white linen pumps are bound together with string, the heels adorned with chef's "boots" or cuffs, and then placed on a platter so that they look like a pair of lamb chops. The cuffs and white shoes remind us of the uniform and headdress of the nanny, and the sculpture can be read on one level as a defiance of authority and the civilizing rule of the governess. Yet at the same time Oppenheim plays on the double meaning of the images as the shoes, paired, can also recall a woman's "chops," or legs. Oppenheim's "getting back" at her nanny apparently hit its mark, as the original was destroyed at the gallery by a woman "in a fit of rage" and was lost until 1967, when Oppenheim made a replica.

The last piece Oppenheim exhibited in Paris before the war was the *Table with Bird's Feet*. This work points to the organic base of much of her work, as she often linked natural images, such as a bird, to typical, functional manmade objects, such as a table. In 1959 she reinterpreted this theme in a different way. For a spring feast given for a group of friends, she served the banquet on the nude body of one of the participants. Although she chose here a woman as a symbol of nurturance, she emphasized that "it was not just men, not a naked woman for men only, but a fertility rite for women and men. A different Easter." Oppenheim repeated this event in December 1959 at Breton's request as a celebration of Eros for the opening of the Exposition Internationale du Surréalisme at the Cordier Gallery in Paris.

Twenty Years of Depression

Oppenheim was forced to leave Paris in 1937. The war and Hitler's anti-Semitism caused her father, of Jewish descent, to give up his medical practice in Germany and return to Switzerland. As a result, he was unable to contribute to Oppenheim's support. After an unsuccessful attempt at jewelry and fashion design, Oppenheim returned to Basel. She studied art restoration for two years and thereafter made her living restoring paintings.

With her return to Switzerland, Oppenheim virtually disappeared from public view for almost 20 years. She had experienced depressions in Paris, and with her return to Basel these depressions became a permanent state. She later described the 1940s and early 1950s as a period of "crisis like many artists go through," but for many years she was unable to produce any art. Gradually, in the mid-1950s, she began working again. In 1956 she had her first Paris one-person show. In 1958 she compiled an autobiographical chronicle consisting of photographs, mementos, and commentary. She also made the model for her first large scale sculpture, *Green Spectator*. Although completed in 1959, *Green Spectator* was based on sketches made in 1933. This method of using ideas and sketches from earlier periods of her life became a regular working procedure and can be seen as her way of integrating past and present time.

In her juxtaposition of natural and organic forms and her use of archetypal images and dream and memory, Oppenheim was often associated with Surrealism and this movement's method of using the unconscious to retrieve universal themes. Indeed, as she once stated, "Artists, poets keep the passage to the unconscious open. . . . The unconscious is the only place from which help and advice can come to us." Yet despite these close ties, Oppenheim's works always emphasize an intuitive interpretation of Surrealist themes. Thus she chose organic, primitive creatures such as serpents, fish, butterflies, or caterpillars as her primary subject matter, often giving new meanings to these images. The serpent, for example, frequently appears in Oppenheim's paintings and sculpture, but in a fashion quite different from Freud or Christian tradition. In her 1972 painting *The Secret of Vegetation,* for example, Oppenheim resurrects the ancient, pre-Christian view of the snake as a divine aspect of nature; that is, as a creative and constructive force rather than a destructive one, as a natural element that joins together spirit and matter. In *Old Snake Nature* the serpent takes on a more three-dimensional presence as it is portrayed with its head peering out of a sack of coal. Again Oppenheim describes the snake as it was understood in ancient cultures—as part of and growing out of the material of nature from which it had been formed.

Oppenheim's work should not be interpreted, however, as advancing a feminist or matrilineal view of creative activity. Rather, like Carl Jung, Oppenheim sought to portray through her work the idea of balance—a balance of the male and female elements, the intellect with the emotive, the intuitive with the objective.

Oppenheim lived a long and creative life, dying in 1985 at the age of 72. She remained active until the time of her death, writing, lecturing, and making art.

Further Reading

The most useful reference on Meret Oppenheim remains a catalogue from an exhibition of her work: *Meret Oppenheim,* Museum der Stadt Solothurn (1974). Another good source is *Meret Oppenheim,* Moderna Museet Stockholm (1967). ☐

J. Robert Oppenheimer

The American physicist J. Robert Oppenheimer (1904-1967) made fundamental contributions to theoretical physics and was director of the atomic energy research project at Los Alamos, N.Mex.

On April 22, 1904, J. Robert Oppenheimer, whose father was a German immigrant and wealthy textile importer, was born in New York City. After attending the Ethical Culture School in New York, where his lifelong devotion to literature, the arts, and science was nurtured, he entered Harvard University in 1922 and completed his bachelor's degree in 3 years. He required only 2 additional years of study at Cambridge University and the University of Göttingen to complete his doctoral degree in 1927.

Following 2 years of postdoctoral study at home and abroad on fellowships, Oppenheimer became associate professor of physics at the California Institute of Technology in Pasadena. Almost immediately, however, he began spending part of each academic year at the University of California at Berkeley, and he simultaneously rose through the academic ranks at both institutions. His teaching and research abilities were so exceptional and his personal magnetism was so great that many of his students followed him in his annual Berkeley-Pasadena pilgrimages, often willingly repeating the courses he offered. In general, by attracting and training an unusually large number of highly competent physicists, Oppenheimer, more than any other individual, was responsible for moving theoretical physics in America from a position of obscurity into one of preeminence in the world.

Oppenheimer's own researches between 1926 and 1942 took root in his extremely insightful exploitation of the recently discovered quantum mechanics of Werner Heisenberg, Erwin Schrödinger, Paul Dirac, Max Born, and others. With Born he developed a now-standard quantum theoretical understanding of molecules and their spectra. He undertook extensive investigations on processes involving transitions to the continuous spectrum, showing, for example, how to understand the photoelectric effect quantummechanically. He explored electron capture and exchange processes, as well as electron-atom collision processes. In 1930 he presented a cogent symmetry argument that was later recognized to be tantamount to the prediction of the positive electron, or positron. He studied the production of cosmic-ray showers. He explored various problems in quantum electrodynamics, as well as the properties and role of the meson in nuclear forces. He helped develop the so-called Oppenheimer-Phillips interpretation of deuteronnuclear reactions, which eventually led to great insight into the structure of the nucleus. In all of these theoretical investigations—and many more could be cited—Oppenheimer displayed his genius in implementing Wolfgang Pauli's conviction that a physicist should concern himself first and foremost with those problems on the very frontiers of current knowledge.

To the general public, Oppenheimer, as a scientist, is best known for his role in directing the development of the atomic bomb at Los Alamos, the laboratory high on a New Mexican mesa at a site he chose. Many of America's foremost physicists were persuaded to come with their families to this isolated laboratory to beat the Germans in the development of the most awesome weapon of destruction in human history. When all of the huge and unique problems were solved, and the test bomb was exploded on July 16, 1945, in the desert near Alamogordo, N. Mex., Oppenheimer was deeply shaken. He thought of the words from the *Bhagavad-Gita:* "If the radiance of a thousands suns/ Were to burst into the sky/That would be like/The splendor of the Mighty One. . . . / I am become Death, the shatterer of worlds." Not much later Hiroshima and Nagasaki were obliterated.

Oppenheimer was a complex man, one who could inspire distrust as well as utter devotion, and one who could commit indiscretions as well as be a scientist of faultless integrity. After the war, his early left-wing sympathies, inflated by Senator Joseph McCarthy and his coterie of witchhunters, made Oppenheimer the defendant in perhaps the most celebrated trial since the time of Galileo. In spite of the fact that Oppenheimer's past associations had aroused no undue concern earlier—he had received the coveted Presidential Medal of Merit in 1946 and had been serving on the highest policy-making committees—his security clearance was revoked, deeply shocking the vast majority of his fellow scientists. Not until 1961, when President John F. Kennedy made the decision to give the Fermi Award to Oppenheimer (it was actually presented in 1963 by President Lyndon B. Johnson), was a significant attempt made to publicly clear Oppenheimer's name. In the interim, Oppenheimer had been serving as the director of the Institute for Advanced Study in Princeton, giving his splendid administrative and technical talents to the young group of highly gifted physicists who had gathered there.

Oppenheimer will remain a subject of study, discussion, controversy, and admiration for years to come. His profound concern for uniting the intellectual community, and humanity in general, is evident from the vast number of lectures and articles he devoted to the subject. He died of cancer in Princeton on Feb. 18, 1967.

Further Reading

The most complete obituary notice of Oppenheimer is by H. A. Bethe in the Royal Society of London, *Biographical Memoirs of Fellows of the Royal Society,* vol. 14 (1968). Considerable biographical information, along with selected writings of Oppenheimer included as an addendum, is in a study of his scientific contributions to atomic theory: Michel Rouze, *Robert Oppenheimer: The Man and His Theories,* translated by Patrick Evans (1964). See also Peter Michelmore, *The Swift Years: The Robert Oppenheimer Story* (1969).

A number of works deal with the dramatic and controversial investigation of Oppenheimer's security status. The reports of the U.S. Atomic Energy Commission in 1954-1955, published as *In the Matter of J. Robert Oppenheimer,* constitute the official record of his trial. Haakon Chevalier, *Oppenheimer: The Story of a Friendship* (1965), is a personal account of the still obscure events of the 1940s. Other books on this aspect of Oppenheimer's life are Joseph and Stewart Alsop, *We Accuse!* (1954); Cushing Strout, ed., *Conscience, Science and Security: The Case of Dr. J. Robert Oppenheimer* (1963); and Philip M. Stern and Harold P. Green, *The Oppenheimer Case: Security on Trial* (1969).

For Oppenheimer's work on atomic energy see J. Alvin Kugelmass, *J. Robert Oppenheimer and the Atomic Story* (1953); Richard G. Hewlett and Oscar E. Anderson, Jr., *A History of the United States Atomic Energy Commission* (2 vols., 1962-1969); and Nuel Pharr Davis, *Lawrence and Oppenheimer* (1968). □

Orcagna

Orcagna (c. 1308-c. 1368) was an Italian painter, sculptor, and architect whose work greatly influenced Florentine and Tuscan art during the late 14th century.

Nothing is known of the early years of Andrea di Cione, called Orcagna. According to a document of June 1368, he fell ill and presumably died later that year. Giorgio Vasari reported that Orcagna was 60 years old at the time of his death; hence, he was born about 1308. In 1343/1344 his name first appeared on the register of the Florentine painters' guild (Arte dei Medici e Speziali) and in 1352 on the register of the stone workers' guild (Arte dei Maestri della Pietra). After 1352 Orcagna was mentioned in numerous documents relating to a number of projects in Florence, including the *Strozzi Altarpiece* in S. Maria Novella and the marble tabernacle in Orsanmichele.

He was *capomastro* of the Cathedral in Orvieto (1359-1362), where he executed the mosaic decorations for the facade.

The signed and dated (1357) altarpiece commissioned in 1354 by Tommaso Strozzi, in the family chapel in S. Maria Novella, is the only painting entirely by Orcagna that has come down to us intact. It is a large polyptych depicting Christ as the Redeemer in the center flanked by (left) the Virgin and St. Thomas Aquinas and (right) John the Baptist and St. Peter. The outermost panels depict (left) St. Catherine and St. Michael and (right) St. Lawrence and St. Paul.

Most scholars view this unusual altarpiece as a conscious effort to return to pre-Giottesque conceptions of religious art. Orcagna rejected the logical and coherent spatial articulation of Giotto and his followers to return to the tense, cramped abstract space of earlier days. He filled the gold openings of the frame with insistently plastic and full forms, often using contradictory devices. The figure of Christ, for example, is brought forward to the foreground plane by his gestures to St. Thomas and St. Peter and simultaneously pushed back in space by the way the adoring angels overlap the seraphim of his mandorla.

The explanation for Orcagna's return to an earlier artistic conception is probably the shattering effect of the plague, or Black Death, of 1348. The survivors of the epidemic interpreted it as evidence of God's anger and vengeance against the moral corruption of mankind. Their efforts to appease Him took the form of returning to the sanctified ways of their ancestors. Artists, too, rejected the realism of their immediate predecessors, Giotto and his school, for the abstraction of late-13th-century art. Orcagna's *Strozzi Altarpiece* is the finest work of the period illustrating this attitude.

The marble tabernacle in Orsanmichele (1355-1359) was built to enclose a painting by Bernardo Daddi and depicts the life of the Virgin in a series of relief panels. The major panel depicts the Assumption of the Virgin and combines relief sculpture with mosaic decoration. According to Vasari, Orcagna learned the sculptor's art from Andrea Pisano, a plausible but unverified theory. Orcagna's sculptural style is close to Andrea Pisano's in its concern for sweeping rhythms and decorative surfaces. Generally the figures have a fullness and plasticity very similar to the painted figures on the *Strozzi Altarpiece.*

At the time of his death Orcagna was working on the *St. Matthew Altarpiece* (Uffizi, Florence) with his brother Jacopo di Cione, who finished the project. Some fragments of frescoes have been attributed to Orcagna, though they are probably by assistants. These include the *Triumph of Death,* the *Last Judgment,* and *Hell* in Sta Croce (ca. 1348), the *Last Supper* and the *Crucifixion* in the refectory of Sto Spirito, and some half-length figures of prophets in the choir of S. Maria Novella.

Further Reading

A valuable discussion of late-14th-century Florentine painting, including an especially good analysis of Orcagna's *Strozzi Altarpiece,* is in Millard Meiss, *Painting in Florence and Siena after the Black Death* (1951). Evelyn Sandburg-Vavalà in-

cludes most of Orcagna's paintings in her books *Uffizi Studies* (1948) and *Studies in the Florentine Churches* (1959). For Orcagna's work as a sculptor see John Pope-Hennessy, *Italian Gothic Sculpture* (1955). □

Francisco de Orellana

Francisco de Orellana (ca. 1511-1546) was a Spanish conquistador and explorer of the Amazon whose name remains somewhat tainted because of the suspicion that he deserted Gonzalo Pizarro in a desperate situation.

Francisco de Orellana a relative of the Pizarros, was born in Trujillo, Estremadura. He evidently reached the New World as a teen-age boy and took part in the Pizarro conquest of Peru, where he lost an eye in battle. In 1538 he fought under Hernando Pizarro at the battle of Las Salinas, where Hernando captured Diego de Almagro, whom he executed. Orellana next went north and founded Guayaquil in late 1538 or early 1539.

He was now immediately subordinate to his kinsman Gonzalo Pizarro, governor of Quito. Gonzalo had orders from his brother Francisco to seek the reported Cinnamon Forests east of the Andes, and Orellana went as second-in-command of the large expedition in 1541. The explorers marched in good order until reaching the Napo River, an Amazon tributary, where food ran low. Orellana either volunteered or was ordered by Pizarro to go farther down the river with a hastily constructed boat and about 60 men to bring back food from a place where friendly Indians reported it to be plentiful. Orellana did obtain food and then, whether by his own decision or compelled by subordinates, decided to follow the main Amazon, now close at hand, to the Atlantic. No one had traversed the river before, but its size convinced the Spaniards that it must emerge at the ocean. Controversy has long gone on as to Orellana's guilt, but the general verdict is that he had intended to desert from the time of leaving Gonzalo.

The adventurers proceeded to the Amazon mouth and then to the Spanish island of Cubagua, which they reached early in September 1542. Many of them then went to Peru, but Orellana traveled to Spain by way of Trinidad, Santo Domingo, and Portugal.

During their descent of the Amazon, Orellana's Spaniards underwent frequent attacks by Indians, and in one region women fought and surpassed males in valor. Gaspar de Carvajal, chaplain of the expedition, describes the women as being very white and tall and doing as much fighting as 10 Indian men. Such formidable strength brought to mind the Amazons of Greek mythology, and the Spaniards gave this name to their land; only afterward was "Amazon" gradually applied to the river.

In Spain, Orellana sought and obtained a concession to explore and govern New Andalusia, meaning roughly the land south of the great river. He sailed from Sanlúcar on

May 11, 1545, with a poorly equipped fleet and accompanied by his wife, Ana de Ayala, whom he had married in Spain. But Orellana died of sickness and fatigue about November 1546, and the fleet went to pieces. Some survivors, including Ana, were rescued later at the island of Margarita.

Further Reading

José Toribio Medina, ed., *The Discovery of the Amazon according to the Account of Friar Gaspar de Carvajal,* translated by Bertram T. Lee and edited by H. C. Keaton (1934), prints the original documents regarding Orellana's expedition and completely absolves him of treachery to Gonzalo Pizarro. Hoffman Birney, *Brothers of Doom: The Story of the Pizarros of Peru* (1942), declares Orellana a traitor. Walker Chapman, *The Golden Dream* (1968), is more lenient. William H. Prescott, *History of the Conquest of Peru* (2 vols., 1848; later editions), considers Orellana a criminal. ☐

Origen

The Christian theologian and biblical scholar Origen (ca. 185-ca. 254) is famous for the originality and power of his mind as well as for his vast learning and prolific writings. He was the most influential Christian theologian before St. Augustine and one of the most controversial Christian thinkers of all time.

Origen, whose full name was Origenes Adamantius, was born of Christian parents, probably in the Egyptian city of Alexandria. Forced to support the family because of his father's martyrdom before Origen was 20 years old, he taught grammar for a time and then became head of the Christian catechetical school in Alexandria. Devoting himself to the duties of this post for the next 12 years or so, Origen adopted notably ascetic habits of life. He extended his own studies to the point of attending the lectures of the Platonist philosopher Ammonius Saccas. During these years Origen also learned Hebrew and began the compilation of his *Hexapla,* famous in the history of textual criticism. It was an edition of the Old Testament in six parallel columns, one each for the Hebrew text, the Hebrew text in Greek characters, and four different Greek versions.

A local outburst of violence against Christians about 215 prompted Origen to leave Alexandria and to journey to Palestine. There his fame had preceded him, and he was asked, though a layman, to preach publicly in church. News of this irregular proceeding reached the ears of Demetrius, the bishop of Alexandria, who forthwith recalled Origen home. Once in Alexandria, Origen began an intense period of literary work facilitated by shorthand writers and transcribers supplied by his wealthy friend and convert Ambrose.

The most famous of Origen's writings from this period was the work *De principiis (On First Principles).* In it he articulated a comprehensive and coherent statement of the Christian doctrines of creation and redemption. Drawing guardedly upon contemporary currents of philosophical and Gnostic speculation, he projected a cosmic history of rational beings, created before the material universe, who fell from their original love of God and who then entered bodies in the material world created by God as a place of corrective education. God's providential care for his rational creatures was brought to a decisive turning point by the Incarnation of His Word in Jesus Christ, whose role was to lead souls freely joined to him in faith and love back to the original state from which they fell in their premundane existence. Origen believed that even Satan and his angels would one day be led back to God, one of his teachings that in his lifetime and in later centuries brought him into disrepute.

About 230, on a journey to a theological disputation in Greece, Origen stopped off in Palestine, where he was ordained presbyter by his admirers, the bishops of Caesarea and Jerusalem. His ordination outside the jurisdiction of Demetrius brought Origen's tense relations with the bishop of Alexandria to a climax. At Alexandria he was formally condemned, a decree not honored elsewhere in the Eastern Church.

Thereafter, Origen lived at Caesarea, where for 2 decades he was active as teacher, preacher, biblical commentator, and Christian apologist. As a teacher of prospective scholars and Church leaders, Origen developed a carefully planned course of studies that proceeded from logic through physics and ethics to theology and the interpretation of Scripture. His sermons abounded in shrewdly critical observations on the state of the Church, including sharp comments on the laxity and venality of bishops. His expositions of Scripture, the main bulk of his vast literary output, were marked by extensive use of allegorical interpretations. Two chief purposes of this were to block any suggestion that unworthy conceptions of God are to be found in the Bible and to display the Bible as offering differing levels of insight according to the varying capacities of men in their gradual progress toward spiritual perfection. According to St. Jerome, Origen wrote about 800 exegetical and apologetic works.

In 250, during the persecution of the Church by Emperor Decius, Origen was imprisoned and tortured. He died in Tyre.

Further Reading

The best work on Origen is Jean Danielou, *Origen* (1955), which includes many quotations from Origen's works. A helpful, if brief, treatment is in Henry Chadwick, *Early Christian Thought and the Classical Tradition: Studies in Justin, Clement and Origen* (1966). An older work, but one from which much can still be learned, is Charles Bigg, *The Christian Platonists of Alexandria* (1886; rev. ed. 1913). □

Vittorio Emmanuele Orlando

The Italian statesman Vittorio Emmanuele Orlando (1860-1952) was the leader of the Italian delegation to the Paris peace talks after World War I and an unsuccessful candidate for the presidency of the Italian Republic.

Vittorio Orlando was born in Palermo on May 19, 1860. His long career in politics brought him into the limelight of national and world affairs, although he played no more than a minor role in the shaping of contemporary history. On the other hand, his career illustrates certain tendencies in Italian politics which are worthy of mention.

Since the unification of Italy there has been a marked tendency for middle-class and intellectual southern Italians to seek an outlet for their ambitions in national government service. Until very recently the rural and impoverished Mezzogiorno region offered pitifully few opportunities for its educated stratum to rise. Quite naturally, once established in Rome, the despised Sicilian or Calabrese politician might well wish to submerge his southern identity — to prove himself more "national" in outlook than his northern colleagues. Thus when Orlando went to the Chamber of Deputies in 1897, he was following, and would continue to follow, a well-worn path.

However, Orlando was luckier than most. He entered the Cabinet in 1903 and thereafter held a number of important ministerial posts until the outbreak of World War I. A fervent supporter of Italian entry into the war, he eventually

was made prime minister, a position which he occupied when he led the Italian delegation at Paris after the 1918 armistice. A famous group photograph of the time shows him poised in amiable talk with his conference colleagues, American president Woodrow Wilson, British prime minister David Lloyd George, and the French war leader Georges Clemenceau. But the smile fled from Orlando's face after Wilson refused to support Italian claims to the Adriatic city of Fiume (later a lodestone for Fascist agitation).

Orlando's patriotic stand first won him domestic plaudits; but his failure to achieve a favorable diplomatic settlement cost him his post in June 1919. However, he remained in the Chamber of Deputies, where, as president of the Chamber, he was representative of a less fortunate political tendency than the movement of southern Italians into national administration. This was the tendency of a large number of conservative and center politicians to look favorably upon the posturings of Benito Mussolini and his Blackshirts during the wave of labor unrest that swept postwar Italy. Their fears heightened by the rise of bolshevism and the Third International, these politicians, Orlando among them, succumbed to Mussolini's propaganda that the "emergency" warranted the formation of a "strong" government that would crack down hard on labor and the left.

When eventually it was revealed that Mussolini (the Duce was now in power) ordered the murder of the Socialist deputy Giacomo Matteotti, Orlando went over into opposition to fascism. In Sicily he attempted to mobilize electoral opposition to Mussolini; but the elections were easily rigged by the Fascists and there were soon no meaningful elections to contest. Orlando then withdrew from politics.

Following World War II, Orlando joined the group of old-line politicians who were attempting, with mixed success, to play a renewed role in the politics of the republic. First as president of the 1946 Constituent Assembly, then as senator, Orlando seemed to have made the transition with marked success. But in 1948 he was defeated by Luigi Einaudi in his bid to become first president of the republic; and he died in Rome only a few years later, on Dec. 1, 1952.

Further Reading

For a discussion of Orlando's career and its political and social background see Denis Mack Smith, *Italy: A Modern History* (rev. ed. 1969), and A. William Salomone, ed., *Italy from the Risorgimento to Fascism* (1970), which has an especially useful bibliography. ☐

Charles D'Orléans

The French prince and poet Charles, Duc d'Orléans (1394-1465), a repeated victim of the political intrigues into which he was born, drew from his tragic life the impetus to write lyrics remarkable for their polish and charm.

The son of Charles VI's brother Louis d'Orléans, Charles d'Orléans was only 13 years old when the Burgundians assassinated his father, thus making him titular head of his family in 1407. His mother, Valentine Visconti, Duchess of Milan, died the following year. In 1415 Charles participated in the Battle of Agincourt, where he was taken captive by the English. Taken to England and held for ransom, the duke remained in captivity until 1440, receiving now painful, now charitable treatment from the English.

When freedom came, Charles's misfortunes did not cease. The cost of his ransom had depleted his resources, and his attempt in 1447 to regain by force the Italian lands he had inherited from his mother failed utterly. Charles ended his years on his estates near Blois, where he formed a literary circle of sufficient renown to attract François Villon. Charles's court was graced by his third wife, the young Marie de Clèves, with whom he had several children, including a son, Louis, who later became King Louis XII of France.

The greatest portion of Charles's writing consists of ballads and rondels. The poet evolved in their use, preferring the ballad in the years before his return to France and the rondel after 1440; that is, Charles moved away from a malleable form that he exploited to the fullest toward an equally malleable form that he treated conservatively. Although no pattern dominates among the ballads, Charles had a marked predilection for the rondel with either a 4-4-5 or 4-3-5 strophic arrangement. Charles also evolved away from the *amour courtois* views of his younger years. His mature verse exhibits an amused, ironic, and, rarely, wistful attitude toward life and its lost pleasures. Only too aware of the vanity of titles and of the gap between the chivalric code and the realities of aristocratic life, Charles produced poetry that participates fully in the malaise of the declining Middle Ages.

Charles's poetry of self-analysis is best known for its ingenious use of allegory. Influenced by *Le Roman de la rose* and by Jean de Garencières, Charles greatly expanded their techniques until triple the number of allegorical characters that appear in *Le Roman de la rose* people his poems. During his period of exile, Hope, Sadness, and Loyalty recurred in his verse, whereas in his later poems Melancholy and Care figured. Initially very artificial, these characters were gradually developed by the poet into a means of self-expression of undeniable sophistication.

Further Reading

Two major studies of Charles are by Norma L. Goodrich, *Charles, Duke of Orleans: A Literary Biography* (1963) and *Charles of Orleans: A Study of Themes in His French and in His English Poetry* (1967). Also useful is John H. Fox, *The Lyric Poetry of Charles d'Orléans* (1969). ☐

Philippe II D'Orléans

Philippe II, Duc d'Orléans (1674-1723), was regent of France during the minority of Louis XV. He failed

in his efforts to reverse the tendency toward absolutism by restoring the power of the nobles.

Philippe II d'Orléans was the son of Philippe I d'Orléans, the second son of Louis XIII. Philippe began a successful military career at the age of 18 during the War of the League of Augsburg. In 1692 he married Mademoiselle de Blois, an illegitimate daughter of Louis XIV. In 1708, after a brilliant campaign in Spain, he was recalled because of suspicions that he was conspiring to replace Philip V, Louis XIV's grandson, on the Spanish throne. Such suspicions, as well as his dissolute life, caused Louis XIV to bar Philippe from the position of regent, one that according to tradition he should have held. However, after the death of Louis XIV, Philippe, with the aid of the nobles and the *parlements,* broke the late ruler's testament and became regent for the young Louis XV.

The regent had a number of praiseworthy qualities. He was intelligent, courageous, generous, sensitive to the arts (he was himself a minor poet), and interested in the sciences, particularly chemistry, which led to rumors that he practiced alchemy. He was tolerant of religious differences and briefly considered restoring the Edict of Nantes, which had granted considerable religious freedom to the Protestants and which Louis XIV had revoked. However, the regent's personal life was far less admirable; immoral and an alcoholic, he surrounded himself with friends whose way of life helped discredit his rule.

Philippe's internal policy was marked by an effort to restore the power of the nobles, which had been severely limited by strong ministers such as Richelieu and Mazarin and by Louis XIV. He returned to the *parlements* the right of remonstrance (the power to protest and to delay royal decrees), which Louis XIV had curtailed. In place of the system of powerful ministers employed by Louis XIV, the regent introduced the institution of *polysynodie,* with councils dominated by the nobles. However, by 1718 the nobles had demonstrated that they were incapable of governing, and the regent reluctantly restored the former system of administration by ministers. In order to reduce the enormous public debt left by Louis XIV's wars, the regent authorized the Scottish financier John Law to establish a royal bank and a company to exploit foreign commerce, the famous ''system'' of Law. The collapse of the system contributed to a decline in the prestige of the regency.

The regent's foreign policy reversed that of Louis XIV. He abandoned the family alliance with Spain and in 1717 signed the Triple Alliance of The Hague with Great Britain and the Netherlands, the great foes of the former ruler. In February 1723 Louis XV was declared to be of age, but the Duc d'Orléans continued in control until his death on Dec. 2, 1723.

Further Reading

There are many popular biographies that stress the personal life of Philippe II, particularly his vices, such as Warren Hamilton Lewis, *The Scandalous Regent: A Life of Philippe, Duc d'Orleans, 1674-1723 and of His Family* (1961). An old but still informative work is James Breck Perkins, *France under the Regency* (1892). For the regent's relationship to Louis XV see Pierre Gaxotte, *Louis the Fifteenth and His Times* (1934).

Additional Sources

Shennan, J. H., *Philippe, Duke of Orleans: Regent of France, 1715-1723,* London: Thames and Hudson, 1979. □